Handbook of
Psychopharmacology

Volume 8
Drugs, Neurotransmitters, and Behavior

Handbook of
Psychopharmacology

SECTION I: BASIC NEUROPHARMACOLOGY
Volume 1   Biochemical Principles and Techniques in Neuropharmacology
Volume 2   Principles of Receptor Research
Volume 3   Biochemistry of Biogenic Amines
Volume 4   Amino Acid Neurotransmitters
Volume 5   Synaptic Modulators
Volume 6   Biogenic Amine Receptors

SECTION II: BEHAVIORAL PHARMACOLOGY IN ANIMALS
Volume 7   Principles of Behavioral Pharmacology
Volume 8   Drugs, Neurotransmitters, and Behavior
Volume 9   Chemical Pathways in the Brain

SECTION III: HUMAN PSYCHOPHARMACOLOGY
Volume 10   Neuroleptics and Schizophrenia
Volume 11   Stimulants
Volume 12   Drugs of Abuse
Volume 13   Biology of Mood and Antianxiety Drugs
Volume 14   Affective Disorders: Drug Actions in Animals and Man

Volume 8
Drugs, Neurotransmitters, and Behavior

Edited by

Leslie L. Iversen
Department of Pharmacology
University of Cambridge

Susan D. Iversen
Department of Psychology
University of Cambridge

and

Solomon H. Snyder
Departments of Pharmacology and Psychiatry
The Johns Hopkins University
School of Medicine

PLENUM PRESS • NEW YORK AND LONDON

Library of Congress Cataloging in Publication Data

Main entry under title:

Handbook of psychopharmacology.

   Includes bibliographies and indexes.
   CONTENTS: — v. 2. Principles of receptor research. — v. 3. Biochemistry of biogenic amines. [etc.]
   1. Psychopharmacology. I. Iversen, Leslie Lars. II. Iversen, Susan D. 1940- III. Snyder, Solomon H., 1938-   [DNLM: 1. Psychopharmacology. QV77 H236]
RC483.H36   615'.78   75-6851
ISBN 0-306-38928-2 (v. 8)

© 1977 Plenum Press, New York
A Division of Plenum Publishing Corporation
227 West 17th Street, New York, N.Y. 10011

All rights reserved

No part of this book may be reproduced, stored in a retrieval system, or transmitted, in any form or by any means, electronic, mechanical, photocopying, microfilming, recording or otherwise, without written permission from the Publisher

Printed in the United States of America

CONTRIBUTORS TO VOLUME 8

JAMES D. BELLUZZI, *Department of Psychopharmacology, Wyeth Laboratories, Philadelphia, Pennsylvania 19101*

MONA ELIASSON, *University of Uppsala, Department of Medical Pharmacology, Biomedicum, Box 573, S-751 23, Uppsala, Sweden*

JEFFREY A. GRAY, *Department of Experimental Psychology, University of Oxford, Oxford, England*

BARTLEY G. HOEBEL, *Department of Psychology, Princeton University, Princeton, New Jersey 08540*

BRUCE HUNTER, *Department of Neuroscience, College of Medicine, University of Florida, Gainesville, Florida 32610*

SUSAN D. IVERSEN, *Department of Experimental Psychology, University of Cambridge, Cambridge, England*

MURRAY E. JARVIK, *Department of Psychiatry, School of Medicine, University of California at Los Angeles, Los Angeles, California 90024, and V. A. Hospital Brentwood, Los Angeles, California 90073*

MICHEL JOUVET, *Department of Experimental Medicine, University Claude Bernard, Lyon, France*

PETER H. KELLY, *Department of Pharmacology, Michigan State University, East Lansing, Michigan 48824*

JAMES L. McGAUGH, *Department of Psychobiology, University of California at Irvine, Irvine, California 92664*

BENGT J. MEYERSON, *University of Uppsala, Department of Medical Pharmacology, Biomedicum, Box 573, S-751 23, Uppsala, Sweden*

ARYEH ROUTTENBERG, *Cresap Neuroscience Laboratory, Northwestern University, Evanston, Illinois 60201*

REBECCA SANTOS-ANDERSON, *Cresap Neuroscience Laboratory, Northwestern University, Evanston, Illinois 60201*

PAULETTE E. SETLER, *Biological Research Division, Smith Kline and French Laboratories, Philadelphia, Pennsylvania 19101*

LARRY STEIN, *Department of Psychopharmacology, Wyeth Laboratories, Philadelphia, Pennsylvania 19101*

DAVID M. WARBURTON, *Department of Psychology, Reading University, Reading R96 2AL, England*

C. DAVID WISE, *Department of Psychopharmacology, Wyeth Laboratories, Philadelphia, Pennsylvania 19101*

STEVEN F. ZORNETZER, *Department of Neuroscience, College of Medicine, University of Florida, Gainesville, Florida 32610*

PREFACE

The first six volumes of the *Handbook* reviewed basic neuropharmacology, drawing on expertise in biochemistry, pharmacology and electrophysiology. The next three volumes focus attention on the functional importance of these basic neuropharmacological mechanisms for normal behavior.

In order to study this interface in the intact functioning organism, appropriate methods for describing and quantifying behavior must be developed. The past twenty years have witnessed a revolution in the study of behavior which has taken us away from the often fruitless theoretical arguments to descriptive behaviorism. Technical achievements in the design of apparatus and the recording of behavior played an important role in these developments, and the resultant behavioral methods have been accepted and found useful in studying the effects of drugs. The development of psychopharmacology as a discipline owes as much to these behavioral methods as it does to the basic neuropharmacological techniques pioneered for *in vitro* studies.

In the first section of Volume 7, an effort has been made to provide reviews both of theory and practice in behavioral science. Milner's chapter deals with the concept of motivation in a theoretical framework. By contrast, the chapters by Morse *et al.* and Dews and DeWeese provide a more descriptive view of the various ways in which aversive stimuli control behavior and the importance of schedules of reinforcement in determining the profile of responding in the animal. The equal importance of observational behavioral methods is well illustrated by Mackintosh *et al.,* and a more detailed treatment of the analysis of *sequences* of behavior is provided by Norton. Other contributors illustrate how a variety of these behavioral approaches and methods may be combined in the analysis of a particular problem. Marshall and Teitelbaum do this admirably for motivation, and Kumar discusses the progress that has been made in developing animal models of certain human behavioral disorders.

In the remaining section of Volume 7, attention is paid to the general factors that determine the profile of behavioral responses in the individual and their potential for modification by drugs. This represents an immensely important and growing area in psychopharmacology. Genetic factors, developmental experience, social experience, and drug experience have been selected for review.

Global descriptions of behavior often seem far removed from the detailed workings of brain neuropharmacology. In Volume 8 this chasm is bridged. In some areas we are beginning to understand how function at the neuronal level is related to overt behavior. This is so in the case of eating, drinking, sex, sleep, and memory, and the volume provides reviews in these areas.

Certain areas, however, remain highly controversial, and it was considered important to represent the unresolved as well as the resolved issues. The neural and neuropharmacological basis of reinforcement is one such problem, and Routtenberg and Stein *et al.* provide provocative reviews from two points of view. An effort has also been made to include reference to more diffuse areas of behavioral control such as behavioral inhibition. Warburton and Gray review this topic from different theoretical positions and illustrate how difficult it is to devise specific behavioral tests for certain nervous functions. Yet it may be that these more global levels of control are of immense importance in behavioral integration.

Finally, in Volume 9 the structural basis of neuropharmacology is considered. Are neuropharmacological systems, for example, a particular class of receptor or neurotransmitter, localized in the brain? And if so, how do we go about unraveling the details of this organization? Histochemical techniques for localizing acetylcholine, catecholamine, and indoleamine pathways in the brain are reviewed and information presented on our current knowledge of the anatomical distribution of these transmitter pathways in the central nervous system. Alternative methods using radioautography and immunofluorescence are also considered. These techniques are already proving to be of immense importance in studying neurotransmitter localization at the neuronal level and, in particular, in the study of novel neuromodulators such as the peptides, where conventional histochemical methods are not available. Lesion techniques have traditionally played an important role in unraveling neural organization and continue to do so in conjunction with the specific histological techniques. The problems associated with lesion techniques are also considered. This volume is a fair reflection of the current state of knowledge regarding the anatomical basis of neuropharmacology and is invaluable to those seeking to understand the basis of behavior and its modification of psychotropic drugs.

L.L.I.
S.D.I.
S.H.S.

CONTENTS

CHAPTER 1

The Role of Prefrontal Cortex in Intracranial Self-Stimulation: A Case History of Anatomical Localization of Motivational Substrates

ARYEH ROUTTENBERG and REBECCA SANTOS-ANDERSON

   1. Introduction 1
   2. Pathways of Intracranial Self-Stimulation: A Three-Step Procedure for Specification 2
      2.1. Mapping 2
      2.2. Lesions at ICSS Sites 5
      2.3. Brain Lesions Which Eliminate Self-Stimulation 7
      2.4. Summary 7
   3. Defining the Input and Output in ICSS 8
      3.1. The Nature of the Wiring Diagram 8
      3.2. The Definition of Input and Output 10
      3.3. Anatomical Localization of Sites Eliciting Drinking by Carbachol and Angiotensin II: The Advantages of Defined Input and Output 10
      3.4. Some Preliminary Attempts at Solution 12
   4. The Central Role of the Frontal Cortex in ICSS 13
      4.1. Initial Map of the Brainstem for ICSS: Dubious Role of the Locus Coeruleus 14
      4.2. ICSS in Frontal Cortex: Medial and Sulcal Cortex ... 16
   5. Relation of Frontal Cortex to Brainstem Self-Stimulation .. 19
   6. Summary 20
   7. References 21

CHAPTER 2

Neuropharmacology of Reward and Punishment

LARRY STEIN, C. DAVID WISE, and JAMES D. BELLUZZI

   1. Introduction 25
   2. Operant Reinforcement 26

  2.1. Pharmacological Evidence Implicating Norepinephrine
    (NE) 27
  2.2. Anatomical Evidence Implicating Norepinephrine 33
  2.3. Self-Stimulation and Brain Dopamine 36
  2.4. Intravenous Self-Administration of Drugs 39
  2.5. Conclusions 40
 3. Operant Punishment 41
  3.1. Pharmacology 41
  3.2. Effects of Benzodiazepines on Monoamine Turnover . 42
  3.3. Benzodiazepines and Brain Norepinephrine 43
  3.4. Benzodiazepines and Brain Serotonin 43
  3.5. Suppression of Behavior by Dorsal Raphe Stimulation
    and Reversal by Oxazepam 47
  3.6. Effects of Repeated Doses of Oxazepam on
    Monoamine Turnover 47
  3.7. Conclusions 48
 4. References 49

Chapter 3

The Psychopharmacology of Feeding

Bartley G. Hoebel

 1. Introduction 55
 2. Putative Neurotransmitters and Food Intake 56
  2.1. Norepinephrine and Epinephrine 56
  2.2. Dopamine 72
  2.3. Serotonin 78
  2.4. Acetylcholine 81
  2.5. Other Influences 85
 3. Anorectic Drugs 86
  3.1. Structure–Function Relationships in Sympathomimetics 87
  3.2. Epinephrine 92
  3.3. Nordefrin: α-Methylnorepinephrine 93
  3.4. Phenethylamine 94
  3.5. Amphetamine 94
  3.6. Phentermine, Phenmetrazine, and Diethylpropion 99
  3.7. Phenylpropanolamine 101
  3.8. Chlorphentermine and Chloroamphetamine 103
  3.9. Fenfluramine 104
  3.10. Social Psychology and Anorectic Drugs 107
 4. Orectic Drugs 110
  4.1. Cyproheptadine 111
  4.2. Tranquilizers 111

4.3. L-Dopa	113
5. References	114

CHAPTER 4

The Neuroanatomy and Neuropharmacology of Drinking
PAULETTE E. SETLER

1. Introduction	131
2. Thirst Receptors	132
3. The Neuroanatomy of Thirst	134
3.1. Hypothalamus	134
3.2. Limbic System and Midbrain	138
4. The Neuropharmacology of Thirst	140
4.1. Cholinergic Systems	141
4.2. Angiotensin	144
4.3. Adrenergic Systems	150
4.4. Other Dipsogenic Substances	151
5. Defense of Body Fluids	151
6. References	152

CHAPTER 5

Pharmacological and Hormonal Control of Reproductive Behavior
BENGT J. MEYERSON and MONA ELIASSON

1. Introduction	159
2. Ontogeny of Sexual Behavior	161
2.1. Hormones and Development of Sexual Behavior: Sexual Dimorphism	161
2.2. Monoamines, Drugs, and Development of Sexual Behavior	172
3. Sexual Behavior in the Adult Subject	175
3.1. Hormonal Regulation of Sexual Behavior in the Female	175
3.2. Hormonal Regulation of Sexual Behavior in the Male	186
3.3. Effects of Psychoactive Drugs on Sexual Behavior	191
4. Parental Behavior	205
4.1. Maternal Behavior	206
4.2. Paternal (Paternalistic) Behavior	212
5. General Conclusions	212
6. References	213

Chapter 6

Neuropharmacology of the Sleep–Waking Cycle

Michel Jouvet

1. Introduction	233
2. The Sleep–Waking Cycle in the Cat	234
3. An Outline of Recent Theories of Sleep Mechanisms	235
3.1. Recent Advances in the Study of Sleep Mechanisms	235
3.2. Classical Neurophysiology of Sleep	236
3.3. "Wet Neurophysiology"	237
4. 5-Hydroxytryptamine and the Sleep–Waking Cycle	240
4.1. Increased Availability of 5-HT to Serotoninoceptive Neurons	240
4.2. Decreased Availability of 5-HT	243
5. Catecholamines and the Sleep–Waking Cycle	251
5.1. Increased Availability of Catecholamines	251
5.2. Decreased Availability of Catecholamines	255
6. Acetylcholine and the Sleep–Waking Cycle	260
6.1. Increased Availability of ACh to Cholinoceptive Neurons	260
6.2. Decreased Availability of ACh	261
6.3. Cholinergic Mechanisms Involved in Paradoxical Sleep	263
7. Pharmacological Alterations of PGO Activity	265
7.1. The Reserpine Syndrome and the PGO System	265
7.2. Pharmacology of PGO Activity	265
7.3. The PGO Method in Pharmacology	268
8. Short-Chain Fatty Acids and the Sleep–Waking Cycle	269
8.1. The Narcotic Effect	269
8.2. Mechanisms of Action	270
9. Antidepressant and Neuroleptic Drugs	271
9.1. Antidepressants	271
9.2. Neuroleptic Drugs	272
10. Hypnotics and Tranquilizing Drugs	272
10.1. Hypnotics	272
10.2. Minor Tranquilizers	273
11. Hormones and the Sleep–Waking Cycle	274
12. Drugs Acting on Protein Synthesis and the Sleep–Waking Cycle	275
12.1. Experimental Evidence	275
12.2. Impossible Interpretation	276
13. Miscellaneous Compounds	277
13.1. Putative Neurotransmitters	277
13.2. Miscellaneous Drugs	278
14. Conclusions	279
15. References	281

CONTENTS

CHAPTER 7

Drug-Induced Motor Behavior

PETER H. KELLY

1. Introduction	295
2. Locomotor Activity	296
2.1. Drug Effects on Locomotor Activity	296
2.2. Neural Mechanisms of the Locomotor-Stimulant Action of Amphetamine	296
2.3. Roles of Transmitters Other than Dopamine in Locomotor Activity	303
2.4. Conclusions	306
3. Stereotyped Behavior	307
3.1. The Drug-Induced Stereotyped Behavior Syndrome	307
3.2. Neural Basis of Amphetamine-Induced Stereotypy	307
3.3. Roles of Transmitters Other than Dopamine in Stereotyped Behavior	311
3.4. Conclusions	312
4. Rotational Behavior	313
4.1. Drug-Induced Circling	313
4.2. Neural Mechanisms of Amphetamine-Induced Circling	314
4.3. Roles of Transmitters Other than Dopamine in Drug-Induced Circling	317
4.4. Conclusions	320
5. References	320

CHAPTER 8

Brain Dopamine Systems and Behavior

SUSAN D. IVERSEN

1. Introduction	333
2. Studies of the Dopamine Pathways and Behavior	337
2.1. Methods of Investigation	337
2.2. Unconditioned Behavior	338
2.3. Conditioned Behavior	344
3. Classical Studies of Striatal Function	356
4. A Synthesis of the Role of DA in the Nigrostriatal Tract	358
4.1. Endogenous DA Asymmetry and Sensory–Motor Coordination	358
4.2. Behavioral Nature of Amphetamine-Induced Motor Changes	362
5. An Overview of Striatal Function	364
5.1. Frontostriatal Interactions	364

5.2. How Does the Striatum Influence Motor Control? 366
5.3. Striatum and Cognitive Function 368
5.4. Nonstriatal Dopamine Systems 369
6. References 374

CHAPTER 9

Stimulus Selection and Behavioral Inhibition

DAVID M. WARBURTON

1. Varieties of Behavioral Inhibition 385
   1.1. Habituation 386
   1.2. Extinction 386
   1.3. Discrimination 387
   1.4. Response Suppression by Aversive Stimuli 388
2. Hypotheses about Neural Mechanisms for Behavioral Inhibition 389
   2.1. Stimulus Selection 389
   2.2. Decreased Activation 390
   2.3. Response Inhibition 390
   2.4. Summary 392
3. Psychopharmacology of Behavioral Inhibition 392
   3.1. Habituation 393
   3.2. Extinction 396
   3.3. Discrimination 400
   3.4. Response Suppression by Aversive Stimuli 410
4. Neurochemical Substrates for the Increases in Responding by Amphetamine, Cholinolytics, and Benzodiazepines 415
   4.1. Amphetamine 415
   4.2. Cholinolytics 417
   4.3. Benzodiazepines 419
5. Mechanisms of Behavioral Inhibition 421
6. Conclusions 424
7. References 425

CHAPTER 10

Drug Effects on Fear and Frustration: Possible Limbic Site of Action of Minor Tranquilizers

JEFFREY A. GRAY

1. Introduction 433
2. Learning Theory Background 434

3.	The Effects of the Barbiturates on Emotional Behavior	439
	3.1. Rewarded Behavior	440
	3.2. Passive Avoidance	442
	3.3. Classical Conditioning of Fear	444
	3.4. Escape Behavior	447
	3.5. One-Way Active Avoidance	447
	3.6. Two-Way Active Avoidance	448
	3.7. Responses Elicited by Aversive Stimuli	451
	3.8. Frustrative Nonreward	452
	3.9. Conclusion	464
4.	The Behavioral Inhibition System	464
5.	The Effects of Ethanol on Emotional Behavior	466
	5.1. Rewarded Behavior	467
	5.2. Passive Avoidance	468
	5.3. Classical Conditioning of Fear	470
	5.4. Escape Behavior	471
	5.5. One-Way Active Avoidance	471
	5.6. Two-Way Active Avoidance	472
	5.7. Responses Elicited by Aversive Stimuli	473
	5.8. Frustrative Nonreward	474
	5.9. Responses to Novelty	475
6.	The Effects of the Benzodiazepines on Emotional Behavior	475
	6.1. Rewarded Behavior	475
	6.2. Passive Avoidance	477
	6.3. Classical Conditioning of Fear	478
	6.4. Escape Behavior	480
	6.5. One-Way Active Avoidance	481
	6.6. Two-Way Active Avoidance	483
	6.7. Responses Elicited by Aversive Stimuli	483
	6.8. Frustrative Nonreward	487
	6.9. Responses to Novelty	489
7.	The Behavioral Effects of the Minor Tranquilizers: An Overview	489
	7.1. Rewarded Behavior	489
	7.2. Passive Avoidance	489
	7.3. Classical Conditioning of Fear	490
	7.4. Escape Behavior	490
	7.5. One-Way Active Avoidance	490
	7.6. Two-Way Active Avoidance	490
	7.7. Responses Elicited by Aversive Stimuli	491
	7.8. Frustrative Nonreward	491
	7.9. Responses to Novelty	491
8.	The Mode of Action of the Minor Tranquilizers in the Central Nervous System: A Hypothesis	492

8.1. The Hippocampal Theta Rhythm	492
8.2. Testing the Frequency-Specific Hypothesis	496
8.3. The Pharmacology of the Theta-Driving Curve	503
9. Conclusions	509
10. References	511

Chapter 11

Modulation of Learning and Memory: Effects of Drugs Influencing Neurotransmitters

Bruce Hunter, Steven F. Zornetzer, Murray E. Jarvik, and James L. McGaugh

1. Introduction	531
1.1. Preliminary Considerations	532
2. Acetylcholine	534
2.1. Physostigmine (Eserine)	535
2.2. Nicotine	536
2.3. Anticholinergic Agents	538
3. Catecholamines	544
3.1. Sympathomimetics	545
3.2. Antiadrenergic Agents	548
4. ECS, Protein-Synthesis Inhibition, and CA	554
5. Serotonin (5-Hydroxytryptamine, 5-HT)	555
6. Neurotransmitter Interactions	558
7. Conclusions	559
8. References	567

Index ... 579

THE ROLE OF PREFRONTAL CORTEX IN INTRACRANIAL SELF-STIMULATION:
A CASE HISTORY OF ANATOMICAL LOCALIZATION OF MOTIVATIONAL SUBSTRATES

Aryeh Routtenberg and Rebecca Santos-Anderson

1. INTRODUCTION

Intracranial self-stimulation remains enigmatic. There is one view that its demonstration lies at the heart of our understanding of the brain substrates of behavior, and there is another, but quite opposite view, that suggests that it is to be dismissed as an artifact, and cannot provide any meaningful insights. Regardless of viewpoint, it does seem refractory to study with the logical building-block approach used in a variety of scientific lines of research. Perhaps the problem is that one does not know the appropriate initiation point. As a consequence, a variety of investigators have begun at quite different starting points.

The problem may be stated briefly: What piece of information do we need to know *first* to build on the analysis of this demonstration? We believe the answer is: the specification of the fiber pathways involved. We must not be content with knowledge of the *spheres* of intracranial self-stimulation (ICSS), but rather the *cells* and their processes must be described. This is particularly important in relation to the goals of this Handbook, since such an approach provides the foundation for determining the transmitter chemistry of the cell and subsequently the specific means by which such systems can be manipulated by pharmacological agents.

In this chapter we propose to detail the anatomical approach used in this laboratory to define ICSS pathways. We shall then describe how such an approach has led to an alternative to the norepinephrine hypothesis outlined by Dr. Stein in the next chapter. This alternative strongly worded is: The focus of self-stimulation is the medial (Routtenberg, 1970) and sulcal (Routtenberg and Sloan, 1972) cortex in the frontal lobe. The weak form of the hypothesis is that this system represents the ultimate elaboration of ICSS and that it is re-represented in the Jacksonian sense (see Taylor, 1931) throughout the neuraxis.

2. PATHWAYS OF INTRACRANIAL SELF-STIMULATION: A THREE-STEP PROCEDURE FOR SPECIFICATION

In this section we outline the methods that we have used to obtain further information concerning the pathways which are involved in ICSS. It is felt that the approach that is most suitable in this case involves the use of *interlocking experiments* rather than using separate experiments with interlocking data; in an interlocking experiment we combine self-stimulation methods with anatomical techniques to provide additional information as to the pathways near the electrode tip which may play a role in ICSS. Thus, we first map ICSS sites in a brain region; we then make lesions at ICSS sites and through the ICSS electrode trace pathways from these loci; finally, we determine the effects on ICSS of ablating the cell bodies or origin of the presumed ICSS pathway.

2.1. Mapping

The first set of procedures that require performance consists of the systematic testing for ICSS of electrodes implanted in a brain area (e.g., brainstem, frontal cortex). The approach that we have used has involved the testing of a single bipolar electrode with a single current level and a single testing session per day with no behavioral shaping. We have tried to use a procedure which is, in some sense, as simple as possible so that comparisons of effects in brain regions do not interact with the procedure used (for additional discussion of this problem, see Routtenberg, 1973). In practice, interactions do exist, but the number of interactions are reduced when this simple behavioral testing procedure is used for mapping ICSS sites. An example of one interaction relates to the seizures generated at certain ICSS loci and not at others. While epileptic activity is not a prerequisite for ICSS (e.g., Mogenson, 1964), it could interfere with the use of the rate measure for comparison of ICSS in several brain regions. The approach which we have taken to reduce this problem is to use a current level which is usually below the epileptic threshold at points where epileptic threshold is lowest, i.e., in subcortical telencephalic sites.

It is the case, however, that there are also certain drawbacks to this rigid testing procedure. First, there can be no procedure which does not, in any absolute terms, interact with the effect of stimulation. The absence of certain procedures, such as behavioral shaping, could indeed interact with the site of stimulation; although not yet resolved, it is possible that ICSS in the region of the locus coeruleus may only be obtained with behavioral shaping (compare Crow et al., 1972, and Ritter and Stein, 1973, with Amaral and Routtenberg, 1975). The second disadvantage of this rigid testing procedure is that due to variability in electrode implantation only a certain percentage of subjects demonstrate ICSS. Perhaps other variations, such as the tissue reaction to the electrode and the behavior of the animal, account, in part, for different response levels observed when electrodes are aimed in the same brain region. Our experience with fine-wire stimulating electrodes suggests that variability in placement accounts for the majority of ICSS response variability.

With the rigid testing methods one can expect, at best, a 75% yield of animals that will self-stimulate. In certain brain regions, this can go down to 20% or 30%. If one uses, however, the ICSS method that is typically employed, in which current level is elevated until the animal shows ICSS behavior, then the yield of ICSS subjects is, of course, much higher. The procedure used in this laboratory may not be readily appealing, therefore, since a certain percentage of animals appear to be of no value, because their electrodes did not yield ICSS. One feels, we suppose, that each animal is worth more when ICSS is demonstrated.

It should be understood that these deficiencies may be more apparent than real. Thus, the use of behavioral-shaping procedures at different current levels considerably complicates the assessment of the relative potency of various brain regions in their ability to support ICSS. Shaping, for example, may reduce differences in ICSS rate among brain regions. The rigid testing procedure which we use, then, does provide certain *relative* advantages. In the case of discarding non-ICSS animals, it should be recognized that such animals represent, in fact, valuable negative instances which are typically not emphasized in studies of ICSS anatomy. It is felt, rather, that knowledge of the negative instances is as important as knowledge of the positive instances. In fact, were all cases positive, one could suspect that the ICSS effect was indeed related to some artifact rather than activation of particular fiber pathways. In short, negative instances define, sharpen, and focus on those regions which are ICSS positive.

It is worthwhile noting for the readers of this *Handbook* that use of the single current level is most valuable in the evaluation of psychopharmacological agents. Such evaluation of ICSS typically uses alterations in threshold as a measure of drug effectiveness. But, as Valenstein (1964) pointed out, and Panksepp and Trowill (1969, 1970) demonstrated, evaluation of the effects of brain stimulation using various current levels can given rise to behavioral contrast effects which may complicate interpretation. In the careful study of stimulus parameters by Wauquier, Niemegeers, and Geivers (1972), contrast effects were also noted, particularly at lower current intensities and smaller pulse widths. In this respect then, use of higher current intensities may cause different stimulus-bound behaviors accompanying ICSS performance. Such motor side effects could interact with drug treatment, i.e., the drug could affect ICSS by altering the motor side effect. We have used our lower intensity, single current, rigid behavioral testing procedure with drug application on certain occasions (e.g., Routtenberg and Bulloch, 1970) and have found that such an approach gives stable controlled baselines against which a drug can be evaluated on an individual day.

The present approach also provides a convenient technique for evaluating the effects of a drug on ICSS behavior derived from different stimulation sites. The recent work of Phillips and Fibiger (1973), for example, which indicates differential effects of *d*- and *l*-amphetamine on ICSS in two brain regions, would be easier to interpret were single current parameters chosen first before evaluation of the effect of various drug dosages at these sites. Thus, the use of different drug dosages, and different current levels at different brain regions, complicates the interpretation of their results. It is possible, for example, that the absence of a potentiating influence of *d*-amphetamine relative to *l*-amphetamine on substantia nigra ICSS was related to use of higher current levels in substantia nigra than in lateral hypothalamus. Their results, however, are sufficiently intriguing so as to warrant further detailed, but simplified, analysis of that approach.

The end result of collecting points of ICSS in a particular brain area is an ICSS map of that region. It is often mistakenly concluded, however, that on the basis of such a map, a particular fiber system can be implicated in self-stimulation. Having obtained and collated mapping data, we believe it is only reasonable to conclude that particular spheres, however limited, can be implicated in ICSS. But no conclusion can be drawn as to the involvement of the particular pathways that support that behavior. This type of conclusion can only be drawn after all steps of the three-stage approach to be discussed in this section are performed. The mapping experiment is still essential, as will be shown later, to the logic of determining the cells or the pathways of ICSS, since it provides a check for subsequent experiments that attempt to describe the pathways that are involved. In addition, because these pathway experiments, to be discussed below, require use of lesions at the sites of stimulation, localization of the electrode tip is blurred sufficiently so that mapping experiments provide the best set of data concerning the sites within the brain which support ICSS.

2.2. Lesions at ICSS Sites

The approach which we have used to obtain an initial view of the particular fiber pathways which may be involved was to make lesions through the electrode following its testing for ICSS, and then trace fiber degeneration from the lesioned area surrounding the tip of the electrode. This basic approach was first used by the Swiss neurophysiologist W. R. Hess (1942), and his co-workers. They had shown that lesions at stimulation sites inducing attack behavior demonstrated the descending pathways associated with this behavior. There were probably several reasons why Hess did not pursue this approach in detail, not the least of which was the Marchi method, used to trace the fiber pathways. This technique is capricious, at best, and does not reveal unmyelinated fiber systems, or preterminal degeneration. Such difficulties have been overcome with the Nauta (1957) and the Fink–Heimer (1967) techniques, which do enable the tracing of unmyelinated fiber pathways and the demonstration of synaptic terminals, respectively.

We have applied these latter techniques, then, making lesions at ICSS sites and tracing fiber degeneration. This approach appears to provide a method by which ICSS pathways can be clearly revealed. In practice, however, such an approach allows the demonstration of several pathways, one or more of which can be associated with ICSS. Thus, following ICSS testing, lesions are made through the ICSS electrodes, and the Nauta or Fink–Heimer procedure is used. We have employed this technique in the study of ICSS pathways in brainstem (Routtenberg and Malsbury, 1969), frontal cortex (Routtenberg, 1970), and posterolateral hypothalamus in rat (Huang and Routtenberg, 1971) and subcortical sites in rhesus monkey (Routtenberg *et al.*, 1971). In such experiments several pathways are typically revealed. On the basis of these data alone, then, there is no good way of deciding which pathways are involved. One can refer back, however, to the mapping data and determine which pathways are more likely involved and which ones are not likely involved. In particular, if a fiber pathway trajectory revealed by lesions at a self-stimulation site passes through a variety of locations which support ICSS, this is compelling indirect evidence for the involvement of that pathway in ICSS. Similarly, a pathway which touches several negative instances of ICSS would be less likely as a candidate for an ICSS pathway. It is, however, an uncertain approach, since one can only note the *association* of a pathway with ICSS. One can view the Fink–Heimer method in the context of lesions at ICSS sites as an approach which gives information as to the fiber pathways and the trajectories which potentially support ICSS. It should be emphasized that the trajectory of the fiber pathways discovered may reveal some interesting congruence with prior mapping data, such that certain fiber pathways may be considered to be more likely involved than others.*

This approach of making lesions at ICSS sites can also be applied to evaluate the role of catecholamine fiber systems in ICSS using the Falck–Hillarp technique for the histochemical demonstration of biogenic amines (Falck, Hillarp, Thieme, and Torp, 1962). This approach was first employed by Dresse (1966) but because of lack of anatomical information, certain erroneous conclusions were drawn (see Clavier, 1973). The logic of such a method is identical with that used with the Fink–Heimer technique, except that the focus of interest is exclusively on catecholamine systems revealed by the Falck–Hillarp technique. Here, too, it is possible to be misled by the results obtained insofar as associations discerned between ICSS sites and the observation of a particular catecholamine bundle may *only* be an association. The ICSS behavior observed may not require the integrity of that particular catecholamine system to maintain ICSS. Indeed, were one to initiate one's study by looking exclusively at the catecholamine fiber systems, one would have quite a limited view of the fiber pathways passing through, near, and under the electrode tip.

Nonetheless, the interlocking evidence supporting the role of catecholamine involvement in ICSS (reviewed by Dr. Stein in the next chapter) has warranted a detailed anatomical study of catecholamine systems and ICSS. For this purpose Clavier and I (1974) made lesions at ICSS sites and studied the retrograde buildup of catecholamines with the histochemical fluorescence technique. Since lesions at self-stimulation sites, which overlap with the catecholamine pathways (Ungerstedt, 1971), would give rise to buildup of catecholamine in the proximal axon, it is possible to draw conclusions with regard to the association of ICSS with the presence or absence of catecholamine fiber system buildup. In addition, decisions as to which catecholamine pathway may be involved can also be facilitated.

One may wonder whether these approaches provide any information in addition to that provided by strict anatomical studies of brain regions associated with ICSS which, of course, did not relate to a functional end point, such as ICSS. Strict morphological studies which describe the hodology of particular brain regions, it may be argued, would be sufficient to provide information on the pathways associated with intracranial self-stimulation. It has been our experience, however, that prior anatomical information, while of considerable use in confirming results obtained with the functional-

---

* Here again the value of using a single current level and a rigid testing procedure can be seen if one obtains similar ICSS rates at both point a and point b, using the same current level. If one also shows that one fiber pathway passes through point a or through point b, there is indirect support for the notion that the ICSS at both points is derived from the very same fiber pathway. If, on the other hand, one had used different current levels and behavioral procedures in which differences in shaping would occur from animal to animal, one might be less secure in drawing this conclusion.

anatomical methods described here, does not usually contain the restricted or localized lesion that can be of particular value in providing a limited set of alternative fiber systems which can then be considered candidate substrates of ICSS. In addition, observation of the trajectory of the axonal systems with one's own set of anatomical material often reveals interesting associations not previously described in the related anatomical material simply because the purposes of such an experiment were somewhat different from those used here. In particular, one is continually looking for points along the axonal trajectory which overlap with ICSS sites that have been described with mapping procedures. In our view, then, the technique of making lesions at ICSS sites and using anatomical methods to determine the ICSS-associated pathways is of considerable value in providing a list of candidate pathways that may be associated with intracranial self-stimulation, which, in turn, provides a stepping stone for proving the association of a particular fiber system with intracranial self-stimulation. To determine which of these pathways may be important to ICSS, we proceed to the third step of our three-stage approach of attempting to prove the necessity of a particular fiber system for ICSS by using a brain-lesion technique to eliminate that behavior.

2.3. Brain Lesions Which Eliminate Self-Stimulation

This experimental approach logically follows the first two paradigms and represents the final proof experiment for evaluation of the fiber pathways which are essential to ICSS. We have emphasized in the previous section that the fiber pathways that are described by anatomical methods can only be said to be *associated* with ICSS, but their necessity must be shown by another set of procedures. We think that the approach to this problem is to run animals on a rigid behavioral testing procedure for intracranial self-stimulation, and then make lesions at the suspected cell bodies of origin of the axonal system under study and observe the consequences of that lesion on self-stimulation. If only one system is involved and one has identified the cell bodies of origin, then it should be the case that the destruction of those cell bodies should substantially eliminate ICSS at points of the map associated with this pathway. Should such a result obtain, it would not mean that all ICSS was derived only from this fiber system or that it is essential for self-stimulation at all locations. But it would mean that this particular fiber system is an essential component. One could evaluate whether it was an essential component to all ICSS by observing the consequences of similar lesions with electrodes placed at a variety of other ICSS locations.

2.4. Summary

The present section has detailed some of the logic of a three-stage paradigm and the procedures to be used to achieve a description of the anatomy of intracranial self-stimulation. In the first stage, a map of the region is produced; in the second stage, pathways from ICSS sites are described. In the third stage, lesions are made at the presumed cell bodies of origin to modify ICSS at sites along the axonal trajectory of these cells. An attempt has been made to avoid reference to particular anatomical issues, since these general views are applied in subsequent sections of this chapter to particular problems which we have encountered. In addition, the present approach may be applied to problems other than ICSS, where localization is of major import.

In historical perspective it may be appreciated that we have evolved in our criterion for what represents sufficient localization of the ICSS effect. The evolution has gone from the specification of the spheres of influence of ICSS to the cells and their processes which are involved. Such an evolution also provides an anatomical basis for evaluation of drug effects on ICSS behavior.*

3. DEFINING THE INPUT AND OUTPUT IN ICSS

3.1. The Nature of the Wiring Diagram

In the preceding section we have discussed techniques for describing the fiber pathways associated with ICSS and the ways in which one might prove the essentiality to ICSS of particular fiber pathways. Such an approach, based on an assumption concerning the nature of wiring in brain, may have some serious limitations. This assumption briefly states that there exists a circuit or

---

* Anatomically specific drug effects on ICSS: One of the principal difficulties with the data on the role of particular transmitters of ICSS has been the evaluation of the consequences to ICSS of peripheral injections of pharmacological agents. These experiments have not been the only ones performed, but there is always considerable difficulty in attempting to evaluate these results since a variety of peripheral or nonspecific central effects may lead to the results obtained. In particular, it has been extremely difficult to associate the application of a drug given parenterally to its influence on a particular brain region. It is certainly misleading to assume that the drug acts exclusively at the region being stimulated by the electrode. It is possible, for example, that the drug is acting on another system, peripheral or central, and then acts or interacts with the electrical stimulation to produce the observed effect. We think it is now possible, given our understanding of the specification of the fiber pathways involved in ICSS, to achieve a greater specificity in the understanding of the application of drugs to an animal with regard to its effect on ICSS. As we know more concerning these fiber pathways, it should be possible to show that the direct manipulation of the transmitter either at the cell body or at the terminals by chemical injection methods (Routtenberg, 1972) will have specific effects on intracranial self-stimulation and that subsequent removal of that drug will be accompanied by specific recovery of intracranial self-stimulation. With little specific information we had begun such an approach several years ago (Routtenberg and Olds, 1966). Anatomically more appropriate studies have recently appeared (Lippa *et al.*, 1973).

a set of pathways connected together which support ICSS and these pathways are connected in some sequence so that they can be interrupted at a certain point. The effect of interruption would be logically the cessation of ICSS. But such an assumption may be incorrect since it is based, in some sense, on the approach used to describe the anatomy and physiology of the visual system. We have no reason to believe that the model of the visual system that is currently used is the appropriate one for the model of limbic-midbrain subcortical mechanisms of intracranial self-stimulation. It is convenient, however, to consider this model as a reasonable first choice.

Consider the following situation: Self-stimulation is supported by two groups of cell bodies which are reciprocally connected and whose axons overlap through most of their trajectory. While there will be some problems in identifying and separating the two, lesions at one point will interrupt ICSS at another point. Similarly, if we have a circuit of neurons which feeds back ultimately on itself, interruption of that circuit at any point should eliminate ICSS. But the problem arises when we have several fiber pathways which are not intimately dependent one on the other, but rather interdigitate at particular locations and diverge and converge at other locations. In such a case, an association with ICSS (second stage) will be extremely difficult to extend to the point of specifying the fiber pathway (third stage). For example, in the model presented in Fig. 1, there are several pathways having no known synaptic interaction but are related to each other only in a spatial sense. If these systems operate independently, their association may be no

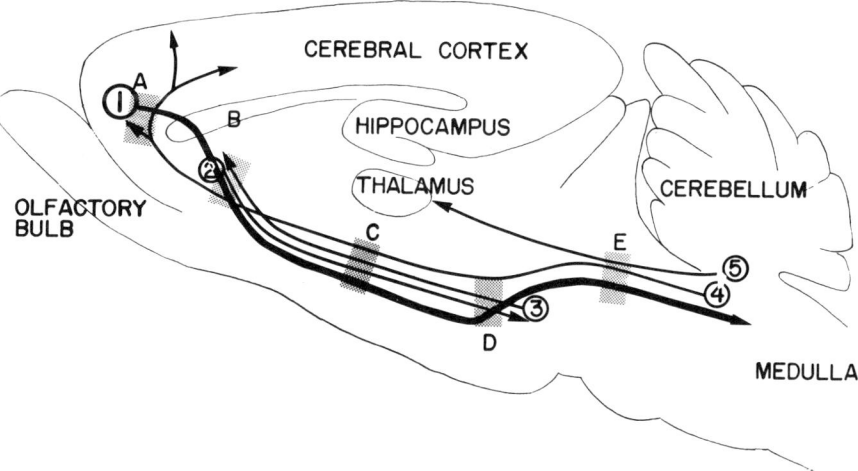

FIG. 1. A schematic summary of pathways that have been associated with ICSS (Routtenberg, 1976b). Numbers 1 to 5 are the cell bodies or origin of these pathways: (1) frontal cortex; (2) caudate nucleus; (3) substantia nigra; (4) locus coeruleus; (5) subcortical cerebellar nuclei. Letters A to E are known ICSS sites: (A) frontal cortex; (B) caudate nucleus; (C) medial forebrain bundle; (D) substantia nigra, pars compacta; (E) dorsal tegmental (peribrachial) region.

different than a line tangent to a curve. Considerable difficulty in the analysis of the fiber pathways critical to self-stimulation will then be present. Although the task appears formidable, it may be possible to determine the relative involvement of each pathway by use of the techniques outlined in the previous section. The results obtained to date have already shown some progress in this regard.

3.2. The Definition of Input and Output

Another difficulty which may impede the progress of specification of the fiber systems involved in ICSS may be related to the input that is used and the output measured. It can be argued that self-stimulation input will remain nonspecific as long as a multiple set of fiber pathways are revealed by electrical stimulation and lesion techniques described earlier.* The problem of nonspecificity of output arises because ICSS can be demonstrated by a variety of instrumental responses, the most common of which is lever pressing. Since the stimulation does not lead to a specific observable behavior, such as, for example, in drinking, to be discussed in the following paragraph, output must be defined in terms which are applicable to the variations of instrumental behavior for obtaining brain stimulation. Thus, the problem of output may be stated in the form of a question: What neural mechanisms need be activated for an animal to perform any one of a variety of responses for brain stimulation?

3.3. Anatomical Localization of Sites Eliciting Drinking by Carbachol and Angiotensin II: The Advantages of Defined Input and Output

It will be seen that though the localization of ICSS mechanisms has improved and been narrowed down, we still cannot state, with any confidence, what precisely are the cells and axons which support ICSS. This may be contrasted with a recent series of studies in this laboratory which has shown that the subfornical organ is the site of action of drinking induced by intracranial injection of carbachol, (Routtenberg and Simpson, 1971; Simpson and Routtenberg, 1972), acetylcholine (Simpson and Routtenberg, 1974), and angiotensin-II (Simpson and Routtenberg, 1973, 1975): In sum, as noted

---

* Recourse to recent anatomical methods which are more specific, such as autoradiographic tracing (Lasek *et al.*, 1968) or retrograde tracing (LaVail and LaVail, 1972), would give only a misleading specificity since the electrical stimulus will influence both axons and cell bodies, whereas presumably with autoradiographic tracing methods, for example, only those pathways from cell bodies will be traced.

by Severs and Summy-Long (1975),

> Simpson and Routtenberg (1973) originally provided evidence that the subfornical organ (SFO) was a site of angiotensin's dipsogenic action. An expanding literature strongly supports this opinion. The following data are noteworthy: (A) The threshold dose for angiotensin-induced drinking after injection into the subfornical organ is at least an order of magnitude lower than any other site or route of peptide administration. (B) Units in the SFO respond to iontophoretic application of angiotensin. (C) Subfornical lesions reduce angiotensin drinking when the peptide is given into the diencephalon, cerebroventricles, or intravenously (pp. 1519–1520).

While some uncertainty exists with regard to the exclusive role of the subfornical organ (see Severs and Summy-Long, 1975; Buggy et al., 1975; Nicolaïdis and Fitzsimons, 1975), we have been able to achieve a better anatomical specification in the case of drinking than in the case of the anatomy of ICSS. Part of the reason for this may lie in the specificity of the input and output of the system under study. Once it was recognized that chemical injection was spreading from sites of application to other sites (Routtenberg, 1967; Routtenberg et al., 1968; Routtenberg and Bondareff, 1969; Bondareff et al., 1970; Bondareff et al., 1971), the search for alternative locations reached via the ventricles (Routtenberg, 1967) or the vasculature (Routtenberg, 1972) was initiated. Thus, like electrical stimulation, the input could be acting at several sites; unlike electrical stimulation, however, the chemical could be expected to act at only a specific set of receptors. The electrical stimulus, it can be easily seen, is unlikely to achieve such selectivity. In sum, the chemical input, once its liabilities are recognized, may be considered more specific than the electrical stimulus.

With respect to output, it is clear that drinking behavior is quite a bit more specific than ICSS behavior; i.e., imbibing water requires a certain specific set of motor components which must be used to achieve intake of water. To achieve brain stimulation, in contrast, an animal can press a lever with his paw, press a button with his finger, poke his nose through a hole, increase or decrease his heart rate, locomote from one side of a tilt cage to another, run down an alley, or stand perfectly still. In short, the subject has to perform an activity specified by the experimenter. It is possible, then, to have the animal obtain brain stimulation with motor activities that have little in common.

I believe that the above considerations illustrate the difficulty with achieving specificity of output with the study of ICSS. The problem does not end simply with the variety of motor outputs that may be contemplated, but one is also forced to consider the variety of neural mechanisms which will be required as determinants of that output. Comparison with the literature on body fluid regulation, again, indicates that there are probably only two major determinants of primary thirst (Epstein et al., 1973), suggesting a far less complicated set of neural mechanisms which will be responsible for the drinking output.

If our analysis is valid, then it will be necessary to take steps to achieve specificity of both input and output in the ICSS paradigm in order to determine the cells and their processes which account for ICSS.

3.4. Some Preliminary Attempts at Solution

Realizing the value of defining the input and output in our work on drinking, we have attempted to reduce the nonspecificity of input and output in our ICSS work. Thus, on the input side we have attempted to use a lower current level and a finer electrode wire to attenuate the problem of the nonspecificity of the electrical stimulus by simply stimulating fewer fibers. It has been our impression that finer electrode wires and lower current levels consistently give less ambiguous anatomical information with respect to mapping. With the use of larger electrodes ICSS is obtained from one electrode at point a but not from another electrode in another animal at the same point. The reason for such differences, although still undiscovered, could be potentially quite important, since it points to several unknown factors related to the ICSS input. In this regard, it is well to recall the pioneering studies of Olds *et al.* (1964), in which they had rats self-inject neurochemicals into the hypothalamus, in an attempt to define the neurochemical or neurohumoral transmitters involved in ICSS. With the advantage of considerably more information concerning ICSS anatomy, it now appears that the choice of the hypothalamus may not have been the most strategic. This self-injection approach, however, might be quite fruitful if used again in other brain regions where the presynaptic terminals and postsynaptic receptors and their transmitter chemistry are known. It seems possible that such an approach could provide a suitable basis for study of ICSS with the use of a defined input.

We have attempted to reduce the potential nonspecificity on the output side by simplifying our behavioral training method. Thus, the rigid behavioral testing procedure we employ complicates less the interpretation of our results, though, as can be well understood, this is a relative gain and hardly an absolute one.*

---

* Specificity of the output is complicated as much by the behavioral testing procedures used as by the theory upon which these behavioral tests are based. Thus, the concept that the fiber pathways that are being studied are those that support reward, reinforcement, and pleasure suggests the possibility that there would be a considerable number of anatomical pathways that would support ICSS behavior. One approach to this problem is to ask the question, "Is there some other, perhaps more specific, function that can be attributed to the fiber pathways which support self-stimulation?" The answer to that question is of course not known. It has been speculated (Routtenberg, 1975a; Routtenberg, 1975b) that these fiber pathways may be important in memory consolidation, i.e., that activity in these fiber pathways forms the basis of the memory consolidation process. While it may be argued that this redefinition of the output of the fiber pathways is no more specific than reinforcement or reward, it does provide an alternative definition which may be of value in delimiting the fiber pathways involved. In addition, one might use both the definition that

4. THE CENTRAL ROLE OF THE FRONTAL CORTEX IN ICSS

In this section we illustrate the application of the approach outlined above which we have used over the past few years. In particular, it is worth emphasizing that we have progressed from the definition of the anatomy of ICSS exclusively on the basis of mapping data, and are moving inexorably toward a definition of the specific fiber pathways involved in self-stimulation. We would suspect that by the end of this decade a rather firm picture of the major fiber pathways which support ICSS will be gained.

In this section, then, we shall discuss some specific experiments that follow the logic of the three-stage approach in the context of particular brain regions under study.

The self-stimulation effect was characterized as being most prominent in the lateral hypothalamus, along the medial forebrain bundle (Olds, 1962). Here the highest rates of bar pressing for the lowest current levels were discerned; more anterior and posterior electrode locations most often resulted in attenuation of the effect. Hence, the lateral hypothalamus became known as the focus of the ICSS system, and this was the system which was studied in detail. While it was comprehensible then to study lateral hypothalamic self-stimulation, it now appears strategic, from an anatomical point of view, to study the fiber pathways which perforate through the hypothalamus (Routtenberg, 1975a). The reason for this became obvious as it was discovered that the cell bodies of origin of the ICSS fibers in the lateral hypothalamus were located primarily outside the hypothalamus. It was not possible, then, to obtain more than several initial clues to the fiber systems when we made lesions at ICSS sites in the lateral hypothalamus itself (Huang and Routtenberg, 1971). Although these results did present a survey of the fiber pathways involved, a better lead on this problem was gained when we began to study the brainstem (Routtenberg and Malsbury, 1969) and anterior forebrain (Routtenberg, 1970) mechanisms of ICSS. These were two lines of research that were proceeding concurrently in this laboratory. Although brainstem and forebrain have in the past not been associated with one another, we believe that present information suggests that the brainstem mechanisms which have been studied in some detail may be related to forebrain mechanisms in the prefrontal cortex. In this section, then, we discuss brainstem ICSS mechanisms; in the next section we discuss the

---

these pathways are involved in reward processes and memory processes, conjointly, to achieve an analysis based on converging behavioral operations. One can determine, then, those fiber pathways which both support ICSS and which are involved in memory consolidation processes. Perhaps such a definition will give a more restricted set of fiber pathways. It should be emphasized that ultimately the goal here is the characterization of the input and output, not of ICSS systems *per se*, but of the pathways which support ICSS.

frontal cortical ICSS system, and in the final section we discuss the relation of the brainstem system to the frontal cortical system.

4.1. Initial Map of the Brainstem for ICSS: Dubious Role of the Locus Coeruleus

Because of the paucity of information in both brainstem and cerebral cortex, this laboratory began to question the view that ICSS should be considered as primarily centered about lateral hypothalamic mechanisms. It was in this context that we began to explore regions posterior to the hypothalamus, first with a mapping experiment. We used one current level and one behavioral testing procedure so as to increase our chances of making reasonable comparisons among brain regions. This study (Routtenberg and Malsbury, 1969) indicated that (a) ICSS could be obtained from sites posterior to the hypothalamus, (b) the sites were not ones which were readily associated with ICSS, (c) at the level of the midbrain, ICSS was observed in the substantia nigra, (d) although placements in this region had been described earlier, no emphasis had been placed on the extrapyramidal-motor nature, rather than limbic nature, of such structures, and (e) ICSS was obtained from electrodes placed in the superior cerebellar peduncle (brachium conjunctivum), the output of the cerebellum. We also found that electrodes along the ascending portion of this peduncle would support ICSS. This tended to give credence to the idea that the brachium was involved in ICSS. In addition, we made lesions at such ICSS sites and, not too surprisingly, we found degeneration using the Nauta (1957) method along the brachium. The trajectory of the axonal system observed overlapped with those sites where we had discovered ICSS. We concluded, then, that the brachium conjunctivum represented a new ICSS fiber pathway.

This conclusion was questioned by Fuxe and Lindbrink (1970) who suggested that certain of the brachium placements where we had obtained ICSS may have overlapped with the dorsal norepinephrine bundle (Ungerstedt, 1971). This alternative hypothesis was certainly not unreasonable, although there were some ICSS points which did not appear to be that close to the dorsal norepinephrine bundle (German and Bowden, 1974).

It seemed reasonable, however, to evaluate this suggestion and subsequent statements of that same issue by Crow et al. (1972), Ritter and Stein (1973), and German and Bowden (1974) by making lesions at ICSS sites in the brachium conjunctivum and following this with histochemical fluorescence of that region. Clavier and I (1974) reasoned that, if ICSS were derived from the dorsal norepinephrine bundle, then all lesions at brainstem ICSS sites should be accompanied by buildup in this norepinephrine bundle. At sites where no ICSS was obtained, buildup may or may not be demonstrated, since in these studies it is possible that the field of stimulation may be less than the extent of the lesion. In this study, then, we did find that use of a larger electrode and a small lesion gave clearer results than use of a smaller electrode and a larger lesion, since with a larger lesion we would likely be damaging considerably more than the field of stimulation.

Clavier and Routtenberg (1974) found that, as suggested, all sites which gave rise to ICSS yielded buildup in the dorsal norepinephrine bundle. Sites which did not yield ICSS at times did not have buildup in the dorsal norepinephrine bundle. It was our conclusion, then, that the norepinephrine bundle was indeed associated with ICSS. These results did not, of course, rule out the possibility that brachium conjunctivum plays an important role in ICSS.

It was clear to us, however, that one further study was required, namely, to destroy the cell bodies of origin of the dorsal norepinephrine bundle, the locus coeruleus, and to observe the effect on ICSS derived from the so-called brachium conjunctivum ICSS location. This is what Clavier set out to do for his doctoral dissertation, fully expecting to severely attenuate ICSS by a locus coeruleus lesion. A perusal of his dissertation proposal indicates how certain he was that such an event would occur.

Clavier discovered, to *our* surprise, that locus coeruleus lesions did not attenuate ICSS from brachium conjunctivum locations that were within or immediately adjacent to the dorsal norepinephrine bundle. Such lesions reduced norepinephrine levels by 85% in the cerebral cortex, with little or no effect on ICSS (Clavier and Routtenberg, 1976a). Such results may not be welcomed by workers who have associated the locus coeruleus with intracranial self-stimulation (Crow et al., 1972; Ritter and Stein, 1973). We have other data (Amaral and Routtenberg, 1975) which indicate that ICSS is not particularly easy to obtain from the locus coeruleus, using our rigid testing procedures. We believe, therefore, that the data that we have gathered to date indicate that the locus coeruleus may not be an essential substrate for ICSS* at our brachium site and that other pathways, not detected by the Falck–Hillarp method, must be given consideration. We feel that such a conclusion is warranted since it is based on a sequence of experiments involving three separate procedures: first, mapping of the region; second,

---

* In the context of describing the self-stimulation pathways as having functions related to memory consolidation (Routtenberg, 1975b), it is interesting that Anlezark et al. (1973) have shown that lesions of the locus coeruleus impair learning in a runway situation. Such results have not, however, been repeated by Amaral and Foss (1975), using essentially the same type of procedure. In addition, Santos-Anderson and Routtenberg (1976) did not obtain disruptive effects by direct stimulation of the locus coeruleus during a one-trial learning situation, a situation in which we have demonstrated disruption when the stimulation is applied to the medial amygdala (Bresnahan and Routtenberg, 1972), substantia nigra, pars compacta (Routtenberg and Holzman, 1973), and prefrontal cortex (Santos-Anderson and Routtenberg, 1976). Thus, the involvement of the locus coeruleus both in ICSS and in learning and memory has been questioned (Routtenberg, 1976a). One might suggest, then, that the functional role of the locus coeruleus has not been described and that at present some controversy exists. It will be of considerable interest to renew the search for the functional importance of the locus coeruleus as a substrate for behavior.

lesions in coordination with anatomical techniques; and third, lesions at the cell body of origin of the suspected fiber system to evaluate its essentiality to self-stimulation. Finally, other laboratories have reported difficulties in demonstrating ICSS in locus coeruleus (Simon *et al.*, 1975) and attenuating ICSS with locus coeruleus lesions (Koob *et al.*, 1976).

Alternative interpretations to such negative findings have been discussed elsewhere (Routtenberg, 1975a; Amaral and Routtenberg, 1975; Clavier and Routtenberg, 1976a), which may yet allow for an essential role in ICSS of the locus coeruleus. Nonetheless, the evidence to date from our laboratory must be viewed as quite negative with respect to locus coeruleus involvement. We believe that the effects on brachium ICSS, which we have obtained following lesions of other brain regions, to be discussed below, indicate a different conception of the ICSS effect and point to a new approach for the integration of self-stimulation anatomy.

The following positive effect of lesions was obtained: Lateral medial forebrain bundle (MFB) destruction caused a marked reduction in ICSS in the brachium conjunctivum region (Clavier and Routtenberg, 1976a). Such a result may be interpreted in relation to the data of Huang and Routtenberg (1971), who showed that lesions at lateral hypothalamic ICSS sites give rise to degeneration which perforated through the brachium conjunctivum at the ICSS region used by Clavier. Thus, it seems possible that the lesions of the MFB are interrupting a descending system from the hypothalamus or, perhaps, more anterior structures. We have not ruled out the involvement or projection of an ascending system, since lesions at brainstem sites of self-stimulation followed by a Fink–Heimer study indicate the presence of degeneration going through the MFB (Clavier and Routtenberg, 1976b). Thus, it is possible that this fiber system, detected by the Fink–Heimer method to ascend through the MFB, may contribute to the effects of such lesions on brachium conjunctivum ICSS. We think it is reasonable to ascribe some portion of the effect to a descending system as well, which has, in fact, been demonstrated by Huang and Routtenberg (1971). In the next section we shall discuss the origins of this descending system.

4.2. ICSS in Frontal Cortex: Medial and Sulcal Cortex

The study of the brainstem indicated that locations distant from the lateral hypothalamus were capable of supporting ICSS. A similar conclusion was drawn from data obtained during exploration of frontal cortex for ICSS. ICSS from anterior forebrain was first described in the Olds' laboratory (Olds and Olds, 1963). If one looked at the map of Olds and Olds (1963), there are placements which are indeed anterior (Plate 3). These anterior placements were close to the septal area and were mistakenly identified as part of the septal area (Routtenberg and Olds, 1963, 1966). Valenstein and Campbell (1966) reported ICSS placements in this anterior region. But it was clear, particularly after the anatomical report of Leonard (1969), that many of our placements were in medial frontal cortex, a region which receives projections from, and sends projections to, the dorsomedial thalamus. These findings suggested, then, that this region was part of the frontal cortex in analogy with the dorsomedial thalamic connections of the primate.

A systematic study of the frontal cortex was carried out (Routtenberg, 1970), first with ICSS mapping and then with lesions at ICSS sites. The first fact noted was that we obtained ICSS from the most anterior regions of the forebrain that had been reported up to that time. Our ICSS points were clustered primarily in the medial portions of the frontal cortex, although this conclusion was rather limited, since we had not explored all of the frontal cortex. It was found, however, that dorsomedial and dorsolateral placements did not support ICSS. In this study it was also shown that ICSS was obtained from the caudate/putamen complex.

Lesions were then made at ICSS sites in frontal cortex, and the pathways were traced using the Fink–Heimer method (Routtenberg, 1970). The projection of the axons from frontal cortex was most interesting since they perforated through the caudate/putamen complex and occupied a position in the lateral edge of the medial forebrain bundle. Perhaps because our lesions were small, we could not trace the degeneration further than the posterior parts of the hypothalamus, but other data (Harting and Martin, 1970; Leonard, 1969) suggest that the fiber pathway does extend into the midbrain. Perhaps the most interesting finding of that study was the location of the axons within the lateral edge of the medial forebrain bundle (or the medial edge of the internal capsule). It was suggested, indeed, that ICSS from the medial forebrain bundle may have been derived, in part, from stimulation of the axons of frontal cortex cell bodies.

We explored the frontal cortex for ICSS in its ventral and lateral portions and discovered a second location in the lateral edge of the frontal cortex, above the rhinal sulcus, an area usually referred to as sulcal cortex, in which ICSS could be demonstrated (Routtenberg and Sloan, 1972). It again was of great interest that this region was the only other location which the dorsomedial thalamus projected to and also which projected, reciprocally, to the dorsomedial thalamus (Leonard, 1969). Additionally, it was shown that the sulcal cortex projected caudally through the lateral edge of the medial forebrain bundle down into the brainstem (Leonard, 1969).

These results indicated that the frontal cortex may play a quite important role in ICSS. A recent series of studies by Edmund Rolls has extended considerably these initial findings and further supports the idea that the frontal cortex plays a vital role in intracranial self-stimulation. In addition, his electrophysiological results suggest an integration of our findings in brainstem with the data gathered in the frontal cortex. Rolls and Cooper (1973) showed that during self-stimulation in lateral hypothalamus, midbrain tegmentum, or the nucleus accumbens, prefrontal cortex neurons were activated, probably antidromically. In addition, such neurons were not activated by stimulation at non-ICSS sites. In a second study in which ICSS sites near the locus coeruleus were studied, it was found that neurons in the prefrontal cortex were antidromically activated. Rolls and Cooper (1974a) indicated that activation of prefrontal neurons by electrodes in the dorsal tegmentum in the region of the locus coeruleus suggests the possibility that the noradrenaline-containing neurons in the locus coeruleus may not be essential for ICSS. This, of course, is consistent with our view (Clavier and Routtenberg, 1976a) discussed earlier. Rolls and Cooper (1974b) have performed the third portion of the three-step procedure outlined before (Section 2) by making reversible lesions of frontal cortex, injecting procaine into the sulcal cortex, and observing its effect on hypothalamic and locus coeruleus ICSS. They have found, indeed, that local anesthetization of sulcal cortex produced a decrease in rate and an increase in threshold for ICSS. Injections into the medial cortex were ineffective. This study, which is of considerable relevance to the present hypothesis, requires replication since the cannula placements which gave rise to attenuation are somewhat medial to the sulcal cortex. In addition, a detailed quantitative study of the effect of procaine injection would be desirable. Finally, the possible nonspecific effects of the injection are of some concern, since unilateral injections had no effect on ICSS, though the evidence that we have obtained (Routtenberg, 1970) indicates a unilateral projection from the site of stimulation down into the hypothalamus. It is possible, therefore, that the ICSS blockade is not specific and is related to some more general action which would affect other behavioral measures as well.

It should be pointed out, nonetheless, that the Rolls and Cooper findings follow the suggested paradigm of experimental procedure, albeit with a somewhat different method than described earlier. It was not necessary for them to perform extensive mapping since it had been done earlier (Routtenberg, 1970; Routtenberg and Sloan, 1972). They traced the pathways from the frontal cortex, using electrophysiological methods, which indicated *association* between the sulcal cortex and brainstem ICSS sites. Finally, they lesioned reversibly the sulcal prefrontal cortex and attenuated ICSS. Such a series of findings strongly supports the view (Routtenberg, 1970) that the frontal cortex plays an important role in ICSS.

One study that places considerable limitations on the just-stated conclusion has been reported by Huston and Borbély (1973). Briefly, they have shown that radical forebrain ablations, so-called partial decerebrations, do not influence the learning of a tail lift or head lift response, reinforced by posterior hypothalamic brain stimulation. These findings raise difficulties for a theory which states that the frontal cortex is critically involved in maintaining ICSS, since the entire frontal cortex was removed. It can be pointed out that the stimulation electrode locations in these experiments are somewhat dorsal to the medial forebrain bundle, and in one case (subject No. 5), its location is dorsomedial. What role the electrode tip locations play cannot be stated, though this may have some bearing on the result. It is to be emphasized that the entire frontal cortex, as well as the remaining cerebral cortex, was no longer intact. Since the animals were tested one day after the lesion, success in conditioning cannot be attributed to reorganization based on the time course of brain plasticity (Raisman, 1969; Lynch et al., 1973). Thus, it seems more likely that other brain structures must play a role. One candidate, in particular, deserves mention, and that is the dorsomedial thalamus. Keene and Casey (1973) have shown that the dorsomedial thalamus responds to rewarding and aversive brain stimulation with physiologically different responses. This is particularly important since Millhouse (1969) has shown that the path neurons extend dorsally from the hypothalamic region of the medial forebrain bundle to the dorsomedial thalamus. Guillery (1959) also described hypothalamic-dorsomedial thalamic connections. Since lesions of the thalamus do not appear to affect hypothalamic self-stimulation (Asdourian et al., 1966), it is reasonable to conclude that the hypothalamus can support ICSS in the absence of the dorsomedial thalamus.

5. RELATION OF FRONTAL CORTEX TO BRAINSTEM SELF-STIMULATION

In this section we propose a summary and integration of existing data with the model shown in Fig. 1 which focuses attention on the prefrontal cortex as both the head end of the ICSS system and the brain region whose axonal trajectory perforates through many ICSS loci throughout the neuraxis. Frontal cortex connections with the dorsomedial thalamus (Leonard, 1969) bestows on it wide access to both sensory and motor cerebral cortical structures. In addition, its projection to the caudate nucleus provides another interface with cerebral cortical brain regions (Kemp and Powell, 1971a, 1971b). Finally, prefrontal cortex projects through the caudate nucleus and lateral hypothalamus (Routtenberg, 1970), and through the substantia nigra (Leonard, 1969), perforating through the brachium conjunctivum, as well, in this descending course (Huang and Routtenberg, 1971; Leonard, 1969). The possibility that this system does project through the locus coeruleus has also been suggested (Rolls and Cooper, 1974a). Figure 1 shows how five well-established self-stimulation regions (designated A–E) attained by mapping can be related directly to the frontal cortical descending fiber system. It is worth noting that the set of ICSS points which German and Bowden (1974) have collated and then associated with the ascending brainstem catecholamine systems may be just as readily associated with this descending frontal system.*

---

* It should be pointed out that the catecholamine involvement in self-stimulation is not denied insofar as the involvement of the substantia nigra and caudate nucleus is suspected, both with regard to self-stimulation placements (e.g., Routtenberg and Malsbury, 1969) and with regard to the effects of 6-hydroxydopamine on self-stimulation (Lippa et al., 1973; Stinus et al., 1975).

In this model of the five fiber systems selected, three or four are depicted as coursing through each of the ICSS regions. If more than one of these systems are important to ICSS at a particular site, but are not functionally connected to one another, it is not difficult to understand why a lesion restricted to one of the systems will not eliminate self-stimulation. On the other hand, other systems may only be *associated* with an ICSS site but are not important to sustain the behavior. One can readily see from this diagram, if the prefrontal system is critical, how lesions in the lateral hypothalamic-medial forebrain bundle area would have a major effect on self-stimulation in the region of the brachium conjunctivum and the locus coeruleus, while neither the brachium or the dorsal norepinephrine bundle would play a major role in self-stimulation (Clavier and Routtenberg, 1975*a*).

6. SUMMARY

The present review has focused on the intracranial self-stimulation effect initially reported by Olds and Milner (1954) as an example of a motivational system whose detailed anatomy is in the process of being characterized. The major point of this review is to indicate the necessity for detailed study of the anatomical aspects of self-stimulation and that merely knowing the location of the electrode tip is not sufficient for characterization of the substrate of intracranial self-stimulation. A sequence of techniques is proposed to give a relatively firm answer as to the pathways serving as substrate for self-stimulation. A three-stage paradigm was presented: mapping, anatomy following lesions at ICSS sites, and ICSS following lesions at cell bodies of origin. The value of specifying the anatomy in the context of psychopharmacological manipulations was indicated. Difficulties in specifying the pathways are discussed, particularly with regard to definition of the input that is the electrical stimulus, and the output that is the reward. It is suggested that the nonspecificity of the input and the variability of the output and its antecedents may present one source of difficulty in reaching the goal of describing the anatomy of self-stimulation.

Specific examples of attempts to describe pathways of self-stimulation focused on brainstem and purported involvement of the locus coeruleus in ICSS. This laboratory has collected data which question this involvement with regard to self-stimulation. A second system which we have investigated, the frontal cortex, was discussed with regard to the importance of this system in self-stimulation. The understanding of self-stimulation has been advanced by moving from the sites where the highest rates of self-stimulation (the most intense behavior) have been demonstrated to the putative cell bodies or origin. We have been studying these systems at locations both in the brainstem and in the most anterior regions of frontal cortex. Finally, an attempt is made to show how frontal cortex and brainstem self-stimulation may be related, and a tentative heuristic anatomical model is presented which summarizes the available facts. Given that several laboratories are working on the problem of localization, it is expected that the model will be suitably evaluated.

In the perspective of the first 20 years of intracranial self-stimulation, it can be readily seen that a considerable amount of information has been accumulated with regard to the sites of self-stimulation, and a beginning is now being made in collating sites and reducing them to a simplifying heuristic, such as is presented in Fig. 1. It is hoped that this type of approach will provide a meaningful organization of the pathways of intracranial self-stimulation leading to a more easily approached system for questions concerning the specific analytic function of these fiber pathways.

7. REFERENCES

AMARAL, D. G., and FOSS, J. A., 1975, Locus coeruleus lesions in learning, *Science* **188**:377–378.
AMARAL, D. G., and ROUTTENBERG, A., 1975, Locus coeruleus and intracranial self-stimulation: a cautionary note, *Behav. Biol.* **13**:331–338.
ANLEZARK, G. M., CROW, T. J., and GREENWAY, A. P., 1973, Impaired learning and decreased cortical norepinephrine after bilateral locus coeruleus lesions, *Science* **181**:682–684.
ASDOURIAN, D., STUTZ, R. M., and ROCKLIN, K. W., 1966, Effects of thalamic and limbic system lesions on self-stimulation, *J. Comp. Physiol. Psychol.* **61**:468–472.
BONDAREFF, W., NAROTZKY, R., and ROUTTENBERG, A., 1971, Intrastriatal spread of catecholamines in senescent rats, *J. Gerontol.* **26**:163–167.
BONDAREFF, W., ROUTTENBERG, A., NAROTZKY, R., and MCLONE, D. G., 1970, Intrastriatal spreading of biogenic amines, *Exp. Neurol.* **28**:213–229.
BRESNAHAN, E., and ROUTTENBERG, A., 1972, Memory disruption by unilateral, low-level, sub-seizure stimulation of the medial amygdaloid nucleus, *Physiol. Behav.* **9**:513–525.
BUGGY, J., FISHER, A. E., HOFFMAN, W. E., JOHNSON, A. K., and PHILLIPS, M. I., 1975, Ventricular obstruction: effect on drinking induced by intracranial injection of angiotensin, *Science* **190**:72–74
CLAVIER, R. M., 1973, Ascending monoamine-containing fiber pathways related to intracranial self-stimulation: histochemical fluorescence study, unpublished master's thesis, Northwestern University, Evanston, Illinois.
CLAVIER, R. M., 1974, Ascending catecholamine fiber systems and brainstem intracranial self-stimulation, unpublished doctoral dissertation, Northwestern University, Evanston, Illinois.
CLAVIER, R. M., and ROUTTENBERG, A., 1974, Ascending monoamine-containing fiber pathways related to intracranial self-stimulation: histochemical fluorescence study, *Brain Res.* **72**:25–40.
CLAVIER, R. M., and ROUTTENBERG, A., 1976a, Brainstem self-stimulation attenuated by lesions of medial forebrain bundle but not by lesions of locus coeruleus or caudal ventral norepinephrine bundle, *Brain Res.* **101**:251–271.
CLAVIER, R. M., and ROUTTENBERG, A., 1976b, Fibers associated with brainstem self-stimulation: Fink–Heimer study, *Brain Res.* **105**:325–323.
CROW, T. J., SPEAR, P. J., and ARBUTHNOTT, G. W., 1972, Intracranial self-stimulation with electrodes in the region of the locus coeruleus, *Brain Res.* **36**:275–287.

DRESSE, A., 1966, Importance du système mesencephalo-telencephalique noradrenergique comme substratum anatomique du comportement d'autostimulation, *Life Sci.* **5**:1003–1014.

EPSTEIN, A. N., KISSELEFF, H. R., and STELLAR, E., 1973, *The Neuropsychology of Thirst*, Winston, Washington, D.C.

FALCK, B., HILLARP, N.-A., THIEME, G., and TORP, A., 1962, Fluorescence of catecholamines and related compounds condensed with formaldehyde, *J. Histochem. Cytochem.* **10**:348–354.

FINK, R. P., and HEIMER, L., 1967, Two methods for selective silver impregnation of degenerating axons, and their synaptic endings in the central nervous system, *Brain Res.* **4**:369–374.

FUXE, K., and LINDBRINK, P., 1970, On the function of central catecholamine neurons—their role in cardiovascular and arousal mechanisms, paper presented at the Congress on the Pharmacology and Physiology of Monoamines in the Central Nervous System, Palo Alto, California.

GERMAN, D. C., and BOWDEN, D. M., 1974, Catecholamine systems as the neural substrate for intracranial stimulation: an hypothesis, *Brain Res.* **73**:381–419.

GUILLERY, R. W., 1959, Afferent fibers to the dorsomedial thalamic nucleus in the cat, *J. Anat.* **93**:403–419.

HARTING, J. K., and MARTIN, G. F., 1970, Neocortical projections to the mesencephalon of the armadillo, *Dasypus novemcinctus*, *Brain Res.* **17**:447–462.

HESS, W. R., 1942, Die stimulations-eliminations-degenerations-Methode in der Hirnforschung, *Verh. Ver. Schweiz. Physiol.*, Juni. Cited by Hess, W. R., 1957, in: *The Functional Organization of the Diencephalon* (J. R. Hughes, ed.), Grune and Stratton, New York.

HUANG, Y. H., and ROUTTENBERG, A., 1971, Lateral hypothalamic self-stimulation pathways in *Rattus norvegicus*, *Physiol. Behav.* **7**:419–432.

HUSTON, J. P., and BORBÉLY, A. A., 1973, Operant conditioning in forebrain-ablated rats by use of rewarding hypothalamic stimulation, *Brain Res.* **50**:467–472.

KEENE, J. J., and CASEY, K. L., 1973, Rewarding and aversive brain stimulation: opposite effects on medial thalamic units, *Physiol. Behav.* **10**:283–287.

KEMP, J. M., and POWELL, T. P. S., 1971a, The site of termination of afferent fibres in the caudate nucleus, *Phil. Trans. Roy. Soc. London* **262**:413–427.

KEMP, J. M., and POWELL, T. P. S., 1971b, The termination of fibres from the cerebral cortex and thalamus upon dendritic spines in the caudate nucleus: a study with the Golgi method, *Phil. Trans. Roy. Soc. London* **262**:429–439.

KOOB, G. F., BALCOM, G. J., and MEYERHOFF, J. L., 1976, Increases in intracranial self-stimulation in the posterior hypothalamus following unilateral lesions in the locus coeruleus, *Brain Res* **101**:554–560.

LASEK, R., JOSEPH, B. S., and WHITLOCK, D. G., 1968, Evaluation of a radioautographic neuroanatomical tracing method, *Brain Res.* **8**:319–336.

LAVAIL, J. H., and LAVAIL, M. M., 1972, Retrograde axonal transport in the central nervous system, *Science* **176**:1416–1417.

LEONARD, C. M., 1969, The prefrontal cortex of the rat. I. Cortical projections of the mediodorsal nucleus. II. Efferent connections, *Brain Res.* **12**:321–343.

LIPPA, A. S., ANTELMAN, S. M., FISHER, A. E., and CANFIELD, D. R. 1973, Neurochemical mediation of reward: a significant role for dopamine?, *Physiol. Behav.* **1**:23–28.

LYNCH, G. S., MOSKO, S., PARKS, T., and COTMAN, C. W., 1973, Relocation and hyperdevelopment of the dentate gyrus commissural system after entorhinal lesions in immature rats, *Brain Res.* **50**:174–178.

MILLHOUSE, O. E., 1969, A Golgi study of the descending medial forebrain bundle, *Brain Res.* **15**:341–363.

MOGENSON, G. J., 1964, Effects of sodium pentobarbital on brain self-stimulation, *J. Comp. Physiol. Psychol.* **58**:461–462.

NAUTA, W. J. H., 1957, Silver impregnation of degenerating axons, in: *New Research Techniques in Neuroanatomy* (W. F. Windle, ed.), Thomas, Springfield, Illinois.

NICOLAÏDIS, S., and FITZSIMONS, J. T., 1975, La dépendance de la prise d'eau induite par l'angiotensine II envers la fonction vasomotrice cérébrale locale chez le rat, *C. R. Acad Sci. Paris* **281**:1417–1420.

OLDS, M. E., and OLDS, J., 1963, Approach-avoidance analysis of rat diencephalon, *J. Comp. Neurol.* **120**:259–295.

OLDS, J., YUWILER, A., OLDS, M. E., and YUN, C. 1964, Neurohumors in hypothalamic substrates of reward, *Am. J. Physiol.* **207**:242–254.

PANKSEPP, J., and TROWILL, J., 1969, Positive and negative contrast effects with hypothalamic reward, *Physiol. Behav.* **4**:173–175.

PANKSEPP, J., and TROWILL, J., 1970, Positive incentive contrast with rewarding electrical stimulation of the brain, *J. Comp. Physiol. Psychol.* **70**:358–363.

PHILLIPS, A., and FIBIGER, H. C., 1973, Dopaminergic and noradrenergic substrates of positive reinforcement: differential effects of *d*- and *l*-amphetamine, *Science* **179**:575–577.

RAISMAN, G., 1969, Neuronal plasticity in the septal nuclei of the adult rat, *Brain Res.* **14**:25–48.

RITTER, S., and STEIN, L., 1973, Self-stimulation of noradrenergic cell group (A6) in locus coeruleus of rats, *J. Comp. Physiol. Psychol.* **85**:443–452.

ROLLS, E. T., and COOPER, S. J., 1973, Activation of neurones in prefrontal cortex by brain-stimulation reward in the rat, *Brain Res.* **60**:351–368.

ROLLS, E. T., and COOPER, S. J., 1974*a*, Connection between the prefrontal cortex and pontine brain-stimulation reward sites in the rat, *Exp. Neurol.* **42**:687–699.

ROLLS, E. T., and COOPER, S. J., 1974*b*, Anesthetization and stimulation of the sulcal prefrontal cortex and brain-stimulation reward, *Physiol. Behav.* **12**:563–571.

ROUTTENBERG, A., 1967, Drinking induced by carbachol: thirst circuit or ventricular modification?, *Science* **157**:838–839.

ROUTTENBERG, A., 1970, Forebrain pathways of reward in *Rattus norvegicus, J. Comp. Physiol. Psychol.* **75**:269–276.

ROUTTENBERG, A., 1972, Intracranial chemical injection and behavior: a critical review, *Behav. Biol.* **7**:601–641.

ROUTTENBERG, A., 1973, Intracranial self-stimulation pathways as substrate for stimulus-response integration, in: *Efferent Organization and the Integration of Behavior* (J. D. Maser, ed.), pp. 263–318, Academic Press, New York.

ROUTTENBERG, A., 1975*a*, Intracranial self-stimulation catecholamine brain pathways and memory consolidation, in: *Nebraska Symposium on Motivation* (J. K. Cole and T. Sonderegger, eds.), pp. 161–182, Univ. of Nebraska Press, Lincoln, Nebraska.

ROUTTENBERG, A., 1975*b*, Significance of intracranial self-stimulation pathways for memory consolidation, in: *Methods in Brain Research* (P. B. Bradley, ed.), pp. 453–474, Wiley, New York.

ROUTTENBERG, A., 1976*a*, Doubts about the locus coeruleus role in learning and the phosphorylation mechanisms it engages in cerebellum, *Nature* **260**:79–80.

ROUTTENBERG, A., 1976*b*, Self-stimulation pathways: origins and terminations—a three-stage technique, in: *Brain-Stimulation Reward* (A. Wauquier and E. T. Rolls, eds.), pp. 31–39, Elsevier, New York.

ROUTTENBERG, A., and BONDAREFF, W., 1969, Histochemical fluorescence as an index of spread of centrally applied chemicals, *Science* **165**:1032.

ROUTTENBERG, A., and BULLOCH, G. C., 1970, Self-starvation and rewarding brain stimulation: effects of chlorpromazine and pentobarbital, *Learn. Motiv.* **2**:83–94.

ROUTTENBERG, A., and HOLZMAN, N., Electrical stimulation of substantia nigra, pars compacta disrupts memory, *Science* **181**:83–86.

ROUTTENBERG, A., and MALSBURY, C., 1969, Brainstem pathways of reward, *J. Comp. Physiol. Psychol.* **68**:22-30.

ROUTTENBERG, A., and OLDS, J., 1963, The attenuation of response to an aversive brain stimulus by concurrent rewarding septal stimulation, *Fed. Proc.* **22**:515.

ROUTTENBERG, A., and OLDS, J., 1966, Stimulation of dorsal midbrain during septal and hypothalamic self-stimulation, *J. Comp. Physiol. Psychol.* **62**:250-255.

ROUTTENBERG, A., and SIMPSON, J., 1971, Carbachol-induced drinking at ventricular and subfornical organ sites of application, *Life Sci.* **10**:481-490.

ROUTTENBERG, A., and SLOAN, M., 1972, Self-stimulation in the frontal cortex of Rattus norvegicus, *Behav. Biol.* **7**:567-572.

ROUTTENBERG, A., SLADEK, J., and BONDAREFF, W., 1968, Histochemical fluorescence after application of neurochemicals to caudate nucleus and septal area *in vivo*, *Science* **161**:272-274.

ROUTTENBERG, A., GARDNER, E. L., and HUANG, Y. H., 1971, Self-stimulation pathways in the monkey, *Macaca mulatta*, *Exp. Neurol.* **33**:213-224.

Santos-Anderson, R., and ROUTTENBERG, A., 1976, Stimulation of rat medial or sulcal prefrontal cortex during passive avoidance learning selectively influences retention performance, *Brain Res.* **103**:243-259.

SEVERS, W. B., and SUMMY-LONG, J., 1975, The role of angiotensin in thirst, *Life Sci.* **17**:1513-1526.

SIMON, H., LEMOAL, M., and CARDO, B., 1975, Self-stimulation in the dorsal pontine tegmentum in the rat, *Behav. Biol.* **13**:339-348.

SIMPSON, J., and ROUTTENBERG, A., 1972, The subfornical organ and carbachol-induced drinking, *Brain Res.* **45**:135-152.

SIMPSON, J. B., and ROUTTENBERG, A., 1973, Subfornical organ: site of drinking induction initiation by angiotensin II, *Science* **181**:83-86.

SIMPSON, J. B., and ROUTTENBERG, A., 1974, Subfornical organ: acetylcholine application elicits drinking, *Brain Res.* **79**:157-164.

SIMPSON, J. B., and ROUTTENBERG, A., 1975, Subfornical organ lesions reduce intravenous angiotensin-induced drinking, *Brain Res.* **88**:154-161.

STINUS, L., THIERRY, A-M., and CARDO, B., 1975, Self-stimulation and local injections of 6-hydroxydopamine into the rat brain. Enhanced behavioural depressive effects of α-methylparatyrosine, *Physiol. Behav.* **3**:19-23.

TAYLOR, J. (ed.), 1931, *Selected Writings of John Hughlings Jackson*, 2 vols., Hodder and Stoughton, London.

UNGERSTEDT, U., 1971, Stereotaxic mapping of the monoamine pathways in the rat brain, *Acta Physiol. Scand.*, Suppl. **367**:1-48.

VALENSTEIN, E. S., Problems of measurement and interpretation with reinforcing brain stimulation, *Psychol. Rev.* **71**:415-437.

VALENSTEIN, E. S., and CAMPBELL, J. F., 1966, Medial forebrain bundle-lateral hypothalamic area and reinforcing brain stimulation, *Am. J. Physiol.* **210**:270-274.

WAUQUIER, A., NIEMEGEERS, C. J. E., and GEIVERS, H. A., 1972, Intracranial self-stimulation in rats as a function of various stimulus parameters. I. An empirical study with monopolar electrodes in the medial forebrain bundle, *Pyschopharmacologia* **23**:238-260.

2

NEUROPHARMACOLOGY OF REWARD AND PUNISHMENT

Larry Stein, C. David Wise, and James D. Belluzzi

1. INTRODUCTION

A hungry pigeon is easily trained to peck at a target to obtain food. A frightened rat, periodically subjected to electrical foot shock, learns equally well to avoid the painful stimulation by pressing a pedal. These demonstration experiments illustrate a high form of behavioral adaptation which Skinner (1938) has termed *operant reinforcement*. The term *operant* emphasizes the fact that the behavior operates on the environment to generate consequences. The term *reinforcement* refers to the fact that the behavior is strengthened when its consequences are favorable or rewarding.

Behavioral analysis suggests that operant reinforcement is based mainly on a knowledge of response consequences and, specifically, on the expectation that a particular act will be followed by a particular reward (Mackintosh, 1974). The mechanism of facilitation is not clearly understood, but motivation and learning may both be involved. On the one hand, expected rewards appear to provide motor facilitation and to increase the readiness to act; on the other hand, past rewards guide response selection by shaping the response repertoire and elevating the probabilities of previously rewarded responses.

A rat may also learn that a pedal press will deliver foot shock or remove food. Since the operant response in these cases has unfavorable consequences, it is not surprising that the behavior becomes weakened or

---

Larry Stein, C. David Wise, and James D. Belluzzi • Department of Psychopharmacology, Wyeth Laboratories, Philadelphia, Pennsylvania 19101.

suppressed (operant punishment). It is tempting to suggest, by analogy to operant reinforcement, that operant punishment depends heavily on the development of negative expectations. According to this view, the anticipation of punishment (or reward loss) reduces the tendency to engage in dangerous or unsuccessful behaviors, both by generating motor inhibition and by providing "no" signals for response guidance. Positive and negative expectations are thus assumed to exert reciprocal actions in the regulation of operant behavior (Table 1).

Although such conceptualizations of operant reinforcement and punishment are useful in psychological investigations of animal learning, these ideas would have a greater impact on neurobiology if it were possible to relate the psychological concepts to a biological substrate. The problem is simplified by the assumption that there are special sets of neurons for reward and punishment, whose identity may be revealed by appropriate behavioral and neurobiological methods. In this chapter, we selectively review data and concepts which offer some evidence of progress toward this goal.

2. OPERANT REINFORCEMENT

Analysis of the structure of the reward system has been facilitated by the discovery that animals will electrically self-stimulate certain regions of their own brains (Olds and Milner, 1954). Like all operant behavior, self-stimulation requires a source of reinforcement for its maintenance. In the absence of other sources of positive reinforcement, the reward for self-stimulation must arise from the neuronal activity that is excited by the electrical stimulus. Although such centrally elicited reward could be an

TABLE 1
The Four Operant Behavior Schedules Generated by Presenting or Withholding a Favorable or Unfavorable Event as a Consequence of the Behavior[a]

Event	Presentation	Omission
Favorable	Positive reinforcement or reward (Facilitates behavior) Catecholamines "Hope"	Nonreward or extinction (Suppresses behavior) Serotonin, acetylcholine "Disappointment"
Unfavorable	Punishment or passive avoidance (Suppresses behavior) Serotonin, acetylcholine "Fear"	Negative reinforcement or active avoidance (Facilitates behavior) Catecholamines "Relief"

[a] Behavioral effects, neurotransmitters, and affective states thought to be associated with the various schedules are indicated.

artifact, it more plausibly represents a direct activation of the brain's normal reinforcement system (Deutsch, 1960; Olds, 1962; Stein, 1964a; Gallistel, 1973). If so, identification of the pathways that subserve self-stimulation would reveal the pathways that subserve reward.

Because the field of stimulation contains diverse neural elements, identification of those neurons which are actually responsible for self-stimulation is largely a matter of inference. Solutions may be based on mapping studies which demonstrate self-stimulation in anatomically coherent systems, and on pharmacological studies which implicate specific neurotransmitters. Anatomical and pharmacological evidence of this kind has produced widespread agreement that catecholamine (CA)-containing neurons in the brain play a critical role in self-stimulation (Stein, 1962, 1968; Poschel and Ninteman, 1963; Arbuthnott, Fuxe, and Ungerstedt, 1971; Crow, 1972a, 1972b; Stinus and Thierry, 1973; Phillips and Fibiger, 1973; Wise et al., 1973; Clavier and Routtenberg, 1974; German and Bowden, 1974; Herberg et al., 1976). Acetylcholine or serotonin systems seem to be associated with the suppression, rather than the facilitation, of self-stimulation (Stein, 1968; Wise et al., 1973), and there is little or no evidence as yet for the direct involvement of other neurotransmitters.

2.1. Pharmacological Evidence Implicating Norepinephrine (NE)

In early studies it was found that self-stimulation behavior is selectively affected by drugs that influence central catecholamine transmission (Stein, 1962, 1964b; Poschel and Ninteman, 1963). Substances that release catecholamines rapidly from functional stores (such as amphetamine, α-methyl-m-tyrosine, or phenethylamine in combination with a monoamine oxidase inhibitor) facilitate self-stimulation. Conversely, drugs that deplete catecholamine stores (reserpine), block catecholamine receptors (chlorpromazine, haloperidol), or inhibit catecholamine synthesis (α-methyl-p-tyrosine) suppress self-stimulation (Fig. 1).

An important role for NE, in particular, was suggested by work with inhibitors of dopamine-β-hydroxylase, the enzyme that converts dopamine (DA) to NE. Systemic administration of disulfiram or intraventricular administration of diethyldithiocarbamate abolished self-stimulation and eliminated the rate-enhancing action of amphetamine (Wise and Stein, 1969, 1970). Intraventricular administration of l-NE after DBH inhibition reinstated self-stimulation and restored the facilitatory action of amphetamine; in control experiments, similar injections of d-NE and DA were ineffective. These observations have been confirmed in recent studies with newer and supposedly more specific DBH inhibitors such as U-14,624, fusaric acid, and FLA-63 (Figs. 2 and 3). In the latter case, however, a dependable behavioral suppression was observed only after prior reserpinization (Franklin and Herberg, 1975). A possible explanation for this uniqueness is that the

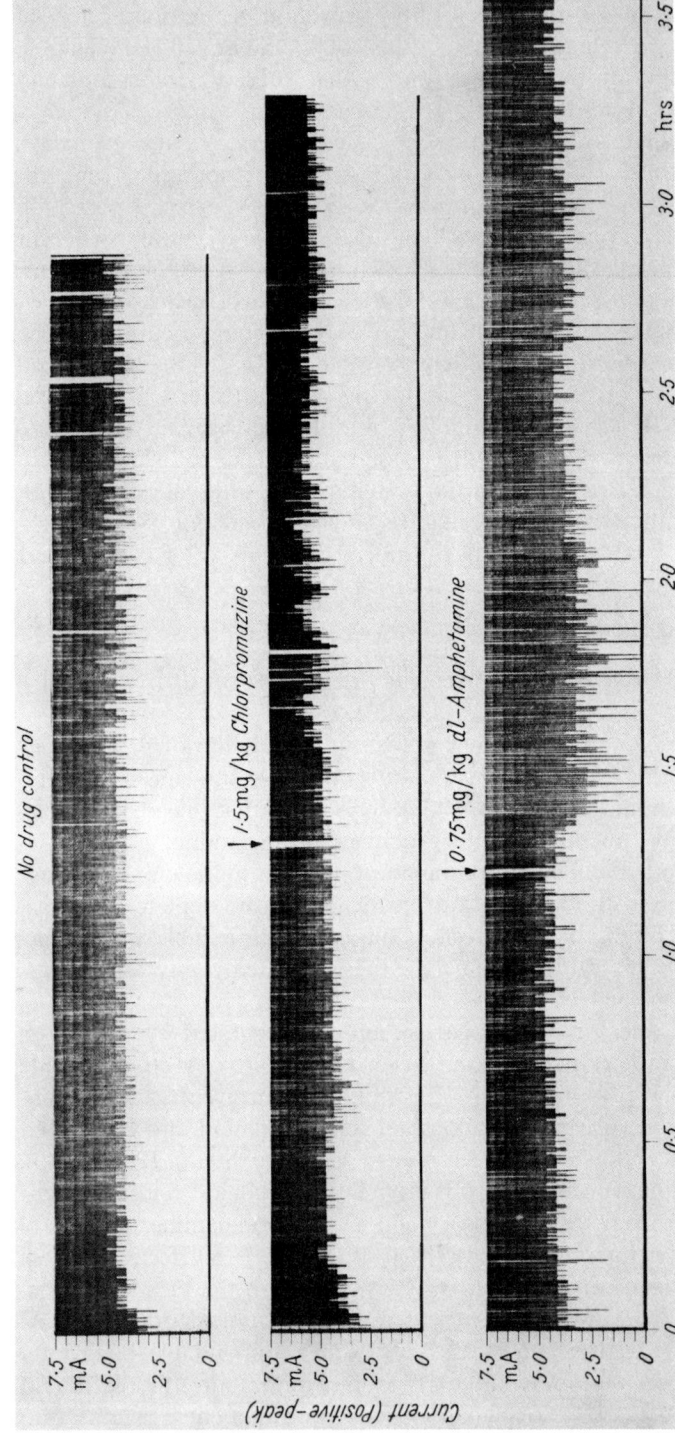

FIG. 1. Two-pedal "current-resetting" test for rate-independent estimation of brain-stimulation reinforcement thresholds. One pedal delivers brain stimulations which decrease stepwise in intensity with successive responses. When the "reward threshold" is reached, the rat operates the second pedal to reset the current (and the recording pen) to the top step (7.5 mA). The jagged edge of the records gives, in sequence, the current intensities at which resets occurred and thus traces the reward threshold throughout the test. The reset response is expedited by chlorpromazine and retarded by amphetamine. These uncharacteristic effects cannot be attributed to nonspecific actions of chlorpromazine and amphetamine, and thus may be best interpreted to reflect elevation and lowering, respectively, of the reward threshold. The ordinal markings indicate the 16 current levels available. From Stein and Ray (1960).

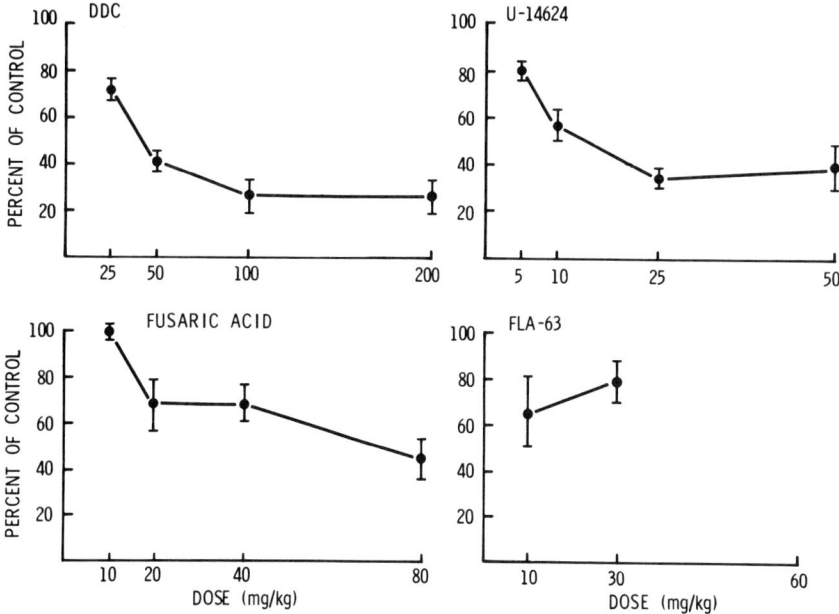

FIG. 2. Dose-related suppression of medial forebrain bundle self-stimulation by dopamine-β-hydroxylase inhibitors (DDC, diethyldithiocarbamate). All drugs were administered 1 hr prior to a daily 2-hr self-stimulation test. Each point is based on data from three to eight rats and shows drug rates as a percent of control for three prior sessions.

blockade of NE synthesis by FLA-63 is of short enough duration that the NE in reserpine-sensitive "reserve" pools can maintain self-stimulation until synthesis recovers (Franklin and Herberg, 1974).

Since DBH inhibitors leave brain DA levels unaffected (or even slightly increased), and since replenishment of depleted transmitter stores by intraventricularly administered NE produces a selective and almost immediate behavioral recovery, the DBH-inhibitor experiments provide the best evidence to date for the conclusion that NE neurons are specifically involved in self-stimulation. This conclusion has been challenged, however, on the grounds that DBH inhibitors may decrease self-stimulation merely by making animals drowsy (Roll, 1970).* Although the suggestion may be valid, the experimental evidence offered in its support was weak. Noting that

* Wise and Stein (1969) considered, and rejected, this idea on the grounds that barbiturates, which produce powerful sedative effects, do not consistently decrease self-stimulation rates and often increase them. Franklin and Herberg (1975) observed no evidence of somnolence or sedation after administration of FLA-63 to rats pretreated 3 or 5 days previously with reserpine, although self-stimulation was virtually abolished. The sedation hypothesis is also inconsistent with early work of Stein and Ray (1960) in which a self-stimulation current-resetting technique was used to demonstrate rate-independent threshold-lowering effects of amphetamine and threshold-elevating effects of chlorpromazine (Fig. 1).

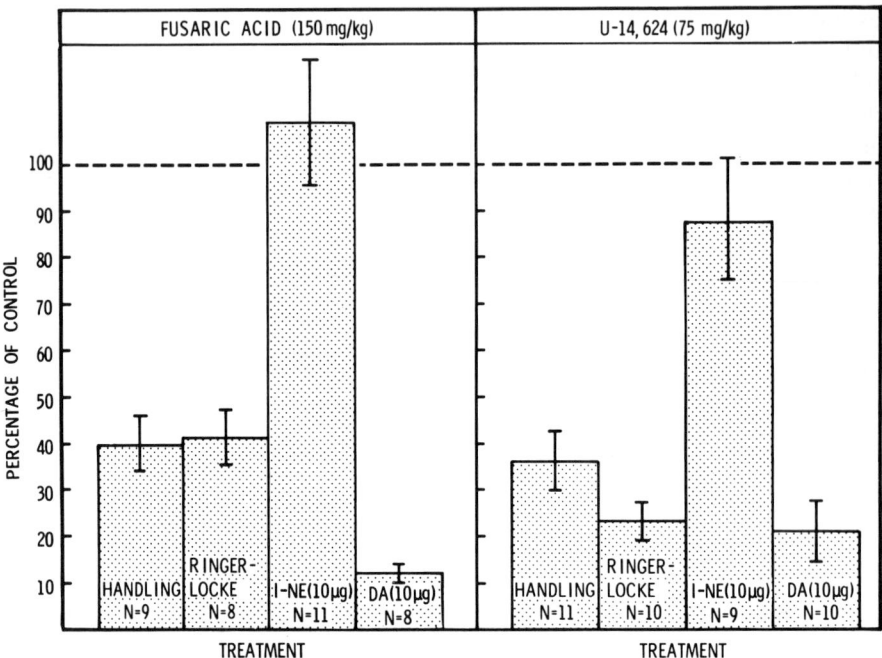

FIG. 3. Suppression of hypothalamic self-stimulation by fusaric acid or U-14,624 and its selective reinstatement by intraventricular administrations of L-norepinephrine (L-NE). Similar injections of Ringer–Locke solution or dopamine (DA) or sham injections were ineffective. Scores indicate self-stimulation rates in the 15-min periods just before and after intraventricular injections as a percent of the undrugged rate in the same time period on a preceding control day. See Fig. 9 for an illustrative experiment with another DBH inhibitor, diethyldithiocarbamate.

disulfiram induced long pauses in self-stimulation, Roll recalculated the response rates under the drug after eliminating the intervals of no response and found, not surprisingly, that the rates were much higher. Since extinction of self-stimulation induces a similar pattern of pausing (during which rats often go to sleep), the same statistical treatment could be used to support the conclusion that reduction of current intensity to zero does not affect reward value, but merely makes rats drowsy.

In another test of the sedation hypothesis, Rolls *et al.* (1974) observed that disulfiram had relatively greater depressant effects on two presumed measures of arousal, spontaneous locomotor activity and spontaneous rearing, than it did on self-stimulation. It was concluded that disulfiram's effects "on self-stimulation reward are relatively nonspecific" (p. 736). The validity of this conclusion obviously rests on the assumption that spontaneous locomotion and rearing are relatively independent of reward effects. It is known, however, that rats eagerly explore novel environments and will even work for the opportunity to do so. It is also a fact that exploration extinguishes rapidly as novelty wears off, and that the rats will go to sleep unless the environment provides a fresh source of positive reinforcement or other significant stimulation. Thus, it is not inconceivable that disulfiram's depressant action on locomotor activity and rearing may reflect in part an accelerated depreciation of the rewarding effects of novel stimulation, due to depletion of reward transmitter. Even the greater susceptibility of locomotion and rearing to the effects of the DBH inhibitor, when compared to that of self-stimulation, is consistent with this suggestion. Direct activation of NE neurons during self-stimulation would release large amounts of transmitter (Stein and Wise, 1969), which would tend to counteract disulfiram's action until NE stores were completely depleted; on the other hand, the drug might easily suppress exploration since NE neurons would be only weakly activated by the mild reward available in the activity tests. Some support for these ideas is provided in the Rolls et al. (1974) paper. Rats allowed to self-stimulate for 2 hr after disulfiram administration (presumably thus inducing transmitter depletion in the reward pathways stimulated) subsequently exhibited a significantly enhanced drug depression, not only in self-stimulation, but in the activity tests as well (Fig. 4).

The NE receptor involved in behavioral reinforcement appears to be of the α-type (Wise et al., 1973). Intraventricular administration of the α-NE antagonist phentolamine, but not the β-antagonist propranolol, reduced the

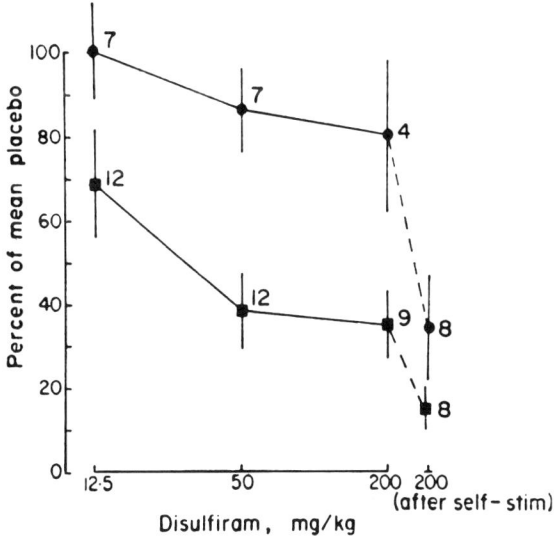

Fig. 4. Dose–response curves of the effects of disulfiram on self-stimulation rate and locomotor activity. Disulfiram attenuates locomotor activity more than self-stimulation rate. The 200 mg/kg (after self-stimulation) condition refers to eight rats allowed to self-stimulate continuously and tested 2 hr after the disulfiram injection on both locomotor activity and self-stimulation. Each point represents mean ± S.E.M.; the number of rats is indicated beside each point. ●, Self-stimulation rate; ■, locomotor activity. From Rolls et al. (1974).

rate of self-stimulation and blocked the facilitatory effect of amphetamine (Fig. 5). Systemically administered thymoxamine, a newly developed α-antagonist, also reduces self-stimulation rates (Herberg et al., 1976). However, phentolamine failed to suppress self-stimulation in an experiment in which rats were reinforced for each pedal press (Lippa et al., 1973). In the two studies that yielded positive results, responses were reinforced only aperiodically at variable intervals; thus, the suppressant potency of α-antagonists would appear to vary inversely with the density of the brain-stimulation reinforcement. In fact, if food-rewarded behavior is simultaneously punished with foot shock in a "conflict" test, the suppressant potency of phentolamine increases 10- to 20-fold (Stein et al., 1973). These observations support the idea that NE and phentolamine may compete for binding at reward receptors. Decreases in the frequency or magnitude of positive stimulation, or the presentations of punishing stimulation, will reduce the concentration of NE at reward synapses (Stein and Wise, 1969); as a

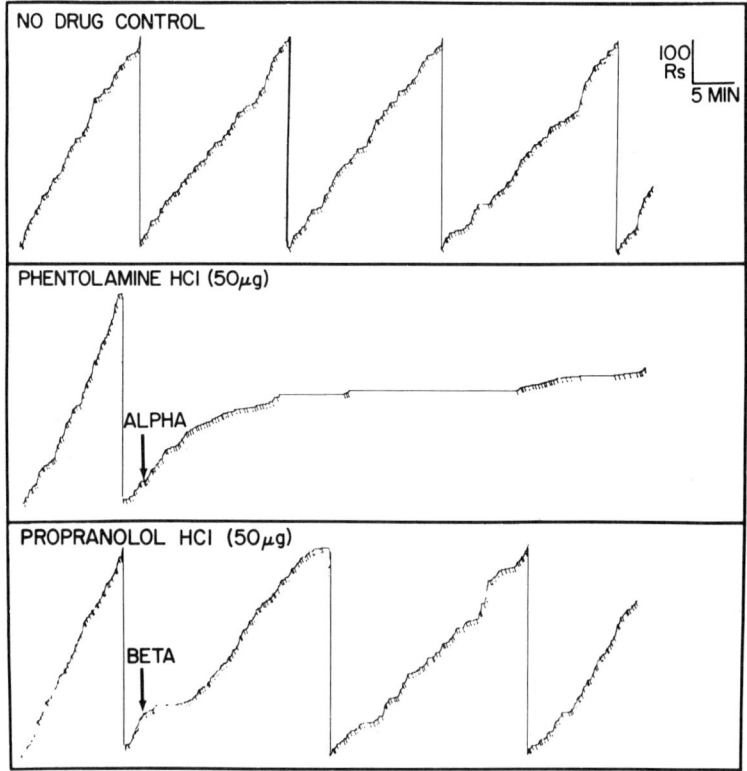

FIG. 5. Selective suppression of self-stimulation by central α-noradrenergic blockade. Phentolamine (α-antagonist) and propranolol (β-antagonist) were injected in the lateral ventricle 15 min after the start of a 75-min test. Pen resets automatically after 500 responses. Variable-interval reinforcement schedule. From Wise et al. (1973).

consequence, such manipulations will favor phentolamine binding and cause an apparent increase in its behavior-suppressant potency.

In other experiments, rewarding brain stimulation or moderate doses of amphetamine given to freely moving rats with permanently indwelling cannulas released NE and its metabolites into brain perfusates (Stein and Wise, 1969). Both treatments caused shifts in the pattern of metabolites toward O-methylated products (see also Glowinski and Axelrod, 1965).

2.2. Anatomical Evidence Implicating Norepinephrine

These pharmacological observations fit nicely with the results of self-stimulation mapping studies on the one hand, and histochemical maps of NE pathways on the other. This histochemical work presently demonstrates three major ascending NE fiber systems in the rat brainstem (Fuxe *et al.*, 1970; Ungerstedt, 1971b; Jacobowitz, 1973; Lindvall and Björklund, 1974). A dorsal pathway originates mainly in the principal locus coeruleus (NE cell group A6 in the classification of Dahlström and Fuxe, 1964) and innervates neocortex, cerebellum, hippocampus, and thalamus (Fig. 6). A ventral

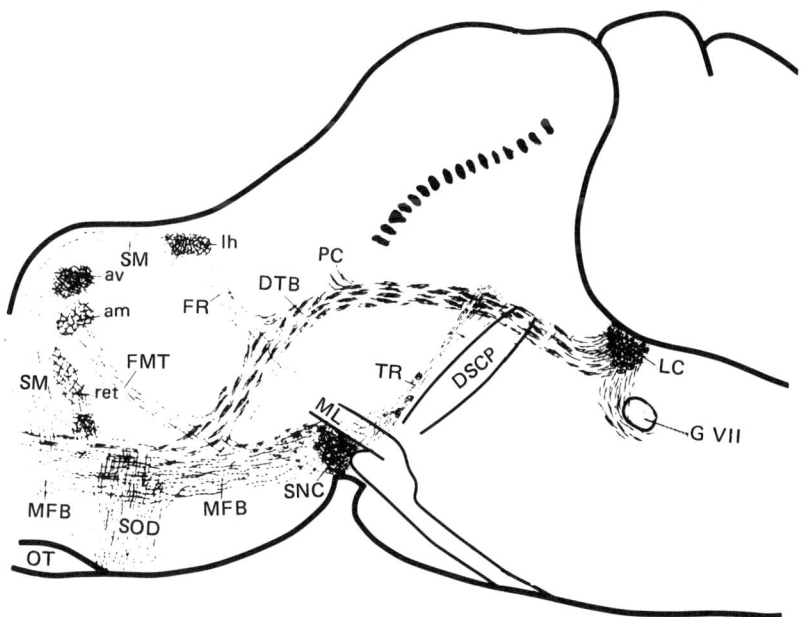

FIG. 6. Semidiagrammatic representation of the dorsal noradrenergic bundle (DTB), originating in the locus coeruleus (LC), and its projections in the diencephalon. The medial part of the medial forebrain bundle (MFB) and cells in the pars compacta of the substantia nigra (SNC) are also included. For other abbreviations, see Lindvall and Björklund (1974).

pathway originates more heterogeneously and mainly from NE cell groups in the medulla oblongata and pons (A1, A2, A5, A6, and A7) and innervates hypothalamus and ventral parts of the limbic system (Fig. 7). And a newly discovered periventricular pathway originates in part from disseminated NE cell bodies in the central gray matter and innervates medial regions of thalamus and hypothalamus (Fig. 8). All three NE ststems may subserve self-stimulation. Early mapping studies and supporting pharmacological evidence suggest that electrodes in the dorsal pathway or its cells of origin in the locus coeruleus support high rates of self-stimulation (Crow *et al.*, 1972; Ritter and Stein 1973). More recently, locus coeruleus self-stimulation has been routinely observed in many different laboratories (Wauquier and Rolls, 1976), but there have also been two negative reports (Amaral and Routtenberg, 1975; Simon *et al.*, 1975). In these latter studies, however, the negative findings may be attributed to the use of very low current intensities and the fact that no behavioral shaping of the response was tried.

High rates of self-stimulation have also been obtained from ventrocaudal sites in the mesencephalic central gray area in the region of the dorsal raphe nucleus (Margules, 1969; Routtenberg and Malsbury, 1969; Liebman *et al.*, 1973) or just rostral to the locus coeruleus (Ritter and Stein, 1973) or in Gudden's ventral tegmental nucleus (Simon *et al.*, 1975). Somewhat lower rates are found in medial regions of hypothalamus, especially nucleus paraventricularus (Atrens, 1973). Although self-stimulation generally is not obtained and mostly aversive effects are reported in more rostral central gray sites (Liebman *et al.*, 1973), these reports can now be taken as evidence that

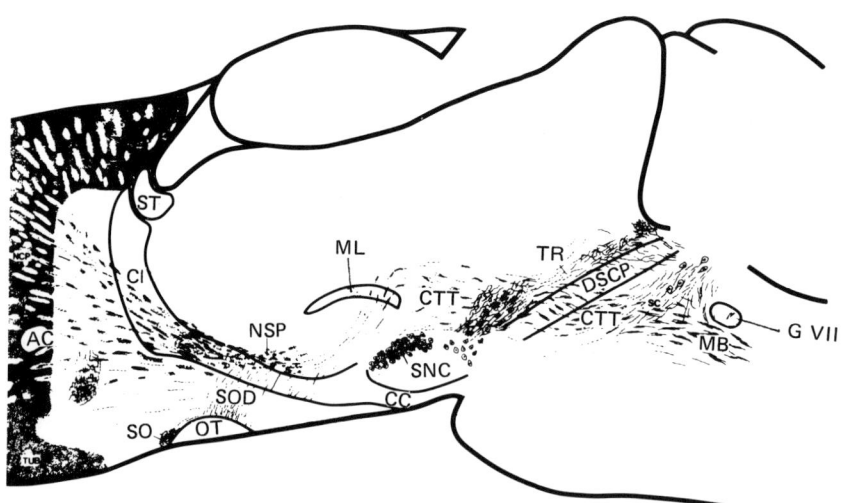

FIG. 7. Semidiagrammatic representation of the ventral noradrenergic bundle (CTT) and its caudal extension (MB). For other abbreviations, see Lindvall and Björklund (1974).

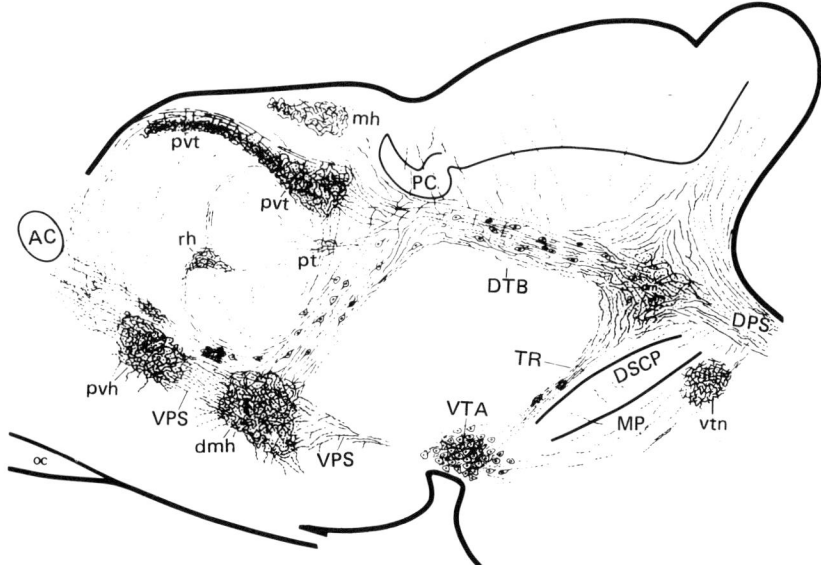

FIG. 8. Semidiagrammatic representation of the periventricular noradrenergic bundle (DPB) rostral to the locus coeruleus, the medial fiber flow of the tegmental radiations (TR), and the catecholamine fibers of the mamillary peduncle (MP). For other abbreviations, see Lindvall and Björklund (1974).

activation of at least some components of the periventricular NE system also yields positive reinforcement.

The role of the ventral NE pathway in self-stimulation, however, is still disputed. Arbuthnott *et al.* (1971) obtained self-stimulation from five electrodes in the ventral bundle at the level of the interpeduncular nucleus; furthermore, they observed in all positive cases (but not in 15 out of 16 non-self-stimulators) an increased turnover of NE on the stimulated side in hypothalamic and limbic system areas innervated by terminals of the ventral bundle. Similar results with slightly more rostral reward placements in the area ventralis tegmenti have also been reported (Stinus and Thierry, 1973). On the other hand, Anlezark *et al.* (1974) and Clavier and Routtenberg (1974) failed to obtain self-stimulation either from within the A1 or A2 areas or from the ascending fibers of the ventral bundle at the level of the locus coeruleus; both groups concluded that their experiments do not support the contention that the ventral bundle of NE neurons is involved in electrical self-stimulation. Recently, Ritter and Stein (1974) mapped the trajectory of the ventral bundle for self-stimulation throughout the region of its separation from the dorsal bundle in the mesencephalon of the rat. Eleven rewarding electrodes were localized in the ventral bundle at sites clearly caudal to all known DA cell groups. Since activation of DA neurons or other NE systems by current spread could probably be ruled out, the positive reinforcement was attributed to NE fibers in the ventral bundle itself. The cells of origin of these positive fibers were not identified, but NE neurons in cell groups A6 and A7 were thought to be likely candidates since these groups supply an important inflow of fibers to the ventral bundle anterior to the locus coeruleus (Lindvall and Björklund, 1974), and since electrodes in the region of both A6 and A7 support high rates of self-stimulation (Crow *et al.*, 1972; Ritter and Stein, 1973).

Finally, the supposition that the caudal NE cell groups (A1, A2, and A5) do not support self-stimulation has recently been called into question by the observation of positive electrodes in dorsal medulla oblongata ventral to and within the solitary nucleus, the caudal aspect of which corresponds to group A2 (Carter and Phillips, 1975). Interestingly, peak response rates were obtained at a relatively high stimulation frequency (200 Hz), while a conventional frequency of 60 Hz yielded rates near nonreinforced levels.

If NE fibers in the ventral bundle in fact support self-stimulation, then it would appear that activation of all three major ascending NE systems in the brain yields positive reinforcement. The evolutionary selection of the NE neuron for reward functions raises interesting questions about the neurochemical characteristics that suit it for this role and the anatomical organization that permits its fulfillment. It is also interesting to consider in what ways reward functions may be differentiated or specialized among the three systems. The innervation of neocortex, hippocampus, thalamus, and cerebellum by the dorsal pathway suggests its involvement in associative thinking and learning (Crow, 1968; Anlezark *et al.*, 1973; Kety, 1970, 1972*a*; Ritter and Stein, 1973; Stein and Wise, 1971); the capacity of neurons in this pathway for regeneration and new growth (Stenevi *et al.*, 1974), and hence for reorganization, supports this suggestion. The innervation of hypothalamus and limbic system by the ventral pathway suggests involvement in motivation, mood, and neuroendocrine function (Olson and Fuxe, 1972; Stein and Wise, 1971; Stein *et al.*, 1972). And the periventricular system's innervations of medial hypothalamus and mesencephalic central gray area suggests, respectively, an involvement in feeding (Liebowitz, 1972) and interactions with pain and punishment systems (Mayer and Liebeskind, 1974; Stein *et al.*, 1973).

2.3. Self-Stimulation and Brain Dopamine

While much evidence suggests that NE neurons are involved in self-stimulation reward, a specific role for DA is less certain. Mapping studies suggest that the DA tracts in the medial forebrain bundle and internal capsule can support self-stimulation, but this evidence is inconclusive because of the close proximity of NE tracts. Thus, Kojima *et al.* (cited in Stein and Wise, 1973) obtained self-stimulation from some electrodes in the internal capsule, particularly from sites surrounding the tip of the crus cerebri; however, maximum rates were only about 20% of the maximum rates obtained from medial forebrain bundle electrodes. The most reinforcing internal capsule placements were located either in medial sites that border on the NE fiber system in the medial forebrain bundle, or in ventrolateral sites just dorsal to the NE projection into the amygdala. Internal capsule self-stimulation was facilitated by d- and l-amphetamine, but d-amphetamine was about nine times more potent. The localization of positive electrodes in the DA cell groups of the substantia nigra and the region around the interpeduncular nucleus is more compelling; in fact, this was the main evidence that led Crow (1972a, 1972b) to suggest that there are DA systems whose activation yields self-stimulation. Unfortunately, even this evidence is confounded by the presence of ascending NE tracts that pass in the close vicinity of, and partly intermingle with, the DA cell groups (Ungerstedt, 1971b; Lindvall and Björklund, 1974). In view of the demonstrated involvement of NE systems in self-stimulation, these tracts represent a potentially important source of reinforcement that should be isolated or excluded as a first step in the verification of the DA hypothesis.

To evaluate the NE contribution to substantia nigra self-stimulation, Belluzzi *et al.* (1975) used surgical, chemical, and pharmacological methods to inactivate the NE, but not the DA, systems in the field of stimulation. In the first experiment, the dorsal, periventricular, and ventral NE fiber bundles were transected by a knife cut extending to the midline just caudal to the interpeduncular nucleus, at a level 2.5 mm posterior and ipsilateral to the rewarding substantia nigra electrode. This level is caudal to all known central DA systems (Ungerstedt, 1971b). Only an ipsilateral cut was thought to be necessary because the NE fibers are mostly uncrossed (Ungerstedt, 1971b); for the same reason, contralateral knife cuts were expected to be largely ineffective and were placed in control rats to assess any nonspecific effects of the brain damage. A retracting, 150-μm stainless steel wire knife was used to transect deep structures with minimum damage to overlying structures (Sclafani and Grossman, 1969; Gold *et al.*, 1973).

Ipsilateral knife cuts through the NE bundles virtually abolished substantia nigra self-stimulation for three days, starting within 1 hr after the operation. Self-stimulation remained suppressed over the next several weeks, although varying degrees of partial recovery were observed in most cases. In a few cases, no recovery was obtained despite efforts to restore the response by priming, reshaping, and increases of current. In contrast, contralateral knife cuts caused only partial suppression of self-stimulation behavior during the first three days, and recovery occurred rapidly. Indeed, by the end of the first week, the response rate in the contralateral group had significantly exceeded that prior to surgery, and, by the end of the second week, had stabilized at about 160% of control.

In both groups, spontaneous circling away from the cut side was observed in almost every case. The circling started immediately after the operation and persisted for at least several days.

In the second experiment, the NE bundles were chemically lesioned, at the same caudal level as before, by local applications of 6-hydroxydopamine (10 µg in 1 µl of saline). Because the toxic drug is selectively taken up and concentrated in catecholamine neurons (Ungerstedt, 1971a), the injections were expected to cause a more specific degeneration of the NE fiber bundles than can be produced by knife cuts. Again, ipsilateral damage to NE systems caused an almost immediate suppression of substantia nigra self-stimulation that persisted, with only partial recovery, throughout the observaion period. The effects of contralaterally injected 6-hydroxydopamine similarly resembled those of the contralateral knife cuts; however, the initial suppressant effect was observed only on the day of injection, and the phase of supranormal response, which again peaked at about 160% of control, appeared several days earlier. In contrast to the persistent contraversive turning which was caused by the knife cuts, only transient ipsiversive turning was observed after the administration of 6-hydroxydopamine.

In a related experiment by Ritter et al. (cited in Belluzzi et al., 1975) the involvement of NE systems in substantia nigra self-stimulation was analyzed pharmacologically by the use of diethyldithiocarbamate (DDC), an inhibitor of dopamine-β-hydroxylase. Subcutaneous injections of DDC (50 to 300 mg/kg) in 21 rats caused dose-related decreases in the rate of substantia nigra self-stimulation, with nearly complete suppression in most cases within 1–3 hr after the higher doses (Fig. 9). During this time the animals were hypoactive but not asleep. Reversal experiments demonstrated that the suppression of self-stimulation by DDC was due to its inhibitory action on DBH and the consequent depletion of NE, and not so some other action unrelated to the metabolism of NE. Intraventricular administration of 10 µg of l-NE hydrochloride restored the suppressed behavior of eight rats within the first 15 min after injection to $114.8 \pm 27.9\%$ of control. Similar injections of Ringer–Locke solution, DA, or chlonidine were ineffective (Fig. 9).

Belluzzi's and Ritter's experiments thus show that electrodes in the substantia nigra lose their ability to support self-stimulation after surgical, chemical, or pharmacological treatments that inactivate NE systems, but leave DA systems relatively unaffected. These findings and the fact that three different approaches produced convergent results strongly suggest that ipsilateral NE fibers of passage play an essential role in the mediation of substantia nigra self-stimulation. The origin of these fibers cannot yet be specified with certainty, but it is probable from recent histochemical evidence (Lindvall and Björklund, 1974) that they mainly involve those components of the dorsal, ventral, and periventricular NE fiber systems which enter the ventral mesencephalon via the tegmental radiations and intermingle with the DA cell bodies and their outgoing fibers.

Whether other sites in the brain may yield "pure" dopaminergic self-stimulation remains to be demonstrated. Ritter and Stein (1974) found that rostrally placed electrodes in the ventral NE bundle (in regions of NE and DA overlap) yielded higher maximum self-stimulation rates than more caudal ventral bundle electrodes in relatively "pure" NE sites. It was

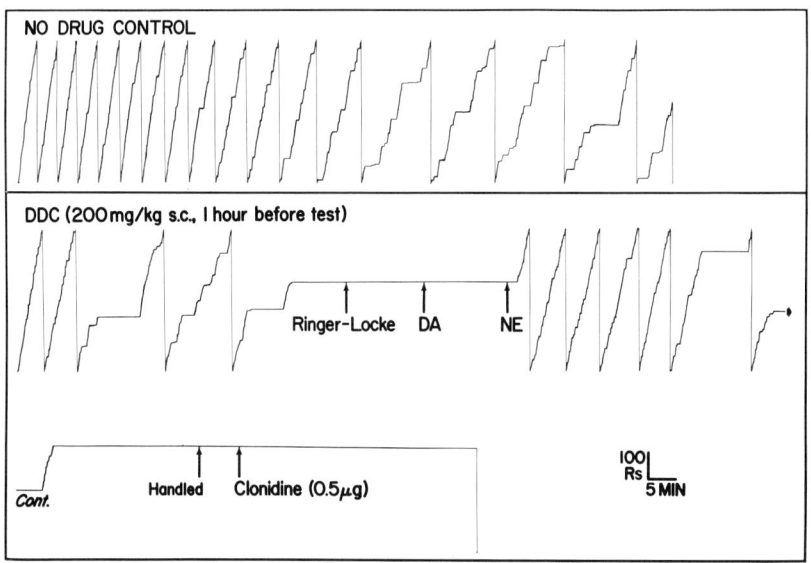

Fig. 9. Suppression of substantia nigra self-stimulation after inhibition of norepinephrine synthesis by diethyldithiocarbamate (DDC) and its selective reinstatement by an injection of *l*-norepinephrine hydrochloride (NE, 10 μg) in the lateral ventricle. Similar injections of Ringer–Locke solution and dopamine (DA, 10 μg) were ineffective. In other animals, similar results were obtained when the sequence of norepinephrine and dopamine injections was reversed. Direct stimulation of noradrenergic receptors by intraventricularly injected clonidine also was without effect, which suggests that presynaptic uptake and replenishment of functional stores of norepinephrine, and not simply restoration of central noradrenergic "tone," is required for the reinstatement of self-stimulation. From Belluzzi *et al.* (1975).

suggested that self-stimulation at the rostral sites may have been enhanced by the simultaneous activation of NE and DA neurons. The possibility that both catecholamines may be involved in rostral mescencephalic self-stimulation may be considered a "weak" form of the DA hypothesis, an idea which is consistent with anatomical and pharmacological evidence (Crow, 1972*b*; Liebman and Butcher, 1973; Lippa *et al.*, 1973; Wauquier and Niemegeers, 1972). The "strong" form of the DA hypothesis holds that the activation of DA neurons alone will yield self-stimulation (Crow, 1972*a*). Although the experiments of Belluzzi *et al.* (1975) would seem to contradict this idea, some support is provided by the demonstration that rats will intravenously self-inject the DA-receptor stimulant apomorphine (Baxter *et al.*, 1974) (Fig. 10).

2.4. Intravenous Self-Administration of Drugs

Rats can be trained to pedal press for intravenous injections of drugs. Catecholamine-facilitating agents, such as amphetamines and cocaine, pro-

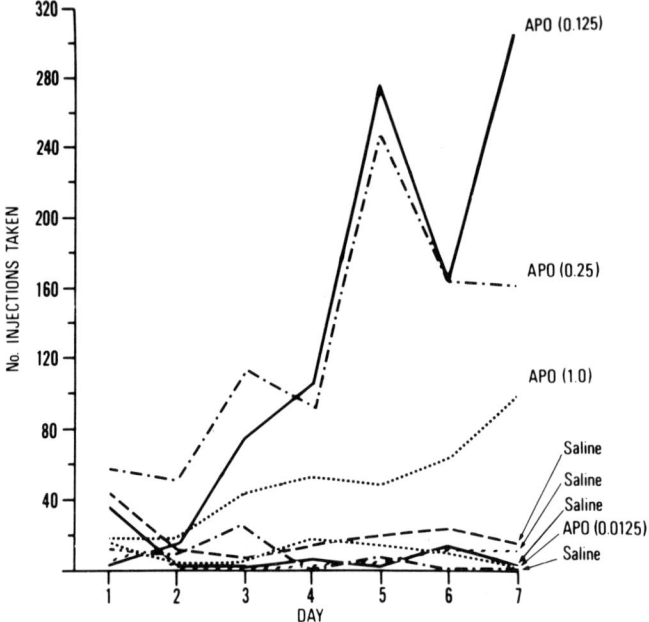

FIG. 10. Acquisition curves of apomorphine (APO) self-administration. Experimentally naive rats had daily access to apomorphine during 22-hr test sessions. A reinforcing effect was obtained at all doses except 0.0125 mg/kg/injection. From Baxter et al. (1974).

vide especially potent reinforcement for self-administration behavior, consistent with the hypothesis that operant reinforcement generally is mediated by CA systems. The reinforcing properties of DA in particular are revealed even more directly by the demonstration that apomorphine, a DA receptor stimulant, is avidly self-administered (Baxter et al., 1974; Davis and Smith, 1975). Intravenous self-administration of apomorphine, unlike that of amphetamine or morphine, is unaffected by CA depletion (Baxter et al., 1976; Davis et al., 1975); however, apomorphine self-injection is blocked by the DA antagonist pimozide (Baxter et al., 1974). Unless reserve stores of NE can be mobilized and released by apomorphine, these experiments thus provide strong support for Crow's suggestion that positive reinforcement can result from DA receptor activation.

Davis et al. (1975) find a similar patern of results with the α-NE agonist clonidine. Self-administration of this agent is unaffected by NE synthesis inhibition but is blocked by the α-antagonist phenoxybenzamine.

2.5. Conclusions

Positive reinforcement of operant behavior is mediated by catecholamine systems in the brain. This conclusion is supported by a consistent pattern of anatomical and pharmacological evidence from studies of brain self-stimulation, and is further supported by studies of intravenous self-administration. In the absence of definitive evidence favoring one catecholamine over the other, the original question of which catecholamine is the more important has given way to a more detailed inquiry into the precise roles of NE and DA systems. Theories of Crow (1972b) and more recently of Herberg et al. (1976), based partly on CA anatomy and partly on CA psychopharmacology, resemble each other in the attribution of motivational or incentive functions to DA systems and reinforcement or memory-generating functions to NE systems. Other important questions that remain concern the degree of overlap in the functions of NE and DA systems, whether these systems act jointly or separately, and the functional specialization of the different DA and NE systems.

3. OPERANT PUNISHMENT

3.1. Pharmacology

The pharmacology of the punishment system has mainly been studied in "passive avoidance" or "conflict" tests (Geller and Seifter, 1960). In this test, hungry rats perform a lever-press response to obtain a sweetened milk reward. The reinforcement schedule consists of punishment and nonpunishment components, alternating approximately every 15 min. On the nonpunishment schedule (3–15 min), a response is rewarded with sweetened milk in infrequent and variable intervals—on the average, once every 2 min. On the punishment schedule (3 min), signaled by a tone, every response is rewarded with milk, but is also punished with a brief electrical foot shock (0.1–0.6 mA, 0.25 sec in duration). The rate of response in the tone period may be regulated by adjustment of shock intensity, and any degree of behavioral suppression may be obtained in well-trained animals. After several weeks of training, stable low rates of response are observed during the punishment periods, and stable high rates in the nonpunishment periods. Drug-induced increases in the rate of punished responses are taken as an index of anxiety-reducing activity, while substantial decreases in the rate of nonpunished responses are taken as an index of depressant activity.

Geller and his associates have studied the effects of different psychotherapeutic drugs in the conflict test. In general, a substantial release of punished behavior is produced only by benzodiazepines and related tranquilizers. Antipsychotic agents (e.g., chlorpromazine) do not have this effect and often cause a further suppression of punished behavior (Geller et al., 1962). Stimulant drugs of the amphetamine type also decrease the frequency of punished behavior. Even morphine, a powerful analgesic, fails to disinhibit punished behavior in this test (Geller *et al.*, 1963; Kelleher and Morse, 1964). This observation and the fact that a well-trained animal usually will cease to respond at the onset of the warning stimulus and before any painful shocks are delivered make it clear that it is not pain itself but rather the threat or fear of pain that suppresses conflict behavior.

In order to determine if the punishment deficit induced by tranquilizers is due to a generalized disinhibition, Margules and Stein (1967) studied the effects of the benzodiazepine derivative oxazepam in several different situations, using different response measures and means of producing response suppression. Oxazepam caused a marked increase in the occurrence of previously suppressed behavior regardless of whether the behavior was inhibited by footshock, nonreward (extinction), punishing brain stimulation, or the bitter taste of quinine. Furthermore, oxazepam caused a substantial disinhibition of feeding in satiated rats. Margules and Stein (1967) concluded that the disinhibitory action of oxazepam and related tranquilizers is clearly a general one, and that tranquilizers may act on a final common pathway for the suppression of behavior. If so, elucidation of the biochemical mechanism of benzodiazepine action could reveal the biochemical nature of the punishment system.

3.2. Effects of Benzodiazepines on Monoamine Turnover

Biochemical and histochemical studies indicate that benzodiazepines and barbiturates decrease the turnover of norepinephrine, serotonin, and other biogenic amines in the brain. Taylor and Laverty (1969) used intraventricular injections of labeled dopamine to study the effect of benzodiazepines on catecholamine metabolism. Significant decreases in norepinephrine and dopamine turnover were obtained in cortex and striate region, respectively. Corrodi *et al.* (1967) found that anesthetic doses of pentobarbital partially blocked the depletion of brain serotonin normally obtained after administration of the tryptophan hydroxylase inhibitor α-propyldopacetamine, and they suggested that pentobarbital probably decreases the activity of serotonin neurons. More recently, Chase *et al.* (1970) demonstrated that diazepam greatly increased the retention of [^{14}C]serotonin in rat brain following an intracisternal injection of labeled serotonin, although the drug had no effect on the uptake of the radioisotope. These findings were taken to suggest that diazepam may interfere with the metabolism of brain serotonin.

Thus, work from several laboratories indicates that benzodiazepines and barbiturates decrease the turnover of norepinephrine, serotonin, and other biogenic amines in the brain. It thus seems reasonable to speculate that the decreased turnover of these substances may be at least partly responsible for the punishment-lessening effects of tranquilizers.

3.3. Benzodiazepines and Brain Norepinephrine

If the punishment-lessening effects of benzodiazepines depend on a reduction of central norepinephrine activity, then other agents that reduce such activity ought also to exert a punishment-lessening effect. Phenothiazine derivatives such as chlorpromazine exert strong central antiadrenergic effects, but do not release punished behavior from suppression (Geller et al., 1962; Cook and Davidson, 1973). Since phenothiazines also antagonize other neurotransmitter actions, the relatively selective α-noradrenergic antagonist phentolamine and the β-noradrenergic antagonist propranolol were used in further tests. Both antagonists failed to release punishment-suppressed behavior in the rat conflict test. Intraventricular injections of propranolol (20–100 μg) had no obvious effects, but intraventricular injections of phentolamine (5–10 μg) strongly suppressed both punished and nonpunished behaviors (Wise et al., 1973). These experiments do not support the idea that disinhibitory effects of tranquilizers depend on noradrenergic blockade. On the contrary, they suggest that α-noradrenergic blockade causes suppression of behavior. Experiments with L-norepinephrine supported this idea. Intraventricular injections of the transmitter produced large increases in the rate of punished responses (Fig. 11); indeed, the punishment-lessening activity of norepinephrine administered intraventricularly compared favorably with that of the benzodiazepines administered systemically. Neurochemical specificity is suggested as D-norepinephrine and dopamine produced only negligible effects (Figs. 11 and 12). Significantly, intraventricular injections of norepinephrine increased rather than decreased the punishment-lessening activity of systemically administered benzodiazepines (Stein et al., 1973); this finding again contradicts the idea that the disinhibitory effects of tranquilizers depend on a reduction of noradrenergic activity.

3.4. Benzodiazepines and Brain Serotonin

If reduction of serotonin, rather than norepinephrine, turnover is involved in the punishment-lessening activity of benzodiazepines, then antagonists of serotonin or inhibitors of its synthesis should counteract the suppressive effects of punishment. Such seems to be the case. Graeff and Schoenfeld (1970) observed very large increases in the punished response rates of pigeons after intramuscular injection of the serotonin antagonists methysergide and D-2-bromolysergic acid diethylamide; the effect "was of the same magnitude as that produced by chlordiazepoxide, diazepam, and nitrazepam" (p. 281). Stein et al. (1973) also obtained punishment-lessening effects with methysergide in the rat conflict test (Fig. 13), and both Geller et al. (1974) and Cook and Sepinwall (1975) observed a similar effect with the

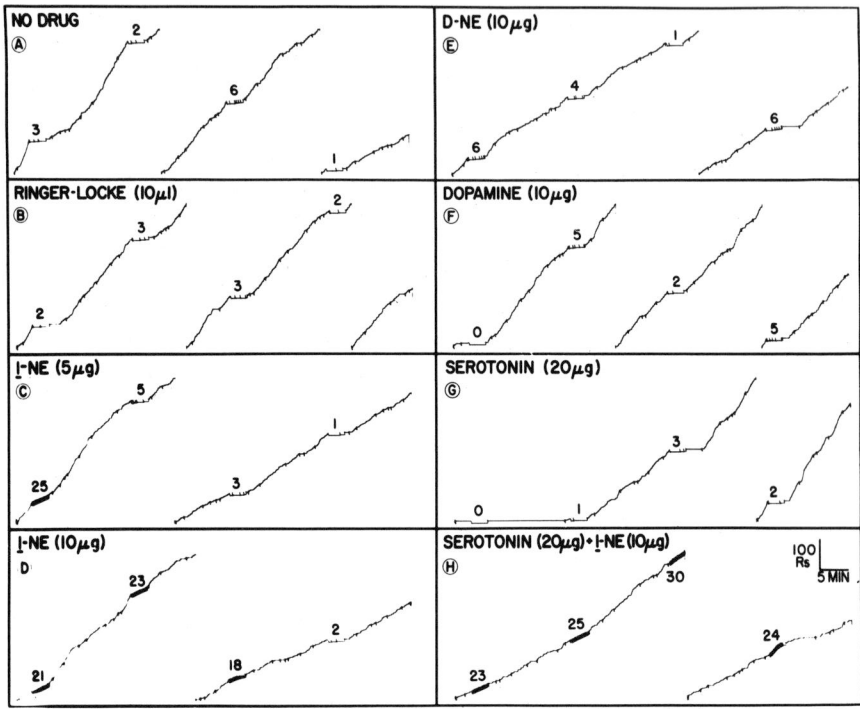

FIG. 11. Effects of various monoamine transmitters in the conflict test (rat WZ32). Hydrochloride salts of all substances were dissolved in 10 μl of Ringer–Locke solution and injected in the lateral ventricle via a permanently indwelling cannula immediately before the start of the test. In this and in subsequent figures, each record represents a complete 72-min session consisting of four 3-min punishment periods (punished responses are numbered) and five unpunished periods of different durations, in which responses are reinforced at variable intervals (on the average, every 2 min). Pen resets automatically after 550 responses. Note especially the dose-related punishment-lessening effect of L-norepinephrine (L-NE) (compare panels B through D), relative inactivity of D-norepinephrine (D-NE) and dopamine (panels E and F), initial suppressant action of serotonin (palen G), and unexpected potentiation of norepinephrine's punishment-lessening effect by serotonin (compare panels D and H). From Stein *et al.* (1973).

serotonin antagonist cinanserin. There are also reports of large releases of punishment-suppressed behavior after administration of the serotonin synthesis inhibitor *p*-chlorophenylalanine (PCPA) (Robichaud and Sledge, 1969; Geller and Blum, 1970; Wise *et al.*, 1973). The time courses of behavioral release and of serotonin depletion after PCPA injection coincide closely, and repletion of serotonin by administration of its precursor 5-hydroxytryptophan reverses the punishment-lessening effect of PCPA (Robichaud and Sledge, 1969; Geller and Blum, 1970; Wise *et al.*, 1973). Finally, Stein *et al.* (1975) obtained a profound, if transitory, release of punished behavior in the

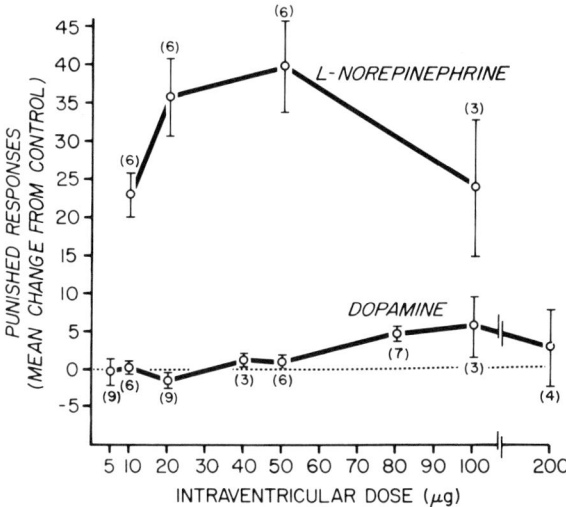

Fig. 12. Dose–response curves of the punishment-lessening effects of intraventricularly administered *l*-norepinephrine and dopamine in the conflict test. Dopamine had negligible activity at all doses tested. Bars indicate S.E.M.; the number of subjects is indicated in parentheses.

rat conflict test after a single intraventricular administration of 5,6-dihydroxytryptamine (100 μg), a drug which destroys serotonin-containing terminals in the brain (Baumgarten *et al.*, 1971). The punishment-lessening effect of 5,6-dihydroxytryptamine peaked on the second day after the injection, but

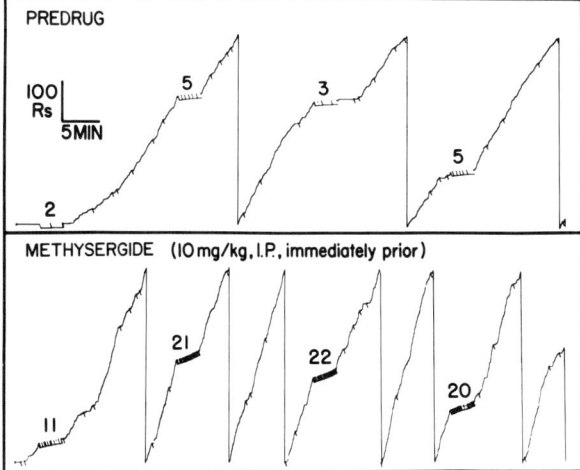

Fig. 13. Punishment-lessening action of methysergide in the rat conflict test. From Stein *et al.* (1973).

virtually disappeared by the fourth day. It may be noteworthy in this regard that Baumgarten *et al.* (1971) found a significant recovery of serotonin in pons-medulla, hypothalamus, and septum 4 days after a single 75-μg intracisternal injection of 5,6-dihydroxytryptamine (although, in spinal cord and neocortex, serotonin levels seemed permanently depleted). The punishment-lessening effects of 5,6-dihydroxytryptamine in the conflict test were relatively selective. Although the unpunished response rate was significantly depressed on the day of the injection, it had recovered almost fully to normal by the second day when punished behavior was maximally disinhibited.

Consistent with these findings, elevation of the concentration of serotonin in the brain by combined administration of 5-hydroxytryptophan and an inhibitor of monoamine oxidase causes suppression of food-rewarded behavior in the pigeon (Aprison and Ferster, 1961). Furthermore, the long-lasting serotonon agonist α-methyltryptamine suppresses punished and unpunished behaviors in the pigeon (Graeff and Schoenfeld, 1970) and rat (Stein *et al.*, 1973). These findings with serotonin agonists, antagonists, PCPA, and 5,6-dihydroxytryptamine support the possible existence of a behaviorally suppressive serotonin "punishment" system, whose activity may be decreased by benzodiazepines and other anxiety-reducing agents.

The suppressant effects of intraventricular serotonin in the rat self-stimulation test generally support these conclusions (Wise and Stein, 1969; Wise *et al.*, 1973). However, for reasons that are not yet clear, the action of serotonin in the conflict test is complex and often triphasic (Wise *et al.*, 1973). Doses of 5–20 μg of serotonin lead to an initial phase of intense behavioral suppression that lasts for 10–20 min, a longer secondary phase of normal response, or, frequently, behavioral facilitation (including release of punished behavior), and, finally, a prolonged period of behavioral suppression, which may persist for 2 days with high doses. Similarly, intracarotid administration of serotonin induces biphasic effects on the electroencephalogram [a brief arousal pattern followed by a longer phase of hypersynchrony (Koella and Czicman, 1966)], and iontophoretic application of serotonin to some spinal neurons cause biphasic changes in their spontaneous firing rate (Weight and Salmoiraghi, 1968). These findings, on a reduced time scale, resemble the effects of serotonin in the conflict experiments, although the acute nature of the preparations makes it difficult to evaluate the possibility of a third phase.

Stein *et al.* (1973) tried to antagonize the punishment-lessening action of oxazepam by intraventricular administration of serotonin. Eight rats received intraventricular injections of either serotonin hydrochloride (5 μg), L-norepinephrine hydrochloride (5 μg), or Ringer–Locke solution (10 μl) immediately before receiving intraperitoneal injections of oxazepam (10 mg/kg). All rats received all drug combinations during 10 days of testing, but in different sequences. In six out of the eight rats, serotonin decreased the anxiety-reducing action of oxazepam, whereas in seven out of the eight rats L-norepinephrine increased the anxiety-reducing effect of the tranquilizer.

3.5. Suppression of Behavior by Dorsal Raphe Stimulation and Reversal by Oxazepam

The foregoing data are consistent with the idea that a serotonin system in the brain mediates the suppressive effects of punishment. If so, and if it were correct to assume that tranquilizers act partly by reduction of serotonin activity, then it might be possible to demonstrate (1) suppression of behavior by direct activation of serotonin systems and (2) antagonism of such directly induced behavioral suppression by administration of tranquilizers.

Stein *et al.* (1973) applied minute quantities (about 5 µg) of crystalline carbachol via permanently indwelling cannulas to the dorsal raphe region of five rats with stable rates of punished and unpunished responses in the conflict test. The dorsal raphe nucleus was selected for initial study because, as one of the two major serotonin cell groups in the midbrain, it is the site of origin of many of the ascending serotonin fibers to the diencephalon and forebrain; furthermore, this nucleus consists almost entirely of serotonin cell bodies (Fuxe *et al.*, 1968). Crystalline carbachol was used for chemical stimulation because powerful suppressive effects on behavior are readily obtained by direct application of this substance to the medial hypothalamic region (Margules and Stein, 1967).

In three out of three cases, application of carbachol to the dorsal raphe nucleus caused marked suppression of both punished and unpunished behaviors within 1–2 min after treatment. In all of these cases, oxazepam reversed the suppressive effects of raphe stimulation on both types of behavior. In two rats, the tip of the cannula penetrated into the reticular formation, about 1 mm lateral or caudal to the dorsal raphe. In these cases, carbachol had a much smaller or negligible suppressive effect on behavior. Although these are only preliminary experiments, the data further support the idea that serotonin neurons in the dorsal raphe nucleus may be involved in the mediation of behavioral suppression.

3.6. Effects of Repeated Doses of Oxazepam on Monoamine Turnover

Studies on animals and man indicate that the anxiety-reducing and depressant actions of benzodiazepines follow different courses during their chronic administration. The depressant action rapidly undergoes tolerance after a few doses (Goldberg *et al.*, 1967), while the anxiety-reducing action fails to show tolerance and may even increase with repeated doses (Margules and Stein, 1968). If the behavioral effects were mediated, respectively, by reductions in norepinephrine and serotonin turnover, then it might be possible to show that benzodiazepine-induced decreases in serotonin turnover will persist with repeated doses, while the decrease in norepinephrine turnover will undergo tolerance.

Wise *et al.* (1972) compared the effects of single or six repeated doses of oxazepam on the turnover of [^{14}C]serotonin and [^{3}H]norepinephrine in the midbrain–hindbrain region of rat brain. In animals treated with a single dose of oxazepam, significant elevations were found in the concentration of [^{14}C]serotonin and [^{3}H]norepinephrine and their major metabolites. In rats treated with repeated doses of oxazepam, there were significant increases only in the concentration of [^{14}C]serotonin and metabolites labeled with ^{14}C, but not of [^{3}H]norepinephrine or metabolites labeled with ^{3}H. Thus, a decrease in norepinephrine turnover in the midbrain–hindbrain region was no longer detectable after six doses of oxazepam, although serotonin turnover was still substantially reduced. In the conflict test, the depressant action of this dose of oxazepam similarly disappears after six daily injections, whereas its anxiety-reducing action persists (Margules and Stein, 1968).

Oxazepam also exerted small effects on serotonin turnover in the diencephalon–forebrain region, but the greatest effects of the drug were concentrated in the midbrain–hindbrain region. This result seems consistent with the observation that intraventricularly administered serotonin is selectively accumulated in the central gray area of the midbrain (Aghajanian and Bloom, 1967), a region frequently associated with punishment and aversive behavior (Fernandez deMolina and Hunsperger, 1962; Olds and Olds, 1963; Stein, 1965). Such considerations focus attention on serotoninergic synapses in the central gray area as possible sites of action for the antianxiety effects of benzodiazepines and related tranquilizers.

3.7. Conclusions

Evidence from the rat conflict test, a widely used animal model of operant punishment, implicates serotonin systems in the neurochemical mechanisms of punishment. This evidence can be summarized as follows:

1. The punishment-lessening effects of benzodiazepines in the conflict test are mimicked by serotonin antagonists (methysergide, cinanserin, bromolysergic acid), serotonin synthesis inhibition (PCPA), and serotonin nerve terminal damage (5,6-dihydroxytryptamine).

2. Punishment effects may be intensified by the serotonin precursor 5-hydroxytryptophan (in combination with a monoamine oxidase inhibitor), serotonin agonists (α-methyltryptamine), or intraventricular injections of serotonin itself. Intraventricularly administered serotonin also antagonizes the punishment-lessening effects of benzodiazepines.

3. Stimulation of the serotoninergic cell bodies in the dorsal raphe nucleus by local application of crystalline carbachol causes intense suppression of behavior. The suppressive effects of raphe stimulation are antagonized by systemic administration of benzodiazepines.

4. In biochemical experiments, the decrease in norepinephrine turnover induced by benzodiazepines rapidly undergoes tolerance, whereas the decrease induced in serotonin turnover is maintained over repeated doses. These results parallel findings in the conflict test which indicate that the depressant action of benzodiazepines rapidly undergoes tolerance, whereas the punishment-lessening action is maintained over repeated doses.

4. REFERENCES

AGHAJANIAN, G. K., and BLOOM, F. E., 1967, Localization of tritiated serotonin in rat brain by electron-microscopic autoradiography, *J. Pharmacol. Exp. Ther.* **156**:23–30.

AMARAL, D. G., and ROUTTENBERG, A., 1975, Locus coeruleus and intercranial self-stimulation: a cautionary note, *Behav. Biol.* **13**:331–338.

ANLEZARK, G. M., CROW, T. J., and GREENWAY, A. P., 1973, Impaired learning and decreased cortical norepinephrine after bilateral locus coeruleus lesions, *Science* **181**:682–684.

ANLEZARK, G. M., ARBUTHNOTT, G. W., CHRISTIE, J. E., CROW, T. J., and SPEAR, P. J., 1974, Electrical self-stimulation in relation to cells of origin of catecholamine-containing neural systems ascending from the brain stem, *J. Physiol.* **237**:31–32.

APRISON, M. H., and FERSTER, C. B., 1961, Neurochemical correlates of behavior. II. Correlation of brain monoamine oxidase activity with behavioral changes after iproniazid and 5-hydroxytryptophan, *J. Neurochem.* **6**:350–357.

ARBUTHNOTT, G., FUXE, K., and UNGERSTEDT, U., 1971, Central catecholamine turnover and self-stimulation behavior, *Brain Res.* **27**:406–413.

ATRENS, D. M., 1973, A reinforcement analysis of rat hypothalamus, *Am. J. Physiol.* **224**:62–65.

BAUMGARTEN, H. G., BJÖRKLUND, A., LACHENMAYER, L., NOBIN, A., and STENEVI, U., 1971, Long-lasting selective depletion of brain serotonin by 5,6-dihydroxytryptamine, *Acta Physiol. Scand. Suppl.* **373**:1–15.

BAXTER, B. L., GLUCKMAN, M. I., STEIN, L., and SCERNI, R. A., 1974, Self-injection of apomorphine in the rat: positive reinforcement by a dopamine receptor stimulant, *Pharm. Biochem. Behav.* **2**:387–392.

BAXTER, B. L., GLUCKMAN, M. I., and SCERNI, R. A., 1976, Apomorphine self-injection is not affected by alpha-methylparatyrosine treatment: support for dopaminergic reward, *Pharm. Biochem. Behav.* **4**:611–612.

BELLUZZI, J. D., RITTER, S., WISE, C. D., and STEIN, L., 1975, Substantia nigra self-stimulation: dependence on noradrenergic reward pathways, *Behav. Biol.* **13**:103–111.

CARTER, D. A., and PHILLIPS, A. G., 1975, Intracranial self-stimulation at sites in the dorsal medulla oblongata, *Brain Res.* **94**:155–160.

CHASE, T. N., KATZ, R. I., and KOPIN, I. J., 1970, Effects of diazepam on fate of intracisternally injected serotonin-C^{14}, *Neuropharmacology* **9**:103–108.

CLAVIER, R. M., and ROUTTENBERG, A., 1974, Ascending monoamine-containing fiber pathways related to intracranial self-stimulation: histochemical fluorescence study, *Brain Res.* **72**:25–40.

COOK, L., and DAVIDSON, A. B., 1973, Effects of behaviorally active drugs in a conflict-punishment procedure in rats, in: *The Benzodiazepines* (S. Garattini, ed.), pp. 327–345, Raven Press, New York.

COOK, L., and SEPINWALL, J., 1975, Behavioral analysis of the effects and mechanisms of action of benzodiazepines, in: *Mechanism of Action of Benzodiazepines* (E. Costa and P. Greengard, eds.), pp. 1–28, Raven Press, New York.

CORRODI, H., FUXE, K., and HOKFELT, T., 1967, The effect of some psychoactive drugs on central monoamine neurons, *Eur. J. Pharmacol.* **1**:363–368.

CROW, T. J., 1968, Cortical synapses and reinforcement: a hypothesis, *Nature (London)* **219**:736–737.

CROW, T. J., 1972a, Catecholamine-containing neurons and electrical self-stimulation. 1. A review of some data, *Psychol. Med.* **2**:414–421.

CROW, T. J., 1972b, A map of the rat mesencephalon for electrical self-stimulation, *Brain Res.* **36**:265–273.

CROW, T. J., SPEAR, P. J., and ARBUTHNOTT, G. W., 1972, Intracranial self-stimulation with electrodes in the region of the locus coeruleus, *Brain Res.* **36**:275–287.

DAHLSTRÖM, A., and FUXE, K., 1964, Evidence for the existence of monoamine-containing neurons in the central nervous system. 1. Demonstration of monoamines in the cell bodies of brain stem neurons, *Acta Physiol. Scand.* **62** (232):1–55.

DAVIS, W. M., and SMITH, S. G., 1975, Self-administration of noradrenergic and dopaminergic agonists, *Neurosci. Abst.* **1**:276.

DAVIS, W. M., SMITH, S. G., and KHALSA, J. H., 1975, Noradrenergic role in the self-administration of morphine or amphetamine, *Pharm. Biochem. Behav.* **3**:477–484.

DEUTSCH, J. A., 1960, *The Structural Basis of Behavior*, University of Chicago Press, Chicago.

FERNANDEZ DEMOLINA, A. F., and HUNSPERGER, R. W., 1962, Organization of the subcortical system governing defense and flight reactions in the cat, *J. Physiol.* **160**:200–213.

FRANKLIN, K. B. J., and HERBERG, L. J., 1974, Self-stimulation and catecholamines: drug-induced mobilization of the "reverse"-pool reestablished responding in catecholamine-depleted rats, *Brain Res.* **67**:429–437.

FRANKLIN, K. B. J., and HERBERG, L. J., 1975, Self-stimulation and noradrenaline: evidence that inhibition of synthesis abolishes responding only if the "reserve" pool is dispersed first, *Brain Res.* **97**:127–132.

FUXE, K., HOKFELT, T., and UNGERSTEDT, U., 1968, Localization of indolealkylamines in CNS, in: *Advances in Pharmacology* (S. Garattini and P. A. Shore, eds.), pp. 235–251, Academic Press, New York.

FUXE, K., HOKFELT, T., and UNGERSTEDT, U., 1970, Morphological and functional aspects of central monoamine neurons, *Int. Rev. Neurobiol.* **13**:93–126.

GALLISTEL, C. R., 1973, The neurophysiology of reward and motivation, in: *The Physiological Basis of Memory* (J. A. Dseutsch, ed.), pp. 176–267, Academic Press, New York.

GELLER, I., and BLUM, K., 1970, The effects of 5-HT on para-chlorophenylalanine (p-CPA) attenuation of "conflict" behavior, *Eur. J. Pharmacol.* **9**:319–324.

GELLER, I., and SEIFTER, J., 1960, The effects of meprobamate, barbiturates, d-amphetamine and promazine on experimentally induced conflict in the rat, *Psychopharmacologia* **1**:482–492.

GELLER, I., KULAK, J. T., JR., and SEIFTER, J., 1962, The effects of chlordiazepoxide and chlorpromazine on a punishment discrimination, *Psychopharmacologia* **3**:374–385.

GELLER, I., BACHMAN, E., and SEIFTER, J., 1963, Effects of reserpine and morphine on behavior suppressed by punishment, *Life Sci.* **4**:226–231.

GELLER, I., HARTMANN, R. J., and CROY, D. J., 1974, Attenuation of conflict behavior with cinanserin, a serotonin antagonist: reversal of the effect with 5-hydroxytryptophan and α-methyltryptamine, *Res. Commun. Chem. Pathol. Pharmacol.* **7**:165–174.

GERMAN, D. C., and BOWDEN, D. M., 1974, Catecholamine systems as the neural substrate for intracranial self-stimulation: a hypothesis, *Brain Res.* **73**:381–419.

GLOWINSKI, J., and AXELROD, J., 1965, Effect of drugs on the uptake, release, and metabolism of H^3-norepinephrine in the rat brain, *J. Pharmacol. Exp. Ther.* **149**:43–49.

GOLD, R. M., KAPATOS, G., and CAREY, R. J., 1973, A retracting wire knife for stereotaxic brain surgery made from a microliter syringe, *Physiol. Behav.* **10**:813–815.

GOLDBERG, M. E., MANIAN, A. A., and EFRON, D. H., 1967, A comparative study of certain

pharmacological responses following acute and chronic administration of chlordiazepoxide, *Life Sci.* **6**:481–491.
GRAEFF, F. G., and SCHOENFELD, R. I., 1970, Tryptaminergic mechanisms in punished and nonpunished behavior, *J. Pharmacol. Exp. Ther.* **173**:277–283.
HERBERG, L. J., STEPHENS, D. N., and FRANKLIN, K. B. J., 1976, Catecholamines and self-stimulation: evidence suggesting a reinforcing role for noradrenaline and a motivating role for dopamine, *Pharmacol. Biochem. Behav.* **4**:575–582.
JACOBWITZ, D. M., 1973, Effects of 6-hydroxydopa, in: *Frontiers in Catecholamine Research* (E. Usdin and H. S. Snyder, eds.), pp. 729–739, Pergamon Press, New York.
KELLEHER, R. T., and MORSE, W. H., 1964, Escape behavior and punished behavior, *Fed. Proc.* **23**:808–835.
KETY, S. S., 1970, The biogenic amines in the central nervous system: their possible roles in arousal, emotion and learning, in: *The Neurosciences: Second Study Program* (F. O. Schmitt, ed.), pp. 324–336, Rockefeller University Press, New York.
KETY, S. S., 1972, The possible role of the adrenergic systems of the cortex in learning, in: *Neurotransmitters* (I. J. Kopin, ed.), pp. 376–389, Williams and Wilkins, Baltimore.
KLÜVER, H., and BARRERA, E., 1953, Method for combined staining of cells and fibers in the nervous system, *J. Neuropathol. Exp. Neurol.* **12**:400–403.
KOELLA, W. P., and CZICMAN, J., 1966, Mechanism of the EEG-synchronizing action of serotonin, *Am. J. Physiol.* **211**:926–934.
KOJIMA, H., RITTER, S., WISE, C. D., and STEIN, L., unpublished data (cited in Stein and Wise, 1973).
LEIBOWITZ, S. F., 1972, Central adrenergic receptors and the regulation of hunger and thirst, in: *Neurotransmitters* (I. J. Kopin, ed.), pp. 327–358, Williams and Wilkins, Baltimore.
LIEBMAN, J. M., and BUTCHER, L. L., 1973, Effects on self-stimulation behavior of drugs influencing dopaminergic neurotransmission mechanisms, *Naunyn-Schmiedebergs Archiv. Pharmacol.* **277**:305–318.
LIEBMAN, J. M., MAYER, D. J., and LIEBESKIND, J. C., 1973, Self-stimulation in the midbrain central gray matter of the rat, *Behavioral Biology* **9**:299–306.
LINDVALL, O., and BJÖRKLUND, A., 1974, The organization of the ascending catecholamine neuron systems in the rat brain as revealed by the glyoxylic acid fluorescence method, *Acta Physiol. Scand. Suppl.* **412**:1–48.
LIPPA, A. S., ANTELMAN, S. M., FISHER, A. E., and CANFIELD, D. R., 1973, Neurochemical mediation of reward: a significant role for dopamine, *Pharmacol. Biochem. Behav.* **1**:23–25.
MACKINTOSH, N. J., 1974, *The Psychology of Animal Learning*, Academic Press, New York.
MARGULES, D. L., 1969, Noradrenergic rather than serotonergic basis of reward in dorsal tegmentum, *J. Comp. Physiol. Psychol.* **67**:32–35.
MARGULES, D. L., and STEIN, L., 1967, Neuroleptics vs. tranquilizers: evidence from animal studies of mode and site of action, in: *Neuropsychopharmacology* (H. Brill, J. O. Cole, P. Deniker, H. Hippinus, and P. B. Bradley, eds.), pp. 108–120, Excerpta Medica Foundation, Amsterdam.
MARGULES, D. L., and STEIN, L., 1968, Increase of "antianxiety" activity and tolerance of behavioral depression during chronic administration of oxazepam, *Phychopharmacologia* **13**:74–80.
MAYER, D. J. and LIEBESKIND, J. C., 1974, Pain reduction by focal electrical stimulation of the brain: an anatomical and behavioral analysis, *Brain Res.* **68**:73–93.
OLDS, J., 1962, Hypothalamic substrates of reward, *Physiol. Rev.* **42**:554–604.
OLDS, J., and MILNER, P., 1954, Positive reinforcement produced by electrical stimulation of septal area and other regions, *J. Comp. Physiol. Psychol.* **47**:419–427.
OLDS, J., and OLDS, M. E., 1963, Approach-avoidance analysis of rat diencephalon, *J. Comp. Neurol.* **120**:259–295.

Olson, L., and Fuxe, K., 1972, Further mapping out of central noradrenaline neuron systems: projections of the "subcoeruleus" area, *Brain Res.* **43**:289–295.

Phillips, A. G., and Fibiger, H. C., 1973, Dopaminergic and noradrenergic substrates of positive reinforcement: differential effects of d- and l-amphetamine, *Science* **179**:575–576.

Poschel, B. P. H., and Ninteman, F. W., 1963, Norepinephrine: a possible excitatory neurohormone of the reward system, *Life Sci.* **2**:782–788.

Ritter, S., and Stein, L., 1973, Self-stimulation of noradrenergic cell group (A6) in the locus coeruleus of rats, *J. Comp. Physiol. Psychol.* **85**:443–452.

Ritter, S., and Stein, L., 1974, Self-stimulation in the mesencephalic trajectory of the ventral noradrenergic bundle, *Brain Res.* **81**:145–157.

Robichaud, R. C., and Sledge, K. L., 1969, The effects of p-chlorophenylalanine on experimentally induced conflict in the rat, *Life Sci.* **8**:965–969.

Roll, S. K., 1970, Intracranial self-stimulation and wakefulness: effects of manipulating ambient brain catecholamines, *Science* **168**:1370–1372.

Rolls, E. T., Kelly, P. H., and Shaw, S. G., 1974, Noradrenaline, dopamine, and brain-stimulation reward, *Pharmacol. Biochem. Behav.* **2**:735–740.

Routtenberg, A., and Malsbury, C., 1969, Brainstem pathways of reward, *J. Comp. Physiol. Psychol.* **68**:22–30.

Sclafani, A., and Grossman, S. P., 1969, Hyperphagia produced by knife cuts between the medial and lateral hypothalamus in the rat, *Physiol. Behav.* **4**:533–537.

Simon, H., LeMoal, M., and Cardo, B., 1975, Self-stimulation in the dorsal pontine tegmentum in the rat, *Behav. Biol.* **13**:339–347.

Skinner, B. F., 1938, *The Behavior of Organisms,* Appleton-Century-Crofts, New York.

Stein, L., 1962, Effects and interactions of imipramine, chlorpromazine, reserpine and amphetamine on self-stimulation: possible neurophysiological basis of depression, in: *Recent Advances in Biological Psychiatry,* Vol. 4 (J. Wortis, ed.), pp. 288–308, Plenum Press, New York.

Stein, L., 1964a, Reciprocal action of reward and punishment mechanisms, in: *The Role of Pleasure in Behavior* (R. G. Heath, ed.), pp. 113–139, Hoeber Medical Division, Harper and Row, New York.

Stein, L., 1964b, Self-stimulation of the brain and the central stimulant action of amphetamine, *Fed. Proc.* **23**:836–850.

Stein, L., 1965, Facilitation of avoidance behavior by positive brain stimulation, *J. Comp. Physiol. Psychol.* **60**(1):9–19.

Stein, L., 1968, Chemistry of reward and punishment, in *Psychopharmacology, A Review of Progress* (D. H. Efron, ed.), pp. 105–123, U.S. Government Printing Office, Washington, D.C.

Stein, L., and Ray, O. S., 1960, Brain stimulation reward "thresholds" self-determined in rat, *Psychopharmacologia* **1**:251–256.

Stein, L., and Wise, C. D., 1969, Release of norepinephrine for hypothalamus and amygdala by rewarding forebrain bundled stimulation and amphetamine, *J. Comp. Physiol. Psychol.* **67**:189–198.

Stein, L., and Wise, C. D., 1971, Possible etiology of schizophrenia: progressive damage to the noradrenergic reward system by 6-hydroxydopamine, *Science* **171**:1032–1036.

Stein, L., and Wise, C. D., 1973, Amphetamine and noradrenergic reward pathways, in: *Frontiers in Catecholamine Research* (E. Usdin and S. H. Snyder, eds.), pp. 963–968, Pergamon Press, New York.

Stein, L., Wise, C. D., and Berger, B. D., 1972, Noradrenergic reward mechanisms, recovery of function, and schizophrenia, in: *The Chemistry of Mood, Motivation, and Memory* (J. L. McGaugh, ed.), pp. 81–103, Plenum Press, New York.

Stein, L., Wise, C. D., and Berger, B. D., 1973, Antianxiety action of benzodiazepines: decrease in activity of serotonin neurons in the punishment system, in: *The Benzodiaze-*

pines (S. Garattini, E. Mussine, and L. Randall, eds.), pp. 299–326, Raven Press, New York.
STEIN, L., WISE, C. D., and BELLUZZI, J. D., 1975, Effects of benzodiazepines on central serotonergic mechanisms, in: *Mechanism of Action of Benzodiazepines* (E. Costa and P. Greengards, eds.), pp. 29–44, Raven Press, New York.
STENEVI, U., BJERRE, B., BJÖRKLUND, A., and MOBLEY, W., 1974, Effects of localized intracerebral injections of nerve growth factor on the regenerative growth of lesioned central noradrenergic neurons, *Brain Res.* **69:**217–234.
STEPHENS, D. N., FRANKLIN, K. B. J., and HERBERG, L. J., 1975, Differing but complementary functions of brain noradrenaline and dopamine in self-stimulation, in: *Proceedings of the 1st International Conference on Brain-Stimulation Reward,* Beerse, Belgium, pp. 79–80.
STINUS, L., and THIERRY, A. M., 1973, Self-stimulation and catecholamines. II. Blockade of self-stimulation by treatment with alpha-methylparatyrosine and reinstatement by catecholamine precursor administration, *Brain Res.* **64:**189–198.
TAYLOR, K. M., and LAVERTY, R., 1969, The effects of chlordiazepoxide, diazepam and nitrazepam on catecholamine metabolism in regions of the rat brain, *Eur. J. Pharmacol.* **8:**296–301.
UNGERSTEDT, U., 1971*a*, Histochemical studies of the effect of intracerebral and intraventricular injections of 6-hydroxydopamine on monoamine neurons in the rat brain, in: *6-Hydroxydopamine and Catecholamine Neurons* (T. Malmfors and H. Thoenen, eds.), pp. 101–127, American Elsevier, New York.
UNGERSTEDT, U., 1971*b*, Stereotaxic mapping of the monoamine pathways in the rat brain, *Acta Physiol. Scand. Suppl. 367* **82:**1–48.
WAUQUIER, A., and NIEMEGEERS, C. J. E., 1972, Intracranial self-stimulation in rats as a function of various stimulus parameters. II. Influence of haloperidol, pimozide and pipampherone on medial forebrain bundle stimulation with monopolar electrodes, *Psychopharmacologia,* **27:**191–202.
WAUQUIER, A., and ROLLS, E. T. (eds.), 1976, *Brain-Stimulation Reward,* North-Holland, Amsterdam.
WEIGHT, F. F., and SALMOIRAGHI, G. C., 1968, Serotonin effects on central neurons, in: *Advances in Pharmacology* (S. Garattini and P. A. Shore, eds.), pp. 395–413, Academic Press, New York.
WISE, C. D., and STEIN, L., 1969, Facilitation of brain self-stimulation by central administration of norepinephrine, *Science* **163:**299–301.
WISE, C. D., and STEIN, L., 1970, Amphetamine: facilitation of behavior by augmented release of norepinephrine from the medial forebrain bundle, in: *Amphetamines and Related Compounds* (E. Costa and S. Garattini, eds.), pp. 463–485, Raven Press, New York.
WISE, C. D., BERGER, B. D., and STEIN, L., 1972, Benzodiazepines: anxiety-reducing activity by reduction of serotonin turnover in the brain, *Science* **177:**180–183.
WISE, C. D., BERGER, B. D., and STEIN, L., 1973, Evidence of α-noradrenergic reward receptors and serotonergic punishment receptors in the rat brain, *Biol. Psychiat.* **6:**3–21.

3

THE PSYCHOPHARMACOLOGY OF FEEDING

Bartley G. Hoebel

1. INTRODUCTION

Studies of behavioral neurochemistry have revolutionized research on feeding. The catalyst was Grossman's (1960) discovery that norepinephrine injected directly into the hypothalamus via a cannula selectively induced feeding behavior in the rat. Then Ungerstedt (1970) showed that depletion of dopamine by intracerebral injection of a selective neurotoxin could mimic part of the classical, lateral hypothalamic, starvation syndrome. The advent of a simple technique for injecting drugs into the brain through implanted cannulas and the realization that the local application of drugs could have meaningful behavioral effects has precipitated a great change in the neuroscientist's approach and thinking. Studies of feeding have been at the forefront of this change.

Evidence has now been marshalled for central nervous system noradrenergic, dopaminergic, serotonergic, and cholinergic influences on food intake. Hand in hand with this progress, the neuropharmacology of systemically injected drugs has come under intensive study in the hope of understanding and improving the agents used to curb food intake in overweight people and to facilitate food intake in those who lack the urge to eat.

This chapter focuses first on neurotransmitters in the control of feeding in mammals and then uses this information as a basis for discussing selected drugs which are thought to cause anorexia or hunger. (For other shorter

---

Bartley G. Hoebel • Department of Psychology, Princeton University, Princeton, New Jersey 08540.

reviews the reader can refer to Hoebel, 1971; Grossman and Sclafani, 1971; Leibowitz, 1972; Cole, 1973a; Heil and Ross, 1973; Singer and Montgomery, 1973; Baile, 1974; Mawson, 1974; Novin *et al.*, 1975; and Hoebel, 1977).

There are a number of interesting discoveries to be discussed. They include observations that norepinephrine-induced feeding is linked to fluid balance; norepinephrine effects on satiety can change with circadian rhythm; amphetamine has both alpha- and beta-adrenergic properties in the hypothalamus and can elicit eating as well as suppress it; hyperphagia may result from depletion of brain norepinephrine or serotonin; and amphetamine loses some of its anorectic effectiveness in norepinephrine-depleted rats, but fenfluramine becomes more effective.

Although most anorectics can act in the brain, some may also act peripherally either directly to alter fat stores or indirectly by releasing satiety signals to the brain. There is new evidence that some of the popular anorectic monoamine derivatives are truly effective in suppressing appetite and causing weight loss in overweight people, even when the drugs are not stimulants, but it will be shown that social, physiological, and personality factors can influence tests of drug efficacy and should be taken into account when clinical decisions are being made.

2. PUTATIVE NEUROTRANSMITTERS AND FOOD INTAKE

2.1. Norepinephrine and Epinephrine

2.1.1. The Discovery of Norepinephrine-Induced Feeding

a. Injection of Crystalline Drugs. MacLean (1957) showed that chemicals in crystalline form applied to the brain could produce localized effects. Grossman, in Miller's laboratory at Yale, improved the technique by implanting a guide shaft to permit repeated application of drugs to precisely the same brain area in a given rat. The guide shaft was lodged with its tip in the lateral hypothalamic area near the fornix where Miller and his colleagues routinely obtained electrically elicited feeding. Grossman chose drugs well known for their neurotransmitter functions in the peripheral nervous system and applied them to this hypothalamic site. The result was feeding in response to noradrenaline application and drinking with cholinergic drugs.

Norepinephrine-elicited feeding began after a few minutes and lasted about one-half hour. The rats consumed several grams of food or sometimes as much as a full day's ration. If the treatment was repeated daily, it was sufficient to cause an increase in body weight. The effective dose was huge; 1–5 μg of crystalline norepinephrine was injected as judged by weighing the inner cannula with and without drug. This not only caused a feeding response but also inhibited drinking. Greater doses caused lethargy (Grossman, 1962a). Norepinephrine was more effective than epinephrine, suggesting that norepinephrine might be the neurotransmitter in a feeding system. Drugs injected systemically to block noradrenergic or cholinergic action strengthened Grossman's conclusions. For example, norepinephrine failed to induce feeding in rats pretreated with ethoxybutamoxane, an adrenergic blocker.

b. Fluid Injections. Aqueous solutions were used by Miller, Gottesman, and Emery (1964) in a dose–response study performed to confirm the main effects of the earlier studies. Increasing doses of norepinephrine produced increased consumption of liquid diet. The threshold dose was 0.8 μg. Other laboratories confirmed the norepinephrine feeding effect and found a broader range of effective sites. Wagner and DeGroot (1963) obtained feeding from the ventromedial hypothalamus; and Coury (1967), working with Fisher (1969), observed the effect throughout much of the limbic system. Booth (1967) used fluid injections through tiny, 34 gauge cannulas and reported that the effect was very reliable, specific to feeding as opposed to drinking, all or none in occurrence, and localized (± 0.1 mm) in structures from the original perifornical hypothalamic site to the lateral septum.

The best source summarizing the first five years of this work is in the meeting proceedings published in the *Annals of the New York Academy of Science* where Grossman (1969), Fisher (1969), Soulairac (1969), and Myers (1969) discussed their extensions of the new discovery.

In the same volume Lehr (1969) raised the possibility that the noradrenergic feeding response might be differentially coded according to the alpha–beta classification. This is a scheme based on peripheral bioassays in which some sympathetic systems, called alpha-adrenergic, are most sensitive to norepinephrine, less so to epinephrine, and least to isoproterenol, whereas other systems, denoted beta-adrenergic, are most sensitive in the reverse order: isoproterenol is more potent than epinephrine, which in turn exceeds norepinephrine (Ahlquist, 1948; Kattus *et al.*, 1970; Innes and Nickerson, 1970). Alpha and beta effects are usually opposing. For example, in their differential action on smooth muscles of blood vessels, alpha-adrenergic drugs cause vasoconstriction and the beta-adrenergic type cause vasodilation. When Lehr and his colleagues suggested alpha–beta coding of feeding, they had already found evidence for such a distinction in the neurochemical control of thirst, but Lehr (1974) maintained that it is not clear whether this distinction is due to peripheral or central systems in the control of thirst. For an overview of modern thirst research, including its pharmacology, see Epstein *et al.* (1973).

2.1.2. Chemical Coding of Behavior in the Brain

This was the title of an influential article in *Science* in which Miller (1965) summarized the great potential for the "chemostimulation" technique in tracing neural circuits. The advantage from the experimentalist's point of view was that it enables one to distinguish separate neural systems, any one of which could be individually stimulated by an electrode or destroyed by a lesion. It was a chance to stimulate or block selectively on the basis of synaptic function. In particular, Miller emphasized that lateral hypothalamic feeding, thirst, and the reward of self-stimulation might have different chemical receptor properties and in that sense be "coded."

The second five years of research on norepinephrine and feeding were dominated by efforts to analyze the new discovery at the synaptic receptor level by distinguishing alpha and beta systems. Booth (1968) suggested that norepinephrine had an alpha-adrenergic action in the brain because norepinephrine-induced feeding could be prevented by hypothalamic injection of an alpha-adrenergic blocker, phentolamine. Moreover, the use of MAO inhibition with nialamide plus tetrabenazine to release norepinephrine at the synapse caused feeding analogous to direct injection of norepinephrine (Slangen and Miller, 1969). Similarly, desmethylimipramine, which blocks reuptake of norepinephrine and increases synaptic norepinephrine concentrations, potentiated feeding following hypothalamic norepinephrine injection (Booth, 1968) and also increased spontaneous feeding (Montgomery et al., 1971).

More recently it has been shown that immediately after 6-hydroxydopamine (6-OHDA) injection to destroy catecholaminergic nerves there is a period of increased feeding, thought to result from catecholamine release during the cellular destruction induced by 6-OHDA (Evetts et al., 1972). Ritter and Epstein (1974) injected norepinephrine in shots as small as 2.5 ng, which prolonged spontaneous meals but did not initiate them. They suggest norepinephrine may normally function in the control of meal size.

Considering all the evidence, there can be very little doubt that endogenous norepinephrine, an alpha agonist, can induce feeding. The next advance was the discovery of beta-adrenergic responses to hypothalamic injections of isoproterenol.

Most of what we know from this technique comes from the laboratories of Margules and Leibowitz who independently tested a battery of alpha- and beta-adrenergic agonists and antagonists. In brief, Margules (1969) found opposing alpha- and beta-adrenergic processes, both of which *suppressed* feeding; the alpha system suppressed feeding in response to postingestional satiety factors, and the beta system suppressed feeding by taste factors. Leibowitz (1970a) found *alpha-adrenergic feeding* and *beta-adrenergic satiety*. These two sets of results are clearly conflicting, but new techniques have been brought to bear on the problem, and some semblance of order is emerging. Dose, cannula site, test diet, and circadian effects may be crucial factors. Adrenergic feeding effects will be discussed, then adrenergic satiety.

2.1.3. Alpha-Adrenergic Feeding

Leibowitz (1970a, 1972) combined the research trends from Miller's and Lehr's laboratories in an elegant series of experiments which demonstrated that alpha-adrenergic agonists (e.g., norepinephrine) caused feeding when injected into the hypothalamus, that this feeding is blocked by alpha blockers (such as phentolamine) delivered peripherally or through the same cannula, and that the feeding is potentiated by beta-adrenergic blockers (propranolol). Epinephrine, which has both alpha and beta effects in the peripheral nervous system, retained its dual role in the central nervous system. Its predominant effect was alpha-adrenergic elicitation of feeding. Thus, either norepinephrine or epinephrine injected into the perifornical region of the hypothalamus in doses of 10–200 nmol increased food intake in *ad lib* fed or food-deprived rats, and the effect was clearly alpha, as opposed to beta-adrenergic. Broekkamp and Van Rossum (1972) injected clonadine, an alpha agonist, and they too observed feeding that was blocked by phentolamine.

Singer and Kelley (1972) obtained similar results with an interesting twist; norepinephrine injected into the hypothalamus on one side of the brain was blocked by the alpha blocker phentolamine on the contralateral side. It was as if the effects of the drugs on the two sides of the brain were integrated at some higher level. The problem of cannulated drugs leaking up the cannula shaft, acting and interacting in the ventricle, is treated by Routtenberg (1972).

Leibowitz (1970b) next localized the norepinephrine effect medial to the fornix in the medial hypothalamic region where one could presume that the noradrenergic synapses might inhibit the classical ventromedial hypothalamic satiety system and thereby disinhibit feeding. Most recently she has localized noradrenergic feeding in two nearby hypothalamic regions, the paraventricular nucleus, and the periventricular nuclei. To accomplish this, fluid injections in nanogram quantities were applied, showing that feeding could be elicited with norepinephrine in concentrations which approach physiological levels (Leibowitz, 1973).

a. Neurochemical Correlates of Food–Fluid Balance. There appears to be a reciprocal interaction between adrenergic and cholinergic influences on ingestive behavior. Grossman (1962b) observed that norepinephrine elicited feeding and inhibited thirst, whereas carbachol produced drinking while inhibiting feeding. This has been confirmed (Singer and Kelly, 1972), but Hutchinson and Renfrew (1967) warn that injection site and deprivation conditions at the time of testing can greatly affect the results. Leibowitz (1972, 1973) suggests that noradrenergic inhibition of drinking is alpha-adrenergic. A physiological parallel to the inhibition of drinking was noted by Blundell and Herberg (1973) in studies showing that primary polydiuresis with dilute urine occurred after hypothalamic injections of norepinephrine. Thus norepinephrine injections can make the rat act behaviorally and physiologically as if excessively hydrated.

On the other hand, it is also well known that when a rat in water balance eats a meal, it drinks and conserves water (Epstein, 1971). Miller and Chien observed that some rats given hypothalamic norepinephrine drank a little water before starting to eat and were slightly antidiuretic (Miller, 1965).

Leibowitz (1973, 1975a) has observed this series of interlocking physiological and behavioral responses using 33 ng of norepinephrine injected in the periventricular or paraventricular nuclei. The rats drank 1-4 ml starting within a minute, then ate 2-5 g starting within 3 or 4 min, and if the cannula was in the supraoptic nucleus antidiuresis occurred (Garay and Leibowitz, 1974). The threshold dose for the feeding component of the response was only 0.04 µg. Pharmacological analysis with adrenergic blockers indicated that the feeding response was alpha-adrenergic and the prior drinking involved both alpha and beta receptors (Leibowitz, 1975b). This is the first evidence for neurochemical control of prandial (mealtime) drinking and water conservation.

We are beginning to see in these neurochemical studies evidence for the neural linkages which chain ingestive behaviors together in the defense of homeostasis. More needs to be done, however, to show that local, endogenous norepinephrine can serve all these functions.

b. Postsynaptic Action: Neurotransmission or Metabolic Modulation. Leibowitz and most other workers have taken the results as evidence for a noradrenergic action on postsynaptic receptor sites of neurons in a feeding control circuit. In other words, norepinephrine acts as a neurotransmitter which activates alpha-adrenergic, postsynaptic receptor sites. Davis and Keesey (1971) have suggested another possibility. Norepinephrine might modify the metabolic rate of cells involved in feeding. As evidence they showed that feeding induced by hypothalamic norepinephrine injections interacted with insulin administration. Insulin-induced hypoglycemia was associated with a marked increase in norepinephrine-induced feeding. Thus, norepinephrine might produce feeding by acting synergistically with insulin to modulate metabolic events in cells which act as feeding control sensors (e.g., glucoreceptors). In any case it is agreed that alpha specificity of feeding caused by norepinephrine or epinephrine is probably the result of coding in the postsynaptic receptor (Davis and Keesey, 1971; Leibowitz, 1972). There is also a possibility that some of the effects are the result of presynaptic end-product inhibition whereby exogenous drugs affect the synthesis and release of endogenous transmitter.

c. Postsynaptic Action: Excitation or Disinhibition. Grossman (1962a) and Miller (1965) originally suggested that norepinephrine might be an excitatory neurotransmitter. This seemed less likely when Leibowitz and Miller (1969) noted that intrahypothalamic chlorpromazine (an aminergic-receptor blocking agent) produced feeding like norepinephrine. In the central nervous system chlorpromazine only mimics norepinephrine in situations in which chlorpromazine has an inhibitory action (Bradley et al., 1966). Therefore, norepinephrine may serve an inhibitory function at the cellular level in the hypothalamus; it might inhibit a neural satiety function, thereby disinhibiting feeding.

When Leibowitz found that the norepinephrine effect on feeding is stronger in the ventromedial than the lateral hypothalamic region, this reinforced the idea that norepinephrine might be inhibiting the well-known ventromedial satiety function rather than exciting the lateral hypothalamic feeding system directly. Coons and Quartermain (1970) found that norepinephrine-induced feeding shared some of the "motivational weakness" known for feeding produced by ventromedial hypothalamic lesions. Norepinephrine-induced feeding was also "finicky" feeding (Booth and Quartermain, 1965). In addition, norepinephrine injected intraventricularly facilitated feeding in rats recovering from lateral hypothalamic lesions. This was interpreted as inhibition of a medial hypothalamic satiety system (Berger *et al.*, 1971). They also found that the alpha feeding effect was sometimes produced by beta block with propranolol. Logically, the alpha-noradrenergic effect was blocked by the alpha blocker phentolamine.

Similarly, phentolamine prevented gourmet rats from eating highly desired meal worms, even though it failed to block this feeding response when induced by deprivation (Broekkamp *et al.*, 1974).

Thus, in many respects it was as if alpha-adrenergic function mimicked a ventromedial hypothalamic lesion. Both disinhibited feeding with signs of finickiness as if both deactivated the same satiety system. As additional evidence, Herberg and Franklin (1972) found that ventromedial hypothalamic lesions eliminated norepinephrine feeding. On the other hand, they point out that not all medial lesions that produced hyperphagia also diminished norepinephrine feeding; so the interpretation of this combined lesion and injection study is not simple. We will have more to say about this later in the light of combined lesions and neurochemical depletion.

As a final bit of indirect evidence for disinhibition, norepinephrine depletion by 6-hydroxydopamine does not eliminate feeding (Ahlskog and Hoebel, 1972), which suggests that norepinephrine is not necessary for feeding. Therefore, when norepinephrine applied through a cannula elicits feeding, it probably does so indirectly as by the inhibition of a satiety function.

d. Norepinephrine Release. Indirect evidence for endogenous norepinephrine release causing feeding was outlined earlier. Direct evidence would be obtained if it could be demonstrated that radioactively labeled norepinephrine was released during feeding. Since norepinephrine injected into the ventricles can diffuse from the ventricles to the relevant synapses, as shown by a change in feeding behavior (e.g., Berger *et al.*, 1971), this also might work in reverse. If so, norepinephrine from the synapses could be recovered from the ventricles as a function of feeding behavior. This has been shown by Myers (1974). Moreover, hypothalamic perfusate from a hungry monkey induced feeding when reinjected into the hypothalamus of a satiated monkey (Yaksh and Myers, 1972).

e. Noradrenergic Feeding in a Variety of Animals. Baile (1974) has summarized the evidence for norepinephrine feeding in sheep and cattle. In all cases in which an alpha antagonist was tested, it blocked norepinephrine-induced feeding or caused satiety by itself. Norepinephrine feeding has also been confirmed in cats (Avery and Nance, 1970) and pigs (Jackson and Robinson, 1971), as well as in monkeys (Sharpe and Myers, 1969; Setler and Smith, 1974). The effect in monkeys was especially convincing. Chair-restricted monkeys started eating within 5 sec of a 21 µg injection of *l*- (not *d*-) norepinephrine injected into the lateral or anterior hypothalamus (Sharpe and Myers, 1969). The effect was decreased by pretreatment with alpha blockers (phentolamine or phenoxybenzamine) but not by beta blockers. Epinephrine also elicited feeding, but not as well as norepinephrine.

f. Summary. There seems to be some agreement in the last few years that norepinephrine injections in the hypothalamus can produce feeding and does so by disinhibition. We can also conclude that the effect, when it occurs, is alpha-adrenergic, not beta-adrenergic, that the relevant synapses are close enough to the ventricles to be reached by diffusion, and that they are heavily concentrated in several regions of the medial and anterior hypothalamus where they function together with other influences controlling thirst and diuresis. Alpha-adrenergic receptors apparently function in short-term maintenance of fluid balance in the oro-gastro-intestinal tract at meal time and in overall osmotic balance as part of physiological and behavioral homeostasis. There is not yet sufficient evidence to be sure that these synapses use endogenous norepinephrine as a neurotransmitter, but much evidence points in that direction.

2.1.4. *Alpha-Adrenergic Satiety*

Margules (1969, 1970) presented the first evidence for a noradrenergic satiety function. His results are very different from those reviewed above. The alpha agonist, norepinephrine, injected into approximately the same perifornical lateral hypothalamic region used by workers in Miller's laboratory produced satiety instead of feeding. Rats taken from their home cages during the nocturnal period of their light cycle were placed in a testing cage with sweetened, canned milk available instead of their usual diet of *ad libitum* chow. Intrahypothalamic *l*-norepinephrine decreased their consumption of milk. The clearest indication of alpha-adrenergic satiety was produced by the alpha blocker phentolamine when injected alone. Milk consumption doubled. The milk, however, had to be sweet, not bitter (Margules, 1970).

Norepinephrine suppressed feeding regardless of whether the milk was sweet or bitter, and this result was antagonized by food deprivation. This led Margules to propose the alpha-adrenergic satiety theory which states that increased concentration of norepinephrine at appropriate hypothalamic synapses enhances the feeding suppressant effect on food intake of physiological satiety cues coming from the digestion of food.

Note that this theory says that alpha *blockers* produce overeating of palatable food like a ventromedial hypothalamic lesion, which is quite the opposite of the earlier discussion in which this was ascribed to norepinephrine. (For a discussion of "finickiness" following hypothalamic lesions, see

Hoebel, 1974.) The best way to remember these two theories is to think in terms of norepinephrine feeding for Leibowitz and norepinephrine satiety for Margules.

a. Circadian Reversal of Norepinephrine Effects. Table 1 summarizes Margules' scheme alongside that of Leibowitz. As a first step toward elucidating these conflicting results, recent work by Margules' group has shown that norepinephrine suppresses feeding when milk is introduced at night, but the same injection at the same brain site in the same rat can enhance milk consumption in the daytime. This confirms with a liquid diet the norepinephrine feeding effect of Grossman, Leibowitz, and others.

Margules *et al.* (1972) propose that norepinephrine may be involved in an endogenous circadian oscillator for feeding, or that norepinephrine released as a consequence of energy homeostasis interacts with oscillating norepinephrine levels to produce satiety at night and feeding in the day.

Stern and Zwick (1973) confirmed the circadian reversal of norepinephrine-induced feeding. They used intraventricular injections. Unfortunately, Armstrong and Singer (1974) obtained opposite results. The three studies used different doses, and so we can draw no general conclusions.

That diurnal cycle can affect, even reverse, drug effects emphasizes the importance of time of day in assessing any drug's action. The reader interested in "chronopharmacology" can refer to the review by Reinberg and Halberg (1971).

b. Noradrenergic Satiety in Other Animals. Norepinephrine injected intraventricularly into cattle produced anorexia which was antagonized by an alpha blocker, phenoxybenzamine (Baille, 1974). In cats, the picture is very incomplete. In one study norepinephrine in the preoptic region blocked feeding and in the anterior hypothalamus increased feeding, unless the dose was too high, in which case feeding decreased. This serves to warn that placement, dose level, and other effects such as body-temperature changes may influence the results on food intake (Milner *et al.*, 1971). There is no evidence favoring any particular interpretation across species.

2.1.5. Beta-Adrenergic Satiety

Peripheral administration of beta-adrenergic drugs pointed to a central beta-adrenergic satiety function. Lehr's group reported that systemic isoproterenol, the beta agonist, decreased food intake. Systemic epinephrine also caused anorexia associated with stupor; however, pretreatment with an alpha blocker, tolazoline, caused aphagia without stupor which the authors attributed to epinephrine's activity on a brain beta-adrenergic satiety function (Conte *et al.*, 1968). They obtained similar results with perifornical hypothalamic injections and, in addition, noted a decrease in feeding from serotonin as well as isoproterenol. Systemic propranolol blocked both (Goldman *et al.*, 1971).

a. Beta-Adrenergic Satiety with Reference to Alpha Feeding. Leibowitz

TABLE 1
Summary of Alpha- and Beta-Adrenergic Effect on Feeding Following Perifornical, Lateral Hypothalamic Injections[a]

Standard food	Test food	Test time	Alpha (norepinephrine)	Beta block (propranolol)	Beta (isoproterenol)	Alpha block (phentolamine)	Laboratory
Pellets	Pellets	Day	↑[b]	↑[b]	↓	↓	Leibowitz
Pellets	Sweet milk	Day	↑[c]	↑↓	—	↓	Stein
Pellets	Milk	Night	↓	↓	↓	↑[d]	Margules
Pellets	Bitter milk	Night	—	↑		↓	Margules

[a] Arrow indicates direction of change in feeding.
[b] In anorectic rats recovering from lateral hypothalamic lesions.
[c] Reverses from decrease to increase in daytime.
[d] Increases day or night.

(1972) presents extensive evidence for a central nervous system beta-adrenergic satiety function. When epinephrine was injected directly into the hypothalamus instead of peripherally, there was feeding but no stupor. When combined with an alpha blocker to unmask epinephrine beta activity the result was anorexia. Therefore, even though epinephrine's dominant effect by itself was to elicit feeding, its dual alpha–beta role was revealed by blocking the feeding effect with phentolamine so that anorexia resulted. This anorexia was most readily seen in the lateral hypothalamus as opposed to the medial region (Leibowitz, 1973). As a more direct test the beta agonist isoproterenol reduced food intake in food-deprived rats, and this effect was blocked by a beta blocker, propranolol, but not by an alpha blocker, phentolamine (Table 1). In short, the beta system acted as a satiety system.

b. Beta-Adrenergic Satiety with Reference to Alpha Satiety. Margules (1970*b*) again used a milk test diet which facilitated manipulation of taste. He observed that isoproterenol only suppressed intake of diet that was bitter. Logically, a beta blocker overcame the bitter taste, and the rat briefly overate.

Another way to see this beta effect was to block alpha receptors. Recall that in the Margules testing situation hypothalamic alpha blockade not only caused hyperphagia on milk, but the animals were also finicky about their milk. He suggested that when the alpha receptors are blocked, only the beta receptors are left open to the action of the neurotransmitter, and therefore the finickiness is perhaps the result of a beta-adrenergic system. Recently Margules and Dragovich (1973) report that phentolamine hyperphagia is reversed by adulterating the food with a negative taste and the rats become hypophagic relative to controls. In sum, phentolamine caused finickiness; that is, both positive and negative overreaction to taste. Phentolamine-induced feeding occurred both day and night; therefore, it was different from norepinephrine feeding in this respect (Table 1).

Both norepinephrine (Booth and Quartermain, 1965) and its blocker phentolamine (Margules and Dragovich, 1973) caused finicky feeding. This suggests that finickiness is related to some other overriding factor in addition to alpha- or beta-adrenergic interactions discussed so far. Numerous possibilities exist. Lesion studies have shown that finickiness can be a function of body weight, diet familiarity, diet palatability, and excitement or emotionality level. Lesion and hypothalamic island studies also tell us that it is possible with various medial and perifornical hypothalamic placements to obtain either hyperphagia or hypophagic, either one with or without finickiness (Hoebel, 1975). Similarly, cannula placement must be crucial in the drug studies and may explain some of the differences between them.

2.1.6. Summary and Cautions

The one fact about which there is general agreement is that norepinephrine can elicit feeding in the rat's daytime. The overall picture as seen from Leibowitz's vantage point is summarized in Table 1 which indicates that in

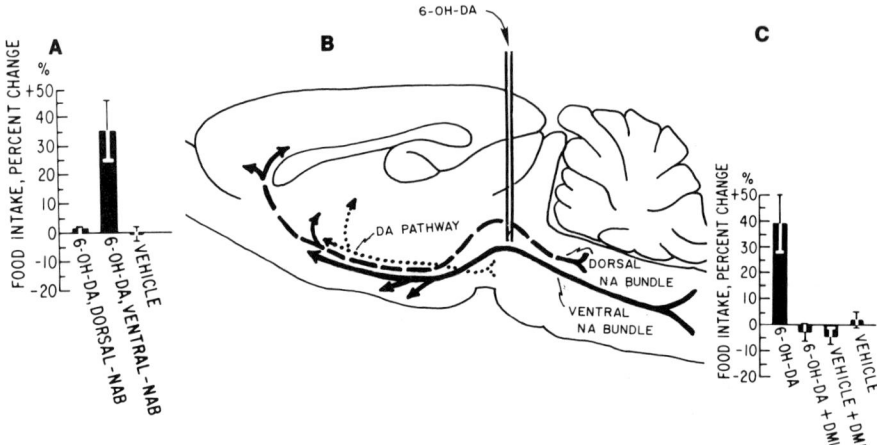

FIG. 1. (A) The selective neurotoxin 6-hydroxydopamine (6-OHDA) depleted the brain of norepinephrine and caused hyperphagia as shown at the left, but only when injected into the ventral, not dorsal, noradrenergic bundle. (B) Side view of the brain showing the ventral and dorsal noradrenergic (NA) bundles and the dopamine (DA) nigrostriatal pathway (after Ungerstedt, 1971). (C) Hyperphagia was prevented by pretreatment with desmethylimipramine which protected the ventral nonadrenergic bundle from 6-OH-DA. From Ahlskog and Hoebel (1972) and Ahlskog (1974).

this scheme there is an alpha-adrenergic feeding function and a beta-adrenergic satiety function. Margules' testing procedures give a different perspective, alpha suppression of feeding by satiety cues and beta suppression by taste (Table 1). The neurotransmitter for the alpha effects is believed to be norepinephrine; and for the beta satiety effects it is unknown. The beta transmitter could conceivably also be norepinephrine, but the recent discovery of epinephrine in nerve terminals of the hypothalamus (Hokfelt et al., 1974) suggests that epinephrine could act in some of the various beta satiety capacities (Leibowitz, 1975b–d).

Some of these diverse alpha and beta effects may be due to the action of sympathomimetics on neurons which are not influenced normally by such drugs or by such concentrations of the drugs under *normal* physiological conditions. Studies with iontophoretic application of norepinephrine to cells during single-unit recording studies have run into difficulties in interpretation which may be related to some of the multiple effects seen with cannulation of large quantities of norepinephrine into the hypothalamus. There is very little assurance that norepinephrine is acting as it should or where it normally would. When the drugs are injected through cannulas which pierce the ventricles, the problems compound but are not insurmountable (Myers and Sharpe, 1968; Myers et al., 1971; Routtenberg, 1972). Singer and Montgomery (1973) review the chemical stimulation techniques in detail and compare chemically elicited behavior to natural, deprivation-induced behaviors. They conclude that effects can be well localized, and that chemical injections can mimic the various internal and external sensory inputs so as to make one behavior or another predominate.

It is only in studies which show a consistent pattern of results using adrenergic agonists and antagonists that one feels fairly confident about the membrane response to the drugs. Even so, proof of consistent membrane receptor properties is not proof of a neurotransmitter; thus, the workers in this field have been cautious in interpreting their results.

It has recently become clear that noradrenergic neurons in both the peripheral and the central nervous system engage in negative feedback control of their own neurotransmitter release. Alpha receptors on the presynaptic nerve terminal respond to norepinephrine by curbing further norepinephrine release (Starke and Montel, 1973; Costa and Meek, 1974). Thus, it may be that norepinephrine delivered by cannula might cause a major shutdown of norepinephrine release. Conversely its effect on the postsynaptic membrane could be chronic depolarization.

Similarly alpha blockers amplify norepinephrine release by blocking the feedback receptor (Starke and Montel, 1973), so that administering an alpha blocker through a cannula could at some doses produce synaptic facilitation instead of blocking it. Some "blocking" agents may also facilitate synaptic transmission by blocking reuptake at certain doses (Cebeddu et al., 1974). Thus, internally consistent schema using alpha and beta agonists and antagonists might under certain circumstances give a series of results which prove the existence of reciprocal alpha and beta functions, but which might be unnatural functions from the behavioral point of view, or natural only at certain times of day or night when endogenous conditions happen to match the conditions imposed by cannulated drugs. In short, there is no dearth of explanations for the variety of behavioral results seen in different testing situations, and it is very difficult to compare results from one laboratory to another. Clearly a task for the future is to discern which conditions are necessary or sufficient for each of the alpha and beta schema that emerge.

The results suggest that norepinephrine serves in several capacities, all of which influence feeding: for example, arousal, circadian oscillation, hypothalamic-releasing-factor control, thirst inhibition, prandial drinking, insulin response, and so forth. Given the multifactor controls over feeding, it is not surprising that the results of brain neurochemical studies are complex. To simplify the problem the newest approach has been to deplete one transmitter at a time and observe the deficits and recovery processes which occur.

2.1.7. Hyperphagia Following Norepinephrine Depletion

The use of 6-hydroxydopamine to deplete catecholamines, combined with histofluorescent evaluation of the effect, has been a boon to many neuroscientists, but its greatest impact has been in the study of feeding. Here neurochemistry, neuroanatomy, and neuropsychology have been combined.

In brief, Ungerstedt (1970, 1971) found that dopamine depletion of the nigrostriatal tract is associated with starvation or anorexia. Ahlskog and Hoebel (1972, 1973) reported that norepinephrine depletion of the ventral ascending noradrenergic bundle is associated with hyperphagia.

The ventral noradrenergic bundle (VNAB) has heavy projections through the lateral hypothalamus and into the medial hypothalamus, and so this was a logical candidate for a role in the control of feeding. To destroy this pathway without also destroying the nigrostriatal path, Ahlskog injected 6-hydroxydopamine into the ventral or dorsal noradrenergic bundles at the level of the oculomotor or trochlear nuclei where the noradrenergic bundles separate from one another and are far enough posterior to the substantia nigra to avoid dopamine cell bodies (Fig. 1B).

Bilateral 6-hydroxydopamine injection in the ventral noradrenergic bundle depleted both dorsal and ventral bundle projection sites, reduced brain norepinephrine to 15% or less, and caused hyperphagia leading to obesity. The effect was not due to dopamine depletion because the brain dopamine levels were normal, fluorescence in the striatum was normal, and pretreatment with systemic desmethylimipramine to block 6-hydroxydopamine uptake into noradrenergic neurons prevented hyperphagia. Desmethylimipramine blocks norepinephrine uptake 1000-fold more than dopamine uptake, so we presume that this drug prevented hyperphagia by protecting noradrenergic nerves. This also provided a control for nonspecific damage by 6-hydroxydopamine (Butcher et al., 1974). Nonspecific damage near the injection site occurred about equally in all cases (Ahlskog, 1974), but it did not cause hyperphagia in desmethylimipramine-protected rats; therefore, the hyperphagia is specifically the result of noradrenergic, or possibly adrenergic, nerve destruction (Fig. 1C).

This new hyperphagia syndrome was attributed to the ventral bundle, not to the dorsal bundle, because dorsal bundle depletion alone failed to produce hyperphagia. In addition, electrolytic lesions placed so as to destroy the ventral bundle alone caused depletion of ventral bundle, not dorsal bundle, projection sites and confirmed the hyperphagic effect. We concluded that the ventral noradrenergic bundle serves, at least in part, as a pathway involved in the inhibition of feeding, and that norepinephrine is a neurotransmitter in a satiety system (Ahlskog and Hoebel, 1973; Ahlskog, 1974).

In spite of our controls for nonspecific damage, recent evidence reported by Lorden et al. (1975) while this chapter was in press raised questions about our interpretation of a strictly adrenergic function. This and other attempts to replicate our results are reviewed by Hoebel (1977).

Hypothalamic knife cuts, using bilaterally asymmetrical lesions to produce an asymmetrical pattern of nonspecific damage and a symmetrical pattern of specific damage, caused hyperphagia and obesity as great as that seen with ventromedial hypothalamic lesions (Kapatos and Gold, 1973). These cuts were made along the trajectory of the ventral noradrenergic bundle, which further suggested that norepinephrine depletion is associated with overeating.

Gold (1973) suggested that classical hyperphagia from ventromedial hypothalamic lesions may result from norepinephrine depletion, and Glick et al. (1973) found that after ventromedial lesions, hyperphagia was proportional to norepinephrine depletion. Our recent evidence suggests that is not the whole story. It is possible to make rats hyperphagic with ventromedial lesions that cause no significant norepinephrine depletion that we could measure in forebrain assays, whereas rats with 95% depletion were typically only half as hyperphagic as ventromedial-lesioned rats (Ahlskog et al., 1975). In addition, the two procedures were additive, not substitutive; ventromedial lesions in norepinephrine-depleted rats caused superhyperphagia. Also, we find that norepinephrine-depleted rats overeat in the night, not in the day as ventromedial rats do (Fig. 2), and are less sensitive, rather than more sensitive, to amphetamine anorexia (Ahlskog and Hoebel, 1973). They also appear to be less finicky to the taste of cheese, saccharine, or quinine added to an oily diet (Ahlskog, 1976). Finally, hypophysectomized rats show hyperphagia after ventromedial lesions but not after norepinephrine depletion (Ahlskog et al., 1974). Therefore, classical hyperphagia seems to be the result of more than just damage to projections of the noradrenergic bundle.

In geese (Auffray et al., 1973) and monkeys (Nicolaidis, personal communication) 6-hydroxydopamine can cause hyperphagia when injected into the ventricles. In monkeys the effect is dose dependent in a way which suggests that hyperphagia gives way to aphagia when the dose is sufficient to deplete the nigrostriatal tract. This serves as a caution that the neurotoxin can have multiple effects whenever injected in such a way as to gain access to

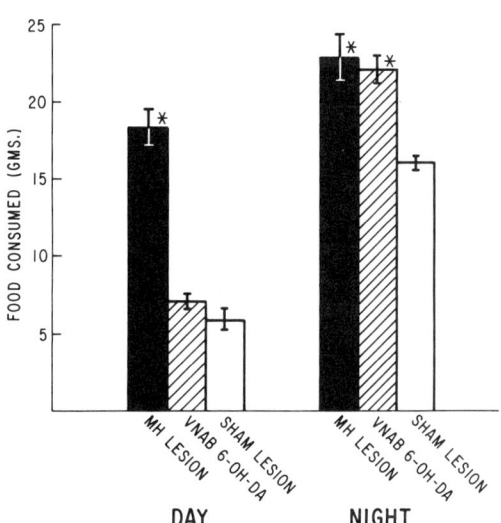

FIG. 2. The rats with ventral noradrenergic bundle (VNAB) injections of 6-OHDA overate as much as the rats with medial hypothalamic lesions at night, but did not overeat in the daytime. From Ahlskog et al. (1975).

a variety of catecholamine systems. Intraventricular 6-hydroxydopa (Richardson and Jacobowitz, 1973) or ventral noradrenergic bundle 6-hydroxydopamine in doses that produced moderate depletion of norepinephrine without loss of dopamine did not cause hyperphagia. Perhaps it is necessary to have fairly complete depletion, or depletion in some particular part of the noradrenergic system, if obesity is to be seen. There is also a possibility that epinephrine pathways are included in the 6-hydroxydopamine hyperphagia phenomenon.

2.1.8. Epinephrine

Hokfelt *et al.* (1974) have succeeded in localizing adrenergic nerves by immunofluorescent identification of the enzyme (phenethylamine-*n*-methyltransferase) which converts norepinephrine to epinephrine. This group points out that the standard histofluorescence technique cannot separate epinephrine from norepinephrine and that although epinephrine is only 5% of total norepinephrine in the brain it may have important behavioral functions that easily could be falsely attributed to norepinephrine. They suggest on anatomical grounds that epinephrine may be involved in feeding or drinking.

If we go back over the literature on noradrenergic feeding and satiety, it is evident that adrenergic synapses may have played a role in generating the results. Grossman (1962*b*) reported that epinephrine elicited feeding, but that norepinephrine did it better. Leibowitz (1972) found that epinephrine could cause feeding (alpha effect) or satiety (beta effect) in the perifornical hypothalamus, and she suggests that epinephrine is ideally suited to be the unknown beta-adrenergic neurotransmitter in her scheme. Margules obtained satiety with epinephrine, and, as mentioned above, Ahlskog and Hoebel's results with 6-hydroxydopamine hyperphagia could have involved destruction of an epinephrine pathway.

2.1.9. Summary and Conclusions

What started out as a simple hypothalamic feeding system with norepinephrine as the excitatory neurotransmitter has turned into norepinephrine disinhibition of feeding, then into Leibowitz's dual norepinephrine alpha-adrenergic disinhibition of feeding interacting with a reciprocally functioning beta-adrenergic system for satiety using an unknown neurotransmitter presumed also to be norepinephrine or epinephrine. But this view is incongruous with Margules' dual noradrenergic satiety theory with its alpha-adrenergic suppression of feeding by postingestional factors at night and beta-adrenergic suppression of feeding by taste factors. Lastly, the experiments on norepinephrine depletion point to a noradrenergic satiety mechanism. Thus, this review has progressed from norepinephrine feeding to norepinephrine satiety. How can the results be integrated into a reasonable picture?

First, it should be noted that norepinephrine feeding and satiety are compatible concepts. If norepinephrine cannulated into the hypothalamus were to produce feeding as a direct excitatory action in a system necessary for feeding, then norepinephrine depletion would have caused starvation. The fact that we observed hyperphagia, not starvation, suggests not only that there exists a norepinephrine system necessary for satiety, but also that when norepinephrine cannulated into the brain produces feeding it does so by a route that is sufficient for eliciting feeding, but not necessary for feeding. For example, norepinephrine feeding and satiety are compatible concepts if norepinephrine induces eating by inhibiting a noradrenergic satiety system.

Second, the systematic designs of Margules and Leibowitz are each internally consistent. Although the overall results disagree, their patterns of results lend strong support to some important principles of catecholaminergic function as originally revealed in the peripheral nervous system and suggest that these principles hold in the central nervous system. The experimental series in both laboratories show that reputed adrenergic agonists and antagonists do, in fact, have opposite effects on the behaviors measured. Phentolamine antagonizes norepinephrine, propranolol antagonizes isoproterenol, and so forth. Moreover, in both experimental series, drugs that block the alpha process have the opposite effect on the beta functions and, vice versa, beta block potentiates alpha functions. Both Margules and Leibowitz attribute this to the existence of both alpha and beta type receptor sites in close proximity such that blocking one forces the neurotransmitter to act on the only other one available.

A number of problems have been mentioned. The neurochemical manipulations that have been discussed must influence not only local, neural systems for feeding but also a host of neuroendocrine systems, other hypothalamic physiological and behavioral control functions such as thirst, temperature, and arousal, and probably also a variety of hypothalamically initiated, peripherally mediated neural controls over metabolic events involving the pancreas, liver, and other organs. In addition, iontophoretic studies have shown that some exogenously applied neurotransmitters may even act where there normally is none present, and transmitter-sensitive sites on the presynaptic membrane may be responsible for some behavioral effects of cannulated drugs. At this stage it is reasonable to suppose that, as the old story goes, investigators with their different views are describing different appendages of the same elephant and giving very different descriptions of the beast.

It clearly is advisable to use physiological doses injected in very small volumes in precisely localized sites, to pay close attention to circadian rhythms, diet palatability and the animal's prior experience, and to manipulate endogenous stores as well as exogenous states whenever possible.

On the basis of the work described, it is concluded that norepinephrine or epinephrine can exert both feeding and satiety functions. The studies of adrenergic receptor agonists, antagonists, reuptake blockers, releasers, depleters, catabolism inhibitors, and perfusates recovered and reinjected make it appear likely that norepinephrine and/or epinephrine serve these functions as neurotransmitters. It is also likely that appropriate neurotransmitter systems that have antagonistic or synergistic effects on each other will have corresponding effects on food intake, and so we turn to dopamine, serotonin, and acetylcholine.

2.2. Dopamine

2.2.1. Anorexia Following Dopamine Depletion

Ungerstedt (1970, 1971) found that 6-hydroxydopamine injected into the nigrostriatal pathway to destroy it caused aphagia and adipsia. Three questions have captivated the interest of researchers. Is the starvation effect following 6-hydroxydopamine a result of dopamine depletion; is the effect the same as the well-known lateral hypothalamic starvation syndrome, and what does this tell us about recovery of brain function after a neurochemical deficit?

Much evidence points to the loss of dopamine as the primary cause of the starvation syndrome after 6-hydroxydopamine injections. (For a review see Zigmond and Stricker, 1974.) When lesions are made along the nigrostriatal tract in the hypothalamus, there is both a decrease of dopamine fluorescence in the more anterior structures and a pileup of fluorescent dopamine in the proximal parts of the interrupted nerves due to axoplasmic transport of dopamine in the transected fiber pathway. Even when electrolytic lesions of the lateral hypothalamus are used, those that cause the greater catecholamine depletion will also cause the greater symptoms of aphagia and adipsia (Oltmans and Harvey, 1972). Although this correlation has been observed, it is not a necessary condition on either theoretical or experimental grounds. Lesions with minimal dopamine loss which happen also to damage other systems involved in feeding might produce a greater deficit than a lesion which caused a great deal of dopamine depletion and very little other damage (Zigmond and Stricker, 1973). In addition, dopamine in a particular subsystem may be the crucial element, not overall striatal dopamine.

Lesions that deplete norepinephrine may compound the deficit by interfering with the noradrenergic feeding function (Teitelbaum *et al.*, 1971; Smith *et al.*, 1972; Richardson and Jacobowitz, 1973), or ameliorate the deficit by interfering with monoamine satiety functions. Some lesions may damage descending fibers such as the motor nerves in the internal capsule and thereby exacerbate feeding deficits. Damage to sensory afferents in the trigeminal system can be involved (Zeigler and Karten, 1974). The situation reflects the state of the art described earlier as part of the norepinephrine story in which greater hyperphagia was observed with electrolytic lesions of the ventromedial hypothalamus than with 6-hydroxydopamine lesions (Ahlskog et al., 1975). Thus the use of 6-hydroxydopamine as a "chemical knife" does not necessarily mean that the experimental surgeon will find a greater deficit.

Nonspecific damage can be extensive (Butcher et al., 1974); however, Ungerstedt's original (1971) and recent reports emphasize that 6-hydroxydopamine can cause relatively little nonspecific damage when compared to electrolytic lesions. The brain tissue some distance from the cannula looks normal except for the loss of individual cells presumed to be catecholaminergic. In the substantia nigra, destruction of cell bodies is seen to progress systematically and selectively in brains time-sampled after the neurotoxin is injected (Ungerstedt, 1974). Smith et al. (1972), studying the results of posterior hypothalamic injection of 6-hydroxydopamine, concurred in the conclusion that the adipsia and aphagia were not likely to be due to nonspecific damage. Caution is still in order, however, because midbrain electrical lesions near but not in the substantia nigra can produce the starvation syndrome, whereas some nigral lesions have no effect on feeding (Wise and Spindler, unpublished).

Zigmond and Stricker (1972) avoided nonspecific nerve damage near the cannula by injecting the 6-hydroxydopamine intraventricularly. Again the syndrome appeared, but it was more subtle. The rats were anorectic but did not have to be tube fed to survive. Intraventricular 6-hydroxydopamine almost completely depleted telencephalic norepinephrine and striatal dopamine. Classical lateral hypothalamic lesions caused nearly complete dopamine depletion but only 50% norepinephrine loss. This led them to suggest that dopamine depletion is a central factor in the loss of appetite. As confirmation, they combined interventricular 6-hydroxydopamine with i.p. injection of a monoamine oxidase inhibitor, pargyline, to protect the neurotoxin from degradation and thus potentiate dopamine depletion according to the technique of Breese and Traylor (1971). The combination of drugs, but not either drug alone, caused prolonged aphagia and adipsia.

When a noradrenergic uptake blocker is administered before intraventricular 6-hydroxydopamine to protect noradrenergic neurons, then dopamine is severely depleted but not norepinephrine. This procedure causes the adipsia and aphagia syndrome and strongly suggests that dopamine is crucial for normal feeding (Cooper and Breese, 1974; Zigmond and Stricker, 1974).

Another approach is to block dopamine synthesis with i.p. α-methyl-p-tyrosine (AMPT) (Zigmond and Stricker, 1973). They used rats recovered from nigrostriatal damage several days after i.p. pargyline plus intraventricular 6-hydroxydopamine, or lateral hypothalamic lesions, and found that AMPT reinstated the food and water intake deficits. The "recovered" rats were very much more sensitive to AMPT inhibition of food intake than normal control rats. The longer it took them to recover from the lesions, the more susceptible they were to AMPT. Thus, these rats were vitally dependent on the synthesis of catecholamine, probably dopamine. AMPT blocks synthesis of norepinephrine and epinephrine as well as dopamine and sometimes makes rats sick or lethargic, so the only reason to assume that AMPT acted specifically on the dopamine system was that the rats with prior dopamine depletion were particularly susceptible. When intraventricular 6-hydroxydopamine was injected so as to deplete norepinephrine but not dopamine, then the anorexia did not appear (Fibiger et al., 1973). Similarly a dopamine-β-hydroxylase inhibitor given to deplete norepinephrine, but not dopamine, failed to depress operant responses for food as usually happens after depletion of both neurotransmitters with AMPT. This suggested again that dopamine deficits can be more devastating to the rat than norepinephrine deficits (Cooper and Breese, 1974). Such examples are complicated, however, because dopamine-β-hydroxylase inhibitors not only decrease norepinephrine but also increase dopamine release, including possible dopamine release from noradrenergic nerves (Anden et al., 1973).

In addition to possible problems involved in depleting the correct subset of dopamine fibers, and damage to other neurotransmitter systems, a great deal depends on the completeness of the depletion because of compensatory supersensitivity of the postsynaptic receptor to transmitter released by the remaining intact nerve terminals. Other compensatory mechanisms may also be available to mitigate the effects of the lesion or change them over time. Nearby pathways may sprout to compensate, or other pathways may be sufficiently redundant to take over the lost functions. In the case where a lesion is made on only one side of the brain, the other side may satisfy the animal's everyday needs. The animal will appear normal until the testing situation is designed to reveal lateralized deficits. The contralateral sensory neglect following unilateral, lateral hypothalamic damage and contralateral sensory enhancement following unilateral ventromedial damage (Marshall and Teitelbaum, 1973; Marshall, 1974) are phenomena which illustrate this point (see the paper by Marshall and Teitelbaum in Volume 7 of this *Handbook*).

Two more general principles need to be kept in mind while interpreting these experiments. First, in multifactor control systems such as feeding, a lesion which damages only certain functions may not produce a noticeable deficit unless the test is designed to reveal it. This is the case with unilateral dopamine-depleted rats or "recovered" rats which subsist quite well on food pellets and water, but appropriate tests can reveal deficits in the ability to eat in the face of severe glucoprivation (Breese et al., 1973), to drink in response to i.p. hypertonic saline (Fibiger et al., 1973), or to respond normally to taste factors (Sorenson et al., 1972). Second, extensive damage sometimes causes less of a deficit than restricted damage. Coscina et al. (1973) combined 6-hydroxydopamine depletion of catecholamines with ventromedial lesions. The catecholamine depletion caused anorexia culminating in a lowered weight level, presumably due to dopamine depletion; subsequent ventromedial lesions caused hyperphagia and a typical increment of body weight starting from the low baseline. The rats with combined lesions showed less hyperreaction to quinine than rats with the ventromedial lesions alone.

2.2.2. Comparison of Dopamine Anorexia and Hypothalamic Lesions Anorexia

Ungerstedt's (1971) study showed that like electrolytic hypothalamic lesions, 6-hydroxydopamine injection can cause inactivity and starvation to the point of death. He suggested that the lateral hypothalamic syndrome might be similar in some ways to Parkinson's disease because both apparently involve loss of nigrostriatal function. Dopamine depletion might be a common factor in Parkinsonian lack of motor initiative and the lack of initiative to eat or drink. Evidence that motor inability is not the sole cause of aphagia is reviewed elsewhere (Hoebel, 1971), but clearly striatal dopamine depletion contributes to the lateral hypothalamic starvation syndrome.

In Ungerstedt's study the extent of dopamine depletion was correlated with hypokinesis and feeding deficits, but not with the most severe motoric effects. He concluded that severe akinesia, catalepsy, and somnolence cannot be specifically attributed to the nigrostriatal pathway (Ungerstedt, 1971, 1974), but perhaps feeding deficits can.

In many subtle respects, the aphagia and adipsia following dopamine depletion is like the lateral hypothalamic syndrome described by Teitelbaum and Epstein (1962). The rats initially refuse all food and water, then gradually begin to eat and drink palatable liquid diets much as an infant does in the early stages of its development. Eventually they recover the ability to regulate their food intake and body weight on ordinary laboratory diet and water (Zigmond and Stricker, 1974). But they persist in their unwillingness to eat in response to severe, even lethal, hypoglycemia caused by insulin (Epstein and Teitelbaum, 1967; Breese *et al.*, 1973) or to short-term glucoprivation induced by the nonmetabolizable glucose analog 2-deoxy-*d*-glucose (Epstein, 1971; Zigmond and Stricker, 1972; Marshall and Teitelbaum, 1973). The rats recovered from LH lesions and 6-hydroxydopamine were also similar to one another in that both could eat in response to a cold environment. This led Marshall and Teitelbaum (1973) to conclude that the deficits after nigrostriatal 6-hydroxydopamine injections are (a) selective in sensory impairment and (b) identical to the deficits which follow lateral hypothalamic electrolytic lesions. Zigmond and Stricker (1974), using intraventricular 6-OHDA injections, emphasized that the deficits observed are a function of the severity of the stress imposed on the animal. Thus 50% dopamine-depleted rats may eat in the cold, but fail to eat as a normal rat would when the environment is even colder. In a variety of ways the deficits were similar to those seen in peripheral sympathectomized rats. Zigmond and Stricker think of them as being centrally sympathectomized, lacking responses to physiological emergencies.

Lateral hypothalamic rats display sensory neglect. They fail to respond to odors, sights, or touch that would elicit an immediate response in normal animals (Marshall et al., 1971). Dopamine-depleted rats are similar (Ungerstedt, 1974). Knowing that their sensory fields for peripheral stimulation are diminished, we can guess that their internal sensory mechanisms suffer the same malady.

Dopamine depletion seems to cause behavioral response deficits without corresponding physiological response deficits (Zigmond and Stricker, 1974). For example, rats that fail to eat in response to 2-deoxy-d-glucose nevertheless mobilize blood sugar. Additional physiological tests are needed before we can accept this as general principle. For now, the point is that dopamine depletion is largely associated with behavioral failure. This syndrome includes, on the one hand, a change in sensory responsiveness to both internal and external cues and, on the other hand, a lack of motor initiation.

As a descriptive synthesis of the results described above, the syndrome might be called a sensory-motor impairment. The next question is whether this is just sensory impairment and motor impairment or sensory-to-motor impairment, i.e., impaired ability to link sensations and responses. Teitelbaum and co-workers have published interesting papers showing that rats recovering from lateral hypothalamic lesions did not learn to avoid food that was associated with poison (Roth et al., 1973), even though they could remember a similar task learned prior to the lesion (Schwartz and Teitelbaum, 1974). They could remember, but not learn. At least they could not learn readily; the limits of this phenomenon have not been tested. It is conceivable, given the parallels drawn above, that this relative inability to make associations involves the nigrostriatal path and loss of dopamine. If so, then we will need to know if this disability applies only to food-cue learning or to learning in general. There are already suggestions of dopamine involvement in general learning (Zis et al., 1974; Ungerstedt, 1974; Cooper and Breese, 1974).

This means that any experimental manipulation which interrupts the nigrostriatal tract or depletes dopamine may cause effects which appear to be feeding deficits, but which may sometimes be more general deficits having to do with hypokinesia, stress, or learning disability. Conversely, those who study learning using food as a reinforcer should be forewarned that this neurochemical impairment may affect the animal's ability to sense the food, to be aroused by the food, to initiate action to get to the food, or to perform the muscle movements needed to chew the food.

2.2.3. Recovery from Brain Damage

Manipulations which accustom the rat ahead of time to the state experienced during the starvation syndrome lessen the severity of the syndrome (Myers and Martin, 1973; Finger et al., 1973). Prelesion weight reduction can eliminate postlesion anorexia, suggesting that body weight regulation is a factor (Powley and Keesey, 1970); prelesion experience with palatable diets can facilitate recovery of feeding on those diets (DiCara, 1970); and most to the point, prelesion treatment with AMPT can eliminate postlesion anorexia, suggesting that AMPT prepares the rat by depleting catecholamines ahead of time and inducing supersensitivity needed for quick recovery after nerve destruction (Glick et al., 1972).

In an effort to show that the supersensitivity responsible for facilitating recovery of function is specifically dopaminergic, Hynes et al. (1973) pretreated nigrostriatal lesioned rats with haloperidol to block dopamine receptor sites without interfering with catecholamine synthesis. Chronic haloperidol injections caused supersensitivity evidenced as augmented apomorphine stereotypy and "wet dog shakes." This pretreatment significantly increased the body weight level reached a week after the lesion. They conclude that dopamine supersensitivity is a factor in recovery of function; they further infer that other preoperative treatments such as reduced body weight may facilitate recovery by facilitating the dopamine system. Some postoperative procedures might also promote dopamine synthesis, such as presentation of highly palatable food (Teitelbaum and Epstein, 1962) or direct lateral hypothalamic stimulation which shortens recovery time (Harrell et al., 1974) and elicits feeding for the first time after the lesion (Hoebel, 1976b). Stricker and Zigmond (1975) review the neurochemistry of aphagia and propose a model for the biochemical basis of the recovery of feeding function.

There is much to do before such a mechanism is confirmed and well understood, but even now the implications are clear and of great potential importance in the preoperative and postoperative care given people suffering brain damage. It appears that postoperative behavioral trauma can be dramatically mitigated or aggravated by drug therapy. Drugs which affect brain catecholamines, perhaps even something as innocuous as a history of systemic sympathomimetic nasal decongestants or anorectics, could conceivably affect recovery of function after damage to catecholamine systems.

2.2.4. Dopamine Inhibition of Feeding

Just as there was strong evidence for both feeding and satiety functions for norepinephrine, results are beginning to appear indicating that the same is true of dopamine. Intracerebral dopamine can reduce feeding (Kruk, 1973) but may also cause lethargy (Hansen and Whishaw, 1973). In addition, dopamine-depletion studies suggest that dopamine provides one of the neurochemical substrates for amphetamine anorexia. Perhaps anorexia can result from too much dopamine as well as too little (Heffner et al., 1975). It is also possible that there are simply a variety of dopaminergic functions, some of which facilitate feeding and some of which reduce it.

In any case, current evidence leads to the conclusion that a dopamine system involving the nigrostriatal tract is necessary for normal feeding.

2.3. Serotonin

Some subset of serotonin neurons is probably necessary for normal suppression of food intake. This tentative conclusion has been reached after reviewing many conflicting results. There are two major factors which tend to confound most experiments; serotonin manipulations often affect the general health of the animal through drastic effects on peripheral serotonergic systems, and there are often a variety of behavioral changes stemming from the central effects of such manipulations. Serotonin is well known for its effects on arousal and REM sleep, temperature regulation, aggressiveness, and mating (Chase and Murphy, 1973). Effects on feeding are often confounded with such changes in arousal level, temperature, hormone states, and also affective or emotional dispositions. There is a general tendency for serotonin to be associated with suppression of all these behavior patterns and with punishment in general (Stein and Wise, 1974). Therefore, one might predict involvement in suppression of feeding responses.

2.3.1. Serotonin Agonists and Antagonists

The serotonin precursor, 5-HTP, injected systemically decreased feeding but not drinking (Joyce and Mrosovsky, 1964). Brain serotonin increased following i.p. 5-HTP in association with decreased food intake (Singer et al., 1971), but the amino acid could be acting peripherally. Nevertheless, intraventricular or lateral hypothalamic 5-HTP and 5-HT also caused anorexia.

Serotonin injected in the perifornical hypothalamus gave mixed results. Goldman et al. (1971) observed decreased feeding; Slangen and Miller (1969) obtained no effect, and Booth (1968) saw a small delayed increase. Baille (1974) reviews the increased feeding his group observed in monkeys and sheep after serotonin injections.

Serotonin agonists, yohimbine (Singer et al., 1971) and fenfluramine, cause anorexia, as will be discussed further on. The serotonin antagonist cyproheptadine increases food intake (Baxter et al., 1970; Opitz et al., 1971; Chakrabarty et al., 1974). Blundell and Leshem (1974) found that either cyproheptadine or another serotonin inhibitor, methylsergide, would disinhibit feeding if given to deprived rats after they finished eating for an hour. They suggest these drugs counteract the elevated serotonin levels in the brain seen after a meal (Fernstrom and Wurtman, 1973).

2.3.2. Dietary Influences

Food intake itself can influence serotonin metabolism. Food-deprived rats had elevated levels of the serotonin precursor, tryptophan, and the serotonin metabolite, 5-HIAA, compared to fasted rats allowed to eat for 2 hr (Perez-Cruet et al., 1972). This does not fit the idea of a serotonergic satiety function and is contrary to the results cited above; different lighting schedules, deprivation conditions, and test diets may account for the different results.

Serotonin levels are a function of dietary tryptophan, not total intake. To the contrary, Wurtman and Fernstrom (1974) report that dietary tryptophan accelerates serotonin synthesis, but that dietary protein has the opposite effect by contributing other amino acids. Similarly, they also tentatively suggest that foods which elevate tyrosine availability in the brain may accelerate catecholamine synthesis. It is conceivable, therefore, that in accordance with the norepinephrine and serotonin satiety theories, dietary intake of monoamine precursors could facilitate the appropriate satiety mechanism and curb further intake of that diet.

2.3.3. Serotonin Depletion

If a serotonergic system in the brain suppresses feeding, then as a more direct test serotonin depletion should cause hyperphagia.

Koe and Weissman (1966) suggested that *p*-chlorophenylalanine (PCPA) produces serotonin depletion by inhibiting its synthesis at the tryptophan hydroxylase step, but there are numerous other effects of PCPA (Chase and Murphy, 1973). Perhaps most troublesome is the PCPA-induced depletion of serotonin in the gut, peripheral organs and blood, as well as in the brain. Gut irritation, phenylketonurea, and diarrhea are not uncommon. There is also a decrease in gastric secretion (Hano *et al.*, 1973). This may explain why some authors have observed a decrease in feeding after i.p. PCPA (Funderburk *et al.*, 1971; McFarlain and Bloom, 1972; Borbely *et al.*, 1973; Panksepp and Nance, 1974; Breisch and Hoebel, 1975), while others report no change in feeding (Sheard, 1969) and others note a slight increase in feeding (Mouret *et al.*, 1968; Ferguson *et al.*, 1969). Nevertheless Sheard (1969) found that a moderate serotonin depletion with i.p. PCPA increased mouse-killing, and there are numerous reports that i.p. PCPA can increase components of male copulatory behavior (see review by Chase and Murphy, 1973.) Hyperactivity and hyperreactivity are also reported after PCPA (Fibiger and Campbell, 1971).

To test the hypothesis that PCPA would cause hyperphagia, a way was needed to deplete brain serotonin without peripheral depletion and the accompanying malaise. One possibility was to cut serotonin pathways. Harvey *et al.* (1963) did this when they lesioned the lateral hypothalamus (medial forebrain bundle) and depleted about half the serotonin in forebrain structures. They also noted norepinephrine depletion. We can assume they interrupted the nigrostriatal pathway, and so with hindsight we would not expect hyperphagia. Another possibility is represented by the effort of Saminin *et al.* (1972) to lesion the raphe, which depleted forebrain serotonin 77% without altering norepinephrine or dopamine levels. This increased feeding slightly but not significantly on a 6-hr feeding schedule.

Researchers studying feeding did not put PCPA into the brain, probably because it is not water soluble. If the methyl ester of PCPA is used so that it is soluble, then we find that an intraventricular injection causes significant hyperphagia and transient increase in body weight (Breisch and Hoebel, 1975). Food intake reaches a peak in three to four days and returns to normal in two weeks (Fig. 3). This is the timing one would expect if the behavioral effect resulted from serotonin depletion as opposed to other effects of PCPA (Brody, 1970). Breisch et al. (1976) find that PCPA-induced hyperphagia occurs mainly in the daytime and is associated with selective depletion of serotonin, not norepinephrine or dopamine. Because hyperphagia after norepinephrine depletion is a nighttime phenomenon (Ahlskog et al., 1975) and the PCPA effect is largely a daytime phenomenon, our working hypothesis is that serotonin, not norepinephrine, is necessary for

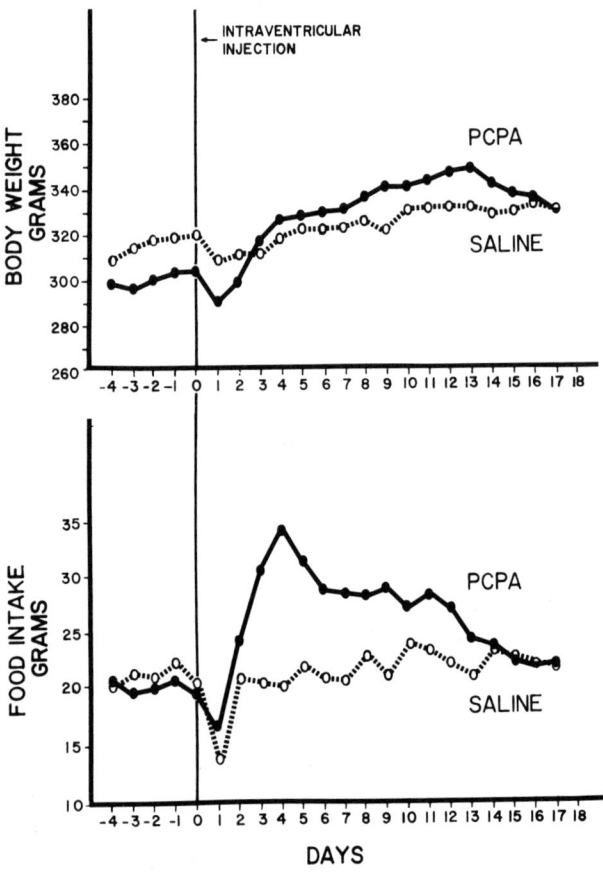

FIG. 3. p-Chlorophenylalanine (PCPA) injected intraventricularly caused an increase in daily food intake and body weight lasting two weeks. From Breisch et al. (1976).

normal suppression of daytime feeding in rats given *ad libitum* food. If so, its depletion by ventromedial hypothalamic lesions might partially account for daytime hypothalamic hyperphagia.

Even if it is correct to classify serotonin as an anorectic neurotransmitter candidate, there is no measure of its relative importance in the repertoire of feeding controls. It is also quite possible that part or all of serotonin's satiety function is nonspecific, having to do with endocrine effects, arousal level, or response dampening as mentioned at the outset. Also, as with all the reputed neurotransmitter mechanisms discussed, the satiety effects of serotonin might be better attributed to some other system with which serotonin interacts. For example, serotonin has been cast in an interactive role with norepinephrine (Everett, 1974), dopamine (Jacobs, 1974), and acetylcholine (Pepeu *et al.*, 1974).*

2.4. Acetylcholine

2.4.1. Cholinergic Inhibition of Feeding

In Grossman's early studies hypothalamic injection of the cholinergic agonist carbachol elicited drinking and inhibited spontaneous feeding. Hypothalamic carbachol also decreases feeding induced by norepinephrine (Grossman, 1962; Singer and Kelly, 1972). This suggested that a cholinergic system inhibits feeding and that the underlying systems for feeding and drinking are mutually inhibitory (Singer and Montgomery, 1973). We have spoken of "satiety systems" in connection with alpha-adrenergic agonists, beta-adrenergic agonists, norepinephrine depletion, and PCPA injections. Satiety, in these studies, is measured several ways: as failure to eat in the presence of food, in terms of past food consumption, and sometimes with special reference to rejection of food on the basis of taste. The role of ACh in satiety is possibly limited to body-fluid balance. Osmotic balance is a function not only of water intake and loss, but also hypertonic food intake and loss. Blood hypertonicity inhibits feeding, and hypotonicity elicits feeding (Smith, 1966). It is logical that at least some circuits of the brain having to do with thirst would also be involved in inhibiting food intake. This appears to be the case of the cholinergic thirst circuit.

It is not clear whether cholinergic drugs injected into the hypothalamus act directly on feeding inhibitory synapses, or whether they activate a drinking circuit that secondarily inhibits feeding in other synapses with unknown characteristics. The cholinergic thirst receptors may well be far from the lateral hypothalamus (Lovett and Singer, 1971) in the subfornical

* Note Added in Proof: The reader is referred to the most recent reviews of serotonin and feeding (Blundell, 1977; Hoebel, 1977) and the New York Academy of Science Conference on serotonin neurotoxins (in prep.).

organ where hypothalamically injected drugs can act by leaking up the cannula shaft into the ventricular fluid (Routtenberg, 1972; Simpson and Routtenberg, 1973). There may be cholinergic synapses in the hypothalamus as well, but we have scant assurance that cholinergic thirst is triggered at the hypothalamic injection site, so we cannot be sure cholinergic inhibition of feeding occurs here either.

There is another problem in that most studies use carbachol as a cholinergic agonist because it is not hydrolyzed as fast as acetylcholine; however, carbachol is known to stimulate axons under some circumstances. Therefore, there may be stronger grounds than usual for doubting that the compound acts only at specific synapses. In search for more convincing evidence, Grossman (1962b) injected the cholinergic blocker atropine into the perifornical hypothalamus, where it failed to increase free feeding even though it did block thirst and increased activity level.

We need to make a distinction between the feeding measured as bar pressing for food and feeding measured as eating freely available food. This distinction will be important in connection with amphetamine's strange capacity to make rats increase their bar pressing for food without eating it. Methylatropine injected into the ventromedial hypothalamus did the same thing; bar pressing to activate a milk dispenser increased, but actual milk intake did not (Margules and Stein, 1967). Cholinergic blockade increased not only operant feeding responses in satiated rats but also operant feeding responses suppressed by foot shock in deprived rats. Therefore, Margules and Stein hypothesized that atropine blocks cholinergic synapses normally involved in suppression of operant behavior. In line with Carlton's (1963) proposal for cholinergic suppression of unrewarded behavior, they suggest that this system suppresses operant behavior in general, not just feeding behavior *per se*.

The evidence for cholinergic satiety is clear in monkeys. In hungry monkeys responding to food, small doses (e.g., 0.7 mol) of carbachol injected in the hypothalamus suppressed feeding in a dose-related fashion, as did acetylcholine or physostigmine. Atropine blocked the effect (Sharpe and Myers, 1969).

Much additional evidence relating to anatomical and chemical specificity has been reviewed recently by Singer and Montgomery (1973), leading them to support Grossman's original hypothesis that cholinergic thirst and adrenergic feeding circuits are mutually inhibitory. They emphasize that their model provides for chronic, mutual inhibition of feeding, drinking, mating, and all other such drives until the physiological conditions for any one of them becomes sufficiently great to activate a behavior pattern while strongly inhibiting all the others. They point out that carbachol can be a stronger inhibitor of norepinephrine feeding than the alpha-adrenergic blocker phentolamine, and presumably thirst can be a stronger inhibitor of feeding than food satiety.

2.4.2. Cholinergic Facilitation of Feeding

a. Cholinergic Agonists. In addition to cholinergic satiety, Singer's laboratory finds evidence for a cholinergic feeding influence. Carbachol injected in the far lateral hypothalamus instead of the usual perifornical lateral hypothalamus site augmented norepinephrine-induced feeding instead of antagonizing it. Further evidence for central cholinergic facilitation of feeding comes indirectly from Stark *et al.* (1971) who report that lateral hypothalamic electrically elicited eating is facilitated by systemic administration of cholinergic drugs that cross the blood–brain barrier (physostigmine, not neostigmine) and is blocked by cholinergic blockers (atropine, not methylatropine). The same drugs influenced the cessation of eating produced by ventromedial hypothalamic stimulation. Physostigmine decreased this form of satiety, and atropine increased it. The authors proposed that a cholinergic system "starts" feeding behavior by an action on the medial and lateral hypothalamus. Instead of electrical stimulation, Sciorelli *et al.* (1972) used perifornical hypothalamic injections of dibutyryl cyclic-AMP and found that it augments feeding in a rat with cholinergic synapses potentiated by physostigmine, but decreases feeding in an animal with cholinergic synapses disabled by atropine. In animals other than rats, cholinergic feeding with hypothalamic injections was reported in rabbits (Sommer *et al.*, 1967), sheep (Forbes and Baile, 1973), and cats (Nance *et al.*, 1971).

b. Cholinergic Mouse-Killing and Feeding. Experience with cholinergic drugs and feeding in our laboratory has been in the context of mouse-killing behavior. Whether or not mouse-killing is a form of predation aimed at food-getting is a matter of debate (Paul and Posner, 1973). Hypothalamic injection of crystalline carbachol and an anticholinesterase, neostigmine, triggered killing in nonkiller rats. Crystalline atropine or graded doses of methylatropine injected in the lateral hypothalamus blocked mouse-killing in killers (Smith *et al.*, 1970; Smith, 1970). There are pitfalls in interpreting the action of any one of these drugs, but the total picture based on all three suggested that a cholinergic mechanism could trigger mouse-killing. Bandler (1971) obtained similar results in which carbachol facilitated mouse-killing, but Lonowski *et al.* (1973), using fluid injections of carbachol, observed decreased mouse-killing. When we tested carbachol, neostigmine, and atropine in a situation allowing the rats to eat pellets, drink water, or run in a running wheel, only running activity was consistently affected by all three drugs, suggesting cholinergic involvement in that behavior (Smith and Hoebel, 1973). Food intake was increased by carbachol and decreased by atropine, as seen also by Capobianco and Mountford (1974), but unaffected by neostigmine. However, Sciorelli *et al.* (1972) have shown that physostigmine will increase feeding if injected in the hypothalamus in combination with dibutyryl cyclic-AMP.

The cholinergic drug pilocarpine has yielded interesting results. Injected systemically, pilocarpine will elicit first-time mouse-killing (Vogel and Leaf, 1972), but Abissi, Meis, and Hoebel (unpublished) find it will not elicit feeding whether injected systemically or into the hypothalamus. It is interesting that pilocarpine can elicit mouse-killing, but not eating, even though pilocarpine killing is facilitated by food deprivation. This is not the place to resolve the role of mouse-killing in the rats's repertoire of feeding behaviors; it is important to note, however, that cholinergic feeding influences might be related to various forms of aggression and general activity level.

    c. Cholinergic Antagonists. Pradhan and Roth (1968) focused on cholinergic blockers. Systemic atropine, scopolamine, or JB329 depressed feeding, drinking, and activity in a photocell cage. The methylated analogs of these drugs, which are less permeable to the blood–brain barrier, failed to give large effects on drinking and activity but did decrease feeding, suggesting that the anticholinergic decrease in feeding was of peripheral origin, presumably due to mouth dryness. Similarly, scopolamine and methylscopolamine decreased feeding (Houser, 1970) and spontaneous activity regardless of deprivation level which was interpreted as a peripheral effect (Adams, 1973). On the other hand, scopolamine was more potent than methylscopolamine in inhibiting feeding produced by deprivation (Glick and Greenstein, 1973) or produced by morphine in morphine-tolerant rats (Oka et al., 1972). Evidently, under the conditions these researchers used to avoid dry mouth a central action of scopolamine occurs. This supports the central cholinergic feeding idea.

    A very indirect, intriguing bit of evidence for cholinergic feeding in the CNS arose as part of a study showing that an increase in acetylcholine synthesis (choline acetylase activity) was correlated with recovery of feeding (behavioral tolerance) after chronic treatment with amphetamine (Ho and Gershon, 1972). This suggested that amphetamine inhibited a cholinergic system somewhere in the neural circuitry controlling feeding. As the system became less sensitive to the effects of repeated amphetamine administration, feeding and acetylcholine activity resumed. Note, however, that amphetamine affects many behaviors, and the correlation between feeding and acetylcholine synthesis is merely circumstantial.

    Turning now to the striatum, Neill and Grossman (1973) suggest that the nigrostriatal dopamine system which is necessary for feeding may act by way of its influence on a striatal, cholinergic system. They blocked cholinergic action by injecting crystalline scopolamine in the striatum of rats and observed a deficit in eating solid food and bar pressing for it, even though the animals would eat liquid diet and press for water. These rats would gnaw the pellets, although they either could not or would not swallow the food while the striation was under the influence of a cholinergic block. This would seem to be closely related to some components of the starvation syndrome seen after depletion of dopamine in the nigrostriatal tract. On the other hand, it may relate to stereotypic gnawing seen in animals with excess dopamine stimulation. At present we can only conclude that acetylcholine–

dopamine balance is important in feeding. (For a review of cholinergic–dopamine inter-regulation see Bartholini *et al.*, 1975.)

d. Tolerance. Russell *et al.* (1971) used the irreversible cholinesterase inhibitor diisopropylfluorophosphate (DFP) to lower cholinesterase activity and thereby potentiate cholinergic activity. This treatment decreased feeding and drinking, as observed earlier by Glow *et al.* (1966). Feeding recovered in about 10 days, suggesting some form of relatively rapid tolerance; drinking took longer to recover. After recovery, when DFP was withdrawn, excess drinking occurred. The tolerance to DFP was classified as behavioral, rather than pharmacological, because cholinesterase had been clamped at a low level by DFP and yet the animals gradually became less sensitive to DFP, i.e., feeding recovered. This behavioral tolerance in DFP rats apparently resulted from a gradual reduction in postsynaptic receptor sensitivity induced by chronic stimulation by acetylcholine that could not be metabolized (Chippendale *et al.*, 1972). The same pattern of results occurs in temperature control: DFP causes cholinesterase inhibition with acetylcholine potentiation followed by cholinergic hypothermia and gradual cholinergic subsensitivity leading to loss of the hypothermic response, i.e., behavioral tolerance resulting from postsynaptic receptor changes secondary to the action of the drug itself (Overstreet *et al.*, 1973).

Because hypothermia would be expected to increase feeding, the decreased feeding observed with DFP cannot easily be attributed to temperature regulation. Because feeding recovered before drinking, the feeding deficit was probably not secondary to dehydration. It would appear, therefore, that a cholinergic system that directly decreases feeding may exist.

2.5. Other Influences

2.5.1. Histamine

There are high concentrations of histamine in the hypothalamus, and a histamine pathway ascends in the medial forebrain bundle (Garbarg *et al.*, 1974), but hypothalamic injections of histamine have not affected feeding (Booth, 1968; Wagner and DeGroot, 1963; Capobianco and Mountford, 1974; Baile, 1974). Recently, however, Clineschmidt and Lotti (1973) report that 1 μg injected intraventricularly will suppress feeding in cats on a 21-h deprivation schedule. The effect may be maintained by repeated injections, or blocked by oral antihistamines. Anorexia did not occur with catabolites of histamine given intraventricularly. The authors suggest histamine may play a role in the regulation of feeding; however, more needs to be done to rule out malaise. In humans, oral histamine taken in doses as high as 64 g caused anorexia associated with a loss of taste sensitivity (Henkin *et al.*, 1972). Again the mechanism is entirely unknown.

2.5.2. GABA

γ-Aminobutyric acid (GABA) has not been studied in any detail since Grossman reported 10 years ago that GABA injected in the amygdala decreased feeding like the cholinomimetic carbachol. In the hypothalamus GABA levels vary with glucose availability, rising during insulin hypoglycemia and falling during alloxan hyperglycemia. Thus, GABA neurons may be in a position to play a role in glucostatic feeding mechanisms (Kuriyama *et al.*, 1973).

2.5.3. Cyclic-AMP and Ionic Balance

Baile (1974) reviews the possible role of cyclic-AMP and ionic balance in relation to feeding. Briefly put, cyclic-AMP injected in the hypothalamus can elicit feeding. Breckenridge and Lisk (1969) implanted crystalline dibutyryl cyclic-AMP into the hypothalamus of mature rats and noted increased feeding and body weight for a few days. Booth (1972) injected 4 nmol of dibutyryl cyclic-AMP in either the lateral or ventromedial hypothalamus of 6-hr deprived rats and found potentiated feeding on flavored food. However, when the rats' preference was tested after 3 days, those that had received lateral hypothalamic injections ate more food than controls, and the ventromedial injected rats ate less. Here then is another caution; ventromedial hypothalamic treatments that increase feeding during the drug action may result in aversion to feeding when tested at a later time. Rindi *et al.* (1972) confirm the cyclic-AMP feeding effect, and the same group finds that the anticholinesterase physostigmine potentiates it. They propose cholinergic mediation of cyclic-AMP-produced ingestive responses (Sciorelli *et al.*, 1972).

A number of studies have tested sodium, potassium, and calcium injections into the hypothalamus for their effect on feeding. Baile (1974) noted that calcium caused feeding in all the species tested. Myers *et al.* (1972) suggest that ionic balance, sodium/calcium, may be correlated with energy balance and establish a set-point by influencing nerve excitability.

3. ANORECTIC DRUGS

The first section of this chapter was written to lay a foundation for the discussion of selected drugs that follows. A number of constraints on this discussion are purposely imposed by such a plan. Most drugs thought to act primarily in the periphery will be excluded. For example, we will not go into the myriad of drugs that affect pancreatic function and thereby glucostasis and feeding. The drugs of greatest interest will be those which, via a central action, are reported to influence perceptions, moods, desires, preferences, appetites, motivations, and thereby food intake.

Some behavior patterns are of overriding importance in the life of the individual animal, particularly eating, breathing, drinking, and temperature regulation. Among this group, feeding is controlled by the greatest variety of physiological factors. Control factors include such diverse signals as stomach distention, cholecystokinin secretion, circulating epinephrine, liver glucose, glucose utilization and glucose level in combination with insulin availability, osmotic factors, possibly circulating fat or protein availability signals, temperature, taste and odors, feelings of sickness or recuperation in combination with food ingestion, reward and punishment contingencies, etc.; the list continues to encompass a wide variety of factors concerned with energy balance. Virtually any drug that can be named will influence at least one of these energy-linked factors and thereby possibly influence feeding. In order to make sense of the psychopharmacology of feeding as a systematic discipline, it is therefore necessary to focus on brain mechanisms which somehow serve as a final common path in the control of feeding behavior. This becomes an attempt to understand certain prototypic drugs in terms of their action on the monoaminergic and cholinergic systems described earlier.

3.1. Structure–Function Relationships in Sympathomimetics

3.1.1. Catecholamines

Table 2 shows most of the better known catecholamines and related compounds including many appetite-suppressant drugs arranged according to their relationship to the basic phenethylamine skeleton. All have a 2-carbon ethyl chain separating the benzene ring from the nitrogen. This is essential for anorectic action in this general type of compound. For an overview of this topic, the review by Innes and Nickerson (1970) is very useful.

The first group are the catecholamines, so called because of an intact catechol moiety consisting of the benzene ring hydroxylated in the 3 and 4 (para) positions. These are neurotransmitters or neurotransmitter substitutes capable of acting directly on catecholaminergic receptor sites. Within this group, hydroxylation of the beta carbon atom transforms the compound from dopamine to norepinephrine and presumably confers noradrenergic as opposed to dopaminergic characteristics to nordefrin and isoproterenol.

a. Nitrogen Substituents. It is interesting that increased substitution on the nitrogen atom is associated with progressive loss of alpha-adrenergic effects and increased beta function as one goes from norepinephrine with no nitrogen side chains to epinephrine with one methyl group, isoproterenol with two, and protokylol with a complex radical hanging on the nitrogen (not shown in Table 2). Isoproterenol and protokylol are almost purely beta-adrenergic in their function; by the same principle, nylidrin in the next group is also a pure beta agonist.

TABLE 2
A Comparison of Catecholamines and Noncatecholamines, Particularly Anorectic Phenethylamine Derivatives[a]

Phenethylamine skeleton	3	4	5	β	α	N
Catecholamines:						
Dopamine[b]	3-OH	4-OH				
Norepinephrine[b]	3-OH	4-OH		OH		
Epinephrine[b]	3-OH	4-OH		OH		CH_3
Epinine	3-OH	4-OH				CH_3
Adrenalone	3-OH	4-OH		O		CH_3
Nordefrin[b]	3-OH	4-OH		OH	CH_3	
Isoproterenol	3-OH	4-OH		OH		$CH(CH_3)_2$
Metaproterenol	3-OH		5-OH	OH		$CH(CH_3)_2$
Noncatecholamines missing one hydroxyl from the ring:						
Tyramine		4-OH				
Phenylephrine	3-OH			OH		CH_3
Metaraminol	3-OH			OH	CH_3	
Hydroxyamphetamine		4-OH			CH_3	
p-Hydroxynorephedrine		4-OH		OH	CH_3	
Nylidrin		4-OH		OH	CH_3	$CH(CH_3)(CH_2CH_2C_6H_5)$
Paredrinol		4-OH			CH_3	CH_3
Synephrin		4-OH		OH		CH_3
Suprifen		4-OH		OH	CH_3	CH_3
Paredrine		4-OH			CH_3	CH_3

Noncatecholamines missing both hydroxyls from the ring:

Compound	Ring	β	α	N-substituents
Phenethylamine[b]				
Amphetamine[b]			CH_3	
Methamphetamine			CH_3	CH_3
Furfenorex			CH_3	$CH_3(CH_2C_4H_3O)$
Benzphetamine			CH_3	$CH_3(CH_2C_6H_5)$
Phentermine[b]			$(CH_3)_2$	
Mephentermine			$(CH_3)_2$	CH_3
Ephedrine[b]		OH	CH_3	CH_3
Phenylpropanolamine[b]		OH	CH_3	
Phenmetrazine[b]		O—	CH_3	—CH_2CH_2
Aminoxaphen		O—	CH_3	NH_2
Diethylpropion[b]		O	CH_3	$(C_2H_5)_2$
Chlorphentermine[b]	4-Cl		$(CH_3)_2$	
p-Chloroamphetamine[b]	4-Cl		CH_3	
Fenfluramine[b]	3-CF_3		CH_3	C_2H_5

[a] Goodman and Gilman (1965); Innes and Nickerson (1970); Biel (1970); Cox and Maikel (1972).
[b] Compounds discussed under their own heading in the text.

3.1.2. Noncatecholamines

a. Loss of Ring Hydroxylation. The next category of anorexic sympathomimetics is arranged as in Goodman and Gilman's text (Innes and Nickerson, 1970) under the general heading of noncatecholamines, meaning they lack one or both ring hydroxyl groups. By virtue of this change in structure at the benzene end of the molecule these drugs lose some of their receptor agonist potency. They do not interact potently with receptors, but they can *release* norepinephrine. This gives them an indirect alpha-adrenergic action by way of norepinephrine release which compensates for the loss of receptor potency.

We have confirmed this principle of indirect action with specific reference to anorexia through our finding that amphetamine loses anorectic potency in rats depleted of norepinephrine (Ahlskog and Hoebel, 1973). The same effect is reported for dopamine-depleted rats (Heffner et al., 1975); therefore, amphetamine acts, in part, by an indirect action on noradrenergic and dopaminergic nerves to curb feeding. As further evidence for presynaptic action in anorexia, relatively high affinity for membrane uptake is necessary for anorectic action.

Structural deviations in the noncatecholamines also cause shifts in peripheral effects on feeding. The noncatecholamines lack the typical epinephrine effect on glycogenolysis, and, even more specifically, loss of the hydroxyl at the 4 position of the benzene ring decreases free fatty acid release. For example, phenylephrine, which is epinephrine without the 4-hydroxyl group, does not release free fatty acid. This is likely part of the reason that phenylephrine is $1/20$th as potent an anorexiant as epinephrine. These drugs also have decreased cardiovascular potency. This allows a 20-fold increase in the tolerable dose of most of these drugs.

b. Alpha Methylation. Higher doses of alpha-methylated compounds can be administered, and this facilitates their entry into the brain. In addition, almost all the noncatecholamines in the list are methylated on the alpha carbon. As a general rule, they fail to be anorectic without the alpha methyl (Beregi *et al.,* 1970). This alpha substituent prevents monoamine oxidase (MAO) from breaking down the drugs rapidly in the gastrointestinal tract, liver, blood, or brain. Therefore, these drugs, such as amphetamine and ephedrine derivatives, are longer lasting, longer acting, and often suitable for oral administration. They also may gain MAO inhibitory properties and are granted the key to membrane uptake and the ability to lock out norepinephrine. If the alpha-carbon methyl is tied to the beta carbon, the compound becomes a 5000-fold more potent MAO inhibitor but loses anorexic power. Therefore anorexia probably does not usually depend on MAO inhibition. To the contrary, some such drugs (pheniprazine) become appetite stimulants. (See review by Biel, 1970.)

Double methylation of the alpha carbon reduced the norepinephrine-releasing properties of amphetamine and the serotonin releasing-properties of *p*-chloroamphetamine.

   c. Beta Hydroxylation. Unfortunately once the drugs are out of the gut and into the brain they often have multiple effects. With regard to appetite suppression, central nervous system arousal is the most troublesome side effect. However, hydroxylation of the beta carbon seems to decrease central nervous system stimulation. For example, methamphetamine is extremely stimulating, but β-hydroxymethamphetamine, i.e., ephedrine, is less exciting. Ephedrine is a compound used for medicinal purposes by the Chinese for 5000 years. It was the starting point for research on phenethylamine analogs in the treatment of cardiovascular disorders, nasal and brochial problems, arousal and learning phenomena, and anorexia. The first problem from the point of view of those interested in feeding was to eliminate arousal effects while retaining anorexia.

   d. Loss of Aminomethyl Group. As one goes down Table 2, the first and simplest modification to ephedrine is elimination of the aminomethyl group giving norephedrine, known as phenylpropanolamine or propadrine. We have studied this drug extensively and find it is a relatively specific anorectic. Judging from norephedrine (i.e., phenylpropanolamine) and normethamphetamine (i.e., amphetamine), the nor-compounds of this group cause less arousal.

   The next group retains the amino side chains, but ties them back to the beta carbon atom. Phenmetrazine is a well-known example.

   e. Substituted Ring Compounds. Finally we come to the new generation of ring-substituted compounds with enhanced beta-blocking action as in the pure alpha agonist methoxamine (Innes and Nickerson, 1970). Some of the halogenated compounds also become depressants instead of stimulants, notably fenfluramine.

   f. Tools of the Trade. Thus, drugs are available with varying excitatory and anorectic potency, and among them it should be possible to find the drug of choice for various therapeutic purposes. However, we are only beginning to comprehend the diversity of behavioral effects of these drugs which almost certainly affect various aspects of behavior in addition to feeding, for example, "aggression," both physiological and behavioral temperature regulation, sexual behavior, and so forth. It may well be that after focusing on the brain action of these drugs in order to understand them and to understand the brain, it will be necessary to reverse the process and seek out the anorectic agents that work on the peripheral metabolic signals of satiety. Only in that way will we be able to use the body's own systems of selectivity for production of clinical anorexia without a multitude of subtle brain neurochemical effects on a wide variety of behaviors.

   The focus of the remainder of this review continues to be on the brain. Only by finding how and where these drugs affect brain feeding systems can we learn how to find drugs which accomplish clinical goals by an action on natural feeding and satiety signals without neurochemical effects. At the same time, studies with drugs such as amphetamine, phenylpropanolamine, and fenfluramine are adding to our knowledge of both biochemical psychopharmacology and social psychopharmacology.

3.2. Epinephrine

Based on the structure–function relationships discussed above, the most interesting appetite suppressants might have alpha methylation to inhibit MAO and confer uptake, beta hydroxylation, no aminomethyl to minimize CNS arousal, and ring substitutions to release fat without effects on hemodynamics. Epinephrine has none of these features and is therefore one of the worst anorectics from a practical viewpoint.

Epinephrine is the prototype of peripherally administered, anorectic catecholamines. Systemically administered epinephrine causes a very pronounced refusal to eat even in hungry animals (Russek, 1971; Russek et al., 1973). This could be in part the result of an action in the liver.

3.2.1. Catecholaminergic Response of Hepatic Glucoreceptors

Russek and his co-workers find evidence that glucoreceptors in the liver influence feeding by sending neural signals to the brain, possibly to the hypothalamus, to signal satiety. Russek and Grinstein (1974) reviewed the evidence that these liver receptors respond to systemic anorectic compounds including catecholamines, glucose, nonmetabolizable 3-O-methyl glucose, and ammonium chloride. They suggest that ammonium chloride mimics the action of ammonium released by catabolism of amino acids. Systemic injections of epinephrine caused rapid and very pronounced refusal to eat with a time course parallel to hyperpolarization of hepatocytes. Russek and Grinstein (1974) suggest that the neural activity generated by these glucoreceptive hepatocytes is the main factor controlling food intake. This activity is a function of intracellular glucose influenced by a number of other factors, such as protein availability, circulating influxes of epinephrine as during stress, and reflex secretion of hepatic norepinephrine and epinephrine triggered by food arriving in the GI tract. In the absence of any of these influences the receptors gradually depolarize until "hunger discharges" are generated and transmitted to the brain.

As a corollary to this theory, we may assume that some peripherally acting phenethylamine derivatives would block the hypothetical hepatic hunger signal by acting directly on the receptors to hyperpolarize them or indirectly by releasing hepatic norepinephrine or epinephrine. This should be particularly true for phenethylamines with alpha-carbon methylation to protect them from MAO. This includes every well-known appetite suppressant in Table 2.

3.3. Nordefrin: α-Methylnorepinephrine

3.3.1. Catecholamine Uptake

Norepinephrine injected systemically is catabolized so rapidly by MAO that its central effects are not clear, but its neurochemical properties have been studied by pretreating the animal with an MAO inhibitor or by adding a methyl side chain to norepinephrine to make it MAO resistant. Fuxe and Ungerstedt (1970) review evidence that *in vitro* α-methylnorepinephrine is taken up by the catecholamine membrane uptake mechanism and accumulated sufficiently to produce fluorescence. This accumulation is extragranular, judging from the occurrence in reserpine-treated, catecholamine-depleted nerves. The accumulation seems to occur in the terminals of both norepinephrine and dopamine nerves. The same thing occurred *in vivo* when α-methylnorepinephrine was delivered intraventricularly. α-Methylnorepinephrine is not an oral anorectic because it does not easily cross the blood–brain barrier, but we can expect from these studies that some appetite-suppressant drugs of the norepinephrine type which do cross the barrier will be taken up by both dopamine and norepinephrine neurons.

3.3.2. Route of Administration

Neural accumulation of injected catecholamines was also demonstrated following the systemic injection of the norepinephrine precursor *l*-dopa, which crosses the blood–brain barrier. Systemic catecholamines that do not cross are nevertheless taken up by dopaminergic nerve terminals in the median eminence which must therefore be outside the blood–brain barrier. Administration within the barrier is possible by intraventricular injection. However, judging by the spread of fluorescing catecholamines, these compounds injected intraventricularly move less than 0.5 ml into surrounding tissue (Fuxe and Ungerstedt, 1970). Thus, the behavioral effects of intraventricular norepinephrine may be due to an action quite close to the ventricle. Leibowitz (1973) suggests that intraventricular norepinephrine elicits feeding by acting in the nearby periventricular and paraventricular nuclei. If this interpretation is correct, then one reason intraventricular injections of norepinephrine produce feeding instead of satiety is because the relevant satiety pathways and terminals are too far from the ventricle. Reports of norepinephrine-induced satiety with intracerebral injections have used cannulas at least 1 mm from the ventricle. Therefore, to influence a noradrenergic satiety system, the drug may have to be delivered directly to the relevant tissue or given systemically with protection from MAO. One such drug might logically be α-methylnorepinephrine with the ring hydroxyl groups removed to get it through the blood–brain barrier; this drug is called phenylpropanolamine and will be discussed shortly.

3.4. Phenethylamine

3.4.1. Competitive Catecholamine Uptake Block

Phenethylamine, the simplest of the noncatecholamines, has both ring hydroxyl groups missing and no side chains. Fuxe and Ungerstedt (1970) report that this noncatecholamine blocks catecholamine uptake, probably by competition for the uptake pump.

3.4.2. Catecholamine Release

Phenethylamine also releases catecholamine from extragranular stores. Amphetamine does the same thing, as does another appetite suppressant, phenmetrazine. Apparently this action is a property of the basic phenethylamine skeleton. Behavioral experiments confirmed the neurochemical findings. Phenethylamine, phenmetrazine, and mephetermine caused arousal and stereotyped sniffing, indicating catecholamine release in rats with reserpine-induced depletion of granular catecholamine stores. α-Methyl-p-tyrosine given to block catecholamine synthesis and thereby deplete extragranular stores prevented the behavioral effects.

In addition to blocking membrane uptake of catecholamines and releasing extragranular stores, the structure of these drugs also confers a degree of direct receptor action either as an agonist or antagonist according to the principles discussed in the section on structure–function relationships.

3.5. Amphetamine

3.5.1. Peripheral vs. Central Anorectic Action

The standard of comparison for anorectic action is d-amphetamine, famous as an appetite suppressant and stimulant, infamous as a drug of abuse. Of the numerous reviews of amphetamine, the following deal primarily with feeding: Cole (1973a), Grossman and Sclafani (1971), Marley and Stephenson (1972), Heil and Ross (1973), and Mawson (1974). A number of explanations of amphetamine anorexia have been offered. For example, anorexia has been explained as activation of responses incompatible with feeding (Carlton, 1963; Uehling and Venator, 1967; Modell, 1972) and by activation of glucose-satiety receptors in the liver (Russek *et al.*, 1973). In addition, there is no longer any doubt that amphetamine anorexia also depends in part on an action in the brain itself. There is overwhelming evidence for central action, illustrated ten ways as follows: (1) Lateral hypothalamic lesions decrease amphetamine anorexia (Carlisle, 1964; Panksepp and Booth, 1973) as do certain amygdala lesions (Cole, 1973b). (2) The hepatic anorectic effect of amphetamine also depends on the brain. As a rat recovers from the lateral hypothalamic lesions, epinephrine anorexia recovers, but amphetamine anorexia does not, suggesting that amphetamine has a separate effect via an unrecovered hypothalamic function (Russek *et al.*, 1973). (3) Ventromedial hypothalamic lesions, on the other hand, either have no effect or enhance anorexia (Stowe and Miller, 1957; Epstein, 1959; Reynolds, 1959; Wishart and Walls, 1973), as do lesions in the anterior hypothalamus (Cole, 1966) and area postrema (Reynolds and Carlisle, 1961). (4) Amphetamine decreases feeding elicited with hypothalamic electrodes (Miller, 1965; Stark and Totty, 1967). (5) Hypothalamic recordings during amphetamine administration show an increase in activity in the ventromedial hypothalamus but not in other areas (Brobeck *et al.*, 1956; Krebs *et al.*, 1969). (6) Amphetamine injected into the hypothalamus can produce satiety (Booth, 1968*b*; Leibowitz, 1972; 1975*c*). (7) Amphetamine anorexia is blocked by central-acting catecholamine-synthesis inhibitors such as AMPT (Leibowitz, 1975*d*) and restored by the catecholamine precursor *l*-dopa (Baez, 1974). (8) Amphetamine releases norepinephrine and dopamine as cited earlier. (9) *d*-Amphetamine is three times as potent as *l*-amphetamine as an anorectic whether it is injected peripherally (Baez, 1974) or centrally (Leibowitz, 1975*d*). (10) Specific depletion of forebrain norepinephrine (Ahlskog and Hoebel, 1972) or dopamine (Heffner *et al.*, 1975) is associated with decreased amphetamine anorexia. The question of central amphetamine anorectic action is settled once and for all.

The next question is how the central action is exerted. The problem is to identify the neurotransmitters or, better yet, specific neurochemical pathways which serve as a substrate for amphetamine anorexia.

3.5.2. *Neurochemistry of Anorexia*

a. Adrenergic Agonists and Antagonists: Amphetamine's Dual Alpha–Beta Effects. In the early days of intracerebral injection when researchers thought that norepinephrine elicited feeding by a direct postsynaptic excitatory action, it was speculated that amphetamine might cause anorexia by disrupting noradrenergic function, as by depolarization block. Booth (1968*b*) suggested this on the grounds that cannula sites for maximum norepinephrine feeding were also the best for amphetamine anorexia. Margules (1970*a*), however, suggested that amphetamine acts on a noradrenergic satiety system. Using local cannula injections, Leibowitz (1972) found that cannulated amphetamine, like epinephrine, caused the greatest decrease in food intake when injected with an alpha-adrenergic blocker, or when injected into the more lateral regions of the hypothalamus. Thus, amphetamine was most effective as an anorectic in beta-adrenergic sites. Conversely, she found that amphetamine, like epinephrine, actually increased food intake when injected with beta blockers or in locations designed to maximize alpha-adrenergic effects. Thus, amphetamine had *both* alpha-feeding and beta-satiety effects.

b. Catecholamine Agonists and Antagonists: Amphetamine's Dual Adrenergic and Dopaminergic Action. Most recently, Leibowitz (1975*c,d*) reports that 0.8

μg of d-amphetamine produced anorexia when injected in the hypothalamus anterior and lateral to the original perifornical site. This central effect, and the effects of amphetamine injected peripherally, were blocked by hypothalamic injection of a beta-adrenergic blocker, propranolol, or the dopamine blocker haloperidol, but not alpha-adrenergic, serotonergic, or cholinergic blockers. These results again suggest that amphetamine anorexia is a beta function, but added that a dopamine satiety substrate is also involved. Similarly, i.p. pimozide, a dopamine blocker, antagonized amphetamine anorexia (Kruk, 1973).

c. *Catecholamine Release and Depletion: Amphetamine's Presynaptic Action.* Amphetamine released norepinephrine (Taylor and Snyder, 1971) in the amygdala (Stein and Wise, 1969) and ventromedial hypothalamus (Carr and Moore, 1969) and also released dopamine (Von Voigtlander and Moore, 1973; Anden and Svensson, 1973). AMPT decreased amphetamine anorexia (Holtzman and Jewett, 1971; Leibowitz, 1975d; Heffner *et al.*, 1975), and anorexia can be restored with l-dopa (Baez, 1974). Therefore, just as the neurochemists working with AMPT and amphetamine in the 1960's concluded that amphetamine produces psychostimulation by presynaptic action (Weissman *et al.*, 1966), we can conclude that amphetamine also produces some of its anorexia by presynaptic action.

In histofluorescence studies, amphetamine in high doses appears to release serotonin as well as norepinephrine and dopamine (Fuxe and Ungerstedt, 1970). Amphetamine also releases all three putative neurotransmitters *in vitro* (Azzaro and Rutledge, 1973). If there is a serotonergic mechanism that curbs feeding, as suggested by Blundell and Lesham (1973) and Breisch and Hoebel (1975), hypothalamic lesions could damage this system as well as the norepinephrine bundles and the nigrostriatal tract. Thus, loss of amphetamine anorexia after lateral hypothalamic lesions could result from damage to any one or two or all three monoamine feeding-suppression systems.

Ahlskog and Hoebel (1973) reported that specific, adrenergic depletion with 6-hydroxydopamine injected in the ventral noradrenergic bundle diminished amphetamine anorexia (Fig. 4). These were potentially hyperphagic rats that were eating normal amounts on a restricted feeding schedule. After 6-hydroxydopamine treatment, the amphetamine dose–response curve was shifted in the direction of less effectiveness, i.e., the rats ate more under amphetamine than they did prior to norepinephrine depletion (Ahlskog, 1974). We concluded that amphetamine acts, in part, by facilitating norepinephrine or epinephrine action in the adrenergic satiety system. This confirmed Margules' view of noradrenergic, amphetamine satiety. It would also fit Leibowitz's beta-adrenergic satiety model if norepinephrine is a beta system transmitter or if we were depleting epinephrine and it is a beta transmitter.

6-Hydroxydopamine given intraventricularly to deplete dopamine by

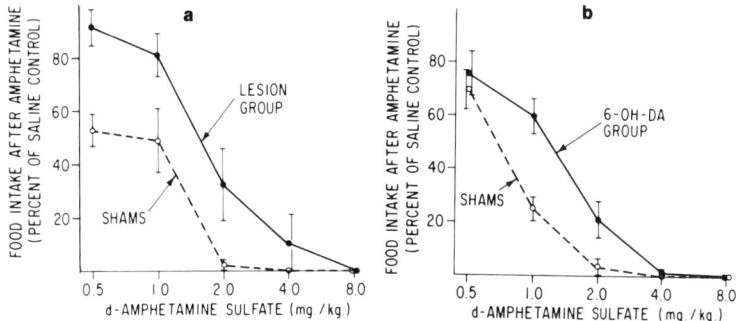

FIG. 4. Lesions (a) or 6-OHDA (b) in the vicinity of the ventral noradrenergic bundle attenuated amphetamine-induced anorexia. From Ahlskog (1974).

90% also diminished amphetamine anorexia. This suggested a dopamine substrate for amphetamine (Heffner *et al.*, 1975). We cannot be sure whether catecholamine depletion renders a substrate unavailable for amphetamine-induced satiety or disinhibits a substrate for amphetamine-induced feeding; the net result would be the observed loss of amphetamine anorexia in either case.

3.5.3. Dissociation of Anorexia and Arousal

a. Dissociation by Blocking or Depletion. Amphetamine's anorectic, hyperthermic, and CNS stimulation effects have been separated on behavioral, pharmacological, and anatomical grounds. In mice the beta-adrenergic blocker propranolol antagonized hyperthermia but potentiated anorexia (Mantegazza *et al.*, 1970). This is contrary to Leibowitz's report (1975c; 1975d) that hypothalamically administered beta blockers antagonized amphetamine anorexia, but in any case the point here is that hyperthermia did not account for the anorexia in mice. Neill and Grossman (1971) gave reserpine to deplete monoamines and were able to decrease amphetamine anorexia without affecting activity level. Similarly, Campbell and Baez (1974) found an anatomical separation in testing rats with lateral hypothalamic lesions. These animals failed to show amphetamine anorexia, but did display normal increases in activity. Amphetamine arousal does not require the lateral hypothalamus and probably involves an action in the reticular arousal system instead. It might be possible, therefore, to find anorectic drugs that suppress feeding in the hypothalamus without reticular activation.

b. Dissociation through Differential Tolerance Effects. Amphetamine effects can also be dissociated on the basis of differential tolerance. In the periphery, sympathomimetic agents have a variety of tolerance effects. For example, amphetamine, ephedrine, and others with an alpha-methyl group show rapid loss of cardiac stimulation (tachyphylaxis) compared to unsubstituted compounds like tyramine. The catecholamines themselves show little or no tachyphylaxis, partly because their metabolites do not compete with the endogenous transmitter. The same considerations apply in the CNS. The clinical implications of central tolerance to amphetamine effects are recognized, but very little is known and interpretation is difficult because tolerance occurs on at least three levels: (1) Tolerance occurs to the direct neural action of the drug. This would happen, for example, if drug-released transmitter acted back to inhibit further synthesis, or if the drug itself were taken up and released as a false transmitter, or if the drug excited the receptor and then blocked its own further action. (2) Tolerance occurs to indirect, neural actions of the drug. Synaptic subsensitivity to cholinergic agonists has been measured along with corresponding supersensitivity to cholinergic blockers in rats treated daily with a cholinesterase inhibitor, DFP, to prevent transmitter degradation. In cholinergic systems of this sort there seems to be no end-product inhibition; the unmetabolized transmitter gradually desensitizes the receptors. This may occur with no overt behavior change. Changes in postsynaptic sensitivity were revealed only when a second test drug was administered (Chippendale *et al.*, 1972). If the test drug was pilocarpine in anorectic doses, feeding was reduced less than usual. Thus, the animal showed "tolerance" to pilocarpine even though it had never received this particular drug before. Amphetamine suppressed feeding as usual, showing that it does not rely on this cholinergic system for its initial anorectic effect (Overstreet *et al.*, 1972). In another experiment, rats given amphetamine repeatedly showed a gradual lessening of anorexia (tolerance) with a corresponding increase in acetylcholine synthesis measured as choline acetylase activity. It is possible that amphetamines, and therefore catecholamines, can modulate acetylcholine synthesis (Ho and Gershon, 1972). (3) There are indirect physiological tolerances, such as gradually reduced duration of hyperthermia (Lewander, 1974), and indirect behavioral tolerances.

Behavioral "tolerance" to anorexia is an ambiguous phenomenon because animals on periodic deprivation schedules become progressively more deprived with repeated amphetamine injections during their only opportunity to feed; therefore, they will have a progressively greater physiological need for food (Panksepp and Booth, 1973). Increasing deprivation may also cause changes in catecholamine levels. Glick *et al.* (1973) found that food deprivation for two days depleted hypothalamic norepinephrine, and modified amphetamine's neurochemical actions. In addition the animals may simply learn to eat more food before it is removed. Thus, tolerance to anorexia becomes synonymous with increasing deprivation levels and learning trials. Proof that behavioral tolerance reflects behavioral adaptation comes from studies showing that amphetamine given daily after eating, instead of before, causes no tolerance to amphetamine anorexia in a subsequent test (Carlton and Wolgin, 1971).

In the test situation used by Magour *et al.* (1974) anorexia disappeared in a week, but body weight remained suppressed and activity remained elevated for about a month before signs of tolerance appeared. Similarly, we have observed a partial return of feeding without a return to the normal rate of body weight gain using daily phenylpropanolamine injections (Chen and Hoebel, unpublished). Therefore, tolerance to amphetamine's effect on feeding may have a different time course than tolerance to amphetamine's effect on activity and body weight. The time it takes a rat to learn to overcome amphetamine anorexia may depend on whether the animal is injected and allowed to eat at night or in the daytime. Our depletion studies (Ahlskog *et al.*, 1975) and the studies of Margules *et al.* (1972) suggest that feeding is suppressed by norepinephrine in the night and perhaps by serotonin in the day (Breisch *et al.*, 1976). Therefore, the severity of amphetamine effects and the rapidity of tolerance to them will probably be found to have a circadian rhythm.

3.5.4. Summary

Amphetamine suppresses food intake, at least in part, by indirect action on noradrenergic or adrenergic, dopaminergic, and, perhaps at high doses, also serotonergic systems in the brain. The adrenergic effect is at least partly beta-adrenergic and is strongest in the lateral, as opposed to medial, hypothalamic area. These findings help explain amphetamine's actions but do not necessarily imply that all the putative monoamine transmitters perform satiety functions under natural conditions. Amphetamine clearly has multiple effects, but anorexia does not seem to be entirely dependent on any one of them. In particular, amphetamine anorexia depends on different mechanisms than amphetamine arousal. Tolerance to amphetamine anorexia is greater than tolerance to weight loss and seems to be adequately explained by physiological-psychological phenomenon independent of presynaptic or postsynaptic changes in catecholamine or cholinergic satiety mechanisms. The most useful indication that anorexia and arousal are separable lies in the fact that some amphetamine derivatives have high arousal potency and low anorectic action, whereas others are highly anorectic but not arousing (Cox and Maickel, 1972). The drugs to be discussed next are all anorectics, but progressively less potent as stimulants.

3.6. Phentermine, Phenmetrazine, and Diethylpropion

3.6.1. Phentermine

This drug is amphetamine with two alpha-methyl groups instead of one. It is similar to amphetamine in anorectic and cardiovascular effects but less potent. It acts in part by releasing catecholamines as one would expect and exhibits tachyphylaxis with amphetamine cross-tolerance (Yelnosky *et al.*, 1969).

There is reasonably good evidence that phentermine is an anorectic in humans. Like amphetamine, it decreased subjective ratings of hunger with a correlated (+0.68) decrease in food intake (Silverstone and Stunkard, 1968; Silverstone, 1972). Even though these are placebo-controlled studies, the subjects may sense side effects and use them as a cue to act according to their expectations. Strangely, people in this type of study often do not report any side effects and may not mention stimulation or euphoria unless asked directly. For example, in a double-blind, one month, clinical test of amphetamine showing a significant 7.3 lb weight loss with the drug vs. 0.5 lb with the placebo, there were no signs of dependency and no reports of stimulation (Sproule, 1969). The same type of result was obtained with phentermine.

3.6.2. Phenmetrazine

Phenmetrazine (Preludin) is a popular anorectic that was designed to "tie back" the nitrogen side chain (Table 2) in the hope of obtaining anorexia without stimulation. However, phenmetrazine is clearly a mild stimulant and has led to misuse in some cases (Bell and Trethowan, 1961), including possible toxic psychosis similar to amphetamine (Kelman, 1965). In rats, it displays cross-tolerance with amphetamine (Lewander, 1974). The norepinephrine reuptake blocker DMI increased both the stimulant and anorectic properties of amphetamine, phentermine, and diethylpropion, but not phenmetrazine, which is metabolized differently from the other three (Menon et al., 1970).

3.6.3. Diethylpropion

Diethylpropion is a new drug with two nitrogen side chains. A list of over 400 references to this drug is available (Riker Laboratories, Inc.). The following experiments will serve as a sample of this extensive literature. Jonsson et al. (1964) compared 10 mg of d-amphetamine to 50 mg of phenmetrazine and 50 mg of diethylpropion. All three drugs had a slight enhancing effect on performance in tests such as flicker fusion frequency, suggesting all three are mild stimulants. There are reports of habitual users, but people who abuse this drug usually take excessive doses (Kelman, 1965).

Double-blind studies have shown that diethylpropion can produce significant weight loss in humans (e.g., Rosenberg, 1961). Often in such studies the compound is bound to a hydrophylic colloid for continual, slow release in the intestine (Tenuate, Dospan). This too has proven effective (Silverstone et al., 1970; Hadden and Lucey, 1961). Testing this long-acting preparation, Silverstone et al. (1968) found that subjective rating of hunger decreased with the first few administrations of the drug, but the effect disappeared. Food intake at home as reported by the subjects showed a long-term decrease. They did not find consistent side effects although they noted some initial restlessness and an increase in reports of mouth dryness. Most recently, Bolding (1974) reported that his patients lost an average of 14.8 lb (8.4%) in 3 months compared to 9 lb (4.7%) on placebo. There were no differences noted in pulse rate, blood pressure, or EKG between the two groups at the end of the study. There were a few side effects reported, but the pattern is difficult to interpret except to suggest that the drug group felt something more than the placebo group. Bolding used diet and exercise counseling as well as strong feedback in the form of wall charts showing weight-loss progress and financial rewards. The office visit charge was waived for weight loss and increased for weight gain. In this setting the drug appears responsible for a mean added weight loss of 4.8 lb in 3 months.

In sum, the drug is effective in producing statistically significant weight loss in patients concerned with their weight, and it causes some signs of moderate stimulation. Unlike methamphetamine, phenmetrazine, chlorphentermine, and fenfluramine, diethylpropion did not raise blood pressure (Woodward and Lucas, 1973). It has been used to treat obesity in people of all ages, including pregnant women, children, and patients with cardiovascular disease (review by Bolding, 1974).

It is clear that each anorexic has its particular idiosyncrasies which may make it the drug of choice in certain circumstances. Phenmetrazine is not potentiated by norepinephrine-uptake blockers; diethylpropion is not hypertensive. Next we need drugs that are less likely to be abused and that might be recommended for animal studies requiring anorexia without arousal.

3.7. Phenylpropanolamine

This drug is amphetamine hydroxylated on the beta carbon to decrease CNS stimulation and make it structurally more similar to norepinephrine. It is norephedrine, sometimes referred to as propadrine.

This drug seems to be relatively free of unwanted side effects. Comparing amphetamine and phenylpropanolamine in rats, Tainter (1944) reported that amphetamine increased oxygen consumption, but phenylpropanolamine did not at the dose tested. Epstein (1959) reported that phenylpropanolamine decreased feeding in rats without overt signs of activity change. Innes and Nickerson (1970) note that it causes relatively little CNS activation. We have confirmed that phenylpropanolamine decreases free feeding in rats (Kornblith and Hoebel, 1976). It also selectively inhibited electrically elicited feeding (Fig. 5) (Hoebel, 1971; Hoebel *et al.*, 1975*a*).

Welsh (1962), reviewing the side effects of antiobesity drugs, compared phenylpropanolamine to ephedrine and concluded that phenylpropanolamine is a strong vasoconstrictor, a weaker bronchial dilator, and a much weaker CNS stimulant. Therefore the primary contraindication is vasoconstriction. This popular compound is sold over the counter to relieve nasal congestion and relax bronchial spasm (e.g., in Propadrine, Contac, Allerest); it is also marketed widely as an appetite suppressant (e.g., Hungrex).

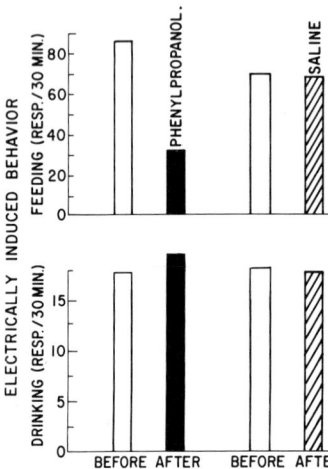

FIG. 5. Phenylpropanolamine (i.p.) inhibited feeding, but not drinking, induced by lateral hypothalamic stimulation. From Hoebel et al. (1975a).

There is surprisingly little literature on phenylpropanolamine's effectiveness in humans (see review by Silverman, 1963). Hirsh (1939) did a case study of phenylpropanolamine taken before meals and reported decreased appetite with no side effects. A comparison of phenylpropanolamine and amphetamine found phenylpropanolamine effective, but the study was not double blind (Colton et al., 1943). Fazekas et al. (1959) failed to get an effect with phenylpropanolamine, but the study was poorly controlled.

We recently found that phenylpropanolamine taken 30 min before a standard lunch given according to Jordan's technique (1966) significantly decreased food intake. This was a double-blind study with interspersed days of drug and placebo with each subject as his or her own control. They drank significantly less liquid diet on drug days and also perceived that they were drinking less judging from subjective ratings of amount consumed. There were no consistently reported side effects, although, as cited earlier, this can occur even with amphetamine. The subjects were recruited through their interest in weight loss (Hoebel et al., 1975b). We replicated this study, again with significant results, but two later studies using an uninformed student population failed to show significant appetite suppression. When the human dose, proportional to body weight, was given to monkeys, it very significantly suppressed food intake (Hamilton and Hoebel, unpublished; Hoebel, 1977).

Weight loss was significantly reduced in a double-blind cross-over study in which people interested in their weight took phenylpropanolamine before each meal at home (Fig. 6). During the first two weeks the placebo almost equaled the drug in producing weight loss, but when the subjects were "crossed over," those who had been on placebo continued to lose weight for the next two weeks with phenylpropanolamine, whereas those who had been on the drug failed to lose any more weight with the placebo (Hoebel et al., 1975c).

It is concluded that this drug can cause decreased appetite and weight loss in a population of people who are likely to use the drug for this purpose, that is, people interested in weight loss. The drug has yet to meet the most stringent test of appetite suppression and weight loss in a population of people who have no interest in weight loss and no knowledge that the drug is sold for that purpose.

3.8. Chlorphentermine and Chloroamphetamine

Chlorine or fluorine added to the benzene ring often decreases arousal in anorectic drugs. Phentermine is amphetamine with two alpha-carbon methyl groups (α-dimethylamphetamine); chlorphentermine (Presate) is, in addition, chlorinated in the para position. Compared to amphetamine, this drug causes rats to work less, instead of more, on a variable interval schedule for food; it decreases locomotor activity but with signs of hyperexcitability (Gylys et al., 1962; Gylys, 1966). Rats will work to self-inject it just as they do amphetamine, phenmetrazine, and diethylpropion (Baxter et al., 1973). In humans it causes anorexia with less arousal than amphetamine (Takacs and Petho, 1969; Ruedy, 1967).

Para-chlorination confers high lipid solubility, promoting entry into the brain and long-lasting effects. The drug is metabolized differently than amphetamine because para-hydroxylation is blocked.

Most intriguing, chlorinated amphetamines lowered brain serotonin

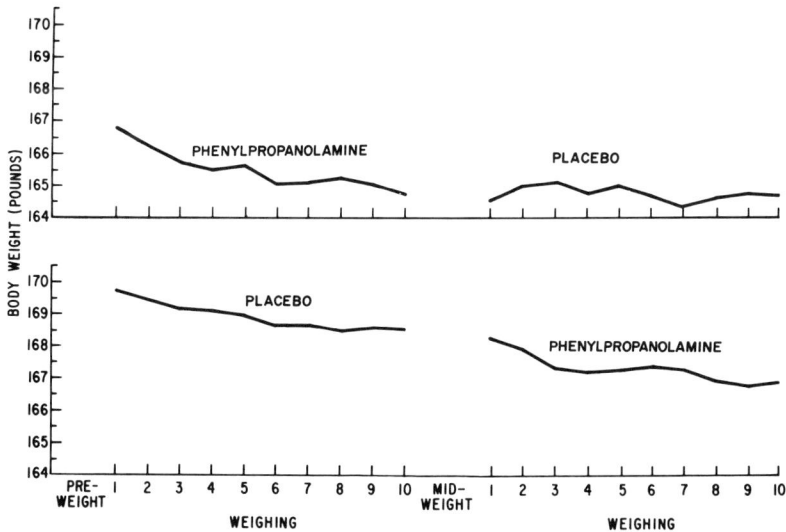

FIG. 6. Phenylpropanolamine taken before meals by people who wanted to lose weight decreased body weight compared to the placebo, particularly during the second ten weighings (second two weeks). From Hoebel et al. (1975c).

levels, although chlorphentermine did not (see reviews by Nielson and Dubnick and by Frey and others in Costa and Garrattini, 1970). This suggests that some halogenated phenethylamines might cause anorexia via brain serotonin. As further support for a serotonergic role, *p*-chloroamphetamine anorexia was blocked not only by AMPT and disulfiram, but also by antiserotonergic drugs, PCPA and cyproheptadine (Frey and Schulz, 1973).

In sum, halogenated amphetamine derivatives seemed to have a new and different mode of action, so there was hope that some would not be stimulants. We turn now to fenfluramine which combines both these features, serotonergic satiety and nonarousal.

3.9. Fenfluramine

3.9.1. Physiological and Behavioral Effects

Fenfluramine has the alpha-methyl group of amphetamine, an ethyl group on the nitrogen, and a trifluoromethyl group on the ring. Noble (1974) has written a useful general review of the drug.

This drug was designed to mobilize fat; it may also block fat storage. In humans, fenfluramine produced a dose-dependent increase in free fatty acid, free glycerol, and ketone levels in plasma, but it decreased triglycerides, suggesting increased fat mobilization and decreased fat synthesis (Pawan, 1969). In rats, free fatty acid release was not observed (Dannenburg and Kardian, 1969). Fenfluramine was $^1/_{20}$ as potent as amphetamine in raising blood pressure in rats and it did not raise body temperature (Bizzi *et al.*, 1970). Rats did not self-inject it (Baxter *et al.*, 1973). Fenfluramine, like chlorphentermine, suppressed feeding without locomotor stimulation (Van Rossum and Simons, 1969). A detailed behavioral analysis showed increased sniffing in spite of decreased eating, drinking, and rearing (Taylor *et al.*, 1971). Unlike amphetamine, fenfluramine blocked cortical activity during reticular stimulation (Foxwell *et al.*, 1969) even though both drugs activated the medial hypothalamus (Foxwell *et al.*, 1969; Khanna *et al.*, 1972).

Fenfluramine is undoubtedly an anorectic. This has been shown in many species including mice, rats, guinea pigs, cats, dogs, cattle (Bizzi *et al.*, 1970; Alphin and Ward, 1969; Chandler *et al.*, 1970; Abdallah and White, 1970; Cox and Maickel, 1972), in monkeys, (Chhina *et al.*, 1971; Tang and Kirch, 1971), and in people (Stunkard *et al.*, 1973). This recent study is particularly interesting because it compares fenfluramine with *d*-amphetamine and a placebo in the same study using 27 subjects per group from six different practicing physicians in an effort to approximate normal usage and add greater control. Fenfluramine and amphetamine led to a 4-lb weight loss in three weeks compared to less than 1 lb for the placebo. More of the subjects reported drowsiness with fenfluramine than for placebo or amphetamine. Fenfluramine also caused more frequent reports of gastrointestonal upsets and dry mouth. Both were associated with some claims of insomnia. There are no reports of addiction in use with over 9 million people (A. H. Robins Co.) and nine monkeys (Woods and Tessel, 1974). Gotestam and Gunne (1971) asked the real experts, experienced human drug abusers, to describe the subjective effects of two anorectics. They said one was a little like amphetamine, and the other, which was fenfluramine, did not feel like amphetamine. Individual differences in response to the drug do exist and the usual caution in interpreting such results is called for (Krengel, 1970).

3.9.2. Neurochemistry

a. Fenfluramine Anorexia via Serotonin. Several studies suggest that serotonin in the brain might mediate fenfluramine anorexia (Costa and Garattini, 1970). Fenfluramine anorexia is decreased by serotonin antagonists (Funderburk *et al.*, 1971; Jesperson and Scheel-Kruger, 1973; Blundell *et al.*, 1973; Clineschmidt *et al.*, 1974), by serotonin cell-body lesions (Samanin *et al.*, 1972), by serotonin depletion with 5,6-dihydroxytryptamine (Clineschmidt, 1973), and by serotonin-reuptake inhibition by chlorimipramine (Jespersen and Scheel-Kruger, 1973).

On the other hand, rats displayed clear anorexia in spite of serotonin depletion with *p*-chlorophenylalanine (PCPA) (Opitz, 1967; Funderburk *et al.*, 1971; Clineschmidt, 1973). Even when PCPA was injected intraventricularly, causing hyperphagia (Breisch and Hoebel, 1975), we detected no loss of fenfluramine anorexia at 3 and 5 mg/kg (unpublished; for recent reviews, see Blundell, 1977 and Hoebel, 1977). From studies such as these it appears that fenfluramine may cause anorexia partly by direct postsynaptic action or by some means not involving serotonin synapses at all.

Fenfluramine is also known to act indirectly by releasing serotonin. It can release some norepinephrine and dopamine, but they are normally catabolized too rapidly to cause hyperactivity (Ziance *et al.*, 1972). The end result of serotonin release is serotonin depletion (Duhault and Verdavainne, 1967; Opitz, 1967). When release is prevented by blocking fenfluramine uptake with chlorimipramine, anorexia is prevented (Ghezzi *et al.*, 1973). Therefore, anorexia following fenfluramine appears to depend in part on serotonin release.

b. Fenfluramine Anorexia via Nonmonoamines: Indirect Evidence. Clineschmidt *et al.* (1974) investigated the issue by testing a range of fenfluramine and amphetamine doses after a variety of blockers. Cyproheptadine, cinanserin, methylsergide, or chlorimipramine diminished fenfluramine anorexia, but only at 6 mg/kg, a high dose of fenfluramine. Catecholamine blocking agents, AMPT or haloperidol, diminished amphetamine anorexia with high, 3 mg/kg, doses of amphetamine. The authors conclude that fenfluramine in high doses acts by way of serotonin, that amphetamine in high doses acts by way of catecholamines, and that in lower doses both drugs cause anorexia via other, nonmonoamine, mechanisms.

The pharmacological dissociation of amphetamine and fenfluramine anorexia strongly suggests the existence of both catecholamine and serotonergic satiety functions as outlined in the first half of this chapter. The low dose effects on nonmonoamine systems suggested by Clineschmidt et al. (1974) would seem to depend very much on the testing situation because other workers have succeeded in diminishing amphetamine anorexia in doses as low as 0.5 mg/kg using AMPT to deplete catecholamines (Baez, 1974) or 6-hydroxydopamine given so as to deplete either norepinephrine (Ahlskog and Hoebel, 1972) or dopamine (Heffner et al., 1975). Blundell et al. (1973) illustrated the importance of long-term feeding tests to reveal biphasic or delayed action of anorectic drugs. It has also been suggested that anorexia may sometimes result from too much of a transmitter as well as too little (Heffner et al., 1975). Thus, interpretation of results is often difficult; broad-range dose–response curves and long-feeding tests with frequent food-intake measurements are advisable.

c. Fenfluramine Anorexia via Beta-Adrenergic Receptors. Systemic injections of fenfluramine, like amphetamine, can counteract feeding produced by hypothalamic injection of norepinephrine (Broekkamp et al., 1974). This could be a behavioral as well as neurochemical competition. If it is a hypothalamic neurochemical effect, then the most logical possibilities are either that fenfluramine via serotonin inhibits noradrenergic feeding, or, in accordance with Leibowitz's scheme, fenfluramine acts as an alpha-adrenergic blocker or beta agonist. The latter possibility is supported by experiments in which beta blockage by propranolol antagonized anorexia produced by serotonin injected peripherally (Goldman et al., 1971).

This suggests that serotonin anorexia is partly beta-adrenergic and that part of the beta satiety function might conceivably be performed by endogenous serotonin. But we know that hypothalamic amphetamine produces beta-adrenergic satiety (Leibowitz, 1972; 1975) and that fenfluramine and amphetamine have different substrates for anorexia according to all the depletion and synaptic blocker studies discussed above and below. Therefore, even if fenfluramine and amphetamine have a beta-adrenergic action in common, fenfluramine must have another anorectic action too. This is a convoluted line of reasoning, but Blundell and Leshem's experiment (1973) brings us straight to the point. Amphetamine or fenfluramine injected in the hypothalamus caused anorexia, but the time course was different for the two drugs, and the relative potencies were inversely related in any given rat. Therefore, there must be some substrate through which anorexia can be produced which they do not share.

d. Differential Effects of Hypothalamic Lesions and Norepinephrine Depletion. Ventromedial hypothalamic lesions do not mitigate fenfluramine anorexia (Bernier et al., 1969), as they do not amphetamine anorexia (Epstein, 1959). However, lateral hypothalamic lesions enhance fenfluramine anorexia, which is the opposite of their effects on amphetamine. Amphetamine anorexia is diminished by the lesion. The anorectic response to amphetamine recovers in time, but the enhanced response to fenfluramine does not change (Blundell and Leshem, 1974).

Norepinephrine depletion with 6-hydroxydopamine lesions of the ascending noradrenergic bundles have the same effects as lateral hypothalamic lesions. Amphetamine loses anorectic effectiveness, and fenfluramine gains (Fig. 7). Apparently norepinephrine depletion removes a substrate for amphetamine anorexia and sensitizes a different one for fenfluramine (Ahlskog et al., 1977; Hoebel, 1976a).

3.9.3. Electrophysiology

Anand's and Oomura's laboratories report that fenfluramine and its opposite, cyproheptadine, have effects on lateral and ventromedial hypothalamic neurons in accord with the lateral-feeding, medial-satiety dichotomy. Cyproheptadine tends to activate lateral cells more than medial ones, and fenfluramine activates medial cells more than lateral cells (Chakrabarty et al., 1967; Khanna et al., 1972; Oomura et al., 1973).

3.10. Social Psychology and Anorectic Drugs

It is clear that in this field placebos can have large effects. In most of the human studies of weight loss that have been cited, the placebo effect was more than half the drug effect. In our study of phenylpropanolamine, for example, the subjects lost weight between getting a medical checkup and starting the study, simply in anticipation of receiving a pill. Then in the first

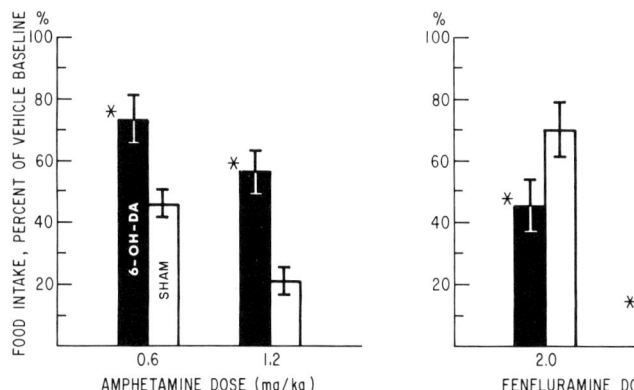

FIG. 7. VNAB lesions with 6-OHDA reduced amphetamine anorexia, i.e., increased food intake (left). The same injections in the same rats augmented fenfluramine anorexia (right). From Ahlskog et al. (1977).

two weeks they lost weight significantly with the drug but, expressed in terms of percent weight loss, it was not significantly different from the subjects taking a placebo. Thus, the study exerted some sort of "consciousness raising" which helped people to lose weight; they used the study as an excuse to start an effective weight loss regimen with no other help. In the subsequent two weeks subjects did have a significantly greater percent weight loss on the drug than on the placebo (Fig. 6).

This example raises three basic problems in anorectic drug testing. First, very few experiments use subjects matched for starting weight, degree of starting overweight, starting height–weight ratio, or any other attempt to make a pound-by-pound comparison of drug and placebo really convincing. Calculation of percent weight loss is a reasonable way of circumventing the problem, but there are several bigger problems.

Schachter and Rodin (1974) and Nisbett (1972) have shown that people who are overweight according to insurance companies' statistics tend to be more susceptible to external cues. They are more likely than nonoverweight people to eat when the clock says eat or when food is sighted and readily available. This tendency to pay attention to stimuli can extend to other aspects of their personality such that they may be better proofreaders, for example. Thus, the testing situation may in many ways influence the response of the subject, and may influence overweight subjects differently from nonoverweight subjects. Matched subjects are clearly advisable. The best way to match subjects is to use each subject as his or her own control, and in a crossover design allow each subject to return to his or her original starting weight for both the drug test and for the placebo test. I am not aware that this has ever been done.

Second, Modell (1972) has suggested that human subjects often eat less in anorectic drug tests because the drug makes them feel different, usually more stimulated, so they can tell when they are taking the drug as opposed to the placebo. They then eat less due to their expectations. Thus, they eat less on the drug, but for reasons irrelevant to a scientific concern with anorexia. This power of suggestion is shown in the Schachter and Singer (1962) experiment in which people were injected with epinephrine to arouse them. Then, if they sat in a waiting room with a euphoric stooge, they were more likely than controls to report euphoria. By contrast, if they waited with a grumpy stooge, they tended to label their feelings as anger. Conversely, Zanna and Cooper (1974) found that people in conflict over what they just wrote in an essay readily attributed their feelings to a pill even though unbeknown to them the pill was a placebo.

We can expect people to act as if they had lost their appetite if a reputed appetite suppressant gives them a different feeling for which they will seek a label (Morris and O'Neal, 1974). If it is an anorectic drug study, even a double-blind, cross-over, matched sample study, they may well label themselves anorectic on drug days. Thus, an important question is whether or not the drug produces a sensation that can be discriminated and labeled by the subjects. Asking the subjects if they feel any side effects is not really sufficient since even amphetamine studies sometimes find no side effects, and yet amphetamine is clearly a stimulant. This is not to say that subjective reports are not valuable; in some cases, they clearly are, as in the instance of the drug R300 (fenisorex), which gave many signs of being an effective appetite suppresant until the subjects reported getting headaches, perhaps as a result of rebound hypertension (Silverstone and Fincham, 1974).

One solution to the side-effect problem is to give the subjects two possibilities to expect. Then, if the drug causes an irrelevant, but labelable state, some subjects will react one way while some react another way, and the net result will be an increase in variance in the data but no significant drug effect on food intake or body weight. Thus, Jordan (personal communication) instructed people in his amphetamine-lunch study that the drug was an antidepressant which might stimulate them into eating more lunch, or that it might suppress their appetite. Under these conditions amphetamine failed to decrease food intake in this pilot study. Similarly we have found twice that phenylpropanolamine decreases food intake at lunch time in Princeton residents concerned about their weight and interested in helping in an appetite study, but failed to affect food intake in Princeton University students interested only in getting paid and who were told that they were being given a nasal decongestant that might make food intake go up or down. We do not know if the failure was due to the dual expectation, to the different motivations of the students, or to their younger, less weighty stage in life, but the point is the same. The way subjects are selected, instructed, and motivated makes such a large difference that any true pharmacological effect on appetite or body weight can be enhanced or masked. This drug does have a true appetite-suppressant effect if we judge by its significant effect on 24-hr food intake in monkeys (Hamilton and Hoebel, unpublished).

The practitioner may choose to enhance the effect with various behavior-modification procedures such as built-in expectations, feedback on progress, group pressures to conform, explanations of obesity morbidity and mortality figures, financial and social rewards, elimination of unnecessary food cues to tempt the subjects, exercise and diet counseling, and so forth. The research scientist, on the other hand, must control as many of these factors as possible. It is also highly advisable to compare the drug under test with other well-known drugs such as d-amphetamine and fenfluramine in order to include both an assessment of the stimulant and depressant effects of the drug.

Finally, even if a drug gives a statistically significant weight loss under the best of test conditions, it may be so small in actual pounds as to be medically insignificant except as a social justification for inducing the big placebo effect. In most studies the difference between the drug effect and placebo effect is just a few pounds after weeks of treatment. Some individuals of course lose a great deal of weight on these drugs, and so generalizations based on trivial mean weight loses may be unfair to them, as long as the drug is so innocuous as to be of no risk to people who take it without achieving weight loss.

Medical significance, as distinguished from statistical significance, is the real problem. There is no concensus as to whether a transient weight loss to "give the heart a rest" is better than no weight loss, or how much weight loss constitutes a beneficial improvement. The one fact known beyond question is life-insured people live longer on the average if they keep their weight down to the level attained in their early twenties (Society of Actuaries, 1960). This can be accomplished by eating less, digesting less, storing less fat, raising the metabolic rate, and so forth. It is not clear which of these means, or combination of means, is safest and most effective. Perhaps the worst thing would be a drug that released and laid down vascular fat regardless of what else it did to appetite. Thus, this chapter on the pharmacology of feeding fails to take into consideration all that is important from a medical point of view. The focus is arbitrarily on food intake and whole-body weight. For a review of obesity as a health hazard, see Sedgwick (1971).

Longevity aside, cosmetic weight loss has its own peculiar benefits, and because personality variables such as "sensory externality" vary with body weight, the patient and patient's close associates may have their own assessment of the social-psychological benefits of weight loss for a given individual.

In sum, the "efficacy" of an appetite-suppressant drug cannot be measured solely in terms of pounds lost compared to placebo; the effect of the placebo and the effect of the pounds are subject to powerful social factors which may be falsely attributed to the drug.

4. ORECTIC DRUGS

Undereating and the consequent abnormally low weight arise in a number of contexts usually grouped together under the name of anorexia nervosa. Endocrine imbalance leading to chronic anorexia is included as well as "mental" or "psychiatric anorexia" (Albeaux-Fernet et al., 1968; Beaumont et al., 1972). A full description of this disorder and the population it strikes is given in the detailed review by Mawson (1974). The main symptom is resolute refusal to eat, with nausea when eating does occur. Mawson proposes that these patients may suffer from loss of catecholamines necessary for feeding, like anorectic rats with lateral hypothalamic lesions. A crude way to boost neurochemical synthesis in rats and presumably in people is with electroconvulsive shock (Kety et al., 1967). Pharmacological approaches include treatment with cyproheptadine, tranquilizers, or l-dopa.

4.1. Cyroheptadine

Cyproheptadine (Periactin) is an appetite stimulant, serotonergic antagonist, and antihistamine. It helps men, women, and children to gain weight as shown in many studies over the last five years (e.g., Mertz and Stelzer, 1969; Noble, 1969; Stiel *et al.*, 1970; Penfold, 1971; Silbert, 1971). It also increases food intake and body weight in rats (Oomura *et al.*, 1973).

On the basis of the previous discussion of serotonin-induced satiety, Mawson's catecholamine theory of anorexia nervosa could be expanded to include serotonin. This also expands the treatments one would consider and makes cyproheptadine a logical possibility. A number of references to cyproheptadine neurochemistry and feeding have already been made in the sections on serotonin and fenfluramine. It is most likely that cyproheptadine augments the appetite in part by antagonizing a serotonergic satiety function in rats and humans.

4.2. Tranquilizers

Anorexia nervosa patients are hyperactive. In the extreme case, this might reflect indirect starvation-induced hyperactivity (Campbell and Fibiger, 1971) or, more likely, a direct neurochemical abnormality in arousal systems. In an effort to treat this symptom, tranquilizers have been used to calm the patients with mixed success. Recently the action of tranquilizers on brain feeding mechanisms has been explored. The minor tranquilizers increase feeding; major tranquilizers have mixed effects.

4.2.1. Minor Tranquilizers: Benzodiazepines: Diazepam and Oxazepam

These drugs are antianxiety, anticonvulsant, antitension agents—in another word, relaxants. Elements of these characterizations seem to be true in both rats and humans. Their effects on feeding result from three interrelated actions, all of which tend to increase food intake.

First, Margules and Stein (1967) describe the action of these drugs in terms of release of punished behavior. This idea is deceptively simple and quite elegant because it may encompass all three actions to be described.

Some stimuli, called negative reinforcers or punishers, decrease the frequency of preceding behavior patterns. This behavior suppression is reversed by oxazepam. That is, oxazepam disinhibits punished behavior, such as milk licking that has been suppressed by foot shock (Margules and Stein, 1967). This explains anxiety reduction as reducing the threat of punishment.

Oxazepam released feeding punished by foot shock, or feeding suppressed by physiological satiety, or even operant feeding responses suppressed by failure of the feeding machine, i.e., response extinction (Margules and Stein, 1967). This is an interesting way of viewing satiety as an active, suppressive process, not just a failure to start eating. I have extended this idea with evidence that satiety can involve an aversion to food which can be measured as responses to escape from hypothalamic stimulation (Hoebel 1975, 1976b).

Second, benzodiazepines such as diazepam (N-methylated oxazepam) initiate feeding in satiated rats (Randall et al., 1960; Poschel, 1971; Margules and Stein, 1967; Wise, 1974; Wise and Dawson, 1974). These drugs apparently disinhibit feeding. This is especially dramatic in the reversal of a learned aversion to a particular food punished by gastric illness. After chlordiazepoxide the hapless rat will eat the taboo food and might die if it were poisonous (Cappell et al., 1972).

The third way these antianxiety drugs relate to feeding is through their ability to relax the strictures of food novelty. Rats given diazepam will eat novel diets they would normally avoid (Poschel, 1971). This was particularly noted in lateral-hypothalamic-stimulated rats that would not eat novel food, but would eat readily under the drug's influence (Soper and Wise, 1971; Wise and Erdmann, 1973). It is not entirely clear how to best describe this effect. Did the brain stimulation make the rats too excited, or too emotional, or too neophobic? Wise and Dawson (1974) review this literature and report experiments suggesting that diazepam may elicit feeding, as opposed to drinking or other behaviors, by specifically blocking a satiety function with little or nothing to do with emotionality or anxiety.

The next question is which of the neurochemical systems we have discussed might be involved. Margules and Stein (1967) suggest that oxazepam mimics atropine or a lesion in blocking a cholinergic system in the ventromedial hypothalamus, thereby releasing punished behavior. More recently Wise et al. (1972) suggest that benzodiazepines decrease anxiety by decreasing serotonin turnover. Dominic (1973) reports decreased serotonin synthesis. Wise and Dawson (1974) link diazepam to the role of serotonin in satiety, but point out that norepinephrine satiety also qualifies because benzodiazepines decrease norepinephrine turnover (Taylor and Laverty, 1969).

Further indirect evidence for catecholamine involvement comes from the observation that one of these drugs, chlordiazepoxide, decreases amphetamine anorexia (Borella et al., 1969) like norepinephrine depletion (Ahlskog and Hoebel, 1973) or dopamine depletion (Heffner et al., 1975). On the other hand, decreased amphetamine anorexia with this tranquilizer might reflect nothing more than a general tendency to eat more food, having nothing to do with catecholamine satiety.

4.2.2. Phenothiazines: Chlorpromazine

These are the "major" tranquilizers which cause sedation like the minor tranquilizers just discussed, but which do not release punished responses

(Margules and Stein, 1967). They do increase behavioral output, but this is clearly nonspecific. For example, chlorpromazine, unlike diazepam, makes rats eat more and also drink more (Reynolds and Carlisle, 1961; Stolerman, 1970; Wise and Dawson, 1974). Leibowitz (1972) reviews the results of chlorpromazine injected into the hypothalamus. Hypothalamic chlorpromazine, like norepinephrine, increased feeding. The effect was blocked by phentolamine, an alpha blocker. Chlorpromazine differed from norepinephrine, however, in that its feeding effect was reduced by blocking catecholamine synthesis. This series of studies suggested that chlorpromazine produced feeding by releasing endogenous transmitter onto alpha-adrenergic receptors.

Chlorpromazine would also seem to be capable of potentiating catecholaminergic satiety as well as feeding, judging from the synergistic action of chlorpromazine and amphetamine in producing enhanced anorexia (Borella et al., 1969). Therefore, its use in anorexia nervosa would seem less appropriate than the antianxiety agents.

4.2.3. Barbiturates: Phenobarbital and Pentobarbital

Jacobs and Farel (1971) noted serendipitously that phenobarbital in a dose that caused arousal also increased feeding in rats. Kuhn (1973) reported hyperphagia following intraventricular injections in cats. Jacobs and Farel reviewed the literature showing that barbiturates can elicit drinking, sexual behavior, and aggression and conclude that a properly chosen dose causes arousal which triggers nonspecific consummatory behavior, including feeding. They offer this as an example of a general principle that arousal in the presence of an appropriate goal object is sufficient to produce consummatory behavior. This is quite different from the major tranquilizer, chlorpromazine, which is also nonspecific, but presumably acts by calming the rat, not arousing it. The barbiturates are also different from the minor tranquilizers, which increased feeding but not drinking.

4.3. L-Dopa

Mawson (1974) reviews L-dopa therapy for Parkinson's disease and proposes its use for anorexia nervosa. This does seem logical in order to boost norepinephrine and dopamine feeding functions. These functions were discovered first and are therefore best known. The problem here, based on the information given in the norepinephrine and dopamine sections of this chapter, is that these neurochemicals serve satiety functions as well. The goal must be to modulate catecholamine function in the correct subsystem. L-Dopa, a precursor to both norepinephrine and dopamine, is probably going to be too nonspecific for a selective effect on food intake.

Acknowledgments

I would like to acknowledge the Hastings Institute of Society, Ethics, and the Life Sciences, and endorse the concept that the task for the future is not just the revelation of brain psychopharmacology, but also the invention of mechanisms of social trust for the ethical use of psychopharmacology (Sollitto and Veatch, 1974).

Work on this review was done in 1974 with the support of Public Health Service Grant MH-08493-12 and National Science Foundation Grant GB-43407.

5. REFERENCES

ABDALLAH, A., and WHITE, H. D., 1970, Comparative study of the anorectic activity of phenindamine d-amphetamine and fenfluramine in different species, *Arch. Int. Pharmacodyn. Ther.* **188**:271–283.

ADAMS, P. M., 1973, The effects of cholinolytic drugs and cholinesterase blockage on deprivation-based activity and appetitive behavior, *Neuropharmacology* **12**:825–833.

AHLQUIST, R. P., 1948, A study of adrenotropic receptors, *Am. J. Physiol.* **153**:586–600.

AHLSKOG, J. E., 1974, Food intake and amphetamine anorexia after selective forebrain norepinephrine loss, *Brain Res.* **82**:211–240.

AHLSKOG, J. E., 1976, Feeding response to regulatory challenges after 6-hydroxydopamine injection into the brain noradrenergic pathways, *Physiol. Behav.* **17**:407–411.

AHLSKOG, J. E., and HOEBEL, B. G., 1972, Hyperphagia resulting from selective destruction of an ascending adrenergic pathway in the rat brain, *Fed. Proc.* **31**:377.

AHLSKOG, J. E., and HOEBEL, G. B., 1973, Overeating and obesity from damage to a noradrenergic system in brain, *Science* **182**:166–169.

AHLSKOG, J. E., RANDALL, P. K., and HOEBEL, B. G., 1975, Hypothalamic hyperphagia: Dissociation from noradrenergic depletion hyperphagia, *Science* **190**:399–401.

AHLSKOG, J. E., RANDALL, P. K., and HOEBEL, B. G., 1977, Noradrenergic neuron destruction: opposite effects on fenfluramine- and amphetamine-anorexia (submitted for publication).

ALBEAUX-FERNET, M., DROMARD, M., DAUMEZON, G., and KESTEMBERG, E., 1968, Mental anorexia: round table discussion, *Rev. Med. Psychosom. Psychol. Med.* **10**:447–460.

ALPHIN, R. S., and WARD, J. W., 1969, Anorexigenic effects of fenfluramine hydrochloride in rats, guinea pigs, and dogs, *Toxicol. Appl. Pharmacol.* **14**:182–191.

ANDEN, N. E., and SVENSSON, T. H., 1973, Release of dopamine from central noradrenaline nerves after treatment with reserpine plus amphetamine, *J. Neural Transm.* **34**:23–30.

ANDEN, N. E., ATACK, C. V., and SVENSSON, T. H., 1973, Release of dopamine from central noradrenaline and dopamine nerves induced by a dopamine-beta-hydroxylase inhibitor, *J. Neural Transm.* **34**:93–100.

ARMSTRONG, S., and SINGER, G., 1974, Effects of intrahypothalamic administration of norepinephrine on the feeding response of the rat under conditions of light and darkness, *Pharmacol. Biochem. Behav.* **2**:811–815.

AUFFRAY, P., MARCILLOUX, J. C., BAHY, C., and ALBE-FESSARD, D., 1973, Hyperphagia induite chez l'oie par injections intraventriculaires de 6-hydroxydopamine, *C. R. Acad. Sci. Paris* **276**:347–350.

AVERY, D. D., and NANCE, D. M., 1970, Behavioral correlates of chemical stimulation in the cat thalamus, *Psychonom. Sci.* **19**:7–8.

AZZARO, A. J., and RUTLEDGE, C. O., 1973, Selectivity of release of norepinephrine, dopamine and 5-hydroxytryptamine by amphetamine in various regions of rat brain, *Biochem. Pharmacol.* **22**:2801–2813.

BAEZ, L. A., 1974, Role of catecholamines in the anorectic effects of amphetamine in rats, *Psychopharmacologia* **35**:91–98.

BAILE, C. A., 1974, Putative neurotransmitters in the hypothalamus and feeding, *Fed. Proc.* **33**:1166–1176.

BANDLER, R. J., 1971, Chemical stimulation of the rat midbrain and aggressive behavior, *Nature (London) New Biol.* **229**:222–223.

BARTHOLINI, G., STADLER, H., and LLOYD, K. G., 1975, Cholinergic–dopaminergic interregulations within the extrapyramidal system, in: *Cholinergic Mechanisms* (P. G. Waser, ed.), Raven Press, New York.

BAXTER, M. G., MILLER, A. A., and SOROKO, F. E., 1970, The effect of cyproheptadine on food consumption in the fasted rat, *Br. J. Pharmacol.* **39**:229P–230P.

BAXTER, B. L., GLUCKMAN, M. I., and SCERNI, R., 1973, Differential self-injection behavior produced by fenfluramine versus other appetite inhibiting drugs, *Fed. Proc.* **32**:754.

BEATON, J. M., and CROW, T. J., 1969, The effect of noradrenaline synthesis inhibition on motor activity and lever pressing for food and water in the rat, *Life Sci.* **8**:1129–1134.

BEAUMONT, P. J. V., BEARDWOOD, C. J., and RUSSELL, G. F. M., 1972, The occurrence of the syndrome of anorexia nervosa in male subjects, *Psychol. Med.* **2**:216–231.

BELL, D. S., and TRETHOWAN, W. H., 1961, Amphetamine addiction, *J. Nerv. Ment. Dis.* **133**:489–495.

BEREGI, L. G., HUGON, P., LEDOUAREC, P. C., LAUBIE, M., and DUHAULT, J., 1970, Structure–activity relationships in CF_3 substituted phenethylamines, in: *Amphetamines and Related Compounds* (E. Costa and S. Garattini, eds.), pp. 21–61, Raven Press, New York.

BERGER, B. D., WISE, C. D., and STEIN, L., 1971, Norepinephrine: reversal of anorexia in rats with lateral hypothalamic damage, *Science* **172**:281–284.

BERNIER, A., SICOT, N., and LEDOUAREC, J. C., 1969, Fenfluramine et amphetamine chez les rats obeses hypothalamiques, *Rev. Fr. Etud. Clin. Biol.* **14**:762–772.

BIEL, J. H., 1970, Structure–activity relationships of amphetamine and derivatives, in: *Amphetamines and Related Compounds* (E. Costa and S. Garattini, eds.), pp. 3–20, Raven Press, New York.

BIZZI, A., BONACCORSI, A., JESPERSEN, S., JORI, A., and GARATTINI, S., 1970, Pharmacological studies on amphetamine and fenfluramine, in: *Amphetamines and Related Compounds* (E. Costa and S. Garattini, eds.), pp. 577–596, Raven Press, New York.

BLUNDELL, J. E., 1977, Is there a role for serotonin (5-hydroxytryptamine) in feeding? *Int. J. Obesity* **1**:15–42.

BLUNDELL, J. E., and HERBERG, L. J., 1973, Primary polyuria accompanies hunger elicited by intrahypothalamic injection of noradrenaline, *Neuropharmacology* **12**:597–599.

BLUNDELL, J. E., and LESHEM, M. B., 1973, Dissociation of the anorexic effects of fenfluramine and amphetamine following intrahypothalamic injection, *Br. J. Pharmacol.* **47**:183–185.

BLUNDELL, J. E., and LESHEM, M. B., 1974, Central action of anorexic agents: effects of amphetamine and fenfluramine in rats with lateral hypothalamic lesions, *Eur. J. Pharmacol.* **28**:81–88.

BLUNDELL, J. E., LATHAM, C. J., and LESHEM, M. B., 1973, Biphasic action of a 5-hydroxytryptamine inhibitor on fenfluramine-induced anorexia, *J. Pharm. Pharmacol.* **25**:492–494.

BOLDING, O. T., 1974, Diethylpropion hydrochloride: an effective appetite suppressant, *Curr. Ther. Res. Clin. Exp.* **16**:40–48.

BOOTH, D. A., 1967, Localization of the adrenergic feeding system in the rat diencephalon, *Science* **158**:515–517.

BOOTH, D. A., 1968a, Mechanism of action of norepinephrine in eliciting and eating response on injection into the rat hypothalamus, *J. Pharm. Exp. Ther.* **160**:336–348.

BOOTH, D. A., 1968b, Amphetamine anorexia by direct action on the adrenergic feeding system of rat hypothalamus, *Nature (London)* **217**:869–870.
BOOTH, D. A., 1972, Unlearned and learned effects of intrahypothalamic cyclic AMP injection on feeding, *Nature (London) New Biol.* **237**:222–224.
BOOTH, D. A., and QUARTERMAIN, D., 1965, Taste sensitivity of eating elicited by chemical stimulation of rat hypothalamus, *Psychonom. Sci.*, **3**:525–526.
BORBELY, A. A., HUSTON, J. P., and WASER, P. G., 1973, Physiological and behavioral effects of parachlorophenylalanine in the rat, *Psychopharmacologia* **3**:131–142.
BORELLA, L. E., PAQUETTE, R., and HERR, F., 1969, The effect of some CNS depressants on hypermotility and anorexia induced by amphetamine in rats, *Can. J. Physiol. Pharmacol.* **47**:841–871.
BRADLEY, P. B., WOLSTENCROFT, J. H., HOSLI, L., and AVANZINO, G. L., 1966, Neuronal basis for the central action of chlorpromazine, *Nature (London)* **212**:1427–1428.
BRECKENRIDGE, B. M., and LISK, R. D., 1969, Cyclic adenylate and hypothalamic regulatory functions, *Proc. Soc. Exp. Biol. Med.* **131**:934–935.
BREESE, G. R., and TRAYLOR, T. D., 1971, Depletion of brain noradrenaline and dopamine by 6-hydroxydopamine, *Br. J. Pharmacol.* **42**:88–99.
BREESE, G. R., SMITH, R. D., COOPER, B. R., and GRANT, L. D., 1973, Alterations in consummatory behavior following intracisternal injection of 6-hydroxydopamine, *Pharmacol. Biochem. Behav.* **1**:319–328.
BREISCH, S. T., and HOEBEL, B. G., 1975, Hyperphagia and transient obesity following intraventricular parachlorophenylalanine, *Fed. Proc.* **34**:296.
BREISCH, S. T., ZEMLAN, F. P., and HOEBEL, B. G., 1976, Hyperphagia and obesity following serotonin depletion with intraventricular parachlorophenylalanine, *Science* **192**:382–385.
BROBECK, J. R., LARSSON, S., and REYES, E., 1956, A study of the electrical activity of the hypothalamic feeding mechanism, *J. Physiol. (London)* **132**:358–364.
BRODY, J. F., 1970, Behavioral effects of serotonin depletion and of p-chlorophenylalanine (a serotonin depleter) in rats, *Psychopharmacologia* **17**:14–23.
BROEKKAMP, C., and VAN ROSSUM, J. M., 1972, Clonidine induced intrahypothalamic stimulation of eating in rats, *Psychopharmacologia* **25**:162–168.
BROEKKAMP, C., HONIG, W. M., PAULI, A. I., and VAN ROSSUM, J. M., 1974, Pharmacological suppression of eating behavior in relation to diencephalic noradrenergic receptors, *Life Sci.* **14**:473–481.
BUTCHER, L. L., EASTGATE, S. M., and HODGE, G. K., 1974, Evidence that punctuate intracerebral administration of 6-hydroxydopamine fails to produce selective neuronal degeneration, *Nauyn-Schmeidebergs Arch. Pharmacol.* **285**:31–70.
CAMPBELL, B. A., and BAEZ, L. A., 1974, Dissociation of arousal and regulatory behaviors following lesions of the lateral hypothalamus, *J. Comp. Physiol. Psychol.* **87**:142–149.
CAMPBELL, B. A., and FIBIGER, H. C., 1971, Potentiation of amphetamine-induced arousal by starvation, *Nature (London) Phys. Sci.* **233**:424–425.
CAPOBIANCO, S., and MOUNTFORD, D., 1974, The effects of drug administration to the lateral hypothalamus: neurochemical coding or nonspecificity, *Bull. Psychonom. Soc.* **3**:179–180.
CAPPELL, H., LEBLANC, A. E., and ENDREYI, L., 1972, Effects of chlordiazepoxide and ethanol on the extinction of a conditioned taste aversion, *Physiol. Behav.* **9**:167–169.
CARLISLE, H. J., 1964, Differential effects of amphetamine on food and water intake in rats with lateral hypothalamic lesions, *J. Comp. Physiol. Psychol.* **58**:47–54.
CARLTON, P. L., 1963, Cholinergic mechanisms in the control of behavior by the brain, *Psychol. Rev.* **70**:19–39.
CARLTON, P. L., and WOLGIN, D. L., 1971, Contingent tolerance to the anorexigenic effects of amphetamine, *Physiol. Behav.* **7**:221–223.
CARR, L. A., and MOORE, K. E., 1969, Norepinephrine: release from brain by d-amphetamine *in vivo*, *Science* **164**:322–323.
CEBEDDU, L., LANGER, S., and WEINER, H., 1974, The relationships between alpha receptor

block, inhibition of norepinephrine uptake and the release and metabolism of ^{3}H-norepinephrine, *J. Pharmacol. Exp. Ther.* **188**:368-385.

CHAKRABARTY, A. S., PILLAI, R. V., ANAND, B. K., and SINGH, B., 1967, Effect of cyproheptadine on the electrical activity of hypothalamic feeding centers, *Brain Res.* **6**:561-569.

CHAKRABARTY, A. S., BHATNAGAR, O. P., and CHAKRABARTY, K., 1974, Feeding behavior of cyproheptadine-treated rats, *Indian J. Med. Res.* **62**:726-730.

CHANDLER, P. T., DANNENBURG, W. N., POLAN, C. E., and THOMPSON, N. R., 1970, Effect of fenfluramine on appetite and lipid metabolism of the young ruminant, *J. Dairy Sci.* **53**:1747-1756.

CHASE, T. N., and MURPHY, D. L., 1973, Serotonin and central nervous system function, *Ann. Rev. Pharmacol.* **13**:181-197.

CHHINA, G. S., KANG, H. K., SINGH, B., and ANAND, B. K., 1971, Effect of fenfluramine on the electrical activity of the hypothalamic feeding centers, *Physiol. Behav.* **7**:433-438.

CHIPPENDALE, T. J., ZAWOLKOW, G. A., RUSSELL, R. W., and OVERSTREET, D. H., 1972, Tolerance to low acetylcholinesterase levels: modification of behavior without acute behavioral change, *Psychopharmacologia* **26**:127-139.

CLINESCHMIDT, B. V., 1973, 5,6-Dihydroxytryptamine: suppression of the anorexigenic action of fenfluramine, *Eur. J. Pharmacol.* **24**:405-409.

CLINESCHMIDT, B. V., and LOTTI, V. J., 1973, Histamine: intraventricular injection suppresses ingestive behavior of the cat, *Arch. Int. Pharmacodyn. Ther.* **206**:288-298.

CLINESCHMIDT, B. V., MCGUFFIN, J. C., and WERNER, A. B., 1974, Role of monoamines in anorexigenic actions of fenfluramine, amphetamine and parachloromethamphetamine, *Eur. J. Pharmacol.* **27**:313-323.

COLE, S. O., 1966, Increased suppression of food intake by amphetamine in rats with anterior hypothalamic lesions, *J. Comp. Physiol. Psychol.* **61**:302-305.

COLE, S. O., 1973a, Hypothalamic feeding mechanisms and amphetamine anorexia, *Psychol. Bull.* **79**:13-20.

COLE, S. O., 1973b, Changes in amphetamine anorexia following amygdala lesions in rats, *Proc. 81 Ann. Conv. Am. Psychol. Assoc.* **8**:1047-1048.

COLTON, N. H., SEGAL, H. I., STEINBERG, A., SHECHTER, F. R., and PASTOR, N., 1943, The management of obesity with emphasis on appetite control, *Am. J. Med. Sci.* **206**:75-86.

CONTE, M., LEHR, D., GOLDMAN, W., and KRUKOWSKI, M., 1968, Inhibition of food intake by beta-adrenergic stimulation, *Pharmacologist* **10**:180.

COONS, E. E., and QUARTERMAIN, D., 1970, Motivational depression associated with norepinephrine-induced eating from the hypothalamus: resemblance to the ventromedial hyperphagic syndrome, *Physiol. Behav.* **5**:687-692.

COOPER, B. R., and BREESE, G. R., 1974, Relationship of dopamine neural systems to the behavioral alterations produced by 6-hydroxydopamine administration into brain, *Adv. Biochem. Psychopharmacol.* **12**:353-368.

COSCINA, D. V., ROSENBLUM-BLINICK, D., GODSE, D. D., and STANCER, H. C., 1973, Consummatory behaviors of hypothalamic hyperphagic rats after central injection of 6-hydroxydopamine, *Pharm. Biochem. Behav.* **1**:629-642.

COSTA, E., and GARATTINI, S. (eds.), 1970, *Amphetamine and Related Compounds*, Raven Press, New York.

COSTA E., and MEEK, J. L., 1974, Regulation of biosynthesis of catecholamines and serotonin in the CNS, *Ann. Rev. Pharmacol.* **14**:491-511.

COURY, J. N., 1967, Neural correlates of food and water intake in the rat, *Science* **156**:1763-1765.

COX, R. H., JR, and MAICKEL, R. P., 1972, Comparison of anorexigenic and behavioral potency of phenylethylamines, *J. Pharmacol. Exp. Ther.* **181**:1-9.

DANNENBURG, W. M., and KARDIAN, B. C., 1969, The effect of fenfluramine and methamphetamine on free fatty acid release in epididymal fat cells of the rat, *Arch. Int. Pharmacodyn.* **177**:196-210.

Davis, J. R., and Keesey, R. E., 1971, Norepinephrine-induced eating—its hypothalamic locus and an alternate interpretation of action, *J. Comp. Physiol. Psychol.* **77**:394-402.

DiCara, L. U., 1970, Role of postoperative feeding experience in recovery from lateral hypothalamic damage, *J. Comp. Physiol. Psychol.* **72**:60-65.

Dominic, J. A., 1973, Suppression of brain serotonin synthesis and metabolism by benzodiazepine tranquilizers, in: *Serotonin and Behavior* (J. Barchas and E. Usdin, eds.), pp. 149-154, Academic Press, New York.

Duhault, J., and Verdavainne, C., 1967, Modification du taux de serotonnine cerebrale chez le rat par les trifluromethylphenyl-2-ethyl-2-ethylaminopropane (fenfluramine 768s), *Arch. Int. Pharmacodyn. Ther.* **170**:276-286.

Epstein, A. N., 1959, Suppression of eating and drinking by amphetamine and other drugs in normal and hyperphagic rats, *J. Comp. Physiol. Psychol.* **52**:37-45.

Epstein, A. N., 1960, Reciprocal changes in feeding behavior produced by intrahypothalamic chemical injections, *Am. J. Physiol.* **199**:969-974.

Epstein, A. N., 1971, The lateral hypothalamic syndrome: its implications for physiological psychology of hunger and thirst, in: *Progress in Physiological Psychology* (E. Stellar and J. M. Sprague, eds.), pp. 263-317, Academic Press, New York.

Epstein, A. N., and Teitelbaum, P., 1967, Specific loss of the hypoglycemic control of feeding in recovered lateral rats, *Am. J. Physiol.* **213**:1159-1167.

Epstein, A. N., Kissileff, H. R., and Stellar, E., 1973, *The Neuropsychology of Thirst: New Findings and Advances in Concepts*, Winston and Company, Washington, D.C.

Everett, G. M., 1974, Effect of 5-hydroxytryptophan on brain levels of dopamine, norepinephrine, and serotonin in mice, *Adv. Biochem. Psychopharmacol.* **10**:261-262.

Evetts, K. D., Fitzsimons, J. R., and Setler, P. E., 1972, Eating caused by 6-hydroxydopamine-induced release of noradrenaline in diencephalon of rat, *J. Physiol. (London)* **223**:35-47.

Fazekas, J. F., Ehrmantraut, W. R., Campbell, K. D., and Negron, M. C., 1959, Comparative effectiveness of phenylpropanolamine and dextro-amphetamine on weight reduction, *J. Am. Med. Assoc.* **170**:1018-1021.

Feldberg, W. S., 1958, Behavioral changes in the cat after injection of drugs into the cerebral ventricle, *Proc. Assoc. Res. Nerv. Ment. Dis.* **36**:401-423.

Ferguson, J., Henriksen, S., Cohen, H. Hoyt, G., Mitchell, G., McGarr, K., Rubenson, D., Ryan, L., and Dement, W., 1969, The effect of chronic administration of para-chlorophenylalanine on the behavior of cats, *Psychophysiology* **6**:211.

Fernstrom, J. D., and Wurtman, R. J., 1973, Control of brain 5-HT content by dietary carbohydrates, in: *Serotonin and Behavior* (J. Barchus and E. Usdin, eds.), pp. 121-128, Academic Press, New York.

Fibiger, H. C., and Campbell, B. A., 1971, The effect of para-chlorophenylalanine on spontaneous locomotor activity in the rat, *Neuropharmacology* **10**:25-32.

Fibiger, H. C., Phillips, A. G., and Clouston, R. A., 1973a, Regulatory deficits after unilateral electrolytic or 6-hydroxydopamine lesions of substantia-nigra, *Am. J. Physiol.* **225**:1282-1287.

Fibiger, H. C., Zis, A. P., and McGeer, E. G., 1973b, Feeding and drinking deficits after 6-hydroxydopamine administration in the rat: similarities to the lateral hypothalamic syndrome, *Brain Res.* **55**:135-148.

Finger, S., Walbran, B., and Stein, D. G., 1973, Brain damage and behavioral recovery: serial lesion phenomena, *Brain Res.* **63**:1-18.

Fisher, A. E., 1969, The role of limbic structures in the central regulation of feeding and drinking behavior. *Ann. N.Y. Acad. Sci.* **157**(2):894-901.

Forbes, J. M., and Baile, C. A., 1973, Increased feeding following injections of carbachol into hypothalamus of sheep, *J. Endocrinol.* **59**:39.

Foxwell, M. H., Funderburk, W. H., and Ward, J. W., 1969, Studies on the site of action of a new anoretic agent, fenfluramine, *J. Pharmacol. Exp. Ther.* **165**:60-70.

FREY, H. H., and SCHULZ, R., 1973, On the central mediation of anorexigenic drug effects, *Biochem. Pharmacol.* **22**:3041–3049.

FUNDERBURK, W. H., HAZELWOOD, J. C., RUCKART, R. T., and WARD, J. W., 1971, Is 5-hydroxytryptamine involved in the mechanism of action of fenfluramine? *J. Pharm. Pharmacol.* **23**:468–470.

FUXE, K., and UNDERSTEDT, U., 1970, Histochemical, biochemical and functional studies on central monoamine neurons after acute and chronic amphetamine administration, in: *Amphetamines and Related Compounds* (E. Costa and S. Garattini, eds.), pp. 257–288, Raven Press, New York.

GARAY, K. F., and LEIBOWITZ, S. F., 1974, Antidiuresis produced by adrenergic receptor stimulation of the rat supraoptic nucleus, *Fed. Proc.* **33**:563.

GARBARG, M., BARBIN, G., FEGER, J., and SCHWARTZ, J., 1974, Histaminergic pathway in rat brain evidenced by lesions of the medial forebrain bundle, *Science* **186**:833–835.

GHEZZI, D., SAMANIN, R., BERNASCONI, S., TOGNONI, G., GERNA, M., and GARATTINI, S., 1973, Effect of thymoleptics on fenfluramine-induced depletion of brain serotonin in rats, *Eur. J. Pharmacol.* **24**:205–210.

GLICK, S., D., and GREENSTEIN, D., 1973, Pharmacological inhibition of eating, drinking and prandial drinking, *Behav. Biol.*, **8**:55–61.

GLICK, S. D., GREENSTEIN, S., and ZIMMERBERG, B., 1972, Facilitation of recovery by α-methyl-*p*-tyrosine after lateral hypothalamic damage, *Science* **177**:534–535.

GLICK, S. D., GREENSTEIN, S., and WATERS, D. H., 1973*a*, Ventromedial hypothalamic lesions and brain catecholamines, *Pharm. Biochem. Behav.* **1**:591–592.

GLICK, S. D., WATERS, D. H., and MILLOY, S., 1973*b*, Depletion of hypothalamic norepinephrine by food deprivation and interaction with *d*-amphetamine, *Res. Commun. Chem. Phathol. Pharmacol.* **6**:775–778.

GLOW, P. H., RICHARDSON, A., and ROSE, S., 1966, Effects of acute and chronic inhibition of cholinesterase upon body weight, food intake and water intake in the rat, *J. Comp. Physiol. Psychol.* **61**:295–299.

GOLD, R. M., 1973, Hypothalamic obesity: the myth of the ventromedial nucleus, *Science* **182**:488–490.

GOLDMAN, H. W., LEHR, D., and FRIEDMAN, E., 1971, Antagonistic effects of alpha and beta-adrenergically coded hypothalamic neurons on consummatory behaviour in the rat, *Nature (London)* **231**:453–455.

GOODMAN, L. S., and GILMAN, A. (eds.), 1965, *The Pharmacological Basis of Therapeutics*, 3rd Ed., pp. 478–486, Macmillan, New York.

GOTESTAM, K. G., and GUNNE, L., 1971, Subjective effects of two anorexigenic agents fenfluramine and An 448 in amphetamine-dependent subjects, *Br. J. Addict.* **67**:39–44.

GROSSMAN, S. P., 1960, Eating or drinking elicited by direct adrenergic or cholinergic stimulation of the hypothalamus, *Science* **132**:301–302.

GROSSMAN, S. P., 1962*a*, Direct adrenergic and cholinergic stimulation of hypothalamic mechanisms, *Am. J. Physiol.* **202**:872–882.

GROSSMAN, S. P., 1962*b*, Effects of adrenergic and cholinergic blocking agents on hypothalamic mechanisms, *Am. J. Physiol.* **202**:1230–1236.

GROSSMAN, S. P., 1964, Behavioral effects of chemical stimulation of the ventral amygdala, *J. Comp. Physiol. Psychol.*, **57**:29–36.

GROSSMAN, S. P., 1969, A neuropharmacological analysis of hypothalamic and extrahypothalamic mechanisms concerned with the regulation of food and water intake, *Ann. N.Y. Acad. Sci.* **157**(2):902–912.

GROSSMAN, S. P., and SCLAFANI, A., 1971, Sympathomimetic amines in: *Pharmacological and Biophysical Agents and Behavior* (E. Furchtgott, ed.), pp. 269–345, Academic Press, New York.

GYLYS, J. H., 1966, Chorphentermine and food-controlled behavior in the rat, *Arch. Int. Pharmacodyn. Ther.* **161**:102–115.

GYLYS, J. A., HART, J. J. D., and WARREN, M. R., 1962, Chlorphentermine, a new anorectic agent, *J. Pharmacol. Exp. Ther.* **137:**365–373.

HADDEN, D. R., and LUCEY, L., 1961, Diethypropion in the treatment of obesity. A crossover trial of long-acting preparation. *Ulster Med. J.* **30:**109–113.

HANO, J., BUGAJSKI, J., and DANEK, L., 1973, The effect of drugs interfering with biogenic amine metabolism on basal gastric secretion in the rat, *Pol. J. Pharmacol. Pharm.* **25:**537–549.

HANSEN, M. G., and WHISHAW, I. Q., 1973, The effects of 6-hydroxydopamine, dopamine and *dl*-norepinephrine on food intake and water consumption, self-stimulation, temperature and electroencephalographic activity in the rat, *Psychopharmacologia* **29:**33–44.

HARRELL, L. E., RAUBESON, R., and BALAGURA, S., 1974, Acceleration of functional recovery following lateral hypothalamic damage by means of electrical stimulation in lesioned areas, *Physiol. Behav.* **12:**897–899.

HARVEY, J. A., HELLER, A., and MOORE, R. Y., 1963, The effect of unilateral and bilateral medial forebrain bundle lesions on brain serotonin, *J. Pharmacol. Exp. Ther.* **140:**103–110.

HEFFNER, T. G., ZIGMOND, M. J., and STRICKER, E. M., 1975, Brain dopamine involvement in amphetamine-induced anorexia, *Fred. Proc.* **34:**348.

HEIL, G. C., and ROSS, S. T., 1973, Agents affecting appetite, *Annu. Rep. Med. Chem.* **8:**42–51.

HENKIN, R. I., KEISER, H. R., and BRONZERT, D., 1972, Histidine-dependent zinc loss, hypogeusia, anorexia and hyposmia, *J. Clin. Invest.* **51:**44A.

HERBERG, L. J., and FRANKLIN, K. B., 1972, Adrenergic feeding: its blockage or reversal by posterior VMH lesions and a new hypothesis, *Physiol. Behav.* **8:**1029–1034.

HIRSH, L. S., 1939, Controlling appetite in obesity, *J. Med.* **20:**84–85.

HO, A. K. S., and GERSHON, S., 1972, Drug-induced alterations in the activity of rat brain cholinergic enzymes. I. *In vitro* and *in vivo* effect of amphetamine, *Eur. J. Pharmacol.* **18:**195–200.

HOEBEL, B. G., 1971, Feeding: neural control of intake, *Annu. Rev. Physiol.* **33:**533–568.

HOEBEL, B. G., 1975, Brain reward and aversion systems in the control of feeding and sexual behavior, in: *Nebraska Symposium on Motivation, 1974* (J. K. Cole and T. B. Sonderegger, eds.), University of Nebraska Press, Lincoln.

HOEBEL, B. G., 1976a, Satiety: hypothalamic stimulation, anorectic drugs, neurochemical substrates, in: *Hunger: Basic Mechanisms and Clinical Implications* (D. Novin, W. Wyrwicka, and G. Bray, eds.), pp. 33–50, Raven Press, New York.

HOEBEL, B. G., 1976b, Brain stimulation reward and aversion in relation to behavior, in: *Brain Stimulation Reward* (A. Wauquier and E. T. Rolls, eds.), pp. 335–372, North-Holland Publishing, Netherlands.

HOEBEL, B. G., 1977, Pharmacologic control of feeding, *Ann. Rev. Pharmacol. Toxicol.* **17:**605–621.

HOEBEL, B. G., HERNANDEZ, L., and THOMPSON, R. D., 1975a, Phenylpropanolamine inhibits feeding, but not drinking, induced by hypothalamic stimulation, *J. Comp. Physiol. Psychol.* **89:**1046–1052.

HOEBEL, B. G., COOPER, J., KAMIN, M. C., and WILLARD, D., 1975b, Appetite suppression by phenylpropanolamine in humans, *Obesity Bariatric Med.* **4:**192–197.

HOEBEL, B. G., KRAUSS, I. K., COOPER, J., and WILLARD, D., 1975c, Body weight decreased in humans by phenylpropanolamine taken before meals, *Obesity Bariatric Med.* **4:**200–206.

HOKFELT, T., FUXE, K., GOLDSTEIN, M., and JOHANSSON, O., 1974, Immunohistochemical evidence for the existence of adrenaline neurons in the rat brain, *Brain Res.* **66:**235–251.

HOLTZMAN, S. G., and JEWETT, R. E., 1971, The role of brain norepinephrine in the anorexic effects of dextroamphetamine and monoamine oxidase inhibitors in the rat, *Psychopharmacologia* **22:**151–161.

HOUSER, V. P., 1970, The effects of adrenergic and cholinergic agents upon eating and drinking in deprived rats, *Psychonomic Sci.* **20:**153–155.

HUTCHINSON, R. R., and RENFREW, J. W., 1967, Modification of eating and drinking: interactions between chemical agent, deprivation state, and site of stimulation, *J. Comp. Physiol. Psychol.* **63**:408–416.

HYNES, M. D., ANDERSON, C., and LAL, H., 1973, Aphagia and adipsia after nigrostriatal bundle (NSB) lesion: facilitation of recovery by blockade of central dopaminergic receptors, *Pharmacologist* **15**:218.

INNES, I. R., and NICKERSON, M., 1970, Drugs acting on postganglionic adrenergic nerve endings and structures innervated by them (sympathomimetic drugs), in: *The Pharmacological Basis of Therapeutics* (L. S. Goodman and A. Gilman, eds.), pp. 478–523, Macmillan, New York.

JACKSON, H. M., and ROBINSON, D. W., 1971, Evidence for hypothalamic and adrenergic receptors involved in the control of food intake of the pig, *Br. Vet. J.* **127**:51–53.

JACOBS, B. L., 1974, Evidence for the functional interaction of two central neurotransmitters, *Psychopharmacologia* **39**:81–86.

JACOBS, B. L., and FAREL, P. B., 1971, Motivated behaviors produced by increased arousal in the presence of goal objects, *Physiol. Behav.* **6**:473–476.

JESPERSEN, S., and SCHEEL-KRUGER, J., 1973, Evidence for a difference in mechanism of action between fenfluramine and amphetamine induced anorexia, *J. Pharm. Pharmacol.* **25**:49–54.

JONSSON, C. O., SJOBERG, L., and VALLBO, S., 1964, Studies in the psychological effects of a new drug (diethylpropion), *Rep. Psychol. Lab. Univ. Stockholm*, No. 174.

JORDAN, H. A., WIELAND, W. F., ZEBLEY, S. P., STELLAR, E., and STUNKARD, A. J., 1966, Direct measurement of food intake in man: a method for the objective study of eating behavior, *Psychosom. Med.* **28**:836–842.

JOYCE, D., and MROSOVSKY, N., 1964, Eating, drinking, and activity in rats following 5-hydroxytryptophan (5-HTP) administration, *Psychopharmacology* **5**:417–423.

KAPATOS, G., and GOLD, R. M., 1973, Evidence for ascending noradrenergic mediation of hypothalamic hyperphagia, *Pharmacol. Biochem. Behav.* **1**:81–87.

KATTUS, A. A., ROSS, G., and HALL, V. E., 1970, *Cardiovascular Beta Adrenergic Responses*, University of California Press, Berkeley.

KELMAN, H., 1965, Addiction to innocuous drugs, *Med. Times* **93**:155–158.

KETY, S. S., JOVOY, F., THIERRY, A. M., JULOU, L., and GLOWINSKI, J., 1967, A sustained effect of electroconvulsive shock on the turnover of norepinephrine in the central nervous system of the rat, *Proc. Nat. Acad. Sci. U.S.A.* **58**:1249–1254.

KHANNA, S., NAYAR, U., and ANAND, B. K., 1972, Effect of fenfluramine on the single neuron activities of the hypothalamic feeding centers, *Physiol. Behav.* **8**:453–456.

KOE, B. K., and WEISSMAN, A., 1966, PCPA: a specific depleter of brain serotonin, *J. Pharmacol. Exp. Ther.* **154**:499–516.

KORNBLITH, C. L., and HOEBEL, B. G., 1976, A dose-response study of anorectic drug effects on food intake, self-stimulation and stimulation-escape, *Pharmacol. Biochem. Behav.* **5**:215–218.

KREBS, H., BINDRA, D., and CAMPBELL, J. F., 1969, Effect of amphetamine on neuronal activity in the hypothalamus, *Physiol. Behav.* **4**:685–691.

KRENGEL, B., 1970, Drugs for obesity, *S. Afr. Med. J.* **44**:682.

KRUK, Z. L., 1973, Dopamine and 5-hydroxytryptamine inhibit feeding in rats, *Nature (London) New Biol.* **246**:52–53.

KUHN, F. J., 1973, Hyperphagia in cats induced by injection of sodium pentobarbital into cerebral ventricles as a method for testing anorectics, *Arzneim. Forsch.* **23**:100–102.

KURIYAMA, K., KIMURA, H., and TACHIBANA, M., 1973, GABA-nergic neurons in lateral hypothalamic area, *J. Cell. Biol.* **59**:180A.

LAWLOR, R. B., TRIVEDI, M. C., and YELNOSKY, J., 1969, A determination of the anorexigenic potential of *dl*-amphetamine, *d*-amphetamine, *l*-amphetamine and phentermine, *Arch. Int. Pharmacodyn. Ther.* **179**:401–407.

Lehr, D., 1969, Discussion of Grossman's and Fisher's papers, *Ann. N.Y. Acad. Sci.* **157**(2):912–916.
Lehr, D., 1974, Neurotransmitter involved in control of water intake, *V International Conference on Physiology of Food and Fluid Intake,* Israel.
Leibowitz, S. F., 1970a, A hypothalamic beta-adrenergic "satiety" system antagonizes an alpha-adrenergic "hunger" system in the rat, *Nature* **226**:963–964.
Leibowitz, S. F., 1970b, Reciprocal hunger-regulating circuits involving alpha- and beta-adrenergic receptors located, respectively, in the ventromedial and lateral hypothalamus, *Proc. Nat. Acad. Sci. U.S.A.* **67**:1063–1070.
Leibowitz, S. F., 1972, Central adrenergic receptors and the regulation of hunger and thirst, in: *Neurotransmitters* (I. J. Koplin, ed.), *Res. Publ. Assoc. Res. Nerv. Ment. Dis.* **50**:327–358.
Leibowitz, S. F., 1973, Brain norepinephrine and ingestive behavior, in: *Frontiers in Catecholamine Research,* pp. 711–713, Pergamon Press, London.
Leibowitz, S. F., 1975a, Pattern of drinking and feeding produced by hypothalamic norepinephrine injection in the satiated rat, *Physiol. Behav.* **14**:731–742.
Leibowitz, S. F., 1975b, Ingestion in the satiated rat: role of alpha and beta receptors in mediating effects of hypothalamic adrenergic stimulation, *Physiol. Behav.* **14**:743–754.
Leibowitz, S. F., 1975c, Amphetamine: possible site and mode of action for producing anorexia in the rat, *Brain Res.* **84**:160–167.
Leibowitz, S. F., 1975d, Catecholaminergic mechanisms of the lateral hypothalamus: their role in the mediation of amphetamine anorexia, *Brain Res.* **98**:529–545.
Leibowitz, S. F., and Miller, N. E., 1969, Unexpected adrenergic effect of chlorpromazine: eating elicited by injection into rat hypothalamus, *Science* **165**:609–611.
Lewander, T., 1974, Effect of chronic treatment with central stimulants on brain monoamines and some behavioral and physiological functions in rats, guinea pigs and rabbits, *Adv. Biochem. Psychopharmacol.* **12**:221–240.
Lonowski, D. J., Levitt, R. A., and Larson, S. D., 1973, Effects of cholinergic brain injections on mouse-killing or carrying by rats, *Physiol. Psychol.* **1**:341–345.
Lorden, J., Oltmans, G. A., and Margules, D., 1976, Central noradrenergic neurons: differential effects on body weight of electrolytic and 6-hydroxydopamine lesions in rats, *J. Comp. Physiol. Psychol.* **90**:127–143.
Lovett, D., and Singer, G., 1971, Ventricular modification of drinking and eating behavior, *Physiol. Behav.* **6**:23–26.
MacLean, P. D., 1957, Chemical and electrical stimulation of hippocampus in unrestrained animals, *Arch. Neurol. Psychiatry* **78**:113–127.
Magour, S., Coper, H., and Fahndrich, C., 1974, The effects of chronic treatment with d-amphetamine on food intake, body weight, locomotor activity, and subcellular distribution of the drug in rat brain, *Psychopharmacologia* **34**:45–54.
Mantegazza, P., Muller, E. E., Naimzada, M. K., and Riva, M., 1970, Studies on the lack of correlation between hyperthermia and hyperactivity and anorexia induced by amphetamine, in: *Amphetamines and Related Compounds* (E. Costa and S. Garattini, eds.), pp. 559–575, Raven Press, New York.
Margules, D. L., 1969, Noradrenergic synapses for the suppression of feeding behavior, *Life Sci.* **8**:693–704.
Margules, D. L., 1970a, Alpha-adrenergic receptors in hypothalamus for the suppression of feeding behavior by satiety, *J. Comp. Physiol. Psychol.* **73**:1–12.
Margules, D. L., 1970b, Beta-adrenergic receptors in the hypothalamus for learned and unlearned taste aversions, *J. Comp. Physiol. Psychol.* **73**:13–21.
Margules, D. L., and Dragovich, J., 1973, Studies on phentolamine-induced overeating and finickiness, *J. Comp. Physiol. Psychol.* **84**:644–651.
Margules, D. L., and Stein, L., 1967, Neuroleptics vs. tranquilizers: evidence from animals of mode and site of action, in: *Neuropsychopharmacology* (H. Brill, ed.), Excerpta Medica Foundation, Amsterdam.

MARGULES, D. L., LEWIS, M. J., DRAGOVICH, J. A., and MARGULES, A. S., 1972, Hypothalamic norepinephrine: circadian rhythms and the control of feeding behavior, *Science* **178**:640–642.

MARLEY, E., and STEPHENSON, J. D., 1972, Central actions of catecholamines, in: *Catecholamines, Handbook of Experimental Pharmacology* (H. Blaschko and E. Muscholl, eds.), pp. 463–537, Springer-Verlag, Berlin.

MARSHALL, J. F., 1974, Exaggeration of contralateral sensorimotor functions after unilateral medial hypothalamic damage in rats, *V. International Conference on Physiology of Food and Fluid Intake,* Israel.

MARSHALL, J. F., and TEITELBAUM, P., 1973, A comparison of the eating in response to hypothermic and glucoprivic challenges after nigral 6-hydroxydopamine and lateral hypothalamic electrolytic lesions in rats, *Brain Res.* **55**:229–233.

MARSHALL, J. F., TURNER, B. H., and TEITELBAUM, P., 1971, Sensory neglect produced by lateral hypothalamic damage, *Science* **174**:523–525.

MAWSON, A. R., 1974, Anorexia nervosa and the regulation of intake: a review, *Psychol. Med.* **4**:289–308.

MCFARLAIN, R. A., and BLOOM, J. M., 1972, The effects of para-chlorophenylalanine on brain serotonin, food intake, and u-maze behavior, *Psychopharmacologia* **27**:85–92.

MENON, M. K., SUBRAMANIAN, K., MENON, N. K., and SHARMA, S. N., 1970, Influence of desmethylimipramine on the appetite-lowering effects of d-amphetamine and other anorectics, *Eur. J. Pharmacol.* **12**:156–160.

MERTZ, D. P., and STELZER, M., 1969, Zum Mechanismus der appetit- und gewichtssteigernden Wirkung von Cyproheptadin, *Klin. Wochenschr.* **47**:1194.

MILLER, N. E., 1965, Chemical coding of behavior in the brain, *Science* **148**:328–338.

MILLER, N. E., GOTTESMAN, K. S., and EMERY, N., 1964, Dose response to carbachol and norepinephrine in rat hypothalamus, *Am. J. Physiol.* **206**:1384–1388.

MILNER, J. S., NANCE, D. M., and SHEER, D. E., 1971, Effects of hypothalamic and amygdaloid chemical stimulation on appetitive behavior in the cat, *Psychonom. Sci.* **23**:25–26.

MODELL, W., 1972, *Drugs of Choice,* Mosby Co., St. Louis.

MOGENSON, G. J., 1973, Changing views of the role of hypothalamus in the control of ingestive behaviors, in: *Recent Studies of Hypothalamic Function* (K. Lederis and K. E. Cooper, eds.), pp. 268–293, Karger, Basel, 1974.

MONTGOMERY, R. B., SINGER, G., PURCELL, A. T., NARBETH, J., and BOLT, A. G., 1971, The effects of intrahypothalamic injections of desmethylimipramine on food and water intake of the rat, *Psychopharmacologia* **19**:81–86.

MORRIS, L. A., and O'NEAL, E. C., 1974, Drug-name familiarity and placebo effect, *J. Clin. Psychol.* **30**:280–282.

MOURET, J., BOBILLIER, P., and JOUVET, M., 1968, Insomnia following PCPA in the rat, *Eur. J. Pharmacol.* **5**:17–22.

MYERS, R. D., 1969, Chemical mechanisms in the hypothalamus mediating eating and drinking in the monkey, *Ann. N.Y. Acad. Sci.* **157**(2):918–932.

MYERS, R. D., 1974, Neurochemical mechanism of temperature regulation and food ingestion, *Adv. Behav. Biol.* **10**:99–114.

MYERS, R. D., and MARTIN, G. E., 1973, 6-Hydroxydopamine lesions of the hypothalamus: interaction of aphagia, food palatability, set-point for weight regulation, and recovery of feeding, *Pharmacol. Biochem. Behav.* **1**:329–345.

MYERS, R. D., and SHARPE, L. E., 1968, Chemical activation of ingestive and other hypothalamic regulatory mechanisms, *Physiol. Behav.* **3**:987–995.

MYERS, R. D., TYTELL, M., KAWA, A., and RUDY, T., 1971, Microinjection of H-3-acetylcholine, C-14-serotonin and H-3-norepinephrine into hypothalamus of rat: diffusion into tissue and ventricles, *Physiol. Behav.* **7**:743–751.

MYERS, R. D., BENDER, S. A., KRSTIC, M. K., and BROPHY, P. D., 1972, Feeding produced in

the satiated rat by elevating the concentration of calcium in the brain, *Science* **176:**1124–1125.
NANCE, D. M., MILNER, J. S., and SHEER, D. E., 1971, Hypothalamic anticholinergic inhibition of eating and drinking in cat, *Psychonom. Sci.* **23:**26–28.
NEILL, D. B., and GROSSMAN, S. P., 1971, Interaction of the effects of reserpine and amphetamine on food and water intake, *J. Comp. Physiol. Psychol.* **76:**327–336.
NEILL, C. B., and GROSSMAN, S. P., 1973, Effects of intrastriatal injections of scopolamine on appetitive behavior, *Pharmacol. Biochem. Behav.* **1:**313–318.
NISBETT, R. E., 1972, Eating behavior and obesity in men and animals, *Adv. Psychiatry Med.* **7:**173.
NOBLE, R. E., 1969, Effect of cyproheptadine on appetite and weight gain in adults, *J. Am. Med. Assoc.* **209:**2054–2056.
NOBLE, R. E., 1974, Fenfluramine: an anorexigenic without stimulant properties, *Obesity Bariatric Med.* **3:**200–209.
NOVIN, D., WYRWICKA, W., and BRAY, G., 1975, *Hunger: Basic Mechanisms and Clinical Implications,* Raven Press, New York.
OKA, T., NOZAKI, M., and HOSOYA, E., 1972, The effect of cholinergic antagonists on increases of spontaneous locomotor activity and body weight induced by the administration of morphine to tolerant rats, *Psychopharmacologia* **23:**231–237.
OLTMANS, G. A., and HARVEY, J. A., 1972, LH syndrome and brain catecholamine levels after lesions of the nigrostriatal bundle, *Physiol. Behav.* **8:**69–78.
OOMURA, Y., ONO, T., SUGIMORI, M., and NAKAMURA, T., 1973, Effects of cyproheptadine on the feeding and satiety centers in the rat, *Pharmacol. Biochem. Behav.* **1:**449–459.
OPITZ, K., 1967, Anorexigene Phenylalkylamine und Serotoninstoffwechsel, *Naunyn-Schmiedebergs Arch. Pharmacol.* **259:**56.
OPITZ, K., WEISCHER, M. L., and KLOSE, L., 1971, Influence of cyproheptadine on food intake in animal experiments, *Arzneim. Forsch.* **21:**957–961.
OTSUKA, 1972, *Folia Pharmacol. Jpn.* **68:**514–520.
OVERSTREET, D. H., HADICK, D. G., and RUSSELL, R. W., 1972, Effects of amphetamine and pilocarpine on eating behavior in rats with chronically low acetylcholinesterase levels, *Behav. Biol.* **7:**217–226.
OVERSTREET, D. H., KOZAR, M. D., and LYNCH, G. S., 1973, Reduced hypothalamic effects of cholinomimetic agents following chronic anticholinesterase treatment, *Neuropharmacology,* **12:**1017–1032.
PANKSEPP, J., and BOOTH, D. A., 1973, Tolerance in depression of intake when amphetamine is added to rat's food, *Psychopharmacologia* **29:**45–54.
PANKSEPP, J., and NANCE, D. M., 1974, Effects of para-chlorophenylalanine on food intake in rats, *Physiol. Psychol.* **2:**360–364.
PAUL, L., and POSNER, I., 1973, Predation and feeding: comparison of feeding behavior of killer and nonkiller rats, *J. Comp. Physiol. Psychol.* **84:**258–264.
PAWAN, G. L. S., 1969, Effect of fenfluramine on blood-lipids in man, *Lancet* **1:**499–500.
PENFOLD, J. L., 1971, Effect of cyproheptadine and a multivitamin preparation on appetite stimulation, weight gain and linear growth. A clinical trial of 40 children, *Med. J. Aust.* **1:**307–310.
PEPEU, G., GAVAU, L., and MULAS, M. L., 1974, Does 5-hydroxytryptamine influence cholinergic mechanisms in the central nervous system? *Adv. Biochem. Psychopharmacol.* **10:**247–252.
PEREZ-CRUET, J., TAGLIAMONTE, A., TAGLIAMONTE, P., and GESSA, G. L., 1972, Changes in brain serotonin metabolism associated with fasting and satiation in rats, *Life Sci.* **11**(Part 2):31–39.
POSCHEL, B. P., 1971, A simple and specific screen for benzodiazepine-like drugs, *Psychopharmacologia* **19:**193–198.
POWLEY, T. L., and KEESEY, R. E., 1970, Relationship of body weight to the lateral hypothalamic feeding syndrome, *J. Comp. Physiol. Psychol.* **70:**25–36.

PRADHAN, S. N., and ROTH, T., 1968, Comparative behavioral effects of several anticholinergic agents in rats, *Psychopharmacologia* **12:**358–366.
RANDALL, L. O., SCHALLEK, W., HEISE, G. A., KEITH, E. F., and BAGDON, R. E., 1960, The psychosedative properties of methaminodiazepoxide, *J. Pharmacol. Ther.* **129:**163–171.
RANDRUP, A., and MUNKVAD, I., 1966, Role of catecholamines in the amphetamine response, *Nature* **211:**540.
REINBERG, A., and HALBERG, F., 1971, Circadian chronopharmacology, *Annu. Rev. Pharmacol.* **11:**455–492.
REYNOLDS, R. W., 1959, The effect of amphetamine on food intake in normal and hypothalamic hyperphagic rats, *J. Comp. Physiol. Psychol.* **52:**682–684.
REYNOLDS, R. W., and CARLISLE, H. J., 1961, The effect of chlorpromazine on food intake in the albino rat, *J. Comp. Physiol. Psychol.* **54:**354–356.
RICHARDSON, J. S., and JACOBOWITZ, D. M., 1973, Depletion of brain norepinephrine by intraventricular injection of 6-hydroxydopa: a biochemical histochemical and behavioral study in rats, *Brain Res.* **58:**117–133.
RINDI, G., SCIORELLI, G., POLONI, M., and ACANFORA, F., 1972, Induction of ingestive responses by cAMP applied into rat hypothalamus, *Experientia* **28:**1046–1049.
RITTER, R. C., and EPSTEIN, A. N., 1974, Brain norepinephrine may control meal size, *V International Conference on Physiology of Food and Fluid Intake,* Israel.
ROSENBERG, B. A., 1961, A double-blind study of diethylpropion in obesity, *Am. J. Med. Sci.* **242:**201–206.
ROTH, S. R., SCHWARTZ, M., and TEITELBAUM, P., 1973, Failure of recovered lateral hypothalamic rats to learn specific food aversions, *J. Comp. Physiol. Psychol.* **83:**184–197.
ROUTTENBERG, A., 1972, Intracranial chemical injection and behavior: a critical review, *Behav. Biol.* **7:**601–647.
RUEDY, J., 1967, Drug therapy in obesity, *Mod. Treatment* **4:**1138–1145.
RUSSEK, M., 1971, Hepatic receptors and the neurophysiological mechanisms of feeding behavior, in: *Neuroscience Research,* Vol. 4 (S. Ehrenpreis, ed.), Academic Press, New York.
RUSSEK, M., and GRINSTEIN, S., 1974, Coding of metabolic information by hepatic glucoreceptors, *Adv. Behav. Biol.* **10:**81–97.
RUSSEK, M., RODRIGUEZ-ZENDEJAS, A. M., and TEITELBAUM, P., 1973, The action of adrenergic anorexigenic substances on rats recovered from lateral hypothalamic lesions, *Physiol. Behav.* **10:**329–333.
RUSSELL, R. W., VASQUEZ, B. J., OVERSTREET, D. H., and DALGLISH, F. W., 1971, Consummatory behavior during tolerance to and withdrawal from chronic depression of cholinesterase activity, *Physiol. Behav.* **7:**523–528.
SAMININ, R., GHEZZI, D., VALZELLI, L., and GARATTINI, S., 1972, The effects of selective lesioning of brain serotonin or catecholamine containing neurones on the anorectic activity of fenfluramine and amphetamine, *Eur. J. Pharmacol.* **19:**318–322.
SCHACHTER, S., and RODIN, J., 1974, *Obese Humans and Rats,* Wiley, New York.
SCHACHTER, S., and SINGER, J. E., 1962, Cognitive, social and physiological determinants of emotional state, *Psychol. Rev.* **69:**379–399.
SCHWARTZ, M., and TEITELBAUM, P., 1974, Dissociation between learning and remembering in rats with lesions in the lateral hypothalamus, *J. Comp. Physiol. Psychol.* **87:**384–398.
SCIORELLI, G., POLONI, M., and RINDI, G., 1972, Evidence of cholinergic mediation of ingestive responses elicited by dibutyryl-adenosine-3′,5′-monophosphate in rat hypothalamus, *Brain Res.* **48:**427–431.
SEDGWICK, J. P., 1971, Obesity—The health hazard of our time, *S. Afr. Med. J.* **45:**362–370.
SETLER, P. E., and SMITH, G. P., 1974, Increased food intake elicited by adrenergic stimulation of the diencephalon in rhesus monkeys, *Brain Res.* **65:**459–473.
SHARPE, L. G., and MYERS, R. D., 1969, Feeding and drinking following stimulation of the diencephalon of the monkey with amines and other substances, *Exp. Brain Res.* **8:**295–310.

SHEARD, M. H., 1969, The effect of PCPA on behavior in rats: relation to brain serotonin and 5-hydroxyindoleacetic acid, **15**:524-528.
SILBERT, M. V., 1971, The weight gain effects of Periactin in anorexic patients, *South Afr. Med. J.* **45**:374-377.
SILVERMAN, H. I., 1963, Phenylpropanolamine—Misused? or simply abused? *Am. J. Pharm.* **135**:45-54.
SILVERSTONE, J. T., 1972, The anorectic effect of a long-acting preparation of phentermine (duromine), *Psychopharmacology* **25**:315-320.
SILVERSTONE, J. T., and FINCHAM, J., 1974, Clinical pharmacology of a new appetite-suppressant compound R800 (fenisorex), *V International Conference on Physiology of Food and Fluid Intake,* Israel.
SILVERSTONE, J. T., and STUNKARD, A. J., 1968, The anorectic effect of dexamphetamine sulphate, *Br. J. Pharmacol.* **33**:513-522.
SILVERSTONE, J. T., TURNER, P., and HUMPHERSON, P. L., 1968, Direct measurement of the anorectic activity of diethylpropion (Tennate Dospan), *J. Clin. Pharmacol. J. New Drugs* **8**:172-179.
SILVERSTONE, J. T., COOPER, R. M., and BEGG, R. R., 1970, A comparative trial of fenfluramine and diethylpropion in obesity, *Br. J. Clin. Pract.* **24**:423-425.
SIMPSON, J. B., and ROUTTENBERG, A., 1973, Subfornical organ: site of drinking elicitation by angiotension II, *Science* **181**:1172-1175.
SINGER, G., and KELLY, J., 1972, Cholinergic and adrenergic interaction in the hypothalamic control of drinking and eating behavior, *Physiol. Behav.* **8**:885-890.
SINGER, G., and MONTGOMERY, R. B., 1973, Specificity of chemical stimulation in the rat brain and other related issues in the interpretation of chemical stimulation data, *Pharm. Biochem. Behav.* **1**:211-221.
SINGER, G., SANGHVI, I., and GERSHON, S., 1971, Exploration of certain behavioral patterns induced by psychoactive agents in the rat, *Commun. Behav. Biol.* **6**:307-314.
SLANGEN, J. L., and MILLER, N. E., 1969, Pharmacological tests for the function of hypothalamic norepinephrine in eating behavior, *Physiol. Behav.* **4**:543-552.
SMITH, D. E., 1970, Killing in the rat: the chemical basis in the lateral hypothalamus, Ph.D. Thesis, Princeton University.
SMITH, D. E., and HOEBEL, B. G., 1973, Wheel-running in rats: possible involvement of a cholinoceptive mechanism, *Int. Res. Commun. Syst. Med. Sci. Libr. Compend.* (73-10), 7-10-13.
SMITH, D. E., KING, M. B., and HOEBEL, B. G., 1970, Lateral hypothalamic control of killing: evidence for a cholinoceptive mechanism, *Science* **167**:900-901.
SMITH, G. P., STROHMAYER, A. J., and REIS, D. J., 1972, Effect of lateral hypothalamic injection of 6-hydroxydopamine on food and water intake in rats, *Nature (London) New Biol.* **235**:27-29.
SMITH, M. H., 1966, Effects of intravenous injections on eating, *J. Comp. Physiol. Psychol.* **61**:11-14.
Society of Actuaries, 1960, Transactions No. 1.
SOLLITTO, S., and VEATCH, R. M., 1974, *Bibliography of Society, Ethics, and the Life Sciences,* Hastings Center Publications, Hastings-on-Hudson, New York.
SOMMER, S. R., NOVIN, D., and LEVINE, M., 1967, Food and water intake after intrahypothalamic injections of carbachol in the rabbit, *Science* **156**:983-984.
SOPER, W. Y., and WISE, R. A., 1971, Hypothalamically induced eating: eating from "non-eaters" with diazepam. *T.-I.-T. J., Life Sci.* **1**:79-84.
SORENSEN, C. A., ELLISON, G. D., and MASUOKA, D., 1972, Changes in fluid intake suggesting depressed appetite in rats with central catecholaminergic lesions, *Nature (London) New Biol.* **237**:279-281.
SOULAIRAC, A., 1969, The adrenergic and cholinergic control of food and water intake, *Ann. N.Y. Acad. Sci.* **157**(2):934-961.

SOUTHGATE, P. J., MAYER, S. R., BOXALL, E., and WILSON, A. B., 1971, Some 5-hydroxytryptamine-like actions of fenfluramine: a comparison with (+)-amphetamine and diethylpropion, *J. Pharm. Pharmacol.* **23**:600–605.
SPROULE, B. C., 1969, Double-blind trial of anorectic agents, *Med. J. Aust.* **1**:394–395.
STARK, P., and TOTTY, C. W., 1967, Effects of amphetamines on eating elicited by hypothalamic stimulation, *J. Pharmacol. Exp. Ther.* **158**:272–278.
STARK, P., TURK, J. A., and TOTTY, C. W., 1971, Reciprocal adrenergic and cholinergic control of hypothalamic elicited eating and satiety, *Am. J. Physiol.* **220**:1516–1521.
STARKE, K., and MONTEL, H., 1973, Alpha-receptor-mediated modulation of transmitter release from central noradrenergic neurones, *Naunyn-Schmiedebergs Arch. Pharmacol.* **279**:53–60.
STEIN, L., and WISE, C. D., 1969, Release of norepinephrine from hypothalamus and amygdala by rewarding medial forebrain bundle stimulation and amphetamine, *J. Comp. Physiol. Psychol.* **67**:189–198.
STEIN, L., and WISE, C. D., 1974, Serotonin and behavioral inhibition, *Adv. Biochem. Psychopharmacol.* **11**:281–291.
STIEL, J. N., LIDDLE, G. W., and LACY, W. W., 1970, Studies of mechanism of cyproheptadine-induced weight gain in human subjects, *Metabolism* **19**:192–200.
STERN, J. J., and ZWICK, G., 1973, Effects of intraventricular norepinephrine and estradiol benzoate on weight regulatory behavior in female rats, *Behav. Biol.* **9**:605–612.
STOLERMAN, I. P., 1970, Eating, drinking and spontaneous activity in rats after the administration of chlorpromazine, *Neuropharmacology*, **9**:405–417.
STOWE, F. R., and MILLER, A. T., 1957, The effect of amphetamine on food intake in rats with hypothalamic hyperphagia, *Experientia* **13**:114–115.
STRICKER, E. M., and ZIGMOND, M. J., 1975, Brain catecholamines and the lateral hypothalamic syndrome in: *Hunger: Basic Mechanisms and Clinical Implications* (D. Novin, W. Wyrwicka, and G. Bray, eds.), Raven Press, New York.
STUNKARD, A., RICKELS, K., and HESBACHER, P., 1973, Fenfluramine in the treatment of obesity, *Lancet* **1**:503–505.
SWANSON, E. F., SCOTT, C. C., LEE, H. M., and CHEN, K. K., 1943, Comparison of the pressor action of some optical isomers of sympathomimetic amines, *J. Pharmacol. Exp. Ther.* **79**:329–333.
TAINTER, M. L., 1944, Actions of benzedrine and propadrine in the control of obesity, *J. Nutr.* **27**:89–105.
TAKACS, L., and PETHO, B., 1969, Clinical experience with a new, amphetamine-unlike appetite reducing drug (desopimon, egyt), *Arzneim. Forsch.* **19**:516–518.
TANG, A. H., and KIRCH, J. D., 1971, Appetite suppression and central nervous system stimulation in the rhesus monkey, *Psychopharmacologia* **21**:139–146.
TAYLOR, K. M., and LAVERTY, R., 1969, The effect of chlordiazepoxide, diazepam, and nitrazepam on catecholamine metabolism in regions of the rat brain, *Eur. J. Pharmacol.* **8**:286–301.
TAYLOR, K. M., and SNYDER, S. H., 1971, Differential effects of d-amphetamine and l-amphetamine on behavior and on catecholamine disposition in dopamine and norepinephrine containing neurons of rat brain, *Brain Res.* **28**:295–309.
TAYLOR, M., LIVESEY, J., DEMPSTER, T., and BUNCE, R., 1971, The effects of acutely administered fenfluramine on activity and eating behavior, *Psychopharmacologia* **21**:165–173.
TEITELBAUM, P., and EPSTEIN, A. N., 1962, The lateral hypothalamic syndrome: recovery of feeding and drinking after lateral hypothalamic lesions, *Psychol. Rev.* **69**:74–90.
TEITELBAUM, P., SATINOFF, E., MARSHALL, J., KOSTUZEWA, R., and JACOBOWITZ, D., 1971, Disturbance in the regulation of body temperature and food intake in rats caused by 6-hydroxydopa, *Pharmacologist* **18**:304.

UEHLING, B. S., and VENATOR, E. R., 1967, Effects of d-amphetamine and pentobarbital on vigilance in the rat, *Psychonom. Sci.* **9**:113–114.

UNGERSTEDT, U., 1970, Is interruption of the nigrostriatal dopamine system producing the "lateral hypothalamus syndrome"?, *Acta Physiol. Scand.* **80**:35A-36A.

UNGERSTEDT, U., 1971, Stereotaxic mapping of the monoamine pathways in the rat brain, *Acta Physiol. Scand. Suppl.* **367**:1–48.

UNGERSTEDT, U., 1974, Neuropharmacology of the control of food intake, *V International Conference on Physiology of Food and Fluid Intake*, Israel.

VAN ROSSUM, J. M., and SIMONS, F., 1969, Locomotor activity and anorexogenic action, *Psychopharmacologia* **14**:248–254.

VOGEL, J. R., and LEAF, R. C., 1972, Initiation of mouse-killing in nonkiller rats by repeated pilocarpine treatment, *Physiol. Behav.* **8**:421–424.

VONVOIGTLANDER, P. F., and MOORE, K. E., 1973, Involvement of nigrostriatal neurons in in vivo release of dopamine by amphetamine, amantadine and tyramine, *J. Pharmacol. Exp. Ther.* **184**:542–552.

WAGNER, J. W., and DEGROOT, J., 1963, Changes in feeding behavior after intracerebral injections in the rat, *Am. J. Physiol.* **204**:483–487.

WEISSMAN, A., KOE, B. K., and TENEN, S. S., 1966, Antiamphetamine effects following inhibition of tyrosine hydroxylase, *J. Pharmacol. Exp. Ther.* **151**:339–352.

WELSH, A. L., 1962, *Side Effects of Anti-obesity Drugs*, C. C. Thomas Co., Springfield, Illinois.

WISE, R. A., 1974, Lateral hypothalamic electrical stimulation: does it make animals "hungry"? *Brain Res.* **67**:187–209.

WISE, R. A., and DAWSON, V., 1974, Diazepam-induced eating and lever pressing for food in sated rats, *J. Comp. Physiol. Psychol.* **86**:930–941.

WISE, R. A., and ERDMANN, E., 1973, Emotionality, hunger and normal eating: implications for interpretation of electrically induced behavior, *Behav. Biol.* **8**:519–531.

WISE, C. D., BERGER, B. D., and STEIN, L., 1972, Benzodiazepines: anxiety-reducing activity by reduction of serotonin turnover in the brain, *Science* **177**:180–183.

WISHART, T. B., and WALLS, E. K., 1973, The effects of anorexic doeses of dextroamphetamine on the ventromedial hypothalamic hyperphagic rat, *Can. J. Physiol. Pharmacol.* **51**:354–359.

WOODS, J. H., and TESSEL, R. E., 1974, Fenfluramine: amphetamine congener that fails to maintain drug-taking behavior in rhesus monkey, *Science* **185**:1067–1069.

WOODWARD, J. K., and LUCAS, R. W., 1973, Differential circulatory effects of various anorexigenic drugs, *Fed. Proc.* **32**:754.

WURTMAN, R. J., and FERNSTROM, J. D., 1974, Dietary control of brain neurotransmitter synthesis, *V International Conference on Physiology of Food and Fluid Intake*, Israel.

YAKSH, T. L., and MYERS, R. D., 1972, Neurohumoral substances released from hypothalamus of the monkey during hunger and satiety, *Am. J. Physiol.* **222**:503–515.

YELNOSKY, J., PANASEVICH, R. E., BORRELLI, A. R., and LAWLOR, R. B., 1969, Pharmacology of phentermine, *Arch. Int. Pharmacodyn. Ther.* **178**:62–76.

ZANNA, M. P., and COOPER, J., 1974, Dissonance and the pill: an attribution approach to studying the arousal properties of dissonance, *J. Pers. Soc. Psychol.* **29**:703–709.

ZEIGLER, H. P., and KARTEN, H. J., 1974, Central trigeminal structures and lateral hypothalamic syndrome in rat, *Science* **186**:636–638.

ZIANCE, R. J., SIPES, I. G., KINNARD, W. J., JR., and BUCKLEY, J. P., 1972, Central nervous system effects of fenfluramine hydrochloride, *J. Pharm. Exp. Ther.* **180**:110–117.

ZIGMOND, M. J., and STRICKER, E. M., 1972, Deficits in feeding behavior after intraventricular injection of 6-hydroxydopamine in rats, *Science* **177**:1211–1214.

ZIGMOND, M. J., and STRICKER, E. M., 1973, Recovery of feeding and drinking by rats after intraventricular 6-hydroxydopamine or lateral hypothalamic lesions, *Science* **182**:717–719.

ZIGMOND, M. J., and STRICKER, E. M., 1974, Ingestive behavior following damage to central dopamine neurons: implications for homeostasis and recovery of function, *Adv. Biochem. Psychopharmacol.* **12**:385–402.

ZIS, A. P., FIBIGER, H. C., and PHILLIPS, A. G., 1974, Reversal by *l*-dopa of impaired learning due to destruction of the dopamine nigro-neostriatal projection. *Science* **185**:960–962.

4

THE NEUROANATOMY AND NEUROPHARMACOLOGY OF DRINKING

Paulette E. Setler

1. INTRODUCTION

Terrestrial animals maintain body fluid balance by controlling both the intake of water and the output of water and solutes by the kidney. Regulatory intake of fluid occurs in response to a homeostatic imbalance or in anticipation of the need for water. Nonregulatory drinking, such as that induced by the availability of highly palatable solutions, also occurs. This discussion will be concerned only with regulatory drinking and primarily with drinking in response to alterations of body fluid volume or concentration.

Body water is distributed between cellular and extracellular compartments; a deficit in either is a sufficient stimulus for drinking, and thirst stimuli arising from a deficit in one compartment are additive with stimuli resulting from deficits in the other major compartment.

Extracellular thirst is caused by a reduction in intravascular volume and is referred to as hypovolemic thirst. Hemorrhage is an obvious cause of hypovolemia which may also be produced experimentally by parenteral injection of a hyperoncotic substance. The hyperoncotic colloid causes plasma (serum) to be withdrawn from the vasculature and sequestered in the area in which the colloid was injected. Thus, a deficit in vascular volume is produced

---

Paulette E. Setler • Biological Research Division, Smith Kline and French Laboratories, Philadelphia, Pennsylvania 19101.

without alteration of cellular or extracellular fluid osmolarity. Water deprivation results in hypovolemia together with cellular dehydration.

2. THIRST RECEPTORS

Stretch receptors in the vascular walls are sensitive to blood volume, and it is assumed, although not experimentally proven, that these volume receptors are one source of input to the thirst mechanisms in the CNS. Another probable indicator of blood volume is the level of circulating angiotensin formed by renin which is released from the kidney in response to hypovolemia or hypotension. Thus, it appears that receptors for monitoring extracellular fluid volume are localized in the periphery and send information to the central nervous system. In contrast, the CNS itself has been identified as the site of receptors monitoring the cellular compartment by responding to cellular dehydration. Cellular dehydration is produced by the movement of water from cells following, for example, water deprivation or injection of hypertonic solutions of osmotically active salts. In 1947 Verney described cells in the ventral diencephalon which behaved as osmometers and functioned as osmoreceptors, activation of which triggered the release of ADH from the posterior pituitary. That these or similar osmoreceptors within the hypothalamus are responsible for the initiation of drinking in response to cellular dehydration was hypothesized by Wolf in 1950. Evidence in support of this hypothesis was contributed by the studies of Andersson (1953) who produced a localized increase in osmotic pressure at several sites within the brain of the goat by injecting small volumes of hypertonic saline through implanted cannulae. Injections of hypertonic saline in the hypothalamus near the third ventricle caused the goats to drink. Injections of iso- or hypotonic solutions were without effect, as were injections of hypertonic saline in the lateral hypothalamus or supraoptic region (Andersson and McCann, 1955). These important experiments served to demonstrate that dehydration of cells within the brain will produce drinking but did not provide identification of those cells. The effective injections were made near or into the third ventricle, and the area of diffusion of the injected solution was not determined. Recent experiments using hypertonic solutions of a number of substances have led Andersson and his co-workers to contend that it is the sodium concentration *per se*, rather than the effective osmotic pressure, to which the brain receptors respond (Andersson *et al.*, 1967a,b). This appears not to be the case for rabbit or rat in which osmoreceptors have been identified in the lateral preoptic area. Peck and Novin (1971) made repeated injections of hypertonic solutions at 49 sites within the rabbit brain. Hypertonic saline was an effective stimulus for drinking at many of these sites. The majority of sites, however, did not meet the criteria for thirst osmoreceptors. Hypertonic solutions other than saline did not produce drinking, and other behaviors, including eating, were also produced by stimulation with hypertonic NaCl at these sites. Few, only six, sites were labeled as osmoreceptive. Those were sites at which hypertonic NaCl and hypertonic sucrose, which, because they do not readily penetrate cells, cause cellular dehydration, were effective stimuli for drinking but at which the hypertonic urea, which easily penetrates cells, was an ineffective stimulus. These six osmoreceptive sites were in close proximity to each other in the preoptic area just lateral and caudal to the anterior commissure. The lateral preoptic area of the rat ventral to the anterior commissure and including the ventral nucleus of the stria terminalis were shown by Blass and Epstein (1971) to be osmosensitive. When injected in this region minute amounts (as little as 1 μl injected bilaterally) of barely hypertonic (0.18 M) saline elicited drinking as did hypertonic sucrose, but not urea. Destruction of the osmosensitive region of the preoptic area of rabbit and rat abolished or attenuated drinking in response to a systemic hypertonic challenge as did hydration of the preoptic area of the rat by injection of distilled water.

At a finer level of analysis single-unit recordings have identified osmosensitive cells in the hypothalamic area. It is generally assumed that these cells are part of the control system for ADH or drinking, but proof is difficult to obtain for the involvement of individual cells in the control of a complex behavior. Vincent and his colleagues (1972) have perfected the technique of single-unit recording in the unanesthetized monkey and have used this preparation to attempt to define the activity of osmosensitive cells during drinking. They defined three types of osmosensitive cells including a group surrounding, but not within, the supraoptic nucleus. These cells displayed a monophasic response to intracarotid saline injection but no response to nonspecific arousal. These cells were proposed to function as true osmoreceptors, to be, in fact, the "osmoreceptors of Verney," the monitors of cellular dehydration which govern the release of antidiuretic hormone. When the animals were allowed to drink, the drinking had an effect on the osmoreceptors opposite to the effect of intracarotid saline. The latency of the cells' response to drinking was too brief to reflect changes in the osmolarity of extracellular fluid. The alteration in rate of firing was, therefore, directly related to the act of drinking and may reflect a direct connection or interaction with the neuronal network controlling drinking. Nonspecific osmosensitive cells which altered firing rates in response to arousal as well as intracarotid injection of saline were found in large number, and a major proportion of these were located in the lateral preoptic area. The firing of one type of nonspecific osmosensitive cell was found to be increased by the osmotic stimulus and by arousal, but depressed during drinking. These cells located in the vicinity of the medial forebrain bundle in the lateral hypothalamus and preoptic area were considered by the authors as the most likely candidates of all of the osmosensitive cells studied for participation in the control of drinking. The distribution of these cells, however, does not suggest that they are coincident with the osmoreceptors studied by Peck and Novin (1971) and Blass and Epstein (1971).

3. THE NEUROANATOMY OF THIRST

The lateral preoptic area has been identified as having an explicit role in the control of drinking, but the neuroanatomy of the remainder of the control system has not been definitively mapped. The neurobiologists' techniques of lesions and stimulation have located a number of areas in the forebrain and midbrain whose activation or deactivation can have a profound effect on drinking. How, or indeed if, each of these areas participates physiologically in the control of daily water intake or the response to a deficit in body fluids is not known. Until very recently most lesion studies were concerned only with the effects of the lesion on daily water intake under normal laboratory conditions. A more subtle analysis of the effect of lesions on responses to specific challenges is required to determine the role of any neural structure in the regulation of body water because, as will be seen in the following discussion, cellular and extracellular thirst mechanisms are to some extent independent of each other yet act in concert to maintain homeostasis. Electrical stimulation can often be a more precise tool than lesions for accurate identification of structures whose activation results in drinking. Rarely, however, have stimulation studies attempted to classify the role of specific structures in the control of drinking, or the interaction of individual structures. Nevertheless, stimulation and lesion analysis of the brain have provided a considerable volume of useful, if not definitive, information.

3.1. Hypothalamus

A fascinating review of the historical developments leading to current concepts of the neuroanatomy of thirst is provided by Fitzsimons (1973a), who points out that in 1881 Nothnagel first designated a thirst center in the brain. Nothnagel suggested that this control center was in the hindbrain wherein the vital centers were located. Somewhat later Paget suggested a cortical site as the thirst center. The suggestions of both Nothnagel and Paget were based on clinical incidences of polydipsia following brain damage caused by injury or disease (Fitzsimons, 1973a). In the beginning of the 20th century interest shifted to the hypothalamus as a result of research on the origin of diabetis insipidus. Beginning in the late 1930's the importance of the hypothalamus in the control of food intake and energy balance was demonstrated (Hetherington and Ranson, 1942; Brobeck et al., 1943; and

Anand and Brobeck, 1951), but it was the observations of adipsia in rats with lateral hypothalamic damage (Teitelbaum and Stellar, 1954) and the induction of drinking by hypothalamic stimulation in the goat (Andersson and McCann, 1955) and in the rat (Greer, 1955) which determined that the hypothalamus had a primary influence on thirst as opposed to an effect secondary to changes in ADH secretion or food intake.

Drinking has been elicited by electrical stimulation of the lateral hypothalamus of the rat (Greer, 1955; Mogenson and Stevenson, 1966, 1967), goat (Andersson and McCann, 1955), dog (Andersson, 1959), monkey (Robinson and Mishkin, 1968), and pigeon (Akerman *et al.*, 1960). Often eating, gnawing, and/or self-stimulation has also been elicited from the same hypothalamic electrode which produced stimulus-bound drinking (Mogenson and Stevenson, 1966; Devor *et al.*, 1970; Cox and Valenstein, 1969; Wise, 1971). When a single electrode elicited both eating and drinking, food intake raised the threshold for stimulus-bound eating but did not alter the threshold for drinking, and vice versa. Overhydration by administration of water into the rats' stomach prior to hypothalamic stimulation reduced the threshold for stimulus-bound drinking (Devor *et al.*, 1970). Adulteration of the drinking water with bitter-tasting quinine depressed hypothalamically elicited drinking whereas sweetening the water increased drinking (Mendelson, 1970). These experiments point out the similarities between stimulus-bound and normal drinking as does the study by Andersson and Wyrwicka (1957) who elicited drinking from hypothalamic electrodes in goats trained to perform a conditioned response to obtain water. These animals performed the same conditioned response when stimulated, indicating that the goats responded to electrical stimulation in the same manner as they responded to normal thirst.

Lesions of the lateral hypothalamus of the rat cause immediate aphagia and adipsia which are overcome through a process of gradual recovery in rats carefully tended and tube fed their daily nutritional requirements for days or even weeks. The recovery proceeds through four discrete stages and culminates in a stage in which the animals maintain normal body weight and water balance when given *ad libitum* access to laboratory chow and water (Teitelbaum and Epstein, 1962) (Fig. 1). Rats ostensibly recovered from lateral hypothalamic damage do not, however, respond normally to deficits in body fluid balance; these animals drink only in order to eat. When deprived of food or when water but not food is available after a period of water deprivation, these rats drink practically nothing but when food is restored the animals take a draught of water with every one or two bites of food in order to enable them to chew and swallow the dry food (Teitelbaum and Epstein, 1962). Inadequate salivary secretion by the lesioned rat may be a contributory cause of this exaggerated prandial drinking (Kissileff and Epstein, 1969; Hainsworth and Epstein, 1966). Rats "recovered" from lateral hypothalamic damage also fail to drink in response to injection of hypertonic saline, to hyperthermia, or to injection of hyperoncotic colloid (Epstein and

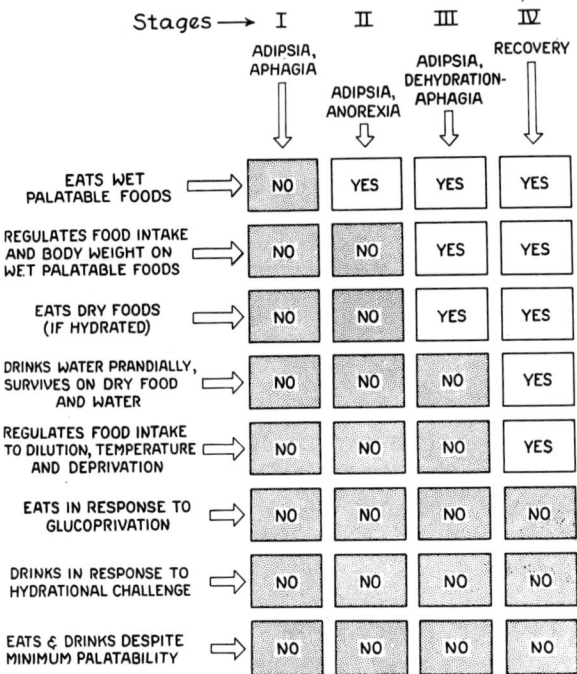

FIG. 1. The four stages of recovery following lateral hypothalamic lesions in the rat. From Epstein (1971).

Teitelbaum, 1964; Stricker and Wolf, 1967), nor do they drink in the heat (Epstein and Teitelbaum, 1964).

The lesions which produce the "lateral hypothalamic syndrome" involve the lateral midhypothalamus, destroy the medial forebrain bundle, and extend laterally into the internal capsule and posteriorly into the subthalamus (Teitelbaum and Epstein, 1962). Lesions in the lateral hypothalamic area which result in long-lasting adipsia without aphagia have also been described in rats (Montemurro and Stevenson, 1957) and in dogs (Andersson and McCann, 1956).

The lateral hypothalamus is a reticulated area of fibers and neuronal cell bodies through which several major fiber bundles pass. The relative importance of hypothalamic neurons and of fibers *en passage* in the production of the regulatory deficits which comprise the lateral hypothalamic syndrome has long been an open controversy (Morrison et al., 1958; Morgane, 1961). Recently the controversy has focused on the possibly critical involvement of monoamine-containing fiber bundles coursing through the hypothalamus to the telencephalon.

Lateral hypothalamic lesions produce partial depletion of telencephalic norepinephrine, dopamine, and serotonin (Heller et al., 1962; Heller and Moore, 1965; Ungerstedt, 1971b) by interrupting fiber tracts which project rostrally from midbrain and/or hindbrain (Andén et al., 1966; Ungerstedt, 1971a). This observation prompted intensive investigation of the regulatory deficits which are produced by selective, 6-hydroxydopamine-induced, degeneration of catecholaminergic pathways and the similarity of these deficits to the lateral hypothalamic syndrome. Depletion of catecholamines by injection of 6-hydroxydopamine into the cerebral ventricles, bilaterally into the substangia nigra, or along the course of the medial forebrain bundle or nigrostriatal tract results in aphagia and adipsia of variable duration followed by recovery of function in stages similar to the stages of recovery which follow electrolytic lesions of the lateral hypothalamus (Ungerstedt, 1971b; Smith et al., 1972; Zigmond and Stricker, 1972, 1973; Breese et al., 1973; Myers and Martin, 1973; Stricker and Zigmond, 1974; Marshall et al., 1974). At the time of recovery, that is, when the animals are once again maintaining a stable body weight on a diet of laboratory chow and water, residual deficits in regulation are still present. The thirst deficits reported from various laboratories include reduced drinking during food deprivation (Smith et al., 1972; Stricker and Zigmond, 1974; Breese et al., 1973; Fibiger et al., 1973; Marshall et al., 1974), reduced water intake following isoproterenol or polyethylene glycol, which are cellular thirst stimuli (Stricker and Zigmond, 1974), or hypertonic saline, an extracellular thirst challenge (Fibiger et al., 1973; Marshall et al., 1974). Catecholamine-depleted rats also showed residual deficits in food intake similar to those produced by lateral hypothalamic lesions (Stricker and Zigmond, 1974; Marshall et al., 1974). One major difference in the residual deficits of the "recovered" catecholamine-depleted rats is that unlike "recovered laterals" they show little finickiness, that is, they fail to show an exaggerated aversion to diets or solutions adulterated with unpleasant-tasting substances (Smith, 1973; Marshall et al., 1974).

In general, the long-term deficits in regulation produced by destruction of catecholamine-containing pathways are less severe than those observed in "recovered laterals" no matter how long the initial stage of aphagia and adipsia or how profound the depletion of catecholamines. The duration of stage I (aphagia and adipsia), however, does seem to be correlated with the degree of catecholamine depletion and more specifically with the degree of dopamine depletion (Zigmond and Stricker, 1973). In contrast, electrolytic lesions in the lateral hypothalamus which cause aphagia and adipsia produce a relatively modest depletion of catecholamines in the forebrain (Zigmond and Stricker, 1973) but include destruction of variable amounts of lateral hypothalamic tissue.

As emphasized by Marshall and his colleagues (1974) in a detailed comparison of the regulatory, sensory, and motor deficits produced by catecholamine depletion and by lateral hypothalamic lesions, selective catecholamine depletion produces a syndrome similar to but not identical to the lateral hypothalamic syndrome. Thus, although the studies discussed above strongly suggest an important role for dopaminergic pathways, the nigrostriatal bundle and/or the mesolimbic dopaminergic bundle, in the regulation of thirst and discount the possibility that the lateral hypothalamus is "the drinking center," it would be premature to disregard the lateral hypothalamus as a part of the regulatory system for water intake.

Lesions of the ventromedial hypothalamus cause hyperphagia and obesity accompanied by relative hypodipsia in spite of an increase in water intake. Ventromedial hyperphagic rats fail to increase their water intake to the same extent as food intake, which results in a reduced water:food ratio and an elevated serum sodium concentration (Stevenson, 1949; Stevenson et al., 1950).

To date, no hypothalamic lesion has caused primary hyperdipsia except in cases of destruction of the median eminence by irritative lesions. Nonirritative radiofrequency lesions at the same site had no effect on water intake (Rolls, 1970).

3.2. Limbic System and Midbrain

Drinking may be altered by lesions and by electrical stimulation in brain sites other than the hypothalamus. Most of these sites are located in the limbic system and mesencephalon. The limbic system functions as a circuit, each member structure capable of influencing every other directly or indirectly. The two major fiber bundles of the limbic system, the fornix and the stria terminals, project, in part, to the hypothalamus and preoptic area carrying fibers from the hippocampus and amygdala, respectively. A second pathway from amygdala to hypothalamus is the ventral amygdalofugal pathway which also carries a massive input from the pyriform cortex. The system is intimately linked with the hypothalamus by the medial forebrain bundle. Thus, the hypothalamus is a part of the circuit by which limbic structures interact, and many of the functions of the hypothalamus are shared by or influenced by limbic structures.

The amygdala strongly influences and interacts with the hypothalamus in the control of endocrine secretions, sexual behavior, the defense alarm reaction, and food intake, and is a rewarding site from which self-stimulation may be elicited. Experimental evidence also suggests that the amygdala influences drinking behavior. The amygdala is not a single nucleus but is a nuclear group for which there is no evidence to support uniformity or even unidirectionality of function, but rather the opposite. Therefore, it is not surprising that experiments in which large, but not necessarily identical, areas of the amygdala are stimulated or destroyed may produce contradictory results. In cats and dogs lesions of the amygdala (often including portions of the pyriform cortex) cause hypodipsia or adipsia usually in conjunction with aphagia. The critical portion of the amygdaloid lesion responsible for adipsia in the dog appears to be the dorsomedial region (Fonberg, 1969). In rats bilateral posteroventral amygdaloid lesions involving mainly the cortical nucleus caused a prominent rise in water intake which was temporary, lasting about eight weeks, but with a time course differing from that of the postlesion hyperphagia. Anterior ventral amygdaloid lesions resulted in hypodipsia and hyperphagia, whereas medial ventral lesions caused hypodipsia with little effect on eating (Grossman and Grossman, 1963). Electrical stimulation of the rat amygdala in the anterior and medial ventral regions produced no reliable changes in drinking behavior but posterior ventral stimulation reduced both food and water intake (Grossman and Grossman, 1963).

The septal area of the limbic system, which is intimately connected with the lateral hypothalamus and with the amygdala by the medial forebrain bundle and the stria terminalis respectively (Raisman, 1966), also exerts a marked influence on water intake. This influence is predominantly inhibitory. Lesions of the septum cause hyperdipsia without an effect on food intake (Harvey and Hunt, 1965), whereas electrical stimulation of the septum reduces *ad libitum* and deprivation-induced drinking with no effect on eating (Wishart and Mogenson, 1970).

Blass and Hanson (1970) have shown that the overdrinking which results from septal destruction meets the criteria for primary hyperdipsia. These authors have shown that rats with septal lesions have normal body fluid volume and composition and although they excrete a large volume of urine, their overdrinking is not secondary to polyuria. Nor is septal hyperdipsia a form of exaggerated prandial drinking; overdrinking persists in the absence of food. Blass and Hanson also showed that rats with septal lesions overrespond to an extracellular thirst challenge, hyperoncotic colloid, but not a cellular thirst stimulus, hypertonic saline. Other thirst stimuli related to extracellular thirst, angiotensin, renin, isoproterenol, and caval ligation also produce greater water intake in rats with septal lesions than in normal rats (Blass *et al.*, 1974). These results have led Blass and his colleagues to suggest that septal lesions remove an inhibitory influence on drinking in response to hypovolemia.

Other interpretations have been advanced to account for septal hyperdipsia. Rats with septal lesions are emotional and aggressive; they show perseveration of responding and fail to suppress punished behaviors. Beatty and Schwartzbaum (1968) have suggested that septal hyperdipsia could be a reflection of response perseveration or nonspecific enhancement of reward. The former is not reconcilable with the data of Harvey and Hunt (1965) which indicated that rats with septal lesions performed as well as controls when low rates of responding were preferentially rewarded by water. Neither hypothesis could account for the failure of septal-lesioned rats to overrespond to hypertonic saline nor for the fact that septal lesions produce only overdrinking, not overeating.

Areas within the midbrain and subthalamus have also been implicated in the control of drinking. Within the midbrain, lesions of the substantia nigra or mesencephalic reticular formation cause adipsia accompanied by aphagia. Following small bilateral lesions of the reticular formation, animals gradually recover from aphagia and adipsia (Parker and Feldman, 1967), but persistent deficits in water regulation have not been investigated. Lesions of the substantia nigra have been discussed in detail above.

The anterior zona incerta within the subthalamic region, like the septal area, has a marked influence on water intake but does not appear to be involved in food intake. Stimulation of the anterior portion of the zona incerta elicits drinking but not eating (Olds *et al.*, 1971; Huang and Mogenson, 1972); in fact, drinking is more readily elicited by stimulation of the zona incerta than by stimulation of the lateral hypothalamus (Huang and Mogenson, 1972). Discrete lesions of the anterior zona incerta reduce water intake with no significant effect on eating (Walsh and Grossman, 1973; Huang and Mogenson, 1974), and when food is unavailable, drinking ceases, suggesting that, like the rat "recovered" from lesions of the lateral hypothalamus, the rat with incertal lesions drinks in order to eat.

The zona incerta may be involved specifically, or at least predominantly, with extracellular thirst. Walsh and Grossman (1974) have observed that drinking in response to an extracellular thirst stimulus was greatly reduced in rats with incertal damage although these rats drank normally in response to hypertonic saline. The zona incerta may selectively facilitate, as the septal area may selectively attenuate, extracellular thirst.

Robinson and Mishkin (1968) have attempted to determine the localization of alimentary responses in the forebrain of the Rhesus monkey by use of electrical stimulation. Drinking was elicited from the preoptic area, lateral hypothalamus, substantia nigra, ventral tegmentum, and neostriatum, all sites previously implicated by the many experiments discussed above. Unexpectedly, however, drinking was most often evoked from cortical areas, specifically the anterior cingulate cortex and neighboring areas.

4. THE NEUROPHARMACOLOGY OF THIRST

This section, devoted to the neuropharmacology of thirst, will deal with attempts to determine by use of drugs the mechanism by which the central nervous system controls drinking behavior. The drugs used are those which modify synaptic neurotransmisson.

Of the many putative neurotransmitters in the central nervous system, the transmitter role has been firmly established for four: norepinephrine, acetylcholine, dopamine, and serotonin. Of these, acetylcholine, norepinephrine, and dopamine appear to participate in the control of fluid intake.

The anatomical localization of the neural systems containing these transmitters has been determined. Using staining methods for cholinesterase and choline acetylase Shute and Lewis (1966) have demonstrated that acetylcholine-containing nerve fibers arise from the central tegmental area and substantia nigra to project to the subthalamus, posterior and lateral hypothalamus, and forebrain. These fibers of the ventral tegmental pathway are joined by axons from cholinergic neurons in the subthalamus, hypothalamus, preoptic area, and globus pallidus.

Functionally, the cholinergic neurons in the central nervous system form part of the extrapyramidal motor system and also play a role in arousal, memory, and control of body water balance.

Swedish histologists using the formaldehyde-induced fluorescence technique have provided an elegant map of the catecholamine-containing neurons in the brain. Noradrenergic neurons originate in the hindbrain and project rostrally to the remainder of the brain stem with major inputs to the hypothalamus and subcortical telencephalon as well as a minor input to the cerebral cortex. Other noradrenergic axons leave the hindbrain to project to the cerebellum and to the spinal cord. Noradrenergic neurons have been implicated in the control of food and water intake, in neuroendocrine regulation, in the mediation of the defense alarm reaction, and may participate in the mediation of brain stimulation reward. Dopaminergic neurons originate in the ventral mesencephalon. Dopaminergic cells in the substantia nigra innervate the striatum, and the remainder of the dopamine-containing cells provide diffuse innervation of the hypothalamus, limbic system, and cerebral cortex. A very small but important group of dopaminergic neurons originates at the base of the third ventricle and sends axons to the median eminence; this pathway participates in the control of the anterior pituitary, but is not known to be concerned with body fluid balance.

An important feature of the topography of all three of these systems, cholinergic, noradrenergic, and dopaminergic, is that they send projections to the hypothalamus, preoptic area, and limbic system and that in so doing all three systems course through the lateral hypothalamic area. All of these are areas which lesion and electrical stimulation studies have shown to be important for the control of drinking behavior.

Strong evidence for a key role of each of these systems has come from the use of chemical stimulation of the brain, specific chemical lesions of catecholaminergic neurons, and the use of drugs which act as selective pharmacologic antagonists to specific neurotransmitters.

4.1. Cholinergic Systems

Since Grossman (1960, 1962a) stimulated drinking in the water-replete rat by implanting crystals of a cholinergic substance directly into the hypothalamus, a large volume of evidence has emerged which indicates that cholinergic neural pathways are involved in the control of water intake. Acetylcholine itself is an effective dipsogen (Grossman, 1962a; Simpson and Routtenberg, 1974) but is so rapidly destroyed by acetylcholinesterase in brain that carbachol, a direct cholinergic agonist not metabolized by cholinesterase, is employed in most studies of cholinergic-induced thirst. The dose–

response curve for solutions of carbachol injected into the lateral hypothalamus of the replete rat is biphasic. The threshold dose for drinking is about 0.9×10^{-10} mol, with the maximum response produced by approximately 24×10^{-10} mol; higher doses have a lesser effect (Miller *et al.*, 1964). Carbachol increases drinking by water-deprived rats as well as by water-replete rats (Grossman, 1962a; Kirkstone and Levitt, 1970; Barrelet, 1974). Inhibitors of cholinesterase also cause drinking when injected into the rat brain (Miller and Chien, 1968; Levitt and Boley, 1970; Winson and Miller, 1970; Simpson and Routtenberg, 1974) and will potentiate the dipsogenic effect of acetylcholine (Grossman, 1962a).

Carbachol-induced drinking shares many of the motivational properties of deprivation-induced drinking. Water-replete rats stimulated to drink by carbachol will perform an operant task to obtain water (Grossman, 1962a; Franklin and Quartermain, 1970) or run a maze (Khavari and Russell, 1966; Kelly and Mountford, 1974). Franklin and Quartermain (1970) showed, however, that doses of carbachol which induce intakes of an amount of water equal to that drunk after 24 hr of water deprivation support a lower rate of bar pressing on a variable interval schedule than is supported by deprivation. Franklin and Quartermain also demonstrated a difference in quinine tolerance between carbachol-treated and water-deprived rats. In contrast, Johnson and Fisher (1973a,b) found no differences between carbachol-stimulated and water-deprived rats in taste preferences for water, sucrose, and quinine. These authors concluded that carbachol can adequately reproduce the motivational and behavioral patterns of water deprivation if the appropriate conditions are provided.

Sites in the brain from which cholinergic drinking may be elicited are listed in Table 1. Fisher and Coury (1962) noted that the cholinergic drinking sites in the rat correspond approximately to the Papez circuit (of emotion) and have called the sites they localized the cholinergic drinking

TABLE 1
Principal Elements of the Cholinergic Thirst Circuit[a]

Dorsomedial hippocampus
Area of the diagonal band
Septum
Reuniens nucleus of the thalamus
Cingulate gyrus
Posterior mammillary nucleus—
  interpeduncular nucleus
Preoptic area
Perifornical hypothalamus
Anterior thalamus
Lateral hypothalamus—MFB
Fimbria of the fornix

[a] Adapted from Fisher and Coury (1962) and Coury (1967).

circuit. The study in which the cholinergic circuit was mapped employed fairly large doses of carbachol and made no attempt to determine the relative sensitivity of the various active sites. Although the manner in which the circuit operates and the interrelationships between the various active sites has not been determined, it has been shown that an intact lateral hypothalamus is required in order to produce a cholinergic drinking response at some extrahypothalamic sites. Lateral hypothalamic lesions placed at sites either positive or negative for carbachol-induced drinking reduced drinking in response to injections of carbachol into the anterior thalamus, septum (Stein and Levitt, 1971), preoptic area, and posterior hypothalamus (Wolf and Miller, 1964). Lesions in other regions of the circuit produced small transient depressions of drinking elicited by carbachol. It must be remembered that lesions, even unilateral lesions, of the lateral hypothalamus produce a number of deficits in ingestive behavior and that these effects, including attenuation of cholinergic thirst, may not be due to interruption of the cholinergic circuit *per se*.

Carbachol-induced drinking is abolished by anticholinergic drugs given centrally or systemically (Grossman, 1962b; Kirkstone and Levitt, 1970; Stein, 1963; Levitt and Fisher, 1966). Adrenergic antagonists do not affect cholinergic-induced drinking nor does depletion of brain catecholamines by 6-hydroxydopamine (Fitzsimons and Setler, 1971; Setler, 1973). In contrast, intracerebral administration of the adrenergic agonists norepinephrine (Setler, 1973) or isoproterenol (Singer and Armstrong, 1973) inhibits drinking in response to carbachol.

Anticholinergic drugs reduce but do not abolish drinking induced by water deprivation (Grossman, 1962b; Block and Fisher, 1970), by injection of hypertonic saline (DeWied, 1966; Block and Fisher, 190), by schedule-induced polydipsia (Burks and Fisher, 1970), and by electrical stimulation of the hypothalamus (Gentil *et al.*, 1971). Neither angiotensin-induced drinking nor isoproterenol-induced drinking is attenuated by anticholinergic drugs except at exceptionally high doses of the anticholinergic (Giardina and Fisher, 1971; Fitzsimons and Setler, 1971); these results will be discussed in greater detail below.

Because (1) acetylcholine is an endogenous neurotransmitter in the central nervous system, (2) cholinergic agents are potent central dipsogens, and because (3) anticholinergic drugs reduce drinking in response to "natural thirst," i.e., deprivation-induced drinking, it has been widely accepted that regulatory drinking is at least partially mediated by a cholinergic thirst circuit. Also, because salt-induced drinking is attenuated by anticholinergic drugs whereas drinking elicited by angiotensin or isoproterenol is not, it has been suggested that the cholinergic thirst circuit may be specifically related to responses to cellular dehydration.

Most of the data which suggest an important role for cholinergic systems in the control of drinking have been obtained from studies in which rats were used. Studies using other species do not support this suggestion.

Cholinergic agents do not produce reliable, dose-related drinking in any other species. Carbachol does elicit drinking when injected into the hypothalamus of the rabbit but not in a dose-related fashion; stimulation of food intake is the predominant effect of most doses (Sommer et al., 1967). In monkeys carbachol causes nausea and vomiting accompanied by inhibition of ingestive behavior (Sharpe and Myers, 1969). Cats display emotional responses after intracerebral administration of cholinergic drugs (Myers, 1964), but drinking has not been observed. Until the problem of species specificity has been resolved, there will be reservations about the overall importance of the cholinergic thirst circuit.

4.2. Angiotensin

Angiotensin II, a potent central dipsogen, in contrast to carbachol, elicits drinking in all species tested including mammals, birds, and reptiles. Angiotensin is believed to play a central role in the physiology of thirst, specifically in extracellular thirst (Fitzsimons, 1969). During hypovolemia, renin is released from the kidney to convert a protein substrate in plasma to angiotensin I, which is, in turn, converted by converting enzyme to angiotensin II, an octapeptide. The renin–angiotensin system is diagrammed in Fig. 2.

All of the known causes of extracellular thirst augment renin secretion and, conversely, elevation of plasma angiotensin levels by administration of either exogenous renin or angiotensin elicits drinking.

Taken together, these observations suggest that angiotensin II formed by renin released in response to hypovolemia is a stimulus for thirst. Fitzsimons (1969) has suggested at least three ways in which angiotensin could cause drinking: (1) by sensitizing vascular volume receptors to hypovolemia, (2) by increasing capillary permeability with a subsequent fall in plasma volume and an exaggeration of hypovolemia, and (3) by a direct

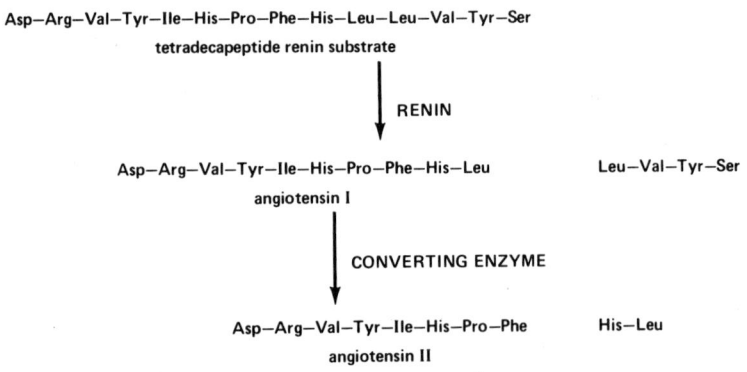

FIG. 2. The biosynthetic pathway for angiotensin II.

action on the central nervous system. The first hypothesis has proved untestable to date. The second is not supported by measurement of hematocrit and plasma volume during the infusion of angiotensin (Fitzsimons, 1969). The third hypothesis has provided an area for fruitful investigation.

Booth first reported in 1968 that angiotensin was an effective central dipsogen, and this fact was firmly established by Epstein et al. (1970) (see also Epstein et al., 1969); nonetheless, acceptance of the third hypothesis has been hindered by the fact that attempts to demonstrate that plasma angiotensin II crosses the blood–brain barrier have consistently failed.

The water-replete rat drinks in response to angiotensin administered intravenously, into the cerebral ventricles or into selected sites in the brain. Fitzsimons and Simons (1969) administered Val^5 angiotensin II by slow intravenous infusion to intact and to nephrectomized rats in test cages in which water was available. Drinking began after infusion of 29.1 μg/kg in intact rats and after 15.7 μg/kg to nephrectomized rats. Epstein and Simpson (1975) found that the threshold for drinking was considerably lower when Ile^5 angiotensin II (the peptide endogenous to the rat) was infused intravenously into intact rats resting in their home cages. Under these circumstances the threshold dose of angiotensin was 25 ng/kg/min with a latency to drinking of 4 to 8 min. Thus drinking occurred after infusion of 100 to 400 ng/kg.

Johnson and Epstein (1975) noted that in rats angiotensin-sensitive sites were often located in proximity to a ventricle or were identified using cannulae which passed through a ventricular space. By autoradiographic monitoring they determined that radiolabeled angiotensin could be detected in the cerebrospinal fluid after injection into brain parenchyma through a cannula which traversed a ventricle. These authors have suggested that angiotensin must gain access to the ventricular system to exert its dipsogenic effect, and they concur with Routtenberg and Simpson that the primary site of the dipsogenic action of angiotensin may be the subfornical organ. Routtenberg and Simpson (1971) and Simpson and Routtenberg (1973) showed that the subfornical organ, a modified ependymal structure in the third ventricle, was especially sensitive to angiotensin and to carbachol. Drinking was elicited by injection of as little as 0.5 ng of angiotensin into the subfornical organ. Lesions of the subfornical organ reduced the drinking response to intracranially administered angiotensin. Although the subfornical organ is exquisitely sensitive to angiotensin, the bulk of the evidence argues against its being the only site for the dipsogenic effect of intracranially administered angiotensin. The reduction of angiotensin-induced drinking following lesions of the subfornical organ is transient and has been attributed to ventricular obstructions (Buggy et al., 1975). The possibility remains that the subfornical organ may be the principal receptive site in the central nervous system mediating the dipsogenic effects of circulating angiotensin (Simpson and Routtenberg, 1975).

The minimal effective dose of Val^5 angiotensin II injected directly into the preoptic area of the rat brain is approximately 1 ng (1 pmol) (Fitzsimons, 1973b). The dose–response curve is monotonic and approximately linear up to a dose of 100 ng at which a plateau is reached. Doses as large as 5 µg have been given into the preoptic area without producing a diminution in the drinking response. No other overt behavioral changes have been reported following administration of doses as large as 4 µg into the rat brain.

The threshold and dose–response relationship for drinking induced by administration of angiotensin II into the lateral ventricle of the cat are similar to those for preoptic angiotensin in rats (Cooling and Day, 1975).

Unlike the dose–response curves for angiotensin-induced drinking in rat and cat, that for the monkey appears to be biphasic. Unilateral injection of angiotensin II into the brain of the Rhesus monkey produced significant drinking at doses of 3 ng and above. Maximal response were achieved at 100 to 300 ng; doses higher than 300 ng produced a lesser response (Sharpe and Swanson, 1974). Injection of large doses of angiotensin into the ventricles of the monkey occasionally produced behavioral excitation which was not seen when angiotensin was injected into brain parenchyma.

Whatever the location of the primary receptor site for angiotensin-induced drinking, the behavioral response to intracranially administered angiotensin appears to require the integrity of neural systems in the hypothalamus and preoptic area. As in the case of carbachol-induced drinking, lesions in the lateral hypothalamus of the rat attenuated drinking in response to the injection of angiotensin II into nonhypothalamic sites (Black et al., 1974; Kucharczyk and Mogenson, 1975). Lesions placed in the dorsomedial aspect of the lateral hypothalamus reduced drinking in response to angiotensin given into the preoptic area and to systemically administered renin and isoproterenol but not to systemically administered hypertonic saline (Kucharczyk and Mogenson, 1975), indicating that deficits in the response to angiotensin were not due to generalized suppression of ingestive behavior but were caused by disruption of an area or pathway specifically related to extracellular thirst.

Pharmacological evidence also supports the idea that angiotensin-induced drinking depends on the integrity of neural systems in the hypothalamus and/or preoptic area which are related to extracellular thirst but not intracellular thirst. At least one of these neural systems appears to be catecholaminergic in nature. Angiotensin-induced drinking is markedly attenuated by partial depletion of brain catecholamines (Setler, 1973; Fitzsimons and Setler, 1975). Significant disruption of the drinking response to angiotensin is produced following treatment with doses of 6-hydroxydopamine which cause only modest depletion of catecholamines. These treatments do not result in aphagia or adipsia. Moreover, the antidipsogenic effect of these modest depletions is specific for angiotensin's dipsogenic effect; the drinking response to carbachol is unaffected (Fig. 3). A similar

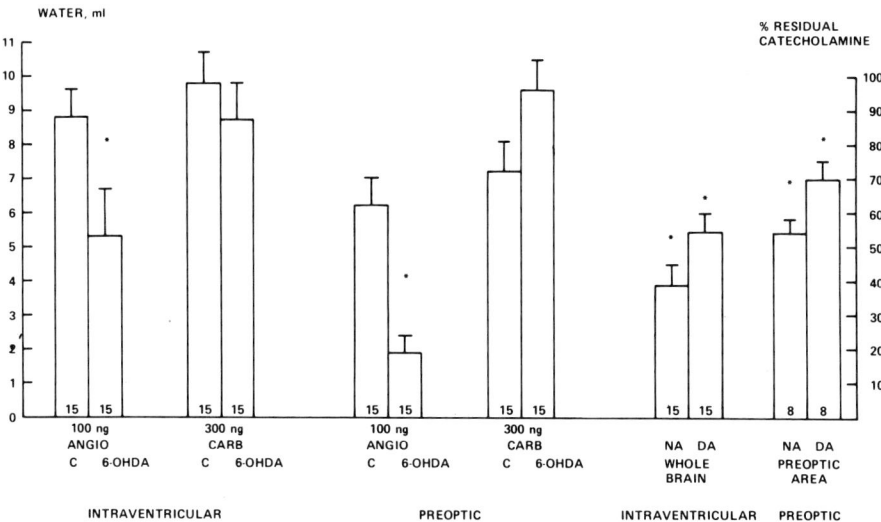

FIG. 3. The amount of water drunk in response to injection of angiotensin II or carbachol into either the lateral ventricle or preoptic area before and after partial depletion of catecholamines by 6-hydroxydopamine (6-OHDA). The number of rats per group is shown within the bars. $p < .05$.

selective inhibition of angiotensin-induced drinking is seen following injection of a catecholamine antagonist into the brain (Setler, 1973; Peres et al., 1974; Fitzsimons and Setler, 1975). Following haloperidol, angiotensin-induced drinking and isoproterenol-induced drinking, both related to extracellular thirst mechanisms, are reduced, whereas salt-induced and carbachol-induced drinking are unaffected. Drinking in response to a mixed stimulus, water deprivation, is also reduced (Fig. 4). Haloperidol more effectively blocks dopaminergic receptors than noradrenergic receptors (Andén et al., 1970). Because angiotensin-induced drinking is reduced by selective depletion of dopamine (Setler, 1973), the effect of haloperidol on the dipsogenic response to angiotensin is probably due to dopamine-receptor blockade. This suggestion is upheld by the observation that angiotensin-induced drinking is not affected by noradrenergic blocking agents except at toxic doses (Fitzsimons and Setler, 1975).

These studies emphasize the differences noted in the section on cholinergic thirst between the sensitivity of angiotensin-induced thirst to various pharmacologic antagonists of central neurotransmitters and the sensitivity of carbachol to the same, and thus emphasize the independence of extracellular thirst from cholinergic thirst systems.

The proposed interaction between extracellular thirst and dopaminergic neural pathways is still hypothetical, and no likely mode of interaction has

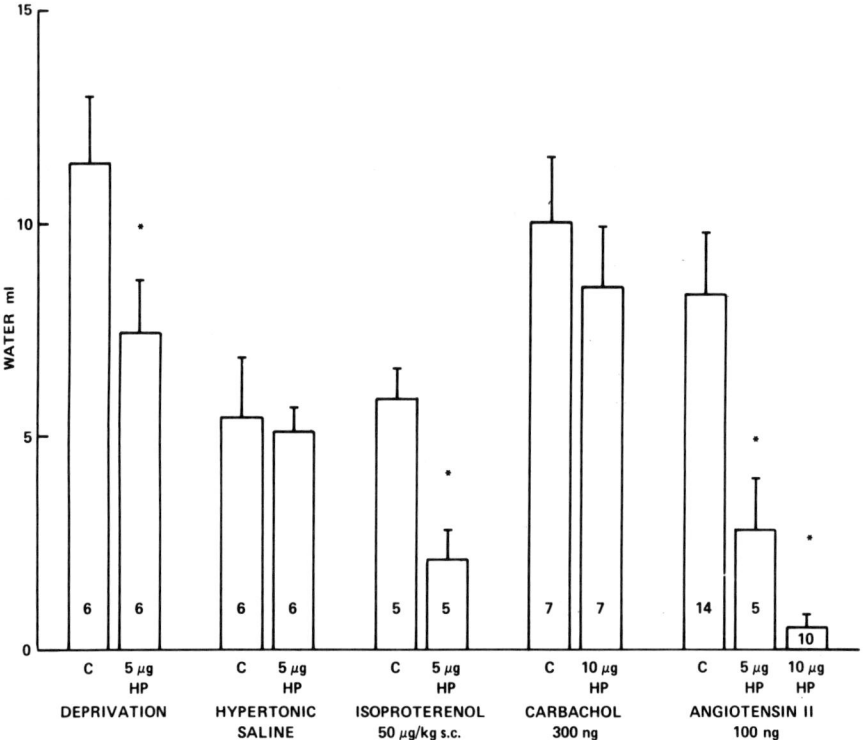

FIG. 4. The effect of injection of 5 µg of haloperidol (HP) on drinking in response to various thirst stimuli. Hypertonic saline (NaCl 2 M) was given i.p., isoproterenol was given s.c., and carbachol and angiotensin II were given into the preoptic area. The number of rats per group is shown within the bars. $p < .05$.

been ascertained. It is known that angiotensin releases and/or inhibits the reuptake of norepinephrine in the peripheral and central nervous system (Hughes and Roth, 1971; Palaic and Khairallah, 1968); it is possible that dopaminergic neurons might be similarly affected by angiotensin. Such a presynaptic mechanism for the angiotensin–dopamine interaction in thirst is rendered untenable by the observation that amphetamine which causes release of presynaptic dopamine is not a dipsogen but may reduce drinking in acute experiments, perhaps because of locomotor activation and induction of stereotyped behavior (Maickel et al., 1970; Soulairac and Soulairac, 1970). Nor is it likely that angiotensin activates dopamine receptors directly; dopamine itself is a relatively weak dipsogen (Fitzsimons and Setler, 1975), as is apomorphine, a dopamine agonist (Fisher, 1973). A direct postsynaptic mechanism is also incompatible with the observation that destruction of dopaminergic neurons reduces the dipsogenic effect of angiotensin. Since angiotensin does not appear to act directly on dopaminergic systems either pre- or postsynaptically, it is tentatively suggested that dopaminergic neuronal systems play an ill-defined permissive role in extracellular thirst.

Angiotensin-induced thirst is most effectively reduced by a specific competitive inhibitor of angiotensin II in brain and peripheral tissues. The inhibitor is Sar^1, Ala^8, angiotensin II, called P113. When infused intravenously, P113 blocks drinking elicited by intravenous administraton of angiotensin II (Tang and Falk, 1974); when given intracerebrally, P113 blocks drinking in response to angiotensin given intracerebrally in rats (Epstein et al., 1973a) and cats (Cooling and Day, 1973), or intravenously in rats (Simpson et al., 1975). Simpson found P113 to be especially effective at blocking drinking to intravenous angiotensin when the inhibitor was given directly into the subfornical organ. Angiotensin-induced drinking is also inhibited by antiserum to angiotensin II (Epstein et al., 1973b).

Drinking may also be elicited by fragments of the angiotensin molecule; dipsogenic efficacy diminishes with diminishing chain length and is essentially absent in the C-terminal pentapeptide and either C- or N-terminal tetrapeptide. This is in agreement with the results of Bumpus and Smeby (1968) who found that the C-terminal hexapeptide carried the essential biological actions of angiotensin. The peptide precursors of angiotensin II and also the enzyme renin elicit drinking (Fitzsimons, 1971). This led Fitzsimons to conjecture that because all of the known biological activities of the renin–angiotensin system are mediated by angiotensin II, the brain must contain all of the substrates and enzymes for synthesis of angiotensin II from the injected precursors. This was found to be true; the brain does have the capacity to synthesize angiotensin II, and in normal animals the renin and angiotensin found in the brain are of local, not renal origin (Ganten et al., 1971; Fisher-Ferraro et al., 1971; Yang and Neff, 1972).

More direct proof of the dipsogenic effect of the precursors of angiotensin II was afforded by the observations that drinking induced by renin substrate is reduced by antiserum to angiotensin II (Epstein et al., 1973b) and that P113 inhibits drinking in response to renin, renin substrate, and angiotensin I as well as drinking in response to angiotensin II (Epstein et al., 1973a). Epstein and his co-workers also found that drinking responses to renin and renin substrate were reduced by a renin inhibitor, Pepstatin, and that the dipsogenic effects of all of the angiotensin precursors and of renin were blocked by an inhibitor of the enzyme which catalyzes conversion of angiotensin I to angiotensin II.

This discussion of the pharmacology of angiotensin-induced drinking has been predominantly concerned with responses to either exogenous angiotensin or angiotensin formed by renin released from the kidney in hypovolemia. The role of the brain isorenin system in thirst and the interaction of this system with the neural systems discussed here are unknown and provide an area for further investigation.

4.3. Adrenergic Systems

Adrenergic neural systems have been implicated in the control of water intake in at least two ways. Lehr and his colleagues (1967) and Leibowitz (1971) have observed that beta-adrenergic agonists induce water intake and proposed that this behavior is mediated by beta-adrenergic receptors in the central nervous system. Subsequent studies showed, however, that the potent beta-adrenergic agonist isoproterenol was a more effective dipsogen when administered systemically than when given directly into the brain (Fisher, 1973; Lehr, 1973). Both Fisher and Lehr have presented evidence that following administration of isoproterenol into the central nervous system, the drug "leaked" into the peripheral circulation in quantities above the threshold amount required to induce a drinking response. Drinking in response to circulating isoproterenol (and to isoproterenol injected into the brain) appears to be mediated to a very large extent by release of renin from the kidney (Houpt and Epstein, 1971), which is under beta-adrenergic control (Ganong, 1973).

Drinking in response to beta-adrenergic stimulants and alpha-adrenergic blocking agents is accompanied by an increase in plasma renin activity (Peskar *et al.*, 1970; Leenen and McDonald, 1974) and abolished by nephrectomy (Houpt and Epstein, 1971; Meyer *et al.*, 1971). Drinking in response to isoproterenol is reduced by a beta antagonist, propranolol (Lehr *et al.*, 1967), which also prevents the isoproterenol-induced release of renin (Meyer *et al.*, 1973). Isoproterenol-induced drinking is also reduced by haloperidol (Fig. 4), which blocks angiotensin-induced thirst, and by antiserum to angiotensin II (Abdelaal *et al.*, 1974). Although most of the available data support the idea that drinking produced by beta-adrenergic agonists is mediated by renin release, there are reports to the contrary. Tang and Falk (1974) failed to inhibit the dipsogenic response to isoproterenol by administration of P113, the competitive antagonist of angiotensin II. It has also been reported that isoproterenol induces drinking in the nephrectomized dog as well as in the intact dog (Fitzsimons and Szczepanska-Sadowska, 1974).

An inhibitory control of drinking by noradrenergic neurons was proposed by Grossman (1962a) because crystals of norepinephrine implanted into the hypothalamus of the rat suppressed drinking induced by water deprivation. Injection of norepinephrine into the brain inhibits drinking in response to some, but not all, dipsogenic stimuli. In addition to deprivation-induced drinking, drinking stimulated by hypertonic saline and by carbachol is reduced by norepinephrine, whereas the responses to angiotensin and to isoproterenol are unaffected (Setler, 1975).

Extracellular thirst stimuli appear to be insensitive to noradrenergic inhibition. The physiological significance of these observations is uncertain; as discussed above, electrolytic or biochemical lesions which produce marked regional or whole-brain depletions of catecholamines usually decrease water intake in response to most dipsogenic stimuli and may cause adipsia. The antidipsogenic effect of intracerebrally administered norepinephrine may be a pharmacologic artifact.

4.4. Other Dipsogenic Substances

Systemic administration of serotonin to rats produces drinking; this behavior change is accompanied by an elevation of plasma levels of renin and angiotensin I, as shown by Meyer and colleagues (1974). These authors also showed that serotonin-induced drinking is prevented by nephrectomy and reduced by those drugs which prevented the serotonin-induced release of renin from the kidney. Serotonin has also been shown to induce drinking (and eating) when given directly into the brain of the monkey (Sharpe and Myers, 1969), but the mechanism underlying the response has not been investigated.

Injection of histamine into the ventricular system (Gerald and Maickel, 1972) or into the hypothalamus (Leibowitz, 1973) caused drinking in water-replete rats. The dipsogenic effect of intraventricular histamine was blocked by systemically administered methapyriline, an antagonist of the H_1-receptor. The only dose of antihistamine used was also shown to markedly inhibit drinking in response to water deprivation (Gerald and Maickel, 1972). The effects of the antihistamines on drinking to other thirst stimuli were not reported.

Nicotine was reported by Myers *et al.* (1973) to be an effective central dipsogen in the monkey; the authors felt that the response was mediated by activation of nicotinic receptors in the brain. This hypothesis has not yet been tested by use of differential blocking agents. Nicotine has many pharmacologic effects on several types of neuronal receptors; included among these are release of catecholamines in the central nervous system (Westfall, 1973) as well as both stimulation and inhibition of nicotinic receptors. It is, therefore, not certain by what mechanism nicotine induces drinking.

5. DEFENSE OF BODY FLUIDS

The body defends its water and electrolyte balance by other mechanisms in addition to the regulation of water intake. Most important are the renal mechanisms which are, in turn, influenced by hormones from the adrenal (the mineralocorticoids) and from the anterior pituitary (antidiuretic hormone). In some species sodium appetite contributes to the maintenance of body fluid composition. The control systems which maintain the constancy of body fluids must also interact with the neural and hormonal mechanisms which participate in the control of blood pressure. Because of these complex interactions the anatomical systems which control drinking behavior and the pharmacological effects of drugs which alter water intake may be expected to influence and be influenced by those mechanisms regulating renal function, salt appetite, and blood pressure.

6. REFERENCES

ABDELAAL, A. E., MERCER, P. F., and MOGENSON, G. J., 1974, Drinking elicited by polyethylene glycol and isoproterenol reduced by antiserum to angiotensin II, *Can. J. Physiol. Pharmacol.* **52**:362-363.

AKERMAN, B., ANDERSSON, B., FABRICIUS, E., and SVENSSON, L., 1960, Observation on central regulation of body temperature and of food and water intake in the pigeon *(Columba linia), Acta Physiol. Scand.* **50**:328-336.

ANAND, B. K., and BROBECK, J. R., 1951, Hypothalamic control of food intake in rats and cats, *Yale J. Biol. Med.* **24**:123-140.

ANDÉN, N.-E., BUTCHER, S. G., CORRODI, N., FUXE, K., and UNGERSTEDT, U., 1970, Receptor activity and turnover of dopamine and noradrenaline after neuroleptics, *Eur. J. Pharmacol.* **11**:303-314.

ANDÉN, N.-E., DAHLSTRÖM, A., FUXE, K., LARSSON, K., OLSON, L., and UNGERSTEDT, U., 1966, Ascending monoamine neurons to the telencephalon and diencephalon, *Acta Physiol. Scand.* **67**:315-326.

ANDERSSON, B., 1953, The effect of injections of hypertonic NaCl solutions into different parts of the hypothalamus of goats, *Acta Physiol. Scand.* **28**:188-201

ANDERSSON, B., 1959, Implantation of electrodes in the hypothalamus of the dog by the diasphenoid route, *Acta Physiol. Scand.* **47**:56-62.

ANDERSSON, B., and MCCANN, S. M., 1955, A further study of polydipsia evoked by hypothalamic stimulation in the goat, *Acta Physiol. Scand.* **33**:333-346.

ANDERSSON, B., and MCCANN, S. M., 1956, The effect of hypothalamic lesions on the water intake of the dog, *Acta Physiol. Scand.* **35**:312-320.

ANDERSSON, B., and WYRWICKA, W., 1957, The elicitation of a drinking motor conditioned reaction by electrical stimulation of the hypothalamic "drinking area" in the goat, *Acta Physiol. Scand.* **41**:194-198.

ANDERSSON, B., JOBIN, M., and OLSSON, K., 1967a, A study of thirst and other effects of an increased sodium concentration in the third brain ventricle, *Acta Physiol. Scand.* **69**:29-36.

ANDERSSON, B., OLSSON, K., and WARNER, R. G., 1967b, Dissimilarities between the central control of thirst and the release of antidiuretic hormone (ADH), *Acta Physiol. Scand.* **71**:57-64.

BARRELET, L. F., 1974, Interactions between peripheral and hypothalamic carbachol stimulation of drinking in the rat, *Eur. J. Pharmacol.* **26**:89-95.

BEATTY, W. W., and SCHWARTZBAUM, J. S., 1968, Consummatory behavior for sucrose following septal lesions in the rat, *J. Comp. Physiol. Psychol.* **65**:93-102.

BLACK, S. L., KUCHARCZYK, J., and MOGENSON, G. J., 1974, Disruption of drinking to intracranial angiotensin by a lateral hypothalamic lesion, *Pharmacol. Biochem. Behav.* **2**:515-522.

BLASS, E. M., and EPSTEIN, A. N., 1971, A lateral preoptic osmosensitive zone for thirst in the rat, *J. Comp. Physiol. Psychol.* **76**:338-394.

BLASS, E. M., and HANSON, D. G., 1970, Primary hyperdipsia in the rat following septal lesions, *J. Comp. Physiol. Psychol.* **70**:87-93.

BLASS, E. M., NUSSBAUM, A. I., and HANSON, D. G., 1974, Septal hyperdipsia: specific enhancement of drinking to angiotensin in rats, *J. Comp. Physiol Psychol.* **87**:422-439.

BLOCK, M. L., and FISHER, A. E., 1970, Anticholinergic central blockade of salt-aroused and deprivation-induced drinking, *Physiol. Behav.* **5:**525-527.

BOOTH, D. A., 1968, Mechanism of action of norepinephrine in eliciting an eating response on injection into the rat hypothalamus, *J. Pharmacol. Exp. Ther.* **160:**336-348.

BREESE, G. R., SMITH, R. D., COOPER, B. R., and GRANT, L. D., 1973, Alterations in consummatory behavior following intracisternal injection of 6-hydroxydopamine, *Pharmacol. Biochem. Behav.* **1:**319-328.

BROBECK, J. R., TEPPERMAN, J., and LONG, C. N. H., 1943, Experimental hypothalamic hyperphagia in the albino rat, *Yale J. Biol. Med.* **15:**831-853.

BUGGY, J., FISHER, A. E., HOFFMANN, W. E., JOHNSON, A. K., and PHILLIPS, M. I., 1975, Ventricular obstruction: effect on drinking induced by intracranial angiotensin, *Science* **190:**72-74.

BUMPUS, F. M., and SMEBY, R. R., 1968, Angiotensin, in: *Renal Hypertension* (I. H. Page and J. W. McCubbin, eds.), pp. 62-100, Year Book Publishers, Chicago.

BURKS, C. D., and FISHER, A. E., 1970, Anticholinergic blockade of schedule-induced polydipsia, *Physiol. Behav.* **5:**635-640.

COOLING, M. J., and DAY, M. D., 1973, Antagonism of central dipsogenic and peripheral vasoconstrictor responses to angiotensin II with Sar^1 Ala^8 angiotensin II in the conscious cat, *J. Pharm. Pharmacol.* **2:**1005-1006.

COOLING, M. J., and DAY, M. D., 1975, Drinking behavior in the cat induced by renin, angiotensin I, II, and isoprenaline, *J. Physiol. (London)* **244:**325-336.

COURY, J. N., 1967, Neural correlates of food and water intake in the rat, *Science* **156:**1763-1765.

COX, V. C., and VALENSTEIN, E. S., 1969, Distribution of hypothalamic sites yielding stimulus-bound behavior, *Brain Behav. Evol.* **2,** 359-376.

DEVOR, M. G., WISE, R. A., MILGRAM, N. M., and HOEBEL, B. G., 1970, Physiological control of hypothalamically elicited feeding and drinking, *J. Comp. Physiol. Psychol.* **73:**226-232.

DEWIED, D., 1966, Effect of autonomic blocking agents and structurally related substances on the "salt arousal of drinking," *Physiol. Behav.* **1:**193-197.

EPSTEIN, A. N., 1971, The lateral hypothalamic syndrome: its implications for the physiological psychology of hunger and thirst, in: *Progress in Physiological Psychology* (E. Stellar and J. M. Sprague, eds.), Vol. 4, pp. 263-317, Academic Press, New York.

EPSTEIN, A. N., and SIMPSON, J. B., 1975, The dipsogenic action of angiotensin, *Acta Physiol. Lat.-Am.* **24:**405-408.

EPSTEIN, A. N., and TEITELBAUM, P., 1964, Severe and persistent deficits in thirst in rats with lateral hypothalamic damage, in: *Thirst* (M. J. Wayner, ed.), pp. 395-406, Pergamon Press, New York.

EPSTEIN, A. N., FITZSIMONS, J. T., and SIMONS, B. J., 1969, Drinking caused by the intracranial injection of angiotensin into the rat, *J. Physiol. (London)* **200:**98-100P.

EPSTEIN, A. N., FITZSIMONS, J. T., and ROLLS (née Simons), B. J., 1970, Drinking induced by injection of angiotensin into the brain of the rat, *J. Physiol. (London)* **210:**457-474.

EPSTEIN, A. N., FITZSIMONS, J. T., and JOHNSON, A. K., 1973a, Peptide antagonists of the renin–angiotensin system and the elucidation of the receptors for angiotensin-induced drinking, *J. Physiol. (London)* **238:**34-35P.

EPSTEIN, A. N., FITZSIMONS, J. T., and JOHNSON, A. K., 1973b, Prevention by angiotensin II antiserum of drinking induced by intracranial angiotensin, *J. Physiol. (London)* **230:**42P-43P.

FIBIGER, H. C., ZIS, A. P., and MCGEER, E. G., 1973, Feeding and drinking deficits after 6-hydroxydopamine administration in the rat: similarities to the lateral hypothalamic syndrome, *Brain Res.* **55:**135-148.

FISCHER-FERRARO, C., NAHMOD, V. E., GOLDSTEIN, D. J., and FINKIELMAN, S., 1971, Angiotensin and renin in rat and dog brain, *J. Exp. Med.* **133:**353-361.

FISHER, A. E., 1973, Relationships between cholinergic and other dipsogens in the central mediation of thirst, in: *The Neuropsychology of Thirst: New Findings and Advances in*

Concepts (A. N. Epstein, H. R. Kissileff, and E. Stellar, eds.), pp. 243–279, Winston, Washington, D.C.

FISHER, A. E., and COURY, J. N., 1962, Cholinergic tracing of a central neural circuit underlying the thirst drive, *Science* **138**:691–693.

FITZSIMONS, J. T., 1969, The role of a renal thirst factor in drinking induced by extracellular stimuli, *J. Physiol. (London)* **201**:349–368.

FITZSIMONS, J. T., 1971, The effect on drinking of peptide precursors and of shorter chain peptide fragments of angiotensin II injected into the rat's diencephalon, *J. Physiol. (London)* **214**:295–303.

FITZSIMONS, J. T., 1973a, Some historical perspectives in the physiology of thirst, in: *The Neuropsychology of Thirst: New Findings and Advances in Concepts* (A. N. Epstein, H. R. Kissileff, and E. Stellar, eds.), pp. 3–33, Winston, Washington, D. C.

FITZSIMONS, J. T., 1973b, Angiotensin as a thirst regulating hormone, in: *Proceedings of the Fourth International Congress of Endocrinology, Washington, D. C., June 18–24, 1972* (R. O. Scow, F. J. G. Ebling, and I. W. Henderson, eds.), pp. 711–716, Exerpta Medica, Amsterdam.

FITZSIMONS, J. T., and SETLER, P. E., 1971, Catecholaminergic mechanisms in angiotensin-induced drinking, *J. Physiol. (London)* **218**:43–44P.

FITZSIMONS, J. T., and SETLER, P. E., 1975, The relative importance of central nervous catecholaminergic and cholinergic mechanisms in drinking in response to angiotensin and other thirst stimuli, *J. Physiol. (London)* **250**:613–631.

FITZSIMONS, J. T., and SIMONS, B. J., 1969, The effect on drinking in the rat of intravenous infusion of angiotensin given alone or in combination with other stimuli of thirst, *J. Physiol. (London)* **203**:45–57.

FITZSIMONS, J. T., and SZCZEPANSKA-SADOWSKA, E., 1974, Drinking and antidiuresis elicited by isoprenaline in the dog, *J. Physiol. (London)* **239**:251–267.

FONBERG, E., 1969, Effects of small dorsomedial amygdala lesions on food intake and acquisition of instrumental alimentary reactions in dogs, *Physiol. Behav.* **4**:739–743.

FRANKLIN, K. B., and QUARTERMAIN, D., 1970, Comparison of the motivational properties of deprivation-induced drinking with drinking elicited by central carbachol stimulation, *J. Comp. Physiol. Psychol.* **71**:390–395.

GANONG, W. F., 1973, Catecholamines and the secretion of renin, ACTH, and growth hormone, in: *Frontiers in Catecholamine Research* (E. Usdin and S. Snyder, eds.), pp. 819–824, Pergamon Press, New York.

GANTEN, D., MINNICH, J. L., GRANGER, P., HAYDUK, K., BRECHT, H. M., BARBEAU, A., BOUCHER, R., and GENEST, J., 1971, Angiotensin-forming enzyme in brain tissue, *Science* **173**:64–65.

GENTIL, C. G., STEVENSON, J. A. F., and MOGENSON, G. J., 1971, Effect of scopolamine on drinking elicited by hypothalamic stimulation, *Physiol. Behav.* **7**:639–641.

GERALD, M. C., and MAICKEL, R. P., 1972, Studies on the possible role of brain histamine in behavior, *Brit, J. Pharmacol.* **44**:462–471.

GIARDINA, A. R., and FISHER, A. E., 1971, Effect of atropine on drinking induced by carbachol, angiotensin and isoproterenol, *Physiol. Behav.* **7**:653–655.

GREER, M. A., 1955, Suggestive evidence of a primary "drinking center" in hypothalamus of rat, *Proc. Soc. Exp. Biol. Med.* **89**:59–62.

GROSSMAN, S. P., 1960, Eating or drinking in satiated rats elicited by adrenergic or cholinergic stimulation, respectively, of the lateral hypothalamus, *Science* **132**:301–302.

GROSSMAN, S. P., 1962a, Direct adrenergic and cholinergic stimulation of hypothalamic mechanisms, *Am. J. Physiol.* **202**:872–882.

GROSSMAN, S. P., 1962b, Effect of adrenergic and cholinergic blocking agents on hypothalamic mechanisms, *Am. J. Physiol.* **202**:1230–1236.

GROSSMAN, S. P., and GROSSMAN, L., 1963, Food and water intake following lesions or electrical stimulation of the amygdala, *Am. J. Physiol.* **205**:761–765.

HAINSWORTH, H. R., and EPSTEIN, A. N., 1966, Severe impairment of heat-induced saliva spreading in rats recovered from lateral hypothalamic lesions, *Science* **153**:1255-1257.

HARVEY, J. A., and HUNT, H. F., 1965, Effect of septal lesions on thirst in the rat as indicated by water consumption and operant responding for water reward, *J. Comp. Physiol. Psychol.* **59**:49-56.

HELLER, A., and MOORE, R. Y., 1965, Effect of central nervous system lesions on brain monoamines in the rat, *J. Pharmacol. Exp. Ther.* **150**:1-9.

HELLER, A., HARVEY, J. A., and MOORE, R. Y., 1962, A demonstration of a fall in brain serotonin following central nervous system lesions in the rat, *Biochem. Pharmacol.* **11**:859-866.

HETHERINGTON, A. W., and RANSON, S. W., 1942, The spontaneous activity and food intake of rats with hypothalamic lesions, *Am. J. Physiol.* **136**:609-617.

HOUPT, K. A., and EPSTEIN, A. N., 1971, The complete dependence of beta-adrenergic drinking on the renal dipsogen, *Physiol. Behav.* **7**:897-902.

HUANG, Y. H., and MOGENSON, G. J., 1972, Neural pathways mediating drinking and feeding in rats, *Exp. Neurol.* **37**:269-287.

HUANG, Y. H., and MOGENSON, G. J., 1974, Differential effects of incertal and hypothalamic lesions on food and water intake, *Exp. Neurol.* **43**:276-281.

HUGHES, J., and ROTH, R. H., 1971, Evidence that angiotensin enhances transmitter release during sympathetic nerve stimulation, *Brit. J. Pharmacol.* **14**:239-255.

JOHNSON, A. K., and EPSTEIN, A. N., 1975, The cerebral ventricles as the avenue for the dipsogenic action of intracranial angiotensin, *Brain Res.* **86**:399-418.

JOHNSON, A. K., and FISHER, A. E., 1973a, Taste preferences for sucrose solutions and water under cholinergic and deprivation thirst, *Physiol. Behav.* **10**:607-612.

JOHNSON, A. K., and FISHER, A. E., 1973b, Tolerance for quinine under cholinergic versus deprivation-induced thirst, *Physiol. Behav.* **10**:613-616.

KELLY, D. L., and MOUNTFORD, D., 1974, The motivational consequences of cholinergic stimulation of the medial septal area, *Physiol. Psychol.* **2**:101-103.

KHAVARI, K. A., and RUSSELL, R. W., 1966, Acquisition, retention, and extinction conditions of water deprivation and of central cholinergic stimulation, *J. Comp. Physiol. Psychol.* **61**:339-345.

KIRKSTONE, B. J., and LEVITT, R. A., 1970, Interactions between water deprivation and chemical brain stimulation, *J. Comp. Physiol. Psychol.* **71**:334-340.

KISSILEFF, H. R., and EPSTEIN, A. N., 1969, Exaggerated prandial drinking in the recovered lateral rat without saliva, *J. Comp. Physiol. Psychol.* **67**:301-308.

KUCHARCZYK, J., and MOGENSON, G. J., 1975, Separate lateral hypothalamic pathways for extracellular and intracellular thirst, *Am. J. Physiol.* **228**:295-301.

LEENEN, F. H. H., and MCDONALD, R. H., 1974, Effect of isoproterenol on blood pressure, plasma renin activity, and water intake in rats, *Eur. J. Pharmacol.* **26**:129-135.

LEHR, D., 1973, Invited comment: comments to papers on "thirst" by Drs. Fisher, Harvey, and Setler, in: *The Neuropsychology of Thirst: New Findings and Advances in Concepts* (A. N. Epstein, H. R. Kissileff, and E. Stellar, eds.), pp. 307-315, Winston, Washington, D. C.

LEHR, D., MALLOW, J., and KRUKOWSKI, M., 1967, Copious drinking and simultaneous inhibition of urine elicited by beta-adrenergic stimulation and contrary effect of alpha-adrenergic stimulation, *J. Pharmacol. Exp. Ther.* **158**:150-163.

LEIBOWITZ, S. F., 1971, Hypothalamic alpha- and beta-adrenergic systems regulate both thirst and hunger in the rat, *Proc. Nat. Acad. Sci. U.S.A.* **68**:332-334.

LEIBOWITZ, S. F., 1973, Histamine: a stimulatory effect on drinking behavior in the rat, *Brain Res.* **63**:440-444.

LEVITT, R. A., and BOLEY, R. P., 1970, Drinking elicited by injection of eserine or carbachol into rat brain, *Physiol. Behav.* **5**:693.

LEVITT, R. A., and FISHER, A. E., 1966, Anticholinergic blockade of centrally induced thirst, *Science* **154**:520-522.

MAICKEL, R. P., COX, R. H., KSIR, C. J., SNODGRASS, W. R., and MILLER, F. P., 1970, Some aspects of the behavioral pharmacology of the amphetamines, in: *International Symposium on Amphetamines and Related Compounds* (E. Costa and S. Garattini, eds.), pp. 747–760, Raven Press, New York.

MARSHALL, J. F., RICHARDSON, J. S., and TEITELBAUM, P., 1974, Nigrostriatal bundle damage and the lateral hypothalamic syndrome, *J. Comp. Physiol. Psychol.* **87:**808–830.

MENDELSON, J., 1970, Palatability, satiation, and thresholds for stimulus-bound drinking, *Physiol. Behav.* **5:**1295–1297.

MEYER, D. K., ABELE, M., and HERTTING, G., 1974, Influence of serotonin on water intake and the renin-angiotensin system in the rat, *Arch. Int. Pharmacodyn. Ther.* **212:**130–140.

MEYER, D. K., PESKAR, B., and HERTTING, G., 1971, Hemmung des durch blutdruchsenkende Pharmaka bei Ratten ausgelösten Trinkens durch Nephrectomie, *Experientia* **27:**65–66.

MEYER, D. K., RAUSCHER, W., PESKAR, B., and HERTTING, G., 1973, The mechanism of the drinking response to some hypotensive drugs: activation of the renin-angiotensin system by direct or reflex stimulation of beta-receptors, *Naunyn-Schmiedebergs Arch. Pharmacol.* **276:**13–24.

MILLER, N. E., and CHIEN, C. W., 1968, Drinking elicited by injecting eserine into preoptic area of rat brain, *Commun. Behav. Biol.* **1:**61–63.

MILLER, N. E., GOTTESMAN, K. S., and EMERY, N., 1964, Dose response to carbachol and norepinephrine in rat hypothalamus, *Am. J. Physiol.* **206:**1384–1388.

MOGENSON, G. J., and STEVENSON, J. A. F., 1966, Drinking and self-stimulation with electrical stimulation of the hypothalamus, *Physiol. Behav.* **1:**251–254.

MOGENSON, G. J., and STEVENSON, J. A. F., 1967, Drinking induced by electrical stimulation of the lateral hypothalamus, *Exp. Neurol.* **17:**119–127.

MONTEMURRO, D. G., and STEVENSON, J. A. F., 1957, Adipsia produced by hypothalamic lesions in the rat, *Can. J. Biochem. Physiol.* **35:**31–37.

MORGANE, P. J., 1961, Alterations in feeding and drinking behavior of rats with lesions in globi pallidi, *Am. J. Physiol.* **201:**420–428.

MORRISON, S. D., BARRNETT, R. J., and MAYER, J., 1958, Localization of lesions in the lateral hypothalamus of rats with induced adipsia and aphagia, *Am. J. Physiol.* **193:**230–234.

MYERS, R. D., 1964, Emotional and autonomic responses following hypothalamic chemical stimulation, *Can. J. Psychol.* **18:**6–14.

MYERS, R. D., and MARTIN, G. E., 1973, 6-OHDA lesions of the hypothalamus: interaction of aphagia, food palatability, set-point for weight regulation and recovery of feeding, *Pharmacol. Biochem. Behav.* **1:**329–345.

MYERS, R. D., HALL, G. D., and RUDY, T. A., 1973, Drinking in the monkey evoked by nicotine or angiotensin II microinjected in hypothalamic and mesencephalic sites, *Pharmacol. Biochem. Behav.* **1:**15–22.

OLDS, J., ALLAN, W. S., and BRIESE, E., 1971, Differentiation of hypothalamic drive and reward centers, *Am. J. Physiol.* **221:**368–375.

PALAIC, D., and KHAIRALLAH, P. A., 1968, Inhibition of norepinephrine reuptake by angiotensin in brain, *J. Neurochem.* **15:**1195–1202.

PARKER, S. W., and FELDMAN, S. M., 1967, Effect of mesencephalic lesions on feeding behavior in rats, *Exp. Neurol.* **17:**313–326.

PECK, J. W., and NOVIN, D., 1971, Evidence that osmoreceptors mediating drinking in rabbits are in the lateral preoptic area, *J. Comp. Physiol. Psychol.* **74:**134–147.

PERES, V. L., GENTIL, C. G., GRAEFF, F. G., and COVIAN, M. R., 1974, Antagonism of the dipsogenic action of intraseptal angiotensin II in the rat, *Pharmacol. Biochem. Behav.* **2:**597–602.

PESKAR, B., MEYER, D. K., TAUCHMANN, U., and HERTTING, G., 1970, Influence of isoproterenol, hydralazine and phentolamine on the renin activity of plasma and renal cortex of rats, *Eur. J. Pharmacol.* **9:**394–396.

RAISMAN, G., 1966, The connexions of the septum, *Brain* **89**:317-348.
ROBINSON, B. W., and MISHKIN, M., 1968, Alimentary responses to forebrain stimulation in monkeys, *Exp. Brain Res.* **4**:330-366.
ROLLS, B. J., 1970, Drinking by rats after irritative lesions in the hypothalamus, *Physiol. Behav.* **5**:1385-1393.
ROUTTENBERG, A., and SIMPSON, J. B., 1971, Carbachol-induced drinking at ventricular and subfornical organ sites of application, *Life Sci.* **10**:481-490.
SETLER, P. E., 1973, The role of catecholamines in thirst, in: *The Neuropsychology of Thirst: New Findings and Advances in Concepts* (A. N. Epstein, H. R. Kissileff, and E. Stellar, eds.), pp. 279-291, Winston, Washington, D. C.
SETLER, P. E., 1975, Noradrenergic and dopaminergic influences on thirst, in: *Control Mechanisms of Drinking* (G. Peters and J. T. Fitzsimons, eds.), pp. 62-68, Springer-Verlag, New York.
SHARPE, L. G., and MYERS, R. D., 1969, Feeding and drinking following stimulation of the diencephalon with amines and other substances, *Exp. Brain Res.* **8**:295-310.
SHARPE, L. G., and SWANSON, L. G., 1974, Drinking induced by injections of angiotensin into forebrain and mid-brain sites of the monkey, *J. Physiol. (London)* **239**:595-622.
SHUTE, C. C. D., and LEWIS, P. R., 1966, Cholinergic and monoaminergic pathways in the hypothalamus, *Brit. Med. Bull.* **22**:221-226.
SIMPSON, J. B., and ROUTTENBERG, A., 1973, Subfornical organ: site of drinking elicitation by angiotensin II, *Science* **181**:1172-1175.
SIMPSON, J. B., and ROUTTENBERG, A., 1974, Subfornical organ: acetylcholine application elicits drinking, *Brain Res.* **78**:49-56.
SIMPSON, J. B., and ROUTTENBERG, A., 1975, Subfornical organ lesions reduce intravenous angiotensin-induced drinking, *Brain Res.* **88**:154-161.
SIMPSON, J. B., EPSTEIN, A. N., and COMARDO, J. S., 1975, Ablation or competitive blockade of subfornical organ (SFO) prevents thirst of intravenous angiotensin, *Fed. Proc.* **34**:374.
SINGER, G., and ARMSTRONG, S., 1973, Cholinergic and beta-adrenergic compounds in the control of drinking behavior in the rat, *J. Comp. Physiol. Psychol.* **85**:453-462.
SMITH, G. P., 1973, Introduction: Neuropharmacology of thirst, in: *The Neuropsychology of Thirst: New Findings and Advances in Concepts* (A. N. Epstein, H. R. Kissileff, and E. Stellar, eds.), pp. 231-241, Winston, Washington, D. C.
SMITH, G. P., STROHMAYER, A. J., and REIS, D. J., 1972, Effect of lateral hypothalamic injections of 6-hydroxydopamine on food and water intake in rats, *Nature (London)* **235**:27-29.
SOMMER, S. R., NOVIN, D., and LEVINE, M., 1967, Food and water intake after intrahypothalamic injections of carbachol in the rabbit, *Science* **156**:983-984.
SOULAIRAC, A., and SOULAIRAC, M.-L., 1970, Effects of amphetamine-like substances and L-DOPA on thirst, water intake and diuresis, in: *International Symposium on Amphetamines and Related Compounds* (E. Costa and S. Garattini, eds.), pp. 819-840, Raven Press, New York.
STEIN, G. W., and LEVITT, R. A., 1971, Lesion effects on cholinergically elicited drinking in the rat, *Physiol. Behav.* **7**:517-522.
STEIN, L., 1963, Anticholinergic drugs and the central control of thirst, *Science* **139**:46-48.
STEVENSON, J. A. F., 1949, Effects of hypothalamic lesions on water and energy metabolism in the rat, *Recent Prog. Horm. Res.* **4**:363-394.
STEVENSON, J. A. F., WELT, L. G., and ORLOFF, J., 1950, Abnormalities of water and electrolyte metabolism in rats with hypothalamic lesions, *Am. J. Physiol.* **161**:35-39.
STRICKER, E. M., and WOLF, G., 1967, The effect of hypovolemia on drinking in rats with lateral hypothalamic damage, *Proc. Soc. Exp. Biol. Med.* **124**:816-820.
STRICKER, E. M., and ZIGMOND, M. J., 1974, Effect on homeostasis of intraventricular injections of 6-hydroxydopamine in rats, *J. Comp. Physiol. Psychol.* **86**:973-994.
TANG, M., and FALK, J. L., 1974, Sar^1-Ala^8 angiotensin II blocks renin-angiotensin but not beta-adrenergic dipsogeneses, *Pharmacol. Biochem. Behav.* **2**:401-408.

TEITELBAUM, P., and EPSTEIN, A. N., 1962, The lateral hypothalamic syndrome: recovery of feeding and drinking after lateral hypothalamic lesions, *Psychol. Rev.* **69**:74–90.

TEITELBAUM, P., and STELLAR, E., 1954, Recovery from the failure to eat produced by hypothalamic lesions, *Science* **120**:894–895.

UNGERSTEDT, U., 1971a, Stereotaxic mapping of the monoamine pathways in the rat brain, *Acta Physiol. Scand. Suppl.* **367**:1–48.

UNGERSTEDT, U., 1971b, Adipsia and aphagia after 6-hydroxydopamine induced degeneration of the nigrostriatal dopamine system, *Acta Physiol. Scand. Suppl.* **367**:95–122.

VERNEY, E. B., 1947, The antidiuretic hormone and the factors which determine its release, *Proc. Roy. Soc. London, Ser. B.* **135**:25–106.

VINCENT, J. D., ARNAULD, E., and BIOULAC, B., 1972, Activity of osmosensitive single cells in the hypothalamus of the behaving monkey during drinking, *Brain Res.* **44**:371–384.

WALSH, L. L., and GROSSMAN, S. P., 1973, Zona incerta lesions: disruption of regulatory water intake, *Physiol. Behav.* **11**:885–887.

WALSH, L. L., and GROSSMAN, S. P., 1974, Effects of zona incerta lesions and knife cuts on water intake following cellular and extracellular dehydration, presented at the Society for Neurosciences, St. Louis, Missouri, October, 1974.

WESTFALL, T. C., 1973, Effects of acetylcholine and the release of H^3-norepinephrine by nicotine and potassium chloride from rat brain slices, in: *Frontiers in Catecholamine Research* (E. Usdin and S. Snyder, eds.), pp. 618–619, Pergamon Press, New York.

WINSON, J., and MILLER, N. E., 1970, Comparison of drinking elicited by eserine or DFP injected into the preoptic area of the rat brain, *J. Comp. Physiol. Psychol.* **73**:233–237.

WISE, R. A., 1971, Individual differences in effects of hypothalamic stimulation: the role of stimulation locus, *Physiol. Behav.* **6**:569–572.

WISHART, T. B., and MOGENSON, G. J., 1970, Reduction of water intake by electrical stimulation of the septal region of the rat brain, *Physiol. Behav.* **5**:1399–1404.

WOLF, A. V., 1950, Osmometric analysis of thirst in man and dog, *Am. J. Physiol.* **161**:75–86.

WOLF, G., and MILLER, N. E., 1964, Lateral hypothalamic lesion effects on drinking elicited by carbachol in preoptic area and posterior hypothalamus, *Science* **143**:585–587.

YANG, H. Y. T., and NEFF, N. H., 1972, Distribution and properties of angiotensin-converting enzyme of the rat brain, *J. Neurochem.* **19**:2443–2450.

ZIGMOND, M. J., and STRICKER, E. M., 1972, Deficits in feeding behavior after intraventricular injection of 6-hydroxydopamine in rats, *Science* **177**:1211–1214.

ZIGMOND, M. J., and STRICKER, E. M., 1973, Recovery of feeding and drinking by rats after intraventricular 6-hydroxydopamine or lateral hypothalamic lesions, *Science* **182**:717–720.

5

PHARMACOLOGICAL AND HORMONAL CONTROL OF REPRODUCTIVE BEHAVIOR

Bengt J. Meyerson and Mona Eliasson

1. INTRODUCTION

Reproductive behavior consists of a sequence of behavior patterns which under natural conditions appear in a certain fixed order. Thus, the copulatory behavior is preceded by the seeking of sexual contact, orientation toward a certain partner, and some form of courtship or sexual presentation. In experimental work the behavior under study must be given a clearcut and precise definition. This means that under experimental conditions, a certain behavior pattern is often studied, isolated, and dissected out from its normal place in the biological sequence of performance. The production of reproductive behavior is achieved by a complicated central nervous integration of environmental and endogenous stimuli. In studying the effects of drugs and hormones on a certain component of the reproductive behavior we also, as far as possible, keep the environmental conditions constant. In the laboratory this means artificial climate (controlled light regimen, temperature, humidity) and diet (standard pellet chow), and that animals are kept in cages with a certain sex ratio and number of cage mates. Our knowledge of how drugs and hormones influence reproductive behavior is based on investigations conducted, under controlled and defined, but also highly artificial, conditions. This fact must be borne in mind when we generalize from the

---

Bengt J. Meyerson and Mona Eliasson • University of Uppsala, Department of Medical Pharmacology, Biomedicum, Box 573, S-751 23, Uppsala, Sweden.

laboratory to the natural state. Obviously a mutual exchange of data must go on continuously between people working in the laboratory and those in the field in order to avoid studies of behavior artifacts which are products of the experimental design.

This overview will be restricted to the effect of hormones and drugs on reproductive behavior in some selected mammalian species, mainly the laboratory rat. The behavior patterns considered are *sexual behavior* and *parental behavior*. Sexual behavior means the urge to seek sexual contact as well as the behavior observed during the copulatory act. Parental behavior includes nest building, behavior in connection with feeding the pups, and patterns displayed to care for the pups in other ways. Both sexual and parental behavior are to a certain extent hormone dependent. Evidence is provided that some elements of reproductive behavior are produced by a local hormonal effect on the CNS. Hormones and drugs could interfere with reproductive behavior by a direct effect on mechanisms involved in the production of the behavior. However, hormones and drugs could also act on the behavior indirectly by an effect on the CNS–pituitary–hormone secretory organ systems, thereby increasing or decreasing an endogenous hormone secretion of significance for the behavior. Figure 1 depicts the possible loci of action. Besides a direct or indirect effect on CNS mechanisms, hormones

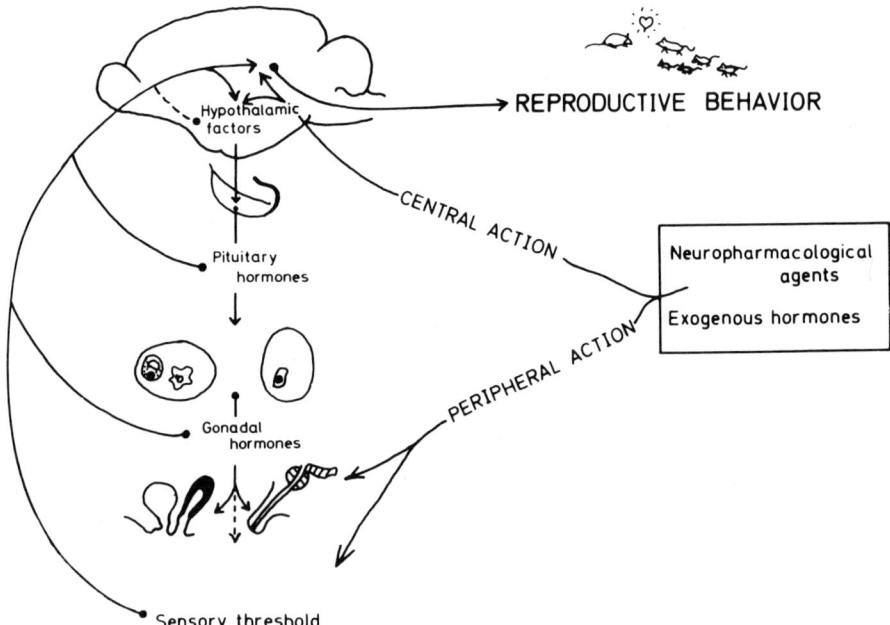

FIG. 1. Schematic diagram of possible loci of action of hormonal or neuropharmacological treatments on reproductive behavior.

and drugs could change a relevant sensory input by acting on peripheral sensory receptors and thereby changing their responsiveness to environmental stimuli.

2. Ontogeny of Sexual Behavior

An overview of the influence of hormones and drugs on the development of structures which mediate the expression of sexual behavior will be given. Reviews in the field have appeared and are referred to in the text below (Whalen, 1971; Goy and Resko, 1972; Money and Ehrhardt, 1972; Goy and Goldfoot, 1973). For basic concepts in the field see Beach (1948) and Young (1961).

2.1. Hormones and Development of Sexual Behavior: Sexual Dimorphism

Although a certain variability occurs between different species, it is easy to distinguish a typical male pattern of the *copulatory behavior* which involves mounting the sexual partner, pelvic thrusting, and intromission and ejaculation behavior. The female characteristics are lordosis (in infraprimate species), tail deviation, and treading or other posture to facilitate penile intromission. These typical motor patterns are easily recognized and only seen in connection with the copulatory act. It should be emphasized, however, that both feminine and masculine reactions are seen in either sex, but the male pattern is more frequent in the genetic male than in the female, and vice versa (see Beach, 1948; Young, 1961). The display of copulatory behavior is to a certain extent dependent on gonadal hormones (see below) and does not normally occur in its full expression until the endogenous hormone production is appropriate for producing the behavior. Elements of copulatory behavior can, however, be seen in certain species also during early adolescence. The adult male is usually capable of mating at any time, whereas the female mammal is characterized by periods of sexual activity. This difference between the sexes is to a certain extent dependent on the cyclic pattern of gonadotropin and ovarian hormone secretion in the female and the tonic hormonal secretion in the male. The copulatory behavior is most likely preceded by a state in which the individual seeks sexual contact and orients toward a partner (see Fig. 3). This condition will in the following be called *sexual motivation*. The attempt to distinguish motivation, in this sense, from the probability that a certain behavioral response like mounting or lordosis will occur is made because we believe the production of the motivational state and the following consummatory response could be controlled by different neuroendocrine and neuropharmacological principles. The existence of heterosexual motivation in the adult subject is indicated by preference studies in some species, and the relationship to gonadal hormones will be discussed in the following sections. It is not clear if there are sex-specific behavior patterns associated with the seeking of sexual contact and sexual orientation.

Accumulating evidence demonstrates that sexual differentiation of the copulatory behavior is influenced by *hormonal* factors. This hormonal influence on sexual differentiation is limited to a particular period of development. Hormonal manipulation during a pre- or neonatal period will influence the proportion of masculine and feminine copulatory behavior of this individual in adulthood.

2.1.1. Genetic Females; Female Copulatory Behavior

Phoenix *et al.* (1959) showed that TP* given to pregnant guinea pigs brought about a female offspring less responsive as adult to the lordotic-behavior-activating effect of estrogen + progesterone. The degree of inhibition of the feminine copulatory behavior was related to TP dosage given to the mothers. Harris and Levine (1962, 1965) showed that female rats treated with TP at 5 days of age failed to display the estrogen + progesterone activated lordotic behavior as adults. These findings have subsequently been confirmed and extended (Barraclough and Gorski, 1962; Grady *et al.*, 1965; Whalen and Edwards, 1967; Hendricks, 1969; Clemens *et al.*, 1970; Dörner, 1970; Pfaff and Zigmond, 1971; Sheridan *et al.*, 1973) and it is today well established that *androgen treatment at an appropriate period of early development* results in the female type of copulatory behavior being less responsive or no longer activated by exogenous EB + progesterone treatment in adulthood, a hormonal treatment which otherwise is effective in producing lordosis in spayed females.

In addition to the rat and guinea pig, this has been shown in the mouse (Edwards and Burge, 1971), hamster (Carter *et al.*, 1972; Coniglio *et al.*, 1973), and dog (Beach and Kuehn, 1970). The evidence of a similar change of dimorphous sexual behavior patterns in primates and humans due to exposure to androgen during a certain developmental period is reviewed by Goy and co-workers (Goy and Phoenix, 1971; Goy and Resko, 1972) and Money and Ehrhardt (1972). Also EB and other steroids (see below) administered neonatally are, in the female rat, effective in suppressing the estrogen + progesterone activated lordosis response in adulthood (Whalen and Nadler, 1963; Levine and Mullins, 1964).

* The following abbreviations are used in this chapter: TP, testosterone propionate; DHT, dihydrotestosterone propionate; EB, estradiol benzoate; 5-HTP, L-5-hydroxytryptophan; 5-HT, 5-hydroxytryptamine; NE, norepinephrine; DA, dopamine; dopa, L-dihydroxyphenylalanine; PCPA, *p*-chlorophenylalanine; α-MT, α-methyl-*p*-tyrosine; DOPS, DL-dihydroxyphenylserine.

2.1.2. Genetic Females; Male Copulatory Behavior

Early reports by Phoenix *et al.* (1959) and Harris and Levine (1962) stated that adult treatment with TP brought about more masculine behavior in the pre- or neonatally androgenized female than in normal female subjects. There are other reports in accordance with these using pre- or postnatal treatment with TP, androstenedione, or EB (Levine and Mullins, 1964; Gerall and Ward, 1966; Ward, 1969; Stern, 1969; Sachs *et al.,* 1973; Sheridan *et al.,* 1973; Södersten, 1973a), but at present it is not quite clear whether all elements of the male copulatory behavior are facilitated in the genetic female by the neonatal hormonal manipulation. Whalen and Edwards (1967) and Whalen *et al.* (1969) found no effect on mounting responses, but there was an increase in intromission frequency. Pfaff and Zigmond (1971) reported that neonatally androgenized female rats were not different from control females in masculine-behavior tests. The diversity in reported effects could be attributed to experimental differences, but clearly the influence of TP on elements of male copulatory behavior in the genetic female has to be analyzed further to be fully understood.

2.1.3. Genetic Male; Male Copulatory Behavior

The intromission and ejaculation type of response of the male copulatory behavior are affected by neonatal castration (Beach and Holz, 1946; Whalen, 1964; Grady *et al.,* 1965). Male rats castrated 1–3 days after birth displayed decreased or complete absence of intromission and/or ejaculatory response to TP treatment in adulthood compared to males castrated two weeks after birth or later. This decrease in the masculine copulatory behavior is prevented by neonatal TP treatment given within the first week of life (Harris, 1964; Larsson, 1966; Whalen and Edwards, 1966, 1967; Beach *et al.,* 1969). The effect of early castration on mounting reactions varies between different reports. It is a consistent finding that mounting behavior is less affected than intromission and ejaculation patterns by early hormonal manipulation. Beach and Holz (1946) found mounts without intromission to increase in day 1 castrated males. According to Whalen and Edwards (1967), males castrated at birth mounted as frequently as males castrated in adulthood, and neonatal TP treatment led to no further effect on adult mounting behavior. A further investigation into this matter should consider a change in sensitivity to different doses of TP in adulthood with respect to the mounting reaction. A decrease in adult sensitivity to TP in this respect is indicated by the data of Larsson (1967).

2.1.4. Genetic Males; Female Copulatory Behavior

Castration of male rats at different ages (Grady *et al.,* 1965; Gerall *et al.,* 1967) revealed that castration at day 1 or 5 brought about a more frequent lordosis response when the males were given estrogen + progesterone treatment as adults. Males castrated at or after 10 days of age were not different from males castrated after puberty in this respect, i.e., did not very often display any lordosis response. Male rats castrated at birth and given TP or estrogen did not display the feminine lordotic patterns as adults (Whalen and Edwards, 1966).

2.1.5. Sexual Motivation

Sexual motivation in the female rat studied in terms of the willingness to cross over an electric grid to reach a sexually active male and also as the preference for a male versus a female in a choice situation (Meyerson and Lindström, 1973a) was modified by neonatal hormone treatment. EB increased the response in both situations in females ovariectomized in adulthood, but no EB-induced response was seen in subjects which had received 1 mg TP per animal at 5 days of age (Meyerson and Lindström, 1973b). In the male golden hamster castrated at birth, sexual preference for a male was induced by EB + progesterone treatment in adulthood. Males castrated as adults did not show any preference on this treatment (Johnson and Tiefer, 1972). In the female dog, the readiness to coital activity is reflected in the sexual presentation and to certain extent also in the social interaction intensity between members of a pair. Beach and Kuehn (1970) found the female dog's presentation response decreased or abolished in pre- and neonatally androgen-treated female beagles. Females exposed to testosterone from early infancy or *in utero* + infancy reacted to ovarian hormones in adulthood with a significant reduction in social interaction to the stimulus male. It was further the author's subjective impression "that several individuals in both of the groups involved appeared to exhibit an increased tendency to avoid or actively reject contact with the stimulus male during the period of hormone treatment."

2.1.6. Factors Which Influence the Effect of Neonatal Hormone Treatment

Most of the available data have been obtained in experiments on the rat. From these data it is concluded that the most consistent finding from experiments on pre- or neonatal hormonal manipulation is an effect on the feminine copulatory behavior (Table 1). Effects on the masculine elements of copulatory behavior exist but are less consistent. Stimulation by the testes or exogenous testosterone proprionate during a certain phase of the development decrease the potential for lordosis response in both sexes. The hypothesis which has emerged from these data is that prior to a period of hormonal differentiation the system which controls mating is essentially feminine (see Fig. 2 for a schematic diagram). If the organism continues to develop through the differentiation period without appropriate hormonal

TABLE 1
The Effects of Neonatal Hormonal Manipulation on Hormone-Activated Copulatory Behavior in the Adult Rat[a]

Sex	Treatment in adulthood	Copulatory behavior pattern	Effect of neonatal manipulation compared to normal pattern			
			Gonadectomy	Gonadectomy + TP	Gonadectomy + EB	TP or EB
Female	TP	Mounting	None	None	None	Increase to none
		Intromission	None to slight	Increase	None	Increase to none
	EB + progesterone	Lordosis	None	Inhibition	Inhibition	Inhibition
Male	TP	Mounting	None to decrease	None	None	None
		Intromission	Decrease	Increase[b]	None	None
	EB + progesterone	Lordosis	Increase	None	None	None

[a] Based on data taken from Barraclough and Gorski (1962); Grady et al. (1965); Whalen and Edwards (1967); Clemens et al. (1969); Pfaff and Zigmond (1971); and Sheridan et al. (1973).
[b] Compared to animal castrated neonatally, but less than normal.

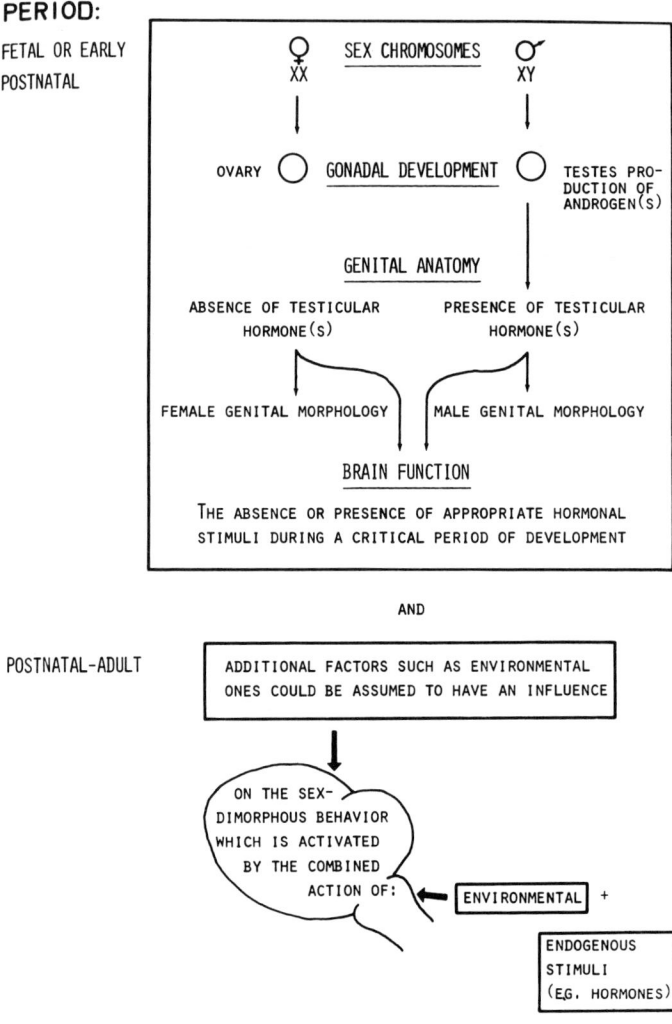

FIG. 2. Diagram to illustrate proposed components in the development of sex-dimorphous behavior. Modified from Money and Ehrhardt (1972).

stimulation, it will later respond in a feminine manner to stimulation with gonadal hormones. With appropriate hormonal stimulation during a critical period of development the adult pattern of sexual behavior will, under the additional factors of environment and genome, become masculine. Available data from experiments on exogenous hormonal influence on the differentiation of sexual behavior in the rat suggest a relationship between the effect of the hormone treatment and the following factors: (a) pre- and/or postnatal period of hormonal exposure; (b) amount of hormone; (c) length of time of hormonal exposure; (d) appropriate type of hormone; (e) extent of dimorphism in the element of hormone-dependent behavior. These factors will now be discussed.

a. The Critical Period of Hormonal Exposure. It is now generally held that the particular period of hormone-induced sexual differentiation is related to the developmental stage of the animal rather than a definite ontogenetic or neonatal age (see Goy and Phoenix, 1971). The exact critical period when testosterone is effective in altering the development of the adult display of the dimorphous behavior in the monkey is not known. In a study by Goy and Phoenix (1971) TP was given from the 39th through 70th or 105th day of gestational age. In the guinea pig, TP is most effective in inhibiting the display of sexual receptivity in the adult female offspring if given to the pregnant guinea pig from days 30–35 of gestation. Given before day 25 or after day 45, no effect or very weak effects were seen (Goy *et al.*, 1964). In the rat this critical period was found to be 0–10 days of age (Goy *et al.*, 1962; Beach *et al.*, 1969). In the rhesus monkey the secretion of testosterone and androstenedione was higher in males than in females during fetal age 100–150 days. The androgen level was not measurable a few weeks after birth and did not reappear until puberty at 3 years of age (Resko, 1970). Androgen concentration in plasma of the male rat was elevated during the first 5 days of life and then declined (Resko *et al.*, 1968).

Is the "critical period" for a certain species and element of behavior the same in genetic males and females? Lordotic behavior was more frequent in males castrated at day 1 than day 5 of age (Gerall *et al.*, 1967). TP was more effective in inhibiting lordosis response in neonatally castrated males when given day 1, 2 than 3, 4 (Beach *et al.*, 1969). In females TP was more effective in inhibiting the estrogen + progesterone activated lordotic behavior displayed in adulthood when given at 4 or 6 days of age than at day 1 or 2 (Clemens *et al.*, 1969). Thus, there are data to indicate that for a particular element of behavior the critical period could be somewhat different between the two genetic sexes. One possible explanation of this could be a difference in the rate of development since the critical period is related to developmental age, with males reaching this age slightly earlier than females.

Within the same species and genetic sex the different neuroendocrine functions which are hormonally influenced during a developmental stage of differentiation exhibit different "critical periods." A good illustration of this is provided by the comparison of the effect of neonatal TP treatment on lordotic behavior and cyclic gonadotropin secretion in the female rat. After neonatal TP treatment females develop a malelike noncyclic gonadotropin secretion. There is an extensive literature to demonstrate that this is caused by neonatal exposure to testicular hormones (Barraclough and Gorski, 1961; Gorski, 1971). The effect of exogenous TP treatment in inducing masculine gonadotropin secretion is achieved when the hormone is given within 2 days of birth (Gorski, 1968). As mentioned above, TP was more effective in inhibiting the lordotic behavior when given at 4–6 days of age. Thus, the optimal time for TP interference is different for gonadotropin and behavioral regulatory mechanisms. It is not known for a given genetic sex if the various behavioral elements influenced by early hormonal manipulation have different critical periods. There is some evidence that the lordotic behavior and the masculine elements of copulatory behavior have different critical periods, but the data are obtained under such different experimental conditions that comparisons are hardly possible.

Thus, an estimate of the critical period of hormonal influence on sexual differentiation must consider (1) the developmental stage of the animal, (2) that for the same element of behavior the period could be different in the two sexes, and (3) that within the same sex, different elements of behavior under hormonal influence could have different critical periods.

The main interest has been focused on the role of the testes in sexual development. Although less certain, prepuberal ovarian influence on sexual development is indicated by some recent data. Dunlop *et al.* (1972) and Gerall *et al.* (1967) reported that male rats castrated and given ovarian implants at birth displayed more feminine copulatory behavior than males which had only been castrated. Females ovariectomized at birth and then injected with TP at 3 days of age displayed less EB + progesterone induced lordosis response in adulthood than females ovariectomized at 20 or 60 days of age (Hendricks and Duffy, 1974). The physiological significance of these data is at present difficult to assess; however a new field for further investigations is opened up.

b. The Amount of Hormone and Appropriate Length of Time of Hormonal Exposure. What is the dose of a neonatal hormone necessary to interfere with the display of the behavior in adulthood for a certain species, genetic sex, and a certain element of behavior? In the female rat the optimal time of neonatal administration of TP for decreasing the adult display of the lordotic response was shown to be day 4–6 of age and the effective dose was 10 μg of TP (Clemens *et al.*, 1969). When the dose was increased to 100 μg the treatment was effective also when given on day 1, 2, 4, or 6, but 500 μg was ineffective when given on day 30.

Sheridan *et al.* (1973) found that a total of 1.0 μg TP but not 0.1 μg TP rendered the female less responsive to estrogen + protesterone treatment as adult. Their treatment was given 0.05 × 2 or 0.005 × 2 during days 1–10. It is not possible to compare the effectiveness of different treatments between different reports. However, the fact that TP or implanted capsules with testosterone (Whalen and Rezak, 1974) is more effective than injection of unconjugated testosterone (Luttge and Whalen, 1970) would speak in favor of the fact that the time during which the tissue is exposed to the androgen is important and that, in addition, the androgen has to be given at a certain critical period. The total amount of hormone necessary to induce androgenization is less when a longer time of exposure is achieved by repeated injection or using esterified androgen derivatives. For comparison with the above-mentioned exogenous doses of hormone the amount of testosterone in plasma for the first 5 days of life in the rat is around 0.027 µg/100 ml (Resko et al., 1968).

c. *Appropriate Type of Hormone.* The fact that neonatal EB treatment also androgenizes the female rat raises the question of other steroid hormones than testosterone secreted by the testes being biologically effective compounds. The possibility that aromatization of testosterone could be involved in the androgenizing syndrome has been investigated (Brown-Grant et al., 1971; McDonald and Doughty, 1972a,b, 1974). Neural tissue from fetal and neonatal rats is capable of converting the testosterone metabolite androstenedione to estrogens (Reddy et al., 1974; Weisz and Gibbs, 1974). The nonaromatizable androgen dihydrotestosterone did not inhibit lordotic behavior when given neonatally (Whalen and Rezak, 1974). A relationship between suppression of lordotic behavior in females and aromatizable or nonaromatizable androgens has, however, not won experimental support (McDonald and Doughty, 1974). Although evidence has been provided that the testes of the male rhesus monkey and rat secrete testosterone during the fetal or neonatal critical period (Resko et al., 1968; Resko, 1970), it is still not elucidated whether the testosterone secreted is the effective androgen stimulus or if some metabolites of testosterone are more effective in producing the sexual differentiation. The neonatal effects of testosterone, given to females or secreted in males, can be inhibited by the androgen antagonist cyproterone (Neumann et al., 1970). The antiestrogen MER-25 was found also to block the sterilizing effect of TP given to 5-day-old female rats (McDonald and Doughty, 1972b). A comparison of the capacity of different steroids to interfere with sexual differentiation reveals that different neuroendocrine functions and elements of behavior have different sensitivity to the androgenization effect of different steroids (see Luttge and Whalen, 1970; McDonald and Doughty, 1974). Cyproterone acetate given to neonatal males was effective in inhibiting the OB- and TP-induced mounting behavior in adulthood, but no effect was seen on the probability of display of the lordosis (Dörner et al., 1971). This could be due to the time of exposure as Ward found that prenatal exposure to cyproterone acetate clearly increased the estrogen + progesterone activated lordosis response (Ward, 1972).

d. *Extent of Dimorphism.* Besides sexual behavior, other sexually dimorphic behavior patterns have been reported to be influenced by the presence or absence of androgen during a critical neonatal period (for a review, see Goy and Goldfoot, 1973). The activities include open-field behavior (Gray et al., 1969; Pfaff and Zigmond, 1971; Quadagno et al., 1972), maternal behavior (Quadagno and Rockwell, 1972; Bridges et al., 1973), cyclic wheel running activity (Harris, 1964), micturation pattern (Berg, 1944; Martins and Valle, 1944), growth rate (Slob et al., 1973), oxygen consumption (Goy, 1968), and aggressive behavior (Conner and Levine, 1969). The effects of early androgen treatment are not restricted to sexual behavior but to dimorphous behavior patterns influenced by gonadal hormones. Sexually isomorphic behavior like the lordosis response in guinea pigs in response to manual stimulation on the day of birth is not influenced by prenatal androgen treatment (Goy and Phoenix, 1971).

2.1.7. Loci of Action

The study of Nadler (1968) who implanted TP in different areas of the neonatal rat brain is consistent with the hypothesis that ventral parts of the brain are implicated in the androgenizing effect of TP. The effect of early hormonal influence on mechanisms involved in sexual differentiation might not only be on cerebral tissue but also at the spinal level and on peripheral gonadal hormone target tissue. Hart (1968b) has shown that spinal male rats, which had been castrated at 4 or 12 days after birth, had a reduced frequency of genital reflexes, pointing to the possibility of sexual differentiation of the spinal cord. Besides an effect on neural tissue, early hormonal stimulation during a critical period of sexual differentiation might also organize peripheral hormone target tissue to respond to hormonal stimulation in adulthood. The neonatally castrated male rat not only exhibits a decrement in certain patterns of copulatory behavior, like intromission and ejaculation, but also shows incomplete penile development on TP treatment in adulthood (Beach and Holtz, 1946; Grady *et al.*, 1965; Whalen, 1968). Furthermore, peripheral target tissue, essential for the copulatory behavior, goes through a critical period of differentiation itself. Thus, the insufficient penile development and decreased sensitivity to testosterone could contribute to the incomplete copulatory behavior in the neonatally castrated male (for further discussion, see Whalen, 1968; Stern, 1969; Beach, 1970).

By convention we think in terms of sexual behavior being activated by testosterone in the male and by estrogen with or without progesterone in the female. In this context it is an important fact that the ovary has the capacity to produce testosterone, and the testes to manufacture estradiol (Saez *et al.*, 1972; Falvo *et al.*, 1972). The amount of sex hormones in the circulation after puberty is, however, quite different in the two sexes. This is mainly due to a sex difference in the gonadal biosynthesis and also in tissue metabolic transformation. The mechanisms that determine this sex difference in the adult pattern of biosynthesis are not well understood. Besides genetic factors the specific biosynthesis might be programmed by the fetal or neonatal androgen secretion. Considering the different loci of sexual differentiation and their relationship to the production of hormone-induced feminine and masculine sexual behavior in adulthood, the differentiation of the sex-steroid biosynthesis, which might play an important role, should not be omitted. Also tissue metabolism of sex steroid hormones could have an important function in this context. The sex difference here is evident at puberty (for a review, see Denéf, 1973) and is also under the influence of neonatal androgen. The sex difference in liver metabolism became smaller, with a change in the male to a pattern more like that of the female, when gonadectomy was conducted at or before 5 days of age. Most effective was castration 10 hr after birth. No difference was seen when castration was performed at 10 days of age (DeMoor and Denéf, 1968; Denéf and DeMoor, 1968). The hypothesis that the differentiation of the liver enzymes at puberty is mediated by pituitary hormones is discussed by Denéf (1973). Animals hypophysectomized and gonadectomized at 25 days of age had a clearly masculine metabolic pattern which was turned into a female pattern by female pituitaries implanted at 35 days of age. The interpretation of these data given by Denéf is that the female pituitary secretion governs a feminine type of liver steroid metabolism. The neonatal androgen action in the male inhibits this pituitary signal.

It seems clear that the effect of early endogenous or exogenous hormonal stimulation, which leads to sexual differentiation, has several loci of action. The dimorphism in sexual behavior as displayed in adulthood is the integration of an action on different hormonal target cells at the cerebral, spinal, gonadal, and peripheral genital levels. In addition we must also consider the significance of secondary processes of differentiation, which appear as a consequence of the endocrine process during the fetal or neonatal critical period, e.g., altered patterns of steroid metabolism. The secondary processes should not only be sought in endogenous events, but also in the interaction with the environment. For instance, in the androgenized female rhesus monkey, dimorphous play patterns are something in between the normal pattern of a female and male (Goy and Phoenix, 1971). This should influence the behavior of, for example, playmates, with consequences for the behavior which will be exhibited in adulthood by the androgenized female. (For clinical aspects on this topic see Money, 1971.)

2.1.8. Mechanism of Action

What is known about the mechanism of action of early androgen treatment on a cellular or subcellular level? Effects on the retention of radioactive sex hormones in brains of adult rats have been reported after neonatal hormone treatment. Androgenized females and genetic males have a lower retention of [^{3}H]estradiol in the hypothalamus than do normal females (Anderson and Greenwald, 1969; Flérko *et al.*, 1969; Green *et al.*, 1969; McGuire and Lisk, 1969; McEwen and Pfaff, 1970). This would be consistent with an altered hormone sensitivity to gonadal hormones and could subsequently explain some of the behavioral effects seen after neonatal hormone treatment. However, Whalen and co-workers have provided data which showed that the differences obtained in male and female cerebral uptake of estradiol disappeared when the experimental animals are matched with respect to body weight (Green *et al.*, 1969). Thus, it has not yet been accepted that a changed retention of sex hormones could contribute to the mechanism of neonatal hormonal differentiation effects.

The role of protein synthesis in the androgenization effect of TP is discussed by Gorski (1973) on the basis of studies of the effects of hypothalamic implants of various agents known to interfere with protein synthesis. Different DNA and RNA synthesis inhibitors did not mimic the action of TP when implanted in the preoptic area of the hypothalamus. When testing to find out if different antibiotics could attenuate the TP action, Gorski and Shryne (1972) found only cycloheximide to slightly reduce the effect of the TP action. There are other results suggesting that protein synthesis might be involved in the sexual differentiation processes. Sex differences and effects of testosterone on brain RNA metabolism and synthesis have been reported in neonatal rats (Clayton et al., 1970; Shimada and Gorbman, 1970; Salamann, 1970; Soriero and Ford, 1973).

2.2. Monoamines, Drugs, and Development of Sexual Behavior

Hypothetically a great number of morphological and neurochemical correlates have been implicated in the process of sexual differentiation. Emphasis will be given to monoaminergic mechanisms as a great deal of evidence suggests that they are involved in both the production of sexual behavior (see below) and the cerebral control of pituitary gonadotropic hormone secretion (for a recent review, see De Wied and de Jong, 1974). The dimorphous pattern of both these functions are under early hormonal influence (see Gorski, 1973).

2.2.1. Ontogeny of Monoaminergic Neurons

Using the technique of fluorescence histochemistry, primordium of monoaminergic neurons can be demonstrated in the rat brain as early as gestation days 12–14. Thus, the differentiation and the development of NA-, DA-, and 5-HT-containing neuron systems is started prenatally (see Olson and Seiger, 1972; Seiger and Olson, 1973). Judging from biochemical evidence there is, during the process of maturation, a translocation of biosynthesizing enzyme activity from regions that contain the cell bodies to the regions that contain the terminals of these neurons. It is assumed that this regional shift of activity, which is seen mainly just after birth, reflects the outgrowth of axons (Lamprecht and Coyle, 1972; Coyle and Axelrod, 1972a,b; Loizou, 1972; Keller et al., 1973). Thus, although the full-term rat fetus has most monoaminergic neuronal pathways well developed, the final complete outgrowth of axons and terminals is a postnatal event and takes place during the first 3 weeks of life. An interesting exception is the catecholamine-containing cell bodies of various hypothalamic areas and nerve terminals in the median eminence region which cannot be histologically demonstrated at all 2–3 days after birth. These neurons rapidly develop during the first weeks of life (Loizou, 1971; Seiger and Olson, 1973). The suggested site of cerebral hormonal action related to sexual differentiation is the hypothalamus (Nadler, 1968; see also Gorski, 1973). The coincidence in time for hormonal sexual differentiation and the development of monoaminergic (hypothalamic) pathways, taken together with the fact that various hormones (thyroid, corticosteroid, and estrogens) are known to influence the biochemical maturation of the brain (Schapiro, 1968; Baláz, 1971; Hudson *et al.*, 1970), leads naturally to the question of whether gonadal hormones could influence sexual differentiation by means of an action on the maturation of neurons specifically involved in the adult display of feminine or masculine hormone-dependent behavior.

2.2.2. Early Sex Differences in Brain Monoamines

Kato reported (1960) that female brains contained more 5-HT than male brains and that it had been found in a preliminary experiment that estradiol (15 μg/g per day for 7 days) increased the brain serotonin content both in young female rats and adult male rats. On the other hand, treatment with testosterone (2 μg/g per day for 7 days) did not change the brain serotonin level in female or young male rats. Ladoski and Gaziri (1970) reported a significant increase in 5-HT concentration in the female rat brain at age 12 days but could find no sex differences at age 1, 4, or 8 days. The combination of biochemical and histochemical analysis of hypothalamic NA and 5-HT in normal and neonatally TP-treated females or castrated male rats revealed no significant change between control and treated subjects at 30 days of age in an investigation by Hyyppä and Rinne (1971). Hardin (1973*a,b*) found that neonatal male brains (2 days of age) synthesized less 5-HT than female brains. No sex difference was found in the monoamine oxidase activity. Sex differences in NA, DA, or 5-HT levels were not statistically significant at age 5 or 10 days, but at age 2 days male brains contained approximately 15% more NA and 37% less 5-HT than did littermate female brains. Females which received TP, 300 μg s.c. at age 5 days had significantly higher NA and lower histamine values at age 10 days compared with oil-treated controls. Also DA and 5-HT increased, but these differences did not reach statistical significance. Giulian *et al.* (1973) demonstrated that female rats have higher 5-HT content than males in forebrain + midbrain measured at days 10, 12, and 14, but that no differences were obtained before or after this period. In 12-day-old subjects treated with estogen or androgen at day 1, the highest 5-HT values were obtained in estogen-treated females and males, and the lowest in untreated males and testosterone-treated females. These authors propose that the transient increase of 5-HT levels in the female brain at day 10–14 reflects an increase in ovarian activity. Estrogen given day 1 should facilitate the development of the 5-HT system, and androgen treatment at the same time should block ovarian function and/or decrease cerebral sensitivity for estrogen. Neither EB nor TP changed the 5-HT levels in 25-day-old females or males when given at or after day 20, indicating that the sensitivity to gonadal steroid effects on brain 5-HT was not permanent. The data and hypothesis are exciting but should be confirmed with further experiments to elucidate the specificity of the changes in 5-HT levels after neonatal hormonal manipulation. Transient sex differences and effects of steroid hormones on amine levels might be related to a sex difference in rate of maturation of the brain.

2.2.3. Alteration of Adult Sexual Behavior by Drugs Given Neonatally

The use of psychopharmacological agents is based upon knowledge of their specific action on certain aspects of neuronal function such as binding to receptor sites, interference with amine-storage mechanisms, or inhibition of enzymes related to biosynthesis or metabolism of biogenic amines. The specificity of the drug action and the rationale for its use require that the neurons have reached an adequate state of maturation, i.e., that the mechanism influenced by the drug has developed. It is evident from the studies of Loizou (1972) and Seiger and Olson (1973) that the neuroblast of the embryonal rat brain could take up amine precursors and react to reserpine and monoamine oxidase inhibitors like the adult neuron. In other words, before completion of the morphological development, synthesis and storage of monoamines is possible in the neuroblast.

There are comparatively few investigations as to the effect of drugs given during the pre- or neonatal period and the effect of this treatment on the adult sexual behavior. The first report is by Tuchmann-Duplessis and Mercier-Parot (1963) who reported that chronic treatment of female rats with the monoamine oxidase inhibitor nialamide led to a female offspring which refused to accept males mounting while displaying vigorous mounting of cage mates themselves. Zucker and Feder (1966) found that female rats neonatally treated with estrogen and reserpine or with estrogen alone had significantly lower scores for lordotic behavior than vehicle-treated controls. Reserpine did not protect female rats from the adverse effect of estradiol. Lehtinen et al. (1972) demonstrated that neonatal administration of reserpine did not alter hormone-induced female sexual behavior in adult female rats. Males needed fewer intromissions to ejaculate than controls. Hyyppä et al. (1972) showed that PCPA given to male and female rats on the second and third and on the fifth and sixth postnatal day brought about only minor changes in the female display of lordotic behavior when the animal had reached adulthood. Male rats injected neonatally with PCPA displayed significantly higher mount and intromission frequencies and shorter intromission and ejaculation latencies.

Neonatal reserpine treatment has been shown to block the development of the pattern of gonadotropin secretion in the male rat (Kawashima, 1964) and in neonatally testosterone-treated females (Kikuyama, 1961) and to decrease pituitary luteinizing hormone contents at 30 and 60 days of age (Carraro et al., 1965). A similar effect was obtained with chlorpromazine treatment in the androgenized female (Kikuyama, 1962). The influence of other drugs like barbiturates and antibiotics on the sexual differentiation of the CNS–pituitary ovarian functions has been described by Gorski (1973) and Arai and Gorski (1968). As will be discussed below, evidence has been provided that there are monoaminergic pathways which mediate inhibition of the hormone-activated lordosis response in ovariectomized female rats (see Section 3.3.2). The possibility of facilitating female copulatory behavior in adult castrated males and neonatally androgenized females by EB in combination with amine depletors like reserpine was investigated by Meyerson (1968a). Ovariectomized rats which have received androgen respond differently to EB than untreated controls, and this difference is not abolished by amine-depleting agents. Reserpine or tetrabenazine treatment was, however, more effective than progesterone in inducing lordosis in EB-treated males castrated as adults. This latter effect is antagonized by the monoamine oxidase inhibitor nialamide (Larsson and Södersten, 1971).

3. SEXUAL BEHAVIOR IN THE ADULT SUBJECT

The hormonal regulation of sexual behavior has been reviewed from many different aspects (Robertson, 1969; Luttge, 1971; Davidson, 1972; Davidson and Levine, 1972; Beyer and McDonald, 1973; Lisk, 1973; Michael, 1973; Diakow, 1974). The different components of sexual behavior are illustrated in Fig. 3.

3.1. Hormonal Regulation of Sexual Behavior in the Female

3.1.1. Characteristics and Measures of Female Sexual Activity

Female coital behavior in different mammalian species consists of a fairly similar behavior repertoire, although some elements of the behavior are different among species. In common laboratory rodents and in some other species such as the rabbit and cat, the display of lordosis (spinal flexion, raised head and perineum) on mounting by a male is the most consistent behavior pattern. In other species the female coital posture is less characteris-

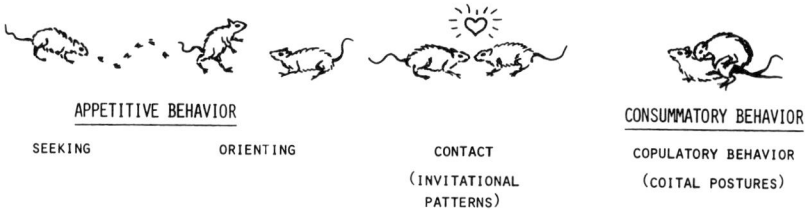

FIG. 3. Different components of sexual behavior.

tic. The female takes a posture adjusted to permit the male to achieve intromission. In the rhesus monkey this means elevation of the buttocks and tensing of the muscles in the straightened hind legs to support the weight of the male, who is mounting the female by being attached to her without contact with the ground. *The coital posture* is, however, only a fraction of the entire pattern displayed by the female in heat. There exists also a great behavior repertoire of *female sexual invitational patterns.* These have a greater variability between different species than the coital behavior, and some of the gestures are not specific to sexual invitation but are components of other social interactions as well. We will also here mention the concept of *sexual attractiveness.* The attractiveness of the female is not necessarily coupled to her sexual receptivity. A highly attractive female may vigorously refuse the male's mating attempts. A female can also present herself in sexual invitation without attracting the male. This is probably a general phenomenon, which can be seen in all mammalian species. It seems to be of great importance in the sexual interaction between pairs of monkeys (see Michael *et al.,* 1972). Hormones and drugs may influence sexual invitations and attractions. The female invitations and attractiveness will influence the vigor of the male sexual approach, a fact which has to be considered in measurements of the female copulatory response. Besides the communication with the female, the male is influenced also by his surroundings. Very few males will copulate in a strange environment. To keep the stimulus situation for the female copulatory response as constant as possible, trained males adapted to the experimental situation should be used. In our studies on the rat and other rodents, the male home cage is used as the test cage to which the female is transferred, and the males have been trained together with estrous females and selected as vigorous mounters. Rabbits are tested in cages to which the male has been adapted, and males are trained with receptive females. Similar procedures have been reported by Michael (1973) as advisable in the study of copulatory behavior in the cat. The preference with which a female will accept different males is ignored under these experimental conditions. In species such as the beagle dog and rhesus monkey (see Beach and Le Boeuf, 1967; Herbert, 1968) individual differences in acceptance of the male seem important. Under conditions where familiarity between the male and the female and partner preference are significant, it is probably advisable to measure the coital activity together with several different kinds of tests of interindividual interaction. This strategy has been employed by Beach in the studies of coital behavior in dogs (1967, 1970) and by Herbert (1970) and Michael and co-workers (see Michael, 1973) in their studies on sexual behavior in the rhesus monkey.

The quantification of the female copulatory response is expressed mainly either as the proportion of mounts by the male which are followed by acceptance or by lordosis (copulatory quotient, lordosis-to-mount ratio L/M, lordosis quotient, acceptance ratio; see Kuehn and Beach, 1963, Edwards *et al.,* 1968; Herbert, 1970) or in terms of the percentage of females which display a positive lordosis response after a certain defined stimulus, e.g., five mounts by two males within 1 min (Meyerson, 1964a). The L/M ratio requires that mounts be performed so far apart that each stimulus situation is independent of the preceding one. If mounts are given with shorter intervals the L/M ratio measures not only the probability of lordosis response but also how often it is possible to elicit the response by repeated stimuli. The central and peripheral nervous mechanisms involved in the initial elicitation of the lordosis response need not necessarily be the same as those mechanisms which make the female respond to repeated stimuli. After repeated mounts the female will reject the male's mounting depending on the interval between mounts and the quality of the preceding mounts. In some studies in the rat the quality of mounts has been made more similar by not permitting intromission, achieved by closing the vaginal orifice of the female partner (Green et al., 1970).

The maintenance of sexual receptivity has been less thoroughly investigated than the copulatory response. In the female golden hamster the duration of the postcopulatory receptivity was found to be a function of ovarian hormones (Carter, 1972; Carter and Porges, 1974).

Most investigations of the effects of hormones on sexual behavior have been concerned with copulatory behavior. Copulatory behavior is relatively easy to define and record as it represents a stereotyped hormone-dependent motor pattern. It can be assumed that copulatory behavior is preceded by a physiological state which brings the subject to seek sexual contact, i.e., *sexual motivation*. We use this terminology fully aware of the risk of confusion. Intervening variables, such as sex drive and motivation, have a dubious function; however, they can be justified if given a precise operational definition. It was thought wise to distinguish the eagerness to seek sexual contact from the frequency of the copulatory behavior. To study the effects of hormones on sexual motivation, different techniques to measure the urge of the female rat to seek contact with a sexually active male have been employed. Details of the techniques used have been described by Meyerson and Lindström (1973a). The *increasing barrier technique* was used to record how much of an aversive stimulus the female was willing to take to reach contact with a sexually active male. In an *open-field method* the animals were observed in a circular observation arena, where a sexually active partner was placed in a mesh cage in the center or periphery of the field. The animal being studied was free to move around, and its location in the arena was recorded. In the *runway-choice method* the choice between a sexually active male and an estrous female was measured in a run-and-choose situation. A straight runway or a T-maze situation have also been used to test sexual motivation in the male rat (Bohus et al., 1975; Whalen, 1961). An operant-conditioning technique on a fixed-ratio basis has also been used to test the willingness of rats (Bermant and Westbrook, 1966) and rhesus monkeys (Michael et al., 1972) to gain access to the other partner's cage for sexual reinforcement.

3.1.2. Endogenous Hormonal Control of the Female Sexual Behavior

In some species reproductive activity occurs during specific seasons of the year, and in other species breeding occurs throughout the year. The effect of season is of course more important in field studies and is diminished when the animal is brought into a laboratory with constant climatic conditions. In most mammalian species, except in the dog and the fox, there is more than one period of sexual activity during the season (polyestrus). The periods of sexual activity are at least in the infraprimate related to a restricted time of the estrus cycle during which male copulatory activity is accepted by the female.

There is a generally accepted view that the preovulatory estrogen secretion is the principal hormonal activator for the female sexual behavior during the estrous cycle of spontaneously ovulating infraprimate species. The endogenous estrogen stage is reflected in the proliferation of the vaginal epithelium or a vaginal discharge whose occurrence is correlated to the female acceptance of the male. Direct measurements of plasma steroid levels have also been reported in a few species. For the relationship between stage of the estrous cycle and sexual responsiveness in rodents, see Brown-Grant (1971), Hardy (1972), and Lisk (1973). The significance of progesterone is indicated by the close coincidence with the onset of estrus and the increase in concentration of plasma progesterone in the rat and guinea pig (Feder *et al.*, 1967, 1968). In the cat there is a highly significant association between the female acceptance of the male coital efforts and the vaginal epithelial pattern (Michael, 1958). The sexual activity in the rhesus monkey can take place throughout the menstrual cycle. Although there is a great variability between different pairs, rhythmic changes could be found in relation to the female menstrual cycle. Michael and co-workers (Michael *et al.*, 1967a; Michael and Welegalla, 1968; Michael *et al.*, 1972) reported that in about 50% of the pairs and cycles in their study there was either a well-defined maximum in sexual activity near mid-cycle with a sharp decline early in the luteal phase and a secondary rise before menstruation, or high levels of activity throughout the follicular phase and very low levels during the luteal phase which remained low to menstruation.

The rabbit differs from the above-mentioned species in that no defined periods of estrus exist. The female rabbit will accept the male's mounting more or less continuously, although there exists some seasonal variability; for a comprehensive review, see Beyer and McDonald (1973).

During the proestrous/estrous state of the estrous cycle, the female rat seeks significantly more contact with the male than during the diestrous state of the cycle, as measured by the techniques for sexual motivation used by Meyerson and Lindström (Meyerson and Lindström, 1973a; Eliasson and Meyerson, 1975). In an operant-behavior situation, a female rhesus monkey pressing a lever in order to obtain access to a male partner, Michael *et al.* (1972) found a marked increase in operant behavior during the time of the menstrual cycle when ovulation could be expected. Using a similar technique, Eaton and Resko (1974) found no significant change in sexual behavior during the ovarian cycle in *Macaca nemestrina*.

3.1.3. Sexual Activity after Gonadectomy

In rodents ovariectomy leads to disappearance of the female display of copulatory response and acceptance of the male's mounting (for references of earlier literature, see Young, 1961). This is also seen in the dog (see Fuller and Du Buis, 1962; Beach *et al.*, 1968) and cat (Michael (1961). In some rhesus monkeys female copulatory behavior persists for prolonged periods after bilateral ovariectomy. The coital activity finally disappears as a product of decreased attractiveness and receptivity of the female (see Michael, 1973 for survey), which is dependent on estrogen.

In the rat, studies of the timing of ovarian secretion associated with mating behavior have been conducted (Schwartz, 1969; Powers, 1970; Rodgers, 1970; Nequin and Schwartz, 1971). Marked inhibition of mating followed ovariectomy performed in proestrous, just before the period of estrogen secretion. Adrenalectomy and ovariectomy in the morning of proestrus prevented mating whereas ovariectomy alone did not. It was suggested that the estrogen secretion necessary for the mating response is completed during proestrus and that progesterone secretion is important. The experiments further suggest that the adrenals are capable of secreting progesterone or progesteronelike steroids effective in substituting for the ovarian progesterone secretion. This is consistent with the finding of Feder and Ruf (1969) who found that progesterone secretion from the adrenal gland could facilitate estrogen-induced lordosis behavior in the female rat. However, lordotic behavior has also been seen in rats under conditions of long periods of estrogen production, such as those induced by exposure to constant light (Hardy, 1970). These animals do not ovulate, i.e., no ovarian progesterone production could be expected, but the effects of adrenal progestine output under these conditions have not been elucidated.

The cyclic increase in the contact sought with a sexually active male by the female rat completely disappears after ovariectomy (Meyerson and Lindström, 1973a).

3.1.4. Induction of Sexual Behavior in the Ovariectomized Female

Sexual receptivity in female mammals disappears sooner or later after ovariectomy. It is possible to induce the behavior again by administration of exogenous gonadal hormones. We will in the following be concerned with:

1. The dose–response relationship of the hormones necessary for the production of copulatory behavior

2. The latency between the injection of the hormone and the appearance of the behavior and the duration of the effect
3. The ability of different estrogens, progestins, and other hormones to produce the behavior

a. Hormonal Induction of Lordotic Behavior. In the rat, guinea pig, hamster, and mouse, estrogen followed by progesterone activates the copulatory response more effectively than estrogen alone (Boling and Blandau, 1939; Dempsey *et al.,* 1936; Beach, 1942*d*; Ring, 1944; Frank and Fraps, 1945). Estrogen alone is effective in inducing sexual receptivity in the rabbit (Bard, 1939; McDonald *et al.,* 1970*a*; Beyer and McDonald, 1973). Estrogen alone can also activate copulatory behavior in female dogs, but the behavior is facilitated by progesterone injection (Beach and Merari, 1970). In the rhesus monkey progesterone seems to depress estradiol-activated sexual activity, the female becoming unreceptive and not attractive to the male (Michael *et al.,* 1967*b*, 1968). Everitt and Herbert (1971, 1975) and Everitt *et al.* (1972) have recently provided evidence that sexual receptivity in the female rhesus monkey is under androgen influence: Ovariectomized and adrenalectomized estradiol-treated females were sexually unreceptive. Sexual presentation and acceptance of male mounting were significantly increased in these subjects by androstenedione or testosterone given s.c. or testosterone implanted directly into the anterior preoptic hypothalamus. In the following, data obtained in the rat will be considered.

The optimum time interval between the estrogen and progesterone injection in the ovariectomized rat is about 26–48 hr. This held true also when estrogens other than EB were used (Meyerson, 1971*a*). Intravenous injection of 100 µg estradiol-17β followed by repeated progesterone injections showed that the lordosis response was obtained from as early as 18 hr after treatment and reached a maximum around 24 hr after the injection (Green *et al.,* 1970).

The ED_{50} dose of EB to produce a lordosis response after a single s.c. injection followed by a maximal dose of progesterone is around 4 µg/kg (Meyerson, 1964*a*, 1971*a*). Investigations using the L/M ratio report a ratio of 0.50 after around 8 µg/kg (Whalen, 1974). When EB is used alone, the dose required for 50% response is more than 25 µg/kg (Meyerson, unpublished). Davidson and co-workers (1968*a*) found a plateau in the response after around 8 days of daily treatment with EB alone and reported that a daily dose of 0.8–3.2 µg EB per rat restored sexual behavior. A similar effect was obtained in similar experiments in adrenalectomized rats (Davidson *et al.,* 1968*b*). EB is more effective than the nonesterified estradiol. The effect of 30 µg of estradiol per animal is about equivalent to the effect of 2 µg EB per animal (Meyerson and Lindström, 1968). A repeated administration of estradiol was far more effective than the same amount given in a single injection. Thus, the target tissue is easier to activate when exposed to the estrogen during an extended time interval. So far we can conclude that in the rat (1) there is a synergistic interaction between progesterone and estrogen in the induction of lordosis response. However, progesterone is not an absolute requirement. (2) The estrogen has to act for a certain time before the behavior can be elicited. This time is a matter of 24 hr or more for optimum effectiveness. (3) It is more effective if the brain is continuously exposed to the estrogen rather than hit with a high peak concentration.

The antiestrogen ethamoxytriphetol (MER-25) competes with estradiol for estrogen binding sites in target tissues (Lerner *et al.*, 1958). Meyerson and Lindström (1968) have shown that MER-25 inhibits the EB-induced lordosis response when the antiestrogen is given 2 or 8 hr after the estrogen treatment. When the antiestrogen is given 24 hr after the EB treatment, it is no longer effective in preventing the lordosis-inducing effect. Similar results were obtained by Arai and Gorski (1968*b*) using the antiestrogen CN-55, 945-27. An explanation of this effect could be that 24 hr after EB treatment the hormone has produced an effect which cannot be disturbed by the antiestrogen, indicating that the estrogen itself at this time is no longer necessary for the production of the behavioral response. Another explanation is that after 24 hr the estrogen had reached intracellular sites at which the antiestrogens were not competitive.

The time taken by different estrogens to produce the lordosis response has been shown to be similar (Meyerson, 1971*a*). Even a nonsteroid estrogen such as the estrogenic carboxylic acid methallenestril requires a time interval of 48 hr between injection and the administration of progesterone to be effective. When the progesterone injection is postponed beyond the optimum time interval of 48 hr after the estrogen injection, there is a slow decline in the response. Ninety-six hours after a single subcutaneous injection of EB at a dose producing 80% response when progesterone is given at 48 hr, almost no response is obtained (Meyerson, unpublished). No further systematic investigations were performed on the duration of the estrogen effect.

Many different estrogens are capable of inducing the lordosis response. Meyerson (1971*a*) used compounds with different stereochemical configuration but with identical physicochemical properties. A comparison of the capacity to produce lordosis response and vaginal epithelial proliferation by these compounds provided evidence that the receptor site in the brain had recognition characteristics for estrogens similar to those of the peripheral binding sites involved in the vaginal cornification process. Similar work using the *cis*-trans isomers of clomiphene has recently been reported (Ross *et al.*, 1973*b*).

The dose of progesterone required to elicit lordosis in estrogen-treated rats varies around 0.1 to 0.5 mg per animal. Progesterone alone is not effective in producing the behavior, and a full response is dependent on the pretreatment with estrogen. Various synthetic progesterone derivatives were tested by Kincl and Dorfman (1961) and were found to activate copulatory behavior in guinea pigs. The capacity of 11 progestins to induce estrous behavior was studied in ovariectomized rats by Meyerson (1967a). No correlation was obtained between the efficiency of the injected progestins to activate estrous behavior and the ability to induce general anesthesia. On the other hand, a positive correlation was revealed on comparison of the data in the estrous-behavior assay and ability to maintain pregnancy in spayed rats. It was suggested that progesterone activates lordotic behavior in the estrogen-treated ovariectomized rat by a specific action on the central nervous system which is different from a general anesthetic effect. The latency between the injection of estrogen and the appearance of lordosis behavior is a matter of many hours. In contrast, the latency between intravenous injection of progestins and appearance of the lordotic behavior in estrogen-treated ovariectomized rats was found to have a median of only 10–30 min (Meyerson, 1972). The latency of the lordosis response after different progestins and progesterone metabolites given intravenously was studied. It was found that progestins with anesthetic capacity such as progesterone and medroxyprogesterone had a longer latency at high doses than at low ones. It was suggested that the true latency for these progestins is masked by the anesthetic property even at doses which did not produce any overt sedative effects. Isopregnenone lacked an anesthetic effect, and the latency obtained was around 10–30 min regardless of the dose given. The effect of ether anesthesia and strychnine on the latency between injection of isopregnenone and the appearance of lordosis response was studied by Carrer and Meyerson (1976). Ether anesthesia (10 min) at the time of isopregnenone injection delayed the appearance of the response. An opposite effect was seen after strychnine treatment.

The isopregnenone data suggest that a certain time is required between the treatment and the appearance of lordotic behavior, which is longer than could be expected if only transport from the circulation to the brain tissue is involved. Progesterone metabolites such as 5α-pregnane-3,20-dione were less effective than progesterone and there was similar latency for the appearance of the first lordosis response after injection. 17α-Hydroxy- and 20α-hydroxy-progesterone are also less effective than progesterone (Langford and Hilliard, 1967; Meyerson, 1972). No systematic investigations of the duration of the progesterone effect are available. A biphasic influence of progesterone has been observed in guinea pigs (Zucker and Goy, 1967; Zucker, 1968); i.e., progesterone increased the intensity of receptivity shortly after administration and subsequently induced a refractory behavioral condition. This biphasic influence of progesterone was not observed in rats given identical hormone treatment (Zucker, 1967). Edwards et al. (1968) have shown, however, that daily injections of progesterone and estrogen lead to continuous high levels of receptivity. In contrast to the former authors, Nadler (1970), using a submaximal dose of estrogen, found that progesterone had a biphasic influence on the sexual receptivity of spayed female rats. The use of suprathreshold amounts of estrogen to induce receptivity might have prevented adequate evaluation of the progesterone influence in the earlier work

(Nadler, 1970). The progesterone treatment necessary for producing the lordosis response in the estradiol-treated spayed female rat can be replaced by certain psychopharmacological agents and by cortical applications of potassium chloride or electric current (see below). Recently it was reported that luteinizing-hormone-releasing factor can induce a lordosis response in estrogen-treated ovariectomized female rats (Moss and McCann, 1973; Pfaff, 1973). The results are of great interest and should initiate many interesting lines of investigation.

b. Induction of Female Sexual Behavior by Androgens. Female copulatory behavior can also be activated in a female animal by testosterone treatment (Table 2). This has been shown in the rat, rabbit, and cat. As with estrogen-induced lordosis behavior, the induction of sexual receptivity in the rat after testosterone propionate requires that progesterone be also given. The action of testosterone is inhibited by prior treatment with an estrogen antagonist (Beyer and Vidal, 1971; Meyerson *et al.*, 1971; Whalen *et al.*, 1972). It has been suggested that testosterone induces sexual receptivity by conversion to estradiol, and this has been shown to occur within the central nervous system of several species including the rat (Ryan *et al.*, 1972). Androstenedione is capable of inducing lordosis in female rats. In contrast, dihydrotestosterone, a metabolite of testosterone which is not converted to estrogenic compounds

TABLE 2

Lordosis Response in Ovariectomized Female Rats and Mounting Behavior in Castrated Male Rats after Administering Estradiol Benzoate (EB) and Testosterone Proprionate (TP) in Combination with Progesterone (PROG) and the Antiestrogen Ethamoxytriphetol (MER-25)[a]

Lordosis response in females			Mounting behavior in males		
Treatment	%	N	Treatment	%	N
EB, 10 μ/kg	0	24	EB, 50 μg/kg	70	44
EB, 5 μg/kg + PROG, 1.0 mg/rat	72	44	Oil blank	33	36
MER-25, 150 mg/kg + EB, 5 μg/kg + PROG, 1.0 mg/rat	13	24	MER-25, 150 mg/kg + EB, 50 μg/kg	24	21
TP, 1 mg/kg	0	24	TP, 0.20 mg/kg	73	37
TP, 1.0 mg/kg + PROG, 1.0 mg/kg	78	23	Oil blank	49	37
MER-25, 150 mg/kg + TP, 1.0 mg/kg + PROG, 1.0 mg/rat	3	23	MER-25, 150 mg/kg + TP, 0.20 mg/kg	41	37

[a] Data taken from Meyerson *et al.* (1971), and Malmnäs and Meyerson (1973). Progesterone was given 48 hr after, and MER-25 injected 2 hr prior, to the EB or TP treatment. Lordosis response was tested 4, 6, and 8 hr after the progesterone injection. Each female was exposed to six mounts on each occasion. If the female displayed a clear-cut lordosis response on at least two mounts, she was classed as responding. The percentages in the table are cumulative mean responses. Mount percent is the percentage of males which mounted an estrous female 48 hr after TP administration. N = number of animals tested.

by mammalian tissue, while peripherally active as an androgen, appears to exert little or no effect on the neural mechanisms controlling sexual behavior. In the female rhesus monkey (see also above) testosterone seems to increase elements such as female presentation, but did not render the female attractive to the male (Trimble and Herbert, 1968; Everitt and Herbert, 1971, 1975; Everitt *et al.*, 1972).

c. Sexual Motivation and Gonadal Hormones. In ovariectomized subjects EB caused an obvious increase in the amount of aversive stimuli the subject was willing to tolerate in order to reach contact with a sexually active male. The female also spent more time sitting close to the male in the open-field arena, and in the runway-choice situation there was an increase in number of trials in which the male was chosen instead of an estrous female (Meyerson and Lindström, 1973a). TP had an effect similar to EB, but the nonaromatizable androgen, dihydrotestosterone benzoate, was ineffective in producing any effect on sexual motivation (McDonald and Meyerson, 1973). The antiestrogen MER-25 inhibited the estrogen-induced response but was only partially effective in blocking the testosterone-induced response. The effect of progesterone differed between the different techniques. No effect was seen in the increasing-barrier method, but there was a slight facilitation of the estrogen-induced response when progesterone was given before the full estrogen response was achieved. In the operant-behavior situation used by Michael *et al.* to test sexual motivation in the female rhesus monkey, a gradual increase in operant behavior was found following administration of graded doses of estradiol to ovariectomized females. The operant response was well correlated with other measures of sexual activity (Michael *et al.*, 1972).

d. The Site of Action of Gonadal Hormones. Experiments using direct implantation of minute amounts of estrogenic hormones into the brain have provided the most conclusive evidence for a central nervous site of action of estrogen in producing its effect on mating behavior. Implants of estrogens into certain areas of the brain induced mating behavior while having no detectable effects on peripheral estrogen target tissues. Harris *et al.* (1958) reported that minute amounts (about 0.1–0.3 mg) of estradiol and stilbestrol esters applied onto the tips of stainless steel needles implanted in different regions of the brain of ovariectomized cats could produce a fully developed mating behavior in the absence of any sign of estrogenic stimulation of the genital tract. The implants were placed in the mammillary region of the hypothalamus. Using similar techniques, comparable results have been obtained in the rabbit (Palka and Sawyer, 1966), rat (Lisk, 1962), hamster (Ciaccio and Lisk, 1973), guinea pig (Morin and Feder, 1974c), and monkey (Michael *et al.*, 1972). Although there is conclusive evidence of a local effect exerted on the brain by the implanted estrogen, the exact site within the brain is not yet fully elucidated. In the rat, implants in the preoptic area of the hypothalamus seem to increase receptivitiy. Recent work by Whalen (1972) has shown that rather large areas of the basomedial brain seem to respond to estrogen in controlling lordosis. In the guinea pig estradiol-sensitive areas have been found in the basal hypothalamus and basal anterior hypothalamic preoptic area (Morin and Feder, 1974c).

As to the effect of progesterone, Ross *et al.* (1971) reported that this hormone facilitated the lordosis response in estrogen-treated rats after unilateral implantation into mesencephalic areas but was rather ineffective at diencephalic locations. However, Powers (1972) provided contradictory results to those of Ross *et al.*, demonstrating that bilateral progesterone implants in the medial basal hypothalamus but not in the mesencephalic reticular formation facilitated the lordosis response. Morin and Feder (1974a) found that progesterone implanted into diencephalic areas (basal from ventromedial hypothalamus into premammillary region) facilitated lordosis response in guinea pigs, whereas implants in anterior preoptic areas had no effect. Progesterone implants in the region of zona compacta in the midbrain substantia nigra had an inhibitory effect on the lordosis response activated by subcutaneous injection of EB + progesterone (Morin and Feder 1974b). The reports on progesterone implantation reveal some technical difficulties regarding the specificity of the progesterone effect, since cholesterol implants in many areas were also effective in producing a response. The lordosis response has also been activated in estrogen-treated spayed female rats by cortical application of potassium chloride (Clemens *et al.*, 1967) and after cortical stimulation (Ross *et al.*, 1973a). The hypothesis was advanced that progesterone may facilitate mating responses by suppressing cortically involved inhibitory activity. For further evidence on inhibitory neural systems, see below (Beach, 1967; Meyerson, 1964a).

Some information as to the site of action of the hormone in inducing sexual receptivity is revealed by the distribution of labeled estrogen taken up and retained by brain tissue. The sites of steroid binding and action in the brain have recently been reviewed by Stumpf and Sar (1973) and McEwen *et al.* (1972).

e. Gonadal Hormones and Sexual Reflexes in the Female. Data indicating that reflexes which are mediated by the spinal cord play an important role in the mating behavior of adult female mammals have been reviewed by Beach (1967). After transection of the spinal cord certain components of the female cat's mating behavior, such as lateral tail deviation and elevation of the pelvis are retained (Bard, 1940). It is also possible to elicit a lordosis-like reflex in spinal female rats. Gonadal hormones did not influence the frequency of occurrence or intensity of this reflex (Hart, 1969). Similar data exist on estrogen and progesterone in spinal female guinea pigs (Dempsey and Rioch, 1939). A lordosis reflex can also be elicited by mechanical stimulation of the cervix in ovariectomized rats. Komisaruk (1971) showed that small doses of estrogen increased the response activated in this way.

f. Hormonal Regulation of the Masculine Sexual Pattern in the Female. A complete masculine copulatory pattern has been demonstrated (Beach, 1942a) in female rats. This behavior was divided into three reactions: (1)

sexual clasp, the female grasping the stimulus animal with her forepaws from the rear but not executing pelvic thrusts; (2) mounts, the rat mounting with pelvic thrusts; the complete pattern includes mounting with final forceful thrust; and (3) rapid dismount. The complete pattern is analogous to the male intromission pattern, and is as a rule accompanied by genital grooming. Androgen administration resulted in a shift in the relative frequencies of the three types of responses to a more complete malelike pattern (Beach, 1942b). Recently Pfaff (1970) found that estrogen stimulates mounting behavior in ovariectomized females. The role of gonadal hormones and mounting behavior in the female rat has been further investigated by Södersten (1972). He reported that in intact 4-day cyclic female rats mounting behavior was displayed throughout the cycle, with the lowest frequencies on the night between proestrus and estrus. Mounting was decreased but not abolished after ovariectomy, and treatment with EB or TP stimulated the display of mounting behavior. Females treated with EB and DHT showed significantly more mounts with pelvic thrusting than females receiving either EB or DHT (Baum *et al.* 1974). The frequency of mounting was not affected by anesthetization of the clitoris and external vagina with lidocain. It was, therefore, concluded that the effects of DHT on estradiol-induced mounting resulted from the action of this androgen on the brain and not from the stimulatory effect which DHT may exert on genital sensory receptors.

3.2. Hormonal Regulation of Sexual Behavior in the Male

3.2.1. Characteristics and Measures of Male Sexual Activity

To determine the hormonal control of sexual behavior in the male, a definition of the different patterns of behavior displayed by the male during the copulatory act is required. Generally we can distinguish four components, namely: (1) a foreplay, followed (2) by the male mounting the female partner, (3) the behavior exhibited in connection with intromission of the penis into the vagina, and (4) behavior displayed in connection with ejaculation. These patterns vary between different species. The foreplay may be a prolonged affair or just a matter of seconds. Intromissions as well as ejaculations can be single or multiple. The reason for such differences has been discussed in terms of differences in genital morphology and socioecological circumstances (Walton, 1952), and several aspects of species differences in the ejaculatory response have been discussed by Ford and Beach (1951) and Beach *et al.* (1966). It is obvious that the individual components of copulatory behavior are not independent. Ejaculation, for instance, is dependent on the pattern of and interval between each intromission, in addition to the total number of intromissions. To obtain an insight into hormonal and drug influences on the different phases of copulatory behavior, a number of parameters have to be measured. The most commonly used are the following:

1. Percentage of animals which display the different components of coital behavior: mount percentage, intromission percentage, ejaculation percentage.
2. Latency between the first mount and intromission, and latency between first intromission and ejaculation and the time between ejaculation and the following intromission (postejaculatory interval).
3. Mount and intromission frequency, i.e., number of mounts and intromissions preceding the ejaculatory behavior pattern.
4. Number of mounts, intromissions per minute.
5. Intromission ratio, which is the proportion of mounts with intromission to the total number of mounts.

3.2.2. Effects of Castration

The clear-cut cyclic nature of the female gonadal hormonal secretions and reproductive functions cannot be seen in the male. However, cyclic variations have been reported in some male sexual functions, such as the volume of the ejaculate, number of sperm cells, spontaneous ejaculation, etc. (for a survey see Kihlström, 1971). In addition, Kihlström and Arrendal have recently obtained data showing an LH secretion cycle of 26–33 days length in human males (personal communication).

Data on the endocrine control of sexual behavior in the male as in the female are obtained mainly by studying the effect of castration and restoration of behavior by exogenous hormone therapy. In contrast to what is found in the female, castration of the male rat is followed by a gradual decline in sexual activity. It is important to realize that the different components of the copulatory behavior pattern disappear at different rates. There are several reports on the disappearance rates of the copulatory pattern of the male rat (Stone 1939; Beach and Holz-Tuckel, 1949; Davidson 1966a; Malmnäs, 1973). There is great variability in different reports and even between different series conducted by the same observer as to the rate of decline of the copulatory patterns after gonadectomy. Generally there is a more-or-less linear decrease in the number of male rats showing the ejaculatory pattern during the first 4–8 weeks after castration. The ability to achieve intromission deteriorates soon after the disappearance of the ejaculatory response. Mounting behavior, i.e., readiness to mount a receptive female, declines more slowly and is seen many weeks after the ejaculatory pattern can no longer be elicited. A similar change of the different components of coital behavior after castration is seen in other rodents such as guinea pig (Grunt and Young, 1952) and hamster (Beach and Pauker, 1949) and also in the rabbit (Stone, 1932). In the cat, dog, and rhesus monkey the survival of the different elements of copulatory behavior is longer. As a rule, a decline in intromission and ejaculatory patterns is apparent within a couple of months, whereas mounting behavior may persist for many years or never show any decline (Rosenblatt and Aronson, 1958; Beach, 1970; Michael and Wilson, 1974). Although the degree of retention of various elements of behavior varies among species and individuals, it is still evident that the behavior is maintained for a remarkably long time, considering that female sexual receptivity disappears almost immediately after ovariectomy. Bloch and Davidson (1968) investigated the possibility that precastration mating experience and adrenocortical androgens contributed to the maintenance of mating behavior following castration in the male rat. Their conclusion was that neither prior sexual experience nor adrenal hormones appeared to be involved in the maintenance of mating behavior following castration. To what extent is the decline in intromission and ejaculation patterns influenced by the effects of castration on seminal vesicles, glans penis, and other penile tissues? Fluoxymesterone and dihydrotestosterone, which exert a strong androgenic effect upon accessory sexual structures, did not restore mating behavior in castrated male rats (Beach and Westbrook, 1968a; Feder, 1971; Whalen and Luttge, 1971; Johnston and Davidson, 1972). Hart (1973) studied the influence of TP and DHT on the sexual reflexes in spinal male rats and found reduced reflexes in DHT-treated subjects in spite of penile stimulation. Testicular atrophy, but no significant decrease of mating behavior, was detected in intact male rats treated for 3 weeks with EB (Södersten, 1973b): Thus, the castrational changes in penile tissue do not seem to be of immediate importance for copulatory behavior. However, this does not exclude the possibility that prepuberal castration or castration during longer time intervals than studied so far cause a morphological change in the penis which could influence sexual behavior.

3.2.3. Induction of Sexual Behavior in the Castrated Male

a. Effect of Testosterone. There is an abundance of data which show that testosterone propionate will maintain and restore normal sexual behavior in adult castrated males (the references given above on effects of castration are also relevant to TP). In order to find a dose of testosterone which will maintain or restore the behavior at a certain response level, the following has to be considered. Each behavior component could have its specific sensitivity to the hormone. The hormone sensitivity for restoring a certain element of the copulatory behavior could be different depending on the time elapsed from castration. In pharmacology this problem is met by using the 50% response level (ED_{50}) as a point of reference. This involves an estimate of the dose of testosterone which maintains a 50% response after the response has declined to this level. Beach and Holz-Tucker (1949) investigated the effects of different concentrations of TP on sexual behavior in castrated male rats by giving daily treatments starting 48 hr after castration. The estimates were based upon tests performed from 2 to 10 weeks after surgery. The different behavioral criteria measured were not equally sensitive to the hormone treatment. Mount latency could be maintained by a dose level of around 25–50 μg/day, while mount percentage was kept between 80–100% on a dose of 25–75 μg. A dose of 500 μg was required for the mount frequency to reach precastration level, and to reach ejaculation at least once in each test the dose required was around 75–500 μg for a 100% response. In Malmnäs' (1973) study the animals were castrated and substitution therapy was initiated at a time when 50% of the animals showed clear-cut mounting behavior. Malmnäs showed that TP given once weekly maintained the mount percentage at a constant level for at least 5 weeks, and a dose–response relationship was obtained at TP doses between 0.05 and 0.20 mg/kg.

Malmnäs also studied the latency to the onset of the hormonal effect. The distribution of the time intervals from the administration of the testosterone to the appearance of the first mount showed a latency of 54 hr and the duration of different doses of TP was found to be dependent on the dose given. The effect of 0.10 mg/kg TP lasted about 5 days, and the effect of 0.40 mg/kg could still be seen after 15 days.

b. Effects of Steroids Other than Testosterone, Peptides, and Antiandrogens. Androstenedione is highly effective in maintaining copulatory behavior when given systemically immediately after castration and also in restoring mating behavior when given a long time after castration (Davidson and Bloch, 1969; Luttge and Whalen, 1970). The testosterone metabolite 5α-androstan-17β-ol-3-one (dihydrotestosterone, DHT) has androgenic effects on the accessory sex organs, can be formed in the hypothalamus (Jaffe, 1969; Rommerts and van der Malen, 1971), but does not prevent the postcastration decline in mating behavior and is unable to restore the behavior in castrated animals (McDonald *et al.*, 1970*b*; Feder, 1971; Whalen and Luttge, 1971; Johnston and Davidson, 1972; Parrott, 1974; Luttge *et al.*, 1975). Also estradiol given to castrated adult rats induce, mating behavior. How close to the TP-induced restoration of the ejaculatory pattern it is possible to come by EB treatment varies in different reports. It seems to be dependent on factors such as the age at castration and time elapsed from castration (Beach, 1942*c*; Davidson, 1969; Pfaff, 1970; Malmnäs and Meyerson, 1973; Södersten, 1973*b*) (see Table 2). Aromatization may be a necessary step in the induction of male sexual behavior by androgens. 19-Hydroxytestosterone is postulated as an early intermediary in the androgen-to-estrogen conversion from testosterone. Parrott (1974) reported that 19-hydroxytestosterone, which has no peripheral effects, did not affect ejaculatory performance in castrated male rats. Johnston *et al.* (1975) found 19-hydroxytestosterone to produce male copulatory behavior 24 hr posttherapy in castrated + adrenalectomized males, but it was less effective in only the castrated subjects. In reports by Baum and Vreeburg (1973) and Larsson *et al.* (1973) EB combined with DHT induced mating behavior indistinguishable from that in other castrates treated with TP. Testosterone-induced heterosexual pursuit and mounting behavior was inhibited by the antiestrogen MER-25 (Malmnäs and Meyerson, 1976). These results suggest that testosterone activation of these elements of the male copulatory behavior is mediated by estrogen receptors.

In peripheral testosterone-sensitive tissues, the synthetic steroid cyproterone acetate has been shown to be effective as an antiandrogen. The weight of the seminal vesicles is reduced (Neumann and von Berswordt-Wallrabe, 1966) and Bloch and Davidson (1967) have demonstrated an inhibition of the testosterone effect on gonadotropin secretion. However, in contrast to the antiestrogen MER-25 (see Table 2), cyproterone does not alter sexual behavior in male rats or guinea pigs (Zucker, 1966; Beach and Westbrook, 1968b; Whalen and Edwards, 1969), nor does this compound given with TP inhibit the increase in wheel-running activity in male rats (Stern and Murphy, 1971).

Bertolini et al. (1968) reported that ACTH injected into the lateral brain ventricle induced "sexual excitement" (penile erection) in male rabbits. The response seemed dependent on testosterone. However, our excitement awaits the data to be statistically evaluated with the use of appropriate control groups.

In a recent study Bohus et al. (1975) demonstrated that the ACTH-like peptide $ACTH_{4-10}$, which lacks adrenocorticotropic activity, increased intromission and ejaculatory latencies in TP-treated castrated male rats. Extinction of a runway response, in a runway with an estrous female as incentive, was delayed by the peptide. No doubt, peptides will open up a new and interesting field of investigation in this area.

c. Site of Action of Testosterone. Intracerebral implantation of testosterone (Davidson, 1966b; Lisk, 1967) resulted in reappearance of a complete pattern of male sexual behavior in castrated male rats in the absence of any histologically demonstrable stimulation of seminal vesicles or prostate. Occasional responses were found following implants in several areas of the brain, but implants in hypothalamic preoptic regions were most effective. The distribution of effective implants agrees fairly well with those areas of the hypothalamus which selectively concentrate and retain testosterone according to autoradiographic studies (Sar and Stumpf, 1973).

d. Sexual Reflexes in the Male. In an extensive study of sexual reflexes in different spinal animals, Hart (1967a, 1968a,b) found that the spinal cord mediates sexual responses similar to some of those exhibited during mating. Hart also found that gonadal hormones had a quantitative influence on the sexual reflexes. There was a pronounced decline in the total number of erections, quick flips, and long flips per 30 min test when testosterone was withdrawn from castrated subjects given daily s.c. injections of TP. The responses were restored by injection of testosterone. Subjects with spinal implants of TP exhibited an increase in sexual reflex activity whereas cholesterol-implanted subjects showed a decline in sexual reflex activity (Hart and Haugen, 1968). These authors suggest that testosterone has a facilitatory influence on sexual reflexes by means of a direct action on spinal neural tissue mediating sexual reflexes.

3.3. Effects of Psychoactive Drugs on Sexual Behavior

3.3.1. Rationales and Strategies

The use of drugs in the field of sexual behavior is based upon the *rationales* below.

a. Neurohumoral Transmission. Evidence has accumulated that various neurohumoral transmitters such as noradrenaline, dopamine, serotonin, ACH, and GABA are essential for central nervous functions. Abundant data are also available demonstrating that the action of many of the modern psychoactive compounds is related to interference with central nervous transmitter mechanisms. As it became clear that hormones activate specific sexual behavior patterns by a local effect on the CNS, the role of transmitter functions in this connection became important and psychopharmacological agents were seen as useful tools for the study of sexual behavior.

b. Compounds Influencing Biosynthesis and Transport of Proteins. The possibility of a hormonal influence on genomic activity leading to changes in protein synthesis has been investigated extensively using many different peripheral steroid target tissues (see Jensen and DeSombre, 1972; Liao and Fang, 1969). Estrogen binding to peripheral target tissues such as the uterus parallels the estrogen-induced uterotropic effect (Terenius, 1965, 1966; Korenman, 1970). Similarly estrogen activation of uterine RNA synthesis is correlated to the extent of accumulation of estrogen in uterus (Jensen and Jacobson, 1962). As more evidence was provided that estrogen was taken up and retained in certain neurons of the CNS, the hypothesis of possible genomic effects of estrogen on CNS tissue emerged. The possibility of hormone-induced formation of proteins relevant to neurotransmitter functions led some laboratories to investigate the effects of drugs which interfere with protein synthesis and transport. The end point of the hormonal effect studied was some element of sexual behavior.

c. Clinical Applications. The third rationale for the investigation of the influence of drugs on sexual behavior is the search for compounds which could be used to increase or decrease human sexual activity and in the pharmacotherapy of sexual disorders. This rationale is the oldest one. A search for so-called aphrodisiacs seems to be as old as mankind.

d. Side Effects. Closely related to the clinical aspect of drugs and sexual behavior is the fourth rationale, namely, to find out how drugs and hormones used for other purposes affect sexual behavior, i.e., exploring side effects of hormones and psychoactive drugs. This rationale has been very much ignored especially in view of the fact that steroid and drug therapies are sometimes used during very long periods of time.

e. Drug Screening. The fifth rationale is common to all drug-behavior experimentation. If certain elements of sexual behavior are found to be related to a certain transmitter system, the behavior is easily defined for use in the future for the testing of new drugs.

The *general strategies* in the use of drugs as tools in the investigation of sexual behavior are, of course, not different from the use of compounds in investigations of any kind of behavior. Some specific factors are, however, involved, as elements of sexual behavior are dependent on hormones. In addition to keeping in mind the effect of drugs on hormonal secretion (see above) the requirements below should be filled.

f. Behavior Parameters and Measures Clearly Defined. Behavior consists of a mosaic of elements. It is essential that the element under study be clearly defined with respect to its overt expression as well as its dependence on and relation to other behavioral components; e.g., the ejaculatory pattern in the male rat is displayed as a prolonged mount, slow dismount, and extended genital grooming. This pattern is easy to recognize. Ejaculation under normal conditions is dependent on intromissions. Thus, drugs could act primarily on the mechanisms directly related to ejaculation, or they could secondarily affect ejaculation by changing, for instance, intromission rates.

g. The Importance of Keeping the Hormone-Induced Response at a Submaximal Level. The fact that the behavior is dependent on hormones requires that the effect of a compound, stimulatory or inhibitory, be studied when the behavior response is maintained at a submaximal level with respect to the hormonal stimulation.

h. The Time of Treatment. Drugs could be administered at a time which permits us to study the effect on the already hormone-induced response or could be given at a time when the hormone-induced response is not yet fully produced. The difference in injection schedule in relation to the hormone treatment could be used as a strategy, but should also be considered when results from different investigations are compared.

Drugs might also affect a hormone-induced response differently at different times during the day–night cycle.

i. The Use of Drugs with a Common Point of Action or Different Point of Action but Equivalent Functional Effects. Almost all drugs have several actions. It is an advantage if several compounds with a common action can be tested on the same behavioral parameter to determine the relationship between a certain action of the compound and its effect on the behavior, e.g., the use of different MAO inhibitors on the lordosis response (see below).

Another strategy in the study of drugs and behavior is the comparison of effects on behavior by compounds with different points of action but a similar or equivalent functional effect, e.g., comparison of the effect of impaired dopaminergic transmission achieved by storage depletion (reserpine), decreased biosynthesis (α-methyltyrosine), and receptor blockage (pimozide). As more knowledge is available, there seems to be less justification for relating behavior to cerebral levels of the presumptive transmitter substances. Dynamic events such as transport mechanisms, receptor sensitivity, *de novo* biosynthesis, turnover rates and release mechanisms from labile storage pools, and finally complicated feedback mechanisms seem to be of more functional significance than just the amount of transmitter substance measurable by techniques available at present. These facts must also be considered when comparison is made between compounds which superficially appear to bring about an equivalent functional state but which have different points of action. The functional state achieved by inhibition of transmitter biosynthesis need not necessarily affect behavior in the same way as receptor blockade. This is particularly important when drugs are used on a repeated dose regimen and for long periods. The acute effects of drugs may be very different from the effects obtained after repeated administration, and effects after single injections may vary dramatically between initial and late effects. Late effects might be undetected in the sense that they sometimes do not show up on overt behavior but could be evident when other compounds are injected at certain time intervals after drug treatment. Depending on the time elapsed from the last drug administration, the same drug could induce different effects. The initial effect of, for example, decreased biosynthesis could be followed by other effects during a phase when feedback mechanisms are at work to overcome the decrease of biosynthesis. This means that besides working out the importance of dose–response relationships we should also consider time–response relationships.

A third strategy is the comparison of behavioral effects using analogous series of compounds. This strategy is classical in pharmacological experimentation in the investigation of receptor configurations. Used in behavioral pharmacology it means that a series of structurally related compounds are tested with respect to different behavioral parameters. An example of this is the comparison of the ability of different progestins to induce lordotic responses, their anesthetic and pregnancy maintenance effects (Meyerson, 1967), and comparison of the activity of different isomers of estrogens in producing lordotic responses and vaginal epithelial proliferation (Meyerson, 1971).

j. Specificity of Drug Action. Coital activity and the expression of sexual motivation requires a certain capacity of the motor functions. Different test situations may be affected differently. The lordosis response can be elicited in an obviously sedated female, while mounting behavior declines already at low levels of decreased locomotor activity. An estimate of motor ability (e.g., in terms of exploratory activity, etc.) is always advisable in order to evaluate a drug-induced effect on sexual performance. Especially when intervening variables (such as sexual motivation) are used, it is necessary to test the specificity of a drug effect by investigating whether the effects obtained could be extended to other intervening variables tested under the same conditions, e.g., change of male incentive for water, etc., in the study of female sexual motivation.

3.3.2. Drugs and Female Sexual Behavior

The characteristics and measures of female sexual behavior have been described above. The effects of drugs on female sexual behavior have been studied mainly in the rat, and the sexual behavior has been measured in terms of lordotic behavior. Attempts to measure drug effects on sexual motivation have recently been reported, but the data are still at a preliminary stage (Meyerson et al., 1974; Meyerson, 1974). To exclude effects of endogenous gonadal hormone production, the effects of different compounds on hormone-activated sexual behavior have been studied in the castrated female given exogenous hormone treatment. This treatment has mainly consisted of EB + progesterone in doses adjusted to induce a certain submaximal response. In some studies, however, estrous behavior has been induced in spayed rats by EB alone. It is at present difficult to determine if the effects of psychotropic drugs on the estrogen + progesterone induced response are in full agreement with effects on the estrogen-alone-activated copulatory behavior and vice versa. Data should, therefore, not be generalized unreservedly between the two preparations.

a. *Monoamines and Female Copulatory Behavior.* We first discuss monoamine oxidase inhibitors and monoamine precursors. A general or more selective increase of CNS monoamines was produced by monoamine oxidase inhibitors alone or with the different monoamine precursors. The first evidence of an antagonistic relationship between CNS monoamines and lordotic response in the estrogen + progesterone treated ovariectomized rat was provided by a study of Meyerson (1964a) using three different monoamine oxidase inhibitors and combining some of them with the monoamine precursors 5-HTP and dopa. It was found that the lordotic response was inhibited, especially by the combination of a monoamine oxidase inhibitor and 5-HTP. This inhibitory effect of monoamine oxidase inhibitors on the lordosis response has also been observed in the hamster, mouse, and rabbit (Meyerson et al., 1973b). When dopa was used instead of 5-HTP, no effect or a brief decline in copulatory behavior was seen. This was more evident in the hamster than in the rat (Meyerson, 1970), but is also seen in the rat when an extracerebral decarboxylase inhibitor is given as well as dopa (Meyerson and Malmnäs, 1977). Analogous recordings of food eaten and the number of meals per hour revealed that the effects seen on the sexual response did not carry over to feeding behavior (Meyerson, 1964a). The inhibitory effect of the monoamine oxidase inhibitor pargyline on the lordosis response was prevented by pretreatment with the serotonin-synthesis inhibitor *p*-chlorophenylalanine (PCPA) or α-propyl-dopacetamide (H 22/54) (Meyerson, 1964c). In contrast, the catecholamine synthesis inhibitor α-methyltyrosine (α-MT) did not prevent the inhibitory effect of pargyline (Meyerson et al., 1973).

Tricyclic antidepressants such as imipramine and related antidepressant drugs which inhibit amine uptake mechanisms reduced the lordosis response. There was no relation between the inhibitory effect on estrous behavior and the ability of different antidepressants to prevent tetrabenazine-induced sedation (Meyerson, 1966a).

We now discuss the receptor-stimulating and receptor-blocking compounds. A variety of compounds are known to act as direct or indirect stimulants of monoamine receptors. An inhibitory effect of LSD on the lordosis response induced by estrogen + progesterone was evident at a dose level of 50 µg/kg i.p. For data on LSD/5-HT receptor action, see Aghajanian (1972a,b), and the paper by Aghajanian et al. in Vol. 6 of this series. A clear cut tolerance to the effect of LSD was observed when LSD was given daily at 100 µg/kg i.p. for 6 days (Eliasson and Meyerson, 1973; Meyerson et al., 1973, Eliasson and Meyerson, 1976). In a recent study Everitt et al. (1975a) found LSD (50 µg/kg) to inhibit the lordosis response induced by estrogen alone; however, a slightly stimulatory effect was achieved at lower dose levels (5-10 µg/kg). A compound related to LSD, methysergide (5-10 mg/kg i.p.), has an inhibitory effect similar to that of LSD when given s.c. (Fechter and Meyerson, unpublished). Apomorphine and piribadil (ET 495) have been found to stimulate CNS dopamine receptors (Ernst, 1967; Andén et al., 1967; Corrodi et al., 1972). Both apomorphine (Meyerson et al., 1974) and piribedil (Everitt et al., 1974) decrease the estrogen + progesterone activated copulatory behavior, while the dopamine-receptor-blocking compound pimozide (Andén et al., 1970a) prevented the effect of apomorphine (Meyerson et al., 1974). Pimozide significantly increased the lordosis:mount ratio in females treated only with estrogen (Everitt et al., 1975), but no significant effect was seen on the estrogen + progesterone activated response (Michanek and Meyerson, 1977). Meyerson (1966b) found that chlorpromazine inhibited the estrogen + progesterone activated lordosis response, an effect which was more pronounced when the hypothermic effect of chlorpromazine was not prevented. α-Amphetamine, p-chloroamphetamine, and fenfluramine decreased the lordosis response in a dose-dependent way (Meyerson, 1968b; Michanek and Meyerson, 1975, 1977; Everitt et al., 1975b). A comparison of the effectiveness of the different amphetamine derivatives in inhibiting the lordosis response and inducing stereotyped behavior revealed that there was no correlation between these effects. This indicates that amphetamine may have different mechanisms of action for inhibiting the lordosis response and inducing stereotyped behavior. The inhibitory effect of α-amphetamine but not those of l-amphetamine, fenfluramine, or p-chloroamphetamine was decreased by pimozide treatment (Michanek and Meyerson, 1975).

Finally, we discuss the amine depletors and synthesis inhibitors. The inhibitory effects of drugs which increase monoaminergic tone suggest the possibility of activating copulatory behavior by the administration of compounds which suppress monoaminergic activity. It must then be kept in mind that in facilitating the copulatory behavior, drugs might augment the hormone-activated response by an effect on neuronal functions directly involved in the production of the behavior and/or exert an indirect influence by an effect on neuroendocrine functions, thereby activating endogenous hormone production. As stated above, it is well established that the combination of estrogen, followed by progesterone (after a certain time), activates copulatory behavior in ovariectomized rats, hamsters, and mice more effectively than estrogen alone. It has now been shown that in ovariectomized estrogen-treated rats reserpine, tetrabenazine, PCPA (Meyerson, 1964b, 1968a: Meyerson and Lewander, 1970; Ahlenius et al., 1972a), and α-MT (Ahlenius et al., 1972b) can substitute for progesterone treatment. The reserpine effect was not obtained in the hamster (Meyerson, 1970), and in the mouse the effect of reserpine was not produced if the animals had been adrenalectomized (Uphouse, 1970). Monoamine-synthesis inhibitors failed to facilitate the lordosis response in adrenalectomized rats (Eriksson and Södersten, 1973). Contradictory results have been found by Everitt et al. (1975a). The implication of adrenals in the activation of lordosis in the estrogen-treated female rat was suggested by Paris et al. (1971), who found that reserpine treatment increased the concentration of plasma progesterone in the ovariectomized rat. Ahlenius et al. (1972b) suggested that this effect was more closely related to the suppression of catecholamine functions than of 5-HT. It is likely that the facilitatory effect on lordotic behavior achieved by amine depletion involves some secretion from the adrenals. This might augment the estrogen-activated behavior. However, there is also evidence that compounds which suppress 5-HT activity facilitate the lordosis response without any adrenal mediation. Recently Zemlan et al. (1973) showed that PCPA, methysergide, and cinanserine (a serotonin antagonist) activated the lordosis response in estrogen-treated ovariectomized + adrenalectomized rats, and similarly Everitt et al. (1975) demonstrated that PCPA as well as α-MT facilitated the lordosis response in ovariectomized and adrenalectomized female rats kept on a daily estrogen maintenance dose. Ovariectomized and adrenalectomized female rhesus monkeys which received PCPA at 75 or 100 mg/kg s.c. every four days were observed to present to the male more frequently, an effect which was reversed by 5-HTP treatment (Gradwell et al., 1975). In the female cat, whose copulatory behavior is not influenced by progesterone, Hoyland et al. (1970) found PCPA to increase treading and rubbing (proestrous behavior) during the nonestrous phase.

b. Effects of Muscarinic Compounds. Muscarinic compounds such as pilocarpine, arecoline, and oxotremorine were found to decrease the estrogen + progesterene activated lordosis response in the female rat and hamster (Lindström and Meyerson, 1967; Lindström, 1972a,b). The effect of pilocarpine was inhibited by atropine but not by methylatropine, indicating that the effect of pilocarpine is probably exerted at a CNS level. The monoamine oxidase inhibitor pargyline prolonged the effect of pilocarpine treatment (Lindström, 1970), whereas blockage of serotonin biosynthesis by PCPA given 8 hr before pilocarpine treatment prevented the inhibitory effect of pilocarpine. The catecholamine-synthesis inhibitor α-MT did not have an analogous effect (Lindström, 1971). It was concluded that the effect of pilocarpine depends on the presence of 5-HT and that the inhibitory effect of pilocarpine on hormone-activated copulatory behavior in the female rat involves muscarinic mechanisms while being mediated by serotonergic functions. Lindström also demonstrated that pilocarpine had a late activating effect on the behavior (Lindström, 1972a). Pilocarpine given instead of progesterone facilitated the behavior. This effect was achieved about 4 hr after the injection of pilocarpine, in contrast to the inhibitory effect which was obtained 30 min after injection. The late effect of progesterone was not achieved in adrenalectomized animals, and it was concluded that the effect was probably due to stimulation of adrenal secretion.

The anticholinergic drug atropine slightly facilitated the lordosis response 3 hr after 0.5 mg/kg. However, no effect was seen after scopolamine (Lindström, 1972b).

c. *Monoamines and Sexual Motivation in the Female Rat.* The different methods employed to measure sexual motivation described above have in some introductory studies been used to investigate the involvement of monoaminergic mechanisms. The treatments used in this investigation were chosen on the basis of a dose regimen which affected locomotor ability only slightly, or not at all. Inhibition of the biosynthesis of serotonin by means of PCPA treatment seems to increase the response in the increasing-barrier technique. This increase was only seen if estrogen was given as well (Meyerson *et al.*, 1973). When no estrogen was given, or if the incentive was water and the animals were water deprived, PCPA treatment decreased the response. The same treatment schedule decreased the time the female was located in the vicinity of the male and the preference for a male versus an estrous female in "run-and-choose" situation (Meyerson, 1975). The role of serotonin in the regulation of sexual motivation in the female rat has to be elucidated by further experiments. However, by using different methods in parallel, it may be possible to find a neuropharmacological profile which can provide evidence for the pathways that are implicated in the condition which brings the animal to seek sexual contact.

d. *Conclusions.* When the available data are taken together (see Table 3), there is good evidence that serotoninergic pathways mediate inhibition of hormone-activated copulatory behavior in the female rat. Increased dopaminergic tone also has an inhibitory effect. Amphetamine facilitated the estrogen-induced lordosis response after pretreatment with pimozide but not after chlorpromazine, which has been interpreted by Everitt *et al.* (1974) as evidence "at best slight" for a facilitatory role of norepinephrine. The possibility that noradrenergic neurons are implicated in the facilitation of certain elements of the copulatory response of female guinea pigs was recently suggested by Crowley *et al.* (1976). LSD and apomorphine inhibited the sexual behavior whereas clonidine increased the duration of the lordosis response. The significance of norepinephrine in the lordosis response is, however, still very uncertain and has to be further elucidated.

There is also evidence that copulatory behavior is inhibited by increased monoaminergic tone in other species such as the hamster, mouse, guinea-pig, rabbit, cat, and rhesus monkey. The specific role of serotonin and other amines in these species has, however, to be further investigated.

TABLE 3
Influence of Neuropharmacological Agents on Hormone-Activated Copulatory Behavior in Gonadectomized Female and Male Rats[a]

Receptor	Main effect achieved on receptor activity	Females		Males	
		Lordosis response	Compounds used	Mount percentage	Compounds used
Serotonergic	Increased	Inhibition	Pargyline + 5-HTP, LSD	Inhibition	Pargyline + 5-HTP LSD
	Decreased	Increased	PCPA	Increased	PCPA
Noradrenergic	Increased	No inhibition	Pargyline + DOPS	Unaffected (?)	Pargyline + MK486 + DOPS, clonidine
	Decreased	Decreased (?)	Chlorpromazine	Unaffected (?)	FLA-63, phenoxybenzamine
Dopaminergic	Increased	Inhibition	Apomorphine, ET-495, pargyline Ro4-4602 + dopa	Increased	Pargyline + MK486 + dopa, apomorphine
	Decreased	Increased	Pimozide, α-MT	Decreased	Pimozide, chlorpromazine, α-MT
Muscarinic	Increased	Inhibition	Pilocarpine, arecholine, oxotremorine	?	
	Decreased	Increased (?)	Atropine	Decreased	Atropine, scopolamine

[a] Data taken from Meyerson (1964a,c); Bignami (1966); Meyerson (1966b); Meyerson and Lewander (1970); Malmnäs (1973); Meyerson et al. (1973, 1974); and Everitt et al. (1975a).

Stimulation of muscarinic receptors apparently decreased female copulation behavior in the rat and hamster. A relationship between CNS cholinergic and monoaminergic mechanisms was obtained in the rat. The fact that PCPA but not α-MT prevented the inhibitory effect of pilocarpine on lordosis response suggests that the effect of pilocarpine in the rat is mediated by serotonergic mechanisms.

What evidence exists for a relationship between gonadal hormones and monoamines in the production of lordosis response in the female rat? It has not been possible to elicit the behavior in ovariectomized females by male mounting unless estrogen is given. In contrast, progesterone treatment can be substituted by suppression of serotoninergic and/or catecholaminergic (dopaminergic) activity. If it can be clearly established that endogenous hormone production is not involved, it will still be an open question as to whether the effect of progesterone is implicated in the monoaminergic inhibitory mechanisms. There are data which could be interpreted as suggesting that progesterone activates lordosis by removing an inhibition (see Section 3.1.4d). However, one of many alternatives is that progesterone facilitates the activation of lordosis, the tonic inhibition thereby being overcome. In a recent overview these hypotheses are further elaborated by Kow, et al. (1975), who add anatomical data to the evidence provided by the pharmacological tools.

There is a number of biochemical and histochemical studies demonstrating that monoaminergic mechanisms are influenced by gonadal hormones (Donoso et al., 1969; Fuxe and Hökfelt, 1969; Lichtensteiger, 1969; Bapna et al., 1971; Tonge and Greengrass, 1971; Kordon and Glowinski, 1972; Wirz-Justice et al., 1974; Everitt et al., 1975b). There are also studies in which gross changes in monoamines have *not* been seen after hormonal treatments appropriate for producing the lordosis response in ovariectomized rats (Meyerson 1964b; Meyerson and Lewander, 1970; Hyyppä and Cardinali, 1973). The changes in monoamines which have been demonstrated might well be specifically related to the hormone activation of sexual behavior. The effects of drugs would indicate this. However, there are many other neuroendocrine functions in which monoamines are implicated (for a review, see De Wied and de Jong, 1974), so it is not yet possible to relate directly the hormone-induced changes in cerebral monoamines to the production of copulatory behavior.

3.3.3. Drugs and Male Sexual Behavior

The effect of drugs on sexual behavior in males has been studied mainly on copulatory behavior in rats, and most recent studies have been concerned with the mounting phase of this behavior.

a. Methodological Considerations. Some investigators have studied the effects of drugs on intact animals, either from a random population or selected sexually sluggish or active individuals. Other studies are performed on castrated males subjected to exogenous testosterone treatment. We must consider that due to the fact that the intact animal is already at a maximal or a minimal overt response level, stimulatory or inhibitory effects, respectively, of a treatment might remain undiscovered. From this point of view there are some advantages in using castrated males maintained at an appropriate response level with respect to the behavior studied. Measurements and characteristics of the male copulatory behavior have been given above. With regard to pharmacological studies the following methodological considerations are suggested (for an applied study, see Malmnäs, 1973). They are based upon experiments on the castrated male rat but could apply also to experiments on other species.

To avoid influences of environmental exploration or emotional reactions to a novel environment on latencies to response, an adequate time of adaptation to the testing environment should be given before the female partner is introduced.

The duration of a test should be based on the distribution of latencies in sexually experienced intact subjects (or other stages of reference). When the distributions of latencies to mount, intromission, and ejaculation are known, the appropriate length of testing can be determined.

The time of testing after hormone injection is based upon the determination of the latency to onset of the response after different doses of the hormone and the duration of the effect of a single hormone injection.

The time between hormone injections is based on the duration of a single hormone injection to avoid cumulative effects and on the dose–response relationship established to find a submaximal response level.

At this stage we have to check again the distribution of the copulatory parameters in subjects kept on the weekly hormonal treatment chosen. After appropriate adjustment of the observation time to cover the latencies, the study on how drugs influence the hormone-activated copulatory behavior can start.

Latency and rate of intromission are very likely to be dependent on the number of mounts performed. Ejaculation is likely to be influenced by the pattern of intromissions. The evaluation of the influence of drugs on intromission and ejaculation must be based upon comparison of experimental and control subjects with equivalent mount responses for intromission comparisons, and similar intromission patterns for ejaculation comparisons.

Most studies are performed using a highly receptive female often stimulated by exogenous hormone treatment. Some laboratories use a high level of estrogen-induced heat (pellet implantation or injection); in other instances estrogen + progesterone is given. The treatment of the female partner is probably not unimportant when comparisons of data from different studies are made. However, in some studies male subjects are used as copulatory partners, and even other species than the tested subjects have been utilized. In studies on male-to-male copulatory behavior 5–10 males are placed, after a certain time of isolation, together in a test cage. The percentage of males exhibiting mounting behavior is recorded. It is up to the experimenter to determine if such a gross technique should be used. However, for screening purposes it might be acceptable. When comparing results from different laboratories, it should be considered that in some studies the experimental subjects are tested as a group. In other studies the interaction between treated and nontreated subjects is observed. The two test situations are obviously different from a stimulus point of view. Unfortunately, in some papers the stimulus situation is not made clear in this respect.

The importance of partner preference in dogs and primates was mentioned earlier.

b. Monoamines and Male Copulatory Behavior. First, we discuss the monoamine oxidase inhibitors and precursors. The effects of monoamine oxidase inhibitors on copulatory behavior in male rats have been tested by Soulairac (1963), Malmnäs and Meyerson (1970, 1971), Tagliamonte *et al.* (1971), Dewsbury *et al.* (1972), and Malmnäs (1973). The great variety of methods used allows only the general conclusion that when significant effects were obtained the direction of the responses was consistently an inhibition of the elements of copulatory behavior. On the other hand, Butcher *et al.* (1969) and Leavitt (1969) found no effect of nialamide and tranylcypromine on copulatory behavior in male rats. However, the doses used were rather small.

Monoamine precursors have been given after pretreatment with a monoamine oxidase inhibitor alone or with an extracerebral decarboxylase inhibitor such as MK 486 or RO4-4602. There is a marked reduction in the number of males mounting after 5-HTP treatment (Malmnäs and Meyerson, 1970, 1972; Tagliamonte *et al.*, 1972a; Malmnäs, 1973). In contrast, the mount percentage significantly increased in analogous experiments with dopa (Malmnäs and Meyerson, 1970; Malmnäs, 1973). Low doses of dopa (2.5 mg/kg) were effective provided pargyline and MK 486 were given as well. No effect was achieved by pargyline and dopa or dopa together with MK 486 (Malmnäs, 1973). However, Da Prada *et al.* (1973a,b) and Tagliamonte *et al.* (1973) reported an increase in mount percentage after RO4-4602 + dopa. Hyyppä *et al.* (1971) found no increase in the number of mounts and intromissions preceding ejaculation responses after RO4-4602 + dopa treatment, and Gray *et al.* (1974) reported an increase in intromission and ejaculation latencies after an analogous treatment but no stimulatory effect. It is, in this connection, important to emphasize that (1) the measures of Malmnäs, Da Prada, and Tagliamonte and co-workers were mount percentage, which is clearly different from the measures of Hyyppä and Gray and co-workers, and (2) the stimulatory effect of dopa was found in males kept at a submaximal response level, in contrast to the findings of Hyyppä and Gray *et al.*, which were obtained in vigorous subjects. The dose of dopa used when combined with a monoamine oxidase inhibitor and extracerebral decarboxylase inhibitor was around 2.5 mg/kg and 100 mg/kg when no monoamine oxidase inhibitor was given. High doses of dopa might displace 5-HT, and some of the stimulatory effects seen in these experiments could have been achieved in this way, as suggested by Da Prada *et al.* (1973).

DL-DOPS given in doses which either did not or did significantly produce overt effects on locomotor activity in both instances failed to change mount percentage (Malmnäs, 1973).

Second, we discuss the receptor-stimulating and receptor-blocking agents. The dopamine-receptor-stimulating agent apomorphine reduced the number of intromissions occurring before ejaculation (Butcher *et al.*, 1969), increased mount percentage and intromission percentage, and shortened mount latency (Malmnäs and Meyerson, 1972; Malmnäs, 1973; Tagliamonte *et al.*, 1973).

In contrast, a marked reduction in mount and intromission percentage was seen after LSD (30–100 µg/kg, Malmnäs, 1973). Bignami (1966) showed that intromission frequency increased and intromission and postejaculatory intervals decreased in a dose-dependent manner after LSD (5 µg/kg). At 50 µg/kg the opposite effect was obtained. A dose-dependent decrease and increase, respectively, was demonstrated. Clonidine, a central noradrenaline receptor stimulator (Andén *et al.*, 1970*b*), had no effect on copulatory behavior except for a slight reduction of mount latency at high doses (30 µg/kg; Malmnäs, 1973).

Male-to-male mounting was increased after treatment with mesorgydin and methysergide (Benckert and Eversmann, 1972), agents which are proposed to have antiserotoninergic properties. The evidence for the antiserotonin effect is, however, scarce.

So far, the results obtained from different laboratories rather consistently demonstrate that in the male rat a selective increase in serotonin decreases the percentage of males mounting, whereas an increase in catecholamines increases the mounting percentage. The apomorphine experiments would be in line with the interpretation that it is dopamine and not norepinephrine which is important in this behavior. This is further evidenced below. The above statement is valid both for male-to-male mounting and mounting of an estrous female. Available data do not allow further conclusions as to a difference in the pharmacology of mounting behavior in relation to sex of the stimulus object. A great range of doses have been used in different laboratories, and parallel studies have also been performed on locomotor activity and other overt behavior patterns (Malmnäs, 1973). In instances where sexual behavior was suppressed this was not necessarily associated with a disturbance in overt behavior.

Third, we discuss the amine depletors and synthesis inhibitors. Since the discovery of Tagliamonte *et al.* (1969), Shillito (1969, 1970), and Sheard (1969) that PCPA increased male mounting, there has been a rapidly growing literature on the effect of PCPA on different aspects of sexual behavior. Again, many different measures of sexual behavior have been used, and the techniques employed vary. The data on PCPA effects on sexual behavior were recently reviewed by Gessa and Tagliamonte (1974). It could be concluded that PCPA produces male-to-male mounting behavior under conditions where in control animals male-to-male mounting was not seen, or was seen at a significantly lower level. There is also a clear-cut increase in mount percentage when females in heat are used as sexual partners (Malmnäs and Meyerson, 1971; Salis and Dewsbury, 1971; Ahlenius et al., 1971; Malmnäs, 1973). In some of these studies the ejaculatory percentage was increased. It has been established that the stimulatory effect of PCPA is also seen after pinealectomy (Tagliamonte et al., 1969) and adrenalectomy (Malmnäs and Meyerson, 1971; Malmnäs, 1973). However, there are data suggesting that PCPA + pargyline-induced male-to-male mounting is dependent on an intact pituitary. The increased mounting was not seen after hypophysectomy (Gawienowski and Hodgen, 1971). Whalen and Luttge (1970) found no significant effect of PCPA on number of mounts and intromissions per ejaculation nor on coital activity preceding satiation. These parameters are apparently different from those on which a stimulatory effect of PCPA has been reported. Of studies in other species than the rat, there is one indicating increased mounting behavior in the rabbit (Perez-Cruet et al., 1971), two reports in which male-to-male mounting was found to be increased in the male cat (Hoyland et al., 1970; Ferguson et al., 1970), and one study in which no increase of male-to-male mounting was found above what was normally seen in untreated cats (Zitrin et al., 1970). In primates, Redmond et al. (1971) found no effects on PCPA on social-sexual presentations and mounting in groups of *Macaca speciosa* containing both sexes. Data on the effect of PCPA in the rhesus monkey has been given above (Everitt and Herbert, 1975). A selective decrease of cerebral 5-HT, achieved by intraventricular injections of 5,6-dihydroxytryptamine, increased the male-to-male mounting in male rats (Da Prada et al., 1972; Gessa and Tagliamonte, 1975). The catecholamine synthesis inhibitor α-MT significantly decreased mount percentage (Malmnäs, 1973). The dopamine-β-hydroxylase inhibitor FLA63 and the noradrenaline-receptor-blocking agent phenoxybenzamine did not affect mount percentage. In contrast, the dopamine-receptor-blocking agent pimozide decreased mount percentage at a dose level where no effect was seen on overt behavior. Pimozide was also effective in inhibiting the stimulatory effect of apomorphine (Malmnäs, 1973).

The amine depletors reserpine and tetrabenazine have been found to facilitate some components of copulatory behavior in male rats in that they reduce the number of intromissions required to attain ejaculation (Soulairac, 1963; Dewsbury and Davis, 1970; Dewsbury, 1972). The mount percentage was, however, decreased; mount latency increased, and no certain effect on ejaculation pattern was found by Malmnäs (1973).

Recently it was reported that amantadine induced penile erection in intact, but not in castrated, male rats (Baraldi and Bertolini, 1974). Atropine prevented this effect. It is at present difficult to interpret this interesting finding as amantadine has many different effects on monoaminergic and cholinergic mechanisms.

c. Cholinergic Mechanisms and Sexual Behavior in the Male. Very few investigations have been performed on the effect of cholinergic drugs on male sexual behavior. The doses used by Soulairac (1963) induced too much motor disturbance to permit an effect on the sexual behavior to be evaluated. In general, anticholinergic compounds (scopolamine, benactyzine, atropine) decreased the number of male rats which mounted receptive females and increased intromission latencies, intervals, and the postejaculatory intervals (Bignami, 1966). From the description of the male behavior in the paper by Bignami it seems as if the anticholinergic compounds decreased initiation of the mounting behavior.

d. Conclusions. Opposite effects of serotonin and dopamine on the activation of copulatory behavior in male rats seem to exist (see Table 3). A selective increase of dopamine facilitates mounting behavior, whereas an opposite effect is obtained by increased serotoninergic tone. The evidence for this hypothesis has been obtained in the male rat. Results in other species supporting the hypothesis are rather scarce.

3.3.4. Compounds with an Effect on Protein Synthesis and Axonal Transport Mechanisms

The hypothesis that protein synthesis is involved in steroid-activated female sexual behavior has been proposed by several investigators (Quadagno *et al.*, 1971; Meyerson, 1971b; Wallen *et al.*, 1972; Kan-wha Ho *et al.*, 1974; Terkel *et al.*, 1973; Whalen *et al.*, 1974). Intracranial implants or infusions of actinomycin D in the preoptic area significantly inhibited estrogen-activated lordosis behavior in ovariectomized rats. Actinomycin D was implanted bilaterally in the preoptic area of the hypothalamus before or after a subcutaneous injection of EB. The steroid-induced sexual receptivity was blocked by this treatment. Implants into the caudate nucleus and systemic actinomycin D had no effect on the behavior. Whether the intracranial implants specifically blocked the DNA-dependent synthesis of RNA or interfered with the estrogen-activated response by a cytotoxic effect has not been fully elucidated. Cycloheximide given subcutaneously (Meyerson, 1973) or into the lateral brain ventricles (Meyerson, 1972) inhibited the estrogen + progesterone activated lordosis response in the female rat. The effect was obtained only if cycloheximide was given before the estrogen injection but not if the protein-synthesis inhibitor was given 24 hr after the estrogen injection. Cycloheximide given intracranially to guinea pigs was found to block the inhibitory action of progesterone on the display of estrous behavior (Wallen *et al.*, 1972). This effect opens the possibility that protein synthesis is involved in the inhibitory effect of progesterone. Actinomycin D implanted into the anterior hypothalamic preoptic region of the diencephalon decreased estrogen-induced wheel-running activity in female rats (Stern and Jankowiak, 1972). Again the inhibitory effect could be a specific effect related to protein-synthesis inhibition or else a nonspecific cytotoxic effect. The fact that the animals look healthy and that the effects are reversible does not prove that the drug acts by protein-synthesis inhibition. The compound could affect cellular functions by other mechanisms of action.

Colchicine has been shown in many studies to inhibit axonal transport mechanisms (Dahlström, 1968; Kreutzberg, 1969; Karlsson and Sjöstrand, 1969). Colchicine given in connection with estrogen treatment inhibited the estrogen-activated lordosis response in ovariectomized rats when colchicine was given in connection with the estrogen treatment but not when given 24 hr later (Meyerson, 1973). The lordotic behavior was inhibited for 48 hr after colchicine treatment but could be activated again at 72 or 96 hr after the injection.

Evidently the investigations on the effect of drugs which interfere with protein synthesis and axonal transport mechanisms on hormone-induced elements of sexual behavior are presently at a stage which would make any conclusion premature.

4. PARENTAL BEHAVIOR

The behavior of parents toward their young is a matter of survival of the species and very likely also plays a crucial role in the development of various aspects of the behavior of the young. We will, however, only be concerned with parental behavior that includes nest building and the behavior toward the young until they are able to obtain food independently of their parents. So far as it is justified to call parental behavior reproductive behavior; in fact, nest building is, in many birds at least, an integrated part of the sexual behavior pattern. Care of the young in connection with term of gestation is very much dominated by the behavior of the female. Data concerning paternal behavior are indeed meager. By analogy with sexual-behavior patterns, males can, of course, also display a response to the young characteristic of the female, i.e., be maternal. As was the case with sexual behavior, most data on the hormonal and pharmacological control of parental behavior have been obtained in laboratory animals, especially the rat. We will, therefore, review the data concerning the hormonal influence on parental behavior of the rat with outviews to other species. Comprehensive reviews in the field have appeared and are referred to in the text below (Mitchell, 1969; Moltz, 1972; Noirot, 1972; Rosenblum, 1972; Zarrow *et al.*, 1972; Lamb, 1975).

4.1. Maternal Behavior

4.1.1. Characteristics of Maternal Behavior

The following behavior patterns are generally looked upon as constituents of maternal behavior. However, it should be mentioned that in some species certain parts of these behavior patterns are lacking and there is a great species variability as to the performance.

1. Nest building. The female collects material to build a nest. In most nest-building species this kind of nest can be distinguished from a sleeping nest.
2. Cleaning. This means cleaning the pups from fetal tissue and licking their bodies.
3. Nursing. The mother takes a characteristic posture which allows the pups to attach to the nipples. The nursing posture also helps to maintain the body temperature of the young.
4. Retrieving. The mother grasps the pups and transports them back to the nest if for some reason they have come outside the nest. Retrieving also includes the pups being deposited in the nest, not only transported and randomly deposited.

Neuroendocrinological investigations of maternal behavior have been concerned mainly with nest building and retrieving. The measures are usually nest weight and style, occurrence, and latency to retrieving when exposed to pups.

4.1.2. The Rat

The rat has a gestation period of 21–23 days. Nest building starts about 24 hr before term. Immediately after parturition, more nest material is collected to form a higher and more compact nest. Cleaning of the pups starts immediately after parturition and at about the same time the mother starts to crouch over the young with adjustment of posture to allow nursing. In the rat there is a characteristic retrieving behavior. It is also possible to induce retrieving in virgin females and males. This requires that the female be kept in the presence of young ("sensitized") for 6–7 days continuously (Rosenblatt, 1967). Although the pattern of behavior is very much the same as that seen immediately after parturition, in nulliparous females it differs from the behavior seen in connection with term of gestation in that it has a latency of several days of exposure to pups. A shortening of this latency by means of hormonal manipulation has been thought to shed some light on the neuroendocrine mechanisms involved in this element of maternal behavior.

The maternal responsiveness of lactating female rats differs from that exhibited after sensitization also with regard to the response displayed in certain specific situations. Bridges *et al.* (1972) found that lactating female rats investigated a T-maze extension of the home cage, retrieving pups placed in the wings of the maze more often than sensitized rats. Similar data were obtained by Quadagno et al. (1974) using a runway.

a. Hormonal Control. Stone (1925) was the first to raise the question of whether hormonal factors were responsible for the maternal reaction. Stone used parabiotic rats, one of which was pregnant and displayed clear-cut maternal behavior. Her partner was found to be completely indifferent. More recently Terkel and Rosenblatt (1968, 1972), using direct injections of plasma, were able to significantly shorten the latency of induction of maternal behavior in the virgin rat. The elements of maternal behavior were induced within 14.5 hr. Twenty-four hours prior to parturition, the mother's blood had not yet attained the capacity to induce the maternal behavior, and 24 hr after parturition it had lost this capacity.

Progesterone in rat plasma begins to increase on day 4 of pregnancy, reaching a maximum concentration on day 14; thereafter the output of the steroid falls slowly until day 20, when the decrease is abrupt (Fajer and Barraclough, 1967; Hashimoto et al., 1968; Wiest et al., 1968). Estrogen rises to a peak value shortly before the day of parturition (Yoshinaga et al., 1969), while prolactin has a low plasma concentration until about day 20 of pregnancy. On the day of parturition, it increases sharply. Other hormonal events also occur during gestation, such as fluctuations in FSH, LH, and oxytocin.

Moltz and co-workers (Moltz et al., 1970) manipulated progesterone, estrogen, and prolactin in an attempt to reduce the latency to retrieving in the nulliparous female rat. Nulliparous females were ovariectomized and given estradiol daily for 11 days, progesterone was given on days 6 through 9, and prolactin was given on the evening of day 9 and the morning of day 10. On the afternoon of day 10 the females were exposed to foster pups. The full spectrum of maternal behavior was recorded (nest building, nursing posture, licking, retrieving) between 35 and 40 hr from the time the pups were first introduced. This is a significant reduction from the average 6–7 days, the typical latency of untreated nulliparae. Zarrow et al. (1971), using a similar technique, found a regimen of estradiol, progesterone, cortisol acetate, and prolactin effective in producing retrieving after 1.4 instead of 4.9 days. Thus, it is concluded that the presence of young can activate the neuronal system mediating the expression of maternal behavior but that these environmental stimulations require a period of 6–7 days to be effective. The hormonal manipulations described above significantly shortened this period. However, the latency was 35–40 hr, which again contrasts with the postpartum behavior of the female rat, who immediately retrieves her young. Recently Leon et al. (1973) reported estrogen to have an inhibitory influence on maternal behavior in the rat and that after long-term removal (8 weeks) of the gonads the maternal behavior was facilitated. Under certain conditions progesterone has been shown to decrease nursing behavior (Moltz et al., 1969).

Hysterectomy during the second half of pregnancy or in virgin rats induced a rapid onset of maternal behavior (Siegel and Rosenblatt 1975a,b). This effect was prevented by ovariectomy but restored in hysterectomized-ovariectomized rats by estrogen. Progesterone had no effect or an inhibitory effect on the estrogen-induced maternal behavior. Rosenblatt and Siegel interpret their data in the following way: "Estrogen acts to stimulate maternal behavior in the experimental preparations under circumstances in which progesterone levels have recently declined and are currently very low." This would correspond to the hormonal situation in which maternal behavior arises prepartum.

The male rat will also display maternal behavior on exposure to foster pups (Wiesner and Sheard, 1933; Rosenblatt, 1967). Again it takes around 6–7 days of exposure to induce the behavior. A significant reduction in exposure time was also achieved by estrogen + progesterone + prolactin treatment in the male. However, even doubling the doses of the hormones did not result in the same short latency as was obtained in the nulliparous female (Lubin et al., 1972). This fact has brought up the question of whether sex differences in hormone-activated maternal behavior are influenced by hormonal manipulation in infancy, by analogy, for example, with copulatory behavior.

Bridges et al. (1973) tested the effect of neonatal TP treatment of female Wistar rats and neonatal castration of males on hormone-induced (estrogen + progesterone + prolactin) retrieving in the home cage and in a T-maze situation. In subjects not neonatally hormonally manipulated, the adult hormone treatment shortened the latency to retrieving in females as well as males (home-cage test). The hormonal response in the T-maze situation was clear cut in females but very weak in males who almost did not retrieve at all. Neonatally castrated males significantly increased T-maze retrieving after hormone treatment in adulthood. Since 94% of sham-castrated, hormone-treated males retrieved in the home cage, it was not possible to detect a further increase by neonatal castration. However, no effect was seen on the latency to retrieving. In neonatally TP treated females there was almost no hormone-induced T-maze retrieving. In contrast, no effect of early TP treatment was seen in the home-cage tests. Thus, the home-cage retrieving in which the sex difference was less pronounced than in the T-maze situation was not influenced by neonatal hormonal manipulation.

Quadagno and Rockwell (1972) reported that neonatal exposure to androgen significantly altered retrieval behavior in the male direction, i.e., fewer females (Long Evans strain) retrieved pups. No normal males exhibited retrieving in this study. However, a significant number of males castrated at birth retrieved. Using the same strain of rats but working in another laboratory, Quadagno (Quadagno et al., 1974) failed to replicate the earlier work. No effect was obtained in this study by neonatal TP treatment. In this latter study males also displayed maternal behavior. It seems from a footnote of the paper that Quadagno returned to his own laboratory and was able to replicate his first data. (See also McCullough *et al.*, 1974.) The last word seems not to have been said. Only dimorphous behavior activated by hormones in adulthood is influenced by hormonal manipulation pre- or neonatally (see above). The sensitized maternal behavior response was not hormone-dependent (Rosenblatt, 1967). The retrieving displayed after estrogen + progesterone + prolactin treatment is apparently hormone-dependent, with a certain difference in sensitivity between the two sexes. Thus, this is what we expect in that only the hormone-dependent retrieving should be influenced by neonatal hormonal manipulation. More experiments have to be performed to show whether this prediction is correct.

Ablation studies and studies concerned with implanted steroid hormones have been performed to establish which brain regions mediate the hormonal influence on maternal behavior. The data are still very scarce in the rat, and no conclusions can be drawn as to a specific central nervous location for the hormonal effect on the maternal behavior. (For a review see Moltz, 1972.)

4.1.3. The Rabbit

The gestation period in the rabbit is 31–32 days. The maternal nest, which is unique to pregnancy, is built a few days before or on the day of parturition. For a description of nest-building behavior, see Ross *et al.* (1963). Licking of the young and nursing starts a few minutes after parturition (Deutsch, 1957; Zarrow *et al.*, 1965). Retrieving is not a common phenomenon in the rabbit (Ross *et al.*, 1959), and it is not clear if nulliparous females will respond maternally after continuous exposure to young.

a. Hormonal Control. There is a progesterone increase on the second day after mating, reaching a maximum value on day 16, and thereafter decreasing to abruptly disappear around parturition. Estradiol and progesterone given for some weeks to ovariectomized females led to maternal nest building. It was necessary to terminate the progesterone treatment some days before the cessation of estradiol. Nest building started 3 days after the progesterone treatment had been withdrawn (see Zarrow *et al.*, 1972). If progesterone and estradiol treatment were stopped simultaneously, nest building did not occur. The estrogen + progesterone treatment given to female rabbits was not effective in producing nest-building behavior in male rabbits. TP during the second half of gestation inhibited maternal nest building and care for the litter (Fuller *et al.*, 1970).

4.1.4. The Golden Hamster

The gestation period is 16 days. Both sexes build nests. A typical maternal nest contains more material than the ordinary nest built by a nonpregnant female or by a male hamster (see Richards, 1967). The maternal nest is built already around day 5–6 of gestation and is progessively improved towards term. There are characteristic maternal behavior parameters such as licking and nursing. Fragments of the maternal complex were exhibited in nulliparous female hamsters exposed to pups of 6–10 days of age.

Hormonal Control. Plasma progesterone does not increase until day 8 of pregnancy, with a maximum peak on day 14 (Lukaszewska and Greenwald, 1970; Leavitt and Blaha, 1970). Decrease of progesterone before parturition is close to term. The effect on nest building of estrogen and progesterone pellets implanted under the skin of ovariectomized nulliparous females (Richards, 1969) was studied. An increase of this behavior was observed only after implantation of both steroids. It did not occur in castrated male hamsters.

4.1.5. The Mouse

The mouse engages in two distinct kinds of nest-building: a sleeping nest and a much larger one built exclusively during pregnancy (Koller, 1955). Lisk and Pretlow (1969) found that progesterone elicited nest building, and there is also some evidence for a synergistic action of estradiol with progesterone. However, high levels of estrogen (Lisk, 1971) and also TP (Gandelman, 1973) inhibited nest building. In contrast to the rat, rabbit, and hamster, nulliparous female mice never having been in contact previously with foster pups respond with maternal behavior within 5 min after presentation of pups (Leblond, 1940; Noirot, 1972). All components of maternal behavior, such as retrieving, licking, and nursing posture, are seen. Also the castrated male displays much the same behavior (Leblond, 1940). Following the neonatal TP treatment to females, and estrogen and progesterone in adulthood, no maternal nest building response was seen (Lisk and Russel, 1972). Facilitation of maternal behavior in the mouse by administration of prolactin into the anterior hypothalamus was reported by Voci and Carlson (1973).

4.1.6 Primates

Systematic studies of the maternal behavior in primates and its dependence on hormonal changes are lacking, but there are a few studies that are indicative.

a. Postpartum Mother–Infant Contact. For a detailed description of the behavior in connection with the parturition in Macacae, see Tinklepaugh and Hartman (1930, 1932) and Rosenblum (1972).

After delivering the infant, the female begins to manually explore the vaginal area, and when the placenta appears in the vagina, it is expelled and eaten. After this the female turns her attention to the newborn, licking her infant, and later on shows more common grooming patterns. After this initial phase a ventral contact position is supported by the mother actively clasping the infant. A gradual decrease in ventral contact takes place during the first four months of life (Hinde *et al.*, 1964; Rosenblum *et al.*, 1964; Kaufman and Rosenblum; 1966; Hinde and Spencer-Booth, 1967). Almost immediately after birth, the infant has oral contact with the nipples. The age at which a complete termination of nipple contact occurs is influenced by many factors (see Simonds, 1965). In the chimpanzee the neonate is not automatically held and carried at the breast area by the mother, and the newborn lacks the coordinated movements necessary to reach the breast (Rogres and Davenport, 1970). Nursing is initiated by a combination of signals of distress in the newborn (squirms, vocalizing), seeking head movements, the suckling reflex, and the mother's reacting to these signals by repositioning the location of the infant on her body until the nipples are found and nursing initiated. Much learning is required for the development of efficient nursing. The reinforcement which according to Rogres and Davenport is responsible for the development of the coordinated behavioral sequence of nursing is the reduction of hunger in the infant and breast tension in the mother.

b. Protective Maternal Behavior. The first regulatory patterns of protective behavior are generally seen at a time approximately coinciding with attempts of the young to leave the mother for a short period, that is, around the second week after birth. Before this time the mother has restrained the infant in a ventral position by clasping it. With some variability between primates, the maternal restraining of the young decreases gradually during the first months and is completely gone after about 45 weeks. There appear to be three different phases in the maternal protection. The first is restraining of the infant from breaking contact with the mother, the second is a close guarding of the infant by the mother moving along and protecting the infant by her body or hand, and the third phase is an increased duration of the infants' excursions. The mother's protective behavior then appears to be watching and attending to the vocalization of the infant. There are very few data as to endogenous factors governing the maternal protection, but as Rosenblum (1972) has pointed out, at the end of the third month of life protective patterns either fall to low levels or virtually disappear, a fact which possibly indicates that some endogenous factor may play a crucial role in the termination of maternal protection. Whether this is a shift of hormonal status and/or only a change in the stimulus characteristics of the maturing infant is not clear. One possibility raised is that the disappearance of the protective behavior is correlated to the infant's decrease in nursing and thereby the altered hormonal status in the mother. In the study of Breuggeman (1973) on parental care in free-ranging rhesus monkeys the care-giving behavior was greater among 2- and 3-year-old females at birth and mating seasons. This could possibly indicate a relationship with the onset of puberty and reproductive cyclicity.

4.1.7. The Effect of Drugs

The influence of drugs on maternal behavior seems at present to be a virgin field for exploration. The technical experience from the experiments on drug action on sexual behavior should guide future experiments in the field. Again we face the problem that drugs can act directly on neuronal mechanisms involved in the production of maternal behavior or indirectly by changing the endocrine control of the behavior. For example, perphenazine, a phenothiazine, could substitute for the progesterone treatment (Moltz *et al.*, 1971) in activation of retrieving in rats. It is difficult at this stage to advance any hypothesis as to how the drug might exert its effect. It is known to release prolactin (Ben-David, 1968); however, effects on neuronal functions directly related to the retrieving behavior are also plausible.

4.2. Paternal (Paternalistic) Behavior

There are comparatively few reports on the behavior between adult males and immatures. The paternal behavior in different primates has been reviewed by Mitchell (1969), and the paternal behavior in the Mongolian gerbil has been described by Elwood (1975). There are very few data which could provide the basis for a view on the hormonal implication in the relation between adult males and infants. Wilson and Vessey (1968) observed exaggerated affectional behavior toward infants in two castrated adult male rhesus monkeys. Similar findings were reported by Breuggeman (1973) studying parental care in a group of free-ranging rhesus monkeys.

5. GENERAL CONCLUSIONS

It is obvious from what has been said that hormones influence the development of, as well as exert control over, reproductive behavior in the adult. Neuropharmacological studies, although in an early phase, have provided interesting evidence for implications of monoaminergic and cholinergic mechanisms in the hormone-activated behavior. Clinical data have, due to consideration of space, not been included. We are convinced, however, that by continuous improvement of psychoendocrine techniques, extending our experiments to several species for the sake of generality, and by multidisciplinary teamwork, our data can provide a fruitful basis for systematic clinical studies.

Acknowledgments

Our appreciation is extended to Mrs. Ann-Mari Kjellberg and Mrs. Mona Nilsson for their skillful and patient preparation of the manuscript.

Studies conducted in this laboratory since 1964 were supported in part by the Swedish Medical Research Council Grant 14X-64-01/10 and by NIH Grant R01-HD4108-01/03.

6. REFERENCES

AGHAJANIAN, G. K., 1972a, LSD and CNS transmission, *Ann. Rev. Pharmacol.* **12**:157–168.

AGHAJANIAN, G. K., 1972b, Chemical-feedback regulation of serotonin-containing neurons in the brain, *Ann. N.Y. Acad. Sci.* **193**:86–94.

AHLENIUS, S., ERIKSSON, H., LARSSON, K., MODIGH, K., and SÖDERSTEN, P., 1971, Mating behavior in the male rat treated with *p*-chlorophenylalanine methyl ester alone and in combination with pargyline, *Psychopharmacologia* **20**:383–388.

AHLENIUS, S., ENGEL, J., ERIKSSON, H., and SÖDERSTEN, P., 1972a, Effects of tetrabenazine on lordosis behaviour and on brain monoamines in the female rat, *J. Neural Transm.* **33**:155–162.

AHLENIUS, S., ENGEL, J., ERIKSSON, H., MODIGH, K., and SÖDERSTEN, P., 1972b, Importance of central catecholamines in the mediation of lordosis behaviour in ovariectomized rats treated with estrogen and inhibitors of monoamine synthesis, *J. Neural Transm.* **33**:247–256.

AMENORI, Y., CHEN, C. L., and MEITES, J., 1970, Serum prolactin levels in rats during different reproductive states, *Endocrinology* **70**:506–510.

ANDÉN, N. E., RUBENSON, A., FUXE, K., and HÖKFELT, T., 1967, Evidence for dopamine receptor stimulation by apomorphine, *J. Pharm. Pharmacol.* **19**:627–629.

ANDÉN, N. E., BUTCHER, S. G., CORRODI, H., FUXE, K., and UNGERSTEDT, U., 1970a, Receptor activity and turnover of dopamine and noradrenaline after neuroleptics, *Eur. J. Pharmacol.* **11**:303–314.

ANDÉN, N. E., CORRODI, H., FUXE, K., HÖKFELT, T., RYDIN, C., and SVENSSON, T., 1970b, Evidence for a central noradrenaline receptor stimulation by clonidine, *Life Sci.* **9**:513–523.

ANDERSON, C. H., and GREENWALD, G. S., 1969, Autoradiographic analysis of estradiol uptake in the brain and pituitary of the female rat, *Endocrinology* **85**:1160–1165.

ARAI, Y., and GORSKI, R. A., 1968a, Protection against the neural organizing effect of exogenous androgen in the neonatal rat, *Endocrinology* **82**:1005–1009.

ARAI, Y., and GORSKI, R. A., 1968b, Effect of anti-estrogen on steroid-induced sexual receptivity in ovariectomized rats, *Physiol. Behav.* **3**:351–353.

BALÁZS, R., 1971, Effects of hormones on the biochemical maturation of the brain, in: Influence of hormones on the nervous system, *Proceedings of the International Society for Psychoneuroendocrinology*, pp. 150–164, Karger, Basel.

BAPNA, J., NEFF, N. H., and COSTA, E., 1971, A method for studying norepinephrine and serotonin metabolism in small regions of rat brain: effect of ovariectomy on amine metabolism in anterior and posterior hypothalamus, *Endocrinology* **81**:1345–1349.

BARALDI, M., and BERTOLINI, A., 1974, Penile erections induced by amantadine in male rats, *Life Sci.* **14**:1231–1235.

Bard, P., 1939, Central nervous mechanisms for emotional behavior patterns in animals, *Res. Publ. Assoc. Res. Nerv. Ment. Dis.* **19**:190-218.

Bard, P., 1940, The hypothalamus and sexual behavior, in: The hypothalamus and control levels of autonomic functions, *Res. Publ. Assoc. Res. Nerv. Ment. Dis.* **20**:551-579.

Barraclough, C. A., and Gorski, R. A., 1961, Evidence that the hypothalamus is responsible for androgen-induced sterility in the female rat, *Endocrinology* **68**:68-71.

Barraclough, C. A., and Gorski, R. A., 1962, Studies on mating behavior in the androgen-sterilized female rat in relation to the hypothalamic regulation of sexual behavior, *J. Endocrinol.* **25**:175-182.

Baum, M. J., and Vreeburg, J. T. M., 1973, Copulation in castrated male rats following combined treatment with estradiol and dihydrotestosterone, *Science* **182**:283-285.

Baum, M. J., Södersten, P., and Vreeburg, J. T. M., 1974, Mounting and receptive behavior in the ovariectomized female rat: influence of estradiol, dihydrotestosterone, and genital anesthetization, *Horm. Behav.* **5**:175-190.

Beach, F. A., 1942a, Execution of the complete masculine copulatory pattern by sexually receptive female rats, *J. Genet. Psychol.* **60**:137-142.

Beach, F. A., 1942b, Male and female mating behavior in prepuberally castrated female rats treated with androgens, *Endocrinology* **31**:373-378.

Beach, F. A., 1942c, Copulatory behavior in prepuberally castrated male rats and its modification by estrogen administration, *Endocrinology* **31**:679-683.

Beach, F. A., 1942d, Importance of progesterone to induction of sexual receptivity in spayed female rats, *Proc. Soc. Exp. Biol. Med.* **51**:369-371.

Beach, F. A., 1948, *Hormones and Behavior*, P. P. Hoelser Inc., New York.

Beach, F. A., 1967, Cerebral and hormonal control of reflexive mechanisms involved in copulatory behavior, *Physiol. Rev.* **47**:289-316.

Beach, F. A., 1968, Factors involved in the control of mounting behavior by female mammals, in: *Reproduction and Sexual Behavior* (M. Diamond, ed.), pp. 83-131, Indiana University Press.

Beach, F. A., 1970, Coital behavior in dogs. VI. Long-term effects of castration upon mating in the male, *J. Comp. Physiol. Psychol. Monogr.* **70**:1-32.

Beach, F. A., and Holz, A. M., 1946, Mating behavior in male rats castrated at various ages and injected with androgen, *J. Exp. Zool.* **101**:91-142.

Beach, F. A., and Holz-Tucker, A. M., 1949, Effect of different concentrations of androgen upon sexual behavior in castrated male rats, *J. Comp. Physiol. Psychol.* **42**:433-453.

Beach, F. A., and Kuehn, R. E., 1970, Coital behavior in dogs. X. Effects of androgenic stimulation during development on feminine mating responses in females and males, *Horm. Behav.* **1**:347-367.

Beach, F. A., and LeBoeuf, B. J., 1967, Coital behavior in dogs. I. Preferential mating in the bitch, *Anim. Behav.* **15**:546-558.

Beach, F. A., and Merari, A., 1970, Coital behavior in dogs. V. Effects of estrogen and progesterone on mating and other forms of social behavior in the bitch, *J. Comp. Physiol. Psychol. Monogr.* **70**:1-22.

Beach, F. A., and Pauker, R. S., 1949, Effects of castration upon mating behavior in the male hamster (*Cricetus auratus*), *Endocrinology* **45**:211-221.

Beach, F. A., and Westbrook, W. H., 1968a, Dissociation of androgenic effects on sexual morphology and behavior in male rats, *Endocrinology* **83**:395-398.

Beach, F. A., and Westbrook, W. H., 1968b, Morphological and behavioural effects of an "antiandrogen" in male rats, *J. Endocrinol.* **42**:379-382.

Beach, F. A., Westbrook, W. H., and Clemens, L. G., 1966, Comparisons of the ejaculatory response in men and animals, *Psychosom. Med.* **28**:749-763.

Beach, F. A., LeBoeuf, B. J., and Rogers, C. M., 1968, Coital behavior in dogs. II. Effects of estrogen on mounting by females, *J. Comp. Physiol. Psychol.* **66**:296-307.

Beach, F. A., Noble, R. G., and Orndoff, R. K., 1969, Effects of perinatal androgen treatment on responses of male rats to gonadal hormones in adulthood, *J. Comp. Physiol. Psychol.* **68**:490-497.

BEN-DAVID, M., 1968, Mechanisms of induction of mammary differentiation in Sprague-Dawley rats by perphenazine, *Endocrinology* **83**:1217-1223.

BENKERT, O., and EVERSMANN, T., 1972, Importance of the anti-serotonin effect for mounting behaviour in rats, *Experientia* **28**:532-533.

BERG, I. A., 1944, Development of behavior: the micturation pattern in the dog, *J. Exp. Psychol.* **34**:343-368.

BERMANT, G., and WESTBROOK, W. H., 1966, Peripheral factors in the regulation of sexual contact by female rats, *J. Comp. Physiol. Psychol.* **61**:244-250.

BERTOLINI, A., GESSA, G. L., VERGONI, W., and FERRARI, W., 1968, Induction of sexual excitement with intraventricular ACTH; permissive role of testosterone in the male rabbit, *Life Sci.* **7**:1203-1206.

BEYER, C., and MCDONALD, P., 1973, Hormonal control of sexual behaviour in the female rabbit, in: *Advances in Reproduction Physiology* vol. 6 (M. W. H. Bishop, ed.), pp. 185-219, Elek Ltd., London.

BEYER, C., and VIDAL, N., 1971, Inhibitory action of MER-25 on androgen-induced oestrous behaviour in the ovariectomized rabbit, *J. Endocrinol.* **51**:401-402.

BIGNAMI, G., 1966, Pharmacological influences on mating behavior in the male rat, *Psychopharmacologia* **10**:44-58.

BLOCH, G. J., and DAVIDSON J. M., 1967, Antiandrogen implanted in brain stimulates male reproductive system, *Science* **155**:593-595.

BLOCH, G. J., and DAVIDSON, J. M., 1968, Effects of adrenalectomy and prior experience on postcastrational sex behavior in the male rat, *Physiol. Behav.* **3**:461.

BOHUS, B., HENDRICKX, H. H. L., VAN KOLFSCHOTEN, A. A., and KREDIET, T. G., 1975, Effect of $ACTH_{4-10}$ on copulatory and sexually motivated approach behavior in the male rat, in: *Sexual Behavior, Pharmacology and Biochemistry* (M. Sandler and G. L. Gessa, eds.), Raven Press, pp. 269-275.

BOLING, J. L., and BLANDAU, R. J., 1939, The estrogen-progesterone induction of mating response in the spayed female rat, *Endocrinology* **25**:359-364.

BOND, V. J., SHILLITO, E. E., and VOGT, M., 1972, Influence of age and of testosterone on the response of male rats to parachlorophenylalanine, *Brit. J. Pharmacol.* **46**:46-55.

BREUGGEMAN, J. A., 1973, Parental care in a group of free-ranging rhesus monkeys (*Macaca mulatta*), *Folia Primatol.* **20**:178-210.

BRIDGES, R., ZARROW, M. X., GANDELMAN, R., and DENENBERG, V. H., 1972, Differences in maternal responsiveness between lactating and sensitized rats, *Dev. Psychobiol.* **5**:123-127.

BRIDGES, R. S., ZARROW, M. X., and DENENBERG, V. H., 1973, The role of neonatal androgen in the expression of hormonally induced maternal responsiveness in the adult rat, *Horm. Behav.* **4**:315-322.

BROWN-GRANT, K., 1971, The role of steroid hormones in the control of gonadotropin secretion in adult female mammals, in: *Steroid Hormones and Brain Function* (C. H. Sawyer and R. A. Gorski, ed.), UCLA Forum Med. Sci., University of California Press.

BROWN-GRANT, K., MUNCK, A., NAFTOLIN, F., and SHERWOOD, M. R., 1971, The effects of administration of testosterone propionate alone or with phenobarbitone and of testosterone metabolites to neonatal female rats, *Horm. Behav.* **2**:173-182.

BUTCHER, L. L., BUTCHER, S. G., and LARSSON, K. 1969, Effects of apomorphine, (+)-amphetamine and nialamide on tetrabenazine-induced suppression of sexual behavior in the male rat, *Eur. J. Pharmacol.* **7**:283-288.

CARRARO, A., CORBIN, A., FRASCHINI, F., and MARTINI, L., 1965, The effect of prepuberal treatment with reserpine on puberty, pituitary luteinizing hormone and the oestrous cycle of the rat, *J. Endocrinol.* **32**:387-393.

CARRER, H., and MEYERSON, B. J., 1976, Effects of CNS-depressants and stimulants on lordosis response in the female rat, *Pharmacol. Biochem. Behav.* **4**:497-506.

CARTER, C. S., 1972, Postcopulatory sexual receptivity in the female hamster: the role of the ovary and adrenal, *Horm. Behav.* **3**:261-265.

CARTER, C. S., CLEMENS, L. G., and HOEKEMA, D. J., 1972, Neonatal androgen and adult sexual behavior in the golden hamster, *Physiol. Behav.* **9**:89-95.

CARTER, C. S., and PORGES, S. W., 1974, Ovarian hormones and the duration of sexual receptivity in the female golden hamster, *Horm. Behav.* **5**:303-315.

CIACCIO, L. H., and LISK, R. D., 1973/74, Central control of estrous behavior in the female golden hamster, *Neuroendocrinology* **13**:21-28.

CLAYTON, R. B., KOGURA, J., and KRAEMER, H. C., 1970, Sexual differentiation of the brain: effects of testosterone on brain RNA metabolism in newborn female rats, *Nature (London)* **226**:810-812.

CLEMENS, L. G., WALLEN, K., and GORSKI, R. A., 1967, Mating behavior: facilitation in the female rat after cortical application of potassium chloride, *Science* **157**:1208-1209.

CLEMENS, L. G., HIROI, M., and GORSKI, R. A., 1969, Induction and facilitation of female mating behavior in rats treated neonatally with low doses of testosterone propionate, *Endocrinology* **84**:1430-1438.

CLEMENS, L. G., SHRYNE, J., and GORSKI, R. A., 1970, Androgen and development of progesterone responsiveness in male and female rats, *Physiol. Behav.* **5**:673-678.

CONIGLIO, L. P., PAUP, D. C., and CLEMENS, L. G., 1973, Hormone factors controlling the development of sexual behavior in the male golden hamster, *Physiol. Behav.* **10**:1087-1094.

CONNER, R. L., and LEVINE, S., 1969, Hormonal influences on aggressive behavior, in: *Aggressive Behavior* (S. Garattini and E. B. Sigg, eds.), pp. 150-163, Excerpta Medica Foundation, Amsterdam.

CORRODI, H., FARNEBO, L. O., FUXE, K., HAMBERGER, B., and UNGERSTEDT, U., 1972, ET 495 and brain catecholamine mechanisms: evidence for stimulation of dopamine receptors. *Eur. J. Pharmacol.* **20**:195-204.

COYLE, J. T., and AXELROD, J., 1972a, Dopamine β-hydroxylase in the rat brain: developmental characteristics, *J. Neurochem.* **19**:449-459.

COYLE, J. T., and AXELROD, J., 1972b, Tyrosine hydroxylase in the rat brain: developmental characteristics, *J. Neurochem.* **19**:1117-1123.

CROWLEY, W. R., FEDER, H. H., and MORIN, L. P., 1976, The role of monoamines in sexual behavior of the female guinea pig, *Pharmacol., Biochem. Behav.* **4**:67-71.

DAHLSTRÖM, A., 1968, Effect of colchicine on transport of amine storage in sympathetic nerves of rat, *Eur. J. Pharmacol.* **5**:111-113.

DA PRADA, M., CARRUBA, M., O'BRIEN, R. A., SANER, A., and PLETSCHER, A., 1972, Effect of 5,6-dihydroxytryptamine on sexual behaviour of male rats, *Eur. J. Pharmacol.* **19**:288-290.

DA PRADA, M., CARRUBA, M., SANER, A., O'BRIEN, R. A., and PLETSCHER, A., 1973a, The action of 5,6-dihydroxytryptamine and L-DOPA on sexual behaviour of male rats, in: *Psychopharmacology, Sexual Disorders and Drug Abuse* (T. A. Ban, ed.), pp. 517-522, North Holland Publishing Co., Amsterdam.

DA PRADA, M., CARRUBA, M., SANER, A., O'BRIEN, R. A., and PLETSCHER, A., 1973b, Action of L-DOPA on sexual behaviour of male rats, *Brain Res.* **55**:383-389.

DAVIDSON, J. M., 1966a, Characteristics of sex behaviour in male rats following castration, *Anim. Behav.* **14**:266-272.

DAVIDSON, J. M., 1966b, Activation of the male rat's sexual behavior by intracerebral implantation of androgen, *Endocrinology* **79**:783-794.

DAVIDSON, J. M., 1969, Effects of estrogen on the sexual behavior of male rats, *Endocrinology* **84**:1365-1372.

DAVIDSON, J. M., 1972, Hormones and reproductive behavior, in: *Reproductive Biology* (H. Balin and S. Glasser, eds.), pp. 877-918, Excerpta Medica Foundation, Amsterdam.

DAVIDSON, J. M., and BLOCH, G. J., 1969, Neuroendocrine aspects of male reproduction, *Biol. Reprod. Suppl. 1* **1**:67.

Davidson, J. M., and Levine, S., 1972, Endocrine regulation of behavior, *Annu. Rev. Physiol.* **34**:375–408.
Davidson, J. M., Smith, E. R., Rodgers, C. H., and Bloch, G. J., 1968a, Relative thresholds of behavioral and somatic responses to estrogen, *Physiol. Behav.* **3**:227–228.
Davidson, J. M., Rodgers, C. H., Smith, E. R., and Bloch, G. J., 1968b, Stimulation of female sex behavior in adrenalectomized rats with estrogen alone, *Endocrinology* **82**:193–195.
De Moor, P., and Denéf, C., 1968, The "puberty" of the rat liver. Feminine patterns of cortisol metabolism in male rats castrated at birth, *Endocrinology* **82**:480–492.
Dempsey, E. W., and Rioch, D. McK., 1939, The localization in the brainstem of the oestrus responses of the female guinea pig, *J. Neurophysiol.* **2**:9–18.
Dempsey, E. W., Hertz, R., and Young, W. C., 1936, The experimental induction of oestrus (sexual receptivity) in the normal and ovariectomized guinea pig, *Am. J. Physiol.* **116**:201.
Denéf, C., 1973, Differentiation of steroid metabolism in the rat and mechanisms of neonatal androgen action, *Enzymes* **15**:254–271.
Denéf, C., and De Moor, P., 1968, The "puberty" of the rat liver. II. Permanent changes in steroid metabolizing enzymes after treatment with a single injection of testosterone propionate at birth, *Endocrinology* **83**:791–798.
Deutsch, J. A., 1957, Nest building behaviour of domestic rabbits under seminatural conditions, *Br. J. Anim. Behav.* **2**:53–54.
De Wied, D., and de Jong, W., 1974, Drug effects and hypothalamic-anterior pituitary function, *Annu. Rev. Pharmacol.* **14**:389–412.
Dewsbury, D. A., 1972, Effects of tetrabenazine on the copulatory behavior of male rats, *Eur. J. Pharmacol.* **17**:221–226.
Dewsbury, D. A., and Davis, H. N., 1970, Effects of reserpine on the copulatory behavior of male rats, *Physiol. Behav.* **5**:1331–1333.
Dewsbury, D. A., Davis, H. N., and Janssen, P. E., 1972, Effects of monoamine oxidase inhibitors on the copulatory behavior of male rats, *Psychopharmacologia* **24**:209–217.
Diakow, C., 1974, Male–female interactions and the organization of mammalian mating patterns, *Adv. Stud. Behav.* **5**:227–268.
Donoso, A. O., de Gutierrez Moyano, M. B., and Santolaya, R. L., 1969, Metabolism of noradrenaline in the hypothalamus of castrated rats, *Neuroendocrinology* **4**:12–19.
Dörner, G., 1970, The influence of sex hormones during the hypothalamic differentiation and maturation phases on gonadal function and sexual behavior during the hypothalamic functional phase, *Endokrinologie* **56**:280–291.
Dörner, G., Phuong, N. T., and Hinz, G., 1971, Influence of chlormadinone acetate on hypothalamic differentiation in male rats, *Acta Biol. Med. Ger.* **26**:105–114.
Dunlop, J. L., Gerall, A. A., and McLean, L. D., 1972, Enhancement of female receptivity in neonatally castrated males by prepuberal ovarian transplants, *Physiol. Behav.* **10**:701–705.
Eaton, G. G., and Resko, J. A., 1974, Ovarian hormones and sexual behavior in *Macaca nemestrina*, *J. Comp. Physiol. Psychol.* **86**:919–925.
Edwards, D. A., and Burge, K. G., 1971, Early androgen treatment and male and female sexual behavior in mice, *Horm. Behav.* **2**:49–58.
Edwards, D. A., Whalen, R. E., and Nadler, R. D., 1968, Induction of estrus: estrogen–progesterone interactions, *Physiol. Behav.* **3**:29–33.
Eliasson, M., and Meyerson, B. J., 1973, Influence of LSD and apomorphine on hormone-activated copulatory behavior in the female rat, *Acta Physiol. Scand. Suppl.* 396, abstr. 129, 1973.
Eliasson, M., and Meyerson, B. J., 1975, Sexual preference in female rats during estrous cycle, pregnancy and lactation, *Physiol. Behav.* **14**:705–710.
Eliasson, M., and Meyerson, B. J., 1977, The effects of lysergic acid diethylamide on copulatory behavior in the female rat, *Neuropharmacology* **15**:37–44.

ELWOOD, R. W., 1975, Paternal and maternal behaviour in the Mongolian Gerbil, *Anim. Behav.* **23**:766-772.
ERIKSSON, H., and SÖDERSTEN, P., 1973, Failure to facilitate lordosis behavior in adrenalectomized and gonadectomized estrogen-primed rats with monoamine-synthesis inhibitors, *Horm. Behav.* **4**:89-98.
ERNST, A. M., 1967, Mode of action of apomorphine and dexamphetamine on gnawing compulsion in rats, *Psychopharmacologia* **10**:316-323.
EVERITT, B. J., and HERBERT, J., 1971, The effects of dexamethasone and androgens on sexual receptivity of female rhesus monkeys, *J. Endocrinol.* **51**:575-588.
EVERITT, B. J., and HERBERT, J., 1975, The effects of implanting testosterone propionate into the central nervous system on the sexual behaviour of adrenalectomized female rhesus monkeys, *Brain Res.* **86**:109-120.
EVERITT, B. J., HERBERT, J., and HAMER, J. D., 1972, Sexual receptivity of bilaterally adrenalectomized female rhesus monkeys, *Physiol. Behav.* **8**:409-415.
EVERITT, B. J., FUXE, K., and HÖKFELT, T., 1974, Inhibitory role of dopamine and 5-hydroxytryptamine in the sexual behavior of female rats, *Eur. J. Pharmacol.* **29**:187-191.
EVERITT, B. J., FUXE, K., HÖKFELT, T., and JONSSON, G., 1975a, Studies on the role of monoamines in the hormonal regulation of sexual receptivity in the female rat, in: *Sexual Behavior: Pharmacology and Biochemistry* (M. Sandler and G. L. Gessa, eds.), Raven Press, New York.
EVERITT, B. J., FUXE, K., HÖKFELT, T., and JONSSON, G., 1975b, Role of monoamines in the control by hormones of sexual receptivity in the female rat, *J. Comp. Physiol. Psychol.* **89**:556-572.
FAJER, A. B., and BARRACLOUGH, C. A., 1967, Ovarian secretion of progesterone and 20α-hydroxypregn-4-en-3-one during pseudo-pregnancy and pregnancy in rats, *Endocrinology* **81**:617-622.
FALVO, R. E., KALTENBAHC, C. C., and PANCOE, W. L., 1972, Determination of testosterone concentration in the plasma of normal and androgen-sterilized female rats, using a competitive protein binding technique, *Neuroendocrinology* **10**:229-234.
FEDER, H. H., 1971, The comparative actions of testosterone propionate and 5-α-androstan-17-ol-3-one propionate on the reproductive behavior, physiology and morphology of male rats, *J. Endocrinol.* **51**:241-252.
FEDER, H. H., and RUF, K. B., 1969, Stimulation of progesterone release and estrous behavior by ACTH in ovariectomized rodents, *Endocrinology* **69**:171-174.
FEDER, H. H., GOY, R. W., and RESKO, J. A., 1967, Progesterone concentration in the peripheral plasma of cyclic rats, *J. Physiol. (London)* **191**:136-137.
FEDER, H. H., GOY, R. W., and RESKO, J. A., 1968, Progesterone concentrations in the arterial plasma of guinea pigs during the oestrous cycle, *J. Endocrinol.* **40**:505-513.
FERGUSON, J., HENRIKSEN, S., COHEN, H., and MITCHELL, G., 1970, Hypersexuality and behavioral changes in cats caused by administration of *p*-chlorophenylalanine, *Science* **168**:499-501.
FLÉRKO, B., MESS, B., and ILLEI-DONHOFFER, 1969, On the mechanism of androgen sterilization, *Neuroendocrinology* **4**:164-169.
FORD, C. S., and BEACH, F. A., 1951, *Patterns of Sexual Behavior,* Harper, New York.
FRANK, A. H., and FRAPS, R. M., 1945, Induction of estrus in the ovariectomized golden hamster, *Endocrinology* **37**:357-361.
FULLER, G. B., ZARROW, M. X., ANDERSSON, C. O., and DENENBERG, V. H., 1970, Testosterone propionate during gestation in the rabbit: effect on subsequent maternal behavior, *J. Reprod. Fertil.* **23**:285-290.
FULLER, J. L., and DU BUIS, E. M., 1962, The behavior of dogs, in: *The Behavior of Domestic Animals* (E. S. E. Hafez, ed.), pp. 415-452, Williams and Wilkins, Baltimore.
FUXE, K., and HÖKFELT, T., 1969, Catecholamines in the hypothalamus and the pituitary gland, in: *Frontiers in Neuroendocrinology* (W. F. Ganong and L. Martini, eds.), pp. 61-83, Oxford University Press, Oxford.

GANDELMAN, R., 1973, Reduction of nest building in female mice by testosterone propionate treatment, *Dev. Psychobiol.* **6:**539.

GAWIENOWSKI, A. M., and HODGEN, G. D., 1971, Homosexual activity in male rats after *p*-chlorophenylalanine-effects of hypophysectomy and testosterone, *Physiol. Behav.* **7:**551–555.

GERALL, A. A., and WARD, J. L., 1966, Effects of prenatal exogenous androgen on the sexual behavior of the female albino rat, *J. Comp. Physiol. Psychol.* **62:**370–375.

GERALL, A. A., HENDRICKS, S. E., JOHNSON, L. L., and BOUNDS, T. W., 1967, Effects of early castration in male rats on adult sexual behavior, *J. Comp. Physiol. Psychol.* **64:**206–212.

GESSA, G. L., and TAGLIAMONTE, A., 1974, Role of brain monoamines in male sexual behavior, *Life Sci.* **14:**425–436.

GESSA, G. L., and TAGLIAMONTE, A., 1975, Role of brain serotonin and dopamine in male sexual behavior, in: *Sexual Behavior, Pharmacology and Biochemistry* (M. Sandler and G. L. Gessa, eds.), pp. 117–128, Raven Press, New York.

GIULIAN, D., POHORECKY, L. A., and MCEWEN, B. S., 1973, Effects of gonadal steroids upon brain 5-hydroxytryptamine levels in the neonatal rat, *Endocrinology* **93:**1329–1335.

GORSKI, R. A., 1968, Influence of age on the response to perinatal administration of a low dose of androgen, *Endocrinology* **82:**1001–1004.

GORSKI, R. A., 1971, Gonadal hormones and the perinatal development of neuroendocrine function, in: *Frontiers in Neuroendocrinology* (L. Martini and W. F. Ganong, eds.), pp. 237–290, Oxford University Press, New York.

GORSKI, R. A., 1973, Perinatal effects of sex steroids on brain development and function, in: *Progress in Brain Research*, Vol. 39, *Drug Effects on Neuroendocrine Regulation*, pp. 149–163, Elsevier, Amsterdam.

GORSKI, R. A., and SHRYNE, J., 1972, Intracerebral antibiotics and androgenization of the neonatal female rat, *Neuroendocrinology* **10:**109–120.

GOY, R. W., 1968, Organizing effects of androgen on the behavior of rhesus monkeys, in: *Endocrinology and Human Behavior* (R. P. Michael, ed.), pp. 12–31, Oxford University Press, New York.

GOY, R. W., and GOLDFOOT, D. A., 1973, Hormonal influences on sexually dimorphic behavior, in: *Handbook of Physiology*, Sec. 7, Vol. 11, Part 1, Chap. 9 (R. O. Greep and E. B. Astwood, eds.), pp. 169–186, Am. Physiol. Soc., Washington, D. C.

GOY, R. W., and PHOENIX, C. H., 1971, The effects of testosterone propionate administered before birth on the development of behavior in genetic female rhesus monkeys, in: *Steroid Hormones and Brain Function* (C. H. Sawyer and R. A. Gorski, eds.), pp. 193–201, UCLA Forum Med. Sci., University of California Press, Los Angeles.

GOY, R. W., and RESKO, J. A., 1972, Gonadal hormones and behavior of normal and pseudohermaphroditic nonhuman female primates, in: *Recent Progress in Hormone Research*, Vol. 28 (E. B. Astwood, ed.), pp. 707–733, Academic Press.

GOY, R. W., PHOENIX, C. H., and YOUNG, W. C., 1962, A critical period for the suppression of behavioral receptivity in adult female rats by early treatment with androgen, *Anat. Rec.* **142:**307 abstr.

GOY, R. W., BRIDSON, W., and YOUNG, W. C., 1964, Period of maximal susceptibility of the prenatal guinea pig to masculinizing actions of testosterone propionate, *J. Comp. Physiol. Psychol.* **57:**166–174.

GRADWELL, P. B., EVERITT, B. J., and HERBERT, J., 1975, 5-Hydroxytryptamine in the central nervous system and sexual receptivity of female rhesus monkeys, *Brain Res.* **88:**281–293.

GRADY, K. L., PHOENIX, C. H., and YOUNG, W. C., 1965, Role of the developing rat in differentiation of the neural tissues mediating mating behavior, *J. Comp. Physiol. Psychol.* **59:**176–182.

GRAY, G. D., DAVIS, H. N., and DEWSBURY, D. A., 1974, Effects of L-dopa on the heterosexual copulatory behavior of male rats, *Eur. J. Pharmacol.* **27:**367–370.

GRAY, J. A., LEON, J., and KEYNES, A., 1969, Infant androgen treatment and adult open field behavior: direct effects and effects of injections to siblings, *Physiol. Behav.* **4:**177–181.

GREEN, R., LUTTGE, W. G., and WHALEN, R. E., 1969, Uptake and retention of tritiated estradiol in brain and peripheral tissues of male, female, and neonatally androgenized rats, *Endocrinology* **85**:373-378.

GREEN, R., LUTTGE, W. G., and WHALEN, R. E., 1970, Induction of receptivity in ovariectomized female rats by a single intravenous injection of estradiol-17β, *Physiol. Behav.* **5**:137-141.

GRUNT, J. A., and YOUNG, W. C., 1952, Differential reactivity of individuals and the response of the male guinea pig to testosterone propionate, *Endocrinology* **51**:237-248.

HARDIN, C. M., 1973*a*, Sex differences and effects of testosterone injections on biogenic amine levels of neonatal rat brain, *Brain Res.* **62**:286-290.

HARDIN, C. M., 1973*b*, Sex differences in serotonin synthesis from 5-HTP in neonatal rat brain, *Brain Res.* **59**:437-439.

HARDY, D. F., 1970, The effect of constant light on the estrous cycle and behavior of the female rat, *Physiol. Behav.* **5**:421-425.

HARDY, D. F., 1972, Sexual behaviour in continuously cycling rats, *Behaviour* **41**:288-297.

HARRIS, G. W., 1964, Sex hormones, brain development and brain function, *Endocrinology* **75**:627-648.

HARRIS, G. W., and LEVINE, S., 1962, Sexual differentiation of the brain and its experimental control, *J. Physiol. (London)* **163**:42P and 43P.

HARRIS, G. W., and LEVINE, S., 1965, Sexual differentiation of the brain and its experimental control, *J. Physiol. (London)* **181**:379-400.

HARRIS, G. W., MICHAEL, R. P., and SCOTT, P. P., 1958, Neurological site of action of stilboestrol in eliciting sexual behaviour, in: *The Neurological Basis of Behaviour* (G. E. W. Wolstenholme and C. M. O'Connor, ed.), pp. 236-251, Churchill, London.

HART, B. L., 1967, Sexual reflexes and mating behavior in the male dog, *J. Comp. Physiol. Psychol.* **65**:388-399.

HART, B. L., 1968*a*, Sexual reflexes and mating behavior in the male rat, *J. Comp. Physiol. Psychol.* **65**:453-460.

HART, B. L., 1968*b*, Neonatal castration: Influence on neural organization of sexual reflexes in male rats, *Science* **160**:1135-1136.

HART, B. L., 1969, Gonadal hormones and sexual reflexes in the female rat, *Horm. Behav.* **1**:65-71.

HART, B. L., 1973, Effects of testosterone propionate and dihydrotestosterone on penile morphology and sexual reflexes of spinal male rats, *Horm. Behav.* **4**:239-246.

HART, B. L., and HAUGEN, C. M., 1968, Activation of sexual reflexes in male rats by spinal implantation of testosterone, *Physiol. Behav.* **3**:735-738.

HASHIMOTO, I., HENDRICKS, D. M., ANDERSON, L. L., and MELAMPY, R. M., 1968, Progesterone and pregn-4-en-20α-ol-one in ovarian venous blood during various reproductive states in the rat, *Endocrinology* **82**:333-341.

HENDRICKS, S. E., 1969, Influence of neonatally administered hormones and early gonadectomy on rats' sexual behavior, *J. Comp. Physiol. Psychol.* **69**:408-413.

HENDRICKS, S. E., and DUFFY, J. A., 1974, Ovarian influences on the development of sexual behavior in neonatally androgenized rats, *Dev. Psychobiol.* **7**:297-303.

HERBERT, J., 1968, Sexual preference in the rhesus monkey *Macaca mulatta* in the laboratory, *Anim. Behav.* **16**:120-128.

HERBERT, J., 1970, Hormones and reproductive behaviour in rhesus and talapoin monkeys, *J. Reprod. Fertil. Suppl.* **11**:119-140.

HINDE, R. A., and SPENCER-BOOTH, Y., 1967, The behaviour of socially living rhesus monkeys in their first two and a half years, *Anim. Behav.* **15**:169-196.

HINDE, R. A., ROWELL, T. E., and SPENCER-BOOTH, Y., 1964, Behaviour of socially living rhesus monkeys in their first six months, *Proc. Zool. Soc. London* **143**:609-649.

HOYLAND, V. J., SHILLITO, E. E., and VOGT, M., 1970, The effect of parachlorophenylalanine on the behaviour of cats, *Br. J. Pharmacol.* **40**:659-667.

HUDSON, D. B., VERNADAKIS, A., and TIMIRAS, P. S., 1970, Regional changes in amino acid concentration in the developing brain and the effects of neonatal administration of estradiol, *Brain Res.* **23:**213-222.

Hyyppä, M., and Cardinali, D. P., 1973, Failure of sex steroid hormones to affect brain serotonin in rats, *Steroids Lipids Res.* **4:**295-301.

Hyyppä, M., and Rinne, U. K., 1971, Hypothalamic monoamines after the neonatal androgenization, castration or reserpine treatment of the rat, *Acta Endocrinol. (Copenhagen)* **66:**317-324.

Hyyppä, M., Lehtinen, P., and Rinne, U. K., 1971, Effect of L-DOPA on hypothalamic, pineal and striatal monoamines and on the sexual behaviour of the rat, *Brain Res.* **30:**265-272.

Hyyppä, M., Lampinen, P., and Lehtinen, P., 1972, Alteration in the sexual behaviour of male and female rats after neonatal administration of *p*-chlorophenylalanine, *Psychopharmacologia* **25:**152-161.

Jaffe, R. B., 1969, Testosterone metabolism in target tissues: hypothalamic and pituitary tissues of the adult rat and human fetus and the immature rat apiphyris, *Steroids* **14:**483-498.

Jensen, E. V., and DeSombre, E. R., 1972, Mechanism of action of the female sex hormones, *Annu. Rev. Biochem.* **41:**203-230.

Jensen, E. V., and Jacobson, H. I., 1962, Basic guides to the mechanism of estrogen action, *Recent Prog. Horm. Res.* **18:**387-414.

Johnson, W. A., and Tiefer, L., 1972, Sexual preferences in neonatally castrated male golden hamsters, *Physiol. Behav.* **9:**213-217.

Johnston, J. O., Grunwell, J. F., Benson, H. D., Kandel, A., and Petrow, U., 1975, Behavioral effects of 19-hydroxytestosterone, in: *Sexual Behavior: Pharmacology and Biochemistry* (M. Sandler and G. L. Gessa, eds.), pp. 227-240, Raven Press, New York.

Johnston, P., and Davidson, J. M., 1972, Intracerebral androgens and sexual behavior in the male rat, *Horm. Behav.* **3:**345-357.

Kan-wha Ho, G., Quadagno, D. M., Cooke, P. H., and Gorski, R. A., 1974, Intracranial implants of actinomycin-D: effects on sexual behavior and nucleolar ultrastructure in the rat, *Neuroendocrinology* **13:**47-55.

Karlsson, J. O., and Sjöstrand, J., 1969, The effect of colchicine on the axonal transport of protein in the optic nerve and tract of the rabbit, *Brain Res.* **13:**617-619.

Kato, R., 1960, Serotonin content of rat brain in relation to sex and age, *J. Neurochemistry* **5:**202.

Kaufman, I. C., and Rosenblum, L. A., 1966, A behavioral taxonomy for *M. nemestrina* and *M. radiata*: based on longitudinal observations of family groups in the laboratory, *Primates* **7:**205-258.

Kawashima, S., 1964, Inhibitory action of reserpine on the development of the male pattern of secretion of gonadatropins in the rat, *Annot. Zool. Jpn.* **37:**79-85.

Keller, H. H., Bartholini, G., and Pletscher, A., 1973, Spontaneous and drug-induced changes of cerebral dopamine turnover during postnatal development of rats, *Brain Res.* **64:**371-378.

Kihlström, J. E., 1971, A male sexual cycle, in: *Current Problems in Fertility* (A. Ingelman-Sundberg and N.-O. Lunell, eds.), pp. 50-54, Plenum Press, New York.

Kikuyama, S., 1961, Inhibitory effect of reserpine on the induction of persistent estrus by sex steroids in the rat, *Annot. Zool. Jpn.* **34:**111-116.

Kikuyama, S., 1962, Inhibition of induction of persistent estrus by chlorpromazine in the rat, *Annot. Zool. Jpn.* **35:**6-11.

Kincl, F. A., and Dorfman, R. I., 1961, Copulatory reflex in guinea pigs induced by progesterone and related steroids, *Acta Endocrinol.* **38:**257-261.

Koller, G., 1955, Hormonale und psychische Steuerung beim Nestbau weisser Mäuse, *Zool. Angew. (Verh. Dtsch. Zool. Ges. Freiburg), Suppl.* **19:**123-139.

Komisaruk, B. R., 1971, Induction of lordosis in ovariectomized rats by stimulation of the vaginal cervix: Hormonal and neural interrelationships, in: *Steroid Hormones and Brain*

Function (C. H. Sawyer and R. A. Gorski, eds.), pp. 127-135, UCLA Forum Med. Sci., University of California Press, Los Angeles.

KORDON, L., and GLOWINSKI, J., 1972, Role of hypothalamic monoaminergic neurons in the gonadotrophin release-regulating mechanism, *Neuropharmacology* **11**:153-162.

KORENMAN, S. G., 1970, Relation between estrogen inhibitory activity and binding to cytosol of rabbit and human uterus, *Endocrinology* **87**:1119-1123.

KOW, L. M., MALSBURY, C. W., and PFAFF, D. W., 1975, Effects of progesterone on female reproductive behavior in rats: possible modes of action and role in behavioral sex differences, in: *Reproductive Behavior* (W. Montagna and W. A. Sadler, eds.), pp. 179-210, Plenum Press, New York.

KREUTZBERG, G., 1969, Neuronal dynamics and axonal flow. IV. Blockade of intraaxonal enzyme transport by colchicine, *Proc. Nat. Acad. Sci. U.S.A.* **62**:722-725.

KUEHN, R. E., and BEACH, F. A., 1963, Quantitative measurements of sexual receptivity in female rats, *Behaviour* **21**:282-299.

KWA, H. G., and VERHOFSTAD, F., 1967, Prolactin levels in the plasma of female rats, *J. Endocrinology* **39**:455-456.

LADOSKY, W., and GAZIRI, L. L. J., 1970, Brain serotonin and sexual differentiation of the nervous system, *Neuroendocrinology* **6**:168-174.

LAMB, M. E., 1975, Physiological mechanisms in the control of maternal behavior in rats: a review, *Psychol. Bull.* **82**:104-119.

LAMPRECHT, F., and COYLE, J. T., 1972, DOPA decarboxylase in the developing rat brain, *Brain Res.* **41**:503-506.

LANGFORD, J., and HILLIARD, J., 1967, Effect of 20α-hydroxypregn-4-en-3-one on mating behavior in spayed female rats, *Endocrinology* **80**:381-383.

LARSSON, K., 1966, Effects of neonatal castration upon the development of the mating behavior in the male rat, *Z. Tierpsychol.* **23**:867-873.

LARSSON, K., 1967, Effects of neonatal castration and androgen replacement therapy upon the development of the mating behavior of the male rat, *Z. Tierpsychol.* **24**:471-475.

LARSSON, K., and SÖDERSTEN, P., 1971, Lordosis behavior in male rats treated with estrogen in combination with tetrabenazine, *Psychopharmacologia* **21**:13-16.

LARSSON, K., BEYER, C., and SÖDERSTEN, P., 1973, Sexual behavior in male rats treated with estrogen in combination with dihydrotestosterone, *Horm. Behav.* **4**:289-299.

LEAVITT, F. I., 1969, Drug-induced modifications in sexual behavior and open field locomotion of male rats, *Physiol. Behav.* **4**:677-683.

LEAVITT, W. W., and BLAHA, G. C., 1970, Circulating progesterone levels in the golden hamster during the estrous cycle, pregnancy and lactation, *Biol. Reprod.* **3**:353-361.

LEBLOND, C. P., 1940, Nervous and hormonal factors in the maternal behavior of the mouse, *J. Genet. Psychol.* **57**:327-344.

LEHTINEN, P., HYYPPÄ, M., and LAMPINEN, P., 1972, Sexual behaviour of adult rats after a single neonatal injection of reserpine, *Psychopharmacologia* **23**:171-179.

LEON, M., NUMAN, M., and MOLTZ, H., 1973, Maternal behavior in the rat: facilitation through gonadectomy, *Science* **179**:1018-1019.

LERNER, L. J., HOLTHAUS, F. J., and THOMPSON, C. R., 1958, A non-steroidal estrogen antagonist 1-(p-2-diethylaminoethoxyphenyl)-1-phenyl-2-p-methoxyphenyl ethanol, *Endocrinology* **63**:295-318.

LEVINE, S., and MULLINS, JR., R., 1964, Estrogen administered neonatally affects adult sexual behavior in male and female rats, *Science* **144**:185-187.

LIAO, S., and FANG, S., 1969, Receptor-proteins for androgens and the mode of action of androgens on gene transcription in ventral prostate, in: *Vitamins and Hormones. Advances in Research and Applications* (R. S. Harris, I. G. Wool, J. A. Loraine, and P. L. Munson, eds.), Vol. 27, pp. 18-90, Academic Press, New York.

LICHTENSTEIGER, W., 1969, Cyclic variations of catecholamine content in hypothalamic nerve cells during the estrous cycle of the rat, with a concomitant study of the substantia nigra, *J. Pharmacol. Exp. Ther.* **165**:204-215.

LINDSTRÖM, L. H., 1970, The effect of pilocarpine in combination with monoamine oxidase inhibitors imipramine or desmethylimipramine on oestrous behaviour in female rats, *Psychopharmacologia* **17**:160-168.

LINDSTRÖM, L. H., 1971, The effect of pilocarpine and oxotremorine on oestrous behaviour in female rats after treatment with monoamine depletors or monoamine synthesis inhibitors, *Eur. J. Pharmacol.* **15**:60-65.

LINDSTRÖM, L. H., 1972a, Further studies on cholinergic mechanisms and hormone-activated copulatory behaviour in the female rat, *J. Endocrinol.* **56**:275-283.

LINDSTRÖM, L. H., 1972b, The effect of pilocarpine and oxotremorine on hormone-activated copulatory behavior in the ovariectomized hamster, *Naunyn-Schmiedeberg's Arch. Pharmacol.* **275**:233-241.

LINDSTRÖM, L. H., and MEYERSON, B. J., 1967, The effect of pilocarpine, oxotremorine and arecoline in combination with methylatropine or atropine on hormone-activated oestrous behaviour in ovariectomized rats, *Psychopharmacologia* **11**:405-413.

LISK, R. D., 1962, Diencephalic placement of estradiol and sexual receptivity in the female rat, *Am. J. Physiol.* **203**:493-496.

LISK, R. D., 1967, Neural localization of androgen activation of copulatory behavior in the male rat, *Endocrinology* **80**:754-761.

LISK, R. D., 1971, Oestrogen and progesterone synergism and elicitation of maternal nest-building in the mouse, *Anim. Behav.* **19**:606-610.

LISK, R. D., 1973, Hormonal regulation of sexual behavior in polyestrous mammals common to the laboratory, in: *Handbook of Physiology*, Sec. 7, Vol. 11, Part 1. *Endocrinology* (R. O. Greep and E. B. Astwood, eds.), pp. 223-260, Am. Physiol. Soc., Washington, D. C.

LISK, R. D., and PRETLOW, R. A., 1969, Hormonal stimulation necessary for elicitation of maternal nest building in the mouse, *Anim. Behav.* **17**:730-737.

LISK, R. D., and RUSSELL, J. A., 1972, Regulation of hormone mediated maternal nest structure in the mouse by neonatal hormone manipulation, *4th International Congress Endocrinologists, Washington, D. C., June 18-24, 1972*, Excerpta Medica Foundation, Int. Congr. Series No. 256, abstr.

LOIZOU, L. A., 1971, The postnatal development of monoamine-containing structures in the hypothalamo-hypophyseal system of the albino rat, *Z. Zellforsch.* **114**:234-252.

LOIZOU, L. A., 1972, The postnatal ontogeny of monoamine containing neurons in the CNS of the albino rat, *Brain Res.* **40**:395-418.

LUBIN, M., LEON, M., MOLTZ, H., and NUMAN, M., 1972, Hormones and maternal behavior in the male rat, *Horm. Behav.* **3**:369-374.

LUKASZEWSKA, J. H., and GREENWALD, G. S., 1970, Progesterone levels in the cyclic and pregnant hamster, *Endocrinology* **86**:1-9.

LUTTGE, W. G., 1971, The role of gonadal hormones in sexual behavior of the rhesus monkey and human: a literature survey, *Arch. Sex. Behav.* **1**:61-88.

LUTTGE, W. G., and WHALEN, R. E., 1970, Dihydrotestosterone, androstenedione, testosterone: comparative systems in male and female rats, *Horm. Behav.* **1**:265-281.

LUTTGE, W. G., HALL, N. R., WALLIS, C. J., and CAMPBELL, J. C., 1975, Stimulation of male and female sexual behavior in gonadectomized rats with estrogen and androgen therapy and its inhibition with concurrent antihormone therapy, *Physiol. Behav.* **14**:65-73.

MALMNÄS, C. O., 1973, Monoaminergic influence on testosterone-activated copulatory behavior in the castrated male rat, *Acta Physiol. Scand. (Suppl.)* **395**:1-128.

MALMNÄS, C. O., and MEYERSON, B. J., 1970, Monoamines and testosterone activated copulatory behaviour in the castrated male rat, *Acta Pharmacol. Toxicol. Suppl.* **28**:67.

MALMNÄS, C. O., and MEYERSON, B. J., 1971, *p*-Chlorophenylalanine and copulatory behaviour in the male rat, *Nature (London)* **232**:398-400.

MALMNÄS, C. O., and MEYERSON, B. J., 1972, Monoamines and copulatory activation in the castrated male rat, *Acta Pharmacol. Toxicol. Suppl. 1* **31**:23.

MALMNÄS, C. O., and MEYERSON, B. J., 1973, Effects of an antiestrogen, MER-25, on testosterone-activated copulatory behavior in the castrated male rat, *Acta Physiol. Scand. Suppl.* **396**:88.

MARTINS, T., and VALLE, J. R., 1944, Hormonal regulation of the micturition behavior of the dog, *J. Comp. Physiol. Psychol.* **41**:301–311.

McCULLOUGH, J., OUADGNO, D. M., and GOLDMAN, B. D., 1974, Neonatal gonadal hormones: effect on maternal and sexual behavior in the male rat, *Physiol. Behav.* **12**:183–188.

McDONALD, P. G., and DOUGHTY, C., 1972a, Comparison of the effect of neonatal administration of testosterone and dihydrotestosterone in the female rat, *J. Reprod. Fertil.* **30**:55–62.

McDONALD, P. G., and DOUGHTY, C., 1972b, Inhibition of androgen-sterilization in the female rat by administration of an antioestrogen, *J. Endocrinol.* **55**:455–456.

McDONALD, P. G., and DOUGHTY, C., 1974, Effect of neonatal administration of different androgens in the female rat: correlation between aromatization and the induction of sterilization, *J. Endocrinol.* **61**:95–103.

McDONALD, P. G., and MEYERSON, B. J., 1973, The effect of oestradiol, testosterone and dihydrotestosterone on sexual motivation in ovariectomized female rats, *Physiol. Behav.* **11**:515–520.

McDONALD, P. G., VIDAL, N., and BEYER, C., 1970a, Sexual behavior in the ovariectomized rabbit after treatment with different amounts of gonadal hormones, *Horm. Behav.* **1**:161–172.

McDONALD, P. G., BEYER, C., NEWTON, B., BRIEN, B., BAKER, R., TAN, H. S., SAMPSON, C., KITCHING, P., GREENHILL, R., and PRITCHARD, D., 1970b, Failure of 5-α-dihydrotestosterone to initiate sexual behaviour in the castrated male rat, *Nature (London)* **227**:964–965.

McEWEN, B. S., and PFAFF, D. W., 1970, Factors influencing sex hormone uptake by rat brain regions. I. Effects of neonatal treatment, hypophysectomy and competing steroid on estradiol uptake, *Brain Res.* **21**:1–16.

McEWEN, B. S., ZIGMOND, E., and GERLACH, J. Z., 1972, Sites of steroid binding and action in the brain, in: *The Structure and Function of Nervous Tissue* (G. H. Bourne, ed.), pp. 205–291, Academic Press, New York.

McGUIRE, J. L., and LISK, R. D., 1969, Oestrogen receptors in androgen or oestrogen sterilized female rats, *Nature (London)* **221**:1068–1069.

MEYERSON, B. J., 1964a, The effect of neuropharmacological agents on hormone-activated estrus behaviour in ovariectomized rats, *Arch. Int. Pharmacodyn.* **150**:4–33.

MEYERSON, B. J., 1964b, Estrus behaviour in spayed rats after estrogen or progesterone treatment in combination with reserpine or tetrabenazine, *Psychopharmacologia* **6**:210–218.

MEYERSON, B. J., 1964c, Central nervous monoamines and hormone-induced estrus behaviour in the spayed rat, *Acta Physiol. Scand. Suppl. 241* **63**:3–32.

MEYERSON, B. J., 1966a, The effect of imipramine and related antidepressive drugs on estrus behaviour in ovariectomized rats activated by progesterone, reserpine or tetrabenazine in combination with estrogen, *Acta Physiol. Scand.* **67**:411–422.

MEYERSON, B. J., 1966b, Oestrous behaviour in oestrogen treated ovariectomized rats after chlorpromazine alone or in combination with progesterone, tetrabenazine or reserpine, *Acta Pharmacol. Toxicol.* **24**:363–376.

MEYERSON, B. J., 1967, Relationship between the anesthetic and gestagenic action and estrous behaviour-inducing activity of different progestins, *Endocrinology* **81**:369–374.

MEYERSON, B. J., 1968a, Female copulatory behaviour in male and androgenized female rats after oestrogen/amine depletor treatment, *Nature (London)* **217**:683–684.

MEYERSON, B. J., 1968b, Amphetamine and 5-hydroxytryptamine inhibition of copulatory behaviour in the female rat, *Ann. Med. Exp. Fenn.* **46**:394–398.

MEYERSON, B. J., 1970, Monoamines and hormone activated oestrous behaviour in the ovariectomized hamster, *Psychopharmacologia* **18**:50–57.

MEYERSON, B. J., 1971a, Optical isomers of estrogen and estrogen inhibitors as tools in the investigation of estrogen action on the brain, in: *Steroid Hormones and Brain Function* (C. H. Sawyer and R. A. Gorski, eds.), UCLA Forum Med. Sci., pp. 237–243, University of California Press, Los Angeles.

MEYERSON, B. J., 1971b, Discussion of the action of steroid hormones on neuronal function, in: *Steroid Hormones and Brain Function* (C. H. Sawyer and R. A. Gorski, eds.), UCLA Forum Med. Sci., p. 263, University of California Press, Los Angeles.

MEYERSON, B. J., 1972, Latency between intravenous injection of progestins and appearance of estrous behavior in the estrogen treated ovariectomized rat, *Horm. Behav.* **3**:1–9.

MEYERSON, B. J., 1973, Mechanisms of action of sex steroids on behavior; inhibition of estrogen activated behavior by ethamoxytriphetol (MER-25), colchicine and cycloheximide, in: *Drug Effects on Neuroendocrine Regulation, Progress in Brain Research*, Vol. 39 (E. Zimmermann, W. H. Gispen, B. H. Marks, and D. de Wied, eds.), pp. 135–148, Amsterdam.

MEYERSON, B. J., 1975, Drugs and sexual motivation in the female rat, in: *Sexual Behavior, Pharmacology and Biochemistry* (M. Sandler and G. L. Gessa, eds.), Raven Press, New York, pp. 21–31.

MEYERSON, B. J., and LEWANDER, T., 1970, Serotonin synthesis inhibition and estrous behaviour in female rats, *Life Sci.* **9**:661–671.

MEYERSON, B. J., and LINDSTRÖM, L., 1968, Effect of oestrogen antagonist ethamoxytriphetol (MER-25) on oestrous behaviour in rats, *Acta Endocrinol.* **59**:41–48.

MEYERSON, B. J., and LINDSTRÖM, L. H., 1973a, Sexual motivation in the female rat. A methodological study applied to the investigation of the effect of estradiol benzoate, *Acta Physiol. Scand. Suppl. 389*, pp. 1–80.

MEYERSON, B. J., and LINDSTRÖM, L. H., 1973b, Sexual motivation in the neonatally androgen treated female rat, in: *Hormones and Brain Function* (K. Lissák, ed.), pp. 443–448, Plenum Press, New York.

MEYERSON, B. J., and MALMNÄS, C. O., 1977, Brain monoamines and sexual behaviour, in: *Biological Determinants of Sexual Behaviour* (J. Hutchinson, ed.), Wiley, London.

MEYERSON, B. J., NORDSTRÖM, E. B., and ÅGMO, A., 1971, Sexual behaviour and testosterone in female rats, *Acta Pharmacol. Toxicol. Suppl. 4* **29**:38.

MEYERSON, B. J., LINDSTRÖM, L., NORDSTRÖM, E. B., and ÅGMO, A., 1973a, Sexual motivation in the female rat after testosterone treatment, *Physiol. Behav.* **11**:421–428.

MEYERSON, B. J., ELIASSON, M., LINDSTRÖM, L., MICHANEK, A., and SÖDERLUND, A. C., 1973b, Monoamines and female sexual behaviour, in: *Psychopharmacology, Sexual Disorders and Drug Abuse* (T. A. Ban, J. R. Boissier, G. J. Gessa, H. Heimann, L. Hollister, H. E. Lehmann, I. Munkvad, H. Steinberg, F. Sulser, A. Sundwall, and O. Vinar, eds.), pp. 463–572, North Holland, Amsterdam.

MEYERSON, B. J., CARRER, H., and ELIASSON, M., 1974, 5-Hydroxytryptamine and sexual behavior in the female rat, in: *Advances in Biochemistry and Psychopharmacology*, Vol. 11 (E. Costa, M. Gessa, and M. Sandler, eds.), pp. 229–242, Raven Press, New York.

MICHAEL, R. P., 1958, Sexual behaviour and the vaginal cycle in the cat, *Nature (London)* **181**:567–568.

MICHAEL, R. P., 1961, Observations upon the sexual behaviour of the domestic cat (*Felix catus* L.) under laboratory conditions, *Behaviour* **18**:1–24.

MICHAEL, R. P., 1973, The effects of hormones on sexual behavior in female cat and rhesus monkey, in: *Handbook of Physiology*, Sec. 7, Vol. 11, Part 1 (R. O. Greep and E. B. Astwood, eds.), pp. 187–221, Am. Physiol. Soc., Washington, D. C.

MICHAEL, R. P., and SCOTT, P. P., 1964, The activation of sexual behaviour in cats by the subcutaneous administration of oestrogen, *J. Physiol. (London)* **171**:154–174.

MICHAEL, R. P., and WELEGALLA, J., 1968, Ovarian hormones and sexual behaviour of the female rhesus monkey (*Macaca mulatta*) under laboratory conditions, *J. Endocrinol.* **41**:417–421.

MICHAEL, R. P., and WILSON, M., 1974, Effects of castration and hormone replacement in fully adult male rhesus monkeys, *Endocrinology* **95**:150.

MICHAEL, R. P., HERBERT, J., and WELEGALLA, J., 1967a, Ovarian hormones and the sexual behaviour of the male rhesus monkey (*Macaca mulatta*) under laboratory conditions, *J. Endocrinol.* **31:**81-98.
MICHAEL, R. P., SAAYMAN, G, S., and ZUMPE, D., 1967b, Inhibition of sexual receptivity by progesterone in rhesus monkeys, *J. Endocrinol.* **39:**309-310.
MICHAEL, R. P., SAAYMAN, G. S., and ZUMPE, D., 1968, The suppression of mating behavior and ejaculation in male rhesus monkeys (*Macaca mulatta*) by administration of progesterone to their female partners, *J. Endocrinol.* **41:**421-431.
MICHAEL, R. P., ZUMPE, D., KEVERNE, E. B., and BONSALL, R. W., 1972, Neuroendocrine factors in the control of primate behavior, in: *Recent Progress in Hormone Research*, Vol. 27 (E. B. Astwood, ed.), pp. 665-706, Academic Press, New York.
MICHANEK, A., and MEYERSON, B. J., 1975, Copulatory behavior in the female rat after amphetamine and amphetamine derivatives, in: *Sexual Behavior, Pharmacology and Biochemistry*, (M. Sandler, and G. L. Gessa, eds.), Raven Press, New York.
MICHANEK, A., and MEYERSON, B. J., 1977, A comparative study of different amphetamines on copulatory behavior and stereotype activity in the female rat, *Psychopharmacologia* (in press).
MITCHELL, G. D., 1969, Paternalistic behavior in primates, *Psychol. Bull.* **71:**399-417.
MOLTZ, H., 1972, Ontogeny of maternal behavior in some selected mammalian species, in: *Ontogeny of Vertebrate Behavior* (H. Moltz, ed.), pp. 263-313. Academic Press, New York.
MOLTZ, H., LEVIN, R., and LEON, M., 1969, Differential effects of progesterone on the maternal behavior of primiparous and multiparous rats, *J. Comp. Physiol. Psychol.* **67:**36-40.
MOLTZ, H., LUBIN, M., LEON, M., and NUMAN, M., 1970, Hormonal induction of maternal behavior in the ovariectomized nulliparous rat, *Physiol. Behav.* **5:**1373-1377.
MOLTZ, H., LEON, M., NUMAN, M., and LUBIN, M., 1971, Replacement of progesterone with a phenothiazine in the induction of maternal behavior in the ovariectomized nulliparous rat, *Physiol. Behav.* **6:**735-738.
MONEY, J., 1971, Clinical aspects of prenatal steroidal action on sexually dimorphic behavior, in: *Steroid Hormones and Brain Function* (C. H. Sawyer and R. A. Gorski, eds.), UCLA Forum Med. Sci., pp. 325-336, University of California Press, Los Angeles.
MONEY, J., and EHRHARDT, A. A., 1972a, Gender dimorphic behavior and fetal sex hormones, in: *Progress in Hormone Research*, Vol. 28 (E. B. Astwood, ed.), pp. 735-754, Academic Press, New York.
MONEY, J., and EHRHARDT, A. A., 1972b, *Man and Woman, Boy and Girl*, Johns Hopkins Univ. Press, Baltimore.
MORIN, L. P., and FEDER, H. H., 1974a, Inhibition of lordosis behavior in ovariectomized guinea pigs by mesencephalic implants of progesterone, *Brain Res.* **70:**71-80.
MORIN, L. P., and FEDER, H. H., 1974b, Hypothalamic progesterone implants and facilitation of lordosis behavior in estrogen-primed ovariectomized guinea pigs, *Brain Res.* **70:**81-93.
MORIN, L. P., and FEDER, H. H., 1974c, Intracranial estradiol benzoate implants and lordosis behavior of ovariectomized guinea pigs, *Brain Res.* **70:**95-102.
MOSS, R. L., and MCCANN, S. M., 1973, Induction of mating behavior in rats by luteinizing hormone-releasing factor, *Science* **181:**177-179.
NADLER, R. D., 1968, Masculinization of female rats by intracranial implantation of androgen in infancy, *J. Comp. Physiol. Psychol.* **66:**157-167.
NADLER, R. D., 1970, A biphasic influence of progesterone on sexual receptivity of spayed female rats, *Physiol. Behav.* **5:**95-97.
NEQUIN, L. B., and SCHWARTZ, N. B., 1971, Adrenal participation in the timing of mating and LH release in the cyclic rat, *Endocrinology* **88:**325-331.
NEUMANN, F., and VON BERSWORDT-WALLRABE, R., 1966, Effects of the androgen antagonist, cyproterone acetate, on the testicular structure, spermatogenesis and accessory sexual glands of testosterone-treated adult hypophysectomized rats, *J. Endocrinol.* **35:**363-371.

NEUMANN, F., VON BERSWORDT-WALLRABE, R., ELGER, W., STEINBECK, H., HAHN, J. D., and KRAMER, M., 1970, Aspects of androgen-dependent events as studied by antiandrogens, *Recent Prog. Horm. Res.* **26**:337-411.
NOIROT, E., 1972, The onset of maternal behavior in rats, hamsters and mice. A selective review, *Adv. Stud. Behav.* **4**:107-145.
OLSON, L., and SEIGER, Å., 1972, Early prenatal ontogeny of central monoamine neurons in the rat: fluorescence histochemical observations, *Z. Anat. Entwicklungsgesch.* **137**:301-316.
PALKA, Y. S., and SAWYER, C. H., 1966, The effects of hypothalamic implants of ovarian steroids on oestrus behavior in rabbits, *J. Physiol.* **135**:251-269.
PARIS, C. A., RESKO, J. A., and GOY, R. W., 1971, A possible mechanism for the induction of lordosis by reserpine in spayed rats, *Biol. Reprod.* **4**:23-30.
PARROTT, R. F., 1974, Effects of 17β-hydroxy-4-androsten-19-ol-3-one (19-hydroxytestosterone) on aspects of sexual behaviour in castrated male rats, *J. Endocrinol.* **61**:105-115.
PEREZ-CRUET, J., TAGLIAMONTE, A., and GESSA, G. L., 1971, Differential effects of *p*-chlorophenylalanine (PCPA) on sexual behavior and on sleep patterns of male rabbits, *Riv. Farmacol. Ter.* **11**:27-34.
PFAFF, D. W., 1970, Nature of sex hormone effects on rat sex behavior: specificity of effects and individual patterns of response, *J. Comp. Physiol. Psychol.* **73**:349-358.
PFAFF, D. W., 1973, Luteinizing hormone-releasing factor potentiates lordosis behavior in hypophysectomized ovariectomized female rats, *Science* **181**:1148-1149.
PFAFF, D. W., and ZIGMOND, R. E., 1971, Neonatal androgen effects on sexual and nonsexual behavior of adult rats tested under various hormone regimes, *Neuroendocrinology* **7**:129-145.
PHOENIX, C. H., GOY, R. W., GERALL, A. A., and YOUNG, W. C., 1959, Organizing action of prenatally administered testosterone propionate on the tissues mediating mating behavior in the female guinea pig, *Endocrinology* **65**:369-382.
POWERS, J. B., 1970, Hormonal control of sexual receptivity during the estrous cycle of the rat, *Physiol. Behav.* **3**:831-835.
POWERS, J. B., 1972, Facilitation of lordosis in ovariectomized rats by intracerebral progesterone implants, *Brain Res.* **48**:311-325.
QUADAGNO, D. M., and ROCKWELL, J., 1972, Effect of gonadal hormones in infancy on maternal behavior in adult rat, *Horm. Behav.* **3**:55-62.
QUADAGNO, D. M., SHRYNE, J., and GORSKI, R. A., 1971, Inhibition of steroid-induced sexual behavior by intrahypothalamic actinomycin-D, *Horm. Behav.* **2**:1-10.
QUADAGNO, D. M., SHRYNE, J., ANDERSON, C., and GORSKI, R. A., 1972, Influence of gonadal hormones on social, sexual, emergence and open field behavior in the rat, *Anim. Behav.* **20**:732-740.
QUADAGNO, D. M., DEBOLD, J. F., GORZALKA, B. B., and WHALEN, R. E., 1974, Maternal behavior in the rat: aspects of concavation and neonatal androgen treatment, *Physiol Behav.* **12**:1071-1074.
REDDY, V., NAFTOLIN, F., and RYAN, K. J., 1974, Conversion of androstenedione to estrone by neural tissues from fetal and neonatal rats, *Endocrinology* **94**:117-121.
REDMOND, D. E., MAAS, J. E., KLING, A., and GRAHAM, C. W., 1971, Social behavior of monkeys selectively depleted of monoamines, *Science* **174**:428-430.
RESKO, J. A., 1970, Androgen secretion by the fetal and neonatal rhesus monkey, *Endocrinology* **87**:680-687.
RESKO, J. A., FEDER, H. H., and GOY, R. W., 1968, Androgen concentrations in plasma and testis of developing rats, *J. Endocrinol.* **40**:485-491.
RICHARDS, M. P. M., 1967, Maternal behavior in rodents and lagomorphs: a review, in: *Advances in Reproductive Physiology*, Vol. 2 (A. McLaren, ed.), pp. 54-110, Academic Press, New York.
RICHARDS, M. P. M., 1969, Effects of oestrogen and progesterone on nest building in the golden hamster, *Anim. Behav.* **17**:356-361.

Ring, J. R., 1944, The estrogen–progesterone induction of sexual receptivity in the spayed female mouse, *Endocrinology* **34:**269–275.
Robertson, H. A., 1969, The endogenous control of estrus and ovulation in sheep, cattle and swine, *Vitam. Horm. (N.Y.)* **27:**91–130.
Rodgers, C. H., 1970, Timing of sexual behavior in the female rat, *Endocrinology* **86:**1181–1183.
Rogres, C. M., and Davenport, R. K., 1970, Chimpanzee maternal behavior, in: *Chimpanzee*. Vol. 3, *Immunology, Infections, Hormones, Anatomy and Behavior* (G. H. Bourne, ed.), pp. 361–388, Karger, Basel.
Rommerts, F. F. G., and van der Malen, H. J., 1971, Occurrence and localization of 5α-steroid reductase, 3α- and 17β-hydroxysteroid dehydrogenases in hypothalamus and other brain tissues of the male rat, *Biochim. Biophys. Acta* **248:**489–502.
Rosenblatt, J. S., 1967, Nonhormonal basis of maternal behavior in the rat, *Science* **156:**1512–1513.
Rosenblatt, J. S., and Aronson, L. R., 1958, The decline of sexual behavior in male cats after castration with special reference to the role of prior experience, *Behaviour* **12:**285–338.
Rosenblum, L. A., 1972, The ontogeny of mother, infant relations in macaques, in: *The Ontogeny of Vertebrate Behavior* (H. Moltz, ed.), pp. 315–367, Academic Press, New York.
Rosenblum, L. A., Kaufman, I. C., and Stynes, A. J., 1964, Individual distance in two species of macaque, *Anim. Behav.* **12:**338–342.
Ross, S., Denenberg, V. H., Frommer, G. P., and Sawin, P. B., 1959, Genetic physiological and behavioral background of reproduction in the rabbit. V. Nonretrieving of neonates, *J. Mammal.* **40:**91–96.
Ross, S., Zarrow, M. X., Sawin, P. B., Denenberg, V. H., and Blumenfield, M., 1963, Maternal behavior in the rabbit under semi-natural conditions, *Anim. Behav.* **11:**283–285.
Ross, J., Claybough, C., Clemens, L. G., and Gorski, R. D., 1971, Short latency induction of estrous behavior with intracerebral gonadal hormones in ovariectomized rats, *Endocrinology* **89:**32–38.
Ross, J. W., Gorski, R. A., and Sawyer, C. H., 1973a, Effects of cortical stimulation on estrous behavior in estrogen-primed ovariectomized rats, *Endocrinology* **93:**20–25.
Ross, J. W., Shryne, J., Gorski, R. A., and Marshall, J. R., 1973b, Effect of clomiphene citrate and its isomers on sexual behavior in ovariectomized rats, *Endocrinology* **92:**1079–1083.
Ryan, K. J., Naftolin, I., Reddy, V. Flores, F., and Petro, Z., 1972, Estrogen formation in the brain, *Am. J. Obstet. Gynecol.* **114:**454–460.
Sachs, B. D., Pollak, E. I., Krieger, M. S., and Barfield, R. J., 1973, Sexual behavior: normal male pattering in androgenized female rats, *Science* **181:**770–772.
Saez, J., Morero, A. M., Dazord, A., and Bertrand, J., 1972, Adrenal and testicular contribution to plasma oestrogens, *J. Endocrinol.* **55:**41–49.
Salaman, D. F., 1970, DNA synthesis in the rat anterior hypothalamus and pituitary: relation of neonatal androgen and the oestrous cycle, *J. Endocrinol.* **48:**125–137.
Salis, P. J., and Dewsbury, D. A., 1971, *p*-Chlorophenylalanine facilitates copulatory behaviour in male rats, *Nature (London)* **232:**300–301.
Sar, M., and Stumpf, W. E., 1973, Autoradiographic location of radioactivity in the rat brain after the injection of 1,2-^{3}H-testosterone, *Endocrinology* **92:**251–256.
Schapiro, S., 1968, Some physiological, biochemical, and behavioural consequences of neonatal hormone administration: cortisol and thyroxine, *Gen. Comp. Endocrinol.* **10:**214–228.
Schwartz, N. B., 1969, A model for the regulation of ovulation in the rat, *Recent Prog. Horm. Res.* **25:**1–43.
Seiger, Å., and Olson, L., 1973, Late prenatal ontogeny of central monoamine neurons in

the rat: fluorescence histochemical observations, *Z. Anat. Entwicklungsgesch.* **140:**281–318.
SHEARD, M. H., 1969, The effect of *p*-chlorophenylalanine on behaviour in rats: relation to brain serotonin and 5-hydroxyindoleacetic acid, *Brain Res.* **15:**524–528.
SHERIDAN, P. J., ZARROW, M. X., and DENENBERG, V. H., 1973, Androgenization of the neonatal female rat with very low doses of androgen, *J. Endocrinol.* **57:**33–45.
SHILLITO, E. E., 1969, The effect of *p*-chlorophenylalanine on social interactions of male rats, *Br. J. Pharmacol.* **36:**193–194P.
SHILLITO, E. E., 1970, The effect of parachlorophenylalanine on social interactions of male rats, *Br. J. Pharmacol.* **38:**305–315.
SHIMADA, H., and GORBMAN, A., 1970, Long-lasting changes in RNA synthesis in the forebrains of female rats treated with testosterone soon after birth, *Biochem. Biophys. Res. Commun.* **38:**423–430.
SIEGEL, H. I., and ROSENBLATT, J. S., 1975*a*, Hormonal basis of hysterectomy-induced maternal behavior during pregnancy in the rat, *Horm. Behav.* **6:**211–222.
SIEGEL, H. I., and ROSENBLATT, J. S., 1975*b*, Progesterone inhibition of estrogen-induced maternal behavior in hysterectomized-ovariectomized virgin rats, *Horm. Behav.* **6:**223–230.
SIMONDS, P. E., 1965, The bonnet macaque in South India, in: *Primate Behavior* (I. DeVore, ed.), pp. 175–196, Holt, New York.
SLOB, A. K., GOY, R. W., and VAN DER WERFF TEN BOSCH, J. J., 1973, Sex differences in growth of guinea pigs and their modification by neonatal gonadectomy and prenatally administered androgen, *J. Endocrinol.* **58:**11–19.
SÖDERSTEN, P., 1972, Mounting behavior in the female rat during the estrous cycle, after ovariectomy and after estrogen or testosterone administration, *Horm. Behav.* **3:**307–320.
SÖDERSTEN, P., 1973*a*, Increased mounting behavior in the female rat following a single neonatal injection of testosterone propionate, *Horm. Behav.* **4:**1–17.
SÖDERSTEN, P., 1973*b*, Estrogen-activated sexual behavior in male rats, *Horm. Behav.* **4:**247–256.
SORIERO, O., and FORD, D. H., 1973, The composition of different regions of the neonatal rat brain in relation to sex, in: *Progress in Brain Research. Neurobiological Aspects of Maturation and Aging* (D. H. Ford, ed.), pp. 309–319, Elsevier, Amsterdam.
SOULAIRAC, M. L., 1963, Étude expérimentale des régulations hormono-nerveuses du comportement sexuel du Rat mâle, *Ann. d'Endocrinol.* **24:**1–98, Suppl. to No. 3.
STERN, J. J., 1969, Neonatal castration, androstenedione, and the mating behavior of the male rat, *J. Comp. Physiol. Psychol.* **69:**608–612.
STERN, J. J., and JANKOWIAK, R., 1972, Effects of actinomycin-D implanted in the anterior hypothalamic-preoptic region of the diencephalon on spontaneous activity in ovariectomized rats, *J. Endocrinol.* **55:**465–466.
STERN, J. J., and MURPHY, M., 1971, The effects of cyproterone acetate on the spontaneous activity and seminal vesicle weight of male rats, *J. Endocrinol.* **50:**441–443.
STONE, C. P., 1925, Preliminary note on maternal behavior of rats living in parabiosis, *Endocrinology* **9:**505–512.
STONE, C. P., 1932, The retention of copulatory behavior in male rabbits following castration, *J. Genet. Psychol.* **40:**296–305.
STONE, C. P., 1939, Copulatory activity in adult male rats following castration and injections of testosterone propionate, *Endocrinology* **24:**165–174.
STUMPF, W. E., and SAR, M., 1973, Hormonal inputs to releasing factor cells, feedback sites, in: Drug effects on neuroendocrine regulation, *Prog. Brain Res.* **39:**53–70.
TAGLIAMONTE, A., TAGLIAMONTE, P., GESSA, G. L., and BRODIE, B. B., 1969, Compulsive sexual activity induced by *p*-chlorophenylalanine in normal and pinealectomized male rats, *Science* **166:**1433–1435.
TAGLIAMONTE, A., TAGLIAMONTE, P., and GESSA, G. L., 1971, Reversal of pargyline-induced

inhibition of sexual behaviour in male rats by *p*-chlorophenylalanine, *Nature (London)* **230**:244–245.
TAGLIAMONTE, A., FRATTA, W., MERCURO, G., BIGGIO, G., CAMBA, R. C., and GESSA, G. L., 1972, 5-hydroxytryptophan, but not tryptophan, inhibits copulatory behavior in male rats, *Riv. Farmacol. Ter.* **3**:405–409.
TAGLIAMONTE, A., FRATTA, W., DEL FIACCO, M., and GESSA, G. L., 1973, Evidence that brain dopamine stimulates copulatory behavior in male rats, *Riv. Farmacol. Ter.* **4**:177–181.
TERENIUS, L., 1965, Uptake of radioactive oestradiol in some organs of immature mice, *Acta Endocrinol.* **50**:584–596.
TERENIUS, L., 1966, Specific uptake of oestrogen by the mouse uterus *in vitro*, *Acta Endocrinol.* **53**:611–618.
TERKEL, J., and ROSENBLATT, J., 1968, Maternal behavior induced by maternal blood plasma injected into virgin rats, *J. Comp. Physiol. Psychol.* **65**:479–482.
TERKEL, J., and ROSENBLATT, J. S., 1972, Humoral factors underlying maternal behavior at parturition: cross transfusion between freely moving rats, *J. Comp. Physiol. Psychol.* **80**:365–371.
TERKEL, A. S., SHRYNE, J., and GORSKI, P. A., 1973, Inhibition of estrogen facilitation of sexual behavior by the intracerebral infusion of actinomycin-D, *Horm. Behav.* **4**:377–386.
TINKLEPAUGH, O. L., and HARTMAN, K. G., 1930, Behavioral aspects of parturition in the monkey (*Macaca rhesus*), *Comp. Psychol.* **11**:63–98.
TINKLEPAUGH, O. L., and HARTMAN, K. G., 1932, Behavior and maternal care of the newborn monkey (*Macaca mulatta*), *J. Gen. Psychol.* **40**:257–286.
TONGE, S. R., and GREENGRASS, P. M., 1971, The acute effects of oestrogen and progesterone on the monoamine levels of the brain of ovariectomized rats, *Psychopharmacologia* **21**:374–381.
TRIMBLE, M. R., and HERBERT, J., 1968, The effect of testosterone or oestradiol upon the sexual and associated behaviour of the adult female rhesus monkey, *J. Endocrinol.* **42**:171–185.
TUCHMANN-DUPLESSIS, M. H., and MERCIER-PAROT, L., 1963, Modifications du comportement sexuel chez des descendants de rats traités par un inhibiteur des monoamineoxyclases, *C. R. Acad. Sci.* **256**:2235–2237.
UPHOUSE, L. L., 1970, Induction of estrus in mice: possible role of adrenal progesterone, *Horm. Behav.* **1**:255–264.
VOCI, V., and CARLSON, N. R., 1973, Enhancement of maternal behavior and nest building following systemic and diencephalic administration of prolactin and progesterone in the mouse, *J. Comp. Physiol. Psychol.* **83**:388–393.
WALLEN, K., GOLDFOOT, D. A., JOSLYN, W. D., and PARIS, C. A., 1972, Modification of behavioural estrus in the guinea pig following intracranial cycloheximide. *Physiol. Behav.* **8**:221–223.
WALTON, A., 1952, Patterns of male sex behavior, *Ciba Found. Colloq. Endocrinol.* **3**:47.
WARD, I. L., 1969, Differential effect of pre- and postnatal androgen on the sexual behavior of intact and spayed female rats, *Horm. Behav.* **1**:25–36.
WARD, I. L., 1972, Female sexual behavior in male rats treated prenatally with an antiandrogen, *Physiol. Behav.* **8**:53–56.
WEISZ, J., and GIBBS, C., 1974, Metabolism of testosterone in the brain of the newborn female rat after an injection of tritiated testosterone, *Neuroendocrinology* **14**:72–86.
WHALEN, R. E., 1961, Effects of mounting without intromission and intromission without ejaculation on sexual behavior and maze learning, *J. Comp. Physiol. Psychol.* **54**:409–415.
WHALEN, R. E., 1964, Hormone-induced changes in the organization of sexual behavior in the male rat, *J. Comp. Physiol. Psychol.* **57**:175–182.
WHALEN, R. E., 1968, Differentiation of the neural mechanisms which control gonadotropin secretion and sexual behavior, in: *Perspectives in Reproduction and Sexual Behavior* (M. Diamond, ed.), pp. 303–340, Indiana University Press, Bloomington, Indiana.

WHALEN, R. E., 1971, The ontogeny of sexuality, in: *The Ontogeny of Vertebrate Behavior* (H. Moltz, ed.), pp. 229-261, Academic Press, New York.
WHALEN, R. E., 1972, Gonadal hormones, the nervous system and behavior, in: *Advances in Behavioral Biology*, Vol. 4, *The Chemistry of Mood, Motivation, and Memory* (J. L. McGaugh, ed.), Plenum Press, New York.
WHALEN, R. E., 1974, Estrogen-progesterone induction of mating in female rats, *Horm. Behav.* **5:**157-162.
WHALEN, R. E., and EDWARDS, D. A., 1966, Sexual reversibility in neonatally castrated male rats, *J. Comp. Physiol. Psychol.* **62:**307-310.
WHALEN, R. E., and EDWARDS, D. A., 1967, Hormonal determinants of the development of masculine and feminine behavior in male and female rats, *Anat. Rec.* **157:**173-180.
WHALEN, R. E., and EDWARDS, D. A., 1969, Effect of the antiandrogen cyproterone acetate on mating behavior and seminal vesicle tissue in male rats, *Endocrinology* **84:**155-156.
WHALEN, R. E., and LUTTGE, W. G., 1970, *p*-Chlorophenylalanine methyl ester: an aphrodisiac? *Science* **169:**1000-1001.
WHALEN, R. E., and LUTTGE, W. G., 1971, Testosterone, androstenedione and dihydrotestosterone: effects on mating behavior of male rats, *Horm. Behav.* **2:**117-125.
WHALEN, R. E., and NADLER, R. D., 1963, Suppression of the development of female mating behavior by estrogen administered in infancy, *Science* **141:**273-274.
WHALEN, R. E., and REZAK, D. L., 1974, Inhibition of lordosis in female rats by subcutaneous implants of testosterone, androstenedione or dihydrotestosterone in infancy, *Horm. Behav.* **5:**125-128.
WHALEN, R. E., EDWARDS, D. A., LUTTGE, W. G., and ROBERTSON, R. T., 1969, Early androgen treatment and male sexual behavior in female rats, *Physiol. Behav.* **4:**33-39.
WHALEN, R. E., BATTIE, C., and LUTTGE, W. G., 1972, Antiestrogen inhibition of androgen induced sexual receptivity in rats, *Behav. Biol.* **7:**311-320.
WHALEN, R. E., GORZALKA, B. B., DEBOLD, J. F., QUADAGNO, D. M., KAN-WHA HO, G., and HOUGH, J. L., 1974, Studies on the effects of intracerebral actinomycin D implants on estrogen-induced receptivity in rats, *Horm. Behav.* **5:**337-343.
WIESNER, B. P., and SHEARD, N. M., 1933, *Maternal Behaviour in the Rat*, Oliver and Boyd, Edinburgh.
WIEST, W. G., KIDWELL, W. R., and BALOGH, K., 1968, Progesterone catabolism in the rat ovary: a regulatory mechanism for progestational potency during pregnancy, *Endocrinology* **82:**844-860.
WILSON, A. P., and VESSEY, S. H., 1968, Behavior of free-ranging castrated rhesus monkeys, *Folia Primatol.* **9:**1-14.
WIRZ-JUSTICE, A., HACKMANN, E., and LICHTSTEINER, M., 1974, The effect of estradiol dipropionate and progesterone on monoamine uptake in rat brain, *J. Neurochem.* **22:**187-189.
YOSHINAGA, K., HAWKINS, R. A., and STOCKER, J. F., 1969, Estrogen secretion by the rat ovary *in vivo* during the estrous cycle and pregnancy, *Endocrinology* **85:**103-112.
YOUNG, W. C., 1961, The hormones and mating behavior, in: *Sex and Internal Secretions* (W. C. Young, ed.), pp. 1173-1239, Williams and Wilkins Co., Baltimore.
ZARROW, M. X., DENENBERG, V. H., and ANDERSON, C. O., 1965, Rabbit: frequency of suckling in the pup, *Science* **150:**1835-1836.
ZARROW, M. X., GANDELMAN, R., and DENENBERG, V. H., 1971, Lack of nest building and maternal behavior in the mouse following olfactory bulb removal, *Horm. Behav.* **2:**227-238.
ZARROW, M. X., DENENBERG, V. H., and SACHS, B. D., 1972, Hormones and maternal behavior in mammals, in: *Hormones and Behavior* (S. Levine, ed.), pp. 105-134, Academic Press, New York.
ZEMLAN, F. P., WARD, I. L., CROWLEY, W. R., and MARGULES, D. L., 1973, Activation of lordotic responding in female rats by suppression of serotonergic activity, *Science* **179:**1010-1011.

ZITRIN, A., BEACH, F. A., BARCHAS, J. D., and DEMENT, W. C., 1970, Sexual behavior of male cats after administration of parachlorophenylalanine, *Science* **170:**868–869.

ZUCKER, I., 1966, Effects of an antiandrogen on the mating behavior of male guinea pigs and rats, *J. Endocrinol.* **35:**209–210.

ZUCKER, I., 1967, Actions of progesterone in the control of sexual receptivity of the spayed female rat, *J. Comp. Physiol. Psychol.* **63:**313–316.

ZUCKER, I., 1968, Biphasic effects of progesterone on sexual receptivity in the female guinea pig, *J. Comp. Physiol. Psychol.* **65:**472–478.

ZUCKER, I., and FEDER, H. H., 1966, The effect of neonatal reserpine treatment on female sex behaviour of rats, *J. Endocrinol.* **35:**423–424.

ZUCKER, I., and GOY, R. W., 1967, Sexual receptivity in the guinea pig: inhibitory and facilitatory actions of progesterone and related compounds, *J. Comp. Physiol. Psychol.* **64:**378–383.

6

NEUROPHARMACOLOGY OF THE SLEEP–WAKING CYCLE

Michel Jouvet

1. INTRODUCTION

There are two main problems related to the neuropharmacology of sleep: Is it possible to induce *physiological* sleep, at will, and for a predetermined duration, with a drug in a normal intact animal? The answer to this question is still negative. Neither in animals nor in man do we have yet the right hypnogenic drug or the combination of drugs which will induce *at any time* and *for any duration* the delicate and harmonious succession of the different stages and states of sleep. However, neuropharmacology has allowed us to dissect some of the intimate mechanisms underlying the sleep–waking cycle since some drugs may suppress both states of sleep, or suppress paradoxical sleep (ps) selectively, or restore physiological sleep in an insomniac cat.

Our answers to these two problems explain the organization of this chapter. First I will summarize the present main theories of sleep. They seem either contradictory or complementary since we do not yet understand the intimate mechanism of sleep. This ignorance is responsible for the absence of any real hypnogenic drug. Thereafter I will outline the results of the neuropharmacological dissection of sleep mechanisms: the results obtained with drugs whose mechanisms of action are rather "specific" will be described first, while the results obtained with other drugs whose central mechanisms of action are unknown or too complex will be summarized later. This review will be devoted exclusively to animal experiments. The following recent symposia or reviews contain references pertinent to the subject: Fuxe and

---

Michel Jouvet • Department of Experimental Medicine, University Claude Bernard, Lyon, France.

Lidbrink, 1973; Hartmann, 1968–1970; Jouvet, 1968, 1969, 1972; King, 1971; Morgane and Stern, 1973; Pichot and Serdaru, 1972; Oswald, 1968; Stern and Morgane, 1974.

2. THE SLEEP–WAKING CYCLE IN THE CAT

Since the chronic cat is the main experimental animal with which most of the recent advances in the neurophysiology and neuropharmacology of sleep have been obtained, I will summarize below the main qualitative and quantitative characteristics of the sleep–waking cycle which have been collected with polygraphic methods using continuous cortical and subcortical recordings together with recording of neck muscle activity and of the eye movements using electrooculographic methods. These recordings have provided us with a broad spectrum of regional electrical activity which is characteristic of the delicate intricacy of the different systems entering into play during physiological sleep. It should be emphasized here that the appearance of cortical spindles or slow waves is not sufficient alone to characterize "slow-wave sleep." Thus, it is evident that the old pharmacological techniques using "barbiturate sleeping time" in rats, or "loss of righting reflexes" in mice, or "behavioral sleep" as dependent variables are no longer useful. The main polygraphic features of the sleep–waking cycle in the cat are shown in Fig. 1. In addition to the alterations of cortical activity, from arousal to drowsiness with some slowing of the frequency of the cortical waves, to stage 1 (with spindles) and stage II (high-voltage 2–3 Hz slow waves), some subcortical patterns also permit us to assume that the slowing of cortical activity belongs to physiological sleep. High-voltage sharp waves appear periodically in the pontine reticular formation, the lateral geniculate, and the occipital cortex (pontogeniculate activity) (PGO). This PGO activity appears either during slow-wave sleep (stage II) (isolated PGO, so-called "slow sleep with phasic activity"), or immediately before and during PS. Paradoxical sleep occurs spontaneously every 25 min during sleep and lasts for 6 min. Thus, I shall use the term "physiological sleep" (after any pharmacological alteration) only if we can record the same periodic and harmonious succession of the states of sleep that are observed under control conditions. *Hypersomnia* would be defined as a state in which *both* SWS and PS increase significantly above the control level, since the quantity of sleep is remarkably constant in laboratory cats recorded under standard conditions. Since many drugs may increase cortical synchronization only (but may suppress isolated PGO or PS), we shall call this state either "increased slow-wave sleep" (if isolated PGO still occurs) or "increased cortical synchronization" if the pattern of cortical activity is different from normal sleep. If this state is accompanied by an obvious behavioral sedation, it will be called "sedation," or "decrease of waking" if it is immediately reversible by an external stimulus; otherwise it will be called "narcosis."

3. AN OUTLINE OF RECENT THEORIES OF SLEEP MECHANISMS

3.1. Recent Advances in the Study of Sleep Mechanisms

Four main concepts are responsible for the recent advances in understanding of the neurophysiological mechanism of sleep since 1958 (see the extensive reviews by Moruzzi, 1972, and Jouvet, 1972).

1. Through the development of continuous polygraphic recordings, it was shown that the quantity of sleep was a biological constant and thus could be used *as a dependent variable* after any neurophysiological or neuropharmacological intervention.

2. Although many lesions of the central nervous system (sometimes as large as the destruction of both caudate nuclei) (Villablanca and Marcus, 1974) do not interfere significantly with the sleep–waking cycle, it has been shown that rather circumscribed lesions can either suppress waking or induce total insomnia or selective suppression of PS. This led, first, to the postulate that there might be some anatomical specificity of sleep systems responsible for the two different states of sleep, and second, to the hypothesis that sleep was an active phenomenon and not merely the absence of wakefulness (passive theory of sleep) (Bremer, 1954; Moruzzi, 1964) since it was possible to induce total insomnia following lesions.

3. The discovery of a state of sleep with fast cortical activity ("activated sleep," "paradoxical sleep," "REM sleep") lent strong support to the active and dualistic theories of sleep. Moreover, the discovery of a long-lasting rebound (up to several days) after instrumental or pharmacological suppression of PS, which could not be explained by classical electrophysiology, paved the way for the entry of "wet neurophysiology" into the field of sleep.

4. The "wet neurophysiology" of sleep (as opposed to classical electrophysiology) has followed two main paths: (a) The first is the revival of the old theory of *hypnotoxin* (Pieron, 1913). Some protein or polypeptide is liberated into the blood, the CSF, or brain during sleep, and it should be possible to characterize a hypnogenic factor: the *humoral theory of sleep*. (b) The long time constant of the sleep–waking cycle, or the rebound of PS, can also be explained by the modern concept of neurotransmitter function (e.g., induction of enzyme synthesis, increased turnover). Since modern methods of histochemistry and biochemistry were available, it became possible to approach, with the help of neuropharmacology, the role of the putative

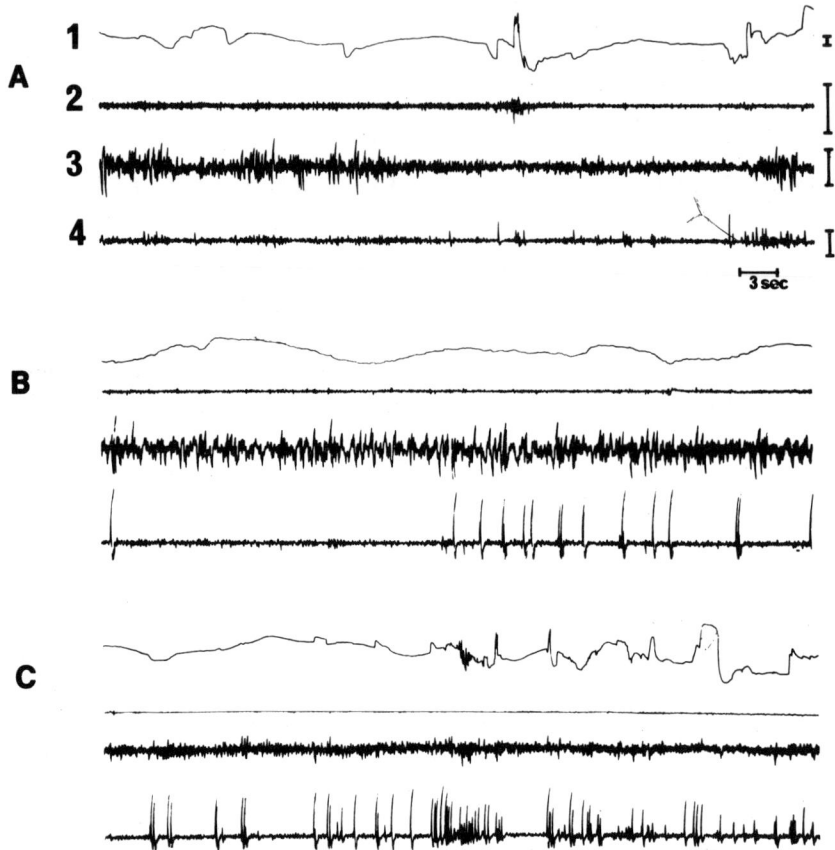

FIG. 1. Main polygraph features of the sleep–waking cycle in the cat. (A) Slow-wave sleep (stage 1) with cortical spindles is followed by a short-lasting cortical arousal with eye movements. (1) Electrooculographic recordings of eye movements; (2) electromyogram of the neck muscles; (3) activity of the frontal cortex; (4) activity of the dorsal geniculate nucleus. Calibration: 3 sec, 50 mV. (B) Slow-wave sleep (stage 2) with cortical spindles and slow wave is followed by slow-wave sleep with phasic activity (PGO). This activity may occur periodically during slow-wave sleep and always heralds the appearance of paradoxical sleep. (C) Paradoxical sleep with its main tonic (fast low-voltage cortical activity, total disappearance of the EMG activity of the neck) and phasic (rapid eye movements and PGO activity) characteristics.

neurotransmitters which could be involved in the regulation of sleep. This led to the development of the cholinergic and monoaminergic theories of sleep.

3.2. Classical Neurophysiology of Sleep

1. Lesions of the ascending reticular system or of the posterior hypothalamus induce a comatose state with cortical synchronization.

2. Structures lying within the isolated cerebrum may account for the reappearance of a sleep–waking cycle in the chronic "cerveau isolé." Then the sleep–waking cycle (excluding PS) *may appear in the absence of any brainstem control.* The ascending reticular system and a group of neurons lying in the posterior hypothalamus are endowed with a tonic activating influence. They are probably concerned with the maintenance of wakefulness.

3. Midpontine pretrigeminal transection, which disconnects lower-brainstem synchronizing structures from the ascending reticular system, considerably enhances wakefulness. Stimulation of the reticular formation of the medulla or of the solitary tract induces EEG synchronization.

4. Preoptic basal forebrain area lesions induce a striking reduction of both states of sleep, while stimulation of this region is followed by EEG synchronization and behavioral sleep.

Thus, the lower brainstem and the basal forebrain area contain structures with an opposing function (to that of the ascending reticular system and posterior hypothalamus) and exert a tonic deactivating influence which leads ultimately to sleep (Moruzzi, 1972).

3.3. "Wet Neurophysiology"

3.3.1. Humoral Theories

a. Blood Factor. Sleep dialysates obtained by extracorporal dialysis in rabbit donors kept asleep by stimulation of the "thalamic sleep area" were injected into the ventricular system of rabbit recipients submitted to quantitative EEG analysis. The hypnogenic material was fractionated by ultracentrifugation and purified by gel filtration, preparative TLC, and high-voltage paper electrophoresis. The delta-sleep (slow-wave sleep) transmitting *factor delta* is a small *peptide,* composed of eight amino acid residues with a molecular weight of about 860. The effective dose for sleep induction is estimated to be 3.3×10^{-10} mol/kg/0.05 ml/25 min (Schoenenberger *et al.,* 1972).

Negative experiments concerning the blood transfer of a sleep factor should also be cited. The transplantation of an isolated dog head to another dog's neck has been carried out successfully recently by Nava *et al.* (1973). The transplanted head remained alive for 4.5 days, showing normal neurologic activity. Periods of wakefulness alternated with those of sleep. The EEG results showed a normal activity in the isolated head, completely independent of the cerebral activity in the receptor dog. Whereas a correlation seemed to exist between the need for feeding and drinking of the implanted head and the appetite and thirst of the host, *the sleep–waking cycle of both was completely independent.*

b. CSF-to-CSF Perfusate. Intraventricular infusion in the rat of 0.1 ml of

CSF from sleep-deprived goats increases the duration of sleep (recorded by EEG) and decreases motor activity for at least 6 hr after the infusion. The sleep-promoting factor (S) has been isolated by ultrafiltration through molecular sieves. Factor S is found in the low-molecular-weight (<500) compounds in CSF from sleep-deprived but not from control goats. The concentration of factor S in CSF increases progressively during the first 48 hr of sleep deprivation (Fencl et al., 1971).

c. Brain-to-Brain Perfusate. Recipient cats were perfused through a push–pull cannula system implanted in the midbrain reticular formation with fluid obtained via a push–pull cannula from sleeping or awake cats. The perfusate extracted from the reticular formation of a sleeping donor increased the duration and decreased the latency of slow-wave sleep in recipient cats, while no effect was seen on PS (Drucker-Colin et al., 1970).

In another series of experiments the same group claimed to have obtained from perfusates from the mesencephalic reticular formation during spontaneous sleep in cats, two peaks of protein in apparent correlation with the spontaneous increase of PS. The perfusate contained proteins at concentrations ranging from 23 to 206 μg/ml. Ultrafiltration analysis indicated that approximately 80% of the proteins were of molecular weight greater than 10^4 and at least 60% were greater than 5×10^4 (Drucker-Colin et al., 1975).

Summing up, there is some evidence that during sleep induced by electrical stimulation of the thalamus in the rabbit, during sleep deprivation in the goat, or during PS in the cat, some polypeptides or proteins might be released into the blood, the CSF, or the brain. These substances have some hypnogenic effects when injected into the CSF or the brain. We still do not know what system is responsible for their synthesis and on what targets they act. These unknown hypnogenic messengers are putative candidates for the final biochemical pathway responsible for sleep.

3.3.2. Neurohumoral Theories

a. Cholinergic Theory. From the work of several groups (Cordeau et al., 1963; Hernandez-Peon et al., 1967; Morgane, 1969), the following picture of two possibly antagonistic cholinergic systems can be schematized: *a sleep system* (in which a local injection of ACh may "trigger" SWS), and a *waking system*. The sleep system is composed of two components: The first component, *a descending component,* closely conforms to the limbic midbrain circuit described by Nauta (1958). An injection of ACh into this circuit is followed by sleep, whereas lesions or atropine injections made *caudally* to the injection of ACh suppress the sleep-inducing effect. This system joins at the pontine level with an *ascending component* originating from the gray substance of the spinal cord.

According to Hernandez-Peon et al. (1967), the cholinergic sleep system would operate as follows: The primary hypnogenic stimuli arise in the peripheral neurons of the ascending and descending segments as, for example, somatic sensory stimuli in the ascending component and conditioned stimuli (arising in the neocortex) in the descending component. These influences converge, then arise in the final pathway to cause a progressively spreading inhibition. As the inhibition begins to ascend, mesencephalic neurons become inhibited. Thus, the thalamic recruiting neurons, now disinhibited, organize the thalamocortical activity which is recorded as spindles and slow waves during SWS. Eventually the wave of inhibition continues to ascend and reaches the thalamic recruiting nuclei. The inhibition of these structures releases the activity of the cortex which becomes rapid during PS. Thus, according to Hernandez-Peon, sleep is not only cholinergic but it is *unitary*. SWS and PS are not separate states but are only different manifestations of the same basic process.

The waking system corresponds to the ascending cholinergic reticular system described by Shute and Lewis (1967) (see also Lewis and Shute, Vol. 9 of this series). Local cholinergic stimulation of this system produces arousal according to Morgane (1969). The cholinoceptive arousal system is topographically dissociated from the descending sleep system in the midbrain, posterior to the interpeduncular nucleus. However, both sleep and waking cholinoceptive systems are topographically intermixed in the medial forebrain bundle and the lateral hypothalamic area, so that in certain regions waking is produced by cholinergic stimulation, while just 1 mm away sleep may follow the same cholinergic stimulation.

b. *The Monoaminergic Theory (Jouvet, 1972)*. The serotonin (5-HT) containing perikarya of the raphe system play a determinant role in the induction of sleep since raphe lesions are followed by an insomnia which is proportional to the extent of the destruction of the raphe nuclei and to the decrease of 5-HT in the terminals. The rostral part of the raphe (N. raphe dorsalis and mostly centralis superior) is mainly involved in the induction of states 1 and 2, while N. raphe magnus and pontis are responsible for the priming mechanisms of PS.

The norepinephrine (NE) containing neurons of the rostral part of the locus coeruleus, ascending in the dorsal noradrenergic pathway, are involved in the maintenance of tonic cortical arousal in addition to cholinergic ascending mechanisms whose topography remains to be discovered. The dopaminergic nigrostriatal system does not play a determinant role in the regulation of the sleep–waking cycle at the EEG level, but is involved in the maintenance of waking behavior.

Paradoxical sleep involves some 5-HT priming mechanisms which are dependent upon nuclei raphe magnus and pontis, whereas its executive noradrenergic and cholinergic mechanisms are located in the dorsolateral part of the pontine tegmentum.

According to the monoaminergic theory, there are reciprocal interactions between the 5-HT and NE systems of neurons. Thus, destruction of the rostral portion of the raphe which leads to insomnia is followed by increased activity of NE neurons ascending in the dorsal NE bundle, while destruction of these latter neurons is followed by increased activity in the rostral raphe system and by hypersomnia.

Thus, two different mechanisms may lead to insomnia: decrease of activity of the raphe system and/or increase of activity of the ascending dorsal NE system. The decrease of waking may also be obtained by two different mechanisms: decrease of activity of the NE system (decreased wakefulness) and/or increased activity in the raphe system (true hypersomnia).

In summary, this theory emphasizes the paramount importance of the brainstem where the monoaminergic (MA) perikarya are located, whereas each level of organization of the brain subjected to the interactions of the systems of 5-HT, CA, and ACh terminals is responsible for the behavioral and EEG aspects of the sleep–waking cycle.

Summing up, it is evident that none of the main theories of sleep can explain entirely the mechanism of the sleep–waking cycle and each theory has its advantages and drawbacks. While it is certainly too early to integrate all of them in a unitary theory, it is possible to explain some of their discrepancies. For example, the hypnogenic role of the preoptic area postulated by classical neurophysiology can be explained by the fact that many 5-HT terminals of N. raphe dorsalis, centralis, superior, and even raphe pontis converge in this area (Bobillier *et al.*, 1975). Thus, insomnia could be obtained *either* by lesion of the perikarya of the rostral raphe nuclei *or* by lesion of the terminals of the 5-HT system in the preoptic region. The monoaminergic theory also does not explain how the 5-HT neurons of the raphe come into play at the beginning of sleep. But it is likely that the hypnogenic role of vagal afferents and solitary tract neurons might be mediated by the raphe (at least for obtaining a tonic cortical synchronization (Puizillout *et al.*, 1974). Finally neurohumoral theories do not give any indication of the postsynaptic events which follow the release of the transmitters. It is possible that some postsynaptic system activated by monoamines or by acetylcholine might synthesize some polypeptides or even proteins which would be the final messengers of sleep. If this hypothesis is true, the infusion of sleep factor delta or factor S should be able to restore both states of sleep in an otherwise insomniac cat after destruction of the raphe system.

4. 5-HYDROXYTRYPTAMINE AND THE SLEEP–WAKING CYCLE

4.1. Increased Availability of 5-HT to Serotoninoceptive Neurons

4.1.1. Action of 5-HT and Its Metabolites

The intravenous injection of 5-HT in chicks, whose blood–brain barrier is permeable to this amine, induces "sleeplike" behavior and cerebral synchronization (Spooner et al., 1968). A "sleeplike" state is also obtained with the deaminated metabolite of 5-HT, 5-hydroxyindolylacetaldehyde (Sabelli and Giardina, 1970), or 5-hydroxytryptophol (Felstein et al., 1970). These results, however, were not confirmed after intraventricular injection of 5-HIAA or intraperitoneal injection of 5-hydroxytryptophol in the cat when using polygraphic recordings (Morgane and Stern, 1973a).

Several attempts have been made to bypass the blood–brain barrier, which is impermeable to 5-HT in mature mammals: local application of 5-HT at the level of the area postrema, which is close to some 5-HT perikarya, or in the ventricles can induce sedation and cortical synchronization or augmentation of the recruiting response in the cat (Koella and Czicman, 1966; Bronzino et al., 1973). Moreover, local injection of 5-HT (Roth et al., 1970) into the arterial circulation which supplies the area postrema and the adjacent medulla increases cortical synchronization, whereas the injection of NE induces cortical desynchronization.

These experiments are difficult to interpret, since it is difficult to know the concentration of exogenous 5-HT in the brain. 5-HT in small quantities may mimic the effects of endogenous 5-HT at the receptor site. But it may also act upon other (nonreceptor) cells through a pharmacological effect, and finally it may be accumulated by other MA neurons (Aghajanian et al., 1966; Fuxe and Ungerstedt, 1968).

4.1.2. Tryptophan

Tryptophan hydroxylase is the rate-limiting step in the biosynthesis of 5-HT. Furthermore, the high K_m observed for tryptophan suggests that the enzyme may not be fully saturated with substrate, so that the overall rate of 5-HT synthesis may be partially dependent upon availability of the substrate (see Green and Grahame-Smith, Chapter 4, Vol. 3). This may explain why loading doses of tryptophan increase the level of brain 5-HT in rats. In the rat, excess tryptophan leads to a small decrease of total sleep duration accompanied by a significant increase in the frequency of PS, whereas a tryptophan-free diet (which also decreases sleep time) decreases the number of PS episodes (Hartmann, 1968).

4.1.3. 5-HTP

This direct precursor of 5-HT readily crosses the blood–brain barrier, and its depressant effects on behavior are well known. The effect of DL-5-HTP depends upon the dose injected. In the cat, at low doses (1–5 mg/kg) there is a slight tendency toward more synchronization (Delorme, 1966).

Large doses (30–50 mg/kg) in the rabbit (Monnier and Tissot, 1958) definitely induce a state of cortical synchronization which lasts continuously for 4–6 hr. However, in the cat PGO activity and PS are totally suppressed for 5–6 hr, after which PS occurs with some rebound (Delorme, 1966). With higher doses, 5-HTP induces a state of sedation followed by excitation (Costa et al., 1960). But since 5-HTP may be decarboxylated in the serotoninergic terminals and may also decrease dopamine (DA) by displacement of DA by newly formed 5-HT in DA terminals (Ng et al., 1970), the effect of high doses of 5-HTP are difficult to interpret. Finally, low doses of 5-HTP have no synchronizing action and do not reverse the total insomnia in raphe-destroyed cats (Pujol et al., 1971). In this case, however, it may be postulated that 5-HTP cannot be decarboxylated in the degenerated 5-HT terminals.

4.1.4. Inhibition of the Catabolism of 5-HT

MAO inhibitors decrease the formation of the deaminated metabolites of both 5-HT and catecholamines. At the same time, they increase 5-HT (and catecholamines) at the receptor level. This fact is probably responsible for the decrease in turnover of central amines (as measured with biochemical techniques) (Macon et al., 1971). MAO inhibitors also decrease the firing of 5-HT nerve cells in the raphe system (Aghajanian et al., 1970). Thus, their mechanism of action is very complex. In the cat, harmaline has an amphetaminelike effect, whereas nialamide and pargyline increase cortical synchronization (Delorme, 1966; Jouvet, 1968). In the rat, nialamide has an activating effect upon the EEG and suppresses sleep.

In addition to their effect on cortical activity, MAO inhibitors have a strong suppressant effect on PS in rats (Mouret et al., 1968b), cats, and monkeys (Reite et al., 1969). Short-lasting suppressions of PS by MAO inhibitors in cats (3–5 days) are not followed by any rebound, whereas long-lasting suppressions (several weeks) are followed by a secondary rebound (Jouvet, 1968) (Fig. 2).

4.1.5. Miscellaneous Drugs Acting on 5-HT

Fenfluramine increases SWS duration but significantly decreases PS in cats (Johnson et al., 1971; Zolovick et al., 1973b). The fenfluramine-induced increase of SWS is facilitated by 5-HTP and blocked by LSD, a central serotonin antagonist (Zolowick et al., 1973).

a. *Drugs Acting on Central 5-HT Receptors.* The *central* effects of peripherally active 5-HT receptor agonists or antagonists are still discussed, since most of these drugs do not induce the striking reduction of firing of 5-HT raphe neurons produced by LSD (Haigler and Aghajanian, 1974). LSD increases cortical synchronization and suppresses PS in the cat (Hobson, 1964), while it has no significant effect in the rat (Bilkova et al., 1971).

Both in rats and cats the injection of dihydroergotamine (1 mg/kg), a putative 5-HT receptor blocking agent, significantly decreases both SWS and PS (Depoortere and Loew, 1971).

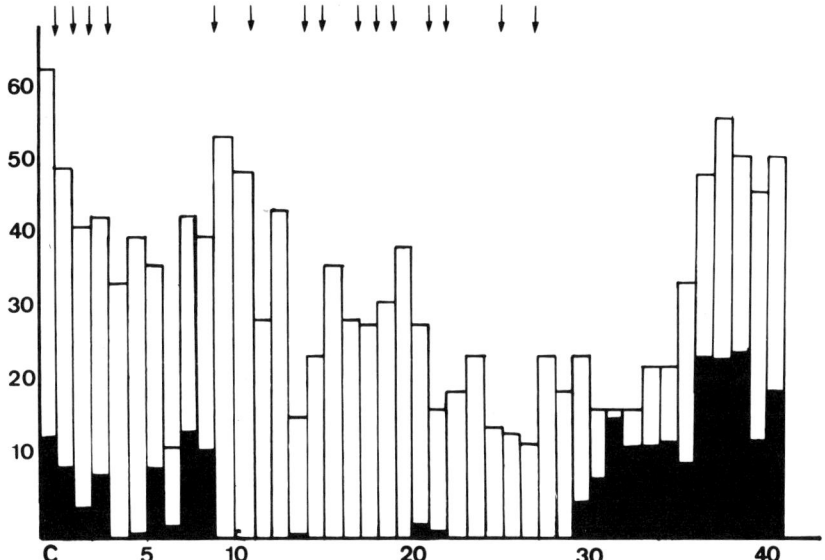

FIG. 2. Suppression of paradoxical sleep by an inhibitor of monoamine oxidase; continuous recording for 40 days in a cat. Ordinate: percentage of SWS (white bars) and PS (black bars) every 24 hr. Abcissa: time (days), on the left. C: control. The arrow signals the day of i.p. injection of phenylisopropylhydrazine (1–4 mg/kg). There is almost total suppression of PS for 20 days and also some decrease of SWS after the 20th day. On withdrawal of the drug, there is first a recovery of PS followed by a secondary rebound. Narcolepsy (direct transition from waking to PS) occurred during the 32–33rd day.

4.2. Decreased Availability of 5-HT

4.2.1. Reserpine

Twenty years ago, the sedative action of reserpine led to the notion of 5-HT as a possible transmitter of the "trophotropic" system (Brodie and Shore, 1957). Among the numerous hypotheses which have been proposed concerning its mechanism of action, the most likely is that reserpine reduces 5-HT storage, presumably by acting on the storage particles and decreasing 5-HT with an increased intracellular catabolism by MAO. Unfortunately reserpine acts similarly upon catecholamine metabolism. This drug has been of paramount importance in sleep physiology, since it permits the study of PGO activity in an acute experiment (see below). Its mechanism of action upon sleep is still controversial. In the cat, reserpine (0.5 mg/kg) suppresses cortical synchronization for 6–8 hr and PS for 1 or 2 days (Matsumoto and Jouvet, 1964). 5-HTP (30–50 mg/kg), which replenishes 5-HT stores, when injected after reserpine is able to restore EEG synchronization almost immediately, whereas dopa (30–50 mg/kg), which replenishes NE stores, hastens behavioral waking and PS. However, this effect was not observed by Stern and Morgane (1973a) after injection of 0.15 mg/kg of reserpine. Moreover, the intraventricular injection of reserpine (0.125 mg) did not alter SWS and even increased PS on the second day. In this case, there was only a small decrease of 5-HT in the brain while CA levels were significantly diminished. The absence of any alteration of sleep after the intraventricular injection of reserpine led Stern and Morgane to postulate that the effects of systemically injected reserpine on sleep may be provoked by autonomic alterations. In rats and rabbits, much higher doses of reserpine, which increase cortical synchronization, are needed to suppress PS (2 mg/kg) (Gottesmann, 1966; Tabushi and Himwich, 1969).

4.2.2. Inhibition of the Biosynthesis of 5-HT

a. 6-Chlorotryptophan. In the rat (Pascalon *et al.*, 1972) the injection of 6-chlorotryptophan (6-CT), a tryptophan hydroxylase inhibitor (McGeer *et al.*, 1967), induced a short-lasting period of reduced PS and SWS, followed by a progressive rebound in both PS and SWS. 5-HTP injection after 6-CT administration did not affect the initial sleep decrease observed, but PS rebound was no longer observed. These results are difficult to interpret since there was no biochemical evaluation of brain amines.

b. p-Chlorophenylalanine. The most potent inhibitor of tryptophan hydroxylase now available is *p*-chlorophenylalanine (PCPA). This drug selectively decreases the level of 5-HT in the rat brain without significantly altering the level of catecholamines (Koe and Weissman, 1966; Gal *et al.*, 1970).

In the adult rat, PCPA induces a decrease of both states of sleep (Torda, 1967). This insomnia is correlated with the fall of cerebral 5-HT, while there are no alterations in catecholamine levels (Mouret *et al.*, 1968a). However, Reschtschaffen *et al.* (1969) found only a small decrease of total sleep time at a time when brain 5-HT was decreased to a very low level. Finally, a reduction in both states of sleep is also observed in the rabbit after injection of PCPA (Florio *et al.*, 1968).

In the monkey, PCPA decreases sleep, but its action varies according to the species. In *Macaca mulatta* (Weitzman *et al.*, 1968), there is mostly a decrease of SWS while PS remains unaltered. In the baboon (*Papio papio* and *Papio hamadryas*) PCPA induces a decrease of sleep duration (mainly stage 2 and 3 and PS). 5-HTP (8 mg/kg) injected 55 hr after pretreatment with PCPA is able to restore normal amounts of both SWS and PS (Bert and Balzamo, 1974).

It is *in the cat* that the action of PCPA on the sleep–waking states has been studied most extensively (Delorme *et al.*, 1966; Mouret *et al.*, 1967; Koella *et al.*, 1968; Pujol *et al.*, 1971; Cohen *et al.*, 1970; Bobillier *et al.*,

1973). After a single injection of 400 mg/kg of PCPA in the cat, no change in behavior or in polygraphic recordings is observed during the first 18–24 hr. This fact demonstrates that the drug itself has no direct pharmacological action upon the brain. Following this period, an abrupt decrease in both states of sleep occurs, and after about 30–40 hr an almost total insomnia appears, associated with a permanent low-voltage, fast cortical activity accompanied by the appearance of permanent PGO waves. Very discrete episodes of PS may appear, either following short episodes of SWS or even directly following waking (narcoleptic episodes). SWS episodes of longer duration gradually reappear at shorter intervals after the 40th hour. Qualitatively and quantitatively normal patterns of sleep are resumed after about 200 hr and there is never any rebound of PS, whatever the duration of its suppression. In smaller doses (200 mg/kg), PCPA reduces mainly stage 2 of SWS (slow wave) without significantly altering stage 1 (spindles) or PS. However, when stage 2 is reduced to 10% or less of control values there is a tendency to a decrease in both stage 1 and PS (Ursin, 1972).

Under the influence of PCPA, a significant correlation has been found to exist between the decrease of SWS and the decrease of cerebral 5-HT, whereas there was no significant alteration of catecholamine levels (Koella *et al.*, 1968; Pujol *et al.*, 1971; Bobillier *et al.*, 1973).

Since PCPA inhibits only the first step of the synthesis of 5-HT at the level of tryptophan hydroxylase, and since the synthesis of 5-HT is still possible from 5-HTP, it is possible to bypass the blocking action of PCPA and thus to reestablish a higher level of 5-HT by injecting 5-HTP. With this procedure, it is possible to manipulate the state of sleep of the animal at will. Thus, a single injection of a very small dose of 5-HTP (2–5 mg/kg) given when the insomnia has reached its maximum is able to restore a quantitatively and qualitatively normal pattern of both states of sleep for 6–8 hr, which is accompanied by a significant increase of 5-HT turnover as shown by the relative increase of cerebral 5-HT and 5-HIAA (Mouret *et al.*, 1967; Koella *et al.*, 1968; Jouvet, 1968; Hoyland *et al.*, 1970; Pujol *et al.*, 1971; Bobillier *et al.*, 1973) (Figs. 3 and 4).

Whereas the insomnia due to the *short-term* administration of high doses of PCPA and its reversibility to normal sleep with very low doses of 5-HTP is a well-established fact, the *chronic* administration of PCPA produces different results. In the cat, daily administration of PCPA for one week leads initially to insomnia, but SWS and PS slowly reappear despite a very low level of brain 5-HT (Cohen *et al.*, 1970). In this condition PCPA has been shown to decrease the turnover of cerebral NE (Stolk *et al.*, 1969). Moreover, the return to cortical synchronization has been observed not only with 5-HTP but also with low dose of chlorpromazine (1–5 mg/kg), although in this case PS did not return to the normal level (Cohen *et al.*, 1973). Fenfluramine also increases cortical synchronization in cats made insomniac with PCPA, and pretreatment with ARH 3009, a potent serotonin antagonist, is effective in blocking the increase of synchronized activity. Thus, Johnson *et al.* (1972)

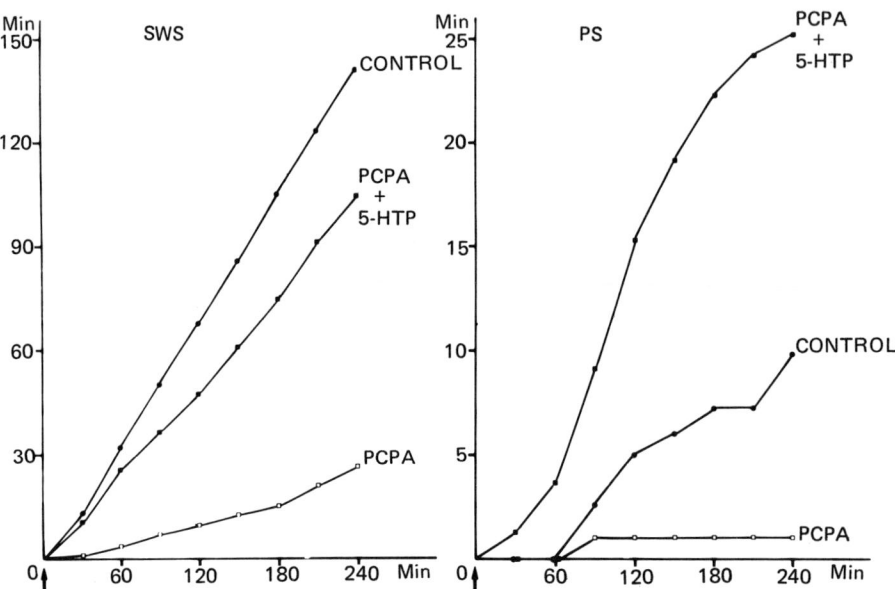

FIG. 3. Effects of *p*-chlorophenylalanine (PCPA) and 5-hydroxytryptophan (5-HTP) on SWS and PS in the cat. Ordinate: cumulative duration of SWS or PS every 30 min. Abcissa: time (minutes). Filled circles: no treatment (8 cats). Filled squares: treatment with 400 mg/kg of PCPA 50 hr before recording and 5 mg/kg of 5-HTP 2 hr before recording (8 cats). Open squares: treatment with 400 mg/kg of PCPA 50 hr before recording (8 cats). The cats were sacrificed at the end of the recording for biochemical measurements of monoamines (see Fig. 4).

have attributed the synchronizing effect of fenfluramine in PCPA-treated cats to a direct action of this drug on tryptaminergic receptors.

Since the suppressant effect of PCPA on sleep and the reversibility to normal amounts of both SWS and PS by a low dose of 5-HTP is one of the *crucial* arguments favoring the role of 5-HT in the mechanism of sleep, these conflicting data must now be discussed in some detail.

The return of a subnormal level of SWS after chronic PCPA treatment in cats with very low levels of brain 5-HT can be explained in a number of ways.

a. The data of Pujol *et al.* (1971) have shown that the *in vivo* inhibition of tryptophan hydroxylase by PCPA in the cat is not total (only 80%). Thus, there is the possibility that a small pool of 5-HT remains and that it may represent the functional pool critical for the return of SWS. It is thus possible that the return of SWS after fenfluramine in PCPA-treated cats could be due to the potentiation of the activity of a small but active residual pool of 5-HT.

b. It is also possible that the initial decrease of 5-HT may have induced a state of supersensitivity in the 5-HT receptors. If this hypothesis is correct, the supersensitivity of the 5-HT receptor could make them sensitive to very minute amounts of 5-HT, since injection of MAO inhibitors (pargyline, 25 mg/kg) does not cause a detectable increase in 5-HT levels in chronically PCPA-pretreated cats (Dement *et al.*, 1970*a,b*).

c. On the other hand, there are some indirect data which favor the role of catecholamines in waking. The possible decrease of the turnover of NE in chronically PCPA-treated cats (Stolk *et al.*, 1969) might thus impair the waking mechanisms. Since waking and sleep may represent the balance between two antagonistic systems, the return to sleep (or mostly the decrease of waking) might be facilitated by the alteration of adrenergic mechanisms.

d. The return to cortical synchronization after chlorpromazine might also be explained either through the effect of chlorpromazine in decreasing catecholamine turnover or through the possible effect of this drug upon 5-

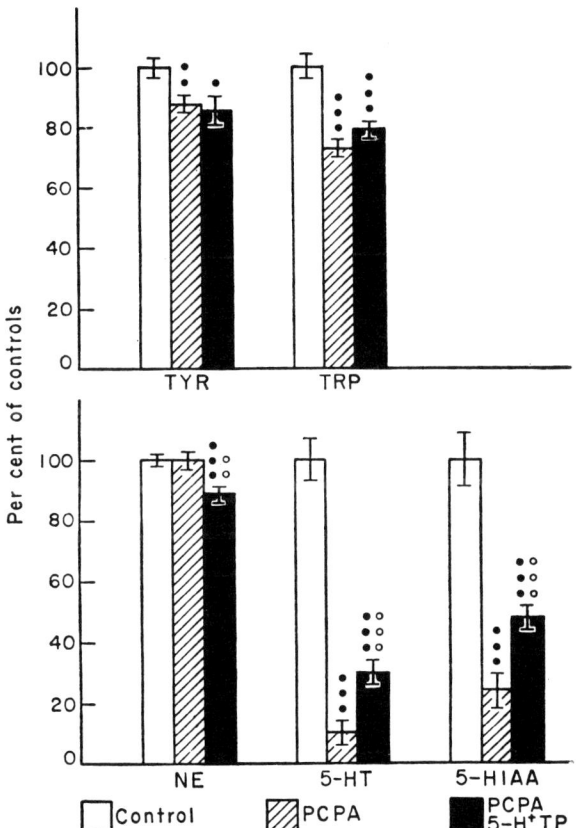

Fig. 4. Effects of 5-HTP (5 mg/kg) and PCPA (400 mg/kg) on monoamine metabolism in the cat telencephalon. Same group as in Fig. 3. The results are expressed in mean percentage ± SEM as compared to controls. The absolute levels (μg/g) for the controls were 0.579 ± 0.011, 0.259 ± 0.018, 0.305 ± 0.028, 5.978 ± 0.267, and 25.729 ± 0.796 for norepinephrine (NE), 5-HT, 5-HIAA, tryptophan (TRP), and tyrosine (Tyr) respectively. Filled circles: ●, $P < 0.05$; ●●, $P < 0.02$; ●●●, $P < 0.005$ as compared with control. Open circles: ○○, $P < 0.002$; ○○○, $P < 0.005$ between the two experimental groups (PCPA and PCPA + 5-HTP).

HT. On the other hand, the fact that PS returns only to half of control levels after chlorpromazine suggests that the cortical synchronization may be the result of a direct pharmacological action of chlorpromazine, a well-known synchronizing drug. Finally, PCPA-induced insomnia can be explained by a hypothesis other than the serotoninergic hypothesis of sleep. Although this is not always the case, the insomnia which follows PCPA treatment is accompanied by bursts of PGO activity during waking. According to Dement et al. (1972), these bursts of activity are accompanied in the cat by behavioral disturbances. Some cats may occasionally attack empty areas in their surroundings. They would also eat voraciously and display aberrant sexual behavior. Thus, the increase of waking could be due to the increase of drive-oriented activities. For Dement et al. (1972), the important role of 5-HT appears to be in the containment of PGO activity to PS and the immediate period which precedes it. The return of sleep in chronic PCPA treatment could reflect the gradual readjustment of other (unknown) systems responsible for sleep to effect some balance.

4.2.3. p-Chloromethamphetamine

p-Chloromethamphetamine was the first drug known to deplete brain 5-HT and its metabolite 5-hydroxyindoleacetic acid selectively without altering catecholamine levels. Its mechanism of action is different from PCPA since it does not act only on the inhibition of 5-HT synthesis but also has a selective neurotoxic action on 5-HT neurons in the brain (Harvey et al., 1975). This drug induces a very marked arousal in the cat which lasts for 16–20 hr (Delorme et al., 1966; Koella, 1969) and is followed by a gradual recovery of SWS (and by an almost permanent discharge of PGO spikes even during waking), whereas PS remains depressed for at least 3 days. However, a subsequent injection of low or high doses of 5-HTP (5–50 mg/kg) is not able to reverse the insomnia but is highly toxic and lethal in the cat.

4.2.4. 5,6-Hydroxytryptamine (5,6-HT)

This drug has a rather selective toxic effect on the serotoninergic system of the rat (Baumgarten et al., 1972). Injection of 5,6-HT directly into the raphe nuclei has no effect on the sleep states or on brain monoamines. However, when 1 mg is injected intraventricularly in the cat it induces temporarily the appearance of PGO spikes during waking, followed by a long-lasting (up to 2 weeks) decrease of both stage 2 and PS which is correlated with the decrease of both 5-HT and 5-HIAA in the telencephalon (Froment et al., 1974). (See Figs. 5 and 6.) These experiments do not solve the problem of the topography of the serotoninergic systems which are involved in sleep mechanisms since the destruction of 5-HT terminals which follows intraventricular injection of 5,6-HT is diffuse.

In summary, in short-term experiments the neuropharmacology of 5-

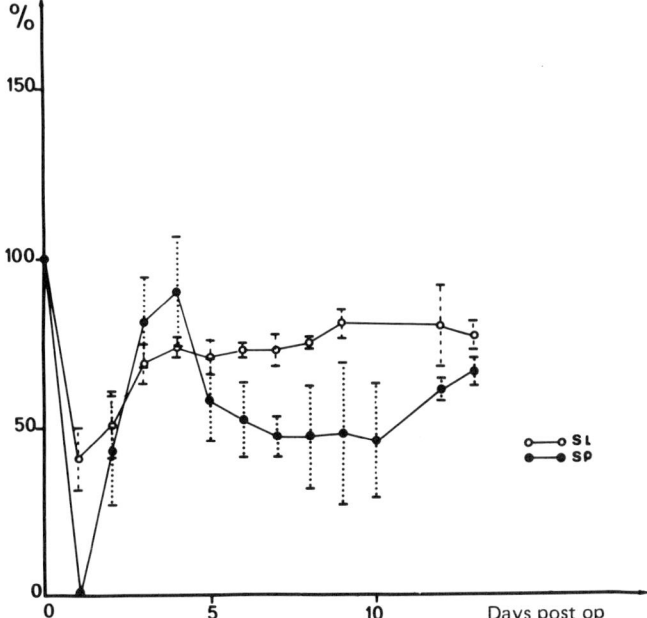

FIG. 5. Evolution of SWS (SL) (open circles) and PS (SP) (filled circles) after intraventricular injection of 5,6-dihydroxytryptamine (5,6-HT) in the cat. Results (mean ± SEM) for six cats are expressed in percentage of the control values for each day of recording. Abcissa: days after injection.

HT has provided a great deal of converging evidence which favors the intervention of 5-HT neurons in both SWS and PS mechanisms, at least in the cat. This does not mean that PS is only dependent on 5-HT since it can also be suppressed by drugs or lesions which do not significantly affect waking or SWS (see below). However, the intricate relationship between the amounts of stage 2 and PS raises the possibility that the mechanisms underlying stage 2 are also necessary for the priming of PS. Thus, we have to make the heuristic distinction between the *priming* mechanisms and the *executive* mechanism of PS. When considering the main results obtained with the drugs acting on 5-HT metabolism, it can be concluded that decreases in cerebral 5-HT turnover (induced by PCPA or 5,6-HT) lead to a decrease of stage 2 and of the rate of appearance of PS, while increases in 5-HT turnover which immediately follow the injection of 5-HTP in PCPA-pretreated cats lead to an increase of SWS and in the frequency of PS episodes. The same phenomenon is observed in the rat during the rebound of PS which follows its previous instrumental deprivation (for 72–96 hr) and is also accompanied by an increase in cerebral 5-HT turnover (Hery et al., 1970). This increase in 5-HT metabolism is not caused by the stress of the

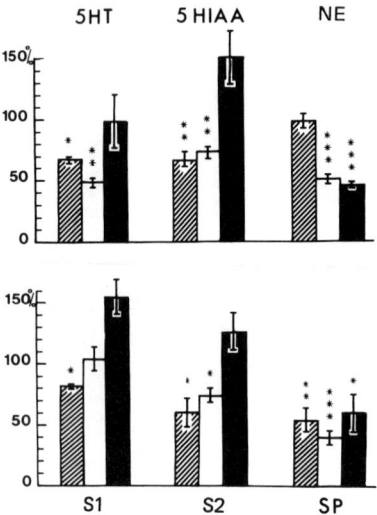

FIG. 6. Biochemical and sleep–waking alterations following intraventricular injection of 6-OHDA or 5,6-HT. Above: percentage of serotonin (5-HT), 5-HIAA, and noripinephrine (NE) in the mesencephalon (as compared with control animals). Below: percentage of stage 1 (S1), stage 2 (S2) and paradoxical sleep (SP) during the 15 days after the intraventricular injection as compared with preinjection control for each group. Oblique hatchings: intraventricular injection of 1 mg of 5,6-HT. White bars: intraventricular injection of 6-OHDA (2.5 mg). Black bars: intraventricular injection of 2.5 mg of 6-OHDA after pretreatment with chlorimipramine (10 mg/kg). Note that SWS decreases only if there is a decrease of 5-HT and 5-HIAA, while PS is decreased in every case. *, $P < 0.05$; **, $P < 0.01$; ***, $P < 0.001$.

deprivation since it is also observed in hypophysectomized rats (Cramer et al., 1973).

These neuropharmacological and biochemical experiments which suggest that a decrease in the rate of 5-HT turnover decreases both SWS and PS, whereas an increase in 5-HT turnover increases SWS and the frequency of PS, are admittedly indirect, but they are corroborated by similar neurophysiological evidence. Indeed, on the one hand, both SWS and PS are suppressed by a total lesion of the raphe system; in this case the striking insomnia may be explained by the decrease in 5-HT turnover *and* the parallel increase in NE turnover in the dorsal NE system (see below). On the other hand, lesions of the dorsal NE bundle at the isthmus are followed by a significant increase in both SWS and PS which is suppressed by PCPA. Biochemical analysis of the forebrain and mesencephalon reveals a significant increase in the turnover and biosynthesis of 5-HT in the rostral raphe system (Blondaux et al., 1975; Petitjean et al., 1975). (See Fig. 7.) Since terminals from NE-containing neurons of the anterior part of the locus coeruleus may be found in the anterior raphe (Loizou, 1969), it is possible that the lesion of the isthmus may have suppressed an inhibitory control on the raphe system and that a true hypersomnia (with increases in both SWS and PS) might be the result of increased 5-HT turnover. *In long-term experiments* there are as yet no satisfactory explanation for the recovery of sleep during chronic PCPA treatment. We have to assume either the development of a postsynaptic supersensitivity to 5-HT or the gradual readjustment of other system(s) of neurotransmitter(s) which would normally play a very limited role.

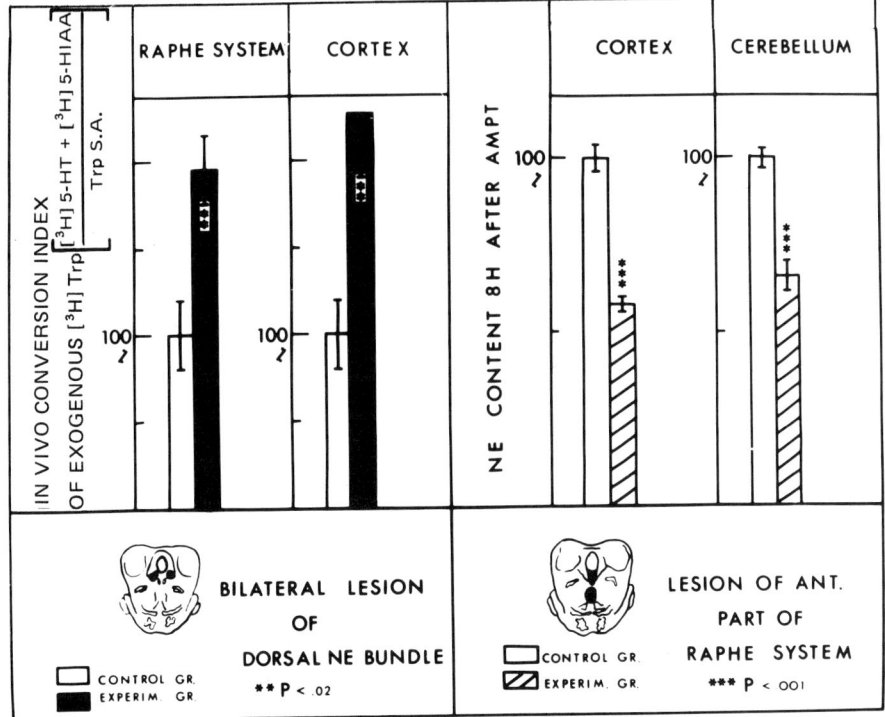

FIG. 7. Biochemical interaction between serotoninergic and dorsal ascending noradrenergic systems. In the left part of the figure are results obtained 48 hr after bilateral lesions of the dorsal noradrenergic bundles. The rate of synthesis of 5-HT was estimated by following the initial accumulation of [^{3}H]5-HT and [^{3}H]5-HIAA endogenously synthesized from [^{3}H]Trp and measuring the conversion index by the ratio

$$\frac{[^3H]5\text{-}HT + [^3H]5\text{-}HIAA}{Trp\ S.A.}$$

Results for the experimental group (black bars) are expressed as a percentage of the mean value for the control group (white bars) ± SEM (five determinations). Values of P were calculated by a t test. The right part of the figure shows NE concentrations in the cortex and cerebellum of control cats (white bars) and raphe-destroyed cats (hatched bars) 8 hr after blockade of NE synthesis by AMPT (200 mg/kg i.p.). Results are expressed as described above. From Pujol *et al.* (1973).

5. CATECHOLAMINES AND THE SLEEP–WAKING CYCLE

5.1. Increased Availability of Catecholamines

5.1.1. *Action of Norepinephrine*

In moderate doses, the intravenous injection of norepinephrine (NE) and epinephrine in the cat produces a cortical activation parallel to an increase of blood pressure. The activating effect of NE is abolished if the mesencephalic reticular formation is lesioned. The possibility was thus considered that the neurons of the reticular activating system might be adrenergic. Thus, at one time, catecholamines were thought to be related to waking (see Dell, 1960–1963).

However, evidence was soon presented that neither epinephrine nor NE crosses the blood–brain barrier to any significant extent in adult animals, except in the hypothalamus (Weill-Malherbe et al., 1959). Moreover, it was shown (Capon, 1959) that direct injections of NE into the carotid artery did not induce arousal (and did not increase blood pressure), whereas other experiments demonstrated that an increased blood pressure, per se, could induce EEG arousal through postulated baroreceptors located in the brainstem reticular formation (Baust et al., 1963).

These experiments led to a reversal of the situation, and, for a period, the catecholamines were considered as "sleep neuromodulators," since in some cases the injection of NE into the cerebral ventricles could induce a "sleeplike" state (Mandell and Spooner, 1968). However, the results of intraventricular injections are difficult to interpret. Very minute amounts of labelled catecholamines may be taken up by noncatecholaminergic neurons (Lichtensteiger and Langemann, 1966; Fuxe and Ungerstedt, 1968). Thus, it is likely that, in some cases, NE may have induced responses on neurons that do not normally respond to catecholamines. This might explain why the effect of NE depends upon the dose injected: Very small doses have a clear-cut behavioral activating effect (Segal and Mandell, 1970; Cordeau et al., 1971; Key, 1975), while larger doses may have a depressant effect.

Intravenous injections of epinephrine, NE, isoproterenol, and dopamine in chicks less than 28 days old (whose blood–brain barrier is permeable to catecholamines) induce EEG and behavioral signs of sleep. On the other hand, direct injections of NE into the brain may induce behavioral sedation without electrocortical synchronization (Key and Marley, 1962; Spooner and Winters, 1966). In adult chickens, in contrast, the same drugs elicit arousal (Dewhurst and Marley, 1965). These results are difficult to interpret since it has not yet been demonstrated that intravenously injected catecholamines are selectively taken up by central NE-containing terminals and immediately released into the synaptic cleft.

5.1.2. L-Dopa

L-Dopa is a precursor for both DA and NE formation in the CNS (see Musacchio, Vol. 3), and it crosses the blood–brain barrier. It is, however, decarboxylated to DA to a considerable extent in the brain capillaries (Constantinidis et al., 1968). Thus, the administration of inhibitors of dopa decarboxylase, which act mainly on the periphery, allows larger amounts of dopa to penetrate into the brain. There is evidence, in cat (Delorme, 1966; Jones, 1970) and rabbit (Monnier and Tissot, 1958), that L-dopa (30–50 mg/

kg) induces a state of arousal which lasts continuously for 5–6 hr. The activating effect of dopa is much enhanced by the peripheral inhibition of dopa decarboxylase (Bartholini et al., 1967). It is possible that L-dopa acts by increasing the amounts of DA or NE in adrenergic nerve terminals. According to Reis et al. (1970) there is indeed a high degree of correlation between the level of NE in the brainstem and the degree of excitement in cats receiving L-dopa. However, many other mechanisms are possible. Thus, part of the exogenous L-dopa may enter 5-HT-containing terminals, in which it can be decarboxylated to DA and can displace endogenous 5-HT from vesicular stores (Ng et al., 1970). This would explain the cortical synchronization which occurs immediately after infusion of a *large* dose of L-dopa (100 mg/kg) in rabbits, which is correlated with a fall in cerebral 5-HT and an increase in 5-HIAA. This cortical synchronization is not observed in PCPA-pretreated rabbits (Gaillard et al., 1974). Thus, as previously with 5-HTP, we are confronted with the problem of the possible "nonspecificity" of the 5-HTP–dopa decarboxylase (see also Musacchio, Vol. 3).

5.1.3. (+)-Erythro-Dihydroxyphenylserine (DOPS)

Both *in vitro* and *in vivo* DOPS may be decarboxylated to NE. In contrast to dopa, injections of DOPS increase both SWS and PS in the rat (Havlicek, 1967). It has been shown by Constantidinis et al. (1975) that (+)-erythro-DOPS enters various brain structures nonspecifically, and that NE is formed in both DA and 5-HT systems. Moreover, (+)-erythro-DOPS produces (+)-norepinephrine and not the naturally occurring (−)-NE. Thus, this drug cannot be considered as a physiological precursor of brain NE, and the neuropharmacological findings obtained with this drug must be interpreted with caution.

5.1.4. Amphetamines

Although its mechanism of action is complex, amphetamine increases the amounts of NE and DA available at some synapses. Amphetamine strongly increases behavioral and EEG arousal (and, of course, suppresses both SWS and PS). This acute suppression has been observed in kittens (Shimizu and Himwich, 1968) and in cats (Jewett and Norton, 1966). Methamphetamine causes similar effects (Wallach et al., 1969). It is likely that the increased motor activity which follows amphetamine injections is mediated through the acceleration of striatal DA turnover (Costa et al., 1972), while the EEG-activating effect may be mediated in the brainstem reticular formation. Indeed, the destruction of the reticular formation or intercollicular transection suppresses amphetamine-induced EEG arousal (Hiebel et al., 1954). Finally, intravertebral injections of amphetamine are not followed by EEG arousal if the basilar artery is tied at the midpontine level (Van Meter and Ayala, 1961).

5.1.5. Inhibition of MAO

The degree of accumulation of endogenous transmitter depends on the species and on the structure of the MAOI. In the rabbit and rat, block of MAO is associated with an increase of CA, sympathomimetic effects are associated with the accumulation of NE, and an almost permanent arousal occurs after nialamide (Mouret et al., 1968b).

If dopa is injected together with an MAOI, this induces an intense excitement with long-lasting cortical arousal in the cat (Jones, 1970) and in the rabbit (Monnier and Graber, 1963).

5.1.6. Inhibition of Catechol-O-methyl Transferase (COMT)

There have been very few studies of the effects of inhibitors of COMT upon the sleep-waking cycle, probably because most COMT inhibitors are very toxic. Tropolone, however, is well tolerated in the cat. This drug is an effective inhibitor of COMT both *in vitro* and *in vivo* (Goldstein et al., 1964). The administration of tropolone alone (100 mg/kg) induces a long-lasting arousal for 6–7 hr, followed by a rebound of both SWS and PS. The administration of dopa (25 mg/kg) and tropolone (50 mg/kg) induces a very dramatic form of behavior. In addition to waking, the cats appear to experience hallucinatory episodes between 1–3 hr after the injection. Continuous arousal is present for about 8 hr. Continuous PGO, which are not related to hallucinations, appear during waking by the sixth hour (Jones, 1972).

5.1.7. Drugs Acting on CA Receptors

Although these drugs do not increase the availability of CA, they will be considered briefly here. Matsumoto and Watanabe (1967) treated cats with phenoxybenzamine and dibenamine (15 mg/kg), two alpha-adrenoceptor blocking agents. There followed a suppression of PS and an increased amount of SWS. Nethalide, a beta-adrenoceptor blocker, caused no changes. In the rat, Hartmann et al. (1973) did not find any alteration of sleep with propranolol (another β-blocker) but they observed an increase of PS and decrease of waking with high doses of phenoxybenzamine (40 mg/kg). The well-known sedative action of clonidine is an indication of its central effects. It is considered to be an α-receptor-stimulating drug. It reduces central NE turnover possibly by a negative feedback mechanism evoked by the stimulation of presynaptic α-receptors. Clonidine is able to induce sedation in cats and even in PCPA-pretreated insomniac rats (Holman et al., 1971). This sedation is prevented by high dose of phentolamine. However, it is not clear if clonidine induces both states of sleep or only decreases wakefulness since there was no continuous polygraphic recordings in this latter study. A possible explanation for the hypnogenic action of clonidine has recently been proposed by Fuxe *et al.* (1974). They found that piperoxane, an alpha-adenoceptor blocking drug, increases EEG waking in the rat. Since it has been shown that there is an epinephrine-containing system of neurons ascending from the medulla in the region of the solitary tract and innervating the NE cell bodies of the locus coeruleus (Hokfelt *et al.*, 1973), Fuxe *et al.* propose that clonidine would act on the inhibitory adrenergic synapses impinging upon the locus coeruleus. Thus, the neurons ascending in the dorsal NE bundle, originating from the locus coeruleus, which are probably involved in the maintenance of EEG waking, would be inactivated.

5.2. Decreased Availability of Catecholamines

5.2.1. Reserpine

Reserpine decreases the availability of both CA and 5-HT, and some of its actions on PS have been reviewed when considering 5-HT mechanisms. In the cat, it induces a sedation in which electrical activity, however, is different from sleep or relaxed wakefulness. This sedation is reversed into normal waking behavior by a subsequent injection of dopa. This suggests that the sedation might be the result of decreased stimulation of postsynaptic neurons by CA, but since reserpine also acts on 5-HT metabolism, the mechanism of its sedative action is still far from being understood.

5.2.2. α-Methyl-dopa

This drug is decarboxylated to form α-methyl-DA which in turn is oxidized to form α-methyl-NE. This substituted NE acts as a false transmitter and depletes NE by displacement. When injected in cats (200 mg/kg) (Dusan-Peyrethon *et al.*, 1968) or in mice (Kitahama and Valatx, 1975), this drug first induces a sedated state, with cortical slowing different from SWS. Then SWS reoccurs, but PS is suppressed for a long time. α-Methyl-dopa has been used to study the putative priming and executive mechanisms of PS (Dusan-Peyrethon *et al.*, 1968). Given every day, in the cat, at a dose of 200 mg/kg during the 2 days of instrumental deprivation of PS, α-methyl-dopa does not suppress the subsequent rebound of PS. Thus, the 5-HT mechanisms which are supposed to be involved in the priming of the rebound are not altered by the drug. However, if α-methyl-dopa is given at the end of the deprivation procedure, it delays the reappearance of the rebound of PS for 14–16 hr. In this case, it must be postulated that the CA terminals are filled with the false transmitter and that, despite normal priming mechanisms (increased turnover of 5-HT), some effector CA neurons are unable to trigger a physiological response from the postsynaptic cells.

5.2.3. Inhibition of CA Biosynthesis

a. Inhibition of Dopamine-β-hydroxylase. This enzyme catalyses the final step in the biosynthesis of NA. The enzyme is inhibited by diethyldithiocarbamate (disulfiram). This drug reduces the NE content of the brain and increases DA. In the cat, disulfiram significantly reduces both waking and PS, whereas striking episodes of atonia or catatonia may appear after chronic administration of the drug (Dusan-Peyrethon and Froment, 1968). Satoh and Tanaka (1973) also found a significant decrease of PS in cats following fusaric acid (40 mg/kg), another inhibitor of dopamine-β-hydroxylase. However, waking was not diminished.

b. Inhibition of Tyrosine Hydroxylase. Tyrosine is converted by tyrosine hydroxylase, a rate-limiting enzyme, into dopa. This enzyme is competitively inhibited by many analogs of tyrosine. At the present time, the inhibitor most widely used in behavioral experiments is α-methyl-p-tyrosine (AMPT), which causes a decrease in cerebral CA, measured by biochemical and histofluorescent techniques. There is considerable evidence, from behavioral observations, that the inhibition of tyrosine hydroxylase which decreases both brain DA and NE induces a state of "sedation" which can be counteracted by a subsequent injection of dopa (Weissman and Koe, 1965).

At the polygraphic level, the effects of AMPT have been studied in rats, cats, and monkeys. Although the effects on PS were different (see below), the common effect observed in all species was decreased behavioral and EEG waking.

The suppressant effect of AMPT upon waking may be obtained even when arousal is dramatically increased by two different experimental methods: injection of amphetamines (Hanson, 1967; Jouvet, 1972) or destruction of the raphe system.

The injection of 200 mg/kg of AMPT was given to raphe-lesioned cats at a time when behavioral and EEG waking was almost permanent. Four to 6 hr after the injection behavioral sedation appeared, together with cortical synchronization. This lasted for 24 hr after which there was a rapid return to behavioral and EEG insomnia. This experiment also provided biochemical evidence that the almost permanent arousal which follows the destruction of the 5-HT-containing neurons of the raphe system might be related to an increased activity of central noradrenergic neurons, since the decrease in brain NE after α-methyl-p-tyrosine was greater in raphe-lesioned cats than in controls (Pujol *et al.*, 1973). Thus, there are many converging lines of evidence which favor an anti-wakefulness role for AMPT. However, the results on PS are still conflicting.

In monkeys, Weitzman et al. (1969) gave AMPT either intraperitoneally or *per os*; they observed a total suppression of PS with a decrease of waking.

In rats, Torda (1968) used implanted crystals of AMPT and also observed a suppression of PS. However, Branchey and Kissin (1970), Hartmann *et al.* (1971), and Marantz *et al.* (1968) did not observe any alteration in either SWS or PS in normal rats, nor did they observe a reduction of PS rebound after previous PS deprivation.

In cats, in the experiments of Iskander and Kaelbling (1970), the drug caused a 50% inhibition of PS during the period of its administration. After the last injection, however, PS increased to 300% above the control level. King and Jewett (1971) reported that several doses of AMPT increased PS in cats. This effect began after 5 hr and lasted for up to 16 hr. The same increases of PS have been observed by Stern and Morgane (1973b) and Henriksen and Dement (1972) after intravenous infusions of 150 mg/kg of AMPT.

Although the results obtained in monkeys suggest the involvement of catecholamine mechanisms in PS, there is contrasting evidence that AMPT does not suppress PS and even increases it in the cat. These results have been taken as solid evidence against a role for CA neurons in PS. Indeed, it has generally been supposed that AMPT acts *only* on CA neurons, since brain 5-HT levels do not change. However, it has been shown recently that this is not the case, since AMPT also increases 5-HT turnover in the cat, as shown by the increase in 5-HIAA in the telencephalon and brainstem at the time of the increase of PS (6 hr after the injection) (Stein *et al.*, 1974). Thus, AMPT may act mostly in the dorsal NE system (as shown by the significant decrease of NE in the region innervated by the dorsal NE bundle, e.g., telencephalon cerebellum) and, at the same time, increases the activity of raphe neurons (as is the case after destruction of the dorsal bundle). Thus, as in the latter case, the increase of PS would be caused by the increased turnover of 5-HT neurons impinging upon either CA neurons or other nonaminergic neurons of the pons.

5.2.4. Pharmacological Destruction of Catecholamine Neurons

The discovery that 6-hydroxydopamine (6-OHDA) could selectively destroy CA neurons has opened a very active field of research (see the most recent reviews by Thoenen and Tranzer, 1973, and Longo, 1973).

a. Intraventricular Injection. In chronically recorded rats, *intracisternal injection of 500 μg 6-OHDA* led to a small decrease in waking while there was a small increase in PS (Hartmann *et al.*, 1971). However, in a more recent study (Matsuyama *et al.*, 1973), intracisternal injection of the same dose of 6-OHDA induced an increase in cortical synchronization for the first 5 days, followed by a small increase in waking. PS was first depressed and returned slowly to 90% of control level. Interpretation of these results is not easy, since the intraventricular injection of 6-OHDA is accompanied, in the rat, by an increased activity in the 5-HT system, as shown by the increase of 5-HIAA and in the rate of biosynthesis of 5-HT (Blondaux *et al.*, 1973). This is another example of the interactions which take place between different monoaminergic systems.

In cats, there have been two studies using about the same dose of *intraventricular 6-OHDA* (2.5–5 mg). The immediate effects were identical: agitation and hypothermia. The agitation was suppressed by pretreatment with α-methyl-*p*-tyrosine and thus can be ascribed to a release of central catecholamines. The chronic effects on the sleep–waking cycle were different. In the study of Laguzzi *et al.* (1972) it was shown that 2–2.5 mg 6-OHDA depleted both cerebral NA and 5-HT. There was no change in cortical synchronization and a decrease in PS. However, when the cats were pretreated with chlorimipramine (an inhibitor of 5-HT uptake), the intraventricular injection of 6-OHDA did not alter brain 5-HT and only cerebral catecholamines were decreased (Petitjean *et al.*, 1972). In this case there was an increase in cortical synchronization for 2 weeks, associated with a decrease in PS. In the second study (Howard and Breese, 1974), 2.4 mg 6-OHDA was injected four times at one-week intervals. Under these conditions there was a definite increase in waking and a small decrease in PS. Although the amount of 6-OHDA injected was higher, there was no change in cerebral 5-HT. In view of the apparent differences in findings, additional work will clearly be necessary in order to define the effects of intraventricular 6-OHDA on the sleep–waking cycle in the cat.

b. Intracerebral injection. In the *rat*, the intracerebral injection of 6-OHDA in the *dorsal* NE bundle led to a decrease in NE terminals in the forebrain. There was a decrease in EEG waking, even during behavioral wakefulness, for the first 4 days, while there were no significant alterations in stage 2 or PS. This decreased waking was significantly correlated with the decrease in cerebral NE. Thereafter a gradual recovery of waking activity started, and total recovery occurred 1 month later (Lidbrink, 1974).

In the *cat*, the administration of 6-OHDA at the level of the *ventral* NE bundle in the mesencephalon caused an increase in both stage 2 and PS. There was a significant decrease in NE in the forebrain and mesencephalon, while 5-HT was also depleted to a lesser extent in the cortex and brainstem. This finding was interpreted as an indication that activation of the ventral NE pathway induces electrocortical arousal, while depletion of amines in this pathway may cause somnolence (Panksepp *et al.*, 1973).

In the dorsolateral part of the pontine tegmentum, the injection of 6-OHDA gave the following results (Buguet *et al.*, 1970): During the first 4 days there was an increase in PGO during waking and SWS, whereas PGO during PS decreased, as did the amount of PS. On the 6th and 7th days, PS and PGO were totally suppressed. In cats killed on the 8th day, there was a significant decrease in NE and 5-HT in the mesencephalon.

Zolovick *et al.* (1973a) also injected 6-OHDA locally into the dorsolateral pontine tegmentum. *The chronic effect* of the treatment was to increase SWS and decrease PS. The biochemical results obtained five weeks after the injection revealed a selective and consistent reduction in cortical and hippocampal NE. However, there were also decreases in forebrain 5-HT, which indicates that 6-OHDA may have destroyed some serotoninergic neurons.

These experiments do not provide crucial proof that *only* CA-containing neurons of the pons are responsible for PS since the nonspecific lesions which follow any direct microinjection of 6-OHDA into the brain might have affected other neurons (Poirier *et al.,* 1972).

Summing up, *in short-term experiments* the neuropharmacological results are almost unanimously in favor of the involvement of CA neurons in waking mechanisms. On the one hand, decreased availability of CA leads to a decrease in wakefulness. On the other hand, increased availability of CA leads to increased waking. The dorsal NE system is involved (although not exclusively) in the maintenance of cortical arousal, while DA mechanisms are probably involved in waking behavior (see Jones *et al.,* 1973). Finally, increased waking caused by other methods (electric shock, stress) is also accompanied by an increased turnover of CA neurons. However, we certainly need additional data in order to understand the intimate mechanisms of action of CA neurons in the broad spectrum of neuronal activities underlying the waking state (learning, memory, emergency situation, etc.).

In long-term experiments, the recovery of a normal sleep–waking cycle within 10–15 days after destruction of the dorsal NE bundle or after intraventricular or intracerebral injections of 6-OHDA, while there is still a permanent depletion of brain CA, can be explained in several ways: In view of the extraordinary capacity of the brain to compensate functionally for the loss of destroyed elements, it is possible that the sprouting of some NE neurons may compensate functionally. The development of postsynaptic supersensitivity may also compensate for the destruction of CA systems. Other interpretations are, however, possible: The acute syndrome observed after intracerebral injections of 6-OHDA might be due to a toxic effect which nonspecifically alters behavior and thus increases waking. Following this period, a normal or subnormal sleep–waking cycle returns in spite of continuing low CA levels because other systems are able to substitute for the curtailed activity of the NE system. This interpretation leads to the concept of biochemical redundancy in the CNS, and to the existence of a multiplicity of pathways which might substitute for each other in cases of emergency for the maintenance of central homeostasis in the sleep–waking cycle (see Longo, 1973).

We have discussed previously the possible role of 5-HT neurons in the priming of PS, and we now discuss the possible role of CA mechanisms in the executive mechanisms of PS. There are converging lines of evidence from neurophysiological experiments that these mechanisms are located in the dorsolateral part of the pontine tegmentum (see Jouvet, 1972). In this region there are numerous CA perikarya belonging to the locus coeruleus, subcoeruleus, and parabrachialis medialis and lateralis. The pharmacological and biochemical results favoring their role in the executive mechanisms of PS in the cat can be summarized as follows: selective suppression of PS by α-methyl-dopa or by inhibition of dopamine-β-hydroxylase (disulfiram, fusaric acid), long-lasting decrease in PS after intraventricular or intrapontine injections of 6-OHDA, and increased turnover of cerebral NE during PS rebound (Pujol *et al.*, 1968). None of these experiments are sufficient to prove that pontine CA neurons are necessary for PS, since it is very easy to suppress PS with drugs which may have other vegetative or central effects (see below). In addition 6-OHDA is not completely specific when injected intracerebrally. Finally, if CA neurons are involved in the executive mechanism of PS, they must impinge directly in the pons, via short axons, to some unknown ascending systems, since destruction of the dorsal, intermediary, and ventral NE pathways does not suppress the stimulation of cortical activity during PS. The absence of any indisputable proof for the participation of NE neurons in the executive mechanism of PS has led to another hypothesis relating *negatively* the functioning of CA neurons with PS. The findings that increased availability of CA causes suppression of PS (as with MAO inhibitors), while decreased availability of CA (as after α-methyl-p-tyrosine) causes an increase in PS, led Hartmann (1970) and Stern and Morgane (1974) to postulate that the function of PS was to maintain a normal functioning of CA systems (maintenance of CA systems theory). In short, during waking, the increased activity of CA systems would lead to synaptic fatigue (decreased availability of free CA) which would generate a daily need for PS. Should CA systems become "fatigued," PS would undergo a compensatory increase, while if there was an excess of CA (after drug treatment), there would be a decreased need for PS. In this case there is no rebound of PS afterwards since the function of PS is taken over by the drug. According to this theory, the decreased PS seen with α-methyl-dopa or 6-OHDA or even with α-methyl-p-tyrosine in monkeys is due to "toxic effects," while the increased turnover of NE which occurs during PS deprivation might be caused by some unspecific effect (stress). Another possible explanation for the apparent negative correlation between CA availability and the amount of PS might be offered by the increasing evidence for a reciprocal interaction between CA metabolism in the dorsal NE system and 5-HT turnover. Thus, decreased availability of CA would be responsible for a compensatory increase in 5-HT activity which would be responsible for the increase of PS (see above). Needless to say, we need much more information concerning possible inter- and intramonoaminergic regulation, and the interaction of monoamines with other transmitters (such as acetylcholine, see below), in order to understand the mechanism of PS. But it is safe to assume that the systemic injection of any drug will not be an adequate method to solve this problem.

6. ACETYLCHOLINE AND THE SLEEP–WAKING CYCLE

6.1. Increased Availability of ACh to Cholinoceptive Neurons

Intracarotidian or intravenous injections of ACh lead to an activation of the EEG (Bremer and Chatonnet, 1949). In addition, physostigmine, nicotine, and prostigmine which increase the activation of cholinergic receptors significantly increase cortical and behavioral arousal in the intact animal (Domino *et al.*, 1968). Since cholinoceptive neurons are present in the brainstem, diencephalon, and cortex, the mechanism of the EEG activation caused by cholinergic agonists is still uncertain. The existence of both muscarinic and nicotinic cholinergic receptors in CNS makes the picture even more complex. Rinaldi and Himwich (1955) and Bradley and Elkes (1957) have suggested that the mesencephalic reticular activating system is cholinergic. Since the cortical arousal caused by nicotine is suppressed by lesions of the mesencephalic reticular formation, it is likely that nicotinic cholinergic agonists act on the brainstem. On the other hand, physostigmine can activate also the "chronic isolated hemisphere preparation" (Villablanca, 1966). This suggests a direct action at the cortical level.

6.2. Decreased Availability of ACh

6.2.1. Inhibition of Synthesis

This can be achieved by hemicholinium 3 (HC3) (Gardiner, 1961). The intraventricular injection of this drug reduces EEG activation and produces a clear-cut dissociation between behavioral arousal and the presence of cortical slow waves (Hazra, 1970; Domino and Stawiski, 1971). The cortical synchronization which follows the inhibition of ACh synthesis with HC3 does not appear after pretreatment with *p*-chlorophenylalanine (Hazra, 1971). This result suggests that some cholinergic neurons might be active during waking and could possibly inhibit 5-HT neurons.

6.2.2. Anticholinergic Drugs: Atropine and Related Compounds (Scopolamine–Hyoscine)

The dissociation produced by atropine and related compounds between a slow cortical activity and waking behavior has been known for a long time (Wikler, 1952). This dissociation, however, is not constant, since fully atropinized cats (2 mg/kg) can be behaviorally asleep when recuperating from previous sleep deprivation (Vimont-Vicary, 1966; Henriksen *et al.*, 1972). On the other hand, the dissociation between cortical slowing and waking behavior may be less dramatic if one considers that in the cat (Rougeul *et al.*, 1969) and monkey (Ricci and Zamparo, 1965) there is a total disruption of conditioned behavior when cortical activity is synchronized after atropine. This may indicate that the subcortical mechanisms which are involved in the maintenance of waking are not impaired by atropine, whereas higher nervous processes (learning, memory) which take place at the neo- or paleocortex are "inhibited" by these drugs. A complicating factor is that these drugs increase cortical ACh release very significantly (see Celesia and Jasper, 1966; Bartolini and Pepeu, 1967).

The data obtained with pharmacological experiments are strongly corroborated by the analysis of ACh release during the sleep–waking cycle. Indeed, in contrast to the monoamines whose release is still very difficult to measure under chronic conditions, the use of bioassay or new biochemical techniques has made the study of the release of ACh at the cortical or subcortical level possible. Thus, the increased waking which follows stimulation of the mesencephalic reticular formation (Celesia and Jasper, 1966) or injection of amphetamine (Pepeu and Bartolini, 1967) is accompanied by an increased release of ACh from the cerebral cortex. Finally, an increased release of cortical (Jasper and Tessier, 1971) and of striatal ACh (Gadea-Ciria et al., 1973) is observed during EEG arousal in chronic cats.

On the other hand, SWS is accompanied by a decreased rate of release of free ACh from the cortex (Celesia and Jasper, 1966; Beani et al., 1968) and from the striatum (Gadea-Ciria et al., 1973).

These correlations, made in different laboratories and under different conditions, are of great importance, since for the first time significant alterations in the rate of release of a neurotransmitter can be associated with the sleep–waking cycle.

Summing up, there is concordant evidence that cholinergic mechanisms act, at the cortical or subcortical level, to mediate cortical arousal. These results support the hypothesis of a waking cholinergic system. However, impairment of cortical arousal by anticholinergic drugs does not suppress *behavioral* waking but strongly impairs learning. Thus, it is likely that some cholinergic intracortical mechanism plays a role in the higher nervous processes which take place during waking. On the other hand, the data favoring the involvement of cortical or subcortical cholinergic mechanisms in slow-wave sleep are not convincing, since neither atropine nor hemicholinium 3 suppresses behavioral sleep, and since there is a decrease in ACh release during cortical synchronization and SWS.

Since NE mechanisms may also participate in the control of tonic cortical arousal through the dorsal NE pathway, it is likely that some interactions take place between ACh and CA mechanisms. Thus, amphetamine, amantadine, and L-dopa which increase CA turnover also increase the cortical outflow of ACh in rabbits, cats, and guinea pigs (Pepeu and Bartolini, 1967). In addition, inhibition of both DA and NA synthesis with α-methyl-p-tyrosine, which leads to cortical synchronization, is accompanied by reduced cortical outflow of ACh in guinea pigs. However, inhibition of NE synthesis with FLA63, a dopamine-β-hydroxylase inhibitor, is accompanied by an increased release of ACh. This finding led Beani et al. (1974) to postulate that it is the DA/NE ratio which is important in the regulation of the cortical release of ACh.

Thus, we are faced once again with the complexity of brain mechanisms.

Which transmitter, or imbalance between transmitters, modulates other transmitters?

6.3. Cholinergic Mechanisms Involved in Paradoxical Sleep

There is much evidence which favors an involvement of cholinergic mechanisms in PS, probably both in its tonic and phasic aspects.

6.3.1. Cholinergic Pontine Induction of Paradoxical Sleep

Normally PS is always preceded by some minutes of slow-wave sleep, and its duration rarely exceeds 10 min. It is, therefore, quite significant that the direct transition from waking into PS or very long-lasting PS episodes (up to 60 min) can be triggered by local injections of ACh or carbachol into the central gray matter in the region of the isthmus or directly into the locus coeruleus area (George et al., 1964; Baxter, 1969). Since the dorsolateral part of the pontine reticular formation is strongly implicated in triggering PS (see Jouvet, 1972), this suggests that there could be cholinoceptive neurons responsible for PS in this area. However, the diffusion of any local injection of ACh or carbachol makes the exact mapping of the areas which respond specifically to cholinergic stimulation difficult. The fact that a direct transition from waking to PS can sometimes be obtained might suggest that direct cholinergic stimulation of the pontine neurons responsible for PS bypasses the "priming" mechanisms of SWS (which are probably serotoninergic). This could indicate that 5-HT mechanisms would normally act first on a cholinergic relay which triggers the "executive" mechanisms of PS.

6.3.2. Pharmacological Alteration of PS

Atropine (1–2 mg/kg) was the first drug found to suppress PS selectively both in its tonic (fast cortical activity, decreased muscle tone) and phasic aspects (PGO activity, rapid eye movements). On the other hand, eserine significantly increases the duration of PS episodes in chronic pontine cats. These findings led to the hypothesis, as early as 1961, that PS might depend upon cholinergic mechanisms (Jouvet, 1961). Identical findings have been obtained in several laboratories (Khazan and Sawyer, 1964; Loizzo and Longo, 1968). The facilitatory action of eserine on PS is *not* observed in chronic animals in which it induces arousal, but only in mesencephalic or pontine preparations. This suggests that cholinergic systems located rostrally to the mesencephalon are mostly involved in arousal mechanisms, while cholinergic neurons located in the pons are directly or indirectly involved in PS. There are in fact numerous possibilities for interactions between cholinergic neurons and monoaminergic neurons (mainly catecholaminergic) in the pons. Such interaction is also suggested by the experiments of Karczmar et al. (1970) in which eserine was able to induce PS in a reserpine-treated cat. The selective suppression of PS by intraventricular injections of hemicholinium 3 (HC3) also favors a cholinergic mechanism (Hazra, 1970; Domino and Stawiski, 1971). Moreover, in the cat, the increased rate of release of ACh from the cortex (Jasper and Tessier, 1971) or the striatum (Gadea-Ciria et al., 1974) during PS suggests that cholinergic neurons in the cortex and striatum are activated during PS. This fact suggests that some cholinergic ascending system might be involved in the mechanism of cortical activation during PS. However, extensive lesions of the mesencephalic tegmentum in the region of the dorsal and ventral tegmental "cholinergic" pathway do not permanently suppress the cortical activation during PS (Jones et al., 1973). Thus, the ascending pathways responsible for cortical activation during PS could be very diffuse, and are probably composed of different systems of neurons which impinge finally on the thalamocortical or cortical cholinergic neurons. Finally, the role of cholinergic mechanisms in triggering the inhibition of muscle tone during PS is still unclear. The inhibition of muscle tone during PS is controlled by a bilateral group of neurons located in the caudal part of the coeruleus complex (Roussel, 1967). The descending pathway responsible for motoneuron inhibition is not yet known, but total cerebellectomy, lesions located in the medial two-thirds of the pontine reticular formation, and lesions of the vestibular nuclei do not prevent muscle inhibition during PS. This suggests that this bilateral (and probably uncrossed) pathway follows a lateroventral route in the pontobulbar region before impinging upon the bulbar inhibitory reticular formation. Since there are no descriptions of any descending "cholinergic" tract in the pons, it is difficult to assume that a purely cholinergic mechanism is responsible for the muscle inhibition during PS. On the other hand, it is possible that this mechanism might be cholinoceptive, since total muscle inhibition either alone (cataleptic attack) or associated with other components of PS is triggered by ACh or carbachol injections in the dorsolateral pontine tegmentum.

Summing up, the involvement of cholinergic mechanisms during PS is demonstrated by the following:

1. Suppressant effect of atropine and hemicholinium 3 and selective induction of PS by eserine in pontine cats
2. Specific triggering of PS by ACh or carbachol directly injected into the pontine reticular formation
3. Increased cortical and striatal release of ACh during PS

The intimate mechanisms which link cholinergic pontine neurons with other transmitters are not yet known, but some additional data may be obtained through the study of PGO activity.

7. PHARMACOLOGICAL ALTERATIONS OF PGO ACTIVITY

The study of PGO activity (which was described in the first part of this paper) belongs to a very specialized field of sleep physiology. However, it is in this field that the most fruitful dialectic exchanges have taken place between pharmacology and neurophysiology. On the one hand, the demonstration that reserpine could induce PGO activity even during waking has permitted its study in acute experiments and thus permitted mapping of the PGO system. On the other hand, the demonstration that PGO activity could be induced or suppressed by numerous drugs acting on brain monoamines has opened a promising new method in neuropharmacology.

7.1. The Reserpine Syndrome and the PGO System

In the cat, reserpine (0.5–1 mg/kg), after a latency of about 90 min, triggers the continuous appearance of PGO at a frequency of 15–30 per minute (Delorme *et al.*, 1965; Jeannerod, 1965; Brooks and Gershon, 1971). This activity is accompanied by discharges in the extraocular muscles and small eye movements. PGO appears continuously either during cortical desynchronization or synchronization. When PS reoccurs after 24 hr, the PGO frequency increases, but the end of the PS episode is followed within a few minutes by a total suppression of the PGO waves. The possibility of recording PGO even in acute experiments in curarized animals made it possible to study their distribution, origin, and organization in more detail than in chronic experiments. From the work of Jeannerod (1965), Laurent *et al.* (1974), and Cespuglio *et al.* (1976), the following picture of the PGO system can be summarized: The bilateral "generators" of PGO activity are situated in the dorsolateral part of the pontine reticular formation. The PGO system related to visual structures ascends in the brainstem in the region of the isthmus dorsally and laterally to the brachium conjunctivum, then sends fibers to the ipsilateral dorsal lateral geniculate nucleus, crosses the midline in the supraoptic decussation, and finally impinges on the controlateral geniculate nucleus. Other axons project to the ipsilateral and controlateral occipital cortices.

7.2. Pharmacology of PGO Activity

7.2.1. 5-HT

5-HT exerts a powerful suppressive action on PGO activity and "closes the gate" of the PGO system (Brooks and Gershon, 1971). Thus, injection of the following drugs, which decrease the availability of 5-HT at synapses, is followed by permanent discharges of PGO waves, either during cortical desynchronization or synchronization: reserpine, *p*-chlorophenylalanine (Delorme *et al.*, 1966; Dement *et al.*, 1972; Koella *et al.*, 1968), *p*-chloromethamphetamine (Delorme *et al.*, 1966; Koella, 1969), and methiothepin—a powerful central 5-HT receptor blocker (Monachon *et al.*, 1972). The same effect immediately follows lesions of the rostral raphe system (Buguet, 1969; Simon *et al.*, 1973; Puizillout *et al.*, 1974), while lesions of the caudal raphe have no effect. On the contrary, any attempt to increase the availability of 5-HT will suppress either spontaneous PGO (in normal cats) or the permanent discharges of PGO in PCPA- or reserpine-treated cats. This suppression has been obtained with 5-HTP, MAO inhibitors (Delorme, 1966), and chlorimipramine—which inhibits 5-HT uptake (Jalfre *et al.*, 1973). LSD, a central 5-HT receptor stimulating agent, also has a powerful suppressant effect (Jalfre *et al.*, 1970; Froment *et al.*, 1971; Henriksen *et al.*, 1972). Methysergide, which is an antagonist of 5-HT at peripheral nonneuronal cells, should also be considered as a central 5-HT agonist since it suppresses PGO activity (Froment *et al.*, 1971; Depoortere and Loew, 1971). Finally, stimulation of the rostral raphe system temporarily suppresses PGO activity during physiological sleep in the cat (Jacobs *et al.*, 1972). Thus, there is converging evidence that some serotoninergic neurons located in the rostral raphe system directly or indirectly exert an inhibitory influence on the hypothetical PGO generator.

7.2.2. Catecholamines

In contrast to 5-HT, the results obtained with pharmacological and neurophysiological alterations of CA metabolism on PGO activity are still conflicting. The following findings favor an involvement of CA neurons in the *generation* of PGO activity: α-Methyl-dopa suppresses both spontaneous or reserpeine-induced PGO waves (Dusan-Peyreton *et al.*, 1968; Delorme, 1966). Dopa increases the frequency of reserpine-induced PGO waves (Delorme, 1966). Tropolone with dopa induces permanent PGO discharges (Jones, 1970). 6-OHDA injected into the dorsolateral pontine tegmentum suppresses PGO activity (Buguet *et al.*, 1969). These findings have led to the hypothesis that deaminated metabolites of CA could be responsible for PGO activity, since these metabolites increase after reserpine and following the combination of dopa with tropolone, while they decrease after MAO inhibition (Jones, 1972).

However, a role for deaminated CA metabolites in neurotransmission has never been established, and the exact localization of the putative CA neurons in the dorsolateral pontine tegmentum (outside the locus coeruleus) has not yet been discovered. Other experiments favor a *suppressant* effect of CA neurons on PGO activity. Clonidine, acting through the stimulation of α-adrenoceptors, reduced the frequency of PCPA-induced PGO waves (Jalfre *et al.*, 1973). Amphetamine, which releases NE, also has the same effect (Jacobs *et al.*, 1972). In addition, lesions of the locus coeruleus are followed, after a latency of several hours, by permanent PGO discharges (Roussel, 1967; Buget, 1969; Jalfre *et al.*, 1974). Thus, it appears possible that some NE-containing neurons of the locus coeruleus may also "close the gate" of the PGO system (as is the case with 5-HT neurons) (Jalfre *et al.*, 1974). However, this possible inhibitory action of CA neurons upon PGO activity is not confirmed by the following findings: Neither the inhibition of dopamine-β hydroxylase with disulfiram, or the inhibition of tyrosine hydroxylase with α-methyl-p-tyrosine, nor the injection of adrenoceptor blocking agents (phenoxybenzamine, phentolamine, propranolol) induced permanent PGO activity, or increased the frequency of the PCPA-induced PGO activity (Jacobs *et al.*, 1972).

7.2.3. *Acetylcholine*

An involvement of cholinergic mechanisms in the generation of PGO waves is probable, but it does not explain all the experimental results.

a. Atropine (2 mg/kg) does not suppress the occurrence of isolated PGO activity in a previously sleep-deprived cat (Vimont-Vicary, 1966), while it considerably decreases the number of bursts of PGO and rapid eye movements (Henriksen *et al.*, 1972).

b. Atropine suppresses the continuous PGO activity which appears after administration of PCPA (Jacobs *et al.*, 1972) and significantly decreases the frequency of PGO activity occurring after reserpine treatment (Delorme, 1966).

c. Eserine increases the frequency of PGO after reserpine administration (Delorme, 1966) and is able to restore PGO activity after its suppression by atropine in PCPA-treated cats (Jacobs *et al.*, 1972).

d. In acute mesencephalic or pontine cats, eserine triggers burst of PGO and eye movements. This bursting is quickly reversed by atropine (Magherini *et al.*, 1971; Matsuzaki, 1969).

This led to the hypothesis that the isolated PGO waves (which are triggered by reserpine and not suppressed by atropine) result from a monoaminergic mechanism, while bursts of PGO would belong to cholinergic mechanism (Pompeiano, 1972).

Summing up, the following model of PGO mechanisms integrates most of the data obtained from pharmacological and neurophysiological experiments: It is possible that the cessation of firing of some raphe neurons (located in the rostral raphe system) at the end of an SWS episode may precipitate the onset of PGO activity (McGinty *et al.*, 1973).

At the same time, some of the locus coeruleus neurons which are involved in waking become silent, and thus another possible inhibitory mechanism acting upon the PGO generator is turned off (this may explain the increased PGO activity which appears after rostral raphe or locus coeruleus lesions or treatment with reserpine and PCPA, or the suppression of PGO activity with 5-HTP, LSD, or with stimulation of the raphe (Jacobs et al., 1973).

Such disinhibition would release the activity of some cells located in the dorsolateral part of the pons. These cells, whose transmitter is still unknown, are not cholinergic, since isolated PGO activity is still observed after high doses of atropine. Secondarily, these neurons would recruit cholinergic cells located in the pontine recticular formation and possibly in the vestibular nuclei. This cholinergic mechanism could be responsible for the bursts of PGO. Finally, both cholinergic and catecholaminergic mechanisms might be involved in other ascending and descending components of PS, but we certainly need additional data, obtained with more sophisticated anatomical and histochemical techniques, in order to understand the delicate agonistic and antagonistic mechanisms which take place between monoaminergic and cholinergic mechanisms during PS.

7.3. The PGO Method in Pharmacology

Most of the preceding data were obtained in chronically recorded cats. However, the recording of PGO activity in acute experiments has become a most powerful method for screening drugs in the pharmacological laboratory. The following example, taken from Monachon et al. (1972), illustrates the heuristic value of PGO recordings in the case of chlordiazepoxide: PGO activity was induced in acute curarized cats by RO4-1284, a benzoquinolizine with reserpinelike monoamine-depleting action, or with PCPA. The effect of chlordiazepoxide on the frequency of PGO waves, which was taken as the dependent variable, was assessed. The drug increased induced PGO activity but did not antagonize the PGO-suppressant effects of 5-HTP. Therefore, it was concluded that chlordiazepoxide did not act on 5-HT receptors. Moreover, the increase in PGO frequency after chlordiazepoxide was similar to the increase obtained after destruction of the locus coeruleus. However, no such pharmacological effect was obtained in the pontine reticular formation after transection of the midbrain. This finding led to the study of the possible involvement of the limbic midbrain circuit, and it was shown that the chronic destruction of the amygdala and septum suppressed the enhancing effect of chlordiazepoxide on PGO. Since atropine acted in a similar way, it was speculated that this drug might activate a possible inhibitory cholinergic pathway descending from the limbic structures to the locus coeruleus. In another series of experiments, Jalfre et al. (1974) investigated the effects of alterations in cerebral GABA metabolism on the same acute induced PGO activity. They found that increases in cerebral GABA (induced by intraventricular injections or by inhibiting its catabolism with aminooxyacetic acid or hydroxylamine) led to an increase only in PCPA-induced PGO activity, but not of RO-4-1284-induced PGO waves (which depletes both 5-HT and CA). They concluded that GABA could have some inhibitory action on the NE system controlling the PGO generator. Although the results of these experiments are largely indirect, they provide us with a new direction in neuropharmacology. Indeed, pharmacologically induced PGO activity, which is at the center of an important biological phenomenon, paradoxical sleep, can be used as a powerful tool in screening many drugs which have potential tranquilizing or antidepressant actions (see below).

8. SHORT-CHAIN FATTY ACIDS AND THE SLEEP-WAKING CYCLE

8.1. The Narcotic Effect

The narcotic effects of short-chain fatty acids (from C4 to C10) were recognized 20 years ago (Samson *et al.*, 1956; Holmquist and Ingvar, 1957). More recently, there has been renewed interest in the C4 compounds: γ-hydroxybutyrate (GOH) and γ-butyrolactone (GBL) (Benda and Perles, 1960; Laborit, 1964). These drugs can induce both states of sleep in normal cats at low doses (50 mg/kg) (Jouvet *et al.*, 1961; Matsuzaki *et al.*, 1964). At higher doses (100 mg/kg), they induce a state of anesthesia both in cats and in rats which is quite different from normal sleep and whose polygraphic pattern is similar to that caused by chloralose (Marcus *et al.*, 1967). The most interesting aspects of the C4 compounds, and also of C5 and C6 compounds, on the sleep–waking cycle (valerate and caproate) (Matsuzaki *et al.*, 1964) are their PS-inducing effect in chronic decorticate, mesencephalic, or pontine cats (Jouvet *et al.*, 1961; Takagi and Matsuzaki, 1968). Under appropriate conditions, these drugs are, with eserine, the only ones currently known to induce typical PS episodes. In order to induce PS, the C4, C5, or C6 compounds must be injected (50 mg/kg), at the earliest, after a refractory period which is equal to half the duration of the PS period. The delay between the intravenous injection and the appearance of PS is shorter after C6 than after C5 or C4, whereas C3 compounds (propiolactone or propiobutyrate) have no effect. That C4–C6 compounds act at the level of the pons is well illustrated by the fact that the effect persists after a mediopontine transection (Matsuzaki, 1969) or is suppressed by a lesion of the dorsolateral pontine tegmentum (Jouvet *et al.*, 1961).

The C4–C6 compounds can counteract the inhibitory effects of atropine on PS in pontine cats, but are unable to reverse the suppressant effects of MAO inhibitors (Delorme, 1966).

8.2. Mechanisms of Action

The numerous mechanisms of action that have been proposed to explain the effect of these drugs can be summarized as follows.

1. Direct action of the fatty acid anion on nerve cells. The fatty acid salts would inhibit the metabolic activity of cerebral tissue as they do in muscle and yeast. This hypothesis was the first proposed to explain their narcotic effects (Samson et al., 1956).

2. Action on cerebral metabolism by affecting the pentose shunt (see Laborit, 1964) or the metabolism of GABA (Godin et al., 1968; Roth and Giarman, 1969).

3. GOH and GBL may also be the precursors of normal constituents of the brain, since GOH is normally found in the brain (Bessman and Fishbein, 1963; Roth and Giarman, 1970).

4. Action on brain ACh. It is also possible that the C4 compounds might be precursors for 2-octylbromoacetoacetate, an organic bromine compound which occurs naturally in the brain and CSF of mammals (Yanagizawa and Yoshikawa, 1968). Indeed, this compound increases PS in the cat at very low doses (0.1 mg/kg) (Torii et al., 1973). Since it has a potent anticholinesterase action, this might explain why GOH increases the level of ACh in the region of the dorsal pontine tegmentum (Giarman and Schmidt, 1963).

5. Action on brain dopamine. GOH increases cerebral DA either by stimulating its synthesis or mainly by blocking its release, whereas it has few significant actions on endogenous levels of either NE or 5-HT (Gessa et al., 1968; Anden et al., 1973). Since it is possible that the region of the locus coeruleus complex contains both ACh and dopamine (Shute and Lewis, 1967; Gerardy et al., 1969) and since there is indirect evidence for the role of these pontine neurons in triggering PS, the triggering effects of C4–C6 compounds might well be related to their regional actions on the pons. In the intact animal the effect on striatal DA could well conceal the pontine effect.

6. Actions on cell membranes. Although the evidence is still indirect, the fatty acid anions may react with membrane lipids and interfere with the movement of critical inorganic ions (Dahl, 1968; Rizzoli and Galzigna, 1970). More specifically, it has been suggested that butyrate molecules may bind to the lecithin of synaptic structures. Butyrate is also capable of binding with 5-HT and DA by forming a molecular interaction complex when it passes through synaptic membranes. The formation of this complex may alter the equilibrium in the synaptic cleft and cause the secretion of additional transmitter, or it may interfere with ACh release. The membrane hypothesis is a very interesting one, since it might also explain the absolute refractory period during which it is impossible to trigger PS either pharmacologically or electrically and during which not enough new transmitter has been synthesized in the terminals. Once a critical level of transmitter has been reached, the fatty acid anions would be able to trigger the release of the transmitter before its normal physiological release. Whatever their intimate mechanism

of action, the short-chain fatty acids, whose blood levels increase after feeding or drinking milk, must certainly be taken into account when considering the possible dietary humoral factors which facilitate the onset of sleep. Thus, due to their probable synergistic action at many levels of the sleep mechanisms, the short-chain fatty acids are good candidates for synthesizing an almost ideal hypnogenic drug.

The first two hypotheses are unlikely since C6 compounds act much more rapidly than C4 compounds.

9. ANTIDEPRESSANT AND NEUROLEPTIC DRUGS

9.1. Antidepressants

Since I have summarized the effects of MAO inhibitors when studying the drugs which act on monoaminergic metabolism, I shall mostly review here the effect of tricyclic antidepressants. In the cat, the administration of a single dose (10–15 mg/kg) of chlorimipramine (Baldy-Moulinier *et al.*, 1969), imipramine, desmethylimipramine (Hishikawa *et al.*, 1965; Wallach *et al.*, 1969), or amitriptyline (Wallach *et al.*, 1969) has a similar effect: an increase in cortical synchronization even during waking and a long-lasting suppression or decrease in PS (for up to 3 days). No rebound occurs following this condition.

However, the *chronic* administration of either cyclazocine or imipramine to cats for 14 days resulted in a complete tolerance to the initial effect (return of PS to baseline level). The abrupt withdrawal of either drug resulted in a significant rebound in PS (Drew *et al.*, 1971).

In rats, Khazan and Sawyer (1964) also reported a decrease in PS after imipramine, while there was no effect with trimipramine.

In rhesus monkey, however, a single dose of imipramine (25 mg/kg) had no significant effect on the sleep states but was, nevertheless, followed by a small rebound of PS during the 2 days following drug administration (David *et al.*, 1974).

The suppressant effects of the tricyclic antidepressants on PS are strongly correlated with their suppressant effects on pharmacologically induced PGO activity (as recorded with the "PGO screening test"). According to Jalfre *et al.* (1972), the potency of these drugs is as follows: Chlorimipramine had the most potent suppressant effect upon RO-4-1284-induced PGO waves. It was followed by imipramine, amitriptyline, protriptyline, chlordesipramine, and desipramine. Iprindole and trimipramine (which has no effect on sleep in rat) had no effect on PGO activity. Thus, it is possible that both the PS and PGO suppressant effects might be due mainly to the inhibitory effects of these drugs on 5-HT uptake (see Iversen, Chapter 7, Vol. 3). The potent suppressant effect of chlorimipramine has been successfully used in man for the treatment of idiopathic narcolepsy [a disease which is often characterized by the abrupt eruption of PS during the waking state (cataleptic attacks)] (Passouant and Baldy-Moulinier, 1970).

9.2. Neuroleptic Drugs

Chlorpromazine (Jewett and Norton, 1966; Wallach et al., 1969) and related drugs, promethazine, perphenazine, and trifluoperazine, have a similar effect on the cat: They increase cortical synchronization without suppressing isolated PGO activity. However, they decrease or suppress PS according to the dose. No PS rebound is observed after single doses or even after chronic administration for 3 weeks (Borenstein et al., 1969). Haloperidol also suppresses PS at high doses in the cat (Monti, 1968), while sulpiride has no significant effects (Borenstein et al., 1969). In contrast to the tricyclic antidepressants, the neuroleptic drugs have no effects on the "PGO screening test" (Jalfre et al., 1972). Thus, their suppressant effects on PS cannot be explained by a possible effect on monoamine uptake, and still remain unexplained.

10. HYPNOTICS AND TRANQUILIZING DRUGS

Every day millions of insomniacs take "sleeping pills." In the USA, per capita consumption of barbiturates in 1948 was 2.4 g. The Department of Health, Education and Welfare (1967) disclosed that retail sales of sedatives and tranquilizers increased by 535% from 1952 to 1963. Thus, it is important to know if "sleeping pills" really induce physiological sleep. Since we deal only with animal experiments here, we refer the reader to the reviews by Oswald (1968), Hartmann (1970), King (1971), and Pichot and Serdaru (1972) which discuss the numerous problems related to the chronic use and abuse of hypnotics and tranquilizers in man (overdose with coma potential, crosstolerance, dependence, abstinence syndrome, the rebound of PS which follows their abrupt withdrawal, with its suite of narcoleptic attacks or nightmares, etc.).

10.1. Hypnotics

In the cat, the neurophysiological action of barbiturates (thiopentone and pentobarbitone) was studied extensively during the reign of the reticular formation in the 1950's. It was shown that barbiturates could induce "sleep" and anesthesia by a special effect on polysynaptic mechanisms in the reticular activating system and by a reduction in nonspecific ascending activating impulses to the cortex (see review by Killam, 1962). At this time, sleep (as an unique state) was considered to be a negative state arising from diminished excitation of the reticular formation (waking system). This concept was simple, elegant, and obeyed following "principle of economy." However, when the existence of synchronizing tonically active sleep-promoting mechanisms in the lower brainstem was discovered (see review by Moruzzi, 1972), it was soon discovered that the injection of thiopentone into the vertebral arteries was able to arouse a sleeping animal, presumably because the drug inactivated the sleep-promoting mechanisms of the lower brainstem (Magni *et al.*, 1959). These experiments together with the discovery of another state of sleep with activated EEG (paradoxical sleep) which was either decreased or totally suppressed by barbiturates exploded the evidence relating barbiturates to a physiological sleep-inducing action. Later experiments performed in chronic cats showed that the effects of barbiturates were dose-dependent: Low doses of thiopental do not suppress PS (Jewett and Norton, 1966). Subanesthetic doses of pentobarbital (Jouvet and Delorme, 1965) cause continuous cortical and subcortical spindles whose pattern is different from stage 1 or 2 sleep. However, provided that the animal is kept in a warm environment, subcortical PGO activity may still occur with the same periodicity as in a normal untreated cat. However, anesthetic doses of thiopental or pentobarbital totally suppress PGO activity and PS in the cat. Finally, pentobarbital (20 mg/kg) in rhesus monkeys may increase stage 2 sleep significantly while it considerably reduces PS for one day. This suppression is followed for 2 days by a PS rebound (David *et al.*, 1974). α-Chloralose, at anesthetic doses (55–65 mg/kg), has a peculiar effect in the chronically recorded cat. It causes for the first 12 h permanent discharges of PGO activity (as with reserpine and PCPA), while there is a very-low-amplitude cortical activity together with spikes. Thereafter, for the next 12 hr cortical activity becomes hypersynchronous and PGO activity occurs only episodically (McGinty and Krenek, 1974). Thus, we have to add α-chloralose to the list of drugs which can act on the PGO system, possibly by decreasing 5-HT and/or CA turnover.

10.2. Minor Tranquilizers

Nitrazepam and diazepam cause a dose-dependent reduction in PS in cats. They also cause long periods of restlessness with unusual fast rhythmic activity in the cortical EEG, so that total sleep time is decreased. When PS reappears, it tends to manifest itself with fewer rapid eye movements (Lanoir and Killam, 1968; Borenstein *et al.*, 1973). In rhesus monkeys nitrazepam has the same PS-suppressant effect on the day of its administration. It is, however, followed by a significant rebound of PS which may last up to 2 days (David *et al.*, 1974). We have reviewed the effects of chlordiazepoxide when studying the "PGO screening test." This drug increases the frequency of

PGO activity possibly by acting on a descending limbic cholinergic system that impinges on the locus coeruleus (Jalfre *et al.,* 1972). However, there is some evidence that chlordiazepoxide may also act directly on the lower brainstem. This drug, or diazepam, when injected into the vertebral artery of rabbits in acute experiments can cause irregularly a "picture similar to PS": activation of the EEG, bursts of eye movements, and total atonia of the neck muscles (Loizzo and Longo, 1968). Thus, this benzodiazepine may have a possible hypnogenic effect on the pontine structures responsible for the induction of PS. Finally Mogadon (7-nitro-5-phenyl-$3H$-1,4-benzodiazepin-2-one, nitrazepam) a well-known "sleeping drug," does not seem to have a true hypnogenic effect, at least in the rabbit. When injected into the vertebral artery it induces, as does thiopental, a true waking behavior with fast cortical activity, while it leads to cortical synchronization when injected into the carotid. These effects are interpreted by Zattoni and Rossi (1967) as a depressant action of the drug on the neuronal systems in the brainstem which have opposite functional roles in the regulation of the sleep–waking cycle.

Summing up, there is no experimental evidence, in rats, rabbits, cats, and monkeys, that hypnotic and tranquilizing drugs have a "physiological" hypnogenic action, since most of them induce a cortical activity different from SWS at the time of their sedative or hypnotic effect and since they have suppressant effects on PS. However, the effect of chlordiazepoxide on PGO activity, and its action on brainstem mechanisms, makes this drug the least "unphysiological" as compared with other hypnotics and tranquilizers. As with short-chain fatty acids, it may be that the path of benzodiazepin derivatives may lead to a putative good "sleep-inducing drug."

11. HORMONES AND THE SLEEP–WAKING CYCLE

Total hypophysectomy does not significantly alter the sleep–waking cycle in the cat, nor the striking hypersomnia which follows lesions of the ascending dorsal NE bundle (Petitjean *et al.,* 1975). Thus, there is solid evidence that the *basic mechanisms* of the sleep–waking cycle do not depend upon hormonal factors. However, there are numerous experiments which favor some reciprocal *regulatory* interactions between the sleep–waking cycle and hormonal release (which may be influenced by the same monoaminergic transmitters which are involved in sleep mechanisms). On the one hand, growth hormone is secreted at the onset of sleep, mainly during SWS in the dog. Prolactin release is also dependent on nocturnal sleep. ACTH secretion is closely related to a basic circadian rhythm, but does not appear to be closely linked to the sleep–waking cycle *per se.* Gonadotrophins (LH and FSH) are randomly secreted during waking and sleep, while testosterone release has been reported to occur in conjunction with PS (see the review by Rubin *et al.,* 1974). Finally, the posterior pituitary also appears to become activated during PS since changes in the volume and osmolarity of the urine suggest the secretion of vasopression during PS. In addition, PS is also accompanied by an increase in the total urinary excretion of 17-hydroxycorticosteroids (Mandell and Mandell, 1965). The latter authors suggested that the function of PS would be the activation of the hypothalamic–pituitary–adrenal system. Thus, PS could be a means of stimulating gluconeogenesis and maintaining the animal's energy-producing mechanisms during the long fast of sleep. On the other hand, the sleep–waking cycle may be influenced by hormones. Sawyer and Kawakami (1961) and Faure (1964) described a strange immediate sequel to coitus in the female rabbit, including a "sleep state with flaccidity and fast cortical EEG." This "EEG after-reaction" has since been recognized as PS and might be related to the postcoital release of LH and FSH (Dufy *et al.*, 1973).

Progesterone (150 mg/kg) injected intraperitoneally can induce both SWS and PS in cat (Heuser, 1967). Crystals of progesterone intracerebrally injected into the preoptic region can also hasten the appearance of PS (Heuser *et al.*, 1967). *Vasopressin* itself can induce PS in the rabbit (Faure, 1964) and cat (Domino and Yamamoto, 1965). The vasopressin effect may explain why injection of hypertonic solutions increases PS by 100–300% in chronic pontine cat with hypothalamic islands, while hypotonic saline suppresses PS (Jouvet, 1965).

Bovine *growth hormone* administered intraperitoneally to cats (Stern *et al.*, 1974) or rats (Drucker-Colin *et al.*, 1975) induces a significant increase in PS. This effect occurs mainly during the first 3 hr.

In the chronic hypophysectomized rat, Valatx *et al.* (1975) found a significant decrease of PS. There was also a decrease in central temperature. When the rats were treated with ACTH or placed in a warm environment, PS rose to control levels. Finally epiphysectomy can chronically disrupt the circadian distribution of PS in rats (Mouret *et al.*, 1974).

Summing up, a large body of evidence suggests the existence of reciprocal interactions between the circadian sleep–waking cycle or the ultradian organization of sleep states and hormonal factors. But these factors do not interfere with the basic mechanisms of sleep which remain unaltered by total hypophysectomy. Thus, hormonal factors can be considered only as ancillary in the regulation of the sleep–waking cycle.

12. DRUGS ACTING ON PROTEIN SYNTHESIS AND THE SLEEP–WAKING CYCLE

12.1. Experimental Evidence

In mice, the subcutaneous injection of cycloheximide (30 mg/kg) increased SWS but significantly reduced the number but not the duration of

PS episodes. Thus, it was postulated that inhibition of protein synthesis might act on the mechanisms which prime PS (Pegram et al., 1973).

In rats, the intraperitoneal injection of anisomycin (5 mg/kg, a dose which produces up to 90% inhibition of protein synthesis) decreased PS for 2–3 hr without alteration of SWS. This effect was not observed if growth hormone was injected together with anisomycin (Drucker-Colin et al., 1975).

In cats, the intraperitoneal injection of puromycin or cycloheximide was followed by decreased PS for 1 day without any secondary rebound. However, the intraventricular injection of cycloheximide, which caused a 75% inhibition of cerebral protein synthesis, did not alter PS on the first day but was followed for 3 days by an 80% increase in PS. No significant effect was obtained with intraventricular puromycin which caused only a 50% inhibition of cerebral protein synthesis (Stern et al., 1972). Finally, in cats, the *per os* administration of chloramphenicol (150 mg/kg) yielded a selective suppression of PS for 10 hr. Thioamphenicol, a closely related analog, had no effect even at a dose four times larger (Petitjean et al., 1975).

These results should be critically evaluated since, at the end of this review, the reader has certainly noted the wide spectrum of drugs which "selectively" suppress PS, the most vulnerable part of the sleep–waking cycle.

Since the suppressant effects of protein synthesis inhibitors on PS are observed only after systemic injections, it is certainly difficult to rule out any peripheral effects. Indeed, the very marked cerebral protein synthesis inhibition which follows intraventricular injections of cycloheximide does not immediately alter the sleep–waking cycle. The long-lasting increase in PS which occurs secondarily after this latter procedure has been related to a return of protein synthesis toward the normal state. According to this hypothesis, PS would be necessary for or correlated with the "recovery of CNS protein synthesis" (Stern et al., 1972).

12.2. Impossible Interpretation

The pharmacological study of protein metabolism during sleep is certainly important, since sleep may represent a period of long-term recovery of the brain which may involve the biosynthesis of macromolecules. But the temporal and structural relationships between macromolecular biosynthesis and sleep states are still unknown. Is this process taking place during SWS or during PS, or both? Are new and specific protein species synthesized during each state of sleep? Indeed, some indirect data indicate that PS may be related to protein synthesis in the brain. There is a high proportion of PS after birth, at a time when maturational processes occur in animals. The high rate of metabolism of the brain during PS (increased blood flow and temperature) is also consistent, with an anabolic process. Finally, the huge increase of PS during withdrawal, after its pharmacological suppression (with MAO inhibitors or tricyclic antidepressant drugs), follows the same time course as the recovery of some enzymes, such as brain acetylcholinesterase after inactivation with organophosphates (Oswald, 1969). However, because of the difficulties of studying protein synthesis by means of administration of single or mixtures of labeled amino acids as precursors, there have been only few reports concerning possible *in vivo* or *in vitro* alterations of the rate of protein synthesis during the sleep–waking cycle. A significant fall in brainstem protein synthesis was observed in total sleep-deprived rats (but the stress of the procedure might have caused the same effect); conversely, the increase of sleep during the recovery seemed to lead to an increase of protein synthesis (Bobillier *et al.*, 1974). This result must be compared with the results of Reich *et al.* (1974) who found a two- or threefold increase in the incorporation of ^{32}P into a phosphoprotein fraction of the rat brain during sleep. Bobillier *et al.* (1973) also reported that the 5-HTP reversal of PCPA-induced insomnia in the cat was associated with the appearance of a high-molecular-weight acidic protein fraction in the telencephalon, and it was hypothesized that the functional release of 5-HT might be related to the synthesis of new protein species. Following another approach in the rabbit, Vitale-Neugebauer *et al.* (1970) found that the pattern of synthesis of high-molecular-weight RNA was influenced by the state of cortical activity prevailing during the period of incorporation of [^{14}C]orotic acid. Finally, a possible link between protein synthesis and sleep may be found in the results of Dolezalova *et al.* (1974). A striking increase (500%) of cadaverine was observed in the brain of "dormant" mice (behaviorally asleep) as compared with waking controls. Although these experiments were interpreted in the direction of the biosynthesis of piperidine (another putative sleep neurotransmitter—see below), the demonstration that some polyamine could increase during sleep is interesting since other polyamines (putrescine, spermidine, spermine) are intimately involved in protein synthesis (see Seiler and Lamberty, 1975).

13. MISCELLANEOUS COMPOUNDS

This last section is a short review of the effects of some putative neurotransmitters and some drugs which defy classification. Some of them, however, may have a future in sleep research.

13.1. Putative Neurotransmitters

13.1.1. GABA

I have briefly considered the possible involvement of GABA in sleep mechanisms when considering the effects of short-chain fatty acids and the "PGO screening test." The increase in brain GABA which follows the continuous intravenous injection of sodium di-*n*-propylacetate is followed by a decrease in PS in rats (Juan de Mendoza *et al.*, 1973). Thus, at the present time, there is still no good evidence for including GABA in the list of putative sleep neurotransmitter.

13.1.2. Histamine

When injected in the rabbit, histamine has a clear-cut waking action (Monnier *et al.*, 1967). The well-known soporific action of antihistamines might be related to the involvement of histaminergic systems in waking. Several antihistamine drugs (chlorpheniramine, tripelennamine) can also suppress PS. But the PS suppressant effects of the antihistamines may not be specific, since these agents also have some anticholinergic actions.

13.1.3. Piperidine

This volatile amine which is synthetized from lysine and cadaverine was recently identified in the brain of the mouse by means of mass spectrography. Moreover, a striking increase in piperidine (up to 3000%) in the brain (and also in the blood (>900%) of dormant mice was demonstrated by Dolezalova and Stepita-Klauco (1974). When injected into the pontine reticular formation (in the very small dose of 10–20 μg), it increased both SWS and PS (100% as compared with saline control) (Miyata *et al.*, 1974). High doses (100–300 μg) were followed by arousal. Injections of piperidine into other brain regions (hippocampus, amygdala, cerebellum) were not followed by sleep. These results were confirmed by Drucker-Colin and Giacobini (1975) who perfused piperidine into the midbrain reticular formation and obtained a significant increase of PS without significant effects on SWS. In both experiments, piperidine was injected into structures which may contain cholinoceptive neurons. Thus, it is possible that the increase of PS might have been due to a true cholinergic effect, since piperidine has a potent nicotinic action. The possibility that piperidine could be a neurotransmitter opens a new and interesting field of research, especially if it is confirmed that its cerebral level is so strikingly elevated during sleep. The increase of blood piperidine during sleep also deserves more study in relation to the possible circulating "sleep factor."

13.2. Miscellaneous Drugs

The ever-increasing use and abuse of hallucinogens or opiates and the need for more fundamental studies concerning their mechanisms of action has had some impact in sleep laboratories, as shown by the results below.

13.2.1. Marijuana

As might have been expected, even cats may enjoy this drug experimentally. Unfortunately, its chronic administration led to some alterations of SWS (decrease of stage 2 and increase of stage 1) which persisted for 30 days after the drug treatment period! (Barratt and Adams, 1973). In rats, tetrahydrocannabinols may also alter PS (mainly by suppressing the cortical activation of PS) (Moreton and Davis, 1973).

13.2.2. Morphine

This opiate causes suppression of PS in rabbits. In rats, self-administration of morphine first suppresses PS, but despite steadily increasing doses (up to 40 mg/kg/hr) both states of sleep may return to normal (Khazan et al., 1967). In cats, morphine (300 µg/kg) induces an arousal lasting for 6 hr which is followed by rebound of PS. The alerting action of morphine can be blocked by naloxone. The mechanism of the morphine-induced wakefulness is not apparent, since the arousal cannot be suppressed either by α-methyl-p-tyrosine or by 5-HTP (Echols and Jewett, 1972). Finally *papaverine* (5 mg/kg) was found by Bauer and Sur (1972) to depress PS temporarily in rats.

13.2.3. Ethanol

That PS can be an exquisitely sensitive index of long-lasting alterations of brain metabolism is shown by the following experiments. When orally administered in naive rats, ethanol (5 g/kg) induced a 30% decrease in PS duration for the 6 hr which followed the alcoholic drink. However, if previously alcoholic rats (which had received the same daily dose of ethanol for 5 weeks, and which were then abstinent for the following 6–8 months) received a test dose of 5 g/kg of ethanol, there was a much more dramatic reduction in PS (~85%) (Gitlow et al., 1973).

13.2.4. Diphenylhydantoin

Cohen et al. (1968) reported that this drug inhibits PS in the cat. This effect is not completely specific since SWS is also depressed. Interestingly, there is no tolerance to the PS suppressant effect, even after 24 days of continuous administration, and no immediate or secondary rebound on withdrawal. The mechanism of this suppressant effect is still obscure.

14. CONCLUSIONS

1. From a practical (clinical) aspect, the lack of any real hypnogenic drug which can induce, physiological sleep at will is the biggest failure of the

neuropharmacology of sleep. It is paralleled by the failure of neurophysiology to provide us with a satisfactory theory to explain the mechanisms of the sleep–waking cycle.

2. However, neuropharmacology has provided us with some fruitful models for explaining *some* of the intimate mechanisms which are involved in the regulation of sleep or waking. These models have been extended by neurophysiology and biochemistry where it has been possible to map out, with histochemistry, the regional distribution of systems of neurotransmitters (monoamines).

3. The role of 5-HT in the induction of slow-wave sleep and the priming of paradoxical sleep in supported by converging lines of pharmacological, physiological, and biochemical evidence. In short-term experiments (days) decreases in 5-HT turnover lead to insomnia, while increases in 5-HT turnover lead to increases in both SWS and PS. However, the return of sleep despite a very low level of 5-HT in long-term experiments with chronic *p*-chlorophenylalanine administration (weeks) is not yet explained.

4. CA mechanisms are involved in waking. This is demonstrated by the increased waking which follows increased availability of CA and by the decreased wakefulness which follows decreased CA turnover. However, the recovery of a normal waking EEG despite a very low level of CA (after intraventricular 6-OHDA) forces us to postulate the intervention of either postsynaptic supersensitivity or the substitution of CA functions by some other systems.

5. The intervention of CA mechanisms in the executive mechanism of PS is still controversial since inhibition of CA synthesis does not always suppress PS. Two explanations are put forward: (a) that the inhibition of CA synthesis leads to increased turnover of 5-HT neurons; (b) that PS is negatively correlated with CA metabolism (maintenance of CA system theory).

6. Cholinergic mechanisms are certainly involved both in cortical arousal and in paradoxical sleep, although there is no evidence for their role in slow-wave sleep. These pharmacological results are, however, difficult to interpret because of our lack of knowledge of the cholinergic pathways in the brain.

7. PGO activity, which heralds and accompanies PS, appears to be an exquisite index for testing the effects of drugs acting on monoaminergic systems, since it can be increased or suppressed by either decreasing or increasing the availability of 5-HT. Some heuristic approaches to the use of the PGO screening test in neuropharmacology are summarized.

8. Short-chain fatty acids still remain the only reliable PS-inducing drugs (in mesencephalic or pontine cats). However, because of their many different mechanisms of action, it is impossible to explain their hypnogenic effects.

9. Antidepressant and neuroleptic drugs both decrease or suppress PS

by different mechanisms (as shown by their differential effects on PGO activity).

10. Neither hypnotics nor tranquilizers have a real hypnogenic effect. α-Chloralose (among hypnotics) and chlordiazepoxide (among tranquilizers) are unique in increasing PGO activity.

11. There are numerous reciprocal interactions between hormonal release and the sleep–waking cycle. However, the role of hormones is not determinant but only ancillary in the basic mechanisms of sleep, since hypophysectomy does not significantly alter sleep.

12. Inhibitors of protein synthesis may suppress PS if systemically injected, or increase it if intracerebrally injected. Because of the difficulties of studying protein synthesis during sleep, it is still impossible to give any explanation to these results and to compare them with the macromolecules which are released into the CSF or in the brain during sleep.

13. Among the miscellaneous compounds which may have some interest in the future, piperidine appears to be the most important since it may act as a neurotransmitter and since its cerebral level increases strikingly during sleep.

15. REFERENCES

AGHAJANIAN, G. K., BLOOM, F. E., LOVELL, R. A., SHEARD, M. H., and FREEDMAN, D. X., 1966, The uptake of 5-hydroxytryptamine-3H from the cerebral ventricles: autoradiographic localization, *Biochem. Pharmacol.* **15**:401–408.

AGHAJANIAN, G. K., GRAHAM, A. W., and SHEARD, M. H., 1970, Serotonin-containing neurons in brain: depression of firing by monoamine oxidase inhibitors, *Science* **169**:1100–1102.

ANDÉN, N. E., MAGNUSSON, T., and STOCK, G., 1973, Effects of drugs influencing monoamine mechanisms on the increase in brain dopamine produced by axotomy or treatment with gammahydroxybutyric acid, *Naunyn-Schmiedeberg's Arch. Pharmacol.* **278**:363–372.

BALDY-MOULINIER, M., DUPRES, G., and PASSOUANT, P., 1969, Organization de la veille et du sommeil au cours du nycthémère chez le chat. Modifications pharmacologiques, *Rev. Neurol. (Paris)* **120**:394–398.

BARRATT, E., and ADAMS, P. M., 1973, Chronic marijuana usage and sleep–wakefulness cycles in cats, *Biol. Psychiat.* **6**:207–214.

BARTHOLINI, G., BIRLARD, W. P., PLETSCHER, A., and BATES, H. M., 1967, Increase of cerebral catecholamines caused by 3,4-dihydroxyphenylalanine after inhibition of peripheral decarboxylase, *Nature (London)* **215**:852–853.

BARTOLINI, A., and PEPEU, G., 1967, Investigations into the acetylcholine output from the cerebral cortex of the cat in the presence of hyoscine, *Brit. J. Pharmacol. Chemother.* **31**:66–74.

BAUER, V., and SUR, R. N., 1972, Studies on the central nervous system actions of papaverine. I. The action on sleep cycle in the rat, *Psychopharmacologia* **26**:263–274.

BAUMGARTEN, H. G., EVETTS, K. D., HOLMAN, R. B., IVERSEN, L. L., VOGT, M., and GAY, W., 1972, Effects of 5,6-dihydroxytryptamine on monoaminergic neurons in the central nervous system of the rat, *J. Neurochem.* **19**:1587–1598.

BAUST, W., NIEMCZYK, H., and VIETH, J., 1963, The action of blood pressure on the ascending reticular activating system with special reference to adrenaline-induced EEG arousal, *Electroencephalogr. Clin. Neurophysiol.* **15**:63–72.

BAXTER, B. L., 1969, Induction of both emotional behavior and a novel form of REM sleep by chemical stimulation applied to cat mesencephalon, *Exp. Neurol.* **23**:220–230.

BEANI, L., BIANCHI, L., SANTINOCETO, L., and MARCHETTI, P., 1968, The cerebral acetylcholine release in conscious rabbits with semi-permanently implanted epidural cups, *Int. J. Neuropharmacol.* **7**:469–481.

BEANI, L., BIANCHI, C., and CASTELLUCI, A., 1974, Correlation of brain catecholamines with cortical acetylcholine outflow behavior and electrocorticogram, *Eur. J. Pharmacol.* **26**:63–72.

BENDA, P., and PERLES, R., 1960, Etude expérimentale de l'abaissement de la vigilance par le gamma butyrolactone, *C. R. Acad. Sci.* **251**:1312–1313.

BERT, J., and BALZAMO, E., 1974, Différenciation des effets de la PCPA sur le sommeil de deux primates appartenant au genre papio, *Electroencephalogr. Clin. Neurophysiol.* **37**:161–166.

BESSMAN, S. P., and FISHBEIN, W. N., 1963, Gamma-hydroxybutyrate, a normal brain metabolite, *Nature (London)* **200**:1207.

BILKOVA, J., RADIL-WEISS, T., and BOHDANECKY, Z., 1971, The influence of low LSD dose administration during sleep in rats, *Psychopharmacologia* **20**:395–399.

BLONDAUX, C., JUGE, A., SORDET, F., CHOUVET, G., JOUVET, M., and PUJOL, J. F., 1973, Modification du métabolisme de la sérotonine (5-HT) cérébrale induite chez le rat par administration de 6-hydroxydopamine, *Brain Res.* **50**:101–114.

BLONDAUX, C., BUDA, M., PETITJEAN, F., and PUJOL, J. F., 1975, Hypersomnie par lésion isthmique chez le chat. I. Etude du métabolisme des monoamines cérébrales, *Brain Res.* **88**:425–437.

BOBILLIER, P., FROMENT, J. L., SEGUIN, S., and JOUVET, M., 1973, Effets de la p-chlorophenylalanine et du 5-hydroxytryptophane sur le sommeil et le métabolisme central des monoamines et des protéines chez le chat, *Biochem. Pharmacol.* **22**:3077–3090.

BOBILLIER, P., SAKAI, F., SEGUIN, S., and JOUVET, M., 1974, The effect of sleep deprivation upon the *in vivo* and *in vitro* incorporation of tritiated amino acids into brain proteins in the rat at three different age levels, *J. Neurochem.* **22**:23–31.

BOBILLIER, P., PETITJEAN, F., SALVERT, D., LIGIER, M., and SEGUIN, S., 1975, Differential projections of nucleus raphe dorsalis and nucleus raphe centralis as revealed by autoradiography, *Brain Res.* **85**:205–210.

BORENSTEIN, P., GEKIERE, F., GRUET-MASSON, J., MENCHIKOFF, F., ALLEGRE, G., and CUJO, P., 1969, Etude comparative de l'effet de trois neuroleptiques majeurs sur l'évolution des tracés de veille-sommeil de chats implantés libres, *Sem. Hop. Paris,* **19**:1271–1300.

BORENSTEIN, P., GEKIERE, F., BRINDEAU, F., CLEAN, M., and ALLEGRE, G., 1973, Etude comportementale et polygraphique de trois benzodiazepines et d'un barbiturique sur le chat implanté libre, *Ann. Med. Psychol.* **2**:13–43.

BRADLEY, P. B., and ELKES, J., 1957, The effects of some drugs on the electrical activity of the brain, *Brain* **80**:77–117.

BRANCHEY, M., and KISSIN, B., 1970, The effect of alpha methylparatyrosine on sleep and arousal in the rat, *Psychosom. Sci.* **19**:281–282.

BREMER, F., 1954, The neurophysiological problem of sleep, in: *Brain Mechanisms and Consciousness* (E. D. Adrian, F. Bremer, and H. H. Jasper, eds.), pp. 137–162, Blackwell, Oxford.

BREMER, F., and CHATONNET, J., 1949, Acétylcholine et cortex cérébral, *Arch. Intern. Physiol.* **57**:106–109.

BRODIE, B. B., and SHORE, P. A., 1957, On a role for serotonin and norepinephrine as chemical mediators in the central autonomic nervous system, in: *Hormones, Brain Function and Behaviour* (H. Hoagland, ed.), pp. 161–176, Academic Press, New York.

BRONZINO, J. D., BRUSSEAU, J. N., STERN, W. C., and MORGANE, P. J., 1973, Power density

spectra of cortical EEG of the cat in sleep and waking, *Electroencephalogr. Clin. Neurophysiol.* **35:**187–192.
BROOKS, D. C., and GERSHON, M. D., 1971, Eye movement potentials in the oculomotor and visual system: a comparison in reserpine-induced waves with those present during wakefulness and rapid eye movement sleep, *Brain Res.* **27:**223–239.
BUGUET, A., 1969, Monoamines et sommeils. V. Etude des relations entre les structures monoaminergiques du pont et les pointes ponto-geniculo-occipitales du sommeil, *Thèse Médecine* (J. Tixier, ed.), p. 214, Lyon.
BUGUET, A., PETITJEAN, F., AND JOUVET, M., 1970, Suppression des pointes PGO du sommeil par lésion ou injection *in situ* de 6-hydroxydopamine au niveau du tegmentum pontique, *C. R. Soc. Biol.* **164:**2293–2300.
CAPON, A., 1959, Nouvelles recherches sur l'effet d'éveil de l'adrénaline, *J. Physiol. (Paris)* **51:**424–425.
CELESIA, G. G., and JASPER, H. H., 1966, Acetylcholine released from cerebral cortex in relation to state of activation, *Neurology* **16:**1053–1064.
CESPUGLIO, R., LAURENT, J. P., and CALVO, J. M., 1976, Organisation anatomique des activités phasiques provoquées par la réserpine au niveau du système oculo-moteur, *Electroencephalogr. Clin. Neurophysiol.* **40:**12–29.
COHEN, H. B., DUNCAN, R. F., and DEMENT, W. C., 1968, The effect of diphenylhydantoin on sleep in the cat, *Electroencephalogr. Clin. Neurophysiol.* **24:**401–408.
COHEN, H. B., FERGUSON, J., HENRIKSEN, S., STOLK, J. M., ZARCONE, V. J., BARCHAS, J., and DEMENT, W., 1970, Effects of chronic depletion of brain serotonin on sleep and behavior, *Proc. Am. Psychol. Assoc.* **78:**831–832.
COHEN, H. B., DEMENT, W. C., and BARCHAS, J. D., 1973, Effects of chlorpromazine on sleep in cats pretreated with para-chlorophenylalanine, *Brain Res.* **53:**363–372.
CONSTANTINIDIS, J., BARTHOLINI, G., TISSOT, R., and PLETSCHER, A., 1968, Accumulation of dopamine in the parenchyma after decarboxylase inhibition in the capillaries of brain, *Experientia* **24:**130–132.
CONSTANTINIDIS, J., GEISSBUHLER, F., GAILLARD, J. M., AUBERT, C., NOVAGUIMIAU, T., and TISSOT, R., 1975, Formation de norepinephrine dans le cerveau du rat après administration de (+)-erythro-3,4-dihydroxyphenylserine, *Psychopharmacologia* **41:**201–210.
CORDEAU, J. P., MOREAU, A., BEAULNES, A., and LAWRIN, C., 1963, EEG and behavioural changes following microinjections of acetylcholine and adrenaline in the brainstem of cats, *Arch. Ital. Biol.* **101:**30–47.
CORDEAU, J. P., CHAMPLAIN, J. DE, and JACKS, B., 1971, Excitation and prolonged waking produced by catecholamines injected into the ventricular system of cats, *Can. J. Physiol. Pharmacol.* **49:**627–631.
COSTA, E., PSCHEIDT, G. R., VAN METER, W. G., and HIMWICH, H. E., 1960, Brain concentrations of biogenic amines and EEG patterns of rabbits, *J. Pharmacol. Exp. Ther.* **130:**81–88.
COSTA, E., GROPPETTI, A., and NAIMZADA, M. K., 1972, Effects of amphetamine on the turnover rate of brain catecholamines and motor activity, *Brit. J. Pharmacol.* **44:**742–752.
CRAMER, H., TAGLIAMONTE, A., TAGLIAMONTE, P., PEREZ-CRUET, J., and GESSA, G. L., 1973, Stimulation of brain serotonin turnover by paradoxical sleep deprivation in intact and hypophysectomized rats, *Brain Res.* **54:**372–375.
DAHL, D. R., 1968, Short-chain fatty acid inhibition of rat brain Na-K adenosine triphosphatase, *J. Neurochem.* **15:**815–820.
DAVID, J., GREWAL, R. S., and WAGLE, G. P., 1974, Persistent electroencephalographic changes in rhesus monkeys after single doses of pentobarbital, nitrazepam, and imipramine, *Psychopharmacologia* **35:**61–75.
DELL, P., 1960, Intervention of an adrenergic mechanism during brain stem reticular activation, in: *Adrenergic Mechanisms. Ciba Foundation Symposium* (J. R. Varre, G. E. W. Wolstenholme, and C. M. O'Connor, eds.), pp. 393–409, Churchill, London.

DELL, P., 1963, Reticular homeostasis and cortical reactivity, in: *Brain Mechanisms* (G. Moruzzi, A. Fessard, and H. H. Jasper, eds.), pp. 82–103, Elsevier, Amsterdam.

DELORME, F., 1966, Monoamines et sommeils. Etude polygraphique neuropharmacologique et histochimique des états de sommeil chez le chat, Thèse Université de Lyon, pp. 168, Imprimerie LMD.

DELORME, F., JEANNEROD, M., and JOUVET, M., 1965, Effets remarquables de la réserpine sur l'activité EEG phasique pontogeniculo occipitale, *C. R. Soc. Biol.* **159**:900–903.

DELORME, F., FROMENT, J. L., and JOUVET, M., 1966, Suppression du sommeil par la *p*-chloromethamphetamine et la *p*-chlorophenylalanine, *C. R. Soc. Biol.* **160**:2347–2351.

DEMENT, W., FERGUSON, J., COHEN, H., and BARCHAS, J., 1970a, Nonchemical methods and data using a biochemical model: the REM quanta, in: *Some Current Issues in Psychochemical Research Strategies in Man* (A. Mandell, ed.), pp. 275–325, Academic Press.

DEMENT, W., ZARCONE, V., FERGUSON, J., COHEN, H., PIVIK, T., and BARCHAS, J., 1970b, Some parallel findings in schizophrenic patients and serotonin-depleted cats, in: *Schizophrenia. Current Concepts and Research* (D. V. Siva-Sankar, ed.), pp. 775–811, PJD Publications, New York.

DEMENT, W. C., MITLER, M., and HENRIKSEN, S. J., 1972, Sleep changes during chronic administration of *p*-chlorophenylalanine, *Rev. Can. Biol.* **31**:239–246.

DEPOORTERE, H., and LOEW, D. M., 1971, Alterations in sleep, wakefulness cycle in rats following treatment with LSD, *Br. J. Pharmacol.* **41**:402–403.

DEWHURST, W. G., and MARLEY, E., 1965, Action of sympathomimetic and allied amines on the central nervous system of the chicken, *Br. J. Pharmacol. Chemother.* **25**:705–728.

DOLEZALOVA, H., and STEPITA-KLAUCO, M., 1974, Piperidine concentration changes in the brain and blood of dormant mice, *Brain Res.* **74**:182.

DOLEZALOVA, H., STEPITA-KLAUCO, M., and FAIRWEATHER, R., 1974, An elevated cadaverine content in the brain of dormant mice, *Brain Res.* **77**:166–168.

DOMINO, E. F., and STAWISKI, M., 1971, Effects of the cholinergic antisynthesis agent HC-3 on the awake–sleep cycle of cat, *Psychophysiology* **7**:315–316.

DOMINO, E. F., and YAMAMOTO, K., 1965, Nicotine: effect on the sleep cycle of the cat, *Science* **150**:637–638.

DOMINO, E. F., YAMAMOTO, K., and DREN, A. T., 1968, Role of cholinergic mechanisms in states of wakefulness and sleep, *Progr. Brain Res.* **28**:113–133.

DREW, W. G., CHAMPLIN, M., and MILLER, L., 1971, Comparison of the effects of cyclazocine and imipramine on the circadian sleep–waking cycle of the cat, *Pharmacology* **6**:339–352.

DRUCKER-COLIN, R. R., and GIACOBINI, E., 1975, Sleep-inducing effect of piperidine, *Brain Res.* **88**:186–189.

DRUCKER-COLIN, R. R., ROJAS-RAMIREZ, J. A., VERA-TRUEBA, J., MONROY-AYALA, G., and HERNANDEZ-PEON, R., 1970, Effect of crossed perfusions of the midbrain reticular formation upon sleep, *Brain Res.* **23**:269–273.

DRUCKER-COLIN, R. R., SPANIS, C. W., COTMAN, C. W., AND McGAUGH, J. L., 1975a, Changes in protein levels in perfusates of freely moving cats: relation to behavioral state *Science* **187**:963–964.

DRUCKER-COLIN, R. R., SPANIS, C., HUNYADI, J., SASSIN, J. F., and McGAUGH, J. L., 1975b, Growth hormone effects on sleep and wakefulness in the rat, *Neuroendocrinology* **18**:1–8.

DUFY, B., VINCENT, J. D., DUFY-BARBE, L., and FAURE, J., 1973, Effects of vaginal stimulation and pituitary hormones on sleep patterns in the female rabbit, *Endocrinology* **92**:1293–1295.

DUSAN-PEYRETHON, D., and FROMENT, J. L., 1968, Effets du disulfiram sur les états de sommeil chez le chat, *C. R. Soc. Biol.* **162**:2141–2145.

DUSAN-PEYRETHON, D., PEYRETHON, J., and JOUVET, M., 1968, Suppression élective du sommeil paradoxal chez le chat par alpha-méthyl-dopa, *C. R. Soc. Biol.* **162**:116–118.

ECHOLS, S. D., and JEWETT, R. E., 1972, Effects of morphine on sleep in the cat, *Psychopharmacologia* **24**:435.

FAURE, J., 1964, Hormones in relation to sleep-wakefulness mechanisms, in: *Endocrinology* (S.

Tayen, ed.), *Proceedings of the Second International Congress of Endocrinologists,* London, 1964, pp. 606–611, Excerpta Medica, Amsterdam.

FELSTEIN, A., CHANG, F. H., and KUCHARSKI, J. M., 1970, Tryptophol, 5-hydroxytryptophol and 5-methoxytryptophol induced sleep in mice, *Life Sci.* **9:**323–329.

FENCL, V., KOSKI, G., and PAPPENHEIMER, J. R., 1971, Factors in cerebrospinal fluid from goats that affect sleep and activity in rats, *J. Physiol. (London)* **216:**565–589.

FLORIO, V., SCOTTI DE CAROLIS, A., and LONGO, V. G., 1968, Observations on the effect of DL-parachlorophenylalanine on the electroencephalogram, *Physiol. Behav.* **3:**861–865.

FROMENT, J. L., ESKAZAN, E., and JOUVET, M., 1971, Effets du LSD et du methysergide sur les états de sommeil du chat, *C. R. Soc. Biol.* **165:**2153–2157.

FROMENT, J. L., PETITJEAN, F., BERTRAND, N., COINTY, C., and JOUVET, M., 1974, Effets de l'injection intracérébrale de 5,6-hydroxytryptamine sur les monoamines cérébrales et les états de sommeil du chat, *Brain Res.* **67:**405–417.

FUXE, K., and LIDBRINK, P., 1973, Biogenic amine aspects on sleep and waking, in: *Sleep. First European Congress on Sleep Research,* Basel 1972 (W. P. Koella and P. Levin, eds.), pp. 12–26, Karger, Basel.

FUXE, K., and UNGERSTEDT, U., 1968, Histochemical studies on the distribution of catecholamines and 5-hydroxytryptamine after intraventricular injections, *Histochemie* **13:**16–28.

FUXE, K., LIDBRINK, P., HOKFELT, T., BOLME, P., and GOLDSTEIN, M., 1974, Effects of piperoxane on sleep and waking in the rat. Evidence for increased waking by blocking inhibitory adrenaline receptors on the locus coeruleus, *Acta Physiol. Scand.* **91:**566–567.

GADEA-CIRIA, M., STADLER, H., LLOYD, K. G., and BARTHOLINI, G., 1973, Acetylcholine release within the cat striatum during the sleep–wakefulness cycle, *Nature (London)* **243:**518–519.

GAILLARD, J. M., BARTHOLINI, G., HERKERT, B., and TISSOT, R., 1974, Involvement of 5-hydroxytryptamine in the cortical synchronization induced by L-dopa in the rabbit, *Brain Res.* **68:**344–350.

GAL, E. M., ROGGEVEEN, A. E., and MILLARD, S. A., 1970, DL-(2^{14}C)-p-chlorophenylalanine as an inhibitor of tryptophan 5-hydroxylase, *J. Neurochem.* **17:**1221–1235.

GARDINER, J. E., 1961, The inhibition of acetylcholine synthesis in brain by hemicholinium, *Biochem. J.* **31:**297–303.

GEORGE, R., HASLETT, W. L., and JENDEN, D. J., 1964, A cholinergic mechanism in the brainstem reticular formation: induction of paradoxical sleep, *Int. J. Pharmacol.* **3:**451–552.

GERARDY, J., QUINAUX, N., MAEDA, T., and DRESSE, A., 1969, Analyse des monoamines du locus coeruleus et d'autres structures cérébrales par chromatographie sur couche mince, *Arch. Int. Pharmacol. Ther.* **177:**492–496.

GESSA, G. L., CRABAI, F., VARGIU, L., and SPANO, P. F., 1968, Selective increase of brain dopamine induced by gamma-hydroxybutyrate: study of the mechanism of action, *J. Neurochem.* **15:**377–383.

GIARMAN, N. J., and SCHMIDT, K. F., 1963, Some neurochemical aspects of the depressant action of γ-butyrolactone on the central nervous system, *Br. J. Pharmacol. Chemother.* **20:**563–568.

GITLOW, S. E., BENTKOVER, S. H., DZIEDZIC, S. W., and KHAZAN, N., 1973, Persistence of abnormal REM sleep response to ethanol as a result of previous ethanol ingestion, *Psychopharmacologia* **33:**135–140.

GODIN, Y., MARK, J., and MANDEL, P., 1968, The effects of 4-hydroxybutyric acid on the biosynthesis of amino acids in the central nervous system, *J. Neurochem.* **15:**1085–1093.

GOLDSTEIN, M., LAUBER, E., and MCKEREGHAN, M. R., 1964, The inhibition of dopamine-β-hydroxylase by tropolone and other chelating agents, *Biochem. Pharmacol.* **13:**1103.

GOTTESMANN, C., 1966, Reserpine et vigilance chez le rat, *C. R. Soc. Biol.* **160:**2056–2061.

HAIGLER, H. J., and AGHAJANIAN, G. K., 1974, Peripheral serotonin antagonists: failure to antagonize serotonin in brain areas receiving a prominent serotonergic input, *J. Neural. Transm.* **35:**257–273.

HANSON, L. C. F., 1967, Evidence that the central action of (+)-amphetamine is mediated via catecholamines, *Psychopharmacologia* **10**:289-298.

HARTMANN, E., 1968, On the pharmacology of dreaming sleep (the D state), *J. Nerv. Ment. Dis.* **146**:165-173.

HARTMANN, E., 1970, The D state and norepinephrine-dependent systems, in: *Sleep and Dreaming* (E. Hartmann, ed.), pp. 308-328, Little Brown, Boston.

HARTMANN, E., BRIDWELL, T. J., and SCHILDKRAUT, J. J., 1971a, Alpha-methyl-paratyrosine and sleep in the rat, *Psychopharmacologia* **21**:157-164.

HARTMANN, E., CHUNG, R., DRASKOCZY, P., and SCHILDKRAUT, J. J., 1971b, Effects of 6-hydroxydopamine on sleep in the rat, *Nature (London)* **233**:425-426.

HARTMANN, E., ZWILLING, G., and LIST, S., 1973, Effects of an alpha-adrenergic blocker on sleep in the rat, in: *Sleep Research* (M. H. Chase, W. C. Stern, and P. L. Walter, eds.), p. 58, Brain Supl. Service, University of California, Los Angeles.

HARVEY, J. A., MCMASTER, S. E., and YUNGER, L. M., 1975, *p*-Chloramphetamine: selective neurotoxic action in brain, *Science* **187**:841-844.

HAVLICEK, V., 1967, The effect of dl-3,4-dihydroxyphenylserine (precursor of noradrenaline) on the ECOG of unrestrained rats, *Int. J. Neuropharmacol.* **6**:83-89.

HAZRA, J., 1970, Effect of hemicholinium-3 on slow wave and paradoxical sleep of cat, *Eur. J. Pharmacol.* **11**:395-397.

HAZRA, J., 1971, Effect of serotonin depletion on HC-3 induced slow wave sleep of cat, *Experientia* **27**:909-911.

HENRIKSEN, S. J., and DEMENT, W. C., 1972, Effects of chronic intravenous administration of α-methyl paratyrosine on sleep in the cat, in: *Sleep Research* (M. H. Chase, W. C. Stern, and P. L. Walter, eds.), Vol. 1, Brain Supl. Service, p. 55, University of California, Los Angeles.

HENRIKSEN, S. J., JACOBS, B. C., and DEMENT, W. C., 1972, Dependence of REM sleep PGO waves on cholinergic mechanisms, *Brain Res.* **48**:412-416.

HERNANDEZ-PEON, R., O'FLAHERTY, J. J., and MAZZUCHELLI-O'FLAHERTY, A. L., 1967, Sleep and other behavioural effects induced by acetylcholinic stimulation of basal temporal cortex and striate structure, *Brain Res.* **4**:243-267.

HERY, F., PUJOL, J. F., LOPEZ, M., MACON, J., and GLOWINSKI, J., 1970, Increased synthesis and utilization of serotonin in the central nervous system in the rat during paradoxical sleep deprivation, *Brain Res.* **21**:391-403.

HEUSER, G., 1967, Induction of anesthesia, seizures and sleep by steroid hormones, *Anesthesiology* **28**:173-183.

HEUSER, G., LING, G., and KLUVER, M., 1967, Sleep induction by progesterone in the preoptic area in cats, *Electroencephalogr. Clin. Neurophysiol.* **22**:122-127.

HIEBEL, G., BONVALLET, M., HUBE, P., and DELL, P., 1954, Analyse neurophysiologique de l'action centrale de la *d*-amphetamine (maxiton), *Sem. Hop. Paris* **30**:1880-1885.

HISHIKAWA, Y., NAKAI, K., HIDENOBU, I., and KANEKO, Z., 1965, The effect of imipramine, desmethylimipramine and chlorpromazine on the sleep-wakefulness cycle of the cat, *Electroencephalogr. Clin. Neurophysiol.* **19**:518-521.

HOBSON, J. A., 1964, The effect of LSD on the sleep cycle of the cat, *Electroencephalogr. Clin. Neurophysiol.* **17**:52-56.

HOKFELT, T., FUXE, K. J., GOLDSTEIN, M., and JOHANZZON, O., 1973, Evidence for adrenaline neurons in the rat brain, *Acta Physiol. Scand.* **89**:286.

HOLMAN, R. B., SHILLITO, E., and VOGT, M., 1971, Sleep produced by clonidine, *Br. J. Pharmacol.* **43**:685-695.

HOLMQUIST, B., and INGVAR, D. H., 1957, Effects of short-chain fatty acid anions upon cortical blood flow and EEG in cats, *Experientia* **8**:331-333.

HOWARD, J. L., and BREESE, G. R., 1974, Physiological and behavioral effects of centrally administered 6-hydroxydopamine in cats, *Pharmacol. Biochem. Behav.* **2**:651-662.

HOYLAND, J., SHILLITO, E., and VOGT, M., 1970, The effect of parachlorophenylalanine on the behaviour of cats, *Br. J. Pharmacol.* **40**:659-667.

ISKANDER, T. N., and KAELBLING, R., 1970, Catecholamines, a dream sleep model and depression, *Am. J. Psychiat.* **127**:43–50.
JACOBS, B. L., HENRIKSEN, S. J., and DEMENT, W. C., 1972, Neurochemical bases of the PGO waves, *Brain Res.* **48**:406–411.
JACOBS, B. L., ASHER, R., and DEMENT, W. C., 1973, Electrophysiological and behavioral effects of electrical stimulation of the raphe nuclei in cats, *Physiol. Behav.* **11**:489–496.
JALFRE, M., MONACHON, M., and HAEFELY, W., 1970, Pharmacological modifications of benzoquinolizine induced geniculate spikes, *Experientia* **26**:691–694.
JALFRE, M., MONACHON, A., and HAEFELY, W., 1973, Drug and PGO-waves in the cat, in: *Proceedings of the First Canadian International Symposium on Sleep* (A. W. McClure, ed.), Roche, Montreal.
JALFRE, M., RUCK-MONACHON, M. A., and HAEFELY, W., 1974, Methods for assessing the interaction of agents with 5-HT neurons and receptors in the brain, *Adv. Biochem. Psychopharmacol.* **10**:121–134.
JASPER, H. J., and TESSIER, J., 1971, Acetylcholine liberation from cerebral cortex during paradoxical (REM) sleep, *Science* **172**:601–603.
JEANNEROD, M., 1965, Organisation de l'activité électrique phasique du sommeil paradoxal. Etude électrophysiologique et neuropharmacologique, Thèse de Médecine (J. Tixiez, ed.), p. 90, Lyon.
JEWETT, R. E., and NORTON, S., 1966, Effects of some stimulant and depressant drugs on sleep cycles of cats, *Exp. Neurol.* **15**:463–475.
JOHNSON, D. N., FUNDERBURK, W. H., and WARD, J. W., 1971, Effects of Fenfluramine on sleep–wakefulness in cats, *Psychopharmacologia* **20**:1–10.
JOHNSON, D. N., FUNDERBURK, W. H., RUCKART, R. T., and WARD, J. W., 1972, Contrasting effects of two 5-hydroxytryptamine depleting drugs on sleep patterns in cats, *Eur. J. Pharmacol.* **20**:80–84.
JONES, B., 1970, The double role of catecholamines in waking and paradoxical sleep: a neuropharmacological model, Ph.D. thesis, University of Delaware.
JONES, B. E., 1972, The respective involvement of noradrenaline and its deaminated metabolites in waking and paradoxical sleep: a neuropharmacological model, *Brain Res.* **39**:121–136.
JONES, B. E., BOBILLIER, P., PIN, C., and JOUVET, M., 1973, The effects of lesion of catecholamine containing neurons upon monoamine content of the brain and EEG and behavioural waking in the cat, *Brain Res.* **58**:157–177.
JOUVET, D., and DELORME, F., 1965, Evolution des signes électriques du sommeil paradoxal au cours de la nacrose au pentobarbital chez le chat, *C. R. Soc. Biol.* **159**:387–390.
JOUVET, M., 1961, Telencephalic and rhombencephalic sleep in the cat, in: *The Nature of Sleep* (G. E. W. Wolstenholme and M. O'Connor, eds.), pp. 188–208, CIBA Foundation Symposium, Churchill, London.
JOUVET, M., 1965, Etude de la dualité des états de sommeil et des mécanismes de la phase paradoxale, in: *Aspects Anatomo Fonctionnels de la Physiologie du Sommeil* (M. Jouvet, ed.), pp. 397–449, Centre National de la Recherche Scientifique, Paris.
JOUVET, M., 1968, Neuropharmacology of sleep, in: *Psychopharmacology. A review of Progress* (D. H. Efron, ed.), pp. 523–540, Public Health Service Publication No. 1836.
JOUVET, M., 1969, Biogenic amines and the states of sleep, *Science* **163**:32–41.
JOUVET, M., 1972, The role of monoamines and acetylcholine-containing neurons in the regulation of the sleep–waking cycle, *Ergeb. Physiol.* **64**:165–305.
JOUVET, M., CIER, A., MOUNIER, D., and VALATX, J. L., 1961, Effets du 4-butyrolactone et du 4-hydroxybutyrate de sodium sur l'EEG et le comportement du chat, *C. R. Soc. Biol.* **155**:1313–1316.
JUAN DE MENDOZA, J. L., GAUTHIER, P., RODI, M., ROUX, R., and GOTTESMANN, C., 1973, Effect of enhanced GABA level in the central nervous system on the different sleep–wakefulness stages in the rat, *C. R. Soc. Biol.* **167**:73–83.
KARCZMAR, A. G., LONGO, V. G., and SCOTTI DE CAROLIS, A., 1970, A pharmacological model

of paradoxical sleep: the role of cholinergic and monoamine systems, *Physiol. Behav.* **5:**175-182.

KEY, G. J., 1975, Electrocortical changes induced by perfusion of catecholamines into the brain stem reticular formation, *Neuropharmacology* **14:**41-52.

KEY, G. J., and MARLEY, E., 1962, The effect of the sympathomimetic amines on behaviour and electrocortical activity of the chicken, *Electroencephalogr. Clin. Neurophysiol.* **14:**90-105.

KHAZAN, N., and SAWYER, C. H., 1964, Mechanisms of paradoxical sleep as revealed by neurophysiologic and pharmacologic approaches in the rabbit, *Psychopharmacologia* **5:**457-462.

KHAZAN, N., WEEKS, J. R., and SCHROEDER, L. A., 1967, Electroencephalographic, electromyographic and behavioral correlates during a cycle of self-maintained morphine addiction in the rat, *J. Pharmacol. Exp. Ther.* **155:**521-531.

KILLAM, E. K., 1962, Drug action on the brain-stem reticular formation, *Pharmacol. Rev.* **14:**175-223.

KING, C. D., 1971, The pharmacology of rapid eye movement sleep, *Advances in Pharmacology and Chemotherapy*, Vol. 9 (S. Garattini *et al.*, eds.), pp. 1-91, Academic Press, New York.

KING, D., and JEWETT, R. E., 1971, The effects of alpha methyltyrosine on sleep and brain norepinephrine in cat, *J. Pharmacol. Exp. Ther.* **177:**188-194.

KITAHAMA, K., and VALATX, J. L., 1975, Action de l'alpha-methyl-dopa sur les rythmes veille-sommeil de souris C57 Br et C 57 B1/6, *Psychopharmacologia* **45:**189-196.

KOE, B. K., and WEISSMAN, A., 1966, *p*-Chlorophenylalanine, a specific depletor of brain serotonin, *J. Pharmacol. Exp. Ther.* **154:**499-516.

KOELLA, W. P., 1969, Serotonin and sleep, *Exp. Med. Surg.* **27:**157-169.

KOELLA, W. P., and CZICMAN, J., 1966, Mechanism of the EEG synchronizing action of serotonin, *Am. J. Physiol.* **211:**926-935.

KOELLA, W. P., FELDSTEIN, A., and CZICMAN, J. S., 1968, The effect of parachlorophenylalanine on the sleep of cats, *Electroencephalogr. Clin. Neurophysiol.* **25:**481-490.

LABORIT, H., 1964, Sodium 4-hydroxybutyrate, *Int. J. Neuropharmacol.* **3:**433-452.

LAGUZZI, R., PETITJEAN, F., PUJOL, J. F., and JOUVET, M., 1972, Effets de l'injection intraventriculaire de 6-hydroxydopamine sur le cycle veille-sommeil du chat, *Brain Res.* **48:**295-310.

LANOIR, J., and KILLAM, E. K., 1968, Alteration in the sleep–wakefulness patterns by benzodiazepines in the cat, *Electroencephalogr. Clin. Neurophysiol.* **25:**530-542.

LAURENT, J. P., CESPUGLIO, R., and JOUVET, M., 1974, Delimitation des voies ascendantes de l'activité ponto-géniculo-occipitale chez le chat, *Brain Res.* **65:**29-52.

LICHTENSTEIGER, W., and LANGEMANN, H., 1966, Uptake of exogenous catecholamines by monoamine-containing neurons of the central nervous system: uptake of catecholamines by arcuato-infundibular neurons, *J. Pharmacol. Exp. Ther.* **151:**400-409.

LIDBRINK, P., 1974, The effect of lesions of ascending noradrenaline pathways on sleep and waking in the rat, *Brain Res.* **74:**19-40.

LOIZOU, L. A., 1969, Projections of the nucleus locus coeruleus in the albino rat, *Brain Res.* **15:**563-566.

LOIZZO, A., and LONGO, V. G., 1968, A pharmacological approach to paradoxical sleep, *Physiol. Behav.* **3:**91-99.

LONGO, V. G., 1973, Central effects of 6-hydroxydopamine, *Behav. Biol.* **9:**397-420.

MACON, J. B., SOKOLOFF, L., and GLOWINSKI, J., 1971, Feedback control of rat brain 5-hydroxytryptamine synthesis, *J. Neurochem.* **18:**323-332.

MAGHERINI, P. C., POMPEIANO, O., and THODEN, U., 1971, The neurochemical basis of REM sleep: a cholinergic mechanism responsible for rhythmic activation of the vestibulooculomotor system, *Brain Res.* **35:**565-569.

MAGNI, F., MORUZZI, G., ROSSI, G. F., and ZANCHETTI, A., 1959, EEG arousal following inactivation of the lower brain stem by selective injection of barbiturate into the vertebral circulation, *Arch. Ital. Biol.* **97:**33-46.

MANDELL, A. J., and MANDELL, M. P., 1965, Biochemical aspects of rapid eye movement sleep, *Am. J. Psychiat.* **122**:391–402.

MANDELL, A. J., and SPOONER, C. E., 1968, Psychochemical research studies in man, *Science* **162**:1442–1453.

MARANTZ, R., RECHTSCHAFFEN, A., LOVELL, R. A., and WHITEHEAD, P. K., 1968, Effect of alpha-methyltyrosine on the recovery from paradoxical sleep deprivation in the rat, *Commun. Behav. Biol.* **2**:161–164.

MARCUS, R. J., WINTERS, W. D., MORI, K., and SPOONER, C. E., 1967, EEG behavioral comparison of gamma-hydroxybutyrate, gamma-butyrolactone and short chain fatty acids in the rat, *Int. J. Neuropharmacol.* **6**:175–187.

MATSUMOTO, J., and JOUVET, M., 1964, Effets de réserpine, DOPA et 5-HTP sur les 2 états de sommeil, *C. R. Soc. Biol.* **158**:2137–2140.

MATSUMOTO, J., and WATANABE, S., 1967, Effects of adrenergic blocking agents, *Proc. Jpn. Acad.* **43**:680–683.

MATSUYAMA, S., COINDET, J., and MOURET, J., 1973, 6-Hydroxydopamine intracisternale et sommeil chez le rat, *Brain Res.* **57**:85–95.

MATSUZAKI, M., 1969, Differential effects of sodium butyrate and physostigmine upon the activities of para-sleep in acute brain stem preparations, *Brain Res.* **13**:247–265.

MATSUZAKI, M., TAKAGI, H., and TOKIZANE, T., 1964, Paradoxical phase of sleep and its artificial induction in the cat by sodium butyrate, *Science* **146**:1328–1329.

McGEER, E. G., McGEER, P. L., and PETERS, D. A., 1967, Inhibition of brain tyrosine hydroxylase by 5-halotryptophans, *Life Sci.* **6**:2221–2233.

McGINTY, D. J., HARPER, R. M., and FAIRBANKS, M. K., 1973, 5-HT-containing neurons: unit activity in behaving cats, in: *Serotonin and Behavior* (J. Barchas and E. Usdin, eds.), pp. 267–280, Academic Press, New York.

McGINTY, D., and KRENEK, T., 1974, REM phenomena during α-chloralose anesthesia in the cat, in: *Sleep Research* (M. H. Chase, W. C. Stern, and P. L. Walter, eds.), Vol. 3, Brain Information Service, p. 61, Brain Res. Inst., University of California, Los Angeles.

MIYATA, T., KAMATA, K., NISHIKIBE, M., KASI, Y., TAKAHAMA, K., and OKANO, Y., 1974, Effects of intracerebral administration of piperidine on EEG and behaviour, *Life Sci.* **15**:1135–1152.

MONACHON, M. A., BURKARD, W., JALFRE, M., and HAEFELY, W., 1972, Blockade of central 5-hydroxytryptamine receptors by methiothepin, *Naunyn-Schmiedeberg's Arch. Pharmacol.* **274**:192–197.

MONNIER, M., and TISSOT, R., 1958, Action de la réserpine et de ses médiateurs (5-HTP-serotonine et DOPA-noradrenaline) sur le comportement et le cerveau du lapin, *Helv. Physiol. Acta* **16**:255–267.

MONNIER, M., and GRABER, S., 1963, Action de la DOPA et du blocage de la monoaminoxydase par l'iproniazid sur le cerveau, Sonderdruck Schw., *Arch. Neurol. Neurochem. Psychol.* **92**:410–414.

MONNIER, M., FALLERT, M., and BHATTACHARYA, I. C., 1967, The waking action of histamine, *Experientia* **23**:21–22.

MONTI, J. M., 1968, The effect of haloperidol on the sleep cycle of the cat, *Experientia* **24**:1143–1144.

MORETON, J. E., and DAVIS, W. M., 1973, Electroencephalographic study of the effects of tetrahydroxycannabinols on sleep in the rat, *Neuropharmacology* **12**:897–908.

MORGANE, P. J., 1969, Chemical mapping of hypnogenic and arousal systems in the brain, *Psychophysiology* **6**:219.

MORGANE, P. J., and STERN, W. C., 1973a, Effects of serotonin metabolites on sleep–waking activity in cats, *Brain Res.* **50**:205–213.

MORGANE, P. J., and STERN, W. C., 1973b, Monoamine systems in the brain and their role in the sleep states, in: *Serotonin and Behavior* (J. Barchas and E. Usdin, eds.), pp. 427–442, Academic Press, New York.

MORGANE, P. J., and STERN, W. C., 1974, Interaction of amine systems in the central nervous system in the regulation of the states of vigilance, in: *Neurohumoral Coding of Brain Function* (R. D. Myers and R. Drucker-Colin, eds.), Plenum Press, New York.

MORUZZI, G., 1964, The historical development of the deafferentation hypothesis of sleep, *Proc. Am. Philos. Soc.* **108**:19-28.

MORUZZI, G., 1972, The sleep-waking cycle, *Ergeb. Physiol.* **64**:1-164.

MOURET, J., FROMENT, J. L., BOBILLIER, P., and JOUVET, M., 1967, Etude neuropharmacologique et biochimique des insomnies provoquées par la p-chlorophenylalanine, *J. Physiol. (Paris)* **59**:463-464.

MOURET, J., BOBILLIER, P., and JOUVET, M., 1968a, Insomnia following p-chlorophenylalanine in the rat, *Eur. J. Pharmacol.* **5**:17-22.

MOURET, J., VILPPULA, A., FRACHON, N., and JOUVET, M., 1968b, Effets d'un inhibiteur de la monoamine-oxydase sur le sommeil du rat, *C. R. Soc. Biol.* **162**:914-917.

MOURET, J., COINDET, J., and CHOUVET, G., 1974, Effet de la pinéalectomie sur les états et les rythmes de sommeil du rat mâle, *Brain Res.* **81**:97-105.

NAUTA, W. J. H., 1958, Hippocampal projections and related neural pathways to the midbrain of the cat, *Brain* **81**:319-340.

NAVA, B., CARBONELL, J., GUTIERREZ, J., ARCE, M., and OBRADOR, S., 1973, Implantes cefalicos en perros. II. Estudios neurologicos y electroencefalograficos, *Rev. Clin. Esp.* **130**:301-306.

NG, K. Y., CHASE, T. N., COLBURN, R. W., and KOPIN, I. J., 1970, L-DOPA-induced release of cerebral monoamines, *Science* **170**:76-77.

OSWALD, I., 1968, Drugs and sleep, *Pharmacol. Rev.* **20**:273-303.

OSWALD, I., 1969, Human brain proteins, drugs and dreams, *Nature (London)* **223**:893-897.

PANKSEPP, J., JALOWIEC, J. E., MORGANE, P. J., ZOLOVICK, A. J., and STERN, W. C., 1973, Noradrenergic pathways and sleep-waking states in cats, *Exp. Neurol.* **41**:233-245.

PASCALON, A., ASHFORD, W., DANSEREAU, J., and MOURET, J., 1972, The effect of 6-chlorotryptophan on sleep in the rat, *Life Sci.* **11**:893-903.

PASSOUANT, P., and BALDY-MOULINIER, M., 1970, Données actuelles sur le traitement de la narcolepsie. Action des imipraminiques, *Concours Med.* **92**:1967-1970.

PEGRAM, V., HAMMOND, D., and BRIDGERS, W., 1973, The effect of protein synthesis inhibition on sleep in mice, *Behav. Biol.* **3**:377-382.

PEPEU, G., and BARTOLINI, A., 1967, Effect of some psychopharmacological agents on acetylcholine release from the cerebral cortex of the cat, *Boll. Soc. Ital. Biol. Sper.* **43**:1409-1411.

PETITJEAN, F., LAGUZZI, R., JOUVET, M., and PUJOL, J. F., 1972, Effets de l'injection intraventriculaire de 6-hydroxydopamine. I. Sur les monoamines cérébrales du chat, *Brain Res.* **48**:281-293.

PETITJEAN, F., SAKAI, K., BLONDAUX, C., and JOUVET, M., 1975a, Hypersomnie par lésion isthmique chez le chat. II. Etude neurophysiologique et pharmacologique, *Brain Res.* **88**:439-453.

PETITJEAN, F., SASTRE, J. P., BERTRAND, N., COINTY, C., and JOUVET, M., 1975b, Suppression du sommeil paradoxal par le chloramphenicol. Absence d'effet du Thiamphenicol, *C. R. Soc. Biol.* **169**:1236-1239.

PICHOT, P., and SERDARU, M., 1972, Psychopharmacologie du sommeil, *Encephale* **4**:1-109.

PIERON, H., 1913, *Le problème physiologique du sommeil*, 520 pp., Masson, Paris.

POIRIER, L. J., LANGELIER, P., ROBERGE, A., BOUCHER, R., and KITSIKIS, A., 1972, Nonspecific histopathological changes induces by the intracerebral injection of 6-hydroxydopamine (6-OHDA), *J. Neurol. Sci.* **16**:401-416.

POMPEIANO, O., 1972, Reticular control of the vestibular nuclei. Physiology and pharmacology, in: *Progress in Brain Research*, Vol. 37 (O. Pompeiano and A. Brodal, eds.), pp. 614-618, Elsevier, Amsterdam.

PUIZILLOUT, J. J., TERNAUX, J. P., FOUTZ, A. S., and FERNANDEZ, G., 1974, Les stades de sommeil de la préparation "encéphale isolé." I. Déclenchement des pointes ponto-

géniculo-occipitales et du sommeil phasique à ondes lentes. Rôle des noyaux du raphé, *Electroencephalogr. Clin. Neurophysiol.* **37:**561–576.
PUJOL, J. F., MOURET, J., JOUVET, M., and GLOWINSKI, J., 1968, Increased turnover of cerebral norepinephrine during rebound of paradoxical sleep in the rat, *Science* **159:**112–114.
PUJOL, J. F., BUGUET, A., FROMENT, J. L., JONES, B., and JOUVET, M., 1971, The central metabolism of serotonin in the cat during insomnia: a neurophysiological and biochemical study after *p*-chlorophenylalanine or destruction of the raphe system, *Brain Res.* **29:**195–212.
PUJOL, J. F., STEIN, D., BLONDAUX, C., PETITJEAN, F., FROMENT, J. L., and JOUVET, M., 1973, Biochemical evidences for interaction phenomena between noradrenergic and serotoninergic systems in the cat brain, in: *Frontiers in Catecholamine Research* (E. Usdin and S. Snyder, eds.), Pergamon, Oxford.
RECHTSCHAFFEN, A., LOVELL, R. A., FREEDMAN, D. W., WHITEHEAD, P. K., and ALDRICH, M., 1969, Effect of *p*-chlorophenylalanine on sleep in rats, *Psychophysiology* **6:**223.
REICH, P., GEYER, S. J., and KARNOVSKY, M. L., 1974, Metabolism of brain during sleep and wakefulness, *J. Neurochem.* **19:**487–498.
REIS, D. J., MOORHEAD, D. T., and MESLINO, N., 1970, Dopa-induced excitement in the cat, *Arch. Neurol.* **22:**31–39.
REITE, M., PEGRAM, G. V., STEPHENS, L. M., BIXLER, E. C., and LEWIS, O. L., 1969, The effect of reserpine and monoamine oxidase inhibitors on paradoxical sleep in the monkey, *Psychopharmacologia* **14:**12–17.
RICCI, G. F., and ZAMPARO, L., 1965, Electrocortical correlates of avoidance conditioning in the monkey. Their modifications with atropine and amphetamine, in: *Pharmacology of Conditioning, Learning and Retention* (M. Y. Michelson and V. G. Longo, eds.), pp. 269–283, Czechoslovak Medical Press, Prague.
RINALDI, F., and HIMWICH, H. E., 1955, Cholinergic mechanism involved in function of mesodiencephalic activating system, *Arch. Neurol. Psychiat.* **73:**396–402.
RIZZOLI, A. A., and GALZIGNA, L., 1970, Molecular mechanism of unconscious state induced by butyrate, *Biochem. Pharmacol.* **19:**2727–2736.
ROTH, G. I., WALTON, P. L., and YAMAMOTO, W. S., 1970, Area postrema abrupt EEG synchronization following close intra-arterial perfusion with serotonin, *Brain Res.* **23:**223–233.
ROTH, R. H., and GIARMAN, N. J., 1969, Conversion *in vivo* of gamma-aminobutyric to gamma-hydroxybutyric acid in the rat, *Biochem. Pharmacol.* **18:**247–250.
ROTH, R. H., and GIARMAN, N. J., 1970, Natural occurrence of gamma-hydroxybutyrate in mammalian brain, *Biochem. Pharmacol.* **19:**1087–1095.
ROUGEUL, A., VERDEAUX, J., and LETALLE, A., 1969, Effets electrographiques et comportementaux de divers hallucinogènes chez le chat libre, *Rev. Neurol. (Paris)* **120:**391–394.
ROUSSEL, B., 1967, Monoamines et sommeils: suppression du sommeil paradoxal et diminution de la noradrénaline cérébrale par les lésions des noyaux locus coeruleus. Thèse de Médecine (J. Tixier, ed.), Lyon, 141 pp.
RUBIN, R. T., POLAND, R. E., RUBIN, L. E., and GOUIN, P. R., 1974, The neuroendocrinology of human sleep, *Life Sci.* **14:**1041–1052.
SABELLI, H. C., and GIARDINA, W. J., 1970, Tryptaldehydes (indoleacetaldehydes) in serotoninergic sleep in newly hatched chicks, *Arzneimittelforschung* **20:**74–80.
SAMSON, F. E., DAHL, N., and DAHL, D. N., 1956, A study on the narcotic action of the short-chain fatty acids, *J. Clin. Invest.* **35:**1291–1298.
SATOH, T., and TANAKA, R., 1973, Selective suppression of rapid eye movement sleep (REM) by fusaric acid, an inhibitor of dopamine-β-oxidase, *Experientia* **29:**177–178.
SAWYER, C. H., and KAWAKAMI, M., 1961, Interactions between the central nervous system and hormones influencing ovulation, in: *Control of Ovulation* (C. A. Villee, ed.), pp. 79–100, Pergamon Press, New York.

Schoenenberger, G. A., Cueni, L. B., Hatt, A. M., and Monnier, M., 1972, Physicochemical characteristics of the hypnogenic factor, *Rev. Neurol.* **126:**427–434.
Segal, D. S., and Mandell, A. J., 1970, Behavioral activation of rats during intraventricular infusion of norepinephrine, *Proc. Nat. Acad. Sci. U.S.A.* **66:**289–293.
Seiler, N., and Lamberty, U., 1975, Interrelations between polyamines and nucleic acids: changes of polyamine and nucleic acid concentrations in the developing rat brain, *J. Neurochem.* **24:**5–13.
Shimizu, A., and Himwich, H. E., 1968, The effects of amphetamine on the sleep–wakefulness cycle of developing kittens, *Psychopharmacol.* **13:**161–169.
Shute, C. C. D., and Lewis, P. R., 1967, The ascending cholinergic reticular system: neocortical, olfactory and subcortical projections, *Brain* **90:**497–520.
Simon, R. P., Gershon, M. D., and Brooks, D. C., 1973, The role of the raphe nuclei in the regulation of ponto-geniculo-occipital wave activity, *Brain Res.* **58:**313–330.
Spooner, C. E., and Winters, W. D., 1966, Neuropharmacological profile of the young chick, *Int. J. Neuropharmacol.* **5:**217–236.
Spooner, C. E., Mandell, A. J., Winters, W. D., Sabbot, I. M., and Cruikshank, M. K., 1968, Pharmacological and biochemical correlates of 5-hydroxytryptamine entry into the central nervous system during maturation, *Proc. West. Pharmacol. Soc.* **11:**98–105.
Stein, D., Jouvet, M., and Pujol, J. F., 1974, Effect of alpha methyl-p-tyrosine upon cerebral amine metabolism and sleep states in the cat, *Brain Res.* **72:**360–365.
Stern, W. C., and Morgane, P. J., 1973a, Effects of reserpine on sleep and brain biogenic amine levels in the cat, *Psychopharmacologia* **28:**275–286.
Stern, W. C., and Morgane, P. J., 1973b, Effects of α-methyltyrosine on REM sleep and brain amine levels in the cat, *Biol. Psychiat.* **6:**301–306.
Stern, W. C., and Morgane, P. J., 1974, Theoretical view of REM sleep function: maintenance of catecholamine in the central nervous system, *Behav. Biol.* **11:**1–32.
Stern, W. C., Morgane, P. J., Panksepp, J., Zolovick, A., and Jalowiec, J. E., 1972, Elevation of REM sleep following inhibition of protein synthesis, *Brain Res.* **47:**254–258.
Stern, W. C., Jalowiec, J. E., and Morgane, P. J., 1974, Growth hormone and sleep in the cat, in: *Sleep Research*, Vol. 3 (M. H. Chase, W. C. Stern, and P. L. Walter, eds.), Brain Information Service, p. 173, Brain Res. Inst., University of California, Los Angeles.
Stolk, J., Barchas, J., Dement, W., and Schauberg, S., 1969, Brain catecholamine metabolism following p-chlorophenylalanine treatment, *Pharmacologist* **11:**258.
Tabushi, K., and Himwich, H. E., 1969, The acute effects of reserpine on the sleep–wakefulness cycle in rabbits, *Psychopharmacologia* **16:**240–252.
Takagi, H., and Matsuzaki, M., 1968, Sleep state and its induction by sodium butyrate in acute "encéphale isolé" and "isolated midbrain pons-medulla" preparations, *Jpn. J. Physiol.* **18:**380–390.
Thoenen, H., and Tranzer, J. P., 1973, The pharmacology of 6-hydroxydopamine, *Annu. Rev. Pharmacol.* **13:**169–180.
Torda, C., 1967, Effect of brain serotonin depletion on sleep in rats, *Brain Res.* **6:**375–377.
Torda, C., 1968, Effects of changes of brain norepinephrine content of sleep cycle in rat, *Brain Res.* **10:**200–207.
Torii, S., Mitsumori, K., Inubushi, S., and Yanagisawa, I., 1973, The REM sleep-inducing action of a naturally occurring organic bromine compound in the encéphale isolé cat, *Psychopharmacologia* **28:**65–76.
Ursin, R., 1972, Differential effect of para-chlorophenylalanine on the two slow wave sleep stages in the cat, *Acta Physiol. Scand.* **86:**278–285.
Valatx, J. L., Chouvet, G., and Jouvet, M., 1975, Sleep–waking cycle of the hypophysectomized rat, *Progr. Brain Res.* **42:**115–120.
Van Meter, W. G., and Ayala, G. F., 1961, EEG effect of intracarotid or intravertebral arterial administration of d-amphetamine in rabbits with basilar artery ligation, *Electroencephalogr. Clin. Neurophysiol.* **13:**382–384.
Villablanca, J. H., 1966, Effects of atropine, eserine and adrenaline in cats with

mesencephalic transection and in the "isolated hemisphere" cat preparation, *Arch. Biol. Med. Exp.* **3:**118–129.
VILLABLANCA, J., and MARCUS, R. J., 1974, Long term sleep–wakefulness effects of caudate nucleus ablation in cats, in: *Sleep Research,* Vol. 3 (M. H. Chase, W. C. Stern, and P. L. Walter, eds.), Brain Information Service, p. 26, Brain Res. Inst., University of California, Los Angeles.
VIMONT-VICARY, P., 1966, La suppression des différents états de sommeil. Etude comportementale, EEG, et neuropharmacologique chez le chat, Thèse Université de Lyon (J. Tixier, ed.), 95 pp.
VITALE-NEUGEBAUER, A., GINDITTA, A., VITALE, B., and GIAQUINTO, S., 1970, Pattern of RNA synthesis in rabbit cortex during sleep, *J. Neurochem.* **17:**1263–1273.
WALLACH, M. B., WINTERS, W. D., MANDELL, A. J., and SPOONER, C. E., 1969, Effects of antidepressant drugs on wakefulness and sleep in the cat, *Electroencephalogr. Clin. Neurophysiol.* **27:**574–581.
WEIL-MALHERBE, H., AXELROD, J., and TOMCHICK, R., 1959, Blood–brain barrier for adrenaline, *Science* **129:**1226–1227.
WEISSMAN, A., and KOE, B. K., 1965, Behavioral effects of L-alpha-methyl-tyrosine hydroxylase, *Life Sci.* **4:**1037–1049.
WEITZMAN, E. D., RAPPORT, M. M., MCGREGOR, P., and JACOBY, J., 1968, Sleep patterns of the monkey and brain serotonin concentration: effect of *p*-chlorophenylalanine, *Science* **160:**1361–1363.
WEITZMAN, E. D., MCGREGOR, P., MOORE, C., and JACOBY, J., 1969, The effect of alpha-methyl-paratyrosine on sleep patterns of the monkey, *Life Sci.* **8:**751–758.
WIKLER, A., 1952, Pharmacologic dissociation of behaviour and EEG "sleep patterns" in dogs. Morphine, *N*-allylmorphine and atropine, *Proc. Soc. Exp. Biol.* **79:**165–261.
YANAGIZAWA, I., and YOSHIKAWA, K., 1968, Microdetermination of bromine in cerebrospinal fluid, *Clin. Chim. Acta* **21:**217–224.
ZATTONI, J., and ROSSI, G. F., 1967, A study of the hypnogenic action of "Mogadon" by selective injection into carotid and vertebral circulation, *Physiol. Behav.* **2:**277–282.
ZOLOVICK, A. J., STERN, W. C., JALOWIEC, J. E., PANKSEPP, J., and MORGANE, P. J., 1973*a*, Sleep–waking patterns and brain biogenic amine levels in cats after administration of 6-hydroxydopamine into the dorsolateral pontine tegmentum, *Pharmacol. Biochem. Behav.* **1:**557–568.
ZOLOVICK, A. J., STERN, W. C., PANKSEPP, J., JALOWIEC, J. E., and MORGANE, P. J., 1973*b*, Sleep–waking patterns in cats after administration of fenfluramine and other monoaminergic-modulating drugs, *Pharmacol. Biochem. Behav.* **1:**41–46.

7

DRUG-INDUCED MOTOR BEHAVIOR

Peter H. Kelly

1. INTRODUCTION

The property of directed movement which most animals possess is a major difference between them and other living things and is largely responsible for their ability to manipulate their environment. In fact, active motor behavior appears to be crucial for perceptual development and learning (Held and Hein, 1963). Here we consider some of the neural mechanisms which underly three types of drug-induced motor behavior. The first of these, locomotor activity, is influenced not only by drugs but by a wide variety of genetic, developmental, hormonal, environmental, motivational, and endogenous rhythmic factors. It is hoped that elucidation of the mechanisms of drug-induced locomotor activity can provide clues as to how some of these other factors might affect locomotor behavior. The second type of activity, stereotyped behavior, is rarely seen in the undrugged animal but is reported to be a striking feature of human schizophrenic behavior (Bleuler, 1950). The third type of behavior, drug-induced circling, is generally studied in animals with some type of unilateral lesion but can be induced in the intact animal (Glick *et al.*, 1976). The behavior is closely related to asymmetric dopaminergic activity in the corpora striata, and its study may reveal functional relationships within the basal ganglia and between them and other brain structures. For reasons of consistency the experiments considered here are mainly restricted to those performed on the rat.

Peter H. Kelly • Department of Pharmacology, Michigan State University, East Lansing, Michigan 48824.

2. LOCOMOTOR ACTIVITY

2.1. Drug Effects on Locomotor Activity

Many different types of drugs can influence locomotor activity, and the effects of a particular drug can depend on the dose administered. For example, barbiturates promote sleep in man and animals, but in lower doses can enhence the locomotor-stimulant effect of amphetamine in rats (Rushton and Steinberg, 1964). The effect of amphetamine-like drugs also depends on their dose. In low doses they increase locomotor activity, whereas at higher doses a stereotyped syndrome of licking, biting, and gnawing appears together with a suppression of locomotor activity. Morphine also stimulates the locomotor activity of rats (Fog, 1970; Ayhan and Randrup, 1973) and mice (Hollinger, 1969; Rethy et al., 1971) in low doses, but suppresses activity as the dose is increased (Sloan et al., 1962; Kumar et al., 1971).

Despite these difficulties, drugs can still be classified into those that predominantly decrease activity and those which predominantly stimulate activity. Most notable among the depressants of activity are the barbiturates, alcohol, neuroleptics, inhibitors of catecholamine synthesis or storage, and cholinomimetic agents. Stimulants of activity include amphetamine and related compounds, cocaine, morphine and other opiates, antagonists of the muscarinic actions of acetylcholine, and nicotinic agonists.

Of the various classes of drugs which increase locomotor activity, the most pronounced stimulant effects are produced by amphetamine and related compounds and cocaine. This observation is reflected in the fact that these compounds are among those which have been most thoroughly studied. In the present section we present results of experiments which indicate that the locomotor stimulant action of d-amphetamine and cocaine may be due to an action on a particular system of neurons in the brain, the mesolimbic dopamine system.

2.2. Neural Mechanisms of the Locomotor-Stimulant Action of Amphetamine

2.2.1. Pharmacological Studies

A variety of pharmacological procedures have been used in an attempt to relate the locomotor-stimulant effect of amphetamine to an action on a particular system of chemically coded neurons. These procedures have included pretreatment with inhibitors of neurotransmitter synthesis or with drugs (e.g., reserpine) which prevent the storage of some neurotransmitters in nerve endings. Other approaches have included attempts to correlate the potencies of the d- and l-isomers of amphetamine in behavioral tests with their pharmacological potencies in releasing or inhibiting the uptake of particular transmitters.

The use of the tyrosine hydroxylase inhibitor α-methyl-p-tyrosine (α-MT) has provided convincing evidence that amphetamine-induced locomotor activity is mediated by release of catecholamines. It has been shown that pretreatment with α-MT, to deplete the brain of noradrenaline (NA) and dopamine (DA), blocks the locomotor-stimulant effect of amphetamine (Weissman et al., 1966; Dominic and Moore, 1969). Depletion of NA and DA in the brain by reserpine pretreatment, however, does not block the amphetamine response (Van Rossum et al., 1962; Smith, 1963). Although these early results with reserpine were taken as evidence for a direct action of amphetamine on catecholamine receptors (Van Rossum et al., 1962; Smith, 1963), it is now generally accepted that they can be explained by the hypothesis that amphetamine-induced locomotor activity is mediated by a small reserpine-insensitive functional pool of transmitter which is rapidly repleted by synthesis. In this respect the action of the amphetamine congeners methylphenidate and pipradrol differs from that of amphetamine. Reserpine blocks the ability of these drugs to stimulate locomotor activity (Smith, 1963; Van Rossum and Hurkmans, 1964; Rech and Stolk, 1970; Scheel-Krüger, 1971), while α-MT is without effect (Aceto et al., 1967; Dominic and Moore, 1969; Scheel-Krüger, 1971; Thornburg and Moore, 1973c). Therefore, pipradrol and methylphenidate may act through a reserpine-sensitive pool of catecholamines, while amphetamine may act by selectively releasing newly synthesized catecholamines.

Since α-MT blocks the synthesis of both NA and DA, it is not possible with this drug to determine the relative importance of NA and DA in amphetamine-induced locomotor stimulation. Pretreatment with dopamine-β-hydroxylase inhibitors to reduce brain NA but not DA has produced variable results. In early experiments the locomotor activity produced by amphetamine or cocaine was blocked by the dopamine-β-hydroxylase inhibitor diethyldithiocarbamate (Pfeifer et al., 1966), while the stereotyped licking, biting, and gnawing was not (Randrup and Scheel-Krüger, 1966). However, there is evidence that some of the behavioral effects of diethyldithiocarbamate are caused by nonspecific effects, rather than by its effects on catecholamine synthesis (Moore, 1969; Thornburg and Moore, 1971). Because of these problems in the use of diethyldithiocarbamate, more recent studies have utilized the dopamine-β-hydroxylase inhibitors FLA-63 or U-14,624. When administered intraperitoneally, both drugs markedly suppress spontaneous locomotor activity (Svensson and Waldeck, 1969; Svensson, 1971b; Von Voigtlander and Moore, 1970; Thornburg and Moore, 1971), and partially suppress the amphetamine-induced locomotor activity of mice (Svensson, 1970). The effects may, however, be related to nonspecific effects of these drugs. When FLA-63 is injected intravenously to avoid peritoneal irritation, the locomotor-stimulant action of amphetamine in rats is not reduced (Corrodi et al., 1970). Thornburg and Moore (1973c) have administered FLA-63 and U-14,624 in the diets of mice as another means of avoiding peritoneal irritation. In doses which inhibited the synthesis of noradrenaline and reduced the concentration of noradrenaline in the brain, these drugs did not significantly decrease spontaneous locomotor activity or amphetamine-induced activity. Addition of α-MT to the diet reduced both spontaneous activity and amphetamine-induced activity (Thornburg and Moore, 1973c). These results therefore indicate that release of dopamine rather than noradrenaline is involved in the locomotor-stimulant action of amphetamine.

In agreement with this hypothesis, low doses of neuroleptics can antagonize amphetamine-induced locomotor activity (Schlechter and Butcher, 1972; Maj et al., 1972). There is considerable agreement that a major mechanism of action of these drugs is blockade of dopamine receptors (Andén et al., 1970; Kebabian et al., 1972; Miller et al., 1974; Iversen, 1975).

The relative potencies of d- and l-amphetamine as stimulants of locomotor activity in vivo and inhibitors of dopamine uptake in vitro are also in agreement with the hypothesis that amphetamine-induced locomotor activity results from an action on dopaminergic neurons, although earlier studies (Coyle and Snyder, 1969; Taylor and Snyder, 1971) were interpreted differently. Recent studies from several laboratories have shown that d-amphetamine is three to five times more potent than l-amphetamine as a stimulant of locomotor activity (Rech and Stolk, 1970; Thornburg and Moore, 1972; Svensson, 1971a; Ellinwood and Balster, 1974), as an inhibitor of dopamine uptake in vitro (Thornburg and Moore, 1973a; Ferris et al., 1972; Svensson, 1971a), and in its ability to release dopamine in vivo (Chiueh and Moore, 1974b). These results are therefore consistent with the idea that locomotor stimulation results from an effect on dopaminergic neurons.

Costa et al. (1972) have examined the effect of a low dose of amphetamine on catecholamine turnover in the rat brain. They reported that a dose of amphetamine which stimulated locomotor activity but which produced no stereotyped licking, biting, or gnawing increased the turnover of dopamine in the brain but not that of noradrenaline. These results are therefore further evidence that dopamine release is involved in amphetamine-induced locomotor excitation.

2.2.2. Lesion Studies

The finding that the chemical analog of the catecholamines, 6-hydroxydopamine (6-OHDA), could be used to selectively destroy catecholamine-containing neurons in the brain (Ungerstedt, 1968; Bloom et al., 1969; Uretsky and Iversen, 1969, 1970; Breese and Traylor, 1970) opened up new approaches in catecholamine research. Despite some claims that 6-OHDA causes considerable nonspecific histological damage (Poirier et al., 1972; Butcher et al., 1974; Evans et al., 1975), biochemical studies have shown no changes in chemical markers of neurotransmitter systems other than those utilizing catecholamines after intraventricular (Bloom et al., 1969; Uretsky and Iversen, 1970; Jacks et al., 1972) or intracerebral (Von Voigtlander and Moore, 1973; Kelly et al., 1977) injections of 6-OHDA.

Several procedures have been used to selectively destroy either noradrenergic or dopaminergic neurons with 6-OHDA. To deplete whole brain dopamine, but not noradrenaline, 6-OHDA has been injected intraventricularly or intracisternally after pretreatment with inhibitors of the catecholamine uptake mechanism of noradrenergic neurons, such as protriptyline (Evetts and Iversen, 1970) or desipramine (DMI) (Breese and Traylor, 1971). To improve the dopamine depletion, pargyline can be included in the pretreatment (Breese and Traylor, 1970, 1971). Noradrenaline can be selectively depleted, although not so completely, by repeated injection of low doses of 6-OHDA (Breese and Traylor, 1971) or by peripheral injections of 6-OHDA into neonatal animals (Taylor et al., 1972). This latter procedure destroys the noradrenergic innervation of some forebrain regions, such as the cortex and hippocampus, without destroying the noradrenergic innervation of more caudal regions. A limitation in the use of intraventricular and intracisternal injections as a means of determining the neural substrate of a behavioral response is that neurons in different systems which use the same transmitter are destroyed. This limitation can be overcome by localized stereotaxic injection of small amounts of 6-OHDA into the nerve terminals, axons, or cell bodies of catecholamine neurons. In the remainder of this section the effects of treatments which produce large-scale depletion of whole-brain noradrenaline or dopamine, or both, on amphetamine-induced locomotor activity will be described. These studies indicate a more important role of dopamine in this behavioral response. The results of experiments in which local microinjections of 6-OHDA have been used to destroy either the mesolimbic dopaminergic neurons or those of the nigrostriatal pathway (Kelly et al., 1975; Iversen and Kelly, 1975; Kelly and Iversen, 1976) will then be described.

When both noradrenaline and dopamine neurons are largely destroyed by intraventricular injections of 6-OHDA into neonate rats (Fig. 1) (Creese and Iversen, 1973) or by injection into adult rats pretreated with a monoamine oxidase inhibitor (Fibiger et al., 1973; Hollister et al., 1974), the locomotor stimulation produced by amphetamine is blocked. Interestingly a large depletion of catecholamines is necessary to achieve this result, and incomplete blockade (Fibiger et al., 1973; Hollister et al., 1974) or no blockade (Evetts et al., 1970) is seen after one 200–250 μg 6-OHDA injection into untreated rats. Hollister et al. (1974) found that 6-OHDA treatments which selectively reduced the whole-brain concentration of dopamine were also able to block amphetamine-induced locomotor activity, while selective reduction of noradrenaline was without effect. Creese and Iversen (1975) have used stereotaxic injections of 6-OHDA into the dorsal and ventral noradrenergic bundles to destroy noradrenergic neurons. They found that these procedures also did not attenuate amphetamine-induced locomotor activity.

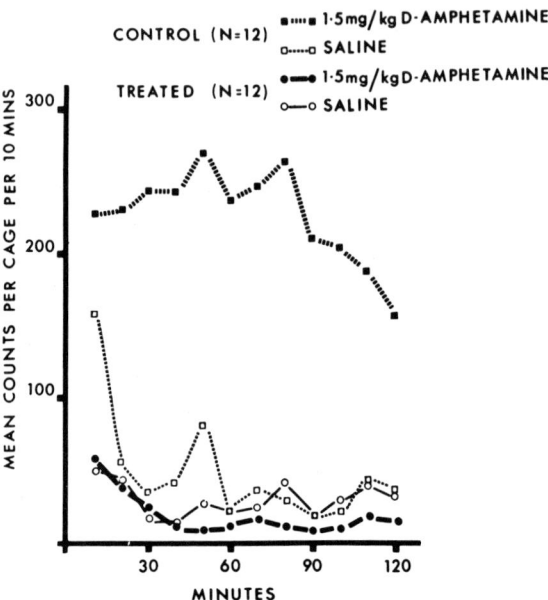

Fig. 1. Locomotor response to saline and 1.5 mg/kg D-amphetamine of adult rats, treated intraventricularly as neonates with 6-OHDA or vehicle control. From Creese and Iversen (1973).

These findings therefore indicated a major role of dopamine neurons and not noradrenergic neurons in amphetamine-induced locomotor activity. The two largest systems of dopaminergic neurons in the brain are the nigrostriatal pathway and the mesolimbic dopamine system (Ungerstedt, 1971b). Nigrostriatal dopaminergic neurons have their cell bodies in the substantia nigra and innervate the caudate-putamen and globus pallidus, while mesolimbic dopamine neurons originate in the A10 group of cell bodies in the ventral tegmentum and innervate the nucleus accumbens and olfactory tubercle (Ungerstedt, 1971b). Kelly et al. (1975) destroyed the mesolimbic or nigrostriatal dopaminergic terminals selectively by localized injection of 6-OHDA into the nucleus accumbens or caudate nucleus. Animals with a 6-OHDA lesion of the nucleus accumbens showed a reduced locomotor-activity response to amphetamine, but an enhanced locomotor response to the directly acting dopamine agonist apomorphine (Fig. 2). The enhanced apomorphine response may result from denervation supersensitivity. Animals with the caudate 6-OHDA lesion showed neither of these changes but showed changes in drug-induced stereotypy. The results of these experiments therefore suggest that release of dopamine from the neurons of the mesolimbic system rather than those of the nigrostriatal system is important for the stimulation of locomotor activity by amphetamine. In addition to destroying mesolimbic dopaminergic terminals, the 6-OHDA lesion of the nucleus accumbens destroyed noradrenergic fibers

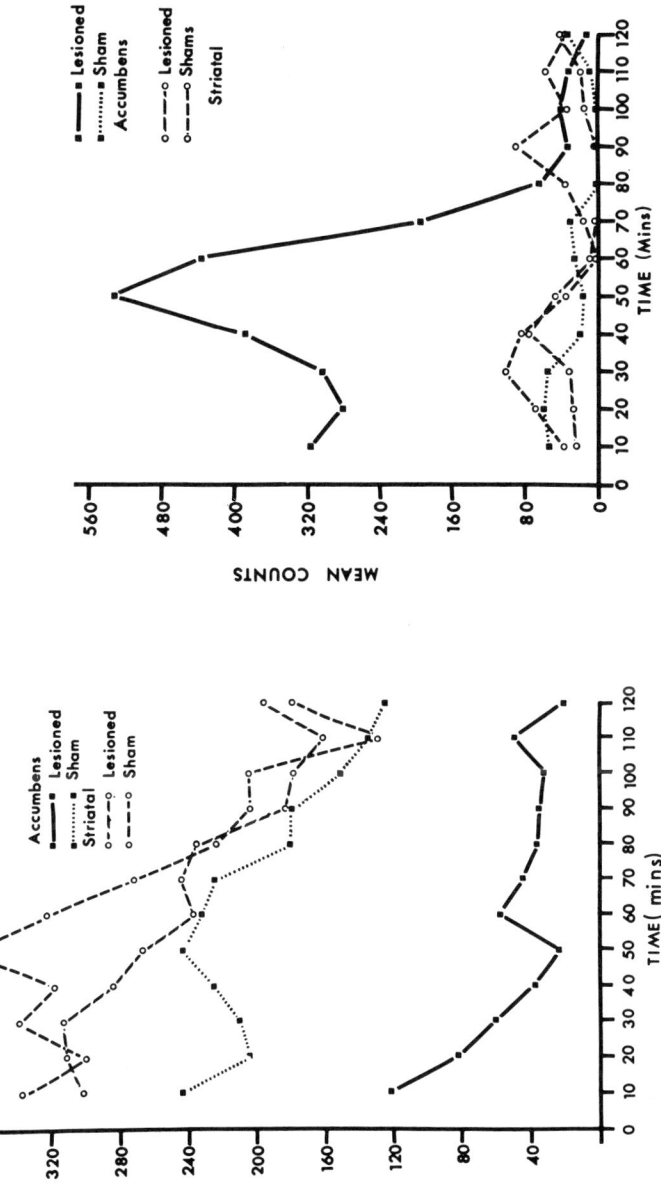

FIG. 2. Locomotor activity response to 1.5 mg/kg D-amphetamine 14 days post-op (left) and 1.0 mg/kg apomorphine 10 days post-op (right). Mean photocell beam interruptions per 10 min for caudate and nucleus accumbens 6-OHDA-lesioned rats and their sham-operated controls. From Kelly *et al.* (1975).

innervating the forebrain. However, desipramine pretreatment before the 6-OHDA lesion prevented this destruction of noradrenergic fibers (Iversen and Kelly, 1975; Kelly and Iversen, 1976), and similar effects on amphetamine- and apomorphine-induced locomotor activity were obtained. The locomotor-stimulant effect of cocaine was also blocked in the lesioned rats (Kelly and Iversen, 1976). These observations therefore suggest that destruction of noradrenergic fibers is not important in the changes in drug-induced locomotor activity observed after 6-OHDA lesions of the nucleus accumbens, and indicate that effects on dopamine release in the nucleus accumbens are involved in the locomotor stimulation produced by both amphetamine and cocaine.

In addition to apomorphine, rats with 6-OHDA lesions of the nucleus accumbens also show an enhanced locomotor-activity response to other drugs which are thought to act as dopamine agonists. Of a series of aporphine alkaloids, (±)-N-n-propylnorapomorphine is much more potent than apomorphine (Kelly et al., 1976a), and (±)-N-n-propylnorapocodeine is also effective. Properties consistent with those of dopamine agonists are also shown by ergometrine (Woodruff et al., 1976), by the rigid analog of dopamine 2-amino-6,7-dihydroxy-1,2,3,4-tetrahydronaphthalene (ADTN) (Woodruff et al., 1976), and by LSD (d-lysergic acid diethylamide) (Kelly and Iversen, 1975). In contrast to 6-OHDA-induced lesions, electrolytic lesions of the nucleus accumbens reduce the locomotor-stimulant action of ADTN (Woodruff et al., 1976).

2.2.3. Intracranial Injections

Injections of dopaminergic agonists into the nucleus accumbens stimulate locomotor activity. This effect was first seen after injections of ergometrine (Pijnenburg et al., 1973), and could be tentatively attributed to stimulation of dopamine receptors after dopamine itself was shown to be effective (Pijnenburg and Van Rossum, 1973; Pijnenburg et al., 1976). Noradrenaline injections into the nucleus accumbens or dopamine injections into the caudate nucleus are much less effective (Pijnenburg and Van Rossum, 1973; Pijnenburg et al., 1975b; Pijnenburg et al., 1976). d-Amphetamine is more potent than dopamine when injected into the nucleus accumbens (Pijnenburg et al., 1976). When injected into the olfactory tubercle dopamine, d-amphetamine and apomorphine also stimulate locomotor activity (Costall and Naylor, 1975; Pijnenburg et al., 1976). Cholera toxin injected into the nucleus accumbens of rats stimulates locomotor activity and adenylate cyclase activity for several days following a lag period (Miller and Kelly, 1975), in agreement with the view that the postsynaptic actions of dopamine in the central nervous system involve activation of adenylate cyclase.

Dopamine antagonists administered either peripherally or into the nucleus accumbens antagonize the locomotor stimulation produced by application of dopamine or its agonists into the nucleus accumbens. For example, the effects of ergometrine or ADTN are antagonized by low intraperitoneal doses of haloperidol or pimozide (Pijnenburg et al., 1973; Elkhawad and Woodruff, 1975). The effects of dopamine in nialamide-pretreated rats are also blocked by peripherally injected neuroleptics, including clozapine and thioridazine (Costall and Naylor, 1976). The effects of dopamine injections into the nucleus accumbens are blocked by haloperidol administered through the same cannula (Pijnenburg et al., 1975b). Similar application of the noradrenergic α-blocker phentolamine potentiates the dopamine effect, for reasons presently unknown, and propranolol, an adrenergic β-blocker, produces a very weak inhibition of the dopamine-induced hyperactivity. Noradrenaline-induced hyperactivity also was not inhibited by propranolol and was potentiated by phentolamine, whereas it was blocked by haloperidol. This may indicate that the effect of noradrenaline injected into the nucleus accumbens is due to an effect on dopamine receptors.

Pijnenburg et al. (1975a) have also examined the effect of catecholamine antagonists, injected into the nucleus accumbens or caudate nucleus, on amphetamine-induced hyperactivity. This hyperactivity was antagonized by the dopamine antagonist haloperidol injected into the nucleus accumbens, but not by phentolamine or propranolol. Haloperidol injected into the caudate nucleus was ineffective in antagonizing amphetamine hyperactivity. These results, in agreement with the previously discussed 6-OHDA lesion studies, provide further support for an important function of the dopaminergic innervation of the nucleus accumbens in amphetamine-induced locomotor activity.

Intraventricular infusions of amphetamine also cause a stimulation of locomotor activity which can be blocked by pretreatment with α-MT (Segal et al., 1974). Unlike the effects of peripherally injected amphetamine, the locomotor-stimulant effect of intraventricular amphetamine is also blocked by reserpine (Segal et al., 1974).

2.3. Roles of Transmitters Other than Dopamine in Locomotor Activity

2.3.1. Serotonin

There is much evidence that a serotoninergic system in the brain inhibits the locomotor activity produced by amphetamine and apomorphine. On the other hand, elevating serotonin (5-HT) synthesis in the brain produces a different kind of hyperactivity syndrome (Grahame-Smith, 1971).

The inhibtory nature of a serotoninergic influence on amphetamine-induced activity is demonstrated by the observations that p-chlorophenylalanine (PCPA), which depletes the brain of 5-HT (Koe and Weissman, 1966) by inhibiting the enzyme tryptophan hydroxylase, enhances amphetamine-induced locomotor activity (Mabry and Campbell, 1973). Similarly, the locomotor-stimulant effect of amphetamine is enhanced in rats with lesions of the raphe nuclei (Neill et al., 1972) which contains the cells of origin of the ascending 5-HT systems (Ungerstedt, 1971b). After intracisternal 5,6-dihydroxytryptamine, a neurotoxic agent which causes a relatively selective destruction of serotoninergic neurons (Baumgarten et al., 1971), amphetamine activity is also potentiated (Breese et al., 1974). This effect, like that of PCPA, is reversed by the serotonin precursor 5-hydroxytryptophan. Breese et al. (1974) also attribute an unexpected inhibition of amphetamine-induced activity by pargyline to an effect on serotoninergic neurons, since both the rise in brain serotonin caused by pargyline and the inhibition of amphetamine-induced locomotor activity were prevented by PCPA pretreatment.

Apomorphine-induced locomotor activity also is potentiated by PCPA (Grabowska et al., 1973) and raphe lesions (Grabowska, 1974) and inhibited by 5-hydroxytryptophan (Grabowska et al., 1973).

The anatomical basis for the inhibition of spontaneous and amphetamine-induced activity by serotonin may be partly the serotoninergic innervation of the hippocampus, although a direct action of 5-HT in the nucleus accumbens is suggested by the observation that 5-HT injected into the nucleus accumbens can antagonize the locomotor-stimulant effect of dopamine injected there (Costall et al., 1976). Lesions of the dorsal hippocampus cause an increase in locomotor activity (Campbell et al., 1971), and raphe lesions cause no further increase in activity in rats with lesions of the dorsal hippocampus (Jacobs et al., 1975a). Similarly, PCPA produces no additional increase in the locomotor activity of rats with dorsal hippocampal lesions (Jacobs et al., 1975a). Mabry and Campbell (1974) suggest that the serotoninergic inhibitory system of amphetamine-induced activity develops between 10 and 15 days of age, which, if this system does involve the hippocampus, is in accord with a report (Moorcroft, 1971) that hippocampal lesions do not increase activity until around 15 days. Also increases in spontaneous activity (Srebro and Lorens, 1975; Jacobs et al., 1974) and in amphetamine-induced activity (Jacobs et al., 1975b) are seen after median raphe lesions, but not dorsal raphe lesions. The serotoninergic innervations of the hippocampus arises predominantly in the median raphe (Lorens and Guldberg, 1974; Jacobs et al., 1974).

2.3.2. Noradrenaline

Intracisternal (Hollister et al., 1974) or localized (Creese and Iversen, 1975) 6-OHDA treatments which selectively deplete the brain of noradrenaline do not block amphetamine-induced locomotor activity. Also dopamine-β-hydroxylase inhibitors do not substantially reduce amphetamine-induced locomotor activity when care is taken to avoid their nonspecific effects (Corrodi et al., 1970; Thornburg and Moore, 1973c). There is, however, evidence that noradrenaline-receptor activation plays a role in the reversal of reserpine-induced suppression of locomotor activity (Andén et al., 1973).

The most direct evidence that activation of noradrenaline receptors can produce locomotor activity comes from intraventricular infusion experiments. Geyer et al. (1972) infused noradrenaline and dopamine intraventricularly into rats. Both compounds stimulated locomotor activity, and noradrenaline was more potent than dopamine. Imipramine, which inhibits the catecholamine-uptake mechanism of noradrenergic but not dopaminergic neurons, blocked the locomotor response to dopamine without affecting the response to noradrenaline. It was therefore suggested that the activity produced by dopamine is due to its conversion to or displacement of noradrenaline after being taken up into noradrenergic neurons. After α-MT, which reduces the amount of noradrenaline available to be displaced without inhibiting the synthesis of noradrenaline from dopamine, the dopamine-induced response was unaltered (Geyer and Segal, 1973). This suggests that the DA-induced hyperactivity is due to the conversion of dopamine to noradrenaline. It is not presently clear how to integrate these data with the large body of evidence implicating dopaminergic, rather than noradrenergic, mechanisms in the locomotor-stimulant action of amphetamine and cocaine.

Intraventricular amphetamine also produced an increase in locomotor activity which could be blocked by α-MT pretreatment (Segal et al., 1974) and by reserpine. In this respect the effect of intraventricular amphetamine differs from that of peripherally injected amphetamine, the effect of which on locomotor activity is not blocked by reserpine (Van Rossum et al., 1962; Smith, 1963).

Both noradrenergic and dopaminergic mechanisms may be involved in the locomotor stimulation produced by 4,α-dimethyl-m-tyramine (H77/77) in rats. The locomotor activity produced by this drug is antagonized by α-MT and by the dopamine-β-hydroxylase inhibitor FLA-63 (Buus Lassen, 1974), although it is not clear whether any attempts were made to minimize possible nonspecific effects of the drugs. H77/77-induced activity is also antagonized by inhibitors of noradrenaline uptake such as desipramine or imipramine (Carlsson et al., 1969; Buus Lassen, 1974) and dopamine-receptor blockers (Buus Lassen, 1974).

2.3.3. Acetylcholine

The muscarinic effects of acetylcholine appear to exert an inhibitory influence on locomotor activity. Cholinomimetic drugs reduce spontaneous locomotor activity and antagonize amphetamine-induced locomotor activity (Fibiger et al., 1970, 1971). Conversely, antimuscarinic drugs increase locomotor activity (Meyers et al., 1964; Payne and Andersson, 1967; Pradhan and Roth, 1968; Thornburg and Moore, 1973b) and potentiate amphetamine-induced activity (Campbell et al., 1969; Fibiger et al., 1970). Thornburg and Moore (1973b) showed that the stimulation of locomotor activity produced by anticholinergic drugs in mice could be reduced by α-MT but not by FLA-63 administered in the diet, suggesting that a dopaminergic system is involved in the mediation of anticholinergic drug-induced locomotor activity.

The antimuscarinic actions of neuroleptic drugs may modify their effects on amphetamine-induced locomotor activity. The neuroleptics thioridazine and clozapine possess both antidopaminergic (Miller et al., 1974) and antimuscarinic actions (Miller and Hiley, 1974). In 11-day-old rats, whose cholinergic neurons are probably not developed (McGeer et al., 1971), they block amphetamine-induced locomotor activity (Miller and Sahakian, 1974) but are ineffective in adult rats. This failure to block amphetamine-induced activity in adult rats is attributed to the display of two opposing actions (antimuscarinic and antidopaminergic) in the control of amphetamine-induced activity.

2.3.4. GABA (γ-Aminobutyric Acid)

One day after injection of an inhibitor of GABA-transaminase, ethanolamine-O-sulfate, into the nucleus accumbens, GABA levels in the nucleus accumbens, olfactory tubercle, and striatum were elevated 3- to 5-fold. At the same time, amphetamine-induced locomotor activity, and that produced by dopamine injected into the nucleus accumbens, was blocked (Pycock and Horton, 1976). These experiments suggest that elevated GABA levels can affect dopamine-mediated locomotor activity, although precise localization of the GABA effect is not yet possible.

2.4. Conclusions

Locomotor activity is stimulated by many drugs, motivational states, and environmental events. The neural basis of most of these effects is unknown. The locomotor stimulation produced by amphetamine, cocaine, and some other drugs, however, appears to depend on release of dopamine from nerve terminals in the brain. This conclusion is based on the effects of altering dopaminergic neurotransmission by synthesis inhibitors or receptor antagonists and by destroying dopaminergic neurons with 6-hydroxydopamine. Stimulation of mesolimbic but not striatal dopamine receptors elicits locomotor activity. The locomotor-stimulant action of amphetamine and cocaine is blocked by bilateral 6-OHDA-induced lesions of the mesolimbic dopaminergic innervation of the nucleus accumbens and olfactory tubercle, and the amphetamine effect is also blocked by bilateral injection of a dopamine antagonist directly into the nucleus accumbens. These experiments strongly implicate the mesolimbic dopamine system in the locomotor-stimulant effects of psychostimulants. The locomotor-stimulant effects of amphetamine appear to be antagonized by serotoninergic mechanisms, by GABA, and by the muscarinic actions of acetylcholine. The anatomical basis of these actions is only partly known. On the basis of experiments with synthesis inhibitors, receptor antagonists, and 6-hydroxydopamine lesions, noradrenergic mechanisms appear to play no role in amphetamine-induced locomotor activity, but intraventricular infusion of noradrenaline does stimulate activity.

3. STEREOTYPED BEHAVIOR

3.1. The Drug-Induced Stereotyped Behavior Syndrome

As the dose of amphetamine administered to a rat is increased, the predominant behavior switches from locomotor activity, which is maximal at fairly low doses, to a stereotyped syndrome of licking, biting, and gnawing behavior. Locomotor activity has often been considered as a less intense form of stereotyped behavior and has been assessed on the same rating scale. The term "stereotyped hyperactivity" has often been used to describe the effects of amphetamine. In the present discussion, however, we will use the term stereotypy to refer only to the sniffing, licking, biting, and gnawing syndrome, as there is evidence that this syndrome has a separate neuroanatomical substrate from that which mediates amphetamine-induced locomotor activity (Ernst and Smelik, 1966; Fog et al., 1967; Pijnenburg and Van Rossum, 1973; Kelly et al., 1975). The evidence that amphetamine-induced stereotyped behavior is mediated by release of dopamine from neurons which innervate the striatum has been extensively reviewed previously (e.g., Randrup and Munkvad, 1970) and will therefore be presented only briefly here. In addition to amphetamine, a variety of other drugs also produce the stereotyped behavior syndrome. These drugs include methamphetamine, methylphenidate, pipradrol, apomorphine, N-n-propylnorapomorphine, LSD-25, and cocaine (Randrup and Munkvad, 1970). Consistent with the view that stereotypy is mediated by a dopaminergic mechanism, many of these drugs have been shown to increase the release of dopamine into a ventriculocisternal perfusate (McKenzie and Szerb, 1968; Chiueh and Moore, 1974a,b, 1975) or to act as dopamine agonists *in vitro* (Miller et al., 1976; Von Hungen et al., 1974).

3.2. Neural Basis of Amphetamine-Induced Stereotypy

3.2.1. *Pharmacological Studies*

In early studies in which reserpine pretreatment was used to deplete neural stores of catecholamines, amphetamine-induced stereotyped behavior was not abolished (Van Rossum et al., 1962; Smith, 1963; Quinton and Halliwell, 1963). This observation led to the suggestion that amphetamine directly stimulates catecholamine receptors (Van Rossum et al., 1962; Smith, 1963). However, the synthesis of dopamine appears to persist after reserpine pretreatment (Andén et al., 1964; Stjärne, 1966; Persson and Waldeck, 1969). Amphetamine could therefore act by releasing newly synthesized catecholamines. This idea received support when it was demonstrated that pretreatment with the tyrosine-hydroxylase inhibitor α-methyl-p-tyrosine (α-MT) abolished the stereotyped activity produced by amphetamine (Weissman and Koe, 1965; Weissman et al., 1966; Randrup and Munkvad, 1966; Stolk and Rech, 1970). α-Methyl-p-tyrosine depletes the brain of both noradrenaline and dopamine (Weissman and Koe, 1965; Weissman et al., 1966) by inhibiting their synthesis.

In order to selectively deplete the brain of noradrenaline by inhibiting the synthesis of noradrenaline from dopamine, animals have been pretreated with inhibitors of dopamine-β-hydroxylase, such as diethyldithiocarbamate (DDC). DDC does not prevent amphetamine-induced stereotypy (Randrup and Scheel-Krüger, 1966) or that produced by dopa (Scheel-Krüger and Randrup, 1967). Noradrenergic α- or β-receptor-blocking drugs are also ineffective antagonists of stereotypy (Randrup et al., 1963; Herman, 1967; Janssen et al., 1965). These studies therefore implicate dopaminergic neurons in amphetamine-induced stereotyped behavior.

Effective antagonists (Janssen et al., 1965; Munkvad and Randrup, 1966) of stereotypy such as the phenothiazines and the butyrophenones are potent antagonists of the effects of dopamine *in vitro* (Kebabian et al., 1972; Miller et al., 1974; Iversen, 1975). In contrast, other sedatives such as meprobamate, chlordiazepoxide, and barbiturates are ineffective antagonists of stereotypy (Munkvad and Randrup, 1966).

3.2.2. Lesion Studies

Mechanical, electrolytic, and 6-OHDA-induced lesions have been used in attempts to elucidate the anatomical basis of amphetamine-induced stereotyped behavior. Most authors agree that amphetamine-induced stereotypy is reduced by bilateral lesions of the neostriatum (Fuxe and Ungerstedt, 1970; Fog et al., 1970; Naylor and Olley, 1972), although Divac (1972) found no effect. It has also been reported that bilateral lesions of the neostriatum abolish apomorphine-induced stereotyped behavior (Fuxe and Ungerstedt, 1970), although others find no effect (Divac, 1972; McKenzie, 1972; Costall and Naylor, 1973a).

Selective destruction of catecholamine neurons by various types of 6-hydroxydopamine (6-OHDA) treatments has produced clearer evidence that nigrostriatal dopamine neurons are involved in amphetamine-induced stereotypy. Amphetamine-induced stereotypy is blocked in rats with large-scale depletions of whole-brain catecholamines produced by administration of 6-OHDA into the cerebrospinal fluid of neonate rats (Creese and Iversen, 1973) or adult rats pretreated with a monoamine oxidase inhibitor (Fibiger et *al.*, 1973). When 6-OHDA treatments which selectively deplete either noradrenaline or dopamine are compared (Hollister *et al.*, 1974; Creese and Iversen, 1975), only rats with destruction of dopamine neurons show blockade of amphetamine-induced stereotypy.

Intranigral injections of 6-OHDA also block amphetamine-induced stereotypy (Creese and Iversen, 1972, 1975; Fibiger *et al.*, 1973). Similar injections of 6-OHDA not only destroy the nigrostriatal dopamine neurons but also cause some damage to the mesolimbic dopamine innervation of the nucleus accumbens and olfactory tubercle (Ungerstedt, 1971c). However, there is no blockade of intense amphetamine-induced stereotypy in rats with extensive destruction of the mesolimbic dopaminergic innervation of the nucleus accumbens and olfactory tubercle (Asher and Aghajanian, 1974; Kelly *et al.*, 1975). In contrast, 6-OHDA lesions of the caudate nucleus produced a reduction of amphetamine-induced stereotypy (Creese and Iversen, 1974; Asher and Aghajanian, 1974; Kelly *et al.*, 1975). The 6-OHDA injection into the caudate nucleus did not damage the dopaminergic innervation of the nucleus accumbens (Kelly *et al.*, 1975) or of the olfactory tubercle (Creese and Iversen, 1974; Kelly *et al.*, 1975). The blockade of stereotypy is apparent from the stereotypy ratings, and by the observation that the suppression of amphetamine-induced locomotor activity observed in animals demonstrating stereotyped behavior is not observed in the caudate 6-OHDA lesion group (Fig. 3).

The globus pallidus may play a role in drug-induced stereotypy. Electrolytic lesions of the globus pallidus block the stereotypy produced by amphetamine, ET495, and apomorphine for at least 6 days following the lesion (Costall and Naylor, 1973a,b, 1974a). Activity in pallidal neurons may therefore facilitate striatal activity or alternatively the output pathways for the expression of striatal dopaminergic activity as stereotypy may involve striatal efferent fibers running to or through the globus pallidus. A similar interpretation concerning the role of the olfactory tubercle may be placed on the observation that suction ablations of the olfactory tubercle decrease apomorphine-induced stereotyped behavior (McKenzie, 1972). However, electrolytic lesions of the olfactory tubercle were not effective in abolishing the more intense elements of stereotypy but reduced the weaker components such as sniffing. Lesions of the central amygdaloid nucleus abolished only the more intense components of amphetamine-induced stereotypy (Costall and Naylor, 1973a, 1974a).

3.2.3. *Intracranial Injections*

Injections of dopamine or anticholinergic drugs directly into the caudate nucleus were shown to elicit sniffing and biting in rats (Fog *et al.*, 1967; Fog and Pakkenberg, 1971), while similar injections into the cortex were ineffective. The syndrome was most pronounced when dopamine and an anticholinergic drug were injected together. The behavioral effect almost certainly

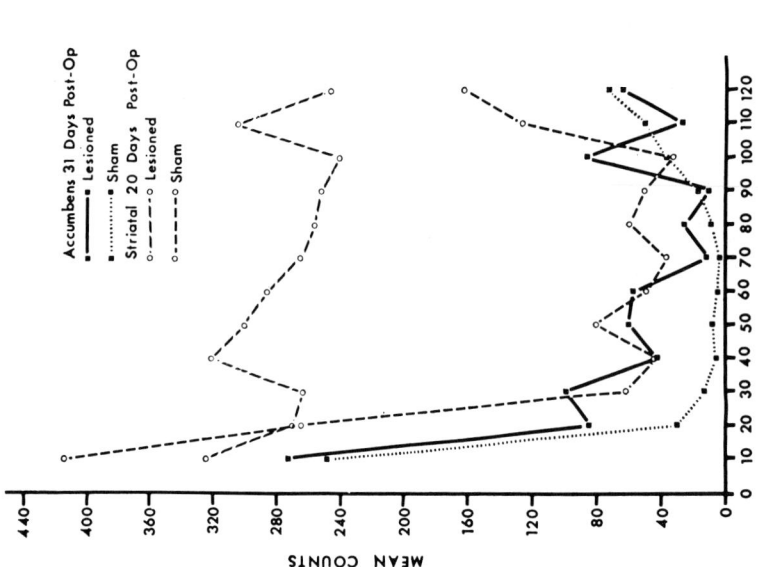
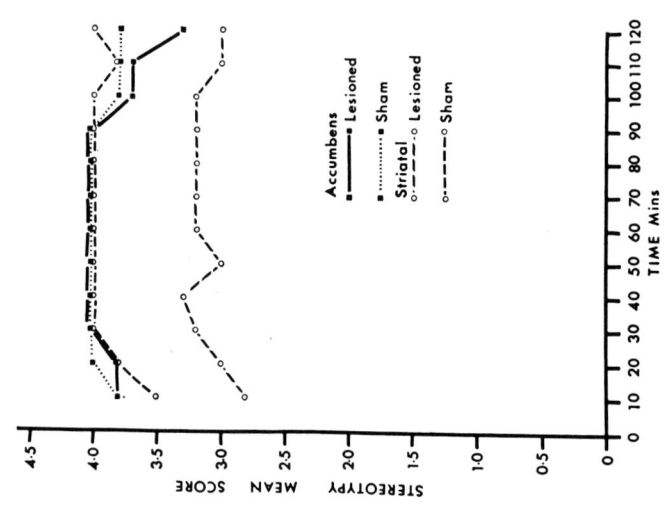

FIG. 3. Stereotypy response (left) and activity counts (right) to 5.0 mg/kg D-amphetamine in caudate and nucleus accumbens 6-OHDA-lesioned rats and their sham controls. From Kelly et al. (1975).

results from an action on the caudate nucleus itself as there is evidence that a variety of dyes, drugs, and neurotransmitters injected in a similar volume (1 μl) are distributed in a sphere of less than 1 mm radius (Myers, 1966; Myers et al., 1971). Ernst and Smelik (1966), using crystalline application of apomorphine or dopa into the caudate nucleus or globus pallidus of rats, also produced a syndrome of "compulsive gnawing."

In contrast to the effects of agonists, neuroleptics administered directly into the striatum produce catalepsy (Tseng et al., 1973) and abolish drug-induced stereotyped behavior (Fog et al., 1968). Pijnenburg et al. (1975c) recently reduced amphetamine- or apomorphine-induced stereotypy by injections of haloperidol into either the caudate nucleus or the nucleus accumbens. While confirming the role of the caudate nucleus in stereotypy, the effect of nucleus accumbens injections contrasts with the effects of 6-OHDA lesions of the nucleus accumbens (Asher and Aghajanian, 1974; Kelly et al., 1975).

3.3. Roles of Transmitters Other than Dopamine in Stereotyped Behavior

3.3.1. Acetylcholine

Data consistent with an antagonistic muscarinic cholinergic influence on amphetamine-induced stereotypy has been reported by Arnfred and Randrup (1968) and Scheel-Krüger (1970). Anticholinergic drugs potentiated the sniffing produced by a low dose of amphetamine, and reversed the neuroleptic blockade of amphetamine-induced licking and biting (Arnfred and Randrup, 1968). In mice, antimuscarinic drugs potentiated apomorphine-induced gnawing (Scheel-Krüger, 1970). Cholinergic agents potentiated the blockade of amphetamine-induced stereotypy produced by a low dose of α-MT (Arnfred and Randrup, 1968).

3.3.2. Serotonin (5-HT)

The role of serotonin in drug-induced stereotypy is less than clear. Methysergide did not affect the amphetamine-induced stereotypy of rats (Randrup and Munkvad, 1964). Also in rats a study by Rotrosen et al. (1972) showed that the stereotypy produced by apomorphine was unaltered by PCPA pretreatment or by the 5-HT antagonist methysergide. Neither was it affected by the 5-HT precursor l-tryptophan. These negative findings cannot be attributed to a "ceiling effect" as the stereotypy produced by the dose of apomorphine used could be potentiated by reserpine pretreatment. Breese et al. (1974) observed no effect of PCPA pretreatment on amphetamine-induced stereotyped behavior in rats. However, in guinea pigs Weiner et al. (1973, 1975) have reported data consistent with an inhibitory action of 5-HT on apomorphine and amphetamine-induced stereotypy. Methysergide slightly reduced the threshold dose of apomorphine necessary to produce stereotypy while 5-hydroxytryptophan increased it slightly.

In contrast to the negative effects on stereotypy of drugs which affect 5-HT mechanisms in rats, electrolytic lesions of the raphe nuclei have been reported to attenuate the stereotypy produced by d- and l-amphetamine, apomorphine, methylphenidate, and piribedil (Costall and Naylor, 1974b).

3.3.3. Noradrenaline

Pharmacological depletion of noradrenaline by DDC does not reduce amphetamine-induced stereotypy (Randrup and Scheel-Krüger, 1966). Destruction of noradrenergic neurons by 6-hydroxydopamine also does not affect amphetamine-induced stereotypy (Hollister *et al.*, 1974; Creese and Iversen, 1975). Noradrenaline does, however, appear to play a role in the stereotypy produced by repeated morphine administration. This stereotypy is blocked by reserpine, α-MT, and FLA-63 (Ayhan and Randrup, 1973). The noradrenaline receptor blockers phenoxybenzamine and aceperone also antagonized the effect of morphine.

3.3.4. GABA (γ-Aminobutyric Acid)

A 3- to 5-fold increase of GABA levels in the striatum and mesolimbic terminal regions produced by injection of ethanolamine-O-sulfate into the nucleus accumbens did not affect the apomorphine-induced stereotyped behavior of rats (Pycock and Horton, 1976). In the guinea pig a smaller increase in whole-brain GABA levels following sodium valproate failed to affect amphetamine-induced stereotypy (Patel *et al.*, 1976).

3.4. Conclusions

The stereotyped licking, biting, and gnawing syndrome can be produced by many drugs, and most of these have been shown to release dopamine in *in vivo* experiments or to act as dopamine agonists *in vitro*. Amphetamine-induced stereotypy is antagonized when dopaminergic neurotransmission is disrupted by synthesis inhibitors, receptor antagonists, or 6-hydroxydopamine-induced lesions. Application of dopamine and anticholinergic drugs directly into the striatum elicits stereotyped behavior. Conversely, amphetamine-induced stereotypy is blocked by injection of neuroleptics into the striatum or by 6-hydroxydopamine-induced lesions restricted to the striatum. These experiments suggest that amphetamine-induced stereotypy is produced, at least in part, by dopamine release from nigrostriatal neurons. Lesion studies also suggest that the globus pallidus, olfactory tubercle, and the central nucleus of the amygdala exert effects on drug-induced stereotyped behavior. There is evidence for antagonism of drug-induced stereotypy by the muscarinic actions of acetylcholine, but presently there is no clear evidence for major effects of noradrenaline, serotonin, or GABA.

4. ROTATIONAL BEHAVIOR

4.1. Drug-Induced Circling

Drug-induced circling after unilateral destruction of nigrostriatal dopamine fibers was first reported by Andén et al. (1966). Large unilateral lesions of the ascending DA fibers or unilateral removal of the neostriatum produced no clear-cut asymmetries in rats, but circling toward the lesioned side was produced by reserpine after nialamide pretreatment. After the dopamine precursor L-dopa, turning was toward the lesioned side in rats with the caudate lesion, but was often toward the unlesioned side after destruction of the ascending dopamine fibers at the level of the crus cerebri. The view that the circling was dependent on unilateral destruction of dopaminergic neurons was strengthened by the use of 6-OHDA to selectively destroy catecholamine-containing neurons. Ungerstedt and Arbuthnott (1970) prepared rats with unilateral 6-OHDA lesions of the substantia nigra and showed that amphetamine provoked marked turning toward the lesioned side. The amphetamine-induced rotation was correlated with the amount of damage to nigrostriatal dopamine neurons (Ungerstedt, 1971c) and could be blocked by drugs with dopamine-receptor-blocking properties such as haloperidol and spiroperidol (Ungerstedt, 1971c). The dopamine agonist apomorphine produced rotation in the opposite direction, i.e., toward the unlesioned side (Ungerstedt, 1971a), which was attributed to postsynaptic supersensitivity of the denervated dopamine receptors. Rotational behavior has been produced in rats with unilateral electrolytic lesions of the substantia nigra (Crow, 1971; Christie and Crow, 1971, 1973). Effective drugs include amphetamines and ephedrines (Christie and Crow, 1971) and cocaine after nialamide pretreatment (Christie and Crow, 1973). The electrolytically lesioned preparation may not be a suitable model for assessing the relative importance of pre- or postsynaptic actions of a drug, however, as it has been reported that both amphetamine and apomorphine provoke ipsilateral circling in this preparation (Costall et al., 1975). This pattern of responses depends upon damage to the substantia nigra pars reticulata (Dray et al., 1975).

Compounds which show the properties of dopamine agonists in the rotation model include ET 495 (Corrodi et al., 1972; Thornburg and Moore, 1974), N-n-propylnorapomorphine (Mendez et al., 1975), diacetylapomorphine (Baldessarini et al., 1975b), a cyclic analog of dopamine, ADTN

(Woodruff et al., 1974a), LSD (Pieri et al., 1974), bromocriptine (Corrodi et al., 1973), and ergometrine (Woodruff et al., 1974b).

4.2. Neural Mechanisms of Amphetamine-Induced Circling

4.2.1. Pharmacological Studies

While amphetamine-induced circling is blocked by the tyrosine hydroxylase inhibitor α-MT (Christie and Crow, 1971; Ungerstedt, 1971c), it is not blocked by the dopamine-β-hydroxylase inhibitor FLA-63 (Christie and Crow, 1971; Ungerstedt, 1971c) and may actually be potentiated (Ungerstedt, 1971c). Reserpine potentiates the effect of amphetamine (Ungerstedt, 1971c), ephedrine (Christie and Crow, 1971), and methamphetamine (Christie and Crow, 1973). This may reflect receptor supersensitivity as the apomorphine-induced circling of rats with unilateral caudate removal is also potentiated by reserpine (Ungerstedt, 1971a). The finding that α-MT but not reserpine blocks amphetamine-induced circling is consistent with an important role of newly synthesized dopamine in the effects of amphetamine. The failure of FLA-63 to block circling excludes an important role of noradrenaline in circling. Neuroleptics are generally potent antagonists of amphetamine- and apomorphine-induced circling (Ungerstedt, 1971a,c; Von Voigtlander and Moore, 1973; Kelly and Miller, 1975; Pycock et al., 1975). Their potencies *in vivo* (Kelly and Miller, 1975) generally correlate well with their potencies as antagonists of the dopamine-sensitive adenylate cyclase of striatal homogenates (Miller et al., 1974). However, clozapine and thioridazine show antidopaminergic activity *in vitro* but do not block amphetamine- or apomorphine-induced circling except at very high doses (Crow and Gillbe, 1973; Muller and Seeman, 1974; Kelly and Miller, 1975; Pycock et al., 1975), possibly because these drugs possess antimuscarinic actions (Stille et al., 1971; Miller and Hiley, 1974; Snyder et al., 1974).

4.2.2. Lesion Studies

Drug-induced circling is observed after electrolytic or 6-OHDA lesions of the substantia nigra (Crow, 1971; Christie and Crow, 1971, 1973; Ungerstedt and Arbuthnott, 1970; Ungerstedt, 1971b,c). Drug-induced circling is also observed after ablation (Andén et al., 1966) or 6-OHDA-induced lesions of the striatum (Von Voigtlander and Moore, 1973). After unilateral 6-OHDA-induced destruction of the mesolimbic dopamine terminals in the nucleus accumbens and olfactory tubercle, rats do not rotate in response to *d*-amphetamine, methamphetamine, or apomorphine (Kelly, 1975) (Fig. 4), while rats with destruction of dopamine terminals only in the striatum show the expected rotational responses. Mesolimbic dopamine neurons, however, do exert a major influence on circling behavior. Bilateral 6-OHDA-induced lesions of mesolimbic dopaminergic terminals reduce the amphetamine-

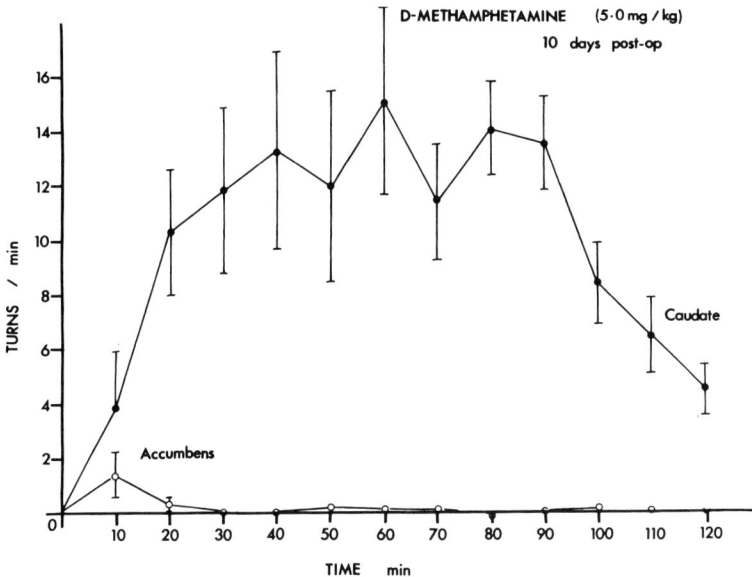

FIG. 4. Turning toward the lesioned side produced by D-methamphetamine (5.0 mg/kg) in rats with a unilateral 6-OHDA lesion of the caudate nucleus or nucleus accumbens. From Kelly (1975).

induced rotation of rats with unilateral 6-OHDA-induced nigrostriatal damage (Fig. 5) (Kelly and Moore, 1976a) and enhance the apomorphine-induced rotation of the same animals. These results suggest that the activity at mesolimbic dopamine receptors can influence circling behavior. A model which we have designed in an attempt to describe the interaction of the mesolimbic and nigrostriatal systems in producing circling behavior is shown in Fig. 6. Signals representing the activity of dopamine receptors in the right and left caudate nuclei enter a comparator. The resultant output, representing the asymmetry of dopaminergic activity in these nuclei, is conducted to an amplifier. The gain of the amplifier is directly related to the activity of dopamine receptors in the nucleus accumbens. The rate of turning is a function of the amplifier output.

This model can be used to explain the results of the experiments depicted in Fig. 5. Considering first amphetamine, the caudate difference signal would be the same for both groups of rats. However, there would be less dopamine for amphetamine to release onto the nucleus accumbens receptors of rats with 6-OHDA-induced destruction of dopamine terminals in this region. The amplifier gain would be low, and amphetamine circling would be reduced (Fig. 7). With apomorphine the caudate difference signal would again be the same for both groups of animals. Apomorphine, however, would have a greater effect on the denervated supersensitive dopamine receptors in the 6-OHDA-treated nucleus accumbens. The ampli-

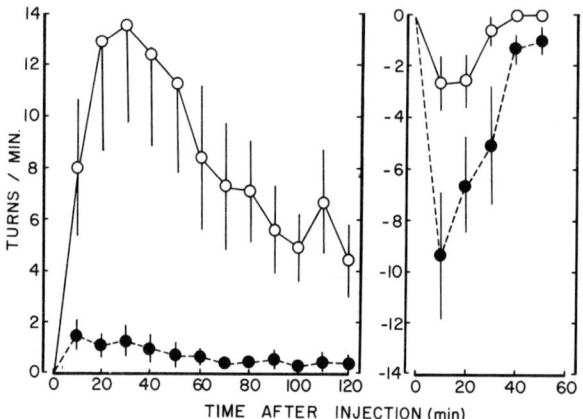

FIG. 5. Turning response to 5.0 mg/kg D-amphetamine (left) or 0.5 mg/kg apomorphine (right) in rats with unilateral 6-OHDA lesions of the caudate nucleus with (filled circles) or without (open circles) additional bilateral 6-OHDA lesions of the nucleus accumbens. From Kelly and Moore (1976a).

fier gain would be high, and apomorphine-induced circling would be enhanced (Fig. 7). Drugs which affect circling rate might therefore do so by effects on mesolimbic dopaminergic mechanisms.

Amphetamine-induced circling has also been reported after unilateral lesions of the raphe nuclei (Costall and Naylor, 1974b) or the mesencephalic reticular formation (Marsden and Guldberg, 1973). These studies bear on the question of the involvement of 5-HT in circling behavior and will be discussed later. After unilateral lesions of the frontal cortex or claustrum, amphetamine also induces rotation (Glick et al., 1976).

4.2.3. Intracranial Injections

Unilateral injections of dopamine or dopamine agonists into the caudate nucleus elicit a tendency to turn away from the injected side (Ungerstedt et

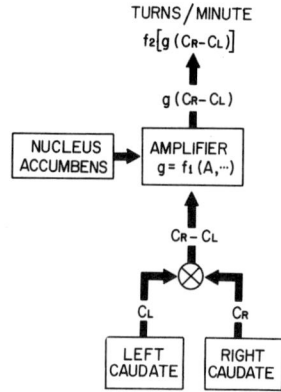

FIG. 6. Model to describe the interaction of nucleus accumbens and caudate nuclei in the production of circling behavior. Signals representing the activity at dopamine receptors in the right or left caudate nuclei (C_R and C_L) are conducted into a comparator. In transforming the resultant difference signal into turning behavior, the signal is amplified. The gain (g) of the amplifier is a function (f_1) of the activity at nucleus accumbens DA receptors (A) and possibly other variables. The resultant turning rate is a function (f_2) of the amplifier output. From Moore and Kelly (1977).

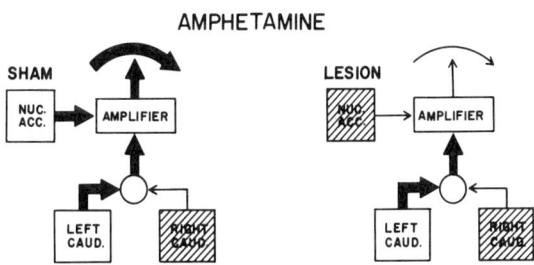

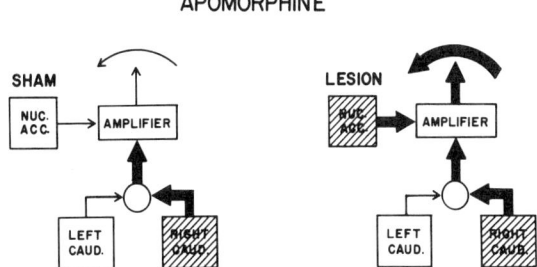

FIG. 7. Actions of amphetamine and apomorphine in a model to describe the role of the nucleus accumbens and caudate nuclei in circling behavior. Shading represents regions of 6-OHDA lesions, and thickness of arrows indicates the magnitude of the signal it represents. From Moore and Kelly (1977).

al., 1969), while unilateral injections into the nucleus accumbens do not (Elkhawad and Woodruff, 1975). Ungerstedt et al. (1969) elicited contralateral turning by unilateral intrastriatal injection of dopamine or apomorphine, and showed that these effects were blocked by bilateral injections of chlorpromazine. Unilateral injections of chlorpromazine elicited ipsilateral turning. The circling response to intrastriatal dopamine injections is enhanced when the nigrostriatal dopamine neurons have been destroyed by injecting 6-OHDA into the substantia nigra (Setler et al., 1976b). This may indicate supersensitivity of the denervated dopamine receptors. After unilateral injections of the cyclic analog of dopamine, ADTN, into the nucleus accumbens, Elkhawad and Woodruff (1975) observed a stimulation of locomotor activity but no circling.

Agents which modify cholinergic function also elicit turning when injected into the striatum. While agonists elicit ipsilateral turning, anticholinergic drugs produce contralateral circling (Costall et al., 1972).

4.3. Roles of Transmitters Other than Dopamine in Drug-Induced Circling

4.3.1. Acetylcholine

In rats with a unilateral 6-OHDA lesion of the substantia nigra the turning produced by amphetamine or apomorphine is antagonized by the cholinergic agonist oxotremorine (Kelly and Miller, 1975). The antimuscarinic drug scopolamine produced weak turning in the same direction as amphetamine (Ungerstedt et al., 1973; Kelly and Miller, 1975) which is blocked by the dopamine antagonist pimozide (Kelly and Miller, 1975). Scopolamine can antagonize the turning produced by neuroleptics (Andén and Bedard, 1971) and antagonizes the blockade of amphetamine-induced circling by neuroleptics (Muller and Seeman, 1974; Setler et al., 1976a). The anticholinergic agent procyclidine potentiates amphetamine-induced circling (Marsden and Guldberg, 1973). These studies therefore indicate an inhibitory interaction of cholinergic and dopaminergic neurons in the regulation of circling. This antagonism may account for the inability of neuroleptics such as thioridazine and clozapine which possess antimuscarinic properties (Miller and Hiley, 1974; Snyder et al., 1974) to block turning (Crow and Gillbe, 1973; Kelly and Miller, 1975) except in very high doses (Muller and Seeman, 1974; Pycock et al., 1975).

There is biochemical evidence that inhibitory cholinergic–dopaminergic interactions could occur both in the striatum and the substantia nigra. In the striatum, nigrostriatal dopamine neurons appear to inhibit cholinergic interneurons. Dopamine antagonists increase the release of acetylcholine from the caudate nucleus (Stadler et al., 1973) and decrease striatal acetylcholine levels (Sethy and Van Woert, 1974; Agid et al., 1974). Dopamine agonists increase striatal levels of acetylcholine (Sethy and Van Woert, 1974). There is also evidence for effects of cholinergic agents applied to the substantia nigra on nigrostriatal dopaminergic neurons (Javoy et al., 1974).

4.3.2. Serotonin (5-HT)

Data concerning the role of 5-HT in circling are conflicting. Andén et al. (1966) observed no circling when the 5-HT precursor 5-hydroxytryptophan was administered to rats with unilateral caudate lesions. Green and Kelly (unpublished data) observed no circling when tranylcypromine and *l*-tryptophan were administered to rats with unilateral 6-OHDA lesions of the substantia nigra, although the treatment produced the usual hyperactivity syndrome and the same animals had previously shown a strong ipsilateral rotational response to methamphetamine. PCPA does not affect the amphetamine-induced circling of rats (Marsden and Guldberg, 1973; Green and Kelly, 1976), enhances that of mice (Milson and Pycock, 1976), but does not affect the apomorphine-induced circling of mice (Milson and Pycock, 1976). L-Tryptophan in a dose which increased forebrain 5-HT levels depressed the apomorphine- and amphetamine-induced circling of mice (Milson and Pycock, 1976). However, a 5-HT antagonist cyproheptadine also depressed apomorphine- and amphetamine-induced circling (Milson and Pycock, 1976). Another 5-HT antagonist, methysergide, had no dose-dependent effects on circling in mice (Milson and Pycock, 1976) but enhanced apomorphine-induced turning in rats (Baldessarini *et al.*, 1975a). LSD, which appears to stimulate 5-HT receptors (Aghajanian *et al.*, 1970), produces turning away from the lesioned side (Pieri *et al.*, 1974), but this may be due to its action as a dopamine agonist as the effect was blocked by haloperidol (Pieri *et al.*, 1974) and LSD shows the properties of a dopamine agonist in other *in vitro* (Von Hungen *et al.*, 1974) and *in vivo* (Kelly and Iversen, 1975) models.

Bilateral lesions of the raphe nuclei do not affect the circling produced by amphetamine in rats with unilateral electrolytic lesions of the substantia nigra (Marsden and Guldberg, 1973) or the asymmetries produced by unilateral striatal injections of dopamine (Costall and Naylor, 1974b).

In contrast to these negative findings, amphetamine has been reported to provoke contralateral circling in rats with unilateral electrolytic lesions of the medial raphe nucleus (Costall and Naylor, 1974b). Marsden and Guldberg (1973) found that circling in this direction was correlated with the lateral extent of the lesion into the mesencephalic reticular formation. Cools and Janssen (1974) used the local anesthetic procaine to produce a reversible block of neural activity in the nucleus linearis raphe of the cat. Unilateral injections provoked ipsilateral head movements. The above results indicate that 5-HT may contribute to asymmetric behavior, but the precise mechanisms clearly require further elucidation.

4.3.3. GABA (γ-Aminobutyric Acid)

There is considerable evidence for the existence of a descending striatonigral pathway in the mammalian brain which uses GABA as an inhibitory transmitter. Striatal ablation or section of striatonigral pathways produce a reduction in the concentration of GABA and its synthesizing enzyme, glutamic acid decarboxylase, in the substantia nigra of several species (Kim *et al.*, 1971; McGeer *et al.*, 1973; Fonnum *et al.*, 1974). Electrical stimulation of the caudate nucleus in barbiturate-anesthetized cats inhibits neurons in the substantia nigra (Precht and Yoshida, 1971). This inhibition is mimicked by the iontophoretic application of GABA (Feltz, 1971; Crossman *et al.*, 1973) and is blocked by the GABA antagonist picrotoxin (Precht and Yoshida, 1971; Crossman *et al.*, 1973). Microinjections of GABA into the substantia nigra increase striatal dopamine levels (Andén and Stock, 1973; Kelly and Moore, 1976b).

In agreement with the inhibitory action of GABA on nigrostriatal neurons suggested by these biochemical studies, the GABA antagonist picrotoxin injected into the substantia nigra provokes contralateral circling (Tarsy *et al.*, 1975). However, GABA and GABA analogs also provoke contralateral circling when injected into the substantia nigra (Kelly and Moore, 1976b). The mechanism underlying this effect is presently not known.

4.3.4. Noradrenaline

Depletion of brain noradrenaline by dopamine-β-hydroxylase inhibitors does not inhibit the drug-induced rotation of rats with unilateral nigrostriatal damage (Christie and Crow, 1971; Ungerstedt, 1971c). Following unilateral electrolytic lesions of the locus coeruleus, amphetamine and apomorphine elicit contraversive circling (Donaldson *et al.*, 1976). It was suggested that the basis of these effects was destruction of a noradrenergic pathway to the substantia nigra, but this hypothesis was not tested by more specific destruction of the noradrenergic projections from the locus coeruleus using 6-OHDA. However, large amounts of noradrenaline injected unilaterally into the substantia nigra did produce contraversive rotation.

4.4. Conclusions

Drug-induced circling occurs after unilateral lesions of several different cerebral structures. The drug-induced rotation of rats with a unilateral 6-hydroxydopamine-induced lesion of nigrostriatal dopamine fibers is unique in that releasers of dopamine such as amphetamine produce rotation in one direction, while directly acting dopamine agonists such as apomorphine produce circling in the opposite direction. These observations closely tie the drug-induced circling of the unilateral 6-hydroxydopamine-treated rat to asymmetry of striatal dopaminergic activity. The contralateral rotation following the directly acting agonists is attributed to supersensitivity of the denervated striatal dopamine receptors. Bilateral destruction of mesolimbic dopamine neurons with 6-hydroxydopamine blocks amphetamine-induced circling and enhances apomorphine-induced circling. Activity at mesolimbic dopamine receptors may affect drug-induced circling as if by amplifying asymmetries of striatal dopaminergic activity. Drugs may therefore modify circling by acting on mesolimbic dopaminergic mechanisms. The muscarinic actions of acetylcholine appear to antagonize both amphetamine and apomorphine-induced circling. Disruption of noradrenergic transmission with synthesis inhibitors or receptor antagonists does not block drug-induced circling. The relationship of activity in serotoninergic and GABA-containing neurons to circling behavior is still equivocal.

5. REFERENCES

ACETO, M. D., HARRIS, G. Y., LESCHER, I. P., and BROWN, T. G., 1967, Pharmacologic studies with 7-benzyl-1-ethyl-1,4-dihydro-4-oxo-1,8-naphthyridine-3-carboxylic acid, *J. Pharmacol. Exp. Ther.* **158**:286–293.

AGHAJANIAN, G. K., FOOTE, W. E., and SHEARD, M. H., 1970, Action of psychotogenic drugs on single midbrain raphe neurons, *J. Pharmacol. Exp. Ther.* **171**:178–187.

AGID, Y., GUYENET, P., JAVOY, F., BEAUJOUIAN, J. C., and GLOWINSKI, J., 1974, Specific aspects of antagonists and agonists of DA receptors on ACh turnover in the rat neostriatum, *J. Pharmacol. Suppl. 1* **5**:59.

ANDÉN, N-E., and BÉDARD, P., 1971, Influences of cholinergic mechanisms on the function and turnover of brain dopamine, *J. Pharm. Pharmacol.* **23**:460–462.

ANDÉN, N-E., and STOCK, G., 1973, Inhibitory effect of gamma-hydroxybutyric acid and gamma-aminobutyric acid on the dopamine cells in the substantia nigra, *Naunyn-Schmiedeberg's Arch. Pharmacol.* **279**:89–92.

ANDÉN, N-E., Roos, B-E., and WERDINIUS, B., 1964, Effects of chlorpromazine, haloperidol and reserpine on the levels of phenolic acids in rabbit corpus striatum, *Life Sci.* **3**:149–158.

ANDÉN, N-E., DAHLSTRÖM, A., FUXE, K., and LARSSON, K., 1966, Functional role of the nigro-neostriatal dopamine neurons, *Acta Pharmacol. Toxicol.* **24**:263–274.

ANDÉN, N-E., BUTCHER, S. G., CORRODI, H., FUXE, K., and UNGERSTEDT, U., 1970, Receptor activity and turnover of dopamine and noradrenaline after neuroleptics, *Eur. J. Pharmacol.* **11**:303–314.

ANDÉN, N-E., STROMBÖM, U., and SVENSSON, T. H., 1973, Dopamine and noradrenaline receptor stimulation: reversal of reserpine-induced sedation, *Psychopharmacologia* **29**:289–298.

ARNFRED, T., and RANDRUP, A., 1968, Cholinergic mechanism in brain inhibiting amphetamine-induced stereotyped behaviour, *Acta Pharmacol. Toxicol.* **26**:384–394.

ASHER, I. M., and AGHAJANIAN, G. K., 1974, 6-Hydroxydopamine lesions of olfactory tubercles and caudate nuclei: effect on amphetamine-induced stereotyped behaviour in rats, *Brain Res.* **82**:1–12.

AYHAN, I. H., and RANDRUP, A., 1973, Behavioural and pharmacological studies on morphine-induced excitation of rats. Possible relation to brain catecholamines, *Psychopharmacologia* **29**:317–328.

BALDESSARINI, R. J., AMATRUDA, T. T., GRIFFITH, F. F., and GERSON, S., 1975a, Differential effects of serotonin on turning and stereotypy induced by apomorphine, *Brain Res.* **92**:158–163.

BALDESSARINI, R. J., WALTON, K. G., and BORGMAN, R. J., 1975b, Esters of apomorphine and N,N-dimethyldopamine as agonists of dopamine receptors in the rat brain *in vivo*, *Neuropharmacol.* **14**:725–731.

BAUMGARTEN, H. G., BJÖRKLUND, A., LACHENMEYER, L., NOBIN, A., and STENEVI, U., 1971, Long-lasting selective depletion of brain serotonin by 5,6-dihydroxytryptamine, *Acta Physiol. Scand. Suppl.* **373**:1–15.

BLEULER, E., 1950, *Dementia Praecox*, International Universities, New York.

BLOOM, F. E., ALGERI, S., GROPPETTI, A., REVUELTA, A., and COSTA, E., 1969, Lesions of central norepinephrine terminals with 6-OH-dopamine: biochemistry and fine structure, *Science* **166**:1284–1286.

BREESE, G. R., and TRAYLOR, T. D., 1970, Effect of 6-hydroxydopamine on brain norepinephrine and dopamine: evidence for selective degeneration of catecholamine neurons, *J. Pharmacol. Exp. Ther.* **174**:413–420.

BREESE, G. R., and TRAYLOR, T. D., 1971, Depletion of brain noradrenaline and dopamine by 6-hydroxydopamine, *Br. J. Pharmacol.* **42**:88–99.

BREESE, G. R., COOPER, B. R., and MUELLER, R. A., 1974, Evidence for involvement of 5-hydroxytryptamine in the actions of amphetamine, *Br. J. Pharmacol.* **52**:307–314.

BUTCHER, L. L., EASTGATE, S. M., and HODGE, G. K., 1974, Evidence that punctate intracerebral administration of 6-hydroxydopamine fails to produce selective neuronal degeneration, *Naunyn-Schmiedeberg's Arch. Pharmacol.* **285**:31–70.

BUUS LASSEN, J., 1974, Evidence for a noradrenergic and dopaminergic mechanism in the hyperactivity produced by 4,α-dimethyl-m-tyramine (H77/77) in rats, *Psychopharmacologia* **37**:331–340.

Campbell, B. A., Lytle, L. D., and Fibiger, H. C., 1969, Ontogeny of adrenergic arousal and cholinergic inhibitory mechanisms in the rat, *Science* **166**:635-637.

Campbell, B. A., Ballantine, P., and Lynch, G. S., 1971, Hippocampal control of behavioral arousal: duration of lesion effects and possible interactions with recovery after frontal cortical damage, *Exp. Neurol.* **33**:159-170.

Carlsson, A., Corrodi, H., Fuxe, K., and Hökfelt, T., 1969, Effects of some antidepressant drugs on the depletion of intraneuronal catecholamine stores caused by 4-α-dimethyl-metatyramine, *Eur. J. Pharmacol.* **5**:367-373.

Chiueh, C. C., and Moore, K. E., 1974a, Effects of α-methyltyrosine on d-amphetamine-induced release of endogenously synthesized and exogenously administered catecholamines from the cat brain *in vivo*, *J. Pharmacol. Exp. Ther.* **190**:100-108.

Chiueh, C. C., and Moore, K. E., 1974b, Relative potencies of d- and l-amphetamine on the release of dopamine from cat brain *in vivo*, *Res. Commun. Chem. Pathol. Pharmacol.* **7**:189-199.

Chiueh, C. C., and Moore, K. E., 1975, Blockade by reserpine of methylphenidate-induced release of brain dopamine, *J. Pharmacol. Exp. Ther.* **193**:559-563.

Christie, J. E., and Crow, T. J., 1971, Turning behaviour as an index of the action of amphetamines and ephedrines on central dopamine-containing neurones, *Br. J. Pharmacol.* **43**:658-667.

Christie, J. E., and Crow, T. J., 1973, Behavioural studies of the actions of cocaine, monoamine oxidase inhibitors, and iminodibenzyl compounds on central dopamine neurones, *Br. J. Pharmacol.* **47**:39-47.

Cools, A. R., and Janssen, H-J., 1974, The nucleus linearis raphe and behavior evoked by direct and indirect stimulation of dopamine-sensitive sites within the caudate nucleus of cats, *Eur. J. Pharmacol.* **28**:266-275.

Corrodi, H., Fuxe, K., Ljungdahl, Å., and Ögren, S-O., 1970, Studies on the action of some psychoactive drugs on central noradrenaline neurons after inhibition of dopamine-β-hydroxylase, *Brain Res.* **24**:451-470.

Corrodi, H., Farnebo, L-O., Fuxe, K., Hamberger, B., and Ungerstedt, U., 1972, ET495 and brain catecholamine mechanisms: evidence for stimulation of dopamine receptors, *Eur. J. Pharmacol.* **20**:195-204.

Corrodi, H., Fuxe, K., Hökfelt, T., Lidbrink, P., and Ungerstedt, U., 1973, Effect of ergot drugs on central catecholamine neurons: evidence for a stimulation of central dopamine neurons, *J. Pharm. Pharmacol.* **25**:409-412.

Costa, E., Groppetti, A., and Naimzada, M. K., 1972, Effects of amphetamine on the turnover rate of brain catecholamines and motor activity, *Br. J. Pharmacol.* **44**:742-751.

Costall, B., and Naylor, R. J., 1973a, The role of telencephalic dopaminergic systems in the mediation of apomorphine-stereotyped behavior, *Eur. J. Pharmacol.* **24**:8-24.

Costall, B., and Naylor, R. J., 1973b, The site and mode of action of ET495 for the mediation of stereotyped behavior in the rat, *Naunyn-Schmiedeberg's Arch. Pharmacol.* **278**:117-133.

Costall, B., and Naylor, R. J., 1974a, Extrapyramidal and mesolimbic involvement with the stereotypic activity of d- and l-amphetamine, *Eur. J. Pharmacol.* **25**:121-129.

Costall, B., and Naylor, R. J., 1974b, Stereotyped and circling behavior induced by dopaminergic agonists after lesions of the midbrain raphe nuclei, *Eur. J. Pharmacol.* **29**:206-222.

Costall, B., and Naylor, R. J., 1975, The behavioral effects of dopamine applied intracerebrally to areas of the mesolimbic system, *Eur. J. Pharmacol.* **32**:87-92.

Costall, B., and Naylor, R. J., 1976, Antagonism of the hyperactivity induced by dopamine applied intracerebrally to the nucleus accumbens septi by typical neuroleptics and by clozapine, sulpiride and thioridazine, *Eur. J. Pharmacol.* **35**:161-168.

Costall, B., Naylor, R. J., and Olley, J. E., 1972, Catalepsy and circling behavior after intracerebral injections of neuroleptic, cholinergic and anticholinergic agents into the caudate-putamen, globus pallidus and substantia nigra of rat brain, *Neuropharmacology* **11**:645-663.

COSTALL, B., MARSDEN, C. D., NAYLOR, R. J., and PYCOCK, C. J., 1975, Differences in circling responses following electrolytic and 6-hydroxydopamine lesions of the nigro-striatal pathway, *Br. J. Pharmacol.* **55**:289-290P.

COSTALL, B., NAYLOR, R. J., MARSDEN, C. D., and PYCOCK, C. J., 1976, Serotonergic modulation of the dopamine response from the nucleus accumbens, *J. Pharm. Pharmacol.* **28**:523-526.

COYLE, J. T., and SNYDER, S. H., 1969, Catecholamine uptake by synaptosomes in homogenates of rat brain: stereospecificity in different areas, *J. Pharmacol. Exp. Ther.* **170**:221-231.

CREESE, I., and IVERSEN, S. D., 1972, Amphetamine response after dopamine neurone destruction, *Nature New Biol.* **238**:247-248.

CREESE, I., and IVERSEN, S. D., 1973, Blockade of amphetamine induced motor stimulation and stereotypy in the adult rat following neonatal treatment with 6-hydroxydopamine, *Brain Res.* **55**:369-382.

CREESE, I., and IVERSEN, S. D., 1974, The role of forebrain dopamine systems in amphetamine induced stereotyped behavior in the rat, *Psychopharmacologia* **39**:345-357.

CREESE, I., and IVERSEN, S. D., 1975, The pharmacological and anatomical substrates of the amphetamine response in the rat, *Brain Res.* **83**:419-436.

CROSSMAN, A. R., WALKER, R. J., and WOODRUFF, G. N., 1973, Picrotoxin antagonism of γ-aminobutyric acid inhibitory responses and synaptic inhibition in the rat substantia nigra, *Br. J. Pharmacol.* **49**:696-698.

CROW, T. J., 1971, The relationship between lesion site, dopamine neurones and turning behavior in the rat, *Exp. Neurol.* **32**:247-255.

CROW, T. J., and GILLBE, D., 1973, Dopamine antagonism and antischizophrenic potency of neuroleptic drugs, *Nature New Biol.* **245**:27-28.

DIVAC, I., 1972, Drug-induced syndromes in rats with large, chronic lesions in the corpus striatum, *Psychopharmacologia* **27**:171-178.

DOMINIC, J. A., and MOORE, K. E., 1969, Acute effects of α-methyltyrosine on brain catecholamines and on spontaneous and amphetamine-stimulated motor activity in mice, *Arch. Int. Pharmacodyn.* **178**:166-176.

DONALDSON, I., MCG., DOLPHIN, A., JENNER, P., MARSDEN, C. D., and PYCOCK, C., 1976, The roles of noradrenaline and dopamine in contraversive circling behavior seen after unilateral electrolytic lesions of the locus coeruleus, *Eur. J. Pharmacol.* **39**:179-191.

DRAY, A., FOWLER, L. J., OAKLEY, N. R., SIMMONDS, M. A., and TANNER, T., 1975, Comparison of circling behavior following unilateral inhibition of GABA-transaminase or discrete electrolytic lesioning in the rat substantia nigra, *Br. J. Pharmacol.* **55**:288P.

ELKHAWAD, A. O., and WOODRUFF, G. N., 1975, Studies on the behavioral pharmacology of a cyclic analogue of dopamine following its injection into the brains of conscious rats, *Br. J. Pharmacol.* **54**:107-114.

ELLINWOOD, E., and BALSTER, R., 1974, Rating the behavioral effects of amphetamine, *Eur. J. Pharmacol.* **28**:35-41.

ERNST, A., and SMELIK, P. G., 1966, Site of action of dopamine and apomorphine on compulsive gnawing behavior in rats, *Experientia* **22**:837-838.

EVANS, B. K., ARMSTRONG, S., SINGER, G., COOK, R. D., and BURNSTOCK, G., 1975, Intracranial injection of drugs: comparison of diffusion of 6-OHDA and guanethidine, *Pharm. Biochem. Behav.* **3**:205-217.

EVETTS, K. D., and IVERSEN, L. L., 1970, Effects of protriptyline on the depletion of catecholamines induced by 6-hydroxydopamine in the brain of the rat, *J. Pharm. Pharmacol.* **22**:540-543.

EVETTS, K. D., URETSKY, N. J., IVERSEN, L. L., and IVERSEN, S. D., 1970, Effects of 6-hydroxydopamine on CNS catecholamines, spontaneous motor activity and amphetamine-induced hyperactivity in rats, *Nature (London)* **225**:961-962.

Feltz, P., 1971, γ-Aminobutyric acid and a caudato-nigral inhibition, *Can. J. Physiol. Pharmacol.* **49**:1113–1115.
Ferris, R. M., Tang, F. L. M., and Maxwell, R. A., 1972, A comparison of the capacities of isomers of amphetamine, deoxypipradrol and methylphenidate to inhibit the uptake of tritiated catecholamines into rat cerebral cortex slices, synaptosomal preparations of rat cerebral cortex, hypothalamus and striatum and into adrenergic nerves of rabbit aorta, *J. Pharmacol. Exp. Ther.* **181**:407–416.
Fibiger, H. C., Lytle, L. D., and Campbell, B. A., 1970, Cholinergic modulation of adrenergic arousal in the developing rat, *J. Comp. Physiol. Psychol.* **72**:384–389.
Fibiger, H. C., Lynch, G. S., and Cooper, H. P., 1971, A biphasic action of central cholinergic stimulation on behavioral arousal in the rat, *Psychopharmacologia* **20**:366–382.
Fibiger, H. C., Fibiger, H. P., and Zis, A. P., 1973, Attenuation of amphetamine-induced motor stimulation and stereotypy by 6-hydroxydopamine in the rat, *Br. J. Pharmacol.* **47**:683–692.
Fog, R., 1970, Behavioral effects in rats of morphine and amphetamine and of a combination of the two drugs, *Psychopharmacologia* **16**:305–312.
Fog, R., and Pakkenberg, H., 1971, Behavioral effects of dopamine and *p*-hydroxyamphetamine injected into the corpus striatum of rats, *Exp. Neurol.* **31**:75–86.
Fog, R., Randrup, A., and Pakkenberg, H., 1967, Aminergic mechanisms in corpus striatum and amphetamine-induced stereotyped behavior, *Psychopharmacologia* **11**:179–183.
Fog, R., Randrup, A., and Pakkenberg, H., 1968, Neuroleptic action of quaternary chlorpromazine and related drugs injected into various brain areas in rats, *Psychopharmacologia* **12**:428–432.
Fog, R., Randrup, A., and Pakkenberg, H., 1970, Lesions in the corpus striatum and cortex of rat brains and the effect on pharmacologically induced stereotyped, aggressive and cataleptic behaviour, *Psychopharmacologia* **18**:346–356.
Fonnum, F., Grofová, I., Rinvik, E., Storm-Mathieson, J., and Walberg, F., 1974, Origin and distribution of glutamate decarboxylase in substantia nigra of the cat, *Brain Res.* **71**:77–92.
Fuxe, K., and Ungerstedt, U., 1970, Histochemical, biochemical and functional studies on central monoamine neurons after acute and chronic amphetamine administration, in: *Amphetamines and Related Compounds* (E. Costa and S. Garattini, eds.) pp. 257–288, Raven Press, New York.
Geyer, M. A., and Segal, D. S., 1973, Differential effects of reserpine and alpha-methyl-*p*-tyrosine on norepinephrine and dopamine induced behavioral activity, *Psychopharmacologia* **29**:131–140.
Geyer, M. A., Segal, D. S., and Mandell, A. J., 1972, Effect of intraventricular infusion of dopamine and norepinephrine on motor activity, *Physiol. Behav.* **8**:653–658.
Glick, S. D., Jerussi, T. P., and Fleisher, L. N., 1976, Turning in circles: the neuropharmacology of rotation, *Life Sci.* **18**:889–896.
Grabowska, M., 1974, Influence of midbrain raphe lesions on some pharmacological and biochemical effects of apomorphine in rats, *Psychopharmacologia* **39**:315–322.
Grabowska, M., Antikiewicz, L., Maj, J., and Michaluk, J., 1973, Apomorphine and central serotonin neurones, *Pol. J. Pharmacol. Pharm.* **25**:29–39.
Grahame-Smith, D. G., 1971, Studies *in vivo* on the relationship between brain tryptophan, brain 5-HT synthesis and hyperactivity in rats treated with a monoamine oxidase inhibitor and L-tryptophan, *J. Neurochem.* **18**:1053–1066.
Green, A. R., and Kelly, P. H., 1976, Evidence concerning the involvement of 5-hydroxytryptamine in the locomotor activity produced by amphetamine or tranylcypromine plus L-DOPA, *Br. J. Pharmacol.* **57**:141–147.
Held, R., and Hein, A., 1963, Movement-produced stimulation in the development of visually guided behavior, *J. Comp. Physiol. Psychol.* **56**:872–876.

HERMAN, Z. S., 1967, Influence of some psychotropic and adrenergic blocking agents upon amphetamine stereotyped behavior in white rats, *Psychopharmacologia* **11**:136–142.

HOLLINGER, M., 1969, Effect of reserpine, α-methyl-*p*-tyrosine, *p*-chlorophenylalanine and pargyline on levorphanol-induced running activity in mice, *Arch. Int. Pharmacodyn.* **179**:419–424.

HOLLISTER, A. S., BREESE, G. R., and COOPER, B. R., 1974, Comparison of tyrosine hydroxylase and dopamine-β-hydroxylase inhibition with the effects of various 6-hydroxydopamine treatments on *d*-amphetamine-induced motor activity, *Psychopharmacologia* **36**:1–16.

IVERSEN, L. L., 1975, Dopamine receptors in the brain, *Science* **188**:1084–1089.

IVERSEN, S. D., and KELLY, P. H., 1975, The use of 6-hydroxydopamine (6-OHDA) techniques for studying the pathways involved in drug-induced motor behaviors, in: *Chemical Tools in Catecholamine Research* (G. Jonsson, T. Malmfors, and C. Sachs, eds.) pp. 327–333, North-Holland/American Elsevier, New York.

JACKS, B. R., DeCHAMPLAIN, J., and CORDEAU, J-P., 1972, Effects of 6-hydroxydopamine on putative transmitter substances in the central nervous system, *Eur. J. Pharmacol.* **18**:353–360.

JACOBS, B. L., WISE, W. D., and TAYLOR, K. M., 1974, Differential behavioral and neurochemical effects following lesions of the dorsal or median raphe nuclei in rats, *Brain Res.* **79**:353–361.

JACOBS, B. L., TRIMBACH, C., EUBANKS, E. E., and TRULSON, M., 1975a, Hippocampal mediation of raphe lesion and PCPA-induced hyperactivity in the rat, *Brain Res.* **94**:253–261.

JACOBS, B. L., WISE, W. D., and TAYLOR, K. M., 1975b, Is there a catecholamine–serotonin interaction in the control of locomotor activity? *Neuropharmacology* **14**:501–506.

JANSSEN, P. A. J., NIEMEGEERS, C. J. E., and SCHELLEKENS, K. H. L., 1965, Is it possible to predict the clinical effects of neuroleptic drugs (major tranquilizers) from animal data? Part 1: Neuroleptic activity spectra for rats, *Arzneim.-Forsch.* **15**:104–117.

JAVOY, F., AGID, Y., BOUVET, D., and GLOWINSKI, J., 1974, Changes in neostriatal dopamine metabolism after carbachol or atropine injections into the substantia nigra, *Brain Res.* **68**:253–260.

KEBABIAN, J. W., PETZOLD, G. L., and GREENGARD, P., 1972, Dopamine-sensitive adenylate cyclase in caudate nucleus of rat brain and its similarity to the "dopamine receptor," *Proc. Nat. Acad. Sci. U.S.A.* **69**:2145–2149.

KELLY, P. H., 1975, Unilateral 6-hydroxydopamine lesions of nigrostriatal or mesolimbic dopamine-containing terminals and the drug-induced rotation of rats, *Brain Res.* **100**:163–169.

KELLY, P. H., and IVERSEN, L. L., 1975, LSD as an agonist at mesolimbic dopamine receptors, *Psychopharmacologia* **45**:221–224.

KELLY, P. H., and MILLER, R. J., 1975, The interaction of neuroleptic and muscarinic agents with central dopaminergic systems, *Br. J. Pharmacol.* **54**:115–121.

KELLY, P. H., and IVERSEN, S. D., 1976, Selective 6-hydroxydopamine induced destruction of mesolimbic dopamine neurones: abolition of psychostimulant induced locomotor activity, *Eur. J. Pharmacol.* **40**:45–56.

KELLY, P. H., and MOORE, K. E., 1976a, Mesolimbic dopamine neurons in the rotational model of nigrostriatal function, *Nature (London)* **263**:695–696.

KELLY, P. H., and MOORE, K. E., 1976b, Actions of GABA, γ-butyrolactone and baclofen (Lioresal) on mesolimbic and nigrostriatal dopaminergic neurons, *Pharmacologist*, **18**:130.

KELLY, P. H., MILLER, R. J., and NEUMEYER, J. L., 1976a, Aporphines 16; action of aporphine alkaloids on locomotor activity in rats with 6-hydroxydopamine lesions of the nucleus accumbens, *Eur. J. Pharmacol.* **35**:85–92.

KELLY, P. H., JOYCE, E. M., MINNEMAN, K. P., and PHILLIPSON, O. T., 1977, Specificity of 6-

hydroxydopamine-induced lesions of mesolimbic or nigrostriatal dopamine-containing terminals, *Brain Res.* **122**:382–387.

KELLY, P. H., SEVIOUR, P. W., and IVERSEN, S. D., 1975, Amphetamine and apomorphine responses in the rat following 6-OHDA lesions of the nucleus accumbens septi and corpus striatum, *Brain Res.* **94**:507–522.

KIM, J. S., BAK, I. J., HASSLER, R., and OKADA, Y., 1971, Role of γ-aminobutyric acid in the extrapyramidal motor system. 2. Some evidence for the existence of a type of GABA-rich strio-nigral neurons, *Exp. Brain Res.* **14**:95–104.

KOE, B. K., and WEISSMAN, A., 1966, *p*-Chlorophenylalanine: a specific depletor of brain serotonin, *J. Pharmacol. Exp. Ther.* **154**:499–516.

KUMAR, R., MITCHELL, E., STOLERMAN, I. P., 1971, Disturbed patterns of behavior in morphine tolerant and abstinent rats, *Br. J. Pharmacol.* **42**:473–484.

LORENS, S. A., and GULDBERG, H. C., 1974, Regional 5-hydroxytryptamine following selective midbrain raphe lesions in the rat, *Brain Res.* **78**:45–56.

MABRY, P. D., and CAMPBELL, B. A., 1973, Serotonergic inhibition of catecholamine-induced behavioral arousal, *Brain Res.* **49**:381–391.

MABRY, P. D., and CAMPBELL, B. A., 1974, Ontogeny of serotonergic inhibition of behavioral arousal in the rat, *J. Comp. Physiol. Psychol.* **86**:193–201.

MAJ, J., SOWINSKA, H., KAPTURKIEWICZ, Z., and SARNEK, J., 1972, The effect of L-dopa and (+)-amphetamine on the locomotor activity after pimozide and phenoxybenzamine, *J. Pharm. Pharmacol.* **24**:412–413.

MARSDEN, C. A., and GULDBERG, H. C., 1973, The role of monoamines in rotation induced or potentiated by amphetamine after nigral, raphe and mesencephalic reticular lesions in the rat brain, *Neuropharmacology* **12**:195–212.

MCGEER, E. G., FIBIGER, H. C., and WICKSON, V., 1971, Differential development of caudate enzymes in the neonatal rat, *Brain Res.* **32**:433–440.

MCGEER, E. G., FIBIGER, H. C., MCGEER, P. L., and BROOKE, S., 1973, Temporal changes in amine synthesizing enzymes of rat extrapyramidal structures after hemitransections or 6-hydroxydopamine administration, *Brain Res.* **52**:289–300.

MCKENZIE, G. M., 1972, Role of the tuberculum olfactorium in stereotyped behavior induced by apomorphine in the rat, *Psychopharmacologia* **23**:212–219.

MCKENZIE, G. M., and SZERB, J. C., 1968, The effect of dihydroxyphenylalanine, phenipra-zine and dextroamphetamine on the *in vivo* release of dopamine from the caudate nucleus, *J. Pharmacol. Exp. Ther.* **162**:302–308.

MENDEZ, J. S., COTZIAS, G. C., FINN, B. W., and DAHL, K., 1975, Rotatory behavior induced in nigra-lesioned rats by N-propylnoraporphine, apomorphine, and *l*-dopa, *Life Sci.* **16**:1737–1742.

MEYERS, B., ROBERTS, K. H., RICIPUTI, R. H., and DOMINO, E. F., 1964, Some effects of muscarinic cholinergic blocking drugs on behavior and the electrocorticogram, *Psychopharmacologia* **5**:289–300.

MILLER, R. J., and HILEY, C. R., 1974, Antimuscarinic properties of neuroleptic drugs and drug-induced parkinsonism, *Nature (London)* **248**:596–597.

MILLER, R. J., and KELLY, P. H., 1975, Dopamine-like effects of cholera toxin in the central nervous system, *Nature (London)* **255**:163–166.

MILLER, R. J., and SAHAKIAN, B. J., 1974, Differential effects of neuroleptic drugs on amphetamine-induced stimulation of locomotor activity in 11-day-old and adult rats, *Brain Res.* **81**:387–392.

MILLER, R. J., HORN, A. S., and IVERSEN, L. L., 1974, The action of neuroleptic drugs on dopamine-stimulated adenosine-3′,5′-monophosphate production in rat neostriatum and limbic forebrain, *Mol. Pharmacol.* **10**:759–766.

MILLER, R. J., KELLY, P. H., and NEUMEYER, J. L., 1976, Aporphines 15; action of aporphine alkaloids on dopaminergic mechanisms in rat brain, *Eur. J. Pharmacol.* **35**:77–83.

MILSON, J. A., and PYCOCK, C. J., 1976, Effects of drugs acting on cerebral 5-hydroxytryptamine mechanisms on dopamine-dependent turning behavior in mice, *Br. J. Pharmacol.* **56:**77–85.

MOORCROFT, W. H., 1971, Ontogeny of forebrain inhibition of behavioral arousal in the rat, *Brain Res.* **35:**513–522.

MOORE, K. E., 1969, Effects of disulfiram and diethyldithiocarbamate on spontaneous locomotor activity and brain catecholamine levels in mice, *Biochem. Pharmacol.* **18:**1627–1634.

MOORE, K. E., and KELLY, P. H., 1977, Biochemical pharmacology of mesolimbic and mesocortical dopamine neurons, in: *Psychopharmacology: A Review of Progress*, Raven Press, in press.

MULLER, P., and SEEMAN, P., 1974, Neuroleptics: relation between cataleptic and anti-turning actions, and role of the cholinergic system, *J. Pharm. Pharmacol.* **26:**981–984.

MUNKVAD, I., and RANDRUP, A., 1966, The persistence of amphetamine stereotypies in spite of strong sedation, *Acta Psychiat. Scand. Suppl. 191* **42:**178.

MYERS, R. D., 1966, Injections of solutions into cerebral tissue; relation between volume and diffusion, *Physiol. Behav.* **1:**171–174.

MYERS, R. D., TYTELL, M., KAWA, A., and RUDY, T. A., 1971, Microinjection of ^{3}H-acetylcholine, ^{14}C-serotonin and ^{3}H-norepinephrine into the hypothalamus of the rat: diffusion into tissues and ventricles, *Physiol. Behav.* **7:**743–751.

NAYLOR, R. J., and OLLEY, J. E., 1972, Modification of the behavioral changes induced by amphetamine in the rat by lesions in the caudate nucleus, the caudate-putamen and globus pallidus, *Neuropharmacology* **11:**91–99.

NEILL, D. B., GRANT, L. D., and GROSSMAN, S. P., 1972, Selective potentiation of locomotor effects of amphetamine by midbrain raphe lesions, *Physiol. Behav.* **9:**655–657.

PATEL, B. C., CROSSET, P., and KLAWANS, H. L., 1976, Failure of increased brain gamma-aminobutyric acid levels to influence amphetamine-induced stereotyped behavior, *Res. Commun. Chem. Pathol. Pharmacol.* **12:**635–643.

PAYNE, R., and ANDERSON, D. C., 1967, Scopolamine-produced changes in activity and in the startle response: implications for behavioral activation, *Psychopharmacologia* **12:**83–90.

PERSSON, T., and WALDECK, B., 1969, The interaction between different metabolic pathways of catecholamines in the brain studied by means of ^{3}H-dopa, *Acta Pharmacol. Toxicol.* **27:**225–236.

PFEIFER, A. K., GALAMBOS, E., and GYÖRGY, L., 1966, Some central nervous properties of diethyldithiocarbamate, *J. Pharm. Pharmacol.* **18:**254.

PIERI, L., PIERI, M., and HAEFELY, W., 1974, LSD as an agonist of dopamine receptors in the striatum, *Nature (London)* **252:**586–588.

PIJNENBURG, A. J. J., and VAN ROSSUM, J. M., 1973, Stimulation of locomotor activity following injection of dopamine into the nucleus accumbens, *J. Pharm. Pharmacol.* **25:**1003–1004.

PIJNENBURG, A. J. J., WOODRUFF, G. N., and VAN ROSSUM, J. M., 1973, Ergometrine-induced locomotor activity following intracerebral injection into the nucleus accumbens, *Brain Res.* **59:**289–302.

PIJNENBURG, A. J. J., HONIG, W. M. M., and VAN ROSSUM, J. M., 1975a, Inhibition of *d*-amphetamine-induced locomotor activity by injection of haloperidol into the nucleus accumbens of the rat, *Psychopharmacologia* **41:**87–96.

PIJNENBURG, A. J. J., HONIG, W. M. M., and VAN ROSSUM, J. M., 1975b, Effects of antagonists upon locomotor stimulation induced by injection of dopamine and noradrenaline into the nucleus accumbens of nialamide-pretreated rats, *Psychopharmacologia* **41:**175–180.

PIJNENBURG, A. J. J., HONIG, W. M. M., and VAN ROSSUM, J. M., 1975c, Antagonism of apomorphine and *d*-amphetamine-induced stereotyped behavior by injection of low doses of haloperidol into the caudate nucleus and the nucleus accumbens, *Psychopharmacologia* **45:**65–71.

PIJNENBURG, A. J. J., HONIG, W. M. M., VAN DER HEYDEN, J. A. M., and VAN ROSSUM, J. M.,

1976, Effects of chemical stimulation of the mesolimbic dopamine system upon locomotor activity, *Eur. J. Pharmacol.* **35:**45–58.
POIRIER, L. J., LANGELIER, P., ROBERGE, A., BOUCHER, R., and KITSIKIS, A., 1972, Nonspecific histopathological changes induced by the intracerebral injection of 6-hydroxydopamine (6-OHDA), *J. Neurol. Sci.* **16:**401–416.
PRADHAN, S. N., and ROTH, T., 1968, Comparative behavioral effects of several anticholinergic agents in rats, *Psychopharmacologia* **12:**358–366.
PRECHT, W., and YOSHIDA, M., 1971, Blockade of caudate-evoked inhibition in the substantia nigra by picrotoxin, *Brain Res.* **32:**229–232.
PYCOCK, C. J., and HORTON, R. W., 1976, Possible GABA-mediated control of dopamine-dependent behavioral effects from the nucleus accumbens of the rat, *Psychopharmacology* **49:**173–178.
PYCOCK, C., TARSY, D., and MARSDEN, C. D., 1975, Inhibition of circling behavior by neuroleptic drugs in mice with unilateral 6-hydroxydopamine lesions of the striatum, *Psychopharmacologia* **45:**211–219.
QUINTON, R. M., and HALLIWELL, G., 1963, Effects of α-methyldopa on the amphetamine excitatory response in reserpinized rats, *Nature (London)* **200:**178–179.
RANDRUP, A., and MUNKVAD, I., 1964, On the relation of tryptaminergic and serotonergic mechanisms to amphetamine-induced abnormal behavior, *Acta Pharmacol. Toxicol.* **21:**272–282.
RANDRUP, A., and MUNKVAD, I., 1966, On the role of catecholamines in the amphetamine excitatory response, *Nature (London)* **211:**540.
RANDRUP, A., and MUNKVAD, I., 1970, Biochemical, anatomical and psychological investigations of stereotyped behavior induced by amphetamine, in: *Amphetamines and Related Compounds* (E. Costa and S. Garattini, eds.), pp. 695–713, Raven Press, New York.
RANDRUP, A., and SCHEEL-KRÜGER, J., 1966, Diethyldithiocarbamate and amphetamine stereotype behavior, *J. Pharm. Pharmacol.* **18:**752.
RANDRUP, A., MUNKVAD, I., and USDEN, P., 1963, Adrenergic mechanisms and amphetamine-induced abnormal behavior, *Acta Pharmacol. Toxicol.* **20:**145–157.
RECH, R. H., and STOLK, J. M., 1970, Amphetamine–drug interactions that relate brain catecholamines to behavior, in: *Amphetamines and Related Compounds* (E. Costa and S. Garattini, eds.), pp. 385–413, Raven Press, New York.
RETHY, C. R., SMITH, C. B., and VILLARREAL, J. E., 1971, Effects of narcotic analgesics upon the locomotor activity and brain catecholamine content of the mouse, *J. Pharmacol. Exp. Ther.* **176:**472–479.
ROTROSEN, J., ANGRIST, B. M., WALLACH, M. B., and GERSHON, S., 1972, Absence of serotonergic influence on apomorphine-induced stereotypy, *Eur. J. Pharmacol.* **20:**133–135.
RUSHTON, R., and STEINBERG, H., 1964, Modification of behavioral effects of drugs by past experience, in: *Animal Behavior and Drug Actions* (H. Steinberg, ed.), pp. 207–218, Churchill, London.
SCHEEL-KRÜGER, J., 1970, Central effects of anticholinergic drugs measured by the apomorphine gnawing test in mice, *Acta Pharmacol. Toxicol.* **28:**1–16.
SCHEEL-KRÜGER, J., 1971, Comparative studies of various amphetamine analogues demonstrating different interactions with the metabolism of the catecholamines in the brain, *Eur. J. Pharmacol.* **14:**47–59.
SCHEEL-KRÜGER, J., and RANDRUP, A., 1967, Stereotyped hyperactive behaviour produced by dopamine in the absence of noradrenaline, *Life Sci.* **6:**1389–1398.
SCHLECHTER, J. M., and BUTCHER, L. L., 1972, Blockade by pimozide of (+)-amphetamine-induced hyperkinesia in mice, *J. Pharm. Pharmacol.* **24:**408–409.
SEGAL, D. S., MCALLISTER, C., and GEYER, M. A., 1974, Ventricular infusion of norepinephrine and amphetamine: direct versus indirect action, *Pharm. Biochem. Behav.* **2:**79–86.
SETHY, V. H., and VAN WOERT, M. H., 1974, Regulation of striatal acetylcholine concentration by dopamine receptors, *Nature (London)* **251:**524–530.

SETLER, P., SARAU, H., and MCKENZIE, G., 1976a, Differential attenuation of some effects of haloperidol in rats given scopolamine, *Eur. J. Pharmacol.* **39**:117-126.
SETLER, P. E., TURNER, K. L., and MALESKY, M. R., 1976b, Production of contralateral rotation by injection of dopaminergic agents and catecholamines into the dopamine-depleted caudate, *Neuroscience Abstr.* **2**:503 (Abstr. No. 726).
SLOAN, J. W., BROOKS, J. W., EISENMAN, A. J., and MARTIN, E. R., 1962, The effect of addiction to and abstinence from morphine on rat tissue catecholamine and serotonin levels, *Psychopharmacologia* **4**:261-270.
SMITH, C. B., 1963, Enhancement by reserpine and α-methyl-DOPA of the effects of d-amphetamine upon the locomotor activity of mice, *J. Pharmacol. Exp. Ther.* **142**:343-349.
SNYDER, S. H., GREENBERG, D. E., and YAMAMURA, H., 1974, Antischizophrenic drugs and brain cholinergic receptors: affinity for muscarinic sites predicts extrapyramidal effects, *Arch. Gen. Psychiat.* **31**:58-62.
SREBRO, B., and LORENS, S. A., 1975, Behavioral effects of selective midbrain raphe lesions in the rat, *Brain Res.* **89**:303-325.
STADLER, H., LLOYD, K. G., GADEA-CIRIA, M., and BARTHOLINI, G., 1973, Enhanced striatal acetylcholine release by chlorpromazine and its reversal by apomorphine, *Brain Res.* **55**:476-480.
STILLE, G., LAUENER, H., and EICHENBERGER, E., 1971, The pharmacology of 8-chloro-11-(4-methyl-1-piperazinyl)-5H-dibenzo[b,e][1,4]diazepine (Clozapine), *Il Farmaco* **26**:603-625.
STJÄRNE, L., 1966, Studies of noradrenaline biosynthesis in nerve tissue, *Acta Physiol. Scand.* **67**:441-454.
STOLK, J. M., and RECH, R. H., 1970, Antagonism of d-amphetamine by alpha-methyl-L-tyrosine: Behavioral evidence for the participation of catecholamine stores and synthesis in the amphetamine stimulant response, *Neuropharmacology* **9**:249-264.
SVENSSON, T. H., 1970, The effect of inhibition of catecholamine synthesis on dexamphetamine-induced central stimulation, *Eur. J. Pharmacol.* **12**:161-166.
SVENSSON, T. H., 1971a, Functional and biochemical effects of d- and l-amphetamine on central catecholamine neurons, *Naunyn-Schmiedebergs Arch. Pharmakol.* **271**:170-180.
SVENSSON, T. H., 1971b, On the role of central noradrenaline in the regulation of motor activity and body temperature in the mouse, *Naunyn-Schmiedebergs Arch. Pharmakol.* **271**:111-120.
SVENSSON, T. H., and WALDECK, B., 1969, On the significance of central noradrenaline for motor activity: experiments with a new dopamine-β-hydroxylase inhibitor, *Eur. J. Pharmacol.* **7**:278-282.
TARSY, D., PYCOCK, C., MELDRUM, B., and MARSDEN, C. D., 1975, Rotational behavior induced in rats by intranigral picrotoxin, *Brain Res.* **89**:160-165.
TAYLOR, K. M., and SNYDER, S., 1971, Differential effects of d- and l-amphetamine on behavior and on catecholamine disposition in dopamine and norepinephrine containing neurons of the rat brain, *Brain Res.* **28**:295-309.
TAYLOR, K. M., CLARK, D. W. J., LAVERTY, R., and PHELAN, E. L., 1972, Specific noradrenergic neurones destroyed by 6-hydroxydopamine injection into newborn rats, *Nature New Biol.* **239**:247-248.
THORNBURG, J. E., and MOORE, K. E., 1971, Stress-related effects of various inhibitors of catecholamine synthesis in the mouse, *Arch. Int. Pharmacodyn.* **194**:158-167.
THORNBURG, J. E., and MOORE, K. E., 1972, A comparison of the locomotor stimulant properties of amantadine and d- and l-amphetamine in mice, *Neuropharmacology* **11**:675-682.
THORNBURG, J. E., and MOORE, K. E., 1973a, Dopamine and norepinephrine uptake by rat brain synaptosomes: relative inhibitory potencies of l- and d-amphetamine and amantadine, *Res. Commun. Chem. Pathol. Pharmacol.* **6**:81-89.
THORNBURG, J. E., and MOORE, K. E., 1973b, Inhibition of anticholinergic drug-induced locomotor stimulation in mice by α-methyltyrosine, *Neuropharmacology* **12**:1179-1185.
THORNBURG, J. E., and MOORE, K. E., 1973c, The relative importance of dopaminergic and

noradrenergic neuronal systems for the locomotor stimulation induced by amphetamine and other drugs, *Neuropharmacology* **12**:853–866.
THORNBURG, J. E., and MOORE, K. E., 1974, A comparison of effects of apomorphine and ET 495 on locomotor activity and circling behavior in mice, *Neuropharmacology* **13**:189–197.
TSENG, L. S., WEI, E., and LOH, H., 1973, Brain areas associated with bulbocapnine catalepsy, *Eur. J. Pharmacol.* **22**:363–366.
UNGERSTEDT, U., 1968, 6-Hydroxydopamine induced degeneration of central monoamine neurons, *Eur. J. Pharmacol.* **5**:107–110.
UNGERSTEDT, U., 1971a, Postsynaptic supersensitivity after 6-hydroxydopamine-induced degeneration of the nigro-striatal dopamine system, *Acta Physiol. Scand. 83* (Suppl. 367):69–93.
UNGERSTEDT, U., 1971b, Stereotaxic mapping of the monoamine pathways in the rat brain, *Acta Physiol. Scand 83* (Suppl. 367):1–48.
UNGERSTEDT, U., 1971c, Striatal dopamine release after amphetamine or nerve degeneration revealed by rotational behavior, *Acta Physiol. Scand. 83* (Suppl. 367):49–68.
UNGERSTEDT, U., and ARBUTHNOTT, G. W., 1970, Quantitative recording of rotational behavior in rats after 6-hydroxydopamine lesions of the nigrostriatal dopamine system, *Brain Res.* **24**:485–493.
UNGERSTEDT, U., BUTCHER, L. L., BUTCHER, S. G., ANDÉN, N-E., and FUXE, K., 1969, Direct chemical stimulation of dopaminergic mechanisms in the neostriatum of the rat, *Brain Res.* **14**:461–471.
UNGERSTEDT, U., AVEMO, A., AVEMO, E., LJUNGBERG, T., and RANJE, C., 1973, Animal models of Parkinsonism, in: *Advances in Neurology*, Vol. 3 (D. B. Calne, ed.), pp. 257–271, Raven Press, New York.
URETSKY, N. J., and IVERSEN, L. L., 1969, Effects of 6-hydroxydopamine on noradrenaline-containing neurones in the rat brain, *Nature (London)* **221**:557–559.
URETSKY, N. J., and IVERSEN, L. L., 1970, Effects of 6-hydroxydopamine on catecholamine-containing neurones in the rat brain, *J. Neurochem.* **17**:269–278.
VAN ROSSUM, J. M., and HURKMANS, J. A. T. M., 1964, Mechanism of action of psychomotor stimulant drugs, *Int. J. Neuropharmacol.* **3**:227–239.
VAN ROSSUM, J. M., VAN DER SCHOOT, J. B., and HURKMANS, J. A. T. M., 1962, Mechanism of action of cocaine and amphetamine in the brain, *Experientia* **18**:229–235.
VON HUNGEN, K., ROBERTS, S., and HILL, D. F., 1974, LSD as an agonist and antagonist at central dopamine receptors, *Nature (London)* **252**:588–589.
VON VOIGTLANDER, P. F., and MOORE, K. E., 1970, Behavioral and brain catecholamine-depleting actions of U-14,624, an inhibitor of dopamine-β-hydroxylase, *Proc. Soc. Exp. Biol. Med.* **133**:817–820.
VON VOIGTLANDER, P. F., and MOORE, K. E., 1973, Turning behavior of mice with unilateral 6-hydroxydopamine lesions in the striatum: effects of apomorphine, L-DOPA, amantadine, amphetamine and other psychomotor stimulants, *Neuropharmacology* **12**:451–462.
WEINER, W. J., GOETZ, C., WESTHEIMER, R., and KLAWANS, H. L., 1973, Serotonergic influences on amphetamine-induced behavior, *J. Neurol. Sci.* **20**:373–379.
WEINER, W. J., GOETZ, C., and KLAWANS, H. L., 1975, Serotonergic and antiserotonergic influences on apomorphine-induced stereotyped behavior, *Acta Pharmacol. Toxicol.* **36**:155–160.
WEISSMAN, A., and KOE, B. K., 1965, Behavioral effects of L-α-methyltyrosine, an inhibitor of tyrosine hydroxylase, *Life Sci.* **4**:1037–1048.
WEISSMAN, A., KOE, B. K., and TENEN, S. S., 1966, Antiamphetamine effects following inhibition of tyrosine hydroxylase, *J. Pharmacol. Exp. Ther.* **151**:339–352.
WOODRUFF, G. N., ELKHAWAD, A. O., CROSSMAN, A. R., and WALKER, R. J., 1974a, Further evidence for the stimulation of rat brain dopamine receptors by a cyclic analogue of dopamine, *J. Pharm. Pharmacol.* **26**:740–741.

WOODRUFF, G. N., ELKHAWAD, A. O., CROSSMAN, A. R., 1974b, Further evidence for the stimulation of rat brain dopamine receptors by ergometrine, *J. Pharm. Pharmacol.* **26:**455–456.

WOODRUFF, G. N., KELLY, P. H., and ELKHAWAD, A. O., 1976, Effects of dopamine receptor stimulants on locomotor activity of rats with electrolytic or 6-hydroxydopamine-induced lesions of the nucleus accumbens, *Psychopharmacology* **47:**195–198.

8

BRAIN DOPAMINE SYSTEMS AND BEHAVIOR

Susan D. Iversen

1. INTRODUCTION

If a monkey is rewarded for pressing a key when a light comes on, there is a considerable delay between the onset of the light and the response to the key. As Evarts (1966) remarks, "What sequence of neural events takes place during the 70-msec delay? An answer to this question would provide a useful clue as to mechanisms of sensorimotor integration."

Physiological psychologists had of course for a number of years studied various aspects of brain organization related to response control (Blakemore *et al.*, 1972). For example, our knowledge of the role of motor cortex, cerebellum, and basal ganglia in the production of specific movements advanced radically in the last 10 years because it became technically possible to study, in the behaving organism, the activity of various classes of motor neurones. However, it is not our purpose to discuss details of the actual motor machinery. (See *Neurosciences Third Study Program,* 1974, for an excellent up-to-date survey of this field.)

It is the aim of this chapter to bring together several lines of neuropharmacological and neuropsychological evidence which suggest that forebrain pathways containing the neurotransmitter dopamine are crucial elements in the neural substrate which allows an animal to emit appropriate responses to meaningful stimuli. There will be no concern with how sensory events activate these pathways or precisely how they, in turn activate, the highly organized motor output systems of the brain.

Susan D. Iversen • Department of Experimental Psychology, University of Cambridge, Cambridge, England.

The impetus to the expanding body of research on forebrain dopamine systems was specific. Three important discoveries in the 1960's focused attention on these neurotransmitter pathways. First, Carlsson (1959) developed biochemical assay methods for quantifying brain levels of the catecholamine neurotransmitters noradrenaline (NA) and dopamine (DA). It quickly became apparent that levels of these two neurotransmitters varied in different brain areas, suggesting localization of these transmitters to specific pathways.

The second crucial development confirmed this impression. The Falck–Hillarp histological technique was developed and with it the possibility of visualizing *in situ* the distribution of catecholamine neurotransmitters in the brain. The method involved exposing sections of *freeze-dried* tissue containing noradrenaline and dopamine to formaldehyde gas. The catecholamines reacted to form fluorescent compounds which with appropriate microscopic techniques were seen to be localized in certain forebrain systems. Dopamine and noradrenaline fluoresce with a similar yellow color, whereas the indoleamine serotonin produces a slightly greener fluoresence. In order to distinguish the distributions of NA and DA, it is necessary to use drugs which interfere with one transmitter rather than another.

Using these methods it was possible by the mid-1960's to publish maps of the brain distribution of NA, DA, and 5-HT (Dahlström and Fuxe, 1965). It was found that whereas NA pathways innervated the cortex and hippocampus, DA was localized to the nigrostriatal pathway. Subsequently more detailed studies by Ungerstedt (1971) revealed that there were three distinct DA pathways; the nigrostriatal, the mesolimbic/cortical, and the tuberculoinfundibular DA systems (Fig. 1). The former systems arise from different cell bodies at the midbrain level. The zona compacta of the substantia nigra (SN) contains the neurons (A9 group) which project in the nigrostriatal tract to the striatum (caudate/putamen), whereas more medially placed neurons in the ventral tegmental area, the so-called A10 cell group, project in the mesolimbic pathway. More recently, it has been demonstrated that a particular group of A10 cells which lie directly above the interpeduncular nucleus form a third distinct pathway, the mesofrontal system which innervates part of the frontal and cingulate cortex. Once it was appreciated that the dopamine pathways were so highly organized and precisely localized within the brain, experiments to determine the functional involvement of these pathways in behavioral control became feasible.

The third discovery concerned Parkinson's disease and encouraged further those interested in the functional role of catecholamine pathways. Parkinsonism is a relatively common neurological condition characterized by specific motor disability in the absence of sensory loss. The cardinal symptoms are severe impairment in the initiation of simple and complex movements and the occurrence of tremor, which tends to be intensified by the intention to move. The two classes of symptom vary in severity in different patients, reflecting, it is thought, the particular etiology of the

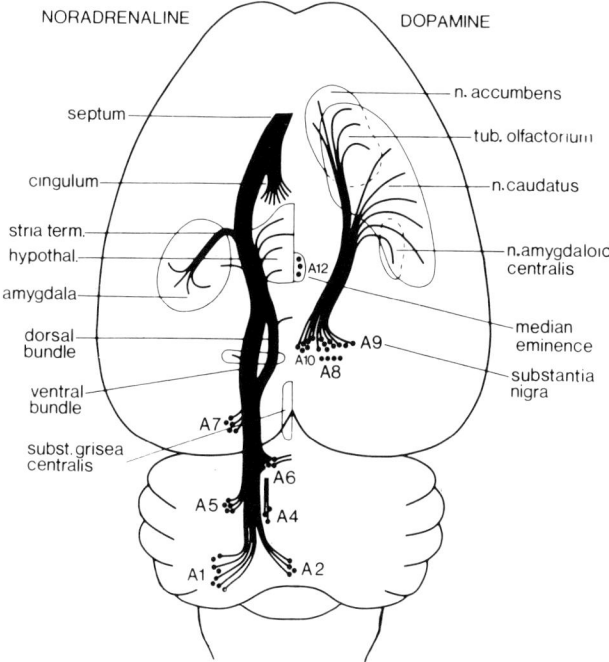

FIG. 1. Horizontal projection of the ascending NA and DA pathways. Reproduced from Ungerstedt (1971).

disease in the patient. Tremor tends to be more severe in idiopathic than in postencephalitic cases, and the opposite is true of the hypokinesia. The discovery that the neurotransmitter DA was present in high concentrations in the striatum prompted investigations of postmortem Parkinsonian brains. After all, the striatum is a crucial element of the extrapyramidal motor system, and Parkinsonism is a motor disorder. In 1960 Erhinger and Hornykiewicz published the observation that in patients who had died with Parkinson's disease there was evidence of degeneration of the nigrostriatal tract. Furthermore, biochemical assay of the striatum revealed that levels of DA and of its synthetic enzymes were drastically reduced.

This important discovery was followed shortly by the introduction of L-dopa therapy for Parkinsonism. The treatment was based on the rationale that if the DA pathways were damaged or functionally inadequate, the raising of brain DA levels by means of treatment with the biochemical precursor L-dopa might improve motor behavior. This indeed proved to be the case particularly in those patients with hypokinesia rather than tremor. It is now generally accepted that in doses of up to 8 mg/day (or higher in some cases), L-dopa can produce a dramatic improvement in the hypokinetic symptoms of Parkinson's disease, and many incapacitated patients have been restored to a normal working life.

There are still unanswered questions regarding the basis of L-dopa therapy and its long-term consequences. It is not clear for example, how the severely damaged nigrostriatal neurons are able to take up and utilize the L-dopa or indeed if it is these neurons which in fact utilize the L-dopa. However, in terms of clinical consequences it would appear that L-dopa is able to reinstate functional levels of neurotransmission in the basal ganglia.

The general acceptance that a specific motor disorder is associated with abnormal dopamine neurotransmission in the basal ganglia generated a body of related research into drugs which interact with these neurochemical processes. The result has been a vast accumulation of knowledge on localized dopamine effects in the CNS, from a biochemical, neuropharmacological, and behavioral point of view.

A considerable body of evidence now exists on the nigrostriatal dopamine system. Equal interest is now being shown in the mesolimbic and mesofrontal systems. However, although a great deal is known about the properties of forebrain DA pathways and that, in the case of one pathway, dysfunction produces a severe motor disorder in man, a more general formulation of the contribution of DA pathways to normal ongoing behavior has not yet been made. Nor is it known how activity in the DA systems is integrated with other aspects of neural control. It is with these matters that the present review is concerned.

Progress has been slow but it is now clear that *spontaneous motor behavior* shown by a rat when it is placed in a novel environment is dependent on the integrity of the *forebrain* DA systems. Depletion of DA reduces such behavior. By contrast, supranormal stimulation of the DA receptors results in a progressive increase in output of this simple motor behavior. Drugs which release DA in the brain such as the stimulant d-amphetamine, or drugs which act as agonists on the DA receptor, such as apomorphine, produce such motor effects and have proved invaluable tools for investigating the functional role of DA systems in motor behavior. Research on *the basis of drug-induced motor behavior* provides one of the few success stories in this area and forms the basis of the preceding review chapter by Peter Kelly. In that chapter results were reviewed which show clearly that drugs which interact with DA systems produce characteristic changes in unconditioned motor behavior and that these changes only occur if the forebrain DA pathways are intact. Increases in spontaneous motor activity, induction of stereotyped species-specific behaviors, and full-body rotational behavior were selected for consideration. The present chapter aims to broaden the discussion of dopamine systems and motor behavior and to provide further evidence that forebrain DA pathways play a crucial role in the expression of conditioned as well as unconditioned responding and to consider more generally the role of dopaminergically innervated structures in forebrain integration.

Although the discovery of dopamine has in a sense brought the striatum back into fashion, it is instructive to realize that a great deal of interest in the 1950s and 1960s focussed on this structure. Striatal function was as much an enigma then as it is now. Reviewing all the classical studies Laursen (1963a) concludes a very long article with the cryptic comment "the function of the corpus striatum is on a high level of integration." The review provides excellent coverage of anatomical, electrophysiological, and lesion approaches to striatal function up to that date. The elucidation of the forebrain dopamine systems in the succeeding 10 years leaves us with the task of trying to reconcile the old and the new. If DA proved to be the only or the most crucial feature of neural organization in the striatum, then of course it would be possible to interpret the older findings in a new way. Clearly this is unlikely to be the case. The striatum is a massive neuronal structure having complex anatomical interactions with many sites other than the substantia nigra (SN) of the midbrain. There may well be aspects of its structural function which are in no sense dependent on the dopamine innervation. Experimental techniques which influence equally *all* the neuronal constituents of the striatum are therefore likely to produce widespread effects which are difficult to ascribe to one or other feature of the structural organization. For this reason, the review will start with experimental approaches which selectively influence dopamine neurotransmission. In a later section some of the older results obtained with less specific methods will be mentioned insofar as they can be reconciled with dopamine function or contribute to the interpretation of the results obtained on the dopamine pathways.

2. STUDIES OF THE DOPAMINE PATHWAYS AND BEHAVIOR

2.1. Methods of Investigation

There are a variety of experimental techniques for interfering with DA transmission, most of which have been referenced in Chapter 7. They may be listed as follows:

a. Prevention of amine storage in the synaptic vesicles, e.g., reserpine or tetrabenazine. These drugs influence NA *and* DA and are therefore most useful when combined with other methods (see technique b).
b. Use of biochemical precursors, e.g., L-dopa, to replenish amine stores depleted with some other drug (reserpine or α-MT).
c. Inhibition of amine synthesis with enzyme blockers, e.g., α-methyl-p-tyrosine which blocks tyrosine hydroxylase and hence depletes brain NA and DA, or FLA-63, an inhibitor of dopamine-β-hydroxylase which preferentially depletes NA. Most useful combined with technique b.
d. Use of antagonists to block receptors. Many neuroleptics, e.g., chlorpromazine, block both NA *and* DA receptors, but there are highly specific DA receptor blockers, e.g., haloperidol and α-flupenthixol.

e. Use of agonists to activate receptors, e.g., apomorphine.
f. Electrolytic or surgical lesions to DA pathways. Difficult to avoid nonspecific damage.
g. Use of specific amine neurotoxin, e.g., 6-hydroxydopamine (6-OHDA) injected into the ventricle or amine neurons. Nonspecific damage is minimal if the dose and injection volume are small.

The validity of any one of these techniques for influencing dopamine transmission is dependent on the use of biochemical or histochemical assay procedures for quantifying the degree of interference with dopamine function. Only with such information can correlations be made between behavior and dopamine activity. For example, in the case of experiments using L-dopa and α-MT, the endogenous levels of amines must be measured in independent groups of animals under the same conditions that behavioral observations were made. As many of the biochemical manipulations result in changes to both NA and DA, brain levels of both amines should be measured.

The success of lesions is verified in the same way. In addition, the use of the lesion technique depends heavily on knowledge of the precise location of amine-containing neurons and their trajectory. Amines are depleted by lesions to the cell bodies, axons, and terminals of the neurons. The severity and duration of the lesion effects may depend on the precise site of the damage, a variable not yet investigated fully. Furthermore, 6-OHDA destroys both DA and NA-containing neurons. Its use as a selective neurotoxin is greatly enhanced by pretreatment with the antidepressant DMI which prevents 6-OHDA uptake by NA neurons. There is no equivalent means of protecting DA neurons when selective NA lesions are required. However, certain regimes of intraventricular 6-OHDA treatments (Cooper *et al.*, 1973a), or intraperitoneal 6-OHDA injections into the neonatal rat (Clark *et al.*, 1972), can be used to preferentially deplete NA systems and in the case of the neonate preparation leave DA systems virtually intact.

2.2. Unconditioned Behavior

Behaviors which ensure the survival of the individual and the species appear in the behavioral repertoire in the absence of specific learning experience. Eating, drinking, mating, and aggression fall within this category of so-called unconditioned behavior. The latter term is viewed warily by some workers as learning clearly plays a role in the refinement of such behavior patterns, if not in their initial expression. Spontaneous motor behavior is another so-called unconditioned behavior which plays an important role in maintaining the animal in a homeostatic relationship with both its external and internal environment. Locomotor activity is a sensitive index of the animal's overall physiological state and responsiveness to the environment. Full-body locomotion achieves movement from place to place and is thus a prerequisite for all forms of specific motivated behavior such as feeding, drinking, mating, or fighting. In addition to being a corollary of motivation in general, locomotor activity also reflects the specific motivation engendered by an interesting and novel environment. In the absence of a specified drive state, rats, for example, locomote in an environment to a varying degree depending on the interest value of the environment and the time for which they have been exposed to it.

Manipulations which influence both NA and DA depress locomotor activity (Rech et al., 1966, 1968). Many experiments have been performed to investigate which of these two systems is the more important with regard to locomotor behavior. It has been a consistent finding of such studies that disruption of dopamine rather than NA transmission attenuates this behavior. Reserpine (Everett and Toman, 1959; Smith and Dews, 1962) and tetrabenazine in rats and mice severely reduce spontaneous locomotor activity. These drugs affect DA and NA, but it was found that the amine precursor, 3,4-dihydroxyphenylalamine (dopa) reverses this depression of motor behavior (Carlsson et al., 1957; Blaschko and Chrusciel, 1960). Dopa raises brain DA but not NA, suggesting that the reinstatement of DA levels is responsible for the reversal of behavior. α-MT also abolishes motor activity, and its effects are similarly reversed by L-dopa (Corrodi and Hanson, 1966; Moore and Rech, 1967; Maj et al., 1971). More recently, Ahlenius and his co-workers have compared systematically the ability of L-dopa to reverse reserpine and α-MT-induced depression of motor behavior. In agreement with earlier workers Ahlenius et al. (1973) find that large doses of L-dopa reverse reserpine and α-MT suppression of spontaneous locomotor activity in mice. Locomotor behavior suppressed by α-MT could, however, be restored with low doses of L-dopa (10–50 mg/kg), which were without effect on reserpine and tetrabenazine suppression. Biochemical studies indicated that after α-MT, L-dopa normalized both NA and DA levels, whereas after reserpine only DA increases were observed. The ineffective reversal of reserpine suppression could be ascribed to the failure of L-dopa to raise NA levels after reserpine pretreatment. This is ruled out by a later study in which, in addition to α-MT, mice were given FLA-63, a dopamine-β-hydroxylase inhibitor which prevents the formation of NA from DA. When subsequently given 10 mg/kg L-dopa, these mice, despite the lack of NA formation, showed the same degree of restoration of locomotor activity as those treated with α-MT alone (Ahlenius, 1974a).

The nature of the activity after low and high doses of L-dopa provides a clue as to why α-MT but not reserpine or tetrabenazine suppression can be reversed by low doses of L-dopa. The restored locomotor activity after α-MT and 10 mg/kg L-dopa appears very normal, whereas the respored behavior after α-MT or reserpine and high doses of L-dopa is abnormal and appears to reflect overstimulation. α-MT leaves the granular storage sites in the synaptic terminal capable of storing and releasing amines; reserpine and tetrabenazine do not. Thus, after α-MT, low doses of L-dopa replenish the granular stores, and this amine is released normally by nerve impulses onto the postsynaptic site. After large doses of L-dopa, the storage granules are rapidly replenished with amine which then overflows into the cytoplasm and floods the postsynaptic receptors. This is reflected in the overstimulation of the behavior observed. After reserpine and tetrabenazine, normal granular amine storage is precluded; only with doses of L-dopa sufficiently high to result in overflow of amine to the receptors is motor behavior restored, and then again it appears overstimulated. Similarly, abnormal locomotor behavior is also seen after high doses of L-dopa in the absence of any drug pretreatment. The rats or mice become aggressive, move in rushes, jump, squeak, and show other signs of hyperactivity. The pattern of results strongly suggest that DA rather than NA underlies the effect of reserpine and α-MT on motor activity, and that the presence of newly synthesized granular stores of DA are required for normal restoration of behavior. There are workers, however, who maintain that NA does play an ancillary role in the motor behavior, although this contribution is difficult to define (Maj et al., 1971; Svennson, 1971).

Neuroleptic drugs block DA receptors and markedly reduce spontaneous activity, hence their basic classification as depressant drugs. Some neuroleptics block both NA and DA receptors, and others are highly potent and specific DA receptor blockers. The selective DA antagonist such as spiroperidol, haloperidol, and α-flupenthixol produce such effects, indicating that DA receptor blockade is a sufficient condition for the block of locomotor behavior.

Persistent blockade of dopamine receptors induced by chronic neuroleptic treatment results in supersensitivity of dopamine synapses as measured experimentally by the response to direct-acting and indirect-acting agonists and is seen clinically as tardive dyskinesia (Klawans, 1973). The stereotyped behavior induced by apomorphine is more intense after chronic haloperidol treatment (Tarsy and Baldessarini, 1973; Gianutsos et al., 1974), and stereotypy can be induced at much lower doses than normal (Tarsy and Baldessarini, 1973). These results suggest that when cut off from normal DA-minergic stimulation, the receptors become supersensitive. As the biochemical consequences of DA receptor blockade are temporary (Matthysse, 1973), they cannot account for this long-lasting change in behavioral responsiveness to apomorphine. A reduction in DA-receptor stimulation can also be achieved with long-term reserpine or α-MT treatment, and in both of these cases the motor response to amphetamine is reported to be enhanced (Stolk and Rech, 1968; Dominic and Moore, 1969; Tarsy and Baldessarini, 1973). A marked increase in *spontaneous* motor activity has been reported after chronic α-flupenthixol treatment (Sahakian et al., 1976).

It appears that the various classes of DA receptors on the DA neuron itself and on the postsynaptic site vary in their responsiveness to blockade by neuroleptics. In an elegant series of studies (Costentin et al., 1975; Protais et al., 1976; Costentin et al., 1977), this fact has been seized upon and used to characterize and identify the DA receptors concerned with particular aspects of behavior, including locomotor activity. Initially the dopamine receptors mediating apomorphine-induced changes in motor behavior and in thermoregulation were investigated. Denervation (Ungerstedt, 1971) or long-term treatment with agents which interrupt dopaminergic transmission, such as neuroleptics, result in hypersensitivity to the action of specific DA agonists, such as apomorphine. Costentin *et al.* (1975) found that a *single dose* of a neuroleptic or of apomorphine also modified the responsiveness of the DA receptors to DA agonists. They selected as their test behaviors for study in the mouse the hypothermic response and characteristic vertical climbing behavior induced by apomorphine. The maximal hypothermic response was induced by 5 mg/kg apomorphine in control mice. One hour after a single treatment with this dose of apomorphine the hypothermia dose–response curve to apomorphine was shifted to the right; i.e., the receptors had become hyposensitive. Although the maximal hypothermia was not modified, the ED 50 for apomorphine increased to 2.8 ± 0.59 mg/kg from a value of 0.35 ± 0.06 mg/kg in controls. After a single dose of haloperidol (0.1 mg/kg) the hypothermia response to apomorphine was not modified. By contrast, a single dose of haloperidol resulted in an enhanced climbing response to apomorphine. The development and decline of the changed hypothermic response and the hyperkinesia followed a similar time course, returning to control levels by 10 days. Thus, the DA receptors mediating temperature and hyperkinesia respond differentially to apomorphine and haloperidol.

In a subsequent study the locomotor response to apomorphine was investigated in more detail. Low doses of apomorphine induce hypokinesia in mice and rats whereas higher doses induce hyperactivity (Costentin *et al.*, 1977). A single dose (5 mg/kg) of apomorphine modifies both of these responses to subsequent doses of apomorphine. The hypokinesia is no longer induced by low (0.15 mg/kg) doses of apomorphine. By contrast, the hyperkinesia is not reduced, but significantly enhanced by apomorphine pretreatment. The effects of *d*-amphetamine are similar to apomorphine in the mouse, low doses producing hypokinesia and high doses hyperkinesia. Apomorphine pretreatment reduces the hypokinetic response and increase the hyperkinetic response to amphetamine. The hypokinesia produced by low doses of DA agonist has been ascribed to stimulation of the so-called "autoreceptors" (Carlsson, 1975), whereas hyperkinesia depends on postsynaptic receptors (Strömbom, 1975). Autoreceptors are now considered to play an important role in regulating synthesis and release of transmitters by nerve terminals. Stimulation of the autoreceptors leads to a diminished synthesis and release of DA and thus a decreased stimulation of postsynaptic receptors. Reduced presynaptic activity would then result in supersensitivity of the postsynaptic receptor, and hence the agonist responses of the postsynaptic site would increase. The depressant effect of apomorphine on the nigrostriatal neurons shows rapid tolerance (Walters *et al.*, 1975), which will account for the loss of apomorphine-induced hypokinesia (autoreceptor effect) and the persistent and enhanced apomorphine hyperkinesia seen after a single dose of apomorphine. Under normal conditions the release of synaptic DA is likely to activate the autoreceptor and hence result in supersensitivity of the postsynaptic receptors. The postsynaptic site would then be more easily activated. Such a mechanism could, after repetitive use of a synapse, result in preferential conduction of nerve impulses in that pathway.

Finally, the experiments with the selective neurotoxin 6-OHDA provide further evidence that disruption of normal-activity DA pathways results in hypokinesia. Bilateral lesions to the SN result in marked hypokinesia (Fibiger *et al.*, 1973; Roberts *et al.*, 1975; Creese and Iversen, 1975). Bilateral lesions to either the dorsal or the ventral NA bundles do not affect locomotor activity (Creese and Iversen, 1975). However, although spontaneous activity is lower when the animals are first placed in the novel environment, the SN-lesioned rats show normal patterns of habituation of the locomotor response (Roberts *et al.*, 1975; Creese and Iversen, 1975). The lesions cited almost certainly damaged both the mesolimbic *and* nigrostriatal DA systems. Subsequently, it has been found that selective lesions to the terminals of the mesolimbic system (destroyed by 6-OHDA injections aimed at the nucleus accumbens) but not of the striatal system produce this attenuation of spontaneous locomotor activity (Iversen and Koob, 1977). Thus, both spontaneous and amphetamine-induced locomotor activity (Kelly *et al.*, 1975) are mediated by the same sector of the dopamine system.

Eating and drinking behavior are abolished by substantial lesions to the substantia nigra. This was originally reported by Ungerstedt (1971) after bilateral 6-OHDA lesions to the SN and has been confirmed subsequently after electrolytic lesions to the SN and 6-OHDA lesions to the nigrostriatal tract, striatum, and lateral hypothalamus (Smith *et al.*, 1972). Intracisternal 6-OHDA in the rat (Breese *et al.*, 1973) also produces aphagia and adipsia provided the rats are pretreated with a monoamine oxidase inhibitor, such as pargyline, to increase the degree of amine depletion induced by 6-OHDA. Intraventricular 6-OHDA in the absence of pargyline did not result in consummatory deficits (Bloom *et al.*, 1969; Uretsky and Iversen, 1970; Breese and Traylor, 1972; Fibiger *et al.*, 1973). Feeding behavior can be directly elicited by electrical stimulation of the lateral hypothalamus. Intraventricular 6-OHDA (Phillips and Fibiger, 1973) and specific DA receptor antagonists such as haloperidol block this behavior, suggesting that induced feeding, like the spontaneous behavior, is mediated by dopamine-containing pathways (Phillips and Nikaido, 1975).

Ungerstedt (1971) suggested that the aphagia and adipsia associated with the classical lateral hypothalamic (LH) syndrome is probably due to damage of the DA-containing nigrostriatal tract at the level of the hypothalamus. The physiological profile of the LH syndrome was described initially by Teitelbaum and Epstein (1962) and studied further by these workers over the years. The "nigrostriatal" feeding syndrome has since been compared on the same measures (Breese *et al.*, 1973; Fibiger *et al.*, 1973; Stricker and Zigmond, 1974). Initially it was felt that DA loss could account for all aspects of the classical LH syndrome. At present, several workers believe that although there is a residual LH syndrome which is not seen after selective DA lesions, most of the LH deficit is reproduced by nigrostriatal damage. It is difficult at present to reconcile the role of DA in feeding with the substantial body of evidence which demonstrates that NA injections into the hypothalamus reliably induce feeding (see Hoebel, Chapter 3 of this volume).

The relationship between amines and behavior may either be studied by varying the amines and observing behavior or by varying behavior and observing amines. Many examples of the former approach have now been described in Section 2.2.

The alternative approach attempts to relate utilization of brain amines, variously measured by brain release (Sparber and Tilson, 1972), rate of depletion (Schoenfeld and Seiden, 1969), rate of turnover (Gordon *et al.*, 1966), or endogenous levels (Kety *et al.*, 1967), to ongoing behavior. With such methods, the relationships described have not been either clear or impressive. However, the techniques themselves are difficult, and this is certainly an approach which warrants further investigation. For example, Gordon *et al.* (1966) found that exposure to cold or forced motor activity increased catecholamine turnover, as measured by the incorporation of radioactively labeled tyrosine. Other workers have found increased turnover of amines associated with motor activity (Corrodi *et al.*, 1968; Stone and DiCara, 1969). Acute aversive stimulation is reported to increase turnover (Thierry *et al.*, 1968), particularly of *newly* synthesized NA (Thierry *et al.*, 1970), and to reduce endogenous concentrations of brain NA (Maynert and Levi, 1964; Bliss *et al.*, 1968), whereas prolonged aversive stimulation causes a rise in NA concentration (Kety *et al.*, 1967), particularly in the hindbrain.

Unfortunately, the kinds of biochemical methods used in these experiments do not permit a distinction to be made readily between DA and NA changes. This remains a challenge for future work. One exception is a study of Sparber and Luther (1970) in which NA, DA, adrenaline, and dopa were assayed after cold exposure of rats designated "active" or "passive" on the basis of measures of exploratory activity. Under standard environmental conditions, active rats had significantly less DA in the brainstem mesencephalon than passive rats, but this difference was equalized after restraint in a cold environment. Presumably the cold stress increased DA levels.

The changes in amine activity in these experiments are not large despite the fact that the behavioral manipulations used are dramatic and severe (repeated electrical shock, forced running, and so on). It is therefore doubtful if, with such methods, it will prove possible to detect and measure variations in amine activity associated with more subtle modifications of behavioral control. Rats behave very differently depending, for example, on the schedule of reinforcement. Are such subtleties of behavior reflected in brain amine levels? Seiden and his co-workers have investigated this problem.

Initially they used α-MT to challenge the amine systems and under the drug condition were able to show that certain schedule-controlled behaviors resulted in greater depletion of brain amines than others. Performance on fixed-ratio (FR) schedules of reinforcement was more affected than performance under fixed interval (FI) reinforcements by equivalent doses of α-MT, which were shown to produce a similar degree of brain amine depletion (Schoenfeld and Seiden, 1969). In an earlier study, behavior generated by an FR 20 schedule was more effective in reducing amine levels than behavior on an FR 10 (Schoenfeld and Seiden, 1967). α-MT also had a greater brain-amine-depletion effect when rats were deprived and working an FI schedule of water reinforcement than when they were left alone in the home environment (Schoenfeld and Seiden, 1969). Using the histofluorescence technique for quantifying levels of brain amine, it has been found that α-MT produces a more marked depletion of amines when rats perform in an avoidance task than when given α-MT in the home cage or α-MT associated with random and meaningless electrical shocks (Fuxe and Hanson, 1967).

Lewy and Seiden (1972) have criticized the use of α-MT in such experiments on the grounds that when a pharmacological agent is used to challenge the amine system, and thus reveal its behavioral responsiveness, the drug rather than the behavior may be producing the biochemical changes. This is an unlikely explanation because in studies of this kind it has been shown that whereas neither behavior manipulation *nor* α-MT by themselves change brain amines, when combined a differential effect of experience is observed (Gordon *et al.*, 1966). However, to counter their own criticism, Lewy and Seiden (1972) performed an experiment in which NA levels were measured in rats after performance on an operant task (FI schedule) for water reward. Operant responding after water deprivation increased brain NA metabolism, whereas deprivation alone did not.

Such observations suggest, to quote from Schoenfeld and Seiden (1969), "that an important determinant of drug action is what, and how much, a subject actually does . . . in the presence of the drug." The same can probably be said of the effect behavior has on brain chemistry. Sparber and Tilson (1972) have reached similar conclusions in their studies relating ongoing behavior with amine release from the brain after an intraventricular injection of radioactively labeled noradrenaline. More labeled amine appeared in a ventricular perfusate when rats were lever pressing on an FR 30 schedule of reinforcement than on an FR 10.

2.3. Conditioned Behavior

Forebrain DA pathways thus appear to be essential for the initiation of normal sequences of unconditioned behavior, certainly insofar as spontaneous locomotor activity, feeding, and drinking are concerned. Do the same dopamine systems play an equivalent role in the initiation and sequencing of conditioned *or* learned motor acts? A rat runs spontaneously in a photocell cage but can learn to run in a photocell cage or wheel in order to obtain food reward. The motor acts or routines are the same in both cases, but in the latter situation the probability of the response has been changed by reinforcement, and learning is said to have occurred. The response of running may be associated with any motivational state in the animal and can be rewarded by food, water, sexual contact, and so on. This is true of any motor act such as a lever press, pedal press, chain pull, or hose pipe bite (Dews, 1958). Furthermore, the pattern of emission of these responses under a given schedule of reinforcement is identical irrespective of the *nature* of the reinforcer or the particular motor response executed. Generality of this kind suggests that there is a common system in the CNS involved in the programming of motor routines. It is clear that motor subroutines are prewired in the tegmental areas of the hindbrain. Von Holst and von Saint Paul (1963) demonstrated in the domestic chicken that discrete electrical stimulation in this area produced species-specific motor-behavior patterns in the absence of any external motivating stimuli. However, under normal conditions it is unlikely that the interplay between motivational states and motor behavior occur only at these lower levels of the brain. As Vanderwolf (1971) comments: "The coupling between a drive state and a voluntary movement is assumed to occur via intermediary mechanisms in the forebrain which establish a 'program' determining the selection of particular motor acts and the sequence in which they are to be performed. Overt behavior results when a program is activated by means of a trigger mechanism, largely located in the diencephalon." The two dopamine systems, activating as they do the striatum and the mesolimbic structures, provide appropriate neural circuitry for such an integrative function. The striatum is located at the "head" of and has strong connections both with other parts of the extrapyramidal motor system and with the thalamocortical motor system, whereas the structures innervated by the mesolimbic DA system have strong connections with the limbic/hypothalamic axis. What then is the evidence that the target sites of the dopamine pathways play a crucial role in the programming of purposeful behavior?

The kinds of studies providing evidence on this point are methodologically similar to those considered under the heading of unconditioned behavior. Drugs and neurotoxins have been used to selectively interfere with the dopamine systems, and in such preparations the acquisition and performance of a variety of learned behaviors have been studied.

2.3.1. Avoidance Behavior

The amine-depleting agent reserpine and the synthesis inhibitor α-MT severely impair the acquisition and performance of shock avoidance responses (Seiden and Carlsson, 1964; Corrodi and Hanson, 1966; Moore and

Rech, 1967), although it is clear that *escape* responses to the shock are unaffected. A number of investigators have studied the ability of L-dopa to reinstate reserpine and α-MT depression of conditioned behavior in mice, rats (Seiden and Carlsson, 1963; Corrodi *et al.*, 1966; Moore and Rech, 1967), and cats (Wada *et al.*, 1963; Seiden and Hanson, 1963). Pretreatment with a monoamine oxidase inhibitor potentiates the effects of L-dopa (Seiden and Carlsson, 1963). The restoration of reserpine-suppressed conditioned avoidance following L-dopa roughly parallels in time the elevation in brain dopamine levels. No increases in brain noradrenaline are found (Seiden and Carlsson, 1964), adding further support to the view that DA loss and recovery correlates with the changes in conditioned responding. This correlation with DA levels was verified in a later paper in which reserpine reversal by L-dopa was studied in two different strains of mice (Seiden and Peterson, 1968). In both strains catecholamines were depleted to the same levels. However, the time of maximal restoration of behavior by L-dopa differed in the two species and coincided with the maximum rise in the DA levels; in strain C 57 this was 5–20 min and in DBA 5–30 min after L-dopa. Thus, behavioral restoration and brain DA levels fell off more rapidly in the C 57 strain.

Ahlenius (1974b) systematically investigated L-dopa reversal of reserpine, tetrabenazine, and α-MT suppression of conditioned avoidance behavior in the same way that spontaneous locomotor activity had been studied. In mice, 10 mg/kg L-dopa completely restored α-MT suppression of avoidance behavior and partially restored the depression induced by treatment with α-MT plus reserpine. In both cases the reversal of suppression did not correlate with the number of intertrial responses in the avoidance box. L-Dopa (400 mg/kg) produced a more complete reversal of suppression induced by α-MT plus reserpine, but in this case there was a correlation with intertrial responses, suggesting that the "restored" behavior differed from that seen after 10 mg/kg L-dopa.

In a modified discrimination situation, mice were required to pass to the safe compartment on presentation of a buzzer via a right black tunnel. Responses to the safe side via the left white tunnel were recorded as incorrect. Escape was not permitted, and a trial was not ended until the correct response was made. On this task 10 mg/kg L-dopa reversed α-MT suppression. L-dopa (200 mg/kg) partially reversed reserpine suppression, but in this case the number of incorrect responses increased as did the number of intertrial responses. Again the reversal by high doses of L-dopa gives evidence of nonspecific activation.

In a further experiment Ahlenius (1974c) used a successive discrimination avoidance task in which rats were required to avoid via the right opening if the lamps in the box were lit and via the left opening if the box was dark. Tetrabenazine suppression on this task was reversed by 100 mg/kg L-dopa, but as well as correct responses the number of both incorrect responses and intertrial responses increased compared with control performance. After α-MT, 10 mg/kg L-dopa completely restored behavior without a significant increase in incorrect responses, whereas the reversal induced by 100 mg/kg L-dopa produced incorrect responses and therefore again appeared to involve nonspecific activation.

The degrees of behavioral restoration in the various conditioned tasks were correlated with endogenous levels of NA and DA after the L-dopa treatments. In several experiments reinstatement of brain levels of NA was excluded as an explanation of behavioral restoration because in additional subjects treatment with FLA-63 (which prevents NA formation from L-dopa) did not modify the degree of L-dopa-induced reversal of behavior. However, it proved difficult in these experiments to make any definitive statement about the level of DA or pattern of NA and DA required for *normal* restored function. The failure of L-dopa to reinstate behavior after reserpine treatment compared with its efficiency after α-MT suggests to Ahlenius that behavior depends not so much on levels of brain amines as on the nature of the storage of those amines. L-Dopa restores amine levels in both the reserpinized and α-MT-treated rat, but in the former case the vesicle storage mechanism remains abnormal and the amines are not available for release by nerve impulses. By contrast, α-MT depletes amines but leaves the amine storage mechanisms normal. When these are replenished by L-dopa, functional release is again possible. Clearly flooding the synapse with amine under abnormal physiological conditions (i.e., the situation with reserpine and 400 mg/kg L-dopa) does not provide the sufficient conditions for normal functional activity of the synapse. Different forms of behavioral control may depend to a varying degree of *normal functional release* of amine. Spontaneous locomotor behavior, successive discrimination-conditioned avoidance, and lever pressing clearly are highly dependent on such a mechanism, hence the ineffectiveness of 10–50 mg/kg L-dopa after reserpine treatment. Simple conditioned avoidance after reserpine, however, is partially restored by such doses of L-dopa, suggesting less dependence on the physiological release of amines.

DA-receptor-blocking agents depress conditioned responding for food-reinforcement (Morse, 1964) shock avoidance and shock escape (Kelleher and Morse, 1964; Iversen and Iversen, 1975). This is true of neuroleptics such as chlorpromazine, which have mixed NA- and DA-blocking activity and of more potent and specific DA antagonists such as spiroperidol and α-flupenthixol, and thus it is difficult to ascribe the global depression seen with neuroleptics to selective interference with one neuropharmacological system rather than another.

However, Janssen and his co-workers have made detailed studies of a wide range of neuroleptics on discriminated Sidman shock avoidance and modifications of this task (Niemegeers *et al.*, 1969) in an effort to rationalize shock avoidance as a suitable test for identifying compounds of potential use as neuroleptics. Among such drugs they report a strong correlation between the attenuation of shock-avoidance behavior and potency of the compounds to block amphetamine-induced stereotyped behavior. As amphetamine stereotypy is mediated specifically by striatal DA receptors, it is reasonable to ascribe the block of avoidance behavior by neuroleptics to the same neuropharmacological substrate. Additional support for this view comes from experiments in which neuroleptic-induced disruption of shock-avoidance behavior can be prevented by pretreatment with L-dopa. Ruiz and Monti (1972) tested rats in a pole-climbing avoidance task and found that pretreatment with L-dopa (80 mg/kg + a dopa decarboxylase inhibitor, T04-4602) changed the degree of suppression of avoidance induced by haloperidol from 100% to 20%. Pretreatment with 1-5-hydroxytryptophan (5-HTP) was without effect. Presumably the raised brain amine levels associated with L-dopa result in release of DA to the postsynaptic site where it competes with haloperidol, and this attenuates neuroleptic blockade of the receptors. In contrast, depletion of brain amines is reported to enhance the depressant effects of neuroleptics (Ahlenius and Engel, 1971a; Jalfre and Haefley, 1971), presumably because competition at the DA receptor is reduced. However, depletion of the terminal amine stores with 6-OHDA does not alter the depressant effect of chlorpromazine, haloperidol, and spiroperidol on continuously reinforced lever pressing (Cooper et al., 1973b).

Since the original studies with neuroleptics were published, it has been repeatedly demonstrated, in a variety of shock-avoidance testing situations, that although the avoidance response is abolished by neuroleptics, shock escape is less affected (Posluns, 1962). This is a dose-dependent effect, and if a sufficiently high dose of neuroleptic is given, then both the response to the conditioned and unconditioned stimuli are reduced. However, with any particular dose the conditioned response is more affected than the unconditioned (Monti and Hance, 1967). Under discriminative shock-avoidance conditions, it can be shown that the escape responses are under normal discriminative control (Ahlenius, 1974b).

Turning now to lesion experiments on the forebrain amine pathways, there is considerable support for the view that DA systems play a critical role in the execution of learned responses. Initially 6-OHDA was used intracisternally, and Breese and his co-workers (see Breese, Volume 1 of this *Handbook*) devised injection regimes and pretreatment procedures to differentially deplete NA as opposed to DA and vice versa, and to deplete these amines by varying amounts.

On a two-way active avoidance task (Cooper et al., 1972a) 2 × 250 μg 6-OHDA given by intracisternal injection 1 week apart severely impeded the acquisition of avoidance responding over 100 trials. Brain amines were reduced by almost 90% in these animals. Pargyline pretreatment increased the effectiveness of 6-OHDA, and the depletion increased to 95%; such rats showed a total failure to acquire avoidance responses. A preferential depletion of DA achieved by pretreatment with DMI before a dose of 200 μg 6-OHDA depleted DA levels to 73% of controls and was without effect on avoidance responding. By contrast, a preferential depletion of NA (to 60%) by three small doses of 6-OHDA (25 + 25 + 50 μg at weekly intervals) enhanced the acquisition of avoidance responding. The experiments of Ahlenius and Engel (1971a; 1972) suggested that NA plays an inhibitory modulatory role on DA systems, and the release of behavior in an avoidance situation after NA depletion is further evidence for this suggestion. In a subsequent study (Cooper et al., 1973a), these results were confirmed and extended by the observation that acquisition of one-way active avoidance and retention of two-way avoidance were also severely impaired by the 2 × 250 μg 6-OHDA treatment. Passive avoidance was unaffected presumably because it does not depend on the initiation of conditioned responses. The degree of DA depletion appears to be the critical cause of the loss of avoidance behavior for the following reasons: (a) After treatment with 1 mg/kg reserpine or 30–50 mg/kg α-MT the preferentially DA-depleted group showed a total loss of avoidance responding, whereas the preferentially NE-depleted group showed only a small performance decrement when treated in the same way (Cooper et al., 1972b). Reserpine depletes NA and DA in both groups, but only in the group already showing DA depletion are the further reductions in DA levels sufficiently severe to impair behavior. (b) After 2 × 240 μg 6-OHDA with DMI pretreatment, DA was depleted to 5% of control levels and NA minimally depleted to 85% of control levels. These rats failed to acquire the avoidance task. This pattern of results demonstrates a critical role of DA in active avoidance acquisition and retention, and this may well be the case for other conditioned behaviors.

The intracisternal use of 6-OHDA taken together with the various dose, pretreatment, and α-MT/reserpine regimes does suggest that DA and not NA mediates avoidance behavior. Efforts have been made to substantiate this claim using local injection of 6-OHDA to lesion particular amine pathways in isolation. Cooper et al. (1974b) compared 6-OHDA lesions to the A10 dopamine neuron cell bodies, NA tegmental pathway, globus pallidus, and caudate/putamen. NA lesions were ineffective but A10 and caudate lesions impaired the acquisition of shuttlebox avoidance. The same two lesion groups were the most sensitive to the effects of α-MT (40 mg/kg). The ventral tegmental lesion reduces forebrain NA as well as DA; however, as α-MT did not have a significant effect on the rats with direct lesions to the NA pathways, the decrements in conditioned behavior may be ascribed to the depletion of DA in the tegmental/striatal DA system.

Fibiger et al. (1974) report that selective bilateral 6-OHDA lesions to the SN result in deficits in the acquisition of a condition-avoidance response and an approach response for food. In a later study (Price and Fibiger, 1975), acquisition of a light discrimination shock *escape* habit was unimpaired and shock-induced flinch and jump thresholds were not elevated by the lesion. The deficit on avoidance is therefore not due to insensitivity to the shock and has therefore been ascribed to a failure to initiate a learned motor response in the avoidance situation. The impairment in avoidance after the selective SN lesion is similar to that observed after treatment with the neuroleptic haloperidol (Fibiger et al., 1975). Both (a) leave escape intact while impairing avoidance, (b) leave the animal capable of showing normal fear responses and, most interestingly, (c) are reduced by overtraining and (d) are reversed by anticholinergic drugs. Overtraining presumably results in heightened functional transmission of the DA synapses, which are thus more resistant to disruption by lesion or antagonist drugs. In the case of the anticholinergics, it is well established that a DA/ACh balance plays a role in striatal function (Stadler *et al.*, 1973). DA-receptor blockade results in overactivity of the ACh component of the balanced system, which presumably contributes to the general striatal dysfunction after neuroleptic treatment. Blockade of this ACh effect with the anticholinergic thus attenuates the functional impact of DA-receptor blockade. The interaction between DA and ACh mechanisms in the mediation of avoidance behavior strongly suggests the involvement of DA receptors in the striatum, rather than in the mesolimbic DA system, where cholinergic interactions seem to be of less functional importance (Iversen, 1977).

2.3.2. *Intracranial Self-Stimulation (ICS)*

Lever pressing to obtain brain stimulation (intracranial self-stimulation, ICS) is a conditioned behavior which has received much attention from those interested in amines and behavior. ICS can be obtained at many sites in the brain, and it has always been anticipated that a definitive plot of these sites would reveal the crucial sites concerned in reinforcement and learning processes. As knowledge accrues, it seems clear that a very widespread circuitry sustains ICS and that activation of the components of this circuit mimic different aspects of the conditioning process. NA pathways have long been implicated in ICS (Stein *et al.*, Chapter 2 of this volume). More recent experiments (Crow, 1972) showed that the forebrain DA pathways also sustain self-stimulation.

Self-stimulation can be sustained at the cell bodies of origin, in the areas of terminal innervation, and probably on the efferent output of dopaminergic systems (for a review, see Routtenberg and Santos-Anderson, Chapter 1 of this volume). Very few of these sites have been extensively investigated with pharmacological manipulators and selective lesions. Many of the experiments for studying the effects of manipulation of brain amines on ICS used lateral hypothalamic self-stimulation electrodes, a site which clearly involves the ascending DA pathways but may also influence NA and 5-HT systems. Within this limited context, depletion of brain amines with α-methyltyrosine (Poeschel and Ninteman, 1966; Black and Cooper, 1970; Liebman and Butcher, 1973; Cooper *et al.*, 1974a) attenuate ICS, whereas inhibition of NA synthesis has not been found as effective (Lippa *et al.*, 1973). Supporting evidence for the importance of DA in ICS comes from studies in which crystalline DA applied to the ventral anterior caudate (Neill *et al.*, 1975) enhanced hypothalamic ICS more than equivalent application of NA; and hypothalamic ICS attenuated with α-MT can be partially restored with systemic injections of the DA agonist apomorphine (Saint-Laurent et al., 1973).

Specific DA-receptor-blocking drugs such as pimozide (Wauquier and Niemegeers, 1972), spiroperidol (Rolls et al., 1974a,b), and haloperidol (Lippa et al., 1973; Phillips et al., 1975) abolish self-stimulation, although the NA-blocking agent phentolamine (Lippa et al., 1973) is without effect. A variety of ICS sites were investigated in a later study (Rolls et al., 1974b), and ICS sustained in the nucleus accumbens, septal area, hippocampus, anterior hypothalamus, and the ventral tegmental area was attenuated by spiroperidol. Free feeding was less affected than ICS, but when rats were required to press a lever for food or water the attenuation was as great as that observed with lever pressing for ICS. The effects of lesions to the DA pathways on ICS behavior have also been studied. Cutting the laterally directed connections of the hypothalamus (and thereby the forebrain DA projections) reduces hypothalamic ICS (Kent and Grossman, 1973). Lesions with 6-OHDA have also been attempted.

Intracisternal 6-OHDA attenuates posterior hypothalamic ICS to a varying degree depending on the extent of the damage of the amine systems (Breese et al., 1971). Various 6-OHDA regimes have been used (Cooper et al., 1974a), as in the study of conditioned avoidance and appetitive behavior. The pargyline + 6-OHDA treatment which severely reduces both DA and NA markedly attenuated ICS. Less complete and acute reductions to DA levels produced only a temporary reduction in ICS, and preferential NA depletion was without effect. α-MT accentuated the decrement in ICS in the group with partial DA loss but was without effect in the preferentially NA-depleted group. Amphetamine increases ICS. This effect is reduced in the 6-OHDA DA-depleted animals but not in the NA group (Cooper et al., 1974a). The neuropharmacological basis of amphetamine-induced increases in ICS was investigated further by treating normal ICS rats with reserpine followed by either α-MT or a selective NA-synthesis inhibitor. Reserpine alone does not abolish amphetamine-induced increases in self-stimulation presumably because a small pool of newly synthesized amine is available for release by the drug. When given amphetamine, the reserpine + α-MT treatment prevented increases in ICS, whereas the reserpine + NA depletion did not. These results together with those obtained after the 6-OHDA lesion demonstrate that DA and particularly newly synthesized DA, rather than NA, mediates ICS and the stimulatory effects of amphetamine on this behavior (Cooper et al., 1974a).

There are a few studies which indicate that the DA innervation of the *ventral caudate* may be the crucial striatal focus of the substrate involved in self-stimulation and other forms of learned behaviors. Application of crystalline 6-OHDA to the ventral anterior head of the striatum depressed lateral hypothalamic self-stimulation, and application of crystalline DA partially restored behavior (Neill et al., 1975), whereas similar placements in the dorsal anterior region were without effect. Avoidance behavior is also impaired by 6-OHDA in the ventral anterior caudate (Neill et al., 1974a) site in very much the same way it is by 6-OHDA lesions to the SN (Fibiger et al., 1974).

Stinus et al. (1975) reported that small 6-OHDA (2 μg in 1 μl) injections in the area ventralis tegmenti (AVT) produced a small decrement in ICS sustained by electrodes at that site. However, when doses of α-MT were administered, which had no effect on control electrode placements, AVT ICS was severely depressed. Similar enhanced sensitivity to the effects of α-MT were seen with lateral hypothalamic α-AVT electrodes after reserpine treatment (Stinus et al., 1976). The time course of recovery of ICS after reserpine correlates better with the pool of newly synthesized amine in the brain than with the overall endogenous level, demonstrating the importance of newly synthesized amines for the maintenance of ICS (Franklin and Herberg, 1974). Efforts are now being made to characterize the nature of the ICS deficit after selective DA lesions.

Selective 6-OHDA lesions to particular amine pathways have now been studied for their effect on ICS. To this end, ICS has been studied at independent sites in the two hemispheres after unilateral DA lesions. Unilateral 6-OHDA infusion into the SN abolishes ICS on the ipsilateral and contralateral electrode using lateral hypothalamic (Ornstein and Huston, 1975) or SN ICS electrode placements (Clavier and Fibiger, 1977). Transecting the lateral border of the hypothalamus (Huston and Ornstein, 1975), which disrupts the nigrostriatal tract, has a similar effect on hypothalamic ICS. However, the results are complicated by other experiments which report that similar lesions to SN region reduce ipsilateral but not contralateral ICS using electrode sites in the caudate nucleus (Phillips et al., 1976), lateral hypothalamus, or locus coeruleus (Koob et al., unpublished findings). The resolution of this discrepancy has important implications in theorizing about the role of dopamine systems in behavior. Contralateral deficits speak for a general role of DA in motor performance, whereas the restriction of the deficit to the ipsilateral electrode suggests that DA pathways have a more specific role in reinforcement and learning (see Section 6).

2.3.3. Appetitive Learning

Appetitive learning tasks have not been studied as intensively as avoidance learning and ICS. In the rat, pigeon, and chick, responding for food on schedules of reinforcement is severely depressed by reserpine, tetrabenazine, and α-MT. In the rat, α-MT depresses performance to a greater degree on an FR 20 than on an FR 10 schedule of reinforcement (Schoenfeld and Seiden, 1967). Responding on fixed-ratio and fixed-interval schedules of reinforcement for water reward is depressed by α-MT, with the FI schedule being more severely affected.

In the rat (Ahlenius and Engel, 1971b), lever pressing for food was abolished equally by tetrabenazine and α-MT treatment, but L-dopa (10 mg/

kg) was capable of restoring only α-MT suppression. After tetrabenazine, doses of L-dopa up to 200 mg/kg failed to restore lever pressing although the animals showed certain signs of activation such as stereotyped activity. Presumably, as in the case of locomotor activity, tetrabenazine pretreatment results in flooding of the synapse with amine after L-dopa treatment, but this neuropharmacological change is not sufficient to restore normal behavior. Lever pressing, like patterned spontaneous activity, is dependent on *the release of stored, probably newly synthesized, amine*.

Neuroleptic drugs produce a marked loss of performance and prevent acquisition of new responses in maze situations and in lever-pressing situations on varying schedules of reinforcement (Morse, 1964). Lever pressing for food or water is as severely depressed as ICS after spiroperidol (Rolls *et al.*, 1974b), suggesting that the DA-receptor blockade is interfering with the execution of complex motor responses. This interpretation is consistent with that offered for the effect of neuroleptics on conditioned shock avoidance (Fibiger *et al.*, 1975).

There are a few studies using 6-OHDA lesions in the study of conditioned appetitive behavior. Intracisternal 6-OHDA does not impair performance in a T-maze or on a schedule of continuous reinforcement (Cooper *et al.*, 1972b, 1973b), although in both experiments subsequent treatment with reserpine or α-MT, in doses which would not normally affect operant responding, severely depressed behavior. Fibiger *et al.* (1974) have attempted to localize operant response deficits to the DA system and report that bilateral 6-OHDA lesions to the SN impair approach responses for food as well as acquisition and retention of shock avoidance behavior tested in the same shuttle-box.

Acquisition of a complex motor task has also been impaired by intracisternal 6-OHDA after pargyline pretreatment (Mason and Iversen, 1974). The rats learned to run through a tube for food, and then the tube was obstructed by a ball which had to be pulled or pushed from the tube. The trial on which it was successfully removed, the time spent trying to remove the ball, and the profile of movements used in attempting the removal were noted. The 6-OHDA-lesioned rats learned more slowly, although their trying time and response repertoire were within the control range. Further localization of this impairment within the amine pathways is now required.

2.3.4. Memory Consolidation

What is the nature of the deficit shown on avoidance and appetitive learning tasks after DA depletion?

In this regard, the observation that disruptive electrical stimulation of the SN impaired retention of a passive avoidance stepdown task is of some interest. Stimulation of the SN (zona compacta) but not of the SN (zona reticulata) or nearby brainstem structures was effective (Routtenberg and Holzman, 1973). The authors comment, "Stimulation of the SNC disrupts the normal physiological activity that occurs during the original learning situation.... We do not believe that the SNC is the site of memory storage but it may be viewed as part of a system important for the memory storage of processed inputs and executed responses." As the SN (z.c.) gives rise to the nigrostriatal DA pathway, this may be construed to infer that normal DA release is a prerequisite if memory storage is to proceed at some other CNS site. However, Fibiger (1977), although able to replicate the Routtenberg and Holtzman findings with electrical stimulation, also reports that bilateral lesions to the nigrostriatal tract which result in massive loss of striatal DA do *not* impair retention of stepdown avoidance. An intact DA containing nigrostriatal pathway does not appear to be essential for memory function.

Similar conclusions were reached by Fibiger *et al.* (1975) in a study of the effects of haloperidol on acquisition of shock avoidance behavior in the rat. Haloperidol at a dose of 0.15 mg/kg/day resulted in a total failure to acquire avoidance over 9 days of training. Such animals were then switched to daily saline injections and, on the first saline day in the avoidance situation, showed performance equivalent to the saline control group which had received saline throughout the previous 9 days of training. Thus, the neuroleptic-treated groups were learning during the 9 days of training under the drug, and this is also borne out by the observation that during the presentation of the CS they urinated, defecated, and showed other signs associated with fear, although they were not able to avoid the ensuing shock. Thus, neuroleptics "do not appear to prevent the animal from learning the significance of the tone with respect to foot shock although they do prevent the motoric expression of this learning" (Fibiger *et al.*, 1975). Posluns' (1962) interpretation of the effects of chlorpromazine on shock avoidance is in agreement with this statement.

It seems more likely that SN electrical stimulation or massive blockade of DA receptors disrupts efferent striatal connections which are essential for learning and performance. There are a number of reports of memory loss after localized brain stimulation in the amygdala (Kesner and Doty, 1968; Bresnaham and Routtenberg, 1972), hippocampus (Shinkman and Kaufman, 1972), caudate nucleus (Wyers *et al.*, 1968; Wyers and Deadwyler, 1971) Haycock *et al.*, 1973; Wilburn and Kesner, 1974), and midbrain tegmentum (Glickman, 1958), and brain lesions to the substantia nigra (Thompson, 1969; Mitcham and Thomas, 1972). No doubt stimulation at these various sites disrupts neural processing in very different ways (Wilburn and Kesner, 1974) which are not apparent from the simple observation that learned behaviors are no longer adequately performed. However, in the case of the striatum it is known that there are striatotegmental and nigrotegmental (Moore *et al.*, 1971) pathways where interference would be likely to impede motor performance. In addition to its dopaminergically mediated motor function, the caudate also serves cognitive functions via its medial thalamic and cortical connections (see Section 5.3). It is therefore not surprising that lesions (Gross *et al.*, 1965) or stimulation (Peeke and Herz,

1971) of the caudate or the medial thalamus (Vanderwolf, 1969) are also reported to produce loss of learned behavior.

2.3.5. General Comments on the Role of DA in Conditioned Behavior

These experiments demonstrate that amine depletions have to be virtually complete before impressive reductions in behavioral efficiency are seen. This is borne out by a variety of earlier studies with 6-OHDA in which minimal disruption of unconditioned (Evetts et al., 1970) and conditioned behavior (Laverty and Taylor, 1970; Laverty and Arnott, 1970; Schoenfeld and Zigmond, 1970; Cooper et al., 1972b) was observed, followed by rapid recovery to normal levels. Indeed, when partial 6-OHDA lesions are made, partial blockade of behavior is not commonly seen. Behavioral output on a conditioned task may actually be enhanced (Cooper et al., 1972a; Schoenfeld and Uretsky, 1972a), as are the behavioral responses to drugs like amphetamine (Evetts et al., 1970; Creese and Iversen, 1972; Roberts et al., 1975), apomorphine (Schoenfeld and Uretsky, 1972b), and L-dopa (Uretsky and Schoenfeld, 1971; Schoenfeld and Uretsky, 1973) which are mediated by the amine systems. Supersensitivity of the receptors to the amine released from the remaining terminals or a compensatory increase in amine turnover in these terminals (Agid et al., 1973) may be responsible for these effects. For these reasons, several laboratories (Harvey, 1965; Cooper et al., 1972b; Iversen and Kelly, 1975; Stinus et al., 1975, 1976) have explored the use of reserpine and α-MT as methods for completing amine depletion after partial damage of the neurons with 6-OHDA. For example, Cooper et al. (1972b) found that in the rat after intracisternal injection of 6-OHDA (200 μg after pargyline) there was no decrement on (a) bar pressing for food on a continuous reinforcement schedule (CRF), (b) shuttlebox avoidance, in agreement with Cooper et al., 1972a, 1973a, and (c) a double T-maze task. However, when these animals were treated with 1 mg/kg reserpine or 25–50 mg/kg α-MT marked decrements in performance on all of these tasks were seen. Disruption of lever pressing for food on a fixed-ratio schedule of reinforcement following reserpine treatment of 6-OHDA lesioned rats has also been reported (Howard et al., 1971).

Although NA is excluded from a central role in the mediation of unconditioned and conditioned behavior, it clearly plays a role, albeit a modulatory one, which is not understood fully at present. Interference with NA pathways enhances amphetamine-induced stereotyped behavior and results in the emergence of increasingly stereotyped responding in the normal animal (Svensson and Waldeck, 1969; Ahlenius and Engel, 1971a,b). The NA modulation would appear, therefore, to be normally inhibitory. In line with this, Ahlenius and Engel (1972) report that in rats performance on a DRL (differential reinforcement of *low* rates of responding) schedule is disrupted by treatment with FLA-63 in much the same way as it is by amphetamine. Both treatments increase functional DA activity, and both decrease interresponse times during DRL-controlled responding. It has been suggested that successful DRL performance depends on stereotyped responses mediating accurate timing behavior. Accelerated stereotyped behavior mediating the delay would effectively shorten intertrial responses and hence distort time perception.

3. CLASSICAL STUDIES OF STRIATAL FUNCTION

The results reviewed in Section 2 suggest that severe depletion of forebrain DA depresses the performance of unconditioned and conditioned motor acts. The deficit is not of a primarily sensory or associative nature; rats discriminate stimuli and learn new behavior patterns after DA pathway lesions, but they are impaired in the initiation of sequences of purposeful behavior. In many of the experiments both the nigrostriatal and the mesolimbic DA systems have been depleted or lesioned, and it is not possible to ascribe the deficits to one DA pathway rather than another. There are, however, a few studies which suggest that the nigrostriatal system is especially central to the programming of motor behavior. It is worth noting that quite independently of pharmacologically oriented studies of the nigrostriatal tract and in some cases long before the DA pathways had been discovered and anatomically defined, disruption of caudate function by classical stimulation and lesion techniques was known to produce deficits similar to those now seen after specific DA lesions.

Buchwald, for example, in an elegant series of papers, studied the electrophysiological and behavioral consequences of electrical stimulation of the caudate nucleus of the cat. Low-frequency stimulation produced a characteristic "caudate-spindle" electrical activity which was correlated with an inhibitory behavioral role of the caudate. Buchwald *et al.* (1961) found that when caudate-spindling was elicited, cats slowed their bar-pressing rate for reward; higher levels of stimulation produced an abrupt cessation of bar pressing, although no abnormal motor behaviors were observed. The results were interpreted to indicate that caudate "stimulation in this frequency range (1 pulse/5 sec to 10 pulses/sec) produces behavioral effects which can be considered as inhibitory, e.g., increased reaction time, cessation of bar pressing, failure to respond to learned cues, inactivation, sleep." Much higher levels of stimulation give evidence of arousal and facilitation, but the inhibitory role is felt to be the usual role of the caudate, a view upheld by other chemical and electrical stimulation and lesion studies. Prolonged disruptive stimulation of the caudate induced by injection of alumina cream produces catatonia, loss of spontaneous movements, and "active catalepsy" in the cat (Spiegel and Szakely, 1961). Crystalline carbachol has been applied to the caudate nucleus (Stevens *et al.*, 1961) of cats where it produces turning behavior followed by a "profound state of quietude" similar to that observed after low-frequency caudate stimulation by Buchwald *et al.* (1961). At this time, shock-avoidance behavior was severely disrupted although shock escape remained intact. These results may be particularly relevant to considerations of the role of DA in the caudate, as there is known to be functional balance between DA and cholinergic mechanisms in normal caudate function (Stadler *et al.*, 1973). Electrical stimulation of the caudate causes a cessation of ongoing eating in the cat (Lineberry and Siegel, 1971) and monkey (Delgado, 1957), and of bar pressing for reward in the monkey (Kitsikis and Rougeul, 1968). In free-moving monkeys in social situations, Delgado *et al.* (1975) find that electrical stimulation of the globus pallidus depresses behavior in the dominant monkey of a pair, making it temporarily the more submissive, again suggestive of a striatopallidal inhibitory influence. A learned motor task involving the initiation and performance of a sequence of discrete motor acts was studied by Wilburn and Kesner (1974) in the cat. The subject was required to remove food from a straight rod or a bent-wire shape. Caudate stimulation (particularly in the anterior ventral region) increased the latency and the time required for successful retrieval of the food. The impairment increased in severity as the current intensity was raised. Videotape analysis of behavior revealed that "During stimulation trials, the most time-consuming errors appeared to involve a failure to organize response components temporally in a productive sequence. The cats repeatedly pawed at an empty rod segment or propelled the food away from themselves." Similar difficulty in suppressing inappropriate responses have been observed on DRL schedules of reinforcement after caudate lesions (Schmaltz and Isaacson, 1968) or stimulation (Deadwyler and Wyers, 1970) and on Sidman avoidance after caudate lesions (Allen and Davison, 1973). Other studies in the literature do not provide such a detailed picture of the nature of the motor impairment but concur with the conclusions of Wilburn and Kesner (1974). Caudate lesions result in profound hypokinesia in the monkey (Davis, 1958), in the cat (Gybels *et al.*, 1967) they interfere with natural movements, such as climbing steps, righting after being dropped, avoiding obstacles and attending to a mouse, and in the rat (Thompson, 1959) they alter avoidance behavior, as do globus pallidus lesions in the cat (Laursen, 1963*b*). Cryogenic lesions to the caudate in the rat (Hansing *et al.*, 1968) interfere with lever-pressing, and in the monkey (Bowen, 1969) they interfere with tracking a lighted moving target with the arm. Of particular interest is an old paper by Rogers (1922) reporting that in the pigeon, removal of the homolog of the striatum impaired the acquisition or retention of the ability to place, in a proper sequence, the patterns of behavior making up the rituals of mating and nesting activity; a deficit reminiscent of that described by Wilburn and Kesner (1974). The reader may question why this section has been included in a chapter on DA and behavior as none of the studies cited make any reference to DA. This is true, but they do define the role of the caudate in motor behavior, and it is quite conceivable that some of the deficits described may have been due to disruption of the nigrostriatal contribution to caudate function. The other reason for their inclusion is educative. Workers sophisticated in the use of pharmacological tools are rarely experts in behavior. In reading the rapidly expanding literature on dopamine, it is difficult to ignore the fact that relatively little advance has been made in defining the precise role of DA in the forebrain organization of behavior. No DA, no behavior—but this does not tell us very much, and clearly it would be foolish to assume that DA pathways have some exclusive role in the generation of behavior. The pathways may serve a very important role in the brain organization required for purposeful behavior, but only with sophisticated behavioral measures will it be possible to understand the integral role of DA in behavior. In this respect, there is much to learn from the older studies of caudate function.

4. A SYNTHESIS OF THE ROLE OF DA IN THE NIGROSTRIATAL TRACT

4.1. Endogenous DA Asymmetry and Sensory–Motor Coordination

A rat with bilateral 6-OHDA lesions of the SN does not show unconditioned motor acts like eating or drinking and is largely hypokinetic. It is also incapable of generating new responses or of performing previously learned ones. This lack of initiation of motor acts is comparable to that seen in Parkinson's disease. However, the lesioned animal is capable of rapid movement if this is required for survival. Ranje and Ungerstedt (1977) report that SN lesioned rats are able to swim in order to escape when submerged in a water maze, although if placed in an ordinary maze with food in one arm they remain incapable of responding. Parkinsonian patients are also reported to be able to move with remarkable speed in dangerous situations. In addition to the lack of motor initiation associated with massive damage to the nigrostriatal system, sensory neglect is also observed in the rat (Ungerstedt, 1971) and cat (Wolgin and Teitelbaum, 1974). This was originally reported by Teitelbaum and Epstein (1962) following bilateral hypothalamic lesions. A *unilateral* lesion to the nigrostriatal DA produces the same deficit, and as this tract passes through the hypothalamus, it is likely that Teitelbaum and Epstein damaged it with their hypothalamic lesion. The syndrome has been reevaluated by Marshall and Teitelbaum recently and described in detail in Chapter 7 of Volume 7 of this *Handbook*. The syndrome associated with unilateral damage to the nigrostriatal system consists of loss of motor efficiency plus generalized sensory neglect on the contralateral side. This results in a postural asymmetry in which the head is turned toward the lesioned side, motor tone and sensory awareness being dominant on that side (i.e., contralateral to the intact nigrostriatal system).

When treated with dopamine-releasing drugs such as amphetamine, locomotion is stimulated and effected by the markedly asymmetrical motor apparatus, and turning toward the lesion side occurs. The sensorimotor function of the nigrostriatal system is thus most dramatically revealed in the asymmetrical preparation. The bilaterally lesioned preparation suffers such a total lack of responsiveness, and it is more difficult to appreciate the impairment. In considering the experimental sensory–motor neglect, it has been pointed out that Parkinsonian patients also show sensory neglect together with their motor deficit. They are observed to use devices to get the responses they are capable of making under better sensory control. For example, they walk more readily and smoothly if lines are drawn on the floor to guide the placing of the feet.

However, it is not necessary to invoke lesions to the nigrostriatal system to appreciate its role in sensorimotor integration. A complementary approach is provided by the studies of Glick and his collaborators studying the role of DA in motor behavior in the normal intact rat, rather than in the lesioned preparation. The rotational behavior seen after amphetamine in the unilateral SN lesioned preparation has been discussed in the previous chapter. Jerussi and Glick (1974) report that normal rats reliably circle to the left or right after varying doses of amphetamine. With lower doses the circling tends to involve the animal rotating on its hind legs with its front paws moving around the surface of the spherical rotometer. At higher doses rats rotate in the tight circles more commonly seen in the SN lesioned preparation. Amphetamine-induced rotation in normal rats suggests, according to the authors, "that there may exist an intrinsic bilateral inbalance in the dopamine content of the nigrostriatal system of normal unoperated rats." Efferent pathways from frontal cortex modulate striatal function, and removal of this cortex results in enhancing motor responses to drugs, like amphetamine, which we know to be mediated by striatal dopamine systems. Glick and Greenstein (1973) have reported that *unilateral* frontal lesions enhance spontaneous and amphetamine-induced rotation because, it is assumed, removal of the influence of frontal cortex results in supersensitivity of the nigrostriatal projection on the lesioned side of the brain. Jerussi and Glick (1975) have subsequently studied rotational behavior induced by apomorphine, the dopamine agonist. Normal rats reliably rotate in one or another direction with doses of apomorphine up to 10 mg/kg. The authors suggest that this result, like that obtained with *d*-amphetamine, reflects the intrinsic asymmetry in dopamine levels in the striatum. Small unilateral lesions to the caudate nucleus result in supersensitivity to dopamine agonists. After such lesions the degree of change in rotation to apomorphine in a given rat depends on the nature of the preoperative rotational behavior in that animal and thus presumably on whether the more or less active striatum was disrupted by the lesion. Rats showed the greatest increase in rotation to apomorphine after the lesion if it had been made ipsilateral rather than contralateral to their preoperative direction of rotation.

Glick *et al.* (1974) went on to investigate the biochemical basis of observed asymmetry in spontaneous and amphetamine-induced behavior. Rats were placed in an apparatus for measuring rotations and treated with either saline or amphetamine (20 mg/kg). Rotations were recorded for 30 min, and then the rats were killed and the striatum assayed fluorometrically to determine the dopamine levels. The results indicated that there was a normal inbalance in the content of dopamine in the left and right striata and that the potentiation of this imbalance by amphetamine is associated with rotation. When the direction of rotation was correlated with the striatal DA levels, it was found that the dopamine levels were significantly lower in the side ipsilateral to the direction of rotation. This effect was greater in the amphetamine-treated rats than in the saline-treated rats. Presumably amphetamine releases more dopamine from the functionally more active nigrostriatal tract (i.e., the one with higher DA levels) and thus produces rotation toward the side of lower functional levels. This is exactly what happens if one nigrostriatal tract is lesioned directly. The dopamine asymmetry in the amphetamine group was not attributed to an unequal distribution of amphetamine in the two sides of the brain. If this were the case, noradrenaline levels in the two sides would also be expected to differ after amphetamine since the drug also effects the storage and release of NA.

Glick has subsequently extended his studies to other aspects of motor behavior. For example, Zimmerberg *et al.* (1974) tested rats in a T-maze situation in which the animals were required to escape from a foot shock by entering either the right or left arm of the maze. Ten consecutive trials with intertrial intervals of 5–15 sec were given, and 92% of the rats showed a side preference under these testing conditions. Biochemical experiments were performed on four more groups of rats: The rats were (1) killed 2 min after 10 trials of preference testing, (2) killed 10 days after testing, (3) killed 2 min after 10 shock trials on which escape into the arms was prevented, and (4) killed 2 min after 10 trials in the maze without shock or the possibility of entering the arms. In both groups tested for preference, dopamine values were higher in the striatum contralateral to the preferred direction than in the ipsilateral striatum. Similarly significant high/low dopamine ratios in groups (3) and (4) suggest that foot shock or learning *per se* does not produce the left/right DA differences. Rather it would seem that the differences reflect intrinsic normal functional differences between the striata which manifest themselves, behaviorally, as spatial motor preferences. Spontaneous rotation was found to correlate with spatial preference in subsequent studies. Rats were first tested in the T-maze for spatial preference and then injected with 1.0 mg/kg *d*-amphetamine and placed in the rotometer. Rats preferentially rotated in the direction of the spatial preference determined in the T-maze, suggesting that "rotation is a stereotyped form of spatial behavior."

Rats show a consistent side preference when offered a choice of two levers in an operant chamber (Glick, 1973). When responding under a fixed-interval 15-sec schedule of water reinforcement, all rats showed a consistent preference for one lever. The effect of *d*-amphetamine in doses of up to 2.0 mg/kg on fixed-interval performance and lever preference was studied, and it was found, particularly at the higher doses, that when the rate of responding to the lever was decreased the strength of the side preference increased. As with the T-maze results, it appears that one of the actions of amphetamine is to produce stereotyped spatial preference presumably by accentuating further the normal asymmetry of the striatal DA system. Thus, under high doses of amphetamine the organism becomes locked in a spatially localized response. Additional discriminative stimuli in a location may further enhance the tendency to direct behavior to that part of the spatial environment. The nature of the response topography demanded in a particular situation also influences the degree of spatial preferences and how it is changed by amphetamine. For example, if rats are responding at a high rate, such as that engendered by fixed-ratio schedules of reinforcement, lever preference is greater (Glick and Jerussi, 1974).

The general model emerging from Glick's work is that there is a normal asymmetry in the striatal DA activity. This results in rotation away from the side of higher activity, spatial preference to the contralateral side, and a preference to make overt motor responses to the contralateral side. It is known from independent studies that a unilateral lesion to the caudate nucleus or globus pallidus selectively blocks lever pressing with the paw contralateral to the lesion.

Contralateral sensory neglect or inattention after unilateral lesions to the nigrostriatal DA system is observed in rats and cat (Frigyesi *et al.*, 1971). (See Chapter 7, Volume 7 of this *Handbook*.) However, the asymmetry revealed by lesions is operational to a lesser degree in the intact animal. A corollary to this idea is the prediction that "artificial" activation of one striatum would make it dominant, would enhance sensory and motor visual attention to the opposite side, and could be used to reverse the direction of the endogenous asymmetry." Zimmerberg and Glick (1975) have used electrical stimulation of the caudate nucleus in the rat to do this. Rats were trained in a two-lever situation to press for water on a continuous-reinforcement schedule. All showed consistent side preferences. Electrodes were then implanted bilaterally in the caudate nuclei, and the surgical procedure was shown not to alter performance or lever preference. The effect of unilateral caudate stimulation on lever-pressing behavior was then observed. Stimulation on the same side as the preferred lever caused a reversal of side preference to the opposite lever. Stimulation of the caudate on the side opposite to the preferred lever had no effect on preference. Thus, an electrically induced increase in activity in one side of the nigrostriatal system results in sensory–motor preference on the opposite side.

There is also evidence from the work of Kitsikis *et al.* (1972) that variations in the endogenous striatum DA levels between animals may account for the great variability of performance shown in certain conditioned-performance tasks. It is known from the basic surgical lesion studies that in the monkey and cat the caudate nucleus plays a role in successful delayed response, delayed alternation, and visual-discrimination behavior. Starting with these observations, Kitsikis *et al.* (1972) investigated in the cat whether delayed-response performance (DR) could be improved by acute or chronic treatment with L-dopa, a drug which, among other effects, raises brain dopamine levels. Two groups of cats were selected, one a *low* performing group unable to learn the delayed-response task within 1000 trials (normal average 300 trials), and another a naive group selected after only 10 training trials. Both groups received a 30 mg/kg capsule of L-dopa after 10 baseline daily training trials, and then ten further test trials were presented 4, 6, 8, and 24 hr after the drug. The acute dose of L-dopa was studied six times, followed by a placebo experiment. Subsequently, chronic L-dopa treatment (50 mg/kg) was investigated. Visual-discrimination performance was investigated in separate groups of cats, and L-dopa was found to have no effect on this behavior. By contrast, acute L-dopa in the low-performing cats resulted in a consistent improvement of DR performance, as measured by errors, 4–8 hr after the L-dopa. There was also a tendency to improvement in the naive cats. In control experiments on naive cats, a dose of 30 mg/kg L-dopa was shown to elevate striatal DA 4–8 hr after the drug treatment. On chronic L-dopa treatment, a gradual improvement in performance was observed over the 7 days, with a return to predrug performance levels 48–72 hr after the cessation of drug treatment. The cats were subsequently killed, and DA, NA, and 5-HT were assayed in many brain areas. The low-performing cats showed significantly lower striatal DA levels but no difference in NA or 5-HT. Thus, the authors claim, "The content of DA in the brain and the level of performance on the delayed-response task appear, in fact, to be closely related."

4.2. Behavioral Nature of Amphetamine-Induced Motor Changes

So far the role of the nigrostriatal tract has been determined by blocking its activity with lesions or drugs. Equally powerful are techniques which increases functional activity. The behavioral consequences of selective electrical activation of the nigrostriatal DA neurons have not been studied in any detail. Amphetamine, however, provides a pharmacological activator, and analysis of the behavioral changes induced by this stimulant (Lyon and Robbins, 1975) may provide an important clue concerning the functional significance of the nigrostriatal DA tract. Low doses of amphetamine release DA and NA widely in the forebrain and result in higher levels of coordinated locomotor activity. However, as the dose increases the animal no longer shows a stimulation of general body movement. Instead, isolated motor acts from the repertoire of the species occur, out of behavioral context and with abnormal frequency. This may be contrasted with the observation that chlorpromazine decreases the frequency of initiation of new motor acts (Bindra and Baran, 1959). As the amphetamine dose increases further, the range of motor acts observed becomes restricted further although the frequency of emission is very high, until eventually the motor stimulation is so intense the organism is incapable of completing the acts and motor tremor is observed. Lyon and Robbins (1975) have considered this phenomenon of drug-induced stereotypy and suggest that as the physiological consequences of amphetamine increase in the CNS the completion of *sequences of motor acts* becomes impossible. Thus, behavior which requires chains of organized motor acts such as grooming and social interaction rapidly become impossible. Acts which can be completed within a shorter period of time are still possible and thus come to dominate the behavior in a highly abnormal fashion. Sniffing, licking, and biting, for example, are constituents of many behavior patterns but occur with a relatively low frequency. Under 5 mg/kg *d*-amphetamine a rat may sniff one point in the cage repetitively for an hour or more. Rats do not show amphetamine-induced stereotypy after striatal DA loss, and therefore it is reasonable to assume that DA release in the striatum is the neuropharmacological trigger for the appearance of stereotyped responding. What we do not understand is how local DA imbalance in the striatum produces this profound change in motor-system oganization. The striatum is itself constituted of many neuronal systems in addition to the nigrostriatal input and is anatomically related to thalamocortical, extrapyramidal, and tegmental motor substrates. The circuit involved in the expression of stereotyped behavior is not known. It seems unlikely that species-specific motor routines are programmed in the striatum, although electrical stimulation of this structure is capable of inducing organized motor patterns. It is known that motor routines can be activated by electrical stimulation of tegmental areas, which may well provide the focus at which forebrain systems influence the output of motor behavior (Hopkins and Niessen, 1976). Although Lyon and Robbins do not pay particular attention to physiological theory, it seems possible that the brainstem could be the final common pathway of the increasing neurophysiological activation induced by amphetamine. Dysfunction within the neuronal circuits mediating specific motor subroutines could account for the constraints on motor output induced by amphetamine, notably the *repetition* of acts which can be *completed within a short period of time*.

A study of amphetamine-induced stereotypy may therefore tell us something of the normal function of DA release in the sriatum. Without DA release, the animal appears unable to modify existing response or initiate new appropriate responses to the environment. Thus, an adequate level of DA modulation in the caudate appears to be the prerequisite for sensorimotor coordination. However, there is no evidence that DA has a role in relating the appropriate response to the prevailing conditions. Presumably many forebrain mechanisms concerned with discrimination, motivation, and emotion have roles to play in the selection process. The caudate may be a site

5. AN OVERVIEW OF STRIATAL FUNCTION

Assuming that the net functional state of the striatum is tonically inhibitory (Buchwald et al., 1961), it may be suggested that motor efficiency depends on some optimum level of this inhibition state. Under- or overinhibition prevents organized motor output although the behavioral symptoms of these two states may be very different (compare, for example, Parkinson's disease and amphetamine psychosis). The inhibitory state of the caudate is dependent, however, on several discrete input systems in addition to the nigrostriatal DA tract, notably from the thalamus and cortex. How these inputs contribute to the steady state of the striatum remains to be explored, and electrophysiological techniques will play an important role here (Hull et al., 1973).

5.1. Frontostriatal Interactions

It is well established, for example, that the frontal cortex plays a modulatory role over striatal function. Lesions to the frontal cortex (particularly the ventral aspect of the frontal lobe) produce, in the monkey, a general release of motor control. Monkeys are hyperactive, and subsequently it was shown in a variety of testing situations that after such lesions animals could no longer control response tendencies, particularly in behavioral situations where reinforcement training had initially encouraged responding. In other words, it appeared that responding could no longer be inhibited (Rosvold and Mishkin, 1961). A number of studies were performed on this frontal "disinhibition syndrome," demonstrating that disinhibition occurred on tasks tested in all sensory modalities, although there was no evidence of a loss of discriminative ability (Mishkin, 1964). Subsequently Iversen and Mishkin (1970), using an auditory behavioral technique devised by Lawicka et al. (1975), localized the response-discrimination impairment further. Bilateral lesions to a sector of the orbital frontal cortex, termed the inferior convexity, and focused on the rim of tissue at the lateral dorsofrontal/orbitofrontal boundary, produced a more severe response-release impairment than equivalent lesions to the remainder of the orbital surface or to the dorsolateral cortex (Lawicka et al., 1975).

In parallel to these experiments, anatomical and behavioral studies were pursued on the areas of the caudate nucleus and limbic system receiving frontal projections. In these structures, lesions to the foci which received projections from the orbital cortex also produced disinhibition deficits.

Object discrimination reversal, a measure of response disinhibition, was impaired by lesions to a region of the caudate nucleus receiving strong projections from the orbital frontal cortex (Divac et al., 1967). Caudate lesions also impair performance on a bar-pressing extinction test (Butters and Rosvold, 1968) previously found to be severely affected by orbitofrontal lesions (Butter et al., 1963). In rats also caudate lesions produce an overresponding impairment in certain behavioral situations (Whittier and Orr, 1962; Kirkby, 1969; Kirkby and Kimble, 1968).

Of particular interest in the present context, frontal lesions in the rat enhance the locomotor and stereotyped responses induced by amphetamine (Iversen et al., 1971). Lesions to the dorsal aspects of the caudate nucleus (Wolfarth, 1974) also have this effect presumably because the frontostriatal projections are damaged. Thus, frontal cortex and SN projection interact in the caudate to determine the level of motor output. This aspect of striatal organization has been taken up in a series of studies by Neill and his co-workers. Frontal lesions and placement of anticholinergic drugs into the ventral caudate (Neill and Grossman, 1970), but not the dorsal caudate, have similar effects on certain behavioral tests, and Neill (1976) suggests that an excitatory (Bloom et al., 1965) ACh link is the final pathway of the frontal influence on the substrate of the striatum. In the same region of caudate, lesions or manipulations of DA terminals interfere with DA-mediated behaviors such as ICS (Neill et al., 1975) and apomorphine (Wolfarth, 1974) and amphetamine stereotypy (Neill et al., 1974b). Electrophysiology studies show that the net outcome of DA release on the postsynaptic membrane is inhibitory (York, 1967). The following model is proposed (Neill, 1976) which will account both for a great deal of recent pharmacological work on the striatum and classical stimulation and lesion work (Fig. 2). Certain predictions can be made, and the references refer to experimental results which fit these predictions.

1. Removal of the origin of the excitatory influence (i.e., frontal cortex

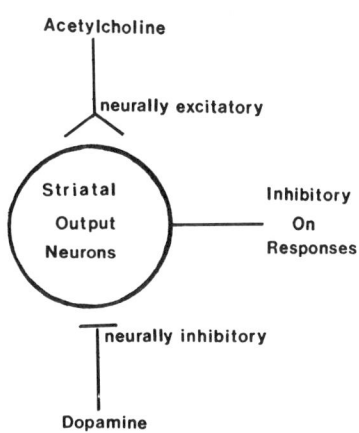

FIG. 2. Model reproduced from Neill (1976) illustrating the frontostriatal projection mediated via an excitatory ACh synapse and the nigrostriatal projection mediated via an inhibitory DA synapse. Both of these influence the intrinsic caudate substrate X which maintains a tonic inhibitory control over output.

or site of passage of fronto/striatal fibers in the dorsal caudate) would produce a predominance of inhibition on X and hence release of behavior (Mishkin, 1964; Butters and Rosvold, 1968) or enhancement of cortically induced motor responses (Liles and Davis, 1969).

2. Removal of excitatory influence on X by pharmacological blockade in the ventral caudate, e.g., scopolamine would also increase inhibition of X and thereby release behavior (Neill and Grossman, 1970).

3. Increase in excitatory influence, e.g., by carbachol, would counter the inhibition of X, and hence the net inhibitory strength of X would increase and behavioral output would be depressed (Stevens et al., 1961).

4. Activation of X by means of electrical stimulation would increase tonic inhibitory influence of caudate and reduce behavioral output (Akert and Anderson, 1951; Buchwald et al., 1961) or inhibit cortically induced motor response (Liles and Davis, 1969).

5. Surgical lesions to be ventral anterior caudate remove part of inhibitory substrate X and result in release of behavior, e.g., on DRL schedules of reinforcement (Neill et al., 1974c).

6. Selective lesion to DA inhibitory influence either by SN (Feltz and de Champlain, 1972) or caudate injection of 6-OHDA results in increased firing of caudate neurons and thus increased inhibitory function of X and reduced behavioral output (Ungerstedt, 1974; Creese and Iversen, 1975).

7. Pharmacological blockade of DA receptors with, e.g., neuroleptics, would mimic the effects of nigrostriatal lesions and reduces behavioral output (see Sections 2.2 and 2.3).

8. Activation of DA inhibitory influences, e.g., by iontophoretic application of DA to the caudate nucleus, or electrical stimulation of SN to release DA (Connor, 1970) increases the inhibition of substrate X and hence reduces its inhibitory state. Increased firing of substrate X (caudate) neurons would be predicted and is reported to occur by Hoffer (cited by Ungerstedt, 1974). Drugs which release DA in the intact animal, e.g., amphetamine, would also result in inhibition of the tonic state of X and thus release behavior.

The foregoing model represents only one of many complex relationships within the striatum. Interactions between chemically coded systems in the striatum have been discovered with pharmacological or biochemical techniques. The anatomical nature of these interactions remain obscure, even in the case of the intensively studied DA/ACh balance.

5.2. How Does the Striatum Influence Motor Control?

This question provides the next challenge to those interested in striatal DA and motor behavior. First of all, there is anatomical data to consider, which emphasizes the complex connections of the striatum both with the thalamocortical motor substrates and with other extrapyramidal structures. It is also clear that the striatum has descending connections which project as far as the ventral tegmental areas where their terminations overlap with brainstem afferents from the limbic areas (Hopkins and Niessen, 1976). Vanderwolf (1971) suggested that this dichotomy of projection indicates striatal control over what he called "voluntary" and "involuntary" acts. The second interesting feature of the striatum concerns the kind of musculature and kind of movements it controls via the extrapyramidal brainstem projections to the spinal cord. In primates, distal musculature, particularly of the digits, is controlled contralaterally by extrapyramidal projections in the lateral brainstem and by the direct pyramidal control of motor neurons, an influence which refines, further, control over this group of muscles. Proximal and axial musculature is controlled bilaterally by the ventromedial brain pathway. Selective lesioning of these brainstem pathways reveals that the lateral system is concerned with discrete movements of the extremities, whereas the ventromedial system is concerned with integrated body-limb movements (Lawrence and Kuypers, 1968). This differentiation is borne out in the split-brain monkey; when visual input is restricted to one hemisphere, the monkey is able to extend the contralateral arm and pick up morsels of food from deep holes, whereas with the ipsilateral arm only gross movements of the limbs toward the baited food wells were possible. Dexterous retrieval of the food with the fingers was not possible (Brinkman and Kuypers, 1973).

Kornhuber (1974) has made a functional, rather than an anatomical, distinction between distal and axial musculature, describing rapid *ballistic* movements controlled predominantly by direct pyramidal control and slow *ramp* movements controlled predominantly by brainstem motor projections. Eye movements and discrete finger or arm movements are ballistic, whereas coordinated movements of the whole limb or body area are ramp.

Body posture, standing up, walking, sitting down, riding a bicycle, knitting, shaving, eating with a knife and fork—all these would be ramp movements depending on bilateral extrapyramidal motor brainstem projections, and all are severely retarded in Parkinson's disease, where a major component of the forebrain extrapyramidal system is known to be dysfunctional.

Electrophysiological work tends to support Kornhuber's functional distinction of movements. In a series of studies Evarts and his co-workers have demonstrated that cerebellar neurons (Thach, 1968) and thalamic (Evarts, 1971) and pyramidal-tract (Evarts, 1966) neurons fire before a fast, direct movement of the limb is made. Indeed it has been suggested that the cerebellum provides the neurophysiological trigger to the cortical pyramidal system.

Neurons in the basal ganglia of cat (Kitsikis *et al.*, 1971) and monkey (DeLong, 1971, 1972) also fire when discrete goal-directed movements are made, for example, to scratch or retrieve food. DeLong has also made a systematic study of such units in the monkey during conditioned limb movements. Neurons in the globus pallidus (DeLong, 1971) and putamen (DeLong, 1972) fire when the monkey alternately pushes and pulls or moves from side to side a lever to obtain food-juice reward. In the putamen, it is also found that slow and fast movements are coded differently by the neurons (DeLong, 1974). Monkeys were trained to grasp a lever and make slow and fast lateral movements between two 1-cm zones, 5 cm apart; the lever had to be held in one zone for 2-6 sec, and when a green lamp came on a slow movement (0.7 sec) had to be made to the opposite zone; after holding in this position, a rapid movement was required back to the starting position when a red light came on. More than 50% of putamen neurons studied discharged preferentially to the slow movement and less than 10% to the fast movements. Such results support an anatomical differentiation of mechanisms responsible for ramp and ballistic movements.

Of course we have no direct evidence that the dopamine-containing innervation of the striatum plays a particular central role in the control of ramp movements. However, Kornhuber (1974) has pointed out that motor behavior dependent on ramp movements, like rising and walking, are especially severely affected in Parkinsonian patients. For this reason it would be interesting to combine pharmacological, iontophoretic, and surgical manipulations of the nigrostriatal tract with the electrophysiological techniques of DeLong. Is it possible, for example, to detect ramp-movement-related activity in the striatum after depletion of the dopamine innervation, or would such responses be modified by reversible inactivation of the nigrostriatal tract. It would also be interesting to know if the DA neurons of the nigrostriatal tract itself show any characteristic firing pattern in relation to ramp movements. Such information would indicate if the nigrostriatal tract merely modulates intrinsic caudate organization or in some way selects caudate output. This no doubt would be technically an extremely difficult experiment to perform because although dopamine neurons in the SN can be identified, and recorded from, they are small neurons and thus less amenable to chronic unit recording procedures. At present perhaps the best we can hope for is further information on the dynamics of the interactions in the caudate.

5.3. Striatum and Cognitive Function

There is thus sufficient evidence to suggest that the striatum serves a modulatory role on motor output constituted partly by a dopaminergic innervation. However, opinion differs as to whether or not striatal lesions impair only motor function. Does the striatum also serve a role in the cognitive aspects of response selection, and if so, is this function dependent in any way on the DA innervation? Divac (1972) points out that there are highly localized cortical inputs to the caudate nucleus from all regions of the cortex, not merely from the response control area of the orbital-frontal cortex. Selective lesions to these caudate foci produce specific *cognitive* deficits identical to those seen after lesions to the cortical area giving rise to the particular striatal afferent pathway. Intracaudate dissociation of this kind has been demonstrated in the rat (Oberg and Divac, 1975), cat (Divac, 1968), and monkey (Divac *et al.*, 1967). The deficits cannot be ascribed either to motor disinhibition or loss of motor initiation. They are therefore considered to be cognitive deficits. Other workers have reached a similar conclusion. Chorover and Gross (1963) and Gross *et al.* (1965) found impairment in rats on a two-lever alternation task which could not be attributed to motor disinhibition.

It remains a challenge to discover if the motor and cognitive roles of the striatum are independent or interdependent aspects of the functioning of this complex structure. It is interesting to note, however, that in the cat low levels of striatal DA are associated with poor performance on the delayed-response task, a cognitive test impaired by dorsolateral frontal lesions and anterodorsal caudate lesions (Divac *et al.*, 1967). L-Dopa treatment improved DR performance in such cats (Kitsikis *et al.*, 1972). Furthermore, L-dopa therapy in Parkinson patients improves the initiation and production of organized motor acts and also improves intellectual functioning (Meier and Martin, 1970; Marsh *et al.*, 1971). Several other workers have hinted at an interdependence of the motor control and the selection process in the caudate (Papeschi, 1972; Wilburn and Kesner, 1974).

Kiksikis and Roberge (1973) have used α-methyl-p-tyrosine to study further the role of catecholamines in the performance of spatial delayed response and visual discrimination behavior, behaviors known on independent evidence (Divac *et al.*, 1967) to be dependent on frontostriatal function. They found that whereas L-dopa treatment improved performance (Kitsikis *et al.*, 1972), α-MT depressed performance on the delayed-response task. Visual discrimination was again not influenced by the drug treatment. However, α-MT alters brain levels of NA and 5-HT as well as DA, and, tempting as it was, the authors were slightly cautious in correlating the loss of performance on delayed response solely with the DA change. In considering why visual discrimination is not affected by L-dopa or α-MT, the authors point out that nonspatial delayed-response testing with the go–no go method is also improved by L-dopa. Both of the delayed-response tasks sensitive to brain amine manipulations require the holding of information for a short period of time. They suggest that perhaps "it may be the neural activity underlying this 'retention' or 'activation' period that is enhanced or impaired by L-dopa and α-MT respectively." If this is so, DA release in the caudate could facilitate cognitive acts in much the same way it does motor acts.

5.4. Nonstriatal Dopamine Systems

The deficits reviewed in Section 2 and synthesized in Sections 4 and 5 were due to damage of the nigrostriatal DA system. The review would be complete if DA were localized exclusively to this forebrain pathway. Although this projection received most attention when the maps of amine distribution were first published (probably on account of Parkinson's disease), it was clear, even then, that there was a second forebrain DA system arising from A10 neurons located medial to the SN and lying dorsal and lateral to the interpeduncular nucleus. Fibers of this system were reported to innervate the nucleus accumbens (NAS), tuberculum olfactorium, and part of the amygdala. Subsequently, Glowinski and his co-workers discovered that DA was also localized in certain sectors of the frontal cortex in the rat. Detailed mapping of the so-called "mesolimbic" and "mesofrontal" or "mesocortical" DA innervations has been contributed by Bjorklund and Lindvall and is reviewed in Volume 9 of this *Handbook*. An updated view of the DA pathways is summarized in Fig. 3.

What then are the roles of the other two dopamine systems? Is there any evidence of biochemical or functional differentiation? Knowledge is fragmentary. On some measures, for example, the biochemical response to dopamine antagonists, both systems respond in the same way (Westernick and Korf, 1975). However, on other measures there may be differences. DA/ACh interactions appear to be of less functional significance in the mesolimbic system than in the striatum (Iversen and Koob, 1977). The changes in DA turnover induced by neuroleptics may differ in the various terminal DA sites. The long-lasting neuroleptic pipotiazine increases DA turnover in the various forebrain sites, but this change persists in the mesocortical area whereas it does not in the nigrostriatal system (Scatton *et al.*, 1977).

Work on the behavioral role of the dopamine systems is just beginning, but there is one interesting lead. 6-OHDA lesions to the mesolimbic/frontal

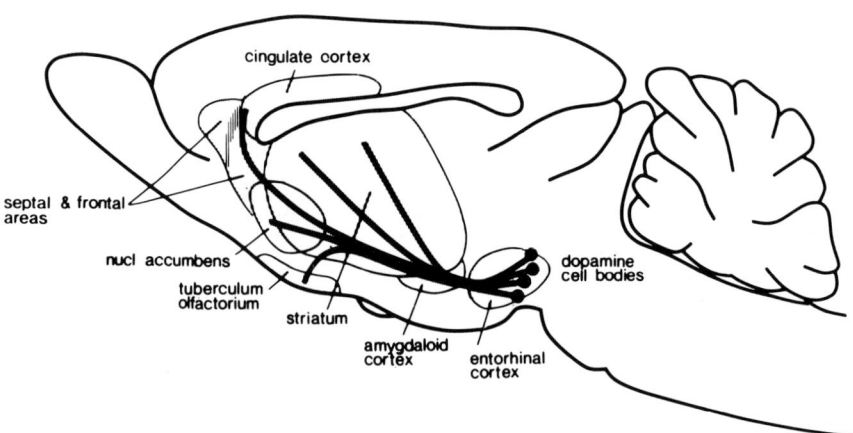

FIG. 3. Lateral view of the ascending DA pathways to (a) striatum: *nigrostriatal*; (b) nucleus acumbens and tuberculum olfactorium: *mesolimbic*; (c) septum, frontal and cingulate cortex: *mesocortical*. Kindly supplied by Ungerstedt.

system (induced by 6-OHDA infusion into the NAS) abolishes the psychomotor stimulation induced by low doses of amphetamine, without any effect on the stereotyped responses seen after high doses. 6-OHDA striatal lesions have an opposite effect on psychomotor stimulation and stereotypy (Kelly *et al.*, 1975). Similarly, local injection of neuroleptic into the NAS blocks amphetamine-induced locomotion, whereas stereotypy is most effectively blocked by striatal injections of neuroleptic (Pijnenburg *et al.*, 1975a,b). If we understood the behavioral implication of amphetamine-induced locomotion, we might understand the role of the mesolimbic system.

The clue to the role of the nigrostriatal system lies in its association with a clinical motor condition and in its massive anatomical relationship with motor circuitries at all levels in the CNS. We do not have clear leads regarding the mesolimbic system. It would appear, however, that although the nucleus accumbens projects to the globus pallidus (Swanson and Cowan, 1975) and thus has access to motor output systems, it also has strong connections with the limbohypothalamic axis and its tegmental projections (Powell and Leman, 1976). This anatomical dissociation is illustrated in Fig. 4 and has led to the speculation (Iversen, 1977) that although both DA systems are concerned in some sense with behavioral arousal, the nigrostriatal system facilitates sensorimotor behavior whereas the mesolimbic system modulates

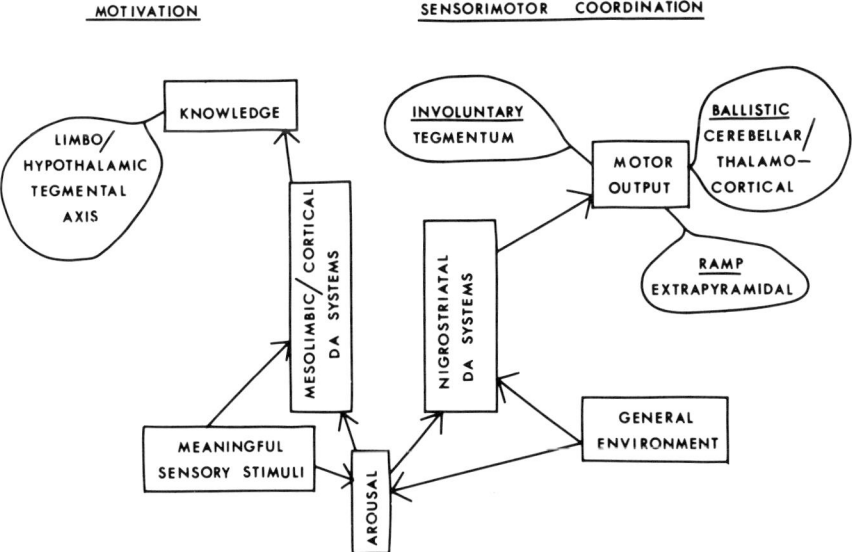

FIG. 4. Stylized diagram illustrating the afferent and efferent relation of the parallel ascending mesolimbic and nigrostriatal DA systems. Specific motivation and sensorimotor coordination are proposed as the functions of these two systems.

affective responses to the environment. This proposal is illustrated in Fig. 4. Purposeful behavior requires sensorimotor integration and direction of appropriate responses to a particular meaningful stimulus. Internal physiological conditions, experience, and the nature of the environment are some of the variables determining the outcome at a particular time. When hungry, the rat searches for food and approaches a stimulus which has been reliably correlated with food presentation. Hunger and recognition of a meaningful stimulus working through the mesolimbic systems select and direct behavior to a given place, but nigrostriatal activation sets the conditions for the appropriate responses to be initiated.

Is there any evidence for a dissociation of this kind? At present the evidence is slim. We need to discover more of the behavioral consequences of *selective* damage to one or another system. The prediction of this model would be that in the absence of both DA mechanisms an animal would not be able to initiate or to direct behavior to an appropriate goal object. In short it would not do anything when placed, for example, in a maze-learning situation. In fact, this is exactly what happens. Fibiger and Ungerstedt report such behavior after 6-OHDA lesions aimed at the SN but which almost certainly result in substantial DA loss from the mesolimbic system as well (Fibiger, personal communication). However, such animals are capable of involuntary escape reactions in aversive situations, supporting Vanderwolf's (1971) contention that involuntary and voluntary responses are initiated via dissociable neural circuits. After generalized block of the dopamine systems with neuroleptic drugs, a similar effect is observed (Hunt, 1956; Herz, 1960). Appetitive and avoidance behavior are impossible, but involuntary escape responses are intact (Posluns, 1962). On this phenomenon, Fibiger *et al.* (1975) comment, "Thus while the animals may not be able to voluntarily initiate the appropriate motor patterns in response to the CS, the onset of the foot shock may induce involuntary reflexive motor responses (e.g., startle, flinch, jump, etc.) which are sufficient to begin the motoric sequences required in the CAR paradigm."

Experiments with a water maze (Ungerstedt and Ljundberg, cited in Ungerstedt, 1974) illustrate a further interesting point. In this test the threat to survival (induced submersion) is sufficiently great to activate the motor initiation system, and swimming occurs. Despite this, the rat is still unable to learn which arm leads to safety (Ranje and Ungerstedt, 1977). It seems probable that this is because the mesolimbic system is severely damaged.

Neuroleptic drugs can also be used to dissociate motor and motivation deficits. Lever pressing for LH (lateral hypothalamic) ICS was attenuated by spiroperidol (Rolls *et al.*, 1974; Mora *et al.*, 1975). Licking to obtain self-stimulation was also impaired by the same dose range of spiroperidol. The observation that licking to obtain water was unaffected (Mora *et al.*, 1975) suggests that spiroperidol effects ICS itself and not just the motor response used to obtain the stimulation. Injection of spiroperidol into the NAS reduced lever pressing ICS by 90% and produced only 10% decrement on an independent measure of motor capacity (Mora et al., 1975). By contrast, equivalent injection into the caudate nucleus reduced ICS by 18% and motor capacity by 38%. These results demonstrate that dopamine receptors are involved in self-stimulation in a way which is not due just to their role in motor behavior and also suggest that the DA receptors mediating motivation and motor performance are also differentially localized. However, the literature on this issue remains highly controversial (see, for example, Fibiger et al., 1976).

Experiments with intracranial self-stimulation which is sustained by DA pathways (see Routtenberg and Santos-Anderson, Chapter 1, this volume) are also yielding interesting results which suggest a dissociation between motivation and motor performance. Fibiger and his co-workers, in an ingeniously designed ICS experiment, studied the effect of unilateral DA pathway lesions ipsi- or contralateral to an ICS electrode placed in the DA substrate. The results vary depending on the particular DA site sustaining self-stimulation. Using caudate ICS electrodes and 6-OHDA lesions to the SN, Phillips et al. (1976) report severe unilateral and mild contralateral decrement in ICS. Similar results have been obtained by Koob et al. (in press) in experiments with lateral hypothalamic and locus coeruleus ICS electrodes and combined unilateral lesions to the A10 and A9 dopamine neurons. It is suggested that these lesions produce both a motor performance and a motivation deficit, the mild motor generalized deficit revealing itself on the contralateral electrode, and the severe motivational impairment showing itself on the ipsilateral side. The neuroleptic studies lead to the prediction that if the motor response to obtain the ICS involved more complex responses, the contralateral deficit would be accordingly greater, and if a simpler response than a lever press was required, it would be less severe. These studies remain to be done. The sites sustaining ICS may also determine whether the deficit is predominantly motor, motivational, or mixed. Clavier and Fibiger (1976), for example, report with nigrostriatal electrodes and an SN lesion an equal deficit contra- and ipsilateral to the electrode, suggesting a mild general performance decrement.

The search is now on for other measures of motivation involving both unconditioned and conditioned responses. However, it is not easy to generate such behavior which can be dissociated from performance measures. Most behavior will, by our definition, involve activation of both DA systems and needs to involve both systems to be efficient. Finally, interest is currently being expressed regarding a specific behavioral role of mesofrontal DA systems (LeMoal et al., 1975; Tassin et al., 1977) which may be dissociable both from the mesolimbic and nigrostriatal systems. Here lies the next challenge in understanding forebrain DA systems and behavior.

6. REFERENCES

AGID, Y., JAVOY, F., and GLOWINSKI, J., 1973, Hyperactivity of remaining dopaminergic neurones after partial destruction of the nigrostriatal dopaminergic system in the rat, *Nature, New Biol.* **245:**150–151.
AHLENIUS, S., 1974a, Reversal by L-dopa of the suppression of locomotor activity induced by inhibition of tyrosine hydroxylase and DA-β-hydroxylase in mice, *Brain Res.* **69:**57–65.
AHLENIUS, S., 1974b, Effects of L-dopa on conditioned avoidance responding after behavioural suppression by α-methyltyrosine or reserpine in mice, *Neuropharmacology* **13:**729–739.
AHLENIUS, S., 1974c, Effects of low and high doses of L-dopa on the tetrabenazine or α-methyltyrosine-induced suppression of behaviour in a successive discrimination task, *Psychopharmacologia* **39:**199–212.
AHLENIUS, S., and ENGEL, J., 1971a, Behavioural effects of haloperidol after tyrosine hydroxylase inhibition, *Eur. J. Pharm.* **15:**187–192.
AHLENIUS, S., and ENGEL, J., 1971b, Behavioural and biochemical effects of L-dopa after inhibition of dopamine-β-hydroxylase in reserpine-pretreated rats. *Naunyn-Schmiedeberg's Arch. Pharmacol.* **270:**349–360.
AHLENIUS, S., and ENGEL, J., 1972, Effects of a dopamine (DA)-β-hydroxylase inhibitor on timing behaviour, *Psychopharmacologia* **24:**243–246.
AHLENIUS, S., ANDEN, N-E., and ENGEL, J., 1971, Importance of catecholamine release by nerve impulses for free operant behavior, *Physiol. Behav.* **7:**931–934.
AHLENIUS, S., ANDEN, N-E., and ENGEL, J., 1973, Restoration of locomotor activity in mice by low-L-DOPA doses after suppression by α-methyltyrosine but not by reserpine, *Brain Res.* **62:**189–199.
AKERT, K., and ANDERSON, B., 1951, Experiemteller Beitrag zur Physiologie des Nucleus Caudatus, *Acta Physiol. Scand.* **22:**281–298.
ALLEN, J. D., and DAVISON, C. S., 1973, Effects of caudate lesions on signalled and nonsignalled Sidman avoidance in the rat, *Behav. Biol.* **8:**239–259.
BINDRA, D., and BARAN, O., 1959, Effect of methylphenidylacetate and chlorpromazine on certain components of general activity, *J. Exp. Anal. Behav.* **2:**343–350.
BLACK, W. C., and COOPER, B. R., 1970, Reduction of electrically rewarded behavior by interference with monoamine synthesis, *Physiol. Behav.* **5:**1405–1409.
BLAKEMORE, C., IVERSEN, S. D., and ZANGWILL, O. L., 1972, Brain functions, *Annu. Rev. Psychol.* **23:**413–456.
BLASCHKO, H., and CHRUSCIEL, T. L., 1960, The decarboxylation of amino acids related to tyrosine and their awakening action in reserpine-treated mice, *J. Physiol. (London)* **151:**272–284.
BLISS, E. L., AILION, J., and SWANSIGER, J., 1968, Metabolism of norepinephrine, serotonin and dopamine in rat brain with stress, *J. Pharmacol. Exp. Ther.* **164:**112–134.
BLOOM, F. E., COSTA, E., and SALMOIRAGHI, G. C., 1965, Anaesthesia and the responsiveness of individual neurones of the caudate nucleus of the cat to acetylcholine, norepinephrine and dopamine administered by microelectrophoresis, *J. Pharmacol. Exp. Ther.* **150:**44–252.
BLOOM, F. E., ALGERI, S., GROPPETTI, A., REVUETTA, A., and COSTA, E., 1969, Lesions of central norepinephrine terminals with 6-OHDA dopamine: biochemistry and fine structure, *Science,* **166:**1284–1286.
BOWEN, F. P., 1969, Visuomotor deficits produced by cryogenic lesions of the caudate, *Neuropsychologia* **7:**59–65.
BREESE, G. R., and TRAYLOR, T. D., 1972, Depletion of brain noradrenaline and dopamine by 6-hydroxydopamine, *Br. J. Pharmacol.* **44:**210–222.
BREESE, G. R., HOWARD, J. L., and LEAHY, J. P., 1971, Effect of 6-hydroxydopamine on electrical self-stimulation of the brain, *Br. J. Pharmacol.* **43:**255–257.

BREESE, G. R., SMITH, R. O., COOPER, B. R., and GRANT, L. D., 1973, Alterations in consumatory behaviour following intracisternal injection of 6-hydroxydopamine, *Pharm. Biochem. Behav.* **1**:319-328.

BRESNAHAM, E., and ROUTTENBERG, A., 1972, Memory disruption by unilateral low level, sub-seizure stimulation of the medial amygdaloid nucleus, *Physiol. Behav.* **9**:513-525.

BRINKMAN, J., and KUYPERS, H. G. J. M., 1973, Cerebral control of contralateral and ipsilateral arm, hand and finger movements in the split-brain rhesus monkey, *Brain* **96**:635-674.

BUCHWALD, N. A., WYERS, E. J., LAUPRECHT, C. W., and HEUSER, G., 1961, The "caudate-spindle." IV. A behavioural index of caudate-induced inhibition, *Electroencephalogr. Clin. Neurophysiol.* **13**:531-537.

BUTTER, C. M., MISHKIN, M., and ROSVOLD, H. E., 1963, Conditioning and extinction of a food-rewarded response after selective ablations of frontal cortex in rhesus monkeys, *Exp. Neurol.* **7**:65-67.

BUTTERS, N., and ROSVOLD, H. E., 1968, The effect of caudate and septal nuclei lesions on resistance to extinction and delayed-alternation performance in monkeys, *J. Comp. Physiol. Psychol.* **65**:397-403.

CARLSSON, A., 1959, The occurrence, distribution and physiological role of catecholamines in the nervous system, *Pharm. Rev.* **11**:490-493.

CARLSSON, A., 1975, Receptor-mediated control of dopamine metabolism, in: *Pre- and Postsynaptic Receptors* (E. Usdin and W. E. Binney, Jr., eds.), Marcel Dekker, New York.

CARLSSON, A., LINDQUIST, M., and MAGNUSSON, T., 1957, 3,4-Dihydroxyphenylalanine and 5-hydroxytryptophan as reserpine antagonists, *Nature (London)* **180**:1200.

CHOROVER, S. L., and GROSS, C. G., 1963, Caudate nucleus lesions: behavioural effects in the rat, *Science* **141**:826-827.

CLARK, D. W. J., LAVERTY, R., and PHELAN, E. L., 1972, Long-lasting peripheral and central effects of 6-hydroxydopamine in rats, *Br. J. Pharmacol.* **44**:233-243.

CLAVIER, R. M., and FIBIGER, H. C., 1976, Recovery of substantia nigra self-stimulation after unilateral 6-hydroxydopamine lesions of the nigrostriatal pathway, in: *Neuroscience Abstracts*, Vol. 2, Part 1, p. 482, Society for Neuroscience Sixth Annual Meeting, Toronto, Canada, Society for Neuroscience, Bethesda, Maryland.

CONNOR, J. D., 1970, Caudate nucleus neurons: correlation of the effects of substantia nigra stimulation with iontophoretic dopamine, *J. Physiol. (London)* **205**:691-703.

COOPER, B. R., BREESE, G. R., HOWARD, J. L., and GRANT, L. D., 1972a, Effect of central catecholamine alterations by 6-hydroxydopamine on shuttlebox avoidance acquisition, *Phys. Behav.* **9**:727-731.

COOPER, B. R., BREESE, G. R., HOWARD, J. L., and GRANT, L. D., 1972b, Enhanced behavioral depressant effects of reserpine and α-methyltyrosine after 6-hydroxydopamine treatment, *Psychopharmacologia* **27**:99-110.

COOPER, B. R., BREESE, G. R., GRANT, L. D., and HOWARD, J. L., 1973a, Effects of 6-hydroxydopamine treatment on active avoidance responding: evidence for involvement of brain dopamine, *J. Pharm. Exp. Ther.* **185**:358-370.

COOPER, B. R., GRANT, L. D., and BREESE, G. R., 1973b, Comparison of the behavioural depressant effects of biogenic amine depleting and neuroleptic aents following various 6-hydroxydopamine treatments, *Psychopharmacologia* **31**:95-109.

COOPER, B. R., COTT, J. M., and BREESE, G. R., 1974a, Effects of catecholamine depleting drugs and amphetamine on self-stimulation of brain following various 6-hydroxydopamine treatments, *Psychopharmacologia* **37**:235-248.

COOPER, B. R., HOWARD, J. L., GRANT, L. D., SMITH, R. D., and BREESE, G. R., 1974b, Alteration of avoidance and ingestive behaviour after destruction of central catecholamine pathways with 6-hydroxydopamine, *Pharm. Biochem. Behav.* **2**:639-649.

CORRODI, H., and HANSON, L. C. F., 1966, Central effects of an inhibitor of tyrosine hydroxylation, *Psychopharmacologia* **10**:116-125.

CORRODI, H., FUXE, K., and HOKFELT, T., 1966, Refillment of the catecholamine stores with

3,4-dihydroxyphenylalanine after depletion induced by inhibition of tyrosine hydroxylase, *Life Sci.* **5**:605-611.

CORRODI, H., FUXE, K., and HOKFELT, T., 1968, The effects of immobilization stress on the activity of central monoamine neurons, *Life Sci.* **7**:107-112.

COSTENTIN, J., PROTAIS, P., and SCHWARTZ, J. C., 1975, Rapid and dissociated changes in sensitivities of different dopamine receptors in mouse brain, *Nature (London)* **257**:405-407.

COSTENTIN, J., MARCAIS, H., PROTAIS, P., and SCHWARTZ, J. C., 1977, Tolerance to hypokinesia elicited by dopamine agonists in mice: hyposensitization of autoreceptors? *Life Sci.*, in press.

CREESE, I., and IVERSEN, S. D., 1972, Amphetamine response in rat after dopamine neurone destruction, *Nature New Biol.* **86**:242-248.

CREESE, I., and IVERSEN, S. D., 1975, The pharmacological and anatomical substrates of the amphetamine response in the rat, *Brain Res.* **83**:419-436.

CROW, T. J., 1972, A map of the rat mesencephalon for electrical self-stimulation, *Brain Res.* **36**:265-273.

DAHLSTRÖM, A., and FUXE, K., 1965, Evidence for the existence of monoamine-containing neurons in the central nervous system. I. Demonstration of monoamines in the cell bodies of brainstem neurons, *Acta Physiol. Scand. Suppl. 232* **62**:1-55.

DAVIS, G. D., 1958, Caudate lesions and spontaneous locomotion in the monkey, *Neurology* **8**:135-139.

DEADWYLER, S. A., and WYERS, E. J., 1970, Effects of interpolated caudate and septal stimulation on DRL performance in rats, *Proceedings of the 78th Annual Conference of the American Psychological Association*, Miami Beach, pp. 241-242.

DELGADO, J. M. R., 1957, Brain stimulation in the monkey, *Fed. Proc.* **16**:29-30.

DELGADO, J. M. R., DELGADO-GARCIA, J. M., AMERIGO, J. A., and GRAV, C., 1975, Behavioural inhibition induced by pallidal stimulation in monkeys, *Exp. Neurol.* **49**:580-591.

DELONG, M. R., 1971, Activity of pallidal neurons during movement, *J. Neurophysiol.* **34**:414-427.

DELONG, M. R., 1972, Activity of basal ganglia neurons during movement, *Brain Res.* **40**:127-135.

DELONG, M. R., 1974, Motor functions of the basal ganglia: single unit activity during movement, in: *The Neurosciences: Third Study Program* (F. O. Schmitt and F. G. Worden, eds.), pp. 319-325, MIT Press, Cambridge, Massachusetts.

DEWS, P. B., 1958, Analysis of psychopharmacological agents in behavioral terms, *Fed. Proc.* **17**:1024-1030.

DIVAC, I., 1968, Effects of prefrontal and caudate lesions on delayed response in cats, *Acta Biol. Exo.* **28**:149-167.

DIVAC, I., 1972, Neostriatum and functions of prefrontal cortex, *Acta Neurobiol.* **32**:461-477.

DIVAC, I., ROSVOLD, H. E., and SZWARCBART, M. K., 1967, Behavioral effects of selective ablation of the caudate nucleus, *J. Comp. Physiol. Psychol.* **63**:184-190.

DOMINIC, J. A., and MOORE, K. E., 1969, Supersensitivity to the central stimulant actions of adrenergic drugs following discontinuation of a chronic diet of α-methyltyrosine, *Psychopharmacologia* **15**:96-101.

EHRINGER, H., and HORNYKIEWICZ, O., 1960, Verteilung von Noradrenalin und Dopamin (3-hydroxytyuamin) im Gerhirn des Menschen und ihr verhalten bei Erkrankungen des extrapyramidalen Systems, *Klin. Wochenschr.* **38**:1236-1239.

EVARTS, E. V., 1966, Pyramidal tract activity associated with a conditioned hand movement in the monkey, *J. Neurophysiol.* **29**:1011-1027.

EVARTS, E. V., 1971, Activity of thalamic and cortical neurons in relation to learned movements in the monkey, *Int. J. Neurology* **8**:321-326.

EVERETT, G. M., and TOMAN, J. E. P., 1959, Mode of action of Rauwolfia alkaloids and motor activity, *Biol. Psychiat.* **2**:75-81.

EVETTS, K. D., URETSKY, N. J., IVERSEN, L. L., and IVERSEN, S. D., 1970, Effects of 6-hydroxydopamine on CNS catecholamines, spontaneous motor activity and amphetamine induced hyperactivity in rats, *Nature (London)* **225**:961-962.

FELTZ, P., and DE CHAMPLAIN, J., 1972, Persistence of caudate unitary responses to nigral stimulation after destruction and functional impairment of the striatal dopaminergic terminals, *Brain Res.* **43**:595-600.

FIBIGER, H. C., 1977, On the role of the dopaminergic nigrostriatal projection in reinforcement, learning and memory, in: *Psychobiology of the Striatum*. (A. R. Cools, A. H. M. Lohman, and J. H. L van den Bercken, eds., pp. 73-83, North Holland Publishing Co., Amsterdam.

FIBIGER, H. C., FIBIGER, H. P., and ZIS, A. O., 1973, Attenuation of amphetamine-induced motor stimulation and stereotypy by 6-hydroxydopamine in the rat, *Br. J. Pharmacol.* **47**:683-692.

FIBIGER, H. C., PHILLIPS, A. G., and ZIS, A. P., 1974, Deficits in instrumental responding after 6-hydroxydopamine lesions of the nigro-striatal dopaminergic projection, *Pharmacol. Biochem. Behav.* **2**:87-96.

FIBIGER, H. C., ZIS, A. P., and PHILLIPS, A. G., 1975, Haloperidol-induced disruption of conditioned avoidance responding: attenuation by prior training or by anticholergic drugs, *Eur. J. Pharmacol.* **30**:309-314.

FIBIGER, H. C., CARTER, D. A., and PHILLIPS, A. E., 1976, Decreased intracranial self-stimulation after neuroleptics or 6-hydroxydopamine: evidence for mediation by motor deficits rather than by reduced reward, *Psychopharmacology* **47**:21-27.

FRANKLIN, K. B. J., and HERBERG, L. J., 1974, Self-stimulation and catecholamines: drug-induced mobilization of the reserve-pool re-establishes responding in catecholamine-depleted rats, *Brain Res.* **67**:429-438.

FRIGYESI, T. L., IGE, A., IULO, A., and SCHWARTZ, R., 1971, Denigration and sensorimotor disability induced by ventral tegmental injection of 6-hydroxydopamine in the cat, *Exp. Neurol.* **33**:78-87.

FUXE, K., and HANSON, L. C. F., 1967, Central catecholamine neurones and conditioned avoidance behaviour, *Psychopharmacologia* **11**:439-444.

GIANUTSOS, G., DRAWBAUGH, R. B., HYNES, M. D., and LAL, H., 1974, Behavioural evidence for dopaminergic supersensitivity after chronic haloperidol, *Life Sci.* **14**:887-898.

GLICK, S. D., 1973, Enhancement of spatial preferences by (+)-amphetamine, *Neuropharmacology* **12**:43-47.

GLICK, S. D., GREENSTEIN, S., 1973, Possible modulating influence of frontal cortex on nigrostriatal function, *Br. J. Pharmacol.* **49**:316-321.

GLICK, S. D., and JERUSSI, T. P., 1974, Spatial and paw preferences in rats: their relationship to rate-dependent effects of d-amphetamine, *J. Pharmacol. Exp. Ther.* **188**:714-725.

GLICK, S. D., JERUSSI, T. P., EATERS, D. H., and GREEN, J. P., 1974, Amphetamine-induced changes in striatal dopamine and acetylcholine levels and relationship to rotation (circling behavior in rats), *Biochem. Pharmacol.* **23**:3223-3225.

GLICKMAN, S. E., 1958, Deficits in avoidance learning produced by stimulation of the ascending reticular formation, *Can. J. Psychol.* **12**:97-102.

GORDON, R., SPECTOR, A., SJOERDSMA, A., and UDENFRIEND, S., 1966, Increased synthesis of norepinephrine and epinephrine in the intact rat during exercise and exposure to cold, *J. Pharm. Exp. Ther.* **153**:440-447.

GROSS, C. G., CHOROVER, S. L., and COHEN, S. M., 1965, Caudate, cortical, hippocampal and dorsal thalamic lesions in rats: alternation and Hebb-Williams maze performance, *Neuropsychologia* **3**:53-68.

GYBELS, J., MEULDERS, M., CALLENS, M., and COLLE, J., 1967, Disturbances of visuo-motor integration in cats with small lesions of the caudate nucleus, *Arch. Int. Physiol. Biochem.* **75**:283-302.

HANSING, R. A., SCHWARTZBAUM, J. S., and THOMPSON, J. B., 1968, Operant behaviour following unilateral and bilateral caudate lesions in the rat, *J. Comp. Physiol. Psychol.* **66:**378–388.

HARVEY, J. A., 1965, Comparison between the effects of hypothalamic lesions on brain amine levels and drug action, *J. Pharmacol. Exp. Ther.* **147:**244–251.

HAYCOCK, J. W., DEADWYLER, S. A., SIDEROFF, S. I., and MCGAUGH, J. L., 1973, Retrograde amnesia and cholinergic systems in the caudate-putamen complex and dorsal hippocampus of the rat, *Exp. Neurol.* **41:**201–213.

HERZ, A., 1960, Drugs and the conditioned avoidance response, *Int. Rev. Neurobiol.* **2:**229–277.

HOPKINS, D. A., and NIESSEN, L. W., 1976, Substantia nigra projections to the reticular formation, superior colliculus and central gray in the rat, cat and monkey, *Neurosci. Lett.* **2:**253–259.

HOWARD, J. L., LEAHY, J. P., and BREESE, G. R., 1971, Some physiological and behavioral consequences of the acute and chronic injection of 6-hydroxydopamine, *Fed. Proc.* **30:**541.

HULL, C. D., BERNARDI, G., PRICE, D. D., and BUCHWALD, N. A., 1973, Intracellular responses of caudate neurons to temporally and spatially combined stimuli, *Exp. Neurol.* **38:**324–336.

HUNT, H. F., 1956, Some effects of drugs on classical (type S) conditioning, *Ann. N. Y. Acad. Sci.* **65:**258–267.

HUSTON, J. P., and ORNSTEIN, K., 1975, Effects of transecting the lateral border of the hypothalamus on self-stimulation, *Neurosci. Lett.* **1:**291–296.

IVERSEN, S. D., 1977, Striatal function and stereotyped behaviour, in: *The Psychobiology of the Striatum*, (A. R. Cools, A. H. Lohman, and J. H. L van den Bercken, eds.,) pp. 99–118, North Holland Publishing Co., Amsterdam.

IVERSEN, S. D., and IVERSEN, L. L., 1975, *Behavioural Pharmacology*, Oxford University Press, New York.

IVERSEN, S. D., and KELLY, P. H., 1975, The use of 6-hydroxydopamine (6-OHDA) techniques for studying the pathways involved in drug-induced motor behaviours, in: *Chemical Tools in Catecholamine Research*, Vol. 1 (G. Jonsson, T. Malmfors, and C. Sachs, eds.), pp. 327–342, North Holland Publishing Co., Amsterdam.

IVERSEN, S. D., and KOOB, G., 1977, Behavioural implications of dopaminergic neurones in the mesolimbic system, in: *Non-striatal Dopaminergic Neurones*, pp. 209–214, Raven Press, New York.

IVERSEN, S. D., and MISHKIN, M., 1970, Perseverative interference in monkeys following selective lesions of the inferior prefrontal convexity, *Exp. Brain Res.* **11:**376–386.

IVERSEN, S. D., WILKINSON, S., and SIMPSON, B., 1971, Enhanced amphetamine responses after frontal cortex lesions in the rat, *Eur. J. Pharmacol.* **13:**387–390.

JALFRE, M., and HAEFLEY, W., 1971, Effects of some centrally active agents in rats after intraventricular injections of 6-hydroxydopamine, in: *6-Hydroxydopamine and Catecholamine Neurons* (S. E. Malmfors and H. Thoenen, eds.), pp. 333–346, American Elsevier Publishing Co., New York.

JERUSSI, T. P., and GLICK, S. D., 1974, Amphetamine-induced rotation in rats without lesions, *Neuropharmacology*, **13:**283–286.

JERUSSI, T. P., and GLICK, S. D., 1975, Apomorphine-induced rotation in normal rats and interaction with unilateral caudate lesions, *Psychopharmacologia*, **40:**329–334.

KELLEHER, R. T., and MORSE, W. H., 1964, Escape behavior and punished behavior, *Fed. Proc.* **23:**808–817.

KELLY, P. H., ROLLS, E. T., and SHAW, S. G., 1973, Functions of catecholamines in brain-stimulation reward, *Brain Res.* **36:**363–364.

KELLY, P. H., SEVIOUR, P. W., and IVERSEN, S. D., 1975, Amphetamine and apomorphine responses in the rat following 6-OHDA lesions of the nucleus accumbens septi and corpus striatum, *Brain Res.* **94:**507–522.

KENT, E. W., and GROSSMAN, S. P., 1973, Elimination of learned behaviour after transection of fibers crossing the lateral border of the hypothalamus, *Physiol. Behav.* **10**:953–963.
KESNER, R. D., and DOTY, R. N., 1968, Amnesia produced in cats by local seizure activity initiated from the amygdala, *Exp. Neurol.* **21**:58–68.
KETY, S. S., JAVOY, F., THIERRY, A. H., JULOV, L., and GLOWINSKI, J., 1967, A sustained effect of electroconvulsive shock on the turnover of norepinephrine in the central nervous system of the rat, *Proc. Nat. Acad. Sci. U.S.A.* **58**:1249–1254.
KIRKBY, R. J., 1969, Caudate nucleus lesions and perseverative behavior, *Physiol. Behav.* **4**:451–454.
KIRKBY, R. J., and KIMBLE, D. P., 1968, Avoidance and escape behavior following striatal lesions in the rat, *Exp. Neurol.* **20**:215–227.
KITSIKIS, A., and ROBERGE, A. G., 1973, Behavioural and biochemical effects of α-methyltyrosine in cats, *Psychopharmacologia* **31**:143–155.
KITSIKIS, A., and ROUGEUL, A., 1968, The effect of caudate stimulation on conditioned motor behavior in monkeys, *Physiol. Behav.* **3**:831–837.
KITSIKIS, A. L., ANGYAN, L., and BUSER, P., 1971, Basal ganglia unitary activity during a motor performance in monkeys, *Physiol. Behav.* **6**:609–611.
KITSIKIS, A., ROBERGE, A. G., and FRENETTE, G., 1972, Effect of L-dopa on delayed response and visual discrimination in cats and its relation to brain chemistry, *Exp. Brain Res.* **15**:305–317.
KLAWANS, H. L., 1973, The pharmacology of tardive dyskinesias, *Am. J. Psychiat.* **130**:82–86.
KOOB, G. F., FRAY, P. J., and IVERSEN, S. D., Self-stimulation from the lateral hypothalamus and locus coeruleus after specific unilateral lesion of the dopamine system, *Brain Res.* (in press).
KORNHUBER, H. H., 1974, Cerebral cortex, cerebellum and basal ganglia: an introduction to their motor functions, in: *The Neurosciences: Third Study Program* (F. O. Schmitt and F. G. Worden, eds.), pp. 267–280, MIT. Press, Cambridge, Massachusetts.
LAURSEN, A. M., 1963a, Corpus striatum, *Acta Physiol. Scand. (Suppl.)* **211**:106.
LAURSEN, A. M., 1963b, Conditioned avoidance behavior of cats with lesions in globus pallidus, *Acta Physiol. Scand.* **57**:81–89.
LAVERTY, R., and ARNOTT, P. J., 1970, Recovery of avoidance behaviour in rats following intraventricular injection of 6-hydroxydopamine, *Proc. Univ. Otago Med. Sch.* **48**:18–20.
LAVERTY, R., and TAYLOR, K. M., 1970, Effects of intraventricular 2,4,5-trihydroxyphenylethylamine (6-hydroxydopamine) on rat behaviour and brain catecholamine metabolism, *Br. J. Pharmacol.* **40**:836–846.
LAWICKA, W., MISHKIN, M., and ROSVOLD, H. E., 1975, Dissociation of deficits on auditory tasks following partial prefrontal lesions in monkeys, *Acta Neurobiol. Exp.* **35**:581–607.
LAWRENCE, D. G., and KUYPERS, H. G. J. M., 1968, The functional organization of the motor system in the monkey. I and II, *Brain* **91**:1–36.
LIEBMAN, J. M., and BUTCHER, L. L., 1973, Effects on self-stimulation behavior of drugs influencing dopaminergic neurotransmission mechanisms, *Naunyn-Schmiedebergs Arch. Exp. Path. Pharmakol.* **277**:305–318.
LE MOAL, M., GALEY, D., AND CARDO, B., 1975, Behavioural effects of local injection of 6-hydroxydopamine in the medial ventral tegmentum in the rat. Possible role of the mesolimbic dopaminergic system, *Brain Res.* **88**:190–194.
LEWY, A. J., and SEIDEN, L. S., 1972, Operant behaviour changes norepinephrine metabolism in rat brain, *Science* **175**:454–455.
LILES, S. L., and DAVIS, G. D., 1969, Interrelation of caudate nucleus and thalamus in alternation of cortically induced movement, *J. Neurophysiol.* **32**:564–573.
LINEBERRY, C. D., and SIEGEL, J., 1971, EEG synchronization, behavioral inhibition and mesencephalic unit effects produced by stimulation of orbital cortex, basal forebrain and caudate nucleus, *Brain Res.* **34**:143–161.
LIPPA, A. S., ANTELMAN, S., FISHER, A., and CANFIELD, D., 1973, Neurochemical mediation of reward: a significant role for dopamine, *Pharmacol., Biochem. Behav.* **1**:23–28.

Lyon, M., and Robbins, T., 1975, The action of central nervous system stimulant drugs: a general theory concerning amphetamine effects, in: *Current Developments in Psychopharmacology*, Vol. 2, pp. 80–163, Halsted Press, New York.

Maj, J., Grabowska, M., and Mogilnicka, E., 1971, The effect of L-DOPA on brain catecholamines and motility in rats, *Psychopharmacologia* **22:**162–171.

Marsh, G. G., Markham, C. M., and Ansel, R., 1971, Levodopa's awakening effect on patients with Parkinsonism, *J. Neurol. Neurosurg. Psychiat.* **34:**209–218.

Mason, S. T., and Iversen, S. D., 1974, Learning impairment in rats after 6-hydroxydopamine-induced depletion of brain catecholamines, *Nature (London)*, **248:**697–698.

Matthysse, S., 1973, Antipsychotic drug action: a clue to the neuropathology of schizophrenia, *Fed. Proc.* **32:**200–205.

Maynert, E. W., and Levi, R., 1964, Stress-induced release of brain norepinephrine and its inhibition by drugs, *J. Pharmacol. Exp. Ther.* **143:**90–95.

Meier, M. J., and Martin, W. E., 1970, Intellectual changes associated with levodopa therapy, *J. Am. Med. Assoc.* **213:**465–466.

Mishkin, M., 1964, Perseveration of central sets after frontal lesions in monkeys, in: *The Frontal Granular Cortex and Behaviour* (J. M. Warren and K. Akert, eds.), pp. 219–237, McGraw-Hill, New York.

Mitcham, J. C., and Thomas, R. K., 1972, Effects of substantia nigra and caudate nucleus lesions on avoidance learning in rats, *J. Comp. Physiol. Psychol.* **81:**101–107.

Monti, J. M., and Hance, A. J., 1967, Effects of haloperidol and trifluperidol on operant behaviour in the rat, *Psychopharmacologia* **12:**34–43.

Moore, K. E., and Rech, R. H., 1967, Reversal of a α-methyltyrosine-induced depression with dihydroxyphenylalanine and amphetamine, *J. Pharm. Pharmacol.* **19:**405–407.

Moore, R. Y., Bhatnager, R. K., and Heller, A., 1971, Anatomical and chemical studies of a nigro-neostriatal projection in the cat, *Brain Res.* **30:**119–135.

Mora, F., Sanguinetti, A. M., Rolls, E. T., and Shaw, S. G., 1975, Differential effects on self-stimulation and motor behaviour produced by microintracranial injections of a dopamine-receptor blocking agent, *Neurosci. Lett.* **1:**179–184.

Morse, W. H., 1964, Effects of amobarbital and chlorpromazine on punished behaviour in the pigeon, *Psychopharmacologia* **6:**286–294.

Neill, D. B., 1976, Frontal-striatal control of behavioral inhibition in the rat, *Brain Res.* **105:**89–103.

Neill, D. B., and Grossman, S. P., 1970, Behavioral effects of lesions or cholinergic blockade of the dorsal and ventral caudate of rats, *J. Comp. Physiol. Psychol.* **71:**311–317.

Neill, D. B., Boggan, W. O., and Grossman, S. P., 1974a, Impairment of avoidance performance by intrastriatal administration of 6-hydroxydopamint, *Pharmac. Biochem. Behav.* **2:**97–103.

Neill, D. B., Boggan, W. O., and Grossman, S. P., 1974b, Behavioral effects of amphetamine in rats with lesions in the corpus striatum, *J. Comp. Physiol. Psychol.* **86:**1019–1030.

Neill, D. B., Ross, J. F., and Grossman, S. P., 1974c, Comparison of the effects of frontal striatal and septal lesions in paradigms thought to measure incentive motivation or behavioural inhibition, *Physiol. Behav.* **13:**297–305.

Neill, D. B., Parker, S. D., and Gold, M. S., 1975, Striatal dopaminergic modulation of lateral hypothalamic self-stimulation, *Pharm., Biochem. Behav.* **3:**485–491.

Niemegeers, C. J. E., Verbruggen, F. J., and Janssen, P. A. J., 1969, The influence of various neuroleptic drugs on shock avoidance responding in rats. I. Nondiscriminated Sidman avoidance procedure, *Psychopharmacologia* **16:**161–174.

Oberg, R. G. E., and Divac, I., 1975, Dissociative effects of selective lesions in the caudate nucleus of cats and rats, *Acta Neurobiol.* **35:**647–659.

Ornstein, K., and Huston, J. P., 1975, Influence of 6-hydroxydopamine injections in the substantia nigra on lateral hypothalamic reinforcement, *Neurosci. Lett.* **1:**339–342.

Papeschi, R., 1972, Dopamine, extrapyramidal system and psychomotor function, *Psychiat. Neurol. Neurochir.* **75:**13–48.

Peeke, H. V. S., and Herz, M. J., 1971, Caudate nucleus stimulation retroactively impairs complex maze learning in the rat, *Science* **173**:80–82.

Phillips, A. G., and Fibiger, H. C., 1973, Deficits in stimulation-induced feeding after intraventricular administration of 6-hydroxydopamie in rats, *Behav. Biol.* **9**:749–754.

Phillips, A. G., and Nikaido, R. S., 1975, Disruption of brain stimulation-induced feeding by dopamine receptor blockade, *Nature (London)* **258**:750–751.

Phillips, A. G., Brooke, J. M., and Fibiger, H. C., 1975, Effects of amphetamine isomers and neuroleptics on self stimulation from the nucleus and dorsal noradrenergic bundle, *Brain Res.* **85**:13–22.

Phillips, A. G., Carter, D. A., and Fibiger, H. C., 1976, Dopaminergic substrates of intracranial self-stimulation in the caudate-putamen, *Brain Res.* **104**:221–232.

Pijnenburg, A. J. J., Honig, W. M. M., and van Rossum, J. M., 1975a, Inhibition of d-amphetamine-induced locomotor activity by injection of haloperidol into the nucleus accumbens of the rat, *Psychopharmacologia* **41**:87–95.

Pijnenburg, A. J. J., Honig, W. M. M., and van Rossum, J. M., 1975b, Antagonism of apomorphine- and d-amphetamine-induced stereotyped behaviour by injection of low doses of haloperidol into the caudate nucleus and nucleus accumbens, *Psychopharmacologia* **45**:65–71.

Poschel, B. P. H., and Ninteman, F. W., 1966, Hypothalamic self-stimulation: its suppression by blockades of norepinephrine biosynthesis and reinstatement by methamphetamine, *Life Sci.* **5**:11–16.

Posluns, D., 1962, An analysis of chlorpromazine-induced suppression of the avoidance response, *Psychopharmacologia* **3**:361–373.

Powell, E. W., and Leman, R. B., 1976, Connections of the nucleus accumbens, *Brain Res.* **105**:389–403.

Price, M. T. C., and Fibiger, H. C., 1975, Discriminated escape learning and response to electric shock after 6-hydroxydopamine lesions of the nigro-neostriatal dopaminergic projection, *Pharmacol. Biochem. Behav.* **3**:285–290.

Protais, P., Costentin, J., and Schwartz, J. C., 1976, Climbing behaviour induced by apomorphine in mice. A simple test for the study of dopamine receptors in striatum, *Psychopharmacology* **50**:1–6.

Ranje, C., and Ungerstedt, U., 1977, Discriminative and motor performance in rats after interference with dopamine neurotransmission with spiroperidol, *Eur. J. Pharmacol.* **43**:39–46.

Rech, R. H., Borys, H. K., and Moore, K. E., 1966, Alterations in behaviour and brain catecholamine levels in rats treated with α-methyltyrosine, *J. Pharmacol. Exp. Ther.* **153**:512–519.

Rech, R. H., Carr, L. A., and Moore, K. E., 1968, Behavioural effects of α-methyltyrosine after prior depletion of brain catecholamines, *J. Pharmacol. Exp. Ther.* **160**:326–335.

Roberts, D. C. S., Zis, A. P., and Fibiger, H. C., 1975, Ascending catecholamine pathways and amphetamine-induced locomotor activity: importance of dopamine and apparent non-involvement of norepinephrine, *Brain Res.* **93**:441–454.

Rogers, F. T., 1922, Studies of the brain stem. VI. An experimental study of the corpus striatum of the pigeon as related to various instinctive types of behaviour, *J. Comp. Neurol.* **35**:15–59.

Rolls, E. T., Kelly, P. H., and Shaw, S. G., 1974a, Noradrenaline, dopamine and brain-stimulation reward, *Pharmacol. Biochem. Behav.* **2**:735–740.

Rolls, E. T., Rolls, B. J., Kelly, P. H., Shaw, S. G., Wood, R. J., and Dale, R., 1974b, The relative attenuation of self-stimulation eating and drinking produced by dopamine-receptor blockade, *Psychopharmacologia* **38**:219–230.

Rosvold, H. E., and Mishkin, M., 1961, Nonsensory effects of frontal lesions on discrimination learning and performance, in: *Brain Mechanisms and Learning* (D. Delfraysne, ed.), pp. 437–444, Blackwell Scientific Publications.

Routtenberg, A., and Holzman, N., 1973, Memory disruption by electrical stimulation of substantia nigra, pars compacta, *Science* **181**:83–85.

Ruiz, M., and Monti, J. M., 1972, Prevention of the haloperidol-induced blockade of a conditioned avoidance response by L-DOPA, *Eur. J. Pharmacol.* **20**:93–96.

Sahakian, B. J., Robbins, T. W., and Iversen, S. D., 1976, α-Flupenthixol-induced hyperactivity by chronic dosing in rats, *Eur. J. Pharm.* **37**:169–178.

Saint-Laurent, J., Leclerc, R. R., Mitchell, M. L., and Miliaressis, T. E., 1973, Effects of apomorphine on self-stimulation, *Pharmacol. Biochem. Behav.* **1**:581–585.

Scatton, B., Boireau, A., Garret, C., Glowinski, J., and Julou, L., 1977, Action of the palmitic ester of pipotiazine on dopamine metabolism in the nigro-striatal, meso-limbic and meso-cortical systems, *Naunyn-Schmiedebergs Arch. Pharmakol.*, **296**:169–175.

Schmaltz, L. W., and Isaacson, R. L., 1968, Effects of caudate and frontal lesions on retention and relearning of a DRL schedule, *J. Comp. Physiol. Psychol.* **65**:343–348.

Schoenfeld, R. I., and Seiden, L. S., 1967, α-methyltyrosine: effects on fixed ratio schedules of reinforcement, *J. Pharm. Pharmacol.* **19**:771–772.

Schoenfeld, R. I., and Seiden, L. S., 1969, Effect of α-methyltyrosine on operant behavior and brain catecholamine levels, *J. Pharmacol. Exp. Ther.* **167**:319–327.

Schoenfeld, R. I., and Uretsky, N. J., 1972a, Operant behaviour and catecholamine-containing neurons: prolonged increase in lever-pressing after 6-OHDA, *Eur. J. Pharmacol.* **20**:357–362.

Schoenfeld, R., and Uretsky, N., 1972b, Altered response to apomorphine in 6-hydroxydopamine-treated rats, *Eur. J. Pharmacol.* **19**:115–118.

Schoenfeld, R. I., and Uretsky, N. J., 1973, Enhancement by 6-hydroxydopamine of the effects of dopa upon the motor activity of rats, *J. Pharmacol. Exp. Ther.* **186**:616–624.

Schoenfeld, R. I., and Zigmond, M. J., 1970, Effect of 6-hydroxydopamine (HDA) on fixed ratio (F.R.) performance, *Pharmacologist* **12**:227.

Seiden, L. S., and Carlsson, A., 1963, Temporary and partial antagonism by L-dopa of reserpine-induced suppression of conditioned avoidance response, *Psychopharmacologia* **4**:418–423.

Seiden, L. S., and Carlsson, A., 1964, Brain and heart catecholamine levels after L-dopa administration in reserpine-treated mice: correlations with a conditioned avoidance response, *Psychopharmacologia* **5**:178–181.

Seiden, L. S., and Hanson, L. C. F., 1963, Reversal of the reserpine-induced suppression of the conditioned avoidance response in the cat by L-DOPA, *Psychopharmacologia* **6**:234–244.

Seiden, L. S., and Peterson, D. D., 1968, Reversal of the reserpine-induced suppression of the conditioned avoidance response by L-DOPA: Correlation of behavioural and biochemical differences in two strains of mice, *J. Pharm. Exp. Ther.* **159**:422–428.

Shinkman, P. G., and Kaufman, K. P., 1972, Time course of retroactive effects of hippocampal stimulation on learning, *Exp. Neurol.* **34**:476–483.

Smith, C. B., and Dews, P. B., 1962, Antagonism of locomotor suppressant effects of reserpine in mice, *Psychopharmacologia* **3**:55–59.

Smith, G. P., Strohmayer, A. J., and Reis, D. J., 1972, Effects of lateral hypothalamic injections of 6-hydroxydopamine on food and water intake in rats, *Nature New Biol.* **235**:27–29.

Sparber, S. B., and Luther, I. G., 1970, Dopamine concentrations in the brain stem-mesencephalon of active rats as compared with passive rats, *Neuropharmacology* **9**:243–247.

Sparber, S. B., and Tilson, H. A., 1972, Schedule-controlled and drug-induced release of norepinephrine-7-^{3}H into the lateral ventricle of rats, *Neuropharmacology* **11**:453–464.

Spiegel, E. A., and Szakely, E. G., 1961, Prolonged stimulation of the head of the caudate nucleus, *Arch. Neurol.* **4**:55–65.

Stadler, H., Lloyd, K. G., Gadea-Ciria, M., and Bartholini, G., 1973, Enhanced striatal acetylcholine release by chlorpromazine and its reversal by apomorphine, *Brain Res.* **55**:476–480.

STEVENS, J. R., KIM, C., and MACLEAN, P. D., 1961, Stimulation of caudate nucleus, *A.M.A. Arch. Neurol.* **4**:47–54.

STINUS, L., THIERRY, A-M., and CARDO, B., 1975, Self-stimulation and local injections of 6-hydroxydopamine into the rat brain: enhanced behavioral depressive effects of α-methyl paratyrosine, *Pharm. Biochem. Behav.* **3**:19–23.

STINUS, L., THIERRY, A. M., and CARDO, B., 1976, Effects of various inhibitors of tyrosine hydroxylase and dopamine beta-hydroxylase on rat self-stimulation after reserpine treatment, *Psychopharmacologia* **45**:287–294.

STOLK, J. M., and RECH, R. H., 1968, Enhanced stimulant effect of *d*-amphetamine in rats treated chronically with reserpine, *J. Pharmac. Exp. Ther.* **158**:140–149.

STONE, E. A., and DICARA, L. V., 1969, Activity level and accumulation of tritiated norepinephrine in rat brain, *Life Sci.* **8**:433–439.

STRICKER, E. M., and ZIGMOND, M. J., 1974, Effects on homeostasis of intraventricular injections of 6-hydroxydopamine in rats, *J. Comp. Physiol. Psychol.* **86**:973–994.

STROMBOM, U., 1975, On the functional role of pre- and postsynaptic catecholamine receptors in brain, *Acta Physiol. Scand. Suppl. 431*, pp. 1–43.

SVENSSON, T. H., 1971, On the role of central noradrenaline in the regulation of motor activity and body temperature in the mouse, *Naunyn-Schmiedebergs Arch. Pharmakol.* **271**:111–120.

SVENSSON, T., and WALDECK, B., 1969, On the significance of central noradrenaline for motor activity: experiments with a new dopamine-β-hydroxylase inhibitor, *Eur. J. Pharmacol.* **7**:278–282.

SWANSON, L. W., and COWAN, W. M., 1975, A note on the connections and development of the nucleus accumbens, *Brain Res.* **92**:324–330.

TARSY, D., and BALDESSARINI, B. J., 1973, Pharmacologically induced behavioural supersensitivity to apomorphine, *Nature New Biol.* **245**:262–263.

TASSIN, J. P., STINUS, L., SIMON, H., BLANC, G., THIERRY, A-M., LE MOAL, M., CARDO, B., and GLOWINSKI, J., 1977, in: *Advances in Biochemical Psychopharmacology*, Vol. 16 (E. Costa and G. L. Gessa, eds.), pp. 21–28, Raven Press, New York.

TEITELBAUM, P., and EPSTEIN, A. N., 1962, The lateral hypothalamic syndrome: recovery of feedig and drinking after lateral hypothalamic lesions, *Psychol. Rev.* **69**:74–90.

THACH, W. T., 1968, Discharge of Purkinje and cerebellar nuclear neurons during rapidly alternating arm movements in the monkey, *J. Neurophysiol.* **31**:785–797.

THIERRY, A-M., JAVOY, F., GLOWINSKI, J., and KETY, S. S., 1968, Effects of stress on the metabolism of norepinephrine, dopamine and serotonin in the central nervous system of the rat. I. Modifications of norepinephrine turnover, *J. Pharm. Exp. Ther.* **163**:163–171.

THIERRY, A-M., BLANC, G., and GLOWINSKI, J., 1970, Preferential utilization of newly synthesised norepinephrine in the brain stem of stressed rats, *Eur. J. Pharmacol.* **10**:139–142.

THOMPSON, R. L., 1959, Effects of lesions in the caudate nuclei and dorsofrontal cortex on conditioned avoidance behaviour in cats, *J. Comp. Physiol. Psychol.* **52**:650–659.

THOMPSON, R., 1969, Localisation of the "visual memory system" in the white rat, *J. Comp. Physiol. Psychol.* **69**(4), Monograph 1–20.

UNGERSTEDT, U., 1971, Stereotaxic mapping of the monoamine pathways in the rat brain, *Acta Physiol. Scand. Suppl. 367*, 1–48.

UNGERSTEDT, U., 1974, Brain Dopamine neurons and behaviour, in: *The Neurosciences: Third Study Program.* (F. O. Schmit and F. G. Worden, eds.), pp. 695–703, MIT Press, Cambridge, Massachusetts.

URETSKY, N. J., and IVERSEN, L. L., 1970, Effects of 6-hydroxydopamine on catecholamine neurones in rat brain, *J. Neurochem.* **17**:269–278.

URETSKY, N. J., and SCHOENFELD, R. I., 1971, Effects of L-DOPA on the locomotor activity of rats pretreated with 6-hydroxydopamine, *Nature New Biol.* **234**:157–159.

VANDERWOLF, C. H., 1969, Effects of medial thalamic damage on initiation of movement and learning, *Psychonomic Sci.* **17**:23–25.
VANDERWOLF, C. H., 1971, Limbic-diencephalic mechanisms of voluntary movement, *Psychol. Rev.* **78**:83–113.
VON HOLST, E., and VON SAINT PAUL, U., 1963, On the functional organisation of drives, *Anim. Behav.* **11**:1–20.
WADA, J. A., WRINCH, J., HILL, D., MCGEER, P., and MCGEER, E. G., 1963, Central aromatic amine levels and behavior, *Arch. Neurol. (Chicago)* **9**:69–89.
WALTERS, J., BUNNEY, B., and ROTH, R., 1975, Piribedil and apomorphine: Pre- and postsynaptic effects on dopamine synthesis and neuronal activity, *Adv. Neurol.* **9**:273–284.
WAUQUIER, A., and NIEMEGEERS, C. J. E., 1972, Intracranial self-stimulation in rats as a function of various stimulus parameters. II. Influence of haloperidol, pimozide and pipamperone on medial forebrain stimulation with monopolar electrodes, *Psychopharmacologia* **27**:191–202.
WESTERNICK, B. H. C., and KORF, J., 1975, Influence of drugs on striatal and limbic homoranillic acid concentration in the rat brain, *Eur. J. Pharmacol.* **38**:31–40.
WHITTIER, J. R., and ORR, H., 1962, Hyperkinesis and other physiological effects of caudate deficit in the adult albino rat, *Neurology* **12**:529–534.
WILBURN, M. W., and KESNER, R. P., 1974, Effects of caudate nucleus stimulation upon initiation and performance of a complex motor task, *Exp. Neurol.* **45**:61–71.
WOLFARTH, S., 1974, Reactions to apomorphine and spiroperidol of rats with striatal lesions: the relevance of kind and size of the lesion, *Pharmacol., Biochem. Behav.* **12**:181–186.
WOLGIN, D. L., and TEITELBAUM, P., 1974, The role of activation and sensory stimuli in the recovery of feeding following lateral hypothalamic lesions in cat, Paper presented at the meetings of the Eastern Psychological Association, Philadelphia, April 1974.
WYERS, E. J., and DEADWYLER, S. A., 1971, Duration and nature of retrograde amnesia produced by stimulation of caudate nucleus, *Physiol. Behav.* **6**:97–103.
WYERS, E. J., PEEKE, H., WILLISTON, J., and HERZ, M., 1968, Caudate/putamen stimulation disrupts memory, *Exp. Neurol.* **22**:350–366.
YORK, D. H., 1967, The inhibitory action of dopamine on neurones of the caudate nucleus, *Brain Res.* **5**:263–266.
ZIMMERBERG, B., and GLICK, S., 1975, Changes in side preference during unilateral electrical stimulation of the caudate nucleus in rats, *Brain Res.* **85**:335–338.
ZIMMERBERG, B., GLICK, S. D., and JERUSSI, T. P., 1974, Neurochemical correlate of a spatial preference in rats, *Science* **185**:623–625.

STIMULUS SELECTION AND BEHAVIORAL INHIBITION

David M. Warburton

One important area of applied psychology is devoted to the development of techniques for eliminating or weakening some responses so that they may be replaced with others. The psychopharmacologist has become involved in the search for drugs that affect response elimination and the neurochemical mechanisms that control inhibition. The term "behavioral inhibition" has been used as a description and as an explanation in psychopharmacology, and some of these uses will be discussed in later sections of this chapter. First, I will discuss some manifestations of behavioral inhibition and consider the possibility that different neurochemical mechanisms may mediate different sorts of inhibition.

1. VARIETIES OF BEHAVIORAL INHIBITION

Inhibition as a psychological term was derived from physiology in which the term refers to arrest of the function of one neural structure by the activity of another. However, the power to execute that function is still retained and can be manifested when the activity of the inhibiting structure is reduced (Brunton, 1883). Working in the physiological tradition, Pavlov adopted this definition as a basis for his discussions of behavioral inhibition.

David M. Warburton • Department of Psychology, Reading University, Reading R96 2AL, England.

This chapter will also be based on this idea, and some examples of behavioral inhibition will make the use of this definition clearer.

1.1. Habituation

Repetition of a novel stimulus usually results in a gradual decrement in its evoked response (Thompson and Spencer, 1966). For example, a novel tone will elicit a startle response, but if it is repeatedly presented the startle response will rapidly decrease until it disappears. This change cannot be due to motor fatigue or to receptor adaptation because of the phenomenon of dishabituation. Dishabituation refers to the return of a full response to the original stimulus when another novel stimulus is given. Konorski (1948) assumes that habituation is due to the formation of inhibitory connections between neural structures so that the excitatory system for the response is suppressed. One interesting habituation phenomenon is "below-zero" habituation (Thompson and Spencer, 1966) in which further habituation trials after the response has disappeared increases the recovery time of the response. This effect provides strong evidence for an inhibitory system which blocks responding.

1.2. Extinction

Once a response has been trained by pairing a conditioned stimulus, e.g., light, with an unconditioned stimulus, e.g., food, the conditioned stimulus will elicit the response, e.g., salivation, when presented alone. However, later repeated presentations of the conditioned stimulus alone results in a loss of the conditioned response. Similarly in operant conditioning, omission of the reinforcer after a period of training results in a decrease in the operant response. Pavlov (1927) proposed an inhibitory system which counteracts the excitatory process established by training. Pavlov believed that extinctive inhibition was one of several kinds of internal inhibition which was a consequence of neural changes at the cortical level.

Konorski (1948) has summarized evidence suggesting that extinctive inhibition is analogous to the habituation process, and that the only difference between extinction and habituation is that the response which becomes habituated is innate and of subcortical origin. Thorpe (1956) agrees with Konorski that the two forms of inhibition may have similar mechanisms and suggests that reinforcement can be looked on as a form of disinhibition.

Evidence against this hypothesis is that "below-zero" extinction has not been observed (Rescorla, 1969). An extinguished conditioned stimulus is not harder to recondition than a novel stimulus, but, on the contrary, a formerly conditioned stimulus reconditions faster than a fresh stimulus. In addition, there is no evidence that an extinguished conditioned stimulus reduces the condition response elicited by another conditioned stimulus. These two facts suggest that in extinction the conditioned stimulus returns to the status of a neutral stimulus and it no longer activates the excitatory system for the response. This idea is in accord with accounts of extinction in operant conditioning proposed by Skinner (1938). He argued that one need postulate only one system with a continuum of response strengths and in extinction "the stimulus is now ineffective in evoking the response, as it was prior to conditioning" (Skinner, 1938, p. 96).

In favor of the hypothesis, several experimenters have found evidence for disinhibition of extinguished responding by a novel stimulus. For example, Brimer (1972) trained rats on a variable-interval schedule and then reinforcement was withheld. When responding had decreased to around 0.5 response per min, a loud noise was given. It was observed that there was a marked increase in responding. Disinhibition has been considered as one of the criteria for determining whether inhibition is operating (Rescorla, 1969; Hearst et al., 1970), and on these grounds we must conclude that inhibition has not been ruled out as a mechanism in extinction.

1.3. Discrimination

In discrimination training, two neutral stimuli are used. In Pavlovian conditioning, one stimulus is paired with the unconditioned stimulus while the other is explicitly unpaired. The organism responds only when the first conditioned stimulus is presented and not when the unpaired stimulus is given; the first stimulus has become a conditioned excitatory stimulus. The second stimulus which was negatively correlated with the unconditioned stimulus becomes a conditioned inhibitory stimulus. Evidence for this assertion is summarized by Rescorla (1969). For example, a conditioned inhibitory stimulus will reduce the response strength elicited by a conditioned excitatory stimulus; this reduction was greater than that produced by a novel stimulus. In addition, a conditioned inhibitory stimulus could be transformed into a conditioned excitatory stimulus only after much longer training than that required by a neutral stimulus. As well as explicit external stimuli becoming conditioned inhibitory stimuli, internal temporal stimuli can also become inhibitors. For example, Pavlov (1927) noticed that when there was a prolonged tone prior to the food, the salivation occurred during the later part of the conditioned stimulus and the amount of salivation increased as the time of presentation of the unconditioned stimulus approached. Pavlov interpreted the finding in terms of an inhibition during the early portion of the stimulus. Evidence in favor of this hypothesis comes from studies that found conditioning slower with a short delay after training with a long-delay stimulus. Konorski (1948) also found that the early portion of long stimulus would reduce the response to a second conditioned excitatory stimulus.

In operant discrimination a subject's responses during one stimulus are reinforced while responses during the other are not reinforced. As a result, the subject responds predominantly during the stimulus associated with reinforcement. Hearst (Hearst et al., 1970; Hearst, 1972) proposed that the stimulus negatively correlated with reinforcement becomes a conditioned inhibitory stimulus; it has the capacity to decrease performance below the level occurring when that stimulus is absent, "below-zero response strength," provided all the conditions that maintain the response, like magnitude of reinforcement and delay of reinforcement, are held constant. Hearst et al. (1970) regard decrements in responding resulting from changes in reinforcement and so on as being more parsimoniously accounted for by variations in an excitatory system.

1.4. Response Suppression by Aversive Stimuli

Aversive stimuli can produce suppression of high-probability responses, and a number of procedures have been developed to investigate this response suppression. The nomenclature of the field is confusing, and so careful definition will be given of each procedure. Punishment will be used to refer to the presentation of an event, consequent upon a response, that reduces the probability of that response. Two types of punishment procedure are passive avoidance and conflict. Passive avoidance is the simple form of punishment schedule where the animal can avoid aversive stimulation by not making the response. In a typical conflict situation the animal is strongly motivated but can obtain reward only at the expense of punishment, and so the animal must choose between avoidance of punishment and drive reduction. This situation clearly has some elements in common with passive avoidance, and some authors have considered conflict studies under the heading of passive avoidance.

In conditioned suppression the aversive stimulation is not contingent upon a response. In this situation, a neutral stimulus is paired with shock and the effects of the conditioned aversive stimulus examined on performance in an appetitively reinforced schedule. Changes in the animal's behavior have no environmental consequences in conditioned suppression, in contrast to passive avoidance and conflict conditioning where changes in the animal's pattern of responding can reduce the aversive consequences.

The suppression of behavior by aversive stimulation could occur by two means. First, an inhibitory mechanism could be activated, and this system reduces the response probability. Second, the aversive stimulation may initiate forms of behavior, such as defensive responses, which compete with the ongoing response and reduce its probability. A combination of the two explanations has been proposed by Mowrer (See discussion in Mowrer, 1960). Mowrer suggests that

> An action, previously strengthened by reward, which is followed by punishment, produces certain stimuli, both internal and external to the organism,

which, by virtue of their contiguity with punishment, take on the capacity to arouse fear; and when the organism subsequently starts to repeat such an action, the resulting fear produces a *conflict* with the drive or motive underlying the original act. If the fear is sufficiently strong, the act will, in consequence, be inhibited, or at least in some fashion modified. (Mowrer, 1960, p. 25; author's italics)

2. HYPOTHESES ABOUT NEURAL MECHANISMS FOR BEHAVIORAL INHIBITION

This section will consider some possible neural mechanisms which could produce the decrements in responding that we have called learned inhibition for explaining inhibition. Two of these, sensory impairment and motor impairment, are uninteresting and will not be considered here. The mechanisms are response inhibition, activation, and stimulus selection; in succeeding sections, evidence for neurochemical bases for these mechanisms will be discussed.

A response-inhibition mechanism would refer to some system which reduced or abolished the response output. An activation mechanism is one that energizes the response. Stimulus-selection system refers to a mechanism which selects from the mass stimuli bombarding the sensory receptors; in other contexts, stimulus selection has been called "attention."

2.1. Stimulus Selection

According to this hypothesis, there is a selection from the various stimulus inputs so that only a subset of environmental stimuli are available for controlling the response output. For example, if an animal is trained with several relevant cues he may learn to use one or two of these cues as discriminative stimuli. Transfer tests can be used to establish which stimuli have been selected. Douglas and Pribram (1966) proposed a hippocampal system which gates out irrelevant aspects of the environment by inhibiting the input along the primary sensory pathways. This inhibitory system was opposed to an excitatory system controlled mainly by the amygdala. Douglas and Pribram postulated that the probability of attention to a stimulus was increased by virtue of its association with reinforcement and other significant events in the environment. The Douglas–Pribram model can be considered to provide a neural basis for Pavlovian theory. In a similar theory, Kimble (1968; 1969) has also emphasized the importance of hippocampal function for inhibition during habituation, extinction, and discrimination. Novel stimuli would elicit cortical arousal via activity in the nonspecific sensory systems of the midbrain and thalamus. An organism would remain attentive to stimuli associated with reinforcement. Repeated presentations of the stimulus in the absence of reinforcement result in the hippocampus inhibiting the nonspecific arousal systems. The organism can switch its attention from that stimulus to new or more important environmental events.

Douglas (1972) has pointed out the parallel between the function of the hippocampus and a brain cholinergic system, and suggested that behavioral inhibition may be mediated cholinergically with the hippocampus as a crucial link in the system. Warburton (1972a) discussed work on cholinergic mechanisms in the brain controlling behavior and concluded that there was a pathway ascending from the reticular formation to the cortex that was important in the selection of stimuli that set the occasion for responses.

The stimulus-selection mechanisms, whatever their locus, could not provide an explanation of the phenomenon of conditioned inhibition because the "gating out" of a stimulus should only make it behaviorally ineffective. It could not produce the below-zero responding obtained in the habituation and discrimination studies.

2.2. Decreased Activation

This mechanism is based on the hypothesis that there is a behavioral activation or arousal mechanism in the brain which energizes response output so that a decrement in activation will result in a decrement in the probability of active responses. The behavioral activation system has been identified with a norepinephrine system in the brain. Brodie and Shore (1957) suggested that it was located in the posterior hypothalamus and was concerned with the control of skeletal muscles involved in active behavior. A related theory was put forward by Olds (1962) and Stein (1964) who proposed a noradrenergic reward system controlling operant behavior which passed through the hypothalamus and was activated by primary reinforcement or stimuli associated with primary reinforcement. The neural pathway assumed to mediate this reward system was the median forebrain bundle.

Activation of such a system can be used to explain response elimination that occurs with decreases in reinforcement magnitude, as in experimental extinction. However, it cannot explain the "below-zero" response strength found after prolonged habituation, prolonged discrimination training, and training with aversive stimuli.

2.3. Response Inhibition

Response inhibition mechanisms could be of several kinds. First, inhibition may involve direct action of some structure on muscle movements or patterns of muscle movements; this mechanism, when triggered, might slow up or even completely stop the response. The arrest of a response in midcourse by stimulation of the globus pallidus and the complete disappearance of the response by caudate stimulation (Ruch *et al.,* 1965) represent neurophysiological examples of this type of mechanism.

A second form of response inhibition is that mentioned by Douglas (1967), the inhibition of learned responses, i.e., of the bonds, connections, or associations between stimuli and responses. One version of this hypothesis (Warburton, 1967) proposed that a cholinergic system is important in the inhibitory control of both competing and dominant responses. A blockage of central neural function by cholinolytics and high doses of anticholinesterases would result in a disinhibition of all responses, but with lower-probability competing responses increasing proportionally more than the higher-probability dominant responses, especially if these higher-probability responses were already at their response ceiling. Once at response ceiling the probability of the dominant response should decrease as the competing responses are increased; an inverted U-shaped dose–response curve for most responses will be the result.

Another version of a mechanism inhibiting response tendencies has been proposed by Mishkin (1964). This mechanism is associated with the frontal cortex and involved in the suppression of competing response set. Thus, a particular mode of response might be appropriate in one situation but inappropriate in another, and correct choice would depend on inhibition of the initial set. For example, in successive learning set problem the previously rewarded choice must be inhibited in order to perform the correct response. Damage to the frontal cortex resulted in perseveration of a central "set" or mode of responding rather than in perseveration of a particular response. This perseveration may produce lowered responding if the original set had a strong "no go" tendency. This hypothesis was adopted by Bignami and Rosić (1970) to explain the performance deficits caused by cholinolytics, and they suggest that there is a cholinergic system which acts on the motor side of the stimulus-response chain to suppress competing response sets.

As we have seen, several theorists have suggested that response inhibition is mediated by the transmitter acetylcholine. This belief is based on the important and influential theory of Carlton (1963), who suggested that there was a catecholamine system in the reticular formation controlling behavioral excitation and an antagonist cholinergic system producing inhibition.

> It thus appeared that some cholinergic system antagonized the diffuse effects of activation and that this antagonism, first, might provide a basis for "selection" of the effects of activation and, second, was related to the extent that certain responses were correlated with non-reinforcement. Thus, level of activation could be viewed as controlling the tendency for *all* responses to occur, whereas an inhibitory cholinergic system would act to antagonize this action on non-reinforced responses. The net result of this interaction would be that changes in activation would result in changes in the likelihood of occurrence of only a *few* responses, those that were reinforced. (Carlton, 1963, p. 27; author's italics)

Carlton's conception of inhibition is very close to the traditional use of the term inhibition in which there is arrest of the function of one system by the activity of another. A response-inhibition system of this sort could provide a mechanism for "below-zero" response strength.

An earlier neurochemical theory of excitation and inhibition was proposed by Brodie and Shore (1957). Behavioral arousal resulted from an increase of the norapinephrine neurons relative to the activity of serotoninergic neurons. Decreased behavioral excitability was the result of predominance of the antagonistic serotonin system. From this theory it could also be predicted that high activity in the serotonin system and low activity in the noradrenergic system could produce "below-zero" response strength.

2.4. Summary

Decrements in responding that have been interpreted as instances of behavioral inhibition could have been the result of changes in three systems, either stimulus selection, or activation, or response inhibition. Decreases to zero could result from the action of any one of the three systems. The "below-zero" response strength, observed in habituation studies and discrimination training, could only result from the function of a response-inhibition mechanism. Two possible neurochemical substrates for response inhibition have been proposed; Carlton (1963) suggested that a cholinergic inhibitory system was opposed to a noradrenergic excitatory system, whereas Brodie and Shore (1957) hypothesized that the noradrenergic excitatory system was antagonized by a serotonin system. The next section will compare these hypotheses.

3. PSYCHOPHARMACOLOGY OF BEHAVIORAL INHIBITION

This section will center on drugs that are presumed to act on the noradrenergic, cholinergic, and serotoninergic pathways in the brain in order to test predictions from the hypotheses of Carlton (1963) and Brodie and Shore (1957). Carlton predicted that "increased activation and decreased cholinergic activity should produce qualitatively similar effects, and conversely, there should be a similarity of decreased activation and increased cholinergic activity" (Carlton, 1963, p. 23). In view of the paradoxical effects obtained with high doses of drugs in rats, I will discuss only studies which have changed cholinergic activity with doses like 0–10 mg/kg of atropine and 0–1.0 mg/kg of scopolamine and manipulated activation with 0–5.0 mg/kg of amphetamine. Brodie and Shore (1957) make a similar sort of prediction that increased noradrenergic activity and decreased serotoninergic activity should have similar effects and that the effect of decreased activity in noradrenergic neurons and of increased activity in serotoninergic neurons would be similar. This prediction will be tested by comparing the changes in behavior produced by low doses of amphetamine and doses of 0–30 mg/kg of chlordiazepoxide. It is believed (Stein *et al.*, 1973) that benzodiazepines such as chlordiazepoxide produce their major effects by changing the functional serotonin in the brain. This belief will be supported by biochemical evidence in Section 4. These drugs will be compared in the behavioral situations mentioned in Section 1 on behavioral inhibition: habituation, extinction, discrimination, including temporal discriminations and response suppression by aversive stimuli. The drug effects will then be examined in relation to the mechanisms of stimulus selection, activation, and response inhibition in order to rule out one or more of these as a possible basis for changes in behavior.

3.1. Habituation

Habituation refers to the phenomenon whereby repetition of a stimulus usually results in a gradual decrease in the response. It is thought to play a part in open-field exploration and spontaneous alternation. Habituation has proved difficult to study in a simple form without being confounded with emotional responses. One of the simplest demonstrations is the startle response which is usually measured by placing the animal in a suspended box connected to a pressure transducer. Amphetamines increase the initial startle response (Kirkby *et al.*, 1972) and impair habituation (Cladel *et al.*, 1966; Kirkby *et al.*, 1972). Thus, increased adrenergic activity enhances the response to novel stimuli and reduces the habituation decrement.

According to Carlton's hypothesis, scopolamine should have similar effects. The evidence on this point is equivocal. Payne and Anderson (1967) found an attenuation of the initial startle response with mg/kg, whereas Warburton observed no initial difference with 0–0.75 mg/kg (Warburton, unpublished), and an enhanced response with the same doses (Warburton and Groves, 1969). Thus, there was evidence in support of Carlton (1963) that intermediate doses of scopolamine may produce loss of behavioral inhibition; however, there was no evidence in these three studies that scopolamine impaired habituation at all.

These results contrast with findings from other studies in which scopolamine decreased spontaneous alternation in a T-maze. Spontaneous alternation is said to be a pure form of habituation (Glanzer, 1953) and "is the very epitome of behavior based on internal inhibition..." (Douglas, 1972, pp. 532–533). In the first drug study using this phenomenon, Meyers and Domino (1964) found that although a saline group alternated at greater than chance level, animals injected with scopolamine alternated at less than chance; this finding has been supported by studies by Douglas and Isaacson

(1966) and Squire (1969). In the study by Squire (1969), physostigmine, a cholinesterase inhibitor which increases the amount of functional acetylcholine, increased spontaneous alternation. These experiments support the idea that the animals which have decreased functional acetylcholine do not habituate in the T-maze and so do not alternate their choices. If this task depends on the animal gating out stimuli as Douglas (1966) suggests, then there seems to be some impairment of stimulus selection in the scopolamine-injected subjects which prevented habituation in this complex situation. In the simple startle situation stimulus selection is not involved and scopolamine had no effect.

This explanation can also be applied to the habituation to a novel environment. Carlton and Vogel (1965) exposed some animals to a novel chamber, whereas others were not exposed; half of the subjects in each group were injected prior to exposure with 0.5 mg/kg of scopolamine. The second part of the study occurred three days later. The animals had been water deprived for 24 hr and then reintroduced into the chamber which now contained a water bottle. Animals which had habituated to the chamber were expected to show a shorter drinking latency than animals which had not habituated or had not been exposed because the unexposed group would spend time exploring prior to drinking. The two saline-injected groups had short latencies, but the scopolamine subjects behaved as if they had never been exposed, as if habituation had not taken place at all. The important feature of this study is that the animals were tested with saline after habituation under scopolamine. If scopolamine had acted on a response-inhibition mechanism, it would have impaired habituation but should have had no effect on the subsequent test session. However, if the scopolamine had interfered with the stimulus input mechanisms, their habituation might be impaired and the effects would carry over to a test session. The group trained under scopolamine did show marked impairment on the test session without the drug, so that the drug could not have had any effect on response output but must have affected the stimulus input; that is to say, the result cannot be explained in terms of scopolamine impairing response inhibition.

Other tests of exploration have studied the choice behavior of rats in maze where one arm led to an "exploratory" box with objects in it, and the other arm to an empty box. Leaton (1968) injected animals with scopolamine and found that they made significantly more exploratory choices than saline-injected controls. When the boxes were reversed, the scopolamine subjects switched their choices and again showed a significantly greater number of exploratory choices. This experiment does not support the response-inhibition hypothesis but provides persuasive support for the conclusion that scopolamine injections impaired an animal's ability to habituate to novelty, as Carlton (1968) suggested. Amphetamine has also been tested in an exploratory box by Robbins and Iversen (1973a). They used a two-compartment apparatus with a main box in which locomotor activity was recorded by means of photocells and an alley in which objects were placed to elicit exploration. Amphetamines decreased exploration and increased locomotor activity, which was the opposite of the results with scopolamine. This finding contradicts the prediction from the original hypothesis of Carlton (1963) that scopolamine and amphetamine would produce qualitatively similar results.

The effects of benzodiazepines on habituation have not been measured directly, but there are several studies that have looked at exploration of an unfamiliar environment. In a T-maze, animals treated with chlordiazepoxide were more active than control subjects during the first 2 min, and less active in the fourth and fifth minutes. This rapid decline was unlike the pattern shown with amphetamine which increases the initial response and retards the decrease in responding (Rushton and Steinberg, 1966). A more recent examination of chlordiazepoxide on exploration used a hole board in which familiarity with the board reduces the number of holes examined in a given time (Nolon and Parkes, 1973). Chlordiazepoxide increased exploration on the first exposure, but not on subsequent occasions. The authors conclude that benzodiazepines act only in removing a factor that limits exploration in a novel situation, i.e., behavioral inhibition by novel stimuli. In contrast, doses of scopolamine had no effect on the initial head poking, but the rate of decrease in responding was slower for the scopolamine group compared with the control group (Feigley and Hamilton, 1971). Measures of the response duration showed that although all groups were responding with head pokes of similar durations at first, the average duration for the control group increased markedly whereas the scopolamine animals were unchanged over the session. The authors conclude that the scopolamine-injected subjects did not habituate as rapidly as the control subjects.

In summary, the effects of amphetamine, the cholinolytics, and chlordiazepoxide on various sorts of habituation are complex, probably on account of differences in the behavioral situation. In general, both amphetamine and chlordiazepoxide increased the initial response to novelty, whereas cholinolytics had no effect. Amphetamine slowed the habituation decrement in all situations, whereas chlordiazepoxide had no apparent effects on the decrement in exploratory habituation. Scopolamine had no effect on the decrement in simple startle situations but retarded the response decrement in exploratory situations, which suggests that different mechanisms may be involved in the two sorts of habituation (Williams *et al.*, 1974). One crucial piece of evidence against the hypothesis that scopolamine was impairing response inhibition came from the study of Carlton and Vogel (1965). They demonstrated that subjects injected with scopolamine prior to habituation behaved as if they had never received training when tested without the drug. This effect on behavior was seen when the drug was not in the body, and so the drug would not have changed response output by impairing a response inhibition mechanism. On the other hand, it would be consistent with scopolamine interfering with the stimulus input during the habituation session.

The evidence from the habituation studies is not consistent with the

Carlton (1963) hypothesis that response inhibition is mediated by a cholinergic system in the brain which is antagonistic to a catecholamine behavioral excitation system. Instead the balance of evidence supports the Brodie and Shore (1957) hypothesis that there is a serotoninergic inhibitory system which is opposed to a norepinephrine excitation system. The one piece of discordant evidence is that amphetamine, which would increase the activity in the norepinephrine system, and chlordiazepoxide, which would decrease activity in the serotonin system, do not have the same effects on the rate of habituation in exploration situations. However, these situations are much more complex behaviorally than other habituation situations and so greater weight can be placed on the other studies.

3.2. Extinction

In Pavlovian conditioning, repeated presentation of the conditioned stimulus without being accompanied by the unconditioned stimulus results in a loss of the conditioned response. Similarly, in operant conditioning omission of the reinforcer after a period of training results in a decrement in the operant response. Below, the effects of drugs on extinguishing responses will be discussed first, and then drug effects on already-extinguished responses. The term extinction has been used rather broadly to include studies where reinforcement was withheld but no external stimulus signaled the changed contingency.

3.2.1. Extinguishing Responses

Work on cholinergic drugs and the extinguishing of Pavlovian conditioned reflexes has been mentioned by Michelson (1961), but no experimental details were given. The only information given in the paper was that atropine and another cholinolytic, parpanite, significantly lengthened the experimental extinction in mice whereas the anticholinesterase paraoxon hastened the decrease in responding. Michaelson concluded that cholinolytics slowed the disappearance of responses whereas increased functional brain acetylcholine speeded up extinction and so a cholinergic system mediates the process of extinctive inhibition.

Drugs were tested by Warburton (1969a) on extinction performance obtained during acquisition of go–no-go alternation (Heise et al., 1969). In this schedule animals were pretrained to press the lever ten times for reinforcement (FR 10) during the trial period. Responding during the intertrial interval postponed the onset of the next trial for 10 sec, so that intertrial-interval responding was extinguished to a low level. When the animals responded on 90% or more of the 480 trials per day for each of five consecutive days, acquisition of alternation was begun. The schedule consisted of odd-numbered trials, in which ten lever presses still resulted in reinforcement and trial termination, and even-numbered trials, in which ten responses did not result in reinforcement and did not terminate the trial. The same discriminative stimulus signaled the beginning of both reinforced and nonreinforced trials, and correct responding depended on the outcome of the preceding trial (Heise et al., 1969). This schedule was selected because it depended on two sorts of extinguished responding. The first type, intertrial-interval responding, was extinguished prior to single-alternation training, and the second type was the nonreinforced responses during the no-go trials which were extinguished during acquisition.

Various drugs and drug combinations were tested on the two sorts of extinction performance, including physostigmine sulfate, atropine sulfate, and amphetamine; the data were analyzed by means of a single statistic, probability of an error, and a descriptive mathematical model of extinction performance. Both atropine and amphetamine increased the mean probability of an error, whereas the physostigmine scores did not differ from control. However, the descriptive model revealed that physostigmine interfered with motor responding and changed the onset trial for extinction, i.e., the trial when no-go response decreased significantly. Low doses advanced the onset trial, i.e., facilitated extinction (Warburton, 1972a), while high doses delayed it (Warburton, 1969a). The extinction rate was the same as for atropine and the control subjects. In contrast, amphetamine both delayed the onset trial for extinction and retarded the rate of decrease in errors.

As mentioned earlier, responding is under the discriminative control of the outcome stimuli persisting from the preceding trial. Thus, the occurrence of reinforcing stimuli on the previous trial is consistently associated with a nonreinforced trial, and the absence of reinforcement always precedes a reinforced trial, provided the rat is responding. Warburton (1972a) reported that the "intensity" of the persisting stimuli was changed by either increasing or decreasing the intertrial interval. It was found that only the onset trial of extinction changed; the mean values decreased with the 5-sec intertrial interval and increased monotonically for the 20- and 40-sec groups in comparison with the 10-sec intertrial interval group. The rate of extinction remained constant for all values of the intertrial intervals examined. In another study (in collaboration with Richard Kolodner), we found that when a specific external cue indicated the reinforced trials, the onset trial advanced significantly but the cue had no effect on the rate of decrease in errors. The behavioral studies suggest that changes in the discriminability of the relevant cue modified the trial when errors started to decrease, and so it does not seem unreasonable to suggest that the initial presolution phase consisted of selection of the relevant stimuli, and that association of stimulus and response occurred during the learning state. The length of this initial phase was reduced by low dose of physostigmine and increased by cholinolytics. These findings are consistent with the hypothesis of a cholinergic system involved in sensory processing described in the last section. The effects of amphetamine were entirely in accord with the hypothesis of a noradrenergic activation system in the brain. The results were similar from the habituation experiment in which amphetamine also retarded the decrease in responding. This provides some pharmacological support for the assertion of Konorski (1948) and Thorpe (1956) that extinction and habituation have some mechanisms in common.

3.2.2. Extinguished Responding

The first article about the effects of drugs on stable extinction performance was by Skinner and Heron (1937). A dose of 0.5 mg, i.e., about 1.0 mg/kg of amphetamine, was injected on the 11th day of extinction. Responding was increased to the rate prevailing during reinforcement. The performance within the session showed little signs of diminishing over the 2-hr session, and so the drug clearly interfered with already extinguished responding. In a latter study, Hearst (1959) trained animals on discrimination with two levers; then they were given 20 sessions of experimental extinction until responding reached a low level. At this time the subjects were injected with scopolamine before each session, and it was found that responding increased to eight times the rate found during the last days of nondrugged extinction. No decrement in performance was obtained after 15 consecutive sessions with scopolamine injections, yet the low levels of responding were restored immediately in the first nondrug session. The finding of increased extinguished responding has been substantiated by Herblin (1968) who trained animals to respond on one lever in a two-lever box and then gave experimental extinction sessions until responding declined to the rate on the nonreinforced bar. When scopolamine was administered, the extinguished responding was "released" so that there was increased pressing on the previously reinforced bar but no change in the rate on the lever that had never delivered reinforcement.

As well as testing extinguished responding after a period of reinforcement, some studies have also examined extinction as part of a multiple schedule in which reinforcement is withheld after a reinforced component without any explicit interoceptive cue to signal the change. An experiment on two rats, published separately by Herrnstein (1958) and Brady (1959), used a four-component schedule consisting of a fixed interval, an unsignaled extinction period, a shock avoidance, and a signaled extinction period in which there were no experimental contingencies in operation. The baseline response rate during the unsignaled extinction period was extremely low, but all the doses of scopolamine up to 1.0 mg/kg produced marked increases in rate during this component in both rats. A third rat was also trained on only the fixed interval and unsignaled extinction components, and the 0.1 mg/kg dose of scopolamine produced similar effects on extinguished behavior as it had during the more complex schedule. A comparable study on a multiple (continuous reinforcement, extinction, and avoidance) schedule (Weissman, 1959) showed that amphetamine also increased extinction responding. Thus, in support of Carlton's hypothesis, amphetamine and scopolamine have similar effects on extinction responding when the experimental extinction is included as one component in a multiple schedule.

The remaining studies to be discussed in this section are special cases of the multiple schedules, but the components are relatively short since they are terminated after the first reinforcement or last a maximum of 10 secs if reinforcement is not delivered. The first one is the single-alternation situation of Heise et al. (1969) that has been discussed earlier in this section. The effects of amphetamine and cholinolytics on extinguished responding have been tested by Heise (unpublished) who demonstrated that intraperitoneal injections of scopolamine, atropine, and amphetamine increased the number of responses on the nonreinforced trials. Injections of atropine directly into cerebral ventricles also increased the number of responses, which showed that this effect was due to the drug acting on the central nervous system. This result was supported by the lack of effect of atropine methyl bromide, which passes through the blood–brain barrier poorly (Warburton, 1969a). Intraventricular injections of amphetamine increased nonreinforced responding as well. In summary, these studies are completely consistent with Carlton's prediction that there is no difference in the behavioral mode of action of amphetamine and cholinolytic drugs.

Another schedule with repeated trials of experimental extinction was designed by Heise et al. (1970). Rats were trained to press during discrete trials; one group was reinforced on every trial, whereas the second was only reinforced on 50% of the trials programmed in a semirandom order. The repeated extinction phase of the study consisted of 10 cycles of reinforcement and extinction; the reinforcement period consisted of about 20 trials during which the 100% group received 20 reinforcements and the 50% group received ten reinforcements, whereas during the extinction period the rat had to stop responding for three trials in order to return to the reinforced component of the cycle. Performance depended on outcome stimuli persisting from the previous trial, and no explicit exteroceptive cue signaled the transition from reinforcement period to withdrawal period. Scopolamine, atropine, chlordiazepoxide, and amphetamine were tested on stable performance measuring the responding during the nonreinforced trials, and it was found that amphetamine, chlordiazepoxide, and the cholinolytics increased extinction responding. Similar results were obtained with atropine during another experiment involving the same procedure (Warburton, 1972b). Greater responding was observed for the 50% group over all doses of amphetamine, chlordiazepoxide, atropine, and scopolamine. Another experiment discussed in Heise et al. (1970) used an explicit cue to signal the transition, and performance was still disrupted by amphetamine, atropine, and scopolamine.

In a related situation (Heise and Lilie, 1970), a lever press during a trial was not reinforced unless it had been preceded by three trials on which no responses had occurred. Lever pressing on trials preceded by less than three nonresponding trials did not produce reinforcement and reset the "count" of the nonreinforced trials. When the rats had learned not to respond during the three "extinction" trials, they were tested with atropine, scopolamine, and amphetamine. It was observed that the drugged rats responded after fewer trials than the control rats, i.e., they showed impaired extinction. This result was obtained with all doses tested, although with atropine the effect decreased with larger doses.

3.2.3. Summary

The effects of amphetamine and cholinolytics on extinguishing responses differ qualitatively; atropine delayed the trial when extinction began but did not change the rate of extinction, whereas amphetamine delayed the onset of extinction and retarded the extinction rate. By contrast, amphetamine, chlordiazepoxide, and cholinolytics all increased responding that had already been extinguished. Thus, there are no grounds for choosing between the rival hypotheses of response inhibition when comparing studies of extinguish*ing* as opposed to extinguish*ed* responses. However, the qualitative difference found in the study of extinguish*ing* responses contradicts the prediction from Carlton's hypothesis and makes it less likely that there is a cholinergic system mediating inhibition. The various results can be reconciled and explained by means of a cholinergic system involved in stimulus selection.

3.3. Discrimination

During discrimination training a response is reinforced during one stimulus and not during another. The effect of training can be assessed from the number of responses in the two conditions. Discrimination baselines have been used extensively both for detecting drug effects and for analyzing the effects of drugs on stimulus control. Two procedures for stimulus presentation have been developed, and these are called the method of successive presentation and the method of simultaneous presentation (Kimble, 1961). As well as differences in stimulus presentation, different procedures have different response requests; these are either go–no-go responses or go–go responses. In simultaneous discriminations, there must be different responses for the two stimuli, so that simultaneous discriminations always involve go–go responding. In successive presentations the animal may be required either to make a response during one stimulus and withhold that response during the other stimulus, i.e., go–no-go responding, or to make the response when one stimulus is present and change that response when the other stimulus is presented, i.e., go–go responses. The go–go method enables the measurement of stimulus preferences, response preferences, response perseveration, and response switching, and is superior to the successive method for assessing whether changes are due to modifications of stimulus control or response inhibition.

3.3.1. Acquisition

Drug studies of discrimination acquisition have not been carried out frequently. The first studies by Whitehouse (1964; 1966) examined the effects of atropine and physostigmine on acquisition of a successive discrimination problem. A right turn was rewarded when the center runway was black with a rough floor and a buzzer sounded, while a left turn was reinforced when the center runway was white with a smooth floor and no buzzer sounded. A dose of 0.05 mg/kg of physostigmine reduced the number of trials to a criterion and significantly reduced the number of errors during the first 70 trials (Whitehouse, 1966). This dose was the same as that facilitating extinction performance in the study of Warburton (1972a). In contrast, atropine retarded acquisition of the discrimination (Whitehouse, 1964; Whitehouse et al., 1964), and Whitehouse showed that the slower acquisition was due to an interference with learning rather than performance of the response. When he partially trained the animals with the drug and stopped injecting, there was not the dramatic improvement in performance that would have been expected if the animal had learned but could not inhibit the error responding (Whitehouse, 1964).

These data were supported by a study by Cox and Tye (1973) which investigated the acquisition of a position discrimination in a T-maze with performance evaluated in terms of trials to a criterion. Small doses of physostigmine, 0.02 and 0.06 mg/kg, produced a significant decrease in the number of trials required to reach a criterion of five successive correct trials, whereas a high dose caused a significant increase. Atropine also caused a significant increase, while methyl atropine and neostigmine which pass through the blood–brain barrier poorly were without effect. These data are consistent with Carlton's hypothesis that a cholinergic system is inhibiting nonreinforced responses, i.e., errors. It is also consistent with the hypothesis that a cholinergic system is involved in stimulus control with reinforcement as a special class of stimuli. In a later study Cox and Tye (1974) showed that the drug effects were not confined to acquisition of the position discrimination, but still occurred when the animals had been trained for eight more days after reaching the criterion and before injecting the drugs.

In a single-alternation maze study, Van der Poel (1972) trained rats to alternate their choices between the left and the right arm during successive trials separated by an intertrial interval of 2 hr. Behavior at all points in the maze, especially exploration, rearing, and intention movements (behavior directed toward one of the maze arms) was recorded. Drug tests were carried out with N-methyl-4-piperidyl cyclopentyl methylethynyl glycolate (PCMG) a short-acting cholinolytic. Injections were given either 20 min before the first trial (Group I), immediately after the first trial (Group II), or 20 min before the second trial (Group III). In order to test for state dependence, another group (Group IV) was tested with injection before both the first and the second trials. An examination of the alternation scores on the second trial showed that the drug affected performance in the groups where the drug was injected before the trial (Groups I, III, and IV). In Group I, the alternation performance was at chance levels even though the drug was not in the body, demonstrating that the drug was not influencing a response-output mechanism. The behavior in the maze was described in a later paper (Van der Poel, 1973), and the most significant observation was the increase in intention movements, suggesting increased conflict. One common cause underlying deficits in alternation and increased "approach–approach" conflict could be an impairment of a mechanism involved in the processing of relevant information, as Van der Poel (1974) suggests.

If the drugs were affecting a mechanism of this sort, it might be predicted that impairment would be increased in discrimination acquisition when irrelevant cues were present, or when multiple relevant cues were available. This was demonstrated by Whitehouse (1967) when he trained rats in a T-maze using a correction procedure in a simultaneous discrimination with relevant visual cues of black or white arms of the maze. The introduction of tactile and auditory irrelevant cues slowed acquisition rate. Injections of atropine slowed acquisition, and there were a larger number of trials to a criterion. In a successive discrimination, where the relevant visual cue was the color of the center alley and the irrelevant cues were tactual and auditory, atropine again retarded the acquisition of the discrimination in terms of trials to a criterion. In a parallel series of experiments with multiple relevant stimuli, Whitehouse (1967) trained rats with visual, auditory, and tactile cues as relevant. The control subjects learned the multicued discrimination faster and with fewer errors than the subjects that were trained with a single cue. Atropine had little effect on the single-cued discrimination, but acquisition was much slower than control in the multicued discrimination.

In an extension of these studies (Warburton, unpublished), rats were trained in an operant situation for four days on a discrimination with two relevant cues. The rats were injected with doses of scopolamine immediately prior to each daily session. The subjects were then given two transfer tests in order to determine the amount that they had learned about the two cues. The first transfer test was proceded by an injection of the dose of drug given during training, while during the second test, given after an intervening day of training, the subjects were not given any drug. Animals that received a placebo during training were injected with scopolamine prior to the second transfer test.

Examination of the acquisition performance showed that scopolamine impaired the acquisition of the discrimination and the animals took more trails to reach a criterion of 75% correct responses. The drug also slowed up the decrease in intertrial-interval responses, another measure of discrimination learning. These results can be interpreted in terms of a two-stage stimulus-selection model of learning. The presolution phase consists of selecting the relevant stimuli, and it will be decreased by any experimental manipulation which increases the probability of a relevant stimulus being selected. One way of achieving this would be to increase the number of relevant stimuli available for selection. When two relevant stimuli are available, some animals will select one cue, and others will select the other cue; it is unimportant which cue is selected because the animal can solve the discrimination in terms of that cue. However, if subjects that were injected with atropine or scopolamine are switching cues more frequently than control animals, then the drugged subjects will show a longer presolution phase. From this hypothesis it would be predicted that control subjects which select the relevant cue and switch less to other cues will learn the problem mainly in terms of that cue and will learn less about other relevant stimuli (see Sutherland and MacIntosh, 1972). This prediction was examined in the transfer tests which showed that animals who learned with two relevant cues did learn something about both cues but that the more a subject learned about one cue the less he learned about the other. An interesting difference was found between the transfer scores of the scopolamine and placebo subjects. Most placebo subjects learned more about one cue than the other, but animals injected with scopolamine tended to respond almost equally in terms of both cues. However, there was no evidence that the group had learned more than the other; the sums of the probability of responding to tone and the probability of responding to light was similar for the two groups. This partial continuity effect was important because it enabled a test of another prediction that animals with quicker learning had learned the problem mainly in terms of one cue. The statistical comparison revealed a significant correlation between a subject's dependence on a single cue and its rate of acquisition which supported this prediction. As a result the scopolamine group, which had less dependence on a single cue, had the slower acquisition rate.

An examination was conducted of the performance on the second transfer test in which subjects that were trained under the drug were tested after a placebo injection and subjects that were injected with saline during training were tested after a dose of scopolamine. Performance for both groups was poorer than when the animals were tested with the same drug as in training; there were fewer responses to the two-cue combination, more intertrial-interval responses, and the probability of responses to the single cues were diminished. These changes are consistent with the hypothesis that discrimination performance had not transferred completely from the drug state to the nondrug state, and vice versa. State dependence has been obtained often in scopolamine studies (see Warburton, 1975b), and the phenomenon seems to be present in these studies. An explanation for the state-dependence effect can be given in terms of scopolamine modifying the mechanisms of stimulus selection so that different stimulus subsets are available to the animal in the drug and nondrug state because of the differences in stimulus selection.

3.3.2. Stable Discrimination Behavior

All behavior is under discriminative control although it may not be programmed by the experimenter and he may not even be able to define the controlling stimulus because it is inside the organism. For example, in simple fixed-ratio schedules (see Ferster and Skinner, 1957), responses are thought to be the stimuli for more responding, because these response-produced stimuli are associated with reinforcement (Keller and Schoenfeld, 1950). These response-produced stimuli must depend on the proprioceptors, but cannot be manipulated directly because they are internal. In simple fixed-interval responding (see Ferster and Skinner, 1957), the discriminative stimuli are usually described merely as internal "temporal" cues.

A study of the effects of amphetamine on fixed-ratio responding was performed by Owens (1960); rats trained on an FR30 schedule were given 1.0, 2.0, and 3.2 mg/kg of d-amphetamine, which decreased the normal high response rate and increased the frequency and duration of pausing following reinforcement. This result was substantiated by Heise (1964). Atropine and scopolamine changed the pattern of responding on FR26 to a steady lower rate, i.e., no pauses after reinforcement, but the effects were small (Boren and Navarro, 1959). In contrast, tests of the cholinolytics and amphetamine in a fixed-interval schedule showed that the increased response rate was due to the drug abolishing the typical temporal pattern of responding with pauses after reinforcement (Boren and Navarro, 1959; Wentink, 1938). Wentink noted that although amphetamine increased the rate, it decreased the consumption of the food pellets, which showed that the response rate changes and motivational effects were independent. The effects of amphetamine on responding have been explained in terms of the overall rate of responding in control conditions (Kelleher and Morse, 1968). A classic experiment by Clark and Steele (1966) demonstrated this phenomenon in a three-component schedule consisting of successive periods of fixed interval, fixed ratio, and no reinforcement. All animals were trained on this schedule, and response rate was high during the fixed-ratio component and low during the nonreinforced component. Amphetamine decreased the response rate during the ratio component, but increased the rate under the two components with the lower rates of responding. Clark and Steele point out that amphetamines must be doing more than disrupting stimulus control of the response patterns, because the response rate during the ratio period often fell below the rates during the interval period of the schedule. A follow-up to this study (McMillan, 1969) using a two-component schedule with various fixed-interval and fixed-ratio parameters showed that the effect was not due to a difference in different types of internal cues in the two schedules, but depended solely on the control-response rate.

Tests of chlordiazepoxide on interoceptive conditioning like fixed interval and fixed ratio have also been carried out. On a fixed-interval schedule, responding consists of a pause after reinforcement, followed by a gradual acceleration in the rate of responding until reinforcement is delivered. Chlordiazepoxide increased response rate and abolished pausing and the acceleration; i.e., it abolished the temporal discrimination (Richelle *et al.*, 1962). In the second experiment reported in this paper Richelle *et al.* injected the drug into animals trained on a differential reinforcement of low-rate schedule. Chlordiazepoxide again disrupted the temporal discrimination; it reduces the delay in responding and increased the lever-pressing rate, in spite of the fact that increased responding delays reinforcement.

Fixed-ratio responding was examined in a two-component schedule consisting of a trial signaled by a light, during which 25 responses delivered a food pellet and terminated the trial (Wedeking, 1968). Each trial was separated by 10 sec of darkness, and responses during the interval were neither punished nor reinforced. Chlordiazepoxide increased response rate during the trials and the number of responses during the intertrial interval. Increased appetite could explain the increased response rate on the ratio but not the disinhibition of the extinguished response during the intertrial interval, and Wedeking (1968) argues that the drug was not disrupting discrimination but was disinhibiting responding. In a related study, Wedeking (1969) tested chlordiazepoxide on a two-lever discrimination where 25 responses on the lever below the light produced reinforcement. Each trial was separated by an intertrial interval as before, and once again the drug increased responding during this period. The drug also increased the number of responses on the correct lever at high doses.

These data on free operant, internally cued discrimination showed that amphetamine, chlordiazepoxide, and scopolamine increased the response rate on fixed-ratio and fixed-interval schedules. Unfortunately, single measures like response rate do not enable the experimenter to say unequivocally whether the drug was impairing stimulus control or interfering with response inhibition. Discrete trial schedules have proved to be more useful in this respect. Accordingly, the rest of this section will be devoted to studies of responding during discrete trials, signaled by an external stimulus.

One procedure, developed by Hearst (1959), used two response levers. Food was delivered by presses on one lever when a tone was on, and food was available on the other lever when a clicking stimulus was presented. Lever pressing between trials did not deliver reinforcement, but delayed the onset of the next trial for 5 sec. Scopolamine was tested using this technique, and it was found that it produced an increase in errors on both levers, and in the number of responses during the intertrial interval. Hearst also examined the occurrence of switching and perseveration. Perseveration was defined as the number of times a subject pressed the same lever twice in a row, whereas switching was the number of times a response on one lever was followed by a response on the other. These measures were made regardless of changes from trial to intertrial interval. He found that the number of perseverations far exceeded the number of switches under scopolamine and that the intertrial-interval responding was characterized by "bursts" of pressing on a single lever. In addition, scopolamine increased the amount of lever pressing on one lever and showed increased lever preference. The results of this study suggest the hypothesis that the drug was interfering with a response-inhibition mechanism by which animals switch from one mode of responding to another. A second experiment tested the hypothesis that the animals could not "hear" the stimuli due to gross sensory deficits produced by scopolamine. No evidence was found that the animals could not discriminate tones and clicks. In a follow-up study to Hearst's experiments, Carlton (1961; described in Carlton, 1963) trained rats on go–go single alternation. Tests with atropine, scopolamine, and amphetamine showed that all these drugs increased perseveration errors; in single alternation there can be no switching errors. These results are in complete accord with the hypothesis of a cholinergic inhibitory system in opposition to a noradrenergic excitatory system.

Evidence against a cholinergic response-inhibition mechanism came from comparisons of internal and external stimulus responding. Cholinergic drugs should have similar effects on performance regardless of the stimuli controlling performance, according to the response-inhibition hypothesis.

Laties and Weiss (1966) attempted to compare drug effects on performance controlled by internal and external cues using two fixed-interval (FI 100 min) schedules. One schedule was the usual fixed-interval schedule where the only cues were temporal stimuli originating with the organism and associated with the passage of time. The other schedule was a fixed interval with a "clock," a sequence of stimuli which varied systematically with time (see Ferster and Skinner, 1957, for a discussion of these schedules). These schedules were presented in a predetermined sequence to three pigeons during the session, and performance was measured using the index of curvature to characterize performance. If there is a steady responding during the interval, the index is small; but if responding is concentrated at the end of the interval, it is high. Amphetamine and scopolamine had large effects on the index for ordinary fixed interval, but had little effect on "clock" fixed interval and, while amphetamine increased the overall rate slightly, scopolamine decreased it. Laties and Weiss take the differential action of drugs on the two schedules as support for the hypothesis that performance controlled by exteroceptive discriminative stimuli is more resistant to drugs than responding behavior controlled by interoceptive stimuli, because the latter control is somehow less precise. However, the different sensitivities of externally and internally cued responding in the Laties and Weiss study can be explained in terms of the controlling stimuli in each condition. In the "interval cue" situation the subjects base their response on a single "temporal" stimulus. In contrast, the experimenter programs the external cue situation by adding an extra external stimulus, the "clock," so that responding is effectively controlled by both an interoceptive and an exteroceptive stimulus. It is not surprising to find that the two situations show differential drug sensitivity. Nevertheless, this experiment does demonstrate that scopolamine can act via stimulus mechanisms rather than directly on response inhibition, because the number of stimuli controlling performance should not make a difference to the latter mechanism.

A direct way of testing the stimulus-selection hypothesis would be to compare performance on discriminations with two exteroceptive cues with performance with a single exteroceptive cue. It would be expected that the discrimination based on two relevant cues would be less sensitive to scopolamine. This prediction was examined using a successive discrimination with either a tone, a light, or a tone and a light as the relevant cues with different amounts of training for two double-cue groups (Warburton, 1974a). After training, all animals were tested for stimulus equivalence by presenting each animal with a set of trials half of which were signaled by each of the remaining two discriminative cues. In order to maintain the original discrimination, retraining trials were given; but responses to the transfer stimuli were neither reinforced nor punished. Following the transfer test, the rats were given one more day of training and then tested with scopolamine at one-week intervals according to a balanced Latin-square design.

The dose–response curves were plotted for the four groups, and it was found that the drug effects were greatest on the single-stimulus groups, and least on the overtrained double-stimulus group. Individual drug-sensitivity indices were calculated from the area under the individual dose–response curves, and a cue-dependence index for each individual in the paired stimulus conditions was calculated from the ratio of the transfer scores to the single stimuli. A correlation was made between these indices, and it was found that the greater the cue-dependence index, i.e., the greater the reliance on more than one cue, the smaller the drug sensitivity. The results from the present study show that this difference probably explains the Laties and Weiss results because there was significantly more impairment produced by scopolamine in the group trained with only one stimulus. In addition, individuals within the double-stimulus groups that responded mainly to one cue were more affected by the drug than subjects responding almost equally to both cues.

This study is supported by a two-trial study by Heise (1975). During the first trial, a cue was presented which set the occasion for a go or a no-go response on the second trial. One group had to discriminate between two tones which determined the response on the second trial. A second group had to respond on the first trial, and the presence or absence of reinforcement was the cue for the second trial responding. The third group discriminated between the two tones and responded for reinforcement on the first trial. The cue for responding on the second trial was the double stimulus of the tone and the presence or absence of reinforcement on the first trial. Scopolamine had the least effect on subjects in the third group, confirming the finding that the number of stimuli can determine the effect of scopolamine.

Although the results of these experiments help to explain the findings of Laties and Weiss (1966), a satisfactory comparison between internal and external cues in the same subject has not been made. This gap was filled by an experiment of Warburton and Heise (1972) who developed a method of training spatial double-alternation responding. Each response was reinforced, correction of errors was prevented, and a discriminative stimulus was placed between each sequence of four responses. Responding on different components of the sequence was controlled by a different set of internal and external stimuli. Thus, the first left response of the double-alternation sequence was controlled by an "external" cue, the intersequence stimulus, whereas performance on the other components of the sequence was controlled by "internal" cues from the previous trial. The second left and first right were controlled by two internal cues, while the second right was under the control of a single internal cue. The extent of this stimulus control could be estimated on the basis of information theory so that the uncertainty associated with each member of the response sequence was measured on a scale ranging from zero (minimum ambiguity and maximum predictability) to one (maximum ambiguity and minimum predictability).

This baseline was used to examine the effects of scopolamine on interoceptively cued responding. It was found that the uncertainty of response increased for all responses, but there was no strong evidence that the interoceptively cued performance was more affected than the exteroceptively cued responding. The increased uncertainty reflected an increase in the total number of errors. The mean number of errors for each dose was divided up into switching errors, i.e., changing levers on successive trials and not being reinforced. The number of errors in each category increased as the total number of errors increased, and the proportions of perseverative and switching errors changed very little with increasing doses of the drug, until at the higher doses the probabilities of both switching and perseveration were nearly equal. This evidence does not agree with the previously discussed findings of Hearst (1959) that scopolamine increased perseveration and response preference. One important difference between the analysis of the data in the two studies was that Hearst calculated perseveration in terms of successive responses on the same lever regardless of whether it was a trial or not. In other words, if the drugged animal did not discriminate the termination of the trial as well as a normal, it would continue responding into the intertrial interval. In the Warburton and Heise study the animal made perseveration and switching errors because it did not discriminate the cues for responding correctly. However, there does not appear to be any strong stimulus specificity in the action of scopolamine on internal as opposed to external cues, which suggests that the drug results in a *general* loss of stimulus control.

In a series of experiments (Brown and Warburton, 1971; Warburton and Brown, 1971; Warburton, 1972), this hypothesis of a generalized loss of stimulus control has been examined extensively. In these studies, discrimination performance was analyzed using the theory of signal detectability. One method of analysis is similar to the "method of free response" used previously by Egan *et al.* (1961) for analyzing the detection of tones occurring at random intervals. In order to partition the number of "yes" responses meaningfully between "hits" and "false alarms," the 3-sec band after the onset of the light was used to measure the probability of correct detections, and the 3-sec interval just prior to the onset of the light as the period used for estimating the probability of a response in the absence of the signal into 3-sec bands. However, making a response in one band may preclude a response being made in a later band, and so a correction must be made by calculating the interresponse times (IRT) in a band per opportunity (OP) of responding in that band. This IRT/OP statistic gives the conditional probability of a response in a band given that the animal reaches the boundary of that interval (Anger, 1956). The conditional probabilities for the hit and false-alarm intervals under the various drug conditions were plotted in order to determine the change in discrimination. In terms of the IRT/OP analysis, it was predicted that a loss of response inhibition would result in an increase of the conditional probability in any interval, while increased response inhibition would reduce these conditional probabilities. However, a loss of stimulus sensitivity would tend to produce equal conditional probabilities in all intervals, whereas improved signal sensitivity would be reflected in a decreased conditional probability of a response before the light onset and an increased probability after the signal.

This analysis was applied to the effect of scopolamine on performance controlled by internal stimulus in differential reinforcement of low rate (Brown and Warburton, 1971). In this schedule the animal's responses must be spaced by more than 15 sec in order to be reinforced. A response less than 15 sec from the last one reset the 15-sec clock. As well as this, the analysis was applied to performance controlled by an external stimulus in light–dark discrimination (Warburton, 1972; Warburton and Brown, 1973) and a paired internal–external cue consisting of a temporal discrimination with added external cue (Warburton and Brown, 1971). It was found that there is a decrease in sensitivity as the dose level increased, with doses as low as 0.0625 mg/kg of scopolamine producing a significant disruption, indicating the sensitivity of the technique. These changes in stimulus sensitivity were not accompanied by any lowering of the animal's response criterion; on the contrary, there was even a tendency for an increase in the criterion with the 0.75 mg/kg dose in the Warburton and Brown (1971) study as a result of fewer "hits" and also fewer "false alarms," probably due to motivational change or motor impairment. These results demonstrated unequivocally that cholinergic blockade modified behavior by reducing the signal-to-noise ratio and by lowering the animal's response criterion. The absence of any decrease in the response criterion contradicted the loss of response inhibition hypothesis which would have predicted an increase in both "false alarms" and "hits."

Parallel studies of amphetamine have been carried out by Robbins and Iversen (1973b) and Warburton and Brown (unpublished). Robbins and Iversen tested with the differential reinforcement of low-rate schedule used by Brown and Warburton (1971). Inspection of the raw data showed that there was a tendency for increases in the conditional probability of responding at all inter-reinforcement times. The signal-detection analysis revealed that the low doses of amphetamine produced response-bias changes without changing the animal's sensitivity to the temporal cues, so that the disruption of internal discrimination performance was secondary to the increased responding. An unpublished experiment of Warburton and Brown, based on the light–dark discrimination of Warburton and Brown (1972), also showed that amphetamine produced a change in response bias without a change in sensitivity to the visual stimulus controlling performance.

3.3.3. Summary

The majority of studies show that amphetamine and the cholinolytics increase nonreinforced responding even when an external stimulus signals the nonreinforced trials. However, some studies provide compelling evidence that amphetamine and cholinolytics do not have the same behavioral mode of action as Carlton's hypothesis demands. The noradrenergic system in the brain seems to be mediating behavioral excitation, but the cholinergic system is not inhibiting responding by antagonizing an excitatory system directly. It seems to be interfering with the selection of sensory stimuli in some way. Some crucial experiments in support of this assertion are the studies which have demonstrated that the number of stimuli controlling performance is an important variable in the effect of cholinolytics. A second set of studies are the signal detection experiments in which cholinolytics changed stimulus sensitivity but not response bias whereas amphetamine changed response bias but not stimulus sensitivity. Unfortunately benzodiazepines have not been tested in either of these sorts of situation. The evidence from the benzodiazepine studies are completely in accord with them acting on an inhibitory system opposed to a noradrenergic excitatory system as Brodie and Shore's (1957) hypothesis requires. More convincing evidence comes from the next studies on response suppression by aversive stimuli.

3.4. Response Suppression by Aversive Stimuli

In Section 1, three procedures were described in which aversive stimulation decreased the probability of responses. The aversive stimulus was contingent upon a response in passive avoidance and conflict but was not contingent upon a response during conditioned suppression. This difference means that a subject can avoid aversive stimulation by not responding in passive avoidance and conflict, but aversive stimulation is unavoidable during conditioned suppression.

3.4.1. Conditioned Suppression

As well as depression of lever-pressing rates during an appetitive schedule by unavoidable shock, responding is also suppressed by a stimulus which has been repeatedly paired with shock. In the original procedure developed by Estes and Skinner (1941), the stimulus precedes the unavoidable shock and responding is suppressed by this cue. Many studies have been performed using this schedule (see Kelleher and Morse, 1968; Millenson and Leslie, 1974), But although results have been conflicting, some generalizations can be made. Amphetamine does not always increase responding that has been suppressed in the presence of the preshock stimulus (Kelleher and Morse, 1968), while acute doses of chlordiazepoxide and other benzodiazepines increase suppressed responding (Millenson and Leslie, 1974).

Rather than quote some of the historical studies, a recent comparison of scopolamine, amphetamine, and chlordiazepoxide (Miczek, 1973b) will be cited. In this study, variable-interval training (VI 30 sec) was given to the rats until responding had stabilized, and then a light was presented irregularly throughout the session. When the light did not disrupt responding, a shock was delivered contiguous with the light, and the shock intensity was adjusted until the response rate was about 25% of the preshock level. Conditioned suppression was not altered by the administration of amphetamine or scopolamine, while chlordiazepoxide markedly reduced conditioned suppression, with the size of the effect increasing with increasing dose of chlordiazepoxide.

In other studies, the stimulus and the shock were paired prior to training on the appetitive schedule. The conditioned aversive stimulus alone was then presented during lever pressing on the appetitive schedule. One example of this procedure examined the recovery of responding after suppression and compared the effects of amphetamine and chlordiazepoxide (Tenen, 1967). Animals were deprived of water and placed in a test chamber and then in a chamber with a drinking bottle and allowed 20 sec of drinking. They were then removed and placed in a dark box where there was flashing light and an intermittent tone which preceded unavoidable shock. The next day, they were allowed to drink undisturbed from the water bottle, but on the third day they were placed in the box and allowed to drink for 20 sec before presentation of the flashing light and intermittent tone. No shock was given and the time that the animals took to return to the bottle and drink for 3 sec, the recovery time, was recorded. Chlordiazepoxide, as well as two other benzodiazepines, diazepam and nitrazepam, produced significantly faster recovery times than the control subjects, in spite of the drugged subject's sedated and flaccid condition. Control studies ruled out the alternative hypothesis that the results were due to a state-dependent learning effect or an increase in thirst motivation. In this study, 1 mg/kg of amphetamine did not produce any significant change in the recovery times.

Scopolamine has also been tested on the acquisition of conditioned suppression of drinking. In the first study (Vogel et al., 1967), deprived rats were allowed to drink freely in a box, with the number of laps being recorded. The following day the animals were returned to the box and given an unavoidable shock paired with a tone so that the tone became a conditioned aversive stimulus. The aversive strength of the tone was determined by returning the animals to the box and allowing them to drink. The tone was then turned on and the suppression of drinking measured. In this study scopolamine administered during the conditioning trials had no effect on performance in the test trial, suggesting that scopolamine did not block the acquisition of conditioned suppression. In contrast, Evans and Patton (1968; 1970), using a similar technique, did find that conditioned suppression was blocked by scopolamine when conditioning occurred in the drug state and subsequent testing was in the nondrug state, but not when both training and testing were under scopolamine. This result was supported by Berger and Stein (1969) and by Avis and Pert (1974) using the technique of Vogel et al. (1967), except the conditioned aversive stimulus was the interior of the box rather than a tone. An examination of the pattern of results in both studies for the four groups (saline–saline, saline–scopolamine, scopolamine–scopolamine, and scopolamine–saline) suggests that the scopolamine was producing state-dependent learning effects, and also impairing the acquisition of conditioned suppression. The large effect observed with the scopolamine–saline group occurred because this was the only group where both actions of the drug were operating. The acquisition impairment cannot be due to a blockade of "fear" because there is very little disinhibition when the animals are tested after an injection of scopolamine. In addition, we have seen that scopolamine also impairs acquisition in nonaversive situations like habituation and discrimination.

3.4.2. Passive Avoidance

The first situation to be described is the step through the passive-avoidance situation where the rat is placed in a compartment connected to a second chamber. The animal is allowed to explore the two compartments and then placed in one chamber and given shock. The animals are then retested 24 hr later, measuring the latency for the animal to enter the shock chamber. Drugs can be administered during the acquisition or retention session. In a study of cholinergic drugs (Bures et al., 1962), physostigmine and atropine had no effect on the initial exploration, but atropine disrupted acquisition, as measured by the latencies at 24 hr. Thus, the drug interfered in some way with input of information to storage, but injections of the drug immediately after training had no effect, showing that consolidation was not impaired. As well as an effect on input, atropine given before the retest trial interfered with retrieval, decreasing latencies. This impairment was not observed after overtraining. Substantially the same effects were obtained with the high doses of physostigmine used in this study. In the study of Bures *et al.* no tests were made of the possibility that there was a state-dependence effect where learning occurred in the drug state but did not transfer to the nondrug state, and *vice versa*. This possibility was studied in a step-down passive-avoidance test by Meyers (1965), and some evidence was obtained for a dependence deficit in an animal trained under saline and tested under the drug.

Similar tests of chlordiazepoxide in a "step-through" passive-avoidance box (Oishi *et al.*, 1972) showed a different pattern of effect; animals trained under chlordiazepoxide showed much lower median latencies than the control group. This result suggests that the drug interfered with acquisition, but this effect was shown to be partly due to state dependence; animals trained under the influence of the drug and tested under the influence of the drug did not differ in terms of median latencies from the control animals trained without drug and tested with drug. However, the percentage of subjects not stepping through in the 3-min test period was 85% for the saline–saline group, 60% for the saline–chlordiazepoxide group, 15% for the chlordiazepoxide–saline group, and 50% for the chlordiazepoxide–chlordiazepoxide group. It can be seen that this drug effect is asymmetrical, with greatest drug effects on acquisition. The authors assume that passive avoidance is the result of conditioned internal inhibition and argue that chlordiazepoxide blocked internal inhibition and produced an impairment of acquisition.

3.4.3. Conflict

In conflict the aversive stimulus is also response contingent, but the stress of aversive stimulation is augmented by the blocked need for food, or other reward. The strength of the approach–avoidance tendencies are measured in relation to each other. One conflict situation developed by Vogel *et al.* (1971) investigated the effects of chlordiazepoxide, amphetamine, and scopolamine on punished drinking behavior. Water-deprived rats were given access to a water bottle, but after 20 licks a foot shock was administered and this was repeated after every 20th lick for the remainder of the 3-min test period. An undrugged rat usually received less than five shocks, but after 8 mg/kg of chlordiazepoxide the number of shocks increased fivefold. It was found that neither amphetamine nor scopolamine increased the number of shocks taken.

Another study which compared scopolamine, chlordiazepoxide, and amphetamine on the same schedule was performed by Miczek (1973*a*). Rats were trained to lever press for food, with reinforcement being delivered at variable intervals with a mean of 30 sec (VI 30 sec). When performance was stable, every 12th response was shocked, with the shock intensity adjusted so that the response rate was about 50% of the prepunishment rate. This intermediate level enabled the detection of both increases and decreases in rate by the drug. Doses of scopolamine ranging from 0.2 to 1.0 mg/kg produced significant decrements in rate, but it must be concluded that the effect is due to a peripheral action of the drug because this effect was obtained with both scopolamine hydrobromide, which enters the brain easily, and scopolamine methyl nitrate, which passes through the blood–brain poorly. Amphetamine produced small changes in responding, with low doses (0.1 mg/kg) increasing the rate during the punished schedule; a high dose of 2.0 mg/kg decreased the punished rate. Chlordiazepoxide increased the punished response rate, showing that it attenuates the suppressive effects of punishment like low doses of amphetamine.

A third conflict situation was devised by Geller and Seifter (1960) to test potential psychoactive drugs. Food-deprived rats were given lever-pressing training on a VI 2-min schedule. Then a tone was given for 3 min to indicate that every lever press was reinforced. After this multiple continuous-reinforcement–variable-interval schedule was well established, conflict was induced by punishing any response during the tone with shock so that animals must balance the positive features of high reinforcement against aversive stimulation. It was found that 0.5 mg/kg amphetamine reduced responding on the conflict trials and on the variable-interval unpunished component (Geller and Seifter, 1960). Chlordiazepoxide increased the responding during the conflict component and so increased the number of shocks (Geller *et al.*, 1962).

3.4.4. Summary

These drug studies on response suppression by an aversive stimulus show a consistent pattern of results. Chlordiazepoxide clearly disinhibited responses that had been suppressed by association with aversive stimulus. Amphetamine had little effect on responding during the suppression periods in many experiments; in the punishment study of Miczek (1973a) there was an increase with small doses (0.1 mg/kg), whereas in the conflict study of Geller and Seifter (1960) there was a significant enhancement of suppression with low doses (0.5 mg/kg). Similarly, scopolamine had little effect on suppressed responding in many of the situations. The positive results obtained in studies of passive avoidance and conditioned suppression can be attributed to state-dependent learning where learning under the influence of the drug did not transfer to the nondrug state. These data provide persuasive evidence for a behavioral inhibitory system that is noncholinergic and is blocked by chlordiazepoxide.

4. NEUROCHEMICAL SUBSTRATES FOR THE INCREASES IN RESPONDING BY AMPHETAMINE, CHOLINOLYTICS, AND BENZODIAZEPINES

4.1. Amphetamine

The neural pathways for reinforcement and the pharmacology of reinforcement are discussed in Chapters 1 and 2 and so only a brief outline will be presented here. Early in the 1960's the behavioral excitation produced by amphetamine was linked to its action on the median forebrain bundle that ascends from the midbrain tegmentum through the hypothalamus to the limbic system and seems to be involved in self-stimulation. In a study on the threshold current levels for self-stimulation, Stein and Ray (1960) found that amphetamine lowered the threshold for stimulation in the median forebrain bundle. The median forebrain bundle has a number of different neurochemical pathways running parallel to one another, and amphetamine has multiple biochemical actions, so it was not certain which biochemical changes in the pathway were related to the behavior. However, studies like those of Stein (1964), which showed that the effect was potentiated by monoamine oxidase inhibitor, leading to an accumulation of norepinephrine, dopamine, and serotonin, and blocked by prior doses of reserpine which depletes norepinephrine, dopamine, and serotonin (Zbinden, 1960), made it likely that the amphetamine's action was mediated by a naturally occurring amine. This finding leads to the multiple working hypothesis that the mediating transmitter system was (a) norepinephrine, (b) serotonin, and (c) dopamine.

These hypotheses were tested when Wise and Stein (1969) administered disulfiram, which blocks norepinephrine synthesis, to rats with electrodes in the median forebrain bundle and suppressed self-stimulation responding. The impairment was abolished by intraventricular injections of l-norepinephrine, the naturally occurring isomer, but not d-norepinephrine, while injections of dopamine and injections of serotonin did not restore the self-stimulation responding. Thus, the reinstatement of the self-stimulation behavior depended on the replenishment of the functional depots with the natural isomer of the transmitter. This implies that l-norepinephrine is the transmitter released during "normal" transmission along the self-stimulation pathway and that amphetamine acts by releasing this transmitter.

There is strong circumstantial evidence from the above studies for the hypothesis that amphetamine is acting to release norepinephrine in the median forebrain bundle. It is also known from fluorescence staining techniques that noradrenergic pathways ascend in the median forebrain bundle and terminate in the hypothalamus, neocortex, and parts of the limbic forebrain including the septal area and the hippocampal formation.

By the same technique, it has been demonstrated that amphetamine released norepinephrine from nerve terminals in these pathways (Carlsson et al., 1966).

In spite of this evidence, the hypothesis was not tested directly until Stein and Wise (1969) implanted electrodes in the median forebrain bundle and a push–pull cannula in the lateral hypothalamus. Injections of radioactive norepinephrine were made intraventricularly, and after 3 hr, when the norepinephrine had been taken up, perfusion was begun in the hypothalamus. Background levels of radioactivity were recorded in the perfusate of unstimulated animals, but application of rewarding stimulation produced large increases in the release of radioactive norepinephrine. Electrodes which did not produce high self-stimulation rates were ineffective in releasing radioactivity. It was found that amphetamine increased the norepinephrine released, giving strong support for the hypothesis that one transmitter in the median forebrain bundle mediating self-stimulation was norepinephrine.

However, there is evidence summarized in Crow (1973) which suggests that dopamine may also be involved in self-stimulation. Crow implanted electrodes in a series of regions around the interpeduncular nucleus which contain dopamine but not norepinephrine. Self-stimulation responding was obtained from electrodes that were close to the dopamine-containing neurons. The neurons run parallel to the norepinephrine-containing neurons in the median forebrain bundle. Spiroperidol, which is believed to be a selective blocker of dopamine synapses and does not affect norepinephrine synapses (Andén et al., 1970), has been tested on self-stimulation in the median forebrain bundle. It was found that this compound markedly reduced responding from 70 to 10 presses per minute (Kelly et al., 1974).

This evidence suggests that the production of responding by self-stimulation is mediated by both norepinephrine and dopamine systems. Crow (1973) argues that the norepinephrine pathology has its origins in the locus coeruleus in the pons and travels dorsally to the cortex while a dopamine pathway passes ventrally from the interpeduncular nucleus to the corpus striatum and the septal area. The nuclei in the corpus striatum are known to be involved in motor control (see Warburton, 1975b), and so it seems reasonable to suggest that this may be a system that is involved in the motor effects of amphetamine. In agreement with this hypothesis, Crow (1973) observed that response-contingent and noncontingent stimulation of the interpeduncular area markedly increased motor activity while stimulation of areas close to the locus coeruleus did not alter responsivity. Pharmacological tests of the hypothesis have proved difficult because of the close relationship between the biochemistry of dopamine and norepinephrine. Recently drugs have been developed which block the synthesis of norepinephrine; these include FLA-63 and U-14,624. A study by Thornburg and Moore (1973) compared the effects on amphetamine's action of pretreatment of these compounds with those of α-methyltyrosine, which inhibits both norepinephrine and dopamine synthesis. It was found that FLA-63 or U-

16,624 did not significantly alter spontaneous activity or amphetamine-stimulated motor activity although the brain contents of norepinephrine were reduced to 50% of control levels. In contrast, α-methyltyroxine decreased spontaneous locomotion and the effects of amphetamine, and inhibited dopamine and norepinephrine synthesis. This suggests that inhibition of dopamine synthesis and not inhibition of norepinephrine synthesis is crucial for the antiamphetamine action of α-methyltyrosine. In other words, amphetamine's locomotor-stimulant action depends on the release of dopamine. It is just possible that the stimulation could depend on the release of dopamine and norepinephrine.

The latter hypothesis was made less tenable by a recent study of Iversen and Kelly (personal communication). They injected 6-hydroxydopamine into the nucleus accumbens septi and corpus striatum in order to destroy the dopamine pathways. Depletion of dopamine was aided by injections of pargyline, a monoamine oxidase inhibitor. In order to prevent damage to the norepinephrine pathways of the forebrain, desipramine was preinjected to block the uptake of the 6-hydroxydopamine into the norepinephrine neurons. It was found that the magnitude of the locomotor response to amphetamine was correlated inversely with the amount of transmitter loss from the dopamine terminals. In particular, it seemed that a lesion in the nucleus accumbens septi prevented an increase in locomotor activity which is usually produced by amphetamine, while a lesion in the corpus striatum blocked the stereotyped motor activity also produced by amphetamine (see also Kelly *et al.*, 1975). Thus, it seems more likely that it is the dopamine pathway to the septal area which is involved in motor activity. The norepinephrine pathways which are also involved in self-stimulation responding seem to be mediating reinforcement (see Crow, 1973).

4.2. Cholinolytics

Evidence summarized in the previous section support the hypothesis that cholinolytic drugs interfere with processes involved in stimulus selection. From neurophysiological studies, there appears to be a generalized arousal mechanism operating on all modalities at the cortex, and it is proposed that this electrocortical arousal forms a background noise which is capable of masking the less intense inputs to the cortex and determines the final behavioral output. This mechanism is a separate system from that maintaining behavioral arousal, and although they are usually coordinated, only electrocortical arousal is modified by cholinergic agents such as anticholinesterases and cholinolytics (Bradley and Elkes, 1953).

The projections of the cholinergic pathways involved in electrocortical arousal and having their origin in the brainstem have been analyzed thoroughly by Shute and Lewis over the last ten years, and their work is summarized in Volume 9 of this *Handbook*. From their studies, it can be seen that there are at least three main systems—two ascending reticular systems and a hippocampal circuit. The ascending reticular systems are the dorsal and ventral tegmental pathways. The dorsal tegmental system projects to the thalamic regions including, at least, some of the primary sensory pathways, and the ventral tegmental system projects to the neocortex and to the diencephalic nuclei. The hippocampal circuit also originates in the ventral tegmental area and projects to the hippocampus, via the medial septal nuclei. From the hippocampus there are noncholinergic efferent fibers returning to the brainstem nuclei from which the three systems originated.

Studies with injections of cholinergic drugs directly into the brain have been carried out (see Warburton, 1972a; 1975b). Solutions of carbachol, a cholinomimetic, and atropine methylbromide were injected bilaterally into, or close to, the ventral tegmental nuclei of the midbrain reticular formation, the origin of the ascending cholinergic pathway to the cortex. The effects of these drugs were examined using stable go–no-go alternation performance that has already been described. The effects of atropine were unequivocal, with an increase in both the internally cued no-go responding and the externally cued intertrial responding at all doses. The effects of carbachol were equivocal; at the lowest dose, 0.10 μg, all animals showed a decrease in errors, i.e., no-go responding and intertrial responding, but, at the two higher doses, 0.20 and 0.40 μg, there were decreases in the reinforced, externally cued, go responding as well.

The effects of atropine can be interpreted as an impairment of internal and external stimulus control. This finding supports the idea that the ventral tegmental pathway is controlling the selection of stimuli by modulating cortical activity. The effects with the lowest doses of carbachol are consistent with this finding. Funderburk and Case (1951) were first to suggest that desynchronization of the cortex was mediated by a cholinergic system. This hypothesis has been supported by the finding that electrocortical arousal produced by stimulation of the tegmental nuclei in the midbrain reticular formation was correlated with a large increase in the rate of release of acetylcholine from the cortex (Kanai and Szerb, 1965). About 15 to 25% of the cortical cells, mainly in the sensory cortex, are excited by direct application of acetylcholine, and this excitation is blocked by atropine and enhanced by physostigmine (Krnjević and Phillis, 1963a,b). Krnjević and Phillis concluded that cortical desynchronization was due to an increase in the random spontaneous activity and that acetylcholine was involved in the control of this activity rather than acting as a mediator from the specific sensory terminals. Administration of acetylcholine directly onto those neurons by microelectrophoresis increased the discharge rate of neurons in the visual cortex after reticular stimulation, as well as the spontaneous discharge rate (Spehlmann, 1969), supporting the conclusion of Krnjević and Phillis. In addition, Spehlmann observed that acetylcholine enhanced the facilitation of visual evoked potentials by mesencephalic reticular stimulation.

As well as the reticulocortical pathway there is also a cholinergic pathway to the limbic system. The hippocampal circuit ascends from the ventral tegmental area via the lateral preoptic, the diagonal band, and the medial septal nuclei to the hippocampus. Although there is little evidence for the involvement of the lateral preoptic nuclei, there is strong support for the importance of the medial septal nuclei and hippocampal formation in mediating stimulus control. Thus, the effects of lesions in the septal area and hippocampal formation closely parallel the changes obtained after attenuation of cholinergic function (Meyers and Domino, 1964; Douglas and Isaacson, 1966). The multiple effects observed after injection of cholinergic drugs into the ventral tegmental nuclei were not found after injection into the hippocampal circuit. In a preliminary report, Warburton and Russell (1969) demonstrated the differential effects of 4.0 μg of atropine and 0.43 μg of carbachol on single alternation when these drugs were introduced into the ventral portion of the hippocampal formation. It was found that atropine increased both no-go and intertrial responding while carbachol reduced both. The hippocampal circuit has its origins in the medial septal nuclei (Shute and Lewis, 1967). Cholinergic stimulation of these nuclei produced increased theta activity in the hippocampal formation analogous to that produced by sensory stimulation (Stumpf, 1965). Stimulation of the septal nuclei with 0.5–5.0 μg carbachol produced a decrease in lever pressing, while similar doses of atropine sulfate increased the response rate (Grossman, 1964) in the same way as intraperitoneally injected atropine. The results of the hippocampal and septal studies confirm that the hippocampal circuit is not a simple negative feedback loop controlling stimulus selection (Warburton, 1975b). If it were, it would have been expected that blockade of the pathway with atropine would have produced effects opposite to those resulting from cholinergic blockade of the ventral tegmental nuclei. Evidence supporting Warburton's results comes from a study by Endroczi et al. (1973) in which they found that injections of acetylcholine directly into the dorsal hippocampus of the cat, which is equivalent to the ventral hippocampus of the rat, did not induce theta activity but did produce transient desynchronization at the cortex. Injections into the dorsal and ventral tegmental areas resulted in neocortical desynchronization for up to half an hour, and also gave rise to marked hippocampal theta activity for 5–10 min. These qualitatively similar results showed a relationship between the hippocampus and the ventral tegmental region in the control of electrocortical activity and stimulus selection.

4.3. Benzodiazepines

Although there are sensitive assay techniques developed for monoamines, very few investigators have studied the effects of the benzodiazepines and other tranquilizers on the synthesis, storage, release, receptor interaction, and inactivation of norepinephrine and serotonin. In a pioneering study

Taylor and Laverty (1969) found that both the major benzodiazepines (chlordiazepoxide, diazepam, and nitrazepam) and the barbiturates did not change the levels of norepinephrine in any part of the rat brain. In addition, there was no evidence for a reduction of reuptake or inhibition of catechol-O-methyltransferase, the inactivating enzyme, showing that inactivation mechanisms were unaffected by these drugs (Taylor and Laverty, 1969). However, the static levels of transmitter are not good indicators of functional transmitter, and so Taylor and Laverty (1973) examined the effect of the three benzodiazepines on norepinephrine turnover in animals stressed with electric shock. This form of stress increased turnover in all regions of the rat brain (Bliss et al., 1968), but Taylor and Laverty found that the benzodiazepines blocked this effect and maintained the norepinephrine levels close to their control values. From the point of view of the neural pathways involved, this effect was maximal in the midbrain sample containing the hypothalamus, and the cortical sample, and least in the brainstem sample.

The depletion of norepinephrine from the cortical and hypothalamic neurons after injection of a norepinephrine-synthesis inhibitor was examined by means of a histochemical fluorescence technique (Corrodi et al., 1971). The animals were stressed by restraining them, which accelerated the depletion of the norepinephrine, but chlordiazepoxide and diazepam reduced the rate of depletion. This result shows that these drugs were probably acting to reduce turnover by blocking release of norepinephrine.

A similar result was obtained when the serotonin neurons were examined after the injection of a tryptophan-hydroxylase inhibitor, which prevented *de novo* synthesis of serotonin. Benzodiazepines reduced the rate of depletion of serotonin in the cortex, but the effects did not occur in all parts of the brain (Lidbrink et al., 1973). The notion that this result might be due to the benzodiazepines blocking serotonin release was supported by the finding that intracisternally injected radioactive serotonin was retained in the brain longer after diazepam (Chase et al., 1970). This finding has been confirmed by single and repeated doses of oxazepam (Wise et al., 1972) which reduced serotonin turnover in the midbrain–hindbrain region, and contrasts with the marked tolerance that developed in the norepinephrine system after repeated doses. This difference in tolerance development can be related to the experiment with oxazepam by Margules and Stein (1968) who found that the slight nonselective decreased responding disappeared after a few days, but the release of suppressed responding in the Geller and Seifter (1960) conflict situation remained unchanged. This circumstantial evidence points to the involvement of a serotonin system in the antianxiety action of the drug.

Direct tests of the hypothesis that it is either the reduction in functional norepinephrine or serotonin which is responsible for the disinhibiting properties of the benzodiazepines have supported the serotonin hypothesis. If it were a reduction of noradrenergic function, then adrenergic blockers should have similar effects as benzodiazepines in the conflict situation of

Geller and Seifter (1960), but tests with the alpha-adrenergic blocker phentolamine and the beta-adrenergic antagonist propranolol injected into the ventricles were negative. Propranolol had no effect, while phentolamine reduced punished and nonpunished responding, showing a nonspecific effect of the latter drug on behavior (Stein *et al.*, 1973). In another set of studies serotonin blockers and a serotonin-synthesis inhibitor were used to produce a reduction of functional serotonin. Methysergide, the antagonist, released the suppressed responding in the conflict situation (Stein *et al.*, 1973). Similar results were obtained with *p*-chlorophenylalanine, the serotonin-synthesis inhibitor, and the suppressed behavior could be reinstated by injecting the precursor 5-hydroxytryptophan to replete serotonin (Stein *et al.*, 1973), as one would have predicted from the other results. In a final test of the hypothesis, Stein *et al.* (1973) injected oxazepam, which released the suppressed responding, and then introduced serotonin directly into the ventricles, which restored the inhibited responding.

The neurochemical pathways on which the oxazepam was acting are not known, although Stein *et al.* (1973) suggested serotonin fibers arising in the dorsomedial tegmental region of the midbrain. These pathways ascend in the median forebrain bundle and terminate mainly in the limbic system including the amygdala and septal area (Dahlstrom and Fuxe, 1964; Andén *et al.*, 1966). Selective damage to this serotonin system can be obtained by injections of a neurotoxic agent, 5,7-dihydroxytryptamine, into the ventromedial tegmentum of rats. Tests of these animals (Tye *et al.*, 1976) indicated that they did not show the normal suppression of responding during a period when all responses were punished by electric shock. There is fragmentary evidence (see Warburton, 1975*b*) that there is serotonin inhibitory input to the motor control system from studies of Parkinson's disease; there seems to be decreased serotonin in the striatum of these patients (Bernheimer *et al.*, 1961). The caudate nucleus and putamen form the neostriatum and the globus pallidus is the paleostriatum. Two reasonable hypotheses are that inhibition of some responses may be mediated by serotonin fibers terminating on the motor control neurons in the striatum or by serotonin fibers which project to the septal area. The studies of Kelly and Iversen that were discussed in Section 4.1 make the septal interaction more likely.

5. MECHANISMS OF BEHAVIORAL INHIBITION

As we saw in the behavioral discussion, it is impossible to consider inhibition in isolation from excitation, and so in this section we will discuss how behavior results from the interactive functioning of three neurochemical systems. The first system is a cholinergic pathway that ascends from the reticular formation to the cortex and seems to be mediating stimulus selection. The second system is a dopamine pathway that passes ventrally through the hypothalamus from the interpeduncular nucleus to the nucleus accumbens septi and appears to be mediating behavioral activation. The third system is a behavioral-inhibition pathway that has serotonin as its transmitter. It has its origins in the tegmental region and projects to the septal area as well. Since the order in which these systems will be discussed will coincide with their involvement in behavior, the first system to be considered will be the cholinergic system mediating the selection of stimuli.

An organism has many sorts of stimuli influencing it while being tested in an experimental situation. From the external environment, stimuli impinge on the exteroceptors, while there are stimuli consequent upon a response which may be experimenter-determined. In addition, responses are influenced by various internal stimuli including response-produced cues and previous "remembered" stimulus sequences. These stimuli may be relevant, irrelevant, or partially relevant for responding. Any response will be determined by a subset of stimuli from these various sources, and disruption of one of these sources in input could impair responding. From the evidence discussed earlier, it is hypothesized that a brain cholinergic system is mediating the selection, from the mass of impinging stimuli, the relevant stimuli which set the occasion for the experimenter-determined "relevant" response and those which set the occasion for inhibiting irrelevant responses.

As we saw in a previous section, the cholinergic selection mechanism seems to be correlated with changes in electrocortical arousal, and based on this evidence, it seems possible that increased cortical activity would produce increased subthreshold excitability with a low level of reticular activation, while a higher level of increased cortical activity would occlude the sensory input (Bremer, 1961), masking the smaller potentials with cortical "noise." The largest potentials will be a function of not only the activity in the cortex but also the modulation that has occurred at successive sites along the primary sensory pathway by, for example, the corticofugal fibers. The ascending cholinergic system makes the final selection of the inputs by masking the smaller ones and so determining the response emitted. Increased activity in this system will usually produce better performance of both acquisition and stable performance by reducing irrelevant sensory stimulation, although very high levels of activity could result in disrupted performance where the relevant stimuli are also masked. Cholinergic blockade produces a different sort of impairment where less intense, irrelevant stimuli are not eliminated and become part of the stimulus subset controlling behavior, so that irrelevant responses, including nonreinforced responses, will occur. However, the cholinergic pathway does not inhibit responses directly: Its action does not account for conditioned inhibition where presentation of the conditioned inhibitory stimulus decreases response strength below the level occurring in its absence. Blockade of the cholinergic selection mechanism will disrupt conditioned inhibition; it does so by interfering with discriminative control.

Once behavior is triggered by the sensory input, then it is energized by an excitatory system which enhances the tendency to respond. The energizing system is believed to be the ascending dopamine pathway running in the median forebrain bundle. Increased release of transmitter in this pathway induces a greater intensity of responding, until either the synapses can no longer function because of a depolarization block (Warburton, 1975b) or the response ceiling is reached for that particular response. Increased activity in the dopamine pathway is produced by reinforcing stimuli and stimuli associated with reward which activate the noradrenergic reinforcement pathway according to Stein and Wise (1970). In particular, the excitatory stimuli were the response-related stimuli, environmental as well as proprioceptive, that have become conditioned excitatory stimuli by association with the unconditioned stimulus of reward (Stein, 1964). As we have seen, the perception of these stimuli will depend on the functioning of the ascending cholinergic pathways. In contrast, Poschel and Ninteman (1971) believe that the noradrenergic pathway is not the actual reward pathway, but is increasing the excitability of a reward system and related motivational structures in the limbic lobe, and so controlling reinforcement and motivational thresholds. For our purposes this distinction is unimportant.

This norepinephrine reinforcement pathway is intimately associated with a serotoninergic pathway running parallel to it in the median forebrain bundle, and Olds (1962) has suggested that fiber bundles mediating punishment effects probably synapse regularly with those yielding positive reinforcement along the median forebrain bundle. The opposition of a serotonin system to the self-stimulation systems was demonstrated in a study by Poschel and Ninteman (1971) in which increased excitation in the median forebrain bundle, as measured by self-stimulation rates, was correlated with depletion of brain serotonin by p-chlorophenylalanine, while decreased excitation in the median forebrain bundle was associated with accumulation of brain serotonin. It is interesting that increased self-stimulation responding occurred even though norepinephrine was depleted to some extent as well. This suggests that the important factor in reinforcement may be the ratio of levels of activity in the two neurochemical systems and not the absolute levels of activity.

In a complementary study on the hypothesis of serotoninergic inhibition of behavioral excitation, Mabry and Campbell (1973) tested the prediction that p-chlorophenylalanine should potentiate amphetamine-induced locomotor activity. The results showed that the drugs acted synergistically to produce activity levels that were greater than those predicted if the drug effects were merely additive. Injections of 5-hydroxytryptophan, the precursor of serotonin, reversed the increase in activity and eliminated the interaction, confirming that serotonin was the important transmitter. These studies provide some evidence that the serotonin inhibitory pathway was not merely blocking the dopamine excitatory pathway so that if activity in the excitatory pathway were low, reduced activity in the inhibitory pathway would have no effect. Thus, there seems to be twin systems modulating behavioral activation, a dopamine pathway controlling excitation and a serotonin pathway subserving inhibition.

These systems can be used to give a partial explanation of the varieties of behavioral inhibition in neurochemical terms. The dopamine pathways mediate behavioral excitation and are modulated by primary and secondary reinforcing stimuli via a norepinephrine system. A novel stimulus will activate the ascending cholinergic pathways, initiating electrocortical arousal and stress-steroid release (Warburton, 1974b). Repetition of the response results in habituation, and it has been suggested (Warburton, 1974b) that habituation depends on the function of the hippocampus, which recognizes regularities in the stimulus input and prevents irrelevant repetitive stimuli from the external and internal environment from activating the ascending cholinergic pathways. When this happens, the stimulus does not elicit any electrocortical response or stress-steroid release. The hippocampus also activates the serotonin inhibitory pathway which produces "below-zero" habituation.

If a positive unconditioned stimulus is paired with the novel stimulus, the noradrenergic pathways of the median forebrain bundle are activated which inhibit stress-steroid release (Warburton, 1974b). Continued pairings of the two stimuli result in conditioning where the previous novel stimulus becomes a conditioned excitatory stimulus which is capable of activating the dopamine pathways and energizing responses via the norepinephrine reinforcement system. When this conditioned excitatory stimulus is no longer paired with the primary reinforcing stimulus, then the ascending cholinergic pathways are again activated and stress steroids are released. Continued presentations of the stimulus alone in experimental extinction will result in it habituating and returning to the same status as a neutral stimulus which does not activate the noradrenergic pathway and the dopamine behavioral activation system.

Aversive unconditioned stimuli excite the serotoninergic pathways of the median forebrain bundle. These pathways inhibit ongoing responding, and this may be replaced by species-specific defensive behavior. It seems that if a stimulus is positively correlated with an aversive unconditioned stimulus, as in conditioned suppression training, or negatively correlated with a positive unconditioned stimulus, as in discrimination training, then the stimulus will become a conditioned stimulus capable of activating the serotoninergic pathways and inhibiting responses.

6. CONCLUSIONS

Habituation, extinction, discrimination, and response suppression by aversive stimuli were given as examples of behavioral inhibition. The behavioral decrement that occurs in habituation can be explained by the operation of a serotoninergic inhibitory system that antagonizes the dopaminergic excitatory pathways. Below-zero habituation is possible because the serotonin pathway is not merely blocking the dopamine excitatory pathway but projects to the same common motor pathway as the excitatory pathway. Below-zero extinction has not been demonstrated so far, and so extinction of responding can be explained parsimoniously in terms of decreases in the activity of the dopamine excitatory system. Discrimination and response suppression are more complicated. A conditioned inhibitory stimulus and an aversive unconditioned stimulus can produce below-zero response strengths, indicating the operation of the serotonin inhibition system, but the perception of the inhibitory stimulus itself depends on the function of a cholinergic stimulus-selection mechanism.

Acknowledgments

This paper was written while I was on leave of absence at Indiana University. The previously unpublished research and the preparation of the manuscript were supported by Public Health Service Grant PHS MH 14658-06. I thank Eliot Hearst, George Heise, John Kelsey, and Sebastian Lazareno for their invaluable comments on the various drafts of the manuscripts.

7. REFERENCES

ANDÉN, N. E., BUTCHER, S. G., CORRODI, H., FUXE, K., and UNGERSTEDT, U., 1970, Receptor activity and turnover of dopamine and noradrenaline after neuroleptics, *Eur. J. Pharmacol.* **11**:303–314.

ANDÉN, N. E., DAHLSTRÖM, A., FUXE, K., LARSSON, K., OLSON, L., and UNGERSTEDT, U., 1966, Ascending monoamine neurons to the telencephalon and diencephalon, *Acta Physiol. Scand.* **67**:313–326.

ANGER, D., 1956, The dependence of interresponse times upon the relative reinforcement of different interresponse times, *J. Exp. Psychol.* **52**:145–161.

AVIS, H. H., and PERT, A., 1974, A comparison of the effects of muscarinic and nicotinic anticholinergic drugs on habituation and fear conditioning in rats, *Psychopharmacologia* **34**:209–222.

BERGER, B. D., and STEIN, L., 1969, An analysis of the learning deficits produced by scopolamine, *Psychopharmacologia* **14**:271–283.

BERNHEIMER, H., BIRKMAYER, W., and HORNYKIEWICZ, O., 1961, Vertielung des 5-Hydroxytryptamins (serotonin) im Gehirn des Menschen und sein Verhalten bei Patienten mit Parkinson-Syndrom, *Klin. Wochenschr.* **39**:1056–1059.

BIGNAMI, G., and ROSIĆ, N., 1970, The nature of disinhibitory phenomena caused by central cholinergic (muscarinic blockade), in: *Proceedings of the VIIth International Congress of the Collegium Internationale Neuropsychologicum*, Prague.

BLISS, E. J., AILION, J., and ZWANZIGER, J., 1968, Metabolism of norepinephrine, serotonin, and dopamine in rat brain with stress, *J. Pharmacol. Exp. Ther.* **164**:122–131.

BOREN, J. J., and NAVARRO, A. P., 1959, The action of atropine, benactyzine and scopolamine upon fixed interval and fixed ratio behavior, *J. Exp. Anal. Behav.* **2**:107–115.

BRADLEY, P. B., and ELKES, J., 1953, The effect of atropine, hyoscyamine, physostigmine and neostigmine on the electrical activity of the conscious cat, *J. Physiol. (London)* **120**:13.

BRADY, J. V., 1959, Differential drug effects upon aversive and appetitive components of a behavioral repertoire, in: *Neuro-psychopharmacology*, Vol. 1 (P. B. Bradley, P. Wencker, and C. Radouco-Thomas, eds.), pp. 275–281, Elsevier, New York.
BREMER, F., 1961, Neurophysiological mechanisms in cerebral arousal, in: *The Nature of Sleep* (G. E. W. Wolstenholme and M. O'Conner, eds.), pp. 30–56, Little, Brown and Company, Boston.
BRIMER, C. J., 1972, Disinhibition of an operant response, in: *Inhibition and Learning* (R. A. Boakes and M. S. Halliday, eds.), pp. 205–227, Academic Press, London.
BRODIE, B. B., and SHORE, P. A., 1957, A concept for a role of serotonin and norepinephrine as chemical mediators in the brain, *Ann. N. Y. Acad. Sci.* **66**:631–642.
BROWN, K., and WARBURTON, D. M., 1971, Attenuation of stimulus sensitivity by scopolamine, *Psychonomic Sci.* **22**:297–298.
BRUNTON, T. L., 1883, On the nature of inhibition and the action of drugs upon it, *Nature (London)* **27**:419–422.
BUREŠ, J., BUREŠOVA, O., BOHDANECKY, Z., and WEISS, T., 1962, Physostigmine-induced hippocampal theta activity and learning in rats, *Psychopharmacologia* **3**:254–263.
CARLSSON, A., FUXE, K., HAMBERGER, B., and LINDGRIST, M., 1966, Biochemical and histochemical studies on the effects of imipramine-like drugs and (+)-amphetamine on central and peripheral catecholamine neurons, *Acta Physiol. Scand.* **67**:481–497.
CARLTON, P., 1963, Cholinergic mechanisms in the control of behavior by the brain, *Psychol. Rev.* **70**:19–39.
CARLTON, P. L., 1968, Brain acetylcholine and habituation, *Progr. Brain Res.* **28**:48–60.
CARLTON, P. L., and VOGEL, J. R., 1965, Studies of the amnesic properties of scopolamine, *Psychonomic Sci.* **3**:261–262.
CHASE, T. N., KATZ, R. I., and KOPIN, I. J., 1970, Effect of diazepam on fate of intracisternally injected serotonin-C^{14}. *Neuropharmacology* **9**:103–108.
CLADEL, C. E., CHO, M. H., and MCDONALD, R. D., 1966, Effect of amphetamine and catecholamines on startle response and general motor activity of albino rats, *Nature (London)* **210**:864–865.
CLARK, F. C., and STEELE, B. J., 1966, Effects of *d*-amphetamine on performance under a multiple schedule in the rat, *Psychopharmacologia* **9**:157–169.
CORRODI, H., FUXE, R. I., LIDBRINK, P., and OLSON, L., 1971, Minor tranquilizers, stress, and central catecholamine neurons, *Brain Res.* **29**:1–16.
COX, T., and TYE, N., 1973, Effects of physostigmine on the acquisition of a position discrimination in rats, *Neuropharmacology* **12**:477–484.
COX, T., and TYE, N., 1974, Effects of physostigmine on the maintenance of discrimination behavior in rats, *Neuropharmacology* **13**:205–210.
CROW, T. J., 1973, Catecholamine-containing neurons and electrical self-stimulation. 2. A theoretical interpretation and some psychiatric implications, *Psychol. Med.* **3**:66–73.
DAHLSTRÖM, A., and FUXE, K., 1964, Evidence for the existence of monamine-containing neurons in the central nervous system. 1. Demonstration of monamines in the cell bodies of the brain stem neurons, *Acta Physiol. Scand.* **62**:Suppl. 232.
DOUGLAS, R. J., 1966, Cues for spontaneous alternation, *J. Comp. Physiol. Psychol.* **62**:171–183.
DOUGLAS, R. J., 1967, The hippocampus and behavior, *Psychol. Bull.* **67**:416–442.
DOUGLAS, R. J., 1972, Pavlovian conditioning and the brain, in: *Inhibition and Learning* (R. A. Boakes and M. S. Halliday, eds.), pp. 529–553, Academic Press, London.
DOUGLAS, R. J., and ISAACSON, R. L., 1966a, Spontaneous alternation and scopolamine, *Psychonomic Sci.* **4**:283–284.
DOUGLAS, R. J., and PRIBRAM, K. H., 1966b, Learning and limbic lesions, *Neuropsychologia* **4**:197–220.
EGAN, J. P., GREENBERG, G. I., and SCHULMAN, A. J., 1961, Operating characteristic, signal detectability and the method of free response, *J. Acoust. Soc. Am.* **33**:993–1007.

ENDROCZI, E., HARTMANN, G., and LISSAK, K., 1963, Effect of intracerebrally administered cholinergic and adrenergic drugs on neocortical and archicortical electrical activity, *Acta. Physiol. Acad. Sci. Hung.* **24**:200–209.

ESTES, W. K., and SKINNER, B. F., 1941, Some quantitative properties of anxiety, *J. Exp. Psychol.* **29**:390–400.

EVANS, H. L., and PATTON, R. A., 1968, Scopolamine effects on a one-trial test of fear conditioning, *Psychonomic. Sci.* **11**:229–230.

EVANS, H. L., and PATTON, R. A., 1970, Scopolamine effects on conditional suppression, *Psychopharmacologia* **17**:1–13.

FEIGLEY, D. A., and HAMILTON, L. W., 1971, Response to novel environment following septal lesions or cholinergic blockade in rats, *J. Comp. Physiol. Psychol.* **76**:496–504.

FERSTER, C. B., and SKINNER, B. F., 1957, *Schedules of Reinforcement,* Appleton-Century-Crofts, New York.

FUNDERBURK, W., and CASE, T., 1951, The effect of atropine on cortical potentials, *Electroencephalogr. Clin. Neurophysiol.* **3**:213–223.

GELLER, J., and SEIFTER, J., 1960, The effects of meprobamate, barbituates, *d*-amphetamine and promazine on experimentally induced conflict in the rat, *Psychopharmacologia* **1**:482–492.

GELLER, J., KULAK, J. T., and SEIFTER, J., 1962, The effects of chlordiazepoxide and chlorpromazine on a punishment discrimination, *Psychopharmacologia* **3**:374–385.

GLANZER, M., 1953, Stimulus satiation. An explanation of spontaneous alternation and related phenomena, *Psychol. Rev.* **60**:257–268.

GROSSMAN, S. P., 1964, Effects of chemical stimulation of the septal nuclei on motivation, *J. Comp. Physiol. Psychol.* **58**:194–200.

HEARST, E., 1959, Effects of scopolamine on discriminated responding in the rat, *J. Pharmacol. Exp. Ther.* **126**:349–358.

HEARST, E., 1972, Some persistent problems in the analysis of conditional inhibition, in: *Inhibition and Learning* (R. A. Boakes and M. S. Halliday, eds.), pp. 5–39, Academic Press, London.

HEARST, E., BESLEY, S., and FARTHING, G. W., 1970, Inhibition and the stimulant control of operant behavior, *J. Exp. Anal. Behav.* **14**:373–409.

HEISE, G. A., 1964, Animal techniques for evaluating anorexigenic agents, in: *Animal and Clinical Techniques in Drug Evaluations* (J. H. Nodine and P. E. Seigler, eds.), pp. 279–282, Year Book Medical Publishers, Chicago.

HEISE, G. A., 1975, Discrete trial analysis of drug action, *Fed. Proc.* **34**:1898–1903.

HEISE, G. A., and LILIE, N. L., 1970, Effects of scopolamine, atropine and amphetamine on internal and external control of responding and nonreinforced trials, *Psychopharmacologia* **18**:38–49.

HEISE, G. A., KELLER, C., KHAVARI, K. A., and LAUGHLIN, N., 1969, Learning of discrete trial, go–no go alternation patterns by the rat, *J. Exp. Anal. Behav.* **12**:609–622.

HEISE, G. A., LAUGHLIN, N., and KELLER, G. A., 1970, Behavioral analysis of reinforcement withdrawal, *Psychopharmacologia* **16**:345–368.

HERBLIN, W. F., 1968, Extinction reversal by scopolamine, *Psychonomic Sci.* **13**:43–44.

HERRNSTEIN, R. J., 1958, Effects of scopolamine on a multiple schedule, *J. Exp. Anal. Behav.* **1**:351–358.

HILLARP, N. A., FUXE, K., and DAHLSTROM, A., 1966, Demonstration and mapping of central neurons containing dopamine, noradrenaline and 5-hydroxytryptamine and their reactions to psychopharmaca, *Pharmacol. Rev.* **18**:727–741.

KANAI, T., and SZERB, J. C., 1965, Mesencephalic reticular activating system and cortical acetycholine output, *Nature (London)* **205**:81–88.

KELLEHER, R. T., and MORSE, W. H., 1964, Escape behavior and punished behavior, *Fed. Proc.* **23**:808–817.

KELLEHER, R. T., and MORSE, W. H., 1968, Determinants of the specificity of behavioral effects of drugs, *Ergeb. Physiol.* **60**:1–56.

Keller, F. S., and Schoenfeld, W. N., 1950, *Principles of Psychology,* Appleton-Century-Crofts, New York.

Kelly, P. H., Rolls, E. T., and Shaw, S. G., 1974, Functions of catecholamines in brain stimulation reward, *Brain Res.* **66:**363–364.

Kelly, P. H., Seviour, P. W., and Iversen, S. D., 1975, Amphetamine and apomorphine responses in the rat following 6-OHDA lesions of the nucleus accumbens septi and corpus striatum, *Brain Res.* **94:**507–522.

Kimble, D. P., 1968, Hippocampus and internal inhibition, *Psychol. Bull.* **70:**285–295.

Kimble, D. P., 1969, Possible inhibitory functions of the hippocampus, *Neuropsychologia* **7:**235–244.

Kimble, G. A., 1961, *Conditioning and Learning,* Appleton-Century-Crofts, New York.

Kirkby, R. J., Bell, D. S., and Preston, A. D., 1972, Effects of methylamphetamine on stereotyped behavior, activity, startle and orienting responses, *Psychopharmacologia* **25:**41–48.

Konorski, J., 1948, *Conditioned Reflexes and Neuron Organization,* Cambridge University Press, Cambridge.

Krnjević, K., and Phillis, J. W., 1963a, Acetylcholine sensitive cells in the cerebral cortex,*J. Physiol. (London)* **166:**296–327.

Krnjević, K., and Phillis, J. W., 1963b, Pharmacological properties of acetylcholine-sensitive cells in the cerebral cortex, *J. Physiol. (London)* **166:**328–350.

Laties, V., and Weiss, B., 1966, Influence of drugs on behavior controlled by internal and external stimuli,*J. Pharmacol. Exp. Ther.* **152:**388–396.

Leaton, R. N., 1968, Effects of scopolamine on exploratory motivated behavior, *J. Comp. Physiol. Psychol.* **66:**524–527.

Lidbrink, P., Corrodi, H., Fuxe, K., and Olsen, L., 1973, The effects of benzodiazepines, meprobamate and barbituates on central monoamine neurons, in: *The Benzodiazepines* (S. Garattini, E. Mussini, and L. O. Randall, eds.), pp. 203–223, Raven Press, New York.

Mabry, P. D., and Campbell, B. A., 1973, Serotonergic inhibition of catecholamine-induced behavioral arousal, *Brain Res.* **49:**381–391.

Margules, D. L., and Stein, L., 1967, Neuroleptics vs. tranquilizers. Evidence from animal behavior studies of mode and site of action, *Neuropsychopharmacology* (A. A. Brill, J. O. Cole, P. Deniker, P. H. Hippius, and P. B. Bradley, eds.), pp. 108–120, Excerpta Medica Foundation, New York.

Margules, D. L., and Stein, L., 1968, Increase of "antianxiety" activity and tolerance of behavioral depression during chronic administration of oxazepam, *Psychopharmacologia* **13:**74–80.

McMillan, D. E., 1969, Effects of d-Amphetamine on performance under several parameters of multiple fixed-ratio fixed interval schedules, *J. Pharmacol. Exp. Ther.* **167:**26–33.

Meyers, B., 1965, Some effects of scopolamine on a passive avoidance response in rats, *Psychopharmacologia* **13:**74–80.

Meyers, B., and Domino, E. F., 1964, The effect of cholinergic blocking drugs on spontaneous alternation in rats, *Arch. Int. Pharmcodyn. Ther.,* **150:**525–529.

Michelson, M. J., 1961, Pharmacological evidence of the role of acetylcholine in the higher nervous activity of man and animals, *Act. Nerv. Super.* **3:**2.

Miczek, K. A., 1973a, Effects of scopolamine, amphetamine and benzodiazepines on conditional suppression, *Pharmacol. Biochem. Behav.* **1:**401–411.

Miczek, K. A., 1973b, Effects of scopolamine, amphetamine, and chlordiazepoxide on punishment, *Psychopharmacologia* **28:**373–389.

Millenson, J. R., and Leslie, J., 1974, The conditioned emotional response (CER) as a baseline for the study of anti-anxiety drugs, *Neuropharmacology* **13:**1–9.

Mishkin, M., 1964, Perseveration of central sets after frontal lesions in monkeys, in: *The Frontal Granular Cortex and Behavior* (J. M. Warren and K. Akert, eds.), pp. 219–237, McGraw-Hill, New York.

Mowrer, O. H., 1960, *Learning Theory and Behavior,* Wiley, New York.
Nolon, N. A., and Parkes, M. W,, 1973, The effects of benzodiazepines on the behaviour of mice on a hole board, *Psychopharmacologia* **29**:277–288.
Oishi, H., Iwahara, D., Yang, Kwo-Man, and Yogi, A., 1972, Effects of chlordiazepoxide on passive avoidance responses in rats, *Psychopharmacologia* **23**:373–385.
Olds, J. E., 1962, Hypothalamic substrates of reward, *Physiol. Rev.* **42**:554–604.
Owens, J. E., 1960, The influence of *dl*-, *d*- and *l*-methamphetamine on a fixed ratio schedule, *J. Exp. Anal. Behav.* **3**:293–310.
Pavlov, J. P., 1927, Conditioned reflexes, Oxford University Press, London.
Payne, R., and Anderson, D. C., 1967, Scopolamine-produced changes in activity and in the startle response: implications for behavioral activation, *Psychopharmacologia* **12**:83–90.
Poschel, B. P. H., and Ninteman, F. W., 1971, Intracranial reward and the forebrain's serotonergic mechanism: studies employing para-chlorophenylalanine and para-chloroamphetamine, *Physiol. Behav.* **7**:39–46.
Rescorla, R. A., 1969, Pavlovian conditioned inhibition, *Psychol. Bull.* **72**:77–94.
Richelle, M., Xhenseval, B., Fontaine, O., and Thone, L., 1962, Action of chlordiazepoxide on two types of temporal conditioning in rats, *Int. J. Neuropharmacol.* **1**:381–391.
Robbins, T., and Iversen, S. D., 1973a, A dissociation of the effects of *d*-amphetamine on locomotor activity and exploration in rats, *Psychopharmacologia* **28**:155–164.
Robbins, T. W., and Iversen, S. D., 1973b, Amphetamine induced disruption of temporal discrimination by response disinhibition, *Nature New Biol.* **245**:145–192.
Ruch, T. C., Patton, H. D., Woodbury, J. W., and Towe, A. L., 1965, *Neurophysiology,* Saunders, Philadelphia.
Rushton, R., and Steinberg, H., 1966, Combined effects of chlordiazepoxide and dexamphetamine on activity of rats in an unfamiliar environment, *Nature (London)* **211**:1312–1313.
Shute, C. C. D., and Lewis, P. R., 1967, The ascending cholinergic reticular system; neocortical, olfactory and subcortical projections, *Brain* **90**:497–520.
Skinner, B. F., 1938, *The Behavior of Organisms,* Appleton-Century-Crofts, New York.
Skinner, B. F., and Heron, W. T., 1937, Effects of caffeine and benzedrine upon conditioning and extinction, *Psychol. Rev.* **1**:340–346.
Spehlmann, R., 1969, Effect of acetylcholine and atropine upon excitation of cortical neurons by reticular stimulation, *Fed. Proc.* **28**:795.
Squire, L. R., 1969, Effects of pretrial and posttrial administration of cholinergic and anticholinergic drugs on spontaneous alternation, *J. Comp. Physiol. Psychol.* **1**:69–75.
Stein, L., 1964, Self-stimulation of the brain and the central stimulant action of amphetamines, *Fed. Proc.* **23**:836–849.
Stein, L., and Ray, O. S., 1960, Brain stimulation reward "thresholds" self-determined in the rat, *Psychopharmacologia* **1**:251–256.
Stein, L., and Wise, C. D., 1969, Release of norepinephrine from hypothalamus and amygdala by rewarding medial forebrain bundle stimulation and amphetamine, *J. Comp. Physiol. Psychol.* **67**:189–198.
Stein, L., and Wise, C. D., 1970, Behavioral Pharmacology of central stimulants, in: *Principles of Psychopharmacology* (W. G. Clark and J. del Giudice, eds.), pp. 313–325, Academic Press, New York.
Stein, L., Wise, C. D., and Berger, B. D., 1973, Antianxiety action of benzodiazepines: decrease in activity of serotonin neurons in the punishment system, in: *The Benzodiazepines* (S. Garattini, E. Mussini, and L. O. Randall, eds.), pp. 299–326, Raven Press, New York.
Stumpf, C., 1965, Drug action on the electrical activity of the hippocampus, *Int. J. Neurobiol.* **8**:77–138.
Sutherland, N. S., and MacIntosh, N., 1972, *Mechanisms of Animal Discrimination Learning,* Academic Press, London.
Taylor, K. M., and Laverty, R., 1969, The effect of chlordiazepoxide, diazepam, and

nitrazepam on catecholamine metabolism in regions of the rat brain, *Eur. J. Pharmacol.* **8:**296-301.

TAYLOR, K. M., and LAVERTY, R., 1973, The interaction of chlordiazepoxide, diazepam, and nitrazepam with catecholamine and histamine in regions of the rat brain, in: *The Benzodiazepines* (S. Garratini, E. Mussini, and L. O. Randall, eds.), pp. 191-202, Raven Press, New York.

TENEN, S. S., 1967, Recovery time as a measure of CER strength: effects of Benzodiazepines, amobarbital, chlorpromazine and amphetamine, *Psychopharmacologia* **12:**1-17.

THOMPSON, R. F., and SPENCER, W. A., 1966, Habituation. A model phenomenon for the study of neuronal substrates of behavior, *Psychol. Rev.* **173:**16-43.

THORNBURG, J. E., and MOORE, K. E., 1973, The relative importance of dopaminergic and noradrenergic neuronal systems for the stimulation of locomotor activity induced by amphetamine and other drugs, *Neuropharmacology* **12:**853-866.

THORPE, W. H., 1956, *Learning and Instinct in Animals*, Methuen, London.

TYE, N. C., IVERSEN, S. D., and EVERITT, B. J., 1976, Release of punished behavior following selective brain 5-hydroxytryptamine depletion, British Association of Psychopharmacology, Cambridge.

UNGERSTEDT, U., 1971, Stereotoxic mapping of the monamine pathways in the rat, *Acta Physiol. Scand. Suppl.* **367:**1-48.

VAN DER POEL, A. M., 1972, Centrally acting cholinolytics and the choice behaviour of the rat, *Prog. Brain Res.* **36:**127-136.

VAN DER POEL, A. M., 1973, Registration of choice direction in a T-maze in rats under the influence of *N*-methyl-4-piperidyl cyclopentyl methylethynyl glycolate (PCMG), a centrally acting cholinolytic, *Psychopharmacologia* **31:**271-290.

VAN DER POEL, A. M., 1974, The effect of some cholinolytic drugs on a number of behavioral parameters measured in the T-maze alternation test: dose-response relationships, *Psychopharmacologia* **37:**45-58.

VOGEL, J. R., HUGHES, R. A., and CARLTON, P. L., 1967, Scopolamine, atropine and conditioned fear, *Psychopharmacologia* **10:**409-416.

VOGEL, J. R., BEER, B., and CLODY, D. E., 1971, A simple and reliable conflict procedure for testing anti-anxiety agents, *Psychopharmacologia* **21:**1-7.

WARBURTON, D. M., 1957, Some behavioral effects of central cholinergic stimulation with special reference to the hippocampus, doctoral thesis, Indiana University, Bloomington, Indiana.

WARBURTON, D. M., 1969a, Behavioral effects of central and peripheral changes in acetylcholine systems, *J. Comp. Physiol. Psychol.* **68:**56-64.

WARBURTON, D. M., 1969b, Effects of atropine sulfate on single alternation in hippocampectomised rats, *Physiol. Behav.* **4:**641-644.

WARBURTON, D. M., 1972a, The cholinergic control of internal inhibition, in: *Inhibition and Learning* (R. M. Boakes and M. S. Halliday, eds.), pp. 431-460, Academic Press, London.

WARBURTON, D. M., 1972b, Effects of atropine sulphate on repeated extinction performance in hippocampectomised rats, *Psychopharmacologia* **23:**348-356.

WARBURTON, D. M., 1974a, The effect of scopolamine on a two-cue discrimination, *Qt. J. Exp. Psychol.* **26:**395-404.

WARBURTON, D. M., 1975a, Modern biochemical concepts of anxiety, *Int. Pharmacopsychiat.* **9:**189-205.

WARBURTON, D. M., 1975b, *Brain, Behaviour and Drugs*, Wiley, London.

WARBURTON, D. M., and BROWN, K., 1971, Scopolamine-induced attenuation of stimulus sensitivity, *Nature (London)* **230:**126-127.

WARBURTON, D. M., and BROWN, K., 1973, The facilitation of discrimination performance by physostigmine sulphate, *Psychopharmacologia* **27:**275-284.

WARBURTON, D. M., and GROVES, P., 1969, The effect of scopolamine on habituation of acoustic startle in rats, *Commun. Behav. Biol.* **3:**289-293.

WARBURTON, D. M., and HEISE, G. A., 1972, The effects of scopolamine on spatial double alternation in rats, *J. Comp. Physiol. Psychol.* **81**:523–532.

WARBURTON, D. M., and RUSSELL, R. W., 1969, Some behavioral effects of cholinergic stimulation of the hippocampus, *Life Sci.* **8**:617–627.

WEDEKING, P. W., 1968, Stimulating effects of chlordiazepoxide in rats on a food reinforced FR schedule, *Psychonomic. Sci.* **12**:31–32.

WEDEKING, P. W., 1969, Disinhibition effect of chlordiazepoxide, *Psychonomic Sci.* **15**:232–233.

WEISSMAN, A., 1959, Differential drug effects upon a three ply multiple schedule of reinforcement, *J. Exp. Anal. Behav.* **2**:271–291.

WENTINK, E., 1938, The effects of certain drugs and hormones upon conditioning, *J. Exp. Psychol.* **22**:150–163.

WHITEHOUSE, J. M., 1964, Effects of atropine on discrimination learning in the rat, *J. Comp. Physiol. Psychol.* **57**:13–15.

WHITEHOUSE, J. M., 1966, The effect of physostigmine on discrimination learning, *Psychopharmacologia* **9**:183–188.

WHITEHOUSE, J. M., 1967, Cholinergic mechanisms in discrimination learning as a function of stimuli *J. Comp. Physiol. Psychol.* **63**:448–451.

WHITEHOUSE, J. M., LLOYD, A. J., and FIFER, S. A., 1964, Comparative effects of atropine and methylatropine on maze acquisition and eating, *J. Comp. Physiol. Psychol.* **58**:475–476.

WISE, C. D., BERGER, B. D., and STEIN, L., 1972, Benzodiazepines: anxiety-reducing activity by reduction of serotonin turnover in the brain, *Science* **77**:180–183.

WISE, C. D., and STEIN, L., 1969, Facilitation of brain self-stimulation by central administration of norepinephrine, *Science* **163**:299–301.

WILLIAMS, J. M., HAMILTON, L. W., and CARLTON, P. L., 1974, Pharmacological and anatomical dissociation of two types of habituation, *J. Comp. Physiol. Psychol.* **87**:724–732.

ZBINDEN, G., 1960, Pharmacodynamics of tetrabenazine and its derivatives, in: *Psychosomatic Medicine* (J. Nodine and J. Moyer, eds.), pp. 443–454, Lea and Fibiger, Baltimore.

10

DRUG EFFECTS ON FEAR AND FRUSTRATION: POSSIBLE LIMBIC SITE OF ACTION OF MINOR TRANQUILIZERS

Jeffrey A. Gray

> *Is the anti-anxiety effect of the benzodiazepines therefore a central anti-adrenergic phenomenon? And if so, what is the role of brain norepinephrine in the chain of events which leads to psychoneurotic fear?*
>
> —Zbinden and Randall (1967, p. 284)

1. INTRODUCTION

This chapter attempts to answer the following linked questions:

1. What is the simplest adequate description of the effects of the "minor tranquilizers" on "emotional behavior" (terms I shall define below)?
2. What underlying psychological processes are altered by these drugs to produce these behavioral effects, and in what way are they altered?
3. On what brain structures or systems do these drugs act to produce these behavioral effects?

In the course of constructing answers to these questions we shall offer a fairly thorough review of certain of the behavioral effects of the minor

---

Jeffrey A. Gray • Department of Experimental Psychology, University of Oxford, Oxford, England.

tranquilizers. In approaching this review, we shall start with the barbiturates, especially sodium amobarbital (SA). The choice of this drug as a starting point is dictated by several considerations: Its behavioral effects are remarkably specific with respect to reinforcement conditions; these effects have been studied in the laboratory in relatively great detail; and they have been investigated with relatively careful theoretical attention paid to the question of the underlying psychological processes affected by the drug. However, we shall see that most of the conclusions applicable to SA are equally applicable to other barbiturates, to ethanol and to the benzodiazepines. These, then, are the drugs covered by the term, "minor tranquilizers" as it is used in this chapter. Considerations of space have made it necessary to exclude meprobamate, which has major similarities with the drugs whose effects are reviewed. Brief mention will be made, however, of Δ^9-tetrahydrocannabinol (THC), the major active principle of cannabis, which also has a number of striking similarities with the minor tranquilizers (Section 8.2, below).

The data I shall draw upon are almost entirely taken from experiments with animals. However, the link between many of these experiments and the clinical effects of the minor tranquilizers in man is quite close. Indeed, psychologists who have studied the effects of SA on rats have often regarded themselves as investigating the changes produced by this drug in emotional states (especially "fear" and "frustration") which are thought to be essentially similar to the emotional states whose control is the aim of clinical intervention with the minor tranquilizers in man. These experiments on rats have usually been conducted within the framework of "learning theory," and it is within this framework that they will be discussed here.

2. LEARNING THEORY BACKGROUND

If we are to make efficient use of this framework, some preliminaries are in order concerning the treatment accorded the emotions within learning theory. As discussed elsewhere (Gray, 1972a, 1975), the most common strategy (e.g., Spence, 1956; Mowrer, 1960; Amsel, 1962; Millenson, 1967; Weiskrantz, 1968) is to treat the emotions as states elicited by instrumentally reinforcing stimuli or by stimuli which have been associated with such reinforcing stimuli. Although the details differ from author to author, this strategy usually forms part of a version of "two-process theory," according to which goal-directed behavior is the outcome of an interaction between two fundamental learning processes, one being classical conditioning (Pavlov, 1927), and the other, instrumental or operant conditioning (Skinner, 1938). The particular version of two-process theory in which it is proposed here to embed the emotions is one I have recently spelled out in some detail (Gray, 1975). The description given of it here can therefore afford to be—as indeed it must be—brief.

According to two-process theory, classical conditioning is concerned with learning the associative relationships between discrete stimulus events (i.e., it is stimulus-stimulus, or S-S, learning), while instrumental conditioning is concerned with the establishment of behavior patterns which affect the organism's exposure to stimulus events (i.e., it is response-stimulus, or R-S, learning). For our present purposes the most important feature of the particular version of two-process theory used here is that the instrumental-learning component of the total learning process is further divided into two varieties, one concerned with maximizing the organism's exposure to rewarding events (as defined by the left column of Table 1), and the other with minimizing the organism's exposure to punishing events (as defined by the right column of Table 1). A "rewarding event" is one which, if it follows upon a particular response, increases the probability of recurrence of that response; a "punishing event" is one which, if it follows upon a particular response, decreases the probability of recurrence of that response.

I have used the phrases "rewarding and punishing *events*" rather than "*stimuli*" advisedly; as we shall see in a moment, these events may be constituted by the termination or omission of stimuli, as well as by their presentation. If, however, we concentrate for the moment on the case of stimulus presentation, we have such obvious instances of rewarding and punishing events as food for a hungry animal or electric shock. The operation of presenting a rewarding event contingent upon a response is termed "reward" and abbreviated in what follows as "Rew." Similarly the operation of presenting a punishing event contingent upon a response is termed "punishment" and abbreviated in what follows as "Pun." These two operations constitute the top row of Table 1, which sets out the various behavioral paradigms which we shall be discussing in this chapter and the terminology applied to them.

These two basic varieties of the instrumental-learning component of the total learning process both combine with the classical-conditioning component in the following way. We suppose that, for a given animal species, there exist stimuli which may act without prior learning as rewards and other stimuli which may act without prior learning as punishments. These stimuli may also act as unconditioned stimuli (UCS) (Pavlov, 1927) in a classical-conditioning paradigm, i.e., one in which the UCS is preceded by another stimulus, the conditioned stimulus or CS. The responses elicited by UCSs are termed "unconditioned responses" or UCRs, and the result of classical conditioning (to a rough approximation) is that the CS comes to acquire the property of eliciting some portion of the total pattern of UCRs elicited by the UCS. When the UCS is provided by a rewarding ("appetitive") or punishing ("aversive") stimulus, classical conditioning may in this manner confer on CSs, themselves not initially rewarding or punishing, "secondary" or "conditioned" appetitive or aversive properties. These secondary appetitive or aversive properties fall into two general classes: "reinforcing" and "motivational." The reinforcing property corresponds to the reinforcing (i.e., re-

TABLE 1
Instrumental Reinforcing Procedures with Unconditioned Reinforcing Events[a]

Procedure	Outcome	
	p(R)↑	p(R)↓
Presentation	Rew (approach)	Pun (passive avoidance)
Termination	Pun! (escape)	Rew! (time-out)
Omission	Pun— (active avoidance)	R̄ēw (extinction)

[a] From Gray (1975). The abbreviations and symbols

```
· · ·   S^{R+}
· · ·

— — —   S^{R-}
— — —
```

are as defined by the intersection of row (procedure) and column (outcome). p(R)↑: Outcome is an increase in the probability of the response on which the reinforcing event is made contingent. p(R)↓: Outcome is a decrease in the probability of this response. Dots and lines indicate those procedures-plus-outcomes which define a stimulus as an S^{R+} or an S^{R-}, respectively. Phrases in parentheses refer to typical learning situations in which the various reinforcing procedures are employed. Rew: reward; Pun: punishment; !: termination; —: omission.

warding or punishing) property of the UCS with which the CS has been paired. Thus, a secondary rewarding stimulus (Rew-CS) increases the probability of recurrence of responses which it follows; and a secondary punishing stimulus (Pun-CS; often called a "warning signal") decreases the probability of responses which it follows. The motivational properties of Rew-CSs and Pun-CSs correspond to (though they are not identical with) the eliciting properties of the UCS (reward or punishment) from which they have been derived. These motivational properties are still very much the subject of empirical research, and their exact nature is not entirely clear. Most of the relevant experimental studies have been carried out by presenting Rew-CSs or Pun-CSs to an animal engaged in instrumentally rewarded behavior or "active-avoidance" behavior (i.e., behavior followed by omission of punishment; see below) and observing the elicited changes in response rate or response vigor. The best established result of such experiments is that a Pun-CS reduces the rate of performance of a rewarded operant. This phenomenon, known variously as the "conditioned emotional response" (CER) or "conditioned suppression," was originally demonstrated by Estes and Skinner (1941), and it has subsequently been much used in drug research.

Further postulates of the present version of two-process theory concern "frustrative nonreward" (Amsel, 1962) and "relieving nonpunishment." Frustrative nonreward ($\overline{\text{Rew}}$) is the operation whereby reward is omitted after a particular response, given that reward has previously followed the same or similar responses and/or that reward is predicted to occur by stimuli (Rew-CSs) to which the animal is currently exposed. Frustrative nonreward is held to have effects on behavior which are in certain respects identical to those produced by punishment, and there is much evidence to support this hypothesis (Wagner, 1966; Gray, 1975). Relieving nonpunishment ($\overline{\text{Pun}}$) is the omission of punishment after a particular response, given that punishment has previously followed the same or similar responses and/or that punishment is predicted to occur by stimuli (Pun-CSs) to which the animal is currently exposed. Nonpunishment is held by the theory to have effects on behavior which are in certain respects identical to those produced by reward. In addition, the termination of reward (Rew!) is thought to be an operation with the same behavioral effects as frustrative nonreward, and the termination of punishment (Pun!) an operation with the same behavioral effects as relieving nonpunishment. These four operations are set out in the bottom two rows of Table 1.

Table 1 can be read in two ways.

First, it defines the behavioral *operations* we have considered above (reward, punishment, termination of reward, termination of punishment, nonreward, nonpunishment). For this purpose, the defining criteria are given by the intersection of the row heading (presentation, termination, or omission of the stimulus) and the column heading (increased or decreased probability of recurrence of the response on which the reinforcing event is made contingent). The entries in the body of the table at a given intersection then define the abbreviations used in this paper to describe the appropriate operations; they also give examples of names typically used to describe the relevant experimental paradigms.

Second, the table may be read as a way of classifying *stimuli*. Thus, there are three ways in which one may test for the appetitive properties of a stimulus: Such a stimulus should increase response probability when its presentation is contingent upon the response, but decrease response probability when its termination or omission is so contingent. Empirically, it is normally the case that any stimulus which passes one test will pass all three. Such a stimulus may be called (using the Skinnerian terminology) a "positive reinforcer" or S^{R+}. Similarly, there are three ways in which one may test for the aversive properties of a stimulus: It should decrease response probability when its presentation is contingent upon the response, but increase response probability when its termination or omission is so contingent. Again (with the possible exception of some kinds of brain stimulation), it is normally the case that any stimulus which passes one test will pass all three. This kind of stimulus is called a "negative reinforcer" or S^{R-}. (The Skinnerian terminology also uses the phrases "positive and negative *reinforcement*." "Positive reinforcement" is the cell abbreviated Rew in Table 1; "negative reinforcement" covers the cells abbreviated Pun! and $\overline{\text{Pun}}$.)

Now it is clear that a classification of *responses* as either maximizing exposure to rewarding events or minimizing exposure to punishing events (the columns of Table 1) is distinct from a classification of *stimuli* as positive or negative reinforcers (the dotted versus the dashed cells of Table 1). It is an empirical question as to which, if either, of these classifications reflects real distinctions in the way the nervous system processes information in different learning situations. As we shall see, however, the behavioral effects of the minor tranquilizers appear to respect the distinction between direction of change in response probability: They alleviate response suppression, whatever its source (the left-hand column of Table 1), while not affecting the acquisition of responses (the right-hand column). Conversely, the behavioral effects of the minor tranquilizers appear to ignore the distinction between positive and negative reinforcers.

Just as the simple operations of Rew and Pun may combine with the classical-conditioning component of the total learning process to produce secondary rewarding and punishing stimuli (Rew-CSs and Pun-CSs), so the more complex operations of omission or termination of reward or punishment may work in the same way. Thus, if an initially neutral stimulus is paired in a stimulus-stimulus sequence with $\overline{\text{Rew}}$, it acquires by classical conditioning secondary aversive properties as a "conditioned frustrative" stimulus ($\overline{\text{Rew}}$-CS). Similarly, if a CS is paired with $\overline{\text{Pun}}$, it acquires secondary appetitive properties as a $\overline{\text{Pun}}$-CS (often called a "safety signal"). Responses followed by $\overline{\text{Rew}}$-CSs, other things being equal, are likely to decline in probability of recurrence; responses followed by $\overline{\text{Pun}}$-CSs are likely to increase in probability of recurrence. With regard to the motivational properties of these types of stimuli, there are indications that those possessed by $\overline{\text{Rew}}$-CSs resemble those of Pun-CSs, and those possessed by Pun-CSs resemble those of Rew-CSs. (Stimuli paired with the termination of reward or punishment have not received much study.)

If the foregoing has inevitably been overcondensed, I hope that it has nonetheless served to introduce the reader to the main lines of division which can be used to fractionate the behavioral effects of the minor tranquilizers. A number of important behavioral processes (e.g., Pavlovian internal inhibition) have not been mentioned at all, since, as far as we know, they are not relevant to this fractionation.

Now, as stated above, the minor tranquilizers are used for the control of emotional states in man, and they are believed to alter emotional states in experimental animals. Furthermore, the emotions are usually treated within learning theory as *states elicited by unconditioned instrumentally reinforcing stimuli or by stimuli which have been associated (by classical conditioning) with such unconditioned reinforcing stimuli.* The most convenient way, therefore, to consider the behavioral effects of the minor tranquilizers is with reference to the kinds of unconditioned or conditioned reinforcers by which the relevant behavior is elicited, reinforced, or motivated. This is the strategy we shall follow, commencing with the barbiturates.

3. THE EFFECTS OF THE BARBITURATES ON EMOTIONAL BEHAVIOR

The case to be argued here is that SA and other barbiturates have little or no influence on the learning or performance of rewarded responses or of active avoidance or escape responses, i.e., all those cases in which the outcome of a learning experiment is the acquisition of new responses. In contrast, these drugs profoundly disturb the ability of an animal to suppress responses which are followed by punishment or nonreward. Further analysis of these drug effects shows that they are not a consequence of any changed effectiveness of the punishing stimulus or of nonreward *per se*: Responses elicited by these two kinds of aversive event are unchanged; and, as already mentioned, there is no disturbance in behavior which is reinforced by the termination or omission of punishing stimuli (escape and active avoidance). This state of affairs may be summarized by saying that the effects of the minor tranquilizers are to reduce the behavioral effects of only *secondary* punishing and secondary frustrative stimuli (Pun-CSs and $\overline{\text{Rew}}$-CSs). To make this conclusion more concrete (and to anticipate data which will be described in detail below), consider a rat in an alley in which entry into a goalbox is followed by electric shock. After one or more experiences of this contingency, stimuli in the startbox and stem of the alley will become Pun-CSs in the presence of which the undrugged animal will suppress the response of traversing the alley toward the goalbox. The major effect of the minor tranquilizers is to impair this type of response suppression.

Now, in the language of the emotions as forged by learning theorists, the state elicited by Pun-CSs is usually termed "fear" (Miller, 1951; Mowrer, 1960), and the state elicited by $\overline{\text{Rew}}$-CSs is termed "conditioned frustration" (Amsel, 1962). Thus, the claim made here may also be stated thus: SA selectively reduces fear and conditioned frustration (Miller, 1964; Wagner, 1966; Gray, 1967, 1971a). Phrased in this way, it offers an easy step to the clinical uses of the minor tranquilizers.

In reviewing the literature which supports this claim, we commence with behavior motivated by reward, on which the barbiturates have little or no effect. In this and succeeding sections, it may be assumed that, unless otherwise stated, the subjects are rats, the drug is SA, the dose of SA is in the range 10–30 mg/kg, and the route of injection is intraperitoneal (i.p.) or subcutaneous (s.c.). The focus of the review is on the effect of *low* doses of the barbiturates: Effects which occur at hypnotic levels only are not of interest.

3.1. Rewarded Behavior

Simple rewarded behavior, such as running an alley or pressing a bar for food or water, is affected by low doses of SA not at all or inconsistently from study to study. Such effects as are observed are more easily attributed to other effects of the drug than to effects on the reward process itself. Thus, reduced rate of performance of an operant may occur when motor incoordination (Rushton *et al.*, 1963) interferes with the actual execution of the response; and increased performance may be observed if the drug reduces the competing influence of fear, especially when the experimental situation is novel to the animal.

In the straight alley with food reward, N. E. Miller's group has variously reported that SA produces faster running on early training trials with no effect at asymptote (Barry *et al.*, 1962; Rosen *et al.*, 1967), or slower running throughout training (Wagner, 1963) and at asymptote (Barry and Miller, 1962, 1965). Capaldi and Sparling (1971a) found no effect of SA administered during late acquisition. Ison and Pennes (1969) observed faster start speeds and slower goal speeds, and Gray (1969), in a very similar experiment, observed no effect on total alley speeds. Still in the straight alley, but using water reward and phenobarbital (doses up to 30 mg/kg), Schmidt and Stewart (1967) found significantly faster running, which they attributed to greater thirst induced by the drug. In the double runway (Amsel and Roussel, 1952), Ison *et al.* (1967), Gray (1969), and Gray and Dudderidge (1971) found no significant changes in running speed under SA, whereas Ludvigson (1967) and Freedman and Rosen (1969) observed significantly slower speeds. Using a food-rewarded jumping response, Gray (1969) obtained significantly shorter response latencies with SA. In a black–white discrimination task, Ison and Rosen (1967) and Caul (1967) obtained the same pattern as Barry et al. (1962) in the straight alley—faster running to the positive stimulus on early trials, but no difference at asymptote.

In the Skinner box, Weissman (1959) saw no effect of pentobarbital (PB) in doses up to 16 mg/kg on responding on a continuous-reinforcement (CRF) schedule. On variable interval (VI) schedules, several investigators have seen only small effects of SA (Barry et al., 1963; Gray, 1964a; Davidson and Cook, 1969; Cook and Davidson, 1973). Similarly, Longoni et al. (1973) found no effect of 20 and 40 mg/kg phenobarbital (PhB). In squirrel monkeys, Hanson et al. (1967) saw increases in VI rate with 5–10 mg/kg PB *per os* (p.o.). In pigeons, Dews (1955b) observed only small changes under PB up to quite high doses (about 20 mg/kg), when substantial decreases in response rate were seen. Increased response rates have often been observed on fixed-interval (FI) and fixed-ratio (FR) schedules in rats given low doses of PhB (Kelleher et al., 1961) and in pigeons given low doses of SA, PhB, or PB (Dews, 1955a, 1956, 1964; Herrnstein and Morse, 1957; Ferster et al., 1962; Waller and Morse, 1963; Laties and Weiss, 1966; Rutledge and Kelleher, 1965; Bignami and Gatti, 1969; McKearney, 1970; McMillan, 1973; Barrett, 1974). The effect observed depends, however, both on dose and on the parameters of the schedule of reinforcement (Kelleher and Morse, 1968). For example, Morse (1962), using SA with pigeons, found substantial rate increases with 5.2 and 10 mg/kg on FR 330, but only a slight increase with 5.2 mg/kg and a steep decrease with 10 mg/kg on FR 33. Similarly, Dews (1955a) reported that the dose of PB at which the pigeon's response rate declined was less on FI than on FR (1 mg/bird vs 4 mg/bird). Many observations support the hypothesis (Dews, 1958; Kelleher and Morse, 1968) that the effect of the drug is a function of the rate at which the response is performed under the no-drug condition. This "rate-dependence" hypothesis will be considered further below.

We come finally to studies of electrical self-stimulation of the brain. Here the barbiturates produce increased response rates when the stimulation produces convulsions. Thus Reid et al. (1964) found consistent rate increases under 15–60 mg/kg PhB; however, their rats had frequent seizures in the undrugged state, and these were controlled by the drug. Mogenson (1964), using PB, confirmed earlier observations of Olds and Travis (1960) and Olds et al. (1957) that this drug (5–20 mg/kg) does not systematically affect response rates; in two of Mogenson's rats which experienced convulsions during self-stimulation, response rate was considerably enhanced by the drug. In opposition to these findings, a dose of 10 mg/kg PB has been reported more recently to reduce self-stimulation by about 30% (Olds and Domino, 1969; Domino and Olds, 1968; Olds and Ito, 1973). Another condition under which the barbiturates facilitate self-stimulation has been described by Reid et al. (1970) and by Wasden and Reid (1968). These workers showed that the overnight performance decrement often seen with self-stimulation can be removed by SA. They suggest that the overnight decrement occurs because the stimulating electrode affects both positive and negative reinforcement pathways, leading to an approach–avoidance conflict, and that SA reduces the avoidance component of this conflict (see below, Section 3.2). Similar effects have been observed with the benzodiazepines (Section 6.1).

We may summarize this section by saying that the only consistent effect of the barbiturates on rewarded behavior is to increase response rates on FI and FR schedules in the Skinner box. However, it will be argued below (Section 3.8.3) that this effect is best understood as the removal of an inhibitory influence of nonreward.

3.2. Passive Avoidance

In contrast to their small and inconsistent effects on rewarded behavior, the barbiturates produce a clear-cut impairment in "passive avoidance" behavior. This term is used to describe the suppression of approach to a particular place (e.g., a box in which reward has previously been delivered) when such approach behavior is punished (e.g., by electric shock). When the experimental paradigm involves punishment of a nonspatial response (e.g., pressing a bar), the resulting response suppression has not commonly been called passive avoidance. However, since there is at present no compelling reason to suppose that the response suppression occurring in the two situations, spatial and nonspatial, is due to different mechanisms (though it has been suggested that fundamental differences may exist: O'Keefe and Nadel, 1974), we shall consider both kinds together.

The effects of SA on passive avoidance in a spatial array were first brought out clearly in Miller's experiments. Bailey and Miller (1952) trained cats to run in an alley for food and then shocked them when they reached the goal. After approach to the food was totally suppressed, SA was injected, which caused the cats to resume approach behavior. Barry and Miller (1962) obtained essentially the same result in a more sophisticated study with rats which were trained before drug administration to associate progressive changes in the length of a "telescope alley" with increasing intensities of shock at the goal (where either food or water reward could be obtained). At the shortest length of alley no shock at all was delivered. SA significantly increased running speed and the number of trials completed when shock was threatened; the effect of the drug was greater, the greater the intensity of the threatened shock; and, on safe trials, it either had no effect or actually decreased running speed. This result was replicated by Barry *et al.* (1962*a*), who further showed that the effect was not simply due to change in drug state from training to testing conditions. An additional control experiment (Miller, 1964) showed that the effects of SA in this situation are the same whether the animal is first trained on the approach response, shock only being introduced later, or whether the order of these two phases of the experiment is reversed. Reductions in passive avoidance have also been reported by Naess and Rasmussen (1958) in thirsty animals shocked through their drinking water, and by Kumar (1971a) in an experiment in which undrugged rats were shocked in one arm of a Y-maze and extinction of the tendency to avoid this arm during free exploration was subsequently investigated with and without drug administration. In Kumar's experiment, doses of SA as low as 3.75 mg/kg (nonsignificantly) and 7.5 mg/kg (significantly) reduced avoidance of the shock-associated arm. However, retest under saline disclosed levels of avoidance not different from those of animals previously exposed to the Y-maze under saline. Thus, although SA reduces the expression of passive avoidance, it appears not to hasten the extinction of the avoidance tendency.

The effects described above do not depend on the use of electric shock to produce the passive avoidance tendency: Morrison and Stephenson (1970) showed that SA (7.5 mg/kg) and PB (3 and 6 mg/kg) reduced avoidance of a single open elevated arm in an otherwise enclosed Y-maze. Nor are they confined to rats and cats: Boissier *et al.* (1968b) punished locomotion in mice and showed that PhB (32 mg/kg, but not 4–16 mg/kg) decreased the resulting degree of suppression of movement.

In the Skinner box, Barry *et al.* (1963) reported that SA substantially reduced the inhibition of food-rewarded barpressing during a tone which signalled intermittent shocks in the vicinity of the bar. In a later experiment, Barry, Etheredge and Miller (1965) suppressed food-rewarded bar pressing by punishing it with shock in the undrugged state, and then showed that injections of SA increased the proportion of animals returning to the lever, no further shocks being given. As in Kumar's (1971a) Y-maze study, further testing under placebo failed to show any hastening of extinction of avoidance of the lever when the animals previously given SA were compared to animals which had only had saline. Results similar to these were reported by Sherman (1967); however, this author's data suggest that some transfer of extinction of avoidance may occur if the drug is withdrawn gradually rather than abruptly.

An important series of experiments in the Skinner box has used a multiple schedule, modeled on that developed by Geller and Seifter (1960), in which periods of relatively low-density positive reinforcement (usually VI) without punishment alternate with periods of relatively high-density positive reinforcement (CRF or FR) coupled with punishment. Such a multiple schedule controls for drug-induced alterations in overall response rate as distinct from changes specific to the punishment contingency. Punished, but not unpunished, responding was significantly increased in rats on this schedule which were given SA or PhB (Davidson and Cook, 1969; Cook and Davidson, 1973). Similar results have been obtained by Geller and Seifter (1960, 1962; Geller, 1964), Ray (1964), Zbinden and Randall (1967), and

Blum (1970) with PB and PhB in the rat; by Morse (1964) with SA in the pigeon; and by Hanson et al. (1967) and McMillan (1967) with PB in the squirrel monkey.

Although the Geller–Seifter schedule controls for general response rate changes unconnected with the punishment contingency, it does not control for the possibility that an increase in response rate observed in the punishment component of the multiple schedule results from a drug effect on low response rates *per se*, no matter how they have been produced. Since there is considerable evidence that drug-induced changes may depend in just this way on preexisting response rates (Kelleher and Morse, 1968), it is important to demonstrate that such an effect does not fully account for the apparent impairment in response suppression produced by barbiturates in the Skinner box. A careful experiment by McMillan (1973) provides such a demonstration. This worker studied pigeons in a multiple FI-5-min–FI-5-min schedule, in one component of which response-contingent shocks were also delivered. Such long fixed intervals generate very different response rates over the duration of the interval. Making use of this fact, McMillan calculated the drug-produced changes in response rate as a function of the undrugged response rate in successive tenths of each FI component. His results showed that 10 and 17.5 mg/kg PB produced greater increases in response rate in the punished than in the unpunished FI component even when the predrug response rates were equated.

Passive avoidance of a nonspatial kind has also been studied outside the Skinner box. Vogel et al. (1971) periodically administered shocks through the drinking tube to thirsty rats licking for water; PB (5 and 10 mg/kg) significantly increased the rate of licking and the number of shocks taken. In dogs, Tamura (1963) observed a resumption of feeding behavior (contingent upon pushing open a door) previously suppressed by shock when PhB (20–50 mg/kg), PB (5–10 mg/kg), or thiopental (5 mg/kg) were injected intravenously.

3.3. Classical Conditioning of Fear

Given the evidence for reduced response suppression in situations involving punishment after barbiturate administration, and given the general context of two-process theory, it would be valuable to have data on the effects of these drugs on the classical conditioning of fear. Data of this kind, however, are sparse and contradictory.

The classic technique for studying the conditioning of fear is the establishment of conditioned suppression or the CER (Estes and Skinner, 1941). In this a CS is paired with an aversive UCS (with no response contingency), and the effects of the conditioning are measured by the reduction the CS produces in the rate of performance of a rewarded operant in the rat, normally bar pressing. The CS-UCS pairings may be conducted while the subject performs this operant (an "on-the-baseline" procedure) or in a separate experimental situation ("off-the-baseline" procedure).

Using an off-the-baseline technique and administering SA during the conditioning phase only, Singh and Eysenck (1960) report results which suggest a reduction in the CER with this drug. But theirs was a complex study of drug antagonism with small groups, and the effect appears to be present in only one of two strains of rats studied. If their result is reliable, it is in any case somewhat surprising, since it suggests, in opposition to the results of Kumar (1971a) and Barry et al. (1965) reviewed above, an effect of SA on learning about aversive stimuli as distinct from the performance of a fear-motivated response.

Lauener (1963) studied the on-the-baseline CER. His results indicate a reduction in conditioned suppression with a number of barbiturates. Since administration was *per os,* it is difficult to compare his doses with other work, but the effective ones appear to have been large: 70 mg/kg SA, 30-45 mg/kg PhB, 100 mg/kg barbital, and 70 mg/kg methylphenobarbital. Furthermore, the conditions of his experiment were less than ideal for demonstrating an effect on classically conditioned fear. The schedule of positive reinforcement was one of differential reinforcement of low rates (DRL), in particular DRL 5 sec (Lauener, personal communication, 1975). This has two disadvantages: First, the barbiturates (and other minor tranquilizers) affect responding on this schedule directly, increasing response rate (see below, Section 3.8.3), an effect which could mimic the alleviation of conditioned suppression; second, CS-shock pairings on a DRL baseline sometimes themselves give rise to an *increase* in response rate (Blackman 1968). Thus, in addition to the problem of possible adventitious punishment effects with the on-the-baseline procedure (Kelleher and Morse, 1968), the use of a DRL schedule as the baseline renders interpretation of drug effects on conditioned suppression particularly hazardous.

Blackman's (1968) data show that the effect of the CER procedure on a DRL baseline is to facilitate responding when a low shock intensity is used and to suppress responding with high shock intensities. De Villiers, Dent, and Gray (unpublished) have used this property of the DRL schedule to test the general hypothesis that SA reduces the effects of Pun-CSs. It was, argued that, if the drug acts in this way, it should counteract both the conditioned acceleration at low shock intensities and the conditioned suppression at high shock intensities. Preliminary results were in accord with this prediction. As pointed out by Millenson and Leslie (1974), the rate-dependence hypothesis (Dews, 1964; Kelleher and Morse, 1968; see previous section) is unable to account for this result. However, the use of an on-the-baseline procedure in this experiment still leaves it inconclusive with regard to the question whether SA reduces *classically* conditioned fear.

Two studies have used a variant of the conditioned-suppression experiment in which the measured operant is drinking. Tenen (1967) trained rats to drink from a bottle, then presented (on the baseline) a CS followed by shock, with no drugs given. His measure of the fear conditioned to the CS was the length of time its presentation on subsequent days (without shock) inhibited drinking. Such inhibition was significantly reduced by injection of 23.7 mg/kg SA on the test days. In contrast, Stein and Berger (1969) reported that a rather larger dose of SA (30 mg/kg), injected before a test session conducted one week after an undrugged off-the-baseline fear conditioning session, significantly *increased* the conditioned suppression of drinking. Stein and Berger's (1969) result is surprising on any count, but it suggests that Tenen's opposite result may have been due to his on-the-baseline conditioning procedure, with its possible contamination by response-punishment effects.

If the conditioned suppression studies do not clearly indicate that the barbiturates produce any reduction in classically conditioned fear, studies using other techniques are no clearer. Kamano et al. (1966b) observed inhibition of movement, defecation, and urination during presentations of a 3-min light which was followed by shock. There was no effect of SA in a dose (20 mg/kg) effective in the passive-avoidance experiments. In a similar experiment, Bindra et al. (1965) found no effect of 30 mg/kg PhB on conditioned immobility. Chi (1965) paired a light with a shock and then tested the "potentiated" startle response to a tone preceded by this light. Controls received the same light–tone combinations in the startle session, but without the previous light–shock pairings. SA was administered on the startle test trials only and significantly reduced the magnitude of the startle response in the group which had the light–shock pairings, while leaving it unaffected in the control group. However, a second control group was tested for the startle response to a 30-V shock, this producing a level of response equivalent to that produced by the light–tone combination in the group with prior fear conditioning. SA reduced the magnitude of the startle response in this second control group as well. Thus, interpretation of Chi's results is equivocal: They could simply indicate that SA affects any startle responses which are above a threshold magnitude. Corson and Corson (1967) reported that PhB (3.5–6 mg/kg per 24 hr p.o.) did not affect a classical-conditioned paw-flexion response in dogs, but did reduce the conditioned cardiac and respiratory responses to the CS. The drug also reduced a cluster of vegetative changes elicited by the general experimental situation in which the conditioning was conducted (involving heart rate, respiration, diuresis, and salivation). This is the best direct evidence available for an effect of the barbiturates on conditioned fear. However, Hidalgo et al. (1968), also studying a conditioned cardiac response in dogs, found effects of PhB only at 20 mg/kg p.o., a dose at which considerable sedation and ataxia were observed.

3.4. Escape Behavior

In contrast to the powerful effects of the barbiturates on passive avoidance, these drugs have no specific effects on other behavior dependent on instrumental contingencies with aversive stimuli. One such form of behavior is escape, in which the unconditioned aversive stimulus is presented to the animal and terminated by its response.

In the straight alley, Barry and Miller (1965) found that SA reduced running speed to escape shock, but this effect was only a little larger than the reduction in running for food also caused by the drug. Schmidt *et al.* (1973) similarly found a reduction in escape speeds with PhB (8–56 mg/kg); but their data show that this effect was almost entirely confined to the first of the five daily trials run by each animal. In a similar experiment, Bindra *et al.* (1965) failed to observe any effect of PhB (30 mg/kg) on escape speed. In the shuttlebox (see below), Mize and Isaac (1962) found a reduction in escape speed with 2.5–10 mg/kg PB, but only by 0.04 sec. In mice a very high dose of PB (41 mg/kg) was necessary to abolish escape responding in the shuttlebox (Cole and Wolf, 1966). Finally, using bar pressing to terminate central electrical stimulation of pain centers in the rat, Olds and Travis (1960) found no systematic effects with 5 or 10 mg/kg PB, but a reduction in response rate with 15 mg/kg.

Although these studies show a slight reduction in escape behavior after barbiturate administration, in most cases this is best explained as a nonspecific effect of sedation or motor incoordination.

3.5. One-Way Active Avoidance

Studies of the effects of barbiturates on active-avoidance behavior (i.e., behavior reinforced by $\overline{\text{Pun}}$) which were published before 1960 have been reviewed by Herz (1960). These early studies tended strongly to the conclusion that active avoidance is systematically affected by these drugs only at sedative or ataxic doses. Subsequent work has reinforced this conclusion.

Thus, Lynch *et al.* (1960) reported that acquisition of a pole-jumping response to avoid shock was improved by 5 and 10 mg/kg SA, 20 mg/kg having no effect, while Domino *et al.* (1965), observing the same response, found impaired acquisition with both 10 and 20 mg/kg, 5 mg/kg having no effect. In the straight alley, Barry and Miller (1965) found a reduction in running speed to avoid shock, but, as already noted, similar reductions in running speed were produced by SA in this experiment not only in escape behavior but also in rewarded approach behavior. Furthermore, their data show that, after a rat had experienced shock during the day's testing (the shock being programmed to occur sometimes at intervals too short for the animal to be able to avoid it), running speed under SA was identical for avoidance and approach behavior. Thus, as in the case of Schmidt *et al.*'s (1973) findings for escape (see above), the most parsimonious account is that the drug produced general sedative effects which were overcome by the first shock of the day.

In the Skinner box a number of experiments have used the Sidman avoidance schedule, on which shocks are programmed to occur at regular intervals unless the subject performs the designated response, thus postponing the next programmed shock for some specified period of time. Heise and Boff (1962) found impaired performance (lower response rate and higher received shock rate) with several barbiturates, but only at high doses: 33 mg/kg PhB, 45 mg/kg hexobarbital, and 12 mg/kg PB. Weissman (1959) similarly found an impairment at 16 mg/kg PB, 8 mg/kg being without effect, and Longoni et al. (1973) an impairment at 40 mg/kg PhB, 20 mg/kg having only insignificant effects. In squirrel monkeys, Cook and Kelleher (1962) state that PhB impaired performance only at doses producing motor impairment. More complex findings have been reported by Bignami et al. (1971) in rats. These workers found that PhB (10–60 mg/kg) generally increased the overall response rate and provoked a *decrease* in the number of shocks taken by animals which, without the drug, were taking many shocks, but an increase in shock rate in animals which, without the drug, were taking only few shocks. They attribute the improved performance produced by the drug in poor performers to a reduction in the response-suppressant effects of shock, i.e., to a reduction in what we have termed passive avoidance. This possibility will be discussed more fully in Section 6.5 on the effects of the benzodiazepines on one-way active avoidance.

Also in the Skinner box, King (1968) trained rats to press one lever for water reward and another to avoid shock, the appropriate response being indicated by a light placed above the corresponding lever. At the lowest of three shock levels used (0.2, 0.6, and 1.0 mA), PB (10 and 20 mg/kg) selectively impaired the avoidance response, but at the other two shock levels both responses were affected equally. Ray (1963) had previously obtained similar results with 7.5–12.5 mg/kg PB. In a later, more elaborate experiment, King (1970) obtained the same essential result with SA. This impaired responding for water and responding to avoid shock to the same degree under three levels of water deprivation. When shock level was varied, shock avoidance was most impaired by SA at the lowest shock intensity. But responding for water was also most impaired by SA at the lowest shock intensity, suggesting, as in the case of the experiments by Schmidt et al. (1973) and Barry and Miller (1965) discussed above, that the effects of the drug were of a sedative nature and could be overcome by the arousing effects of shock.

3.6. Two-Way Active Avoidance

The previous section was concerned with "one-way" active avoidance. This term is used to distinguish the procedures involved from the kind of "two-way" active avoidance which is studied in the shuttlebox. The latter, as we shall see, almost certainly involves in fact a conflict between active and passive avoidance. In a typical shuttlebox experiment the animal is on one side of the two-compartment apparatus when the warning signal (Pun-CS) is presented. At some fixed time after onset of this stimulus, shock is presented to the animal's feet, unless it has by then moved to the other side of the apparatus. If it is still on the original side, it can terminate ("escape") the shock by now running to the other side. The warning signal is itself normally terminated by a cross to the other side, whether on successful avoidance trials or on escape trials. The active-avoidance response, then, is crossing to the other side of the box than the one in which the animal finds itself when the warning signal is presented. But this response takes the animal back to the side from which it has run away on the previous trial. It is natural to suppose that the animal will experience some reluctance to return to the danger area from which it has just fled. More formally, the stimuli making up that side of the box, through their association with shock, will have become Pun-CSs and therefore capable of reducing the probability of occurrence of behavior which they follow. Thus, in the shuttlebox there are two conflicting responses: the active-avoidance response of crossing to the other side, reinforced by $\overline{\text{Pun}}$, by the termination of the explicit Pun-CS constituted by the warning signal, and by the termination of shock on escape trials; and the passive avoidance response of keeping away from that side of the box, reinforced by the implicit Pun-CSs constituted by the stimuli on that side.

This analysis, which has been advanced by a number of previous writers (e.g., McCleary, 1966; Lubar and Numan, 1973), is supported both by direct experimental manipulation of factors in the shuttlebox situation (Freedman et al., 1974) and by the fact that a number of diverse factors affect passive avoidance and shuttlebox avoidance in opposite directions. Thus, Maudsley-reactive (MR) rats, bred for high fearfulness in the open-field test (Broadhurst, 1960; Gray, 1971a), show greater passive avoidance (Weldon, 1967; Ferraro and York, 1968) than Maudsley-nonreactive (MNR) rats, bred on the same test for low fearfulness, but poorer shuttlebox avoidance (for references, see Gray and Lalljee, 1974). Fuller (1970) has reported a similar negative correlation between the efficiency of passive and of shuttlebox avoidance across four inbred strains of mice. The role of genetic factors in the determination of shuttlebox avoidance has been further demonstrated in a diallel cross study of rats by Wilcock and Fulker (1973). These workers showed that there are two separate genetic influences, each with directional dominance, one for poor performance on early avoidance trials, the other for good performance on later trials; they suggest that the first of these influences favors the development of a conditioned emotional response leading to freezing or immobility. Other factors which affect passive and shuttlebox avoidance in opposite directions are sex, the less fearful females (Gray, 1971b) showing poorer passive and better shuttlebox avoidance (for references, see Gray and Lalljee, 1974); early handling, which reduces fearfulness (Levine, 1962a,b) and improves shuttlebox avoidance (for references, see Gray and Lalljee, 1974); and lesions to the hippocampus (Douglas, 1967) and septal area (Lubar and Numan, 1973; Dickinson, 1974), which again impair passive and improve shuttlebox avoidance.

In the light of this evidence, one might expect the barbiturates, which as we have seen impair passive avoidance, to improve performance in the shuttlebox. Just this result has been reported for SA by Powell et al. (1965), Kamano et al. (1966a), Martin et al. (1967), and (nonsignificantly) Kamano et al. (1966b). The second of these experiments examined the effects in male Wistar rats of doses of SA from 5 to 40 mg/kg; the greatest facilitation was produced by 20 and 30 mg/kg, 40 mg/kg giving rise to a decline in performance. In other experiments (Martin et al., 1966; Powell et al., 1967) these workers showed that the dose–response curve varies in different strains and in the sexes, conforming to the following generalization: The more fearful the population studied (as assessed by defecation in the open-field test), the higher the dose of SA which produces maximum facilitation of shuttlebox avoidance. On the assumption (supported by the data reviewed in the preceding paragraph) that the more emotional the animal the greater is the passive-avoidance tendency which must be overcome by the drug, this is an intelligible pattern of results. Thus, Powell et al. (1967) found that shuttlebox performance was facilitated by 20 mg/kg SA and impaired by 40 mg/kg in the more emotional Tryon S_1 strain, but impaired by both doses of SA in the less emotional Tryon S_3 strain. Within the two strains, the performance of the more emotional males was facilitated by the 20 mg/kg dose and impaired by the 40 mg/kg dose, while that of the less emotional females was impaired by both doses. Using Wistar rats, Martin et al. (1966) selected high- and low-fearful groups on the basis of open-field behavior and found that 10–40 mg/kg SA facilitated shuttlebox performance in the high-fearful group, but had no effect on the performance of the low-fearful group.

Presumably the impairments observed by these workers are due to the general sedative effects of the barbiturates; if there is only a weak passive-avoidance tendency for the drug to break up, as in animals of low fearfulness, the role of these sedative effects would be more prominent. In conformity with this deduction, Gupta and Holland (1969) found an impairment of shuttlebox performance with quite low doses of SA (11 and 15 mg/kg) in the MNR, but not the MR, strain. However, there is a discrepancy between this result and the finding reported by Powell (1967) that 30 mg/kg SA had no effect on shuttlebox performance in either Maudsley strain. In mice, shuttlebox performance has been reported (Cole and Wolf, 1966) to be impaired under PB, but the ED_{50} (i.e., the dose effective in 50% of animals) was almost as high as the dose which abolished escape responses to the shock (33 vs 41 mg/kg).

3.7. Responses Elicited by Aversive Stimuli

One possible account of the reduction caused by the barbiturates in passive-avoidance behavior is that the impact of the unconditioned aversive stimulus (usually shock) is itself in some way reduced. This account is rendered unlikely by the relative lack of effect of these drugs on escape and one-way active avoidance, and by their complex effects on two-way active avoidance; it is definitely eliminated by studies of their effects on responses elicited by shock and other aversive stimuli.

Most studies in this field have examined aggressive behavior elicited in paired male animals which are either shocked or are brought together after a previous period of isolation. The majority have used mice and either PB or PhB. These have shown either no effect of the drug (Yen *et al.*, 1959; Kletzkin, 1969; Christmas and Maxwell, 1970; Cole and Wolf, 1970) or impairments only at seizure-preventing (Tedeschi *et al.*, 1959; Chen *et al.*, 1963) or sedative and ataxic (Janssen *et al.*, 1960; Gray *et al.*, 1961; Cole and Wolf, 1966; Sofia, 1969) doses. In rats, Christmas and Maxwell (1970) found no effect on shock-induced fighting of SA up to very large doses (200 mg/kg p.o.). In mink, aggressive reactions to handling were not reduced by 25 mg/kg PB (Bauen and Possanza, 1970). The only exception to the general trend of these findings is a report by Valzelli *et al.* (1967) that isolation-induced fighting in mice was reduced by low doses (5 mg/kg) of PB, PhB, or hexobarbital. In opposition to this finding must be set three reports that low doses of the barbiturates may actually facilitate aggressive behavior. Crowley (1972) observed increases in the duration of shock-induced fighting in rats given 5 or 10 mg/kg PhB; at doses from 20 to 40 mg/kg no change was recorded in the duration of fighting, and at 80 mg/kg a reduction in fighting due to ataxia and lethargy was recorded. Also in rats, Silverman (1966) found an increase in isolation-induced fighting with 2.5–10 mg/kg SA and 2.5–5 mg/kg PB. Finally, in mice, Le Douarec and Broussy (1969) found increased isolation-induced fighting with 5 mg/kg PB and reduced fighting with 40 mg/kg; intermediate doses produced ambiguous results.

It seems reasonable to conclude that barbiturates reduce aggressive reactions to shock and other aversive stimuli only at sedative doses, while sufficiently low doses may reveal a facilitatory effect. Thus, the reduction in passive avoidance produced by the barbiturates cannot be attributed to a general loss of effect of unconditioned aversive stimuli. On the contrary, it is possible that the increased aggression seen at low doses reflects decreased passive avoidance (of the aversive stimuli provided by the partner in the fight). This possibility does not seem to have been investigated.

The data so far reviewed, then, suggest that the barbiturates reduce in a highly selective manner the response suppression caused by punishment. In the context of two-process learning theory, passive avoidance represents a response to Pun-CSs, that is, to the stimuli which regularly precede or accompany the making of the punished response. In contrast, escape and aggressive behavior are directly elicited by the unconditioned punishing stimuli themselves. Thus, one possible implication of this pattern of observations is that the physiological substrates which mediate instrumental responses to unconditioned and conditioned aversive stimuli, respectively, differ from each other, and that the barbiturates act on the one which mediates responses to the latter, but not the former, kind of stimuli.

This kind of fundamental distinction between the processes mediating unconditioned and conditioned responses to aversive stimuli is also indicated by other observations. It is generally true of classical-conditioned responses that these conform to a modified version of Pavlov's (1927) original stimulus-substitution hypothesis: the properties acquired by a CS as a result of classical conditioning are properties also possessed by the UCS used to establish the CR (Gray, 1975). The case where the UCS is an aversive stimulus is, however, a clear exception to this rule. An electric shock elicits as UCS a great deal of activity (running, jumping, etc.) and noise (squealing) in the rat; but a CS which has been followed by such a UCS elicits exactly the reverse—immobility and silence (Myer, 1971). Similarly, a shock may elicit aggressive behavior if a suitable object of aggression is present, but a CS paired with such shock inhibits such aggressive behavior (Baenninger, 1967; Myer, 1971). Heart rate and respiration have also been seen to follow a similar pattern of inverse sign of change. In human subjects, for example, the cardiac response to shock is acceleration, but to a CS signaling shock it is decleration (Notterman et al., 1952; Obrist et al., 1965). Thus, CSs signaling punishment appear to activate a different behavioral system from the one which mediates responses to punishment itself.

It is possible, however, that the true distinction is not between unconditioned and conditioned aversive stimuli, as proposed here, but between aversive stimuli on the surface of the body (including that most common UCS, electric shock) and aversive stimuli perceived through distance receptors (such as the usual auditory and visual CSs). The latter hypothesis has been strongly argued by Myer (1971). If it is correct, it might then be more plausible to suppose that the barbiturates act upon a brain system specialized for the receipt of aversive stimuli through the distance receptors. The choice between the two hypotheses requires more experimental research, both with and without drugs. For the remainder of this chapter, it will be assumed that the relevant distinction is between conditioned and unconditioned stimuli, and that the barbiturates selectively reduce responses to Pun-CSs.

3.8. Frustrative Nonreward

We come now to the last of the primary reinforcing events set out in Table 1, $\overline{\text{Rew}}$ or frustrative nonreward. There are a large number of experiments which show that the behavioral effects of frustrative nonreward are reduced by the barbiturates. Most of the experimental situations employed involve both $\overline{\text{Rew}}$ itself and $\overline{\text{Rew}}$-CSs, conditioned frustrative stimuli. However, at the end of this section (Section 3.8.5), we shall consider some experiments which suggest that, as in the case of punishing stimuli, the principal effect of the barbiturates is on responses to conditioned stimuli, $\overline{\text{Rew}}$-CSs.

3.8.1. Resistance to Extinction

The simplest situation involving nonreward is extinction of a response previously rewarded on a CRF schedule. In the straight alley injection of SA during such extinction retards extinction (Barry et al., 1962b; Stretch et al., 1964; Ison and Rosen, 1967; Gray, 1969; Capaldi and Sparling, 1971b; Capaldi et al., 1971; Dudderidge and Gray, 1974). Barry et al. (1962) found that when animals given SA in extinction were shifted to placebo for further unrewarded trials, there was no carry-over of the drug-induced increased running speed to the placebo state. This finding parallels those of Barry et al. (1965) and Kumar (1971a) in passive-avoidance situations. No exactly comparable experiments seem to have been performed in the Skinner box. With animals trained on a repeated extinction task in this apparatus, no effects of 5 or 10 mg/kg PB or 20 or 30 mg/kg PhB were seen by Heise et al. (1970) or Stein (1964).

More complex effects are found when the response is rewarded on a partial-reinforcement (PRF) schedule. If a random 50% schedule is used in the straight alley, it is often found that at the end of training PRF animals run faster than CRF animals, especially in the start and run sections of the alley (Goodrich, 1959; Haggard, 1959). This "partial-reinforcement acquisition effect" (PRAE) is abolished by SA, which brings the speed of the PRF group down to the level of CRF-trained animals (Gray, 1969; Capaldi and Sparling, 1971a) or even below (Wagner, 1963). Sometimes, however, the PRF group, which usually runs slower than the CRF group at the beginning of the experiment, continues to do so to the end of training. Such a "reversed PRAE" was also reduced by SA, though not to a statistically significant extent, in an experiment by Ison and Pennes (1969).

The injection of SA during training on a PRF schedule also has important effects on subsequent resistance to extinction. It is well known that animals trained on a PRF schedule subsequently display greater resistance to extinction than animals trained on CRF (Lewis, 1960). Injections of SA during training reduce (Ison and Pennes, 1969; Gray and Dudderidge, 1971), abolish (Gray, 1969; Capaldi and Sparling, 1971a), or even reverse (Gray, 1972) this "partial-reinforcement extinction effect" (PREE) when extinction trials are run without the drug. This alteration of the PREE is due to changes in the drugged PRF condition relative to undrugged PRF controls, the performance of CRF animals being essentially unchanged by the drug. Using a discrimination learning task in a Grice box, McGonigle et al. (1967) have reported a similar reduction of resistance to extinction when

SA was given during PRF acquisition; however, no CRF controls were used in this experiment.

Abolition of the PREE by SA during training is a rather dramatic finding,* since the PREE itself is a large and robust phenomenon. It is possible that it is an instance of drug dissociation or "state-dependent learning" (Overton, 1966), but several points may be urged against this interpretation. First, the drug evidently blocks learning about nonreward in the PRF group, but does not affect learning about reward in either CRF or PRF animals. Thus, the state dependence, if it exists, is behaviorally selective. However, selective state dependence of a similar kind has been observed before (Bindra et al., 1965). More importantly, abolition of the PREE by SA is unlikely to represent dependence of learning about nonreward on the *stimulus* state provided by the drug, since it is known that considerable changes may be produced in the animal's internal and external environment between training and extinction without abolishing the PREE (Ross, 1964).

If the effect of SA on the PREE were an instance of state dependence, one would expect such dependence to be symmetrical, i.e., that transfer from placebo in training to drug in extinction would have the same effect as transfer from drug to placebo. Essentially this result was obtained by Ison and Pennes (1969), who reported that both kinds of transfer abolished the PREE in the start section of the alley, but Gray (1969), measuring only total alley speeds, reported abolition of the PREE in the drug–placebo case, with a less complete reduction of the PREE in the placebo–drug case. The state-dependence hypothesis also predicts that there will be no effect of SA on the PREE if both training and extinction are carried out under the drug. This is the result reported by Ison and Pennes (1969); but Gray (1969) found a reduction in the PREE in this condition which was as great as that observed in the placebo–drug condition. As we shall see below, the difference between Ison and Pennes' (1969) observations and those of Gray (1969) are best attributed to the different numbers of trials used for acquisition in the two experiments. But it is clear from Gray's (1969) results that symmetrical state dependence does not necessarily accompany abolition of the PREE by SA in training. It is therefore a more reasonable hypothesis that this effect of the drug reflects an attenuation of behavioral responses to nonreward.†

---

* Recently, Dyck et al. (1975) have investigated the analogous "partial-punishment effect," i.e., increased resistance to continuous punishment produced by training under a partial punishment schedule. In agreement with the data on the PREE, they found that SA given during partial-punishment training abolishes the partial-punishment effect.

† Some authors have considered the possibility of "asymmetrical" state dependence, in which the transfer of learning from drug to placebo is reduced, but the transfer from placebo to drug is essentially normal (Berger and Stein, 1969), and several such instances have been described (e.g., Berger and Stein, 1969; Holloway, 1972). However, an examination of the model proposed by Berger and Stein(1969) to account for such findings shows that this description is in no important way different—except in being more general—from the hypothesis proposed here.

If SA is injected during extinction (and not in training) after acquisition on a PRF schedule, it may sometimes (Gray, 1969; Gray and Araujo-Silva, 1971) but not always (Stretch et al., 1964; Ison and Pennes, 1969) *reduce* resistance to extinction, whereas, as we have seen, injected during extinction after CRF it increases resistance to extinction. What may be a similar phenomenon has been described in the Skinner box by Griffiths and Thompson (1973, 1974): injection of 20–24 mg/kg PB at the start of extinction after training on FR 20 reduced the large burst of responding seen in early extinction in control animals. However, the large dose used in these experiments renders comparison with the SA runway studies difficult. It has been suggested (Gray, 1969) that the reduction of resistance to extinction produced by SA injected after PRF training is due to a blockage by the drug of the cues from conditioned frustration which, according to Amsel's (1962) theory of the PREE, become, after PRF training, discriminative stimuli (S^D) for performance of the rewarded response. On this view the most likely reason for the discrepancy between the results obtained by Stretch et al. (1964) and Ison and Pennes (1969), on the one hand, and Gray (1969) on the other, is the different numbers of training trials used in the three experiments (30, 40, and 64, respectively). The larger number of training trials used by Gray would have more completely counterconditioned the cues from conditioned frustration to their role as S^Ds for performance of the rewarded running response. It is in agreement with this interpretation that SA increased resistance to extinction after the 30 training trials of Stretch et al. but had no effect on resistance to extinction after Ison and Pennes' 40 trials.

The need to take into account such experimental details as these, and the power of frustration theory in dealing with them, is brought out again by an interesting experiment by Capaldi et al. (1971). These workers first showed that a shift from spaced-trial acquisition (24-hr intertrial interval, ITI) to massed-trial extinction (3–4 min ITI) virtually abolished the PREE, reducing in particular the resistance to extinction of PRF-trained rats. They argue convincingly that this effect is due to the fact that massed extinction trials cause a greater emotional response (frustration) than spaced extinction trials; and, furthermore, that, since frustration declines with time since nonreward, the level of frustration during massed-trial extinction was greater than the level which had become counterconditioned as an S^D for running on the nonreward/reward transitions of spaced-trial acquisition. From this account and the hypothesis that SA reduces the emotional effects of $\overline{\text{Rew}}$, they predicted—and found—that injection of this drug during massed extinction after spaced acquisition would *increase* the PREE by reestablishing the relatively low level of frustration under which the PRF animals had learnt to run. Thus, while Gray (1969) found that SA in extinction reduced resistance to extinction in PRF-trained rats and thereby reduced the PREE, and Capaldi et al. (1971) found the reverse effects, both findings are intelligible within the general context of frustration theory (Amsel, 1962) and the hypothesis that SA reduces the emotional effects of nonreward.

3.8.2. Discrimination Learning

It is clear from the foregoing that SA is remarkably effective in antagonising the effects of nonreward as measured by resistance to extinction. The same effective action appears when one considers discrimination learning. In a black–white successive discrimination in a spatial array, Ison and Rosen (1967) found that SA impaired the animal's ability to withold the response to the negative stimulus, while not altering responding to the positive stimulus. In the straight alley, Guillamon and Gray (unpublished) trained rats on a fixed alternating reward/nonreward schedule, so that they ran fast on rewarded trials and slow on nonrewarded ones; injection of SA caused them to run faster on the nonrewarded trials without affecting speed on rewarded trials. In an ingenious variant of this type of experiment Howard and McHose (1974) used a double-alternation procedure (Rew, Rew, Rew, Rew, Rew, Rew, . . .) in which an odor trail left by a "donor" animal served as the cue to the experimental animals as to whether the current trial was to be rewarded or not (Ludvigson and Sytsma, 1967; McHose, 1967). Administration of SA to the *donor* animals abolished the patterned running (fast on rewarded trials, slow on nonrewarded ones) otherwise shown by the *experimental* animals. This result suggests that SA prevents the release of a pheromone occasioned by frustrative nonreward.

Inability to withhold response to the negative stimulus in successive discriminations after administration of PB has been reported in the Skinner box in rats (Weissman, 1959), pigeons (Blough, 1957), and squirrel monkeys (Hanson *et al.*, 1967). Gray (1964a), however, found no effect of SA in rats. In cats, Schallek *et al.* (1972) found that 20 mg/kg PhB increased responses to the negative but not the positive stimulus for a milk-rewarded door-opening response. In rhesus monkeys, Bakay Pragay *et al.* (1969) reported an increase in errors of commission on a matching-to-sample task under 10 and 15 mg/kg secobarbital. The ability to withhold responses to the negative stimulus is also impaired when such responses are punished by postponement of the opportunity to obtain reward (a "time-out" procedure), as shown by McMillan (1967) using 1–3 mg/kg PB with squirrel monkeys. In a simultaneous black–white discrimination with rats, a measure of choice failed to show any effect of SA, though response speed to the incorrect stimulus was higher under the drug (Caul, 1967). However, in the same experiment, SA significantly retarded reversal of the discrimination. Caul (1967) attributes this result to the attenuation by the drug of the effects of nonreward at the beginning of reversal learning. Since there was no effect of the drug on initial acquisition of the discrimination in this experiment, the effect on reversal learning could not be attributed to a reduced ability to discriminate the cues. Similar, but nonsignificant, findings were reported by Meltzer *et al.*

3.8.3. Intermittent Schedules in the Skinner Box

The attenuation by the barbiturates of the behavioral effects of $\overline{\text{Rew}}$-CSs probably underlies the effects of these drugs, documented in Section 3.1, on simple FI and FR schedules in the Skinner box. As pointed out by Staddon (1970, 1972), the delivery of reward on these schedules constitutes a signal that reward will *not* be available for further responding for some period of time. It is this role of reward as a $\overline{\text{Rew}}$-CS which probably gives rise to the diminished rates of response which immediately follow reward (the postreinforcement pause on FR schedules and the initial segment of the "scallop" on FI schedules). Thus, any attenuation of behavioral control by $\overline{\text{Rew}}$-CSs should lead to a reduction in the FR postreinforcement pause and an increase in response rate particularly in the early part of the FI scallop. There is good evidence in support of that part of this deduction which applies to the effects of the barbiturates on behavior maintained by FI schedules (Dews, 1956, 1964; Rutledge and Kelleher, 1965; Laties and Weiss, 1966; McKearney, 1970; McMillan, 1973). Indeed, it has been shown in several experiments that the increase in response rate produced by the barbiturates on FI schedules is inversely proportional to the control response rate (Dews, 1964; McKearney, 1970; McMillan, 1973; Barrett, 1974).

This observation has been interpreted as showing that barbiturates increase low rates of response *per se,* irrrespective of the nature of the factors giving rise to the low rate (Dews, 1964; Kelleher and Morse, 1968). In an elegant test of this rate-dependence hypothesis, Dews (1964) devised an experiment in which a stimulus (the house light) was present or absent on a fixed alternating schedule during successive equal segments of a long FI. The stimulus was never present when reward was finally delivered and thus constituted an explicit $\overline{\text{Rew}}$-CS, as indicated by the fact that the subjects (pigeons) produced extremely low response rates in its presence. In the absence of the house light, response rates were similar to those controlled by an ordinary FI schedule; i.e., they grew steadily as the interval progressed. Dews now argued that, if SA selectively increases response rates which are kept low by the inhibitory effects of nonreward, this drug should produce greater increments during the house-light segments of the FI than would be expected merely on the basis of the response rates observed in those segments. In fact, the increments in response rate produced by 20 and 33 mg/kg SA were not greater than those observed for segments of the fixed interval which, without the house light, produced equally low control rates of response. Knowledge of the control response rate was alone sufficient to predict the increment produced by the drug, irrespective of the presence or absence of the explicit $\overline{\text{Rew}}$-CS.

From this result Dews (1964) concludes that there is no specific antagonism between SA and the behavioral changes produced by nonreward. This conclusion is, of course, contradicted by the evidence summarized in the previous two sections, only some of which is itself interpretable within the rate-dependence hypothesis. However, Dews' argument can be seen to be mistaken, once it is remembered that the whole of the fixed-interval behavior is under the control of a second $\overline{\text{Rew}}$-CS—the delivery of the previous reward—which fades as the interval progresses (Staddon, 1970, 1972). Thus, the control rate of response, both in the presence and the absence of the house light, reflects the degree of inhibitory control exercised by $\overline{\text{Rew}}$-CSs. It is therefore to be expected that the rate-incremental effects of a drug which counteracts such inhibitory control will be proportional to the extent to which that control is present.

There are in any case other observations which render rate dependence untenable as a general account of the effects of the barbiturates. We have already discussed McMillan's (1973) experiment showing that the drug-produced increment in a punished FI was greater than in an unpunished FI with control response rate equated (Section 3.2). Barrett (1974) used a conjunctive schedule in which pigeons had to complete both an FR requirement on one key and an FI requirement on another. There was a rate-dependent rate-increasing effect of PB (3–12 mg/kg) on both schedules, but the rate increase on FI was systematically greater than the increase from the same control rate on FR. Other exceptions to the rate-dependence hypothesis appear to be due to the degree of exteroceptive stimulus control to which the behavior is subject. Thus, McKearney (1970) repeated Dews' (1964) experiment but varied the stimuli used to signal nonreward: When it was a house light, the rate-dependent result found by Dews was obtained again; but when it was on the response key itself, the increase in response rate produced by SA was actually *less* during the segments when this stimulus was present than the increase in other segments of the FI matched for control rate. A similar result was reported by Laties and Weiss (1966) in a comparison between a simple FI schedule and one with an added exteroceptive "clock": Presence of the exteroceptive stimuli indicating the elapsed proportion of the FI prevented the rate increase produced by PB from reaching the magnitude predicted by pure rate dependence.

Another schedule in which there is an implicit $\overline{\text{Rew}}$-CS is that of differential reinforcement of low rates. The requirement of this schedule is that the subject allow at least t seconds to elapse between successive responses for reward to be obtained. Thus, the making of a response (and the delivery of reward if the response is successful) provides stimuli which predict nonreward for any further responses till t seconds have passed. It is not surprising, therefore, that the barbiturates (PB and PhB) disrupt DRL performance in the rat, especially by increasing the proportion of responses made at short interresponse intervals (Sidman, 1956; Kelleher and Cook, 1959; Kelleher *et al.*, 1961; Stretch and Dalrymple, 1968). In the pigeon also, Dews (1960) found an increased response rate when PB was administered to animals responding on a DRL schedule. Furthermore, the increase in rate produced by the drug was greater the *higher* the control rate—the converse of the prediction from the rate-dependence hypothesis.

3.8.4. Incomplete Reduction of Reward

The barbiturates reduces the behavioral effects not only of complete removal of reward, but also of reduction in reward to a nonzero level. This has been demonstrated by Rosen *et al.* (1967) in an experiment on the Crespi (1942) depression effect. This phenomenon is observed in a group of rats trained on a high reward in the straight alley and then shifted to a low reward. Such animals reduce their running speed after the shift to the level of controls which were always run with the low reward, and, over the first few postshift trials, to a level actually lower than this. It is the latter "undershoot" which constitutes the depression effect, and it was specifically this which was blocked by SA (Rosen *et al.*, 1967). The drugged animals, however, did adjust their running speed down to a level appropriate to the lower postshift reward. Thus, an animal injected with SA is able to process the information that reward has been reduced and adjust its performance accordingly; but the emotional consequences of reduction in reward, which appear to be reflected in the depression effect (Crespi, 1942), are blocked by the drug.

Crespi (1942) also described an "elation effect" when animals are shifted from low to high reward. As in the case of reward downshift, two separate changes take place after reward upshift: The animals adjust their running speed to a level equal to that of animals always trained on the high reward, and there is an initial and temporary "overshoot" to a level higher than this. It is the overshoot which constitutes the Crespi elation effect. Ison and Northman (1968), using Crespi's classic runway situation, failed to find an elation effect with SA, but the results do not unequivocally demonstrate the presence of an elation effect in the undrugged controls. Using an operant analog (Baltzer and Weiskrantz, 1970) of the two Crespi effects, however, Ridgers and Gray (1973) showed that SA, in the same animals at the same time, reduced the depression effect but did not alter the elation effect. As in the Rosen *et al.* (1967) study, SA did not alter the animal's ability to adjust its response rate to reward size; only the undershoot produced by unexpected reward reduction—and not the overshoot produced by unexpected reward increase—was blocked by the drug. In contradiction of the Ridgers and Gray (1973) findings, however, Rabin (1975) has recently reported the abolition of the elation effect in Crespi's original runway situation, using sucrose quantity and concentration as the reward variable. Baltzer and Weiskrantz (personal communication) have also found that amobarbital, chlordiazepoxide, and diazepam significantly attenuated both the depression and the elation effects in rats in the Baltzer and Weiskrantz (1970) situation.

3.8.5. The Aftereffects of Nonreward

In sharp contrast to the sensitivity to barbiturates of other situations involving $\overline{\text{Rew}}$, the situation first introduced to demonstrate the behavioral effects of this operation—Amsel and Roussel's (1952) double runway—has remained obstinately refractory. In the double runway the rat encounters two alleys, with two goalboxes, sequentially. In the first goalbox it is rewarded on a random PRF schedule; in the second, on CRF. It has been frequently observed that the speed of running in the second alley after nonreward in the first goalbox is greater than the speed of running after reward there, and that it is greater than the speed of running in the second alley demonstrated by controls either always or never rewarded in the first goalbox (Amsel and Roussel, 1952; Wagner, 1959; Gray and Dudderidge, 1971). This "frustration effect" (FE) was taken by Amsel (1958) to reflect the summation of a "frustration drive," with the drive motivating approach to the second goalbox, or, more simply, the invigorating effects of frustrative nonreward. However, other interpretations are possible. It might reflect the aversive effects of $\overline{\text{Rew}}$, so that the animal is both running toward the second goalbox and away from the first (Gray, 1975). Staddon (1970) has offered an interpretation of the FE according to which reward in the first goalbox signals a period of time when reward will not be available, thus reducing performance vigor; but whereas this explanation fits well with Staddon's own studies of operant analogs of the FE (Staddon and Innis, 1969), it does not apply so easily to the original Amsel and Roussel situation.

Whatever the correct explanation of the FE, it is clear that it is unaffected by SA in doses which have profound effects in other situations involving $\overline{\text{Rew}}$. Such negative findings have been reported by Ison *et al.* (1967), Freedman and Rosen (1969), Ludvigson (1967), Gray (1969), and Gray and Dudderidge (1971). The Gray and Dudderidge (1971) experiment went on to investigate extinction (with no further drug injections) in the first half of the double runway. The same animals which had showed no effect of SA on the FE when this drug was actually in the circulation nonetheless showed the usual attenuation of the PREE measured subsequently without the drug. Thus, the drug was undoubtedly present in quantities sufficient to reduce other behavioral effects of nonreward at the time that the FE was unchanged. It is relevant to note that lesions to the septal area and to the hippocampus, which as we shall see below reduce other behavioral effects of $\overline{\text{Rew}}$-CSs and Pun-CSs in much the same way as does SA, also leave the FE unchanged (Swanson and Isaacson, 1969; Mabry and Peeler, 1972; Dickinson, 1972, 1974).

The immunity of the FE to SA obviously requires explanation. One possibility (Gray, 1969) is that it represents a pure aftereffect of $\overline{\text{Rew}}$ and involves no $\overline{\text{Rew}}$-CSs (i.e., it is an unconditioned frustration effect with no conditioned frustration). One might then be able to conclude, as in the case of Pun and Pun-CSs, that SA affects behavioral responses only to *conditioned* stimuli signaling the primary aversive event. This hypothesis has some evidence in its favor, but other evidence goes against it.

In its favor are some of the experiments which have investigated the effects of SA on the PREE. Analysis of the mechanisms at work in the PREE strongly suggests that this phenomenon can be produced in two different ways (Black and Spence, 1965; Spence et al., 1965; Sutherland and Mackintosh, 1971). In one (the "intertrial" route), the animal subjected to a PRF schedule comes to use the immediate aftereffects of $\overline{\text{Rew}}$ as cues for the performance of the partially reinforced response (Capaldi, 1967). In the other (the "intratrial" route), there are two processes: First, stimuli emanating from the experimental environment become $\overline{\text{Rew}}$-CSs and evoke a state of "conditioned frustration"; second, internal stimuli from this state become cues for the performance of the partially reinforced response (Amsel, 1962). Now, in most experimental situations the PREE is undoubtedly produced by both routes. However, it is possible to maximize the degree to which one or another is involved by manipulating a number of experimental parameters. It appears that the intertrial route is favored by short intertrial intervals, few trials and large rewards, and the intratrial route by the converse of these conditions (Black and Spence, 1965; Spence et al., 1965). If SA attenuates the behavioral effects of $\overline{\text{Rew}}$-CSs but not those of $\overline{\text{Rew}}$ itself, the drug should block the PREE optimally under those conditions which favor the intratrial route.

Existing data tend to fit this expectation. The experiments by Ison and Pennes (1969) and Gray (1969) were almost identical, except for the number of trials during acquisition, which were 40 and 64, respectively. The blocking of the PREE by SA was much greater in Gray's experiment (the larger number of trials favoring the intratrial route). Ziff and Capaldi (1971) used conditions which undoubtedly favor the intertrial route: only six trials, a short intertrial interval (1.5 min), and a large reward (18 pellets). Their experiment is so far the only report of a complete absence of effect of SA during training on the PREE. In contrast, Dudderidge, Gray, and de Wit (unpublished; see Gray, 1972) used conditions maximally favorable to the intratrial route: a 24-hr ITI, making it unlikely that the intertrial route could be used at all. The effects of SA during training on the PREE in this experiment were dramatic: The drugged PRF group actually extinguished significantly faster than the drugged CRF group (which, as usual in these experiments, did not differ from the undrugged CRF controls). This "reversed PREE" may indicate that the nonrewarded trials were obliterated so totally by the drug that performance in extinction was a direct function of the number of rewarded trials (19 and 10 in CRF and PRF groups, respectively).

Two findings however, disturb this consistent pattern.

Gray (1969) directly tested the hypothesis that SA does not alter the behavioral effects of $\overline{\text{Rew}}$ in an experiment using Adelman and Maatsch's (1956) jump-out procedure. In this, rats are first trained in a straight alley on

CRF. They are then placed on extinction and allowed to escape from the goalbox by jumping onto a ledge. They learn to do this more rapidly, and subsequently show greater resistance to forced extinction of the ledge-jumping habit, than animals rewarded for jumping with food (Adelman and Maatsch, 1956). There is reason to suppose that the animals jumping out of the now-empty goalbox during extinction of the running response are escaping the aversive effects of $\overline{\text{Rew}}$. In that case, the jump-out response, like the FE, may reflect only the aftereffects of $\overline{\text{Rew}}$, with no contribution from $\overline{\text{Rew}}$-CSs. If so, it should be unaffected by SA. However, Gray (1969) showed that injections of SA slowed down the learning of the jump-out response in the extinguished animals, although in animals rewarded for the jump-out response with food, learning was actually improved by the drug.

This result weakens the hypothesis that the direct aftereffects of nonreward are not affected by SA. However, the jump-out response may not be a pure index of such aftereffects. Unlike the FE, which may appear at full strength almost immediately after the first nonrewards experienced by the animal (e.g., Gray, 1969), the jump-out response shows a definite learning curve (Adelman and Maatsch, 1956; Gray, 1969). It is possible that this learning curve reflects, at least in part, the acquisition by the goalbox of secondary aversive properties.

A more definite challenge to the hypothesis that SA affects only responses to $\overline{\text{Rew}}$-CSs is posed by an experiment of Capaldi and Sparling (1971a). These investigators ran PRF animals on a schedule in which, on some days, nonrewarded trials occurred before rewarded trials, so that there were (in Capaldi's terminology) "N–R transitions"; on other days nonrewarded trials occurred only after rewarded trials, and there were no N–R transitions. According to Capaldi's (1967) theory of the PREE, which emphasizes the intertrial route, it is only on N–R transitions that the aftereffects of nonreward can become S^Ds for performing the rewarded response, and therefore only these transitions contribute to the increased resistance to extinction of PRF-trained animals. Capaldi and Sparling (1971a) therefore injected SA in some animals only on days containing N–R transitions and in others only on days not containing N–R transitions. In the former case, the PREE was attenuated; in the latter it was unaffected. Thus, in direct contradiction to the other results reviewed above, this experiment suggests that SA reduces responses to the direct aftereffects of $\overline{\text{Rew}}$ and has no other consequences.

One possible explanation for this result is that the design of Capaldi and Sparling's (1971a) experiment could have allowed animals to learn an association between N–R transitions and being in either a drugged or an undrugged state. (There is much evidence that drug states can indeed act as stimuli in this way: Overton, 1966.) Thus, animals given N–R transition under SA might have run slowly in extinction under saline because they had learnt that saline was a cue for only N–N transitions, i.e., for continued nonreward after a single nonrewarded trial. The details of Capaldi and

Sparling's (1971a) results actually fit this interpretation well; but only further research can resolve the issue.

Guillamon and Gray (unpublished) directly tested Capaldi and Sparling's (1971a) hypothesis that SA blocks the aftereffect of nonreward by examining the effect of this drug on the "patterned running" generated by a single alternation schedule of reward and nonreward in the straight alley. On such a schedule, rats develop the pattern of running fast on R (reward) trials and slow on N (nonreward) trials. In terms of Capaldi's aftereffects theory, therefore, the aftereffect of nonreward is a cue for the fast running on R trials, while the cue for slow running on N trials is the aftereffect of reward. Thus, if SA blocks the aftereffect of nonreward, the consequence should be a reduction in running speed on R trials. Such an effect was not observed after injection of SA in Guillamon and Gray's experiment. Instead, patterned running was eliminated because the drug greatly increased running speeds on N trials. This result is consistent with the hypothesis that SA influences conditioned frustration. On this view, the aftereffect of reward acts as the conditioned stimulus for conditioned frustration, and the drug reduces the inhibitory effect of this state on the instrumental response.

One further finding is relevant to the argument of this section. James (unpublished) has investigated the effects of SA on performance in the schedule devised by Khavari (1969). This is a discrete-trial schedule in the Skinner box in which the contingencies are of two kinds. After a trial which eventuates in reward, the probability of reward for pressing the bar on the following trial is 0.5. After a trial which eventuates in nonreward, the probability of reward for pressing the bar is zero, and it remains at zero until the animal refrains from responding for one trial. After a trial on which the animal does refrain from responding, the probability of reward for bar pressing reverts to 0.5. Thus, the animal has to use the aftereffect of nonreward as a cue to withhold responding on the next trial; the aftereffect of reward, in contrast, is a cue to respond on the next trial. According to James' findings, SA selectively impairs the animals's ability to withhold responding on trials following nonreward. Taken on its own, this finding could suggest an impairment in the control of behavior by the aftereffects of nonreward; taken in conjunction with Guillamon and Gray's findings described in the previous paragraph, however, it suggests that the critical variable is not the cue for the behavior (aftereffect of reward or of nonreward), but the nature of the behavior for which it is a cue (withholding a response followed by nonreward or making a response followed by reward).

There is, however, one further observation in James' experiment which once again raises the possibility of an influence of the drug on aftereffects as such. James varied the interval between trials and found that SA impaired performance only when this was 30 sec or more; at 20 sec, performance was unaffected. He suggests, therefore, that the drug influences the memory for nonreward, which is, of course, very similar to Capaldi's notion of an aftereffect of nonreward. Furthermore, he points out that experiments on the FE in the double runway have all employed a detention time in the first goalbox which is less than 30 sec. Thus, it remains possible that one might demonstrate an effect of SA on the FE with a longer detention time. Clearly, the question whether SA influences the aftereffect of nonreward remains open.

3.9. Conclusion

We may conclude this review of the effects of the barbiturates on emotional behavior by offering a tentative answer to the first of the three questions to which, as indicated in the Introduction, this chapter is addressed. The simplest adequate description of the behavioral changes produced by these drugs is that *they selectively antagonize the behavioral effects of Pun-CSs and $\overline{Rew}$-CSs*. In subsequent sections we shall see whether this description fits equally well the effects of ethanol and the benzodiazepines.

4. THE BEHAVIORAL INHIBITION SYSTEM

In the preceding section we have concentrated on showing that low doses of the barbiturates, especially SA, selectively antagonize the behavioral effects of Pun-CSs and $\overline{Rew}$-CSs, without paying any particular attention to the nature of these effects or to the psychological processes which might underlie them. The most obvious description of these effects—and, indeed, the one which is necessarily true if one is correctly to describe a stimulus as "punishing"—is that responses followed by Pun-CSs and $\overline{Rew}$-CSs come to be reduced in probability or are "suppressed." But clearly response suppression of this kind is not the whole of the story. It could not, for example, give rise to the PRAE, in which, as we have seen, animals trained with a random mixture of rewarded and nonrewarded trials reach an asymptotically higher performance level than animals trained with rewarded trials alone; nor could it account for the similar increment in response vigor sometimes seen when a response is both rewarded and punished, as compared to a response given the same number of rewards alone (Fowler and Miller, 1963). Is it possible to obtain a more adequate description of the psychological processes to which Pun-CSs and $\overline{Rew}$-CSs give rise and which, presumably, are in some way impaired by SA?

I have considered this question in detail elsewhere (Gray, 1975; Gray and Smith, 1969), and I shall here only summarize the conclusions reached there. These conclusions constitute a brief description of what I have called "the behavioral inhibition system" (BIS) (Gray, 1975, 1976).

As noted above, the nature of the conditioned response to Pun-CSs is in many respects not only different from, but actually opposed to, the unconditioned response to an aversive UCS. In this respect, classical conditioning with an aversive UCS constitutes a clear-cut exception to the modified stimulus substitution rule (Gray, 1975) according to which conditioned stimuli acquire, as the result of classical conditioning, only properties also possessed by the UCS with which they are paired. Nonetheless, in other respects classical conditioning with an aversive UCS appears to conform to the usual laws of classical conditioning, and, furthermore, such classical conditioning is able to confer on an initially neutral stimulus much the same response-suppressive capacity as can be derived from actually punishing the same response (Church et al., 1970). These facts led the writer to propose (Gray, 1971a) that there is a special "behavioral inhibition system" which is innate in its response outputs but is activated only by particular kinds of conditioned stimuli, notably Pun-CSs. The animal, as it were, knows (innately) how to respond to stimuli which warn of danger, but has to learn (by classical conditioning) which stimuli convey such warnings.

How, then, does an animal respond to Pun-CSs? Still summarizing conclusions for which the arguments are presented elsewhere, one may answer this question thus: by suppressing any ongoing operant behavior (whether maintained by Rew or $\overline{\text{Pun}}$); by increasing attention to the environment, especially novel features of it; and by incrementing the level of arousal (Gray, 1964b), so that whatever activity is finally undertaken is undertaken with a higher vigor than would otherwise have been the case. The first and last of these changes, and the way in which they interact with each other, have been specified more exactly in a mathematical model outlined by Gray and Smith (1969).

By the "behavioral inhibition system," then, is meant a system which produces these basic kinds of output upon receipt of Pun-CSs. The formation of the Pun-CSs themselves is thought to take place according to the same general processes as are involved in other forms of classical conditioning. But the behavioral inhibition system is not activated only by Pun-CSs. Another class of stimuli with the same capacity is that of $\overline{\text{Rew}}$-CSs. As reviewed by Gray (1967, 1975; see also Wagner, 1966, 1969), the similarities between the behavioral properties of Pun-CSs and $\overline{\text{Rew}}$-CSs are so great as to warrant the hypothesis that these two kinds of stimuli are functionally equivalent, i.e., that they act upon a common psychological system. More tentatively, there is a third class of stimuli one can add: that of novel stimuli (Gray, 1975). These too suppress ongoing operant behavior and classical conditioned responses (the latter effect being termed "external inhibition" by Pavlov, 1927); they increase attention (directed to themselves in the "orienting reflex": Sokolov, 1960); and they increase level of arousal (Sokolov, 1963; Vinogradova, 1961).

If the BIS is activated by novel stimuli, as well as by Pun-CSs and $\overline{\text{Rew}}$-CSs, then given the effects of SA on behavior caused by the latter two stimulus classes one might expect this drug also to impair the behavioral effects of novel stimuli. There are experiments which support this hypothesis.

Ison et al. (1966) used a procedure in which rats are placed in the stem of a T-maze, separated by glass partitions from the two arms, of which one is black and one white. After 3 min the rat is removed, one of the arms is changed so that they are now both black or both white, the partitions are removed, and the rat is returned to the stem of the maze. Normal rats respond by preferentially entering the arm whose brightness has been changed (Dember, 1956). Ison et al. (1966) found that SA significantly reduced this tendency to approach novelty, the drugged animal choosing randomly between the two arms.

McGonigle et al. (1967) reported similar observations on the effects of SA on learning about novel stimuli. In their experiment rats were trained on 50% random PRF for choosing the positive cue (black vs white) in a Grice box, the negative cue being unrewarded. They were then shifted to a combined-cue discrimination (black vs white and horizontal vs vertical stripes) in which the old positive cue remained positive. During this stage of the experiment half the animals received SA. Finally, transfer tests were conducted with only horizontal and vertical cues and no drug. Animals which had received SA during the combined-cue phase of the experiment failed to demonstrate any learning of the novel cue, although controls chose correctly on 81% of transfer trials.

A third procedure used to study responses to novelty is simple spontaneous alternation. On successive runs in a T-maze rats tend to alternate their choice of arms. This tendency is significantly reduced by SA (Grandjean and Båttig, 1962; McNaughton, unpublished). However, Sinha et al. (1958), using a version of this procedure in which the animal was first given zero, one, two, or three forced runs to one side of the T-maze, found no effect of SA when no forced runs preceded the alternation trial; with prior forced running, they found an *increase* in alternation under SA. The reason for this discrepancy is unknown, but it may be connected with the use by these authors of the selectively bred MR and MNR strains. We have already seen that the response of the Maudsley strains to SA in the shuttlebox is variable and unusual (Powell, 1967; Gupta and Holland, 1969); we shall see later that the MNR strain has acquired electrophysiological differences from its Wistar forebears which may underlie unusual behavioral responses to the minor tranquilizers.

We may therefore conclude this section with a tentative answer to the second question posed in the Introduction: *The barbiturates exercise their tranquilizing effects on behavior by antagonizing the behavioral inhibition system.*

5. THE EFFECTS OF ETHANOL ON EMOTIONAL BEHAVIOR

In this and the following section the argument is extended to other drugs with similar effects to those of the barbiturates. Now that the behavioral principles which apply to the barbiturates have been set out, it will be possible to review the behavioral effects of these other drugs more rapidly. We commence with ethanol. As in the section on the barbiturates, it may be assumed that, unless otherwise stated, the subjects are rats and the route of injection i.p.; the most commonly used doses with rats are in the range 1000–1500 mg/kg, and dose will be specified only if it is important or departs radically from this range. Again, it is the effects of relatively low doses of ethanol which are of interest.

5.1. Rewarded Behavior

The effects of ethanol on simple rewarded behavior are small and inconsistent. In the straight alley it has been reported to produce faster running on early trials, possibly due to reduced fear of the novel apparatus (Barry et al., 1962b; Nelson and Wollen, 1965). At asymptote, running speed has been reported variously to be unaffected by ethanol (Barry et al., 1962b; Barry and Miller, 1962, 1965), to be decreased (Nelson and Wollen, 1965; Barry and Miller, 1965, with 1800 mg/kg), or to be increased (Grossman and Miller, 1961). Conger (1951) measured the physical strength of pull exerted against a restraining harness in rats trained to run in an alley for food reward: Ethanol failed to alter strength of pull, although in a parallel experiment it substantially reduced the strength of an avoidance response. In cats, Masserman and Yum (1946) and Masserman et al. (1945) found that complex chains of food-rewarded responses were disturbed by ethanol, although simpler responses were not affected. Miller and Miles (1936) made similar observations in rats in a complex maze: Ethanol injected after training was complete decreased running speed, increased variability of performance, and increased errors. However, the increase in errors is probably best attributed to a loss in the effectiveness of nonreward for entering blind alleys.

In the Skinner box, Barry (1968) found that the latency to first barpress (to turn on an illumination condition associated with reward) was shortened by ethanol, whereas Moskowitz and Asato (1966) found an increase in the latency of a discriminated bar press for food. Studying more conventional schedules in this apparatus, Hendry and Van Toller (1964) found no effect of ethanol on CRF response rate. Cook and Davidson (1973) found virtually no effect of the drug on VI response rate over the range 125–1000 mg/kg, though there was a reduction at 2000 mg/kg. FI rate was found to be increased, but nonsignificantly, by Freed (1972). FR rate was increased by 200 and 400 mg/kg, unaffected by 800 mg/kg, and decreased by 1200 and 1600 mg/kg (Holloway and Vardiman, 1971). In cats, FR performance has also been found to be increased by 800 mg/kg p.o. (Goldman and Docter, 1966).

There have been several studies of the effects of ethanol on reward processes as measured by self-stimulation. Vrtunski et al. (1973) found an increased response rate with 800 mg/kg, no effect with 1200 mg/kg, and reduced response rate with 1600 mg/kg; the duration of the bar-press response was an increasing function of the dose, and the peak force of the response showed a similar trend. Olds (1966) found a reduced response rate with 1500 mg/kg, yet Crow (1970) found no effect with 1880 mg/kg.

5.2. Passive Avoidance

The effects of ethanol on passive avoidance in a spatial array are as consistent as those on rewarded behavior are not. In two classic studies Masserman and his collaborators (Masserman et al., 1945; Masserman and Yum, 1946), working with cats, punished a complex chain of food-seeking behavior (crossing a barrier, closing a switch, and opening the lid of a food well) with shock or an air blast. This treatment produced an inhibition of the food-seeking behavior in undrugged animals, but this inhibition was lessened by ethanol whether the drug was administered during the initial exposure to punishment or subseuqent to suppression of the rewarded responses. Smart (1965) conducted a partial replication of Masserman's work, with shock presented either for the instrumental response or after actual commencement of eating, but presented no shock during the test trials with ethanol. There was no effect of ethanol (120 mg/kg by stomach tube) on the suppression of food-seeking behavior, but there were reductions under the drug in a number of "neurotic" patterns of behavior, as also observed in Masserman's experiments (e.g., resisting being put in the apparatus, attempts to escape from it).

Smart's failure to replicate Masserman's basic result is unlikely to be due to his omission of shock on the drug-test trials, since Conger (1951), in another well-known study, used this design with rats in the straight alley, giving ethanol after suppression of running by shock was complete. The drug significantly enhanced resumption of running. In a second experiment Conger used the strength-of-pull technique to measure the intensity of the avoidance tendency established by shock in the goalbox. Rats were shocked in the goalbox and allowed to run out of it toward the other end of the alley. Ethanol significantly reduced the force exerted against the restraining harness half-way along the alley. As noted above, the same technique revealed no effect of ethanol on the strength of rewarded approach to the goalbox. In a third experiment Conger tested the possibility that his results were due to the change of drug state inherent in the designs of the first two experiments. To do this he trained rats to discriminate between sober and intoxicated states by punishing running to food under one state but not the other. It was considerably easier for the rats to make the required discrimination when ethanol accompanied the safe trials than when the significance of the drug was reversed. Thus, in addition to the cue properties of the drug, there was a direct reduction of behavioral inhibition by the drug.

Conger's basic result has been repeated in several other experiments with the rat. Barry and Miller (1962) used the "telescope alley" described in the section on barbiturates (Section 3.2) and obtained the same result with ethanol as with SA: the drug increased the speed and distance that the rat ran to a goalbox containing both food and the threat of shock, and its effect was greater the greater the threatened intensity of shock. On safe trials, however, i.e., one on which the shortest alley threatened no shock, the drug actually reduced running speed. To control for drug-produced stimulus change in the Barry and Miller (1962) experiment, Grossman and Miller (1961) used a 2 × 2 factorial design: ethanol or saline during training combined with ethanol or saline during testing. The drugged rats ran further and faster toward the conflicted goal whether the drug state during training had been ethanol or saline. Three further successful replications of Conger's result have been reported by Freed (1967, 1968, 1971). In his first report Freed (1967) compared doses of 500, 1000, and 1500 mg/kg and also measured blood alcohol concentration: maximum approach toward the conflicted goal occurred at a blood alcohol concentration of 0.11%. In his 1968 paper he used an alley with a lever in the goalbox and administered shock either for bar pressing or upon eating the food delivered by the bar press: in both cases ethanol reduced passive avoidance. A failure to affect passive avoidance was reported by Harris et al. (1964); but this was a complex experiment in which the punished behavior was itself a one-way active avoidance response. More complicated results were reported by Holloway (1972) using two further kinds of passive avoidance situation. In a one-trial dark-avoidance task with a 2 × 2 factorial design (drug vs saline on the shock trial, drug vs saline on the test trial) 1500 mg/kg ethanol on the shock trial impaired passive avoidance whether or not the drug was also present on the test trial. In a punished step-down task, also using a 2 × 2 factorial design, a similar effect of the drug was found only in the drug (training)–saline (test) condition. In neither of Holloway's (1972) experiments was there much effect of ethanol administered on the no-shock test trials after saline during the shocked training trials, nor was there any effect of a lower dose of ethanol (500 mg/kg).

In three experiments species other than cats or rats have been used. MacInnes and Uphouse (1973) have shown that ethanol (1500–3000 mg/kg) reduces passive avoidance in mice punished for entering a dark compartment. Raynes et al. (1968) found impaired passive avoidance in Siamese fighting fish immersed in an ethanol solution (285 mg/100 ml H_2O) and shocked for attacking a target fish. Tamura (1963), using a situation like Masserman and Yum's (1946), observed resumption of a previously punished feeding response in dogs injected with a 30% ethanol solution (0.9 ml/kg) intravenously. Thus, the impairment produced by ethanol in passive avoidance in a spatial array is found in a variety of species and with a variety of punished responses.

In the Skinner box, in contrast, ethanol has not so far been found clearly to reduce passive avoidance. There are two positive reports of such an effect, both using the Geller–Seifter schedule described in the section on the barbiturates (Section 3.2). Freed (1972) found that ethanol, voluntarily ingested by the rat in unknown quantities as a result of schedule-induced polydipsia (Falk, 1971), increased response rate during early exposure to the punished part of the schedule; however, with increased exposure to the situation the difference between ethanol and control conditions disappeared. Cook and Davidson (1973) found a clear reduction of the suppressive effects of punishment, along with an actual decrease in the rate of unpunished responding, with 1000 and 2000 mg/kg ethanol p.o. Against this must be set two negative reports. Barry *et al.* (1963) used a situation in which periods of safe VI responding were interrupted by periods during which a tone of increasing intensity was sounded. Intermittent unpredictable shocks were delivered during this tone, of an intensity correlated with the intensity of the tone, when the animal approached the vicinity of the bar. Whereas SA reduced the suppression of bar pressing during the tone, 1200 mg/kg ethanol further decreased the rate of response. An even greater reduction in response rate was seen during safe periods, so it is probable that Barry *et al.* were merely observing a general sedative effect. It seems unlikely, however, that this explanation can account for Hendry and Van Toller's (1964) finding that a range of doses of ethanol (500–2000 mg/kg) all produced similar decreases in response rate in rats whose bar pressing was rewarded with water on CRF but also punished with shock on FR 10 or 20. Such decreases were not seen in two control rats given CRF water only.

Clearly, the effects of ethanol on punished responding in the Skinner box warrant further attention. The fragility of the results so far obtained is all the more surprising in that Vogel-Sprott (1967) has reported positive results in an operant experiment with human subjects: administration of 1000–1600 mg/kg ethanol reduced the suppression of button pressing (rewarded with pennies) caused by punishment with shock.

5.3. Classical Conditioning of Fear

Lauener (1963), in a study of the on-the-baseline CER discussed in the section (Section 3.3) on the barbiturates, found no effect of a range of doses of ethanol (200–1600 mg/kg p.o.), even though a range of barbiturates was effective in the same study. Cicala and Hartley (1967) studied the off-the-baseline CER, giving ethanol (600–1200 mg/kg) either during the CS–shock pairings or during test sessions or both; there was no significant effect of the drug on the CER under any of these conditions. In cats, Goldman and Docter (1966) saw an alleviation of the off-the-baseline CER under the drug (800 mg/kg p.o.), but this could be accounted for by the increase it also produced in the baseline response rate. Thus, experiments on conditioned suppression are consistent in showing no effect of ethanol on classically conditioned fear.

Other techniques have, however, disclosed effects of ethanol on conditioned fear. Anisman (1972) gave rats CS–shock pairings on one side of a shuttlebox under drug or placebo; controls were treated the same except that shocks were omitted. All rats were then given standard shuttlebox training with the CS as warning signal, half under ethanol and half under placebo factorially combined with drug or placebo in the classical-conditioning phase of the experiment. The results showed that the initial classical conditioning improved avoidance learning (presumably by conferring conditioned fear-eliciting properties on the CS) and that this facilitation was blocked by ethanol during the conditioning session. A second experiment, by D. R. Williams, is reported briefly by Miller and Barry (1960): Ethanol (750–2250 mg/kg) reduced the potentiated startle response, i.e., the increase in the magnitude of the startle to a tone when this is preceded by a light that has been paired with shock. The startle response to the tone without the light was unaffected by the drug. Other findings (Gibbins *et al.*, 1971; Section 5.7 below) also show that the unconditioned startle response is not reduced by ethanol. In contrast to these two positive reports, Hidalgo *et al.* (1968) found only slight effects of 500 mg/kg ethanol p.o. on a conditioned cardiac response in dogs. Thus, the question whether ethanol has any reliable effect on the classical conditioning of fear remains unresolved.

5.4. Escape Behavior

In the rat, Barry and Miller (1965) found reductions in shock-cscape running speed in the straight alley wtih 1200 and 1800, but not 600 mg/kg, ethanol; but these effects were not different from the effects on rewarded running speed. Skurdal *et al.* (1975) also found a reduction in escape running speed with 1200 mg/kg. In the mouse, Deutsch and Roll (1973) found no effect of ethanol during training on a choice shock-escape response, but improvement during retraining under ethanol on the same task whether initial training had been under ethanol or saline. In goldfish, Scobie and Bliss (1974) reported increased swimming to escape shock when the fish were immersed in an ethanol solution. Thus, the available data do not suggest any consistent effect of ethanol on escape behavior.

5.5. One-Way Active Avoidance

Active avoidance in several one-way tasks has been found not to be affected by ethanol: discriminated bar pressing (Graham and Erickson, 1974), pole-climbing (Chittal and Sheth, 1963; Banerjee, 1971), and jump-up (Holloway, 1972; Holloway and Wansley, 1974). When impairments were seen in these tasks, it was at high doses, e.g., 4000 mg/kg (Graham and Erickson, 1974, bar pressing) or 3200 mg/kg (Newman *et al.*, 1972, jump-up).

In a Sidman avoidance task in the Skinner box Reynolds and van Sommers (1960) found improved performance with a dose of 1500 mg/kg and impaired performance with 2900 and 3700 mg/kg, whereas Heise and Boff (1962) found impaired performance with 1300 mg/kg.

5.6. Two-Way Active Avoidance

Ethanol has been reported to facilitate shuttlebox performance in rats, mice, and goldfish, especially during the initial stages of learning.

In rats, earlier experiments failed to find any effect of ethanol on performance in the shuttlebox (McMurray and Jaques, 1959; Broadhurst and Wallgren, 1964; Walgren and Savolainen, 1962). More recently, facilitation has been observed, either slight (Crow, 1966), substantial (Holloway, 1972), or very marked (Chesher, 1974; Izquierdo et al., 1974). The earlier negative reports may be perhaps attributed to dose (1000 mg/kg in Mc-Murray and Jaques' experiment as against 1500 and 2000 mg/kg in Holloway's and Chesher's experiments), to the use of the Maudsley strains by Broadhurst and Wallgren, and to the administration of the drug when training was complete (and the passive avoidance component therefore already overcome) in Wallgren and Savolainen's experiment. In the latter experiment the drug produced an impairment in performance, but only at doses above 2000 mg/kg. A more definite discrepancy to the general pattern of results is provided by Anisman's (1972) report that a dose of 1200 mg/kg retarded shuttlebox avoidance learning over the first 20 trials, this effect having disappeared by trial 30. There is no obvious reason for the difference between Anisman's results and those reported by Crow (1966), Chesher (1974), Holloway (1972), and Izquierdo et al. (1974).

In mice, Anisman and Waller (1974) used an automated Y-maze task which shares with the shuttlebox the feature that the subject has to keep returning to the area from which it has just fled. Ethanol (1200 mg/kg) improved performance over the first 30 trials, but had no effect when administered on the second day of training (60 trials/day). Ethanol on day 1 of training, however, impaired learning of the correct response (entry into the illuminated arm of the Y), as indicated by performance on day 2.

There are several reports of ethanol-produced facilitation of shuttlebox performance in goldfish (Scobie and Bliss, 1974; Petty et al., 1973; Bryant et al., 1973). In the studies by Petty et al. and Bryant et al. only 20 trials were run, so the facilitation occurs on early acquisition trials. These investigators obtained facilitation whether shuttling was reinforced by shock avoidance or light avoidance. In the Scobie and Bliss (1974) experiment, two days' training were conducted at 100 trials/day; the effects of ethanol were marked during the first day, but considerably reduced on the second day. In none of these experiments did the facilitation of shuttling appear to reflect merely drug-induced increases in general activity. Goldfish have also been studied in an automated Y-maze in which incorrect responses are punished when the fish bumps into a transparent barrier. Ryback's (1969) data from this task, as reanalyzed by Scobie and Bliss (1974), show a significant facilitation by ethanol. Since the goldfish studies were carried out by immersing the fish in an ethanol solution, conventional doses cannot be given for these experiments. The solutions successfully used ranged from 350 mg/100 ml H_2O to 865 mg/100 ml in the various experiments. However, Ryback and Ingle (1970) and Ryback (1969) found an impairment in the Y-maze task with a solution of 650 mg/100 ml; this impairment was obtained after two hours' exposure to the ethanol solution but not after six hours' exposure.

5.7. Responses Elicited by Aversive Stimuli

It is clear from the foregoing that, like the barbiturates, the effects of ethanol on instrumental responding with aversive reinforcement consist principally and perhaps solely in a reduction of passive-avoidance behavior, together with an improvement in two-way active avoidance which is probably a consequence of this change in passive avoidance. The question arises therefore whether the reduction on passive avoidance may be due to a general reduction in the felt intensity of aversive stimuli. However, the evidence is against this possibility.

Gibbins *et al.* (1971) found a *reduction* in the flinch and jump thresholds to electric shock with chronic administration of relatively large doses of ethanol (> 3000 mg/kg), though it seems that this was due to adaptation to shock taking place in the controls rather than to an actual lowering of threshold in the drugged rats. In goldfish a definite reduction in the threshold intensity of electric shock eliciting a body twitch was observed by Scobie and Bliss (1974) with ethanol solutions of 350–1100 mg/100 ml. Raynes *et al.* (1968) have reported similar findings in Siamese fighting fish.

Aggressive responses to aversive stimuli are reduced by ethanol only in relatively large doses. Thus, Křsiak and Borgesová (1973) observed a reduction in aggressive behavior in paired male rats of which one was treated with 1200 or 3000 mg/kg ethanol p.o.; however, all social activities were equally reduced by these drug treatments. In contrast, using shock-elicited fighting, Weitz (1974) observed increased aggression with 600 and 1200 mg/kg, but not with 1800 mg/kg. Increased aggressive behavior has also been observed when one male mouse was introduced into the home cage of another, both having received 25 mg/kg ethanol (Chance *et al.*, 1973). In cats in which defensive aggression was elicited by electrical stimulation of the ventromedial hypothalamus, MacDonnell *et al.* (1971) found shorter latencies to a hissing response after 370 mg/kg and longer latencies after 1500 mg/kg ethanol. Similarly, aggressive display was increased in Siamese fighting fish immersed in low concentrations (258 mg/100 ml H_2O), but decreased in fish immersed in high concentrations (650 mg/100 ml), of an ethanol solution

(Raynes et al., 1968; Raynes and Ryback, 1970). Similar observations were made with Convict Cichlid fish by Peeke et al. (1973). Thus, these various studies concur in suggesting a facilitatory effect of ethanol in low doses on aggressive responses to aversive stimuli, with impairments only occurring as part of a nonspecific sedation.

5.8. Frustrative Nonreward

There have been regrettably few studies of the effects of ethanol on behavioral responses to nonreward. The results so far reported, while suggestive of an antagonistic action on these responses, are inconclusive.

In the straight alley Barry et al. (1962b) found that resistance to extinction after CRF was increased by 1200 mg/kg ethanol injected during extinction, whether acquisition had been conducted under ethanol or placebo. In an earlier experiment, however, Miller and Miles (1936) had found the reverse effect—slower running speed—when they injected rats with 800 mg/kg ethanol during extinction of a complex maze-running response. Nelson and Wollen (1965) have reported abolition of the PRAE in the straight alley with 1200 mg/kg ethanol. As in the similar findings with SA (Wagner, 1963; Gray 1969), the performance of the two drugged groups was similar to that of the undrugged CRF animals, indicating that the invigorating effect of the nonrewarded trials in the PRF condition had been blocked by the drug. Surprisingly, given this result, Taylor et al. (1968) were unable to alter the PREE by administration of 1200 mg/kg ethanol during acquisition, extinction taking place without the drug. Since the comparable design has large and reproducible effects with SA (see above), this experiment should be repeated.

There are virtually no data available from discrimination-learning tasks. Blough (1956) found that errors were increased in a conditional discrimination in the Skinner box when pigeons were given 1600 mg/kg ethanol. In the Miller and Miles (1936) rat experiment, ethanol injected during rewarded performance in their complex maze similarly increased errors (entry into blind culs). Both these results are suggestive of a reduced effect of nonreward for incorrect responses under the drug, but fall far short of demonstrating such an effect.

The final line of evidence suggestive of reduced effects of nonreward under ethanol comes from a consideration of the influence of ethanol on schedule-controlled behavior in the Skinner box. As we have seen (Section 5.1), there is some evidence that low doses of ethanol increase response rates on FR. It is unfortunate that FI has hardly been studied, since this schedule shows up very clearly the effects both of the barbiturates and of the benzodiazepines. Somewhat more attention has been paid to DRL performance. Earlier studies reported little effect of ethanol up to 1000 mg/kg (Sidman, 1955; Laties and Weiss, 1962). Sanders and Pilley (1973) also saw no effect up to this dose, but found that higher doses (1300–1700 mg/kg) shifted the distribution of interresponse intervals toward shorter values, as also seen for the barbiturates on this schedule. Holloway and Vardiman (1971) and Holloway and Wansley (1973) found a rather different dose–response relationship, but the same basic effect: Significant response rate increases were observed at doses from 400 mg/kg to 1000 mg/kg, with rate decreases at 1500–1600 mg/kg.

5.9. Responses to Novelty

The only relevant experiment known to the reviewer is by Cox (1970), who found a reduction in spontaneous alternation in rats treated with 2000 mg/kg ethanol.

This brings to a close our review of the effects of ethanol on emotional behavior. We shall postpone summarizing the results of this review until we have made a similar examination of the behavioral effects of the benzodiazepines.

6. THE EFFECTS OF THE BENZODIAZEPINES ON EMOTIONAL BEHAVIOR

6.1. Rewarded Behavior

In the straight alley, speed of running for food on CRF is reduced by chlordiazepoxide (CDP) in doses of 5–20 mg/kg (Barry and Miller, 1965; Iwahara, Iwasaki *et al.*, 1966; Tessel and Lash, 1968; Rosen and Tessel, 1970). Wanner and Bättig (1965) made similar observations, but also noted improvements in performance with 2.5 mg/kg CDP.

In the Skinner box, Fowler (1974) saw no effect of 2.5–10 mg/kg CDP on CRF response rate in rats. Using a larger dose, 25 mg/kg, Stolerman (1971) found a slight reduction in rate. On FR schedules, CDP produces rate increases in rats over the range 0.5 to 15 mg/kg, with rate reductions occurring at 20 mg/kg (Bainbridge, 1968; Wedeking, 1968; Thomas, 1973). Wedeking (1973) failed to find on FR 10 the response rate increases he had previously (Wedeking, 1968) observed on FR 25, but he did find prolonged responding to satiation with 2.5 and 5 mg/kg CDP. In squirrel monkeys, Cook and Catania (1964) found little change in FR performance with 2.5–5 mg/kg CDP, but substantial drops in rate at 20–40 mg/kg. Response rate increases are also caused in rats on FI schedules by CDP over the range 5–40 mg/kg (Richelle *et al.*, 1962; Djahanguiri and Richelle, 1963; Richelle and

Djahanguiri, 1964; Fontaine and Richelle, 1969). Similar results with CDP on FI schedules have been obtained in cats by Richelle (1962, 1969) and in squirrel monkeys by Cook and Kelleher (1962) and Cook and Catania (1964). In pigeons, Bignami and Gatti (1969) found only unsystematic overall rate changes on FI with 5–40 mg/kg CDP or 0.5–5 mg/kg diazepam (DZP). However, both drugs increased the proportion of responses emitted during the early part of the fixed interval. McMillan (1973), also studying pigeons on FI, found no effect with up to 3 mg/kg CDP, 1 mg/kg DZP, or 56 mg/kg oxazepam (OZP), with rate reductions occurring at 5.6–10 mg/kg CDP, 3 mg/kg DZP, and 100 mg/kg OZP. Rats on VI schedules do not show consistent rate changes under CDP except for reductions at comparatively high doses (Geller *et al.*, 1962; Fontaine and Richelle, 1969; Cook and Davidson, 1973; Sepinwall *et al.*, 1973; Miczek, 1973*b*). Similar lack of consistent effect on VI response rates is shown by DZP (Miczek, 1973*b*) and temazepam (Longoni *et al.*, 1973). CDP has also been reported to be without consistent effect on VI response rates in squirrel monkeys (Cook and Davidson, 1973; Miczek, 1973*b*), as has DZP (Miczek, 1973*b*). Margules and Stein (1968) reported strong suppression of VI responding in rats given 20 mg/kg OZP, but tolerance to this effect developed within seven days and it did not appear at all in animals previously exposed to this and other benzodiazepines.

Domino and Olds (1972) studied self-stimulation in rats. Facilitation was found at 2.5 mg/kg and 5 mg/kg CDP; at 40 mg/kg depression was found. At intermediate doses individual differences were noted, animals with high control rates tending to show greatest facilitation under the drug. No effect was found on the threshold current able to sustain self-stimulation. Gandelman and Trowill (1968) found no effect on the speed of acquisition of self-stimulation behavior of 15 mg/kg CDP. An earlier report by Olds (1966) had indicated that the effects of the benzodiazepines depend in part on the placement of the electrode. With placements in the posterior hypothalamus, facilitation of self-stimulation was found with CDP and DZP, both at 5 mg/kg; however, with placements in the anterior hypothalamus, Olds (1966) observed a reduction in response rate with CDP and facilitation with DZP. Results reported by Margules and Stein (1967) suggest that the facilitatory effects of the benzodiazepines on self-stimulation may depend on a reduction in an aversive component of the brain stimulation. These workers found particularly strong facilitation of responding with OZP given to rats which had shown mixed positive and negative reactions to the stimulation. This hypothesis has received strong support from a study by Panksepp *et al.* (1970). They divided their rats into ten which showed response rate increases under 15 mg/kg CDP and six which showed rate decreases: Eight of the former group, but only one of the latter, subsequently learned to escape from experimenter-applied stimulation at the same brain sites. These workers also observed that rats whose response rate for suprathreshold brain stimulation was depressed by CDP nonetheless showed rate increases under the drug at threshold currents. They attribute this finding to a reduction by the drug of the aversive effects of frustration; this is plausible since CDP increases resistance to extinction of self-stimulation (Gandelman and Trowill, 1968; see below, Section 6.8).

Overall this pattern of results does not suggest any consistent effect of the benzodiazepines on reward processes. The rate increases on FI and FR schedules are similar to those seen with the barbiturates and will be discussed again in the section on frustrative nonreward. Unlike the barbiturates, however, CDP seems rather consistently to depress running speed in the straight alley.

6.2. Passive Avoidance

While the evidence is not as impressive as in the case of the barbiturates and ethanol, it is reasonably well established that the benzodiazepines reduce passive avoidance in a spatial array. Morrison and Stephenson (1970) found that avoidance of one open arm of an otherwise enclosed elevated Y-maze was significantly reduced by 60 mg/kg CDP and 6-24 mg/kg DZP, but this effect was not produced by 7.5-30 mg/kg CDP or by 3 or 12 mg/kg DZP. Kumar (1971b), also studying rats in a Y-maze, established fear of one arm by shocking the animal in it; avoidance of this arm was reduced (though the effect was small) by 7.5 and 15 mg/kg CDP; 30 mg/kg, however had the reverse effect, perhaps by making the rats generally inactive. Oishi *et al.* (1972) used a two-compartment apparatus in which passive avoidance of the smaller one was set up by shocking the rat there when it entered. Retention tests were carried out two and three days later. On the acquisition trial and on each retention test the rats were given either 20 mg/kg CDP or saline in a 2 × 2 × 2 factorial design. CDP on the one shock trial reduced passive avoidance on both subsequent retention tests; CDP on the retention tests themselves did not have this effect; and asymmetrical state-dependence occurred, passive avoidance being least in the groups switched from drug in acquisition to saline during retention testing. In mice, Fuller (1970) found a reduction in passive avoidance (staying on one side of a two-compartment apparatus on penalty of shock) with 5-20 mg/kg CDP in four different strains, the drug effect increasing with increasing baseline levels of activity in these strains. Boissier *et al.* (1968b) also found that suppression of movement by shock in the mouse was alleviated by CDP (8-16 mg/kg) and DZP (1-4 mg/kg); higher doses (32 mg/kg CDP and 8 mg/kg DZP) did not have this effect.

In contrast to the small amount of experimental effort invested in the examination of the effects of the benzodiazepines on passive avoidance in spatial arrays, and the small effects observed in them, there is a large and consistent literature on the effects of these drugs on punishment in the Skinner box. Much of this work has used variants of Geller and Seifter's (1960) schedule (see Section 3.2). It has regularly been found in rats that the benzodiazepines (CDP, DZP, OZP, nitrazepam, medazepam, and others) reduce the punishment-produced suppression of responding (Geller *et al.*, 1962; Geller, 1964; Margules and Stein, 1967, 1968; Goldberg and Ciofalo, 1969; Davidson and Cook, 1969; Blum, 1970; Cannizaro *et al.*, 1972; Cook and Davidson, 1973; Rudzik *et al.*, 1973; Stein *et al.*, 1973; Robichaud *et al.*, 1973; Miczek, 1973a; Sepinwall *et al.*, 1973). This increase in punished response rate, furthermore, is not accompanied by similar increases in the unpunished component of the multiple schedule, which is normally unchanged up to high doses, when decreases in rate are seen. Doses at which rate increases are seen in the punished component with little or no change in the unpunished one have been reported for CDP as 2.5–40 mg/kg p.o., with DZP and OZP being, respectively, approximately 3.5 and 1.8 times more potent on a milligram-per-kilogram basis (Cook and Davidson, 1973; Sepinwall *et al.*. 1973).

The studies cited above were performed with rats; but similar findings have been reported for squirrel monkeys (Cook and Catania, 1964; Hanson *et al.*, 1967), pigeons (Wuttke and Kelleher, 1970; McMillan, 1973), and pigs (Dantzer and Roca, 1974). That the effect of the benzodiazepines on punished responding is not merely an instance of rate dependence (Dews, 1958; Kelleher and Morse, 1968) has been shown by Cook and Catania (1964) with monkeys and by McMillan (1973) with pigeons. In these reports it was shown that, although in both punished and unpunished components the increase in response rate induced by CDP was greater the lower the predrug rate, nonetheless punished responding increased more than unpunished responding matched for response rate. Miczek (1973a) similarly found in rats that CDP produced greater rate increases for behavior suppressed by punishment than for behavior of an equivalent control rate produced by nonreward.

Other techniques in the Skinner box besides the Geller–Seifter procedure have also been used to demonstrate attenuation of punishment-produced response suppression by the benzodiazepines (Zbinden and Randall, 1967; Miczek, 1973a, experiment 1; Sepinwall *et al.*, 1973, experiment 2; Bremner *et al.*, 1970). Outside the Skinner box another nonspatial task (suppression of drinking by shocks administered through the drinking tube) was used by Vogel *et al.* (1971) to show the same basic effect in rats given CDP (6 and 8 mg/kg), DZP (2 and 4 mg/kg), and OZP (3–12.5 mg/kg), and by Miczek (1973a) in squirrel monkeys given CDP (1–10 mg/kg).

6.3. Classical Conditioning of Fear

The effects of the benzodiazepines on the classical conditioning of fear are less clearly established than their effects on punishment.

Most of the positive reports have come from studies of the on-the-baseline CER in rats, though even in this situation negative findings have been reported by Fontaine and Richelle (1969) using 2–12 mg/kg CDP. Cicala and Hartley (1967) gave CDP either during CER training (10 mg/kg) or during CER testing without shock (5, 7.5, or 10 mg/kg) in a 2 × 2 factorial design. The effect on the CER of the drug given at either time approached but did not attain significance ($p < 0.1$). More definite reductions in the CER were reported by Lauener (1963), on a DRL baseline (Section 3.3), and by Miczek (1973b), with doses of CDP from 5 to 40 mg/kg. Miczek (1973b) included an important control by showing that the drug had no effect on "positive" conditioned suppression, i.e., the reduction in response rate seen when the UCS signaled by the CS is an appetitive one. Thus, the reduction in conditioned suppression produced by CDP is specific to an aversive UCS. Tenen (1967) used drinking as his baseline and used a single CS–shock pairing. Drugs (31.6 mg/kg CDP, 17.8 mg/kg DZP, and 10 mg/kg nitrazepam) were administered before a no-shock testing session, and all produced significant reduction in the suppression of drinking. In a second experiment, Tenen (1967) injected CDP either before the CER training session or before both the training and the testing sessions; the former procedure produced only an insignificant reduction in the CER (as in Cicala and Hartley's experiment), the latter a significant reduction. Thus, Tenen's (1967) two experiments between them suggest an effect of CDP on the expression of conditioned fear, but not on its conditioning. Consistently with this view, Holtzman and Villareal (1969) observed a reduction in the CER when rhesus monkeys were given 4 mg/kg DZP after long training had produced a stable level of 80–90% conditioned suppression. This was also the general procedure followed by Lauener (1963) and Miczek (1973b) in their experiments.

The on-the-baseline CER experiments, then, suggest that the benzodiazepines reduce the expression of conditioned fear. Exactly the opposite conclusion is suggested by the results of Scobie and Garske (1970), working with the off-the-baseline CER. Like Tenen (1967), these investigators used drinking as the baseline operant, but the CS–shock pairings were carried out with the drinking tube removed from the apparatus. CDP (12 mg/kg) was administered either before the conditioning session or before a no-shock testing session. There was a significant reduction in conditioned suppression when the drug was given before conditioning, but no effect when it was given before testing. In a second experiment the same pattern of results was found for an off-the-baseline CER with bar pressing as the operant. Furthermore, a group given CDP both before the conditioning session and the test session was also significantly less suppressed than controls, and so the effect of the drug given before conditioning was not an instance of drug dissociation. Stein and Berger (1969) used essentially the same design as Scobie and Garske's (1970) first experiment and administered OZP (20 mg/kg) or another benzodiazepine, Wy 4036 (0.5–2 mg/kg), only before the test session, which was conducted a week after the off-the-baseline training session. Like Scobie and Garske (1970), they found no evidence for a reduction in the expression of conditioned fear—indeed, the reverse was the case, for these drugs significantly *increased* conditioned suppression of drinking. This surprising effect was not produced by 15 or 25 mg/kg CDP, which left conditioned suppression unaltered.

These two off-the-baseline CER experiments, then, do not support the notion, suggested by the on-the-baseline experiments, that the benzodiazepines reduce the expression of conditioned fear. Instead Scobie and Garske's (1970) results suggest that there is an effect of CDP on the conditioning of fear. However, Chisholm and Moore (1970), also studying an off-the-baseline procedure, though of a rather different kind, found no such effect. These workers trained rabbits in a shuttlebox and interspersed off-the-baseline conditioning sessions with a CS+ followed by shock and a CS− not followed by shock. CDP (12 mg/kg) was administered before these conditioning sessions. In the test sessions (without the drug) presentation of the CS+ together with the warning signal for the shuttle response decreased response latency in control animals, and the CS− used in the same way increased response latency. Neither of these effects was altered by CDP during the conditioning sessions.

There have been two studies of the classical conditioning of autonomic responses to aversive stimuli under CDP. Yamaguchi and Iwahara (1974), using differential conditionng in rats, found that 20 mg/kg of this drug had very slight effects on the conditioned heart-rate response to the CS+ and none at all on the conditioned respiratory response. Such effects as were observed consisted of increased responding to the CS−. Hidalgo *et al.* (1968), studying a simple conditioned cardiac response in dogs, found this to be blocked by CDP (10–20 mg/kg p.o.) and DZP (10 mg/kg p.o.). But the authors note that these doses produced visible signs of ataxia and sedation.

If these various studies are looked at together, the one consistent finding is that the benzodiazepines reduce the expression of fear in the on-the-baseline CER (Lauener, 1963; Miczek, 1973b; Tenen, 1967; Holtzman and Villareal, 1969). However, the failure to reproduce this finding in the off-the-baseline studies (Scobie and Garske, 1970; Stein and Berger, 1969; Chisholm and Moore, 1970) leaves open the possibility that it is due to an attenuation by the drug of adventitious punishment effects.

6.4. Escape Behavior

In the straight alley, Barry and Miller (1965) found a reduction in speed of shock escape when 5–15 mg/kg CDP was injected after training was complete, but this change was identical to that produced in food-approach behavior. Cicala and Hartley (1965) found only insignificant reductions in escape speed when 5–10 mg/kg CDP was administered on the second two days of training; when the drug was given on the first two days of training, a more substantial reduction in running speed was obtained with 10 mg/kg, 5 mg/kg still being without effect. In a running wheel, Gluckman (1965) also found a reduction in speed of escape with 5 and 10 mg/kg CDP, but DZP was facilitatory up to a dose of 5 mg/kg and oxazepam had no systematic effect up to 30 mg/kg; the latter two drugs produced impairments only at 10 and 40 mg/kg, respectively. In mice, Cole and Wolf (1966) found the ED_{50} for blocking escape responding in the shuttlebox to be very high, 415 mg/kg. Finally, Panksepp (1971), using aversive electrical stimulation of the hypothalamus in rats, found no systematic effect on bar-press escape responding of 10 mg/kg CDP, though Panksepp et al. (1970) found reductions in speed of escape under 15 mg/kg CDP. Thus, the only systematic effect of the benzodiazepines on escape responding appears to be a reduction in running speed with CDP, and this is similar to the effect of this drug on rewarded running behavior (Section 6.1).

6.5. One-Way Active Avoidance

In the straight alley, Barry and Miller (1965) found only slight reductions in running speed when 5–15 mg/kg CDP was administered after training was complete. However, Iwahara and Takahashi (1971) found that 20 mg/kg CDP injected during the initial training trials on a similar task significantly slowed running behavior. In a black–white discrimination, Iwahara and Matsushita (1971) found no effect of 20 mg/kg CDP on correct choices, but there was again a small reduction in speed of response. In a pole-climbing task, CDP (10–15 mg/kg) was found to affect performance only at doses at which ataxia was also seen (Chittal and Sheth, 1963). In the running wheel, Gluckman (1965) found no systematic effect on avoidance performance of CDP (2.5–10 mg/kg) or DZP (1.25–10 mg/kg), although performance was impaired by OZP (10–40 mg/kg).

A number of studies have investigated the effects of the benzodiazepines on Sidman avoidance in rats in the Skinner box. The results have generally disclosed a facilitatory effect at low doses, especially in animals which perform poorly in the undrugged state, followed by depression at high doses, especially in animals with good performance in the undrugged state (Bignami et al., 1971; Takaori et al., 1969).

Thus, Heise and Boff (1962) reported that 2–10 mg/kg DZP produced an increase in Sidman avoidance response rate, whereas from 13 mg/kg up a decrease was seen. The rate of shocks received was increased at doses of 10 mg/kg DZP and above. In the same experiment, CDP produced a response rate decrease above 13 mg/kg and a shock rate increase above 4 mg/kg. Fontaine and Richelle (1969) found only rate decreases with CDP, the dose at which this effect was seen varying from 4–30 mg/kg in different rats. Studying the same avoidance schedule in a circular runway, however, these workers found facilitation of the running response at doses of CDP up to 18 mg/kg, with a reduction in responding only at 40 mg/kg or above. Returning to the Skinner box, Davidson (1970) reported improved Sidman avoidance with doses of 12–40 mg/kg CDP. Using temazepam, Longoni et al. (1973)

found no effect of 5 mg/kg, but doses from 10 to 40 mg/kg increased shock rate. Some order can be brought into this picture by taking account of differences between individual animals. Takaori et al. (1969) noted that the rate of response was increased in rats with a low control rate by 1.25-10 mg/kg DZP, 2.5-10 mg/kg nitrazepam, or (insignificantly) 5-40 mg/kg CDP. In addition, nitrazepam decreased the shock rate. In rats with a good control performance, in contrast, response rate was decreased and shock rate was increased by 2.5-10 mg/kg of either CDP or nitrazepam; CDP reduced response rate in these animals at 40 mg/kg and increased shock rate at 10-40 mg/kg. Similar findings were reported by Gatti and Bignami (1969) and Bignami et al. (1971). These workers reported that 10-60 mg/kg CDP and 1-20 mg/kg DZP reduced shock rate in rats with high shock rates under control conditions, but increased shock rate in rats with low control shock rates. The impairment in the performance of the good avoiders was significant only at higher doses (60 mg/kg CDP and 2 mg/kg DZP) than the improvement in the performance of the poor avoiders (20 mg/kg CDP and 1 mg/kg DZP).

Bignami et al. (1971) suggest that the improvement in Sidman avoidance seen in these experiments is due to an attenuation by the benzodiazepines of the suppressant effects on responding of "shock." In view of the effects of shock and Pun-CSs, respectively, on behavior (discussed in Sections 3.7 and 4), this hypothesis is perhaps better expressed as an attenuation of the suppressant effects on responding of the apparatus cues associated with shock. Bignami and de Acetis (1973) tested the hypothesis by varying certain parameters of the avoidance task. They found that 20-40 mg/kg CDP was able to counteract the increased difficulty in Sidman avoidance produced by a change in these parameters thought likely to increase response suppression; but the drug did not facilitate performance when the schedule was made more difficult in other respects.

Biphasic relationships between benzodiazepine dose and change in bar-press avoidance performance have also been reported in species other than rats. In mice, Sansone et al. (1972) found that acquisition of a discriminated bar-press avoidance response was facilitated by 5 mg/kg CDP (especially during early trials) and retarded by 15 mg/kg, 10 mg/kg being without effect. Since the drug reduced intertrial responses at all doses, the observed facilitatory effects could not be attributed to a general increase in activity. In squirrel monkeys on a Sidman avoidance schedule, Scheckel and Boff (1967) reported increased response rates under 2.5-7.5 mg/kg DZP p.o., with reduced rates above 10 mg/kg; with CDP (10-40 mg/kg) only rate reductions were seen. Cook and Kelleher (1962) also observed an impairment in Sidman avoidance in squirrel monkeys given CDP, but only at doses (20 and 40 mg/kg) which produced ataxia.

From these various studies of one-way active avoidance, it seems possible to conclude that impairments in performance are only seen under the benzodiazepines as a result of general sedation or ataxia. Improvements are sometimes seen at low doses, especially in the Skinner box and especially in animals whose performance in the undrugged state is poor. It seems likely, as suggested by Bignami et al. (1971) and Bignami and de Acetis (1973), that these improvements are due to an attenuation by the drug of the suppressant effects of Pun-CSs on operant responding.

6.6. Two-Way Active Avoidance

Performance in the shuttlebox is facilitated by benzodiazepines, especially during early acquisition. This has been reported by Sachs et al. (1966) with 15 mg/kg CDP, over the first 40 trials; Henriksson and Järbe (1971) with 10 mg/kg DZP, over the second ten-trial session; Iwahara (1971) with 20 mg/kg CDP; Cannizzaro et al. (1972) with 2.5 mg/kg medazepam, over the first 150 trials; Robichaud et al. (1973) with 10 mg/kg CDP in mice; and Fuller (1970) with 5–20 mg/kg CDP, also in mice. Kamano and Arp (1964) found no effect of CDP in the drinking water of rats (approximately 24 mg/kg). When the drug is given after training is complete, however, disruption of performance may be seen (Sachs et al., 1966, with 15 and 30 mg/kg CDP; Chisholm and Moore, 1970, with 10 and 15 mg/kg CDP in rabbits). This pattern is broken by the report of Goldberg et al. (1973), who found in mice that CDP (1.25–20 mg/kg) had no effect when injected during initial acquisition of shuttling, but gave rise to substantial improvement in performance when injected after 500 trials had already been completed. At the high end of the dose range, Cole and Wolf (1966) report the ED_{50} of CDP for the abolition of shuttlebox avoidance in mice as 140 mg/kg.

6.7. Responses Elicited by Aversive Stimuli

The benzodiazepines do not have analgesic effects at doses typically used in the behavioral studies reviewed here (Christmas and Maxwell, 1970; Sternbach et al., 1964; Gluckman, 1965). Conversely, the Geller–Seifter punishment schedule, which is so effective at demonstrating the antianxiety effects of the benzodiazepines, does not show the same effects for morphine, which is of course a powerful analgesic (Geller et al., 1963; Kelleher and Morse, 1964).

With regard to aggressive behavior elicited by aversive stimuli, the picture is more complex. It was originally reported that the benzodiazepines had strong taming effects (Randall, 1960, 1961; Randall et al., 1961; Heuschele, 1961; Heise and Boff, 1961). In recent years this conclusion has been questioned (DiMascio, 1973). It is clear that reduction in aggression is observed with moderate to high doses of benzodiazepines, but there is conflicting evidence as to whether these effects are specific to aggressive behavior or nonspecific changes due to general sedation or muscular incoordination. If they are specific to aggression, it is also not clear whether all forms of aggressive behavior are affected by the drugs or only aggression with a strong component of fear (Hoffmeister and Wuttke, 1969).

Many of the early reports of reduced aggressiveness under the benzodiazepines involved measurement of the animal's response to various forms of "provocation" by the experimenter. With this technique, reduced aggressive behavior has been observed in rhesus, squirrel, and cynomolgus monkeys given CDP or DZP (Randall, 1960; Randall et al., 1960, 1965; Heise and Boff, 1961; Scheckel and Boff, 1967; Delgado, 1973), in cats given DZP (Langfeldt and Ursin, 1971), and in mink given CDP, DZP, and OZP (Bauen and Possanza, 1970). It is difficult in procedures such as these to disentangle aggressive behavior elicited by unconditioned aversive stimuli from fearful behavior elicited by stimuli predictive of such unconditioned stimuli, a distinction which is, of course, basic to our theme (Section 3.7). We shall not therefore consider these studies in detail.

Another series of studies has used electric shock as the UCS to elicit fighting behavior in paired male animals. Christmas and Maxwell (1970) found this type of aggression reduced in rats given CDP (ED_{50} = 35 mg/kg), DZP (ED_{50} = 28 mg/kg), OZP (ED_{50} = 14 mg/kg), or nitrazepam (ED_{50} = 3.8 mg/kg), and also in mice given the same four drugs (ED_{50} = 4.7, 2.1, 4.5, and 1.2 mg/kg, respectively). Similar values were found by Sofia (1969) in mice: ED_{50} = 4.2 mg/kg CDP and 0.9 mg/kg DZP. Randall et al. (1965), however, report higher values of ED_{50} in mice: 40 mg/kg CDP, 10 mg/kg DZP, and 40 mg/kg OZP. In rats again, Quenzer et al. (1974) found reduced aggression with CDP at 15 mg/kg, a small effect also being seen at 5 mg/kg. However, Manning and Elsmore (1972) saw a reduction in shock-elicited fighting only with 40 mg/kg CDP, 10 and 20 mg/kg producing only small changes; these authors noted that their rats appeared distinctly sedated after the effective dose of 40 mg/kg.

A further series of studies has used isolation-induced aggressive behavior, seen when the isolates are brought together in groups of two or more. This type of aggression has been reported to be reduced in mice by 5–15 mg/kg CDP, 7–15 mg/kg DZP, 7.5–15 mg/kg OZP, 7.5–15 mg/kg nitrazepam, and 7.5–25 mg/kg medazepam (Valzelli et al., 1967; Valzelli and Bernasconi, 1971; Valzelli, 1973; Scriabine and Blake, 1962; Sofia, 1969; DaVanzo et al., 1966). However, Le Douarec and Broussy (1969) did not see clear signs of reduced aggression with CDP at doses below 20 mg/kg; and rather high values of ED_{50} are reported for this drug by Sofia (1969) (23 mg/kg) and Cole and Wolf (1966) (52 mg/kg). In contrast, Boissier et al. (1968a) found about 30% suppression of fighting in grouped mice given as little as 1–2 mg/kg DZP.

Given this wide range of effective doses found in experiments on both shock- and isolation-induced aggression, it is not surprising that controversy has arisen as to whether the observed reductions in fighting are specific to this form of behavior or the consequence of a more general sedative or ataxic effect. Different investigators have used different techniques to evaluate the degree to which such general changes take place. Some have claimed that they occur significantly only at doses higher than those at which the changes in aggressive behavior are seen (Zbinden and Randall, 1967; Scheckel and Boff, 1967; Cole and Wolf, 1966; Christmas and Maxwell, 1970); others have claimed the reverse (Hoffmeister and Wuttke, 1969; DaVanzo et al., 1966; Sofia, 1969). It is clear that in many of the reported experiments the effective doses for reduction have been quite high (see above).

They have also been rather variable. In an effort to bring some order into this confusion, Hoffmeister and Wuttke (1969) have suggested that defensive aggression (i.e., behavior aimed at warding off an attack) is reduced by the benzodiazepines, whereas pure attack behavior is not. These authors further suggest that fighting produced by foot shock is defensive aggression, whereas the behavior of an isolated animal toward an intruder is pure attack. In support of this distinction, Hoffmeister and Wuttke (1969) found the ED_{50} for suppression of shock-induced fighting in mice to be 10 mg/kg CDP p.o., while for isolation-induced fighting it was as high as 93 mg/kg, well above the ED_{50} found in their experiments for ataxia in an inclined screen test (33 mg/kg). However, although Hoffmeister and Wuttke's (1969) value for the ED_{50} of CDP on shock-induced fighting is reasonably comparable to the results of other similar experiments on mice, the value of 93 mg/kg is very high compared to other reports on isolation-induced fighting (see above). A further experiment reported by Hoffmeister and Wuttke (1969) showed that 10 mg/kg CDP p.o. reduced defensive aggression in cats (elicited by the experimenter's gloved hand), whereas 31 mg/kg was insufficient to alter male–male fighting. The first part of this result is in line with the reports, briefly mentioned above, of the marked taming effects of the benzodiazepines when "provocation" techniques have been used with other species. Langfeldt and Ursin (1971) also report reduced defensive aggression in cats given 1 mg/kg DZP; however, flight responses to the provocation (with a stick) were not reduced by the drug, as Hoffmeister and Wuttke's hypothesis might lead one to expect. Better support for Hoffmeister and Wuttke's hypothesis was provided by Sofia (1969). He found that shock-induced fighting was reduced in mice by doses of CDP and DZP of 4.2 and 0.9 mg/kg, respectively; the comparable values for isolation-induced fighting were 23.5 and 11.1 mg/kg, respectively, above the values of ED_{50} for ataxia as measured on the rotarod test (9.2 and 7.1 mg/kg). Nonetheless, in view of the variability in the effective doses found in studies both of isolation- and shock-induced aggression (see above), further careful experimentation is clearly needed before this problem can be resolved.

Further complications have been introduced by recent studies which have demonstrated *increased* aggressive behavior when low doses of the benzodiazepines are used, usually on a chronic basis. Since these increases have been seen with isolation-induced fighting (shock-induced fighting not having yet been studied in the same way), these results are consistent with Hoffmeister and Wuttke's (1969) hypothesis that the aggression-reducing effects of the benzodiazepines are confined to shock-induced fighting or other varieties of "defensive" aggression.

Thus, Fox and Snyder (1969) fed mice for six days on a diet containing 0.01% DZP; this regime substantially increased the level of isolation-induced aggression. Similar results were obtained by Fox et al. (1970) when mice were fed a diet containing 0.03% CDP, by Fox et al. (1972) using a diet containing 0.005% nitrazepam or 0.02% flurazepam, and by Guaitani et al. (1971) using a diet containing 0.006–0.03% N-methyldiazepam, DZP, or OZP. The daily dose of drug consumed in these experiments is difficult to compare with acute doses, but it is probably effectively lower than those which have produced reductions in aggressive behavior. It is not possible to decide from these experiments, however, whether the important variable is size of dose or chronicity of treatment. One experiment suggests that it is dose. Miczek (1974), studying fighting in rats competing over a food supply, observed increased aggressive behavior with acute doses of 2.5 and 5 mg/kg CDP; 10 mg/kg was without effect, and 20 mg/kg reduced aggression. Isolation-induced aggression was also increased by acute treatment with CDP in two species of grasshopper mice, but at quite high doses: 15 and 27 mg/kg (Cole and Wolf, 1970).

Experiments which have examined the effects of the benzodiazepines on aggressive behavior elicited by central electrical stimulation do not help resolve the issues raised in this section. Panksepp (1971) found that 10 mg/kg CDP exerted a strong depressant effect on hypothalamically elicited attack in rats; neither bar-press escape from this stimulation nor the unconditioned flight elicited by it was systematically affected by the drug. However, Baxter (1964) found no systematic effect of 5–20 mg/kg CDP on hypothalamically elicited hissing in cats; he did observe, however, a rather mysterious rise in thresholds for hissing over days in his drugged animals, an effect not seen in saline-injected controls.

In conclusion, there is more evidence for a reduction of aggressive behavior by the benzodiazepines than for such an effect with the barbiturates or ethanol. This effect, however, may be confined (apart from nonspecific sedative or motor changes) to types of aggression in which fear is a prominent component, as when the animal is provoked by the experimenter, or shock-induced fighting. Furthermore, there is clear evidence that low doses of the benzodiazepines, usually administered on a chronic basis, increase isolation-induced fighting. The latter effect deserves further study, especially to see whether dose or chronicity of administration is the important factor, and whether other forms of aggression are also susceptible to it. It may also be of considerable clinical and social importance (DiMascio, 1973; Editorial, 1975; Lynch et al., 1975).

6.8. Frustrative Nonreward

Studies of the influence of the benzodiazepines (mainly CDP) on behavioral responses to nonreward are consistent in showing an attenuation of these responses. Rapidity of extinction after CRF is reduced by CDP both in the straight alley (Tessel and Lash, 1968; Iwahara et al., 1967) and in the Skinner box (Heise et al., 1970; Fowler, 1974), the effective doses so far employed ranging from 5 to 20 mg/kg. In the Iwahara et al. (1967) experiment some animals were given the drug both in training and in extinction (as also in Tessel and Lash's experiment), while others were drugged only in extinction. The latter design produces reliable increases in resistance to extinction with SA (Section 3.8.1); but the drug-dissociation effect (Overton, 1966) was so great (see below) in the Iwahara et al. experiment that their results do not permit any conclusion about the effects of CDP on runway extinction when this design is used. Gandelman and Trowill (1968), however, used this design successfully in a study of the effects of 15 mg/kg CDP on extinction of barpressing for electrical stimulation of the hypothalamus: Resistance to extinction was increased when the drug was present during extinction, whether or not it had also been administered during acquisition, and there were no effects of administering the drug during acquisition alone.

In successive discrimination learning in the Skinner box, a number of investigators have reported increased responding in the presence of the negative stimulus in rats (Margules and Stein, 1967, with 10 mg/kg OZP; Wedeking, 1968, 1969, with 0.5–10 mg/kg CDP; Davidson, 1970, with 10 and 20 mg/kg CDP), cats (Schallek et al., 1972, with 10 mg/kg CDP), squirrel monkeys (Hanson et al., 1967, with 12 and 36 mg/kg CDP p.o.), and Japanese monkeys (Hasegawa et al., 1973, with 20 mg/kg CDP). Wedeking's (1968) results might have reflected an overall increase in response rate, since rates during the positive stimulus (reinforced on an FR schedule) were also increased by the drug. In his 1969 experiment, however, correct responses were increased by 5 mg/kg CDP and decreased by 10 mg/kg, although both these doses increased responses to the negative stimulus. Similarly, in the study by Hanson et al. (1967), response rate during the positive stimulus (reinforcement on VI) was increased by 12 mg/kg CDP and decreased at 36 mg/kg, but both these doses increased response rate in the negative stimulus. In contrast to these positive results, Miczek (1973a) observed only insignificant rate increases during the negative stimulus in rats given 10–33 mg/kg CDP. Since the design of his experiment was essentially the same as that of Hanson et al., it is not clear why Miczek's results differ from those of other workers in this field.

Returning to the straight alley, Iwahara et al. (1966) reported a slight reduction in the PRAE with 10 mg/kg CDP and its abolition with 20 mg/kg. The further study by this group of the PREE (Iwahara et al., 1967) is difficult to interpret owing to the strong drug-dissociation effect observed. The design was a 2 × 2 × 2 factorial one (CRF vs PRF, drug or placebo in training, drug or placebo in extinction), the drug again being 20 mg/kg CDP. However, the fall in running speed on the first day of extinction in all groups which experienced a change in drug condition was so great that it is difficult to evaluate rate of extinction in these groups. However, it is clear from inspection of the graphs of Iwahara *et al.* (1967) that the PREE was less in the drug (in training)–drug (in extinction) condition than in the placebo–placebo condition, as is also the case for SA (Gray, 1969). This experiment deserves repetition with a dose of CDP smaller than 20 mg/kg.*

There have been two experiments on the Crespi depression effect. Rosen and Tessel (1970), using 1 or 15 food pellets as reward in the straight alley, were able to eliminate the depression effect with 5 and 10 mg/kg CDP, but not 2.5 mg/kg, the drug being injected throughout both pre- and postshift testing. Preshift running speed under the drug was significantly greater in the high than in the low reward condition, indicating that, as is also true for SA (Rosen *et al.*, 1967; Ridgers and Gray, 1973), the drug does not affect the basic perception of reward magnitude. Vogel and Principi (1971), using sucrose (4 or 32%) as the reward and licking as the response, injected 8 mg/kg CDP postshift only. This treatment increased the depressed performance of the down-shifted (32–4%) group to the level of the unshifted (4–4%) controls. A further test day without the drug indicated no carryover from the drug day; this result resembles that found for the effects of SA on extinction (Barry *et al.*, 1962b).

As already mentioned (Section 6.1), response rate increases are produced by the benzodiazepines in the Skinner box in animals trained on FR (Bainbridge, 1968; Wedeking, 1968; Thomas, 1973) and FI (Richelle, 1962, 1969; Richelle *et al.*, 1962; Djahanguiri and Richelle, 1963; Richelle and Djahanguiri, 1964; Cook and Kelleher, 1962; Cook and Catania, 1964; Fontaine and Richelle, 1969). The rate increase on FI is in part due to an increased proportion of responses being emitted early in the fixed interval (Richelle, 1962, 1969; Richelle *et al.*, 1962; Richelle and Djahanguiri, 1964; Cook and Catania, 1964; Fontaine and Richelle, 1969), and this effect may be observed even where there is no overall rate increase under the drug (Bignami and Gatti, 1969). In Cook and Catania's (1964) experiments with squirrel monkeys given CDP (10–15 mg/kg), the disruption of the FI scallop was seen whether the reinforcement was food or termination of shock. However, given the postulated equivalence between termination of negative reinforcers and presentation of positive ones (Gray, 1975; Section 2), this finding is not incompatible with the view that disruption of the FI scallop is due to a reduction in the response-suppressant effects of $\overline{\text{Rew}}$-CSs (Section 3.8.3). Rate increases, with an increase in the proportion of short interresponse intervals, have also been observed on DRL schedules after CDP in rats (Richelle *et al.*, 1962; Sanger *et al.*, 1974) and pigeons (McMillan and Campbell, 1970), though in the latter case the effect was not consistently

---

* Feldman and Gray (unpublished) have recently been able to attenuate greatly the PREE with 5 mg/kg CDP given either in training alone or in both training and extinction.

seen in all birds. As explained earlier (Section 3.8.3), all these changes in performance in the Skinner box under various intermittent schedules of reinforcement are consistent with a drug-produced reduction in the inhibitory effects of $\overline{\text{Rew}}$-CSs, though they do not constitute very direct evidence for such a reduction.

6.9. Responses to Novelty

The only finding of direct relevance to the question whether the benzodiazepines impair reactions to novelty is that CDP reduces spontaneous alternation in the rat (20 mg/kg: Grandjean and Bättig, 1962; Iwahara *et al.*, 1972) and the ferret (5 and 7.5 mg/kg: Hughes and Greig, 1975). However, Douglas and Scott (1972) failed to affect spontaneous alternation with 10 or 50 mg/kg nitrazepam orally administered to rats.

7. THE BEHAVIORAL EFFECTS OF THE MINOR TRANQUILIZERS: AN OVERVIEW

In this section we briefly summarize the conclusions reached in the previous four sections concerning the behavioral effects of the minor tranquilizers.

7.1. Rewarded Behavior

When a range of rewarded behavior patterns is investigated, none of the drugs reviewed is found to have consistent effects which can be interpreted as an alteration in basic reward processes. Self-stimulation studies confirm this conclusion. It is consistently found that response rates are increased on certain kinds of intermittent schedule in the Skinner box (FI, FR, DRL), though there is a shortage of data on the effects of ethanol in this respect. However, the most likely explanation for these effects is that they are due to a reduction in the response-suppressant effects of $\overline{\text{Rew}}$-CSs. The benzodiazepines (or rather CDP, since only this has so far been studied in this connection) appear to slow running speed in the straight alley in a way which is not characteristic of the barbiturates or ethanol.

7.2. Passive Avoidance

The minor tranquilizers all reduce passive avoidance in spatial arrays. This effect is less dramatic in the case of the benzodiazepines than the barbiturates and ethanol, a fact which is possibly connected with the more marked depressant effects of the former on running behavior (see preceding paragraph). In the Skinner box and other nonspatial tasks, the barbiturates and benzodiazepines again reduce passive avoidance (i.e., the effects of punishment). Ethanol, in contrast, has not been clearly shown to reduce passive avoidance in such situations.

7.3. Classical Conditioning of Fear

None of the minor tranquilizers has yet been shown unequivocally to affect the conditioning of fear or the expression of fear that has been purely classically conditioned (i.e., with no possibility of adventitious punishment effects). The most consistent finding has been that the benzodiazepines reduce the expression of fear in the on-the-baseline CER; but this effect has not been reproduced in studies of the off-the-baseline CER.

7.4. Escape Behavior

None of the minor tranquilizers appears to have consistent and specific effects on escape behavior.

7.5. One-Way Active Avoidance

None of the minor tranquilizers appears to have consistent and specific effects on one-way active avoidance. Both the barbiturates and the benzodiazepines may improve performance in Sidman avoidance tasks in the Skinner box when given in low doses, especially to animals which perform poorly in the undrugged state. As suggested by Bignami *et al.* (1971), this pattern of results is probably best understood as reflecting a drug-produced reduction in the response-suppressant effects of Pun-CSs. Insufficient data are available for ethanol in Sidman avoidance tasks in the Skinner box.

7.6. Two-Way Active Avoidance

All the drugs reviewed have been shown to improve performance in the shuttlebox, especially at low doses, especially during early acquisition, and especially (in the case of SA, as shown by the experiments of Kamano and collaborators) in highly fearful animals. This pattern of results strongly suggests that the observed effects are due to a reduction under the drug of the passive-avoidance component of the conflict involved in shuttlebox procedures (Section 3.6).

7.7. Responses Elicited by Aversive Stimuli

The effects of the minor tranquilizers on passive avoidance behavior cannot be attributed to a general reduction in the effects of aversive stimuli. Responses elicited by aversive stimuli do not typically show a reduction under these drugs except when sedative or ataxic effects come into play. Aggressive responses have been reported to be facilitated by low doses of barbiturates, ethanol, and the benzodiazepines, though it is possible that, in the latter case, chronicity of drug treatment is the important variable rather than dose. Only in the case of the benzodiazepines is there evidence for an antagonistic effect on aggressive behavior, but it is not yet clear whether such effects can be seen with all types of aggression. In spite of the large number of studies of aggressive behavior after administration of benzodiazepines, there are still considerable ambiguities in the data.

7.8. Frustrative Nonreward

Much the greatest volume of experimental work on frustrative nonreward has been concerned with the barbiturates, especially SA. This has shown very clearly, and across a wide variety of situations, that responses to nonreward are substantially reduced. Studies of the effects of the benzodiazepines (mainly CDP) confirm this conclusion. Data for ethanol are sparse and inconclusive, though an antagonistic effect on responses to nonreward is suggested. It is not yet clear whether the effects of the minor tranquilizers are due to an attenuation of responses to the primary event of $\overline{\text{Rew}}$ or an attenuation of responses to $\overline{\text{Rew}}$-CSs or both. This is a much harder problem to tackle experimentally than the equivalent question concerning Pun and Pun-CSs, and only in the case of SA are there as yet relevant data. These suggest that the effect of the drug is confined to an attenuation of responses to $\overline{\text{Rew}}$-CSs, but the issue remains open.

7.9. Responses to Novelty

All the drugs examined (SA, ethanol, CDP) reduce spontaneous alternation. Only in the case of SA have other techniques been used to investigate responses to novelty. These have confirmed the implication of the spontaneous-alternation experiment in showing reduced reactions to novel stimuli.

The above may be taken as a summary behavioral profile of the minor tranquilizers. The degree to which it is applicable to all of the drugs reviewed is remarkable (though there are several points at which more data are needed with regard to the effects of one or another drug on one or another procedure). The only major qualifications necessary, with regard to a particular drug, in constructing this summary are: (1) the benzodiazepines appear to slow rewarded running speed more than the other drugs; (2) ethanol has not been shown definitely to reduce passive avoidance in nonspatial situations; and (3) the benzodiazepines may have more specific antagonistic effects on aggressive responses than do the barbiturates and ethanol.

As already discussed in connection with the barbiturates (Section 4), this profile is consistent with the hypothesis that the minor tranquilizers selectively antagonize the behavioral effects of Pun-CSs, $\overline{\text{Rew}}$-CSs, and (more tentatively) novel stimuli. It is not entirely excluded that the benzodiazepines also reduce some of the responses directly elicited by Pun (certain forms of aggressive behavior; see above). However, they cannot affect responses to Pun generally, or they would presumably alter escape and one-way active-avoidance behavior, and this does not occur. Nor is it clearly established that the minor tranquilizers do not also affect responses directly elicited by $\overline{\text{Rew}}$; this problem requires more experimental attention. It was also pointed out in Section 4 that the data on the barbiturates can be accommodated by the hypothesis that these drugs antagonize the behavioral inhibition system, which responds to inputs (Pun-CSs, $\overline{\text{Rew}}$-CSs, and novel stimuli) by suppressing ongoing operant behavior (whether reinforced by Rew or $\overline{\text{Pun}}$), by increasing attention to novel features of the environment, and by incrementing the level of arousal. The data on ethanol and the benzodiazepines allow this hypothesis to be extended also to these drugs.

8. THE MODE OF ACTION OF THE MINOR TRANQUILIZERS IN THE CENTRAL NERVOUS SYSTEM: A HYPOTHESIS

In the Introduction, three questions were posed. The third remains as yet unattacked: On what brain structures or systems do the minor tranquilizers act to produce their effects on emotional behavior? We might now rephrase this question as: What is the physiological substrate of the behavioral inhibition system?

8.1. The Hippocampal Theta Rhythm

I have proposed a hypothesis in answer to this question previously (Gray, 1970, 1972a). According to this hypothesis, the physiological substrate for the BIS consists of a number of linked structures in the limbic system, especially the septal area and the hippocampus, and its functioning is indicated by the occurrence of a hippocampal theta rhythm (Stumpf, 1965) in a particularly frequency band (lying, in the rat, around 7.7 Hz). The behavioral effects of the minor tranquilizers are then due to an impairment in the control exerted by the septal area (Stumpf, 1965) over the hippocampal theta rhythm specifically in that frequency band. In the present section I shall outline this hypothesis, and the evidence on which it is based, once more; but I shall also present new evidence which allows the hypothesis to be taken one stage further. This evidence, which is largely from unpublished experiments in my own laboratory, suggests that septal production of a hippocampal theta rhythm is facilitated selectively at 7.7 Hz by noradrenergic inputs to the hippocampus traveling in the dorsal ascending noradrenergic bundle from the locus coeruleus (Ungerstedt, 1971); that this facilitation is removed by the minor tranquilizers; and that this impairment of conduction in the projection from the locus coeruleus to the hippocampus underlies the tranquilizing effects of these drugs.

The hippocampal theta rhythm consists of trains of regular, high-voltage slow waves, in the frequency range 3–8 Hz in the cat and dog, but in a higher range, 5–12 Hz, in the rat and rabbit, which can be recorded from macroelectrodes throughout the hippocampal formation, including the dentate gyrus and subiculum (Green and Arduini, 1954; Stumpf, 1965; Vanderwolf *et al.*, 1975; Kemp and Kaada, 1975; Gray, 1972*b*; Bland *et al.*, 1975). There is good evidence that the pacemaker cells for the hippocampal theta rhythm are located in the medial septal area (Stumpf, 1965; Gray and Ball, 1970; Gray, 1971*c*). The hypothesis that the behavioral effects of the minor tranquilizers are due to an action on this septohippocampal system was motivated in the first instance by the similarities between the behavioral changes produced by the administration of SA, on the one hand, and those produced by lesions to the septal area (McCleary, 1966; Lubar and Numan, 1973; Dickinson, 1974) and the hippocampus (Douglas, 1967; Kimble, 1969) on the other. The assumption that all three treatments act by virtue of a disruption of the hippocampal theta rhythm provides a parsimonious explanation for these similarities.

This hypothesis was sharpened up after some simple experiments in which Gray and Ball (1970) recorded the electrical activity of the hippocampus in free-moving rats exposed to reward and nonreward for running down an alley. We observed that there were predictable relations between the frequency of the theta rhythm and the rat's behavior. When the rat was engaging in such "fixed action patterns" as eating, drinking, grooming etc., the theta rhythm was rather irregular and tended to be about 6–7 Hz. When the animal was traversing the runway toward a well-learned goal, the theta rhythm was of very high amplitude and frequency (typically 9–10 Hz). When the rat was either exploring a novel environment or exposed to frustrative nonreward in the goalbox, the theta rhythm was of an intermediate frequency which averaged 7.7 Hz. These observations have been replicated by Kimsey *et al.* (1974). Frequency-specific relations between behavior and hippocampal theta, although of different kinds in different experimental situations, have also been observed in cats (Elazar and Adey, 1967) and dogs

(Lopes da Silva and Kamp, 1969; Kamp et al., 1971). Based on the observations of Gray and Ball (1970), the hypothesis which has guided the work reported here is that the operation of the BIS involves a hippocampal theta rhythm in an intermediate frequency band centered on 7.7 Hz; and that the minor tranquilizers alter behavior by impairing the functioning of the theta rhythm in this frequency band (Gray, 1970).

This is by no means the only hypothesis about the functional significance of the hippocampal theta rhythm. Indeed there are at least six or seven others (too many certainly to review here), most of which are a good deal more popular than this one. Currently the most favored is probably Vanderwolf's (1971). He believes that the hippocampal theta rhythm is related to voluntary movement, and he has amassed a considerable body of evidence (mostly of a correlational variety, juxtaposing an observed theta rhythm with an observed form of behavior) in support of this hypothesis (Vanderwolf et al., 1975). Other evidence in support of a relation between hippocampal theta comes from Black's (1975) ingenious experiments on the operant conditioning of theta. However, there are two reasons why this hypothesis, especially if it is taken to mean that the hippocampus is concerned actively with the organization of voluntary movement, cannot be correct. First, even within the domain of data which have provided most support for Vanderwolf's hypothesis, there are many well-authenticated observations of hippocampal theta rhythms accompanying immobility in rats (Black, 1975; Gray 1971c), cats (Kemp and Kaada, 1975), and rabbits (Vanderwolf et al., 1975). Faced with these recalcitrant data, Vanderwolf et al. (1975) have recently altered the initial hypothesis into one which postulates two separate theta-producing systems. We shall return to this more elaborate hypothesis below. Second, and more difficult to deal with, is the fact that lesions to the hippocampus do not impair voluntary behavior, however this is defined. Rewarded behavior, one-way active avoidance, etc., are typically unaltered by such lesions, and two-way active avoidance is actually improved (Douglas, 1967; Kimble, 1969).

There are several ways in which it might be possible to reconcile Vanderwolf's voluntary-movement hypothesis with the effects of hippocampal lesions. [Vanderwolf himself appears not to have worried about the problem, though it has been considered by Altman et al. (1973), O'Keefe and Nadel (1974), and Black (1975).] One way is to suppose that the hippocampus is itself inhibited during the occurrence of the hippocampal theta rhythm. In this way the absence of the hippocampus (after a lesion) would be similar to the state in which a theta rhythm occurs, and voluntary movement could occur in both. On this view, one would need also to suppose that the active function of the hippocampus is to *inhibit* voluntary movement, and that this function is normally discharged when the hippocampus is displaying electrical activity other than theta. Although this is a tenable position, I have discussed elsewhere reasons for believing it to be wrong (Gray, 1970). A second way is more complicated. But it offers the advantage that it reconciles

Vanderwolf's hypothesis—and, more importantly, the data which support this hypothesis—not only with the effects of hippocampal lesions, but also with data which support the frequency-specific hypothesis of the functional significance of hippocampal theta (Gray, 1970).

According to the frequency-specific hypothesis, theta frequency has to be divided into three bands. The lowest of these (less than about 7 Hz in the rat) is related to fixed action patterns (eating, drinking, grooming, etc.). The highest (above about 8 Hz) is related to approach behavior, i.e., to instrumental behavior which is directed either to the attainment of reward or to the active avoidance of punishment (Gray, 1975). The middle frequency band (between about 7 and 8 Hz) is related to the functioning of the BIS as it has been described in this chapter (see Gray, 1975, 1976).

Now the first thing to note about this hypothesis is that it is not as different from Vanderwolf's voluntary-movement hypothesis as at first appears. In the highest frequency band, indeed, the two hypotheses become very hard to distinguish. It is not clear to me how Vanderwolf defines "voluntary" movement; but the only satisfactory understanding of this term I can reach myself is that it is movement directed to attainment of reward or the avoidance of punishment. If that is so, then in the highest frequency band the two hypotheses are identical. In the lowest frequency band such conflict as at one time divided the two hypotheses has been removed by Vanderwolf's recent jettisoning of the assumption that there is a unitary significance to the theta rhythm. He now proposes the existence of two frequency bands (Vanderwolf *et al.*, 1975). One of these, with frequencies above 7 Hz, is related to voluntary movement, the other, with frequencies below 7 Hz, is not. Where there is a real conflict between the two hypotheses is in the middle frequency band. According to Vanderwolf, frequencies above 7 Hz are associated with voluntary movement (albeit movement of low vigor, since he believes that theta frequency increases as the amplitude of movement increases); according to the present writer, in contrast, frequencies between 7 and 8 Hz reflect the activity of a system whose chief function is to *inhibit* voluntary movement.

How can we reconcile these two hypotheses? And how can we reconcile the fact that hippocampal lesions have no effect on voluntary movement with the correlation between high theta frequencies and voluntary movement?

Let us suppose that the major function of the hippocampus is to inhibit various kinds of behavior, as is indeed indicated by the lesion literature (Douglas, 1967; Kimble, 1969). Suppose further that these kinds of behavior belong to two fundamentally different classes: fixed action patterns and instrumental (voluntary) behavior dependent on reward or avoidance of punishment. Finally, we suppose (Fig. 1) that inhibition of voluntary-behavior systems is accomplished when the hippocampal theta rhythm is present at low frequencies (<8 Hz), and that inhibition of fixed action patterns is accomplished when the hippocampal theta rhythm is present at high frequencies (>7 Hz); it follows that at frequencies between 7 and 8 Hz both

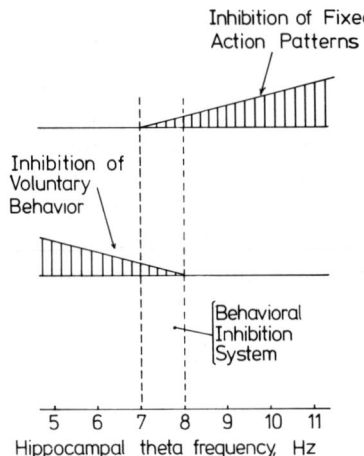

FIG. 1. Proposed relation of hippocampal theta frequency to behavioral inhibition. For explanation, see text.

voluntary behavior and fixed action patterns are inhibited, i.e., the BIS is in operation. This hypothesis accounts for the observed correlations between high theta frequencies and voluntary movement and low theta frequencies and fixed action patterns (Vanderwolf, 1971; Vanderwolf et al., 1975; Gray and Ball, 1970); for the lack of effect on voluntary movement, and general disinhibitory effects, of hippocampal lesions (Douglas, 1967; Kimble, 1969); and for the way in which various brain systems appear to exercise a rather precise control over hippocampal theta frequency (see below).

8.2. Testing the Frequency-Specific Hypothesis

We have tested the frequency-specific hypothesis in several ways, all revolving round septal control of hippocampal theta. The object of investigation is the free-moving rat with a stimulating electrode implanted permanently in the medial septal area and a recording electrode in the dorsomedial subiculum. Through the latter electrode a hippocampal theta rhythm may be recorded which is in exact phase with the theta rhythm simultaneously recorded in CA 1 within the hippocampus proper (Rawlins, unpublished). By delivering trains of short (0.5 msec) square-wave pulses to the medial septal area at frequencies within the theta range, it is possible artificially to drive the hippocampal theta rhythm, in the sense that one wave is driven by each pulse (Gray and Ball, 1970; Gray, 1972b; James et al., in press); by using a high-frequency train (above about 70 Hz), it is possible artificially to block the theta rhythm (Gray et al., 1972a); and by making electrolytic lesions confined to the medial septal area, it is possible to permanently abolish hippocampal theta (Donovick, 1968; Gray, 1971c). We have used these techniques to test the particular hypothesis that the hippocampal theta rhythm at a frequency of about 7.7 Hz (the observed hippocampal response to nonreward in the runway: Gray and Ball, 1970) is part of the physiological system which mediates the behavioral effects of nonreward.

From this hypothesis, the following predictions can be made: (1) Septal driving of a 7.7-Hz theta rhythm during extinction after CRF will facilitate extinction. This prediction was verified by Gray (1972b). (2) Septal driving of a 7.7-Hz theta rhythm on a random 50% schedule during CRF acquisition will mimic the PREE; i.e., it will increase subsequent resistance to extinction. This prediction was verified by Gray (1972b). More recently Glazer (1974) has verified a similar prediction: He showed that training rats by instrumental procedures to produce 7.7-Hz theta to obtain reward increased the resistance to extinction of a subsequently learned lever-pressing response, a phenomenon which mimics the generalized PREE described by Ross (1964). (3) Septal blocking (by high-frequency stimulation) of the naturally occurring theta response to nonreward on a random 50% PRF schedule will reduce resistance to extinction. This prediction was verified by Gray et al. (1972a). (4) Lesions to the medial septal area will reduce the PREE both by increasing resistance to extinction in a CRF group and by decreasing resistance to extinction in a PRF group. This prediction was verified by Gray et al. (1972b) and by Henke (1974), though in the latter experiment lesions were of the total septal area. Similar findings have been reported by Donovick (1968) and Butters and Rosvold (1968).

However, it was a different way of investigating the frequency-specific hypothesis which led to the particular findings to which the remainder of the chapter is devoted. Gray and Ball (1970) plotted the threshold current able to drive the hippocampal theta rhythm from the medial septal area as a function of the frequency of the stimulating current. The effects on this "theta-driving curve" of SA, administered to free-moving male rats in the dose and manner known to be behaviorally effective (20 mg/kg i.p., 10 min before a 30-min test session), are shown in Fig. 2. There are two things to note in this figure. The first is that the drug is very selective in its action: The threshold at 7.7 Hz is raised, but thresholds at frequencies above and below this value are unaltered. This is a striking confirmation of the hypothesis that SA produces its behavioral effects by impairing the hippocampal theta rhythm specifically in the middle frequency band. The second is that the curve obtained from the undrugged rat has a minimum threshold or "dip" at this same frequency, 7.7 Hz. This is a highly reliable phenomenon in the male rat (James et al., in press), though, as we shall see, it does not occur in females. Furthermore, it is a common feature of the minor tranquilizers that they eliminate the 7.7-Hz dip. Figure 3 shows the results we have recently obtained for another dose of SA (15 mg/kg), CDP (5 mg/kg), and ethanol

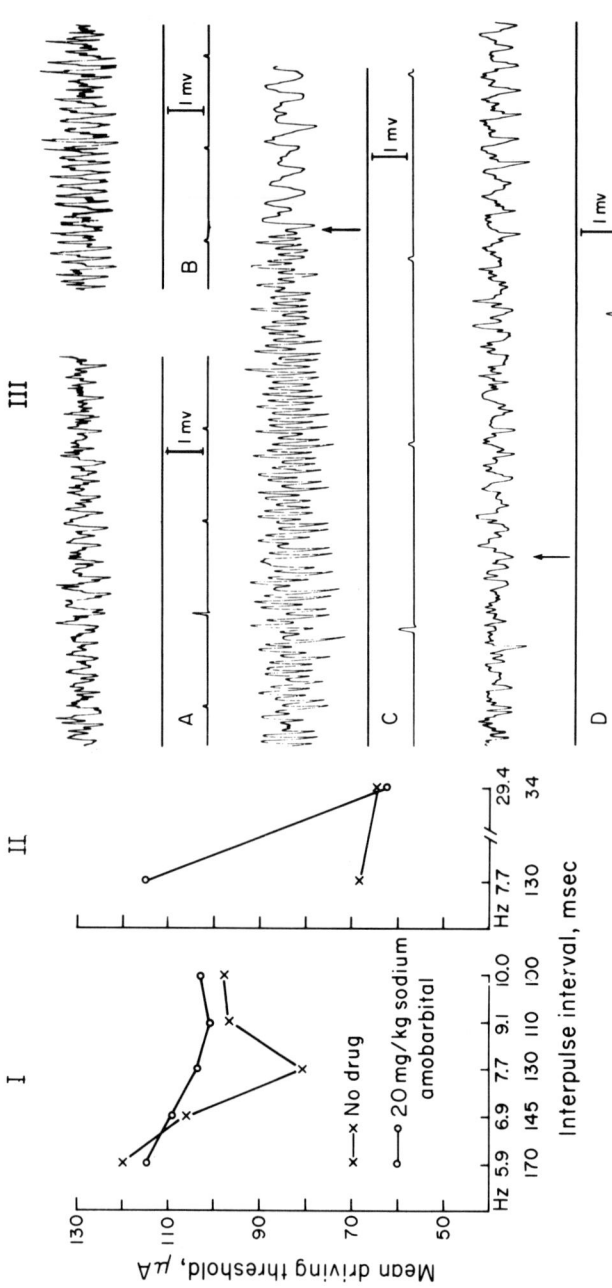

FIG. 2. Effect of 20 mg/kg sodium amobarbital on threshold for septal driving of hippocampal theta rhythm as a function of driving frequency (i.e., on "theta-driving curve") in two groups (I and II) of five rats. (III) Examples of driven hippocampal response. Bottom channel: time in seconds. A: Driving current 5.9 Hz, 175 μA; B: 10 Hz, 150 μA; C: 29.4 Hz, 150 μA (arrow marks termination of stimulation); D: 7.7 Hz, 60 μA (arrow marks start of stimulation). From Gray and Ball (1970).

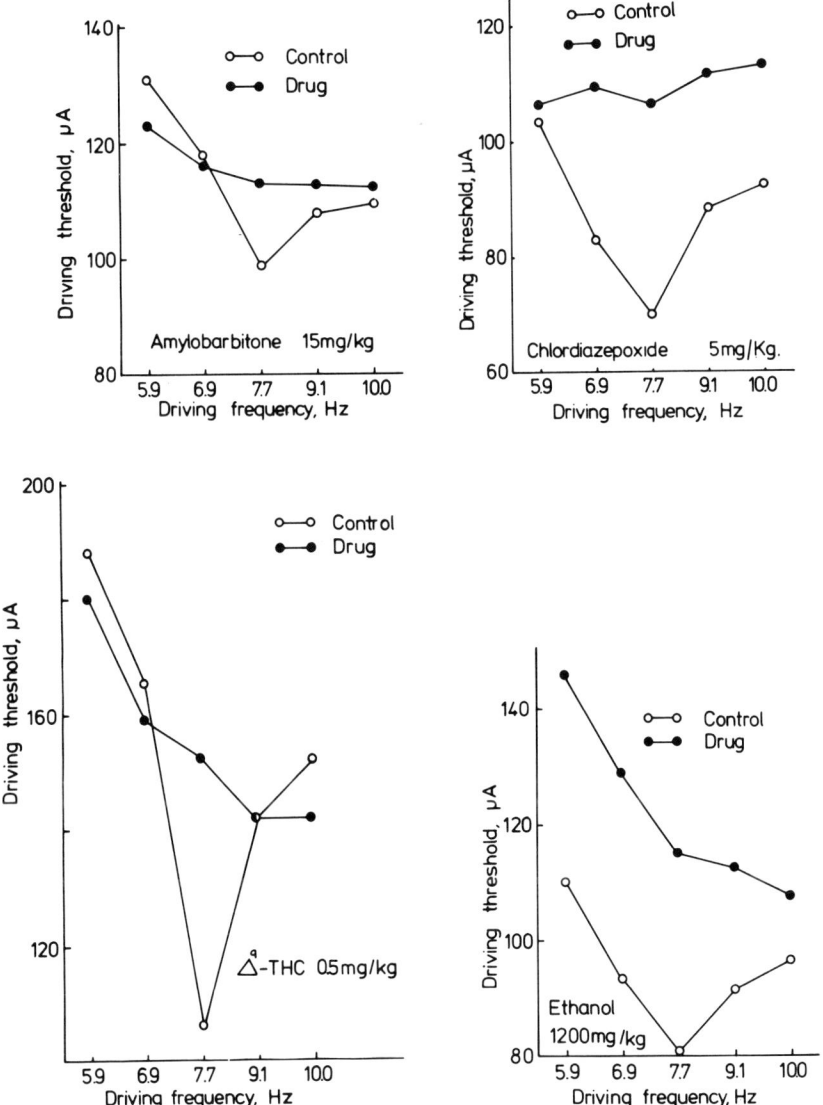

FIG. 3. Effects of four drugs which impair behavioral inhibition on the theta-driving curve. From Gray et al. (1975).

(1200 mg/kg) (Gray et al., 1975). In each case the threshold at 7.7 Hz is significantly lower than at any other frequency in the control condition, but significantly lower only than the threshold at 5.9 Hz in the drug condition.

Figure 3 also shows the effects on the theta-driving curve of 0.5 mg/kg Δ^9-tetrahydrocannabinol (THC), the major active principle of cannabis (Drewnowski and Gray, unpublished). It can be seen that the effects of this drug are remarkably similar to those of the minor tranquilizers. Similarities between the action of THC and that of the barbiturates and alcohol have been noted by a number of writers (e.g., Friedman and Gershon, 1974; Newman et al., 1972; Kubena and Barry, 1970; Gill et al., 1970). Given the theory being developed here and the results shown in Fig. 3, the prediction naturally follows that THC should have the same effects on emotional behavior as the minor tranquilizers. We have conducted two experiments on the effects of THC (0.5 mg/kg) on responses to nonreward (Drewnowski and Gray, 1975). As predicted, the drug blocked the PRAE and the PREE; blockage of the PREE occurred both when the drug was given in training and placebo in extinction, and when the drug was given in training and in extinction. The observed pattern of results was closely similar to that found with SA (Section 3.8.1): The drugged PRF animals behaved during both acquisition and extinction like control CRF animals, as did the drugged CRF animals. Thus, these experiments show that THC, like the minor tranquilizers, blocks the behavioral effects of nonreward. They also demonstrate that it is possible to predict the behavioral effects of drugs from their effects on the theta-driving curve.

A striking demonstration of the power of the reverse direction of prediction—from behavior to the theta-driving curve—has emerged from work we have done on the Maudsley strains. These strains have been mentioned at several points in this chapter, and the reader is by now aware that the MR and MNR strains have been selectively bred for, respectively, high and low fearfulness as measured by defecation in the open-field test (Broadhurst, 1960; Gray, 1971a). Compared to the MR strain, MNR rats show poorer passive avoidance (Weldon, 1967; Ferraro and York, 1968) and improved shuttlebox avoidance (many experiments; for references, see Gray and Lalljee, 1974). There are unfortunately no data available on responses to Rew-CSs, but many other experiments support the hypothesis that the MNR strain is generally more fearful than the MR strain (Gray, 1971a). It is pertinent to note that, although Broadhurst (1960) conducted a bidirectional selective breeding experiment, his results indicate that the major response to selection occurred in the MNR strain. It is also relevant to what follows that one consequence of the selective breeding in both strains has been that the sex difference in open-field defecation which is present in the unselected Wistar rat (males defecating more) has disappeared (Broadhurst, 1960; Gray, 1971a,b).

The behavioral profile of the MNR strain may be described as similar to that of an unselected rat which has been administered a minor tranquilizer. It follows from this description that one might expect to find in the MNR strain a theta-driving curve which lacks the 7.7-Hz minimum. This is indeed the case. But before setting out the data we have obtained on this point, it is necessary to digress into the subject of sex differences.

The data shown in Figs. 2 and 3 relate exclusively to male rats. In female rats which have not been drugged, the 7.7-Hz minimum, which is such a stable feature of the results obtained in male rats (it is absent in less than 10% of these), is missing (Drewett et al., in press). This surprising sex difference is shown in Fig. 4, which also displays our findings with regard to the role played in it by gonadal hormones. The theta-driving curve obtained from female rats is unaffected by the estrous cycle or ovariectomy; the curve obtained from male rats, however, changes to one characteristic of females 7–11 weeks after castration (Drewett et al., in press). Finally, as shown in Fig. 5, daily injections of testosterone propionate (TP), in doses around 250 μg/day, were sufficient to restore the castrated male rats' theta-driving curves to ones typical of intact males in 2–3 days; and somewhat more prolonged treatment with slightly higher doses also altered the curves obtained from females to ones typical of males (Drewett et al., in press). Owing to the slow disappearance of the 7.7-Hz dip after castration and its comparatively slow reappearance after treatment with TP (2–3 days compared to 5–10 min for the effect of SA to appear), it is not possible to say whether the effects of the

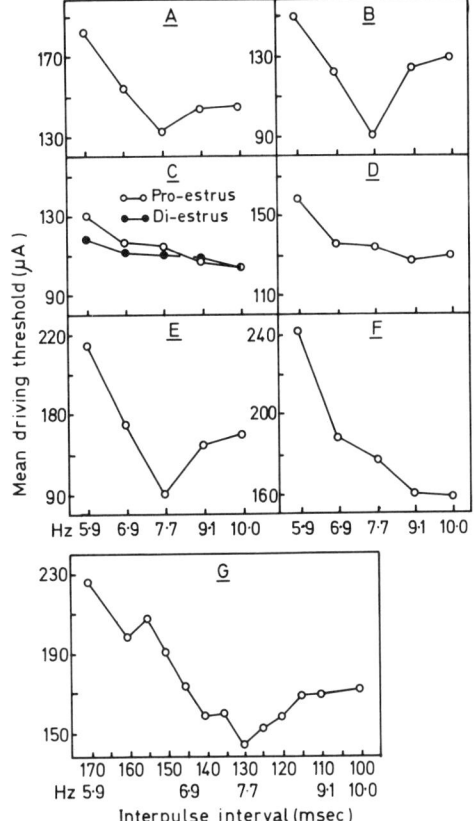

FIG. 4. Thresholds for septal driving of hippocampal theta rhythm as a function of stimulation frequency. A: Mean of five Wistar male rats; B: single male rat; C: mean of four females during proestrus and diestrus; D: mean of six ovariectomized females; E: mean of three male rats tested at 49, 59, and 69 days after castration, respectively; F: mean of same three male rats as in E, tested at 70, 79, and 72 days after castration, respectively; G: results from single intact male tested with 5-msec increments of interpulse interval (abscissa). From Drewett et al. (in press).

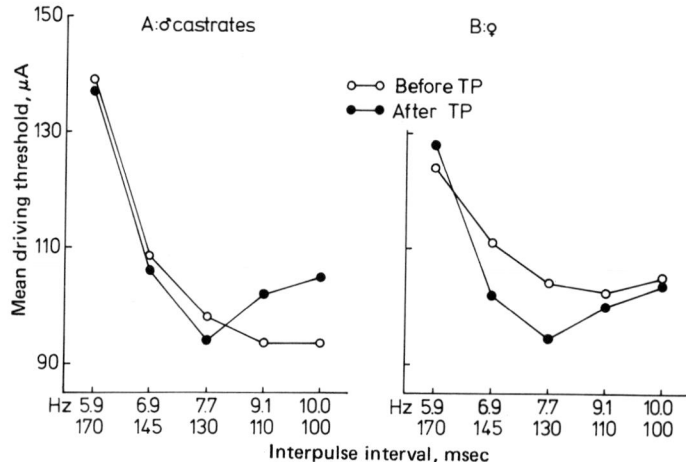

FIG. 5. Effect of daily injection of testosterone proportionate (TP) on theta-driving curve in castrated male rats (A) and ovariectomized female rats (B). From Drewett et al. (in press).

hormone are due to a fall in the threshold at 7.7 Hz, to a rise in threshold at other frequencies, or both. But it is clear that the presence of a 7.7-Hz dip is dependent on testosterone.

This is the situation in Wistar and Sprague–Dawley rats. But when we investigated the Maudsley strains (which were bred from an original parental population of Wistars) a different picture emerged (Drewett et al., in press). Males from the MR strain show the 7.7-Hz minimum; males from the MNR strain do not—like female Wistars, they give rather variable results which average out as shown in Fig. 6. Furthermore, when we injected MR females with TP in quite low doses, the theta-driving curve was altered to one typical of males, with a 7.7-Hz minimum; but very large doses of the hormone were ineffective in this respect in females from the MNR strain (Fig. 6).

These results suggest two important conclusions. First, the shape of the theta-driving curve is under the control of testosterone. The function discharged by this control and the route by which it is exercised are so far unknown. Nonetheless, the fact that it exists at all indicates that the theta-driving curve, though obtained under artificial experimental conditions, reflects important physiological influences. Second, selective breeding for low fearfulness in the MNR strain has produced changes in the theta-driving curve which resemble those produced by the minor tranquilizers in unselected rats. This strengthens the possibility that the effects of these drugs on the theta-driving curve and their effects on emotional behavior are causally linked.

8.3. The Pharmacology of the Theta-Driving Curve

Given the common effect of the minor tranquilizers on the theta-driving curve (Fig. 3), our next step was to determine whether this could be mimicked by other drugs with better-understood neurochemical actions. In this way one might get a clue as to the neural pathways involved.

A natural first hypothesis was that cholinergic mechanisms might be involved. There is good evidence that the projection from the medial septal nucleus to the hippocampus consists of cholinergic fibers (Lewis and Shute, 1967; Mellgren and Srebro, 1973), and also evidence that some of the inputs

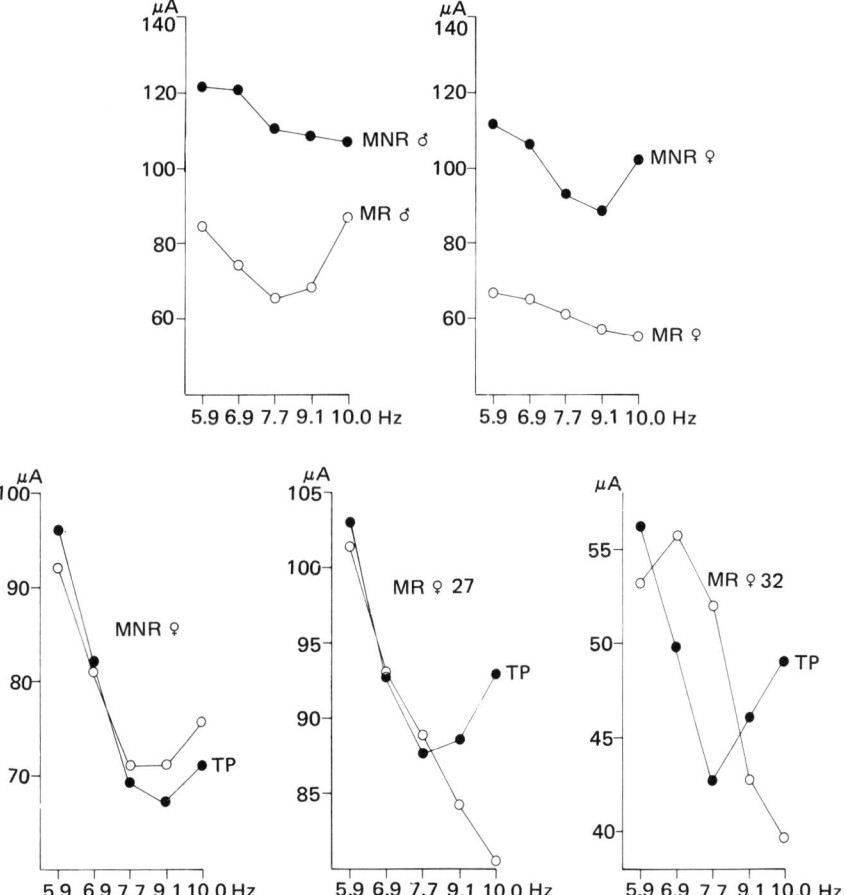

FIG. 6. Theta-driving curves in untreated Maudsley-reactive (MR) and nonreactive (MNR) males and females (above), and in a group of four MNR females and two individual MR females before and after daily injection of testosterone proportionate (TP) (below). From Drewett et al. (in press).

to the medial septal area are themselves cholinergic (Shute and Lewis, 1967). There is also evidence that anticholinergic drugs may interfere with relevant forms of behavior whether injected systemically (Carlton, 1963; Warburton, 1972) or directly into the septal area (Kelsey and Grossman, 1969; Grossman, 1972). In contrast, the anticholinesterase physostigmine facilitates the theta rhythm (Stumpf, 1965) and produces some behavioral changes which are opposite in sign to those produced by the minor tranquilizers (Bureš et al., 1962; Glazer, 1973). Thus, one might expect anticholinergic drugs to act on the theta-driving curve like the minor tranquilizers, and cholinomimetic drugs to have the reverse effect. However, Fig. 7 shows that neither scopolamine nor physostigmine, in behaviorally effective doses, have effects which lend themselves to this kind of interpretation (McNaughton et al., in press). Scopolamine (0.5 mg/kg) slightly raises thresholds in a frequency-nonspecific manner; and, while physostigmine (0.05 mg/kg) produces a kind of frequency-specific effect, this is because it *fails* to affect 7.7 Hz while lowering thresholds at other frequencies. Larger doses of scopolamine, to be sure, are capable of blocking septal production of theta entirely (Stumpf, 1965; Macadar et al., 1970), but this is not the effect produced by the minor tranquilizers. It should be noted that the results shown in Fig. 6 also fail to

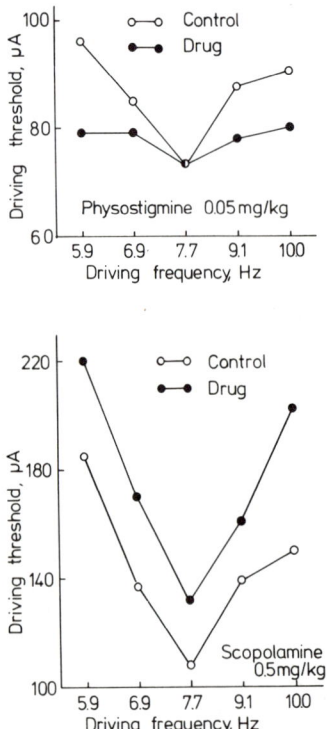

FIG. 7. Effects of 0.05 mg/kg physostigmine and 0.5 mg/kg scopolamine on the theta-driving curve. From McNaughton et al. (in press).

support the view, advanced by Vanderwolf et al. (1975), that the theta rhythm consists of two functionally (Section 8.1, above) and pharmacologically distinct frequency bands, of which the lower only (up to 7 Hz) is cholinergic. On this view, one might have expected scopolamine to raise, and physostigmine to lower, thresholds selectively at the low frequencies, and this did not occur. There is, of course, no reason to suppose that our technique of driving theta from the septum is sensitive to all the influences which affect theta, though we shall see that it has proved very sensitive to other frequency-specific effects. But it should also be noted that Brücke et al. (1957) found that scopolamine does not change the frequency of the theta rhythm elicited by reticular stimulation in rabbits. This observation has been replicated in free-moving rats by McNaughton (unpublished) with both scopolamine and atropine: Different stimulus currents reliably elicited different theta frequencies over the range 5–10 Hz, and these relationships were unaffected by the anticholinergic drugs up to doses which completely blocked theta.

A second likely candidate as the neural basis of the action of the minor tranquilizers is a serotoninergic mechanism. The neurotransmitter 5-hydroxytryptamine (5-HT) has been implicated in the control of behavioral inhibition in psychopharmacological studies (Dominic, 1973; Weissman, 1973; Mabry and Campbell, 1974), and Stein et al. (1973) have explicitly proposed that the behavioral effects of the benzodiazepines are due to an antagonistic action on a serotoninergic "punishment" system whose postulated functions are very similar to those allotted here to the BIS. In a test of this possibility, we used p-chlorophenylalanine (PCPA) (300 mg/kg three days before test) to block 5-HT synthesis (Koe and Weissman, 1968), with the results shown in Fig. 8 (McNaughton et al., in press). Rather than selectively increasing the theta-driving threshold at 7.7 Hz, as do the minor tranquilizers, PCPA selectively reduced the threshold at every frequency other than 7.7 Hz. Furthermore, injection of 5-hydroxytryptophan (5-HTP), from which 5-HT is synthesized in PCPA-blocked animals (Koe and Weissman, 1968), restored the theta-driving curve to normal, showing that the effect of PCPA was indeed due to a blockage of 5-HT synthesis. It is interesting to note that the effects of PCPA and physostigmine (Fig. 7) are qualitatively similar, suggesting that theta-driving thresholds above and below 7.7 Hz are the net outcome of a cholinergic facilitatory influence and a serotoninergic inhibitory one. The anatomical possibilities for the latter influence are not hard to find: There are major serotoninergic projections from the raphe nuclei in the brainstem to both the septal area and the hippocampus (Ungerstedt, 1971; Dahlström et al., 1973; Aghajanian et al., 1973).

Unable to mimic the effects of the minor tranquilizers on the theta-driving curve by interfering with either cholinergic or setotoninergic transmission, we turned our attention to the catecholamines. While neither dopamine nor noradrenaline has previously been linked with behavioral inhibition, noradrenaline has been implicated in emotional behavior and

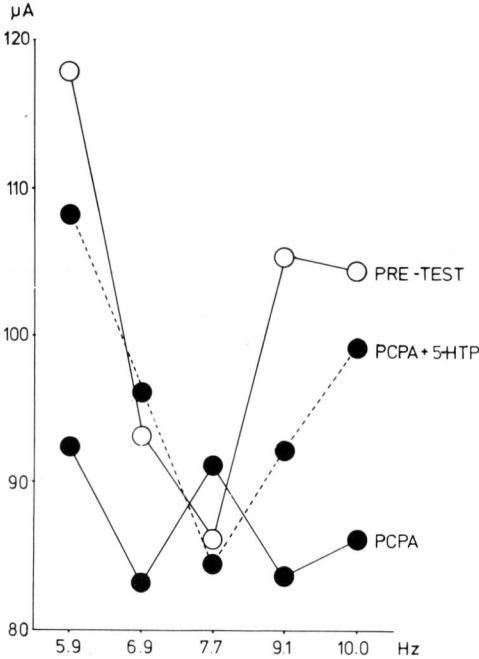

FIG. 8. Effect of *p*-chlorophenylalanine (PCPA) (300 mg/kg, 3 days before test) and subsequent 5-hydroxytryptophan (5-HTP) (40 mg/kg, 45 min before test) on the theta-driving curve. From McNaughton *et al.* (in press).

stress reactions (Schildkraut and Kety, 1967). To test the possibility of catecholamine involvement, McNaughton *et al.* (in press) investigated the effects on the theta-driving curve of haloperidol, which is a receptor blocker for both catecholamines (Andén *et al.*, 1970), and of α-methyl-*p*-tyrosine (α-MPT), which blocks their synthesis (Andén *et al.*, 1966; Corrodi and Hanson, 1966). As shown in Fig. 9, both these treatments affected the theta driving in the same way as the minor tranquilizers, abolishing the 7.7-Hz minimum by selectively raising thresholds at this frequency. To distinguish between the roles played by dopamine and noradrenaline, we further injected the α-MPT-treated animals with dihydroxyphenylserine, which restores noradrenaline but not dopamine levels (Corrodi and Fuxe, 1967). This completely normalized the theta-driving curve (Fig. 9), showing that the important action of haloperidol and α-MPT was the blockage of a noradrenergic mechanism.

Given this information, and the great advances made in recent years in our knowledge of the neuroanatomy of central noradrenergic pathways (Ungerstedt, 1971; Livett, 1973), it is possible to ask reasonable questions concerning the locus of action of the minor tranquilizers in the brain. Noradrenergic fibers appear all to originate in the midbrain and brainstem and thence to ascend to higher structures. In their ascent they separate into two bundles. The ventral bundle collects fibers from many nuclei of origin and distributes them mainly to the hypothalamus. The dorsal bundle collects from only one nucleus, the locus coeruleus, and distributes in the main to the neocortex, the cerebellum, and the hippocampus (Ungerstedt, 1971), and also to the medial septal area (Segal and Landis, 1974). Thus, the dorsal bundle is the obvious candidate for the site of action of the minor tranquilizers on the theta-driving curve, especially as there is already evidence from neurochemical studies that the benzodiazepines and the barbitur-

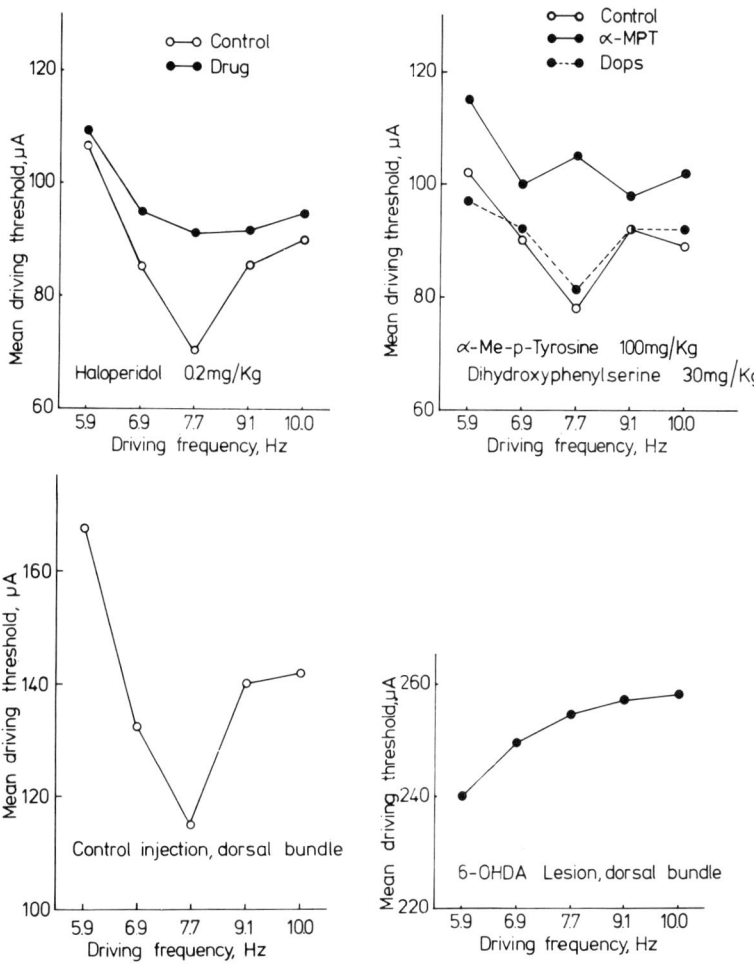

FIG. 9. Effects of haloperidol, α-methyl-*p*-tyrosine (α-MPT), dihydroxyphenylserine (DOPS) given after α-MPT, and 6-hydroxydopamine (6-OHDA) lesions to the dorsal ascending noradrenergic bundle on the theta-driving curve. From Gray *et al.* (1975) and McNaughton *et al.* (in press).

ates reduce neuronal activity and noradrenaline turnover in this pathway (Corrodi et al., 1971; Lidbrink et al., 1972).

In order to examine this possibility, Kelly, McNaughton, and I (Gray et al., 1975) destroyed the dorsal bundle by injecting into it a neurotoxin, 6-hydroxydopamine, which is specific for dopaminergic and noradrenergic fibers (Ungerstedt, 1968). Subsequent biochemical assay showed that this treatment reduced hippocampal levels of noradrenaline by 98%, indicating a virtually complete lesion of the noradrenergic innervation of this structure, while there was no change in hypothalamic or striatal levels of dopamine (which would be expected to fall if the 6-hydroxydopamine had also destroyed the ventral bundle, since this carries the ascending dopaminergic neurons as well as other noradrenergic fibers). Animals treated in this way and subsequently implanted with electrodes showed a theta-driving curve with no sign of a minimum threshold at 7.7 Hz (Fig. 9). Thus, the noradrenergic innervation of the hippocampus and/or septal area from the locus coeruleus appears selectively to facilitate septal driving of the hippocampal theta rhythm at a frequency of 7.7 Hz; and it seems very likely that the selective rise in the 7.7-Hz threshold produced by the minor tranquilizers is due to an impairment produced by these agents in the activity of this pathway.

From this conclusion it is a small step to the hypothesis that the *behavioral* effects of the minor tranquilizers are due to an action on the dorsal bundle. One prediction from this hypothesis is that the behavioral effects of lesions to the dorsal bundle should resemble the effects of the minor tranquilizers. Just such results have been obtained by Mason and Iversen (1975). The dorsal bundle was destroyed by local injection of 6-hydroxydopamine, which produced virtually total depletion of cortical and hippocampal noradrenaline. Rats treated in this way showed no impairment in the acquisition of a running response for CRF food reward, but a greatly increased resistance to extinction. A similar increase in resistance to extinction was observed with a bar-pressing response, also on CRF food reward. Finally, rats with dorsal-bundle lesions showed slower inhibition of responding to the negative stimulus in a light/dark successive discrimination (Mason and Iversen, 1977). These effects, of course, can all be produced by injections of the minor tranquilizers.*

These data then point to the dorsal ascending noradrenergic bundle as the physiological substrate (or at least part of it) of the BIS and as the most important site of action of the minor tranquilizers. This conclusion is in line with a number of earlier observations. Zbinden and Randall (1967), on the basis of drug-antagonism studies, raised the possibility that "the antianxiety effect of the benzodiazepines is a central antiadrenergic phenomenon." Histofluorescence studies of turnover of brain noradrenaline have shown that stress increases turnover especially in forebrain structures (which are

---

* Owen, Boarder, Gray, and Fillenz (unpublished) have similarly abolished the PREE by lesioning the dorsal bundle.

innervated via the dorsal bundle), and that this increase is counteracted by benzodiazepines, barbiturates, and ethanol (Corrodi et al., 1966, 1971; Lidbrink et al., 1972). Another relevant fact is that all the drugs we have considered in this chapter are known to depress "fast-wave" or "rapid-eye-movement" sleep, e.g., the barbiturates (Oswald et al., 1963; David et al., 1974), the benzodiazepines (Hartmann and Cravens, 1973; Oswald et al., 1973), ethanol (Rundell et al., 1972; Yules et al., 1966), and THC (Wallach and Gershon, 1973; Freemon, 1974). There is evidence that this mode of sleep is controlled by the locus coeruleus, the nucleus of origin of the dorsal bundle (Jouvet, 1969, 1974). Thus, the action of the minor tranquilizers on rapid-eye-movement sleep is also consistent with the hypothesis that they impair conduction in the dorsal bundle.

However, though the results we have obtained by interfering with noradrenergic brain systems are clear-cut and offer, at least in embryo, a satisfying and coherent story, it would be a mistake to bury the possibility of serotoninergic involvement in the BIS on the grounds that PCPA does not alter the theta-driving curve in the same way as the minor tranquilizers. Indeed, if we put together the results shown in Fig. 7 for this drug with those shown in Fig. 8 for α-MPT, we see that the shape of the theta-driving curve in the undrugged male animal depends on the joint influence of serotoninergic and noradrenergic mechanisms, presumably acting on the final common path constituted by the cholinergic projecton from the medial septal nucleus to the hippocampus (Lewis and Shute, 1967; Mellgren and Srebro, 1973). Frequencies above and below 7.7 Hz appear to be inhibited by a serotoninergic mechanism, while 7.7 Hz is facilitated by noradrenergic neurons traveling in the dorsal bundle. It is possible that the critical feature of the action of the minor tranquilizers is not that they raise the threshold at 7.7 Hz, but that they alter the shape of the curve so that the minimum threshold is no longer at this frequency. It is also possible that these drugs act on forebrain systems *both* of a noradrenergic nature [as suggested by the present data and those of Corrodi et al. (1971) and Lidbrink et al. (1972)] *and* of a serotoninergic nature [as suggested by Stein et al. (1973)], rather than on noradrenergic systems alone. We do not yet know whether our own techniques can distinguish between these possibilities.

9. CONCLUSIONS

In this chapter we set ourselves the aim of answering three questions concerning the minor tranquilizers. To these three questions the answers have been as follows.

1. The simplest adequate description of the effects of the minor tranquilizers on emotional behavior is that these drugs selectively reduce the behavioral effects of CSs which have been paired with punishment (Pun-CSs), CSs which have been paired with frustrative nonreward ($\overline{\text{Rew}}$-CSs), and novel stimuli.

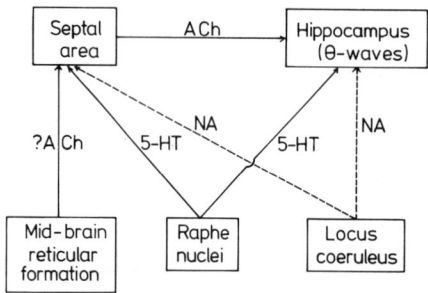

FIG. 10. Structures, pathways, and neurotransmitters which influence the occurrence and frequency of the hippocampal theta rhythm. ACh: acetylcholine. 5-HT: 5-hydroxytryptamine. NA: noradrenaline. For explanation, see text.

2. The psychological processes altered by these drugs are those which make up the "behavioral inhibition system" (BIS). This system responds to Pun-CSs, $\overline{\text{Rew}}$-CSs, and novel stimuli by suppressing ongoing operant behavior (whether maintained by reward or the avoidance of punishment), by increasing attention to the environment, especially novel features of it, and by increasing the level of arousal. All these outputs of the BIS are reduced by the minor tranquilizers.

3. The brain structures on which the minor tranquilizers act (and which form the physiological substrate of the BIS) comprise the medial septal area, the hippocampus, and a number of afferent pathways to these two areas which influence the occurrence and frequency of the hippocampal theta rhythm. These structures and pathways are summarized in Fig. 10. The most important mode of action of the minor tranquilizers appears to be an impairment of the noradrenergic input to the hippocampus and medial septal area from the locus coeruleus. In the rat, this input apparently facilitates septal production of the hippocampal theta rhythm selectively at about 7.7 Hz; the minor tranquilizers block this facilitation. The minor tranquilizers also impair conduction in serotoninergic pathways which apparently inhibit septal production of the hippocampal theta rhythm selectively at frequencies above and below 7.7 Hz. It is possible that the behavioral properties of the minor tranquilizers arise from the capacity of these drugs to interfere with both forebrain noradrenergic and forebrain serotoninergic mechanisms, and thus to alter the functioning of the septohippocampal system.

Acknowledgments

I am grateful to all my colleagues who have allowed me to cite their unpublished data: R. F. Drewett, A. Drewnowski, A. Guillamon, D. T. D. James, P. Kelly, N. McNaughton, S. Owen, J. N. P. Rawlins, and J. Stewart. We have received generous support in gathering these data from the Medical Research Council and the Smith, Kline and French Foundation. The paper was prepared while the author held a Social Science Research Fellowship from the Nuffield Foundation.

10. REFERENCES

ADELMAN, H. M., and MAATSCH, J. L., 1956, Learning and extinction based upon frustration, food reward, and exploratory tendency, *J. Exp. Psychol.* **52:**311–315.
AGHAJANIAN, G. K., KUHAR, M. J., and ROTH, R. H., 1973, Serotonin-containing neuronal perikarya and terminals: differential effects of p-chlorophenylalanine, *Brain Res.* **54:**85–101.
ALTMAN, J., BRUNNER, R. L., and BAYER, S. A., 1973, The hippocampus and behavioral maturation, *Behav. Biol.* **8:**557–596.
AMSEL, A., 1958, The role of frustrative nonreward in non-continuous reward situations, *Psychol. Bull.* **55:**102–119.
AMSEL, A., 1962, Frustrative nonreward in partial reinforcement and discrimination learning: some recent history and a theoretical extension, *Psychol. Rev.* **69:**306–328.
AMSEL, A., and ROUSSEL, J., 1952, Motivational properties of frustration. I. Effect on a running response of the addition of frustration to the motivational complex, *J. Exp. Psychol.* **43:**363–368.
ANDÉN, N.-E., BUTCHER, S. G., CORRODI, H., FUXE, K., and UNGERSTEDT, U., 1970, Receptor activity and turnover of dopamine and noradrenaline after neuroleptics, *Eur. J. Pharmacol.* **11:**303–314.
ANDÉN, N.-E., CORRODI, H., DAHLSTRÖM, A., FUXE, K., and HÖKFELT, T., 1966, Effects of tyrosine hydroxylase inhibition on the amine levels of central monoamine neurons, *Life Sci.* **5:**561–568.
ANISMAN, H., 1972, Fear reduction and active avoidance learning after alcohol administration during prior CS-shock exposure, *Q. J. Stud. Alcohol* **33:**783–793.
ANISMAN, H., and WALLER, T. G., 1974, Effects of alcohol on discriminative active avoidance behavior in mice, *Q. J. Stud. Alcohol* **35:**439–444.
BAENNINGER, R., 1967, Contrasting effects of fear and pain on mouse killing by rats, *J. Comp. Physiol. Psychol.* **63:**298–303.
BAILEY, C. J., and MILLER, N. E., 1952, The effect of sodium amytal on an approach–avoidance conflict in cats, *J. Comp. Physiol. Psychol.* **45:**205–208.
BAINBRIDGE, J. G., 1968, The effect of psychotropic drugs on food reinforced behavior and on food consumption, *Psychopharmacologia* **12:**204–213.
BAKAY PRAGAY, E., MIRSKY, A. F., and ABPLANALP, J. M., 1969, The effects of chlorpromazine and secobarbital on matching from sample and discrimination tasks in monkeys, *Psychopharmacologia* **16:**128–138.
BALTZER, V., and WEISKRANTZ, L., 1970, Negative and positive behavioural contrast in the same animals, *Nature (London)* **228:**581–582.
BANERJEE, U., 1971, Acquisition of conditioned avoidance response in rats under the influence of addicting drugs, *Psychopharmacologia* **22:**133–143.
BARRETT, J. E., 1974, Conjunctive schedules of reinforcement I. Rate-dependent effects of pentobarbital and d-amphetamine, *J. Exp. Anal. Behav.* **22:**561–573.
BARRY, H., III, 1968, Prolonged measurements of discrimination between alcohol and nondrug states, *J. Comp. Physiol. Psychol.* **65:**349–352.
BARRY, H., III, and MILLER, N. E., 1962, Effects of drugs on approach–avoidance conflict tested repeatedly by means of a "telescope alley," *J. Comp. Physiol. Psychol.* **55:**201–210.
BARRY, H., III, and MILLER, N. E., 1965, Comparison of drug effects on approach avoidance and escape motivation, *J. Comp. Physiol. Psychol.* **59:**18–24.

BARRY, H., III, MILLER, N. E., and TIDD, GAIL E., 1962a, Control for stimulus change while testing effects of amobarbital on conflict, *J. Comp. Physiol. Psychol.* **55:**1071–1074.

BARRY, H., III, WAGNER, A. R., and MILLER, N. E., 1962b, Effects of alcohol and amobarbital on performance inhibited by experimental extinction, *J. Comp. Physiol. Psychol.* **55:**464–468.

BARRY, H., III, WAGNER, S. A., and MILLER, N. E., 1963, Effects of several drugs on performance in an approach–avoidance conflict, *Psychol. Rep.* **12:**215–221.

BARRY, H., III, ETHEREDGE, E. E., and MILLER, N. E., 1965, Counterconditioning and extinction of fear fail to transfer from amobarbital to nondrug state, *Psychopharmacologia* **8:**150–156.

BAUEN, A., and POSSANZA, G. J., 1970, The mink as a psychopharmacological model, *Arch. Int. Pharmacodyn.* **186:**133–136.

BAXTER, B. L., 1964, The effect of chlordiazepoxide on the hissing response elicited via hypothalamic stimulation, *Life Sci.* **3:**531–537.

BERGER, B. D., and STEIN, L., 1969, Asymmetrical dissociation of learning between scopolamine and Wy 4036, a new benzodiazepine tranquilizer, *Psychopharmacologia* **14:**351–358.

BIGNAMI, G., and DE ACETIS, L., 1973, An investigation on the nature of continuous avoidance deficits: differential response to chlordiazepoxide treatment, *Pharmacol. Biochem. Behav.* **1:**277–283.

BIGNAMI, G., and GATTI, G. L., 1969, Analysis of drug effects on multiple fixed ratio 33–fixed interval 5 min. in pigeons, *Psychopharmacologia* **15:**310–332.

BIGNAMI, G., DE ACETIS, L., and GATTI, G. L., 1971, Facilitation and impairment of avoidance responding by phenobarbital sodium, chlordiazepoxide and diazepam—the role of performance baselines, *J. Pharmacol. Exp. Ther.* **176:**725–732.

BINDRA, D., NYMAN, K., and WISE, J., 1965, Barbiturate-induced dissociation of acquisition and extinction: role of movement-initiating processes, *J. Comp. Physiol. Psychol.* **60:**223–228.

BLACK, A. H., 1975, Hippocampal electrical activity and behaviour, in: *The Hippocampus: A Comprehensive Treatise* (R. L. Isaacson and K. H. Pribram, eds.), Plenum Press, New York.

BLACK, R. W., and SPENCE, K. W., 1965, Effects of intertrial reinforcement on resistance to extinction following extended training, *J. Exp. Psychol.* **70:**559–563.

BLACKMAN, D., 1968, Conditioned suppression or facilitation as a function of the behavioural baseline, *J. Exp. Anal. Behav.* **11:**53–61.

BLAND, B. H., ANDERSEN, P., and GANES, T., 1975, Two generators of hippocampal theta activity in rabbits, *Brain Res.* **94:**199–218.

BLOUGH, D. S., 1956, Technique for studying the effects of drugs on discrimination in the pigeon, *Ann. N.Y. Acad. Sci.* **65:**334–344.

BLOUGH, D. S., 1957, Some effects of drugs on visual discrimination in the pigeon, *Ann. N.Y. Acad. Sci.* **66:**733–739.

BLUM, K., 1970, Effects of chlordiazepoxide and pentobarbital on conflict behavior in rats, *Psychopharmacologia* **17:**391–398.

BOISSIER, J.-R., GRASSET, S., and SIMON, P., 1968a, Effect of some psychotropic drugs on mice from a spontaneously aggressive strain, *J. Pharm. Pharmacol.* **20:**972–973.

BOISSIER, J.-R., SIMON, P., and ARON, C., 1968b, A new method for rapid screening of minor tranquilizers in mice, *Eur. J. Pharmacol.* **4:**145–151.

BREMNER, F. J., COBB, H. D., and NAGY, T. J., 1969, Comparison of the effect of two minor tranquilizers on escape behavior, *Psychon. Sci.* **17:**159–160.

BREMNER, F. J., COBB, H. D., and HAHN, W. C., 1970, The effect of chlordiazepoxide on the behavior of rats in a conflict situation, *Psychopharmacologia* **17:**275–282.

BROADHURST, P. L., 1960, Applications of biometrical genetics to the inheritance of behaviour, in: *Experiments in Personality*, Vol. 1, *Psychogenetics and Psychopharmacology* (H. J. Eysenck, ed.), pp. 1–102, Routledge and Kegan Paul, London.

BROADHURST, P. L., and WALLGREN, H., 1964, Ethanol and the acquisition of a conditioned avoidance response in selected strains of rats, *Q. J. Stud. Alcohol* **25**:476-489.

BRÜCKE, F., SAILER, S., and STUMPF, CH., 1957, Pharmakologische Beeinflussung der Frequenz der Hippocampustätigkeit während retikulärer Reizung, *Arch. Exp. Pathol. Pharmakol.* **231**:267-278.

BRYANT, R. C., PETTY, F., WARREN, J. L., and BYRNE, W. L., 1973, Facilitation by alcohol of active avoidance acquisition performance in the goldfish, *Pharmacol. Biochem. Behav.* **1**:523-529.

BUREŠ, J., BOHDANECKÝ, Z., and WEISS, T., 1962, Physostigmine-induced hippocampal theta activity and learning in rats, *Psychopharmacologia* **3**:254-263.

BUTTERS, N., and ROSVOLD, H. E., 1968, Effect of caudate and septal nuclei lesions on resistance to extinction and delayed alternation, *J. Comp. Physiol. Psychol.* **65**:397-403.

CANNIZZARO, G., NIGITO, S., PROVENZANO, P. M., and VITIKOVÀ, T., 1972, The relationship between inhibitory factors and behaviour after treatment with medazepam, *Arzneim.-Forsch.* **22**:772-776.

CAPALDI, E. J., 1967, A sequential hypothesis of instrumental learning, in: *The Psychology of Learning and Motivation*, Vol. 1 (K. W. Spence and J. T. Spence, eds.), pp. 67-156, Academic Press, New York and London.

CAPALDI, E. J., and SPARLING, D. L., 1971a, Amobarbital and the partial reinforcement effect in rats: isolating frustrative control over instrumental responding, *J. Comp. Physiol. Psychol.* **74**:467-477.

CAPALDI, E. J., and SPARLING, D. L., 1971b, Amobarbital vs. saline extinction following different magnitudes of consistent reinforcement, *Psychon. Sci.* **23**:215-217.

CAPALDI, E. J., BERG, R. F., and SPARLING, D. L., 1971, Trial spacing and emotionality in the rat, *J. Comp. Physiol. Psychol.* **76**:290-299.

CARLTON, P. L., 1963, Cholinergic mechanisms in the control of behavior by the brain, *Psychol. Rev.* **70**:19-39.

CAUL, W. F., 1967, Effects of amobarbital on discrimination acquisition and reversal, *Psychopharmacologia* **11**:414-421.

CHANCE, M. R., MACKINTOSH, J. H., and DIXON, A. K., 1973, The effects of ethyl alcohol on social encounters between mice, *J. Alcoholism* **8**:90-93.

CHEN, G., BOHNER, B., and BRATTON, A. C., JR., 1963, The influence of central depressants on fighting behavior in mice, *Arch. Int. Pharmacodyn.* **142**:30-34.

CHESHER, G. B., 1974, Facilitation of avoidance acquisition in the rat by ethanol and its abolition by α-methyl-*p*-tyrosine, *Psychopharmacologia* **39**:87-95.

CHI, C. C., 1965, The effect of amobarbital sodium on conditioned fear as measured by the potentiated startle response in rats, *Psychopharmacologia* **7**:115-122.

CHISHOLM, D. C., and MOORE, J. W., 1970, Effects of chlordiazepoxide on discriminative fear conditioning and shuttle avoidance performance in the rabbit, *Psychopharmacologia* **18**:162-171.

CHITTAL, S. M., and SHETH, U. K., 1963, Effect of drugs on conditioned avoidance response in rats, *Arch. Int. Pharmacodyn.* **144**:471-480.

CHRISTMAS, A. J., and MAXWELL, D. R., 1970, A comparison of the effects of some benzodiazepines and other drugs on aggressive and exploratory behaviour in mice and rats, *Neuropharmacology* **9**:17-29.

CHURCH, R. M., WOOTEN, C. L., and MATTHEWS, T. J., 1970, Discriminative punishment and the conditioned emotional response, *Learn. Motiv.* **1**:1-17.

CICALA, G. A., and HARTLEY, D. L., 1965, The effects of chlordiazepoxide on the acquisition and performance of a conditioned escape response in rats, *Psychol. Rev.* **15**:435-440.

CICALA, G. A., and HARTLEY, D. L., 1967, Drugs and the learning and performance of fear, *J. Comp. Physiol. Psychol.* **64**:175-178.

COLE, H. F., and WOLF, H. H., 1966, The effects of some psychotropic drugs on conditioned avoidance and aggressive behaviors, *Psychopharmacologia* **8**:389-396.

COLE, H. F., and WOLF, H. H., 1970, Laboratory evaluation of aggressive behavior of the grasshopper mouse (*Onychomys*), *J. Pharm. Sci.* **59**:969–971.

CONGER, J. J., 1951, The effect of alcohol on conflict behavior in the albino rat, *Q. J. Stud. Alcohol* **12**:1–29.

COOK, L., and CATANIA, A. C., 1964, Effects of drugs on avoidance and escape behavior, *Fed. Proc.* **23**:818–835.

COOK, L., and DAVIDSON, A. B., 1973, Effects of behaviorally active drugs in a conflict-punishment procedure in rats, in: *The Benzodiazepines* (S. Garattini, E. Massini, and L. O. Randall, eds.), pp. 327–345, Raven Press, New York.

COOK, L., and KELLEHER, R. T., 1962, Drug effects on the behavior of animals, *Ann. N.Y. Acad. Sci.* **96**:315–335.

CORRODI, H., and FUXE, K., 1967, The effect of catecholamine precursors and monoamine oxidase inhibition on the amine levels of central catecholamine neurons after reserpine treatment or tyrosine hydroxylase inhibition, *Life Sci.* **6**:1345–1350.

CORRODI, H., and HANSON, L. C. F., 1966, Central effects of an inhibitor of tyrosine hydroxylation, *Psychopharmacologia* **10**:116–125.

CORRODI, H., FUXE, K., and HÖKFELT, T., 1966, The effect of ethanol on the activity of central catecholamine neurones in rat brain, *J. Pharm. Pharmacol.* **18**:821–823.

CORRODI, H., FUXE, K., LIDBRINK, P., and OLSON, L., 1971, Minor tranquilizers, stress and central catecholamine neurons, *Brain Res.* **29**:1–16.

CORSON, S. A., and CORSON, E. O'L., 1967, Pavlovian conditioning as a method for studying the mechanisms of action of minor tranquilizers, in: *Neuropsychopharmacology, Proceedings of the 5th International Congress, Colleguium Internationale Neuropsychopharmacologicum* (H. Brill *et al.*, eds.), pp. 857–878, Excerpta Medica Foundation, International Congress Series, No. 129.

Cox, T., 1970, The effects of caffeine, alcohol, and previous exposure to the test situation on spontaneous alternation, *Psychopharmacologia* **17**:83–88.

CRESPI, L. P., 1942, Quantitative variation of incentive and performance in the white rat, *Am. J. Psychol.* **55**:467–517.

CROW, L. T., 1966, Effects of alcohol on conditioned avoidance responding, *Physiol. Behav.* **1**:89–91.

CROW, L. T., 1970, Alcohol state transfer effects with performance maintained by intracranial self-stimulation, *Physiol. Behav.* **5**:575–577.

CROWLEY, T. J., 1972, Dose-dependent facilitation or suppression of rat fighting by methamphetamine, phenobarbital, or imipramine, *Psychopharmacologia* **27**:213–222.

DAHLSTRÖM, A., HÄGGENDAL, J., and ATACK, C., 1973, Localization and transport of serotonin, in: *Serotonin and Behavior* (J. Barchas and E. Usdin, eds.), pp. 87–96, Academic Press, New York.

DANTZER, R., and ROCA, M., 1974, Tranquilizing effects of diazepam in pigs subjected to a punishment procedure, *Psychopharmacologia* **40**:235–248.

DA VANZO, J. P., DAUGHERTY, M., RUCKART, R., and KANG, L., 1966, Pharmacological and biochemical studies in isolation-induced fighting mice, *Psychopharmacologia* **9**:210–219.

DAVID, J., GREWAL, R. S., and WAGLE, G. P., 1974, Persistent electroencephalographic changes in rhesus monkeys after single doses of pentobarbital, nitrazepam and imipramine, *Psychopharmacologia* **35**:61–75.

DAVIDSON, A. B., 1970, Facilitory effects of chlordiazepoxide on behavior of rats, *Proceedings of the 78th Annual Convention of the American Psychological Association*, pp. 807–808.

DAVIDSON, A. B., and COOK, L., 1969, Effects of combined treatment with trifluoperazine–HCl and amobarbital on punished behavior in rats, *Psychopharmacologia* **15**:159–168.

DELGADO, J. M. R., 1973, Anti-aggressive effects of chlordiazepoxide, in: *The Benzodiazepines* (S. Garattini, E. Mussini and L. O. Randall, eds.), pp. 419–432, Raven Press, New York.

DEMBER, W. N., 1956, Response by the rat to environmental change, *J. Comp. Physiol. Psychol.* **49**:93–95.

DEUTSCH, J. A., and ROLL, S. K., 1973, Alcohol and asymmetrical state-dependency: a possible explanation, *Behav. Biol.* **8**:273–278.

DEWS, P. B., 1955a, Studies on behavior. I. Differential sensitivity to pentobarbital of pecking performance in pigeons depending on the schedule of reward, *J. Pharmacol. Exp. Ther.* **113:**393–401.

DEWS, P. B., 1955b, Studies on behavior. II. The effects of pentobarbital, methamphetamine and scopolamine on performances in pigeons involving discriminations, *J. Pharmacol. Exp. Ther.* **115:**380–389.

DEWS, P. B., 1956, Modification by drugs of performance on simple schedules of positive reinforcement, *Ann. N.Y. Acad. Sci.* **65:**268–281.

DEWS, P. B., 1958, Studies on behavior. IV. Stimulant actions of methamphetamine, *J. Pharmacol. Exp. Ther.* **122:**137–147.

DEWS, P. B., 1960, Free-operant behavior under conditions of delayed reinforcement. I. CRF-type schedules, *J. Exp. Anal. Behav.* **3:**221–234.

DEWS, P. B., 1964, A behavioral effect of amobarbital, *Naunyn-Schmiedebergs Arch. Exp. Pathol. Pharmakol.* **248:**296–307.

DICKINSON, A., 1972, Septal damage and response output under frustrative nonreward, in: *Inhibition and Learning* (R. A. Boakes and M. S. Halliday, eds.), pp. 461–496, Academic Press, London.

DICKINSON, A., 1974, Response suppression and facilitation by aversive stimuli following septal lesions in rats: a review and model, *Physiol. Psychol.* **2:**444–456.

DIMASCIO, A., 1973, The effects of benzodiazepines on aggression: reduced or increased? *Psychopharmacologia* **30:**95–102.

DJAHANGUIRI, B., and RICHELLE, M., 1963, Effet d'un traitement prolongé au chlordiazepoxide sur un conditionnement temporel chez le rat, *J. Physiol. (Paris)* **55:**136–137.

DOMINIC, J. A., 1973, Suppression of brain serotonin synthesis and metabolism by benzodiazepine minor tranquilizers, in: *Serotonin and Behavior* (J. Barchas and E. Usdin, eds.), pp., 149–156, Academic Press, New York.

DOMINO, E. F., and OLDS, M. E., 1968, Cholinergic inhibition of self-stimulation behavior, *J. Pharmacol. Exp. Ther.* **164:**202–211.

DOMINO, E. F., and OLDS, M. E., 1972, Effects of d-amphetamine, scopolamine, chlordiazepoxide and diphenylhydantoin on self-stimulation behavior and brain acetylcholine, *Psychopharmacologia* **23:**1–16.

DOMINO, E. F., CALDWELL, D. F., and HENKE, R., 1965, Effects of psychoactive agents on acquisition of conditioned pole jumping in rats, *Psychopharmacologia* **8:**285–289.

DONOVICK, P. J., 1968, Effects of localized septal lesions on hippocampal EEG activity and behavior in rats, *J. Comp. Physiol. Psychol.* **66:**569–578.

DOUGLAS, R. J., 1967, The hippocampus and behavior, *Psychol. Bull.* **67:**416–442.

DOUGLAS, R. J., and SCOTT, D. W., 1972, The differential effects of nitrazepam on certain inhibitory and excitatory behaviors, *Psychon. Sci.* **26:**164–166.

DREWETT, R. F., GRAY, J. A., JAMES, D. T. D., MCNAUGHTON, N., VALERO, I., and DUDDERIDGE, H. J., in press, Sex and strain differences in septal driving of hippocampal theta rhythm as a function of frequency: Effects of gonadectomy and gonadal hormones, *Neuroscience*.

DREWNOWSKI, A., and GRAY, J. A., 1975, Influence of Δ^9-tetrahydrocannabinol on partial reinforcement effects, *Psychopharmacologia* **43:**233–237.

DUDDERIDGE, H. J., and GRAY, J. A., 1974, Joint effects of sodium amylobarbitone and amphetamine sulphate on resistance to extinction of a rewarded running response in the rat, *Psychopharmacologia* **35:**365–370.

DYCK, D. G., LUSSIER, D., and OSSENKOPP, K.-P., 1975, Partial punishment effect following minimal acquisition training: sodium amobarbital and the stimulus properties of early punished trials, *Learn. Motiv.* **6:**412–420.

EDITORIAL, 1975, Tranquilizers causing aggression, *Br. Med. J.*, No. 5950, pp. 113–114.

ELAZAR, Z., and ADEY, W. R., 1967, Electroencephalographic correlates of learning in subcortical and cortical structures, *Electroencephalogr. Clin. Neurophysiol.* **23:**306–319.

ESTES, W. K., and SKINNER, B. F., 1941, Some quantitative properties of anxiety, *J. Exp. Psychol.* **29:**390–400.

FALK, J. L., 1971, The nature and determinants of adjunctive behavior, *Physiol. Behav.* **6:**577–588.
FERRARO, D. P., and YORK, K. M., 1968, Punishment effects in rats selectively bred for emotional elimination, *Psychon. Sci.* **10:**177–178.
FERSTER, G. B., APPEL, J. B., and HISS, R. A., 1962, The effects of drugs on a fixed-ratio performance suppressed by a pre-time-out stimulus, *J. Exp. Anal. Behav.* **5:**73–88.
FONTAINE, O., and RICHELLE, M., 1969, Etude comparative chez le rat des effets de la chlorpromazine et du chlordiazepoxide sur une série de programmes à renforcement positif et à renforcement négatif, *Psychol. Belg.* **9:**17–29.
FOWLER, H., and MILLER, N. E., 1963, Facilitation and inhibition of runway performance by hind- and forepaw shock of various intensities, *J. Comp. Physiol. Psychol.* **56:**801–805.
FOWLER, S. C., 1974, Some effects of chlordiazepoxide and chlorpromazine on response force in extinction, *Pharmacol. Biochem. Behav.* **2:**155–160.
FOX, K. A., and SNYDER, R. L., 1969, Effect of sustained low doses of diazepam on aggression and mortality in grouped male mice, *J. Comp. Physiol. Psychol.* **69:**663–666.
FOX, K. A., TUCKOSH, J. R., and WILCOX, A. H., 1970, Increased aggression among grouped male mice fed chlordiazepoxide, *Eur. J. Pharmacol.* **11:**119–121.
FOX, K. A., WEBSTER, J. C., and GUERRIERO, F. J., 1972, Increased aggression among grouped male mice fed nitrazepam and flurazepam, *Pharmacol. Res. Commun.* **4:**157–162.
FREED, E. X., 1967, The effect of alcohol upon approach–avoidance conflict in the white rat, *Q. J. Stud. Alcohol* **28:**236–254.
FREED, E. X., 1968, Effect of alcohol on conflict behaviors, *Psychol. Rep.* **23:**151–159.
FREED, E. X., 1971, Alcohol and conflict: role of drug-dependent learning in the rat, *Q. J. Stud. Alcohol* **32:**13–28.
FREED, E. X., 1972, Alcohol and conflict: the role of self-intoxication in a punishment discrimination by rats, *Q. J. Stud. Alcohol* **33:**756–768.
FREEDMAN, P. E., and ROSEN, A. J., 1969, The effects of psychotropic drugs on the double-alley frustration effect, *Psychopharmacologia* **15:**39–47.
FREEDMAN, P. E., HENNESSY, J. W., and GRONER, D., 1974, Effects of varying active/passive shock levels in shuttle box avoidance in rats, *J. Comp. Physiol. Psychol.* **86:**79–84.
FREEMON, F. R., 1974, The effect of Δ^9-tetrahydrocannabinol on sleep, *Psychopharmacologia* **35:**39–44.
FRIEDMAN, E., and GERSHON, S., 1974, Effect of Δ^8-THC on alcohol-induced sleeping time in the rat, *Psychopharmacologia* **39:**193–198.
FULLER, J. L., 1970, Strain differences in the effects of chlorpromazine and chlordiazepoxide upon active and passive avoidance in mice, *Psychopharmacologia* **16:**261–271.
GANDELMAN, R., and TROWILL, J., 1968, Effects of chlordiazepoxide on ESB-reinforced behavior and subsequent extinction, *J. Comp. Physiol. Psychol.* **66:**753–755.
GATTI, G. L., and BIGNAMI, G., 1969, Effects of chlordiazepoxide, diazepam, phenobarbital, meprobamate and phenytoin on continuous lever pressing avoidance with or without warning stimulus, in: *Proceedings of the 6th International Congress, Collegium Internationale Neuropsychopharmacologicum*, pp. 255–256, Excerpta Medica Foundation, International Congress Series, No. 180.
GELLER, I., 1964, Relative potencies of benzodiazepines as measured by their effects on conflict behavior, *Arch. Int. Pharmacodyn.* **149:**243–247.
GELLER, I., and SEIFTER, J., 1960, The effects of meprobamate, barbiturates, *d*-amphetamine and promazine on experimentally induced conflict in the rat, *Psychopharmacologia* **1:**482–492.
GELLER, I., and SEIFTER, J., 1962, The effects of mono-urethans, di-urethans and barbiturates on a punishment discrimination, *J. Pharmacol. Exp. Ther.* **136:**284–288.
GELLER, I., KULAK, J. T., JR., and SEIFTER, J., 1962, The effects of chlordiazepoxide and chlorpromazine on a punishment discrimination, *Psychopharmacologia* **3:**374–385.

GELLER, I., BACHMAN, E., and SEIFTER, J., 1963, Effects of reserpine and morphine on behavior suppressed by punishment, *Life Sci.* **4:**226–231.

GIBBINS, R. J., KALANT, H., LeBLANC, A. E., and CLARK, J. W., 1971, The effects of chronic administration of ethanol on startle thresholds in rats, *Psychopharmacologia* **19:**95–104.

GILL, E. W., PATON, W. D. M., and PERTWEE, R. G., 1970, Preliminary experiments on the chemistry and pharmacology of cannabis, *Nature (London)* **228:**134–136.

GLAZER, H. I., 1973, The effects of increased acetylcholine levels during feeding on subsequent acquisition and extinction of bar pressing, *Physiol. Psychol.* **1:**333–336.

GLAZER, H. I., 1974, Instrumental conditioning of hippocampal theta and subsequent response persistence, *J. Comp. Physiol. Psychol.* **86:**267–273.

GLUCKMAN, M. I., 1965, Pharmacology of oxazepam (Serax), a new anti-anxiety agent, *Curr. Ther. Res.* **7:**721–740.

GOLDBERG, M. E., and CIOFALO, V. B., 1969, Effect of diphenylhydantoin sodium and chlordiazepoxide alone and in combination on punishment behavior, *Psychopharmacologia* **14:**233–239.

GOLDBERG, M. E., HEFNER, M. A., ROBICHAUD, R. C., and DUBINSKY, B., 1973, Effects of Δ^9-tetrahydrocannabinol (THC) and chlordiazepoxide (CDP) on state-dependent learning: evidence for asymmetrical dissociation, *Psychopharmacologia* **30:**173–184.

GOLDMAN, P. S., and DOCTER, R. F., 1966, Facilitation of bar pressing and "suppression" of conditioned suppression in cats as a function of alcohol, *Psychopharmacologia* **9:**64–72.

GOODRICH, K. P., 1959, Performance in different segments of an instrumental response chain as a function of reinforcement schedule, *J. Exp. Psychol.* **57:**57–63.

GRAHAM, D. T., and ERICKSON, C. K., 1974, Alteration of ethanol-induced CNS depression: ineffectiveness of drugs that modify cholinergic transmission, *Psychopharmacologia* **34:**173–180.

GRANDJEAN, E., and BÄTTIG, K., 1962, Die Wirkung verschiedener Psychopharmaka auf die spontane Alternation der Ratte, *Helv. Physiol. Pharmacol. Acta* **20:**373–381.

GRAY, J. A., 1964a, The effects of pipradrol hydrochloride and sodium amylobarbitone on operant responding in a discrimination situation, *Psychopharmacologia* **6:**417–434.

GRAY, J. A., 1964b, Strength of the nervous system and levels of arousal: a reinterpretation, in: *Pavlov's Typology* (J. A. Gray, ed.), pp. 289–366, Pergamon Press, Oxford.

GRAY, J. A., 1967, Disappointment and drugs in the rat, *Adv. Sci.* **23:**595–605.

GRAY, J. A., 1969, Sodium amobarbital and effects of frustrative non-reward, *J. Comp. Physiol. Psychol.* **69:**55–64.

GRAY, J. A., 1970, Sodium amobarbital, the hippocampal theta rhythm and the partial reinforcement extinction effect, *Psychol. Rev.* **77:**465–480.

GRAY, J. A., 1971a, *The Psychology of Fear and Stress*, Weidenfeld and Nicolson, London; McGraw-Hill, New York.

GRAY, J. A., 1971b, Sex differences in emotional behaviour in mammals including man: endocrine bases, *Acta Psychol.* **35:**29–46.

GRAY, J. A., 1971c, Medial septal lesions, hippocampal theta rhythm and the control of vibrissal movement in the freely moving rat, *Electroencephalogr. Clin. Neurophysiol.* **30:**189–197.

GRAY, J. A., 1972a, The structure of the emotions and the limbic system, in: *Physiology, Emotion and Psychosomatic Illness* (R. Porter and J. Knight, eds.), pp. 87–130, Associated Scientific Publishers, Amsterdam.

GRAY, J. A., 1972b, Effects of septal driving of the hippocampal theta rhythm on resistance to extinction, *Physiol. Behav.* **8:**481–490.

GRAY, J. A., 1975, *Elements of a Two-Process Theory of Learning*, Academic Press, London.

GRAY, J. A., 1976, The behavioural inhibition system: a possible substrate for anxiety, in: *Theoretical and Experimental Bases of the Behaviour Therapies* (M. P. Feldman and A. Broadhurst, eds.), pp. 3–41, Wiley, London.

GRAY, J. A., and ARAUJO-SILVA, M. T., 1971, Joint effects of medial septal lesions and amylobarbitone injections in the rat, *Psychopharmacologia* **22:**8–22.

Gray, J. A., and Ball, G. G., 1970, frequency-specific relation between hippocampal theta rhythm, behavior, and amobarbital action, *Science* **168**:1246–1248.

Gray, J. A., and Dudderidge, H., 1971, Sodium amylobarbitone, the partial reinforcement extinction effect and the frustration effect in the double runway, *Neuropharmacology* **10**:217–222.

Gray, J. A., and Lalljee, B., 1974, Sex differences in emotional behaviour in the rat: correlation between open field defecation and active avoidance, *Anim. Behav.* **22**:856–861.

Gray, J. A., and Smith, P. T., 1969, An arousal-decision model for partial reinforcement and discrimination learning, in: *Animal Discrimination Learning* (R. Gilbert and N. S. Sutherland, eds.), pp. 243–272, Academic Press, London.

Gray, J. A., Araujo-Silva, M. T., and Quintão, L., 1972a, Resistance to extinction after partial reinforcement training with blocking of the hippocampal theta rhythm by septal stimulation, *Physiol. Behav.* **8**:497–502.

Gray, J. A., Quintão, L., and Araujo-Silva, M. T., 1972b, The partial reinforcement extinction effect in rats with medial septal lesions, *Physiol. Behav.* **8**:491–496.

Gray, J. A., McNaughton, N., James, D. T. D., and Kelly, P. H., 1975, Effect of minor tranquilisers on hippocampal theta rhythm mimicked by depletion of forebrain noradrenaline, *Nature (London)* **258**:424–425.

Gray, W. D., Osterberg, A. C., and Rauh, C. E., 1961, Neuropharmacological actions of mephenoxalone, *Arch. Int. Pharmacodyn.* **134**:198–215.

Green, J. D., and Arduini, A. A., 1954, Hippocampal electrical activity in arousal, *J. Neurophysiol.* **17**:533–557.

Griffiths, R. R., and Thompson, T., 1973, Effects of chlorpromazine and pentobarbital on pattern and number of responses in extinction, *Psychol. Rep.* **33**:323–334.

Griffiths, R. R., and Thompson, T., 1974, Pentobarbital facilitated extinction: effects of different schedules of drug withdrawal, *Pharmacol. Biochem. Behav.* **2**:331–338.

Grossman, S. P., 1972, Cholinergic synapses in the limbic system and behavioral inhibition, *Res. Publ. Assoc. Res. Nerv. Ment. Dis.* **50**:315–326.

Grossman, S. P., and Miller, N. E., 1961, Control for stimulus-change in the evaluation of alcohol and chlorpromazine as fear-reducing drugs, *Psychopharmacologia* **2**:342–351.

Guaitani, A., Marcucci, F., and Garattini, S., 1971, Increased aggression and toxicity in grouped male mice treated with tranquilizing benzodiazepines, *Psychopharmacologia* **19**:241–245.

Gupta, B. D., and Holland, H. C., 1969, An examination of the effects of stimulant and depressant drugs on escape/avoidance conditioning in strains of rats selectively bred for emotionality/non-emotionality, *Psychopharmacologia* **14**:95–105.

Haggard, D. F., 1959, Acquisition of a simple running response as a function of partial and continuous schedules of reinforcement, *Psychol. Rep.* **9**:11–18.

Hanson, H. M., Witoslawski, J. J., and Campbell, E. A., 1967, Drug effects in squirrel monkeys trained on a multiple schedule with a punishment contingency, *J. Exp. Anal. Behav.* **10**:565–569.

Harris, H. E., Piccolino, E. B., Roback, H. B., and Sommer, D. K., 1964, The effects of alcohol on counter-conditioning of an avoidance response, *Q. J. Stud. Alcohol* **25**:490–497.

Hartmann, E., and Cravens, J., 1973, The effects of long term administration of psychotropic drugs on human sleep. VI. The effects of chlordiazepoxide, *Psychopharmacologia* **33**:233–245.

Hasegawa, Y., Ibuka, N., and Iwahara, S., 1973, Effects of chlordiazepoxide upon successive red–green discrimination responses in Japanese monkeys, *Macaca fuscata, Psychopharmacologia* **30**:89–94.

Heise, G. A., and Boff, E., 1961, Taming action of chlordiazepoxide, *Fed. Proc.* **20**:393.

Heise, G. A., and Boff, E., 1962, Continuous avoidance as a base-line for measuring behavioral effects of drugs, *Psychopharmacologia* **3**:264–282.

HEISE, G. A., LAUGHLIN, N., and KELLER, C., 1970, A behavioural and pharmacological analysis of reinforcement withdrawal, *Psychopharmacologia* **16**:345–368.

HENDRY, D. P., and VAN TOLLER, C., 1964, Fixed-ratio punishment with continuous reinforcement, *J. Exp. Anal. Behav.* **7**:293–300.

HENKE, P. G., 1974, Persistence of runway performance after septal lesions in rats, *J. Comp. Physiol. Psychol.* **86**:760–767.

HENRIKSSON, B. G., and JÄRBE, T., 1971, Effects of diazepam on conditioned avoidance learning in rats and its transfer to normal state conditions, *Psychopharmacologia* **20**:186–190.

HERRNSTEIN, R. J., and MORSE, W. H., 1957, Effects of pentobarbital on intermittently reinforced behavior, *Science* **125**:929–931.

HERZ, A., 1960, Drugs and the conditioned avoidance response, *Int. Rev. Neurobiol.* **2**:229–277.

HEUSCHELE, W. P., 1961, Chlordiazepoxide for calming zoo animals, *J. Am. Vet. Med. Assoc.* **139**:996–998.

HIDALGO, J., TARLETON, W. A., DILEO, R. J., and THOMPSON, C. R., 1968, Effect of drugs on the cardiac conditioned response of dogs, *Behav. Res. Ther.* **6**:461–471.

HOFFMEISTER, F., and WUTTKE, W., 1969, On the actions of psychotropic drugs on the attack and aggressive–defensive behaviour of mice and cats, in: *Aggressive Behaviour* (S. Garattini and E. B. Sigg, eds.), pp. 273–280, Excerpta Medica Foundation, Amsterdam.

HOLLOWAY, F. A., 1972, State-dependent effects of ethanol on active and passive avoidance learning, *Psychopharmacologia* **25**:238–261.

HOLLOWAY, F. A., and VARDIMAN, D. R., 1971, Dose–response effects of ethanol on appetitive behaviors, *Psychonom. Sci.* **24**:218–220.

HOLLOWAY, F. A., and WANSLEY, R. A., 1973, Factors governing the vulnerability of DRL operant performance to the effects of ethanol, *Psychopharmacologia* **28**:351–362.

HOLLOWAY, F. A., and WANSLEY, R. A., 1974, Motivational parameters in ethanol-induced state dependent dissociation of avoidance learning, *Physiol. Psychol.* **2**:71–74.

HOLTZMAN, S. G., and VILLAREAL, J. E., 1969, The effects of morphine on conditioned suppression in rhesus monkeys, *Psychon. Sci.* **17**:161–162.

HOWARD, G. S., and MCHOSE, J. H., 1974, The effects of sodium amobarbital on odor-based responding in rats, *Bull. Psychon. Soc.* **3**:185–186.

HUGHES, R. N., and GREIG, A. M., 1975, Spontaneous alternation in ferrets following treatment with scopolamine, chlordiazepoxide and caffeine, *Physiol. Psychol.* **3**:153–156.

ISON, J. R., and NORTHMAN, J., 1968, Amobarbital sodium and instrumental performance changes following an increase in reward magnitude, *Psychon. Sci.* **12**:185–186.

ISON, J. R., and PENNES, E. S., 1969, Interaction of amobarbital sodium and reinforcement schedule in determining resistance to extinction of an instrumental running response, *J. Comp. Physiol. Psychol.* **68**:215–219.

ISON, J. R., and ROSEN, A. J., 1967, The effects of amobarbital sodium on differential instrumental conditioning and subsequent extinction, *Psychopharmacologia* **10**:417–425.

ISON, J. R., GLASS, D. H., and BOHMER, H. M., 1966, Effects of sodium amytal on the approach to stimulus change, *Proc. Am. Psychol. Assoc.* **2**:5–6.

ISON, J. R., DALY, H. B., and GLASS, D. H., 1967, Amobarbital sodium and the effects of reward and nonreward in the Amsel double runway, *Psychol. Rep.* **20**:491–496.

IWAHARA, S., 1971, Effects of drug-state changes upon two-way shuttle avoidance responses in rats treated with chlordiazepoxide or placebo, *Jpn. Psychol. Res.* **13**:207–218.

IWAHARA, S., and MATSUSHITA, K., 1971, Effects of drug-state changes upon black–white discrimination learning in rats, *Psychopharmacologia* **19**:347–358.

IWAHARA, S., and TAKAHASHI, T., 1971, Effects of drug-state changes upon starting and running responses in a straight runway in shock-motivated rats, *Psychologia* **14**:193–199.

IWAHARA, S., IWASAKI, T., NAGAMURA, N., and MASUYAMA, E., 1966, Effect of chlordiazepoxide upon partially-reinforced behavior of rats in the straight runway, *Jpn. Psychol. Res.* **8**:131–135.

Iwahara, S., Nagamura, N., and Iwasaki, T., 1967, Effect of chlordiazepoxide upon experimental extinction in the straight runway as a function of partial reinforcement in the rat, *Jpn. Psychol. Res.* **9**:128-134.

Iwahara, S., Oishi, H., Yamazaki, S., and Sakai, K., 1972, Effects of chlordiazepoxide upon spontaneous alternation and the hippocampal electrical activity in white rats, *Psychopharmacologia* **24**:496-507.

Izquierdo, J. A., Merlo, A. B., Chemerinski, E., and Billiet, M., 1974, Effects of ethanol and sherry on the performance of a conditioned response in the rat, *Pharmacol. Biochem. Behav.* **2**:317-323.

James, D. T. D., McNaughton, N., Rawlins, J. N. P., Feldon, J., and Gray, J. A., in press, Septal driving of hippocampal theta rhythm as a function of frequency in the free-moving rat, *Neuroscience*.

Janssen, P. A. J., Jageneau, A. H., and Niemegeers, C. J. E., 1960, Effects of various drugs on isolation-induced fighting behavior of male mice, *J. Pharmacol. Exp. Ther.* **129**:471-475.

Jouvet, M., 1969, Biogenic amines and the states of sleep, *Science* **163**:32-41.

Jouvet, M., 1974, The role of monoaminergic neurons in the regulation and function of sleep, in: *Basic Sleep Mechanisms* (O. Petre-Quadens and J. D. Schlag, eds.), pp. 207-236, Academic Press, New York.

Kamano, D. K., and Arp, D. J., 1964, Effects of chlordiazepoxide (Librium) on the acquisition and extinction of avoidance responses, *Psychopharmacologia* **6**:112-119.

Kamano, D. K., Martin, L. K., and Powell, B. J., 1966a, Avoidance response acquisition and amobarbital dosage levels, *Psychopharmacologia* **8**:319-323.

Kamano, D. K., Martin, L. K., Ogle, M. E., and Powell, B. J., 1966b, Effects of amobarbital on the conditioned emotional response and conditioned avoidance response, *Psychol. Rec.* **16**:13-16.

Kamp, A., Lopes da Silva, F. H., and Storm van Leuwen, W., 1971, Hippocampal frequency shifts in different behavioural situations, *Brain Res.* **31**:287-294.

Kelleher, R. T., and Cook, L., 1959, Effects of *d*-amphetamine, meprobamate, phenobarbital, mephenesin, or chlorpromazine on DRL and FR schedules of reinforcement with rats, *J. Exp. Anal. Behav.* **2**:267.

Kelleher, R. T., and Morse, W. H., 1964, Escape behavior and punished behavior, *Fed. Proc.* **23**:808-817.

Kelleher, R. T., and Morse, W. H., 1968, Determinants of the specificity of behavioral effects of drugs, *Ergeb. Physiol.* **60**:1-56.

Kelleher, R. T., Fry, W., Deegan, J., and Cook, L., 1961, Effects of meprobamate on operant behavior in rats, *J. Pharmacol. Exp. Ther.* **133**:271-280.

Kelsey, J. E., and Grossman, S. P., 1969, Cholinergic blockade and lesions in the ventromedial septum of the rat, *Physiol. Behav.* **4**:837-845.

Kemp, I. R., and Kaada, B. R., 1975, The relation of hippocampal theta activity to arousal, attentive behaviour and somato-motor movements in unrestrained cats, *Brain Res.* **95**:323-342.

Khavari, K. A., 1969, Effects of central versus intraperitoneal *d*-amphetamine administration on learned behavior, *J. Comp. Physiol. Psychol.* **68**:226-234.

Kimble, D. P., 1969, Possible inhibitory functions of the hippocampus, *Neuropsychologia* **7**:235-244.

Kimsey, R. A., Dyer, R. S., and Petri, H. L., 1974, Relationship between hippocampal EEG, novelty and frustration in the rat, *Behav. Biol.* **11**:561-568.

King, A. R., 1968, Drug effects in rats on approach and avoidance behavior at varying drive levels, *Physiol. Behav.* **3**:935-939.

King, A. R., 1970, Drive related effects of amylobarbitone and chlorpromazine on appetitive and aversively controlled behaviour in the rat, *Physiol. Behav.* **5**:1365-1371.

Kletzkin, M., 1969, An experimental analysis of aggressive-defensive behavior in mice, in:

Aggressive Behaviour (S. Garattini and E. B. Sigg, eds.), pp. 253–262, Excerpta Medica Foundation, Amsterdam.

KOE, B. K., and WEISSMAN, A., 1968, The pharmacology of para-chlorophenylalanine, a selective depletor of serotonin stores, in: *Advances in Pharmacology*, Vol. 6B (S. Garattini and P. A. Shore, eds.), pp. 29–47, Academic Press, New York.

KRŠIAK, M., and BORGESOVÁ, M., 1973, Effect of alcohol on behaviour of pairs of rats, *Psychopharmacologia* **32**:201–209.

KUBENA, R. K., and BARRY, H., III, 1970, Interactions of Δ^1-tetrahydrocannabinol with barbiturates and methamphetamine, *J. Pharmacol. Exp. Ther.* **173**:94–100.

KUMAR, R., 1971a, Extinction of fear. I. Effects of amylobarbitone and dexamphetamine given separately and in combination on fear and exploratory behaviour in rats, *Psychopharmacologia* **19**:163–187.

KUMAR, R., 1971b, Extinction of fear. II. Effects of chlordiazepoxide and chlorpromazine on fear and exploratory behaviour in rats, *Psychopharmacologia* **19**:297–312.

LANGFELDT, T., and URSIN, H., 1971, Differential action of diazepam on flight and defense behavior in the cat, *Psychopharmacologia* **19**:61–66.

LATIES, V. G., and WEISS, B., 1962, Effects of alcohol on timing behavior, *J. Comp. Physiol. Psychol.* **55**:85–91.

LATIES, V. G., and WEISS, B., 1966, Influence of drugs on behavior controlled by internal and external stimuli, *J. Pharmacol. Exp. Ther.* **152**:388–396.

LAUENER, H., 1963, Conditioned suppression in rats and the effect of pharmacological agents thereon, *Psychopharmacologia* **4**:311–325.

LE DOUAREC, J. C., and BROUSSY, L., 1969, Dissociation of the aggressive behavior in mice produced by certain drugs, in: *Aggressive Behaviour* (S. Garattini and E. B. Sigg, eds.), pp. 281–295, Excerpta Medica Foundation, Amsterdam.

LEVINE, S., 1962a, Psychophysiological effects of infant stimulation, in: *Roots of Behavior* (E. L. Bliss, ed.), pp. 246–253, Hoeber, New York.

LEVINE, S., 1962b, The effects of infantile experience on adult behavior, in: *Experimental Foundations of Clinical Psychology* (A. J. Bachrach, ed.), pp. 139–169, Basic Books, New York.

LEWIS, D. J., 1960, Partial reinforcement: a selective review of the literature since 1950, *Psychol. Bull.* **57**:1–28.

LEWIS, P. R., and SHUTE, C. C. D., 1967, The cholinergic limbic system: projections to hippocampal formation, medial cortex, nuclei of the ascending cholinergic reticular system, and the subfornical organ and supraoptic crest, *Brain* **90**:521–540.

LIDBRINK, P., CORRODI, H., FUXE, K., and OLSON, L., 1972, Barbiturates and meprobamate: decreases in catecholamine turnover of central dopamine and noradrenaline neuronal systems and the influence of immobilization stress, *Brain Res.* **45**:507–524.

LIVETT, B. G., 1973, Histochemical visualization of peripheral and central adrenergic neurones, in: *Catecholamines* (L. Iversen, ed.), *Br. Med. Bull. Suppl.* **29**(2):93–99.

LONGONI, A., MANDELLI, V., and PESSOTTI, I., 1973, Study of anti-anxiety effects of drugs in the rat, with a multiple punishment and reward schedule, in: *The Benzodiazepines* (S. Garattini, E. Mussini, and L. O. Randall, eds.), pp. 347–354, Raven Press, New York.

LOPES DA SILVA, F. H., and KAMP, A., 1969, Hippocampal theta frequency shifts and operant behaviour, *Electroencephalogr. Clin. Neurophysiol.* **26**:133–143.

LUBAR, J. F., and NUMAN, R., 1973, Behavioral and physiological studies of septal functions and related medial cortical structures, *Behav. Biol.* **8**:1–25.

LUDVIGSON, H. W., 1967, A preliminary investigation of the effects of sodium amytal, prior reward in G_1, and activity level on the FE, *Psychon. Sci.* **8**:115–116.

LUDVIGSON, H. W., and SYTSMA, D., 1967, The sweet smell of success: apparent double alternation in the rat, *Psychon. Sci.* **9**:283–284.

LYNCH, M. A., LINDSAY, J., and OUNSTED, C., 1975, Tranquilizers causing aggression, *Br. Med. J.*, No. 5952, p. 260.

Lynch, V. C., Aceto, M. C. G., and Thoms, R. K., 1960, Effects of certain psychopharmacologic drugs on conditioning in the rat. I. Avoidance-escape conditioning, *J. Am. Pharm. Assoc.* **49:**205-210.

Mabry, P. D., and Campbell, B. A., 1974, Ontogeny of serotonergic inhibition of behavioral arousal in the rat, *J. Comp. Physiol. Psychol.* **86:**193-201.

Mabry, P. D., and Peeler, D. F., 1972, Effect of septal lesions on response to frustrative nonreward, *Physiol. Behav.* **8:**909-913.

Macadar, O., Ring, J. A., Monti, J. M., and Budelli, R., 1970, The functional relationship between septal and hippocampal theta rhythm, *Physiol. Behav.* **5:**1443-1449.

McCleary, R. A., 1966, Response-modulating functions of the limbic system: initiation and suppression, in: *Progress in Physiological Psychology*, Vol. 1 (E. Stellar and J. M. Sprague, eds.), pp. 209-272, Academic Press, New York.

MacDonnell, M. F., Fessock, L., and Brown, S. H., 1971, Ethanol and the neural substrate for affective defense in the cat, *Q. J. Stud. Alcohol* **32:**406-419.

McGonigle, B., McFarland, D. J., and Collier, P., 1967, Rapid extinction following drug-inhibited incidental learning, *Nature (London)* **214:**531-532.

McHose, J. H., 1967, Patterned running as a function of the sequence of trial administration, *Psychon. Sci.* **9:**281-282.

MacInnes, J. W., and Uphouse, L. L., 1973, Effects of alcohol on acquisition and retention of passive-avoidance conditioning in different mouse strains, *J. Comp. Physiol. Psychol.* **84:**398-402.

Manning, F. J., and Elsmore, T. F., 1972, Shock-elicited fighting and delta-9-tetrahydrocannabinol, *Psychopharmacologia* **25:**218-228.

Margules, D. L., and Stein, L., 1967, Neuroleptics vs. tranquilizers: evidence from animal behavior studies of mode and site of action, in: *Neuropsychopharmacology, Proceedings of the 5th International Congress, Collegiuum Internationale Neuropsychopharmacologicum* (H. Brill et al., eds.), pp. 108-120, Excerpta Medica Foundation, International Congress Series, No. 129.

Margules, D. L., and Stein, L., 1968, Increase of "anti-anxiety" activity and tolerance of behavioral depression during chronic administration of oxazepam, *Psychopharmacologia* **13:**74-80.

Martin, L. K., Powell, B. J., and Kamano, D. K., 1966, Effects of amobarbital sodium on avoidance performances of rats differing in emotionality, *Proceedings of the 74th Annual Convention of the American Psychological Association*, pp. 125-126.

Martin, L. K., Powell, B. J., and Kamano, D. K., 1967, Mediation of shock- and drug-produced effects on avoidance responding, *Psychonomic Sci.* **9:**3-4.

Mason, S. T., and Iversen, S. D., 1975, Learning in the absence of forebrain noradrenaline, *Nature (London)* **258:**422-424.

Mason, S. T., and Iversen, S. D., 1977, Effects of selective forebrain noradrenaline loss on behavioural inhibition in the rat, *J. Comp. Physiol. Psychol.* **91:**165-173.

Masserman, J. H., and Yum, K. S., 1946, An analysis of the influence of alcohol on experimental neuroses in cats, *Psychosom. Med.* **8:**36-52.

Masserman, J. H., Jacques, M. G., and Nicholson, M. R., 1945, Alcohol as a preventive of experimental neuroses, *Q. J. Stud. Alcohol* **6:**281-299.

McKearney, J. W., 1970, Rate-dependent effects of drugs: modification by discriminative stimuli of the effects of amobarbital on schedule-controlled behavior, *J. Exp. Anal. Behav.* **14:**167-175.

McMillan, D. E., 1967, A comparison of the punishing effects of response-produced shock and response-produced time out, *J. Exp. Anal. Behav.* **10:**439-449.

McMillan, D. E., 1973, Drugs and punished responding. I. Rate-dependent effects under multiple schedules, *J. Exp. Anal. Behav.* **19:**133-145.

McMillan, D. E., and Campbell, R. J., 1970, Effects of d-amphetamine and chlordiazepoxide on spaced responding in pigeons, *J. Exp. Anal. Behav.* **14:**177-184.

McMurray, G. A., and Jaques, L. B., 1959, The effects of drugs on a conditioned avoidance response, *Can. J. Psychol.* **13**:186-192.

McNaughton, N., James, D. T. D., Stewart, J., Gray, J. A., Valero, I., and Drewnowski, A., in press, Spetal driving of hippocampal theta rhythm as a function of frequency in the male rat: drug effects, *Neuroscience*.

Mellgren, S. I., and Srebro, B., 1973, Changes in acetylcholinesterase and distribution of degenerating fibres after septal lesions in the rat, *Brain Res.* **52**:19-36.

Meltzer, D., Merkler, N. L., and Maxey, G. C., 1966, Discrimination reversal under sodium pentobarbital, *Psychon. Sci.* **5**:413-414.

Miczek, K. A., 1973a, Effects of scopolamine, amphetamine and chlordiazepoxide on punishment, *Psychopharmacologia* **28**:373-389.

Miczek, K. A., 1973b, Effects of scopolamine, amphetamine and benzodiazepines on conditioned suppression, *Pharmacol. Biochem. Behav.* **1**:401-411.

Miczek, K. A., 1974, Intraspecies aggression in rats: effects of d-amphetamine and chlordiazepoxide, *Psychopharmacologia* **39**:275-301.

Millenson, J. R., 1967, *Principles of Behavioral Analysis*, Macmillan, New York.

Millenson, J. R., and Leslie, J., 1974, The conditioned emotional response (CER) as a baseline for the study of anti-anxiety drugs, *Neuropharmacology* **13**:1-9.

Miller, N. E., 1951, Learnable drives and rewards, in: *Handbook of Experimental Psychology* (S. S. Stevens, ed.), pp. 435-472, Wiley, New York.

Miller, N. E., 1964, The analysis of motivational effects illustrated by experiments on amylobarbitone, in: *Animal Behaviour and Drug Action* (H. Steinberg, ed.), pp. 1-18, Churchill, London.

Miller, N. E., and Barry, H. III, 1960, Motivational effects of drugs: methods which illustrate some general problems in psychopharmacology, *Psychopharmacologia* **1**:169-199.

Miller, N. E., and Miles, W. R., 1936, Alcohol and removal of reward: an analytical study of rodent maze behavior, *J. Comp. Psychol.* **21**:179-204.

Mize, D., and Isaac, W., 1962, Effects of sodium pentobarbital and d-amphetamine on latency of the escape response in the rat, *Psychol. Rep.* **10**:643-645.

Mogenson, G. J., 1964, Effects of sodium pentobarbital on brain self-stimulation, *J. Comp. Physiol. Psychol.* **58**:461-462.

Morrison, C. F., and Stephenson, J. A., 1970, Drug effects on a measure of unconditioned avoidance in the rat, *Psychopharmacologia* **18**:133-143.

Morse, W. H., 1962, Use of operant conditioning techniques for evaluating the effects of barbiturates on behavior, in: *First Hahnemann Symposium on Psychosomatic Medicine* (J. H. Nodine and J. H. Moyer, eds.), pp. 275-281, Lea and Febiger, Philadelphia.

Morse, W. H., 1964, Effect of amobarbital and chlorpromazine on punished behavior in the pigeon, *Psychopharmacologia* **6**:286-294.

Moskowitz, H., and Asato, H., 1966, Effects of alcohol upon the latency of responses learned with positive and negative reinforcers, *Q. J. Stud. Alcohol* **27**:604-611.

Mowrer, O. H., 1960, *Learning Theory and Behavior*, Wiley, New York.

Myer, J. S., 1971, Some effects of noncontingent aversive stimulation, in: *Aversive Conditioning and Learning* (F. R. Brush, ed.), pp. 469-536, Academic Press, New York and London.

Naess, K., and Rasmussen, E. W., 1958, Approach-withdrawal responses and other specific behaviour reactions as screening tests for tranquillizers, *Acta. Pharmacol. Toxicol.* **15**:99-114.

Nelson, P. B., and Wollen, K. A., 1965, Effects of ethanol and partial reinforcement upon runway acquisition, *Psychon. Sci.* **3**:135-136.

Newman, L. M., Lutz, M. P., Gould, M. H., and Domino, E. F., 1972, Δ^9-tetrahydrocannabinol and ethyl alcohol: evidence for cross-tolerance in the rat, *Science* **175**:1022-1023.

NOTTERMAN, J. M., SCHOENFELD, W. N., and BERSH, P. J.,1952, Conditioned heart rate response in human beings during experimental anxiety, *J. Exp. Psychol.* **45**:1-8.

OBRIST, P. A., WOOD, D. M., and PEREZ-REYES, M., 1965, Heart rate during conditioning in humans: effects of UCS intensity, vagal blockade and adrenergic block of vasomotor activity, *J. Exp. Psychol.* **70**:32-42.

OISHI, H., IWAHARA, S., YANG, K-M., and YOGI, A., 1972, Effects of chlordiazepoxide on passive avoidance responses in rats, *Psychopharmacologia* **23**:373-385.

O'KEEFE, J., and NADEL, L., 1974, The hippocampus in pieces and patches, in: *Essays on the Nervous System: A Festschrift for Professor J. Z. Young* (M. R. Bellais and E. G. Gray, eds.), Oxford University Press, Oxord.

OLDS, M. E., 1966, Facilitatory action of diazepam and chlordiazepoxide on hypothalamic reward behavior, *J. Comp. Physiol. Psychol.* **62**:136-140.

OLDS, M. E., and DOMINO, E. F., 1969, Comparison of muscarinic and nicotinic cholinergic agonists on self-stimulation behavior, *J. Pharmacol. Exp. Ther.* **166**:189-204.

OLDS, M. E., and ITO, M., 1973, Effects of chlorpromazine, chlordiazepoxide and pentobarbital on neuronal excitability in the medial forebrain bundle during self-stimulation behavior, *Neuropharmacology* **12**:1117-1133.

OLDS, J., and TRAVIS, R. P., 1960, Effects of chlorpromazine, meprobamate, pentobarbital and morphine on self-stimulation, *J. Pharmacol. Exp. Ther.* **128**:397-404.

OLDS, J., KILLMAN, K. F., and EIDUSON, S., 1957, Effects of tranquillizers on self-stimulation of the brain, in: *Psychotropic Drugs* (S. Garattini and V. Ghetti, eds.), pp. 235-243, Elsevier, New York.

OSWALD, I., BERGER, R. J., JARAMILLO, R. A., KEDDIE, K. M. G., OLLEY, P. C., and PLUNKETT, G. B., 1963, Melancholia and barbiturates: a controlled EEG, body and eye movement study of sleep, *Br. J. Psychiat.* **109**:66-78.

OSWALD, I., LEWIS, S. A., TAGNEY, J., FIRTH, H., and HAIDER, I., 1973, Benzodiazepines and human sleep, in: *The Benzodiazepines* (S. Garattini, E. Mussini, and L. O. Randall, eds.), pp. 613-625, Raven Press, New York.

OVERTON, D. A., 1966, State-dependent learning produced by depressant and atropine-like drugs, *Psychopharmacologia* **10**:6-31.

PANKSEPP, J., 1971, Drugs and stimulus-bound attack, *Physiol. Behav.* **6**:317-320.

PANKSEPP, J., GANDELMAN, R., and TROWILL, J., 1970, Modulation of hypothalamic self-stimulation and escape behavior by chlordiazepoxide, *Physiol. Behav.* **5**:965-969.

PAVLOV, I. P., 1927, *Conditioned Reflexes* (G. V. Anrep, translator), Oxford University Press, London.

PEEKE, H. V. S., ELLMAN, G. E., and HERG, M. J., 1973, Dose-dependent alcohol effects on the aggressive behavior of the convict cichlid *(Cichlasoma nigrofasciatum), Behav. Biol.* **8**:115-122.

PETTY, F., BRYANT, R. C., and BYRNE, W. L., 1973, Dose-related facilitation by alcohol of avoidance acquisition in the goldfish, *Pharmacol. Biochem. Behav.* **1**:173-176.

POWELL, B. J., 1967, Prediction of drug action: elimination of error through emotionality, *Proceedings of the 75th Annual Convention of the American Psychological Association,* pp. 69-70.

POWELL, B. J., MARTIN, L. K., and KAMANO, D. K., 1965, Effects of amobarbital sodium and meprobamate on acquisition of conditioned avoidance, *Psychol. Rep.* **17**:691-694.

POWELL, B. J., MARTIN, L. K., and KAMANO, D. K., 1967, Relationship between emotionality, drug effects, and avoidance responses in Tryon S_1 and S_3 strains, *Can. J. Psychol.* **21**:294-300.

QUENZER, L. F., FELDMAN, R. S., and MOORE, J. W., 1974, Toward a mechanism of the antiaggression effects of chlordiazepoxide in rats, *Psychopharmacologia* **34**:81-94.

RABIN, J. S., 1975, Effects of varying sucrose reinforcers and amobarbital sodium on positive contrast in rats, *Anim. Learn. Behav.* **3**:290-294.

RANDALL, L. O., 1960, Pharmacology of methaminodiazepoxide, *Dis. Nerv. Syst. Suppl.* **21**:7-10.

RANDALL, L. O., 1961, Pharmacology of chlordiazepoxide (Librium), *Dis. Nerv. Syst. Suppl.* **22**:7–15.

RANDALL, L. O., SCHALLEK, W., HEISE, G. A., KEITH, E. F., and BAGDON, R. E., 1960, The psychosedative properties of methaminodiazepoxide, *J. Pharmacol. Exp. Ther.* **129**:163–171.

RANDALL, L. O., HEISE, G. A., SCHALLEK, W., BAGDON, R. E., BANZIGER, R. E., BORIS, A., MOE, R. A., and ABRAMS, W. B., 1961, Pharmacological and clinical studies of Valium (TM), a new psychotherapeutic agent of the benzodiazepine class, *Curr. Ther. Res.* **3**:405–425.

RANDALL, L. O., SCHECKEL, C. L., and BANZIGER, R. F., 1965, Pharmacology of the metabolites of chlordiazepoxide and diazepam, *Curr. Ther. Res.* **1**:590–606.

RAY, O. S., 1963, The effects of tranquilizers on positively and negatively motivated behavior in rats, *Psychopharmacologia* **4**:326–342.

RAY, O. S., 1964, The effect of central nervous system depressants on discrete-trial approach–avoidance behavior, *Psychopharmacologia* **6**:96–111.

RAYNES, A. E., and RYBACK, R. S., 1970, Effect of alcohol and congeners on aggressive response in *Betta splendens*, *Q. J. Stud. Alcohol Suppl.* **5**:130–135.

RAYNES, A. E., RYBACK, R., and INGLE, D., 1968, The effect of alcohol on aggression in *Betta splendens*, *Commun. Behav. Biol. Pt. A.* **2**:141–146.

REID, L. D., GIBSON, W. E., GLEDHILL, S. M., and PORTER, P. B., 1964, Anticonvulsant drugs and self-stimulating behavior, *J. Comp. Physiol. Psychol.* **57**:353–356.

REID, L. D., WASDEN, R. E., and COURTNEY, R. J., 1970, Reinforcing limbic system stimulation and sodium amytal, *Psychon. Sci.* **18**:47–48.

REYNOLDS, G. S., and VAN SOMMERS, P., 1960, Effects of ethyl alcohol on avoidance behavior, *Science* **132**:43–44.

RICHELLE, M., 1962, Action du chlordiazepoxide sur les régulations temporelles dans un comportement conditionné chez le chat, *Arch Int. Pharmacodyn.* **140**:434–449.

RICHELLE, M., 1969, Combined action of diazepam and *d*-amphetamine on fixed-interval performance in cats, *J. Exp. Anal. Behav.* **12**:989–998.

RICHELLE, M., and DJAHANGUIRI, B., 1964, Effet d'un traitement prolongé au chlordiazepoxide sur un conditionnement temporel chez le rat, *Psychopharmacologia* **5**:106–114.

RICHELLE, M., XHENSEVAL, B., FONTAINE, O., and THONE, L., 1962, Action of chlordiazepoxide on two types of temporal conditioning in rats, *Int. J. Neuropharmacol.* **1**:381–391.

RIDGERS, A., and GRAY, J. A., 1973, Influence of amylobarbitone on operant depression and elation effects in the rat, *Psychopharmacologia* **32**:265–270.

ROBICHAUD, R. C., SLEDGE, K. L., HEFNER, M. A., and GOLDBERG, M. E., 1973, Propranolol and chlordiazepoxide on experimentally induced conflict and shuttle box performance in rodents, *Psychopharmacologia* **32**:157–160.

ROSEN, A. J., and TESSEL, R. E., 1970, Chlorpromazine, chlordiazepoxide and incentive-shift performance in the rat, *J. Comp. Physiol. Psychol.* **72**:257–262.

ROSEN, A. J., GLASS, D. H., and ISON, J. R., 1967, Amobarbital sodium and instrumental performance following reward reduction, *Psychon. Sci.* **9**:129–130.

ROSS, R. R., 1964, Positive and negative partial-reinforcement extinction effects carried through continuous reinforcement, changed motivation, and changed response, *J. Exp. Psychol.* **68**:492–502.

RUDZIK, A. D., HESTER, J. B., TANG, A. H., STRAW, R. N., and FRIIS, W., 1973, Triazolobenzodiazepines, a new class of central nervous system depressant compounds, in: *The Benzodiazepines* (S. Garattini, E. Mussini, and L. O. Randall, eds.), pp. 285–297, Raven Press, New York.

RUNDELL, O. H., LESTER, B. K., GRIFFITHS, W. J., and WILLIAMS, H. L., 1972, Alcohol and sleep in young adults, *Psychopharmacologia* **26**:201–218.

RUSHTON, R., STEINBERG, H., and TINSON, C., 1963, Effects of a single experience on subsequent reactions to drugs, *Br. J. Pharmacol.* **20**:99–105.

RUTLEDGE, C. O., and KELLEHER, R. T., 1965, Interactions between the effects of methamphetamine and pentobarbital on operant behavior in the pigeon, *Psychopharmacologia* **7**:400-408.

RYBACK, R. S., 1969, State-dependent or "dissociated" learning with alcohol in the goldfish, *Q. J. Stud. Alcohol* **30**:598-608.

RYBACK, R. S., and INGLE, D., 1970, Effect of ethanol and bourbon on Y-maze learning and shock avoidance in the goldfish, *Q. J. Stud. Alcohol Suppl.* 5, pp. 136-141.

SACHS, E., WEINGARTEN, M., and KLEIN, N. W., JR., 1966, Effects of chlordiazepoxide on the acquisition of avoidance learning and its transfer to the normal state and other drug conditions, *Psychopharmacologia* **9**:17-30.

SANDERS, S. H., and PILLEY, J., 1973, Effects of alcohol on timing behavior in rats, *Q. J. Stud. Alcohol* **34**:367-372.

SANGER, D. J., KEY, M., and BLACKMAN, D. E., 1974, Differential effects of chlordiazepoxide and d-amphetamine on responding maintained by a DRL schedule of reinforcement, *Psychopharmacologia* **38**:159-171.

SANSONE, M., RENZI, P., and AMPOSTA, B., 1972, Effects of chlorpromazine and chlordiazepoxide on discriminated lever-press avoidance behavior and intertrial responding in mice, *Psychopharmacologia* **27**:313-318.

SCHALLEK, W., KUEHN, A., and KOVACS, J., 1972, Effects of chlordiazepoxide hydrochloride on discrimination responses and sleep cycles in cats, *Neuropharmacology* **11**:69-79.

SCHECKEL, C. L., and BOFF, E., 1967, Effects of drugs on aggressive behavior in monkeys, in: *Neuropsychopharmacology, Proceedings of the 5th International Congress, Collegium Internationale Neuropsychopharmacologicum* (H. Brill *et al.*, eds.), pp. 789-795, Excerpta Medica Foundation, International Congress Series, No. 129.

SCHILDKRAUT, J. J., and KETY, S. S., 1967, Biogenic amines and emotion, *Science* **156**:21-30.

SCHMIDT, H., JR., and STEWART, A. L., 1967, Acute effects of phenobarbital upon a locomotor response, *Physiol. Behav.* **2**:403-407.

SCHMIDT, H., JR., MAHONEY, G. J., and KENNEDY, M. A., 1973, Acute effect of phenobarbital on escape behavior, *Physiol Behav.* **10**:19-22.

SCOBIE, S. R., and BLISS, D. K., 1974, Ethyl alcohol: relationships to memory for aversive learning in goldfish (*Carassius auratus*), *J. Comp. Physiol. Psychol.* **86**:867-874.

SCOBIE, S. R., and GARSKE, G., 1970, Chlordiazepoxide and conditioned suppression, *Psychopharmacologia* **16**:272-280.

SCRIABINE, A., and BLAKE, M., 1962, Evaluation of centrally acting drugs in mice with fighting behaviour induced by isolation, *Psychopharmacologia* **3**:224-226.

SEGAL, M., and LANDIS, S. C., 1974, Afferents to the septal area of the rat studied with the method of retrograde axonal transport of horseradish peroxidase, *Brain Res.* **82**:263-268.

SEPINWALL, J., GRODSKY, F. S., SULLIVAN, J. W., and COOK, L., 1973, Effects of propranolol and chlordiazepoxide on conflict behavior in rats, *Psychopharmacologia* **31**:375-382.

SHERMAN, A. R., 1967, Therapy of maladaptive fear-motivated behavior in the rat by the systematic gradual withdrawal of a fear-reducing drug, *Behav. Res. Ther.* **5**:121-129.

SHUTE, C. C. D., and LEWIS, P. R., 1967, The ascending cholinergic reticular system: neocortical, olfactory and subcortical projections, *Brain* **110**:497-539.

SIDMAN, M., 1955, Technique for the assessment of drug effects on timing behavior, *Science* **122**:925.

SIDMAN, M., 1956, Drug-behavior interaction, *Ann. N.Y. Acad. Sci.* **65**:282-302.

SILVERMAN, A. P., 1966, Barbiturates, lysergic acid diethylamide, and the social behaviour of laboratory rats, *Psychopharmacologia* **10**:155-171.

SINGH, S. D., and EYSENCK, H. J., 1960, Conditioned emotional response in the rat. III. Drug antagonism, *J. Gen. Psychol.* **63**:275-285.

SINHA, S. N., FRANKS, C. M., and BROADHURST, P. L., 1958, The effect of a stimulant and a depressant drug on a measure of reactive inhibition, *J. Exp. Psychol.* **56**:349-354.

SKINNER, B. F., 1938, *The Behavior of Organisms*, Appleton-Century-Crofts, New York.

SKURDAL, A. J., ECKARDT, N. J., and BROWN, J. S., 1975, Effects of alcohol on escape learning

and on regular and punished extinction in a self-punitive situation with rats, *Physiol. Psychol.* **3:**29-34.
SMART, R. G., 1965, Effects of alcohol on conflict and avoidance behavior *Q. J. Stud. Alcohol* **26:**187-205.
SOFIA, R. D., 1969, Effects of centrally active drugs on four models of experimentally-induced aggression in rodents, *Life Sci.* **8,** Part 1:705-716.
SOKOLOV, YE. N., 1960, Neuronal models and the orienting reflex, in: *The Central Nervous System and Behaviour* (M. A. B. Brazier, ed.), 3rd Conference, pp. 187-276, Josiah Macy Jr. Foundation, New York.
SOKOLOV, YE. N., 1963, *Perception and the Conditioned Reflex*, Pergamon Press, Oxford.
SPENCE, K. W., 1956, *Behavior Theory and Conditioning*, Yale University Press, New Haven.
SPENCE, K. W., PLATT, J. R., and MATSUMOTO, R., 1965, Intertrial reinforcement and the partial reinforcement effect as a function of number of training trials, *Psychon. Sci.* **3:**205-206.
STADDON, J. E. R., 1970, Temporal effects of reinforcement: a negative "frustration" effect, *Learn. Motiv.* **1:**227-247.
STADDON, J. E. R., 1972, Temporal control and the theory of reinforcement schedules, in: *Reinforcement: Behavioral Analyses* (R. M. Gilbert and J. R. Millenson, eds.), pp. 201-262, Academic Press, New York.
STADDON, J. E. R., and INNIS, N. K., 1969, Reinforcement omission on fixed-interval schedules, *J. Exp. Anal. Behav.* **12:**689-700.
STEIN, L., 1964, Reciprocal action of reward and punishment mechanisms, in: *The Role of Pleasure in Behavior* (R. G. Heath, ed.), pp. 113-139, Harper and Row, New York.
STEIN, L., and BERGER, B. D., 1969, Paradoxical fear-increasing effects of tranquilizers: evidence of repression of memory in the rat, *Science* **166:**253-256.
STEIN, L., WISE, C. D., and BERGER, B. D., 1973, Anti-anxiety action of benzodiazepines: decrease in activity of serotonin neurons in the punishment system, in: *The Benzodiazepines* (S. Garattini, E. Mussini, and L. O. Randall, eds.), pp. 299-326, Raven Press, New York.
STERNBACH, J. H., RANDALL, L. O., and GUSTAFSON, S R., 1964, 1,4-benzodiazepines (chlordiazepoxide and related compounds), in: *Psychopharmacological Agents*, Vol. 1 (M. Gordon, ed.), pp. 137-224, Academic Press, New York.
STOLERMAN, I. P., 1971, A method for studying the influences of drugs on learning for food rewards in rats, *Psychopharmacologia* **19:**398-406.
STRETCH, R., and DALRYMPLE, D., 1968, Effects of methylphenidate, pentobarbital and reserpine on behavior controlled by a schedule of interresponse time reinforcement, *Psychopharmacologia* **13:**49-64.
STRETCH, R., HOUSTON, M., and JENKINS, A., 1964, Effects of amobarbital on extinction of an instrumental response in rats, *Nature (London)* **201:**472-474.
STUMPF, C., 1965, Drug action on the electrical activity of the hippocampus, *Int. Rev. Neurobiol.* **8:**77-138.
SUTHERLAND, N. S., and MACKINTOSH, N. J., 1971, *Mechanisms of Animal Discrimination Learning*, Academic Press, London and New York.
SWANSON, A. M., and ISAACSON, R. L., 1969, Hippocampal lesions and the frustration effect in rats, *J. Comp. Physiol. Psychol.* **68:**562-567.
TAKAORI, S., YADA, N., and MORI, G., 1969, Effects of psychotropic agents on Sidman avoidance response in good- and poor-performed rats, *Jpn. J. Pharmacol.* **19:**587-596.
TAMURA, M., 1963, The effects of some central nervous system depressants on conflict behavior in dogs, *Jpn. J. Pharmacol.* **13:**133-142.
TAYLOR, A., LEHR, R., BERGER, D. F., and TERRY, C. A., 1968, Effects of alcohol on the partial reinforcement effect, *Psychon. Sci.* **11:**371-372.
TEDESCHI, R. E., TEDESCHI, D. H., MUCHA, A., COOK, L., MATTIS, P. A., and FELLOWS, E. J., 1959, Effects of various centrally acting drugs on fighting behavior in mice, *J. Pharmacol. Exp. Ther.* **125:**28-34.

TENEN, S. S., 1967, Recovery time as a measure of CER strength: effects of benzodiazepines, amobarbital, chlorpromazine and amphetamine, *Psychopharmacologia* **12**:1-7.

TESSEL, R. E., and LASH, S., 1968, Effects of chlordiazepoxide on the acquisition and extinction of a running response, *Proceedings of the 76th Annual Convention of the American Psychological Association*, pp. 149-150.

THOMAS, J. R., 1973, Amphetamine and chlordiazepoxide effects on behavior under increased pressures of nitrogen, *Pharmacol. Biochem. Behav.* **1**:421-426.

UNGERSTEDT, U., 1968, 6-hydroxydopamine-induced degeneration of central monoamine neurons, *Eur. J. Pharmacol.* **5**:107-110.

UNGERSTEDT, U., 1971, Stereotaxic mapping of the monoamine pathways in the rat brain, *Acta. Physiol. Scand.* **82**:Suppl. 367, 1-48.

VALZELLI, L., 1973, Activity of benzodiazepines on aggressive behavior in rats and mice, in: *The Benzodiazepines* (S. Garattini, E. Mussini, and L. O. Randall, eds.), pp. 405-417, Raven Press, New York.

VALZELLI, L., and BERNASCONI, S., 1971, Differential activity of some psychotropic drugs as a function of emotional level in animals, *Psychopharmacologia* **20**:91-96.

VALZELLI, L., GIACALONE, E., and GARATTINI, S., 1967, Pharmacological control of aggressive behavior in mice, *Eur. J. Pharmacol.* **2**:144-146.

VANDERWOLF, C. H., 1971, Limbic diencephalic mechanisms of voluntary movement, *Psychol. Rev.* **78**:83-113.

VANDERWOLF, C. H., KRAMIS, R., GILLESPIE, L. A., and BLAND, B. H., 1975, Hippocampal rhythmical slow activity and neocortical low voltage fast activity: relations to behavior, in: *The Hippocampus: A Comprehensive Treatise*, Vol. 2 (R. L. Isaacson and K. H. Pribram, eds.), pp. 101-128, Plenum Press, New York.

VINOGRADOVA, O. S., 1961, *The Orienting Reflex and Its Neurophysiological Mechanism*, Akad. Pedagog. Nauk, Moscow (in Russian).

VOGEL, J. R., and PRINCIPI, K., 1971, Effects of chlordiazepoxide on depressed performance after reward reduction, *Psychopharmacologia* **21**:8-12.

VOGEL, J. R., BEER, B., and CLODY, D. E., 1971, A simple and reliable conflict procedure for testing anti-anxiety agents, *Psychopharmacologia* **21**:1-7.

VOGEL-SPROTT, M., 1967, Alcohol effects on human behaviour under reward and punishment, *Psychopharmacologia* **11**:337-344.

VRTUNSKI, P., MURRAY, R., and WOLIN, L. R., 1973, The effect of alcohol on intracranially reinforced response, *Q. J. Stud. Alcohol* **34**:718-725.

WAGNER, A. R., 1959, The role of reinforcement and non-reinforcement in an "apparent frustration effect," *J. Exp. Psychol.* **57**:130-136.

WAGNER, A. R., 1963, Sodium amytal and partially reinforced runway performance, *J. Exp. Psychol.* **65**:474-477.

WAGNER, A. R., 1966, Frustration and punishment, in: *Current Research on Motivation* (R. M. Haber, ed.), pp. 229-239, Holt, Rinehart and Winston, New York.

WAGNER, A. R., 1969, Frustrative nonreward: a variety of punishment? in: *Punishment and Aversive Behavior* (B. A. Campbell and R. M. Church, eds.), pp. 157-181, Appleton-Century-Crofts, New York.

WALLACH, M. B., and GERSHON, S., 1973, The effects of Δ^8-THC on the EEG, reticular multiple unit activity and sleep of cats, *Eur. J. Pharmacol.* **24**:172-178.

WALLER, M. B., and MORSE, W. H., 1963, Effects of pentobarbital on fixed-ratio reinforcement, *J. Exp. Anal. Behav.* **6**:125-130.

WALLGREN, H., and SAVOLAINEN, S., 1962, The effect of ethyl alcohol on a conditioned avoidance response in rats, *Acta Pharmacol. Toxicol.* **19**:59-67.

WANNER, H. U., and BÄTTIG, K., 1965, Pharmakologische Wirkungen auf die Laufleistung der Ratte bei verschiedener Leistungsbelohnung und verschiedener Leistungsanforderung, *Psychopharmacologia* **7**:182-202.

WARBURTON, D. M., 1972, The cholinergic control of internal inhibition, in: *Inhibition and Learning* (R. A. Boakes and M. S. Halliday, eds.), pp. 431-460, Academic Press, London.

WASDEN, R. E., and REID, L. D., 1968, Intracranial stimulation: performance decrements and a fear-reducing drug, *Psychon. Sci.* **12:**117–118.
WEDEKING, P. W., 1968, Stimulating effects of chlordiazepoxide in rats on a food reinforced FR schedule, *Psychon. Sci.* **12:**31–32.
WEDEKING, P. W., 1969, Disinhibition effect of chlordiazepoxide, *Psychon. Sci.* **15:**232–233.
WEDEKING, P. W., 1973, Comparison of chlordiazepoxide and food deprivation in rats on a fixed-ratio satiation schedule, *Physiol. Behav.* **10:**707–710.
WEISKRANTZ, L., 1968, Emotion, in: *Analysis of Behavioral Change* (L. Weiskrantz, ed.), pp. 50–90, Harper and Row, New York.
WEISSMAN, A., 1959, Differential drug effects upon a three-ply multiple schedule of reinforcement, *J. Exp. Anal. Behav.* **2:**271–287.
WEISSMAN, A., 1973, Behavioral pharmacology of *p*-chlorophenylalanine (PCPA), in: *Serotonin and Behavior* (J. Barchas and E. Usdin, eds.), pp. 235–248, Academic Press, New York.
WEITZ, M. K., 1974, Effects of ethanol on shock-elicited fighting behavior in rats, *Q. J. Stud. Alcohol* **35:**953–958.
WELDON, E., 1967, An analogue of extraversion as a determinant of individual behaviour in the rat, *Br. J. Psychol.* **58:**253–259.
WILCOCK, J., and FULKER, D. W., 1973, Avoidance learning in rats: genetic evidence for two distinct behavioral processes in the shuttle-box, *J. Comp. Physiol. Psychol.* **82:**247–253.
WUTTKE, W., and KELLEHER, R. T., 1970, Effects of some benzodiazepines on punished and unpunished behavior in the pigeon, *J. Pharmacol. Exp. Ther.* **172:**397–405.
YAMAGUCHI, K., and IWAHARA, S., 1974, Effects of chlordiazepoxide upon differential heart rate conditioning in rats, *Psychopharmacologia* **39:**71–79.
YEN, C. Y., STANGER, R. L., and MILLMAN, N., 1959, Ataractic suppression of isolation-induced aggressive behavior, *Arch. Int. Pharmacodyn.* **123:**179–185.
YULES, R. B., FREEDMAN, D. X., and CHANDLER, K. A., 1966, The effect of ethyl alcohol on man's electroencephalographic sleep cycle, *Electroencephalogr. Clin. Neurophysiol.* **20:**109–111.
ZBINDEN, G., and RANDALL, L. O., 1967, Pharmacology of benzodiazepines: laboratory and clinical correlations, *Adv. Pharmacol.* **5:**213–291.
ZIFF, D. R., and CAPALDI, E. J., 1971, Amytal and the small trial partial reinforcement effect: stimulus properties of early trial nonrewards, *J. Exp. Psychol.* **87:**263–269.

11

MODULATION OF LEARNING AND MEMORY: EFFECTS OF DRUGS INFLUENCING NEUROTRANSMITTERS

Bruce Hunter, Steven F. Zornetzer, Murray E. Jarvik, and James L. McGaugh

1. INTRODUCTION

Drugs have been utilized for many years as experimental tools in the analysis of the biological mechanisms underlying behavior. An assumption implicit in this approach is that an assessment of the actions of various drugs on behavior, coupled with knowledge of mechanisms of drug action, will provide important information concerning the neurobiological bases of behavior.

A variety of pharmacological agents including general anesthetics, depressants, and analeptics have been used to investigate learning and memory. There are several general reviews of the effects of many of these agents on learning and memory processes (Herz, 1960; McGaugh and Petrinovich, 1965; Essman, 1971; Jarvik, 1972; Dawson and McGaugh, 1973; McGaugh, 1973).

Bruce Hunter and Stephen F. Zornetzer • Department of Neuroscience, College of Medicine, University of Florida, Gainesville, Florida 32610. *Murray E. Jarvik* • Department of Psychiatry, School of Medicine, University of California at Los Angeles, Los Angeles, California 90024, and V. A. Hospital Brentwood, Los Angeles, California 90073. *James L. McGaugh* • Department of Psychobiology, University of California at Irvine, Irvine, California 92664.

This chapter focuses on recent evidence concerning the effects on learning and memory of drugs which influence cholinergic, catecholaminergic, and serotoninergic neurotransmitter systems. Our coverage is not exhaustive, but rather emphasizes recent findings of studies of drug influences on the storage of recently acquired information.

1.1. Preliminary Considerations

The neuropharmacological analysis of memory processes is complicated by the fact that the effects of drugs on learning and memory depend upon numerous experimental variables including species, age, task, and level of training. In addition, a number of other variables, unique to pharmacological investigations, may influence the outcome of a particular experiment. These pharmacological variables include dose–response relationships, route of drug administration, peripheral versus central drug action, rate of drug uptake, drug toxicity, and possible chronic effects such as the development of drug tolerance. The potential confounding effects of these variables in pharmacological studies of associative processes have been carefully considered previously (McGaugh and Petrinovich, 1965).

Four stages of the memory process are commonly assumed: (1) sensory registration or acquisition, (2) storage or consolidation, (3) maintenance, and (4) retrieval. Interest in the neurobiological mechanisms of memory is generally concerned with the latter three stages. At least three approaches have been used in the analysis of the effects of drugs on associative processes: (A) One approach involves the administration of drugs prior to acquisition training. In this experimental condition, potential drug effects on associative processes are particularly confounded by possible alterations in performance, due to drug-induced changes in sensory or motor processes. (B) A second approach involves the administration of drugs prior to training, and the assessment of effects on retention at some later time when the drug is assumed to no longer directly influence behavior. However, the basis of drug effects on learning are not easily determined with this experimental procedure. In particular, alterations in retention could be due to drug effects on nonspecific processes, such as arousal or attention, which may influence sensory registration rather than memory storage processes *per se*. If sensory registration is altered, then memory storage may also be altered as a consequence. Thus, this procedure does not differentiate between potential disruptive-facilitative effects on acquisition as opposed to subsequent storage, maintenance, or retrieval processes. (C) A third approach involves the administration of drugs shortly following training, at a time when memory storage processes are assumed to be maximally susceptible to modulating influences (McGaugh, 1966). The animals are then tested later when they are not directly under the drug's influence. Only with this approach can possible nonspecific performance effects such as alterations in attentional processes during training be eliminated. Using this experimental procedure, differences between drug and control groups can be attributed to alterations in processes involved in memory storage.

Unfortunately, a number of drugs exert their effects on neurotransmitter systems only after a significant delay following administration. For example, p-chlorophenylalanine (PCPA), a tryptophan hydroxylase inhibitor, results in maximal depletion of brain serotonin approximately 3 days following a single injection (Koe and Weissman, 1966). In view of the evidence that memory storage processes are normally susceptible to modulation within a period of minutes or hours following training, it is apparent that agents such as PCPA cannot be utilized effectively with the posttraining treatment paradigm.

In studies of drug influences on learning and memory, it is essential to control for the possibility that the behavioral effects might depend upon the drug state during training or testing. The state-dependent phenomenon, originally observed by Girden and Culler (1937) and subsequently investigated and popularized by Overton (1966, 1974), arose from the basic observation that retention deficits are sometimes found when drug conditions during training and testing are not identical. A typical experiment investigating state dependence might use four groups in which drugs are administered as follows: (1) control vehicle prior to training and testing (ND-ND); (2) drug prior to training and vehicle prior to testing (D-ND); (3) vehicle prior to training and drug prior to testing (ND-D); and (4) drug prior to training and testing (D-D). Such experiments have yielded several patterns of results (Overton, 1974). Three patterns are particularly important in determining the nature of drug-induced memory deficits and are summarized in Table 1.

In the first pattern, deficits are observed in the D-ND and D-D condition. These results show that memory has been disrupted and imply a disruption of acquisition, although potential effects on subsequent stages of memory cannot definitely be ruled out. In the second pattern, deficits are observed only when the drug conditions during training and testing are

TABLE 1
Patterns of Results Observed in State-Dependence Experiments

Patterns	Performance at time of retention test[a]				Probable memory stage affected
	ND-ND	D-ND	ND-D	D-D	
1	Good	Poor	Good	Poor	Acquisition
2	Good	Poor	Poor	Good	Storage
3	Good	Poor	Good	Good	Acquisition or acquisition and storage

[a] Abbreviations used: ND, no-drug condition; D, drug condition.

reversed (ND-D and D-ND). This is the classical state-dependent or symmetrical dissociation, and this pattern of results indicates a modification of postacquisitional memory processes in view of the good retention shown by the D-D group. Symmetrical dissociations have been considered to reflect state-dependent retrieval failures (Spear, 1973). Retrieval failure used in this sense implies that the memory is present in the brain, i.e., has been stored, but cannot be "retrieved" during retention testing. When considered on a mechanistic level, however, it is apparent that state-dependent memory deficits could be attributed to either drug-induced *alterations* in memory storage *or* retrieval processes. As Table 1 shows, memory has not been eradicated (as indicated by the performance of the D-D group), but has been altered (as indicated by the performance of the D-ND group). While state-dependent learning has received considerable attention, the underlying neural mechanisms remain largely unknown (Bliss, 1974). Overton (1964) hypothesized that the memory trace itself is state-dependent. According to this notion, symmetrical dissociations reflect abnormal memory storage. Retrieval processes could remain normal, but the stored information is only *retrievable* when the state of the trace is identical during training and testing. Others have provided an explanation based on the stimulus properties of drugs (Otis, 1964). Thus, drug-induced stimuli become an important part of the training situation. State-dependence, therefore, becomes a special instance of a stimulus-generalization decrement and might be considered as a case of pure retrieval deficit.

In the final pattern of results seen in Table 1, memory deficits are observed only in the D-ND group. This is the asymmetrical or one-way dissociation. Here it is difficult to distinguish between deficits in acquisition or storage processes. Further experiments are generally warranted to clarify this issue. Specifically, good retention in the D-D group might reflect drug-induced facilitation of performance at the time of testing. Such facilitation might only be demonstrable under conditions of poor initial acquisition. This facilitation may not be apparent in the ND-D group because good acquisition resulted in a ceiling effect on testing performance. Thus, if an agent produces a one-way dissociation, it should be determined whether that agent facilitates the performance of poorly learned responses. If so, then poor retention of D-ND groups can be attributed to a deficit in acquisition. If such facilitation cannot be demonstrated, then asymmetrical dissociations may reflect a combined moderate deficit in acquisition together with a weak state-dependent effect. This discussion provides a basis for interpreting the various experiments considered below which have examined state-dependent memory formation.

2. ACETYLCHOLINE

Among the substances proposed as central nervous system neurotransmitters, acetylcholine (ACh) has probably received the most experimental attention in relation to learning and memory. The relative emphasis on a cholinergic substrate for associative processes emerged largely from the clinical observation of the behavioral effects of compounds such as atropine, scopolamine, and physostigmine, all of which are known to influence peripheral as well as central cholinergic synaptic transmission.

A number of compounds that alter normal cholinergic activity have been used in the study of associative processes. The compounds can be classified into two categories: (1) the cholinergic agonists including the cholinesterase inhibitors such as physostigmine, and cholinomimetic agents, such as nicotine; and (2) the anticholinergic compounds of which the muscarinic blocking agents atropine and scopolamine have received the most attention.

2.1. Physostigmine (Eserine)

Physostigmine, a reversible cholinesterase inhibitor, as well as the cholinomimetics arecoline and pilocarpine, have been found to depress the performance of well-learned active-avoidance responses (Pfeiffer and Jenney, 1957; Goldberg et al., 1965) as well as operant performance with appetitive or aversive reinforcement (Pradhan and Mhatre, 1970). Physostigmine-induced depression of performance is not limited to associative responses, since similar doses also depress food intake, water intake, and spontaneous motor activity. The behavioral depression exerted by physostigmine may be in part dependent upon peripheral actions of the drug. Rosecrans and Domino (1974) have recently found that neostigmine, a quaternary cholinesterase inhibitor, in doses having little effect on brain ACh or AChE, caused a depression of a pole-jump avoidance response.

The effects of physostigmine upon performance during acquisition appear to be both dose- and task-dependent. For example, physostigmine (0.05 mg/kg) facilitated the acquisition of an appetitive T-maze discrimination response (Whitehouse, 1964), whereas identical doses were reported to disrupt the acquisition of a two-way avoidance response (Rosic and Bignami, 1970). Similarly, increased errors produced by physostigmine, in a go–no-go avoidance discrimination, were interpreted as indicating a disruption of the active avoidance but a facilitation of the passive avoidance components of this task. On the other hand, in doses comparable to those resulting in suppression of well-learned responses (0.25–0.50 mg/kg), physostigmine impaired the acquisition of active- and passive-avoidance learning (Bures et al., 1962; Cardo, 1959).

When administered prior to training in a single-trial inhibitory avoidance task with retention assessed 24 hr later, physostigmine (0.5 mg/kg) produced retention deficits (Bohdanecky and Jarvik, 1967). The nature of this memory deficit was subsequently investigated by Gardner et al. (1972). Using the state-dependent paradigm, these investigators found that physostigmine produced an asymmetrical dissociation for a passive-avoidance response; i.e., deficits were observed only in the D-ND condition. Deutsch (1973), on the other hand, reported that diisopropylfluorophosphate (DFP), also a cholinesterase inhibitor, facilitated performance during retention in poorly trained animals. The good retention in the D-D group found by Gardner *et al.* (1972) above might be attributed to facilitation of a weakly learned habit.

The conclusion that physostigmine affects memory-storage processes is more clearly supported by experiments in which treatments were administered following training. For example, posttrial physostigmine affected the retention of a variety of tasks (Stratton and Petrinovich, 1963; Doty and Johnson, 1966; Greenough *et al.*, 1973; Izquierdo *et al.*, 1973). Stratton and Petrinovich (1963), using rats from the S_1 and S_3 strains, found that daily posttrial administration of physostigmine facilitated retention of an appetitive maze-learning problem (Lashley III maze). The maximum doses at which posttrial facilitation was observed were 0.50 mg/kg for the S_1 and 0.75 mg/kg for the S_3 strain. However, disruption was observed in both strains with doses of 1.0 mg/kg.

Interest in the effects of physostigmine on rats of the S_1 and S_3 strains emerged from the findings of Krech and co-workers (Krech, Bennett, Rosenzweig, and associates). The results of Stratton and Petrinovich (1963) have been interpreted as indicating that memory-storage processes, or their susceptibility to modification, differ in these two strains. This approach has been extended recently to include an examination of the effects of posttrial physostigmine administration on rats reared in enriched environments versus rats reared in isolation. Differing environmental experience resulted in a different response to drug administration (Greenough *et al.*, 1973). Rats reared in enriched environments required a lower dose for facilitation than rats reared in isolation, a result which can be compared to those of Stratton and Petrinovich. The recent report of a physostigmine-induced deficit (0.40 mg/kg) in retention of an appetitive brightness-discrimination response (Miller *et al.*, 1971) appears attributable to chronic effects on food motivation rather than to a disruption of memory storage processes, since drug-treated rats did not differ from controls until after 40–50 days of drug treatment.

2.2. Nicotine

The cholinergic substrates of memory processes have also been studied through the use of various cholinomimetic agents. Of the compounds within this general category, nicotine has received the most experimental attention. The cholinergic activity of this substance is restricted to "nicotinic" receptors (as opposed to muscarinic). In addition, nicotine is known to stimulate catecholamine release peripherally (Volle and Koelle, 1970). Nevertheless, nicotine has been observed to exert actions on learning and memory processes similar to those of physostigmine. Nicotine at low doses facilitated, and at high doses disrupted, the performance of a well-learned pole-jump avoidance response (Domino, 1965). Nicotine also facilitated the acquisition of shuttle-box avoidance, maze learning, and two-choice visual discrimination behavior, when administered prior to training (Robustelli, 1963; Bovet et al., 1966; Bovet-Nitti, 1969). In one series of experiments, nicotine injections 15 min prior to training enhanced shuttle-box avoidance acquisition in six strains of mice (Bovet et al., 1966). Interestingly, in the latter study, impairment of learning was observed in two strains of mice which initially exhibited superior shuttle-box avoidance learning.

Posttrial nicotine treatment has been shown to result in facilitated retention of a variety of tasks (Garg and Holland, 1968, 1969; Garg, 1969; Battig, 1970; Evangelista et al., 1970; Erickson, 1971). Battig (1970) found that pretraining or posttraining nicotine treatment facilitated memory for a maze problem. Similar results were obtained for a lever-press avoidance response (Erickson, 1971). In this latter study, nicotine bismethiode, a quaternary nicotine derivative, failed to influence memory for the avoidance response. On the other hand, Evangelista et al. (1970) reported that the quaternary nicotinic-blocking agent hexamethonium partially antagonized the facilitatory effects of posttrial nicotine on shuttle-box avoidance learning. Clearly further research is warranted on the question of peripheral versus central actions of nicotine in the modulation of memory-storage processes.

Some experiments have shown disruptive effects of posttrial nicotine. Garg and Holland (1969) reported that posttrial nicotine (0.8 mg/kg) administration facilitated retention of an appetitive Hebb–Williams maze response in rats, but produced a trend toward disruption of an aversive shuttle-box avoidance response. A possible interpretation of these results is that the excitatory CNS effects of nicotine depend upon the degree of arousal produced by a given conditioning procedure. If this is the case, then nicotine administered following an appetitive task might be expected to produce a lower level of CNS excitability than the same doses of nicotine given after an aversive task. In this view, the combined effect on CNS excitation might be expected to follow the well-documented inverted U-shaped relationship between learning and level of arousal (Malmo, 1967). Such an interpretation is supported by subsequent experiments showing that posttrial nicotine injections in considerably lower doses than those used by Garg and Holland (1969), specifically 0.1 mg/kg (Erickson, 1971) or 0.2 mg/kg (Evangelista et al., 1970), facilitated retention of discrimination lever-press avoidance and shuttle-box avoidance responses, respectively.

In summary, both physostigmine and nicotine affect memory-storage processes. At low doses, posttrial administration of these compounds facilitates memory storage, perhaps by enhancing consolidation processes (McGaugh and Petrinovich, 1965; Dawson and McGaugh, 1973), whereas higher doses result in memory disruption.

The mechanisms through which these compounds produce enhancing and disrupting actions on memory processes are not clear. Further, the differential role of either muscarinic or nicotinic components of central cholinergic systems in mediating these actions remains an important question for future research. Interestingly, different doses of cholinomimetic agents and cholinesterase inhibitors produce quite different effects on rhythmic brain electrical activity. At low doses of these drugs, a classical EEG arousal response (cortical desynchronization and hippocampal theta activity) is normally observed in rats (Stumpf, 1965; Domino et al., 1968). At high doses, these compounds produce hypersynchrony and eventually seizure activity (Karczmar, 1974). This latter effect appears to be related to cholinergic synaptic blockade since (1) atropine antagonizes the effects and (2) in the case of AChE inhibitors, recovery coincides with diffusion of ACh away from receptor sites, an increase in "bound" as opposed to "free" ACh, and a regeneration of AChE activity (Karczmar, 1974). The extent to which this synaptic blocking action of excessive ACh is related to the disruption of memory-storage processes produced by high doses of these cholinergic agonists is not clear. A determination of the electrographic effects of posttrial physostigmine or nicotine administration may provide a clarification of this problem.

2.3. Anticholinergic Agents

The role of cholinergic systems in associative processes has also been studied with drugs which disrupt cholinergic synaptic transmission. The most extensively used anticholinergic drugs in studies of memory processes have been the muscarinic blocking agents atropine and scopolamine.

2.3.1. Effects on Performance during Acquisition

The centrally acting muscarinic blocking agents atropine (10–50 mg/kg) and scopolamine (0.5–1.0 mg/kg) have been found to disrupt the acquisition of active avoidance (Herz, 1960), successive discrimination (Whitehouse, 1964), maze (Pazzagli and Pepeu, 1964), and passive-avoidance responses (Meyers, 1965; Dilts and Berry, 1967). The quaternary derivatives methyl scopolamine and methyl atropine, which penetrate into the CNS less readily, have generally proved ineffective (Herz, 1960). On the other hand, scopolamine facilitated the acquisition of a two-way avoidance response (Suits and Isaacson, 1968; Rech, 1966, 1968; Barrett et al., 1974; Oliverio, 1968). The effects of scopolamine on two-way avoidance appear to be dependent upon baseline performance level (Rech, 1966, 1968), since rats with an initially poor level of performance were greatly facilitated, whereas rats with superior two-way avoidance performance were disrupted. Thus, the actions of these muscarinic blocking agents upon performance during acquisition, as is the case with the performance of well-learned responses (Longo, 1966), appear more contingent upon such variables as the response requirements of a given task, rather than upon alterations in generalized memory processes. In this regard the effects of muscarinic blocking agents resemble those of large bilateral hippocampal lesions, since comparable results have been observed with spontaneous alternation, habituation, extinction, DRL, passive-avoidance, active-avoidance, and shuttle-box avoidance responses (cf. Pradhan and Dutta, 1971).

2.3.2. Effects on Performance at the Time of Retention Testing

When anticholinergic drugs are administered prior to training but retention is measured some time later (i.e., when the drug effects have subsided), deficits in performance have been observed. Buresova *et al.* (1964) found that atropine (6 mg/kg) disrupted the retention of a passive-avoidance response in rats. This effect was greatest when the injection-training interval was 20 min, a time at which the maximal alterations in EEG activity were observed. Atropine and scopolamine produce a well-documented dissociation between behavior and EEG, consisting of the appearance of synchronous high-voltage slow waves without concomitant induction of behavioral sleep or drowsiness (Longo, 1966). Scopolamine has also been found to disrupt the retention of a pole-jump avoidance response (Gruber *et al.*, 1967) and passive-avoidance responses in rats (Bohdanecky and Jarvik, 1967) and mice (Calhoun and Smith, 1968). That this effect was mediated by central anticholinergic actions was supported by the failure of methyl scopolamine to disrupt retention (Bohdanecky and Jarvik, 1967). Furthermore, physostigmine, but not the quaternary cholinesterase inhibitor neostigmine, was effective in reversing the scopolamine deficit.

These findings suggest that a reduction in muscarinic cholinergic activity results in impaired acquisition of information. The extent to which the effect is related to impairments in sensory registration as opposed to memory-storage or retrieval processes has been the subject of considerable attention, perhaps since several experiments originally failed to demonstrate effects with posttrial scopolamine treatments (Bohdanecky and Jarvik, 1967; Calhoun and Smith, 1968). Using the state-dependent 2 × 2 factorial design, several investigators failed to demonstrate state-dependent properties with a passive-avoidance response (Meyers, 1965; Stark, 1967; Calhoun and Smith, 1968), while others (Gruber *et al.*, 1967) found that scopolamine produced an asymmetrical dissociation for a pole-jump avoidance response.

In a comprehensive series of experiments, Berger and Stein (1969) found that scopolamine produced an asymmetrical dissociation for a conditioned lick-suppression response. These results are not easily understood either as a function of a deficit in sensory registration or state dependence. Under most conditions anticholinergic agents do not facilitate the performance of weakly learned responses (Herz, 1960; Pazzagli and Pepeu, 1964). Therefore, the effect does not appear attributable to impaired acquisition alone. Berger and Stein (1969) have argued that scopolamine produces both a moderate acquisition deficit and state dependence. According to this view, retention deficits should be observed in the D-ND condition, where both factors would be presumed to operate. This assumption has been supported by subsequent findings. Higher doses of scopolamine (300 mg/kg) administered to mice in a single-trial inhibitory avoidance task resulted in subsequent retention deficits in both the D-ND and ND-D conditions (Gardner et al., 1972). This pattern of results reflects a two-way or symmetrical dissociation. However, mice in the ND-D group were significantly less impaired than those in the D-ND condition. This pattern of results would appear to support the view that scopolamine produces moderate deficits in sensory registration as well as alterations in memory storage and/or retrieval processes.

Scopolamine has long been considered clinically to be an amnesic agent (Koelle, 1970). However, as outlined above, this amnesic property appears to be anterograde, since several studies failed to demonstrate amnesic effects when scopolamine was administered following training (Bohdanecky and Jarvik, 1967). Recently, using a single-trial passive-avoidance task with a retention test cutoff latency of 600 sec, Glick and Zimmerberg (1971) found that high doses of scopolamine (5–20 mg/kg) produced retrograde amnesia (RA) when administered up to 1 hr posttraining. Furthermore, these effects were shown to be time-dependent, since injections 6 hr following training had no effect. Weissman (1967) has also reported that a variety of anticholinergic agents produce RA, although distinctly less than that observed following electroconvulsive shock (ECS). Weiner and Messer (1973) examined the effect of posttrial bilateral intrahippocampal injections of scopolamine (6 μl) on the retention of a single-trial inhibitory-avoidance response. Using a 120-sec cutoff latency, scopolamine-injected rats were identical to controls when retention tests were conducted 1 to 3 days following training. However, a progressively increasing deficit was found in the scopolamine-treated rats at training–test intervals of 5, 7, or 10 days. Taken together, these results suggest that posttraining reduction in muscarinic cholinergic activity can produce an impairment in memory-storage processes.

On the other hand, posttrial administration of low doses of atropine (2–10 mg/kg) have been reported to facilitate the retention of a shuttle-box avoidance response (Evangelista and Izquierdo, 1971). These results introduce the interesting possibility that, as was the case with ACh agonists, ACh antagonists may also produce a bidirectional action on memory-storage processes. It should be kept in mind that atropine exerts effects on ACh activity which are much less potent than those of scopolamine (Longo, 1966). Thus, the facilitative doses of atropine are functionally very much lower than those of scopolamine which are reported to disrupt memory (Glick and Zimmerberg, 1971).

In summary, drugs which depress muscarinic cholinergic synaptic transmission produce the following alterations in acquisition and retention: (1) a disinhibitory action on motor responsivity leading to task-dependent alterations in the performance of well-learned responses; (2) moderate effects on acquisitional processes (most likely by means of alterations in sensory registration or on central attentional processes); (3) a moderate drug dissociation or state-dependent effect; (4) RA when administered shortly following training; and (5) a disruptive influence on the maintenance of long-term memory. The extent to which these latter two posttrial anticholinergic actions are due to alterations in (i.e., state dependence), as opposed to eradication of, memory storage has not been investigated. Furthermore, the potential facilitatory effects of low doses of anticholinergic agents merits further investigation.

2.3.3. Effects of Cholinergic Drugs Administered Prior to Retention Testing

An unusual approach to the study of cholinergic mechanisms of associative processes has involved the administration of cholinergic drugs prior to retention testing (Deutsch, 1971, 1973).

Several original experiments utilized similar procedures (Deutsch et al., 1966; Deutsch and Leibowitz, 1966; Weiner and Deutsch, 1968). Rats were initially trained in a Y-maze task either to escape foot shock or for appetitive reinforcement. No drugs were administered during the initial training. Twenty-four hours prior to a retention test, intrahippocampal injections of the cholinesterase inhibitor diisopropylfluorophosphate (DFP) were administered. DFP injections 1–3 days posttraining had no effect on retention. However, beginning 5 days posttraining and extending to 14 days, DFP produced a progressively greater amnesia for the Y-maze response. These effects presumably constituted alterations in retrieval, since the amnesia was shown to be temporary, indicating that the original memory remained unaffected. At 28 days posttraining, when the retention of control rats was poor as a function of forgetting, DFP resulted in facilitated retention. Intrahippocampal injections of scopolamine produced effects on retention which were nearly opposite to those exerted by DFP (Deutsch and Rocklin, 1967; Weiner and Deutsch, 1968).

The drug effects observed in these experiments cannot readily be attributed to nonspecific performance effects, since both disruption and facilitation have been observed depending upon the training–retention interval. Nor are the drug effects task specific, since they have also been demonstrated for T-maze (Squire, 1970) or passive-avoidance responses (Hamburg and Fulton, 1972). The effect has been demonstrated predominantly in rats, but has also been observed in mice (Squire, 1970). Finally, the effect does not depend upon intrahippocampal injections, since comparable results have been obtained with systemic injections of physostigmine (Squire, 1970; Hamburg and Fulton, 1972).

Taken together, the results of Deutsch and co-workers have been interpreted as indicating that learning produces changes in central cholinergic synaptic transmission. Specifically, it has been hypothesized (Deutsch,

1973) that cholinergic synapses normally increase conductivity in a progressive fashion following training up to a certain level, thereafter declining in conductivity as a function of forgetting. This hypothesis follows from the above data if it is assumed that synaptic block occurs as a function of excessive transmitter concentrations around the postsynaptic membrane. This assumption has been formulated from well-known clinical observations. Anticholinesterase therapy in patients suffering from myasthenia gravis ameliorates the symptoms of muscular weakness, whereas similar doses administered to normal individuals causes paralysis (Koelle, 1970). Thus, under conditions of low cholinergic sensitivity, potentiation of ACh presumably restores normal transmission. When cholinergic sensitivity is normal, potentiation of ACh results in synaptic block and a depression of effective synaptic transmission.

However, important questions have been raised by recent studies in regard to the data upon which this hypothesis was based. One question concerns the extent to which cholinergic agents influence retention by peripheral versus central actions. Squire et al. (1971) found that physostigmine-induced effects on retention were antagonized by methyl scopolamine. These results are difficult to reconcile in view of the presumed exclusive central actions of intracerebrally administered cholinergic drugs. Since quaternary agents have been presumed to cross the blood–brain barrier with difficulty, they have been widely used as a control for the peripheral actions of ACh agonists and antagonists. Under most conditions these agents have produced little effect on associative processes. However, Evangelista et al. (1970) reported that posttrial administration of hexamethonium, a quaternary nicotinic blocking agent, facilitated the retention of a shuttle-box avoidance response. The possibility that quaternary agents possess some central actions, which are demonstrable under certain conditions, cannot be ruled out. This possibility is illustrated by a recent experiment which examined the uptake of [^{3}H]atropine sulfate and [^{3}H]methylatropine sulfate into the brain 30 min after systemic injections (Witter et al., 1973). Both compounds appeared to enter the brain slowly, with the uptake of atropine approximately three times greater than that for methylatropine. It was concluded that central blockade of muscarinic cholinergic receptors was possible following systemic injection of atropine or methylatropine.

Of perhaps even greater significance are the recent findings of George and Mellanby (1974), who observed that intrahippocampal control injections identical to those used in many of Deutsch's original experiments (cf. Deutsch et al., 1966) produced deficits in the Y-maze escape task regardless of training–retest interval. Thus, the natural forgetting observed at 28 days in the Y-maze task (Deutsch et al., 1966) may instead result from nonspecific damage to the hippocampus produced by large injection volumes. While these results (George and Mellanby, 1974) raise serious questions about the early studies of the Deutsch group (Deutsch et al., 1966; Deutsch and Leibowitz, 1966; Weiner and Deutsch, 1968) as well as subsequent theories

(Deutsch, 1973), they remain difficult to reconcile with replications of this phenomenon using systemic injections of physostigmine (Squire, 1970; Hamburg and Fulton, 1972).

Whether or not these hypotheses concerning ACh and memory are valid, the findings from Deutsch's laboratory remain important for general theories of memory. Most theories of memory have focused on events which occur shortly after the training experience, and stable long-term memory has been assumed to be complete by at least 24 hr when retention is normally assessed. However, the results of the experiments reviewed above constitute strong evidence for the conclusion that memory processes continue to change in a dynamic fashion over a time course measurable in days following the training experience.

2.3.4. Electroconvulsive Shock and ACh

Another approach used to study the relation between cholinergic mechanisms and memory involves the examination of the effects of known memory disruptive agents on central cholinergic activity. For example, electroconvulsive shock (ECS) has been shown to affect endogenous ACh levels in a temporally related manner. Thus, during the ECS-produced behavioral convulsion both "free" and "bound" ACh increase markedly in the brain (Richter and Crossland, 1949). This change is reflected by increased ACh in cerebrospinal fluid and appears to be a characteristic feature of all convulsant activity (Fink, 1966). In the postconvulsive state, brain ACh rapidly declines and is accompanied by measurable increases in turnover (Richter and Crossland, 1949). Essman (1973c) has reported that following a single ECS treatment in mice, the concentration of ACh in the cerebral cortex declines rapidly to a minimum at 10 min, thereafter recovering slowly to control levels nearly 2 hr post-ECS.

ECS has also been shown to alter brain AChE activity. Adams *et al.* (1969) found that a single ECS treatment increased the concentration of soluble cholinesterase by approximately 21% in the rat brain. At 24 hr following ECS treatment, cholinesterase activity remained nearly 6% above control. Unfortunately the assay system used in this study did not differentiate between AChE and other neural cholinesterases. Recently, Essman (1973c) reported that ECS does not alter total AChE activity, but results in an 11% increase in soluble as opposed to bound AChE. Essman concludes from these data that ECS may alter the distribution of AChE within functional pools, presumably by disrupting membrane-bound AChE. The significance of this change in enzymatic compartmentation for overall evaluation of the effects of ECS on ACh activity remains unclear.

Since ECS produces dramatic alterations in ACh activity, the possibility exists that ECS-induced RA may result from a state-dependent effect. At least two distinct state-dependent models of ECS amnesia have been postulated. Nielson (1968) suggested that ECS produces aberrations in neural activity which persist for days following the training experience. Since most experiments have tested for retention 24 hr posttraining, Nielson assumed that the brain condtions during testing are different from those during training. Such a model would predict spontaneous recovery as the effects of ECS subsided. However, little spontaneous recovery occurs following ECS, and little evidence has accumulated in support of this hypothesis (McGaugh and Herz, 1972). A second model involves a more conventional view of state-dependent phenomena and focuses on ECS-induced changes associated with the training experience itself. Using the state-dependent paradigm in which ECS is administered either pre- or posttraining and either prior to or not prior to retention testing, some authors found the evidence for an ECS-state-dependent effect to be conflicting (McGaugh and Landfield, 1970; Thompson and Neely, 1970; Gardner et al., 1972). Miller et al. (1972) have demonstrated that ECS administered in this fashion prior to retention testing may function like a "remainder" stimulus, since the recovery from amnesia was found to be permanent. A state-dependent model predicts that the recovery would be temporary.

The possibility that ECS produces state dependence has been further explored by examining the relationship between ECS, cholinergic drugs, and associative processes. Davis et al. (1971) found that ECS-induced RA for a one-trial passive-avoidance response was reversed by scopolamine but enhanced by physostigmine, each administered prior to retest. The results provide support for the hypothesis that posttrial decreases in ACh activity produce a state-dependent condition resulting in an apparent ECS-induced amnesia. However, in this experiment retention testing was conducted 4 hr posttraining, when short-term memory processes may still have been operating. Recently, Albert et al. (1974) failed to replicate these effects using a conditioned lick-suppression task in which the training–retest interval was 24 hr. Since scopolamine both depresses water intake (Pradhan and Dutta, 1971) and produces a significant latency increase in nonshocked control rats in this experiment, interpretation of the Albert et al. (1974) data is at best difficult.

In summary, these findings indicate that the effects of ECS on memory may be related to alterations in ACh activity. In some cases, ECS has been found to exert actions on memory-storage processes which closely resemble those of cholinergic agents. The extent to which the various effects of ECS, in particular RA, develop as a function of alterations in cholinergic systems remain to be clarified.

3. CATECHOLAMINES

The findings of many recent studies suggest that memory processes are affected by drugs which affect catecholamines (CA). Many drugs which influence central adrenergic activity exert effects on both dopamine (DA) and norepinephrine (NE). Although a number of pharmacological strategies have recently been developed to differentiate between potential alterations in DA as opposed to NE, these methods have, as yet, not been carefully applied to the study of memory-storage processes.

3.1. Sympathomimetics

Several classes of compounds are assumed to exert actions on behavior that are related to a generalized facilitation of adrenergic activity. These compounds include CA precursors (L-dopa), agents which block CA reuptake (imipramine), and agents which stimulate CA release (amphetamine). Most of the CA precursors and CA reuptake blocking agents have received only limited attention with respect to possible involvement in memory processes. On the other hand, considerable attention has been given to the actions of amphetamine on memory processes. Amphetamine appears to exert its actions *primarily* by stimulating the release of CA (Sulser and Sanders-Bush, 1971). Amphetamine exerts a wide variety of actions on the performance of well-learned responses which are remarkably similar to those exerted by the ACh antagonists atropine and scopolamine. Specifically, amphetamine appears to disrupt performance in tasks requiring some degree of response suppression. For example, efficient performance under DRL or fixed-interval schedules is disrupted by amphetamine administration (Dews and Morse, 1961). This effect appears to be dose-dependent (Bignami and Gatti, 1969). Amphetamine has also been reported to disrupt the acquisition and performance of a passive-avoidance response (Cardo, 1959).

On the other hand, amphetamine (0.3–2.0 mg/kg) facilitates the acquisition of active-avoidance learning (Satinder, 1971; Powell and Hopper, 1971; McGaugh and Petrinovich, 1965; Rech, 1966; Barrett et al., 1974). Discrimination learning has also been shown to be facilitated at low doses and impaired at higher doses (Rensch and Rahmann, 1960).

When amphetamine is administered prior to training and retention is assessed sometime later, acquisition is sometimes facilitated, while little or no effect is seen on the retention test (Rech, 1966; Potts et al., 1970; Sansone and Renzi, 1971). Since performance during acquisition is ordinarily enhanced in these studies, the lack of effect on retention has been attributed to a stimulus change or generalization decrement, particularly since facilitation of retention has been observed either after low doses of amphetamine or when the dose was gradually decreased rather than abruptly terminated (Kulkarni, 1968; Barrett et al., 1974). Furthermore, if amphetamine is administered both prior to training and retention testing, enhanced retention is observed (Roffman and Lal, 1971). This recall-stimulating property has been used to study the neuropharmacology of amphetamine (Roffman and Lal, 1972). In this study amphetamine was administered prior to training of a platform-jump avoidance response. Retention testing was conducted 8 days later after administration of amphetamine alone, or coupled with various other drugs. Thus, reserpine effectively disrupted the excitatory action of amphetamine upon recall, an effect which was reversed by concurrent administration of L-dopa (200 mg/kg) *and* 5-hydroxytryptophan (5-HTP). Neither drug alone was effective in reversing the actions of reserpine. The finding that precursor replacement of both CA and serotonin was necessary to reverse the depressive actions of reserpine implies that amphetamine may stimulate recall performance by a mechanism which may include both of these systems. The role of CA in the stimulatory action of amphetamine was further implicated by the finding that concurrent administration of amphetamine and α-methyl-*p*-tyrosine (α-MPT) reversed the amphetamine-induced enhanced recall. L-Dopa (200 mg/kg) alone also produced a similar facilitation of retention test performance. While these results indicate an important role for CA, independent manipulation of serotoninergic systems also influenced the stimulatory action of amphetamine. Both PCPA and cyproheptadine (2 mg/kg), a serotoninergic receptor blocking agent, reversed the stimulatory amphetamine action. This rather exhaustive study of Roffman and Lal (1971) indicates that amphetamine may have recall-stimulating properties via a neural mechanism which in some way involves both catecholaminergic and serotoninergic systems.

Amphetamine, like the ACh antagonists, appears to exert actions on performance during acquisition which are contingent upon the response requirements of a given task. On the other hand, amphetamine influences memory storage processes in a fashion similar to that of ACh agonists. Numerous experiments have demonstrated facilitatory effects on the storage of information when amphetamine is administered shortly following a training experience. Posttrial amphetamine facilitates the retention of an avoidance-discrimination response (Doty and Doty, 1966). The effects of amphetamine on discrimination problems appear to be related to the complexity of the task. Hall (1969) has shown that posttrial amphetamine failed to affect retention of a two-choice visual-discrimination task and yet facilitated retention of a three-choice discrimination task. Amphetamine has additionally been reported to facilitate passive-avoidance retention. Johnson and Waite (1971) found that posttrial methamphetamine (5 mg/kg) facilitated retention of a single-trial inhibitory avoidance response. This effect was not apparent until 7 days following training. Drug-treated rats were indistinguishable from controls when the training–retest interval encompassed 1, 3, or 5 days. These results suggest that amphetamine may facilitate the maintenance of stored information.

Amphetamine, like physostigmine and nicotine, exerts a dose-dependent bidirectional action on memory-storage processes. Krivanek and McGaugh (1969) reported that posttrial amphetamine administration (0.5–2.0 mg/kg) facilitated retention of an appetitive discrimination response in mice, while doses of 2.5 mg/kg proved ineffective. On the other hand, higher doses of amphetamine (3–50 mg/kg) produced RA for a single-trial inhibitory avoidance response (Weissman, 1967). As was the case with nicotine, amphetamine appears to interact with the level of arousal produced by a given task. Thus, doses of amphetamine (2 mg/kg) which produced RA for a single-trial inhibitory avoidance response were without effect on a single-trial appetitive task (James, 1975). While repeated posttrial amphetamine injections reportedly disrupt memory (Breda et al., 1969), these effects may be attributed to chronic effects of amphetamine since memory was facilitated during early training in this study.

Recently, Evangelista and Izquierdo (1970) found that amphetamine (2 mg/kg) administered 10 min prior to training facilitated acquisition but not retention of a shuttle-box avoidance response. On the other hand, immediate posttrial injections (2 min) of identical doses of amphetamine facilitated retention assessed 5 days later. These results are quite similar to those reviewed previously. However, when combined pretrial and posttrial amphetamine injections were administered, performance of the shuttle-box avoidance response was indistinguishable from performance in rats receiving only posttrial treatments. All the above findings provide support for the view that the neurobiological effects underlying the influence of amphetamine on acquisition may be different from those which affect memory-storage processes.

Crabbe and Alpern (1973) reported an unusual effect of amphetamine. Mice were trained in a brightness-discrimination task. Beginning 24 hr after training, mice received daily amphetamine injections (1 mg/kg) for 5 days. Forty-eight hours after the last injection, retention of the discrimination response was assessed. This regimen resulted in a significant amphetamine-induced impairment of retention. These results were interpreted as indicating that chronic amphetamine administration disrupts the long-term storage of memory. Interestingly, this effect is not characteristic of all CNS stimulants since strychnine or pentylenetetrazol, administered in a similar fashion, facilitated retention (Crabbe and Alpern, 1973).

The results of the experiments in which amphetamine is administered shortly following a training experience have been interpreted as indicating that amphetamine facilitates the consolidation or storage of recently acquired information. Furthermore, amphetamine exerts a dose-dependent bidirectional action on consolidation, since memory disruption is observed at higher doses. In these respects amphetamine appears to be remarkably similar to the ACh agonists physostigmine and nicotine. Amphetamine has also been shown to produce an EEG arousal reaction (vis à vis, cortical desynchronization and hippocampal theta). Several investigators have commented, however, on differences between the electrographic effects of amphetamine and the ACh agonists (cf. Stumpf, 1965). Furthermore, simultaneous administration of physostigmine and amphetamine has been shown to be antagonistic with respect to effects on cortical EEG (Barnes, 1966). Differences between the mechanisms of action of these two classes of compounds, particularly with respect to their similar actions on memory-storage processes, will be discussed more fully below.

3.2. Antiadrenergic Agents

Depletion of CA by tyrosine hydroxylase inhibition (α-MPT), disruption of vesicular storage with reserpine, or disruption of synaptic transmission via receptor blockade by chlorpromazine (CPZ) or haloperidol has generally been found to depress performance of well-learned responses. While this effect has been demonstrated primarily in experiments using a variety of active-avoidance tasks (Seiden and Hanson, 1964; Hanson, 1965; Rech et al., 1966), similar effects have been reported for passive avoidance and appetitive instrumental or runway approach tasks (Carlson et al., 1965; Iwahara et al., 1968). More extensive reviews of these findings are available elsewhere (Herz, 1960; Dews and Morse, 1961; Essman, 1971; Seiden et al., 1973).

More recent research has focused on the relative conribution of NE or DA to the disruption of avoidance learning. For example, Seiden and Peterson (1968) found that reserpine (2.5 mg/kg) when administered 20 hr prior to testing disrupted shuttle-box performance in rats. This effect was reversed by L-dopa (400 mg/kg). This L-dopa-produced reversal most likely occurred as a function of its conversion to DA or NE, since Ro-4-4602, a dopa-decarboxylase inhibitor, blocked the L-dopa-produced reversal. Of interest was the additional observation that the time course of L-dopa reversal was highly correlated with restoration of normal levels of DA. These results suggest that DA may be preferentially important for the performance of avoidance responses. However, it is possible that a rapid turnover of NE prevented significant NE accumulation following L-dopa administration. This possibility has been partially confirmed, since disulfiram, an inhibitor of dopamine-β-hydroxylase, resulted in a 50% inhibition of the L-dopa reversal of reserpine-induced avoidance suppression (Seiden et al., 1973).

The relative contributions of DA or NE to associative processes have been investigated recently using 6-hydroxydopamine (6-OHDA). Intraventricular (Lenard and Beer, 1975a) or intracisternal (Cooper et al., 1973; Howard et al., 1974) administration of 6-OHDA as well as 6-OHDA microinjections into the substantia nigra (Fibiger et al., 1974a; Price and Fibiger, 1975) or caudate nucleus (Neill et al., 1974) have been shown to disrupt acquisition of conditioned avoidance and simple appetitive-response tasks. The deficit in conditioned avoidance responding has been attributed to a disruption of conditioned voluntary motor responses (Price and Fibiger, 1975), a facilitation of incompatible response tendencies such as freezing (Lenard and Beer, 1975a), or a combination of both (Beer and Lenard, 1975).

Evidence for an apparent preferential role of DA in the disruption of avoidance responding has emerged from the studies of Fibiger et al. (1974b).

6-OHDA microinjections into the substantia nigra *pars compacta* disrupted active-avoidance acquisition and was found to result in depletion of striatal DA along with a reduction in tyrosine hydroxylase activity. However, nigral 6-OHDA injections also depleted hypothalamic NE, perhaps by simultaneous destruction of the ventral NE bundle. Control animals in which the ventral noradrenergic bundle was preferentially destroyed by 6-OHDA injections caudal to the substantia nigra displayed normal conditioned avoidance acquisition. Similar disruption of avoidance acquisition has been reported after 6-OHDA injections into the caudate nucleus (Neill *et al.*, 1974). These results suggest a possible preferential role of DA, as opposed to NE, in the acquisition of avoidance responses, a view which has also found support in studies where intracisternal 6-OHDA infusions produced an apparent preferential depletion of whole-brain DA levels (Cooper *et al.*, 1973; Howard *et al.*, 1974). On the other hand, Lenard and Beer (1975*b*) have recently reported that the disruption of avoidance learning induced by intraventricular 6-OHDA infusion was reversed by administration of either DA or NE agonists. Furthermore, the use of intracerebral implantation of 6-OHDA as a tool for the specific destruction of CA neurons has been seriously questioned by recent morphological studies which have characterized the lesions produced by 6-OHDA as being largely nonspecific (Poirier *et al.*, 1972; Sotelo *et al.*, 1973; Evans *et al.*, 1975).

The question of whether DA has a preferential role in normal learning has been further obscured by the finding that bilateral electrolytic lesions of the locus coeruleus (LC) disrupt the acquisition of an appetitive runway response (Anlezark *et al.*, 1973), although this finding was not observed using an appetitive T-maze discrimination response (Amaral and Foss, 1975). Recently, Zornetzer and Gold (1976) found no effect of LC lesions upon acquisition of an inhibitory avoidance response. Interestingly, immediate posttrial lesions of the LC in mice dramatically extended (by at least 40 hr) the period of susceptibility of recent memory to ECS-produced disruption. Since the dorsal NE bundle arises principally from the LC (Fuxe *et al.*, 1970), these results imply an important role for at least certain NE pathways in the normal elaboration of memory processes.

Pretraining administration of antiadrenergic agents has been found to exert mixed effects on the retention of learned responses. Several experiments have failed to observe any effects of CPZ (White and Subowski, 1969), reserpine (Essman, 1971), or α-MPT (Ahlenius, 1973; Saper and Sweeney, 1973) on the retention of a variety of learned responses. However, the effects of antiadrenergic agents on memory may be particularly sensitive to the interval between drug administration and training. For example, White and Suboski (1969) found that CPZ (1–10 mg/kg) failed to effect the retention of a one-trial discriminated avoidance response when administered 2 hr prior to training. Similarly, reserpine (2.0 mg/kg) administered 1 hr prior to training failed to alter retention of a passive-avoidance response assessed 24 hr later (Essman, 1971). On the other hand, when CPZ was administered 10 min prior to passive-avoidance training, retention test performance was significantly disrupted (Johnson, 1969). This effect of CPZ, however, may in part result from state dependence (Otis, 1964), although CPZ appears to exert appreciably smaller dissociational properties than ACh antagonists or barbiturates (Overton, 1966).

The possibility that the interval between drug administration and training may be crucial in the disruption of memory formation was further supported by the experiments of Essman (1971) who examined the effects of α-MPT (100 mg/kg) administered 0–8 hr prior to training of a passive-avoidance response. In all cases, retention was assessed 24 hr following training. Memory disruption was observed only when the drug–training interval was 4 hr, corresponding to the time of maximal depletion of brain CA. Smaller doses of α-MPT (30 mg/kg) have been shown to interact in a complex fashion with foot-shock intensity in influencing retention of a passive-avoidance response in mice (Hall and Mayer, 1975). Thus, when foot-shock intensity was low (0.16 mA), pretraining α-MPT facilitated retention of the passive-avoidance response, whereas identical doses disrupted memory at high foot-shock intensities (1.6 mA).

The nature of the memory impairment produced by α-MPT has recently been investigated using the state-dependent paradigm (Zornetzer et al., 1974). Mice were trained and/or tested in a single-trial inhibitory avoidance task 4 hr subsequent to the administration of α-MPT (100 mg/kg). Retention deficits were observed only when the drug conditions during training and testing were reversed (i.e., D-ND and ND-D). These results suggest a two-way or symmetrical dissociation. It is clear that the α-MPT-induced memory disruption cannot be attributed to a deficit in sensory registration or acquisition, as indicated by the retention performance of the D-D group. Rather, it appears that α-MPT produces an alteration (as opposed to disruption) of those processes involved in the normal storage of information. These results furthermore replicate and extend the findings of Essman (1971) and serve to emphasize the importance of the drug administration–training interval in the analysis of the effects of drugs on memory formation.

Several recent experiments have demonstrated that, when initiated shortly following training, blockade of CA synaptic transmission or depletion of CA stores result in a disruption of memory-storage processes. CPZ has been shown in certain cases to serve as an effective memory disruptive agent. Doty and Doty (1964) reported that CPZ disrupted memory for a single-trial active-avoidance response. This effect was shown to be time-dependent, since CPZ injections 1–2 hr after training failed to influence memory. Johnson (1969) found that CPZ (0.5–3.5 mg/kg) administered 30 sec to 10 min after training disrupted retention assessed 24 hr later. Memory for a classically conditioned fear response was shown to be unaffected by CPZ (Palfai and Cornell, 1968).

Additional evidence suggesting a role of CA in memory storage has emerged from the studies of Dismukes and Rake (1972). Posttrial reserpine (1.5 mg/kg) disrupted retention of a shuttle-box avoidance response in mice assessed 8 days later. This effect was not observed when the training–reserpine interval was 24 hr. The reserpine-induced RA was reversed by simultaneous injections of L-dopa (100 mg/kg), but not 5-hydroxytroptophan (5-HTP), indicating that the RA was attributable to a reduction in CA and not serotonin. Furthermore, PCPA (316 mg/kg) administered 3 days prior to shuttle-box training failed to influence retention assessed 14 days later. The importance of CA in normal memory storage was further emphasized by the disruption of memory produced by posttrial diethyldithiocarbamate (DDC), a dopamine-β-hydroxylase inhibitor, or dichloroisoproterenol (DCI), a β-adrenergic blocking agent. The memory disruptive property of posttrial DCI has been replicated by Merlo and Izquierdo (1971). Interestingly, propranolol, also a β-adrenergic blocking agent, has been reported to disrupt memory for a passive-avoidance response (Cohen and Hamburg, 1975), but produced memory facilitation when administered shortly following training in a shuttle-box avoidance task (Merlo and Izquierdo, 1971).

The procedure of administering reserpine together with CA and serotonin precursors shortly following training has more recently been used in a study using an inhibitory (passive) avoidance task (Rake, 1973). In this study posttrial reserpine (3 mg/kg) was also found to disrupt memory when tested 8 days later. However, unlike the findings of the shuttle-box avoidance study, both L-dopa and 5-HTP were effective in reversing the reserpine-induced RA. Furthermore, PCPA (300 mg/kg) administered in four doses during a three-day interval prior to training facilitated retention of the inhibitory avoidance response assessed 14 days later. This PCPA-induced facilitation of memory was blocked by posttrial 5-HTP administration. Thus, serotonin may also be important in the normal storage of recently acquired information (Knoll, 1974). The results of these studies (Dismukes and Rake, 1972; Rake, 1973) are difficult to compare directly since different strains of mice as well as different doses of reserpine were used in each experiment. Nevertheless, the interesting possibility emerges that different neurochemical systems may participate in processes involved in the storage of different types of information.

The above results strongly implicate CA in at least some aspect of memory-storage processes. However, the role of NE or DA in normal memory formation remains obscure. Several recent studies have shown that RA is produced by DDC. Randt *et al.* (1971) found that DDC (250 mg/kg) interfered with memory in mice when administered shortly before or immediately after training in an inhibitory avoidance task. This dose significantly lowered NE levels within 30 min following administration. Comparable findings have been obtained in subsequent studies (McGaugh *et al.*, 1975; Haycock *et al.*, 1977a). In this latter study, which used a different strain of mice, impairment was found with posttrial doses of DDC greater than 900 mg/kg. A dose of 900 mg/kg produced decreases in NE levels which lasted for up to 8 hr. DA levels were significantly increased during the first 30 min following the DDC injections. However, doses which did not affect memory did not significantly influence either NE or DA. Comparable results have also been obtained in studies using rats (Haycock et al., 1977b). Posttrial administration of DDC produces RA in an inhibitory avoidance task (McGaugh et al., 1975) as well as an active-avoidance task and a visual-discrimination task (Spanis et al., 1977). At doses which affect retention (680 mg/kg), NE was reduced for 24 hr, but DA levels were not significantly influenced. It appears that normal memory storage does not occur in a state of NE depletion. These studies do not rule out the possibility that altered memory storage (i.e., state dependence) may occur under such conditions. DDC administered up to 3 hr prior to training also disrupted passive-avoidance retention in rats. Hamburg and Cohen (1973) reported that administration of DDC prior to retention testing did not ameliorate the retention deficit produced by DDC administered prior to training. This finding suggests that the effects of DDC are not the result of state dependence, but rather are due to a disruption of acquisitional processes.

Determination of the basic effect of DDC on memory is a complicated matter since DDC has many effects. DDC is a chelating agent and therefore might be expected to influence a wide variety of enzyme systems in the CNS. In any case, it can hardly be considered that DDC is a specific inhibitor of dopamine-β-hydroxylase. Recently Randt et al. (1973) reported that DDC administered at doses which produce memory disruption (Randt et al., 1971) induced seizurelike activity consisting of high-voltage spiking and slow-wave activity (2–5 Hz) in the cortex and reticular formation of mice, beginning 15 min after injection. In addition, significant alterations in visual evoked potentials recorded from the dorsal hippocampus were observed. In a further examination of this effect, McGaugh et al. (1975) investigated the relationship between RA and brain-seizure activity in individual rats with implanted electrodes. Their findings indicated that while doses of DDC which produce seizures in some animals also produce RA, memory impairment was also found in animals which did not have seizures.

The findings of a recent study by Stein et al. (1975) support the view that the effect of DDC on memory is due to NE depletion. In this study the impairing effects of pretrial injections of DDC on retention were eliminated by intraventricular administration of NE immediately after training. It is not yet known whether this effect is specific to NE or whether comparable effects can be obtained with other treatments. Thus, considerable research remains to be done in clarifying the basis of the memory disruption produced by DDC.

The role of NE in the conversion of labile to stable memory has been recently investigated by Zornetzer and Gold (1976), who reported that immediate posttrial electrolytic lesions of LC in mice resulted in an extended susceptibility period of newly formed memory to ECS-produced RA. Thus, RA for an inhibitory avoidance task was produced at 40 hr after learning.

More recently, Zornetzer and Appelton (1977) reported that this extended susceptibility period persisted for at least 168 hr after initial learning. Also in this study, it was shown that LC lesions delayed by 6 hr after learning resulted in no extension in the susceptibility gradient; i.e., such lesions had no effect on normal memory and also did not create a condition of increased susceptibility to disruption. These results further implicate the importance of NE in memory processing.

Recent attempts to explore the potential role of NE in memory-retrieval processes similar to that hypothesized for ACh (Deutsch, 1973) have utilized the paradigm where drugs are administered prior to retention testing at differing training–retest intervals. In a passive-avoidance task, both DDC (Hamburg and Cohen, 1973) and propranolol (Cohen and Hamburg, 1975) disrupted retention test performance regardless of the training–retest interval. These results stand in contrast to those observed following administration of ACh agonists using an identical paradigm (Hamburg and Fulton, 1972). However, the use of a retest cutoff latency of 30 sec in the passive-avoidance task may have obscured potential actions of DDC or propranolol on retention by the introduction of an artificially low cutoff level. The extent to which modification of NE may influence retrieval in a manner similar to that for ACh (Deutsch, 1973) remains an important problem for further research.

In summary, several studies indicate that depletion of CA depresses performance of avoidance responding and also, when initiated shortly following training, produces memory disruption. One curious feature of this literature has been the several instances where CA depletion initiated prior to training failed to influence memory formation (White and Suboski, 1969; Ahlenius, 1973; Saper and Sweeney, 1973; Hall and Mayer, 1975). These reports are particularly puzzling, since posttrial administration of many antiadrenergic compounds produces RA. Recent findings of facilitation of avoidance learning with posttrial propranolol (Merlo and Izquierdo, 1971) or DDC (Haycock *et al.*, 1977a) injections are also puzzling. A determination of the conditions where CA depletion results in anterograde, as well as retrograde, actions on memory formation remains an important question for further research.

In general, the effects of antiadrenergic agents on rhythmic brain electrical activity in relation to associative processes has not yet been systematically studied. As noted above, DDC appears to induce cortical and reticular abnormal EEG activity. α-MPT produces cortical high-voltage slow-wave activity in cats (Shellenberger, 1971). In addition, this latter study also reported that α-MPT reduced the cortical desynchronizing action of reticular stimulation while potentiating caudate-induced cortical slow-wave and spindle activity. CPZ and reserpine appear to exert more complex effects. These agents, particularly CPZ, produce differential effects on the classical EEG arousal reaction, suppressing cortical desynchronization with little alteration in hippocampal theta activity (Stumpf, 1965). Furthermore, CPZ and reserpine have been shown to induce paroxysmal activity in limbic areas, particularly in the hippocampus and amygdala (Stumpf, 1965). Thus, CA depletion appears to be associated with a slowing of EEG activity. The extent to which the mechanism of action of sympatholytic agents in producing RA is related to the development of paroxysmal activity in isolated brain regions remains to be investigated.

4. ECS, PROTEIN-SYNTHESIS INHIBITION, AND CA

The effects of ECS on brain CA have been extensively studied. The majority of the experiments, however, have focused on the actions of multiple ECS treatments. These studies have sought to establish correlations between the antidepressant properties of electroconvulsive therapy and CA, and the research is guided by the general hypothesis that affective disorders are associated with disorders of CA metabolism.

The possibility that ECS-induced memory disruption is related to alterations in CA has not as yet been carefully investigated. Some experiments have studied the effects of a single ECS treatment on CA levels. ECS appears to result in a mobilization of CA leading to both an increased turnover and a small, but significant, decline in endogenous NE (Schildkraut and Draskoczy, 1974). The degree of NE depletion is much smaller than that found for ACh. This result may be due to an effect on the reuptake mechanism thought to terminate synaptic NE action. This hypothesis is supported by the finding that pre-ECS administration of desmethylimipramine significantly increased the degree of NE depletion (Schildkraut and Draskoczy, 1974). ECS has also been shown to increase the turnover of DA (Engel et al., 1968). However, findings remain controversial, since others (cf. Papeschi et al., 1974) have failed to observe changes in endogenous NE or DA levels following ECS. This discrepancy may be due to the fact that different procedures were used in these conflicting studies and the procedures may analyze different functional CA pools. However, the majority of evidence appears to favor the view that ECS increases the turnover and rapidly depletes a small functional pool of CA, perhaps with little immediate effect on a large storage pool. It is interesting that doses of pentylenetetrazol, which produce convulsions and memory disruption, also result in a small depletion of NE (Palfai et al., 1974).

There is also recent evidence suggesting that protein-synthesis inhibitors which impair memory storage may act through influences on CA. This suggestion emerged from the observations of Roberts et al. (1970) who found that administration of imipramine, amphetamine, or tranylcypromine prior to retention testing ameliorated the amnesia produced by intracerebral puromycin. The interaction between protein-synthesis inhibition and CA has been strengthened by the finding that cycloheximide inhibits tyrosine hydroxylase, the rate-limiting step in CA synthesis (Flexner *et al.*, 1973). Botwinick and Quartermain (1974) have recently reported that preretention-test administration of pheniprazine or pargyline, both monoamine oxidase inhibitors, reversed an apparent amnesia produced by cycloheximide. These agents were equally effective in reversing retention deficits resulting from pretrial administration of DDC. These results were interpreted as indicating that both cycloheximide and DDC disrupt retrieval processes as opposed to memory-storage processes. However, it has previously been shown that cholinergic agonists facilitate retention performance in poorly trained animals (cf. Deutsch, 1971). Thus, it seems possible that MAO inhibitors, like the cholinergic agonists, might restore memory by acting upon a weakened memory trace of a partially amnesic animal.

Finally, Barondes and Cohen (1968) found that cycloheximide administered prior to T-maze escape training disrupted memory for the experience when tested for retention 7 days later. Foot shock, corticosteroids, or amphetamine administered up to 3 hr following training reversed the cycloheximide-induced amnesia. In support of these findings, Mah and Albert (1975) have found that ECS-induced amnesia for a conditioned lick-suppression response was reversed by amphetamine (1 mg/kg) immediately, but not 6 hr following ECS. This evidence together with other observations (cf. McGaugh and Herz, 1972) has led to the postulation of a short-term memory process which is resistant to the disruptive effects of ECS or protein-synthesis inhibitors and which persists for several hours following a training experience. Furthermore, the results indicate that normal protein synthesis together with a moderate level of arousal are required for the formation of long-term memory. Of importance for the present discussion is the possibility that a portion of the effects of posttrial amphetamine on memory storage may be secondary to alterations in the level of arousal. This hypothesis will be considered more extensively below.

5. SEROTONIN (5-HYDROXYTRYPTAMINE, 5-HT)

The least extensively studied putative neurotransmitter in relation to processes involved in learning and memory is 5-HT. This relative lack of information may be a reflection of the few drugs known to exert specific actions on central 5-HT levels. Nevertheless, evidence has accumulated implicating 5-HT in memory-storage processes. Depletion of forebrain 5-HT either by PCPA or by lesions restricted to the raphe nuclei has been reported to result in facilitation of the performance and acquisition of two-way avoidance responses (cf. Tenen, 1967; Lorens, 1973; Lorens and Yunger, 1974; Steranka and Barrett, 1974). For example, Lorens and Yunger (1974) found that ablations of the medial and/or the dorsal raphe nuclei in the rat resulted in a 33–57% reduction in forebrain 5-HT levels and a facilitation of the acquisition of a shuttle-box avoidance response. These effects may well be alterations in performance rather than memory-storage processes. This interpretation is suggested by the findings that PCPA disrupts performance of a passive-avoidance response (Stevens *et al.*, 1969; Riege, 1971). However, this result remains controversial (Brody, 1970).

It was originally suggested that the PCPA-induced facilitation of avoidance behavior resulted from an increase in reactivity to novel stimuli (Tenen, 1967). Other investigations have emphasized the possible contributions of 5-HT in the modulation of behavioral suppression. For example, Carlton and Advokat (1973) found that PCPA increased startle-response amplitude, an effect which was attributed to a slowing in the rate of habituation, although others have failed to observe an effect of PCPA on habituation (cf. File, 1975). Steranka and Barrett (1974) observed that raphe lesions increased activity, decreased response latencies in a discriminated avoidance task, and also decreased the number of errors. These investigators argued that a depletion of 5-HT markedly attenuated shock-induced behavioral suppression thereby facilitating active-avoidance performance.

Increased brain 5-HT has been shown to depress performance of schedule-controlled responses (Aprison and Hingter, 1970). In these experiments 5-HT was elevated by systemic administration of the precursor 5-HTP. Administration of 5-HTP also depresses active-avoidance acquisition and/or performance (Joyce and Hurwitz, 1964; Roffman and Lal, 1971).

As noted previously, alterations of 5-HT systems have been reported to modify long-term memory formation. While 5-HTP proved ineffective in reversing a reserpine-induced RA for a shuttle-box avoidance response in mice (Dismukes and Rake, 1972), replacement of forebrain 5-HT by 5-HTP administration reversed an amnesia produced by reserpine for a passive-avoidance response (Rake, 1973). In addition, PCPA administered prior to training facilitated memory for a passive-avoidance response assessed 14 days later. These results suggest the possibility that 5-HT may be somewhat specifically involved in the formation of memory for passive-avoidance learning.

Additional evidence for involvement of serotonin in memory-storage processes comes from Essman's studies of the relationship between 5-HT and ECS-induced RA (Essman, 1970, 1971, 1973*a,c*). Essman reported that 5-HTP administration 1 hr prior to training in a single-trial inhibitory avoidance task impaired performance during a retention test conducted 24 hr later. More recently, Essman (1973*b*) reported that posttrial intrahippocampal microinjections of 5-HT produced RA for a passive-avoidance response in mice. This effect was shown to be time dependent, since RA was not observed when training–treatment intervals of 16–32 min were used. These microinjections were shown to result in increases in whole-brain 5-HT content (60–100%). In order to test the specificity of the intrahippocampal 5-HT-induced memory disruption, similar microinjections of NE were administered shortly following passive-avoidance training (Essman, 1973*b*). Although NE failed to produce memory disruption, it is difficult to interpret these results because of the criterion which was used for evidence of RA (defined as a retention test step-through latency of less than 10 sec). This criticism is particularly important, since 20% of the NE-treated mice exhibited criterion RA, as compared to 80% of the 5-HT-treated subjects. Finally, intrahippocampal 5-HT was reported to inhibit protein synthesis as measured by decreases in the rate of incorporation of [^{14}C]leucine into brain protein. Protein-synthesis inhibition was observed in each of several brain regions including the cortex, basal ganglia, diencephalon, midbrain, and, to a lesser extent, the cerebellum.

Evidence for a role of 5-HT in memory processes has also emerged from studies of the effect of ECS on endogenous levels of 5-HT. A single ECS treatment produced an elevation in the content of 5-HT which appeared to reach a peak approximately 10 min post-ECS, remaining elevated for several hours (Essman, 1973c). The increased 5-HT was accompanied by a decreased rate of 5-HT turnover. The increase in 5-HT appears to be greatest in the diencephalon, as compared to cortical or midbrain fractions. Furthermore, decreases in the rate of appearance of 5-HIAA, a 5-HT metabolite, after monoamine oxidase inhibition were also greatest in the midbrain and diencephalic regions. This suggests that the increased 5-HT following ECS treatment may arise predominantly from activity in subcortical structures.

Recently Leonard and Rigter (1975) observed that a foot-shock-induced rise in the concentration of 5-HT in the rat hippocampus was reduced by CO_2 treatment which also produced amnesia for a passive-avoidance response. The reduction was not observed at training–CO_2-treatment intervals which did not produce RA for the passive avoidance response (Rigter et al., 1975). Furthermore, significant correlations were observed between hippocampal 5-HT levels and short-term memory decay following CO_2 treatment (Van Eys et al., 1975). These results further strengthen the association between memory-disruptive treatments and 5-HT.

These results suggest that 5-HT is in some way important for the normal storage of recently acquired information. One property of the biochemistry of serotoninergic systems that has received little consideration in studies of 5-HT and behavior is the extent to which alterations of 5-HT content result in the formation of abnormal metabolites that may act as false transmitters in other neurochemical systems. Biochemical evidence has accumulated suggesting that 5-HT or 5-HTP may be taken up into cells normally containing CA. They are metabolized there abnormally and disrupt CA activity by acting as a false transmitter substance (cf. Chase and Murphy, 1973). Thus, enhancement of neural 5-HT might be expected to result in some degree of disruption of normal activity in CA neurons. More research is needed to determine the extent to which alterations in memory which are related to increases in levels of 5-HT can be attributed to disruption of CA systems.

As is the case with ACh and CA, various drugs which alter 5-HT levels in the brain also produce alterations in rhythmic brain electrical activity. For example, PCPA is known to depress slow-wave sleep and to produce instead an insomnia together with a potentiation of low-voltage high-frequency cortical EEG activity (cf. Jouvet, 1969). On the other hand, administration of 5-HTP (50–100 mg/kg) produces a behavioral sedation together with the appearance of high-voltage slow waves in the cortex of monkeys (Macchitelli et al., 1966). The extent to which these alterations in electrographic activity may account for alterations in memory-storage processes will be considered below.

6. NEUROTRANSMITTER INTERACTIONS

Understanding the complex manner in which neurotransmitter systems are distributed and organized in the central nervous system continues as an important research area in the neurobiological sciences. The reciprocal innervation of target organs in the autonomic nervous system by acetylcholine and norepinephrine provides, of course, one of the more simplistic models of neurotransmitter interactions. In the peripheral nervous system it seems likely that acetylcholine may modulate the release of norepinephrine, perhaps through the presence of nicotinic and muscarinic receptors on presynaptic adrenergic nerve terminals (Volle and Koelle, 1970). Some evidence suggests similar cholinergic–adrenergic interactions in the CNS (cf. Westfall, 1974), although the functional significance of such interactions remains obscure.

In the CNS it would appear that the potential for even more complex interactions exists, particularly with the addition of multiple neurotransmitter systems (Krnjevic, 1974). Only a few experiments have examined the potential interactions of various neurotransmitters in mediating the storage of recently acquired information. As we noted above, Roffman and Lal (1972) reported that the stimulatory action of amphetamine on the retention-test performance of a jump-avoidance response was antagonized by concurrent administration of α-MPT or cyproheptadine, a serotoninergic receptor blocking agent. These investigations suggested that the action of amphetamine in stimulating recall may involve an initial activation of CA neurons, whose projections end upon serotoninergic cells.

Evidence also suggests a potential interaction between CA and ACh in the modulation of associative processes. Orsingher and Fulginiti (1971) found that the stimulatory action of nicotine or amphetamine on the acquisition of a shuttle-box avoidance response in rats was blocked by pretreatment with α-MPT. It may be that the effects of nicotine on associative processes result from an action on cholinoceptive neurons which subsequently modulate activity in CA neurons. However, Evangelista and

Izquierdo (1970) reported that memory facilitation produced by amphetamine was antagonized by atropine. Furthermore, Fibiger *et al.* (1974*b*) have found that the disruption of acquisition of an active-avoidance response produced by haloperidol was reversed by concurrent atropine or scopolamine treatment. These latter results suggest a more complex interaction between ACh and CA in associative processes.

While we have chosen to limit the scope of this chapter to a consideration of the role of ACh, CA, and 5-HT in memory processes, it is likely that several other putative neurotransmitters are also important. For example, some evidence indicates that GABA and glycine may be important for normal memory storage. It has long been known that the CNS stimulants strychnine and picrotoxin influence memory processes (McGaugh and Petrinovich, 1965; McGaugh, 1973) and that these compounds are known to result in a reasonably specific blockade of glycine and GABA postsynaptic receptors, respectively. Furthermore, it appears likely that feedback from peripheral hormonal secretion (Barondes and Cohen, 1968) or through the release of pituitary hormones (de Wied, 1974; de Wied *et al.*, 1975; Van Wimersma Greidanus *et al.*, 1975) may influence memory processes by acting upon cellular excitability either directly or indirectly by modulating the release of neurotransmitters. The ultimate complexity of the potential interactions between these neurochemical systems is illustrated by recent studies which have correlated the effects of nicotine on avoidance behavior with pituitary-adrenal activity and hippocampal 5-HT concentrations (Balfour and Morrison, 1975). Understanding of the manner in which each of these putative neurotransmitters and hormones interact in the modulation of memory-storage processes awaits extensive future research.

7. CONCLUSIONS

The evidence summarized in the present review provides a basis for the conclusion that alterations in ACh, CA (particularly NE), and 5-HT can modulate the storage of recently acquired information. Treatments which selectively depress cholinergic and adrenergic activity generally disrupt memory-storage processes. Similar memory-disruptive properties have been ascribed to treatments which enhance 5-HT activity. These effects have each been shown to be time dependent. Thus, their primary action appears to be on memory-storage processes. Conversely, treatments which enhance ACh or CA generally facilitate memory-storage processes. These effects have been shown to be both time dependent and dose dependent and can readily be described according to an inverted U-shaped dose–response function. Nicotine, physostigmine, and amphetamine are all regarded as CNS stimulants, and their effects upon memory closely resemble other compounds within this general category (cf. McGaugh and Petrinovich, 1965; McGaugh, 1973).

Treatments which deplete 5-HT also appear to facilitate memory formation. Here it remains unclear whether the effect can be attributed to potentiation of acquisitional processes as opposed to specific memory-storage processes. We are not aware of any instances where a careful examination of the effects of posttrial administration of 5-HT antagonists have been studied.

ECS results in depletion of endogenous ACh and NE together with an elevation of 5-HT. Correlations have been reported between ECS-induced RA and alterations in serotoninergic and cholinergic systems. Furthermore, similar correlations have been established between the memory-disruptive properties of protein-synthesis inhibition and CA. The extent to which the mechanisms of these classical memory-disruptive agents are related to modification of the neurotransmitters is an important issue in memory research.

The formation of stable long-term memory appears contingent upon the maintenance of activity in cholinergic and adrenergic systems as well as perhaps some degree of inhibition of ongoing activity in serotoninergic pathways. The striking observation that memory is susceptible to modification by alterations in each of these neurotransmitter systems poses a difficult problem of interpretation. Although considerably more elaborate hypotheses might be generated, two somewhat distinct interpretations emerge: The first is that compounds which alter specific neurotransmitter systems act *directly* upon the memory trace. This hypothesis assumes that the complex biological organization underlying memory involves several pathways, perhaps with each being distinctly coded neurochemically. In this sense the neural representation of the training experience, the proverbial engram or memory trace, may be subserved by multiple pathways involving ACh, CA, and 5-HT as the transmitter substances. Thus, drugs which alter specific neurotransmitter systems may act directly upon components of the memory trace during the labile phase of formation, when strength is still low, to produce selective facilitation or disruption. While this view is not unrealistic, it has no direct support. A second more general hypothesis centers on an explanation based upon drug effects on nonspecific processes which may serve to modulate the strength of the memory trace. According to this view, manipulations of ACh, CA, or 5-HT *indirectly* influence memory-storage processes by their common actions upon other nonspecific neural processes subserving arousal functions.

With regard to the second hypothesis, an initial question is the extent to which nonspecific arousal participates in the modulation of memory-storage processes. Such conceptual variables as arousal, motivation, and reinforcement have long been considered crucial for effective and efficient learning and subsequent performance. An organism's arousal level can be modulated by a variety of interacting factors, including adrenal output, pituitary hormones, and intensity of environmental (both exteroceptive and interoceptive) stimulation of the reticular activating system. Some investigators have suggested that memory-facilitating agents might act as a consequence of their effects on arousal rather than by specific and direct effects on the memory trace *per se* (cf. Bloch, 1970: Dawson and McGaugh, 1973). In general, however, few have considered the possible significance of alterations in nonspecific arousal systems as a potential mechanism of action of agents which produce memory disruption.

Recently Gold and McGaugh (1974) proposed a theory of memory formation which provided a role for nonspecific arousal processes. Their "single-trace dual process" view of memory storage hypothesizes the following steps in the formation of a trace: A training experience initiates the formation of a memory trace, perhaps involving perseverative neural processes, which forms the neural representation of the memory for the specific experience. The training experience also initiates a second process—a nonspecific physiological response, which is a direct consequence of the experience. For example, in an aversive task, foot shock would result in increased CNS arousal levels together with peripheral hormonal secretion. According to this theory, these nonspecific physiological responses serve in a feedback role to modulate the ultimate strength of the memory trace by initiating a brain state which promotes the growth or consolidation of the trace. According to this view, the ultimate strength of the memory can be related to the strength of the nonspecific physiological response to the reinforcing conditions initiated by the training experience. Thus, under conditions where the nonspecific physiological response is normally small (e.g., low foot shock) or is disrupted (e.g., ECS or cycloheximide), the trace will rapidly decay and is soon forgotten. The Gold and McGaugh theory assumes that memory is susceptible to modification by alterations in (1) the initial formation of the memory trace and/or (2) the nonspecific physiological response to the training experience.

The evidence reviewed in the present paper is consistent with the hypothesis that alterations in cholinergic, adrenergic, and serotoninergic systems modify memory-storage processes by modulating the nonspecific physiological response to the training experience. First, and perhaps foremost, is the finding that each of these neurotransmitters has been implicated in central arousal processes. Traditionally, though perhaps inappropriately, two major variables have been considered to reflect the state of an organism's arousal level: behavioral activity and electrocortical activity. Drugs which produce electrocortical arousal (i.e., low-voltage high-frequency activity), whether by potentiation of ACh or NE or depletion of 5-HT, also produce generalized facilitation of memory formation. Conversely, compounds which depress electrocortical arousal, whether by depletion of ACh or NE or by potentiation of 5-HT, have been shown to be effective memory-disruptive agents. It is worth noting that the actions of such compounds on electrographic activity and memory appear to be independent of their actions upon behavioral arousal. Thus, for example, cholinergic agents, which produce a dissociation between electrocortical activity and behavioral arousal, produce a similar dissociation between effects upon the performance of previously learned responses and memory-storage processes in a fashion consistent with their actions upon electrocortical activity as opposed to actions upon behavioral arousal. Extreme caution should be taken in interpreting the above conclusions, since pharmacological manipulation of putative neurotransmitters exert widespread effects on brain function in addition to actions upon arousal processes. Clearly, theoretical formulations relating putative neurotransmitters to memory-storage processes await continued research on the mechanisms of action of drugs used to alter the transmitter functioning.

Apart from evidence indicating a direct or indirect role of ACh, CA, and 5-HT in arousal processes, other findings also support the hypothesis that changes in nonspecific physiological processes constitute a mechanism by which neurotransmitter-specific agents can modulate memory formation. The dose–response curves for the effects of physostigmine, nicotine, and amphetamine on memory all have an inverted U-shaped function. Moreover, the inverted U-shaped dose–response curves appear to be contingent upon the degree of nonspecific arousal produced by a given training experience. Thus, for example, doses of nicotine found to facilitate memory for a shuttle-box avoidance response (Evangelista et al., 1970) are considerably lower than those facilitating memory for an appetitive maze problem (Garg and Holland, 1969). Krivanek (1971) and others (Gold and McGaugh, 1974) have commented upon similar relationships observed for other CNS stimulants. While nicotine, physostigmine, and amphetamine produce seizure activity at higher doses (cf. Stumpf, 1965), memory disruption in these instances may occur in part at least as a consequence of the deleterious properties of excessive arousal levels. Studies examining the effects of training parameters and dose–response curves upon memory processes with concurrent evaluation of electrophysiological measures of neural activity may provide a clarification of these issues.

The nonspecific physiological response to the training experience also appears to depend upon hormonal mediation. Posttrial systemic injections of epinephrine (Gold and van Buskirk, 1975), vasopressin, or ACTH (Gold et al., 1975) produce a similar inverted U-shaped dose–response curve on memory for a conditioned lick-suppression response. These effects also were shown to depend upon foot-shock intensity, presumably demonstrating an interaction with task-dependent arousal. Finally, the work of Barondes and Cohen (1968) appears pertinent to this discussion. As mentioned above, these authors found that increases in nonspecific arousal, whether induced by foot shock, corticosteroids, or amphetamine, if administered within 3 hr following training, effectively antagonized the amnesic properties of protein-synthesis inhibitors. It is tempting here to ascribe a portion of the amnesic properties of protein-synthesis inhibitors like cycloheximide to effects on nonspecific arousal systems.

Typically, cholinergic antagonists have been reported to disrupt memory-storage processes (Glick and Zimmerberg, 1971). Evangelista and Izquierdo (1970) reported that atropine facilitated memory for a shuttle-box avoidance response. These data, while puzzling, could be explained by actions upon nonspecific arousal systems. In this latter study, rats received 60 massed-practice training trials in a shuttle-box avoidance task. Five days later, control animals showed little evidence of retention. This seemingly peculiar result might be explained on the basis of excessive arousal levels which were generated by the training procedures, and which resulted in an interference with efficient information processing. Atropine or other agents resulting in a moderate depression of electrocortical arousal, under these training conditions, might facilitate memory formation by lowering peak arousal level.

The findings are, however, somewhat more complex than this analysis suggests. Evangelista and Izquierdo (1970) reported that using the massed-practice training paradigm described above, amphetamine also facilitated memory. Concurrent administration of atropine antagonized the memory facilitative properties of amphetamine. More research is needed in order to understand the complex way in which drug interactions influence behavior in general, and memory-storage processes in particular.

The extent to which drugs can alter arousal level may depend upon the level of CNS excitability at the time of drug administration. It is interesting in this regard that atropine, in doses which normally produce cortical synchrony, result instead in cortical desynchronization when administered to animals pretreated with seizure-producing doses of cholinesterase inhibitors (Karczmar, 1974).

The hypothesis that drugs influence memory by modifying arousal systems appears to have good foundation. If this view is correct, what *specific* roles do ACh, CA, and 5-HT assume in arousal systems? Since the pioneering studies of Moruzzi and Magoun (1949), the reticular formation has been regarded as the neural region largely responsible for modulating arousal and states of consciousness. Despite considerable interest in this problem, the nature of the neurochemical substrates of the ascending reticular activating system (ARAS) remains unclear. One popular view is that the ARAS is essentially adrenergic (Killam, 1968). In discussing the evolutionary significance of a system of information processing critically dependent upon environmental contingencies, Kety (1970) outlined a role for arousal in memory-storage processes similar to the single-trace dual process recently proposed (Gold and McGaugh, 1974). Kety argued that certain properties of central noradrenergic systems make them particularly suitable for mediating the effects of arousal on memory processes. Apart from the observations that several compounds which act directly upon central CA also influence arousal, other evidence implicates NE in arousal processes. Foremost among this evidence are studies demonstrating that alterations in states of arousal produce concomitant changes in parameters of NE utilization. For example, foot-shock stress has been shown to increase the turnover of central NE (cf. Glowinski, 1972) while cold stress has been shown to potentiate the disruptive properties of α-MPT upon shuttle-box avoidance acquisition (Orsingher and Fulginiti, 1971).

Fluorescence histochemical studies indicate that NE-containing cell bodies are localized in lateral portions of the pontine and medullary reticular formation principally in the LC (cf. Fuxe et al., 1970). These cell bodies send projections, predominantly via the medial forebrain bundle to widespread areas of forebrain. In the case of the dorsal ascending noradrenergic bundle, the major projection areas appear to be the cortex and hippocampus. In the cortex the ascending noradrenergic fibers form numerous axodendritic and axosomatic synapses (Fuxe et al., 1968) in a fashion likened to diffuse nonspecific cortical afferents described by Scheibel and Scheibel (1967) and regarded as a likely system for mediating reticulocortical modulation. Iontophoretic studies suggest that cells in the cortex and hippocampus are generally inhibited by NE (Nelson et al., 1973; Segal and Bloom, 1974a). Furthermore, Segal and Bloom (1974b) recently reported that electrical stimulation of the LC produces inhibition of ongoing firing in pyramidal cells of the hippocampus. Thus, activation of a pathway known to contain NE appears to produce actions similar to iontophoretic administration of NE. It is interesting in this regard that electrical stimulation of LC in cats produces the classical EEG arousal reaction, consisting of cortical desynchronization and hippocampal theta activity (Macadar et al., 1974).

Kety (1970) has also suggested a potential role of NE in modulating nonspecific macromolecular synthesis. Evidence (Siggins et al., 1971; Segal and Bloom, 1974a,b) suggests that a portion of the effects of NE upon cells may be mediated by activation of cyclic adenosine monophosphate (cAMP). The theoretical model of Bloom and associates (cf. Cooper et al., 1974) proposes that NE facilitates cAMP production by stimulating a membrane-bound adenyl cyclase receptor. cAMP in turn is thought to activate protein kinase, thereby increasing protein synthesis.

Activation of these NE pathways during states of arousal might facilitate macromolecular synthetic cellular machinery, perhaps most importantly at those synapses recently activated as a consequence of training. If it is assumed that the arousal system is essentially noradrenergic, then what role do ACh and 5-HT play in arousal? Many investigators have assumed that cholinergic and serotoninergic systems influence arousal indirectly by modulating activity in ascending NE pathways. For example, Campbell and associates (Campbell et al., 1969; Mabry and Campbell, 1973, 1974) provided strong developmental evidence suggesting that descending cholinergic and serotoninergic pathways, arising from the frontal cortex and hippocampus respectively, serve an inhibitory role upon an adrenergic system mediating behavioral arousal. Others have devised even more complicated models in which 5-HT pathways modulate activity in an ACh system, which ultimately acts upon an excitatory noradrenergic arousal system (Swonger and Rech, 1972).

The nature of the neurochemical substrates of the reticular formation however, remain controversial. Shute and Lewis (1967) and others (cf. Rinaldi and Himwich, 1955) have maintained that reticulocortical arousal is mediated, in part at least, by activity in a diffuse reticulodiencephalic cholinergic system. However, as noted by Krnjevic (1974) in a comprehensive review, little conclusive evidence has as yet accumulated indicating an *essential* role of ACh or NE in mediating the actions of the ascending reticular activating system.

Others have taken an alternative theoretical position, hypothesizing a more complex interaction between noradrenergic and cholinergic systems in mediating reticulocortical arousal (Longo, 1968; Karczmar, 1974). Important evidence for this theoretical position were the observations of Barnes (1966) who reported that physostigmine and amphetamine produce antagonistic, as opposed to synergistic, actions on reticulocortical arousal.

As yet little attention has been given to the possibility that arousal may be mediated by ascending parallel neurochemical systems. Those same properties outlined by Kety (1970), which make central CA systems particularly suitable for mediating effects of arousal on memory, also appear to be shared to a great extent by both ACh and 5-HT. Thus, significant numbers of ACh-containing cell bodies have been localized in the ventral tegmental area (Shute and Lewis, 1967). Similarly, 5-HT-containing cell bodies have been located in the various raphe nuclei (cf. Fuxe *et al.*, 1971). Each of these brainstem systems send projections via the medial forebrain bundle to widespread areas of forebrain. The ascending NE, ACh, and 5-HT pathways project to overlapping, but not identical, areas of the forebrain. Studies examining the effects of iontophoretic application of NE, ACh, and 5-HT have shown that each is capable of influencing spontaneous firing rates of cells in the cortex and hippocampus (Nelson *et al.*, 1973; Segal and Bloom, 1974a), as well as other widespread areas of forebrain (cf. Krnjevic, 1974). Finally, both 5-HT and ACh may be capable of influencing macromolecular synthesis. The work of Essman (1970) demonstrating an inhibitory action of 5-HT upon protein synthesis has already been discussed. Further, it appears that ACh may stimulate macromolecular synthesis by activation of cyclic-guanosine monophosphate (Kuo *et al.*, 1972).

From the above evidence it appears that NE, ACh, and 5-HT each potentially possess properties which make them suitable candidates for mediating the effects of arousal on memory processes. A parallel-processing model of neurochemical arousal also appears to account more adequately for certain aspects of interactions between drugs and memory, particularly the phenomenon of state dependence. For example, α-MPT has been shown to produce a state-dependent symmetrical dissociation for a passive-avoidance response (Zornetzer *et al.*, 1974). Reduction of levels of CA which presumably disrupt nonspecific physiological responses to the training experience does not appear to constitute a sufficient condition for the eradication of memory. Clearly, under conditions of depleted CA during training, memory is not stored normally since retention is normal only when the drug condition during training is reinstated prior to testing. Such results prove difficult to reconcile with the hypothesis outlined by Kety (1970). Rather, it appears that a more complex organization of processes involved in memory storage must be entertained, perhaps involving multiple redundant pathways. State-dependent memory formation therefore may be more clearly understood in a formulation involving multiple parallel neurochemical pathways. Thus, the pattern of arousal may be more important than the ultimate behavioral expression of arousal. Specifically, the pattern of arousal, the neural representation of which depends upon the pattern of activity generated by reticular ACh, NE, and 5-HT systems, may become an integral component of the stored information. It is this patterned brain state, present at the time of storage, which might need to be reproduced or at least approximated at the time of retrieval in order for the stored information to be elaborated. While the neural mechanisms responsible for state-dependent learning remain far from being satisfactorily understood (Bliss, 1974), state-dependent memory formation must be considered in any biological theory of memory.

We have suggested that drugs which affect neurotransmitter systems may modify memory indirectly by influencing nonspecific arousal processes which serve to modulate memory storage. Such a hypothesis may be of little more than heuristic value, for on a mechanistic level it may be impossible to separate nonspecific arousal processes from specific memory processes. At the conceptual level, arousal has traditionally been considered distinct from memory processes, and it appears that at least for the present a continuation of this distinction is useful. In this regard it seems reasonable to assume, as has Jarvik (1972), that systemically administered drugs act more directly upon nonspecific neural processes, like excitability, than upon specific aspects of information storage.

An experimental approach that might serve to clarify potential nonspecific as opposed to specific drug actions upon memory processes might utilize drug microinjections into discrete brain regions. Intrahippocampal microinjections of 5-HT or scopolamine administered shortly following training disrupted memory for an inhibitory avoidance response (Weiner and Messer, 1973; Essman, 1973b). In these studies the use of large injection volumes (5–10 μl) precludes a convincing demonstration of a localized action of scopolamine or 5-HT within the hippocampus (Myers, 1971). Such fluid volumes increase the degree of chemical diffusion and furthermore raise the potential for chemical activation of diffuse ascending nonspecific arousal systems. Nevertheless, these results provide a promising basis for further research. This microneuropharmacological technique coupled with discrete localized electrical brain stimulation might serve to provide a powerful approach to the study of the neurobiology of memory.

We have considered those studies which examined the effects of drugs altering ACh, CA, or 5-HT on memory processes. It is apparent that cells using these putative neurotransmitters contribute in some way to the normal processing of information. However, in addition to these a number of other putative neurotransmitters have also been described in the literature. For example, considerable evidence suggests the potential roles of glutamic acid, γ-aminobutyric acid, and others as CNS neurotransmitters (Krnjevic, 1974). To date, little evidence has accumulated implicating these substances in memory processes (McGaugh and Petrinovich, 1965; McGaugh, 1973; Dawson and McGaugh, 1973). Future experiments, no doubt, will begin to uncover an even more complex picture than that portrayed in the present paper. The results summarized in this review serve to emphasize a most promising approach in the study of the neurobiological correlates of memory.

Acknowledgment

Preparation of this paper was supported in part by NIMH Biological Sciences Training Grant 2T01-MH10320-10 (Bruce Hunter is a research trainee at the Center for Neurobiological Sciences at the University of Florida), Research Grant MH26608 (to Murray E. Jarvik), and Research Grant MH12526 (to James L. McGaugh).

8. References

Adams, H. E., Hoblit, P. R., and Sutker, P. B., 1969, Electroconvulsive shock, brain acetylcholinesterase activity and memory, *Physiol. Behav.* **4:**113–116.

Ahlenius, S., 1973, Inhibition of catecholamine synthesis and conditioned avoidance acquisition, *Pharmacol. Biochem. Behav.* **1:**347–350.

Albert, D. J., Mah, C. J., and Bose, W. B., 1974, The effect of scopolamine on the amnesia induced by electroconvulsive shock, *Pharmacol. Biochem. Behav.* **2:**443–446.

Amaral, D. G., and Foss, J. A., 1975, Locus coeruleus lesions and learning, *Science* **188:**377–378.

Anlezark, G. M., Crow, T. J., and Greenway, A. P., 1973, Impaired learning and decreased cortical norepinephrine after bilateral locus coeruleus lesions, *Science* **181:**682–684.

Aprison, M. H., and Hingten, J. M., 1970, Neurochemical correlates of behavior, *Int. Rev. Neurobiol.* **13:**325–342.

Balfour, D. J. K., and Morrison, C. F., 1975, A possible role for the pituitary-adrenal system in the effects of nicotine on avoidance behavior, *Pharmacol. Biochem. Behav.* **3:**349–354.

Barnes, C. D., 1966, The interaction of amphetamine and eserine on the EEG, *Life Sci.* **5:**1897–1902.

Barondes, S. H., and Cohen, H. D., 1968, Arousal and the conversion of "short-term" to "long-term" memory, *Proc. Nat. Acad. Sci. U.S.A.* **61:**923–929.

Barrett, R. J., Leith, N. J., and Ray, O. S., 1974, An analysis of the facilitation of avoidance acquisition produced by d-amphetamine and scopolamine, *Behav. Biol.* **11:**189–203.

Battig, K., 1970, The effect of pre- and post-trial application of nicotine on the 12 problems of the Hebb-Williams Test in the rat, *Psychopharmacologia* **18:**68–76.

Beer, B., and Lenard, L. G., 1975, Differential effects of intraventricular administration of

6-hydroxydopamine on behavior of rats in approach and avoidance procedures: reversal of avoidance decrements by diazepam, *Pharmacol. Biochem. Behav.* **3:**879–886.

BENNETT, E. L., KRECH, D., and ROSENZWEIG, M. R., 1964, Reliability and regional specificity of cerebral effects of environmental complexity and training, *J. Comp. Physiol. Psychol.* **57:**440–441.

BERGER, B. D., and STEIN, L., 1969, An analysis of the learning deficits produced by scopolamine, *Psychopharmacologia* **14:**271–283.

BIGNAMI, G., and GATTI, G. L., 1969, Analysis of drug effects on multiple fixed ratio 33–fixed interval 5 min in pigeons, *Psychopharmacologia* **15:**310–332.

BLISS, D. K., 1974, Theoretical explanations of drug-dissociated behaviors, *Fed. Proc.* **33:**1787–1796.

BLOCH, V., 1970, Facts and hypotheses concerning memory consolidation, *Brain Res.* **24:**561–575.

BOHDANECKY, Z., and JARVIK, M. E., 1967, Impairment of one-trial passive avoidance learning in mice by scopolamine, scopolamine methylbromide, and physostigmine, *Neuropharmacology* **6:**217–222.

BOTWINICK, C. Y., and QUARTERMAIN, D., 1974, Recovery from amnesia induced by preretest injections of monoamine oxidase inhibitors, *Pharmacol. Biochem. Behav.* **2:**375–379.

BOVET, D., BOVET-NITTI, F., and OLIVERIO, A., 1966, Effects of nicotine on avoidance conditioning of inbred strains of mice, *Psychopharmacologia* **10:**1–5.

BOVET-NITTI, F., 1969, Facilitation of simultaneous visual discrimination by nicotine in four inbred strains of mice, *Psychopharmacologia* **14:**193–199.

BREDA, J. B., CARLINI, E. A., and SADER, N. F. A., 1969, Effects of chronic administration of amphetamine on maze performance of the rat, *Br. J. Pharmacol.* **37:**79–86.

BRODY, J. F., 1970, Behavioral effects of serotonin depletion of *p*-chlorophenylalanine (a serotonin depletor) in rats, *Psychopharmacologia* **17:**14–33.

BURES, J., BOHDANECKY, Z., and WEISS, T., 1962, Physostigmine-induced hippocampal theta activity and learning in rats, *Psychopharmacologia* **3:**254–263.

BURESOVA, O., BURES, J., BOHDANECKY, J., and WEISS, T., 1964, Effect of atropine on learning, extinction, retention and retrieval in rats, *Psychopharmacologia* **5:**255–263.

CALHOUN, W. H., and SMITH, A. A., 1968, Effects of scopolamine on acquisition of passive avoidance, *Psychopharmacologia* **13:**201–209.

CAMPBELL, B. A., LYTLE, L. D., and FIBIGER, H. C., 1969, Ontogeny of adrenergic arousal and cholinergic inhibitory mechanisms in the rat, *Science* **166:**635–637.

CARDO, B., 1959, Action of dextrorotatory amphetamine and of eserine on conditioned flight and a phenomena of discrimination, *J. Physiol.* **51:**845–860.

CARLSON, N. J., DOYLE, G. A., and BIDDER, T. G., 1965, The effects of *dl*-amphetamine and reserpine on runway performance, *Psychopharmacologia* **8:**157–173.

CARLTON, P. L., and ADVOKAT, C., 1973, Attenuated habituation due to *p*-chlorophenylalanine, *Pharmacol. Biochem. Behav.* **1:**657–664.

CHASE, T. N., and MURPHY, D. L., 1973, Serotonin and central nervous system function, *Ann. Rev. Pharmacol.* **13:**181–197.

COHEN, R. P., and HAMBURG, M. D., 1975, Evidence for adrenergic neurons in a memory access pathway, *Pharmacol. Biochem. Behav.* **3:**519–523.

COOPER, B. R., BREESE, G. R., GRANT, L. D., and HOWARD, J. L., 1973, Effects of 6-hydroxydopamine treatments on active avoidance responding: evidence for involvement of brain dopamine. *J. Pharmacol. Exp. Ther.* **185:**358–370.

COOPER, J. R., BLOOM, F. E., and ROTH, R. H., 1974, *The Biochemical Basis of Neuropharmacology*, Oxford University Press, New York.

CRABBE, J. C., and ALPERN, H. P., 1973, Facilitation and disruption of the long-term store of memory with neural excitants, *Pharmacol. Biochem. Behav.* **1:**197–202.

DAVIS, J. W., THOMAS, R. K., and ADAMS, H. E., 1971, Interations of scopolamine and physostigmine with ECS and one-trial learning, *Physiol. Behav.* **6:**219–222.

DAWSON, R. G., and McGAUGH, J. L., 1973, Drug facilitation of learning and memory, in: *The Physiological Basis of Memory* (J. A. Deutsch, ed.), pp. 77–111, Academic Press, New York.

DEUTSCH, J. A., 1971, The cholinergic synapse and the site of memory, *Science* **174:**788–794.

DEUTSCH, J. A., 1973, The cholinergic synapse and the site of memory, in: *The Physiological Basis of Memory* (J. A. Deutsch, ed.), pp. 59–77, Academic Press, New York.

DEUTSCH, J. A., and LEIBOWITZ, S. F., 1966, Amnesia or reversal of forgetting by anticholinesterase depending simply on time of injection, *Science* **153:**1017–1018.

DEUTSCH, J. A., and ROCKLIN, K. W., 1967, Amnesia induced by scopolamine and its temporal variations, *Nature (London)* **216:**89–90.

DEUTSCH, J. A., and ROLL, S. K., 1973, Alcohol and asymmetrical state-dependency; a possible explanation, *Behav. Biol.* **8:**273–278.

DEUTSCH, J. A., HAMBURG, M. D., and DAHL, H., 1966, Anticholinesterase-induced amnesia and its temporal aspects, *Science* **151:**221–223.

DE WIED, D., 1974, Pituitary-adrenal system hormones and behavior, in: *The Neurosciences, Third Study Program* (F. O. Schmitt and F. G. Worden, eds.), pp. 653–666, MIT Press, Cambridge, Massachusetts.

DE WIED, D., BOHUS, B., and VAN WIMERSMA GRIEDANUS, T. B., 1975, Memory deficit in rats with hereditary diabetes insipidus, *Brain Res.* **85:**152–156.

DEWS, P. B., and MORSE, W. H., 1961, Behavioral pharmacology, *Annu. Rev. Pharmacol.* **1:**145–174.

DILTS, S. L., and BERRY, C. A., 1967, Effect of cholinergic drugs on passive avoidance in the mouse, *J. Pharmacol. Exp. Ther.* **158:**279–285.

DISMUKES, R. K., and RAKE, A. V., 1972, Involvement of biogenic amines in memory formation, *Psychopharmacologia* **23:**17–25.

DOMINO, E. F., 1965, Some behavioral actions of nicotine, in: *Tobacco Alkaloids and Related Compounds* (U.S. Von Euler, ed.), pp. 145–162, Pergamon Press, Oxford.

DOMINO, E. F., YAMAMOTO, K., and DREN, A. T., 1968, Role of cholinergic mechanisms in states of wakefulness and sleep, *Brain Res.* **28:**113–133.

DOTY, B. A., and DOTY, L. A., 1964, Effect of age and chlorpromazine on memory consolidation, *J. Comp. Physiol. Psychol.* **57:**331–334.

DOTY, B. A., and DOTY, L. A., 1966, Facilitative effects of amphetamine on avoidance conditioning in relation to age and problem difficulty, *Psychopharmacologia* **9:**234–241.

DOTY, B. A., and JOHNSTON, M. M., 1966, Effects of post-trial eserine administration age and task difficulty on avoidance conditioning in rats, *Psychonomic Sci.* **6:**101–102.

ENGEL, J., HANSON, L. C. F., ROOS, B. E., and STRÖMBERGSSON, L. E., 1968, Effect of electroshock on dopamine metabolism in the rat brain, *Psychopharmacologia* **13:**140–144.

ERICKSON, C. K., 1971, Studies on the mechanism of avoidance facilitation by nicotine, *Psychopharmacologia* **22:**357–368.

ESSMAN, W. B., 1970, Some neurochemical correlates of altered memory consolidation, *Trans. N. Y. Acad. Sci.* **32:**948–973.

ESSMAN, W. B., 1971, Drug effects and learning and memory processes, *Adv. Pharmacol. Chemother.* **9:**241–330.

ESSMAN, W. B., 1973a, Neuromolecular modulation of experimentally-induced retrograde amnesia, *Confin. Neurol.* **35:**1–22.

ESSMAN, W. B., 1973b, Age-dependent effects of 5-Hydroxytryptamine upon memory consolidation and cerebral protein synthesis, *Pharmacol. Biochem. Behav.* **1:**7–14.

ESSMAN, W. B., 1973c, *Neurochemistry of Cerebral Electroshock,* Wiley, New York.

EVANGELISTA, A. M., and IZQUIERDO, I., 1971, The effect of pre- and post-trial amphetamine injections on avoidance responses of rats, *Psychopharmacologia* **20:**42–47.

EVANGELISTA, A. M., GATTIONI, R. C., and IZQUIERDO, I., 1970, Effect of amphetamine, nicotine and hexamethonium on performance of a conditioned response during acquisition and retention trials, *Pharmacology,* **3:**91–96.

EVANS, B. K., ARMSTRONG, S., SINGER, G., COOK, R. D., and BURNSTOCK, G., 1975,

Intracranial injection of drugs: comparison and diffusion of 6-OHDA and guanethidine, *Pharmacol. Biochem. Behav.* **3**:205-217.

FIBIGER, H. C., PHILLIPS, A. G., and ZIS, A. P., 1974a, Deficits in instrumental responding after 6-hydroxydopamine lesions of the nigro-striatal dopaminergic projection, *Pharmacol. Biochem. Behav.* **2**:87-96.

FIBIGER, H. C., ZIS, A. P., and PHILLIPS, A. G., 1974b, Haloperidol-induced disruption of conditioned avoidance responding: attenuation by prior training or by anticholinergic drugs, *Eur. J. Pharmacol.* **30**:309-314.

FILE, S. E., 1975, Effects of parachlorophenylalanine and amphetamine on habituation of orienting, *Pharmacol. Biochem. Behav.* **3**:979-983.

FINK, M., 1966, Cholinergic aspects of convulsive therapy, *J. Nerv. Ment. Dis.* **24**:475-484.

FLEXNER, L. B., SEROTA, R. G., and GOODMAN, R. H., 1973, Cycloheximide and acetoxycycloheximide inhibition of tyrosine hydroxylase activity and amnestic effects, *Proc. Nat. Acad. Sci. U.S.A.* **70**:354-356.

FUXE, K., HAMBERGER, B., and HÖKFELT, T., 1968, Distribution of noradrenaline nerve terminals in cortical areas of the rat, *Brain Res.* **8**:125-131.

FUXE, K., HÖKFELT, T., and UNGERSTEDT, U., 1970, Morphological and functional aspects of central monoamine neurons, *Int. Rev. Neurobiol.* **13**:93-126.

GARDNER, E. L., GLICK, S. D., and JARVIK, M. E., 1972, ECS dissociation of learning and one-way cross-dissociation with physostigmine and scopolamine, *Physiol. Behav.* **8**:11-15.

GARG, M., 1969, The effect of nicotine on two different types of learning, *Psychopharmacologia* **15**:408-414.

GARG, M., and HOLLAND, H. C., 1968, Consolidation and maze learning. A further study of post-trial injections of a stimulant drug (nicotine), *Neuropharmacology* **7**:55-59.

GARG, M., and HOLLAND, H. C., 1969, Consolidation and maze learning: a study of some strain/drug interactions, *Psychopharmacologia* **14**:426-431.

GEORGE, G., and MELLANBY, J., 1974, A further study on the effect of physostigmine on memory in rats, *Brain Res.* **81**:133-144.

GERMAN, D. C., and BOWDEN, D. M., 1974, Catecholamine systems as the neural substrate for intracranial self-stimulation: a hypothesis, *Brain Res.* **73**:381-419.

GLICK, S. D., and ZIMMERBERG, B., 1971, Comparative learning impairment and amnesia by scopolamine, phencyclidine and ketamine, *Psychon. Sci.* **25**:165-166.

GIRDEN, E., and CULLER, E. A., 1937, Conditioned responses in curarized striatal muscle in dogs, *J. Comp. Physiol. Psychol.* **23**:261-274.

GLOWINSKI, J., 1972, Some new facts about synthesis, storage and release processes of monoamines in the central nervous system, in: *Perspectives in Neuropharmacology* (S. H. Snyder, ed.), pp. 349-404, Oxford University Press, New York.

GOLD, P. E., and MCGAUGH, J. L., 1976, A single-trace two-process view of memory storage processes, in: *Short-Term Memory* (D. Deutsch and J. A. Deutsch, eds.), Academic Press, New York.

GOLD, P. E., and VAN BUSKIRK, R. B., 1975, Facilitation of time-dependent memory processes with posttrial epinephrine injections, *Behav. Biol.* **13**:145-153.

GOLD, P. E., VAN BUSKIRK, R. B., and MCGAUGH, J. L., 1975, Effects of hormones on time-dependent memory storage processes, in: *Progress in Brain Research*, Vol. 42, *Hormones, Homeostasis and the Brain* (W. H. Gispen, Tj. B. van Wimersma Greidanus, B. Bohus, and D. deWied, eds.), pp. 210-211, Elsevier, Amsterdam.

GOLDBERG, M. E., JOHNSON, H. E., and KNAAK, J. B., 1965, Inhibition of discrete avoidance behavior by three anticholinesterase agents, *Psychopharmacologia* **7**:72-76.

GOLDSTEIN, M., and NAKAJIMA, K., 1967, The effect of disulfiram on catecholamine levels in the brain, *J. Pharmacol. Exp. Ther.* **157**:96-102.

GREENOUGH, W. T., YUWILER, A., and DOLLINGER, M., 1973, Effects of post-trial eserine administration on learning in "enriched" and "impoverished" reared rats, *Behav. Biol.* **8**:261-272.

GRUBER, R. P., STONE, G. C., and REED, D. R., 1967, Scopolamine-induced anterograde amnesia, *Neuropharmacology* **6**:186–190.

HALL, M. E., 1969, Effects of post-trial amphetamine and strychnine on learning as a function of task difficulty, *Behav. Biol.* **4**:171–175.

HALL, M. E., and MAYER, M. A., 1975, Effects of alpha methyl-para-tyrosine on the recall of a passive avoidance response, *Pharmacol. Biochem. Behav.* **3**:579–582.

HAMBURG, M. D., 1967, Retrograde amnesia produced by intraperitoneal injection of physostigmine, *Science* **156**:973–974.

HAMBURG, M. D., and COHEN, R. P., 1973, Memory access pathway: role of adrenergic versus cholinergic neurons, *Pharmacol. Biochem. Behav.* **1**:295–300.

HAMBURG, M. D., and FULTON, D. R., 1972, Influence of recall on an anticholinesterase-induced retrograde amnesia, *Physiol. Behav.* **9**:409–418.

HAYCOCK, J. W., VAN BUSKIRK, R. B., and McGAUGH, J. L., 1977*a*, Facilitation of two-way active avoidance retention performance in mice by posttraining administration of diethyldithiocarbamate (in press).

HAYCOCK, J. W., VAN BUSKIRK, R. B., and McGAUGH, J. L., 1977*b*, Disruption of memory processes in rats by catecholamine agents: neurobiological correlates, *Behav. Biol.* (in press).

HANSON, L. C. F., 1965, The disruption of conditioned avoidance response following selective depletion of brain catecholamines, *Psychopharmacologia* **8**:100–110.

HERZ, A., 1960, Drugs and the conditioned avoidance response, *Int. Rev. Neurobiol.* **2**:229–277.

HOWARD, J. L., GRANT, L. D., and BREESE, G. R., 1974, Effects of intracisternal 6-hydroxydopamine treatment on acquisition and performance of rats in a double T-maze, *J. Comp. Physiol. Psychol.* **86**:995–1007.

IWAHARA, S., IWASAKI, T., and HASEGAWA, Y., 1968, Effects of chlorpromazine and homofenazine upon a passive avoidance response in rats, *Psychopharmacologia* **13**:320–331.

IZQUIERDO, J. A., BARATTI, C. M., TORRELIO, M., AREVALO, L., and McGAUGH, J. L., 1973, Effects of food deprivation, discrimination experience and physostigmine on choline acetylase and acetylcholine esterase in the dorsal hippocampus and frontal cortex of rats, *Psychopharmacologia* **33**:103–110.

JAMES, D. T. D., 1975, Post-trial *d*-amphetamine sulfate and one-trial learning in mice, *J. Comp. Physiol. Psychol.* **89**:626–635.

JARVIK, M. E., 1972, Effects of chemical and physical treatments on learning and memory, *Annu. Rev. Psychol.* **23**:457–486.

JOHNSON, F. W., 1969, The effects of chlorpromazine on the decay and consolidation of short-term memory traces in mice, *Psychopharmacologia* **16**:105–114.

JOHNSON, F. W., and WAITE, K., 1971, Apparent delayed enhancement of memory following post-trial methyl-amphetamine hydrochloride, *Experientia* **27**:1316–1317.

JOUVET, M., 1969, Biogenic amines and states of sleep, *Science* **163**:32–41.

JOYCE, D., and HURWITZ, H. M. B., 1964, Avoidance behavior in the rat after 5-hydroxytryptophan (5-HTP) administration, *Psychopharmacologia* **5**:424–430.

KARCZMAR, A. G., 1974, Brain acetylcholine and seizures, 1974, in: *Psychobiology of Convulsive Therapy* (M. Fink, S. Kety, J. L. McGaugh, and T. A. Williams, eds.), pp. 251–270, Wiley, New York.

KETY, S. S., 1970, The biogenic amines in the central nervous system: their possible roles in arousal, emotion and learning, 1970, in: *The Neurosciences, a Second Study Program*, pp. 324–336, Rockefeller Press, New York.

KILLAM, E. K., 1968, Pharmacology of the reticular formation, in: *Psychopharmacology. A Review of Progress* (D. W. Efron, ed.), PHS Publ. 1863, pp. 411–446, U.S. Government Printing Office, Washington, D.C.

KNOLL, J., 1974, Modulation of learning and retention by amphetamines, in: *Symposium on*

Pharmacology of Learning and Retention (J. Knoll and B. Knoll, eds.), pp. 73–81, Akademiai Kiado, Budapest.

Koe, B. K., and Weissman, A., 1966, *p*-Chlorophenylalanine: a specific depletor of brain serotonin, *J. Pharmacol. Exp. Ther.* **154**:499–516.

Koelle, C. B., 1970, Anticholinesterase agents, 1970, in: *The Pharmacological Basis of Therapeutics* (L. S. Goodman and A. Gilman, eds.), pp. 442–465, Macmillan, Toronto.

Krivanek, J., 1971, Facilitation of avoidance learning by pentylentetrazol as a function of task difficulty, deprivation and shock level, *Psychopharmacologia* **20**:213–229.

Krivanek, J., and McGaugh, J. L., 1969, Facilitatory effects of pre- and post-trial *l*-amphetamine administration of discrimination learning in mice, *Agents Actions* **1**:36–42.

Krnjevic, K., 1974, Chemical nature of synaptic transmission in vertebrates, *Physiol. Rev.* **54**:418–540.

Kulkarni, A. S., 1968, Facilitation of instrumental avoidance learning by *d*-amphetamine: an analysis, *Psychopharmacologia* **13**:418–425.

Kuo, J. F., Lee, T. P., Reyes, P. L., Walton, K. G., Donnelly, T. E., and Greengard, P., 1972, Cyclic nucleotide-dependent protein kinases, *J. Biol. Chem.* **247**:16–22.

Lenard, L. G., and Beer, B., 1975a, 6-hydroxydopamine and avoidance: possible role of response suppression, *Pharmacol. Biochem. Behav.* **3**:873–878.

Lenard, L. G., and Beer, B., 1975b, Modification of avoidance behavior in 6-hydroxydopamine-treated rats by stimulation of central noradrenergic and dopaminergic receptors, *Pharmacol. Biochem. Behav.* **3**:887–893.

Leonard, B. E., and Rigter, H., 1975, Changes in brain monoamine metabolism and carbon dioxide induced amnesia in the rat, *Pharmacol. Biochem. Behav.* **3**:775–780.

Longo, V. G., 1966, Behavioral and electroencephalographic effects of atropine and related compounds, *Pharmacol. Rev.* **18**:965–996.

Longo, V. G., 1968, The pharmacology of the EEG arousal reaction; an appraisal of past and present concepts, in: *Psychopharmacology: A Review of Progress* (D. H. Efron, ed.), PHS Publ. 1863, pp. 447–452, U.S. Government Printing Office, Washington, D.C.

Lorens, S. A., 1973, Raphe lesions in cats: forebrain serotonin avoidance behavior, *Pharmacol. Biochem. Behav.* **1**:487–490.

Lorens, S. A., and Yunger, L. M., 1974, Morphine analgesia, two-way avoidance and consummatory behavior following lesions in the midbrain raphe nuclei of the rat, *Pharmacol. Biochem. Behav.* **2**:215–221.

Mabry, P. D., and Campbell, B. A., 1973, Serotonergic inhibition of catecholamine-induced behavioral arousal, *Brain Res.* **49**:381–391.

Mabry, P. D., and Campbell, B. A., 1974, Ontogeny of serotonergic inhibition of behavioral arousal in the rat, *J. Comp. Physiol. Psychol.* **86**:193–201.

Macadar, A. W., Chalupa, L. W., and Lindsley, D. B., 1974, Differentiation of brainstem loci which effect hippocampal and neocortical electrical activity, *Exp. Neurol.* **43**:499–514.

Macchitelli, F. J., Fischetti, D., and Montanelli, N., 1966, Changes in behavior and electrocortical activity in the monkey following administration of 5-hydroxytryptophan, *Psychopharmacologia* **9**:447–456.

Mah, C. J., and Albert, D. J., 1975, Reversal of ECS-induced amnesia by post-ECS injections of amphetamine, *Pharmacol. Biochem. Behav.* **3**:1–5.

Malmo, R. B., 1967, Motivation, 1967, in: *Comprehensive Textbook of Psychiatry* (A. Freedman and H. I. Kaplan, eds.), pp. 172–180, Williams and Wilkins, Baltimore.

McGaugh, J. L., 1966, Time-dependent processes in memory storage, *Science* **153**:1351–1358.

McGaugh, J. L., 1973, Drug facilitation of learning and memory, *Annu. Rev. Pharmacol.* **13**:229–241.

McGaugh, J. L., and Herz, M. J., 1972, *Memory Consolidation*, Albion Publishing Company, San Francisco.

McGaugh, J. L., and Landfield, P. W., 1970, Delayed development of amnesia following electroconvulsive shock, *Physiol. Behav.* **5:**1109–1113.

McGaugh, J. L., and Petrinovich, L. F., 1965, Effects of drugs on learning and memory, *Int. Rev. Neurobiol.* **8:**139–196.

McGaugh, J. L., Gold, P. E., Van Buskirk, R., and Haycock, J., 1975, Modulating influences of hormones and catecholamines on memory storage, in: *Progress in Brain Research*, Vol. 42, *Hormones Homeostasis, and the Brain* (W. H. Gispen, Th. B. van Wimersma Greidanus, B. Bohus, and D. deWied, eds.), pp. 151–162, Elsevier, Amsterdam.

Merlo, A. B., and Izquierdo, J. A., 1971, Effect of post-trial injection of beta-adrenergic blocking agents on a conditioned reflex in rats, *Pxychopharmacologia* **22:**181–186.

Meyers, B., 1965, Some effects of scopolamine on a passive avoidance response in rats, *Psychopharmacologia* **8:**111–119.

Meyers, B., Roberts, K. H., Riciputi, R. H., and Domino, E. F., 1964, Some effects of muscarinic cholinergic blocking drugs on behavior and the electrocorticogram, *Psychopharmacologia* **5:**289–300.

Miller, L., Drew, W. G., and McCoy, D. F., 1971, Effects of post-trial injections of scopolamine and eserine on acquisition of a simultaneous brightness discrimination, *Psychol. Rep.* **29:**1147–1152.

Miller, R. R., Malinkowski, B., Puk, G., and Springer, A. D., 1972, State-dependent models of ECS-induced amnesia in rats, *J. Comp. Physiol. Psychol.* **81:**533–540.

Moruzzi, G., and Magoun, H. W., 1949, Brainstem reticular formation and activation of the EEG, *EEG Clin. Neurophys.* **1:**455–473.

Myers, R. D., 1971, Methods for chemical stimulation of the brain, 1971, in: *Methods in Psychobiology* (R. D. Myers, ed.), pp. 247–280, Academic Press, New York.

Neill, D. B., Boggan, W. O., and Grossman, S. P., 1974, Impairment of avoidance performance by intrastriatal administration of 6-hydroxydopamine, *Pharmacol. Biochem. Behav.* **2:**97–103.

Nelson, C. N., Hoffer, B. J., Chu, N. S., and Bloom, F. E., 1973, Cytochemical and pharmacological studies on polysensory neurons in the primate frontal cortex, *Brain Res.* **62:**115–133.

Nielson, C. H., 1968, Evidence that electroconvulsive shock alters retrieval rather than memory consolidation, *Exp. Neurol.* **20:**3–20.

Oliverio, A., 1968, Effects of nicotine and strychnine on transfer of avoidance learning in the mouse, *Life Sci.* **7:**1163–1167.

Orsingher, O. A., and Fulginiti, S., 1971, Effects of alpha-methyl tyrosine and adrenergic blocking agents on the facilitating actions of amphetamines and nicotine on learning in rats, *Psychopharmacologia* **19:**231–240.

Otis, L. S., 1964, Dissociation and recovery of a response learned under the influence of chlorpromazine or saline, *Science* **143:**1347–1348.

Overton, D. A., 1964, State-dependent or "dissocated" learning produced with pentobarbital, *J. Comp. Physiol. Psychol.* **57:**3–12.

Overton, D. A., 1966, State-dependent learning produced by depressant and atropine-like drugs, *Psychopharmacologia* **10:**6–31.

Overton, D. A., 1974, Experimental methods for the study of state-dependent learning, *Fed. Proc.* **33:**1800–1813.

Palfai, T., and Cornell, J. M., 1968, Effects of drugs on consolidation of classically conditioned fear, *J. Comp. Physiol. Psychol.* **66:**584–589.

Palfai, T., Kurtz, P., and Gutman, A., 1974, Effect of metrazol on brain norepinephrine: a possible factor in amnesia produced by the drug, *Pharmacol. Biochem. Behav.* **2:**261–262.

Papeschi, R., Randrup, A., and Munkvad, I., 1974, Effect of ECT on dopaminergic and noradrenergic mechanisms. II. Effect on dopamine and noradrenaline concentrations and turnovers, *Psychopharmacologia* **35:**159–168.

PAZZAGLI, A., and PEPEU, G., 1964, Amnesic properties of scopolamine and brain acetylcholine in the rat, *Neuropharmacology* **4**:291–299.

PFEIFFER, C. C., and JENNEY, E. H., 1957, Inhibition of conditioned response and the counteraction of schizophrenia by muscarinic stimulation of the brain, *Ann. N.Y. Acad. Sci.* **66**:753–764.

POIRIER, L. J., LANGELIER, P., ROBERGE, A., BOUCHER, R., and KITSIKIS, A., 1972, Nonspecific histopathological changes induced by intracerebral injection of 6-hydroxydopamine (6-OHDA), *J. Neurol. Sci.* **16**:401–416.

POTTS, W. J., MORSE, D. L., COOPER, B. R., and BLACK, W. C., 1970, The effect of magnesium pemoline, tricyanoaminopropene and d-amphetamine on discriminated avoidance performance in rats as a function of age, *Psychonomic Sci.* **20**:141–143.

POWELL, B. J., and HOPPER, D. J., 1971, Effects of strain differences and d-amphetamine sulphate on avoidance performance, *Psychonomic Sci.* **22**:167–168.

PRADHAN, S. N., and DUTTA, S. N., 1971, Central cholinergic mechanisms and behavior, *Int. Rev. Neurobiol.* **4**:173–232.

PRADHAN, S. N., and MHATRE, R. M., 1970, Effects of two anticholinesterases on behavior and cholinesterase activity in rats, *Res. Commun. Chem. Pathol. Pharmacol.* **1**:682–690.

PRICE, M. T. C., and FIBIGER, H. C., 1975, Discriminated escape learning and response to electric shock after 6-hydroxydopamine lesions of the nigro-striatal dopaminergic projection, *Pharmacol. Biochem. Behav.* **3**:285–290.

RAKE, A. V., 1973, Involvement of biogenic amines in memory formation: the central nervous system indole amine involvement, *Psychopharmacologia* **29**:91–100.

RANDT, C. T., KOREIN, J., and LEVIDOW, L., 1973, Localization of action of two amnesia producing drugs in freely moving mice, *Exp. Neurol.* **41**:628–623.

RANDT, C. T., QUARTERMAIN, D., GOLDSTEIN, M., and ANAGNOSTE, B., 1971, Norepinephrine biosynthesis inhibition: effects on memory in mice, *Science* **172**:498–499.

RECH, R. H., 1966, Amphetamine effects on poor performance of rats in a shuttlebox, *Psychopharmacologia* **9**:110–117.

RECH, R. H., 1968, Effects of cholinergic drugs on poor performance of rats in a shuttlebox, *Psychopharmacologia* **12**:371–383.

RECH, R. H., BORYS, H. K., and MOORE, K. E., 1966, Alterations in behavior and brain catecholamine levels in rats treated with alpha methyltyrosine, *J. Pharmacol. Exp. Ther.* **153**:412–419.

RENSCH, B., and RAHMANN, H., 1960, Einfluß des Pervitins auf das Gedächtnis von Goldhamstern, *Arch. Ges. Physiol.* **271**:693–704.

RICHTER, D., and CROSSLAND, J., 1949, Variation in acetylcholine content of the brain with physiological state, *Am. J. Physiol.* **159**:247–255.

RIEGE, W. H., 1971, One-trial learning and brain serotonin depletion by parachlorophenylalanine, *Int. J. Neurosci.* **2**:237–240.

RIGTER, H., VAN EYS, G., and LEONARD, B. E., 1975, Hippocampal monoamine metabolism and the CO_2 induced retrograde amnesia gradient in rats, *Pharmacol. Biochem. Behav.* **3**:781–785.

RINALDI, R., and HIMWICH, H. E., 1955, Cholinergic mechanisms involved in function of mesodiencephalic activating system, *Arch. Neurol. Psychiat.* **73**:396–402.

ROBERTS, R. B., FLEXNER, J. B., and FLEXNER, L. B., 1970, Some evidence for the involvement of adrenergic sites in the memory trace, *Proc. Nat. Acad. Sci. U.S.A.* **66**:310–313.

ROBUSTELLI, F., 1963, Azione delle nicotina sull'apprendimento dell ratto nel labirinto, *Rend. Accad. Naz. Lincei Cl. Sci. Fis VIII* **34**:703–709.

ROFFMAN, M., and LAL, H., 1971, Facilitatory effect of amphetamine on learning and recall of an avoidance response in rats, *Arch. Int. Pharmacodyn.* **193**:87–91.

ROFFMAN, M., and LAL, H., 1972, Role of brain amines in learning associated with "amphetamine-state," *Psychopharmacologia* **25**:195–204.

ROSECRANS, J. A., and DOMINO, E. F., 1974, Comparative effects of physostigmine and neostigmine on acquisition and performance of a conditioned avoidance behavior in the rat, *Pharmacol. Biochem. Behav.* **2**:67–72.

ROSENZWEIG, M. R., KRECH, D., and BENNETT, E. L., 1960, A search for relations between brain chemistry and behavior, *Psychol. Bull.* **57**:476–492.

ROSENZWEIG, M. R., BENNETT, E. L., and KRECH, D., 1964, Cerebral effects of environmental complexity and training among adult rats, *J. Comp. Physiol. Psychol.* **57**:438–439.

ROSIC, N., and BIGNAMI, G., 1970, Depression of two-way avoidance learning and enhancement of passive avoidance learning by small doses of physostigmine, *Neuropharmacology* **9**:311–316.

SANSONE, M., and RENZI, P., 1971, Shuttle-box avoidance behavior of hamsters: a further investigation of the effects of amphetamine and methylphenidate, *Pharmacol. Res. Commun.* **3**:113–119.

SAPER, C. B., and SWEENEY, D. C., 1973, Enhanced appetitive discrimination learning in rats treated with alpha-methyltyrosine, *Psychopharmacologia* **30**:37–44.

SATINDER, K. P., 1971, Genotype-dependent effects of d-amphetamine sulphate and caffeine on escape-avoidance behavior of rats, *J. Comp. Physiol. Psychol.* **76**:359–364.

SCHEIBEL, M. E., and SCHEIBEL, A. B., 1967, Structural organization of nonspecific thalamic nuclei and their projection toward cortex, *Brain Res.* **6**:60–94.

SCHILDKRAUT, J. L., and DRASKOCZY, P. R., 1974, Effects of electroconvulsive shock on norepinephrine turnover and metabolism: basic and clinical studies, in: *Psychobiology of Convulsive Therapy* (M. Fink, S. Kety, J. L. McGaugh, and T. A. Williams, eds.), pp. 143–170, Wiley, New York.

SEGAL, M., and BLOOM, F. E., 1974a, The action of norepinephrine in the rat hippocampus. I. Iontophoretic studies, *Brain Res.* **72**:79–97.

SEGAL, M., and BLOOM, F. E., 1974b, The action of norepinephrine in the rat hippocampus. II. Activation of the input pathway, *Brain Res.* **72**:99–114.

SEIDEN, L. S., and HANSON, L. C. F., 1964, Reversal of the reserpine-induced suppression of the conditioned avoidance response in the cat by L-dopa, *Psychopharmacologia* **6**:239–244.

SEIDEN, L. S., and PETERSON, D. D., 1968, Reversal of the reserpine-induced suppression of the conditioned avoidance response by L-dopa: correlation of behavioral and biochemical differences in two strains of mice, *J. Pharmacol. Exp. Ther.* **159**:442–428.

SEIDEN, L. S., BROWN, R. M., and LEWY, A. J., 1973, Brain catecholamines and conditioned behavior: mutual interactions, in: *Chemical Modulation of Brain Function* (H. C. Sabelli, ed.), pp. 261–275, Raven Press, New York.

SHELLENBERGER, M. K., 1971, Effects of alpha-methyltyrosine on spontaneous and caudate-induced EEG activity and regional catecholamine concentrations in the cat brain, *Neuropharmacology* **10**:347–357.

SHUTE, C. C. D., and LEWIS, P. R., 1967, The ascending cholinergic reticular system: neocortical, olfactory and subcortical projections, *Brain* **90**:497, 521.

SIGGINS, G. R., HOFFER, B. J., and BLOOM, F. E., 1971, Studies on norepinephrine-containing afferents to Purkinje cells of rat cerebellum. II. Evidence for mediation of norepinephrine effects by cyclic-3′,5′-adenosine monophosphate, *Brain Res.* **25**:535–553.

SOTELO, C., JAVOY, F., AGID, Y., and GLOWINSKI, J., 1973, Injection of 6-hydroxydopamine in the substantia nigra of the rat. I. Morphological study, *Brain Res.* **58**:269–290.

SPANIS, C. W., HAYCOCK, J. W., HANDWERKER, M. J., ROSE, R. P., and MCGAUGH, J. L., 1977, Disruption of retention performance in rats by diethyldithiocarbamate: task differences, *Psychopharmacologia* (in press).

SPEAR, N. E., 1973, Retrieval of memory in animals, *Psychol. Rev.* **80**:163–194.

SQUIRE, L. R., 1970, Physostigmine: effects on retention at different times after brief training, *Psychonomic Sci.* **19**:49–50.

SQUIRE, L. R., GLICK, S. D., and GOLDFARB, J., 1971, Relearning at different times after training as affected by centrally and peripherally acting cholinergic drugs in the mouse, *J. Comp. Physiol. Psychol.* **74**:41–45.

STARK, L., 1967, The inability of scopolamine to induce state-dependent one-trial learning, *Fed. Proc.* **26**:613.

STEIN, L., BELLUZZI, J. D., and WISE, C. D., 1975, Memory enhancement by central administration of norepinephrine, *Brain Res.* **84**:329–335.

STERANKA, L. R., and BARRETT, R. J., 1974, Facilitation of avoidance acquisition by lesion of the median raphe nucleus: evidence for serotonin as a mediator of shock-induced suppression, *Behav. Biol.* **11**:205–213.

STEVENS, D. A., FECHTER, L. D., and RESNICK, O., 1969, The effects of *p*-chlorophenylalanine, a depletor of brain serotonin, on behavior. II. Retardation of passive avoidance learning, *Life Sci.* **8**:379–385.

STRATTON, L. O., and PETRINOVICH, L., 1963, Post-trial injections of an anticholinesterase drug and maze learning in two strains of rats, *Psychopharmacologia* **5**:47–54.

STUMPF, C. H., 1965, Drug action on electrical activity of the hippocampus, *Int. Rev. Neurobiol.* **8**:77–138.

SUITS, E., and ISAACSON, R. L., 1968, The effects of scopolamine hydrobromide on one-way and two-way avoidance learning in rats, *Neuropharmacology* **7**:441–446.

SULSER, F., and SANDERS-BUSH, E., 1971, Effects of drugs on amines in the CNS, *Annu. Rev. Pharmacol.* **11**:209–230.

SWONGER, A. K., and RECH, R. H., 1972, Serotonergic and cholinergic involvement in habituation of activity and spontaneous alternation of rats in a Y-maze, *J. Comp. Physiol. Psychol.* **81**:509–522.

TENEN, S. A., 1967, The effects of para-chlorophenylalanine, serotonin depletor, on avoidance acquisition, pain sensitivity and related behavior in the rat, *Psychopharmacologia* **10**:240–219.

THOMPSON, C. I., and NEELY, J. E., 1970, Dissociated learning in rats produced by electroconvulsive shock, *Physiol. Behav.* **5**:783–786.

VAN EYS, G., RIGTER, H., and LEONARD, B. E., 1975, Time dependent aspects of CO_2 induced amnesia and hippocampal monoamine metabolism in rats, *Pharmacol. Biochem. Behav.* **3**:787–793.

VAN WIMERSMA GREIDANUS, TJ. B., DOGTEROM, J., and DEWIED, D., 1975, Intraventricular administration of anti-vassopressin serum inhibits memory consolidation in rats, *Life Sci.* **16**:637–644.

VOLLE, R. L., and KOELLE, G. B., 1970, Ganglionic stimulating and blocking agents, in: *The Pharmacological Basis of Therapeutics* (L. S. Goodman and A. Gilman, eds.), pp. 585–600, Macmillan, Toronto.

WEINER, N. I., and DEUTSCH, J. A., 1968, Temporal aspects of anticholinergic- and anticholinesterase-induced amnesia for an appetitive habit, *J. Comp. Physiol. Psychol.* **66**:613–617.

WEINER, N. I., and MESSER, J., 1973, Scopolamine-induced impairment of long-term retention in rats, *Behav. Biol.* **9**:227–234.

WEISSMAN, A., 1967, Drugs and retrograde amnesia, *Int. Rev. Neurobiol.* **10**:167–198.

WESTFALL, T. C., 1974, Effect of muscarinic agonists on the release of ^{3}H-norepinephrine and ^{3}H-dopamine by potassium and electrical stimulation from rat brain slices, *Life Sci.* **14**:1641–1652.

WHITE, O. A., and SUBOSKI, M. D., 1969, Resistence of one-trial discriminated avoidance to chlorpromazine, *Psychopharmacologia* **16**:25–29.

WHITEHOUSE, J. M., 1964, Effects of atropine on discrimination learning in the rat, *J. Comp. Physiol. Psychol.* **57**:13–15.

WHITEHOUSE, J. M., 1966, The effects of physostigmine on discrimination learning, *Psychopharmacologia* **9**:183–188.

WITTER, A., SLANGEN, J. L., and TERPSTRA, G. K., 1973, Distribution of ^{3}H-methyl-atropine in rat brain, *Neuropharmacology* **12**:835–841.

ZORNETZER, S. F., and GOLD, M., 1976, The locus coeruleus: its possible role in memory consolidation, *Physol. Behav.* **16**:331–336.

ZORNETZER, S. F., and APPELTON, S., 1977, The Locus Coeruleus and memory processing in: *Sleep, Dreams and Memory* (W. Fishbein, ed.), in press.

ZORNETZER, S. F., GOLD, M. S., and HENDRICKSON, J., 1974, Alpha-methyl-*p*-tyrosine and memory: state dependency and memory failure, *Behav. Biol.* **12**:135–141.

ZORNETZER, S. F., GOLD, M., and BOAST, C. A., 1977, Neuroanatomical localization and the neurobiology of sleep and memory, in: *The Neurobiology of Sleep and Memory* (J. L. McGaugh and R. R. Drucker-Collin, eds.), pp. 185–225, Academic Press, New York.

INDEX

Acceptance ratio, 176
Acetylcholine, 27, 81-85, 140-143, 260-264, 267-270, 305-306, 311, 317, 318, 365, 391, 419, 534-535, 543, 544, 553, 554, 558-560
   and arousal, 562
   and circling, 317-318
   and EEG activation, 260
   and shock, electroconvulsive, 543-544
   and sleep, 262-264
Acetylcholinesterase, 277
Acquisition, 401-404
   of active avoidance, 349
   and performance, 538-539
Acts
   behavioral, 363
   involuntary, 367
   motor, 363
   repetitious, 363
   voluntary, 367
ACTH, 190, 592
Actinomycin D, 204
Action
   anorectic, central *vs.* peripheral, 94-95
   loci of, 170-171
   mechanism of, 171-172
   modulation of, 60
   neurotransmission, 60
   postsynaptic, 60-61
Activation
   behavioral, 390
Activity, locomotor, 338
Adenosine monophosphate, cyclic (cAMP), 86
   dibutyryl, 83
Adipsia, 342
   following dopamine depletion, 75
Adrenalectomy, 179
Adrenalone, 88

Adrenergic system, neural
   alpha
      agonist, 95
      blocker, 59, 62
         feeding, 58-62, 64
         satiety theory, 62-63
         sympathetic, 57
         and water intake, 150-151
   beta, 57
      agonist, 95
      blocker, 59
      satiety, 63-65
Aggression
   defensive, 485-486
   unconditioned, 338
Allerest, 101
Alley
   straight, 447, 453
   telescope, 442, 469
Alumina cream, injected, 356
Amantadine, 203, 262
Amine, biogenic (*see also* separate compounds), 42, 174, 347, 353
γ-Aminobutyric acid (GABA), 86, 268, 277-278, 306, 312, 319, 559
2-Amino-6,7-dihydroxy-1,2,3,4-tetrahydronaphthalene, 302
Aminomethyl group, loss of, 91
Amitriptyline, 271
Ammonium chloride, 92
Amobarbital, sodium, *see* Sodium amobarbital
Amphetamine, 27, 28, 33, 39, 82, 84, 89, 90, 91, 94-99, 195, 197, 253, 262, 267, 296-303, 305, 307, 313, 315, 318, 319, 341, 355, 359, 393-395, 397, 399, 400, 404-406, 409, 411, 413-417, 545-547, 554, 555, 559, 563

Amphetamine (cont'd)
  anorexia, 94, 95, 97, 99, 106, 107, 112
  and atropine, 559
  and avoidance, 545
  chlorinated, 103
  and EEG arousal, 253
  and food intake, 99
  and locomotion, 296-303
  and memory, 563
  and motor changes, 362-364
  and performance, 361
  psychosis, 364
  and rotation, 359, 360
  and sleep, 253
  tolerance to, 98
  and transmitter release, 96
AMPT, see α-Methyl-p-tyrosine
Amygdala, 138, 139
Amylobarbitone, 299
Androgen, 169, 171, 175, 183, 186
  exposure to, 162
  induction of female sexual behavior by, 162, 183
Androstenedione, 163, 183, 189
Angiotensin, 10-12, 132, 144-150
Anisomycin, 276
Anorexia nervosa, 68, 90, 94-95, 110
  by beta-adrenergic receptor, 106
  arousal and dissociation of, 97-99
  catecholamine theory of, 111
  and dopamine depletion, 72-76
  and drugs, 92, 108
  by fenfluramine, 107
  and hyperactivity, 111
  neurochemistry, 95-97
  by nonmonoamine, 105
  by serotonin, 105, 106
  and sympathomimetics, 90
  tolerance, behavioral to, 98
  treatment, 110
Antiadrenergic agents, 548-554
Antiandrogens, 189
Anticholinergic drug, 204, 538-544
Anticholinesterase therapy, 542
Antidepressant, 271-272, 554
  tricyclic, 271
Aphagia, 75, 342
Apomorphine, 148, 195, 197, 202, 203, 301, 307, 311, 341, 355, 359, 365
  self-administration, 39, 40
ARAS, see Ascending reticular activating system
Arecoline, 196, 535
Ascending reticular activating system (ARAS), 563

Atropine, 82, 84, 127, 203, 204, 261-263, 267, 268, 396, 397, 399-403, 406, 412, 419, 535, 538-540, 559, 562, 563
Atropine methyl bromide, 399, 418
Attack behavior, 5, 485
Attractiveness, sexual, 176
Autoreceptor, 341
Arousal, central nervous system, 91
  by amphetamine, 97
  cortical, 262
  EEG, 253
  level of, 465
  mechanism, 390
Avoidance, 345-352
  active, 437, 538
    one-way, 447-448, 471-472, 481-483, 490
    two-way, 448-450, 472-473, 483, 490
  behavior, 473
  passive, 41, 388, 412-413, 442-444, 446, 468, 470, 473, 477, 478, 481, 489-490, 538
  in shuttlebox, 449
  Sidman shock, 347, 357, 448, 472, 482
  two way task, 348
AVT, see Tegmentum, area ventralis
Axon, transport mechanism, 204-205

Barbiturate, 113, 273, 296, 308
  and fear, 446
  and response, 457
  and sleeping time, 234
  as tranquilizer, 466
Barrier technique, 177
Baseline procedure, 445
Behavior
  aggressive, 338, 452, 484-486
  attack, 5, 485
  avoidance, see Avoidance
  and brain dopamine systems, 333-384
  choice in maze, 394
  circling, 295, 315
  coding, chemical, in brain, 57-58
  conditioned, see Conditioning behavior, Pavlov, Skinner
  conflict, 42
  copulatory, 162-164
  decrement, differential, as a measure of, 373
  deficit, 76
  discrimination, stable, 404-410
  and dopamine pathways, 333-384
  drinking, see Drinking
  eating, 338, 342
  emotional, 439-464, 475-489
    and ethanol, 466-475

Behavior (cont'd)
  escape, 447, 471, 480, 481, 490
  ethanol, 467, 468, 471
  extinction, 387
  fighting, 484-486
  inhibition system (BIS), 385-431, 464-466
    varieties, 385-389
  learned, loss of, 355
  locomotor (see also motor), 295
  maternal, 206-212
  in maze, 394
  motor, 76, 338, 339, 362-364, 366, 373
    drug-induced, 295-331, 336
    spontaneous, 336
  mouse-killing, 83
  operant, 26, 40
  and pain, 42
  parameters, 192
  parental, 160, 205-212
  paternal, 212
  protective, maternal, 206-212
  punishment, 437
    nonpunishment, 437
    operant, 26, 41, 388-389
  purposeful, 372
  reduction, 473
  reproductive, 159-232
  rewarded, 435, 437, 440-443, 459, 467-468, 475-477, 489
  rotational, 313-320
  in schizophrenia, 295
  sexual
    in adult, 175-205
    development, 172-175
    female (see also Lordosis), 152, 164, 172, 174-186, 194
      and drugs, 193-199
      and hormones, 161-172
    male, 159-164, 174, 177, 186-190, 199-204
      cholinergic mechanism, 204
      and drugs, 199-204
    motivation, 164, 177, 184
    ontogeny, 161-175
  shock, see Shock
  stereotyped, 295, 307-313, 363
    amphetamine-induced, 307, 308, 312
  theory of two-process, 434-435
  training methods, 3, 12
  unconditioned, 338-344
    aggression, 338
    drinking, 338
    eating, 338
    mating, 338
Benactyzine, 204

Benzodiazepin, 41-46, 111, 395, 410, 419-421, 434, 475-489
  and avoidance, passive, 477-478, 481
  and electrode placement, 476
  and fear, 478-480
  listed, 478
  and monoamine turnover, 42
  and self-stimulation in rat, 476
BIS, see Behavior inhibition system
Blood factor, 237
Body fluids, 151-152
Box
  of Grice, 453
  shuttle, 449, 450, 472, 483
  of Skinner, 441-444, 448, 456-459, 463, 467, 470, 472, 474-478, 487, 488
Brachium conjunctivum, 14, 15
Brain
  damage, 76-77, 134
  mapping, 2-5
  stem, 13-16, 19-20
  wiring in, 8
Bromocriptine, 314
D-2-Bromolysergic acid diethylamine, 43
Brunton (1883), 385
Bundle, ventral noradrenergic (VNAB), 34, 68, 69, 97
γ-Butyrolactone (GBL), 269, 270

Cadaverine, 277
Cannabis, 434
Cannula, 56, 66, 67
Capaldi's theory (1967), 462, 463
Carbachol, 10-12, 47, 59, 81-83, 141-144, 146, 147, 263, 356, 418, 419
  and drinking, 10, 142, 146
Carlton's theory (1963), 391, 392, 395, 400, 401
Castration, 163, 171, 187-190
Catalepsy, 311
Catecholamine, 40, 67, 87-89, 92-96, 137, 242, 247, 251-260, 266-267, 280, 544-554, 558-560
  and arousal, 562
  and brain neurons, 141
  depletion, 137, 143
  neurotransmitter, 334
Catechol-O-methyl transferase (COMT), 254, 420
Cell, osmosensitive, 133
Central nervous system
  biochemical redundancy in, 259
  dopamine effects in, 336
  vast knowledge of, 336
CER, see Conditioned emotional response

Cerebellum, 367
Chemostimulation technique, 57
α-Chloralose, 269, 273
p-Chloramphetamine, 103-104, 195
Chlordiazepoxide, 43, 112, 268, 273, 274, 308, 395, 399, 405, 411, 413, 414, 420, 459, 475-483, 486, 487, 499
Chlorimipramine, 105, 266, 271
p-Chloromethamphetamine, 248, 266
p-Chlorophenylalanine (PCPA), 44, 79, 80, 105, 162, 174, 194, 196, 197, 199, 202, 203, 244, 246, 261, 266, 304, 318, 421, 506, 533, 546, 551, 558
6-Chlorotryptophan, 244
Chlorphentermine, 101, 103-104
Chlorpromazine, 28, 41, 43, 60, 112, 113, 174, 195, 247, 248, 272, 347, 354, 363, 548-550, 553
Choline acetylase, 84
Cholinergic system, 422
  agonist, 83
  antagonist, 84
  and desynchronization of cortex, 418
  feeding inhibition, 81-83
  and mesencephalon, 263
  mouse-killing, 83
  and neuron, 141, 260, 263
    pathway, 141
  sex behavior, 204
  sleep theory, 236, 238, 264, 280
  and thirst, 82, 141-144
  waking hypothesis, 262
Cholinolytic, 417-419
Cinanserin, 44, 105, 196
Circadian reversal, 63
Circling behavior, drug-induced, 295, 313-320
  amphetamine-induced, 314-317
  and injection, intracranial, 316-317
  and lesions, 314-316
  neural mechanism of, 314-317
Clonidine, 40, 202, 254, 266
Clozapine, 303, 306, 314, 318
Cocaine, 39, 296, 302, 307, 313
Coding, chemical
  of behavior in the brain, 57
Cognitive function and striatum, 368-369
Coitus, posture of, 176
Colchicine, 205
Conditioned emotional response (CER)
  baseline of, 445, 470, 478, 479, 480
Conditioning behavior, 344-356
  classical, 434, 435
  of fear, 444-446

Conditioning behavior (cont'd)
  operant, 396, 434-435
  Pavlovian, 387, 396
Conflict, 413-414
  approach–approach, 402
  definition of, 413
Contac, 101
Contact, postpartum
  mother–infant, 210
Control
  hormonal, 178-179, 207, 209, 210
  multifactorial, 67
  neurochemical, 60
  stimulus, hypothesis, 409
Copulatory quotient, 176
Cord, spinal, 190
Cortex
  frontal, 13-19, 18, 364
  medial, 16-19
  prefrontal, 19
  self-stimulation, 1-24
  sulcal, 16-19
  synchronization, 234
  trigger for, 367
CPZ, see Chlorpromazine
Cream of alumina injection, 356
Crespi effect of
  depression, 459, 488
  elation, 459
Current, use of, 4
Curve, theta-driving, 497, 500-502, 506
Cyclazocine, 271
Cycloheximide, 172, 204, 275, 276, 554, 555
Cyproheptadine, 78, 104, 105, 107, 110, 111, 318, 546, 558
Cyproterone acetate, 169, 190

DCI, see Dichloroisoproterenol
DDC, see Diethyldithiocarbamate
Dehydration, cellular, 132
2-Deoxy-d-glucose, 75
Desimipramine, 299, 302, 305
Desmethylimipramine, 58, 66, 271
Desynchronization of cortex, cholinergic, 418
DFP, see Diisopropylfluorophosphate
DHT, see Dihydrotestosterone propionate
Diacetylapomorphine, 313
Diazepam, 42, 43, 111, 112, 273, 274, 420, 459, 476, 481-486
Dibenamine, 254
Dibutyryl cyclic AMP, see Adenosine monophosphate

INDEX

Dichloroisoproterenol, 551
Diencephalon, 33
Diethyldithiocarbamate, 27, 29, 39, 297, 308, 551-555
Diethylpropion, 100-101
  and weight loss in humans, 100
Differentiation, sexual, hormone-induced, 167
Dihydroergotamine, 242
Dihydrotestosterone, 188
  benzoate, 184
  propionate, 162, 186, 188, 189
L-Dihydroxyphenylalanine (L-Dopa), 93, 96, 110, 113-114, 162, 194, 201, 244, 252-256, 262, 266, 308, 311, 339, 340, 346-348, 353, 355, 362, 369, 545-548, 551
L-Dihydroxyphenylalanine decarboxylase, 252, 253
DL-Dihydroxyphenylserine, 162, 202, 253, 507
5,6-Dihydroxytryptamine (see also 5-Hydroxytryptamine), 45, 46, 105, 203, 249, 304, 421
Diisopropylfluorophosphate, 85, 541
4,α-Dimethyl-m-tyramine (H77/77), 305
Dimorphism, 169
  sexual, 161-172
Diphenylhydantoin, 279
Discrimination, 387-388, 398-410
  acquisition, 401-404, 456-457
Dishabituation, 386
Disinhibition, 60, 61, 386, 387
  frontal syndrome, 364
Disorders, affective, 554
Disruption, 554
Dissociation, 97
  of motivation and motor performance, 373
Disulfiram, 27, 30, 31, 104, 267, 415
L-Dopa, see L-Dihydroxyphenylalanine
Dopamine, 30, 36-40, 44, 45, 68, 72-77, 87, 88, 96, 97, 136, 140, 148, 162, 173, 202, 242, 252, 253, 270, 297-300, 303, 305-308, 335-363, 365, 366, 369-373, 415, 416, 548, 549, 551, 554
  and behavior, 337-356
Dopamine-β-hydroxylase, 256, 262, 267, 304
  inhibiter, 29
DL-DOPS, see DL-Dihydroxyphenylserine
Douglas—Pribram model, 389
DR, see Delayed response performance
DRL, see Reinforcement, differential, of low rates

Drinking (see also Thirst), 10-12, 131-158, 338-342
  acetylcholine-induced, 10
  angiotensin-induced, 10, 146
  behavior, unconditioned, 338
  carbachol-induced, 10
  control of, 134
  elicited by electrical stimulation, 135
  isoproterenol-induced, 147
  neuroanatomy of, 131-158
  neuropharmacology, 131-158
  nonregulatory, 131
  regulatory, 131
DRL, see Differential reinforcement of low rate
Drugs, 172-175, 192, 212
  anorectic, 86-110
  anticholinergic, 538-544
  antidepressant, 271-272, 280
  and behavior, 191-205
  cholinergic, 541-543
  cholinolytic, 417-419
  crystalline, injected, 56
  dipsogenic, 151
  neuroleptic, 272, 280
  orectic, 110-114
  screening, 191
  and sexual behavior, 199-204
  and sleep—waking cycle, 275-277
  specificity, 193
  tranquilizing, 272-274
DZP, see Diazepam

Eating, as unconditioned behavior, 338, 342
EB, see Estradiol benzoate
Effect
  Crespi depression, 459, 488
  behavior, 508
  frustration, 460
  punishment, partial, 454
  reinforcement, partial, 453, 454, 461
Electroconvulsive shock, see Shock, electroconvulsive
Electrophysiology, 107
Elimination, of response, 390
Emotion within learning theory, 439-464
Environment, strange
  refusal to copulate in, 176
Ephedrine, 89, 90, 91, 97, 101, 313, 314
Epilepsy threshold, 3
Epinephrine, 56-72, 87, 88, 92, 252, 562
Epinine, 88
Ergometrine, 302, 314

(+) Erythrodihydroxyphenylserine (DOPS), see Dihydroxyphenylserine
Escape behavior, 447, 467, 471
Eserine, see Physostigmine
Estradiol, 170, 171, 173, 183, 184, 209
Estradiol benzoate, 162-164, 169, 175, 180, 181, 183, 186, 204
Estrogen, 173, 178-184, 191, 207, 210
  followed by progesterone, 180
Estrous cycle, 178
Ethamoxytriphetol, 169, 181-184, 189
Ethanol, 279, 434, 466-475, 499
Ethanolamine-O-sulfate, 306
Ether, 182
Ethoxybutamoxane, 57
Excitation
  action, postsynaptic, 60
  theory, neurochemical, 392
    evidence for, 396
Extinction, 386-387, 396-400, 453-456

Falck—Hillarp histological technique, 6, 334
Fatty acid, short-chain, 280
FE, see Frustration effect
Fear
  conditioning, classical, 444, 446, 470-471, 478-480, 490
  definition, 440
  drug effects on, 433-529
Feeding
  alpha-adrenergic, 58-63
  beta-adrenergic, 63
  control, 87
  norepinephrine-induced, 60
  psychopharmacology of, 55-129
Fenisorex, 129
Fenfluramine, 78, 89, 91, 101, 104-107, 195, 242, 246
Fiber degeneration, 5
Fighting, induced
  by isolation, 485-486
  by shock, 485-486
Finickiness, a concept, 65
Fink—Heimer technique, 5
FLA-63, 203, 297, 298, 305, 314, 339, 347, 353, 416
Flinch response, 473
Fluoxymesterone, 188
α-Flupenthixol, 340, 347
Flurazepam, 486
Food-fluid balance, 59
Forebrain, 13, 16
  radical ablation, 18
Frontostriatal interactions, 364-366

Frustration, 440, 460
  conditioned, 461
  drug effects on, 433-529
Function
  cognitive, 368-369
  frontal cortex, 364
Fusaric acid, 30

GABA, see γ-Aminobutyric acid
Globus pallidus, 309
Glucose, 92
  receptor in liver, 92
Glutamic acid decarboxylase, 319
Glycine, 559
Gnawing, compulsive, 311
  apomorphine-induced, 311
Goat, sleep-deprived, 238
Go—go method, 400
Goldfish, shuttlebox performance of, 472
Gonadectomy, 179
Gonadotropin, 161, 167, 274
Gray's hypothesis, 493
Grice box, 453
Growth hormone, bovine, 275

Habituation, 386, 393-396
Hallucination, 254
Haloperidol, 77, 96, 105, 147, 148, 272, 303, 311, 319, 341, 348, 349, 354, 506, 507, 548, 559
Hamster, Golden, 209-210
Hemicholinium, 261, 264
Hexobarbital, 448, 451
5-HIAA, 78, 257
Hippocampus
  dorsal, 304
  theta, 495
Histamine, 85, 151, 278
Hormone
  amount, 168
  exposure
    critical, 167
    time, 168
  gonadal, 184, 185
  growth, 275
  neonatal, 164-170
  ovarian, 161
  regulation, 185
  secretion, 161
  sexual, 161-172
    in female, 175-186
  type, 169
HP, see Haloperidol
5-HT, see 5-Hydroxytryptamine

Humoral theory, 237-238
  of sleep, 235
Hungrex, 101
Hydroxyamphetamine, 88
γ-Hydroxybutyrate (GOH), 269, 270
17-Hydroxycorticosteroid, 275
6-Hydroxydopa, 70
6-Hydroxydopamine (6-OHDA), 38, 58, 66-70, 72-75, 96, 97, 107, 137, 143, 146, 147, 257, 258, 260, 266, 298, 299, 305, 309, 313, 317, 342, 348-353, 355, 358, 370-372, 417, 508, 548, 549
  as a chemical knife, 73
5-Hydroxyindolylacetaldehyde, 241
5-Hydroxyindolacetic acid, 248
Hydroxylation
  beta, 91
  loss of ring, 90
β-Hydroxymethamphetamine, 91
19-Hydroxytestosterone, 189
5-Hydroxytryptamine(5-HT), 27, 42-48, 63, 78-81, 96, 99, 105, 136, 140, 151, 162, 173, 196, 197, 202, 203, 239, 240-250, 253-258, 263-266, 280, 303-304, 311-312, 318-319, 334, 350, 415, 420, 421, 505, 533, 555-560, 562
5,6-Hydroxytryptamine, 248-250
5-Hydroxytryptophan, 44, 46, 78, 162, 194, 201, 241-242, 246, 304, 318, 348, 421, 505, 506, 546, 551
5-Hydroxytryptophol, 241
Hyoscine, 261-263
Hyperactivity
  starvation-induced, 111
  stereotypes, 307
Hyperdipsia
  primary, 139
  septal, 139
Hyperkinesia, 341
  apomorphine-induced, 342
Hyperphagia, 66-70, 73, 80
Hypersomnia, 234, 240
Hypnotics, 272, 274, 281
  and tranquilizing drugs, 272-274
Hypnotoxin theory, 235
Hippocampus, theta, 495
Hypokinesia, 335, 341
  apomorphine-induced, 342
Hypothalamus, 4, 65, 68, 134-138, 187, 342, 343
  lateral, 16, 55, 135, 136, 143
    classical syndrome, 242-243

Hypothalamus (cont'd)
  lesions in, 73, 75-76, 136, 143
  ventromedial, 57, 73
Hypothesis
  frequency-specific, 495-502
  rate dependence, 441, 457, 458
  stimulus selection, 407
  stimulus substitution, 452
  voluntary movement, 495
Hysterectomy, 208

ICSS, see Self-stimulation, intracranial
Imipramine, 194, 271, 305, 545, 554
Impairment, sensory motor, 76
Inhibition
  behavioral, 392-414
    excitation, 423
    hypotheses, 389-392
    mechanism, 421-424
      neural, 389-392
    pathways of, 421-422
    psychopharmacology, 392-414
    varieties of, 385-389
  concept of, 392
  conditioned, 390
  external, Pavlovian, 465
  internal, Pavlovian, 439
  of protein synthesis, 554-555
  response, 390-392
  a term, 385
  theory, 392
Injection
  alumina cream, 356
  of crystalline drugs, 56-57
  fluid, 57
  intracerebral, 258
  intracisternal, 257
  intracranial, 302-303, 309-311
  intraventricular, 75, 257
  self-administration, 39-40
Input, chemical
  more specific than electrical stimulus, 11
  value of defining, 12
Insomnia, 240, 248
Insulin, 60
Interaction
  frontostriatal, 364-366
  of neurotransmitters, 558-559
  reciprocal, 59
Interlocking experiment, 2
Interval, fixed, 406
Intromission, 176
Ionic balance, 86
Isopregnenone, 182

Isoproterenol, 57, 63-65, 87, 88, 137, 143, 150, 252

JB*329*, 84
Jump response, 440, 462, 473

Learning
  appetitive, 352-353
  discrimination, 456-457, 487
  model, 403
  modulation, 531-577
  R-S, 435
  S-S, 435
  Skinner box, *see* Box
  theory, 434-439
    emotion in, 439
Lesion
  caudate, 357, 365
  chemical, *see* 6-Hydroxydopamine
  frontal, 365
  intracranial self-stimulation sites, 5-7
  studies, 298-302, 308-309
  technique, 338
  unilateral, 358, 373
  ventromedial, 61, 69
Lethargy, 77
Limbic system, 138-140
Locomotor activity, 295-307, 338
Locus coeruleus, 14-16, 33
  lesion, 15, 267
  self-stimulation, 14-16, 18
Lordosis, 175, 176, 182
  female characteristics, 161
  to mount ratio, 176, 177
  quotient, 176
  response, 164, 169, 180, 181, 185
LSD, *see* Lysergic acid diethylamide
Lysergic acid diethylamide (LSD), 195, 197, 202, 242, 302, 307, 314, 319

Male
  castrated, 188-190, 200
  copulation, 163-164
MAO, *see* Monoamine oxidase
Marchi method, 5
Marijuana and sleep, 279
Mating as unconditioned behavior, 338
Maze learning, 372, 401
Medazepam, 478, 483, 484
Membrane cell, 270
Memory
  analysis, 532
  and arousal, 565
  consolidation, 353-355
  disruption, 554

Memory (*cont'd*)
  formation, theory of, 560-561
  loss, 354
  mechanism, neurobiological, 532
  modulation, 531-577
  storage, 555-557, 561
Meprobamate, 308
MER-*25*, *see* Ethamoxytriphetol
Mesencephalon, 138
Mesogydin, 202
Metaproterenol, 88
Methamphetamine, 89, 91, 307, 314, 318
Methapyriline, 151
Methiothepin, 266
Methoxamine, 91
Methylation, alpha, 90
Methylatropine, 196
N-Methyldiazepam, 486
α-Methyldopamine, 255, 260, 266
α-Methylnorepinephrine, 93, 255
Methylphenidate, 307
N-Methyl-4-piperidyl cyclopentyl methyl-ethynyl glycolate (PCMG), 401
Methylscopolamine, 84
α-Methyltryptamine, 46
α-Methyl-p-tyrosine (AMPT), 73, 74, 162, 192, 194, 196, 199, 203, 256, 258, 260, 267, 297, 298, 305, 308, 314, 339, 340, 344-346, 349-355, 369, 416, 417, 506, 507, 546, 548-550, 553, 558, 563
Methysergide, 43, 45, 78, 105, 195, 202, 266, 318, 421
Midbrain, 138-140
  MK-*468*, 201
Monkey, 478
Monoamine, 172-175, 194, 201, 248
  neuron, ontogeny of, 172-173
  turnover, 42, 47-48
Monoamine oxidase, 90, 174, 194
  inhibitor, 58, 242, 254
Monoaminergic theory of sleep, 236, 239
Morphine, 41, 84, 279, 296, 483
Motivation, sexual, 161, 164
Motor behavior (*see also* Locomotor), 76, 338, 339, 362-368, 373
  drug-induced, 236, 295-331, 362-364
Mouse, 210
  killing behavior, 83
Movement
  ballistic, 367
  directed, 295
  ramp, 367, 368
Muscarinic compound, 196
Muscle tone, 262, 264

Myasthenia gravis, 542

NA, *see* Noradrenaline
Narcotic effect, 269-271
Nauta technique, 5
Neostigmine, 535
Nest building, 206
Nethalide, 254
Neural system, 58
Neurochemical correlates of food-fluid balance, 59
Neuromodulator of sleep, 252
Neuron, *see also* Neurotransmitter, 26
  dopaminergic, 298
  firing, 367
  monoaminergic, 172-173
Neuropharmacology
  of punishment, 25-53
  of reward, 25-53
  of sleep, 233
Neurophysiology, 235, 237-240
Neurotransmitter (*see also* separate compounds), 303-306, 311-312, 334, 531-577
  function, 235
  interaction, 558-559
  putative, 277-278
    and food intake, 56-87
  release, 67
  specific, 27
Nialamide, 58, 174, 175, 201, 254, 313
Nicotine, 151, 260, 261, 536-538, 546-547
Nigrostriatal system, 343, 358-364, 371
Nipple contact, 211
Nitrazepam, 43, 273, 411, 420, 478, 486
Nitrogen substituents, 87
Nonpunishment, 437
Nonreward, frustrative, 437, 452-464, 474-475, 487-489, 491
  aftereffects, 460-464
Noradrenaline (NA), 173, 258, 297, 299, 303-305, 312, 320, 334, 335, 340, 342, 343, 346-353
Noradrenergic bundle
  dorsal, 33
  ventral, 68
Noncatecholamine, 90-92
  can release norepinephrine, 90
Nordefrin, 87, 88, 93
Norephedrine, 91
L-Norepinephrine (NE), 14, 15, 27-37, 42, 43, 45, 56-72, 74, 87, 90, 96, 99, 106, 107, 136, 140, 143, 148, 150, 162, 202, 239, 244, 251-254, 415, 416, 548-554, 557, 560, 563, 564

Normethamphetamine, 91
Novelty, response to, 475, 489, 491-492
Nucleus
  accumbens, 302, 303
  caudate, 356, 365
Nursing, 206
Nylidrin, 87, 88

Obesity as health hazard, 110
6-OHDA, *see* 6-Hydroxydopamine
Orotic acid, 277
Output
  specificity, 12
  value of defining, 12
Ovariectomy, 179-186, 188, 208
Overtraining, 350
  passive avoidance, 413
Oxazepam, 42, 46, 48, 111, 112, 420, 421, 476, 481, 484, 486, 487
Oxotremorine, 196
OZP, *see* Oxazepam

Papez circuit of emotion, 142
Paredrine, 88
Paredrinol, 88
Pargyline, 73, 194, 196, 201, 299, 304, 348, 353, 555
Parkinson's disease, 75, 334, 335, 358, 364, 367-369, 421
Parpanite, 396
Pathway
  behavioral inhibition, 422
  cholinergic, 421, 424
  dopamine, 421, 423, 424
  neural, 415
  norepinephrine reinforcement, 423
  serotoninergic, 423
Pavlov, 385-387, 396, 435, 439, 465
PCPA, *see* p-Chlorophenylalanine
Pentobarbital, 42, 113, 273, 441, 448, 451
Pentose shunt, 270
Pentylenetetrazol, 547, 554
Peptide, 189
Performance acquisition, 402
  go–no-go, 418
  in shuttlebox, *see* Box
  stable extinction, 396, 398
Perfusate
  brain-to-brain, 238
  central nervous system to central nervous system, 237
Periactin, 111
Perphenazine, 272
PGO, *see* Pontogeniculate activity
Pharmacology, 41-49, 296-298, 307-308

Phenethylamine, 89, 92, 94
    releases catecholamine, 94
Phenethylamine-N-methyltransferase, 70
Pheniprazine, 555
Phenmetrazine, 91, 94, 100, 107
Phenobarbital, 113, 440, 441, 448, 451
Phenothiazine, 112-113
Phenoxybenzamine, 40, 63, 203, 254, 267
Phentermine, 99-100, 103
Phentolamine, 32, 43, 59, 61, 62, 64, 65, 113, 254, 267, 303, 351, 421
Phenylephrine, 88, 90
Phenylpropanolamine, 91, 99, 101-103, 107
Physostigmine, 83, 118, 260, 261, 263, 264, 267, 269, 394, 397, 401, 412, 413, 504, 535-537, 542, 546, 547
Picrotoxin, 559
Pig, 478
Pigeon, 478
Pilocarpine, 83, 84, 98, 196, 197, 535
Pimozide, 40, 96, 192, 195, 197, 203, 303, 318, 351
Piperidine, 277, 278, 281
Piperoxane, 255
Pipradrol, 307
Piribedal, 195
Polydipsia following brain damage, 134
Polygraphy recordings, 235
Polyethylene glycol, 137
Pontogeniculate activity (PGO), 234, 265-269, 273, 280
PRAE, see Reinforcement–acquisition effect, partial
PREE, see Reinforcement–extinction effect
Preludin, 100
Presate, 103
Primate, 210-211
Procyclidine, 318
Progesterone, 165, 170, 175, 178-185, 194, 207, 209, 210, 275
Progestin, 182
Prolactin, 207, 274
Promethazine, 272
Propadrine, 91, 101
Propranolol, 32, 59, 63, 65, 96, 97, 106, 150, 254, 267, 303, 421, 551, 553
α-Propyldopacetamide, 194
α-Propyldopacetamine, 42
(±)-N-n-Propylnorapocodeine, 302
(±)-N-n-Propylnorapomorphine, 302, 307, 313
Prostigmine, 261
Protein synthesis, 191, 204-205, 275-277, 281

Protriptyline, 299
Protokylol, 87
Provocation technique, 485
Psychology, social, 107-110
Psychosis, amphetamine-induced, 364
Punishing–rewarding events, 435
Punishment, 437
    neuropharmacology, 25-53
    operant, 26, 41-49, 388-389
    partial, 454
    response suppression, 388-389
Puromycin, 276, 554

Rabbit, 209
Rat, 206-209, 256, 478
Receptivity, postcopulatory
    duration of, 177
Recording, polygraphic, continuous, 235
Reflex, sexual, 190, 465
Reinforcement, partial, 453, 454, 461
    acquisition, 453
    extinction, 453
        Capaldi's theory, 462
Reinforcement, operant, 25-41
    differential, of low rates (DRL), 445
    fixed interval, 344
    fixed ratio schedule, 344
Reinforcer
    negative, 438
    positive, 438
Renin, 132, 144, 150
Reproductive behavior, 159-232
Reserpine, 97, 174, 175, 196, 203, 243, 244, 255, 265, 266, 305, 314, 339, 340, 345, 346, 349, 352, 355, 415, 551, 555
Responding, see Response
Response behavior
    amphetamine-induced, 404
    conditioned emotional (CER), 437
    decrements, 392
    delayed, 362
    elimination of, 390
    extinguished, 396-400
    free, 409
    hormone-induced, 192
    inhibition, 390-392
    jump, 440, 462, 473
    spatial double alternation, 408
    startle, 393
    stereotyped, 363
    suppression, 388-389, 410-414
    unconditioned, 435
Retention testing, 539-543

Retrieval, 534
  failure, 534
Retrieving, 206
Reversal of object discrimination, 365
Reward behavior, 435, 437, 440-443, 459, 467-468, 475-477, 489
  neuropharmacology, 25-53
Rhythm, hippocampal theta, 492-496
Ring compounds, substituted, 91
Ring hydroxylation, loss of, 90
RO4-4602, 201
Rotational behavior (see also Circling), 313-320
  apomorphine-induced, 313-317
Route, intratrial, 461
Runway, double, 460

SA, see Sodium amobarbital
Satiety
  alpha-adrenergic, 62-63, 65
  beta-adrenergic, 58, 63-65
  nonadrenergic, 63
  systems, 81
  theory, 62
Schedules, multiple, 339, 444
  partial reinforcement, 453
  Sidman avoidance, see Avoidance
  simple fixed-ratio, 404
Schizophrenia, stereotyped behavior in, 295
Scopolamine, 84, 204, 263, 318, 393-395, 400-409, 411-414, 504, 505, 535, 538-540, 542, 559
Season, effect of, 178
Sedation hypothesis, 29
  test of, 30
Self-stimulation, 1-24, 26, 27, 34-38, 350-352, 365, 441
Sensory motor coordination, 358-362
Sensory neglect, 76
Serotonin, see 5-Hydroxytryptamine
Sexual, see Behavior, sexual
Shock, 452
  avoidance, 357
  electrical, 443, 484
  electroconvulsive, 543-544, 554-555, 560
  electrical, 443, 484
  escape, 357
  paired with stimulus, 411
  unavoidable, 411
    paired with a tone, 412
Shuttlebox, see Box
Single-trace dual process, 561
Skinner extinction behavior, 387
Skinner box, see Box

Sleep
  activated, 235
  is active, 235
  behavioral, 234
  cholinergic, 238
  hypnogenic, 238
  main concepts of, 235-236
  monoaminergic theory of, 236, 239
  neuromodulator, 252
  neuropharmacology, 233
  neurophysiology, 236-237
  "wet," 237-240
  paradoxical, 235, 239, 263-264, 273
  physiological (PS), 234, 250, 256-258, 263, 264, 276
  REM, 235
  slow wave (SWS), 234, 237, 250, 255, 262, 263, 280
  theories, recent, 235-240
  —waking cycle, 233-293
    and fatty acids, 269-271
    and hormones, 274-275
    neuropharmacology, 233-293
Sleeping pills in the U.S.A., 272
Sodium amobarbital, 434, 440, 445, 453, 455, 456, 459, 461, 463, 464, 497
Spiroperidol, 313, 347, 351, 372
Starvation syndrome, 55, 72
Stereotypy syndrome, 295, 307-313, 363
  by amphetamine, 307-311
  drug-induced, 307-311
  transmitters in, 311-312
Steroid, 189
Stilbestrol, 184
Stimulation, electrical
  aggressive behavior elicited by, 486
  self-stimulation, see Self-stimulation
Stimulus
  aversive, 388, 410-414, 451-452, 473-474, 483-486, 491
  conditioned, 411-412
  classifying, 438
  conditioned
    aversive, 411
    excitatory, 387
    inhibitory, 387
  excitatory conditioned, 387
  external, 387, 407
  inhibitory conditioned, 387
  internal, 387
  multiple relevant, 402
  novel, 386
  outcome, 397
  Pavlov, 435

Stimulus (*cont'd*)
  persisting, 397
  presentation-produced, 400
  reinforcing, 397
  relevant, multiple, 402
  response-produced, 404
  selection hypothesis, 389
  unconditioned, 386, 435
Strength, below zero response, 388, 392
Striatum, 336, 337, 345, 364-379
  classical studies, 356-358
Strychnine, 182, 547, 559
Subfornical organ, 11, 145
Substantia nigra, 4, 33
Substrate, motivational, 1-24
Sulpiride, 272
Superhyperphagia, 69
  alpha, 66
  of appetite, 66, 92
  by aversive stimuli, 388-389, 391, 410-414
  beta, 66
Suprifen, 88
Sympathetic system, 57
Sympathomimetics, 87-92, 545-548
Synephrin, 88
System
  alpha, 58
  beta, 58

T-maze, 466
Tail deviation, 161
Task, two-way avoidance, 348
Tegmentum, area ventralis (AVT), 352
Tegmentum, pontine, dorsolateral, 259
Temazepam, 476
Testis, 168
Testosterone, 162-164, 167-173, 183-190, 208, 274, 502
Tetrabenazine, 58, 175, 196, 203, 339, 346, 352, 353
Δ^9-Tetrahydrocannabinol (THC), 434, 499
Thalamus, dorsomedial, 19
Theta-driving curve, 497, 500-509
THC, *see* Δ^9-Tetrahydrocannabinol
Therapy
  anticholinesterase, 542

Therapy (*cont'd*)
  L-dopa, 335, 336
  electroconvulsive, 554
Thiopentone, 272
Thioridazine, 303, 306, 314, 318
Thirst, 81, 131
  neuroanatomy, 134-140
  neuropharmacology, 140-151
    first reported (1881), 134
  receptor, 132-134
Thymoxamine, 32
Tolazoline, 63
Tolerance, 85
Tranquilizer (*see also* separate compounds), 42, 111-113, 281, 508
  minor, 111-112, 273-274, 433-529
  and behavioral effects, 489-492
Transition N-R, 462
Transmission, neurohumoral, 191
Transmitter, *see* Neurotransmitter
Tranylcypromine, 201, 318, 554
Treading water, 161
Tremor, 334, 335
Trifluoperozine, 272
Trophotropic system, 243
Tropolone, 254, 266
Tryptophan, 78, 241, 318
Tryptophan hydroxylase, 241, 245, 246, 303
Tyramine, 88, 98
Tyrosine, 79, 256, 343
Tyrosine hydroxylase, 256, 257, 267

U-*14,624,* 297, 298, 416
Undereating, 110

Vasopressin, 562
VNAB, *see* Bundle, ventral noradrenergic
Voluntary movement hypothesis, 494, 495

Waking system, 238-240

Y-maze, 472, 477
Yohimbine, 78

Zona incerta, 140

RC
483
M36
v.9

DEC 8 1977